Library of
Davidson College

SELECTION OF TEACHERS AND SUPERVISORS IN URBAN SCHOOL SYSTEMS

New York City Commission on Human Rights

COMMISSIONERS

Eleanor Holmes Norton
Chairman

David H. Litter
Vice Chairman

Jerome M. Becker

Irving Chin[1]

Gilbert Colgate, Jr.

Joseph R. Erazo[2]

Eleanor Clark French

Dr. Archibald F. Glover

Murray Gross

Rabbi Harry Halpern

Rabbi Bernard Mandelbaum[3]

Rt. Rev. Richard B. Martin[2]

Cornelius McDougald

Dr. Sergio S. Pena[3]

Cleveland Robinson[3]

Julia Rodriguez[1]

Rose Ann Scamardella[1]

Doris Turner[1]

Celia M. Vice[1]

Preston David
Executive Director

HEARINGS AND RESEARCH STAFF

Brooke Aronson, *Director*
Mildred Zander
Florence Cromien
Edith Lyrton
Rosalie La Capra

[1]Appointed after hearings
[2]Resigned after hearings
[3]Term expired after hearings

SELECTION OF TEACHERS AND SUPERVISORS IN URBAN SCHOOL SYSTEMS

A Transcript of the Public Hearings Held Before the New York City
Commission on Human Rights, January 25-29, 1971

Including the Recommendations of the Commission

Edited by
Paul Tractenberg
*Rutgers University School of Law, Newark, N.J.
and Special Counsel to the Commission for the Hearings*

Special Preface by
John V. Lindsay
Mayor of the City of New York

Foreword by
Eleanor Holmes Norton
Chairman, New York City Commission on Human Rights

1972
AGATHON PUBLICATION SERVICES, INC.
NEW YORK, N.Y.

371.1
T759s

© by Agathon Publication Services, Inc.
150 Fifth Avenue
New York, N.Y. 10011

ALL RIGHTS RESERVED

Library of Congress Catalog Card Number: 72-81915

ISBN Number: 0-87988-001-5   73-1560

TABLE OF CONTENTS

	page
Special Preface by John V. Lindsay	vii
Foreword by Eleanor Holmes Norton	ix
Editor's Preface by Paul L. Tractenberg	xiii

Hearings held January 25, 1971
    List of Witnesses   facing page xvi
    Transcript of Hearings   1

Hearings held January 26, 1971
    List of Witnesses   facing page 138
    Transcript of Hearings   139

Hearings held January 27, 1971
    List of Witnesses   following page 321
    Transcript of Hearings   322

Hearings held January 28, 1971
    List of Witnesses   facing page 508
    Transcript of Hearings   509

Hearings held January 29, 1971
    List of Witnesses   following page 581
    Transcript of Hearings   582

Appendix A: Summary and Recommendations	711
Appendix B: Prepared Testimony Submitted in Writing	731
Appendix C: Statements Submitted After the Hearings	744
Topic Guide	781
Subject Index	787
Index of Witnesses	795

SPECIAL PREFACE

By John V. Lindsay

    Educational issues stand near the center of urban problems. Too often, however, concern leads only to aimless conflict as debate becomes dissension. Rancor and recrimination obscure the facts, and efforts toward effective reform may be paralyzed by hostility and polarization. The City Commission on Human Rights held its hearings on the hiring and promotion practices of our city's school system to offer an alternative to such counterproductive conflict, and to provide a more positive and fruitful means for approaching the urgent problems of our schools. It succeeded admirably. Its efforts might be taken as a model for those who seek to resolve these problems.
    The result of the Commission's efforts is a new contribution to the difficult field of personnel selection in the nation's troubled urban schools with the new challenges presented to them by class and race. Only after listening to the week-long testimony of school officials, educational authorities, parents, teachers, and paraprofessionals; only after reading the mass of supplementary material brought to light by the hearings, did the Commission make conclusions and issue recommendations, in its thoughtful and enlightening summary. It has thus made an important and exemplary contribution to bettering the quality of educational debate in New York City and in the country.
    Finding the right personnel is just one aspect of the critical situation confronting New York City's schools and those throughout the nation. This crisis demands the kind of tough, objective examination of issues made by the Commission. Indeed the Commission's analysis is a model of what is needed if we are to move toward the solution of the larger problems of our cities. We must be willing to reassess old methods and re-examine old ideas. We must be willing to experiment and change.
    Too often, the unquestioned acceptance of what worked in the past has thwarted the search for what will work today. For a long time, for example, the belief persisted that teachers, as professionals, should not unionize to protect their own interests and the interest of better education. Once that idea was rejected, and teachers everywhere began to organize, they were able not only to improve their own situation, but to make teaching a more secure and rewarding profession, to attract needed staff and to assure our schools of qualified and adequate personnel. Today, as urban schools face awesome challenges, teachers are reconsidering their exclusive role in the classroom, and have welcomed the effective use of a valuable teammate, the paraprofessional. When used in

conjunction with professional staff and given adequate training and supervision, paraprofessionals can be critical in easing the burden teachers feel from overcrowded classrooms and children with special needs. At the same time, a paraprofessional program can help upgrade the skills of the participants, providing a source of recruitment for professional personnel. New York City has already brought 15,000 paraprofessionals into the city's classrooms, and is looking for ways to use them more effectively and to help them grow professionally. Our teachers have also supported curriculum changes, and other innovations which will help to upgrade the schools and provide improved education for urban children.

But to speak of quality education seems futile when the continuation of even adequate education is put in question by the financial crisis that is strangling our schools as it cripples our cities. This crisis, the result of rising costs and shrinking local revenues, has curtailed essential programs and services, not to mention the stifling of experimental programs. For the first time, the lack of funds threatens to close some urban schools altogether.

When the National Education Association surveyed 63 of the nation's largest school systems in the fall of 1971, it found that two-thirds of them were operating under "crisis conditions." And the crux of the crisis in the cities is the continued reliance on local financing, based on a deteriorating property tax base, which cannot hope to keep up with the soaring costs of urban education. Cities pay more for their schools because of higher construction costs, higher salaries, and the higher cost of educating larger proportions of poor, disadvantaged and non-English speaking children. And the tax base of many cities is dwindling.

This situation can be alleviated only when the state assumes greater financial responsibility for local schools. As it stands now, state aid to education is both inadequate and inequitable. States pay only an average 40% of education costs, and because of outmoded aid formulas, give more per capita aid to suburban schools than to disadvantaged central city schools. Obviously, reforms in the state role in school financing is crucial. Some states have already begun to move to relieve localities of the tax burden. In Hawaii, the schools are presently funded entirely from statewide sources. Minnesota has increased its share of school support from 50 to 65 per cent. The governor of Michigan has suggested sweeping reforms to shift the burden from the localities to the state. All states must accept more responsibility for the cost of running our schools, but we also need a similar commitment from the federal government to provide more resources for meeting the soaring costs of urban education.

Each of these and other problems of our schools must be faced with the dilegence and objectivity reflected in the Commission's hearings on the recruitment and upgrading of those who teach our children. For the teacher stands at the center of our expectations from our schools. And our schools are critical to the improvement of our cities and the future of our country. I commend to you the pages of testimony and conclusions that follow as a tough-minded approach to facing some of our most serious problems.

John V. Lindsay
Mayor of the City of New York

FOREWORD

By Eleanor Holmes Norton

    The New York City Commission on Human Rights initiated these hearings to determine the reason for the surprisingly poor representation of Blacks and Puerto Ricans on the professional staff of New York City's school system. As our investigation proceeded and as our hearings developed, however, it became clear that we were dealing not simply with a question of possible discrimination. Rather we found that we had tackled a matter of great complexity with far-reaching implications for education in the schools of the nation's cities: that of how to develop and recruit a corps of teaching personnel best able to cope with the formidable problems of educating the children who have inherited our deteriorating cities.
    Teachers have too often gotten short shrift in discussions and debates on the problems of education. Today's teacher bears the enormous burden of trying to educate youngsters caught in deteriorating urban conditions. Yet few teachers have been prepared to handle this burden; teacher training and preparation have not kept pace with the astonishingly rapid transformation of our pupil population. As our central cities continue to absorb more and more minority and poor people, many of them migrants from rural areas in the South or Puerto Rico, our school systems have had to handle increasingly more children with special problems and needs. Many come from severely deprived backgrounds; many do not speak English. They are making unique and compelling demands on school systems that have not yet changed to respond to their needs.
    To be sure, city schools have always had the task of educating and assimilating immigrant groups. But never before has that task been so formidable. Earlier immigrant groups did not send their poorest, most deprived children to school, at least not for very long. They were needed to work to add to meagre family earnings in a period in which unskilled jobs were plentiful for those with little education. The "drop-out" in pre-technological society did not necessarily lack a future, as he does today. Now that society has accepted the responsibility of educating all children--even the poorest--and of offering equal opportunity to all, the task is immeasurably greater. Yet little has been done to prepare teachers for these changes, to prepare them for this new task.
    Our hearings were less concerned with the precise number of minority teachers than with the adequacy of teacher preparation and selection in view of this changing situation. The fact that there were, indeed, so few minority teachers in New York City served

as the initial indicator of what turned out to be a larger and more formidable problem. For teaching has traditionally been, among the professions, the one most open to blacks and other minorities. The teaching tradition among minorities was clearly seen in their significant inclusion in virtually every large urban school system.

The contrasting situation in New York (only 9% of our teachers were black and less than 1% Puerto Rican) raised serious questions about the entire system of personnel selection, questions which were illuminated by the testimony at the hearings. Much of this testimony came from people within the system--the Chancellor, other school and union officials, supervisors, teachers, and representatives of community boards--all of whom evidenced an impressive commitment to improve education in their acknowledgment and analysis of the faults of the system and their willingness to work to remedy them. But the hearings gained national significance from experts and school officials that came from across the nation: from other urban systems, from the Educational Testing Service, and from colleges and universities which train teachers.

After studying their testimony and that of the defenders of the system, the Commission concluded that the poor minority showing was not due to conscious and deliberate discrimination, but to a <u>de facto</u> exclusion of minority groups that was a reflection of the <u>rigidities</u> that infected the entire personnel system. This system was judged, in the words of New York City School Chancellor Harvey Scribner, to be "antiquated, outmoded and inconsistent with both contemporary educational requirements and the concept of decentralized schools." Originally designed to exclude from the educational system those not suited to teach, its effect under current conditions was to exclude not only the traditional minority groups, but anyone who thought differently from those who designed and conducted the licensing examinations. Described by one expert as "so inbred as to be sociological incest," the examination process embodied a cultural and geographic bias hardly consistent with the flexibility and innovation demanded by rapidly changing conditions.

The hearings also raised serious doubts about the validity of the examinations as instruments to ensure selection of those best suited to teach. It could not be shown that they tested those qualities necessary for good teachers, nor that performance on the tests was in any way an indication of future success in teaching. It became clear that the best that could be said about the examination system was that it screened out incompetents. But surely the exigencies of urban education today require more--that ways be found to screen <u>in</u> the best potential talent to educate inner-city children now so inadequately served, that ways be found to recruit and select those with the special knowledge, skill, interest, and devotion. There was virtually unanimous agreement among the experts who testified that such qualities cannot be easily evaluated by a written examination; that they are best judged by objective observation and evaluation of personnel during training and on the job. Developing such performance-based criteria has already become a major goal of the best school systems throughout the country.

The Commission's recommendations for New York City schools were comprehensive. It suggested the discontinuation of the Board of Examiners in its present form, and the adoption of an alternative method of selection, relying on state certification for initial screening of applicants, with community school boards exercising ultimate responsibility for selection of staff based on professionally sound and objective selection criteria and procedures. To ensure objectivity, it recommended that the central Board of Education develop appropriate policy guidelines to guarantee protection of due process to all applicants and personnel. Such guidelines are necessary to preclude the possibility of reliance on irrelevant criteria such as race, religion, origin, attitude toward unions, political beliefs, and the like. Witnesses testified that thus far bias had not been a factor in teacher selection under New York's decentralized school system. The hearings, in fact, brought forth no concrete evidence to justify fears of inevitable bias, corruption and disorder in the event that the school system changed to another selection system, especially one depending on decentralized selection, which is presumed by some to be vulnerable to local pressures. This Commission will require that the law against discrimination always be adhered to as the school system tries to find and employ those teachers who can do the best job of educating our children, whatever their race, religion, background or beliefs. These hearings convinced us that this could not be done without significant changes in the training selection of teachers.

Soon after the Commission issued its analysis of the hearings, our findings were in effect confirmed by an independent action by the U.S. District Court for the Southern District of New York, ruling in the case of Chance and Mercado vs. Board of Examiners et al., Federal Judge Walter Mansfield found the examinations used to select supervisory personnel were discriminatory in effect and issued a preliminary injunction forbidding the further administration of exams, the issuance of new eligibility lists and the use of existing lists to fill supervisory posts. At the beginning of the school year, the Board of Education approved a new policy to enable New York's decentralized school districts to fill acting supervisory posts during the period of the injunction. Under the interim system candidates are eligible for these posts "if they meet eligibility requirements for the most recent appropriate supervisory examination or if they possess appropriate state certification." Other provisions include the formulation by the Board of written guidelines for the selection and assignment of acting supervisory personnel, provisions for the development of performance criteria for evaluation of personnel, and for the periodic evaluation of the on-the-job performance of such personnel.

These new provisions coincide with several recommendations made by the Commission in its report on the hearings. The broadening of eligibility requirements, with increased reliance on state standards, is an especially commendable move toward greater flexibility, toward a system that will bring in more qualified candidates, rather than serve merely to exclude the totally unqualified. The provisions for the development and use of job performance criteria, too, show a commitment to finding new and better ways to evaluate supervisory candidates and personnel. We commend the Board on taking these first important steps toward changing its recruitment and selection practices. To complete such change requires a great effort, which has now been begun.

There will be problems, there will be mistakes, but it is better to err while working toward a more competent and open system than to opt for the safety of an old, inadequate and demonstrably unsatisfactory system. It is in the interests of such constructive reform that the Commission held its hearings and offered its analysis and recommendations. We hope that our effort will serve to help all cities facing similar problems in their efforts to provide better education.

Eleanor Holmes Norton
Chairman, New York City Commission on Human Rights

EDITOR'S PREFACE

    The public hearings of the New York City Human Rights Commission concerning teacher selection were held daily during the week of January 25, 1971, at the New York County Lawyers Association, 14 Vesey Street. To encourage attendance, a day care facility was provided nearby. A live broadcast of the complete hearings was carried on WNYC, the radio station of New York City.
    The 140 witnesses during the five full days and several evenings of testimony covered virtually the entire spectrum of those involved and interested in public education. They came from around the country as well as from New York City and State. They addressed themselves to every facet of the selection of teachers and their supervisors, and responded to questions from the Chairman of the Human Rights Commission, the Commissioners and Special Counsel to the Commission for the hearings.
    The first major segment of the hearings consisted of testimony from representatives of the New York City school system describing current employment practices from their particular perspectives. During the first day and a half, the hearings took up consecutively the interrelationships among the City Board of Education, the Chancellor's office, the Board of Examiners and community school boards and their staffs; recruitment practices, including special programs directed at recruiting Black and Spanish-speaking candidates; and selection and appointment practices. The witnesses during this segment included Murry Bergtraum and Isaiah Robinson, then President and Vice-President of the City Board of Education; Chancellor Harvey B. Scribner; Gertrude E. Unser, then Chairman, Jay Greene and Murray Rockowitz, two other members of the Board of Examiners; John J. Theobald, a former Superintendent of Schools; Peter Strauss and Philip Kaplan, chairmen of two community school boards; Edythe Gaines and Andrew Donaldson, two community superintendents; Irving Flinker, a junior high school principal; Wendy Lehrman, an elementary school teacher; and Theodore Lang, former Deputy Superintendent in charge of personnel, and a number of his staff members.
    The second segment of the hearings consisted of testimony from representatives of organizations actively involved in New York City public education. Each of these witnesses had been asked to evaluate the current employment practices of the school system and to suggest improvements. Witnesses who participated during this day-long segment included Albert Shanker, President of the United Federation of Teachers; Walter Degnan, President of the Council of Supervisory Associations; Victor Gotbaum, Executive Director of District Council 37, American Federation of State, County and Municipal Employees; Blanche Lewis, President of the United

Parents Association; Eugene Callender, President of the New York Urban Coalition; Hector Vazquez, Executive Director of the Puerto Rican Forum; Louis Nieves, Executive Director of Aspira, Inc.; Rose Falcon, Teacher Coordinator, Parent Leadership Program, United Bronx Parents; and Ira Glasser, Executive Director of the New York Civil Liberties Union.

The third segment of the hearings consisted of a full afternoon of testimony from testing experts about the use and validity of written tests in the employment of teachers and supervisors. The witnesses were Stephen J. Pollak, former Assistant Attorney in charge of the Civil Rights Division of the U.S. Department of Justice; James R. Deneen, Senior Program Director for Teacher Examinations, Educational Testing Service; Richard Barrett, Office of Admissions Services, CUNY; and Robert Thorndike, Professor of Psychology, Teachers College, Columbia University.

The fourth segment of the hearings consisted of testimony from academic and other education experts who evaluated current teacher training, recruitment, selection and promotion practices and discussed alternatives. Witnesses included John H. Fischer, President of Teachers College, Columbia University; Doxie Wilkerson, Chairman of the Department of Curriculum and Instruction, Yeshiva University; Laurence Iannaccone, Professor of Education Administration, University of Toronto; Marilyn Gittell, Director of the Institute for Community Studies, Queens College; Lillian Weber, Professor of Education, City College; Judith Rothschild, Director of the Urban Leadership Development Program, School of Continuing Education, New York University; Robert A. Dentler, Director of the Center for Urban Education; and Harold Haizlip, Headmaster of the New Lincoln School.

The fifth and last segment, on the final day of the hearings, consisted of testimony about developments in state certification and in employment practices of other large urban school districts. Witnesses included officials of the U.S. Office of Education, the National Education Association, and state education departments of four states. Ewald B. Nyquist, New York State Commissioner of Education submitted a statement. Also participating were Joseph Manch, Superintendent of Schools of Buffalo and Aubrey McCutcheon, Deputy Superintendent in charge of staff relations of the Detroit school system.

During the more than ten hours of public testimony at the hearings, 69 witnesses with broad experience in New York City educational and human rights matters were heard. They included a former member of the Board of Education, community superintendents, community school board members, past and present principals and teachers, parents and students, representatives of education and human rights organizations and many other concerned citizens. Organizations that testified included the Citizens Committee for Children, United Black Caucus of Teachers, the Queens Jewish Community Council, Inc., the Central Brooklyn Neighborhood College and Education Action Program, the Italian-American Civil Rights League, and the New York Chinese Community Council.

The tone of the hearings was remarkable. In recent years, public discussion of New York City education issues often has been characterized by outright rancor and irrationality. In marked contrast, during the Commission's hearings, virtually every witness made careful, factual statements and responded fully and openly to questions, despite some heated exchanges. Not a single disruption of any kind occurred. Every witness was treated with courtesy by the audience, whatever point of view his or her statement reflected.

This high level of decorum, together with the thoughtful preparation of the entire range of witnesses, permitted the hearings to meet their dual goals of developing detailed information about current New York City practices and about innovative alternatives.

The result is, therefore, a document of unique value to students of public education from all disciplines. It provides, perhaps for the first time, an in-depth picture of the total selection process of a major urban school system--the way it is designed to work, its shortcomings, its efforts to change. The transcript also offers insights into alternative systems which are being discussed or tried. But more than that, it captures the deep concern and emotion of a wide range of people about the state of public education in urban school systems and about the extent to which teacher selection methods may hold the key to success or failure.

Because the transcript is such a valuable resource, I have conceived of the editor's task as very limited; essentially to clarify ambiguities and to correct obvious errors in transcription. Changes have been kept to a bare minimum so that as much of the substance and flavor of the hearings as possible could be preserved. For example, there has been no effort to make all of the testimony grammatically perfect and little effort to attain consistency of usage. Where changes were necessary, I have attempted to maintain the flow of the testimony even though occasionally problems in transcription made it impossible to make use of small fragments of testimony.

The appendixes to this volume were selected with an eye toward supplementing and complementing the transcript of the hearings. Appendix A consists of the Commission's Summary of Conclusions and Recommendations based upon the hearings. They were part of a complete analysis of the hearings, entitled <u>Equal Employment Opportunity and the New York City Schools</u>, issued by the Commission on May 4, 1971.

Appendix B consists of material submitted to the Human Rights Commission after the hearings expressly for inclusion in the record, in some cases by witnesses who could not attend and in others to supplement or clarify testimony actually offered. Appendix C consists of letters and supplementary documents submitted to the Commission after the hearings were concluded.

The appendixes do not include the voluminous material submitted to the Commission by officials of the New York City Board of Education and Board of Examiners in response to requests from the Commission. Those materials will be made available to researchers at the Commission's offices, 80 Lafayette Street, New York, New York 10005.

Editor's Preface

I am indebted to many persons for making this book possible. I am particularly grateful to Eleanor Holmes Norton, Chairman of the New York City Commission on Human Rights, Preston David, its Executive Director, and Brooke Aronson, Chief of the Research Division, who conceived of the hearings, carried them out and appreciated their importance. Their cooperation and support were indispensable. The other members of the Research Division, Mildred Zander, Rosalie La Capra, Florence Cromien and Edith Lynton were helpful at every juncture and my research assistant, Marilyn Morheuser, discharged varied and demanding responsibilities with skill and good spirits.

Paul L. Tractenberg

HEARINGS HELD JANUARY 25, 1971

Witnesses in Order of Appearance

                Testimony starts

Murry Bergtraum	page 5
Gertrude Unser	15
Harvey Scribner	32
John Theobald	40
Peter J. Strauss	46
Edythe J. Gaines	50
Irving Flinker	58
Theodore H. Lang	66
Frederick H. Williams	82
John P. King	92
Daisy Hicks	104
James Watkins	115
Vernal Pemberton	121
Gladstone Atwell	124
Joan Burton	130

THE CHAIRMAN: All over America school issues stir people of all origins and backgrounds as no other issues do. Whether it is school desegregation in Mississippi, school bussing in Michigan, sex education in Iowa, or hiring practices in New York, school issues are joined on all sides with unmatched fervor.

No democracy will endure which bemoans such debate. Nor will a people survive who are unable to summon strong feelings about their children.

These hearings are an attempt by government to search for answers to questions citizens have a right to ask of it. For it is government to whom citizens have entrusted our most vital functions, and it is government to whom citizens must look for the facts about their operations. A government which fails to use its fact-finding powers fairly and objectively to find answers to urgent questions necessarily leaves its citizens to their own devices.

The City Commission on Human Rights could not escape its responsibility in the case of the public school system, even if it desired to do so. While most of the troublesome issues that vex our schools fall outside the Commission's province, this one falls squarely within it. The one-third of New York City's population that is Black and Puerto Rican is barely included among the teachers and principals employed in a school system where more than half the children are from these minority groups. Under the Commission's mandate, we must find the reasons why.

For if we do not, the very integrity of government is thrown into issue. Ask any large private employer in this city about the school system's record, and it will complain that if the Commission is content, it has a double standard--one for private and one for public employers. The best way to undermine government efforts to command fair employment in the city at large would be for government to give the impression of less than even-handed concern, or that government winks at the rest of government while setting higher standards for private employers.

The fact is that many industries and companies in the private sector in this city are far ahead of the school system in meeting their obligations to reverse hiring patterns that have historically resulted in few minority group employees. A recent City Commission investigation of 27 major companies in New York City resulted in a 50 per cent increase in minority group employees in a nine month period. Private business made these gains as a direct result of our investigation even before the completion of signed agreements between themselves and the Commission. We would hope that our investigation of the city's school system would spur similar efforts.

We have called these hearings because we do not know how to explain the gap between the rapidly improving situation for minority group people in private business and their painfully slow progress in the public school system. By now it has been demonstrated that confusion and anger in the minority communities remain so long as we who have the power to find answers shun the search that can be the basis for solutions that are fair to all.

Yet nothing is more important than that these hearings be vigorous in their commitment to fact-finding and objectivity. For too long this issue has been confused by rancorous charges and lawsuits, which left the basic questions untouched. It is time to let the facts speak for themselves, for facts have an eloquence rhetorical statements most often lack.

We have placed such great emphasis on getting factual data that we have engaged special counsel, whom I will introduce later, to do most of the interrogation of invited witnesses. As a former attorney for the Board of Education, he has the necessary knowledge and background to bring out the facts, and he has prepared himself exhaustively for these hearings.

We regard the fact-finding quality of these hearings as their unique contribution, because despite hardened views on all sides most citizens have never had the opportunity to hear and judge the facts. If the facts were apparent, these hearings would be superfluous. If the answers to this problem were simple, these hearings would be unnecessary. If the blame for the small numbers of Blacks and Puerto Ricans in the school system were clear, these hearings would be redundant. We have taken this issue to public hearing only because we believe the reasons for this problem are complex, that the roots are historical, and that the responsibility is widespread.

Thus the search for scapegoats has no place here, for no complex phenomenon of long duration can be explained by a select list of villains. This problem is systematic, not dependent upon any set of personalities. We must spend this week in trying to understand the intricacies and origins of a system which--no doubt without malicious intent--has taken on the trappings of exclusiveness.

Only an understanding of the way the employment and promotion system works can explain the most troublesome question of all: Why New York alone among the major cities of this country fails to employ minority group people in its school system in significant numbers. To be sure, no city has a really good record in employment of Spanish-speaking teachers, although New York trails even here. The indication that something is wrong is most apparent if we compare the city's figures on Black teachers and supervisors with other large cities. For example, in Chicago, as in New York, a little over half the children are from minority groups, but so is one-third of the teachers. Roughly these same proportions are also found in Philadelphia just down the coast. Across the river in Newark, 72 per cent of the children and 36 per cent of the teachers are Black. In Detroit the figures are 61 per cent Black students and 41 per cent Black teachers, and in Los Angeles 23 per cent Black students and 14 per cent Black teachers.

I cite these figures only to point up the strange and unique position this city is in, not to suggest that there is any proper racial or ethnic ratio. Indeed, in the other large cities there is no necessary identity or other relationship between the number of Black teachers and Black students. Too many factors influence job selection and promotion for this to be the case. But the other cities do reveal a pattern we might rightly expect to result in the natural course: that, whatever the specific proportion, significant numbers of minority group teachers and supervisors are to be found where there are significant numbers of minority children.

Of course, it is not unusual to find minority group people under-represented in public employment in this country. But it is unusual to find that they have not become principals and teachers. The reasons for this are historic. Traditionally teaching was the one profession open to ambitious and talented Blacks. The other professions that traditionally had offered upward mobility to hard-working immigrants and the union jobs that paved the way for so many others were closed tight to the Black slave immigrants and their despised progeny.

But in the South, the system of segregated schools ironically created a demand for Black teachers and supervisors. Thus teaching became the classic profession for Blacks. When large numbers migrated North, teaching was the only tradition in professional life they brought with them, except for the ministry which could absorb only a few. To be sure, it took some time for Northern Blacks to convert the Southern teaching tradition into Northern jobs; but, as the figures I have quoted bear out, only in New York City, among those cities that absorbed large numbers of Black migrants, have they failed in the long run to reestablish themselves in the teaching profession.

These proceedings will hear testimony from anyone in the public desiring to present facts, explanations or conclusions, but it would be foolish to regard the hearings as a panacea. We are concerned with but one of the countless problems that plague New York's school system, which, like every major system in the country, faces awesome problems for which no one has the answers. We believe that the racial and ethnic personnel problem can be separated out as one that is capable of solution and that this Commission can work cooperatively with the school system to find answers, as we have with private industry.

I am pleased to note that the school system, under Board Chairman Murry Bergtraum, under former Superintendent Irving Anker, and under Chancellor Harvey Scribner, has cooperated with us in this investigation ever since it was announced last summer.

It should not be forgotten that even if the ethnic and racial personnel system is eliminated as a troublesome problem for the school system, the Board of Education will be left with the accumulated problems inherited over years of urban decay, and that many of these problems naturally fall hardest upon the majority of the school children who happen to be Black and Puerto Rican. It will be important for those who testify to remember that only the racial and ethnic personnel question is before this Commission as a matter of jurisdiction. But that is more than enough. We must turn all our energies this week upon it, for it festers as a deep cause of discontent in the schools this year comparable to the place student rights and disorders occupied last year. While the scope of these hearings is narrow, we should not underestimate their value in helping to devise ways to eliminate this issue from the long list of problems our schools face. The Commission will sit down with school personnel when the report on these hearings is completed, for these hearings are only so good as the positive solutions they elicit and the move toward remedies they inspire.

Let me say a final word about the confusion that may exist in the minds of some citizens as to whether this investigation implies that the school system turns away minority people who seek jobs. Like the search for scapegoats and villains to explain the low figures, the implication that we are concerned with bigotry is equally simplistic and false. The problem is far more complicated than that. It is time that Northerners ceased judging their actions with regard to minority people by standards developed in the South where exclusion based expressly and overtly on race has been the rule. The courts have long made it clear that practices which have the effect of excluding groups, even if that is not their intent, fall within the purview of the law. Thus Northerners have a far more difficult job than Southern whites.

New York industry, public and private, must examine its practices with fresh and self-critical vision to see if it fails to take account of the many different groups and conditions to be found in a pluralistic society. Minority people can hardly be expected to believe the majority when it admonishes them to leave the streets and work within the system when they find the system closed or open to only a small number.

I do not know what these hearings will uncover. But I do know that we seek the common end of educating children while being fair to those who teach and supervise them. I do know that a school system based on merit and fairness will not tolerate any but the highest and most objective standards for selecting personnel. I do know that there is every reason to believe that minority group parents, whose children fare so poorly in the public schools, will be the least likely to judge teachers by their color or other irrelevant factors. No teacher can depend upon his racial or ethnic background to prove his fitness. That, too, is against the law. But Blacks and Puerto Ricans, like the large ethnic groups that preceded them as migrants to this city deserve a place in the school system to which they commit so many of their children.

I would like at this time to ask the commissioners who are sitting here to identify themselves. Would you start at my left.

COMMR. COLGATE: Gilbert Colgate.

COMMR. MANGINO: Frank P. Mangino.
COMMR. FRENCH: Eleanor Clark French.
COMMR. GLOVER: Archibald Glover.
COMMR. HALPERN: Harry Halpern.
COMMR. BECKER: Jerome Becker.
COMMR. GROSS: Murray Gross.
MR. DAVID: Preston David, executive director.
THE CHAIRMAN: I would like to formally open these hearings and introduce special counsel, Mr. Paul Tractenberg, a former counsel for the Board of Education and now a professor at Rutgers Law School.

Without further ado I would like to call the first witness, President Murry Bergtraum, President of the Board of Education.

MR. BERGTRAUM: Mrs. Norton, Commissioners, first I must read into the record a letter from the Corporation Counsel to the Chairman of the Commission on Human Rights.

"Dear Mrs. Norton: It has been brought to my attention that the President of the Board of Education, the Chancellor of the Board of Education and other personnel of the Board of Education and members of the Board of Examiners have been requested by you to appear at hearings to be conducted by your Commission during the week of January 25th, 1971. According to a letter from you to Mr. Murry Bergtraum, President of the Board of Education, dated January 6, 1971, these hearings will be conducted 'on the employment and promotion practices in the New York City public school system.'

"Your letter further states, 'The hearings will examine current methods and alternate models of recruitment, selection, appointment and promotion of teachers and supervisors to assess the effectiveness and fairness of these methods. In particular, the hearings will focus on the effectiveness of the employment and promotion processes on minority group professionals. They are designed to deal factually and effectively with these complex and controversial methods.'

"As I have indicated to you and to Mr. Paul Tractenberg who I understand will conduct the major portion of the questioning, the aforementioned persons are most anxious to cooperate fully with your inquiry. I have expressed to you and to Mr. Tractenberg, however, the concern of this office with the possibility that these individuals will be asked questions relating to matters which are before the United States District Court in the case of Chance against the Board of Examiners.

"As you know, the Chance case raises questions concerning the testing procedures of the Board of Examiners for supervisory personnel. In accordance with Canon 20 of the Canons of Professional Ethics, I have advised President Bergtraum, Chancellor Scribner and other personnel of the Board of Education and Examiners who will be testifying in their official capacities, that they should respectfully decline to answer questions concerning the testing procedures of the Board of Examiners insofar as those questions relate to supervisory personnel and to alleged acts or practices of discrimination or alleged failure on the part of the

Board of Examiners to fulfill their statutorily mandated duty to test for merit and fitness.

"This office has no objection to personnel of the Board of Education and Examiners testifying with regard to all other aspects of recruitment and testing practices of the Boards of Education and Examiners.

"I would very much appreciate your announcing at the start of the hearing that the pendency of the Chance case might impose certain inhibitions on Boards of Education and Examiners personnel with regard to the testing practices of the Board of Examiners for supervisory personnel.

"I am certain you share my desire that the integrity of the judicial proceedings involved in the Chance case should not be impaired by the important hearings which your Commission will be conducting. Sincerely, Norman Redlich, First Assistant Corporation Counsel."

THE CHAIRMAN: Let me say for the record that this Commission has all along been aware that the Board of Education, along with the Board of Examiners and their personnel have been sued in a suit testing the Board of Examiners' system of tests. I have spoken at the highest level with the Corporation Counsel's Office. It is my view that the strictures that might be implied from the suit are narrow, and that we, of course, would not wish in any way to intrude upon a matter now in litigation.

The matter before us is the broad policy question, not the narrow legal question, surrounding the employment of minority people in the system.

I am pleased to acknowledge the letter and to acknowledge that these hearings can proceed without intruding upon those issues raised in the letter of the Corporation Counsel.

I am also pleased to welcome counsel from the Corporation Counsel's Office. I shall ask him to identify himself for the record.

I have instructed counsel here, Mr. Tractenberg, that questions directly related to the suit are to be excluded from the questioning before us and he has informed me that that will not in any way hinder our efforts to get facts here.

Would counsel from the Corporation Counsel's Office identify himself for the record, please.

MR. BERNIKOW: My name is Leonard Bernikow, Assistant Corporation Counsel.

THE CHAIRMAN: Let me make my final statement, because we are aware of this problem. Questions have been prepared with the problem in mind and we do not anticipate that there will be questions asked to which counsel will have to take exception although, of course, we understand that that is his individual duty.

We want to say, however, for the record, that we have prepared questions with this problem in mind and do not anticipate it will be necessary for witnesses to decline to answer questions.

MR. BERGTRAUM: I'll come to the main and important subject. I'm a layman, and this is the first time in my life I've ever testified, although I have testified hundreds of times, with counsel at my side. I can't help but say that I wish that there were no Chance case, because it does have some sort of psychological effect as I talk about the subject but I hope to be able to surmount the, as you say, narrow legal problems involved.

First, I want to say that in the letter from the Commissioner, there was a question as to what the Board of Education considers its responsibilities.

I do want to say, as a context for everything that follows, that I consider it the highest responsibility of the Board of Education to educate the children entrusted to its care. And secondary to that must be all other obligations, so that, theoretically, and this is not the existing case but I do want to make a theoretical point, theoretically, if the responsibility to educate children were in conflict with any other legal responsibility, I, as President of the Board of Education, would have to consider the proper education of children as the primary responsibility and let the courts decide as to the clash of legal objectives which might occur.

Now, in that context, what I'm saying is that the children are entitled to the best education and supervision which can be obtained, and that that is our primary responsibility, and that sometimes in some of these discussions that does tend to get a bit obscured.

However, when this Board of Education took office, and before the Commission on Human Rights was looking at it, one of our first concerns and one of our first questions was the question so ably put by the Chairman as to the reason for the rather small number of minority personnel employed in the New York City School System. As we look at the problem, however, we realize that the question was possibly not so much in the terms of minority or nonminority.

Strangely enough, the question that comes out of this question is a much more important and valid one. The question is, are we recruiting into teaching and supervisory positions the types of personnel best suited to teach the urban child and that is not even a question of minority or nonminority. It is a question of the training and focus and requirements. The total question of the fact that we have a new problem in education, new problems, and are the people we are recruiting best trained and properly trained to meet that problem. And we soon came to the conclusion that if we concentrated on that problem, the question of minority employment would, in our opinion, soon solve itself because the type of recruitment, and the type of training of personnel, which would concentrate on reaching the urban child would almost automatically eliminate those systematic practices which in a sense eliminated from consideration, not by any deliberate act but by the nature of the process, many people, minority and nonminority, who would make an impact, a better impact on the vast problem which we face. That is the philosophy with which we have approached the total process of training and recruitment.

For example, when we started to discuss the requirements, and this is not a subject of the lawsuit, the requirements in the examination for promotion to elementary principal, we found that the historic type of requirements imposed, in our opinion, would exclude fairly large numbers of people in the system and outside who, while they might not have the specific accumulation of credits or time required, might make most effective elementary school principals.

And the drastically changing, and I resent the press reports which talked about lowering--we weren't lowering, we were expanding and maybe upgrading--requirements to make it possible for people who didn't have their time served or their credit served, but who might possibly make a contribution and a significant contribution would be admitted.

So that we changed those requirements, and we vastly increased the possibility for members of the staff and people outside to participate in that examination, and that was a positive step.

In the same context, we have been looking at every one of our recruiting practices and our training practices, and our requirement practices, so that the system opens up--again, I say not necessarily just for a minority--but opens up to people who may have gained experience which would be valuable to the school system but in contexts which were not within the traditional, formal context of exam-taking requirements.

We think that dramatic changes will result from this change alone. I must comment on the Commission's comparison between the rapidity of change in private industry and the slow pace in not only the Board of Education, but many other public agencies, and point out that I happen to have a dual role. I earn my living really in private industry and I'm also President of the Board of Education, and if I, in private industry, want to cooperate with the Commission on Human Rights, it's rather a simple problem. All I have to do is call in the Department of Personnel, my personnel manager who is responsible to me, and go over with him the tests he is using, if he does use tests in his recruiting practices, and simply by direction say tomorrow morning, "You stop doing this." And it is done. And six months later you can have substantial progress.

In the Board of Education or in any other city agency, I face --I'm not saying properly, but I just want to say what I face--I face, number one, the State Constitutional provision on merit and fitness, and then I face the Civil Service Law, and then I face the City Charter and the legislative acts, so that between my setting of a policy and its execution, there may be a long road, and I might need to change three or four or seven or ten legislative acts and rules and regulations and so on, so that I'm the same person in two contexts.

In one, I can move quickly and in the other one, I am constrained to move quite slowly.

The question of recruitment of teachers is most interesting. The Decentralization Law recognized the problem, but recognized it in a way which I think is possibly the worst way although it was a legislative compromise and I understand what the legislators were doing. What it says is, in certain districts, the 40 per cent with the lowest reading scores, you can go out and recruit by the National Teacher Exam as opposed to all other districts which have to use the existing system. The point, obviously, is that if the National Teacher Exam is valid and some other system is invalid, in one district, it's invalid in all districts, and that failure in reading should not become the goal you have to seek in order to use a different system of recruiting.

I understand the Legislature, I'm not criticizing what happened. This was a compromise of one caucus with another.

Fortunately, we have been participating in conferences on the recruiting of teachers where the State Education Department is talking about setting up a new method of certification, and let me warn you that certification alone is inadequate to recruit teachers for New York City because that is also just the accumulation of courses.

But, there is a concept now of having statewide certification which might include some form of statewide examination equivalent to the one given for the Bar, not as difficult, I hope, or for other professions; and once a person was certified to teach any place in the state, that person would be available to teach any place in this state, including New York City, and I am heartily for that.

I do question, however, why it should take three years. We were told it will take three years to make this change in the state education requirements. I question three years. If it is valid, it should be able to be done at once and immediately; and I think that all of this is a state problem and that this Commission could do a service by questioning this since it will drastically affect New York City which, after all, educates half the children in the state.

I also want to point out that this Board and the Chancellor, and he will speak for himself, feel that the real examination process for teachers or for supervisors should be on the job, and that accountability for performance during a probationary period is more important to insure quality of performance than any other method, so that examination processes which go into elaborate systems of trying to forecast performance on the job, might very well not direct themselves to these subjects and that the process of being able to direct to another profession persons who do not perform on the job, should be looked at because in New York today, and this is the whole state, it is extremely difficult to use the probationary period as a performance period.

I am deliberately staying away from generalities, trying to direct my talk to specific problems. You might ask what has all this got to do with the basic question which has to do with increasing the employment of minorities in the New York system.

I want to avert to the way I opened this. I said theoretically if increasing that employment didn't give kids a better education, I would not be interested. But what I am saying to you is that it's my opinion that the concentration and that the emphasis on formalistic training, formalistic requirements, long periods of service which are no good for minorities or for nonminorities are the basic reason why in New York City we have these low ratios, and I think that if we set up a system which recruited and brought in people who are tested and then tested by their performance, that this in itself would increase the proportion of minorities because I don't believe, and nobody could convince me that any group in this city has a larger proportion of people who are qualified to teach than any other group and that if there is a disproportion, a large part of that disproportion has to be created by the operation of some form of systems or examinations which do not produce not only the results of increasing minority employment, but do not produce the results of recruiting into the system and keeping in the system people who can meet the problem of today which is different from the problem of ten years ago, and that is the problem of the urban child.

Incidentally, I also urge that attention be paid to the kind of curricula which exist in the schools of education in this city and throughout the country, because my feeling is that many minority college students seeing the formalistic system of those courses are turned off and do not go into teaching, because of the fact that they feel immediately that the total curricular structure in education doesn't relate to what they are and to where they came from and to what they want to do.

I think with that, I welcome questions.

THE CHAIRMAN: Before Mr. Tractenberg begins to ask you questions, I think you may have been relating your concern with your over-all responsibilities which obviously are paramount in educating children.

I think you may have left an impression that is not what you mean to leave. When you say that if recruiting more minority people didn't enhance the goal of an educational system, you are not concerned with it. I'm sure you will agree that integrating the schools in the South not only may not have helped in educating children, but may have set back that process somewhat in the South. That section of the country has been forced to go through a tumultuous change because we believe that it is important, first of all, for a democracy to be fair to people, and I'm wondering if you want to go on record in the North as saying we are not as concerned with fairness as with whatever the specific mandate may be under the law.

MR. BERGTRAUM: Commissioner, the difficulty with making philosophic points is just what you say. You are absolutely correct.

If you listen to the rest of the development, what I am saying is, I think that proper procedures will automatically produce the result. I just said philosophically--I'm trying to make a very important point, which is that there is no downgrading involved in recruiting larger numbers of minorities, and I am sure you will agree. There are people in this city who seem to think that there is some sort of overcompensation which has to result in order to increase the number of minorities. The point I am making is that I think that the reason minority ratios are so low in New York City has to do with our emphasis on the wrong standards, and that that emphasis on the wrong standards produces difficulties with all children in New York City.

That is all I am trying to say.

THE CHAIRMAN: Mr. Tractenberg.

MR. TRACTENBERG: Mr. Bergtraum, I want to focus on what I think is at the core of your remarks for a minute. You have suggested that if the best people to teach urban children are, in fact, recruited, that the present problem of a small percentage of minority people on supervisory staffs would cure itself.

Does that suggest that minority teachers have some advantage in their capacity to reach urban children?

MR. BERGTRAUM: No, I wouldn't even make that judgment. That is a statement again, which I think tends to be misleading. I don't know whether the question specifically in any classroom is the question of whether the teacher is a minority teacher or not. I'm simply saying that pursuing that road leads us into discussions which promote division in the city and are unnecessary.

I am saying I think, with the traditions of minority groups and majority groups, that if the recruiting of teachers and supervisors were based on their ability to reach children and the testing process was during the probationary period and there was less emphasis on formal credits and more on performance, that minorities or majorities would automatically fall into place.

I don't think there is any group in New York City which has a monopoly on its ability to teach and that is what is suggested by the figures in the Board of Education today.

But, I would not accept the other thesis because I don't know. There has been no research on it, and I don't think it's important. I think it's almost an argument which tends to obscure the real facts.

The facts are that it is the standard, the formalistic emphasis on certain kind of training which has kept the minorities in this city--and it is not necessary to get into these questions about lowering standards, raising standards, whether there shall be an image. I would say it's darn good for children to see Blacks or Puerto Ricans not only in teaching positions but in positions throughout the city because it says to them that this is something they can aspire to. We, for example, have brought in professionals from Puerto Rico to travel around the schools so the Puerto Rican children can understand that Puerto Ricans are in the highest level of government, not in New York City, as they should be, but in Puerto Rico. That, yes, but whether that directly relates to teaching is another question, and it's not important.

MR. TRACTENBERG: Mr. Bergtraum, you stated that the Board of Education, at its own instance some time ago, began to evaluate the requirements for promotion to elementary school principal.

MR. BERGTRAUM: And other jobs.

MR. TRACTENBERG: That is one, I gather, of some 1,200 licenses that exist. Is there any kind of systematic study in existence to evaluate the requirements for all those licenses?

MR. BERGTRAUM: Systematic in this form:

Every time an examination is ordered we review the requirements. When there is no examination--that is the system.

In other words, as each exam is ordered, we are looking at the requirements for that examination.

MR. TRACTENBERG: That may take some time then to work through 1,200 licenses.

MR. BERGTRAUM: Yes, but the other thing is slightly academic. If the examination isn't ordered the requirements are meaningless. The systematic review isn't the point.

MR. TRACTENBERG: Does that suggest as to every examination given since this Board of Education has been in office there have been substantial revisions made in the job qualifications?

MR. BERGTRAUM: If those revisions were called for. There are many requirements which are fine, existing requirements.

I'll give you another example. We dramatically revised the requirements for examiner. The Board of Examiners has assistant examiners and senior examiners and so on, and that is Civil Service, rather than a Board of Education position, and when we looked at the requirements for those positions, we found that they were completely inbred.

If you weren't an educator you couldn't possibly compete and we immediately opened that up so that people from all over the nation in personnel positions could compete in that examination.

That is another example that comes immediately to mind.

MR. TRACTENBERG: One can then at least assume that every examination that's been given since this Board of Education has been in office has been reviewed to determine whether the job qualifications are pertinent to educating urban children.

MR. BERGTRAUM: I would assume most of them have. You and I both know better than ever to say about the Board of Education, to make a positive statement that everything has been done because it's like every other bureaucracy; and you are aware of the fact that many things have happened that certainly, I, as President, would not have been aware of.

MR. TRACTENBERG: At least the policy of the Board of Education is that it should be reviewed for every examination.

MR. BERGTRAUM: That's right.

MR. TRACTENBERG: When we talk about qualifications, is that the same thing as job analyses, on the basis of which the Board of Examiners constructs exams?

MR. BERGTRAUM: I'm not familiar enough to be able to answer that. I just can't get into what you're asking me because of the restriction.

MR. TRACTENBERG: You can talk about it in the teacher context, which isn't restricted.

MR. BERGTRAUM: It wouldn't be pointed in the teacher context because the requirements for teachers are not elaborate. It's a dual question, one of which goes into the Chance case.

MR. TRACTENBERG: All I am really asking is whether the re-evaluation that the Board of Education has directed as a matter of policy, in fact, works its way through to the requirements on the basis of which the Board of Examiners construct their examinations for teachers, not for supervisors.

MR. BERGTRAUM: I must decline to answer. I would hope so.

MR. TRACTENBERG: Mr. Bergtraum, you talked about the special 40 per cent recruiting provision that is included in the Decentralization Law and you pointed out a certain inconsistency that you find.

Which way do you personally come down on it? It seems to me there are two possible readings. Either it's a reflection of the failure of the present system of selection, or it may suggest something else.

MR. BERGTRAUM: My position on this is very clear. I favor a system of statewide certification which has in it some form of exam process. I don't understand the question.

MR. TRACTENBERG: Does that mean a written examination?

MR. BERGTRAUM: Yes, some form of written examination. But what I'm talking about is administered by the State Education Department in this context.

MR. TRACTENBERG: Assuming that the State, in fact, revises its certification procedures, you would really favor no additional New York City apparatus designed to impose additional requirements.

MR. BERGTRAUM: For teachers I would favor no additional apparatus. I don't see any reason for New York City--once the State's standards are no longer today's certification standards --for getting into the act and just complicating the process.

MR. TRACTENBERG: You talked about probation as being an integral part of the selection process and the use to which the probationary period should be put in evaluating on the job performance. Yet, if I heard you right, you said the probationary period cannot now be used for that purpose.

I wonder if you could amplify. I think that's an important point.

MR. BERGTRAUM: I think that there are too many restrictions, both by the Commissioner and by union contract and by statute, on probationers.

In other words, while I fully believe in civil rights and due process and everything else for a teacher who has reached tenure, I think that the probationary period must be considered part of the examination process, always should be part of the examination process, and that in that context, even though injustice might result, that a person should be able to be, in a sense, passed or failed as if they passed or failed the examination or certification based on their superior's assessment of their performance with some minor safeguards but no elaborate process where it becomes an adversary proceeding between attorneys and so on as if they were tenured.

If there is a distinction between tenure and nontenure, that's where it should be. That's where we should get rid of people who can't teach and not by constructing examinations which never really test the ability to teach anyway, which is only demonstrated in a classroom situation.

MR. TRACTENBERG: That, I think we agree, involves a rather dramatic change, not only in State law but also in the Board of Education's own regulations for the probationary period.

MR. BERGTRAUM: I don't think the change is that dramatic. I don't think there is that much in the law. I don't think the State's statutes do this. I think it's an overlay of some Commissioner's rulings. Some are in the other direction. For example, the Commissioner has ruled that provision for hearings cannot be bargained in the collective bargaining agreement although some school boards have hearings for probationers on termination.

I think that could be worked out rather quickly, if there was an agreement on the philosophy, and would not necessarily require revision in the State law.

I think it can be done below that level.

MR. TRACTENBERG: One final question.

I think the answer is perhaps almost implied from things you have said.

In your judgment, has the division of responsibility in the selection area among the Board of Education, the Chancellor and his staff, the Board of Examiners, and community boards and their superintendents affected the implementation of your policies or contributed to the difficulty of screening into the system people who have a real capacity to teach urban school subjects and urban children?

MR. BERGTRAUM: Let me answer you positively.

I would favor a system where there was a certifying authority and an appointing authority and I don't think that there should be layers in between. What I am saying then, is, if appointments are going to be at the local level, there should be a certifying authority and it doesn't matter whether in one case it's the Board of Examiners or State Education Department, and so on, and in the other case, the community superintendent, the local school board and all the intervention of intervening layers is detrimental, counterproductive, has no purpose except to perpetuate bureaucracy and I am also opposed to that.

I also want to enter into the record something else which has to do with the minority problem, just for the theory.

The appointing authority is not the community superintendent. Many people misunderstand that. He needs the consent of his local board, community board, but nobody can ever be appointed unless he says so. The community board can't make the appointment.

What I am saying is, at one place a certifying authority, the other place a community superintendent backed by his board and no intervening layers, no necessity for them whatsoever.

MR. TRACTENBERG: If I understand this comment, this would change the current system of central assignment of teachers?

MR. BERGTRAUM: I see no reason for not changing that.

MR. TRACTENBERG: I have no other questions.

COMMR. COLGATE: I have so many questions to ask I don't know where to begin, so I'm not going to start today. I will hope that you might consider it possible to be available to us after we have learned a great deal which we are going to learn in these hearings and then we will be able to ask these questions.

MR. BERGTRAUM: The Board of Education, the President, Chancellor, and the staff are completely and fully available on this subject. We welcome your interest and your concern. We want to help. We think that this is a question of crucial importance. We hope that large steps will be taken towards a solution this year. We think it should not be delayed and we would be delighted to work with you and I want to thank you for having me here.

COMMR. HALPERN: The next person to testify is Miss Gertrude Unser, Chairman of the Board of Examiners.

MISS UNSER: These hearings are being held at a time when there is a dramatic change in process for a number of reasons, which I think may have been touched upon. One is that increasing numbers of teachers and supervisors are in current examinations, most especially in the current elementary school principal examination in which an eligible list is expected shortly.

Because of the revised requirements governing this examination, because of the numbers of persons who have participated in seminars, we anticipate that the number of minority group principals licensed as a result of this exam will be infinitely greater than has ever happened before.

Also, it is well known that because of increased pension legislation, very large numbers of supervisors--some have estimated as many as 50 per cent of the current staff in the next four years--will be leaving the service, a great many this September. This again will open up opportunities for the appointment of minority group members in numbers hitherto unknown.

I am glad to be able to give this Commission and the public some information about an institution about which I think there has been much misinformation, probably more misinformation than about almost any other public agency.

I was asked to consider the statutory background and the relationships between the Board of Examiners and other aspects of the school system. The Board of Examiners is a statutory body. It is established in state law. It has the duty to hold examinations whenever necessary, to examine all applicants who are required to be licensed and to prepare all necessary eligible lists.

The Board of Examiners itself is a reform institution. It was a direct outgrowth of the passage of the Pendleton Act which created Civil Service reform.

Following the passage of that Act, the New York State Constitution was amended to provide that appointments and promotions in the State shall be made according to merit and fitness, to be ascertained as far as practicable by examination, which as far as practicable shall be competitive.

When the Board of Examiners was established, the practice of buying and selling jobs in the New York City school system was an open scandal; and some people, even influential newspapers, say nowadays things are different. You don't have to worry about scandals, corruption or padding the public payroll. That was long ago, but now human nature is different.

Can anyone seriously believe that influence, patronage, raiding the public treasury, the desire for power are any the less operative today than they were in that time? If you think that, just read the daily press. Huge salary increases have been given to appointed officials at a time when low-paid Civil Service employees were being fired in the name of economy.

A high city official was recently convicted of taking bribes. Even appointments to judgeships are openly discussed as patronage plums and only a week ago the New York Daily News carried a lead editorial revealing that a recently appointed city official had brought a large number of his political aides on to the city payroll.

The Board of Examiners has sometimes been referred to as autonomous, implying that it was answerable to no one. All of the decisions of the Board of Examiners are reviewable, both by the Commissioner of Education, by the courts and in recent years in certain specific instances by human rights commissions.

The Board of Examiners has independence only with respect to its legally mandated function of determining the content of examinations and of rating these examinations. In every other respect it is subject to the Board of Education. The Board of Education designates the kind and the degrees of licenses which are to be required. The Board of Education establishes the eligibility requirements for the licenses. The Board of Education formulates the duties for the positions which determine the content of the examinations. The Chancellor determines which examinations are to be called and when.

The function of the Board of Examiners then is to administer a system of professional personnel selection on the basis of merit and fitness alone. Every procedure professes to be in favor of merit. But when you get into definitions and explanations, you frequently find that the definitions used cover the same tired, old system of secret, subjective selection. The concept of merit which the Board of Examiners has attempted to carry out for all these years is far more comprehensive than that.

I think it is important that I explain to you briefly what we consider to be absolutely essential features of a merit system and to indicate, with one or two illustrations, how these features can and are perverted. If any one of these essential features is perverted, the entire merit system is perverted. It is possible to preserve the appearance of merit and destroy the essence of it.

The first essential that we consider necessary is absolute openness, open filing, open announcement. The qualifications required of persons who seek positions on the public payroll, the exact scope of the examination, the pass marks required must be clearly defined, must be openly advertised so that all may have an equal opportunity to apply.

Why do we think this is so essential? I think you can readily see that if qualifications are determined in camera without the open participation of interested professional groups, they can be hand tailored so that certain individuals or certain groups may be either favored or excluded.

Not too many years ago, within the memory of many persons still serving within the school system, you couldn't even apply for a high school principal's examination unless you had the approval of an associate superintendent, and just a few months ago, a high official in the Board of Education saw absolutely no reason why we felt that there had to be a minimum of at least a three-week period for filing and for advertising a high supervisory examination. He felt that could easily be done over a weekend. All you had to do, you knew whom you wanted, you called him up and you said, "Come on in, take the exam."

The second essential that we feel characterizes the true merit system is that all procedures be fully documented and reviewable. The Board of Examiners goes far beyond private industry, far beyond what is required by law of many other public agencies, including community school boards, in supplying to rejected applicants a detailed and documented statement of the reasons for their rejection. In every aspect of the examination process, be it written test, interview test, medical appraisal, or any other part, a person who is turned down is entitled to know exactly why he was found not qualified.

We make use of no confidential reports on people. If we receive an adverse report on a person's service, the contents of that are made known to the applicant. The applicant is given an opportunity to come in and state his side of the case. He is given time after that to submit any additional documents, anything he wishes to, to support his case.

I ask you to contrast this kind of openness and documentary reviewability procedures with a statement I read just a few days ago which had been passed out by a local school board member in which he suggested that parents groups and other community groups or individuals ought to have the right to submit confidential recommendations on the candidacy of individuals for the job of principal.

I ask you to contrast these procedures with the experience of 2,200 Black and Puerto Rican persons who applied for Fordham internships. Of these, 60 were selected and to this very day the other 2,140 minority group applicants do not know why they were rejected and others chosen instead.

A third essential is the right of appeal, the right to review by higher authority. Applicants who fail any part of the examination have the right to appeal to the Board of Examiners for review of their case. We process, on the average, 600 appeals each year. On an average, 15 to 20% are granted. Applicants who still feel aggrieved may appeal to the Commissioner of Education. They may appeal to the courts. Applicants have never hesitated to use these rights and the Board of Examiners considers them an integral part of the examination process. But, when selection is based on undefined, unpublicized, informal procedures, whether by a single community superintendent or a community school board, what rights do rejected applicants have? When a community school board recently appointed as a principal a teacher whose sister was a member of the school board, where did rejected applicants turn for redress?

Fourth essential: confidentiality. The examining process should be free from all undue pressure by the maintenance of absolute confidentiality not only with respect to the applicant, but with respect to the Examiners. We have developed procedures to insure the utmost confidentiality. I don't want to take too long to go into detail, because I think much of this is known. Written papers are rated without the applicant's identity being known. The same safeguards apply to appeals procedures. No one is permitted to participate to test an applicant if he has some contact, personal or professional, one way or the other.

No one knows in advance who is going to examine whom so there are no secret telephone calls, no secret blackballing of people. There is no dropping of a word in the ear for or against anyone.

The fifth essential is the professional development and administration of examinations. Examinations should be developed by experienced professionals who have been carefully briefed and carefully trained so as to obtain the utmost possible degree of objectivity and reliability in rating. Examination questions should be closely related to the duties of the job and not to some such thing as whether or not you support the UFT.

When the Fordham interns were selected, the ones I referred to previously, there was a committee of two people who in one single day interviewed 40 applicants.

Recently a community school board interviewed 38 applicants for junior high school principalship in one single evening. Maybe these people have superior powers of insight and intuition, but the Board of Examiners does not believe that professionals can be selected in quickie three or four minute interviews.

The sixth essential: the members of the Examining Board must themselves be selected solely on the basis of merit. They must have tenure and appropriate status if they are to be protected against undue influence and pressure.

How can this be perverted? If examiners are designated by politicians or any other official or if their term of office is dependent on their receptivity to pressure, there can be no true merit system. Similarly, provisional appointees who may be hand-picked for whatever reason, who have no tenure, are not in a position to withstand improper pressures. The independence of the Examining Board to establish the scopes of the examinations and the standards of selection must be protected by law.

The power to determine the scope goes to the very heart of the merit system. If anyone can coerce an examining board into omitting certain tests, into giving no test at all, into deciding that the sole selection criterion is to be a review of some credential submitted, then there is no true merit system.

Since these hearings deal with minority employment, I want to say just a word on that subject, and that is that the greatest single barrier to minority employment in the school system has been the lack of opportunity to qualify. Until very recently a very minute percentage of the Black population of the city was able to meet the degree requirement. As recently as 1967, Blacks constituted two per cent of the graduating class of the City University and of that two per cent, an even smaller percentage prepared for teaching.

The situation with regard to Puerto Ricans was even worse, but the point that I think we should take hope in is that this situation is changing very rapidly and very dramatically. As greater numbers of minority group people are admitted into the City University and receive degrees, they are going to fill ranges of teaching and supervisory staff and they are going to do it on their merit.

They don't have to have any lowering of standards and they don't have to have any elimination of examinations. To suggest that they do I think is an insult to their abilities.

So far, I have spoken about the legal safeguards which we believe are necessary if the awarding of jobs on the public payroll is not to deteriorate into a spoils system. But I don't want to leave the impression that the purpose and main functioning of the Board of Examiners is solely to prevent this sort of thing. It has another and a far more positive aspect and purpose.

It is a means of attracting superior people, people who owe their jobs to no one, and who reject the debasement of seeking preferment for personal, political, religious, racial or whatever reason you want to mention.

It is the best guarantee for fair treatment for all individuals and all minorities including those who have no special friends in high places.

The day is coming, in fact, I believe the day is here when Blacks and Puerto Ricans are entering the profession in such numbers that they are competing against each other for jobs, just as the 2,200 minority people competed for the Fordham internships, and the safeguards that I have stressed protect them and will continue to protect them as they have protected all other minorities in the past.

I would like to close by reading a few excerpts from an article written by a former superintendent of schools. The title, I believe, was "How Shall Teachers Be Chosen," and after an opening sentence in which he spoke about the attitude of the public towards teachers, he said, "The natural result of this generally accepted view was the appointing of teachers by citizen committees who were too often swayed by prejudice, favor, or political and religious considerations.

"We are slowly, but surely, realizing the necessity of another method of appointment and promotion that will relieve the teacher from humiliation and the schools from the incubus of political management.

"Two plans have been somewhat widely tried. Appointment

by a single expert, supervisor or superintendent, and appointment as the result of competitive examination. Appointment by a superintendent has been known to lead to the displacement of an honest and fearless official, and a substitution of one who is subservient to political control and is not likely to be extended.

"Appointment by competitive examination, on the other hand, while it may not attract the right persons to the right places, is slowly but surely gaining ground. It has raised the standard of scholarship and professional equipment among teachers.

"As a general rule, it attracts the best from among a mass of applicants for a given position, and it preserves the self-respect of the individual teacher because it frees him from the necessity of begging or cringing for a position and enables him to feel that he obtains an appointment or promotion solely upon his own merits.

"As communities awake to the necessity of delivering their schools from the abhorrent influences of political and ecclesiastic patronage, we may live to see the rapid spread of competitive examinations in appointing and promoting teachers."

This was written by former Superintendent William H. Maxwell, in 1904, and I submit to you that every word is as true and as applicable today as it was when it was written then.

THE CHAIRMAN: Miss Unser, is it your view that the standards for teachers as set by the Board of Examiners are the highest standards?

MISS UNSER: We don't set the standard for teachers. We set the standard for passing examinations.

THE CHAIRMAN: In relation to the examination system is what I have reference to.

MISS UNSER: The highest compared with what?

THE CHAIRMAN: Compared with other parts of the country.

MISS UNSER: I believe that our examinations have selected persons who have the basic information, basic knowledge and skills that one expects of beginning teachers.

THE CHAIRMAN: In light of the difficulty the school system is encountering with respect to the actual education of children as revealed by their test scores, is there any reason to believe that the standards, as set through the examination process, in fact produce the best teachers?

MISS UNSER: Well, you know, I do not accept the commonly stated view that the teachers have failed, that they are failures. I think the New York City school system over the years has produced excellent results, and, taking figures in any national competitions, that is still true. That many children in ghetto areas and many children in minority groups are not succeeding as well in school as they should is unfortunately true not only in New York City, but all over the country, and certainly it is not a function only of teaching personnel.

I believe there are many, many other factors such as socio-economic factors, motivation, facilities that are provided, family stability, pupil mobility. All of these things are very significant in a child's success in school, not only the quality of teacher or supervisor.

It isn't quite so simple as that, that you can say the child fails, therefore, off with the head of the teacher. I don't think anyone really thinks that.

THE CHAIRMAN: Let me ask you a question about the figures on college graduates you cited. Are you aware that every Northern city in the country until very recently was faced with that situation because there were very few minority group people coming through the typical Northern colleges? Some Northern people went South to school. Some boards of education established relationships with colleges that tended to have large numbers of minority group students. In any case, certainly in every other Northern city this problem of few college graduates has not resulted in few minority teachers. How, therefore, can we accept that the fact that the City College was graduating so few meant that there was no other way for our system to recruit minority teachers in light of what other cities appeared to have been doing, given the same situation we find here in New York with respect to the number of people graduating from college who are from minority groups.

MISS UNSER: Like all other large cities, most of our teacher applicants come from the local colleges, and this is true not only in New York but everywhere. Certain cities were located near large and reputable colleges that had predominantly Black students. They drew upon them. Certain cities, as I think you know, had segregated schools. They had Black principals in Black schools, White principals in White schools. When they were forced to desegregate they had a great many Black principals on hand whom they appointed to other schools that were now desegregated.

THE CHAIRMAN: I am talking about Northern cities, Miss Unser. The only figures we have relied upon are from Northern systems.

MISS UNSER: It was the Board of Examiners who first proposed that there be recruitment efforts made, and the Board of Examiners first went with a team down into Southern cities to try to recruit persons so that we have made great efforts in this way.

THE CHAIRMAN: Have you found teachers recruited from Southern schools and from other schools outside of the city are, in fact, able to go through the examination process with ease?

MISS UNSER: Those who meet the eligibility requirements set by the Board of Education have, I believe, in their performance, not differed materially from others.

THE CHAIRMAN: Are there significant numbers of minority teachers we have in the system, have any significant number of them come from an out-of-town recruiting process?

MISS UNSER: Yes. We have examined in Washington, we have examined in Nashville, we have examined in Puerto Rico. The number of applicants has not been as great as we would like to see it; I believe very likely possibly because of the eligibility requirements. They have, so far as we know, not differed materially in their results in the examination as compared with other groups.

THE CHAIRMAN: Mr. Tractenberg?

MR. TRACTENBERG: Miss Unser, let me just say at the outset, we will not be asking you very many questions about the validity of examinations and that's not to be regarded by you or anyone else as evidence that I accept at face value much of what appears in your statement, but rather that Dr. Greene, I gather, will be available for testimony tomorrow morning and I had intended to focus with him on the examination process.

I do have some questions which will touch on it, however. Miss Unser, do you agree that, although human nature may not be different now, that the supply of teachers may differ from time to time; that is, if you can't find enough people with teaching licenses is there really that much of a potential for patronage?

MISS UNSER: I think there always is. We are approaching, I think, a period of great oversupply of teaching candidates right now.

In fact, we are in it.

MR. TRACTENBERG: That's not true generally, is it?

MISS UNSER: I believe nationwide.

MR. TRACTENBERG: I mean all licenses.

MISS UNSER: There are some licenses in which there are shortages but appointments have been made much more slowly, eligible lists are piling up. Economic conditions have been such that persons are finding fewer opportunities in private industry and, I think, we are rapidly approaching the point where we are going to have far more persons applying for teaching jobs available.

Frankly, even if that were not so, if there were enough jobs to go around for everyone, the dangers I have pointed out, patronage, manipulation, exist all the time. I could give many illustrations. I'll mention just one. Not too long ago a superintendent of schools was at a convention. He met a young man in California; he was very much impressed with him. He was in data processing. He brought him back, wanted to give him a job, and wanted us to give him a rubber stamp approval. We gave the person a proper examination and it so happened that he was not successful and the superintendent was furious. In fact, he put him on the job in some way anyway, provisionally or what have you, and after a year he was so disenchanted with his performance that he fired him and said to us, "Gosh, I'm awfully glad you didn't give him a permanent license so he would have gotten tenure."

I don't know whether that answers your question.

MR. TRACTENBERG: Only partially. Let me ask a different aspect of it.

If patronage is so rampant, is there any reason to believe that, in fact, the Board of Examiners itself is free from patronage. As I'm sure you are aware, there have been many charges made that at least the overall system of selection and examination as it is presently constituted is not one that is free of patronage. Perhaps not exactly in the sense that you were discussing, but in other respects.

I will turn to that in a moment and try to get your reactions to assertions that have been made in that regard, but I do want to establish what I think is a fundamental question first, and that is, whether there is a written statement of the philosophy of the Board of Examiners which you hold up as evidence of the direction in which the Board is currently moving.

MISS UNSER: I don't know what you mean by a written statement of philosophy.

MR. TRACTENBERG: I have in front of me a copy of a statement of philosophy written by Dr. Vandenberg, who was the Chairman of the Examiners some years ago, 1934 I believe, in which he sets forth a rather careful statement of philosophy, as he calls it, establishing the mission of the Board of Examiners as he saw it.

If there is no updating of that, no current--

MISS UNSER: I think we are all basically in agreement with the things which I have said about what we consider to be the essential purpose of it and the essential features of the merit system.

MR. TRACTENBERG: Let me be more specific and address myself to Dr. Vandenberg's statement.

He said, for example, that the Board of Examiners endeavors to select from among its applicants those who appear to show the greatest promise of long and superior service to the public school children.

Is that still a fair statement of your own philosophy?

MISS UNSER: Yes, I think so.

MR. TRACTENBERG: Do you find that consistent with the emphasis you place on preventing patronage which certainly implies screening out incompetents, not screening in superior people?

MISS UNSER: I see no contradiction between eliminating opportunities for patronage and selecting the best persons from among those who apply. If you are implying there is some contradiction between these two statements, I don't see it.

MR. TRACTENBERG: I think there may be. One of your critics said that mediocrity objectively tested is no particular improvement over the spoils system. What I am really getting at is the basic philosophy which animates the Board of Examiners. Is it to identify and select superior people or simply to eliminate from the total group those who are incompetent?

MISS UNSER: I thought I had made it clear in my statement that we felt that our objective was to give a fair shake to everybody to select persons who have the knowledge and the ability that are necessary for performance on the job. I don't know the date of the Vandenberg quotation you have read, but it is possible that at a time when there were a thousand applicants for the job, that the Board of Examiners conceived of its duty to select the very, very topmost among the huge number who were applying.

For a great many years that has not been our practice. We

believe that every person who demonstrates that he is fit for a job should be licensed. In fact, in some situations in which there is just one job available, like a directorship, we say we are not interested in how many jobs are available.

If three people demonstrate that they are fit for the job, we will list three. If 30 demonstrate they are fit, we will list 30. Everyone who has proved his fitness to begin the duties of the position is entitled to be licensed.

MR. TRACTENBERG: I think the reason that this is a particularly important issue is, in part, based on what the President of the Board of Education has just said this morning; that in his view the requirements involved in the selection process have screened out the very kind of people that have been sought, that is, people who have a particular capacity to teach urban children in urban school settings.

MISS UNSER: Well, people make statements like this as if the inability to answer questions on the subject that you are supposed to teach ipso facto means that you are going to be a great human relations expert.

I have never found that to be true in my 35 years of experience in the school system.

MR. TRACTENBERG: Of course the converse doesn't follow; that is, simply because you can answer questions about your subject matter doesn't mean you can teach your subject matter.

MISS UNSER: No, it does not, but there is certain knowledge a teacher has to have if he is going to teach a subject. I think, too, if I may add here, the concept that a merit system or that our examinations are pencil and paper tests only is an incorrect one. We do test for some of the personal characteristics which we believe are essential to a teacher. In our interview tests we judge the verbal facility which is very closely related to a teacher's success.

We attempt to judge certain traits of personality. We attempt to appraise a person's skill in dealing with situations that may create intergroup tensions. So that it is not just a pencil and paper test.

MR. TRACTENBERG: I am sure you are aware, Miss Unser, that there are a variety of private coaching courses which prepare people for different examinations which you administer. Do you have any reaction to them in general? Do they serve a useful function?

MISS UNSER: There were, in the past, coaching courses. Some were good, some were bad. Some of the persons who took these coaching courses did learn something about teaching and supervision that they should have probably learned elsewhere and hadn't.

However, the Board of Examiners suggested originally that there ought to be professional seminars, not to teach people for examinations, because there is no special knowhow or expertise to take this kind of exam as compared to anything else. There is no way of doing it. We suggested that professional seminars be set up to increase the professional competence of minority group applicants so that they would be better prepared to be successful in examinations.

MR. TRACTENBERG: In view of your last comment, particularly, I would like to read to you and get your reaction to a page which is among the notes handed out in one of the coaching courses held quite recently, last fall.

MISS UNSER: What coaching course do you mean? One of the professional Board of--

MR. TRACTENBERG: Private coaching course. Some of the advice given includes the following:

Number one, if in doubt about any item include it, the marking key does not provide penalties for errors, no matter how foolish.

MISS UNSER: I would like to comment on them as you go along.

All I have to do is to read the statement we hand out with every one of our short answer tests and we say that.

MR. TRACTENBERG: I think this was directed to the essay test.

Is it true there is a marking key which ticks off items that have to be included but makes no reference to deduction of points for other items?

MISS UNSER: I think I ought to decline to answer that, since it refers to the rating of essay type questions in supervisory examinations and is related--

MR. TRACTENBERG: Are there any essay type questions on teacher examinations?

MISS UNSER: Very few. Practically none.

MR. TRACTENBERG: Could you address yourself to the very few. I'm sure you have rating keys on those.

MISS UNSER: I think they are all short answer type questions. You know, I might say there are only one or two coaching courses left, and we are not responsible for what some coaches may be saying in an effort to drum up business.

MR. TRACTENBERG: I wasn't suggesting that you were responsible for them. I think it is interesting how people who are within the system, licensed people, view the examination process. This is a coaching course advertised in the United Teacher, among about 20 others, in an issue fairly recently. Let me just go on, though.

Among the other hints given are, "Don't waste time erasing, simply cross out. Remember, time is of the essence."

Next, "Shall I use mnemonics?"

"Yes, these constitute an integral facet of your successful examination technique. The mnemonics we will provide, used in accordance with the techniques prescribed and the subject matter presented, will do much to insure your success in this examination."

And on the following page is a sample. The word "match" and it suggested every answer include the ingredients of "match," "M," methods and materials; "A," administration; "T," teachers;

"C," children, curriculum, and community; and "H," home.

Do you have a reaction, not in terms of the Board of Examiners being responsible in any direct way for this, but simply about this as a perception of how people see your exams and ways in which they can tutor people to pass them?

MISS UNSER: Well, time is of the essence, they say.

Our examinations naturally do have a certain time limit so that everybody can be examined under equal conditions. As far as mnemonics are concerned, I think they are pretty stupid. I don't think they do anybody any good, but people go around studying in any kind of way they feel like.

We can't stop them if they have faith in that sort of thing. I never took a coaching course in my life. I never failed an exam in my life. I didn't think it was necessary to go through that sort of thing, but if people make money out of it and other people think it will help them, we can't stop them. I don't think it reflects our philosophy at all.

MR. TRACTENBERG: Do you regard it as a wasteful by-product of the examination system?

MISS UNSER: I certainly do not. I think there are coaching courses all over for people who think they should have some help. We have always refused to use anyone who was engaged in coaching as an examination assistant. We have never supported--

MR. TRACTENBERG: Let me just stop you--

MISS UNSER: I don't think they are an integral part of the examination system. I don't think you need to take a coaching course to do well.

MR. TRACTENBERG: I think we will hear more testimony from future participants. I want to point out that your bylaws say anyone who has conducted a private coaching course in the past three years is excluded; but presumably if a person conducted one four years ago he would be eligible to be an assistant examiner; and, similarly, someone who is currently serving as an assistant examiner would be fully eligible under your own bylaws to be head of a private coaching course immediately after his connection with you is severed.

MISS UNSER: If he so desired, we couldn't stop him.

MR. TRACTENBERG: Isn't it true there have been a few instances in which you had to remove assistant examiners because it became known they were running coaching schools while serving in that capacity?

MISS UNSER: I know of no such instance.

MR. TRACTENBERG: I will come up with the names by tomorrow for Dr. Greene.

Let me touch briefly on one other aspect of the system which is involved in what we have been discussing.

Another part of Dr. Vandenberg's philosophy was that the Board of Examiners regards itself as a group of specialists. I think he went on and said it regards itself as a group of specialists constantly studying an extremely complex problem and keeping constantly in touch with the realities of the school system.

I want to get at this question by first asking what requirements in addition to passing a Civil Service examination members of the Board of Examiners have to meet.

MISS UNSER: They have to meet educational and supervisory requirements, similar to or the same as would entitle one to assume certain--

MR. TRACTENBERG: Does that involve expertise in test construction, psychometrics, and the like?

MISS UNSER: There were requirements in that, yes. The questions on the examination were very searching in that aspect.

MR. TRACTENBERG: You regard yourself, then, as a test expert?

MISS UNSER: I don't regard myself as a psychometric expert because I don't know what that really means, but I regard myself as having been qualified by probably the most difficult Civil Service examination ever given to serve on the Board of Examiners. Teaching, supervisory experience was required, a very searching examination.

MR. TRACTENBERG: Would you mind telling us for the record what the areas of specialty of the four members of the Board of Examiners are? What was their background as teachers and supervisors?

MISS UNSER: Mr. Denn was a teacher of English, chairman of English, junior high school principal and senior high school principal.

MR. TRACTENBERG: Could you speak up a little?

MISS UNSER: Mr. Denn was a teacher of English and chairman of English, a junior high school principal and senior high school principal--

MR. TRACTENBERG: I'm really interested in the area of subject matter expertise. Mr. Denn was then an expert in English.

MISS UNSER: He was an expert in junior high school and senior high school administration as well.

Dr. Rockowitz, I think, has the same qualifications except he hasn't served as a senior high school principal because he was appointed to the Board of Examiners before he was appointed to the other position.

Dr. Greene, chairman of English, chairman of academic subjects.

I think he also became an examiner before he became a high school principal.

My background is teacher and chairman of English.

MR. TRACTENBERG: So for the group heading this group of specialists, we have four people, each of whose background is in English.

MISS UNSER: It so happens at this time, yes. There had been others. We had an examiner who was an expert in psychology. We had others who had different backgrounds.

MR. TRACTENBERG: But at the moment at least, the Civil Service process, that has caused the constitution of the Board of Examiners as it is, has resulted in four people, all of whom have the same background area of English.

MISS UNSER: As teachers and supervisors, yes.

MR. TRACTENBERG: Does the specialization in other areas come from your permanent staff, that is, do you have a range of expertise available to you in terms of your permanent staff members?

MISS UNSER: We have a range of expertise available to us that is far greater than our permanent staff members. We have thousands of persons within and without the school system in state education departments, in universities, from other disciplines, from the social sciences, from psychologists, from industry, whom we call upon.

MR. TRACTENBERG: Let's just talk for a moment, if we can, about permanent staff. Let me ask a pointed question. What portion of your permanent staff consists of teachers and supervisors assigned to you?

MISS UNSER: The entire professional staff consists of persons assigned to us, because as long as I can remember, we have urged that there be regularly licensed positions. In 1961 the State Education Law was amended to provide for such positions but the Board of Education in its wisdom never saw fit to call for these examinations.

MR. TRACTENBERG: Does that mean that the permanent staff members assigned to you have not gone through any competitive examination process which demonstrates their qualifications to do the work they do as examiners?

MISS UNSER: That is right.

As a matter of fact, we have been urging for years that these examinations be held and they never were held. We feel that the persons we have do an extremely good job but we would like to see a permanently licensed staff with some permanence of their status.

MR. TRACTENBERG: Do these people also work teachers' and supervisors' hours?

MISS UNSER: No.

MR. TRACTENBERG: They don't have an extended summer vacation?

MISS UNSER: They don't work the same hours as teachers and supervisors. They are entitled to vacations, yes.

MR. TRACTENBERG: Doesn't that cause some problems with your administrative operation? I gather from your suggestion that they should be examined and licensed on the basis of their service with the Board of Examiners, that you have some preference to have a staff that doesn't have lengthy summer vacations, for example--

MISS UNSER: We have always believed that for any kind of permanent job there should be competitive examinations with regularly licensed personnel filling those positions and certainly it would have been highly inconsistent for us to have advocated anything different for our own staff, from what we advocate for all other positions.

It wasn't a question of vacation or anything like that.

MR. TRACTENBERG: If I understand you correctly then,

among your permanent full-time staff you have no test expert. You have only people whose competence is in teaching and supervision of teaching.

MISS UNSER: We have persons who are highly qualified in their fields. Many of them are supervisors who have had extensive training in measurement, educational measurement, test construction. We call upon the services of others who are highly qualified in these areas.

MR. TRACTENBERG: On the permanent staff there are no people who, by background, are especially trained to construct examinations.

Is that a fair statement?

MISS UNSER: No, I don't think it is. I think we have given them a great deal of training. I think many of them in the course of their professional experience have taken courses and have gained sufficient training. We have one person on our staff who is regularly used by the State Department of Education in construction of regents examinations. Others have served with national testing agencies, called in as experts in their fields. I do not think that is a fair statement.

MR. TRACTENBERG: But that is not a requirement of the position.

MISS UNSER: It is not.

MR. TRACTENBERG: You also have a substantial number of temporary assistants. I think your budget of something over three million dollars includes something approaching two million dollars for temporary assistants. Is there any examination or licensing process which determines their qualifications to fill these jobs as examination assistants.

MISS UNSER: There is no examination or licensing process for this temporary, occasional service.

MR. TRACTENBERG: How are they selected if there is no merit and fitness examination?

MISS UNSER: We select them from among thousands of persons available. We make a very careful investigation into their background. We examine recommendations; we solicit recommendations.

MR. TRACTENBERG: There aren't any secret calls at night involved in those recommendations, are there?

MISS UNSER: No, there are not.

MR. TRACTENBERG: Doesn't it strike you as somewhat inconsistent? I'm not attaching blame because you have told me it is the Board of Education which has failed to provide for examinations which you recommended, but doesn't it strike you as somewhat inconsistent to come here and argue for the continuation of a merit system and examination process for teachers and supervisors in 1,200 licenses throughout the system and then to administer that system by people who themselves have met no particular requirements and certainly have not taken examinations to demonstrate their capacity to work in the Board of Examiners constructing and grading exams?

MISS UNSER: We have spoken about the necessity for a

merit system for permanent public employment. We use the system in the calling upon experts for particular jobs which every other agency uses, trying to find the persons most highly qualified to do that kind of work. We use people--for example, if we are conducting an examination for social worker, we may call upon the heads of institutions, we may call upon supervisors in that field, persons who already, by examination, have demonstrated their expertise in this field.

Now, if you believe that the Board of Examiners should conduct examinations for all the thousands of persons whom it calls upon, sometimes a few times, sometimes more frequently to assist in the construction of some part of an examination, that I think is hardly consistent with persons who believe that you can appoint for any kind of job without any examination.

MR. TRACTENBERG: You have turned my question around without answering it.

I asked you whether you thought it was consistent to use as your only full-time staff in constructing examinations which are required of virtually all personnel in the system, people who themselves have taken no examination, nor passed any other specified set of requirements which demonstrate particular background or skills in test construction.

I'm not asking for fault. Do you think it is inconsistent? It seems to me a yes or no is all that is required.

MISS UNSER: I think I answered that question before, that for years we have said that we should like to have as our permanent assistants on the staff persons who were regularized, who had been examined for these positions.

MR. TRACTENBERG: The answer is yes, it is inconsistent?
MISS UNSER: No, it is not inconsistent on our part.
MR. TRACTENBERG: I didn't say on your part.
MISS UNSER: We have been refused the staff that we have asked for, and we have therefore used the best possible persons available within the school system.

Ever since 1961 the position of assistant examiner has been in the State Education Law but the Board has never moved to call for examination for these positions.

THE CHAIRMAN: I think counsel is suggesting that by virtue of the fact that you called for such examinations in your own shop you do find it inconsistent with the general rule, or else you wouldn't have found the necessity to call for examinations in your own shop.

MISS UNSER: We believe there should be such regular positions. Yes, I have said that.

MR. TRACTENBERG: I have many more questions, but I think we are running even later than one would expect of a hearing of this kind. I hope, if questions persist as Mr. Colgate suggested to Mr. Bergtraum, that Miss Unser or other members of the Board of Examiners would be willing to speak with us further about them.

THE CHAIRMAN: The Board of Examiners has not supplied the Commission with all of the material it asked to be supplied.

We understand the reason for that is staff difficulty in compiling these materials. We are therefore directing the Board of Examiners within the next two weeks to provide us with that material.

We do understand that you have such problems and therefore we will give you two weeks from today to provide us with that information.

MISS UNSER: I would ask that you be specific about what information it is that you have not received.

THE CHAIRMAN: Miss Unser, I think you are aware of what information you have provided from a list of ten items we have submitted. If you would like us to let you know precisely what information has not been received, we will be glad to provide you with a further list.

MISS UNSER: I would appreciate that, thank you.

COMMR. COLGATE: I do have one question, Miss Unser, and it is a very simple one, I guess.

From the President's testimony and your testimony, I'm quite confused as to who in the school system is supposed to go out and convince people that they should become teachers.

In other words, to recruit. Who goes out and recruits? Who goes out and says we want the best in our school system?

MISS UNSER: Until ten or 12 years ago, I think there was almost nothing done in the way of recruitment and it was a member of the Board of Examiners who said, "We ought not to just sit here and wait for people to come here. We ought to go out and try to get people from other places."

And, for a period of several years someone from the school system on an informal basis was assigned to us to assist in doing this.

Now, I don't know the precise date but some years ago, a more formal recruitment bureau with a director and a staff was set up by the Board of Education, and put under the jurisdiction of the Deputy Superintendent for Personnel, and we were told that we were not to concern ourselves with recruitment.

COMMR. COLGATE: The answer to the question then, is, there is a Deputy Superintendent of Personnel who supervises a recruiting bureau?

MISS UNSER: Right, and Director of Recruitment and a staff. Does that answer the question?

COMMR. COLGATE: That answers my question.

THE CHAIRMAN: You may be excused, Miss Unser.

We have a great many important witnesses this morning and later today, and we are running behind schedule.

For the benefit of the stenographer, in the name of humanity, I have to call a five minute break at this point to enable him to rest his fingers.

The next witness is Chancellor Harvey Scribner. I am going to call these hearings to order in five minutes.

Let me also announce there is a day care facility available around the corner to the left, 225 Broadway.

(Whereupon, a short recess was taken.)

THE CHAIRMAN: May I ask the Chancellor of the school system, Dr. Harvey Scribner to take his seat.

Let me announce again a child care facility is available around the corner to the left, 225 Broadway, 18th floor, room 27.

DR. SCRIBNER: I had a paragraph in my testimony which pointed to the problems involved in the court case. I will not bother to read it again, but I think it has been said several times.

My opening statement will be confined to general remarks concerning the current system of licensing professional personnel of the schools in New York City. In my remarks I will give my views as to the implications of the system relative to provision of optimum learning opportunities for all the young people of this city.

I will leave to others testimony as to the detailed workings of the system as well as data related to recruitment, selection, and promotion. The School Decentralization Law passed in 1969 by the New York State Legislature was, in my opinion, an historical act for the schools of New York City. Despite any flaws and inconsistencies which it may contain, the Act is the most encouraging legislative development in public education in New York City at this time.

By decentralizing management control of the elementary, intermediate, and junior high schools in this city the Act gave to parents new hope of gaining greater and more direct control over the schools which educate their children and for which they pay. There is no doubt in my mind that educational decisions which deal with the destiny of youth ought to be made with the participation of parents.

The process of decentralization is far from complete. The process has only begun. It will require some years to accomplish fully. It will be a painful process, marked by occasional battles and frustrations. One should not expect the carving up of long centralized power to be a serene act, but the significant fact is that the city has begun to move in the direction of high promise.

One of my top priorities as Chancellor is the fostering of decentralization. For this reason, I have exercised restraint in directly involving my office this school year in the resolution of local disputes which in my opinion ought to be resolved at the level of the community school board.

I have been reluctant to enter into such disputes for fear of harming the concepts of decentralization in the long run. Perhaps the most critical element in the process of enabling a youngster to learn is the quality of teaching available to him. Thus, the paramount responsibility of the community school boards of New York City is the same as that of all other school boards in this country, the selection of staff for the schools of their districts.

No greater single power is possessed by any school board, for the selection of staff is the one act which determines in the final analysis the character and the quality of the schools. This power to select staff dwarfs by comparison all other powers possessed by school boards.

It is a power and responsibility which school boards ought not to take lightly and an authority which ought not to be unnecessarily diluted by the policies of other public agencies.

If the power is taken lightly, the risk is ineffective, unresponsive, and mismanaged educational programs. If the authority is diluted, the board is constrained in the area of its foremost responsibility, and the mechanism by which the public may hold the board accountable for its acts is severely impaired. For if the board is not empowered to freely select the staff of the schools it manages, it can't logically be held accountable for the management of those same schools.

In this city the selection of professional school staff is still, in essence, a centralized process. Although the community school boards select teachers and supervisors for their schools, the list of candidates from which they make their selection is defined by the centralized licensing system.

They are limited to the selection of teachers from centrally promulgated lists of ranked candidates and to the selection of supervisors and principals from unranked lists.

In both cases the lists are comprised of candidates who have successfully met the academic and experience requirements stipulated centrally.

In both cases, the candidates have also successfully passed centrally created and centrally administered tests.

In short, the present system of licensing is a form of city certification by us laid on top of state certification.

In many respects it is far more intricate and much less flexible than state certification. This kind of licensing system is peculiar in this state to the schools of New York City and, to a lesser extent, Buffalo. Nationally, I would estimate that 99 per cent of all school boards rely on state certification and their own good judgment.

It is my personal hope that this philosophy will soon prevail in New York City for until the community school boards, those people closest to students and parents, are empowered to staff their schools on the basis of state certification and their own judgment, as to competence and professional potential, these boards will operate with severe and undue constraints. They will not be fully responsible for the total management of the schools under their jurisdiction and no mechanism for holding these boards fully accountable for the effectiveness of their schools can be devised.

Under the terms of the State Education Law, the Board of Examiners is empowered to examine all candidates for teaching and supervisory positions in the New York City schools. It is empowered to determine their merit and fitness, to develop the written and oral examinations which it administers, and to certify to the Chancellor those candidates who in its sole determination meet the requirements for local licensing.

Licenses are issued by the Chancellor to those individuals so certified.

Under the law, the Chancellor does not possess discretionary powers in the issue of licenses. He can't refuse to grant a license to an individual certified by the Board of Examiners and he can't issue a license to a person not certified by the Board of Examiners.

The Decentralization Law permits a community school board to select its top, and i repeat, its top professional leader, that is, the community superintendent, without regard to city eligibility lists. I want to repeat that sentence. I think it is important to get it into the record.

The Decentralization Law, the law under which we are acting right now, permits a community school board to select its very top professional leader, that is, the community superintendent, without regard to city eligibility lists.

In appointing its superintendent, the board is empowered to hire anyone possessing an appropriate state certificate. The city licensing system is thus bypassed. That is the very top position. The law also permits a community school board to bypass the city licensing system, in the selection of new teachers, for those schools whose reading scores fall within the lowest 40 per cent of the city's schools.

I want to get this point across. That person who is going to make the top decisions, who is going to be the educational leader, who is the top man working for the community board, can be selected on the basis of his having state certification and his acceptability to the local board of education. Then, in the wisdom of that same Legislature, they said that if your schools are badly off to the point that they fall in the lower 40 per cent bracket in reading, we will bypass the Board of Examiners again, and you can go out into the field and get people who have passed the National Teacher Examination.

I think that is an important point. I hope I have made it. Because the precise system of licensing severely limits the schools of this city in selecting professional staff, the system in its existing form, I believe, is self-defeating. For example, the present list of eligible candidates for appointment as high school principals is comprised of approximately 12 names. We have 12 names from whom we may select the next high school principal.

Without deprecating the professional ability of the candidates on this list, it is patently absurd to limit the search for high school principals for New York City to that list. It's a decimated list of a dozen candidates who qualified for that list on the basis of an examination given more than two and a half years ago. The kind of system which sets such limits does not serve the best interests of youth, I believe.

The present system, moreover, requires that when a new list of eligibles for high school principals is promulgated, it is for four years. If the list is issued sometime this year, all principals appointed from that time until some point in 1975 would be named from that list. That list would constitute the total pool of candidates for four years, which is to say, that all principalships would be filled from among only those individuals who happened to be in New York City in 1971, when the examination was administered, who happened to choose to take the examination, who also pass it and who then choose to wait up to four years for an appointment which conceivably might never come.

I would submit that in the search for a high school principal in, say, 1974, in the search for the top leader for perhaps a volatile high school, it is unrealistic to confine the search to a three-year old list of candidates, none of whom may have had actual experience as a high school principal.

I would also submit that in 99 per cent of the situations in the United States, you are not confined, restrained to this kind of a system.

I would also submit to you as a part of this record, we ought to take a look today at some of the problems we have, and ask ourselves if any of it, if any of it, just a bit of it, may be contributed by this particular situation.

My comments here today are not designed to criticize the intent or the professionalism of the Board of Examiners, nor are my remarks intended to reflect on the qualifications or competence of those individuals who have gained appointment to the New York City schools by virtue of the existing licensing system, or of those now on the list awaiting appointment. My comments are directed at a system of licensing which, however useful it has been in helping to eliminate a spoils system since creation of the Board of Examiners more than 70 years ago, is now antiquated, outmoded, and inconsistent with both contemporary educational requirements and the concept of decentralized schools.

The licensing system in question is in need of substantial and immediate reform. It is my personal hope that the State Legislature, which in its wisdom provided community school boards the vitally necessary flexibility to select their superintendents and which in its wisdom provides the boards similar flexibility to hire teachers for schools with the lowest reading scores would now extend the flexibility to include the full complement of professional staff in all the schools of New York City.

THE CHAIRMAN: Have any Commissioners a question before we turn this over to counsel?

COMMR. HALPERN: Dr. Scribner, do you advocate the abolition of the Board of Examiners?

DR. SCRIBNER: I don't think the Board of Examiners' function should be that of determining who is to be appointed as a teacher in New York City. I presume, I must answer your question, to abolish it in terms of its present functions, yes.

COMMR. HALPERN: The New York Times, on January 9th quoted Commissioner Nyquist as saying he goes along with the idea of Chancellor Scribner for the abolition of the New York City Board of Examiners. I just wanted to know whether perhaps the Times had misquoted you. The Times sometimes does misquote.

THE CHAIRMAN: Any other questions?

I apologize for asking a question which is off the subject of these hearings because there will be witnesses who will testify from the public and therefore the Chairman sets a bad example going off the subject matter, but out of consideration for a group of people from the public group, I have consented to ask you this question although it is outside the jurisdiction of these hearings and outside the jurisdiction of the Commission although we hope to have jurisdiction over this matter soon, because a bill is pending in the City Council.

With those apologies, I want to ask you if you might briefly answer this question.

I have been presented with some statements of a young man, two people, who allege that they were denied jobs in the city school system because it was alleged that they had homosexual tendencies.

Is it the policy of the school system to deny jobs on that basis and, if so, how do you discover whether or not the person does, in fact, have such tendencies?

DR. SCRIBNER: I think the recommendations to our departments about those who receive licenses have already been determined by the Board of Examiners and I couldn't speak for them.

THE CHAIRMAN: Your office has nothing to do with administering of such a rule, if there is such a rule?

DR. SCRIBNER: Commissioner Norton, I am not aware of any. There may be others along who can speak better to that item than I. I am not aware of it.

THE CHAIRMAN: Perhaps we might get that information somewhere else.

DR. SCRIBNER: Or I can search it for you.

THE CHAIRMAN: We will be in touch with your office after these hearings.

Mr. Tractenberg.

MR. TRACTENBERG: Chancellor Scribner, obviously what you have suggested involves legislative action, as you have indicated. Assuming such action is not forthcoming, to what extent do you think there is some room for reform within the current system? I have in mind a couple of possibilities which I will mention and I would be interested in your reaction to.

The first is the special provision you mentioned, the so-called 40 per cent provision, which permits schools or boards representing schools with low reading scores to go outside of the current selection and examination process.

I have seen quoted in newspaper accounts statistics that suggested that some 5,000 out of the 8,000 anticipated vacancies for next year might be filled through this 40 per cent provision.

Do you think that is a realistic figure? Do you think the provision itself is as meaningful as that figure would suggest?

DR. SCRIBNER: I would say that it is a high figure. The estimate that someone gave to me would be nearer 2,000, but again who knows who is going to leave, how many vacancies there will be and from which schools it will happen.

I can't answer any more specifically than that.

MR. TRACTENBERG: But aside from the numbers you obviously feel that the use of this provision will not adequately meet the needs of the community districts?

DR. SCRIBNER: No, that answers only a part of it.

Again even that is too restraining. I don't know why a suburban town, which has all the people who fled from the inner city, can operate a school system for their children, where they can go hire the person they want to teach in that school, and yet the city youngsters are denied from their boards of education to have that privilege.

There is something about this that doesn't square.

MR. TRACTENBERG: Has patronage or the spoils system been a problem in school systems you've been involved in?

DR. SCRIBNER: I've never been privileged to work in a community where I was able to practice nepotism or the kinds of things I believe are a part of the spoils system. I don't believe the public would permit it to happen. Once a month you stand before that public for accountability.

MR. TRACTENBERG: You have recently been quoted as deploring the major shortage of bilingual teachers. I gather if the account is correct you have either proposed or will propose special legislation which will carve that area out from the regular examination process.

Is that accurate?

Do you have any ideas or are there specific reasons why the current system isn't meeting this critical need?

DR. SCRIBNER: You are not accurate on the legislative aspect of it, but I'll be glad to answer the question why I haven't prepared the legislation. I believe--it's not my belief, it was brought to us at a public hearing--that one of the most serious problems in New York City today is the problem of non-English speaking youngsters. I feel that one should be able to put into that classroom, first of all, a bilingual person. If communication, rapport, and participation is a part of what we want youngsters to do in the learning process, then obviously first of all we need a teacher who can communicate with youngsters and, therefore, I think that is a high priority.

As for the legislation, as I believe the parent community should be involved in the employment of its personnel, in a strong advisory capacity in the operation of the school system, I also think it's their responsibility to get legislation if they believe in these causes.

MR. TRACTENBERG: I have just a couple of more questions and I'll shortcut them because we are running so late.

I would like your reaction to a couple of specific questions aimed at powers that you possess either independently, or with reference to the Board of Education under the State Education Laws or the Board of Education's own bylaws, and I would like some evaluation from you as to the extent to which this power really gives you any opportunity to reform the system and the extent to which it may have been used.

I have in mind such things as the following:

You have the express power under the State Education Law, the new Decentralization Act, to promulgate minimum education and experience requirements for all teacher and supervisory positions in the school system, so long as they are not below the state requirements.

Have you personally set new minimum requirements since

you've come into office and, if so, are they at or above the state standards?

DR. SCRIBNER: The promulgation of qualifications for a particular exam, the one that comes to my attention is the new high school examination which is coming right up. Beyond that, either the qualifications were promulgated before I got here or at a time when I was too new to understand what was going on.

Therefore, I've only participated in the high school exam that is coming up.

MR. TRACTENBERG: But you will have a personal input in terms of those qualifications?

DR. SCRIBNER: Yes.

I don't assume that to be power. I think my power in New York City is to attempt to get the public to question systems to see whether or not they are serving the youngster who is depending upon that system, or someone else who is a part of that system.

MR. TRACTENBERG: Clearly these suggestions go only to making some modification in the current system rather than replacing it with a new system which I understand you--

DR. SCRIBNER: Obviously, a power to determine the qualifications to secure a license. If you believe the licensing system itself is too restraining, it is not a power that I would accept as being a true bit of power that one could exercise. It's a small corner so far as I am concerned.

MR. TRACTENBERG: You could say the minimum standards are state standards and by doing that at least not impose any additional standards beyond the examination process.

DR. SCRIBNER: I think I am able to do that, yes.

MR. TRACTENBERG: Similarly, you have the power under the Decentralization Law, with the approval of the City Board, to create and abolish titles in all positions in the teaching and supervisory service. As has been pointed out there are something in excess of 1,200 licenses currently in existence.

Have you thought about or is there in the works any action on behalf of you or through your staff which would somewhat lower the number of licenses presently in existence?

I presume by doing that, it would lower the number of necessary examinations.

DR. SCRIBNER: It would seem to me we have far too many distinctions in terms of licenses, but beyond that point, I haven't anything specific.

THE CHAIRMAN: Counsel, just for the record, when you use the word "licenses," you are saying that within the New York City Public School System, that there are 1,200 different positions that one can get only through taking an examination?

What does 1,200 licenses mean?

MR. TRACTENBERG: As I understand it, there are 1,200 different positions, each of which is the subject of a separate license. Not each of them requires an examination, but the vast preponderance do.

DR. SCRIBNER: Mr. Counsel, I would suggest when Dr.

Lang is in, you might--I wouldn't want to overly generalize the situation. Those may be licenses secured through Civil Service and other arrangements. I am not sure where they all come from and I don't think you do, nor do I want to distort the record.

MR. TRACTENBERG: I have just two more comments along the same vein.

One change effected by the Decentralization Law relates to the nomination or approval of examination assistants.

The provision now provides that such examination assistants have to be nominated or approved either by the Chancellor or a community superintendent.

Is this a power that you have used thus far or is it a power you might use to influence the kind of examination assistants who are servicing the Board of Examiners?

DR. SCRIBNER: I think it's a power I have. It's not one I used. A list of names is submitted to me and I sign off on them, yes.

MR. TRACTENBERG: There is no actual check?

DR. SCRIBNER: No. It shows the faith I have in the person who submits the names.

MR. TRACTENBERG: Is he a member of your own staff?

DR. SCRIBNER: No, they come from the Board of Examiners, I believe.

MR. TRACTENBERG: Just one final question.

According to a rather old decision of the Commissioner of Education, the Superintendent of Schools, and I presume you now succeed to that authority, can require the Board of Examiners to submit reports, data, and other material to him for evaluation.

Is this again a power that you have exercised or would consider exercising in the future?

DR. SCRIBNER: Here again, I may have that power, and I am sure the Board of Examiners would respond if I asked them for this kind of data.

I have not exercised it at this point.

MR. TRACTENBERG: That is all I have.

THE CHAIRMAN: With respect to the powers, Dr. Scribner, that you may have, and apparently you haven't had the opportunity to exercise all of your mighty power, is it your intention to exercise more of that power with respect to the discretion which has been brought out?

The last three or four questions indicate where the Chancellor might move without other authority.

DR. SCRIBNER: To be perfectly frank, I am weighing my responsibility very seriously in the listing of the requirements for those who might be eligible for the high school principal exam. I think that answers your question. Otherwise, I have handled these automatically because of my newness to the position, but now comes one that I have a responsibility for which I shall take very seriously.

I like it much better than power, frankly.

MR. TRACTENBERG: I have just one further thing.

You or a designee of yours is actually a member of the Board of Examiners.

DR. SCRIBNER: Yes.

MR. TRACTENBERG: I assume you have not sat personally.

DR. SCRIBNER: I have not, but I am sure I will be invited and I plan to fulfill that role too.

THE CHAIRMAN: Thank you, Dr. Scribner. You may be excused.

We are running extraordinarily late and I am afraid we are going to have to go through lunch.

There are important witnesses who have come here, and for the benefit of the Commissioners you may wish to go and come, because I think I'll go through the lunch period. I will not keep witnesses waiting any longer.

The next witness is Dr. John Theobald, former Superintendent of Schools, now Executive Vice-President, New York Institute of Technology.

DR. THEOBALD: Madame Chairman, and members of the Commission, I should like first to enthusiastically echo the Chancellor's comments regarding the role of the parent and the local community in the affairs of schools. This is one of the big problems that we have had in New York because in a city of eight million people with a thousand schools and some 50,000 or 60,000 teachers, a superintendent who tried to see all his schools and who visited two schools a day, which wouldn't be a very thorough visit, would still take one and a half years to get around.

Quite obviously, the notion that a superintendent in a city of this size can be an operating administrator of the schools is nonsense. The schools must be operated primarily on a local basis, responsive to the needs of the local community, and meeting the ambitions of the parents as they support the schools.

This, of course, is a big change from what we had in my day. It is interesting to note that I did try twice to decentralize when I was Superintendent. Politically it couldn't be done at that time. I thank God it has been done now and I salute the Chancellor for the way in which he has handled himself to move so as to augment the roles of his local boards and his local superintendents.

The next thing that concerns me as I look at the problems, and believe me, you don't spend a lifetime in New York City and then just because you move out you stop worrying about it. As I watch, we have been through a period of ten years of getting rid of this board and that board and instead of getting better, we have gotten worse, and the basic reason, I think, is that no one power, no one board, no one authority in a system this vast can make the difference between good education and education that has become outmoded.

I should like, therefore, if I may, to take just a couple of minutes for some history. Our system was founded in 1898. Prior to that it was a group of local school districts. Dr. Unser didn't overemphasize one bit the highhanded crookedness that went on in appointment and promotion in those days. Desperately needed was some law and order in the whole business of teacher appointments and promotion.

The requirements to teach at that time were one year of teacher training school beyond high school. The curriculum, pretty much a classical curriculum. What do I mean by that? I mean that instead of the electives we have today and the subjects that have to do with today's life, they had Latin and Greek. The rest of the curriculum was substantially what we still have.

They talked a great deal, as we do, about the business of developing each individual to his maximum. But, it wasn't so. Basically, the system was a system that was predicated on the concept that a man could learn all there was to know in a lifetime and so every pupil got a dose of this, a dose of that, and a dose of the next thing in the hopes some of them would go on and learn all there was to know.

The net result, of course, most of you went through it, was a straight elimination procedure. You either ran the course at the same rate as the others, or you dropped out of the race.

If you failed, they made you run it over.

I submit you didn't run any better the next time than you did the first time because you hadn't gotten any more help. All that happened, basically, was you became convinced that you were "dumb" and therefore you lost your interest in schooling; and, fortunately, since it had no relationship to outside life, you went into business and did all right and quite possibly and probably became very successful.

Over the years there have been attempts to change. One of the earliest was in the first year or two of the system. I think you probably all know the name of Julia Richmond. One of the high schools bears her name.

She was a principal of that day, and she developed the unique notion of not having a fixed amount of weeks for the youngsters in her school. The youngsters who could move more rapidly she pushed through more hurriedly, and they got a longer summer vacation and they loved it. They didn't get bored with the rest. The youngsters who were slow got two or three weeks or whatever they needed extra, and, instead of failing, they made the grade for the next class.

Superintendent Maxwell tried very hard to get that accepted by the system but they would not take it. It died.

The next major change, the really major change, probably occurred back in 1935. At that time, working very closely with Teachers College--and there were some giants there at the time --there was an attempt to develop a curriculum, it was known as the Activity Program, a curriculum that gave a youngster a chance to follow that youngster's interest and to learn the necessary things in the process of pursuing that interest.

They did this in 70 schools. They took the teachers and the supervisors of those schools, and for two years they sent them through courses at the colleges and in our own system, in order to learn how to operate this way because it was a different way to run.

Then they had an impartial state inquiry and came up with a very healthy, favorable report, as a result of which the procedure was mandated upon the rest of the city with little or no preparation. It fell flat on its face. It resulted in a system that had no demand for performance; you were promoted on the basis of age; I. Q. became a kind of a tell all. If a youngster had a high I. Q., there was no use wasting your time on him.

We moved a youngster in one case from 72 to 132. This is from rather low grade moron to beginning to push the genius class. Don't tell me these things can't change, they can. The average teacher was not prepared to handle them. One of the finest experiments of the day.

I think there are lessons in this. I think as you look at the problems today, your chief problem is that we know that you can't learn everything you should know in a lifetime, or everything there is to know in the world. Therefore, I think we ought to do away with the concept of a lock step of everybody learning the same thing. We ought to stop thinking about anything as the one key to further education and then we ought to start thinking about the youngster's appetite being whetted in one direction or another and lead him down the safe path of saving that appetite, and in the process, demand performance.

This can be done but it needs a totally different operation in the classroom. It needs teachers skilled to whet the appetite and carry it on. Let me point out to you now that very, very few of our youngsters come to us in the first grade not wanting to come to school. They are eager. By the fifth grade, most of them don't want to stay any more.

I submit basically it is because they are not getting in school those things that they are interested in learning about. We ought to start them developing intellectual capacity, rather than mimicking factual data which they can pick up in any book at any time they need it, once they learn how to read and communicate properly.

I think we are talking about a different kind of a teacher world. This brings me to the whole problem of personnel. Right now we have moved teacher requirements up to masters degree, temporary certificate with a baccalaureate degree and some ten or 12 credits in teacher education. This is far beyond what we had when the system and the Board of Examiners started. We measure in our teacher examination pretty much the same things that youngsters supposedly learned at college.

I submit I would like to see somebody make a correlation study between our examination in New York City and college grades. Do adjustment for college rigors, and we can make those, and I think you will find the examination was not testing anything new. I submit to you if it is not, it is quite a barrier to some people coming to the city when they can go right outside the city, get just as fine a salary, potentially fewer problems in the public atmosphere at least, and do it on the basis of an interview.

I do not mean by that that I don't think there is a role for an examination. But I think this role comes in not as a written examination that repeats the college work, but rather as a determination as to whether or not the youngster, before he becomes a tenured teacher, has met the demand of classroom performance; and I think this is a combination of judgment of peers, judgment of supervisors, and somebody within the system, meaning a group, that has to give some supervision to see that it is done in proper and reasonable fashion.

The reason for that latter to me is very clear. Dr. Scribner says we ought to leave it entirely within the local district and if I were talking about local districts that are not part of a bigger situation, I would agree. I submit to you in our system, unless you give tenure within a city rather than a district, and the law now provides that, you would have no real tenure; and so there has to be some overview to see that adequate standards, minimum standards are met. I think there is a major job to be done here. It is not a light job but it is a different job than the job of written examinations for coming in.

I would go into the promotion procedure with much the same attitude. I believe the judgment of peers and the judgment of supervisors as to whether or not you have done a good job where you are, and whether or not in their judgment you have the skills to try a more advanced job, is about as accurate a measurement as you can get. It is done in your public colleges; it meets the Civil Service requirements if it is properly set up.

I would say yes, you may want to give examinations in administration or something else in addition to that, to augment it. But again, I think promotion should be based to a large extent on job performance measurement by peers and supervisors, plus whatever else the central authority feels is necessary for certification--and it would be a very parallel certification to the State rather than an eligible list in the sense that you have to take off in the traditional Civil Service fashion.

I think, to be perfectly honest with you, that unless we do some of these things, our whole school structure is going down the drain because I can't see a society continuing to support a school program that is not, in the eyes of the people, meeting the needs of the society for people who can carry it on prosperously and well.

This is a new concept in terms of objectives of education. It is no longer the kind of thing that could be saved with a classical education, but in the history of this system, we have had two significant changes.

One was the establishment of a Board of Examiners at the very beginning, and the other was the Activity Program. All of the others, and there were a number of others tried, were relatively minor and generally failed because of lack of orientation of teachers beforehand.

This brings me to my last point.

I don't believe there has been nearly adequate cooperation between the system and the colleges. This works both ways. The system, for the most part, has been negative on college students coming in for student teaching. When I say "negative," they have a system--they had in my day, I'm an oldtimer now, though I think they still have it--where it is the principal's judgment whether or not he wanted student teachers.

Colleges in general tried to put their youngsters into the "better schools," and the net result was, we didn't have anybody who knew how to work in a ghetto school.

One of the things that I did, I'm sorry to say it was dropped but it worked successfully, at the time I came to the city--I had been President at Queens and I worked out a program at Queens College where we took youngsters and they did their student teaching in the so-called difficult schools--was to assign special teachers whose only function was to work with those youngsters, help them learn how to handle the classes in those schools, and work with their faculty so that the faculty knew what the problems were that the youngster was having, and better than 85 per cent of those youngsters requested to remain in the so-called difficult schools when they got their degrees.

I say to you this can be done, it has to be taught. You can't assume that the traditional program of teacher education prepares a youngster for it. I would go a step much further than student teaching.

I would begin by taking a freshman in the teacher education program and assigning him at least half time as a teacher aide in a school. I would bring the classes away from the campus and down to a local spot where there was no wasted time in traveling in between places. Not in every school, but if you had it in one district you would save hours of travel time and you could very readily have a youngster work half a day, take courses half a day, and without any trouble, finish his full program in four years.

I know because I have worked it out in detail. Then I would move that youngster along to assisting supervisors and then move them to the beginning of teaching and, finally, the last year I would have them teaching full time and spending two or three hours in seminar discussion about their classroom experiences in the afternoon, after 3:00. I think in this case we could get youngsters who knew the problems of the schools, who were able to relate the philosophy of operation that they learned in college to the problems of the day.

I'm reminded of a very humorous and yet sad story about the difference between what you get in a college classroom and what you get on the firing line.

This is the story of a man whose name I will not mention because he is very well known. It is a true story. He studied under Dr. John Dewey and he became an education reporter and finally he and his wife were able to scrape together enough money to buy a new home. They weren't able to furnish it for two years but finally they got to that point and he got ready to come home the night the painting and redecorating was finished and he was quite excited and he came in and found his two little girls, four and six, had scribbled all over the freshly painted wall.

He said, "I was furious and I thought of all the things Dr. Dewey told me and I held myself in check. Then I went up about two weeks later to see Dr. Dewey, and I told Dr. Dewey how proud I was to hold myself in check. His answer was 'Ben, they scribbled all over your newly painted wall and you did nothing? You ought to have your head examined.' "

These are the impressions a college student gets in college and what a professor really means to convey, and we desperately need people who will have the classroom experience as they are ready to start on their teacher program.

I have talked too long. I am ready for questions.

THE CHAIRMAN: I would like to move quickly to counsel's questions because of our mounting time problem.

MR. TRACTENBERG: In part they constitute reassurance, that I understood the import of your remarks correctly.

Do I gather that you don't believe the Board of Examiners-- more than that, the whole selection process as it is now constituted--ought to be continued in its current form?

DR. THEOBALD: This is not realistic.

Number one, it should seek the most qualified candidates that make applications. I think we should get the best people out of those candidates, and I think we ought to be measuring classroom performance and not a lot of stuff that they have already passed in college.

MR. TRACTENBERG: I gathered from your statement that you think state certification is sufficient basis at least for provisional licensing.

DR. THEOBALD: I wouldn't give tenure on it, but certainly initial appointment. Understand, I think there are other things that have to be examined into. I think there are questions of moral turpitude, questions of health and a number of things of that sort, but these are relatively routine.

MR. TRACTENBERG: I think you have raised something that has not yet really come up in any detail and I am sure we will be getting to it in later testimony, and that is the relationship between the school system and the teacher education programs. Particularly pertinent, I think, because according to the statistics I have seen, City University alone accounts for some 60 to 65 per cent of the teachers that come into New York City schools each year.

DR. THEOBALD: And the rest of them are probably 90 per cent from other schools in the city or immediately around it.

MR. TRACTENBERG: The only thing I want to raise is whether the Office of Personnel in the school system and the teacher college programs might, in fact, go a long way toward even predicting performance in the classroom.

DR. THEOBALD: I think that a much greater exposure to the schools while a youngster is studying in college will result in very much better performance. It may result in some of them dropping out, but those, I think, will be better off dropped out because they will find it isn't for them.

But I would like to see a teacher who isn't frightened the first day she steps into the classroom, who knows how to handle the obstreperous youngster and all the rest of it.

Frequently, the first couple of days make or break a teacher.

MR. TRACTENBERG: That is all I have.

THE CHAIRMAN: Thank you, Dr. Theobald. I want to say

for the record, this kind of historic overview from a man who had the highest responsibility in the school system is particularly important for these hearings, especially to make clear that the problem we are talking about didn't just arise yesterday.

Thank you very much.

The next witness is Mr. Peter J. Strauss, Chairman, Community School Board No. 2 in Manhattan.

MR. STRAUSS: Good afternoon, Commissioners.

As the Chairman said, I am presently President of Community School Board No. 2 in Manhattan. I was formerly a member of the predecessor board which ceased to exist on July 1st of last year when community school boards were established under the Decentralization Law.

I want to stress that my remarks represent my own views, and I don't necessarily speak for my board or any of my staff.

I believe the goal of the personnel system should be to select those professionals most qualified to assist children to learn. I believe while we have thousands of competent, exciting, and creative professionals in New York City, they are here in spite of our present personnel system, not because of it.

It will be expressed many times during these hearings that there are only a handful, I believe the number is something like nine or 11, Black and Spanish-speaking licensed principals in this system.

I find this to be a shocking statistic. Equally disturbing is the small percentage of Black and Spanish-speaking teachers in our schools although this figure has improved in recent years.

I do not think it is necessary to dwell on the question as to whether these facts result from intentional discrimination. They speak for themselves. I think we must look to the future and eliminate the causes of this failure. I maintain the failure of all of us not to provide meaningful bilingual education is an act of discrimination, and a personnel system that does not have employees to deal with this, is ipso facto deficient.

My school district has 22,000 elementary and junior high school pupils. There are 21 elementary schools, five junior high schools, 1,170 teachers. We employ 26 principals and 40 assistant principals.

As you can see, even though it is one of the 31 so-called decentralized districts, it ranks as the third or fourth largest school district in the State of New York.

Under the Decentralization Law we are given the responsibility for the educational programs in our district. We are elected officials, accountable to our community for the success or failure of our children. Although we are to be held accountable through the elective process for their performance we have little voice in the selection of our pedagogical staff. We are accountable for the failures of the system over which we, in fact, have little influence. The Decentralization Law provides that each community must appoint teachers for all schools and programs under its jurisdiction who are assigned to the district by the Chancellor from competitive eligible lists.

Thus, although there is some language in the statute that the Chancellor is to give weight to our choices, in reality teachers are simply assigned to our district. Aside from the recent questionnaires sent out by the Board of Examiners, we have absolutely no voice in the development of the standards used by the Board of Examiners for licensing teachers. As to supervisors, while we now have some choice, the choice is limited as are the tools at our command for making an intelligent selection.

Generally, when a supervisory vacancy exists, the position is advertised through the Department of Personnel channels and applications are received by the community superintendent.

Usually, particularly in the case of a low-income neighborhood school, the number of applicants is not large. The Department of Personnel gives us no material whatsoever concerning candidates. We must request resumes and make whatever investigation we wish on our own.

Most boards now involve parents and, when they wish, they participate in the teacher screening process.

I have participated as a member of former Local School Board 2 and the present Community School Board in the selection and appointment of principals in about eight schools.

On the basis of my experience, comparing those persons interviewed who hold a principal's license with other supervisors we have interviewed or worked with who didn't have such licenses, it is my considered judgment that the holding of a license granted under the existing Board of Examiners' procedures is not a true test of the qualifications of supervisory personnel.

Rather, I believe it has discouraged the most qualified from success.

I believe, in effect, the Board of Examiners discriminates against competence, that the present system is an anti-merit system and many qualified educators, Black, Spanish-speaking, Chinese, are left back.

I want to return to the role of community school boards in the selection process. We are at present probably not doing better. Our tools are limited and our experience is short. The individual interview process is unsafe.

Among the dangers is the possibility that political or other improper criteria will be used to discriminate against qualified professionals. This should not and need not occur if fair and reviewable standards are developed.

A better method is needed. To accomplish this I would like to make the following recommendations:

    1. Greater latitude in choice is needed. The pool of talent from which the community school board should be able to draw should be larger than the list promulgated by the Board of Examiners. Intensive study is necessary to determine how the minimums should be established. A revised method of state certification might be one possibility.

    2. The community school board should be required to develop objective, rational and reviewable--I think that is

important--reviewable employment criteria which would supplement the minimum standards.

All segments of the community, including the professional unions, should participate. The resources of the Board of Examiners should be placed at the disposal of each community school board.

3. Once employment criteria are developed a mechanism should be established to insure that they are properly applied by the community school board and, I might add, the central Board.

4. Community school boards should be trained and techniques should be provided so that they can intelligently apply the employment criteria.

In fact, the technology of industry should be tapped. It has not been today.

5. Appointment and licensing should be more greatly related to performance. I fully agree with the Chancellor that this is the direction in which we should be moving.

6. Other avenues for professional advancement must be provided for our teachers. Too many great teachers have been forced to become mediocre supervisors because it was the only route to economic and professional success.

Many persons who are opposing reform express concern that if community school boards are given that much freedom, race will become the criterion. I think this is an insult to the millions of parents in the city who are interested in one thing: the better education of their children.

On occasion, when I have participated jointly with parents in the interview of principal candidates, they have been the first to reject one of their own if they doubted his competence.

My experience has led me to believe the vast majority of New Yorkers will agree that belonging to a particular ethnic group is not a qualification for the position, but it may be one of many criteria under certain circumstances.

THE CHAIRMAN: What are the boundaries of your school district?

MR. STRAUSS: We are on the east side from about 100th Street to 14th Street, west side, from 59th to the Battery, and we take in Two Bridges up on the east side again.

We have about 500,000 registered voters. That gives you an idea what the population is.

THE CHAIRMAN: The majority of those children are not minority group children, then?

MR. STRAUSS: The breakdown is about 25% Chinese, 25% Black, 30% Spanish-speaking, and the balance the so-called others.

It's a fairly diverse district.

THE CHAIRMAN: I take it your comments with respect to what you would like to see in teachers and supervisors come from a broad experience and are not based specifically on the racial or ethnic make-up of the school district but what you have seen as the need for professionals.

MR. STRAUSS: I would share President Bergtraum's comments. I think that he was saying if this system truly brought out merit, eventually we would see in the supervisory and in the teaching staff a fair ethnic make-up; and I believe very strongly if the system was a true one that measured merit, that is what we would have.

May I comment on the question of how assistant examiners are appointed because it is one of the things that has always distressed me very much, that in a system which defended itself by arguing it was so fair and objective, the very people who did the examinations were chosen in a system of patronage.

The way you get to earn that $3,000 or $4,000 a year as an assistant examiner is really by whom you knew downtown. I've had experiences where principals and assistant principals have complained to me that because of some personal run-in with somebody who made the selections, they are no longer employed as assistant examiners.

That might bear some future questioning by counsel.

MR. TRACTENBERG: I have just a couple of questions, Mr. Strauss. Because I think it is frequently referred to as one of the great virtues of the Decentralization Law, I want to come back to the special 40 per cent hiring provision and particularly your reactions to it as President of a community school board.

Do you anticipate it will give you much flexibility?

MR. STRAUSS: If we are going to have budget cutbacks and the economy is as bad as it is, so that people are not going to leave the teaching profession, I don't even know if any of our schools which fall within the 40% group will have a large number of openings.

I don't think it is going to be a significant tool at all.

MR. TRACTENBERG: Assuming you have openings, do you have any budget funds to do your own recruiting?

MR. STRAUSS: We don't have the budget funds, and I think it's difficult for us even to go out and do a fair and decent job in hiring. We don't have the facilities.

I think the Chancellor is correct, that the Board of Examiners' functions are obsolete, but I would suggest they could have a role and that could be as a service agency to the community school board. They have the budget and should have the technical resources to be able to provide us with the facilities to make more intelligent decisions as we go along.

It might be they could almost, in a sense, be a consulting agency for the community school boards.

MR. TRACTENBERG: There are a variety of other ways people have suggested, even under the current system, getting around the examination process. For example, the Board of Examiners' own bylaws provide that under emergency circumstances, if the Chancellor so recommends, special licenses can be granted.

Have you had occasion within your district to ask for the exercise of such an emergency power?

MR. STRAUSS: We are considering it now in one special situation. For example, there is no such thing as a special intermediate school license. It seems to me the technique of requesting the Chancellor for the creation of a special position for something like that could be a vehicle that would give us greater flexibility.

In the case of the Park East High School, we have been working with community groups to develop a whole new, broad concept, that the school should not simply be a high school but a comprehensive education center which would serve not only the high school but the community. And the leader of that center would not be a high school principal, but director of the comprehensive center, and we are considering asking for the creation of a new position.

I think this is simply reacting on an ad hoc basis to a particular need in a particular situation, and while we may do it in some cases, and may be able to do it if the courts support us, I don't think it's the long run answer.

I think we need much more drastic reform.

MR. TRACTENBERG: That is all I have.

THE CHAIRMAN: Our next witness is Dr. Edythe J. Gaines, Community Superintendent, School District No. 12, Bronx.

DR. GAINES: Madame Chairman, honorable members of the Commission, and ladies and gentlemen, the work you are about and for which these hearings are being set up is crucially important for our city. In spite of it, the people of the city still believe, and rightfully so, that the quality of life in the city is intimately related to the quality of education delivered to the children and youth. Education is preeminently a people business. What happens in schools depends largely on what kind of people we have there and what those people do there. Thus the question of how we can obtain, hire, fire, upgrade, utilize and develop school personnel, is a central question in the quest for quality education for our children.

I am among those who take the position that our present practices and procedures are counterproductive of that goal. How can I illuminate the problem without being overly wordy or technical? After long consideration I decided to do it by anecdote, just take it from the seat in which I sit and see how it feels to be there.

We have junior high schools which are overly large, one in particular, the one I will talk about, over 2,000 children, a staff of over 140, plus auxiliary personnel raising the faculty to well over 200.

It is a large scale, complex organization. The evidences of school failure are quite pronounced. What kind of person do we need to lead such an organization. Clearly an extraordinary person. Perhaps we need a swashbuckling type, but certainly not a plodding person who just manages to keep on going until he got to a position.

We need an unusual person, a person with executive abilities, a person with knowledge of the best ways of educating children, a knowledge of how to get other people to do it.

We set about the task of looking for the man or woman who

could do this job. We did a number of things but one in particular. We placed an advertisement in a newspaper. That caused a great deal of stir because we simply asked for the kind of person we have been looking for and indicated who could apply.

We included, of course, those who had a license as a principal in the New York City School System, but indicated you could have other kinds of qualifications.

It wasn't very soon after that we received a letter from the Chancellor reminding us that our only legal choice was limited to a person who was on the eligible list. Our only legal choice. Of course, we had invited people from the eligible list and I think I would like to talk for a minute about the eligible list.

The eligible list consists of the names of 91 people listed in alphabetical order. Subsequent to that there was a supplementary list of 18 names. This makes a total pool of talent, from which we might legally select a principal, of 109 people. On that list there was one Black person and one Puerto Rican. Many of the people on that list have subsequently been placed. I don't really know how many of the 109 are left, but the original pool was 109. Let's look at how you came to be one of the 109.

At the time this group of people took the examination--and the examination was given in November 1964, that means the examination was given six years ago--at the time that they took it, they had to have had either eight years of teaching experience under regular licenses in the New York City school system, and among those eight years had to be three years as a regular licensed principal of an elementary school, or they had to have had five years as a regularly licensed assistant principal or other supervisor, and in order to qualify for that you had to have been a regularly licensed teacher for at least five years.

Consequently, if everything were absolutely perfect, you could not have been eligible without having been in the New York City school system 14 years.

In point of fact--I studied that list recently--none of the people on the list met that theoretical minimum. There were four who began their regular service in the New York City school system 17 years ago. Most of them had begun their service 20 to 25 years ago, and one candidate began his service 40 years ago.

Thus the talent pool to which we are legally restricted is made up of people who, number one, can't possibly be from outside of New York City. You must come from New York City and you must have been here at least 18 years ago. You must have been in the system as a regularly appointed person 18 years ago. Excepting for two people, you can't have anybody who is either Black, Puerto Rican, Chinese or a whole lot of other ethnic groups. You certainly can't be young. It is very unlikely that the person is the product of a training program that is recent, one that has to do with the newest ways of educating children.

What was the result of our search? We did receive one applicant who was on the eligible list. Consequently, our legal choice is now reduced to one person. Would any organization, looking for the person to fill its most crucially important position, restrict itself to one eligible person? That would be insanity, and yet, legally, that is the only alternative open to us, that is, to have a regularly assigned principal.

What would happen if we chose a person who was not eligible, according to this procedure? The picture gets very unclear at this point. It seems you could appoint him as an acting principal and he can serve for three months at whatever salary he has, if he is a teacher, and then retroactively they begin to pay him as a principal, but this could only go on for one year.

At the end of the year, it isn't clear what is supposed to happen. How can you invite a person under such uncertain circumstances? It would be insulting. Suppose a person, however, was not a teacher in the New York City school system, the person you want to select.

Now, it is not clear at all what you have to do. He has to have a file number, so apparently you have to send him down to get a substitute teacher's license, so we could even pay him at all. At the moment it is unlikely he would be licensed as a substitute teacher because they say they are not giving special licenses to anybody until they have eliminated or exhausted the alternate lists for teachers. I don't know exactly how we can get him on at all. It is a mystery.

Let me tell you about some of the kinds of people who have come to us who are ineligible. There was a man who scored 99 percentile on his Graduate Record Examination. One of the reasons to have a Board of Examiners examination is to determine intellectual ability. He clearly has that.

I would doubt any sizable percentage presently on the eligible list scored 99 percentile on their Graduate Record Exams. For those of you who don't know quite what that means, it means only one per cent of the nation scores higher than this person does, only one per cent of those who take an examination of this kind. He stands in the top one per cent of the intelligencia. He is in his early 30's and now a principal of a high school in Puerto Rico. We don't have to speculate whether or not he can be a principal or do the job. We have a performance that can be viewed, observed, judged, measured, and there is something sad about it. He is ineligible.

There was another man who has been successful managing a program of basic education of adults who were school dropouts, and he is turning those people into functional literates and capable citizens. He is doing that through procedures that innovative schools are trying to adopt.

Here again, we have a track record, something we can look at and observe, something we don't have to speculate about. He is ineligible.

There was a man who is currently running a residential school for troubled children, almost all of whom come from the slums of New York City and from the public schools in those areas. Almost all of the young people there are Black and Puerto Ricans. The rest are poor white.

Here is a person whom we don't need to speculate about in

terms of what he would do if he were principal with troubled children. We can look to see. He has shown us what he is doing, shown us how he rebuilt the ego of children, and you see how he engenders ethnic pride. He is ineligible.

The one eligible person who applied has never served as a principal or head of school. He has served as an assistant principal but could not identify for us a single educational program that he personally introduced. Nor could he identify a single teacher whom he could claim credit for developing. Nor could he specify any learning results for children that could be directly traceable to his efforts. He is the only eligible available to us under the law.

Let me say one other thing about the principal.

Never in the history of the New York City school system, never in the history of the so-called merit system, has ever there been a time when a person was guaranteed a position, if he passed an examination. Not until now. Even under the most centralized portion of our experience, you were not guaranteed a job if you passed the examination, even when you had to select from the first three, no one was guaranteed he would be hired. Not until now.

Let's say that I was the first on the list, and let's say I wasn't so good and everybody in the system knew that, despite the fact I passed the exam. I would have to be presented as among the first three and I could be passed over and they would pick the second or third and then I became one of the next three and I could be passed over, and so passed on over until I was never hired.

That was the experience, that was true.

Now, under decentralization where we are supposed to have improved the situation, we are for the first time guaranteeing if you passed the exam you will get a job and at the salary indicated.

In point of fact, everybody on the previous elementary school principals' list earns the salary of a principal even though not performing the functions of a principal. Now, until the junior high school principals' list is exhausted no new list may be promulgated, and you may not legally assign anyone from outside that eligibility list.

Let's take a look at how it feels to be a community superintendent trying to assist principals in staffing their schools with teachers. Again I shall do it by anecdote.

We had a secondary school in which we needed a teacher of business subjects. There was not such a teacher available through the regular procedures. Central assignment could not provide us with a teacher in business subjects. We found a beautiful young woman, extraordinarily well qualified in business subjects. In addition, she was bilingual and could communicate with our children. She lacked, according to the statement of the Department of Personnel, sufficient education courses.

I reviewed her record and found at least several courses I thought should be classifiable as education courses. Several of them were courses in Puerto Rican history, culture and background. They said these were not education courses and could not be accepted as such, although it is my conviction that before too long this will be a required area of competency for the professional staff. But at present it isn't, and therefore she could not qualify.

They therefore didn't permit us to hire her and the children then had to be taught their business education subjects by a licensed social studies teacher who knew little about typing. This is called the merit system.

We had a teacher come to us from Los Angeles. He had recommendations, as we say back home, yea long. All of them superb. Clearly an outstanding teacher and a teacher who had outstanding leadership qualifications and other qualities as well.

First, he had to take an examination and that meant some time had to elapse. He came to us in September and so we had to start the procedures by which he could be licensed.

In the meantime he has a family; he has to earn a living, but he was willing to sacrifice something because he felt we had something good going, and the program we wanted him for was a program he wanted to be in.

While awaiting being called for the examination, he taught as a volunteer. We could not place him in the classroom under any other circumstances.

Finally, after some weeks, an examination was called, he went down to take it. It had at that time a short answer portion and an essay portion. It turned out to be--and I recognized the exam when I saw it--that they had pulled an old exam out and gave him that. It happened to be that on the short answer part most of the questions dealt with New York City and you almost had to be a native to do it. He was failed on the examination, therefore, as a result of his score on the short answer.

He was then told he would have to wait six weeks before he could take another examination, and he simply couldn't afford it.

To make a long story short, he is now one of the outstanding teachers and head of a department in an outstanding suburban school system, and we lost him.

Another example: we desired to be a bilingual district. In order to be so we need teachers who at least know Spanish. The Board of Education tells us they have a shortage of regular licensed teachers who speak Spanish and could not supply our needs.

In a district where close to 60 per cent of the pupils come from Spanish-speaking homes, we have a talent pool of people who can teach Spanish although they may not have the other qualifications. We thought we could find a route by which they could travel called the certificate of competency. We would not ask that the person be licensed for everything but just be given a certificate of competency so they can teach Spanish.

The answer was: you will not be permitted to give a certificate of competency examination in any field in which another licensed exam is given.

It's sort of like <u>No Exit</u>, no way out. You are just blocked at every turn.

One other example: we believe the classroom of today and the classroom of tomorrow is a place where a teacher can't be alone, that at the very least there should be a team of a teacher and a paraprofessional, and if that team is going to work effectively together they ought to be trained together, not separately.

So we devised, under the Educational and Professional Development Act, a proposal for the joint training of teachers and paraprofessionals.

We were fortunate because developing any proposals means you are going into a kind of lottery, and we won and the program is funded.

We specified 50 per cent of the teachers to be in that group were to be former Peace Corps volunteers and 50 per cent were to be teachers who lived in the community, and the paraprofessionals had to live in the community and all had to commit themselves to learn to work as a team and be a bilingual team.

Those are pretty high standards. We were able to fulfill all of that and, indeed, with the cooperation of Fordham University, developed really a quite excellent program of joint training.

Then we came down to licensing time. We couldn't get any of them licensed. This was September of the past year. It came down to other people who were on various lists that have to be exhausted first before you can license those. We finally worked out some procedure by which we called them intern teachers, and after several weeks of negotiations we managed to get them licensed. But in the meantime we couldn't open the school for which they were to be the core personnel, and we had to leave the children elsewhere, and they din't get the school under way until close to October over a technicality of this kind.

What have I been trying to say is the system is rigid. It provides us with an extraordinarily restricted talent pool. It is unnecessarily xenophobic.

Not just anti-Black and anti-Puerto Rican, but anti-outsider. It is artificially determined, not based on performance. Indeed, I think all of us have been saying if the exam could prove that you really would produce the person who could do the job, we would probably live with it, but since there is no particular relationship between ability to do the job and the exam, we have to ask for alternatives.

The procedures are unnecessarily cumbersome, dehumanized, and dehumanizing. We believe people behave as they are treated. If you see how teachers are treated coming through that process, you would not be surprised that they are system-oriented. They feel they are cogs in a wheel. The whole thing is predicated on the notion, "If you have seen one, you have seen them all."

The thing is unnecessarily centralized. We can't select the staff we need for our unique needs. What could we do if our system became more open? We could recruit our own staff. Therefore, we could seek staff in less restrictive talent pools. We would not have to go to Puerto Rico or the South to find the people we are looking for. They are right in our own backyard.

If the system were open, we would be advised the people we need are very close to us. We can have staff that meets our unique needs. I am not only talking about the ethnic or bilingual thing. I am talking also about people who understand what open learning is about and who want to be a part of that and so on.

We could hire a staff in a much more dignified manner. Our parents would meet the staff, carry them through the summer--June, July and August--have dinner at their homes, help them to find places to live. I can't imagine that the staff wouldn't be three times as good if they could sit down to a soul dinner and talk with parents.

We could devise truly meaningful staff development programs locally arranged. We could devise and implement staff utilization programs, by which we could maximize their abilities and minimize their weaknesses. We would not have to go on the false assumption that teachers have to be all things to all pupils at all times.

We could make our schools more human and humane institutions which would develop not only our children, but everybody in the system, including teachers, assistant principals, principals, and even community superintendents.

We could have a self-actualizing system. I didn't come here to play a Virginia Woolf game, get the guest or get the Board of Education or get the Board of Examiners.

This is really not what we are trying to do. Nor am I interested in a sensational story or newspaper headlines or some salving of our feelings.

I came here, and I think you came here, because there is a problem and the problem cries out for solution. I hope that the Commission hearings will result in positive actions that will make it possible for us to reach the dreams that I mentioned in the last portion of my address.

Thank you.

MR. TRACTENBERG: I have a few questions if I may.

How long have you been connected with the New York City public school system?

DR. GAINES: I became a substitute teacher in 1945, a regular teacher in 1948, an assistant principal in 1955, a principal in 1959, and superintendent in 1967, I think.

MR. TRACTENBERG: Presumably you have accumulated a series of licenses.

DR. GAINES: I have taken them all and have also been an assistant examiner and know the system from inside and out.

MR. TRACTENBERG: I gather at least some of what you say is based upon personal experience with the system.

DR. GAINES: All of it. And as a very successful candidate. Therefore, no sour grapes.

MR. TRACTENBERG: I have only just a couple of questions further about provisions which I have talked about with Mr. Strauss and Chancellor Scribner, that have been held up as providing flexibility with the system, as a way to permit community boards and their superintendents to avoid the formalities of the full examination process I just wondered what your reaction was, particularly to the special 40 per cent hiring provision.

I assume it would apply to some of your schools.

DR. GAINES: Yes, it does. I think Peter Strauss was absolutely right in his assessment. But in spite of the limited possibility of having places to be filled that way, we are going to go full speed ahead in the hope that even on a limited basis we could make a difference.

I think, as you probably know, the 40 per cent was a political compromise, and it should be viewed as just that. It was a political compromise during the haggling about what would go into the Decentralization Law. Like any other compromise it has certain ridiculous aspects to it.

Let's say if three of the schools in our district are not eligible because of the way they corrected the scores, and you want to institute a bilingual program in those three schools and you are not able to get bilingual staff from the Board of Education, they would become eligible anyway.

I don't know if I have answered you as comprehensively as you wanted to hear. Basically, we don't know yet how much of an opportunity we are going to have to use it. It looks as if it will be limited, but we feel we should use even that limited opportunity to try to break through it.

MR. TRACTENBERG: The provision provides that community boards have this special appointment power between October 1st and May 1st. What I have always been curious about is whether you really know by May 1st with any precision what vacancies you will have for the following September.

DR. GAINES: That is an excellent question. I hope you will ask it of Mr. Lang. It also says if you are not able to get personnel by the regular procedure, you may use the alternate procedure.

However, you do not know whether or not you are going to get personnel by the regular procedure until sometime in August, which is after the time by which you could have used the alternate procedure.

MR. TRACTENBERG: You are answering affirmatively. Number one, you don't know what vacancies you have with any precision, and number two, you may have to wait until the regular procedure--

DR. GAINES: The first one is correct and the second one is you do not know whether or not the regular procedure is going to provide you with the personnel you need until after the time limit on the option is up.

MR. TRACTENBERG: Thank you.

THE CHAIRMAN: I just want to say for the record the testimony which you called anecdotal is the best example I have heard this morning of what public hearings can do because you chose not to speak in generalities but to speak in the specifics that only anecdotes speak and I found it most knowledgeable testimony.

I also want to reiterate that counsel has expressed on the record Dr. Gaines' credentials because indeed she has been fully licensed every step of the process.

Therefore, and although she is a Black person who holds the highest position outside of the central hierarchy, one that is not licensed, it is important to know she speaks from the point of view of someone who has passed every hurdle that there is to pass and has made every hurdle that there is to make, and, therefore, her testimony comes particularly untainted and particularly from the broadest kind of experience.

I only regret she told us she got her license in 1945 because no one could possibly have guessed that by looking at her.

DR. GAINES: My grandchildren will attest to it.

(Applause.)

THE CHAIRMAN: Before Mr. Flinker begins his testimony, let me announce again that we have arranged for a child care facility around the corner, 225 Broadway, 18th floor, Room 27. You should tell people in the community that it is possible to come to these hearings even if they have to care for small children because there is a facility available to care for them during the time that the parents are here.

Mr. Flinker, Principal of George Gershwin Junior High School in Brooklyn.

MR. IRVING FLINKER: Madam Chairman, Commissioners, Ladies and Gentlemen, it is my belief, as it is most of those who preceded me, that the system of selecting teachers in New York City is outmoded, obsolete, and unresponsive to the needs of our children at the present time.

In industry, when a corporation president finds that his machinery is outdated and uneconomical, he is quick to change that machinery so that it is efficient and brings in the dividends. Certainly we can do no less for our children.

The original plan of establishing a Board of Examiners was based on the premise that New York City children should have only the best qualified teachers. The conditions of labor supply and children's needs at the turn of the century were far different from those prevailing today. The size of our system, current State certification standards, decentralized control, and the special needs of inner city children require a re-evaluation of our teacher selecting system.

The examiners are so far removed from the classroom that they have no conception of the current needs of disadvantaged children. The paramount need of these children is to learn to read; the vast majority of ghetto schools average a year or more below grade level in reading. Yet the eligibility requirements for teaching in the elementary or secondary schools do not include a methods course in teaching reading. To become eligible for the license of Teacher of English as a second language a candidate must have completed six semester hours in the structure of modern English or introductory linguistics or methods of comparative analysis or phonetics and phonemics, but no course in methods of teaching reading.

The Board of Examiners sets up such a barrier between teacher applicant and school as to discourage the candidates from taking the test and to frustrate the school principals who have uncovered positions.

Early in September, 1969, hundreds of teachers stormed the corridors of the Examiners' offices protesting the delay in processing the July 3rd examinations. Aware of this situation many principals nominated these qualified applicants for per diem certificates to fill their vacancies about five days before school opened. Because of an inefficient system, tied in knots by red tape, principals waited from one to two weeks to fill their vacancies with these teachers who had applied three months earlier for the jobs. In the meantime classes went uncovered. Results of the August, 1969 examinations were still not available by the middle of January, 1970.

When a principal asks for an explanation he is told that more applicants took the test than were expected, and that the processing took a long time. In my school a substitute teacher took the regular teacher's examination in French in November, 1968 but was not informed of passing until January 20, 1970.

The processing of examinations is so cumbersome and confused that one regular examination is given before the results of the previous test are released. For example, the same applicants who took the industrial arts examination or the high school mathematics examination in October, 1969, sat for these tests again in January, 1970, because the processing of the first tests was incomplete. When a system of teacher selection requires needless second testing, the symptoms of disintegration are clear. There is evident neither consideration of applicants' morale nor regard for taxpayers' money. The result of such an uncoordinated procedure, so frustrating to teacher applicants, is to impede the natural flow of graduate students into the city's schools.

Despite the elaborate examining process many principals doubt that the merit system achieves its purpose. No study has been conducted within the past half century to confirm or negate the Examiners' claims of validity or reliability of their tests. There has been widespread dissatisfaction among the city's principals for the past decade with the caliber of newly appointed teachers. On the other hand, many a principal can point to at least one excellent substitute teacher on his staff who was failed in a regular examination. A number of principals believe that the examinations do not test what they are supposedly designed to test, namely potential teaching ability.

According to the Board of Examiners the merit system depends essentially on the ability of an applicant to pass a written examination and an interview test. The appraisal of record is of very little significance; it is not accorded any numerical rating or weight. A Phi Beta Kappa record and excellent experience ratings would not help a candidate who fails the written or interview tests by five points.

A large number of appeals results from the faulty administration and rating of these tests. When the applicant is provided with an objective standard answer he is often successful in challenging the failing score, with the help of a professional appeals writer. In the case of interview and performance tests, the appellant invariably was turned down because no objective standard answer was available or provided, despite the fact that these tests are reputed to be objective and competitive.

For many years candidates have protested against the arbitrary judgments of assistant examiners in interview tests. In the written tests applicants' papers are identifiable only by number. In the oral tests the candidate is identified by name. It is possible, therefore, that for one reason or another examiners' judgments may be prejudicial and discriminatory.

To lessen this element of arbitrary judgment, candidates have repeatedly requested that a stenographic or electronic records be made of the applicant's presentation and answers at the interview, as well as of the questions put to him. Too often the examiners' notes were fragmentary and incomplete because long-hand writing is much slower than fluent speech. Yet the Board of Examiners obdurately refused to change the traditional practice until they were compelled by an act of the state legislature to use tape recordings.

Interview tests are generally given by two or three examiners to assure the candidate of valid judgments. However, since the panel administers the test cooperatively the summary judgment is made in unison, not independently. A more reliable method would require that the two or three examiners test the candidate independently, and that their individual ratings be averaged. The use of three examiners is predicated on the premise that independent judgment will be exercised and used as a check, one against the other. Yet the opportunity to confer about the candidate's performance immediately after the test negates the element of independent judgment, for in any conference a meeting of minds is reached because of the influence and persuasion of the persons present.

Assistant examiners are chosen to help administer the tests on the basis of the license held. Chairmen of mathematics departments, for example, help to administer tests for math teachers. The license to serve as teacher or supervisor in a special field is considered, ipso facto, enough qualification to construct and administer tests to teacher and supervisory applicants. No inquiry is made into the actual competence, personal qualities, or special skills of the assistant examiners. A very small percentage of these assistant examiners has ever had a single graduate course in personnel selection or management. The preliminary briefing given to the assistant examiners is minimal and leaves much to be desired for administering an objective examination.

It is my belief that among a group of assistant examiners selected to conduct an interview test the variability of expectancy and standards is so wide as to negate the reliability, validity, and objectivity of the entire examination process. The larger the number of assistant examiners employed in an interview test the wider is the variability of the standards. The quality of these examiners' judgments varies as does the quality of their administrative skills.

Is it not more logical, therefore, that the determination of an applicant's fitness for a teaching job should be made by the principal of the school where the vacancy exists?

The merit system is known to interfere with the efficient administration of a school. According to law, personnel vacancies must be filled by one of the top three candidates on the eligible list. This practice often displaces a teacher in a school who is filling the position very competently in a substitute or acting capacity, for example, acting guidance counselor, but may be too low on the list to qualify for the number of available vacancies. The new person needs a period of adjustment and may turn out to be less effective than the displaced counselor. This situation has applied as well to teachers and supervisors.

While the written and interview tests are generally scheduled for evenings and holidays, the physical and medical examinations are invariably given on school days. Substitute teachers taking regular teacher examinations and regular teachers taking supervisors' examinations are excused with pay for an entire day to submit to a thirty-minute physical exam. The Board of Examiners is apparently indifferent to the monetary cost (about $50 per candidate) and insensitive to the loss of continuity of instruction that children must suffer. The per diem substitute, when it is possible to obtain one, generally makes little progress in instruction and causes a deterioration in class discipline which may affect the school decorum.

The members of the Board of Examiners have all had supervisory experience and are well aware of the harmful effects of teacher absenteeism, especially in today's schools. The former superintendent of schools, supervisors' organizations, and individual principals have requested the Board of Examiners to reschedule physical tests of all teaching personnel for late afternoons, evenings, holidays, and Saturdays. The Examiners' answer to such pleas was "For the same reasons that patients find it necessary to schedule physical and medical examinations during doctors' office hours we find it necessary to schedule physical and medical examinations during the day." Such an answer reveals neither logic nor sensitivity to school needs.

This attitude of disinterest in school needs is also exemplified in the Examiners' practice of requiring thousands of candidates to report for physical exams after they were failed in one or more parts of a supervisor's examination. In such cases, also, children lose valuable instruction and the city thousands of dollars.

In most school districts in the country, teachers are ultimately selected by the principal of the school where the vacancies exist. After a preliminary screening the personnel officer refers the applicant to the school principal for an interview. As the administrator of a large organization the principal knows the type of person specifically needed by his pupils with respect to personality, academic training, and experience. Selecting employees for particular jobs is a managerial function in every office, business, or plant.

The school principal is well aware of the need to select personnel who will respond positively to his training program. Having had a major share in the selection of his teachers, he must assume full responsibility for the quality of his teachers. If the caliber of teaching in his school is good, he deserves full credit for successful selection and effective teacher-training. If the converse is true there is something wrong with his choice of teachers or with his supervision or with both. In any case he bears full responsibility for the level of teaching in his school.

In New York City, on the other hand, a principal receives from a central bureau a teacher in whose selection he had no part. Within a few weeks he knows whether he is stuck with a dud or has struck it rich with a gem. The fact that the teacher passed through a time-consuming screening process does not assure the principal of strong teaching potential in his new recruit. Principals frequently complain of scrapings off the bottom of the barrel. In fact, one principal recently remarked, "Judging from my new recruits, I believe that the bottom of the barrel has been scraped clean through." The New York City principal is in a position to disavow full responsibility for the quality of teaching in his school because he did not select his teachers.

Actually, the new teachers are selected by school principals who are employed as assistant examiners to write test questions, to rate papers, and to conduct interviews. Principals and other licensed supervisors earn an additional $100 on holidays and on Saturdays for eight hours of examining inclusive of lunch hour. The successful candidates (a very high proportion) are very seldom appointed to the schools of their individual examiners. While this system is impersonal, it is extravagant and deprives the building principal of his right to choose his own teachers. The money wasted in this system of teacher selection can better be used in teacher-training programs.

The administration of written teacher examinations by the Board of Examiners is costly, time-consuming, and questionable as to effectiveness as an evaluative instrument. If a written test is required, the use of the National Teacher Examination would be more efficient in this city and more readily available to applicants all over the country. Minimum scores and eligibility requirements may be set by a personnel officer who would refer acceptable candidates to the school principals in need of teachers. Interminable delays between parts of examinations and establishing eligible lists would be avoided so that school administrators would have their new crop in May, instead of weeks after the opening of the school year.

For decades school administrators in New York City have complained bitterly that the prolonged examinations for regular teachers impedes their planning the fall school organization. Because examinations take from six months to one year, lists of eligible teachers are not promulgated until July or in many cases not before November. Teaching programs tailored to highly competent and talented substitute teachers are broken up or given to raw recruits who displace the teachers whom the principal had previously trained. Displaced substitute teachers must now scrounge around for vacancies or take any leftover openings from the central assignment unit. Is it any wonder that the city loses many excellent teachers to private and suburban schools where the screening process is more efficient and timely?

The need to re-evaluate and streamline the system of teacher selection is obvious to school principals and superintendents. Yet their supervisor associations have been reluctant to ask for change because of fear of a breakdown of standards and of probable community pressure for employment of favorite sons. Whatever changes are effected can be so constructed as to maintain present eligibility standards and to minimize local pressure for nepotism.

In the April, 1970 issue of Clearing House, I wrote an article on teacher recruitment and selection in New York City. In this article I presented abstracts of the Examiners' statistical reports for the period 1964-1967 and drew the following conclusions:

Formal, protracted examinations discourage many teacher applicants. Large number of applicants withdraw from the examination before completing all parts.

The cost in money and time is not warranted by the low productivity. The percentage of failures in the twelve most popular examinations ranged from 2% for teacher in vacation playground to 28% for teacher in the junior high school. In only one other exam, teacher in the high school, was the failing rate over 20%. Where the screening should have been exceedingly fine, for example, in the elementary school principal examination, the failure rate (14%) was abysmally low.

The examination standards were more rigorous for applicants seeking junior and senior high school positions. Inasmuch as all children need good teachers, especially younger, more impressionable children, one can't but question the escalation of the standards in relation to the educational ladder.

It is significant, also, that the degree of selectivity was considerably less in examinations for substitute teachers than in the regular license tests. Yet, the Examiners were fully aware that most substitute teachers are employed on a "permanent" basis. If a person was good enough to be employed as a substitute teacher of children for one year, he is good enough to serve for thirty years. In 1963 and in 1968 closed examinations for regular licenses were given to substitute teachers and their success in passing was phenomenal.

The success of the substitute teachers in these special examinations mandated by the New York State Legislature indicate that the school principals continue the selection process begun by the Examiners. The school administrators go one step further and train those substitute teachers who give practical evidence of teaching potentiality.

In view of this condition one may question the high rates of failure among applicants for regular junior and senior high school positions. A very large number of these failures are working successfully as substitute teachers in the secondary schools. The validity and reliability of these teacher examinations have been repeatedly questioned by many people.

A more effective method of staffing the schools is to grant conditional licenses after a quick qualifying test. More responsibility should be placed upon the school principal to determine a person's qualifications for the job. Written and oral tests are artificial and academic, and too often reject excellent potential teachers. There is no better test of a person's teaching ability than actual performance in a classroom.

A principal's approval of a conditional license-holder after one year of observation should validate the license and enable the teacher to obtain tenure after two additional years. Should a new teacher prove incompetent the principal may have the option to release this person within one year. Such a teacher should have one additional opportunity to prove her competence in another school.

The law establishing the Board of Examiners is too restrictive for the size and diversity of the New York City school system. In its place we need a method of teacher recruitment and selection which is more efficient, simpler, and more responsive to the special needs of each community.

COMMR. FRENCH: Thank you very much.

MR. TRACTENBERG: Mr. Flinker, just a couple of questions, if I may.

How long have you been in the New York City school system?

MR. FLINKER: I was appointed as teacher of common branches to Public School 80 in Brooklyn in 1937.

MR. TRACTENBERG: And you have been in the system ever since?

MR. FLINKER: Yes.

MR. TRACTENBERG: Presumably you, too, have accumulated a fair number of licenses during that period. Isn't that so?

MR. FLINKER: Yes, I have my quota of licenses. I moved from the elementary schools into the secondary schools. I took the examination for the license as teacher of history in the junior high school and teacher of economics in the senior high school, then went on--served in both capacities--went on to the license as assistant principal. I served in that capacity for five years, became an elementary school principal, served there for two years, and then junior high school principal since 1953.

MR. TRACTENBERG: Presumably your remarks are colored not only by your experience as a principal and the difficulties you have encountered in getting teachers, but by your own reaction to the examination process as you personally witnessed it?

MR. FLINKER: Yes, my opinions and conclusions are drawn from my own extensive experience in the system.

MR. TRACTENBERG: Mr. Flinker, what is the approximate racial composition of your school, the student population?

MR. FLINKER: We have a Black population of 53%, Puerto Rican group of about 23%, and others approximately 22%.

MR. TRACTENBERG: How does the racial composition of the faculty compare with that?

MR. FLINKER: It is predominantly white. We have eight Black teachers. I have tried many, many ways to attract and retain Black and Puerto Rican teachers, but we have been unable to obtain enough.

MR. TRACTENBERG: Is the absence of bilingual teachers --some of the white teachers, of course, may be bilingual--a problem in your school with approximately a quarter of the pupils Puerto Rican?

MR. FLINKER: Yes, we have a problem in filling the need for bilingual teachers. None are ever sent to our school, although we definitely need them.

MR. TRACTENBERG: Let me just address one or two questions to the system which you have proposed, that is a system of provisional licensure, a year's trial on the job.

Do you think that this system would lead to widespread patronage, a spoils system if you will?

MR. FLINKER: No, I believe that a set of criteria would serve to provide a large pool of qualified applicants. I don't believe that a community school board would risk the welfare of the children with any politicking or nepotism or nomination of favorite sons. I think that the welfare of the children would be placed first.

MR. TRACTENBERG: And two final questions.

One, would you consider state certification a sufficient basis for this provisional license or would you like something else in addition to it?

MR. FLINKER: I would consider state certification as minimal, and I would, in addition, add those necessary requirements that will especially meet the needs of the children in the community.

For example, in a bilingual neighborhood we must have teachers who are trained to meet the needs of these children, and therefore, certain courses must be taken.

I would certainly want to add a course in the teaching of reading, which is not specified as part of the state requirements, and, of course, in human relations, which is part of the New York City requirement at the present time.

MR. TRACTENBERG: And, finally, your recommended system would be largely dependent on the ability of principals and community boards to really appraise the job performance of teachers during this one year provisional period.

Have you any reason to believe that they would, in fact, discharge that responsibility since it is possible under the current system for a principal and his community board or community superintendent to discharge a probationary employee any time during the first three years of his service?

MR. FLINKER: It is possible, but it is more difficult under the present system because the teacher comes to the school with a license granted by an authoritative body, namely, the Board of Examiners. The principal has greater difficulty validating his objections to dismiss the teacher when the teacher comes with such a license.

However, it is much easier for a principal to replace a substitute teacher who does not have the regular license, and, therefore, I believe that the provisional license would be tantamount to a substitute license and would enable the principal to make the change more readily.

MR. TRACTENBERG: Is such replacement of substitutes fairly frequently done within the current system?

MR. FLINKER: Yes, they are done frequently in the case of substitute teachers.

MR. TRACTENBERG: I don't have any further questions.

COMMR. FRENCH: Excuse me, you said there are eight black teachers in your--

MR. FLINKER: There are eight Black teachers in my school.

COMMR. FRENCH: Our Chairman was called out unexpectedly, and I would like to say to you what I know she would, if she was here, as she did to Dr. Gaines, that it is the greatest help to have you offer testimony that is so specific and from one who has been on the firing line and knows the problem in all its complexity. We thank you.

Mr. Lang?

DR. THEODORE H. LANG: As requested, Commissioner French, I have a statement, which I will read.

COMMR. FRENCH: Yes.

DR. LANG: I was asked to prepare it.

I have a little difficulty in reading it because I didn't bring my reading glasses along with me. I'll hold it way out in front of me.

I wish the Commission success in its efforts to search into ways of improving the ethnic balance in the New York City school system. This has been the objective of the Board of Education and the Office of Personnel for the five and a half years that I have been associated with the school system and for several years prior thereto. An objective and impartial review by another agency may identify legal and practical steps and techniques not apparent to those busily engaged in this field over the years. Although I am leaving the Board of Education, I am sure that I can say that we will look forward eagerly to positive and constructive suggestions from your Commission.

The role of the Office of Personnel in regard to the staffing of the schools can be discussed under the major headings of Recruitment and Training and License Requirements. In all our efforts in these areas in the past five years, one of our consistent goals has been to bring more Black and Puerto Rican teachers and supervisors into the system.

I should like first to discuss recruitment on the teacher level:

1. General Field Recruitment:
   This program is conducted intensively, both within the metropolitan area and around the part of the country east of the Mississippi River.

   A good portion of this effort has been focused on minority groups. Because of the relative paucity of minority group candidates in the metropolitan area colleges, we added, a few years ago, field recruitment at Negro colleges or centers contiguous to them and, in addition, recruitment trips to Puerto Rico. This program developed into a combination recruitment and field examination approach in order to attract more minority group applicants by removing as much involvement as possible.

   We advertise in newspapers and magazines likely to reach the minority group publics, both Black and Puerto Rican. In addition, invitations to join our staff have been carried over radio stations directed to the minority group public.

   Field visits to Puerto Rico have been conducted in conjunction with the Unit on the Recruitment and Training of Spanish-speaking Teachers.

   The Board of Education has recently approved a proposal from this office which will permit us to reach 100,000 college seniors on a direct mail basis. The 150 colleges with largely minority group enrollment will be included in this mailing.

2. Special Joint Employment Recruitment Program (Board of Education/United Federation of Teachers):
   This program started this year. As a result, we are visiting colleges attended primarily by Black students. The specific goal of this program is to increase the number of minority group staff in our school system and to integrate the new teachers on a system-wide basis. As of the present moment, we have approximately 1,000 predominantly Black candidates awaiting examination by the Board of Examiners. As part of this program new series of posters, brochures and films have been developed designed to attract Blacks and Puerto Ricans into the system. The recruitment staff has been tripled. We will be attending conferences and conventions frequented mainly by minority group teachers as prospective teachers.

3. The New National Teacher Examination Program authorized by the Decentralization Law will apply to those schools falling in the lowest 40% based on reading scores. This will go into effect this year with earliest appointments to be made in September, 1971. Teachers recruited for these schools will be exempted from competitive examinations and will be exempted from taking the Board of Examiners examination. They will take, instead, the NTE and will have to meet other standards of fitness in regard to health and character. This new approach gives community school boards much greater flexibility and allows simpler and more effective and more aggressive recruitment of Blacks and Puerto Ricans. This will also enable such community school systems to extablish training relationships with colleges and to follow through by giving priority of consideration for appointments to the students they have trained.

In regard to pre-service training programs for teachers, I state that we have sought funds from every possible source to implement as many programs as possible for pre-service training of Blacks and Puerto Ricans. I have made available to you a booklet, entitled "Programs and Projects 1969/70 of the Division of Recruitment, Training and Staff Development," which lists many of these programs. Here I will select a few for brief comment as follows:

1. Intensive Teacher Training Program:

This program was conducted in the summers of 1967 and 1968, providing for 12 education credits to college graduates. It was a crash program intended to meet the severe teacher shortages at that time, with instructions to the universities involved to give priority of consideration to Blacks and Puerto Ricans.

2. TENET:

This special program conducted with City College during the school year included two categories of candidates:

    a) College graduates needing education credits.

    b) Applicants who met all requirements but teaching experience.

About 25 Black and Puerto Rican candidates (50% of the group) are included among those presently completing this program.

3. TEMPUS:

This parallels the TENET program but it is a Masters Degree program for the candidates. This is an ongoing program which includes minority group candidates. It includes 50 Spanish-speaking participants next year.

4. Recruitment and Training of Spanish-speaking Teachers:

In this program we seek out in New York and Puerto Rico Spanish-speaking candidates who have been certified or are interested in teaching in the New York City schools and with enough college background to enable us to provide in a reasonable time the additional training needed to enable them to pass the examination for license and to succeed in teaching in New York City. In the past two years, 183 participants in this program obtained licenses in our system, about 223 are pending licenses and another 222 are still in the program.

5. Veterans in Educational Service:

This program provides for paraprofessional employment and college training for selected veterans in elementary schools and in high schools. About 50% of the present 41 are minority group members.

6. Career Ladder Program--Career Opportunities Program:

As with the veterans, these programs provide for college training for paraprofessionals and will lead to a degree and qualifications for teaching license. These programs are fairly new but include almost 1,400 persons, about 80% minority group. We expect this program to grow to over 3,000 trainees as a result of collective bargaining agreements.

7. POWER:

Applicants for license who needed assistance in written or oral English were offered remediation and counseling through this program. Since we have a relatively larger number of minority group staff in the substitute status, this program helps us in our efforts to increase the percentage of regularly licensed Black and Puerto Rican personnel.

On the supervisory level our primary efforts have been directed toward the professional seminars. In 1964 and 1965, the first such professional seminar was held in preparation for the license for Assistant Principal, Elementary Schools. In April, 1967, because of the success of the first effort, the Professional Promotional Seminars were regularized and assigned to the Office of Personnel. Since then we have been giving these seminars for every promotional examination. These seminars were established for the purpose of improving the opportunities of minority group staff to prepare for higher license. Dr. Dennis Hayes will be reporting to you on the numbers involved and the ethnic counts.

I indicated to you that another major responsibility of the Office of Personnel is in regard to recommendations for changes in license requirements. In connection with supervisory examinations held in the past three years, numerous changes in license requirements have been recommended and put into effect primarily for the purpose of increasing the numbers of Blacks and Puerto Ricans who would be eligible for these license examinations, without in any way, in our judgment, diminishing the quality of the resulting eligible list. Thus, there have been reductions in unnecessarily high experience requirements. There has been the acceptance of substitute experience and experience as an acting supervisor instead of insisting upon experience as a regular teacher or as a regular supervisor. There has also been the acceptance of such internship programs as the Fordham Urban Administrative Internship Program. As a result of these changes many more Blacks and Puerto Ricans have been eligible to take these examinations than would otherwise have been true.

On the teacher level, new licenses have been established, such as Teacher of Common Branches (Bilingual), Teacher of Early Childhood Education (Bilingual), Bilingual Professional Assistant; and others are in process, namely Guidance Counsellor (Bilingual) and School Secretary (Bilingual).

Now, let us take a look at the results of these programs. I must admit that results have been very disappointing to those of us who have exerted so much effort to advance this objective.

The balance of this discussion on results will apply primarily to Black teachers because the first ethnic count by the Board of Education of Puerto Ricans was taken in March, 1969. Insofar as Blacks are concerned, the percentage of Blacks in the system increased from 8.2% in 1963 to 8.8% in 1966 to 9.1% in 1969. This is disappointing indeed. However, a deeper analysis indicates a substantial increase in the number of Black teachers in absolute numbers from an estimate of 3,500 in 1963 to 5,395 in 1969, representing an increase of approximately 54% from 1963 to 1969. This compares with the increase of non-Black teachers from an estimate of 38,700 in 1963 to 53,713 in 1969 representing an increase of approximately 39% from 1963 to 1969.

We made an ethnic count of the supervisory staff only in the years 1966 and 1969. Lumping together appointed supervisors and acting supervisors, we still have a very disappointing figure of approximately 4% Black supervisors in 1966 and only approximately 8% in 1969. However, it is to be noted that there has been an actual increase of Black supervisors from 162 in 1966 to 341 in 1969, representing an increase of 110%. The increase in non-Black supervisors was from 3,581 in 1966 to 3,899 in 1969 or approximately 9%. I caution you that in these figures the Blacks are more heavily represented in the acting posts percentage-wise than they are in the appointed posts. Acting principals have been paid the principal's salary. Acting intermediate supervisors have not.

In thinking about the reasons for the slow growth of Blacks in the system and the small percentages of Blacks and Puerto Ricans in the system, I offer the following:
1. The percentages of college graduates who are Blacks and Puerto Ricans are much smaller than their percentages in the adult population; and in the teaching profession we have been drawing only from college graduates.
2. In the past five years, private industry and governmental jurisdictions and governmental agencies have entered into competition with us for the relatively small number of Black and Puerto Rican college graduates who are available.
3. We do not know the impact of our selection system in New York City as compared with the systems in other sections of the country.

Looking to the future, there are prospects which may make a significant difference in meeting this problem in the next five years.
1. The paraprofessional training program on the collegiate level will be training thousands of Blacks and Puerto Ricans for teaching.
2. The newly implemented open-admissions policy of the City University will significantly increase the percentages of Blacks and Puerto Ricans among college graduates.
3. The National Teacher Examination alternative to the Board of Examiners will give up to 45% of our schools much greater flexibility.
4. Hopefully, there should be both a continuation of and a greater extension of the efforts of the Board of Education, including the Joint Board of Education/UFT Recruitment Program which should capitalize on the other factors described above.

I believe the facts are now favorable for a steady growth in the numbers of Black and Puerto Rican teachers and supervisors in the school system so that that system will be more representative of the people which it serves. I believe further that this can be done with maintenance of quality standards if we allow the above forces to mature over the next five years without pressing for immediate results in a one or two year period of time. May I remind you that over a period of six years we increased the number of Black teachers by 50%. Yet because of the general growth of the system and the small base from which we began, this represented at most a small advance of approximately 1% of the entire system.

Our best efforts within the limited resources made available to the Office of Personnel in the past five years have resulted in measurable but small growth in the percentages of minority staff members in the school system. This has not been adequate for the needs of the system. Special recruitment and training efforts directed towards minority group members are essential, are fully justified, and serve the public good in the best sense. It is not possible, because of strictures in regard to discussion of the selection process, to discuss changes which may be desirable in the selection of teachers and supervisors for the City of New York.

Thank you, Mrs. Norton.

THE CHAIRMAN: Any questions by the Commission?

COMMR. COLGATE: Mr. Lang, I am rather distressed at the figures that you gave me. Had you not, I was going to ask for them.

It seems that in the last five or six years you have been recruiting into the public school system of New York City in the neighborhood of 300 Black and/or Puerto Rican teachers per year.

Is my arithmetic--

DR. LANG: I think your arithmetic is wrong.

COMMR. COLGATE: Wrong?

DR. LANG: Yes.

COMMR. COLGATE: Just let me refresh your testimony.

You said that in 1963 there were 3,500 Black and Puerto Rican teachers and in 1969 5,395. The difference is 1,895 and divided by six years it is approximately 330 a year.

Do you still maintain that my arithmetic is wrong?

DR. LANG: Yes, because there are Blacks leaving the system every year, just as there are whites leaving the system every year.

COMMR. COLGATE: What is the turnover?

DR. LANG: I would estimate that we bring into the system somewhere between 800 and a thousand Blacks and Puerto Ricans, and that the--

COMMR. COLGATE: Three times that many.

DR. LANG: I would estimate that, yes.

COMMR. COLGATE: Maybe--

DR. LANG: I would estimate we bring into the system over 10% Blacks and Puerto Ricans and we bring in every year somewhere between 8,000 and 10,000 into teachers. There's a large turnover in the teaching system, Mr. Colgate.

COMMR. COLGATE: Because, on that basis you brought in

about 1,895 Black and Puerto Rican teachers and about 14,000 white teachers in the same period of time, which would indicate that you have hired about 5,000 Black, and about 45,000 white teachers over the same period of time.

Just so that I get the figures pretty much in mind, is that about what it is?

DR. LANG: Yes.

COMMR. COLGATE: I am not trying to pin you down, Mr. Lang, just trying to get a feel for the process.

DR. LANG: Well, there are somewhere between 8,000 and 10,000 teachers coming in each year, beginning teachers. Of that figure, I would estimate somewhere between ten and 13% are Black and Puerto Rican and then they are leaving--we don't have an ethnic count as they leave--and I just gave you the actual counts that we had in 1969, March '69, and the actual counts that we made in 1966.

COMMR. COLGATE: You mentioned that your recruitment staff has been tripled, if I recall your testimony.

How many people were on your recruitment staff and how many are on it now?

DR. LANG: Those figures, I think were made available to the Commission, and Mr. Williams will be testifying in more detail--

THE CHAIRMAN: We have those figures. We did get some data from Mr. Lang's office earlier.

DR. LANG: Yes.

COMMR. COLGATE: It was just a matter that I don't have them.

DR. LANG: From a financial point of view, I think we had $100,000 a year for recruitment prior to this year and this year we're closer to $500,000. $400,000 to $500,000 is in the Joint UFT/Board of Education Recruitment Program.

COMMR. COLGATE: You mentioned that you had been placing advertisements in newspapers and magazines, and I was just wondering, what I was getting to, what sort of budget you had for that.

DR. LANG: Well, prior to this last year, we had around--somewhere around $30,000 to $40,000 for that kind of expense. This year, with the UFT program, we will have significantly more than that, closer to $100,000; but, again, I'd rather have those figures given to you in writing, have them researched and be absolutely accurate. I'm just speaking here from recollection.

COMMR. COLGATE: Very well.

I have no further questions.

THE CHAIRMAN: Mr. Tractenberg.

MR. TRACTENBERG: Dr. Lang, you mentioned in your testimony a number of programs, most of which I think you say had been designed to increase the number of Black and Puerto Rican teachers and supervisors.

Are all of those programs still in operation?

DR. LANG: All of those programs are still in operation except the Intensive Teacher Training Program, which is budgeted for but has not been needed in past years. The Intensive Teacher Training Program did not have the primary purpose of bringing in Blacks and Puerto Ricans; it had a primary purpose of fully staffing the schools. We anticipated in 1966 the schools would be short 3,000 teachers, and we went out to get them; and in 1967 we anticipated we would be short 2,000 teachers, and we went out to get them. However, in the process of getting them, New York City University and State University were told by us that when there were qualified Blacks available and qualified Puerto Ricans available, to take them, not to go for the higher grades or the highest marks in school but first to accept qualified Blacks and Puerto Ricans, because that was the greatest need of the school system.

MR. TRACTENBERG: What was the effect of that program? Were a substantial number of Black and Puerto Rican teachers brought into the system?

DR. LANG: The program was successful in staffing the schools, and the city schools have been well staffed numerically since 1966. There has been a teacher in front of every classroom from the first day at the beginning of the term, and the teachers have been available throughout the school year.

I don't have an ethnic count of the product of the I.T.T.P. I can not give it to you now and we have to look to see if it exists.

MR. TRACTENBERG: Because, as you may be aware, there have been many charges made that that was a program that, in fact, consisted largely of white applicants trained at a specially quick rate to teach, and that most of them sent to Black and Puerto Rican schools.

DR. LANG: Well, I don't think that that--I don't recall that change at all. I do recall the resistance that there was to the program in the first year of the program because most of the products of the I.T.T.P. program had gone into the special service schools, but that resistance disappeared.

In the second or third year of the program there was no resistance to the program, or communities were not displeased with the program at all.

MR. TRACTENBERG: Let me ask you a couple--

DR. LANG: I don't recall at any time any change on an ethnic basis in regard to the program about the ethnic composition of the program.

MR. TRACTENBERG: Let me ask you a fundamental question.

How would you characterize the portion of the overall personnel selection process which resides under the jurisdiction of your Office of Personnel?

What components of the overall process are under other control and what kind of coordination is there?

DR. LANG: Our responsibilities are, as I pointed out in my remarks, primarily recruitment, which means going out to bring in candidates; training, both pre-service and post-entry training; and the matter of the license requirements.

It is important that the selection and the pre-service training work closely with--rather the recruitment and pre-service training work closely with--the selection process, so we must work very closely with the Board of Examiners, and we must have their cooperation in these programs if they are to be successful.

MR. TRACTENBERG: And in your judgment there has been an adequate level of cooperation?

DR. LANG: Well, in my judgment, after necessary periods of discussion, sometimes fairly extended, we have generally been getting the cooperation of the Board of Examiners.

MR. TRACTENBERG: Does the Board of Examiners play some role in the recruitment process?

DR. LANG: They do not, except, of course, for the fact that they do rule on whether the recruits are qualified or not. So that a recruit who wishes an authoritative ruling on whether or not he or she is qualified would have to go to the Board of Examiners. They do not otherwise play any role in the recruitment process except as advisors to us.

In the NTE program we will be able to work more freely without the Board of Examiners, working directly with community superintendents, and we are now. We have met with the community superintendents, and we are meeting with their staff to work out the details of this kind of recruitment program, which will give the community superintendents and their principals a great deal of decision-making power in the selection of the persons who will go into their schools.

MR. TRACTENBERG: Since you mention that, let's talk about it.

I assume you are referring to the 40% hiring provision?

DR. LANG: It's 40% this year, and in future years it's 45%.

MR. TRACTENBERG: I asked a question of Dr. Gaines as a community superintendent, and she wasn't sure of the answer and suggested that I ask you. The question is: the law stipulates that the appointment authority expires on May 1st for the following year, and I asked Dr. Gaines whether she, as a community superintendent, would know by May 1st with any level of precision at all how many vacancies she would have for the following September, and she said she would not know with any precision.

From your vantage point does that seem to be a common practice?

DR. LANG: No, I think that if we work closely with the community superintendents, based upon experience, we can anticipate a safe number of--based upon experience, we can project an estimated number of--vacancies for a district; and I think that we can work out a figure that they can operate with.

MR. TRACTENBERG: But it is a best guess rather than a precise figure?

DR. LANG: We have been going out in the field and making commitments for employment in the past few years. That's how we staffed the schools. We have been going out in the schools in April and May making commitments. Now the community superintendent will have to do it. But it will be based upon information from principals who can anticipate vacancies. Then when you group it together statistically for thirty schools in a district, I think you can develop a working figure that you can go ahead and make appointments. I don't think it will stop the program.

MR. TRACTENBERG: Is there any reason of personnel administration that would suggest that this appointment authority of the community boards should expire on May 1st?

DR. LANG: Well, I don't know the reason for that. You'll have to ask the legislative body.

COMMR. COLGATE: From your point of view you are not aware of any?

DR. LANG: No, I would support an amendment. As I sit here, without having a chance to reflect too deeply, I don't understand why there should be that limitation; but I do want to point out to you and Dr. Gaines that in the following September, in the event there are vacancies, that you are not restricted, and then you can bring in persons throughout in the examinations immediately.

There are two parts to the law. One is appointments to meet projected needs for the following September. The next part is appointments in the current school year to meet immediate needs.

MR. TRACTENBERG: But that presupposes, of course, that there are qualified people around in September who have not committed themselves to other positions.

DR. LANG: Well, that supposes it, and that is always true. There are always some people around who haven't committed themselves. It all becomes a matter of numbers, but certainly there should be a way if there is somebody around and if there is a need; there should be some way to bring them in directly and immediately, and the NTE law permits that.

MR. TRACTENBERG: As I read the statute, it seems to suggest that the threshhold qualification for appointment under this provision is higher than at least one of the routes for certification under the regular provision. That is, it seems to require as a threshhold that the particular person have the education and experience requirements for certification, which I believe is a Master's Degree.

Isn't there an escape valve from the requirement for persons going through the regular certification process?

DR. LANG: I don't--you do not require a Master's Degree for State certification. There are two kinds of certification. One is provisional certification; the other is permanent certification. Permanent certification for most teaching positions is a baccalaureate degree. But you are right in a different way. The state certification requirements are slightly higher than the license requirements of the Board of Education.

MR. TRACTENBERG: So that, in fact, this special hiring provision excludes from the ability of community boards the appointment of people who could be licensed regularly, because it imposes higher standards?

DR. LANG: That may be possible, yes. There's a slight point there that you have that may require attention and maybe legislation.

Incidentally, it's not generally known.

MR. TRACTENBERG: It probably is now. Dr. Lang--

DR. LANG: As a matter of fact, I don't think you knew it when you said it. You were talking about something else.

MR. TRACTENBERG: How successful is the school system at the moment in filling all vacancies with fully licensed, regular teachers? I don't mean just a teacher in front of a classroom but someone fully licensed.

DR. LANG: Well, it is very successful in meeting those needs. There are no new substitutes coming into the system. The only persons coming into the system now are persons from regular lists, with the exception of a small number of temporary, per diem teachers. Others are coming in regularly, and we are eminently successful in that regard.

MR. TRACTENBERG: Does that suggest you will ultimately phase out substitute teachers entirely?

DR. LANG: Yes, that's in the cards. Under the contract with the United Federation of Teachers, two consecutive contracts now, there will be no further substitute license given for teachers; there will be only regular licenses.

MR. TRACTENBERG: I want to touch on a couple of other areas, if I may. One is the question of whether and to what extent the establishment of eligibility requirements for taking examinations is a function of your office.

DR. LANG: Well, as I indicated, the Office of Personnel is the principal advisor to the Chancellor in regard to license requirements.

MR. TRACTENBERG: Mr. Bergtram, in his testimony this morning, suggested that since his Board of Education has been in office he believes that they have established a policy under which every set of eligibility requirements for examinations which have been given since his Board took office has been reviewed and substantially modified to reflect the needs of urban school districts. Does that sound familiar to you?

DR. LANG: Well, as I said myself, in the past three years in regard to every supervisory license, we have had a critical review and analysis of how many Blacks and Puerto Ricans would be eligible under the existing requirements and how the requirements can be changed to bring in more Blacks and Puerto Ricans, maintaining a quality list; and there have been a significant number of changes made. But, of course, all these changes take time until persons come in with a license. It just doesn't take time, but there have been a significant number--from the inside it looks like a revolution, from the outside it looks like nothing happens--and when you look at the figures it is very slow progress.

MR. TRACTENBERG: Has that analysis been carried out for teachers' eligibility requirements as well?

DR. LANG: Well, on elementary teacher requirements we meet state certification requirements a little lower than that for provisional, for our minimum certification. So that we--our requirements for teachers have, on the whole, not been higher than state certification requirements as long as I can remember. There have been no significant changes in that regard. It is mostly on a supervisory level that we have had significant changes.

MR. TRACTENBERG: Are eligibility requirements the same thing as the description of duties or job analyses on the basis of which the Board of Examiners constructs its tests?

DR. LANG: Well, eligibility requirements deal with the training that a person is required to have. Statements of duties and job analyses describe the tasks that the person has to perform. The Board of Examiners uses all three. They are bound by the requirements that are fixed by the Board of Education and they take the duty statements which are set up by the Chancellor and use those as a guide for the examinations.

MR. TRACTENBERG: Is your office the arm of the Chancellor which prepares those descriptions of duties?

DR. LANG: That is correct.

MR. TRACTENBERG: How do you go about compiling such a description for a teaching position?

DR. LANG: Well, I don't recall sending them down on teaching positions themselves. I recall someone sending them down on supervisory positions. I don't recall that we have been asked for the statements or duties of a teacher.

MR. TRACTENBERG: So far as you know, the Board of Examiners has no statements of duties for teaching personnel?

DR. LANG: I have not seen--I have not seen a statement of duties for a teacher in the past five years. I guess we assume we have knowledge of what a teacher does when the Board of Examiners has knowledge of it. They may be in the record though.

MR. TRACTENBERG: I see.

DR. LANG: They probably are in the record. They probably have them down in the Board of Examiners.

MR. TRACTENBERG: Doesn't that suggest to you a slight breakdown in the system?
What I gather you are suggesting is that in your five and a half years in the school system there has never been a new set of job descriptions for teaching personnel?

DR. LANG: That's correct, not for teaching personnel, for teachers.

MR. TRACTENBERG: Teachers?

DR. LANG: Yes. For supervisory personnel it is customary to send down a statement for every license, every examination.

MR. TRACTENBERG: So that presumably the qualifications for teachers--

DR. LANG: Not qualifications, the requirements. The requirements are fixed in the bylaws. Statements of duties are not. They are administratively prepared and approved and go down to the Board of Examiners. The Board of Examiners uses them for examinations. I don't recall sending one down in regard to a teacher license in recent years.

MR. TRACTENBERG: The thinking which prevailed at least five and perhaps more years ago as to what the duties of a teacher were, insofar as you know, is still the prevailing view of what the duties of teachers are in the system, and it is on that basis that teacher examinations are constructed?

DR. LANG: Well, I won't answer that question in regard to how teacher examinations are constructed nor what the judgment of the Board of Examiners is in regard to what the duties of a teacher are. They'll have to answer that themselves.

MR. TRACTENBERG: But isn't it your responsibility, the responsibility of the Chancellor, ultimately to devise that statement of duties?

DR. LANG: I would say that we do have a responsibility to devise the statement of responsibilities and send it down, yes.

MR. TRACTENBERG: But you have not felt that responsibility involved updating any of the teacher statements of duties in at least the last five years?

DR. LANG: That's correct.

That doesn't mean it shouldn't be done now, but I have not up to this point.

MR. TRACTENBERG: Is your office also involved in the assignments of teachers?

DR. LANG: Yes.

MR. TRACTENBERG: So that once an eligible list is produced by the Board of Examiners the actual act of parcelling out teachers among the various community districts is a function of your office?

DR. LANG: That's correct.

MR. TRACTENBERG: Do you have any written policies which state the factors you have taken into account or the sequence in which assignments are made?

DR. LANG: Well, there is a--there are the guidelines of the Board of Education in regard to assignment. What we do now is send the lists out to the community boards. The community boards review the lists and indicate the persons that they want to appoint, and also they can indicate the persons they don't want sent to them. Those are then compiled centrally and assignments are made by the Office of Personnel, giving each community system whom it wants, if it is legally possible to do it.

MR. TRACTENBERG: That means that technically each appointment has to come from among the top three. How does that work if, for example, Community District 1 says that the people they want rank number one, number 500 and number 1000 on this list?

DR. LANG: Well, we have, you recall, been able to use up a list at one time; so therefore, we can give each board precisely whom it wants, if it knows, and if they need 50 teachers and they have identified 30 that they want, the Office of Personnel will fill in with the additional 20, in order from the list.

MR. TRACTENBERG: The ranked list is in effect a qualifying list? It does not matter where on the list particular people fall?

DR. LANG: When we are able to appoint an entire list, and we try to do that, that is correct. We treat it as a qualifying list, allowing the community boards to pick anywhere on the list; but everyone on the list then is appointed, so no one has a complaint.

MR. TRACTENBERG: But let's assume only 75% of any given list is appointed. The community board which wants someone in the bottom 25% would have its desires frustrated?

DR. LANG: That's correct. We would then draw a line and notify the community boards to "Indicate your preference up to a certain number on the eligible list," and within that number we would honor their request. If it's below that number, we could not because of the requirements of a competitive eligible list.

MR. TRACTENBERG: Has the time taken to promulgate lists caused you any problems in terms of this central assignment function? Have you had vacancies in schools which couldn't be filled because of particular lists which had not yet been established by the Board of Examiners?

DR. LANG: I think yes, yes.

MR. TRACTENBERG: Is that a common problem?

DR. LANG: It takes time to bring out an eligible list. So that is an inevitable problem, unless you can have instantaneous lists. If a list takes six months, then you may have a list in progress while you have vacancies. If a list takes three months, you still will have vacancies while a list is in progress.

MR. TRACTENBERG: How do you normally--

DR. LANG: It normally takes the Board of Examiners-- again, this is something they should be telling you about themselves--I would say from six to eight months to bring out a teacher list. It takes longer for supervisors' lists.

MR. TRACTENBERG: But from your point of view of having basic responsibility for administering the personnel apparatus, it is a problem?

DR. LANG: It is a problem when the lists are not available when needed. Of course, the Board of Examiners will always tell me that they are working very, very hard, and they bring these lists out in order, and they will consult with me on the order that we prefer. So that we will determine the priorities for them as to what list to process first, dependent upon the needs of the system as we see it.

MR. TRACTENBERG: How do you ordinarily deal with the problem created if there is a need in community districts which have vacancies and a list not yet promulgated? Are the people who are applicants somehow assigned there on a substitute license?

DR. LANG: Well, we met that problem as soon as we entered into an agreement with the United Federation of Teachers eliminating substitute licenses. That eliminated the possibility of an emergency substitute license where we could bring somebody in to fill a need as the need developed without waiting for months to establish an eligible list. We have established a per diem teacher's certification, which is radically different from the old substitute license, and this enables us to, if there is a teacher needed and there is a person available who meets the requirements, we are able to put them in that spot within a few days.

MR. TRACTENBERG: Again, this presupposes that the person is willing to take the job on that basis rather than on a fully licensed basis?

DR. LANG: Yes.

We will canvass the candidates and find out who is willing. We will canvass those on the list and ask them if they want it. We will advise, if necessary, to bring in persons for a temporary per diem teacher's certificate, but we have been able--again, I say this with pride--to fill in the staff of the city school system, and there's 60,000 teachers strong; so that at any one time, any one day, there are fewer than one hundred vacant positions.

In addition, of course, there is what we call absentee teacher reserve, which is a number of teachers above the authorized budget. These teachers are available as a pool to replace absent teachers on that day. That's above and beyond, so that actually we have been well staffed numerically. I am not talking about qualitatively. But, of course, you can staff better qualitatively when you are staffed quantitatively because then you can begin to weed out less competent teachers which you can't do when you have a quantitative shortage.

MR. TRACTENBERG: Just a few more questions--I want to catch you before you leave the school system.

DR. LANG: I left already. You brought me back.

MR. TRACTENBERG: Dr. Lang, approximately what percentage of teachers in the system or teachers recruited each year come from the New York metropolitan area?

DR. LANG: Well, I really don't have any figure on that. I believe that the great majority come from the New York metropolitan area. I would guess that over 90% come from the New York metropolitan area.

MR. TRACTENBERG: I have heard the figure 60 to 65% for those who come from City University.

DR. LANG: I guess that sounds accurate. Of course, we have, in addition to the City University, about 25 other colleges and universities that serve us.

MR. TRACTENBERG: Focussing for a minute on City University, in view of the great percentage of New York City public school teachers who come from there, is there some procedure whereby fairly regular feedback is received by your office about the qualities of particular applicants? I gather that the teachers colleges tend to produce rather detailed personnel data files on each of the students who complete their course.

Is that reviewed by someone on your staff as a part of the selection process?

DR. LANG: My staff doesn't do the selecting. The determination of fitness is made by the Board of Examiners. To the best of my knowledge, they do not use those dossiers or records or folders of student teachers or students in teaching preparation programs.

We do have those records available and make them available to community superintendents if they wish to use them in regard to their choice from among those on the eligible list, and Mr. Brooks of my office is liaison with the schools, the colleges and our schools, in that regard.

MR. TRACTENBERG: You have access to them although the Board of Examiners may not use them?

DR. LANG: Yes, I think they should be used. I think they should be used more, and I think they will be used extensively in what I call the NTE alternative to the Board of Examiners. I think they will be used.

MR. TRACTENBERG: Two final things, Dr. Lang.

Number one, in your judgment should the probationary period be an important part of this continuing process of recruitment and selection of personnel, and, to the extent that your office has any role in this area, is it now being used in any meaningful way?

DR. LANG: I would say, to answer your first question, yes. I would agree with some of the things I heard earlier today that the only way to really know whether a teacher is a good teacher is by giving him the opportunity to teach and observing him as he teaches. So I say that the probationary period is of critical importance.

I would say that the school system has used the probationary period very little in the past, too little, in my opinion, and I think it is being used more in the last year than in prior years because of the general activity and local initiative. I think that decentralization will have an impact on the view of probationers and whether they should stay in the system.

We have seen the fundamental of that. It is at least double.

MR. TRACTENBERG: And, finally, perhaps you can view this as your valedictory, I wonder if you have any suggested improvements in the personnel system which you think would both make administratively simpler the kind of job that you have been in for five and a half years and which would better serve the school children of the city by producing more people able to teach them well. We would be especially interested in your view of state certification as to the basis of this progress.

DR. LANG: Well, I have enthusiastically seized the opportunity of the NTE alternative to the Board of Examiners. I would really like to say what it does for our system.

I hope that it will bring better qualified teachers, as well as more Blacks and Puerto Ricans into the system. It will be closer to the practices of other school systems, giving the principal more authority in the determination of his staff, involving the principal in the selection of the teacher and the principal then having greater sense of responsibility in the training of the teacher.

I would like to see that tried as it will be, and I would like to see it evaluated, to see if we can get better teachers that way than through the old selection method.

I do think that the making of a good teacher will happen more after appointment in the classroom under the supervision of his colleagues and teacher trainers. I think there ought to be a lot more effort spent in teacher training during the first two and three years of the service of a teacher. I don't think--the colleges have not demonstrated yet--that they can bring a student to the point where he will be more than a, at most, a beginning teacher needing a lot of support and a lot of assistance and a lot of further training. I don't think you can teach a pilot how to fly on ground and I don't think you can teach a teacher how to teach outside the classroom.

MR. TRACTENBERG: Thank you.

THE CHAIRMAN: Thank you, Dr. Lang.

MR. FREDERICK H. WILLIAMS: Frederick H. Williams, Assistant Superintendent, Division of Recruitment, Training, and Staff Development, Office of Personnel.

Mrs. Norton, ladies and gentlemen, since the last school year, I have had a continuing specific responsibility in the area of ethnic ratio of staff. Consequently, I look forward to the constructive suggestions which may develop from these hearings with respect to increasing the number of minority group professionals on our staff.

I have been on the staff of the Office of Personnel since September, 1969, as Assistant Superintendent in charge of the Division of Recruitment, Training, and Staff Development. Prior to that, I was Director of Human Relations and then Assistant Superintendent in charge of the Office of Intergroup Education. In these latter capacities, I was very concerned with the same problem.

Through all the years, relatively little has been accomplished in comparison to the effort made. While there has been growth in absolute numbers of Blacks and Spanish-speaking personnel, the growth in total staff has been such as to leave the percentages unaffected.

The additional methods of selection of personnel established in the Decnetralization Law, the increasing number of paraprofessionals in the career ladder, are encouraging signs.

Since Dr. Lang has already spoken and did so from the vantage point of one familiar with the development and progress of these individual programs, I will try to avoid repeating his comments.

I regard the increase in minority group staff teachers and supervisors as a major goal of the Division of Recruitment, Training and Staff Development and of each unit of the Division. I included this in the published statement of continuing objectives of the Division for this year.

Incidentally, I believe it important that the staff of the Office of Personnel itself reflect our effort in this direction. Since my assignment to head the Division, I have recruited minority staff for key positions to seek better ethnic balance.

Though not included in my divisional responsibility, I have alerted the Deputy Superintendent to staffing matters involving ethnic distribution. For example, I instituted a review of the situation in a bureau outside the Office of Personnel where the racial division of staff generally coincided with the division in levels of work.

Some of the staff of the Division of Recruitment, Training, and Staff Development are included among those you have invited to this hearing. However, let me give you a quick view of all of the units in the Division. I have added some data as appendices to this statement in response to some of the questions contained in Mrs. Norton's letter of invitation. If additional specifics are wished, I will try to supply them for you afterwards.

One of the attachments gives a picture of the budgets over the past three years. The administrative organization of the programs into units has been reshaped as program needs changed. However, the groupings in the tax levy budgets have been about the same. The units handling all pre-service training, training of appointed teachers and executive development are grouped together and share some services. Generally speaking, each of these units has two or three professional staff members and between one and three administrative staff members. The Recruitment Bureau is set out separately, as is the In-service Bureau and the Divisional Office. The Auxiliary Education Career Unit and the Unit on the Recruitment and Training of Spanish-speaking Teachers are and have been funded by federal and state funds. From time to time additional funded projects are devloped but usually are of short duration.

The Recruitment Bureau seeks to meet our objective through the regular field recruitment program and through the Joint Employment Recruitment Program established in the last school year, as a result of the collective bargaining agreement with the United Federation of Teachers. Attached are statistics with regard to the progress of this program.

The Unit on Recruitment and Training of Spanish-speaking Teachers focusses on the two functions contained in its title. The abysmally slow progress in increasing the supply of needed bilingual teachers has been frustrating. The data on the progress to date is attached.

There is a unit on pre-service training which coordinates such programs as student teachers, apprentice teachers and teacher interns. These programs are largely arranged between community districts and colleges. Here, our office acts as a liaison, a facilitator, et cetera.

This unit also conducts a program in the improvement of oral and written English for those substitute teachers or prospective teachers who failed the teacher examination. A large proportion of those who have attended these courses have been Black.

Professional Promotion Seminars are also under the jurisdiction of this unit. The inception of this program a few years ago provided us with the first major breakthrough in our efforts to increase the number of Blacks in supervisory positions. Approximately 135 Blacks and Puerto Ricans were successful out of a total of 700 licensees as assistant principals in elementary schools.

The original program in the Professional Promotion Seminar was specifically designed to overcome many obstacles the minority group applicant usually had in preparing for a supervisory examination. The preparation was too costly; it was conducted in an area far removed from his home or school; it was not sufficiently sensitive to the needs of Black applicants. When I received my present assignment, I undertook to restore some of these features which had not been given the priority I think they deserved.

The Unit on Training Appointed Teachers coordinates the training efforts to provide support for the new or inexperienced teacher. The major parts of the program are: the After-School Study Program for new teachers and the establishment of the position of teacher trainer. Of course, we do not select participants, and by and large we don't select instructors or teacher trainers. When there is an opportunity to select from among the total group for some special purpose, it is standard policy that such a selection represent each of the major social and ethnic groups in the city.

There is a unit on in-service programs. Again, this unit has little direct application to improvement of ethnic proportions on staff.

The Executive Development Program contains two parts. One has provided an internship for newly-licensed principals. The participants in this program have reflected the paucity of Blacks and Puerto Ricans who have been licensed at this level. The second part of the Executive Development Program provides the opportunity for appointed principals and directors to think through the current needs in urban education and to discuss ideas and innovations to meet those needs. Upon my assignment, I requested some community superintendents to include Black and Puerto Rican principals and acting principals in their selections for this program.

The Auxiliary Education Career Unit coordinates the training efforts for the paraprofessionals of our schools. This is one of the most promising sources of Black and Puerto Rican teachers and other staff in related educational fields.

In all programs of these bureaus and units, it is my responsibility to stimulate awareness of the importance of the objective to the improvement of the effectiveness of our educational process.

My responsibility includes, also, removing obstacles to increasing the number of Black and Puerto Rican staff; advising the Deputy Superintendent and other officials in this regard; suggesting additional ideas by which we may increase the number of Blacks and Puerto Ricans on staff and by which the selection process could be made more sensitive to minority group candidates and less subject to particular cultural orientation.

Examples of this would include: working with the Deputy Superintendent for Personnel to make the eligibility requirements for the elementary school principal examination less restrictive; seeking ethnic mix in the interviewing panels used by the Office of Personnel.

All of this, however, has added up to very little movement towards our objective. Each stage in the total process in the preparation of a teacher has fewer and fewer Blacks and Puerto Ricans than the previous stage. In so many aspects of our national life, a process is built up in such a way that it supports the exclusion of minority groups, exclusion to which every facet of life contributes. The process is then strengthened by a labyrinth of laws, rules, regulations, practices, etc. We then engage in the exercise of how to avoid or evade or dodge around these very rules.

It is not surprising that this method produces small results despite the sincere effort of many people. More fundamental change is needed in the process itself rather than the search for ways around it.

Decentralization provides us with opportunity to work cooperatively with the community school districts.

The Decentralization Law, incidentally, has other new methods of selection than the use of the NTE and does permit the community school district in which is located one of the schools in the 40% bracket to select from persons who are on eligible lists without regard to rank as an additional method of selection.

In establishing new relationships with community school districts, I have scheduled meetings with district recruiters and other district officials to discuss ways to meet our mutual goals. The Recruitment Bureau will conduct in-service training at these sessions.

These are just two of a series of such cooperative efforts. I have asked Mr. Santiago, Coordinator of the Unit on Recruitment and Training of Spanish-speaking Teachers to meet with community superintendents and bilingual school principals to plan for a more comprehensive proposal for next year.

My responsibility will be to seek that process which will provide for effective teaching by a qualified staff more representative of the community it serves.

Thank you.

THE CHAIRMAN: Mr. Tractenberg?

MR. TRACTENBERG: Mr. Williams, you said that one part of your job was to remove obstacles that stood in the way of Blacks and Puerto Ricans becoming professional personnel in the system, teachers and supervisors, and you also stated that the results in terms of accomplishment have been rather marginal over the past few years.

I assume that means that you have, in fact, identified certain obstacles that you are in the process of trying to remove.

Could you just indicate some of the obstacles that you have come into contact with?

MR. WILLIAMS: Well, let me give you just the example which has already been posed, just to illustrate.

In trying to determine what the needs might be, to encourage and provide more incentive for Blacks and Puerto Ricans to take the supervisory examinations, we sat down to figure out what some of the blocks were, and it was determined that the process of preparation definitely was a bar. We established that this bar caused failure of many to succeed in the examination. It proved to be a discouragement to even try.

MR. TRACTENBERG: When you say "preparation," are you referring to the--

MR. WILLIAMS: I'm talking about the study, yes, the coaching courses which were preferential elements, some time back, which are still used, and where the Board now undertakes to provide the necessary training and preparation for the examination. And all of the little facts around this, such as the location of the seminar centers as against the location of the coaching courses, things of this nature.

MR. TRACTENBERG: Mr. Williams, if one steps back from the system a bit, doesn't it seem a little ludicrous that one arm of the bureaucracy is creating examinations which another arm of the bureaucracy has to spend dollars to prepare people to take?

MR. WILLIAMS: As long as you are speaking about a large enough bureaucracy. They are all pieces together but not the same pieces necessarily.

MR. TRACTENBERG: But you agree that either there is a lack of coordination, or in effect two parts of the system are, in a sense, working one against the other?

MR. WILLIAMS: I'm not quite sure that I would characterize it in exactly those terms, but I did, in my talk, speak about the fact that this is a national phenomenon that exists in many of the institutions that have come into being in this country, where, in terms of this growth and development, it turns out, you know, that minorities are excluded; and around the institutional establishment is built a whole framework of laws and rules and regulations without regard to the facts of what is excluded.

Then comes a process of, well, being aware of this. What do you do about it? And, so, one way is to see how can I avoid the very things that were put into effect.

Do you say, why don't you just remove them? I don't know, I'm not wise enough to give you the total answer on that, but I know that this is not something that is totally unusual here.

THE CHAIRMAN: It is unusual with respect to principals and teachers if we look at other cities, isn't that so, Mr. Williams?

Some of it is true, I will acknowledge that you are perfectly right, that systems grow up; you can see them everywhere. We are particularly interested that this hasn't been the case with teaching and supervising professionals in the public school systems of this country, the major cities, except here. We are trying to understand why that kind of system would have grown up here where it has not grown up elsewhere.

MR. WILLIAMS: I'm not sure that this would be entirely accurate. I do think it is accurate that other cities certainly had a better proportion, by and large, and have out of the awareness of the past few years been able to obtain an even better proportion of minority group staff than we have been able to in New York City. But I do think that what I'm speaking about is probably preferential treatment in most of the large urban centers of the country, though, ten or twelve years ago, certainly, with very few exceptions.

THE CHAIRMAN: Can you point to any specific factor present today in New York which, in your judgment, may be responsible for our problem here, whereas the problem seems to be taking care of itself much more quickly in other cities? Can you point to any specific factors in our overall system, or elsewhere in the city, that might be responsible for our singular situation here?

MR. WILLIAMS: I could conjecture, Mrs. Norton, but I hope you will permit me not to. There are certain obvious reasons, I would say, and, in all honesty, I haven't established the cause and effect relationship statistically that would allow me to make a statement as to specifically what it is. So, unless you insist on it--

THE CHAIRMAN: I will allow that answer. I ask it of you only because of your chief responsibility in training and development. I thought that that might have put you closer in touch with cause and effect than other people who come here to testify.

MR. WILLIAMS: Well, it may have put me closer to the scene of the difficulty, but not necessarily given me the opportunity or the wherewithal to establish a cause and effect relationship, at least up to this point.

MR. TRACTENBERG: Let me ask him a pointed question which may avoid some of the philosophical issues.

I understand that recruiters for the Detroit school system are able to offer positions on the spot to anybody in the top 50% of his graduating class in an accredited teacher training institution who makes a favorable impression in the campus interview.

I assume there is no comparable provision in New York?

MR. WILLIAMS: Yes.

I don't want to appear cagey on this. Undoubtedly an examination process, per se, is an additional hurdle to overcome for anyone. All I'm saying is that, in terms of establishing this as a hurdle that is more significant for Blacks and Puerto Ricans as against others, there is not much evidence.

MR. TRACTENBERG: Certainly your recruiters come back from schools and there's feedback about why they are not getting as many applicants as they would like.

MR. WILLIAMS: Right.

MR. TRACTENBERG: Would you think that given the Detroit method, for example, your recruiters wouldn't be at an enormous disadvantage if they said, "Yes, you come in and take one of our exams, and six or eight months later we will get you onto a list"?

MR. WILLIAMS: Yes, I would think that having had the opportunity to be more specific and definite about being able to employ a person, without them having to go through some additional steps, would be an aid in the recruitment process, and particularly with respect to Blacks and Puerto Ricans, and that's why we're looking forward so hopefully to the new method of selection which allows us to do this more on the spot.

MR. TRACTENBERG: Wasn't there tried--and may still be in effect, although I have not heard about it recently--one day walk-in examinations which were designed to expedite the process?

MR. WILLIAMS: There was some time back, although I wasn't in the office at the time and I'm not sure of all the details, but I believe it was in the nature of a substitute examination, a substitute or temporary substitute examination, which now is no longer used simply because this whole substitute category is being phased out as per the agreement that exists.

MR. TRACTENBERG: But, so far as you know, there is nothing along the lines of structuring a comparable examination for certain regular teaching licenses?

MR. WILLIAMS: A one-day examination for regular teaching licenses?

MR. TRACTENBERG: Right.

MR. WILLIAMS: No, I know of no such intention.

MR. TRACTENBERG: Mr. Williams, what, at least approximately, is the ethnic composition of your own division, which, after all, has a major responsibility in providing applicants generally, and certainly as you've suggested, Black and Puerto Rican applicants?

MR. WILLIAMS: Let me give it to you, if you will, approximately, simply because I don't have these specific numbers here.

There are about twenty-five professional staff members in the division.

MR. TRACTENBERG: Incidentally, when you say "professional," does that mean that they are--

MR. WILLIAMS: They are pedagogical, I should say.

MR. TRACTENBERG: As in the case of the Board of Examiners these are teachers and supervisors assigned to carry out duties within your division?

MR. WILLIAMS: That's correct.

MR. TRACTENBERG: And they do not take an examination dealing with any facets of their work with you?

MR. WILLIAMS: A couple have, not in all cases, but in particular instances where they are in charge of a special, unique function whereby it is determined that that should be established by license or certification, then that is done. We have a Director of the Bureau of Educational Staff Recruitment, for example, who is a licensed director. We have a Director of the Auxiliary Educational Career Unit Program who is a certified director, but, in most cases, we are talking about principals or assistant principals who are assigned to perform the duties involved.

MR. TRACTENBERG: Are there any professional personnel employees in your division, people with a background and specific training in personnel administration?

MR. WILLIAMS: Yes. We have--there are approximately --three or four personnel examiners or assistant personnel examiners who are part of it.

MR. TRACTENBERG: But the great bulk of your professional staff are people who grew up in the system in an entirely different capacity?

MR. WILLIAMS: That's correct, yes.

MR. TRACTENBERG: Okay, sorry to detour you. You were going to describe the ethnic composition.

MR. WILLIAMS: That's correct.

I was going to give you a figure. Out of approximately twenty-five of the pedagogical personnel there are seven Blacks and approximately five Puerto Ricans.

MR. TRACTENBERG: How many of them are specifically involved in minority recruitment efforts?

MR. WILLIAMS: Well, those in the recruitment bureau are particularly involved, and there are four, I believe, in the bureau. This is approximately accurate.

MR. TRACTENBERG: And those are--

MR. WILLIAMS: Directly involved in recruitment.

MR. TRACTENBERG: Those are included in the twenty-five?

MR. WILLIAMS: Yes, sir.

MR. TRACTENBERG: Let me touch on two or three more areas, if I may.

MR. WILLIAMS: Surely.

MR. TRACTENBERG: Number one, I don't think it's really been made clear in the course of the morning and afternoon exactly what triggers the recruitment efforts of the Board of Education and in particular your division. That is, is there some determination of an anticipated number of vacancies which will determine the scope of your recruiting efforts, or is it purely a budgetary matter, or is it neither of those?

MR. WILLIAMS: Well, it's probably all or more. There is a manpower projection which is made yearly to try and give us the best estimate of what the needs will be in the different areas in the school system, at the different levels, and at the different license areas.

Recruitment is pitched to that to some degree, that is, general recruitment. But we're speaking here about a specific goal which is apart from general recruitment, and that is what do we do about increasing the minority group staff. Those efforts are not dependent upon any manpower projection. Those efforts have been going on and we will increase them. So that is not dependent on the factors you mentioned.

MR. TRACTENBERG: I assume it is dependent on budget to some extent though?

MR. WILLIAMS: Correct, of course. We're limited there.

MR. TRACTENBERG: You have talked about future methods, at least in general. Are there particular things that you anticipate will be tried in the near future to improve the performance of your division in terms of recruiting more minority candidates?

MR. WILLIAMS: I don't have any brand new plan in mind, Mr. Tractenberg. Is that correct?

MR. TRACTENBERG: Yes.

MR. WILLIAMS: I will, however, be searching out not only from my own thinking but from the thinking of anyone whom I think can make a contribution as to what other modes, approaches and efforts could be made. Well, in particular, they have been trying to see whether or not the efforts already set into motion in terms of the new selection procedures established by decentralization will be helpful or successful, whether these are ways that we might expand on or add to or whatever.

MR. TRACTENBERG: But I gather from both Dr. Lang and yourself that substantial faith is being placed in the new recruitment and selection process provided by the Decentralization Law.

MR. WILLIAMS: Yes. I'll say at least hope--and I hope it will be faith. We do think it will make a contribution. We do think it is an improvement over the more limited ways of selecting we have now.

MR. TRACTENBERG: One or two final lines of questions, if I may.

What portion or proportion of your efforts in the recruitment area are directed at supervisory positions, that is, trying to get people from outside the system?

MR. WILLIAMS: There has been some effort in terms of advertising and examination places--that is, the advertising done in places other than New York City and making contacts at different conferences and conventions. And here again there will be particular reference directed to those places where we might have a potential for getting minority group applicants.

MR. TRACTENBERG: What proportion of your advertising would you say presently goes into publications that are directed principally at minority group audiences?

MR. WILLIAMS: I do have some figures on that which I have obtained from the Recruitment Bureau which is charged with that responsibility.

The percentage--the one specific question asked--in publications which have predominantly minority group readership, and reading from 1967-68 up to the present year, would be 33%, 45%, 50% and 81%. For publications used for--

MR. TRACTENBERG: So, then, 81% of your advertising dollars, if you will, are now going into publications that are aimed at a minority group audience?

MR. WILLIAMS: That's correct.

MR. TRACTENBERG: Finally, Mr. Williams, I suppose one other--wait, actually you were in the process of answering an earlier question, so I should let you finish that, the percentage of your manpower, dollars, whatever, aimed at recruiting supervisory as opposed to teaching personnel.

MR. WILLIAMS: Well, it's very difficult to try and give a figure on that. There is a relatively small amount, I would say, devoted to that. We do make a particular effort where there is a large and popular examination coming up, such as for elementary school principal. We have recruited in Puerto Rico, for example, for that particular examination. We'll be running orientation courses down there for that examination. But, by and large, it is restricted to advertisements, flyers, noise at conventions or audiences, and not any intensive effort in other urban centers, for example, to attract people.

MR. TRACTENBERG: Has there ever been a substantial number of candidates for any supervisory license who have not come out of the system?

MR. WILLIAMS: Not to my knowledge, although I must caution you again that I don't speak with a great deal of historical knowledge.

MR. TRACTENBERG: The final thing I want to just ask you about in general is the Fordham program, which I gather is another program designed to increase the number of minority group supervisory personnel.

I assume that the Board of Education through your division has made an input in that program in money, perhaps staff, and otherwise.

Is that a fair characterization?

MR. WILLIAMS: Yes. I wasn't there at the time, but I am familiar with the fact that the Office of Personnel worked with the program.

MR. TRACTENBERG: How successful has that program been in your judgment in terms of actually getting Blacks and Puerto Ricans into the assistant principal and principal positions?

MR. WILLIAMS: To the best of my knowledge, the vast majority of persons who completed the program are in supervisory positions. I saw a report from Fordham, which probably could be made available to the Commission, which would indicate the position that the person had on entrance into the program and the position he now holds, and my recollection is that there was a substantial number who hold higher level positions now.

MR. TRACTENBERG: From your point of view then, it was a successful program?

MR. WILLIAMS: It was a successful program for a number of different reasons, Mr. Tractenberg, and quite apart from what you're referring to, because it had the effect also of breaking some new ground in terms of the kind of programs needed to be put together in developing urban administrators, even apart from color and ethnic background, but also, of course, honing in on the particular problem we have in New York of the paucity of minority group supervisors. That was another reason, but I consider the first item I mentioned also to be very significant.

MR. TRACTENBERG: Is that program, so far as you know, or any comparable program still in existence?

MR. WILLIAMS: Well, the Fordham program for the development of urban administrators is in existence. That particular facet of it which was supported by the Ford Foundation is not any longer in existence.

MR. TRACTENBERG: Is this kind of program so promising that your division definitely might support it?

MR. WILLIAMS: The division is actually proposing a program for the development of administrators through internship. The new state regulations require that our beginning administrators have an internship before they can be appointed. Consequently we see a responsibility to try and develop one through the school system, and we're in the process of developing these plans now for submission to the Chancellor.

MR. TRACTENBERG: I don't have any more questions.
THE CHAIRMAN: Mr. Williams, one final question. This whole problem, of course, touches very much upon your area as an assistant superintendent, et cetera, and as your remarks have made clear, you have found it frustrating that the numbers of minority people did not increase as you desired, and you have been disappointed in this. You also testified, however, that you are unable to say what the cause is as to these failures in the school system.

I'd like to question you on that. The figures you gave clearly showed the concern of your department; 81% of the advertising dollar going to minority publications and media. Without pinpointing cause and effect, without studying whether or not a program is, in fact, producing the result desired, you might go from even the vast majority of the money to complete money in a minority group newspaper and media without any results, because you would not know whether the problem was getting to people in their communities.

Do you feel it is your responsibility or the responsibility of any other department to make recommendations in the school system, to whomever they might be made with respect to how feasible certain programs are--after a study of those programs --so that you might be less frustrated and the minority community might be less frustrated with the failure of the efforts so far produced?

MR. WILLIAMS: Mrs. Norton, regardless of whoever else may have this responsibility, I certainly consider it the responsibility of an office engaged in recruitment and training to make clear to the officials of the school system what that office views as the difficulty that is barring our reaching the objective that we have. I certainly think it to be our responsibility.

THE CHAIRMAN: Why have you not then, Mr. Williams, made a study and evaluation as to which techniques and programs are successful, which are less successful, which are not successful?

MR. WILLIAMS: I can only plead, Mrs. Norton, that I haven't been on the scene long enough to be able to set such an apparatus into motion. We are looking at what we have. I am trying to examine what has been done and possibly looking for what additional can be done, looking to what might be suggested as helpful and profitable and what might be said not to be resulting in anything significant. But I can't quite tell you that I've had sufficient time to do this in the office.

MR. TRACTENBERG: I take it then you are prepared, or your office is prepared, to evaluate the system, to see where the problem specifically is, and that you do regard that as a function of your office?

MR. WILLIAMS: Oh, yes, yes.

THE CHAIRMAN: Any more questions from anyone else? Thank you very much, Mr. Williams.

Mr. King, you may proceed.

DR. JOHN P. KING: Ladies and gentlemen of the Commission, I am very grateful for the opportunity of appearing before you this afternoon. I have felt like a private commission on human rights since 1940, at which time I was appointed as an assistant principal and was the only one in Brooklyn. It's been a sort of a Lone Ranger set-up over the years.

I was in the school system for some thirty-nine and a half years serving on every teaching and supervisory level through that of Executive Deputy Superintendent of Schools, which was the second command post in the Board of Education as it was then organized.

During that time I was privileged to have been appointed in 1940 as an assistant principal and the only one in Brooklyn, the only Black in Brooklyn, the only identifiable Black. At that time I resolved to do something about the situation that existed. There were probably seven or eight assistant principals who were Black, and probably half that number were identifiable as such in the school system; and I felt that the number certainly worked an inequity and disservice to the children of the City of New York.

It is probable that there were 300,000 Black and Puerto Rican youngsters in New York City at that time, that is, in 1940. The number has grown now so that it's probably close to 600,000.

It meant to me then that, having been the beneficiary of the largess of the Board of Education that enabled me to become an assistant principal, I ought to assume the responsibility to see to it that other Blacks and Puerto Ricans had a similar opportunity. I did.

Immediately after I was appointed an assistant principal I started coaching courses, not out of altruism but in order to supplement my salary as an assistant principal, and I had a family to take care of. It was the game that was played in those days. If one wanted to become a supervisor or if one wanted to become a teacher, he had to match wits with the Board of Examiners with the help of a coaching course. Coaching courses even in those days for the teaching position made about $100 as a fee.

There were a great many who had found it easy to get the $100 but there were many Blacks who did not find it so easy. I, therefore, spent a great deal of time contacting churches, fraternities, sororities and the rest encouraging people to come into the school system; by that I mean, some of the Blacks and Puerto Ricans who were either eligible or who had the promise of becoming eligible.

Earlier in the testimony of the previous speaker, the question was asked, "What are some of the factors that contributed to the small number, probably eight licensed principals in New York City now out of some nine hundred odd, eight who are Black or Puerto Rican?"

At that time the people who were unable to pay for the courses to enable them to pass the examination were invited, Blacks and Puerto Ricans, to take my courses for free. At least, they paid the other fellow who was my partner, and my contribution was to let them come in at half rates. I didn't want to accept the funds from them.

Unfortunately, we had a very small number of teachers who were Black. That is one of the factors, Mrs. Norton, that you inquired about. We had very few Black teachers in the system, comparatively. There were probably, back in 1940, oh, 30,000 or 35,000 teachers and supervisors in the city schools, and of that number there were probably 2,000 or 2,500 who were Black Puerto Rican? Practically no Puerto Ricans; the number was negligible.

Now in order to become a principal, one had to have experience as a teacher. So the problem was first to increase the number of Black and Puerto Rican teachers if we're ever going to have any sizable number of Blacks and Puerto Ricans in supervisory ranks.

It was difficult to get Blacks and Puerto Ricans to take examinations, even those who were within the system, and who were otherwise eligible. In the first place, they had to complete certain course requirements which involved courses in administration and supervision, and many of these were family people who did not have the means to pay for those courses or the time. I found in talking with hundreds of the women, Blacks who were teaching, that they simply couldn't do it. They had home responsibilities. They did not have husbands who had incomes sufficient to permit their hiring domestic help, so they were taking care of their own families. Those who were better off and fortunate enough to have gotten a husband through professional school who was now practicing medicine or law or what have you, those women withdrew from the system and gave their time to their families. So it was a matter of money in some instances that deterred many of the few Blacks in the system from taking the examinations for promotion and from taking the courses. That was an important factor.

Now there were very few men, comparatively, particularly in the elementary and junior high schools, back in 1940, and in surveying the situation then, it was clear that the vast majority of those who became principals were men. Well, there were few men in the system compared with the number of women and there were even fewer, by proportion, Black men in the system.

It meant then that we had to increase the basic pool in order to arrive at some point in the future where there was an appreciable number of Blacks and Puerto Ricans.

Well, after some years passed, we found that there was an increasing number of Blacks coming into the system, not at a rapid enough pace to have any meaningful impact on the needs of children in the Black communities, but they were coming in slowly.

The recruitment programs were not as effective and as successful as they might have been, partly because of an indifference at the top. I do not think that it was a matter of discrimination, I think it was simply a matter of indifference. The philosophy was that anybody has an opportunity in New York, and if you don't take advantage of that opportunity, then it's your loss. Unfortunately, it was not the loss to the individual but it was the loss to the children of our public schools.

I tried to encourage people to take coaching courses that I was giving for the principalship. I never had more than three out of over a hundred, never more than three Blacks or Puerto Ricans in any of the coaching courses that I gave, even though those people were invited to come in without charge for my part of the fee. Coaching courses ran from $250 to $350, and a great many people were discouraged by that.

Many others were discouraged because of rumors that went about that people of color would never survive the intensive examination. I went around as an exhibit trying to assure them that color was no regard in my case and shouldn't be in theirs. I wasn't passing in those days either.

The number of people that I was able to get into the coaching courses with the help of Alpha Phi Alpha fraternities, some of the sororities, particularly Delta Kappa, which is a national sorority of Black teachers did not yield very many.

It wasn't until late in the fifties after the Court decision that we were able to make any real breakthrough. With the help of Daisy Hicks, and a number of organizations like the Urban League, NAACP and UFT we were able to start Operation Reclaim. Operation Reclaim grew out of a note that I took of an article that appeared in the New York *Times* reporting that there had been 2,700 desegregated school districts in the South. I was very distraught to hear this, and I investigated it further. In no one of these 2,700 desegregated districts were Black teachers moved from their Black schools into any of the so-called integrated school settings. That meant that there were thousands, literally thousands, of teachers who were now shoveling coal or hay or doing other menial jobs and who couldn't get a teaching job for love nor money--let's say for money. There wasn't much love lost in that area.

I talked with a number of my friends and got some promises of assistance and set up what we called Operation Reclaim, which made it possible for us with funds provided from a variety of sources, particularly organizations, civil rights groups and others, to arrange for the transportation of these people who had been desegregated out of a job, to come up to New York City with the group that we were working with--and we called it our own private underground railway. We had several hundred people who came up and for whom we were able to get services that would enable them to pass the examination for license as substitutes and, subsequently, with the help of instructors, professors at some of the city colleges, private and public, we were able to get them the kind of assistance that they needed in order to match wits with the Board of Examiners, and many of them were licensed as a result of it.

Many of them had taken the substitute exam, worked at it for a while. They were housed by teachers here. Some of them members of Phi Delta Kappa sorority. They had no homes. One fellow came up in a boxcar. He had four children, and he was told by his superintendent that he had no place for one of the new breed.

I had the pleasure of suggesting an arrangement after that fellow came up here without a dime and was housed at the YMCA in Harlem for some six weeks while he was getting enough to live on, and then he started paying them back. He had no place for board or keep. We set up an arrangement where private homes were used to house many of these people. Their transportation was paid.

Some of them had to slip out under the cover of darkness, and it was one of the most thrilling experiences that I had during my forty years with the school system. I had my own private underground railway, and there were droves of other teachers, Blacks who, while we could not put them into this program and give them the financial support that we wanted to, were able to come up by their own devices and get some assistance from some of the same people that worked with our Operation Reclaim. They subsequently became teachers, and I would guess that the number ran well over a thousand that we were able to bring up in that fashion; and it was a chain reaction that set in.

So that eventually the number of Blacks and Puerto Ricans in the school system grew to probably somewhere in the neighborhood of 8,000. Now that is a base number that is very important, because if you take the number of teachers in the system, you have about 65,000 teachers. Of those 65,000 teachers, if 8,000 are Black, then the balance will not all be taking examinations for promotion, and the percentage of Blacks who take the examination for promotion will certainly never exceed the percentage of whites, so that the situation will be a long time in being corrected.

Now one of the previous speakers felt terribly frustrated. I don't feel frustrated in the least. When I was the only principal, the only Black principal, in New York City I felt hopeful that some day I might be instrumental in increasing the number to some eighty principals of color in New York City.

Now there were many years that transpired where very little could be done with the system, and you had to play the game within the system or forget it. You could change it eventually, probably during the lifetime of my grandchildren, but in the meantime you played the game the way it is, and that I tried to do. Number one was to increase the number of Black and Puerto Rican teachers within the city. I set up Operation Prima, not for proselytizing people from Puerto Rico--that was completely unfair. I had a program down there called Operation Understanding, where we exchanged teachers for the purpose of building better relationships and giving some of our New York City teachers and supervisors some insight into the needs of Puerto Rican children in New York City; and we were not going, during the time that I was serving as a deputy superintendent, to raid their schools to bring their teachers up here. But what we did was try to raid the factories where a great number of these Puerto Ricans who had served in the schools as teachers in Puerto Rico were now serving as people who would be putting handles on pocketbooks or some equally challenging professional job in a factory.

All of these people were under-employed, and many of them

had the credentials. They were graduates of the universities of Puerto Rico. Many of them were graduates of universities here but still weren't able to get a professional job in any of the schools in New York City.

I then worked with a number of people at headquarters, some of them sitting here today, to corral as many of these people as possible and give them the assistance that they needed to pass examinations.

The examinations in some instances caused problems because of the language problem. It took some doing with the Board of Examiners to set up different, not lower, but different standards, and it was difficult to convince them that these people were bilinguists. They spoke two languages. Most of the candidates they examined in one language because the person could speak only one language. However, they did come along after a while with the help of the Superintendent and some of the Board members, Clarence Senior, in particular. We also set up the position of auxiliary teacher, a position which enabled us to get a number of these underemployed Puerto Rican university graduates into the system.

At the beginning the number was small, and ultimately we were able to regularize the position so that these people had the position of regular teachers, and then it took another three, four, five years to convince the bureaus that be down there that they had a right to a supervisory post in the city school system. We then created--with the blessing of the Board of Education and others and the great help of Clarence Senior at that time, we were able to create--a post of supervisor of bilingual teachers, and that is one of the few supervisory level positions that the Puerto Rican teacher has access to. These teachers are now known as bilingual teachers, and there are over 200 such. It is not frustrating although there ought to be many more.

It is encouraging to find that where there were none over a few years back we now have over 200 bilingual teachers. We now have over 200 bilingual guidance counselors, not nearly enough, but we didn't have one guidance counselor who was going to talk to thousands and thousands of Puerto Rican children who could speak the language.

We now have the beginning of a fairly substantial number of guidance counselors who can relate to these youngsters. There have been some moves made.

Now, some reference was made to the Professional Promotional Seminars. I think it would help the perspective of the Commission to know how that seminar got started.

Some of these things happened because of changes in the law. Some of them happened because of changes in people. Now, that Professional Promotional Seminar was set up in my office at the time I was Deputy Superintendent as a result of my calling the people who were conducting coaching courses. I want no bouquets for this, because it was a tremendous satisfaction to me to have had some part in getting 135 Black and Puerto Rican, identifiable Black and Puerto Rican, assistant principals on that list.

But the way that that was set up was not through channels in the division of this or division of the other. It was from setting up a luncheon for the people who were conducting coaching courses at about $350 a throw for people who wanted to become assistant principals and principals. They were friends that I had known, friends, some of them in quotes, friends that I had known for a great many years. They came into my office to sit around the table and have lunch, and I told them at that time that I had been privileged to serve as a coach as they had and had reaped some of the monetary rewards as they had through the years but that I was going to start almost immediately to set up a coaching course conducted by the Board of Education, and it would be conducted for free, except that I was going to recommend that $10 be charged for materials which wouldn't begin to pay for the mimeographing, but I wanted the people to have some stake in it. When you get something for nothing, it's worth about that.

However, that professional seminar was set up in name that day with the coaches, and the coaches were not particularly happy about losing this rather lucrative source of income. But they were realistic, and I said that we are now going to put the coaches pretty much out of business.

Now, I told them, in compensating you for this I am going to hire or have the Board hire a number of you as coaches, we're not going to call you coaches, give you a nice fancy name, but we'll have not a coaching course but a Professional Promotional Seminar, and we're going to place it in seventeen different places in this town that will fit in with the law, so that nobody will have any case to take into court against the Board for showing favoritism. But I'm going to place it in schools where there is a predominance of Black teachers and some where there are Puerto Rican teachers because there are so few Puerto Rican teachers who were eligible at that time. They're going to be in those schools, in those areas. Why? Because if we make it easy for those Black teachers to get to the seminar, we'll get more of them there. There are going to be seventeen of them distributed around the city in that fashion. They're open to Blacks, whites, Mexicans, anything you want, so that it's going to be completely safe from any questions of legality in the use of public funds. And, those professional seminars were set up in that fashion at that time.

Now, if we had waited for some division or office to have set up some such professional seminar I doubt that they would ever have been set up. They were subsequently, at the time of my retirement some four years ago, taken over by the Personnel Division and, thank fortune, expanded to include licenses in others than the principalship and assistant principalship.

Now, you might ask why the assistant principals? The assistant principals, because here is another factor; for a number of years no one could become a principal of an elementary school who had not served as assistant principal.

Well, now, you say, was that prejudice or bias. It didn't have to be. It's like so many things in our society. You don't have to have a discriminatory action because you have some de facto actions that make it unnecessary.

Now, if you had in the City of New York some thirteen or fifteen assistant principals of color, Blacks, then you didn't have to worry about very many of them becoming principals of schools because there are only thirteen or fifteen eligible to take the examination. It was that simple.

So that our problem was to get a larger number of Black assistant principals, Black and Puerto Rican assistant principals, if we were ever going to get any sizable number of principals, because at that time the requirement was that you have service for at least two years as an assistant principal before you become eligible for taking the principal's examination.

I am not saying that it was unfair. I am saying that it was unfortunate for the children of this city, which is to me more important than being unfair. I say that it was an ineffective kind of school administration, and it was done more or less behind the scenes.

Now, I mention that because there has to be somebody in a top level post at headquarters who is going to be sensitive to this kind of thing and who is going to pick up the slack in many, many ways on a very informal and friendly basis, friendly in quotes, to see to it that if one is going to become eligible for a supervisory post that nothing is going to be put in the way deliberately or inadvertently.

I have spoken of some of the historical elements here. I would like to more or less summarize by saying that one of the best things that has happened to this town is decentralization, particularly in this area. If we were going to change the situation--and I'm not saying do away with the Board of Examiners, that's inconsequential. I don't think the Board of Examiners can measure--and I think they would admit it--that they can measure the qualities necessary for an effective administrator in any one of the schools in our urban ghetto areas. You can't measure them. They're God-given endowments in part. They are qualities that are completely abstract and intangible, and there is no instrument available to measure those qualities.

Now, you can measure rote memory that one person has and weigh that against the memory that somebody else has of facts and history--of facts and geography and the other subjects of the curriculum--but it has nothing to do with the ability of a principal to go in and relate to his community and relate to his children and relate effectively to his teachers and give the whole operation leadership. You can't measure those qualities.

Now, I say again, by way of summary, that we can thank the State Legislature and all other interested parties for decentralizing the schools of this city. That will make it possible now for the selection of top personnel in that community by the community board rather than by the persons charged with such responsibilities at so-called central headquarters. (Some refer to it more euphemistically as the Pentagon.) I would prefer to see the selection made in the districts, and when those selections are made in the districts then what happened yesterday will be more or less typical.

I was privileged to share in the tribute that was paid to some twenty-five Black principals in Brooklyn, Black acting principals who were selected by the community because the community had faith that they could relate to the children, that they had the qualities necessary to make the children's lives more productive, more rewarding, more meaningful educationally; and if they don't they know that the community who selected them will be just as quick to get rid of them.

Now, the difficulty in the other setup where people are recruited and selected on the basis of some rather extravagant examination of a person's ability to memorize facts--and I know that it can be done that way because in giving coaching courses over the years my partner and I could guarantee that the person would pass that examination if he did the things that we asked him to do in memorizing the necessary mnemonics and other devices.

At that time, in the coaching courses, I was preparing people to pass an examination. I was not preparing people for the principalship. I was not being paid to do that.

At Fordham University I fortunately am being paid for preparing principals, and it's an entirely different job. It's not preparing people to cross swords with the Board of Examiners.

Now, the Board of Education, the State Education Department representatives, the superintendents of schools and Fordham University were fortunate enough to be able to get the Ford Foundation grants which enabled us to prepare 60 fellows as part of an already established program for preparing urban principals. Of those 60, a good many of them are now serving in some of the high supervisory posts.

The question was asked: Will this be continued?

The program was in operation before the Ford Foundation moneys came into it, and the program will continue to be in operation even after the Ford Foundation and other foundations are no longer interested. They are--the persons who are taking the program leading to the State certificate--people who in some instances have gotten moneys from a variety of other sources. We have no arrangements at Fordham that would proscribe or prohibit the entrance of anyone who gets the money from the Chinese consulate, if he wants to, or some Indian development. We will be very happy, our registrar and bursar would be very happy to receive those funds.

Now, the recommendations that I make, number one, is that we make a determined effort--for a number of obvious reasons it's unnecessary to go into--to get people on the Board of Education, in the highest position on the professional staff, to think in terms of getting Blacks and Puerto Ricans and other minority group members into supervisory posts because of the fact that it will have an effect on the way children learn. They are people who are familiar with the style of life, their style of learning, and they need to be in those posts where they can give leadership to some teachers, a great many teachers who are not as alert and as aware of the differences in life style, differences in learning style. If we can get those people to think about it, that's the starting point.

I think that the examination should be an oral examination, an oral interview as it is in other parts of the state. I don't think that there is any written test that anyone could devise that would validly measure the competence or even the potential of a person to serve as a successful principal, particularly in the schools where there are many, many disadvantaged children who have different ways of learning but have just as great a potential as they have in Riverdale or Jackson Heights if they had the kind of teacher that knew how to extract from them the competence that God gave them.

The next consideration is how would you hold these people accountable?

I think that the local community, the local school districts, which in most instances are larger than most of the school districts outside of New York City, in New York State, and other states, should have the responsibility and the authority to select these persons who have demonstrated in the oral interview that they can communicate effectively--and that's all you can measure. You cannot measure a person's integrity in an interview; you cannot measure a person's leadership potential in an interview; you cannot measure any of these other abstract qualities which must be present for a principal to be effective. Therefore, the interview should concern itself with measuring one's ability to communicate effectively with community, with children, with parents. Having established that fact and having the state certificate--having in other words passed all of the necessary courses--then that person would be selected from a list, not a competitive examination. A competitive examination is a figment of the imagination. A competitive examination is completely invalid and unreliable.

To establish a list of qualified people from whom the community can select is the way that it's done throughout this country, and we do not have a monopoly on successful education in New York City. There are some people who would, I'm sure, endorse that position.

THE CHAIRMAN: Excuse me, counsel, did you get a chance to ask any questions? Is this in consequence of a question?

MR. TRACTENBERG: No.

THE CHAIRMAN: We're running a half-hour over in testimony, so maybe counsel will want to ask you something. Can you finish shortly?

DR. KING: I'll finish in one minute. I want to apologize for taking so much time, but I have been doing the kind of investigation that this Commission has addressed itself to for twenty-five years. It's a little difficult to telescope it into a half-hour.

THE CHAIRMAN: Actually, I'm very sympathetic to your position, Mr. King, as a Black person who found himself alone in a system for so many years and has spent so much of that time trying to help other Black and Puerto Rican people get into the system, I understand that to ask you to give us a brief recount of what you do is to ask the impossible.

In any case, I think we'd like to have it on record--why don't you complete? You say you can do it in a few minutes. Maybe counsel will want to ask you a question. Then we can have it on the record.

DR. KING: I just want to make one last statement.

That is to the effects that I have no feeling that what happened in this town that prevented Blacks and Puerto Ricans from reaching the higher supervisory posts is as a result of deliberate planned discrimination. I think that it's worse. It is not unfairness. It is indifference, because no efforts have been made; no sincere and consistent efforts have been made to search out and to assist those people in getting into such posts.

I have no beef against the Board of Examiners. I think that the Board of Examiners did what comes naturally or should have come naturally over the years. I don't think that at this point that it makes much difference whether there is or there isn't the Board of Examiners. I think that it makes the difference if the Board of Examiners addresses itself to the task at hand, and that is in assisting the superintendents and local school boards in making the evaluation of the people on probation in supervisory posts. A principal is selected and appointed by the community board, and during those three years that he is on probation the Board of Examiners might well assist, but not by taking over the whole job, the superintendents and others in evaluating his capability. I think that would be a good function for the Board of Examiners.

Another good reason to have them around is for the conduct of the oral interview examinations or assist in conducting them. I think there are a number of places where the Board of Examiners would fit in, and I do not place at the doorstep of the Board of Examiners the culpability for the failure in this particular aspect of our personnel problem. I don't think it's their fault. I think they were doing what this society imposes on people to do, and they were the victims of that.

THE CHAIRMAN: Counsel, do you have any questions?

MR. TRACTENBERG: I just have one or two, Dr. King.

Let me just say first that I was very interested in your comments about the coaching courses. I had a little colloquy with Miss Unser of the Board of Examiners this morning about what the coaching courses might have to say about the nature of the examination, and I think much of what you have said has been very enlightening from the point of view of one who structured a coaching course.

I would assume that coaching courses are still very much a factor in passing examinations in New York City?

DR. KING: Well, I don't know that your assumption is quite correct. I know that the coaching courses now for the licenses as principal and assistant principal are having an almost negligible effect, because they are getting the same thing from more knowledgeable people in the seminars.

MR. TRACTENBERG: Does that indicate that the Board of Education's own seminars are really directed at teaching people how to take the exam rather than being good supervisors?

DR. KING: Well, the purpose of the seminar is to get people through the examinations. Whether it should be or shouldn't be, that's the purpose of the seminar, as I saw it.

Now I would be interested in the kind of principals who come out of that examination, of course.

MR. TRACTENBERG: Just one or two questions about the Fordham program requirements.

I gather you were in charge of that?

DR. KING: We had a troika that was running it, the chairman of the department, the dean and I.

MR. TRACTENBERG: Were you personally involved in the process of selecting the interns who participated?

DR. KING: Yes.

MR. TRACTENBERG: I assume you did not use any kind of a written examination to make those selections?

DR. KING: We used no written examination. We made an evaluation of record as the Board of Education should be doing now in selecting its principals. We then invited them in for an interview, and the interview was a weighted interview; we interviewed the things that we felt were measurable, and we had some 1,500 out of which we selected twenty in the last group for fellowships, 1,500 applicants.

MR. TRACTENBERG: Is it your feeling that once these interns graduate from the program that they are then fully qualified to be supervisors in the school system?

DR. KING: I'm glad you asked that question, because it is not only my opinion that they are fully qualified but many of the superintendents and the parents and community leaders that they have worked with share my optimism.

MR. TRACTENBERG: What proportion of the graduates of the program are now, in fact, in either assistant principal or principal positions?

DR. KING: About 75%, and others are in other types of positions in federally subsidized programs and the like.

MR. TRACTENBERG: Are the 75% in acting positions or fully licensed?

DR. KING: Some have become fully licensed. Three became community superintendents. Unfortunately, the program we had planned was a little richer than we intended, and they ended up as community superintendents instead of principals. We had to cut it back some. They are fully licensed.

We have a number who are serving as deputy superintendents, that is, deputy to the community superintendents, perhaps a half dozen such. Then we have four or five who took a closed examination for junior high school principal who were successful in that. That was some eight people who were involved in that examination.

The others are all in acting capacities, because the existing list which was exhausted not too far back, as you recall, has about 80 people now sitting in the schools as assistant principals but being paid the salaries of principals on the elementary principal's list, so that the people who were products of our program have to wait until these people are appointed as principals before they're even going to be considered.

MR. TRACTENBERG: I gather despite the fact that these people went through your own program, it was necessary for them to take the regular examination in order to qualify as a fully licensed principal or assistant principal?

DR. KING: Most were urged to take the examination for principal of an elementary school, because we don't know how long they will continue as acting principals when legal action has been taken by various organizations which have a different kind of stake in this thing.

MR. TRACTENBERG: That's all I have.

THE CHAIRMAN: Thank you very much, Mr. King.

We have very much appreciated your coming to tell us about what has been a long and distinguished career in the school system.

DR. KING: Thank you for hearing me.

THE CHAIRMAN: Mrs. Daisy Hicks, Coordinator, Joint Employment Recuitment Program, Board of Education.

MRS. HICKS: Madam Chairman, Commissioners, ladies and gentlemen. I am very happy to see that these hearings are being held because I hope out of this will come some guidelines for most of us who are involved in recruiting to follow.

Athough the New York City school system has been a leader in the field of education, the most innovative approach to education is youth.

I do not feel that this same leadership will be shown in the area of integration, regardless of the procedures now in use by the Board of Examiners or the NTE, unless guidelines are spelled out for New York.

It is asking too much for the head of the school system to defend himself from the discrimination that is involved regarding minority groups; that is, they are the last to be hired and the first to be fired.

The federal government is fully aware that very few businesses or institutions have adopted fair employment policies in hiring and firing, unless a watchful eye is focused on the situation.

In the case of the New York City Board of Education, assistance must be given. That is for the good of the student we attempt to train.

I was asked to give you some historical data as to how I was involved in the recruiting picture for the last three years, and I am going to attempt to do so. And I can say why I feel we need guidelines regardless of the amount of nonsense and regardless of who is conducting the program. I still say, unless we get some guidelines, I just don't feel we are going to meet with the success that we are trying to achieve.

I joined the educational staff in 1966. At that time recruiting schedules focussed on recruitment of candidates from schools located in areas above the Mason-Dixon Line.

Mr. John Nolan, a co-worker of mine, worked under Dr. Gross, our Director, and he headed the recruiting staff. All active recruiters were given recruiting assignments by Mr. Nolan. Recruiters were assigned to large minority enrollment areas such as Washington, D.C. As you know, we have a large university there. Baltimore and Atlanta, Georgia, too, and we have the Atlanta complex and North Carolina, and all of these 15 colleges located in North Carolina, and we were given permission to go and recruit in four of them.

I would like to interject here that in many instances the failure to assign recruiters to visit colleges is due to the lack of cooperation on the part of the placement directors in giving Mr. Nolan, the coordinator of recruitment, a recruiting date. I am happy to state that this past year we visited the campuses of these particular colleges and recruited a large number of canidates.

Time is a factor here. At the present time I think things are moving; the placement directors are a little more receptive to us than at the time we started.

In 1968, the Board of Education staff improved, introduced a cooperative relationship with the Board of Examiners, and made it possible for interested, eligible candidates to be given all facets of the examination in the field.

The examination consisted of about 115 short answer questions, a written essay, and a 30-minute interview. This examination normally took a minimum of four hours for each candidate. The applicant had to pay a fee of $3. This fee excluded many minority group students because many of them did not choose to gamble with the $3, which they could ill afford to pay, on the chance they might get the job.

In 1969, the $3 fee for applicants was discontinued. At that time it was also agreed that results from the National Teachers Examination could substitute for the short-answer questions, but the rest remained.

I would like to consider that I played a role in helping to get rid of the $3 fee charged applicants in the field, for this fee was a frustration, because far too often, when assembling students to be examined, I would discover that either they were not aware that they had to pay the fee or found themselves in the worse plight of just not having the money.

There was a college in North Carolina with 40 candidates who assembled to take the examination and only ten of them had the $3 fee. To permit them to participate in the examination, I loaned 30 students $3 each. At least ten of them paid me back. The money was a handicap which we faced in having to use this plan.

In that phase of our field recruiting we did not go to each individual campus and test candidates but set up examining centers in each state. This procedure worked well in the metropolitan areas but presented a problem in areas where public transportation was not provided.

This situation applied in those areas where the schools serviced Blacks and Puerto Ricans, where they were located.

In the 1969-70 school year, Mr. Nolan, whom I referred to before, gave me the assignment to recruit in certain colleges in the following states: North Carolina, West Virginia, and Georgia.

At this time I decided that the best results might be achieved if we had members of the Board of Examiners on the scene to examine interested and eligible candidates as they were screened. Some went, with the permission of the Director, and the claim of the Board of Examiners is that they were able to visit over 20 colleges in the assigned area and tested over 150 eligible candidates for license.

Recruiting assistance was made available through the support given by Mr. James Watkins, who I know will testify later. He was the Director at that time of the Afro-American Teaching Association. Mr. Watkins was authorized by District 13, funded at the time by the Urban Coalition, to accompany me on recruiting trips and screenings; that is, of Black and Puerto Rican candidates for areas where there was a critical shortage of teachers.

Mr. Watkins' presence gave added support needed to convince candidates that the New York City school system might give them a teaching position.

At this time he was prepared to offer positions to those candidates who he felt would make a good adjustment, and who would have an opportunity to participate in the teacher training program in the summer of 1970 so that these prospective teachers were prepared for their teaching roles.

However, the limitation given as to the subject areas in which candidates would be screened in the field excluded many eligible candidates from taking examinations in the field.

We were only permitted to examine candidates in the following subject areas: the common branches, which as you know is the education from early childhood; junior high school; and high school English.

Many of the young people, out of desperation for securing a license, although they had applied in other subject areas, signed up to take one of these examinations. This was perfectly permissible because they met the requirements. However, a large number of these candidates failed to file, and this is where a lot of confusion comes in, for the National Teacher Examination in the subject area and may have taken the rest of the examination with us. But that made their total score invalid.

Regardless of this, I am happy to report that about 20 of these 150 candidates are now assigned to District 13 in Brooklyn.

Mr. Watkins was able to get the Board of Examiners to issue a per diem certificate to those prospective teachers who had consistently passed the examination phase of the process but failed to secure a regular license because of their failure to meet all of the requirements.

This brings me to the topic of the Joint Recruitment Program which, as many of you have heard, was born as the result of the bargaining procedure between the New York City Board of Education and the United Federation of Teachers.

In April 1970, the Joint Recruitment Program was put into operation. I was appointed by the Board of Education to coordinate the program. The sum of a half million dollars was allocated for the purpose of integrating teaching in the New York City schools. A number of proposals was authorized by the Committee, which consisted of Dr. Lang, who many of you heard this afternoon; Mr. Fredrick Williams, who testified also; and Dr. Gerald Rosenberg; Miss Sandra Feldman; and Mr. Dan Sanders, Assistants to the President of the United Federation of Teachers; and the President, Mr. Albert Shanker.

These are the people who make up the policy committee for this program. When the program was launched, an ethnic count of the professional staff revealed that three whites and three Blacks had been assigned to recruit members of minority groups. Then subsequently it was changed. We now have three Blacks and two whites; one of the whites left the staff. Both of our white staff members have a sufficient work record, as bilingual teachers, and also have a keen interest in the Spanish-speaking community.

These six positions in this program were given to the Board of Examiners for the purpose of providing a liaison relationship between the recruiting and the examination effort.

A rough estimate of the total cost of the professional staff assigned to the group on a full-time basis comes to around $90,000 a year. The salary of the two secretaries assigned to the program brings the total cost of personnel to over $100,000 a year.

There are no part-time workers on the payroll of the Joint Recruitment Program at the present time.

However, in order to carry out our goal of a recruiting center in 5 areas, where there are recruitment and training of Blacks and Puerto Ricans, we will have to employ at least five recruiters and five secretaries on a part-time basis for setting up recruiting centers in Philadelphia, Pennsylvania, where we will have someone on the premises all the time to really give the people information on our needs for minority groups. Also, we are going to have centers in North Carolina, and in San Juan, Puerto Rico, and in Atlanta, Georgia. The sum of $15,000 has been allotted by the policy committee for paying salaries and other incidental expenses connected with the recruiting centers.

At this time I will share with you a brief account of the efforts made to date by the Joint Recruitment Program in carrying out the goal we are to achieve, which is, a better ethnic balance; a professional staff so that the school system would reflect the minority communities and have better quality people; to establish recruiting centers in many areas of this country, therefore providing an opportunity for experienced teachers to join the New York City school system; also, to recruit prospective teachers on the college campuses with special emphasis on recruitment of minority groups; also, to provide an information system which will help all the staff become informed of the advancement opportunities available in the school system.

In order to get this program on the road, we felt that we

would have to really make an effort to sell New York and really to do a good job in that respect, to make members of minority groups feel that we are very sincere. So we designed posters which would give the impression of minority group members. I have some with me here which I will show you. So that we would be communicating with the Blacks and Puerto Ricans, we designed all of these posters, and they have really gone over big in the community.

We were able to get the people on the campuses really to remember us. We designed a film which depicted the positive as well as the negative aspects of New York City. The recruiters on each campus purchased new office space, and we did this so that when the person came into his area he would be received in a very receptive and enjoyable way.

We designed two bulletins which we send out and which present more pictures of minority groups in teaching roles. The total cost involved was less than $25,000.

After making all this preparation, the Joint Recruitment Program began in 1970. The first trip took us to West Virginia.

We had many unforeseen circumstances in this program; I had only one staff member other than myself capable of driving a car (and, by the way, this is a skill that is required in order to have recruiting in areas that are located in the South and in Puerto Rico), and having all new recruiters who had to be trained, having a valuable staff member become ill and remain off the job for four months, and having to handle new itineraries because members of the Board of Examiners were unable to join the recruiters as planned. The Board of Examiners will only give the oral interview and a written essay, so we had to go to 56 of the 76 colleges that we were scheduled to visit without the Board of Examiners. In spite of these handicaps, on November 5th, 1970, one month after our program was launched, recruiters were recruiting at 53 of the 76 colleges listed on our itinerary and had signed up over 1,000 candidates who filed applications to be examined.

After the Christmas vacation the Joint Recruitment Program was setting up a schedule for the purpose of screening candidates; we filed these applications in the field. After much complaining and a get-together with the Board of Examiners just two weeks ago, the factors which operate to prevent members of the Board of Examiners from going with the staff recruiters to college campuses were cleaned up; and after much work, we had a schedule so that we would revisit 56 of the schools and include others, so that we would be able to examine on 76 campuses. But the cost of the recruiting effort for the Joint Recruitment Program will almost be doubled by having to make two trips to 53 of the 76 colleges for the purpose of the examination of recruits.

Now, as to the screening of candidates, the limit placed on the Joint Recruitment Program of being able to screen in the field candidates in only four subject areas meant that only 390 of these 1,000 candidates could receive licenses under the Board of Examiners, which meant that over 600 of them would be lost if we weren't careful. In order for the school system not to miss the opportunity to employ candidates, we made it to other areas, and I will refer the names of these other candidates who could work to Mr. Nolan who can coordinate the program by having prospective teachers there, at the schools, use the NTE alone. This is what we referred to there. It was agreed that districts in the 40% lowest reading scores in the area could use the NTE alone.

The plan for screening candidates in the field by use of the NTE exclusively had been made and we came to the use of the National Teacher Examination. However, it did make the following provision: it made all candidates qualified by the NTE, regardless of the year, eligible for licenses to teach in New York schools.

Now, I expect a lot of confusion there even though we had told them about it.

The NTE alone requires a score of only 1,000, whereas the person who comes in under the plan we have previously had to use has to have over 1,000 as a score.

In October 1970, several candidates came from Puerto Rico and I was successful in recruiting over 150 candidates but in order for these candidates to have more of a chance of securing a license, I had requested and received permission for the examination to be administered by the Board of Examiners in Puerto Rico.

At this time we gave in Puerto Rico the same examination that we gave here, like common branches. There was no change but now we have a bilingual teachers common branch; so I requested that these examinations be given there in place of the ones we had given before.

In order to make certain that there is an on-going effort, I am now in the process of securing the services of a part-time recruiter in Puerto Rico. I anticipate one recruiter to start working on a part-time basis around the middle of February. This person will have the responsibility to work with Spanish-speaking members on an on-going basis.

Decentralization has put a new dimension on our recruiting arena. Now community districts are asking that they be a part of the screening process in order to screen candidates for the New York City school system. In order to service the recruiting needs of the school districts, I have and will continue to work and help, and they have asked us for the candidates that are recruited.

For the districts we are representing, we are helping district representatives carry out their roles, and I have taken the following steps:

I have made information available to all district representatives who have a turn recruiting and examining for the Joint Recruitment Program. From January 25th to April 24th I have estimated the cost of each trip so that I will be able to tell that at a glance, and I know who joins the Joint Recruitment Program.

Also, I have made housing and transportation available for orientation programs for new teachers. And I have designed more rules to assist in keeping meaningful records of recruiting efforts.

As coordinator of the Joint Recruitment Program I see as my role that they give me an opportunity to evaluate the effectiveness of our recruiting program from time to time. On the basis of these findings, I have made the following recommendations to the Board of Examiners: that if they work with us that they make an effort to see that our examining teams reflect the integration we are trying to bring about in our teaching staff; that the examination for the candidates be given after the candidates report to the posts; and that the bilingual teachers be given examinations administered in areas where they are tested by bilingual people.

Although staff members in the Joint Recruitment Program devote a large portion of their working time to efforts to carry out the goal of their field recruiting examination, this is not done with the rest of our teaching staff.

I think this is important because so often we have heard that --it is just like you are going away from home to take care of somebody else's house when you haven't done it too well in your own home. We have a system whereby we can keep our own staff informed of educational goals, and we have tried to register as many members of minority groups as we can, and we are using this card file to advise them of educational opportunities, and from time to time we hand out final applications for examination. On the bais of the information we have available to us, we let them know.

I know we recently informed many people of a bilingual background of the fact that we were having a bilingual teacher examination. We also told the people who were in the category of substitutes; we let them know that they had to file, and we will give them an application to come in.

There is another thing we hope to try for new teaching staff now. Before I leave the subject I would like to mention the fact that we have also established a referral service. We find that a large number of minority group members come to New York and they haven't the slightest idea of how to get into our school system. What we have set up as part of the Joint Recruitment Program is a service wherein we send interested candidates directly to a school with a letter of introduction so that no individual will be a nonentity in this situation.

Since October we have accuired over 200 Black and Puerto Rican individuals for positions allied to teaching.

I said that the entire recruiting effect is one that requires following-up and one in which you have to really be a counselor, especially since some of you are minority group members in the school system. This is not a line which we can learn so easily from each other, so some of us in the field have to serve and share the time. This is what I have tried to do in the Joint Recruitment Program as a result of the overall picture which we are attempting to achieve.

MR. TRACTENBERG: Just for my information, does the Joint Recruitment Program now effectively substitute for the Board's prior recruitment?

MRS. HICKS: No. I didn't make myself clear. As I

pointed out, we have two programs going in the bureau here. One is coordinated by Mr. Nolan, with the use of the NTE exclusively, which is a carry-over from the old program which is operating there.

MR. TRACTENBERG: Is that aimed at out-of-town recruitment exclusively?

MRS. HICKS: No, none of these programs are out-of-town exclusively. We have a possibility of covering schools anywhere in the city.

MR. TRACTENBERG: What proportion of your time is devoted to the out-of-town recruiting efforts?

MRS. HICKS: Well, I would say at least 70%. We have made a special effort because I think all of us are aware of the fact that at the present time we have a big job to do. We have many people right here in the city who need to be moved, too. That is another step that we can take.

MR. TRACTENBERG: How long has the Board been engaged in out-of-town recruitment in a substantial way?

MRS. HICKS: Well, I would say for the past 10 years. It started out before we got the examiners to go in the field and it was more of a public relations kind of situation up until 1966, around that time. Then the Board of Examiners joined and we could do something about it, but, briefly, it was trying to make people aware of the fact that New York City wanted them. That is 10 years ago but in the last seven years we could go in and say, "We can give you a license."

MR. TRACTENBERG: From the testimony we had earlier, both this morning and this afternoon, apparently the percentage of the minority teachers in the school population has barely increased over the last seven or eight years. Does it reflect in any way on the subject of out-of-town recruitment?

MRS. HICKS: Well, let me see. I think it would have to reflect on the subject. If you do not get what you are going after it certainly reflects on it. What you have to look at is what I would like to say about this whole recruiting picture. I think that it is really no one's fault. I think that we have actually come into the situation where there is an awareness and there is a desire but I think before we are going to be successful the people we are trying to recruit must believe us. That is what I was trying to bring out. That just wouldn't give us any break because New York City--we just didn't really have the most beautiful image out there in the hinterlands, you know. We have to be realistic about this and I have to stand on my head and I have to tell the recruiters to be aggressive, don't sit in the recruiting booth and wait for them to come to you. I told them, "You must go out and get them," or we wouldn't have a following, you know. You can go into the places and sit there all day and you can come back to New York but you have to be aggressive and that is exactly what we had to do, not only to sell New York but to get out there and to go back and show faith, that we were sincere, by coming to those campuses and examining them.

MR. TRACTENBERG: You said you had identified a thousand minority applicants but I assume they are still a long way from getting into the school system.

MRS. HICKS: You are right.

MR. TRACTENBERG: Are there some natural hurdles that could substantially reduce the number?

MRS. HICKS: There are some major hurdles and number one, we can make sure that the examiners should show up there. We have to make sure that those candidates are aware of the fact that they are coming back on this certain date, and there is a lot of work involved in this. We have to make sure they understand what is required of them and these hurdles we must overcome or keep coming back with a certain number of candidates, that is all, but we have to do it.

MR. TRACTENBERG: When the Board of Examiners officials actually go to the campus and administer an examination, I presume they don't notify the applicant on the spot or even shortly thereafter whether they have passed and are put on the list. There is still a substantial time lag.

MRS. HICKS: Well, they have to collate all of the phases of the examination before they can tell the applicant whether he has passed or failed. If it is a written essay or oral interview or something and he has to get a physical, you know, and when they get all of that together, then they can tell the applicant but it would present difficulties to do otherwise.

MR. TRACTENBERG: You will be going back to many of these campuses in February or March?

MRS. HICKS: Well, from January to April we will be going back to every one.

MR. TRACTENBERG: Has the Board of Examiners given you a particular date by which the eligible lists will actually be promulgated?

MRS. HICKS: Yes, they are supposed to be ready by September. These people in the field are supposed to be eligible as of September 1st. Now they are supposed to have it ready by that time or before that.

MR. TRACTENBERG: But, until September, you won't actually be able to offer jobs to these people.

MRS. HICKS: Well, I have hopes. Now I can't predict what they are going to do, but normally they do have them. This type of an examination they are supposed to give priority. I think that priority will be given in correcting these papers now, so you and I can just hope together.

MR. TRACTENBERG: Do you find that you and your recruiters labor under disadvantages compared to recruiters from other places?

MRS. HICKS: We do have competitive things but there is no place like New York City, so we really don't have a problem. I don't think that too many people who come to New York say, "No, I don't want any part of this." A large percentage of those we meet in the field (after having been in New York working in the summer and many of them have come up here on their holidays) want to come here. They also have an advantage from the salary standpoint, too, and all they have to do is quote it. From where we stand on what the beginning salary will be, we do get a lot of recruits. And from the standpoint that a large percentage of minority group candidates are eager to get involved in the problems we have in the inner city, it is not so much just money, either.

They want to think that they are making a contribution of helping their own to get out of the situation that they have been in, and they say to me, "Mrs. Hicks, will I be able to work with the youngsters in the inner city, right in the inner city?" This is what I hear, because the dedication to these youngsters is there, and we have so many youngsters who fall in this category, who are among the disadvantaged of the inner city, that we do not have too much of a problem selling New York.

MR. TRACTENBERG: All right.

MRS. HICKS: From time to time things change, you know. As you will recall, this is the method today. The youth today want to become involved. I would not have said that in years past, in fact, in many of the years gone by. I think this is the mode today. I can't say that something today is a reflection of the years gone by.

MR. TRACTENBERG: Will the out-of-town recruitment program and the Joint Recruitment Program as now constituted produce a substantially greater number of minority group teachers in the school system?

MRS. HICKS: To a degree. I am not a mystic, but I prefaced my remarks by saying that I thought we needed guidelines, you know, and we are going to have to have them, too, because we can come up with any program but it is only going to be so successful if you further those guidelines; and the Board itself has not told us what the guidelines are. But, so far as I am concerned, I don't see it, no.

THE CHAIRMAN: I found your opening remarks about the need for guidelines and indeed your own view of what fair employment is interesting because of the tendency not to understand what fair employment means.

I am a little worried, however, about the Joint Recruitment Program because of some testimony heard earlier in the day which indicated that quite apart from minority group people there is a deterrent because people feel that there are certain courses they have to take and because until recently almost 50% of the teachers were not regularly licensed.

Is there not some problem in encouraging minority people to come here because they may come here and they may teach in some sort of unlicensed way and find that they ultimately, just like those people who live here, are not able to get into the system? Is this a problem? Would you anticipate that?

MRS. HICKS: Well, I have not really anticipated that, but I feel that this could be a factor. It is true that we do try to look at examples, and common sense would tell us to not put ourselves out on a limb and no one of us is getting anywhere. But, as I said here earlier, I think that if this operates with the average

Black American, that he feels that maybe it is different from time to time and I think that the time is really right now, with the kind of effort being made by all the agencies, that this Black American should begin to think in a positive way about the opportunities here in New York City. Also, that for someone coming from the state of Alabama or from the Midwest or from some other school system, it is realistic for him to believe that if he comes here he can get through the various procedures and he will become licensed.

We realize, of course, the opportunities could be a little bit better now with the NTE, but I don't look at this as an answer, because, as you know, the National Teacher Examination is another examination based on things like all the examinations we had to face. It is not based on norms where the Black man or the Puerto Rican American were included, so I don't like the NTE as an answer to bring in more minority people. But, the NTE is given in a large number of states and many minority candidates would normally take it anyway. The only thing that I can say is that the applicant out there from these various states will actually think that under the NTE he will have more of an opportunity coming in than under the previous procedure.

MR. TRACTENBERG: Even with the use of the NTE aren't there a number of other things applicants have to go through?

MRS. HICKS: Well, not with the NTE exclusively. Otherwise, we will have this thing and that, and he could report to districts where there is a school which falls in the 40% category, and he could report there and be screened. I think this will encourage many of them to come.

The only thing I do feel--and it is interesting to me--is that we are reaching for the NTE while many schools which have tried to integrate their staff are getting rid of the NTE because they found that it really screens out Blacks. They are now getting rid of it.

MR. TRACTENBERG: Won't you explain why you are optimistic that using the NTE rather than the Board of Examiners' tests, will permit you to get more Black teachers into the school system?

MRS. HICKS: Well, I found many candidates confused because of the NTE and the Board of Examiners' tests. We can never get the actual procedures clear with the out-of-town people as to what they will have to do in order to get a license using this procedure.

If he knew that he had to take the Board of Examiners oral interview and the written essay, if he knew he had to take the NTE in the field that would be fine, but there seems actually to be some confusion as to whether he could be taken into the area where we were giving examinations, and as a result a large percentage of them fail.

MR. TRACTENBERG: Has is also been borne out by your experience that the Board of Examiners' examination effectively screens out a higher percentage of Black applicants?

MRS. HICKS: Well, I don't know about that. I don't want to give you false information about that.

MR. TRACTENBERG: Can you give us some idea of the kind of guidelines that you think would be useful? You mentioned guidelines a few times. Can you expand on that and give us some idea?

MRS. HICKS: Well, in most instances where segregation has taken place and integration of the staff takes place, I think some agency has come in and given guidelines and I think all of us agree that we must say that you are going to have to integrate your staff. If there is an insight on the part of the people involved it may help them to submit guidelines, and in most cases they had to submit guidelines on how they were going to go about doing certain things.

THE CHAIRMAN: Yes, that is true. Many school systems have moved and what we have to do in New York City is to present an affirmative plan to have integration as in other school systems.

MRS. HICKS: That's right.

THE CHAIRMAN: I have one more question. It has to do with the City College enrollment. Until now it would appear from your testimony that you concentrated your efforts out of town. I think the bulk of it is out of town, and that may in part have to do with the fact of the City College enrollment. Do you believe that it would be appropriate, now that there are many more Blacks and Puerto Ricans going to college, in light of the fact that many of them may believe that the school system is not receptive to them, that your office should set up a relationship with the City College that would encourage some people to choose teaching early so that we might begin to get from them a pool of minority people from our city?

MRS. HICKS: This is being done. We have the future teachers clubs which are under the direction of Lola Gentry, and she is not only going to the colleges, but she is moving down to the high school level to plan there so that they will begin to think of this as a career. So we have actually started in that phase.

I hope that a genuine effort will be made, especially on the college level, to make sure those youngsters get the counsel they need and the information they need as to the advantages of going into teaching, and this is the kind of thing we have. We have to get into the heads of these youngsters so that they will realize, as you say, certain advantages, and I am sure Miss Gentry will be doing more of this if she is not doing it already.

THE CHAIRMAN: Thank you very much, Mrs. Hicks.

Mr. James Watkins, who is on the staff of the Afro-American Teachers Association.

MR. WATKINS: Madam, Chairman, ladies and gentlemen and staff, my name is James Watkins. I was formerly a director of the teacher recruitment program for the Afro-American Teachers Association. I am currently a member of the teacher recruiting staff of District 13. I might say in all fairness that the modest success of our recruitment effort last year was due to the committee, and a great deal of thanks to Dr. Lyons, Dr. Brooks, Mr. Williams, and the Board of Examiners and Dr. Greene.

I came into the teaching profession by the back door, from a school system where I was put to read in a one-room school that housed all the grades and in a segregated school system, Madam, where we didn't always learn. But we did learn how to read.

It is very sad to say that in the New York City school system where there is all this money, all of these requirements, the educational system for the Black and Puerto Rican community is a total failure. According to the Times reporter, 53% are reading below grade.

Just to give you a little bit of background, so that you understand me perfectly.

I was in the United States Navy for four years, and I was in the segregated school system of Baltimore, and then there was the conflict. I worked for 12-1/2 years as an airplane mechanic for Lockheed Industries. As a matter of fact, I worked on the late President Kennedy's airplane when he was assassinated.

I then went into the teaching profession with dedication and, as I recall, I had to go into a classroom trying to learn what was going on and how to inculcate the students. What the teachers talked about was what their stocks were doing and things like that. So I decided to work in an all-Black school in Brooklyn where the last New York State test results showed that 100 of our eighth grade students did not possess basic competency in mathematic skills.

There were similar results in reading and 67% of our ninth grade students did not have reading competency. I agree with Dr. Kenneth Clark when he stated that reading ability determines academic performance of pupils and the competency of the teachers and their attitude of acceptance or rejection of their pupils.

I recommended that the Afro-American Teachers Association form a coalition to develop teacher programs for District 13 which, it has been said, was successful.

At the conclusion of my recruitment efforts I wrote this letter, which I wish to have as a public record, dated May 28, 1970, to Mr. Joseph Monserrat, President of the Board of Education of New York City.

"Dear Sir: This letter is to point out Board of Education teacher licensing procedures, which severely handicapped this year's efforts to recruit Black and Puerto Rican teachers. Therefore, in spite of the Board of Education's avowed goal to recruit Black and Puerto Rican teachers, less than 92 out of 1,000 teachers will be indigenous to New York City's minority group student population.

Although there are severe shortages of teachers in the disciplines of science, mathematics, foreign languages, English, women's physical education, home economics and industrial arts, the Board of Education accepted the National Teacher Examination of January 4th for teachers of early childhood, common branches, mathematics and language arts in the Day and Junior High Schools only. We reiterate, there is no test to determine how well a person will teach except that of on-the-job performance. The exam given does not test competence or attitudes. In addition, it appears that the National Teacher Examination will be as effective a deterrent to minority group members becoming part of the New York City teaching staff as was the Board of Examiners' short-answer test."

As an aside, let me say this is especially so because of the May 1 hiring deadline for the NTE alternative. The National Teacher Examination at least should be used until October 1st. Also, it should be used in those areas where the majority of the students read below grade as opposed to the 40% schools. It is my understanding that the 40% figure in the City of New York occurs with something like 30% of the students reading under grade level which is quite a difference; whereas, some 60% of the schools are reading below grade level.

"Most examinations given by the Board of Examiners border on sheer pedantry. Yet, there are many individuals assigned to teach in Black and Puerto Rican communities, who do not meet state certification." (This is borne out by Dr. Lang, who said that some had been given licenses to teach subjects they have never had educational experience in.) Through the chicanery of multiple qualifications and testing, which can be applied discriminatorily, thousands have been given licenses to teach subjects for which they do not have educational expertise; for example, Alternate "B," common branches--one needs a degree and 12 credits in education courses, as opposed to Alternate "A" where one must have the full sequence of educational courses (24 credits) including student teaching. Thus, the qualifications go from the sublime to the ridiculous, and our children are assigned draft dodgers and/or incompetents to teach them in their most formative years.

"The effect of assigning the majority of these teachers, licensed under Alternate "B" to Black neighborhood schools is tantamount to depriving Black children of their constitutional rights to equal education according to the Fourteenth and the Fifteenth Amendments and the 1964 Civil Rights Act. The emphasis of the Board of Examiners on pedantic qualifications must be changed to that of certifying teachers who meet New York State requisits for licensing. This is, by far, more preferable than the 773-type closed examination for substitute teachers recently approved by the New York State Legislature. By legislative act, the short-answer portion of the New York City teachers examination is eliminated."

I would like to digress here for a moment. Public Law 773 does not make sense. 773 states that a teacher can be a substitute teacher and may take an oral interview test for any examination as long as it is on a junior high level. In other words, if I had experience in teaching and I wanted a license to teach mathematics, I could so apply.

"Approximately one-third of New York City's regularly licensed teachers never took the Board of Examiners written short-answer test. The licensing procedures are, therefore, just sacrosanct, but subject to remarkable changes when the educational establishment deems it so.

"Drastically limited recruitment, restricted administering of the National Teacher Examination, different course requirements and examinations for New York City substitutes, and other applicants, and a Kafkaesque oral examination combined to assure the continued unconscionable delay in hiring Black and Puerto Rican teachers for our New York City schools. It is obvious, nevertheless, that we must always ask the question, 'Why must we go to the courts or to the streets to obtain rights for the Black and Brown manchild that the non-Black child is born with?

"At your earliest convenience, I would appreciate an appointment with you and the interim Board of Education to discuss your response to this letter and to personally clarify any questions you may have. We wish the appointment prior to initiating Federal Court action and the requesting of a Congressional investigation of the New York City school system.

"Very truly yours, James A. Watkins, Director."

We have had limited responses from the New York City Board of Education. We had response from other interested groups and we know that court action is a possibility here.

I wonder, why haven't the federal government and the Department of Health, Education and Welfare, or your Justice Department, come into the New York City school system, which is so bad.

I have no duty to spare you about the Black-Puerto Rican count and I have no qualm whatever to say what your major role is. We feel too few Blacks and Puerto Ricans are teaching in the City of New York because of the Board of Examiners.

However, we must also wonder why the Board of Examiners has this power.

We live in a nation which is the richest in the world and possibly in the history of mankind, and yet white people go to bed hungry in Appalachia and Black people go to bed hungry also, and it must have something to do with the normal procedures and the ability of this country. I would hope and I would recommend to this Commission the following steps to correct, at least in New York City, the gross injustices.

My first recommendation is that state certification is certainly sufficient and that no Board of Examiners could possibly determine whether a person can do a job in the school system.

Secondly, I recommend what I refer to as a planned program budget system. I give you the reason for this statement. There were times, if you can remember, when the reason for not admitting Black and Puerto Rican children was that they were not integrated. Some time later it was just that we could not educate them because they were culturally deprived. Either we don't know how to educate them or we do not have enough money. A planned program budget system would demand that each school, each administration and each member of the staff develop the objectives of their instructional program--the lessons they try to teach. Define the teachers, the class, how the class is to be evaluated and the cost of such a program.

This would get to the instructional system and get it out of the Middle Ages and bring it up to modern technology.

I think that each school district should have maximum ability to change what is currently a bad situation. I think the emphasis on teachers' training should be, rather, teacher orientation as opposed to teacher training.

Last but not least, if we cannot make constructive change, that the federal or state government should supervise the New York City school system.

That is all.

THE CHAIRMAN: Mr. Tractenberg?

MR. TRACTENBERG: You actually accompanied the Board of Education's recruitment teams to locations outside of the New York City area, didn't you?

MR. WATKINS: That is correct, yes. You see, the reason why we did this was that whenever the Board of Education and the Board of Examiners were asked why aren't there more Black and Puerto Rican teachers, they claimed they couldn't find them. So I went along, and they had me find them.

MR. TRACTENBERG: What is your opinion about the way the Board of Education recruitment teams operated in these out-of-state locations?

MR. WATKINS: Well, as I said before, I worked with Mrs. Hicks and her recruitment efforts and had some trouble being in a location just one day and suggested that we take two days, and I cannot say too much about the operation. I do feel that the major handicap, as I said before, I am not hesitant to declare that it is the Board of Examiners. You are sitting there and I am examining you with respect to a teaching position, and this is another examiner over here, and we are firing questions at you like in a third degree. Many of the teachers will get up and walk out for they would not want to be subjected to this.

I am saying that this type of prejudice is not the type of prejudice that we should use in this modern day, especially when they have shortages in so many areas and also they are operating under a difficult handicap, being able to recruit on their own.

MR. TRACTENBERG: Mrs. Hicks seemed to feel that using the NTE rather than the Board of Examiners written test would be an improvement. Do you agree with that?

MR. WATKINS: Well, the National Teacher Examination allows us to have a far wider group of people to work with. For example, formerly, if you had to take the New York City examination you would have had to come to New York. With the National Teacher Examination you take it anywhere.

MR. TRACTENBERG: But would you prefer that there be no written test?

MR. WATKINS: Well, the Educational Testing Service, which administers and develops the National Teacher Examination, says that those examinations are an attempt to see what that teacher should remember from his professional training.

MR. TRACTENBERG: And had the candidates, while you interviewed them in the South, advanced to a far enough point through the selection process to know how they are faring in the process?

MR. WATKINS: Well, we had quite a problem with that. Out of the people that we recruited last year, there were something like 124 people that I was acquainted with. There were 120 Blacks and four whites, and by September 1st the Board of Examiners had finally recommended for licenses three whites.

MR. TRACTENBERG: So that none of the 120 Black interviewees that you personally saw were licensed as of September?

MR. WATKINS: No.

MR. TRACTENBERG: When had you interviewed them?

MR. WATKINS: Well, some of them were interviewed back in March and April.

MR. TRACTENBERG: Did they take the examination on the campuses?

MR. WATKINS: Yes, they did.

MR. TRACTENBERG: So that the problem was not getting to New York for the examination. They had already taken it.

MR. WATKINS: Yes, that's right.

MR. TRACTENBERG: Does that mean they have never been licensed or placed on the list then?

MR. WATKINS: Well, what they were able to do is that those who had passed the Board of Examiners examination, written and oral, were able to get per diem licenses. We licensed some 20-odd of them.

MR. TRACTENBERG: Mrs. Hicks mentioned that the score on the NTE required by the Board of Examiners is 1100.

MR. WATKINS: Yes.

MR. TRACTENBERG: But I think it has been said that the pass score for other purposes is 1000?

MR. WATKINS: Well, perhaps it is a little confusing. There are two separate ways in which you could get into the New York City school system using the National Teacher Examination. Under one, the Board of Education and the UFT have joined and agreed to recruit minority group students and for this purpose 1000 is the passing mark.

MR. TRACTENBERG: Who decided that?

MR. WATKINS: I presume the Board of Examiners did.

MR. TRACTENBERG: Go ahead.

MR. WATKINS: Well, they have, further, the Decentralization Law. For those schools where the reading scores are in the bottom 40%, you may recruit teachers solely through the use of the National Teachers Examination. There, the pass marks are 508 and 535 in the two parts, or a composite of 1000. So there are two different ways to come into the New York City school system under the NTE.

MR. TRACTENBERG: Is there any sense in the distinction between the 1000 score and the 1100 score?

MR. WATKINS: Well, in all fairness, it has been referred to as institutionalized racism.

THE CHAIRMAN: That is to say perhaps not overtly.

MR. TRACTENBERG: The only other thing I have is whether you have any particular recommendations that you would like to make to the Commission, perhaps about the guidelines that Mrs. Hicks said would be useful.

MR. WATKINS: I would say New York City should have the same prerogatives to hire teachers as all other communities in the State of New York with the exception of Buffalo--state certificates should be more than sufficient.

MR. TRACTENBERG: Thank you very much.

THE CHAIRMAN: Thank you very much. I want to say for the record, when an activist in the minority community joins with a public agency, as Mr. Watkins has done, instead of screaming on the outside, he is to be congratulated, even though he testified here that they had not one single Black person from these recruitment efforts who has actually been licensed by the school system.

I want to put this on the record because minority people have been admonished that there are ways to work within the system, and I think Mr. Watkins's association has diligently been in search of those ways. I only hope that your efforts will prove more fruitful in the future and I congratulate you for your efforts in this troubled period.

MR. WATKINS: Thank you very much.

THE CHAIRMAN: The next witness is Mr. Vernal Pemberton. He is a Fordham internee and is Assistant to the Superintendent, District 4, Manhattan.

There are still a few important witnesses to come.

All right, Mr. Pemberton.

MR. PEMBERTON: I should try to condense my remarks because I am aware of the lateness of the hour, but since I am the only Fordham intern here who has gone through the Fordham program, to the best of my knowledge, I would like to give you a short chronology of what happened to the Fordham interns because I think it is self-explanatory.

On November 17, 1967, the Board of Education issued a special circular, Number 37, entitled "Ford Foundation Scholarship."

I have a copy which I am submitting to the Commission, and it stated in brief--in fact, I will quote one short paragraph.

"The Ford Foundation has announced a grant of funds to Fordham University for scholarships for Negro and Puerto Rican teachers and supervisors with experience on the high school level. This is to enable them to study to become principals or assistant principals. The program was developed cooperatively by Fordham University, the State Department of Education and the New York City school system."

Now, when this notice appeared on the bulletin board, I was, at that time, a licensed assistant principal, licensed through the regular Board of Examiners process. Now, I applied and I was fortunate to be one of 20 persons chosen from 900, I understand, for this fellowship.

Now I would like to say before I forget that 15 of the 20 chosen were licensed Board of Education supervisors. This is important.

Let me tell you briefly what the Fordham program was all about. First, we had three courses in a series on relationships and on improving the learning-teaching process.

The part of the program that was more significant than the course situation was the field experience. For instance, we made a study of the Mount Vernon school system. We visited it. We visited such agencies as the Community Resource Center which is under the aegis of the City University. We worked on materials there with Black and Puerto Rican culture and history. We visited places such as May's Department Store. That is, we visited the administrative end of May's Department Store, the Equitable Bank, Metropolitan Hospital Community Health Center, Equitable Insurance Company; and the administration is more similar than different, be it a school or a bank or whatever.

We had guest lectures. The educational director of CBS gave a short course within a course. We all went away for several days with Dr. Nobel of NYU. We visited Marshall McLuhan's laboratory, and we spent a day there.

The second semester we concentrated on policy and procedures in the administration of urban schools. Since the program actually began in February, the second semester was the semester that began in September and, of course, was terminated the following February.

Running concurrently with the principal course was, of course, the internship. We were assigned to different schools throughout the city.

At the same time this occurred there was a teachers' strike. Many of us were very active with community groups in opening schools and in working in schools. This probably caused a great deal of disaffection to take place between us and certain other groups in the city.

During the internship of group 1, group 2 came into being and there was articulation between groups 1 and 2. We had people such as Mr. Johnson, who is now teaching a course in Black history at Fordham, and we worked with him. In other words, groups 1 and 2 shared expertise.

Now, I should have said that during the summer that came between the two semesters many of us worked in various programs. I headed a program in the schools in District 12, in the Bronx, which was entitled "Black and Puerto Rican History and Culture."

I worked with a number of community groups, with people, with the parents association. After working with them, I was approached by the then-called local school board of District 2 and asked if I would consider being the principal of Junior High School 136, in the Bronx, which is one of the schools in which I worked.

I have here a letter, dated September 9th, 1968, inviting me to a second screening interview and this is from Dr. Gaines--who testified here this morning, I understand--stating that the first interview was successful, and that I would meet a larger group and that group was composed of community people. In fact, it included high school students from Morisania High School.

Subsequent to that I have here a letter, dated September 18th.

"I am nominating you for the principalship of the Damount School, Junior High School 136. I am requesting that the Superintendent, Mr. Donovan, take all steps to have you licensed for the junior high school principalship at the earliest possible time."

Now, during this time--well, say about September 18th--when Dr. Gaines tried to get me licensed as a principal of this school, and community people did help, I went with various other interns of the Fordham program to see the persons who were liaison persons at the Ford Foundation to get their support in pressuring Dr. Donovan to license me and other people who were designated by various other communities as principals or principal designates of other schools.

A committee of us also went from the Fordham program to visit Dr. Donovan, and we pointed out certain facts. For instance, the Superintendent had the power to give a qualifying examination for a certain percentage of the persons who were eligible to take a certain supervisory examination, and I pointed this out. But because of various pressures on him at that time, he refused to do so.

So now you get to December 2nd and Dr. Gaines is reiterating, "The local school board and I have nominated you for the principalship of Junior High School 136."

That is the beginning of the letter and it was suggested that I familiarize myself with the school. I did do that. In fact, I worked with a committee of teachers and we formulated a set of goals and plans. I have a copy of those.

I also have a copy, for your information, of my internship plan, the kind of thing that we had in the internship.

Well, it seemed that no matter how much pressure was put upon the Superintendent, I was not licensed as principal of that school. Other persons were not licensed as principals of the schools that they were chosen by community people to head, and this, in spite of the fact that the original Board circular read that the program was designed to create principals and assistant principals. I point out again that 15 of us were already licensed assistant principals, so that for us to go through a year's internship program was all for naught, if we were not then to be licensed principals.

I would like to recommend to this Commission that supervisors and teachers be chosen on the basis of performance-based criteria. I do not feel that the Board of Examiners, as presently constituted, can or will achieve the needed changes. I do not feel that one can apply for leadership. I feel that the Board of Examiners may have the idea that one fills out an application, takes an examination and, perhaps, decides that he can be a leader, and that he applies for leadership.

I think that this is supported by the fact, as Dr. King brought out, that three persons from the Fordham program were chosen by communities to be community superintendents. In fact, three of the five minority group persons who are now superintendents came out of the Fordham program. Many of the acting principals came out of the Fordham program. I think think demonstrates that leadership emerges from certain situations, and one cannot apply for leadership.

I will end my remarks there.

THE CHAIRMAN: Thank you very much. Perhaps counsel may have some questions for you.

MR. TRACTENBERG: Yes, I have a few brief questions.

MR. PEMBERTON: All right.

MR. TRACTENBERG: If you had not gotten through the Fordham program would your timetable for moving up to a principalship have been any different?

MR. PEMBERTON: Not at all, no. In fact, although I have gone through the program, I have taken the recent elementary school principal's examination. In fact, I was one of the many persons who applied for the junior high school program which was cancelled about a year ago after having attended seminars.

MR. TRACTENBERG: In your judgment, did your participation in the Fordham program enhance your chances of receiving a principal's license without having to take the examination?

MR. PEMBERTON: No, not at all.

MR. TRACTENBERG: Do you think, in general, that given other circumstances, a program like the Fordham program would be a good way to attract minority supervisors to the school system?

MR. PEMBERTON: Well, I think it would be excellent and I think the fact--it was Dr. King who stated it--that well over a thousand persons applied each time, can be compared to the Board's lack of success in recruiting minority group people in other cities and in the other programs that were recently described.

Here you have a large number of people who know that there are only 20 fellowships. Apparently, they see some value in this program, in this kind of program which is based on performance, where you serve an internship and the community gets a chance to see you perform in their schools. That is the kind of program that should be.

MR. TRACTENBERG: I have nothing else.

THE CHAIRMAN: Thank you very much, Mr. Pemberton.

MR. PEMBERTON: Thank you.

THE CHAIRMAN: Could I call next Mr. Gladstone Atwell, Director, Auxiliary Educational Career Unit, Board of Education.

Go ahead, Mr. Atwell.

MR. ATWELL: I want to thank you and the Commissioners for inviting me. I would prefer to answer any questions but I have a statement and then I will answer some of the questions that are put to me. Approximately 15,000 paraprofessionals are now employed by the Board of Education in the following job titles: family worker, family assistant, family associate, parent program assistant, teacher aide, educational assistant, educational associate, auxiliary trainer and community liaison worker.

Most of these paraprofessionals are employed in elementary schools, from pre-kindergarten through grade 2. Some districts have decentralized programs extending from grade 3 through grade 9.

Salary schedules have been agreed to between the unions representing paraprofessionals and the Board of Education. The majority of those employed are in the assistant category, which is the second level of the career ladder.

The Board of Education does not maintain an ethnic breakdown. However, an estimate would be that approximately 48% are Black, 16% Puerto Rican, and 36% other.

The Career Program began in October of 1967 with the employment of 1,100 educational assistants in the kindergartens. The program was a joint venture of the Board of Education, Human Resources Administration, and the City University. Prior to the beginning of this Career Program, paraprofessionals were employed in pre-kindergarten programs and in some special programs in local districts.

At the inception of the program, recruitment was agreed to by District Council 37, Board of Education, and the Council Against Poverty. 50% of those recruited for the Career Program were to be upgraded from current employees such as, school lunch workers and school aides, and the remainder were to be referred by the community progress corporations to the local school principal, who was the ultimate hiring authority. Since this was a federally funded program under Title I, it was confined to disadvantaged areas which ensured our recruiting persons from the community. To further guarantee employment of persons from the community, there was a prerequisite for hiring, which was that a person must live in the community of the school in which he worked.

Currently, there is an in-service training program to provide immediate skills to the paraprofessionals. This training is mandated under Title I federal guidelines. In addition, approximately 750 are currently enrolled in courses at community colleges of the City University. Their tuition is provided by the Manpower & Career Development Agency of the Human Resources Administration.

An additional 465 are in the Career Opportunities Program which is confined to the Model Cities communities, with priority for participation being that the person lives in the Model Cities community or works with the children in schools in Model Cities communities. These 465 paraprofessionals are enrolled in seven colleges. This program provides for a B.A. degree within a four-year period, if the person is able to achieve it.

The Career Program, sponsored by the Human Resources Administration and the City University is a 64 credit A.A. degree program in the community colleges. However, the maximum number of credits taken during any school year is between 15 and 20. When the paraprofessionals complete the two-year program, they are supposed to be eligible for transfer to the senior colleges of the City University.

Since New York City employs so many paraprofessionals, there is never a recruitment problem, but rather a selection problem, as we do not have enough career programs to satisfy all persons desirous of attending. However, it is my understanding that a career program is to be established under the agreements between the Board of Education and the UFT, and the Board of Education and District Council 37. This is to include a summer career training program of either college level courses or preparation for high school equivalency.

To date, five paraprofessionals from the original Career Ladder Program have graduated. These were students who had prior college credits. No one has achieved the A.A. degree. However, it is anticipated that a good number will receive the A.A. degree in June 1971 and/or August, 1971. Of the five graduates, four are currently employed in the school system, and one is in graduate school.

The Board of Education, in agreement with the Human Resources Administration, provides for five hours of released time for the 750 paraprofessionals currently attending the original program. The five hours released time is equally shared by the H.R.A. and the Board of Education. The Career Opportunities Program also provides a certain amount of released time which is totally supported by community school district funds. The amount of time depends upon the actual hours the individual attends college. However, it has been agreed that it should not exceed the five hours supplied to other paraprofessionals. Currently, released time is provided only to paraprofessionals who are attending one of the college programs.

At this time, the Board of Education does not pay for college courses. Those enrolled in college are supported by the H.R.A. or Career Opportunities Program funds out of the Office of Education, Washington, D.C.

Persons involved in the Career Program sponsored by the H.R.A. are part of the original Career Program which began in October, 1967. Those involved in the Career Opportunities Program were selected by Career Opportunities Program Councils in the local Model Cities communities.

Again we must stipulate that there is an understanding that a career program will be instituted for those paraprofessionals covered by the agreements between the Board of Education and the UFT, and the Board of Education and District Council 37.

The Board of Education and/or community school districts have provided in-service training for paraprofessionals employed in the schools or in some instances provided special college courses. Most often, this is totally funded through federal funds. However, many of the paraprofessionals are employed utilizing, not only the federal funds, but also state urban funds.

There is very little tax levy funds involved in either employment or career development of paraprofessionals.

Very few staff members are assigned to the paraprofessional program. Centrally, three staff members are assigned, and these three staff members have responsibility for the coordination of all college programs involving paraprofessionals, providing materials, drawing up a curriculum for the training of paraprofessionals, training the trainers of paraprofessionals, and for disseminating important information concerning the good and welfare of paraprofessionals.

Every evaluation done of this unit's function has stated that the staff is totally inadequate to perform the functions that they do. There is some surprise that so much has been accomplished for the good and welfare of paraprofessionals over the last four years with such an inadequate staff.

THE CHAIRMAN: Mr. Tractenberg?

MR. TRACTENBERG: I hope you will bear with me. This is a highly technical area, and I think it is important, and I would like to proceed with your indulgence.

First of all, in your judgment, is the basic philosophy of the paraprofessional program to employ people in paraprofessional positions or is it a more important goal that they move up the Career Development Ladder and ultimately become teachers?

MR. ATWELL: Well, it is one of the services to children. Therefore, that is our ultimate goal, but additionally, it is also an opportunity to recruit minority group persons. There is no question about that. In our opinion, it will take a little too long to get to the high ladder and achieve the goals we want.

MR. TRACTENBERG: You said that the only paraprofessionals who have completed the career ladder were those who had previous college experience?

MR. ATWELL: Yes, some of them came to us with a certain amount of college. I do have figures in the office that approximately 25% of the people did have college training prior to coming into the program.

MR. TRACTENBERG: That is in the entire paraprofessional program?

MR. ATWELL: Well, some of them had already some college.

MR. TRACTENBERG: What proportion of all the paraprofessionals are in the Career Development Program?

MR. ATWELL: Less than one-third.

MR. TRACTENBERG: Do you know offhand what the ethnic breakdown is of that one-third?

MR. ATWELL: Well, I would estimate that in the college program originally 70% of the people--a majority, I would say, since they recruited them from certain areas--70 or 80% would be Puerto Ricans and Blacks.

MR. TRACTENBERG: You indicated that the Board of Education itself makes rather limited financial contributions, if any. Does it at least pay for college tuition?

MR. ATWELL: Not at this time. I understand that there is an agreement, however, under the new contracts with the U.F.T. and District Council 37 that an additional, I think, 2,000 will be attending the Career Program and that they will be supported by the Board of Education.

MR. TRACTENBERG: Let me return for a minute to the statement that it takes too long, in your judgment, for paraprofessionals to work up the Career Development Ladder to become teachers. The four who have completed college are also becoming fully licensed as teachers. Have they passed the examination?

MR. ATWELL: Yes, they did.

MR. TRACTENBERG: It is necessary, I assume, for them to go through the regular licensing procedure, although they have been in the school system working for so many years?

MR. ATWELL: As things stand right now, yes.

MR. TRACTENBERG: Do you regard that as a substantial problem?

MR. ATWELL: Well, I would say, that after a person has been employed in the school system for five or six years, getting a degree, that his experience alone would be valuable, and I think that it should count for something.

MR. TRACTENBERG: His on-the-job performance is not considered in any way as part of the process?

MR. ATWELL: No.

MR. TRACTENBERG: At least so far as the Board of Examiners is concerned?

MR. ATWELL: Well, they have to take the examination, yes.

MR. TRACTENBERG: There is not even an evaluation of record such as would take place in the case of a supervisor?

MR. ATWELL: No, not at this time.

MR. TRACTENBERG: Do you have any ideas, Mr. Atwell, about how the procedures might be expedited? How could paraprofessionals move up the career ladder to become teachers more likely?

MR. ATWELL: Well, we have two programs right now. One program is moving at this time. It should take them 12 years but you have to be agreeable to give them credit for work experience as well as providing additional courses for credit which reduces the time it would take to go through college. The original thing started out in 1967, and it was four years before any substantial number received a degree. At that rate, it would take eight years, and I think anyone would be dissatisfied with a period of eight years.

MR. TRACTENBERG: Do the paraprofessionals have released time from their job to take college courses?

MR. ATWELL: Yes, up to 15 hours.

MR. TRACTENBERG: A week?

MR. ATWELL: Yes.

MR. TRACTENBERG: And what would their normal work week be, 30 hours?

MR. ATWELL: 25 to 30 hours.

MR. TRACTENBERG: So, given that period of time, they will have a rather limited amount of time for college work, is that right?

MR. ATWELL: That's right.

THE CHAIRMAN: He said eight years?

MR. TRACTENBERG: Yes.

MR. ATWELL: Well, I meant the people who began, the professionals, the first gang who will be in the year 1971.

THE CHAIRMAN: In college for eight years?

MR. ATWELL: No, I meant there will be many of them at that rate.

THE CHAIRMAN: They will have spent eight years taking college courses?

MR. ATWELL: Yes.

THE CHAIRMAN: A lawyer going to night school can become a graduate of a law school in four rather than three years. In other words, by going part time, he takes an extra year. In your own view, what would be an appropriate amount of time for a paraprofessional, who is similarly going to school part-time, to take to finish?

MR. ATWELL: Well, I went to night school and I would say between five and six.

THE CHAIRMAN: Go ahead.

MR. TRACTENBERG: In your view, Mr. Atwell, do the current institutions of higher education serve adequately the purposes of the Career Development Program? That is, do they have methods which are fairly well-tailored to your needs?

MR. ATWELL: I don't know what they are tailored to. They try to tailor it to meet the paraprofessional working in the school. Some of the private colleges have done better and they guarantee 10 individuals in a year.

MR. TRACTENBERG: Would you have one working on a team arrangement with the paraprofessional, student-teacher, and a teacher, and so forth?

MR. ATWELL: This is a kind of experiment and it speeds up the process, you know. They have specific credit for working with the group as well as other credits.

MR. TRACTENBERG: So that you have had a kind of mixed experience and some schools have been good and some have not, is that right?

MR. ATWELL: Yes.

MR. TRACTENBERG: As far as paraprofessionals are concerned, does the accumulation of college credit get reflected in different job responsibilities or higher salary?

MR. ATWELL: Yes, as in the contract now there is a difference between the salary grades, you know. It is still based on college credits, you know.

MR. TRACTENBERG: But the responsibilities are--

MR. ATWELL: Well, it is supposedly, yes, and you have to go into the community and some schools will be oriented differently, you know.

MR. TRACTENBERG: You must get some feedback.

MR. ATWELL: Yes, but it would depend upon the administration of the school.

MR. TRACTENBERG: Finally, while I think you may have already at least implied the answer, don't you think that there should be a special selection process for paraprofessionals which would give more emphasis to evaluating performance and thereby make it easier for them to reach their ultimate goal of becoming teachers?

What would you advocate based on your personal experience?

MR. ATWELL: Well, I would prefer performance criteria.

MR. TRACTENBERG: Well, if someone has been, as indicated earlier, in the school situation four or five years would that change your view?

MR. ATWELL: Well, again, in any situation I think performance criteria would be the best.

THE CHAIRMAN: We are at least an hour over the time scheduled. These hearings are carried live over WNYC, so that you are reaching far more people than have been in this room and your testimony is particularly important to our record and what these hearings are about.

Mrs. Joan Burton?

MRS. BURTON: Yes.

THE CHAIRMAN: You are from P.S. 134, Queens?

MRS. BURTON: Good evening, ladies and gentlemen. I have been a paraprofessional since March, I should say since February, 1968. I entered the college program in March, 1968, and it was hard to get into, you know. I had to know the right person and I was fortunate in knowing the right person.

The original requirement of becoming a paraprofessional was that I live in what was called a poverty area in Astoria, Queens. My information about the program actually came through a leaflet, a new leaflet with black writing on it, which said that Council 37 wanted to come into disadvantaged areas and bring out the people, you know, and raise them up to a certain level.

Well, I didn't consider myself poor, even though the people around me did, but I was fairly tired of working with a machine that did not talk back to you and I was tired of bosses' abuses; and I had children by then, and I wanted a good education for them and I didn't want them to have the kind of education that I had although it wasn't the public school system. It was the Catholic school system, and that was just as bad.

I think the children did not enjoy their education, and I wanted it to be just as much enjoyment as a lollipop or a romp in the park; and I wanted it to be something more than I had, and I volunteered through Head Start. So getting to this program and what it was about, my children were enrolled in it and I continued doing volunteer work until I found that I couldn't take the business world any longer. I wanted to join the system.

I started out as a school aide in junior high school and the principal told me about a career program. They came to my house and told me about it and I applied for it and somebody was my benefactress, I would say.

The Career Program offered me the opportunity to go to college. When I graduated in 1958 from Catholic high school I did not want to see that school again, ever, but I wanted to get out into the world. To do anything worthwhile there you had to have a piece of paper--a college degree. It was good in any profession you wanted. I wanted to teach and I wanted, you know, cupid hitting my heart, and there was a cupid's bow hitting my heart.

The teacher that I first had I hated her guts. She was an abomination to the teaching profession. She worked but she didn't have to run out every 15 minutes to smoke a cigarette. Her breath smelled like a tobacco field in Virginia but not quite as sweet and the children couldn't learn from her, and I asked myself, "Do I want my children to have a teacher like that?"

So I figured, "Well, the only way to keep my children from coming under the auspices of one like that is to become a teacher."

I have done community work and gotten quite involved in the Astoria area. I knew it inside-out and I knew all the local bosses and I knew when to cross and when not to cross up through the Poverty Council and Board of Education and the local President.

I must tell you, too, that Mr. Atwell had mentioned a job description for the paraprofessional program. It changed the title around. Whatever it was, I don't know, but I was given that job. It paid $140 a week and the principal, Mrs. Sullivan, from P.S. 171, who is no longer there, thank God, she gave me the application and she said, "I think you would like to have this job."

Well, I didn't know what she meant by that. She couldn't tell me what the job description was because she didn't know, but it was a plum and those were handed to those you thought were in your vest pocket. I like to talk but I don't want to talk too much to the wrong people. I guess she thought I was in her vest pocket.

I worked the hell out of myself during that six weeks in that summer program. Like having pregnant mothers that I didn't know going on the trips with me and paying transportation expenses out of my own pocket that I never received. I was told to send it back to Proccacino. I went back to the Board of Education and looked for checks for employees and some of my own checks, too, I might add, and I worked for it, too.

When the time came, I went back to P.S. 171 and the principal said that I stabbed her in the back, and I assume that I was supposed to have sold my soul for $140 a week for six weeks; and then I was supposed to walk out when it ended and anyone in that area was a thing of charm.

And I don't say that the teacher who teaches my child has to love him like I do but to teach a child you have to have a certain amount of sensitivity, feeling and friendliness and I did not see too much of that in the school area where I worked. I watched so-called educated people, and if that's what having a paper means, to be educated in theory only and not in practice, then I don't want to be educated that way. I don't want any languages talked to me. I can learn them by watching the people around me, by watching so-called educated people.

I just watched a man function like that last week. My son's own school which I had to take him out of and I have seen, to be more positive, people who are educated but who do not know how to adapt what they have learned to, I would say, some human aspect, to children that are involved.

Just to give you an idea of how much I wanted to be a teacher. When I first entered college, there was no released time, and my first class was at 5:30. I was living in Astoria and I was three blocks away from the school and I would leave at 3:15. And when I say "leave" I left with blisters on my feet. I would run up the block or down, and first I would pick up my children because I would not allow them to go to the schools that I worked in. I would make dinner and lay out the homework, lay out the clothes for the next morning, and run for the bus. Usually, I didn't get home until about 11:30.

I moved in December 1968, to Laurelton, Long Island. I was going to college at night and getting home a quarter to one and my husband would say to me, "You're going to get killed. Somebody is going to jump you." I was a little tired and I said, "If they jump me, I wouldn't even know it, anyhow." But, nevertheless, I had good instructors, and however I tired I might have felt, when I got to class, I worked hard because the people were good and they looked out for me, for my interest, as best as possible and for that I was very grateful.

When I was about ready to find a job, I had stayed out of the work force a year. In other words, the two years I worked in Astoria were not transferable. The experience that I had gained in the classroom--and the experiences were good and bad, but the children were taught, you know that--none of this was transferable. The project that I had instituted in the classroom, and different things that I had done, and the putting up with those teachers, it didn't count for anything.

THE CHAIRMAN: What do you mean by "not transferable"?

MRS. BURTON: Well, usually when you worked in private industry, for instance, or even in the Board of Education, if you have worked in a particular school district and you want to move into another district, all you have to do is apply and give them your resume of what you did in the past.

I didn't have much of a resume but, nevertheless, I had worked with children and I enjoyed what I did and I volunteered my time to work with them, as well as being paid for it. But when I applied to District 29, I was told that my experience was not transferable, that I had to start all over again and the whole process of reapplying, too, and I did that.

I did eventually get a job in P.S. 24, and I suppose the man upstairs moved it along for me, because it has been the best assistance I ever had. I had been allowed almost full teaching responsibility--not that of a teacher in the classroom or I am left by myself or nothing like that--but I had been allowed to show myself and the children and the teachers and the administrative staff what I can do.

I know I can teach. I feel that. But society says you have to have a piece of paper, so I continued school. It takes me an hour and forty-five minutes to travel from where I live in Laurelton, to my school in Brooklyn, Kingsboro.

Now, you might say, "Why are you going to Brooklyn?" When I entered the program all of the other courses had already started and Kingsboro's were the only ones that had not started yet, and it had an opening. So if you want a position bad enough you can go where it is, and I did not really think it was going to take me too long to get there. I had to find a great deal of time and energy, but I believe it is worth it so far as experience that I had gotten in the classroom.

In coming here I wanted to ask several different paraprofessionals because I realize I am not speaking just for me. Whatever my problem has been, there are others that have had such experiences as I have had.

There are women in this class 50 years of age. They haven't been in school for 29 years. One woman in particular raised her children, sent them to Teachers College and now she is going back herself. She is a straight A student. She is 50 years old and she wants to be a teacher. And in this situation, in any kind of a program as insensitive as this program has been, she has to want to do something, she has to want to achieve a goal.

Trying to get people who live in certain areas? It isn't always as easy as it may sound or as it may have been put forth.

You have to realize that in filling paraprofessional programs, the majority of them have faults. There are the children and the husband, too. You might put the children to go with the husband. There is a fairly different psychology factor involved there; and sometimes it ends up with a broken home and a broken marriage, and you wonder sometimes if it is all worth it, when you are trying to teach someone else's children and you have in the back of your mind whether or not you might be putting your own problems into what you have in mind.

I tried to be logical and sometimes cold as well. When my children grow up, they are going to have a life of their own, and I wanted something to fall back on other than just a pot and pan and possibly a husband I haven't talked to for a year. And I am trying to bring the three of them together, the home, the school, and the job and make it all worthwhile to me. Consequently, I would like the Board of Education and the union and the Human Resources Administration to make it all worthwhile, too.

The Board of Education is a non-entity as far as I am concerned. It is a place I have been told about. The only time I have had occasion to visit it is to get money and to search through the pile of boxes for the checks they inadvertantly forgot to put entries or social security numbers on, and that is the extent of my visiting time.

There are positive aspects so far as training and orientation that we get, but it isn't enough. There is an orientation session once a month and we have requested assistance in different areas and all that has been told to us is that they will try.

I believe it is insincere. I believe that my claim is wanting them to provide us services that we have asked for. I think they understand when we say that we don't feel as though our courses are relevant, because if I take a course in modern literature, you can teach me about the Bible, but it doesn't teach a child how to read and it is wasting my time.

I am 30 years old and I don't expect to, and I don't want to go up to my teaching position in a wheelchair and see right where I am going and if I wanted to get a Master's, I can just forget it.

Naturally, it is my first goal. Nobody knows the problems of the Black child and the Puerto Rican person like I do.

There are those who go into more intricate statements but when you see a child hungry, when you see a child cold or when you see a child uneducated or labelled, not just a child, but a specific color of a child, you know how you feel, and I can think back to my own time when I was the only Black one in the classroom. And the people, all the Negroes and Puerto Ricans were asked, "How are you going to practice birth control?" I said that I am going to and what happened? It is subordination. Well, I am only told that I will produce something that I believe in. Thse children are being told the same thing.

We are teaching robots and the thing that could have happened with the educational system was the paraprofessional, because she comes in with a feeling for the community. She comes in with a feeling of the home life, the inadequacies in it, the shortcomings of her husband or her own shortcomings or her own lack of education, her own inability to motivate. But the average Black parent that I know, and the average Puerto Rican parent, they want their child educated in the best possible way.

When I do something I believe in it thoroughly. I believed in the Poverty Program and I want to believe in it. I believed in the paraprofessional program. I am not going to continue, however, because I don't believe any more, and I don't believe in it because of the simple reason that it is taking too long.

Programs are being instituted by Model Cities, or whatever it is, and I feel as though I am left behind. As I said, I put in the time and the hours, and I wouldn't just do this. In fact, I have been a student in college and I am telling you something, that I wanted this very badly.

I have a child that is an under-achiever, for lack of a better word. He doesn't read, but he was reading when I taught him. He was reading, and he had the benefit of Head Start, and he had the benefit of a private nursery. And he went into the school system and they destroyed him.

They tell me he is fresh, disruptive, and disorganized and all I see, not because he is my child, but I see him as I see a lot of the other Black male children, as expressing himself, and the System wants to produce a stagnant Black male like we already have. I don't want a stagnant Black male growing up, but an educated one.

It is the same thing with my daughter. I don't want her to be characterized and the only way that it is going to happen is for her to have a good teacher.

When a paraprofessional comes into a room, she sees that a child is competent or not, because, just like every teacher is not a competent teacher, a paraprofessional is not a paraprofessional, and when the paraprofessional is in the classroom she provides the minority children with guidance. I think it is the white child who is being left out in not having a paraprofessional in the classroom and four toes and four heads, as the old saying goes, and these are whole children who are suffering under the same educational system, for the children are suffering under it.

I think two years ago one of the New York poverty writers,

I don't remember her name, wrote about better high schools and the kind of caliber of educated student that they had. They did not have a high caliber, they did not have much. They knew the effect, but that is all. There was no warmth, no feeling or understanding or anything behind it.

I would like to see this program accelerated, accelerated by allowing the paraprofessional who has shown she definitely wants to achieve something of a goal, that of being a teacher, by allowing her the time she needs to study, by allowing her the days she needs to take her regular courses. Three days in a classroom and two days in college should be a minimum.

There should be more observations of teachers. That is, teachers should be observed more, and every paraprofessional that I spoke to in my school felt the same way as I do.

If you observe the teacher and you evaluate her, help her toward self-improvement, you should realize that the paraprofessional is there for the child, too. Why not provide her with the same kind of basis for self-improvement? The paraprofessional does not want to hear constantly that she is not doing a good job. She wants to know how to do a good job.

When programs are instituted she wants to know how to implement those programs, wants to use machines. Tell us how to use them. Don't give us a five-minute thing and say, "There it is," and if you got it, you got it, and she is supposed to help the child.

I am interested in the child. I will work with the teacher now in a program in kindergarten. I can't say that I have been lucky in the choice of teachers, but I have been told that we will put you with her, so that she wouldn't tear down the class and destroy the children. That is supposed to make me feel good, but it is not bad because I knew that I was there to help.

Teachers tell me that a "C" makes you just as good a teacher as an "A." I want to be the best. That is why I waited 10 years before I entered college.

The young teacher that comes into the average school system has no children. She doesn't know anything about holding the children, wiping a snotty nose or a child who wets his pants. She comes straight to school, maybe she had sisters or brothers that she had to do that for, but it isn't the same thing, like holding a child that you know, that you want to learn.

It isn't the same thing like knowing how to have a child, knowing the pain that goes with having one. A young teacher has to bring that with her into the classroom and all she brings with her is the textbook.

Thank you.

THE CHAIRMAN: Thank you, Mrs. Burton.
MR. TRACTENBERG: I have a few questions, Mrs. Burton.
MRS. BURTON: All right.
MR. TRACTENBERG: Do you think that your work experience in the classroom has served in any meaningful way to prepare you for ultimately being a teacher?
MRS. BURTON: Yes, I think it has taught me what I don't want to be, for one thing. It opened a new world for me as far as

children are concerned, what the educational system is doing to them, for them, and about them. I have seen good teachers but only at a distance. I never had an opportunity to learn from one. The classroom prepares you. It is up to the person whether it prepares you the right way or the wrong way.

MR. TRACTENBERG: You mentioned in the course of your remarks a few of the major obstacles that you and other paraprofessionals--

THE CHAIRMAN: Just a moment. You have been talking about classroom performance. You said that when you transferred you didn't have anything that was transferable.

MRS. BURTON: Yes.

THE CHAIRMAN: Are you saying that during the two years you were not evaluated on your performance in the classroom by anyone?

MRS. BURTON: Well, I was supposed to be evaluated once. I never had anyone to prevent me from doing anything as far as the paraprofessional program is concerned when I first started.

THE CHAIRMAN: Are paraprofessionals, every six months or every year or something like that, are they evaluated by, let us say, the teachers they are assisting or by the principal or any one of this kind?

MRS. BURTON: Well, in the college program I have been evaluated through the system. That is the four-credit course that I take in which we receive two credits from the theory part, and two credits from the classroom experience.

THE CHAIRMAN: I am now referring only to your work; you work in a school as a paraprofessional, which is apart from your college education.

MRS. BURTON: Yes.

THE CHAIRMAN: Is there a process through which a teacher evaluates you, your program?

MRS. BURTON: No.

THE CHAIRMAN: There is no evaluation whatsoever?

MRS. BURTON: Well, in the school that I am working in now, P.S. 134, there is an administrative staff. A lot of things depend on the administrative supervisor as far as the paraprofessional is concerned.

I happen to be working under a very good administrative staff. Last year I worked in the planning program under Mr. Gordon, from Columbia, and several people did come in and observe me then but that was only because of the plan I was working on. They were quite pleased with it and that is as far as the observation went.

THE CHAIRMAN: I want to get this on the record. When a student goes to college from high school, there is no way that anybody can tell in advance what kind of teacher this person is going to be, but with respect to a paraprofessional it is different. Before being qualified as a teacher and licensed, I take it that it would be possible to have some idea of what kind of teacher that person is going to be because one could evaluate her on the job through those years of her program.

MRS. BURTON: Well, that would be ideal, yes, if it were done, but it isn't being done now. The only time in particular where paraprofessionals get help is through the once-a-month orientation that we have, or, if we are aggressive enough to go tell the assistant principal what our problems are or to ask for assistance from the curricular supervisor. But, as far as regular observation or evaluation is concerned, there is no such thing.

THE CHAIRMAN: All right.

MRS. BURTON: And the paraprofessionals that are not going to college would also like to know how they are doing with the job they are doing. We have paraprofessionals that just go to college but they like what they are doing. They like dealing with children and they feel that the only way that they can know that they are doing a good job is if someone comes in and tells them. If they go wrong, tell them that, too. We don't want to bring in incompetent paraprofessionals along with incompetent teachers, either.

It is just making a bad situation worse.

THE CHAIRMAN: All right, Mr. Tractenberg.

MR. TRACTENBERG: You mentioned in your comments a few major obstacles that you passed with your program. What do you think other paraprofessionals that are talking about it think the main problems with this program are now?

MRS. BURTON: Well, you can start with the Board of Education. The released time has been cut from five hours to 2-1/2 hours, I believe. Just traveling time--say for instance in Queens alone, which is usually two fares and you have to take two buses from the area you live or work at in Queens--would take a good part of that 2-1/2 hours.

In order to remain in Kingsboro, where the instructors who have shown an interest in my goals are teaching, I have had to give up my lunch. We have a 50-minute lunch, but I get 20 minutes. That is voluntary, of course, because it is the only way I can pay back the time that I owe these people, as I figured it out, with my assistant principal. Otherwise, I would be taking 7-1/2 hours.

This is traveling and time sitting in the classroom. That has nothing to do with study time. I had reports to do, book reports to do. We have courses in history, too, and one is American history and it involves reading six books practically from cover to cover. The Afro-American history course involves three large texts to read, cover to cover, and this seminar involves the early childhood book, a handbook guide, which is a piece of material to get through, believe me. The time that they have given us may look like a lot, because they went full time and they, I am sure, read something else. But doing it and raising a family, and trying to do a good job, and trying to carry on and keep your health, and trying to study, it is impossible to do in five hours.

MR. TRACTENBERG: Are there also financial problems involved?

MRS. BURTON: Well, when I first started in the program there was a stipend of $65 for each paraprofessional. That stipend was supposed to cover carfare and/or baby-sitting fees. The average baby-sitter fee two years ago ran you about $20 a week and now I don't know any baby-sitter that you can get away with less than $65. It came in handy, but it was nowhere near being enough. And as far as salary is concerned, I received a 10-cent raise because I had 30 credits and if that is all it is worth to the Board of Education, they could keep their 10 cents and so with the union.

I happen to disagree with the way the union and the Board of Education have locked in the paraprofessionals. We are the ones who are paying. As far as the union is concerned, I have nothing to say about them, nothing.

Although it is all under Title I, under so-called financial benefits--if you can call 10 cents an hour a benefit--they are not doing me any favor. They really didn't, and they didn't do any other paraprofessionals a favor, either. And all they did was split up the paraprofessional ranks between two unions and they are laughing over the fools they made out of us.

If there is going to be a union for paraprofessionals, there should be a paraprofessional union.

I cannot see how people in negotiating can pay the bill for me when they are already representing the professionals. What if they and I disagree? How are they going to represent me? And I say the professional has been paying longer than I have been paying, too.

Am I going to be a second class citizen in the union? No thanks.

I did say that 10 cents an hour was bad, but a little less won't hurt me.

THE CHAIRMAN: All right. Mr. Tractenberg?

MR. TRACTENBERG: I have nothing else.

THE CHAIRMAN: I want to thank you very much for coming here to tell us of your views as one who works in the school system, and it is an important commentary. I appreciate your waiting for us.

Thank you.

MRS. BURTON: Thank you.

THE CHAIRMAN: These hearings are due to reconvene tomorrow at 9:30 a.m. I am going to try to reconvene tomorrow at 9 o'clock to get an earlier start.

I want to announce that we are having, through all this, a child-care facility for people during the hours of these hearings. It is located around the corner from the hearings. The hearings are at 14 Vesey Street and the child-care center is at 225 Broadway, on the 18th floor, Room 27.

For parents who might not be able to attend the hearings during the day, we will have evening hours.

Adjourned until tomorrow morning at 9 o'clock.

- - - - -

(Whereupon, the hearing was adjourned at 7 p.m. to Tuesday, January 26, 1971, at 9 o'clock.)

HEARINGS HELD JANUARY 26, 1971

Witnesses in Order of Appearance

	Testimony starts
Jay E. Greene	page 139
Murray Rockowitz	164
Isaiah E. Robinson	189
Philip Kaplan	197
Andrew G. Donaldson	203
Victor Gotbaum	214
Dennis Hayes	218
Lloyd B. Hunter	225
Wendy Lehrman	229
Ira Glasser	235
Louis Nieves	241
Eugene Callender	246
Irving Chin	252
Rhoda Karpatkin	258

Continued on next page

Rose Falcon	264
Louis Caban	267
Doris Conklin	268
Cecil Forster	278
Morris Seltzer	279
Cynthia Jenkins	281
Dorothy Anderson	282
Joseph F. Valletutti	284
Rita Linquist	286
Elliott Zeitlin	288
Faith Ringgold	293
Carmen Snead	297
Frances Moses	300
Arnold Rothbaum	303
Ruth Buck	306
David Weiner	311
P. Hillman	314
Peter Saltz	316
Reuben Gordon	317

THE CHAIRMAN: We are opening the second day of hearings into the hiring practices of the Board of Education of the City of New York.

I want to announce that there is a child care facility available, free, for parents who wish to attend these hearings. The facility is located around the corner from the hearing.

The hearings are taking place at 14 Vesey Street, Manhattan. The child care center is at 225 Broadway, Room 27, the 18th floor.

Any parent may leave his child there during the times these hearings are going on.

These hearings will go into the evening today in order to accommodate testimony from the public during the late afternoon and evening hours when the public is more likely to be able to come forward to testify because that would be after working hours.

The first witness this morning is Dr. Jay E. Greene, member, Board of Examiners.

Dr. Greene.

DR. GREENE: I must apologize for this delay on my part. I thought that our time was ten o'clock. Forgive me also if I'm not very sharp today. Yesterday was our 30th wedding anniversary and I had a number of people and I was going through some notes, but examiners have anniversaries too. I hope I do provide the answers the Commission wants. If not, you can call me back on a nonholiday.

I would like to clarify today some of the specifics. Yesterday the Chairman of the Board of Examiners, Miss Unser, gave you an over-all view and went into very few specifics. I would like today to go into and to clarify some of the specifics of the selection procedures of the Board of Examiners and I would like to go into similar specifics on some of the alternatives that have been suggested and that are being considered.

So far as our Board of Examiners' procedures are concerned, unfortunately many individuals and persons who have formed judgments and even those who testified here are expressing judgments that are based upon the Board of Examiners' selection procedures of ten, 20, or 30 years ago.

Indeed, our learned counsel here, Mr. Tractenberg, yesterday read a statement from Mr. Vandenberg of the Board of Examiners of 1934 and asked whether this was still a philosophy or the guidepoint of the Board of Examiners.

We unfortunately are in a position, and many of the people who are in supervisory positions or who are teachers, remember procedures that were employed during depression days and are not aware of the great changes that have taken place in our procedures.

Moreover, there are individuals who have testified here who had an unsatisfactory experience with the Board of Examiners at one time or other, some recently, and who have a feeling of bitterness and who have not kept pace with changes, and of course their point of view should be presented here, but I think it should be balanced and there should be an awareness of the built-in hazards of the profession of examining.

Our selection process today, so far as teachers are concerned, usually consists of a three-hour written test. That includes about two hours of short-answers in the subject the individual is supposed to teach and about one hour in written English.

There is also a physical, medical examination and, of course, a review of record. That is what the examination consists of today.

Excuse me, there is an interview test as well.

The rationale in the use of the tests, the written tests, is that there is a body of professional knowledge and subject matter knowledge that would be what teachers have studied in college and they ought to have minimum knowledge or minimum competence in this area.

After all, if a would-be teacher has attended college, has taken a teacher-preparation course, has wanted to teach mathematics, that teacher ought to know something about mathematics and know something about the profession of teaching. And teaching is a profession, as is any other profession.

They have taken examinations of various kinds in colleges and it is no great or horrendous thing to say that such applicants ought to be able to pass a test in their subject, ought to be able to demonstrate minimum proficiency in written English, ought to be able to converse with reasonable clarity on a professional subject.

In New York City, we have people who come from all parts of the country who apply for teaching positions. We don't know what the standards of their colleges were and in many cases they have attended many colleges, taking a course here and there, and we don't know what their background preparation is. There is great diversity.

Therefore, we have this yardstick of a reasonable written test of their background knowledge and information and their ability to communicate orally.

Our standards are not what they used to be during the Vandenberg days of the depression of screening in only the top ten out of a thousand who used to apply and I, along with the others, do recall that these were the unfortunate standards of the depression days where a thousand people took the examination I took for teacher-in-training and about 30 passed.

Those standards would be ridiculous to apply today. The vast majority, perhaps 80 percent, 70 percent, are successful the first time and more are successful as they improve themselves.

So there is an entirely different yardstick that is employed today, but a necessary one.

You would be amazed to see some of the deficiencies that applicants who have degrees, and some of them have master's degrees, some of their deficiencies in their own subject, written English, and literacy. Unless you are familiar with the results that cross your desk, it is almost difficult to believe that this is so.

There are applicants who want to teach mathematics who don't possess knowledge of mathematics of an average 13-year youngster in our junior high schools. Some of the ratings we've had in tests varied from 90 to 20 percent.

In written English there are some amazing examples of illiteracy. I can read just a few from the records of people who have state certification.

Here is one sentence from one paper, for example: "In presenting their project the teacher is able to focus more attention to each child individually periodically. The teacher should plan a trip around each project choosen and present by the group."

Another example: "This problem is well known by the teacher than nobody else. The father and mother going to work every day, children leving alone by themselves in the house grow up without love and respect for nobody."

I have no intention of impugning people by reading the samples. There are many factors which make one person write this way and others write better, but we would not be improving the education of children in our city, and that's my responsibility, if we licensed all teachers who have state certification, for these samples came from people with state certification yet they write that way.

I believe that these people who write this way, many of them, may have been unfortunate in their education. I believe that as adults they can remedy this and they have remedied this as adults. The army, for example, in their intensive training programs showed how highly-motivated adults could remedy deficiencies of whatever kind in academic background.

I don't think the public wants us to license people who are illiterate and deficient at the time they apply to us. We are concerned with minimal standards of competence. We are aware that there is a probationary period and when that change took place in our philosophy, if you wish to call it, it was with the understanding that the probationary period would be more efficiently utilized and that, therefore, instead of screening off the highest percentage, we could aim for what is regarded as minimal competence, minimal knowledge for a beginning teacher to walk into a classroom. But there is an ocean of difference between minimal competence and illiteracy and lack of competence, hostility to children and inability to communicate on the level of children.

There is an ocean of difference between that minimum we look for and, by the way, it is not we examiners, four people who look for it, but professionals from the field who work with children, who are our agents in the selection process, who look for these minimum essentials.

We have made a number of significant changes in our procedures in recent years that I would like you to be familiar with.

In the first place, there has been a tremendous speedup in the examination procedure. There was a time when an examination for a regular license took a year, sometimes two years, and that was unconscionable.

We said we could cut the time if you give us additional staff, if you do more with the probationary period so our initial screening can be reduced. This was with an agreement with the Board of Education somewhere in 1965 where we took a long step in the streamlining of the examination procedures, omitting a teaching test, for example, omitting the essay questions in teaching on the promise that the probationary period would be made use of in a proper way. That utilization of the probationary period never occurred and it is one of the problems we may go into later.

But, there has been a speed-up in the processing. For example, 6,000 or so students who are lower seniors will take our common branches examination in November. The list will come out in March or early April. That's four months for the processing of 6,000 applications, not with a short-answer test alone, but with interviews for each of them, review of record, written English test, short-answers, to assure their minimum competence. Four months, 6,000.

I don't know any other examining body in the country or possibly in the world that can match a record of speed and a record of some comprehensiveness to that extent. Other examinations are similarly reduced in the time factor.

Second change: Examinations are now given while would-be teachers are lower seniors in college so the list is issued before they graduate, in March or April, and they can be offered appointments at that time. We were handicapped in recruiting, prior to this change, because our lists and our examinations were applying to graduates and you can't have them wait or wait as substitutes while you complete your examination. This was the second change.

A third change: The separate oral English test was abandoned. The standards, whatever they were at one time because New York City, and you will recall as I do, was at one time the ridicule of the rest of the country who talked about New Yorkeese, Brooklyneese; and all sorts of things were done to improve the speech of the people. This is a city where immigrants came and so perhaps the standards were unreasonable at that time, Dr. Vandenberg's time or earlier, where there was a separate oral English examination.

We do not have a special oral English test. Our goal now is an interview test of ability to communicate so that children will clearly understand the teacher, so adults will clearly understand. There is no bar on an accent. At one time there were all sorts of hazards in the oral English test. That is no longer true.

We now have a critical score concept in our examinations. In other words, we recognize the written test itself has weaknesses and that to screen people out on a written test at 60 percent instead of 55 or instead of 50 may not be justified because personal factors are important. Therefore, we have said if 60 is the passing mark, we'll have 50 as your cutoff point and the person who does better in the interview, if they get a 70 in the interview and 50 in the written, below the passing mark, an average 60, will come through. This critical score concept is an introduction of flexibility into the examining process without discarding standards, but with recognition of the fact that it is possible to compensate in one area for some weakness in another and still do an adequate job.

We have shortened the written English test in order to be able to give the entire test, written and interview in one day, in a four-hour period. The total test.

We have omitted parts of the test as I indicated earlier, the essay test and teaching test, so that we are doing a different type of screening.

We are using improved machines for the rating of tests, machines under our control, less expensive, that will speed up the process. We have IBM machines for addressing, for preparing lists.

We have improved our selection of test items. Our process for testing questions brings us closer to the job needs. At one time, and this goes back years, we dealt in vague principles of teaching.

Test construction, measurement, indicates the closer you can come to the need of the job, not only the direct needs of working with children, but the needs of working with adults and other colleagues, the more apt you are to have content or construct validity.

We have liberalized the physical standards and medical standards so we are more liberal than any other testing body in the entire world or country. Some of the liberalizations are as follows:

Overweight cases. The question of weight was one we looked into because there was no proven evidence that people who are overweight are likely to be less effective in the classroom. And so that factor was removed.

We at one time had stringent hearing requirements and we said a person who needs a hearing aid can't serve in the classroom because suppose he loses it, what will he do. People don't lose hearing aids that readily and so we have abandoned that flaw.

Arrangements are made to permit diabetics to teach. Individuals who have had a history of possible cancer are permitted to teach. Individuals who have sight deficiencies, even blind people, are permitted to teach. Individuals who are orthopedically handicapped are permitted to teach.

I received phone calls from other jurisdictions, friends of mine in personnel selection in other cities throughout the country, asking me how we have gone about the licensing of blind teachers, how they have performed, what standards we use, and they are asking me the same questions about orthopedically handicapped and other aspects. We have been on the forefront in the sense of opening the doors not only to minority groups, but to people who are handicapped physically.

We now record interviews and make tape recordings available to applicants. What other jurisdiction in selection will do that, so that an individual who is turned down by us because he was unsatisfactory in the interview or unsatisfactory in record which includes an interview, can get a copy of the tape of his interview for three to five dollars and sit down with whatever experts he wishes and say, "Did they rate me fairly, was I treated fairly, was I discriminated against?" I don't know any other jurisdiction who will do that.

Are they proposing that for the community selection of principals or teachers, to have an interview or recording of that interview which would be made available? I haven't heard that mentioned as an alternative.

We do not use confidential reports. We don't believe an individual should be blackballed by a hidden accuser. We believe that if an individual is going to be given an adverse report that will interfere with his record, that will deprive him of a teaching opportunity, that he should be aware of what the accusation is and, to the extent that we will use it, aware of the individual who is making the accusation. What other jurisdiction will make that available in private industry or in public selection anywhere in the country?

I want to tell you there are individuals who have given us adverse reports and we have called them and said we couldn't use this unless you permit us to release this to the applicant. They say, "We don't want to get into difficulty, possible lawsuits, strike that from the record."

This standard is unusual, but we believe it is fair, and we believe the City Commission on Human Rights will believe that this is fair and will consider this in a total evaluation of our procedures.

We make available for our short-answer examinations, the answer keys. In the essay questions we make available the detailed rating scheme that was used so that an applicant who is turned down will know the reason why.

The greatest hazard in terms of people who have gone up against "the system," up against discrimination--and I have as an individual and a great many people have faced "the system" and discrimination--the greatest hazard is secret procedure in selection and determination. Don't call us, we'll call you. You apply, you are greeted with a smile, you are asked questions and you hear nothing further. That is and has been, in the main, the evil, the cause of discrimination in the long run and in the short run. And we have striven to avoid that sort of thing.

Other improvements. In 1967 the Legislature restructured the Board of Examiners. We were a Board of nine and now we are a Board of five.

This was done in cooperation with, or at the instance of, the Board of Education which believed that more changes, innovations, could occur if there were fewer examiners, where you have less discussion, less disagreement, but you could get action as a result.

Dr. Greene

So, the Chairman of the Board of Examiners, under this law, was given increased responsibility for the management of the operation in an effort to get increased efficiency. This was a major change few people are aware of.

We have used walk-in examinations. This is No. 15 on my list. Walk-in examinations where a person can come in on a single day and be examined completely and go out by the end of the day to the school that wanted him in the first place. Now, that's a sort of service cooperation that communities and schools may need. This is to fill emergency vacancies in schools which could not be filled from lists. We are still on a procedure, particularly at the beginning of terms or other times, of that one-day or two-day procedure.

In September and October there were instant needs in schools, and there were 1500 referrals in a six-week period to us by districts who had picked people, recruited people who are not on lists, who are interested in teaching, whom they wanted in their district, referred them to us to check their minimum competence, to begin teaching children the next day. In one day, two days, three days, these 1500 or 1600 were licensed and sent back to schools, that is, those who were regarded as satisfactory. There were some who were not, properly so.

I've read you examples of some of the people we turned down, at least of some of their writing.

Another area in which we were criticized, which was not our fault, is the area of substitutes. At one time 33 percent of our staff were substitutes, four or five years ago. This was properly a scandal. Initially this was done to save money as far back as the LaGuardia administration. Substitutes were paid less than regulars. There were other factors.

The solution was simple we said. Don't ask us to give examinations for substitutes and you won't have any more.

That simple solution took a long time to bear fruit. Finally the UFT insisted in the contract that the examinations for substitutes be discontinued, and they were discontinued.

Now the 33 percent has been decreased tremendously. The figures I have seen are somewhere around 12 or 15 percent, and the change was made only about three years ago.

So that some of the criticisms we have received have not been our fault. We are a service agent of the Board of Education. We are a ruler, a yardstick, an examining body, an impartial, professional examining body.

And yet because, I suppose, it's easy to get scapegoats, we have been the scapegoat, and one Superintendent of Schools said to me one time, "You know, if the only reason we had for paying your salaries was that we could blame you for things in personnel, you would be earning your salary." Whether in jest or not, there is a good deal of truth in it.

The changes have been made, while maintaining the fundamental principles of impartiality, the essentials of a merit system.

Our shortcomings are known. They were mentioned here.

In reaching and stretching, we were blamed for the shortcomings of a coaching system. But all our shortcomings are noted and if the counsel will ask me questions, I'll go into that. If you want to become a lawyer, can't you take a coaching system? If you want to get into college, aren't there coaching courses for college boards? Does that mean the examinations themselves are worse than something else? Does that mean the law boards should be discontinued?

It's almost like blaming the weather bureau, in a sense, for bad weather because the weather bureau predicts the weather or indicates what the weather is. In a sense this may be the role of the Board of Examiners as an examining body saying, "Yes, you do meet these requirements, these are professional requirements," or, "No, you don't."

Let's examine with similar detail some of the alternatives that have been proposed because we have gone into a great deal of detail on the Board of Examiners, and we'll go into some detail, and we should, because we believe, again, open disclosure is the best safeguard that the public and minority groups and everybody else has.

Let's have some open disclosure on these alternatives and some of the specific details on those, too, because it is very easy to give a glib generalization on some of the others.

Let's take state certification which has been indicated as an alternative. This is the reliance of Dr. Scribner as he indicated yesterday.

What is state certification? State certification is obtained by writing a letter and enclosing a transcript and a fee. And nobody sees you and nobody questions you; nobody knows whether you have a criminal record or whether you are healthy or not healthy.

By return mail in a year or two or three you get your certificate. And there was a time in Albany where you couldn't get a phone call through because they were two years behind, and this was a statewide schedule which didn't reach us because we don't use the State. But the New York State Teachers Association was outraged because they couldn't get phone calls answered. They were outraged because there was an admission that they hadn't opened letters for six months.

That's one of the realities of the state certification approach. State certification officials themselves declare state certification is no guarantee of quality, no measure of quality.

It performs a different function and necessary function. I don't want to impugn the function. It performs the function which says people who want to teach must have some preparation. What the preparation is, they are not able, for whatever reason, to define in as much detail, but without state certification we would be in tremendous difficulty, and that was devised in its time to meet a felt need.

The interesting thing about state certification is this: If you want to become a lawyer, you take state boards, or a beautician or mortician. To become a teacher, no exam. Nothing. Credentialling courses, counting credits.

In New York City it was felt this was not enough, that there ought to be an examination, and the states now are considering introducing an examination, at least Dr. Nyquist and other state commissioners are now talking about an examination, and Dr. Scribner said he believed in it, and Mr. Bergtraum said this is what ought to be done.

You know, when you look for a simple solution, it's very easy to say this is the answer until you go into the details of it. They are proposing that the State Education Department be used for certification, and then we wouldn't have to worry.

Let's have a look at that. Commissioner Nyquist, who knows some of the details, said it would take a year or two. Some of our people said why can't we do it right away.

How long does it take to prepare a test? Here are some of the problems. First, what would the test consist of? Would it be a short-answer test, written English? Would it be an interview? Would it be a teaching test? The State of New Jersey has been working on this and they call it now performance-based certification.

I have attended some conferences. Incidentally, I'm past president of the National Association of School Personnel Administrators, and so I have a fairly good knowledge of what is happening, what the problems are elsewhere.

What they're talking about is performance based certification throughout. The State of New Jersey has been working for a year trying to decide what tests to give. Their State Department sent to me to find out what tests we give and they were very much impressed.

When I said we analyze the job, they said, "We've been trying to do that, but we don't know what the criteria are." There are so many differences and variables about a good teacher. A good teacher may be good in one community and not good in another.

There are people who spend 25 and 30 years to define and see whether there is a basic method of a good teacher that every teacher should have. That's one of the difficulties.

The State would also have to decide--there are 1200 different teaching licenses--should they use one test, or 1200. Can you use the same test for a teacher of English or Spanish or a teacher of mathematics or should you use a different test for a teacher of shop work, health education, science, biology, or music, or fine arts? You can't use one test. Now this begins to add up.

If they had 1200 tests or whatever number, if they included an interview, they would get the same complaints that the Board of Examiners face. There is nothing that would be magical about their tests that would avoid charges of discrimination. There are states that have tried tests for certification, and they have been accused of discrimination. The tests are too hard and take too long, the same criticisms we face.

You would face it next year with state tests if they use it. Dr. Nyquist knows he would run into this. They have enough complaints now without an examination.

If you attend, and you have an opportunity, the American Association of School Administrators, come to Atlantic City in February; and if you sat down and heard some of the complaints about state certification throughout the country, the same criticism we face with examinations goes to all certification authorities. They are most unpopular.

Why? Because they insist people need course requirements and the communities say no. We have a person and he's short these two credits, but you won't certify him. You are in opposition to community control, and so the state certification authorities catch it all over the country because they are too technical, because they insist on course credits, because there are delays in certification.

The City of Los Angeles 12 years ago was similar to New York City in that they had their own examining body and did their own certifying. That is, they did eligibility themselves.

Twelve years ago to save money they said, we'll do our own examining but turn eligibility over to the state to save money, and they did that. For three years they saved money, but then there were tremendous complaints, and those in charge were dissatisfied because it used to take them forever to get approval from the State on eligibility. Letters went to the state. They had people waiting for teaching jobs; they couldn't be certified.

They were sorry they had given that up. And yet we in New York City, who have in a sense local control over eligibility and selection, want now to turn it over to the state. Not that it's going to make any improvements, but it seems like an easy change.

Isn't that contrary to the idea of local control or community control? Here we have an open book. If you want changes in eligibility, the Board of Education can make it. You can have delegations, hearings of this sort, and bring changes. Why should you want to move this to the State? What would you gain?

So much for state certification and I could say more. State certification doesn't even guarantee courses. They have a business they call excusive default where, if a community has a teacher who doesn't have a single professional course and they want him, they say we can't get a teacher with training, therefore we want him.

So they have teachers who are what they call substandard teachers. And the New York State Teachers Association, the upstate group, every year passes resolutions deploring the number of teachers who are substandard on these below standard certificates of the state and saying we must get rid of them. It's the same situation we had with substitutes in our city when we were trying to make changes.

If they have this opportunity of excusive default, that means anybody with influence doesn't have to meet state standards. If he has the right connections, he can get a job because he has the right connections.

Let's look at some other alternatives, in some detail, as we should.

Dr. Scribner says why should we have an examination system.

Other school systems in the State and many cities in the country don't; the city where he came from, Teaneck, New Jersey, didn't have any. The population of Teaneck was somewhere around 25,000, of many other cities maybe 10,000 or 15,000.

Should we talk about whether other cities have it or not? Is that the proper criterion for a reasoning man or reasoning group? Isn't it better to say let's do it because other cities are doing it and their programs are better than ours? He doesn't say that.

Let's see what other cities there are. Each of our community districts will not be a Teaneck with 20,000 or 25,000 people. Each of our 30 districts will have a 250,000 population, 30,000 children in the schools, 2,000 teachers. That's quite a large size community.

It is very easy in that situation, through influence, to get some teachers in one school or another among the 2,000 in order to do favors for people.

We are now talking of Jersey City; Jackson, Mississippi; Yonkers, Scranton, Syracuse, and others in the area of 250,000 population. The whole State of Vermont has 411,000, which isn't much larger than one of these districts.

But in these districts, if people were to say that their selection system is better than ours because they have free reign, that might make more sense. That isn't the argument. It is merely they have complete freedom or flexibility and therefore we should do it, follow what they want.

Let's examine this phrase "flexibility" which is a public relations word and sounds wonderful. I think you ought to want to examine it rather than merely accept it. If means you have a right to choose anybody that you want because you say that if you are the boss, head of the unit, you are accountable and if you are accountable, you ought to have the right to choose the staff.

That sounds wonderful on the face of it. But, this is the timeworn argument that existed before Civil Service, because every department head in public employment said that too.

The head of a fire department might say you can't hold me responsible for the fire department unless you let me choose all the firemen, lieutenants, the sergeant, and the head of the police department, the schools, the architecture department. And then what happens when that head is changed?

Then the new head comes in. The new head doesn't want these people. He didn't pick them. There is no flexibility any more. He wants them out. That's the spoils system.

If you want that flexibility, that's what it leads into. And that's one of the things the public and legislature and, I believe, the majority of people in this city do not want in the school system. We haven't had it. I don't believe they want it.

Let's see whether we've had any indications of that in New York City.

We have a community superintendent in New York City. He picks his principals; he picks his staff. He was picked by the local school board. The local school board changed. There was an election less than a year ago, so the principal who was wonderful to the previous community superintendent or the community superintendent who was wonderful is no longer wanted, and he is out.

We've seen that in a number of our districts. There are two districts where there are black principals, for example, who were regarded as highly satisfactory, eminently satisfactory, by their previous bosses. But the local school board changed and the new community superintendent is there and he wants flexibility, so he wants them out. He may want some teachers out. We've seen that happen in districts too.

What you begin to have there is not an education system with some stability, with people who are professionally chosen, who can be brought up on charges if they are incompetent. But you have a spoils system or else you have people coming in who really don't have flexibility.

I'll tell you what happens as was told to me by friends of mine in other cities and as I know happens. If you have a vacancy for a principal under this flexibility word, and you have free choice, you look around among the people who have been close to you and you say, "This fellow, he has driven me to work, he is a good yes man. I can count on him, he'll do things. I can call him; I'll move him into the job."

So, really, when Dr. Scribner says he doesn't want to choose among 12 on the list, he wants to choose from the whole world or the country, the reality of that so-called flexibility is that the person who makes the choice makes it from a very small group of those he knows or those who are recommended to him or those who are forced upon him by influence.

Just as you examine our procedures on reality and practicability, you ought to examine these alternatives in the same way on practicability and what actually happens in practice. The people who are picked under those conditions throughout the country, in Yonkers, Syracuse, and the other places are people who are yes men.

I don't believe the people here are naive. Can you believe that individuals who have free choice will choose somebody as a principal or in a top position who has been a thorn in his side, who has been a person who has rocked the boat?

The truth is, the person who picks an individual picks him in his own image. This has been borne out by research. If one man does a selection, they are in his image, the sort of person he wants. When the top man goes, this person may be out of tune.

This goes back to the 1800's. Do you remember "The Pinafore"? "How do you advance yourself?"--Gilbert and Sullivan. "By polishing the brass of the upper brass," in the mid-1800's.

That hasn't changed very much in 1970. Human nature hasn't changed very much either. We actually, with our procedures, provide a larger pool than is provided under this flexibility.

Dr. Scribner mentioned 12 who are on the present eligible list for high school principal. There are lists which, because we invite open applications from everybody and have an examination, run into the hundreds.

The assistant principal, elementary school had a list of 700 to choose from. And if this 700 is a qualifying list, then a community board could choose any one of 700; whereas under the so-called flexibility, in reality, they have a choice of five. Among these 700 are nay sayers, iconoclasts, innovators, because they were not picked because they were yes men, and close and good followers. They were picked because they demonstrated their merit.

The next principal list, in terms of the performance we've seen so far, will show a list of I don't know how many. It ought to be surely above a thousand, 1500. Each school, each community will have a choice among a thousand, among 1500 in reality and not just people who are yes men.

Look at the reality of our staff under the Board of Examiners and the principals. We have been told about inbreeding in New York City. The truth is we have more diversity in our staff than any other place because of the nature of our selection process.

We have people who are for the Board of Examiners, people who hate us, who believe we are the worse possible thing. I stand in debates, and I don't want to mention names, with people who are at the opposite spectrum. The staff who were leading opponents of ours in Ocean Hill, including the head person, were people we licensed. Some of the people who were supposed to be militants against the establishment completely, people we licensed.

There is no criterion in terms of personality in that sense. There is a fair and objective appraisal.

As a matter of fact, our selection procedures, what is our reputation among personnel people out of the city when I have asked them for an informal evaluation? The answer has been: your people who are licensed are good professionals, they know their stuff; and then their voice drops a bit and they say, but you know, so many of them are too darn independent in their thinking.

This is the label of our staff that we on the Board of Examiners have selected. We think it's a good label. We would hate to see it be tossed overboard so that we could follow Yonkers, Syracuse, Jersey City, Jackson, Mississippi, and a host of others. And I haven't heard anybody tell us that these are ideal educational systems.

Madam Chairman, I'm taking a longer time than you planned, but I believe that there is so little known about the Board of Examiners and I believe that we are in a sense a key in this investigation, a rather important one, and so I hope you'll bear with me.

THE CHAIRMAN: I'm going to do that.

I believe the fact is that you are a key here, and you ought to be given the full time.

DR. GREENE: Thank you very much.

Let's look at another alternative, NTE. This is also regarded as the preferred method. Let's use state certification say some, and some say NTE, National Teacher Examination.

I think we ought to look at the National Teacher Examination and learn some of the specifics. I want to say at the outset I have the utmost respect for the National Teacher Examination. I think it's a good examination; it is prepared by professionals very carefully, very honestly. In fact I'm a member of their National Advisory Commission, and so I know a good deal about it, and, I repeat, I have the utmost respect for it.

It is now suggested that the NTE be used because it would be better, would increase the number of minority people in the school system, we're told, open the gates to more teachers, give us more flexibility, the whole host of adjectives of public relations. In fact, we use NTE.

We believe where we cannot reach with our test, NTE can reach. And for the past three years we have said anybody who has an NTE score, which is the equivalent of our score, we'll take it in place of our written test, and it has helped recruitment. We have every desire and every plan to use it.

When the State Legislature in Albany passed the Decentralization Law they put into the law that the NTE may be used. They asked me about it and I said, "We're using it, it's a valuable test, but we ought to know some of the things about it that make us believe under some circumstance it is better to use our tests."

For example, the NTE written test is a seven and a half hour test, four and a half hours in the morning, three hours in the afternoon. A full day. I did not know whether you knew that.

Secondly, to file for the NTE test there is a fee of $13. Daisy Hicks yesterday testified she had difficulty in some cases, and it was sad because applicants for our license didn't have a $3 fee. And so we urged that that $3 fee be abandoned. But, there is a $13 fee to take the NTE examination. That is a consideration.

Another factor is the NTE is, after all, a test also. This NTE examination has been criticized in Southern states as discriminatory. It has been used improperly in some Southern states to discriminate in the matter of salary. If you got a certain score on the NTE, you qualified for the next step on the salary schedule. But they were aware when they were doing it that there was a substantial part of their faculties in the segregated schools who wouldn't get that high mark on the NTE, and so it was consciously used in that sense for discrimination.

But it is, after all, a test. And if you use it, you will find the same complaint against that test as against our test. It's no better than our test in some ways. In some ways it is better, in some ways it is not.

You should know that only about 10 percent of the education graduates take the NTE. So if we used the NTE, you would find that four out of five of the people you wanted to employ would not have taken the NTE test because it is not used that widely. And then you would have to have some process for screening them to get them into the city school system if you believed there was some minimum requirement in subject matter, if you believed there was some minimum requirement in literacy.

NTE doesn't make tests in the host of 1200 licenses. They have it in common branches. They just began it in library, for example, and in physical education. They don't have it in a host of tests. You would have to have some means of selection other than that.

I'll get to the matter of costs again.

THE CHAIRMAN: May I know about how much longer you would take, because there are other witnesses.

DR. GREENE: I think 20 minutes more.

THE CHAIRMAN: There will be cross-examination after. I need to know--Mr. Tractenberg, is your examination, your prepared examination plus examination based on the testimony, going to be fairly lengthy?

MR. TRACTENBERG: My examination was going to be extensive even before Dr. Greene began. It will be considerably more extensive now.

THE CHAIRMAN: Dr. Greene, I want you to get everything in the record that you have come to say, but let me ask you to the extent you can condense it, will you do that.

DR. GREENE: I'm trying to do that, Madam Chairman, to the extent I can. I appreciate your desire to be fair and give us additional time. I'll try to condense a bit.

Again on NTE, the matter of costs. We have 6,000 people in New York City taking one examination for teacher in elementary schools called common branches.

We can prepare the short-answer test for about $5,000, grade it, prepare all the questions, administer it, and so on. But for 6,000 people, to pay the $13 fee, $75,000 would be the cost of it. So, you have an additional cost of about $70,000. It is less expensive for us to use our tests locally in the City of New York and that's not only in the 6,000, but bear in mind we examine 50,000. So there is a considerable saving in terms of our own tests.

Furthermore, with our tests, which is a three-hour plus interview, in four hours we can conduct a whole test of an individual, whereas the NTE, just the written alone, is seven and a half hours.

So that if we go out on the road, for example, in recruitment, if individuals have not taken the NTE, we can examine individuals on the road as they appear and put them through the selection process.

So, we have advantages over the NTE and they have the same shortcomings we do plus some additional ones.

Another point, in view of learned counsel's questions yesterday. I guarantee if the NTE was used, there would be coaching courses for it very shortly. If jobs are involved and people are serious about it, there would be coaching courses and they would be hard-pressed because they have a limited number of forms of their test. They have an A Form, B Form, perhaps seven or eight forms, and the question of their security would be a difficult one.

We have an unlimited number of forms. We prepare a new test for every examination and have greater security.

In fact we wanted to use the NTE form in our principal's examination just held, the short-answer test, but we were afraid because we said with 2,000 some applicants, with all sort of drives, connections, and so on, we're not sure we could maintain the security once it became known we're going to use their exam.

I'll just condense the next part. You have asked about the preparations of our examination, whether the examiners are measurement experts.

The answer is yes, the examiners are measurement experts. The fact we were English teachers initially doesn't mean we were unable to develop the knowledge in the field of measurement. We were tested on that, a very vigorous examination by the Civil Service Commission. We've gone into the field, we've lived in the field and we are measurement experts.

I think you have to understand this about our selection procedures. When you talk about measurement experts in a broad sense, we are not preparing intelligence tests for national consumption. We are not preparing national aptitude tests or tests of social significance or specialized general tests of personality in which you have the specialized testing people.

We are preparing what you may call achievement tests in subject to know whether a math teacher knows enough math to teach math, whether a math teacher can in an interview be able to communicate and show he can teach math on the level of children, that he knows how to work with groups.

And this type of testing situation, when you're dealing with 1200 different license areas and where you believe that the best test is the test that gets closest to the teaching specialty, is one that is carried on with the advice of measurement experts, with the guidance of testing experts, but to a major degree by people who are experts in supervision in the particular field, who work with beginning teachers, know what to look for, who teach the subject, who supervise the subject.

There is a whole different approach. This is a complex discussion. I don't know whether we want to get into it, but we may if counsel wishes to ask further questions.

What is our role in recruitment? This is one of the questions that was posed. The recruiter going out into the district, persuades them to come in and so on.

We are an examining body. At one time we said we should be given the responsibility for recruitment. We'll go out, do the recruitment and it will be one job.

Superintendent Jensen believed this should be done. But the latest superintendents and the Board of Education said no, we want you merely to be the examining body; the recruitment will be done by the Bureau of Personnel. Let them go out, encourage people to come in, advertise our virtues, advertise opportunities. And you go in with a fair test, in an objective and impartial way do the testing.

That's our relationship. We are willing to cooperate fully because we believe we are a service agency to the Board of Education. We believe there is a considerable influence. We believe we are a service agency and should be to the community boards. Exactly how that's going to be spelled out under the Decentralization Law, we're not sure. We want to meet with the community board to see what their ideas are on this subject and the ways in which we can and will cooperate. We have asked for such meetings with the community boards and I am hopeful these meetings will be held because we are a service agency in that regard.

We have made suggestions in recruitment. We have made a number of suggestions. We were the first ones to suggest that we go to other cities such as Washington, D.C. and Nashville and administer tests there. In fact when we first made the suggestions we were criticized in the press by representatives of minority groups for making that suggestion.

I want to go briefly into the matter of statistics which Madam Chairman has mentioned and she said the statistics are dismal, diastrous, deplorable so far as New York City is concerned.

In a sense, you know, with statistics, you have to analyze. They are red flags which show you there is a problem here, it ought to be investigated. But they are not indications of fault one way or another, and the fact that there are percentage statistics of one type or another does not mean that the Board of Examiners has been responsible for holding people out as we have tried to indicate.

The statistics are just as bad in places without any examinations. Worse, in fact.

The other day, yesterday, the New York *Times* carried an article about the Police Department, their statistics. In the Police Department three or four years ago five percent of their staff were Black. Now after tremendous efforts in recruitment, 7.5% are Black.

We're told nine to ten percent of our teachers are Black. Just look at that. To be a policeman, you don't have to have a college degree, you don't have to have professional training; and yet their figures, 7.5% of their staff. Civil Service, no Board of Examiners.

Statistics are important, as I say. And they should say what's happening here, what can we do about it, and to that extent the Human Rights Commission is on the right track. But I'm afraid maybe one or two of them, because of these statistics, formed a prejudgment that it is the fault of the Board of Examiners.

We'll try to show the way to cure the statistics is not by eliminating the wrong body and doing worse, but by seeing what can be done in a proper sense by keeping whatever is good.

Take the City University, a faculty of thousands, complete flexibility in choosing. What is their percentage of Blacks. I would assume, on the basis of my familiarity, I have no statistics, that they have fewer because a degree is required, majoring in a specialty, and they have tenure of staff, and that probably their percentage figures are worse than ours.

State universities, colleges outside of New York City, have faculties of thousands. I would hazard a guess that their percentage ratio is more disastrous, Madam Chairman, than ours, to use a term you have indicated.

The important thing under our procedure is this: There has been a tremendous acceleration in the numbers of Blacks coming in as teachers in New York City under the Board of Examiners, qualified under a merit system and that number-wise in a shortage area, we are probably better than any other city in the country.

For example, in New York City there may be 6,000 Black and Puerto Rican teachers, and the percentage is very low. The number, 6,000, is significant.

Los Angeles has a higher percentage, but they dont' have 6,000. They have 4,000. Chicago has more, 7,000. Detroit has fewer, 4,400 as against 6,000. Philadelphia has 3,600.

When you deal in a shortage commodity--we're not talking about the elementary and junior high schools, but we're talking about those who come before us--they had been fewer in number, but nevertheless we do have 6,000, and we do have a tremendous acceleration on the supervisory level, and there will be dramatic changes each month that new lists come out in the City of New York.

And that's true on the supervisory level where percentagewise we are lower. But where they have ten or a hundred on all levels of supervisory positions, we have several hundred. The figures are changing drastically.

Our feeling has been that the approach in increasing the numbers--and we have shown that this works--is not to say, as unfortunately the lawsuit of this group representing a faction of the NAACP has said, it is not fair to use tests of social studies or English for principals, because these tests discriminate against Blacks. We don't believe that's true. We believe that it is possible to supply reasonable standards in a merit system and that people of all groups, Blacks, Puerto Ricans, of any nationality, any religion, will come through in significant numbers. We have demonstrated that.

We believe the handicaps people may have had in their early schooling can be overcome by seminar sessions, so long as they believe they have a fair opportunity, a fair challenge, and they're willing to roll up their sleeves. And they are, if they believe there is a fair opportunity. As adults they can master academic handicaps and meet standards on the same par with anybody else. We have demonstrated that in these numbers and in the greater numbers that are coming through.

I think this is a better example to give to the rest of the country, and I think the rest of the country will be moved by our example and what we do in this case, not lowering standards, but keeping standards and opening the doors of opportunity and making these opportunities really available as they have not been.

Another alternative that has been suggested is the internship. Someone came in and said put people in under conditional licenses. If they do well on the job, let them stay.

That's fine if you don't have enough teachers. What do you do if you have ten teachers and five jobs? How do you pick the five interns? How do you pick the five out of the ten provisionals or conditionals to go in? You must wind up with some impartial selection system in order to pick the interns.

I could tell you a good deal about that internship program at Fordham which is a wonderful thing in opening the door to opportunity for Blacks. I'm glad it exists, and I was on the advisory committee and applauded it. But I know how the 20 interns were selected for the program. I'm aghast because they were selected in a way that we believe is unconscionable. It's the secret way. They didn't interview 2,000 people. They went over the applications and tossed some aside in the way in which colleges do their selection.

For heaven's sake, we should not go through the secret procedures of the colleges. If you want to get your children into a college and you wonder on what basis they made the selection, two from this school, two from that, so much of that religion and so many of them. This method which has been used should not be used in the selection of teachers.

There are three steps in the selection procedures we believe in. First, the preparation by the college, second, an impartial selection procedure, and third, a probationary period. All are important. We urge all three be considered, no one part more important than the other.

Yesterday the Decentralization Law was mentioned, and criticized. Learned counsel in a leading question said, "How is it possible that the legislature could say that 40% of the teachers could be chosen one way and the other 60% chosen in another way? If one way is better, why didn't they go one way? If the other is better, why didn't they go for that?"

The truth is, this was really a compromise, and the State Legislature, in its wisdom, foresaw all sorts of problems if this were tried even on a 40 percent basis. And they were unwilling to shut the door to possible abuses or the needs of the school system.

Here are some of the problems they foresaw in the question of how this 40 percent approach would work. They said to themselves, and they knew not everybody takes the NTE, they said if we just say the 40 percent can use the NTE, what will happen if people don't take the NTE, how will they use them? So we'll have to say the Board of Examiners can use an alternative, go to the Board of Examiners and get a special test. So, let's try to see what percentage of the NTE people there are and how that works.

They did not know to what extent the community boards of their own volition would prefer to use the procedures of the Board of Examiners after trying the NTE and after running into difficulty. And they wanted to see how this would work, very properly and very responsibly.

They were concerned about the qualifying lists. They said in the future, examinations for chairmen, assistant principals, and principals should be qualifying. That means if you have a list of a thousand, the community board can choose any one of the thousand.

They were concerned about how this would work out. Does this mean instead of 2,200 people chasing around for influence in order to get jobs what has been accomplished is that you now have a thousand people who were going through this process of seeking influence? They weren't sure how this would work. Would this lead to a spoils system? Would this lead to evils which they couldn't anticipate?

And so they made the charge and said well, we're going to give the community boards a tremendous amount of power. We're going to let them pick the community superintendent and give them a free choice, but we don't know how that will work, and they were unwilling to shut the door completely by saying everything overboard, everything is free choice. So it was a compromise in that sense.

They were concerned about the expense also with these local boards. I said we have 50,000 teachers applying to us. What will happen in New York City if there are 30 community boards and we know there are 50,000 people who want jobs? Are the 50,000 people going to apply to Local School Board 1 and also to Local School Board 2 and 3 and 4? Is each local school board going to screen 50,000, or a thousand who are on the principal's list, or 1500 on an assistant principal's list?

They couldn't see how that would work. Or, if we have City College or Hunter College and you have 30 different school boards, each one with a topnotch recruiting unit, two, three people in each district, three top recruiters, high salaried people, should each of the 30 go to Hunter College and give them pep talks to come to their unit? We would have 30 different high-powered recruiters in Hunter College alone because that's where 67 percent of our teachers come from. Next week they go to Brooklyn and next week to Staten Island.

The Legislature wasn't sure how that was going to work. They were unwilling just to toss the whole thing overboard and let's throw out what has been tried, what has flaws, what we have corrected. They were unwilling to do that.

So there is logistic problems--

THE CHAIRMAN: Dr. Greene, what am I to do about the fact that the Vice-President of the Board of Education is here and he was scheduled for ten o'clock and that every other witness this morning has come and that my counsel has not been allowed to ask you a question.

I want to say for the record that it has been implied this Commission may have prejudged--

DR. GREENE: Not the Commission.

THE CHAIRMAN: Or the public.

I think by allowing you to go on for more than an hour and 15 minutes where we have asked witnesses to prepare for ten or 15 minutes, we have indicated we would take any testimony, but I don't know how much longer I can go on and what to do about the witnesses to come after you.

DR. GREENE: I'll draw a period to what I want to say now.

MR. TRACTENBERG: I'm in a bit of a quandary, Madam Chairman. I would estimate the nature of the questions I have would take a minimum of an hour.

THE CHAIRMAN: Let me call a recess for five minutes. It will be no more than five minutes.

(Short recess taken at this time.)

THE CHAIRMAN: I want to say that other witnesses who are scheduled for this morning, it is most graciously understood that it was necessary in the first place to give Dr. Greene the time he needed and deserved, and that it is necessary in the light of the time needed for counsel to ask him questions of some length, based on his testimony, and therefore I want to especially thank Mr. Isaiah Robinson, the Vice-President of the Board of Education, who has consented to wait and also the other witnesses, Mr. Philip Kaplan, Dennis Hayes, Miss Wendy Lehrman, and Mr. Lloyd Hunter.

MR. TRACTENBERG: Dr. Greene, I hope we can conduct this as if it were a short-answer and not an essay part of the examination.

I think I ought to say one thing as a preface. I don't know that it has been actually articulated, but I think it underlies the whole purpose of these hearings, and that is that this inquiry is not to determine whether a system of merit ought to be replaced by a system not based on merit, but rather what system of merit will operate most efficiently and economically and expeditiously.

THE CHAIRMAN: You should add "fairly" to that.

MR. TRACTENBERG: And fairly. That's really the direction in which many of my questions will go.

First of all, I was glad that you raised something which I think corrects the record from yesterday in Miss Unser's testimony. I had asked whether there was an essay portion of the teacher examinations and, I believe after a conference, it was decided there were no longer essay portions on the teacher examinations.

I understood you to say that the teacher examinations do contain an essay portion. Is that right?

DR. GREENE: No, I said they had been dropped. We may be using a few in trade subjects, but the essay in teacher examinations has been abandoned.

MR. TRACTENBERG: At what point were they abandoned?

DR. GREENE: In 1966, as part of the discussion with the Board of Education in streamlining the procedures, we dropped the teaching test and essay questions for teacher licenses.

MR. TRACTENBERG: I have here copies of some exams which date from 1970 and they all appear to have essay portions.

DR. GREENE: Are you talking about the written English part?

We do have a part which we rate for written English or literacy, in a sense you might call it. We do pose a question, and we say this will be rated not for content, but for written English. That's a one-hour test. We do not have essay questions in scholarship or in methodology.

MR. TRACTENBERG: In any event there are essay questions which have to be graded--

DR. GREENE: Not marked for content. They're rated for basically can a person communicate acceptably, in accordance with minimum standards in written English.

MR. TRACTENBERG: Is there a rating key of some kind for that?

DR. GREENE: Yes. We can make that available.

MR. TRACTENBERG: Is there a model answer as well?

DR. GREENE: If a word is misspelled, there is a model answer for it in the dictionary. In grammar books there are model answers--incomplete sentences, capitalization. I'm not sure we're talking about the same thing, counsel.

MR. TRACTENBERG: I have seen a set of instructions which go to examiners. I'm not sure whether it applies to the supervisory exams. If it does, I understand you have some inhibition about answering.

DR. GREENE: Those are in supervisory examinations only.

I'm glad we cleared the confusion. I was thinking one thing and you another.

MR. TRACTENBERG: I want to turn to some of the things you said because I think they raise important issues.

First of all, isn't it true, Dr. Greene, that something in excess of 90 percent of all the teachers in the New York City school system come from colleges in New York City or immediately adjacent to New York City?

DR. GREENE: Yes.

MR. TRACTENBERG: Don't about 65 percent come from the City University itself?

DR. GREENE: Yes.

MR. TRACTENBERG: Does the Board of Examiners have any way by which it has cooperative efforts with the City University which would permit it to determine the standards used at City University for graduating people in the teacher education program?

DR. GREENE: We have a council, where we meet with all the colleges in the metropolitan area, and they ask us questions, and we ask them questions, and that is a coordinating body.

It's called the Advisory Council of Colleges in Teacher Education.

MR. TRACTENBERG: Does this permit you to find out enough about the standards that apply in City University and some of the other teacher colleges to be able to ascertain that someone who graduates from this program with a good record in fact meets the minimal standard that you say is your present philosophy?

DR. GREENE: In a general sense we meet with them. They're doing different things. But we don't discuss the particulars of every one of the hundreds of their graduates. We don't discuss the particular records of each.

One or two of the samples of illiteracy I read to you, one came from a person with a master's degree at Hunter. So we do discuss in general with them and in the over-all.

MR. TRACTENBERG: Don't they keep a detailed dossier on all their education students?

DR. GREENE: The college placement offices have a booklet on each student who is in their full program. These are comments by instructors, and these are confidential comments by instructors which the students never see.

We have had experiences where some wonderful people, by being nay sayers, ran afoul of some instructor who proceeded to blackball them by having an adverse comment in the folder. And

Dr. Greene 161

we question the reliability of these secret, confidential statements.

And furthermore, the colleges don't have them for people who take part-time courses and there are large numbers who do. I would say that a third of our staff coming in are not coming in--maybe it's a larger number than that--through a full program where they have such dossiers.

MR. TRACTENBERG: Do I understand you to say in cases where the dossiers exist you do not use them as part of the review of record?

DR. GREENE: We review them with a grain of salt. We do other investigation, and we know their shortcomings.

MR. TRACTENBERG: But you do use them and nevertheless--

DR. GREENE: We don't use the dossier. We get a summary report on one of our own forms where the registrar or official checks on our form pretty much in summary what appears in the dossier.

MR. TRACTENBERG: You have apparently found them not sufficiently helpful to eliminate the need for a written examination to test minimum competency of people coming out of the City University.

DR. GREENE: That's right.

MR. TRACTENBERG: I assume it suggests--

DR. GREENE: You said you want short answers.

MR. TRACTENBERG: I assume that suggests something about the character of teacher education in the City University then.

DR. GREENE: I think City University is in the forefront of teacher education. But that doesn't mean that all their young people, with their host of faculty, host of problems, that they can give the sort of guarantee, the sort of impartiality and selection for public employment that we need.

MR. TRACTENBERG: If the function of the Board of Examiners has become one of screening out incompetence and illiterates, what percentage of the candidates you see would you say fall under that category?

DR. GREENE: I would rather express it as saying screening in those with minimum ability, minimum, to begin teaching.

MR. TRACTENBERG: I don't think it means anything different. But what percentage are not screened in?

DR. GREENE: It varies from subject to subject, license to license. There are examinations with people through a full program.

If I had to make an average, nowadays, I would say that possibly 20 percent of those applying are unsuccessful. It varies from subject to subject.

MR. TRACTENBERG: By definition that means they don't meet minimum competency standards to teach?

DR. GREENE: Yes. That includes the record, written test, physical, and an interview.

MR. TRACTENBERG: How many of these incompetents have a substitute license?

DR. GREENE: We don't issue substitute licenses any more. We don't examine for them.

MR. TRACTENBERG: You do issue per diem certificates.

DR. GREENE: Temporary per diem certificates are issued to people who take a written English test and an abbreviated interview. And we know that they are probably less competent than those in the regular examination, but we have the safeguard that they will stay only to the end of the term and that they must file for the regular examination, so that we are not about to perpetuate the abuse of permanent substitutes.

You have to have a speedy way of getting people through your examining procedure into the school. You do take some risk. They may take the regular examination. They may fail, but you say to them we're going to use you because we have no alternative for a limited period of time.

MR. TRACTENBERG: Dr. Greene, if the guiding purpose under which you operate is to screen in those with minimal competence, and that's the way the examination process is geared, does it make any sense at all to have a ranked list for teachers?

DR. GREENE: Yes, it does make sense.

Let's say you have a list of a hundred. Where the whole list is appointed, it may make less difference except a community board may say I want to know about these people. I want to know before I ask for these people whether they were in the upper 20 percent in your examination or in your lower 20 percent. So where the whole list is appointed, even there it makes sense in guidance of the communities or the principal or the community superintendent.

Where you don't appoint the whole list, you have to have a fair way of appointing people.

MR. TRACTENBERG: It seems to me that's a little dishonest, isn't it, Dr. Greene? That is, your test is geared only to determine minimum competency and in fact one of your testing experts said, "All that the testing program seems to do is to evaluate the standing of the applicants on what would be the most universal minimum professional performance criteria."

How can you say that in view of that kind of an evaluation it makes sense to rank them? You're not aiming at ranking them, or distinguishing superior from less superior.

DR. GREENE: You're using general terms. I would rather stick with what the test is and does show.

The test shows the people at the top of the list have demonstrated a greater knowledge of their subject, greater knowledge of professional information. And that knowledge entitles them to be at the top of the rank, and that information ought to be available to local school boards.

If you must appoint people because you don't have a hundred jobs, you have only ten jobs, and you have to pick ten out of a hundred, then I would say it is probably safest to pick people from the upper range than from the lower range. Certainly it is fairest.

MR. TRACTENBERG: Safer in what sense? Let's stop on that one for a minute.

DR. GREENE: There is a compendium of research data in 1970, the U.S. Office of Education, by Mr. Coleman, who is famous and a number of other research people, Hanichek of MIT, Henry Levin of Stamford Center for Research in Teaching. And they issued a 173-page summary of a study, in which it is claimed on the basis of research, that the most important single criterion for teachers is verbal facility.

Verbal facility is one of the factors that is measured in our examination. Since reading this research, and there have been others before it, I made the statement that if you had no other criterion, if you had to make your judgment on that, it would be safer to choose from the upper realm. And then I added also the fairness concept in public employment, in Civil Service, where it is fairer to appoint numerically from a list and let the others wait their turn, than just to have free choice by influence.

MR. TRACTENBERG: Since we've gotten into this, let me proceed along this line and I'll return to a sort of seriatim list of comments.

Let me ask you, since you enjoyed my reference to history yesterday, and I'm a history major and not an English major--

DR. GREENE: But you are an attorney. We were English teachers and became examiners.

MR. TRACTENBERG: Let me read you a couple of questions and see whether they sound familiar to you.

"1) How far does success in the written examination indicate actual future success in the position for which the examination is held?

"2) What relation is there between ranking on an eligible list and success in actual later service?

"3) Is it possible to establish standardized tests and forms for some of the positions in our system?

"4) What relation exists between general intelligence, success in exams, and ability displayed in teaching and supervisory positions?

"5) Do examinations for teachers really measure teaching ability as demonstrated in the quality of service subsequent to appointment?"

DR. GREENE: Let me say, before Dr. Rockowitz responds, you have very difficult questions in terms of validity and we'll try to answer it in a sense. Dr. Rockowitz will.

These are important questions, but we had one conference on that subject, June 1967, teacher selection methods, where we had a number of experts such as Don Medley, who came and told us some of the things and in a general sense, the question--I think I can answer all of your questions in a shorter way.

The question of validity is a very complex problem when you're dealing with human feelings, particularly when you want to say here's a test that guarantees something about human behavior.

There are so many variables, say the experts, in teaching, so many value systems. A teacher may be successful in one situation, not successful in another. Successful under one chairman or principal and not successful under another. Successful as far as some children are concerned, not so far as others.

There are so many variables in determining this. It's not like the behavior of a mouse that you can condition and say when you ring a bell the mouse will run through the maze. You can predict that very well. But, it doesn't apply to human beings that much.

And so in all the areas of human endeavor where they have had tests, they have said predictive validity is one type of validity. The most we can do is say we can build in content validity, face validity, simulation validity. This is what the Army did in preparing pilots, they simulated the things the pilot had to do.

Now, we gather experts and they tell us what is the minimum a teacher should have apart from personal qualities.

A teacher should know the subject he wants to teach, have professional information how to handle children. A teacher should be able to communicate orally. And they say build this into your examination, and then you will know that the teachers have this.

Then you have the 1970 studies which turn up a correlation with verbal facility so that Coleman himself, and I'll use his words, "Further, one of the most important measures of teacher effectiveness is the teacher's verbal skills."

This was in summarizing all the research. You take this research and you try to build it in.

But in the sense of predictive validity, National Teacher Examinations declare that they do not have predictive validity for their tests. And they have a test that is prepared, that they work on, for two or three years and have one test, Form A, Form B. And in their announcements and advertisements they say their tests have no predictive validity and should not be used with that assumption because it is not possible until you get a clearer definition of the criteria, of the variables in the criteria, it is not possible to have such a measure, but they say use it as a guide in your selection, plus other things.

Now, Dr. Rockowitz.

DR. ROCKOWITZ: I'm the examiner in charge of research and was placed in charge of research in 1967 as a result of the reorganization of the Board of Examiners.

I would like to inform the Commission that the research unit of the Board of Examiners consists of two people, an associate and an assistant, and we have tried desperately to get additional personnel.

We talked about the length of lists. For example, it takes four to six months to get a list out.

I became involved in an effort to automate our procedures, to get out lists within four to six weeks, and I got bids from various computer organizations to do so. And those bids are sitting on the desk because money has not been made available to carry out the automation we sought.

So that within the limited ability of a small research unit we've gone into the questions Mr. Tractenberg has asked.

Dr. Greene has handled this concept of predictive validity--

MR. TRACTENBERG: I think we--

DR. ROCKOWITZ: I have your questions. I can answer them.

MR. TRACTENBERG: I think it's interesting to know where those questions came from. You may or may not know this. They were in the 27th Annual Report of the Board of Examiners dated 1924-1925.

What I would like to know is whether you have attempted to answer any of those questions in 1970.

DR. ROCKOWITZ: The questions that you ask deal with the nature of validity of examinations.

We have filed, in connection with the Chance case, and I'll be very happy to make available to the members of the Commission the briefs we filed that deal with this question, if you wish that.

Purportedly the briefs deal solely with supervisory examinations, but the same validation procedures are followed in connection with both teaching and supervisory examinations. I do not hesitate to discuss these generally because there is nothing to hide in this matter. The facts are that these things are under litigation and are a part of the lawsuit.

Now so far as validity is concerned, there are many schools of thought in connection with the questions--

MR. TRACTENBERG: Pardon me, but I really think we could proceed more efficiently if we raised the questions and you responded. I don't mean to be impolite.

What I'm trying to get at is whether there has ever been a study with respect to teacher examinations in New York City which deals with the question of predictive validity, that is, whether someone who scores high on the test is likely to be a better teacher than someone who scores lower or fails the test.

DR. ROCKOWITZ: For supervisors, yes; for teachers, no.

MR. TRACTENBERG: That's incredible. The question was posed by the Board of--

DR. ROCKOWITZ: Your judgment of incredibility is a subjective judgment.

MR. TRACTENBERG: Admittedly.

DR. ROCKOWITZ: The question is: Is predictive validity the sole type of validity?

You assume that the only way to justify the validity of an examination is by going into the field to see how a person does after the exam.

We don't say that.

MR. TRACTENBERG: I didn't say that either.

DR. ROCKOWITZ: You are assuming, isn't it incredible no predictive validity studies were done.

I say to you other kinds of validity studies were done and the kind of validity we emphasize and that has been applauded by such experts as Robert Thorndike and others of Teachers College is content validity.

Let me give you an example of the difference between predictive and content validity, and I think your assumption is ill-founded.

In the giving of a stenographic or typing type of examination, and this illustration was the one used by Dr. Thorndike, if you give a test that tries to get at the natural flair and aptitude of people in terms of manual dexterity in general, you are dealing with a predictive test that tests aptitude and is likely to be transferred into the activity in the field.

We conduct content validity tests. We take a candidate for a stenographic or secretarial position, and we give that candidate dictation, such as she would likely get on the job, and we ask that person to transcribe two letters and type those letters in the format that the secretary would present them to a principal or to anyone else in the school who gave her that job.

Now, that is a proficiency test, which affords a view of content validity. Can the person who goes into the job show that that person has the skills at this point in time, not any time in the future?

We don't claim that. But at this point in time, this person has the necessary know-how and savvy and ability to carry on the skills of the position.

Now we also add--this is my final point on that--we also add that if you want to find out what happens after the person begins to teach, let's say we say as of January, 1971, he has certain knowledge and competency and he gets assigned to a school, the only really true way you can get at whether that person is functioning well as a teacher is an on-the-job probationary review of his performance through criteria that have to be developed.

MR. TRACTENBERG: Let me make a couple of responses and get your reactions to a couple of things.

First of all, I don't believe I said predictive validity was the only type of validity. Let me read you from the affidavit of one of your own experts in testing.

"The approach used by the Board of Examiners in determining the validity or relevance of its test consists essentially of a strategy which relies on the judgment of experts and consensus among them as to what constitutes an appropriate test item.

"The level of validity that may be achieved in this regard is implicit in the procedures used for developing tests, that is, starting with a series of job specifications and assigning expert practitioners the task of writing appropriate items."

As an aside, I'll get back to both of those items in determining the level of content validity.

"But that procedure is limited to the best guess of experts. Without studies of predictive validity, that is, assessment of how well the tests select individuals who function successfully on the job, the very assumption of what constitutes expertise in any given field cannot be fully tested."

That's the testimony of your own expert in testing.

DR. ROCKOWITZ: You're dealing with testimony now and the testimony is at the heart of the court litigation.

You are also very dangerously getting into highly technical and complex matters that sound very bad for the layman but are accepted by the professionals.

The best-guess technique of a pool of experts is a legitimately used research criterion all over the country, not only in education, but elsewhere. The best guess, the word "guess" sounds awful--

MR. TRACTENBERG: I didn't write it. Your expert did.

DR. ROCKOWITZ: You will find it in the research literature, but the point is, this best guess is a professional estimation based on the pooling of knowledge and judgment of experts. It is not just a guess somebody makes in attempting to find an answer without knowledge.

I don't know who determines how deeply we go into the matters that are at litigation. You are reading from affidavits. You are getting into the court case in great detail.

I don't want to avoid it because again, as I said, the Board of Examiners is on the record in connection with what it does to validate exams. We have conducted over 20 studies in the last couple of years and they were made available to the court.

Are you going to arrogate the prerogatives of the court?

MR. TRACTENBERG: I believe there is an opinion of counsel which was read into the record at the outset which indicated that this hearing could properly address itself to any matters dealing with teacher examinations.

My question was directed solely to teacher examinations. Your answer is, you have never conducted a predictive validity study with respect to teaching jobs.

DR. ROCKOWITZ: We have built into the examinations content validity so far as teaching examinations are concerned.

MR. TRACTENBERG: And your own expert in a general statement--

DR. ROCKOWITZ: I don't think we ought to discuss that. It is a matter of the court record. You may have that record from the briefs and affidavits that were presented.

I think you are getting substantively into the content of the examinations because there is a very close correlation between validation of teaching and supervisory examinations.

MR. TRACTENBERG: I'll be glad to defer--

COMMR. COLGATE: I believe you are represented by counsel. I ask you to respond specifically and briefly to counsel's questions. If your counsel advises you that you may not answer a particular question, counsel on this side will rephrase it for you.

DR. GREENE: Counsel, your question is, have we made a predictive study of the teacher examinations.

The answer has to be that if you define predictive study in a sense in which it is defined as one type of validity, we have not.

But the record should also show, and I think this is just as important, not merely to say yes or no, but to know what has been done, that no other teacher agency or other testing agency for selection of people has made a predictive validity study because they have maintained this type of study is impossible. I think the record should show that.

MR. TRACTENBERG: I think the record should also show that according to my information, the Philadelphia school system is at this very moment engaged in a predictive validity study under which they have hired 200 people who fell below their cut-off line on an examination, expressly for the purpose of determining whether the people--this has nothing to do with the ranked list, this is people who fail the examination--whether there was any evidence at all that those people were not every bit as good in the classroom as people who had passed the teacher examination.

DR. GREENE: I think you would agree it is too early to evaluate their study.

We have also said, up to now, and I don't know the results of the Philadelphia study, no other group selecting human beings for jobs has made a successful predictive study they were satisfied with, that is, for teaching jobs.

MR. TRACTENBERG: They have made studies though.

DR. GREENE: There have been frustrating predictive validity studies. They tried to study whether marks in college would predict a good teacher and they found there was no correlation between marks in college and success in teaching.

They made a study of whether pupil-teaching marks correlated with success on the job, and found there was no correlation.

Thus far it has been frustrating and the reason they believe it is frustrating is that the criteria of teacher success and performance are too variable, too much based on other things to have any sort of useful study that will stand up.

MR. TRACTENBERG: Dr. Rockowitz did mention, and because it is within the litigation I won't pursue it, but he mentioned there was a predictive validity study pertaining to supervisors.

You have felt it was possible to undertake such a study in certain cases and have not made that effort with respect to teachers?

DR. ROCKOWITZ: Mr. Tractenberg, it is enormously difficult to carry on predictive validity studies. I would like to ask you one question to illustrate the difficulty. At what time in the future will you pick to correlate how well the teacher did on the examination with his performance? After he has served one year, five years, ten years, 20 years?

The man changes, conditions change. The weakness of predictive validity is that it assumes there is one absolute type of prediction that is going to be made, that this man will be good forever, in all circumstances.

That's poppycock. All predictive validity can tell you really and honestly is that within a very short period of time after assuming the job there may be a correlation. Nobody has demonstrated it yet.

What point in time would you judge we should ask for a predictive validation? After the man has served one year, three years, 20 years?

Suppose he deteriorates or suppose he is a late-bloomer and emerges into a fantastic teacher. What point in time would you suggest?

MR. TRACTENBERG: I assume that's why you have psychometricians available to you.

DR. GREENE: Mr. Tractenberg, did we imply that we believed the first three people, for example, on the list, or first two are better than the next four in terms of teaching ability or supervisory ability?

I don't believe we have.

MR. TRACTENBERG: Then the record ought to be clear that the ranking of people on the exam, insofar as the Board of Examiners is concerned, has no correlation to their likely performance on the job.

DR. GREENE: I haven't said that either.

I have said that the ranking indicates that on the tests we have used for the people who use the ranking, these are the people who did best.

MR. TRACTENBERG: This does not represent a prediction on your part.

DR. GREENE: We don't have evidence on that.

MR. TRACTENBERG: I gather you don't plan to acquire that evidence.

DR. GREENE: We have tried. We didn't have a research staff at all until three years ago. We pleaded for one every year. Now we have two people.

There are individuals in colleges throughout the country on tremendous grants who have been trying to lick this problem and haven't been able to.

MR. TRACTENBERG: My recollection, I won't bother checking now, is that the quote from the 1924-25 Annual Report of the Board of Examiners had to do with the establishment of a research facility in the Board at that time.

DR. GREENE: We asked for it in the budget. It was turned down in 1924 all the way up to 1963, and we were given one research assistant and in 1968 another one. Hardly enough in today's climate. Hardly enough to do more than get guidance from the colleges.

MR. TRACTENBERG: You agree if you had a larger staff through more budget funds, you could have made more extensive efforts to validate the tests.

DR. GREENE: We have pleaded for that. There are so many problems that we really ought to go into. The percentage of our budget allocated for research is abysmal as compared to other organizations.

MR. TRACTENBERG: What is your budget for this current year?

DR. GREENE: We have one research associate and one assistant. I would say, therefore, it's about $40,000.

MR. TRACTENBERG: Out of a total budget of how much?

DR. GREENE: About three million.

MR. TRACTENBERG: Doesn't it seem the proportions are a little askew? Wouldn't it make sense to spend more to find out whether the tests are valid and a little less on giving them?

DR. GREENE: I agree we should have more research and go into matters of validity, whether predictive or content, but certainly improving on our selection procedures.

DR. ROCKOWITZ: Mr. Tractenberg, we now have in the Board of Examiners a computerized analysis of short-answer questions. This computerized analysis of short-answer questions was obtained by us free of charge from the University of Connecticut Educational Research Center through the offices of our research staff because no money was available to develop one locally, and the principles that are applied to item analysis are universal. So we have a means now of running through the responses to every short-answer question through computers to determine certain key information about them.

The fact that we have a very tiny budget for research doesn't mean that the ingenuity of the examiners and of the staff have not made available to the New York City Board of Education, free of charge, the results of research carried on at other institutions, and I just gave you one example.

MR. TRACTENBERG: I assume you would agree with me that it is unfortunate more research funds are not available so you could do more extensive research into the questions of validity.

Let me move on.

You have talked now about the reasons why it has not been possible to conduct predictive validity studies.

I want to explore a bit, based in part on testimony received yesterday, the question of your standard--content validity.

You claim teacher examinations have been content validated, that is, that they test an applicant's ability to respond to things which will be part of his duties as a teacher.

I assume, as your expert points out, that is contingent on at least two things: number one, having adequately and fully identified the duties which he is likely to have to discharge in his position; and number two, the availability of sufficient expertise in the development of the questions, that is the so-called best guess of experts.

Is that a fair statement?

DR. GREENE: Yes.

MR. TRACTENBERG: Dr. Lang, in testifying yesterday, said during his tenure of five and a half years as Deputy Superintendent in charge of the Office of Personnel, he was unaware of there having been any updating of the description of duties for any teaching license.

Would you mind telling us who in your judgment is responsible for preparing this description of duties.

DR. GREENE: When an examination is prepared, we bring in experienced principals, college personnel and we often begin by saying what are the problems that teachers will be facing, what are the problems teachers face? Let us prepare questions based upon the problems teachers face and the knowledge that they should have in today's climate.

So that although we have not received updated statements of duties of teachers from Dr. Lang, we are kept up-to-date by our method of constructing and preparing examinations through the advice of people in the colleges, and the advice of supervisors in the schools. And the result is, because we prepare a new test for each examination, the questions, the approach, the content, the standards, the judging, the things we look for are current with what teachers are expected to do.

MR. TRACTENBERG: Is this a responsibility you have assumed because the Board of Education failed to discharge its responsibility, or is this a responsibility that you have had all along, that is, the creation of the description of duties?

DR. GREENE: It's a responsibility we assume because of the mechanics of working.

There are many examinations called for and we could say to Dr. Lang, give us an updated list for each of these examinations, but we have not done that on the teaching level. We have worked with the people in the field.

On the supervisory levels, or a special situation, we do ask for the statement of duties.

MR. TRACTENBERG: When you say you find out from people in the field, does that include people like community superintendents, community board members, teachers in the field, or is this the core of experts you draw upon?

DR. GREENE: To the extent that principals reflect what the superintendent says, we do include that, and we may also meet with superintendents, we attend meetings and discussions.

MR. TRACTENBERG: Does that mean you rely on the principals rather than--

DR. GREENE: We bring in a panel to work on the examination. They would include supervisors who are in the field, and they may be principals or chairmen, and college people, and we have the benefit of their discussion. And we attend meetings of all kinds in which there is discussion of the new role of the teacher, the role of working with paraprofessionals, for example, which is a new role; or in the bilingual problem, which is different from what it used to be; the role of the teacher vis-a-vis the community.

So, all these side duties are reflected in the selection because of the people who come to us and our attendance at meetings and listening to people talk.

But I would certainly say that it has merely been a shortcut. I don't believe we have been derelict in getting the facts, but we haven't gone through a procedure, and they haven't bothered sending it.

MR. TRACTENBERG: Your role as a service agency would have been simplified though if in fact the Board of Education supplied you with upgraded descriptions of duties, wouldn't it?

DR. GREENE: Every time they ask us for an examination, they should send us such a statement. We would be delighted to have it.

MR. TRACTENBERG: Are you satisfied the panel of experts you have drawn upon for the preparation of each exam is sufficiently in touch with the real needs in the school system?

DR. GREENE: We hope so.

MR. TRACTENBERG: How large is the panel, for example?

DR. GREENE: It would vary with the test. It would usually be somewhere between five and nine people. It might be a larger number than that.

MR. TRACTENBERG: Those who are in the school system are brought in as temporary assistants?

DR. GREENE: And people from colleges and sometimes people from industry for trade subjects or other areas where they can be helpful.

MR. TRACTENBERG: We talked a bit, Miss Unser and I, yesterday, about the selection process which applies both to your full-time staff and temporary assistants.

I have an interesting document I would like to get your reaction to. It is a newsletter of the Association of Assistant Principals containing minutes of a meeting attended by you and Dr. Rockowitz to talk about the matter of assistant examiners.* I'll just mention a few interesting things.

First of all, the opening statement says that Dr. Rockowitz opened the meeting by telling the committee that since the first meeting, September, 1969, he and Dr. Greene have been assigned to work on this problem.

He stated that since there has been a tremendous increase in in the pay for assistant examiners, the job has become more and more desirable.

Then there is a statement attributed to Dr. Rockowitz, that those called from outside of the system either retired or from colleges were called because--there are three reasons given, and they are in the alternative--one, because they live close to the Board of Education; two, because they have special competencies; or three, because they are available at odd hours. A few more things.

Dr. Rockowitz--again, this is attribution, you can speak to the accuracy of it--stated he would look into the issue of people who are willing to serve but have not been called.

Dr. Greene stated he would look into the question of why junior high school assistant principals are rarely used in examining teacher candidates.

Finally, Dr. Rockowitz again is attributed as having summarized: Number one, "to the extent possible, with availability as the only criteria, in-system people will be used as examiners." Number four, "a system will be devised to involve all interested persons who have not been used to date."

In light of these reported reactions to a meeting that you both attended, I would be interested in your evaluation of the screening process that you use in determining who should sit on these panels to give you input of what the current duties of teachers are.

DR. GREENE: In our selection process the use of examination assistants is known. We do get complaints from individuals. We get complaints from organizations, and we do sit down and talk to them.

What we have is professional selection. If we have 1200 different licenses, you must similarly know we have thousands of people who are used as temporary assistants.

At one time, as indicated in the minutes, this was not very desirable. Up to 1967 they used to get $8 an hour. We ran an examination in the evening for four hours, 5:30 to 9:30, they would get $32 for that evening's work.

*See letter from Beatrice Neu, pp. 750-751.

In addition, they would have to have dinner out, didn't get home until eleven o'clock, and we used to have to plead with people to come and serve, and they did it as a professional contribution.

As was indicated in the minutes, now the compensation is higher and people want it.

MR. TRACTENBERG: What is the compensation now?

DR. GREENE: $13.70 an hour as of this past September.

MR. TRACTENBERG: About $100 a day.

DR. GREENE: It is higher as compared with earlier. Now more people are interested in serving than there were, and we've been having meetings because we are now saying we don't want to get into the business of being charged with patronage.

Dr. Rockowitz and I were set up as a committee to see what can be done in all practicality to insure a fair and proper procedure in this matter, which is again an open book, and you have minutes, and we're happy that you have them.

So, as one of our procedures, we had a preliminary meeting with this group that was critical and--

MR. TRACTENBERG: Why were they critical, if I may ask?

DR. GREENE: There were complaints by individuals that they hadn't been used. They would say I'm a principal or assistant principal or from a college and nobody uses me, and they write to their association.

We should sit down probably and defend our situation.

MR. TRACTENBERG: Before you and Dr. Rockowitz were appointed a committee, how were people selected? Was there any basis for their grievance?

DR. GREENE: People were selected as examination assistants because they had the know-how. They were recommended to the Examiners or unit head, or they wrote in, and there was an investigation of their background, their training.

We got reports on them from their supervisors, and they were listed. And then they were tried, and those who did pretty well were called by unit heads, and we've had such a turnover in unit heads, and we don't usually tell them whom to use or not. So you had a system of rotation among those who were approved.

It takes skill to prepare short-answer questions. It takes skill to interview someone, as you know, particularly as a lawyer, conducting an interview. Some have that skill and some don't. Those who have tended to be used more often.

Now newcomers come along and properly they want to serve, and we do introduce newcomers each year, but some newcomers "weren't called" and protested.

We just wondered if there should be a more formal way other than occasionally having people write to us or have recommendations.

The State Legislature took cognizance of this, and they decided all people we use as of 1969 must be nominated or approved by community superintendents or by the Chancellor.

MR. TRACTENBERG: The Chancellor in his testimony indicated he merely rubber-stamped the list sent over by the Board of Examiners.

DR. GREENE: There are thousands of names. We could not stop in midstream all our examinations in 1969, with a host of other problems, and say now let's really turn this up and over.

It does take time and we have to, meanwhile, continue to use the hundreds of people who have served satisfactorily, while we develop some procedure that will be free of any taint and fairer.

Thus far, however, we have said to our units, use rotation so far as practicable. That was an instruction to the units, and we've made particular efforts to bring minority group people in.

I have a two-page description of the procedure that I'll be glad to leave with you. We have had meetings. There are dissatisfactions, and they're open.

If we need a person at a particular time, and we know he is on the list and satisfactory, but as to choosing him at the time, between him and someone in the Bronx, we would have to choose the fellow nearby assuming their competence is equal.

MR. TRACTENBERG: Do we really have anything other than the good faith of the members of the Board of Examiners on which to base a conclusion that in fact people were fairly selected to be examination assistants? There is no written test.

DR. GREENE: There hasn't been a written test.

MR. TRACTENBERG: No particular background requirements.

DR. GREENE: Dr. Rockowitz tells me that in some areas there are tests as in psychology and so on, but by and large there was no written test.

The way this developed, initially the examiners themselves did all the interviewing and test preparations. This goes back a good many years. Then there were too many tests for them, and they were given full-time assistants who did the whole job. And then there were too many people applying, and others were brought in. And because there was an unwillingness to set up permanent jobs for these others--and not only that, but because you couldn't have thousands of people--you needed to tap individuals who are in English, math, in science in order to have content validity in your testing operation. And it wouldn't do any good to add 50 people because they didn't have the special knowledge and you needed them for special situations.

So the members of the Board of Examiners, through recommendations and so on, began to use people on that basis. There was no charge of patronage at that time.

If charges are made, if this is believed in any way to make it better and fairer, and that's the purpose of the committee and the meeting, we'll--

MR. TRACTENBERG: Don't you agree that it seems somewhat inconsistent to argue that we can't replace the Board of Examiners because what would happen is that we would be thrown back on the good will and integrity of community board members who interview applicants whereas at the same time you are agreeing with me, I think, that up to the time you and Dr. Rockowitz rather recently were appointed to head a committee, all we had to rely on in terms of the capacity and honesty and ability of examination assistants is the integrity of the Board of Examiners?

DR. GREENE: There is an inconsistency except for this one point.

We're not dealing with people who want career jobs. They don't want a job as a teacher, or as a principal, that is. We're dealing with people who come in for a few hours when the test is given and they serve.

In terms of the procedures you may have to set up, if you want to use an examination for that sort of service, there is a question of whether it is worth doing. If there is public dissatisfaction with the way it is being done, then it is worth doing. But if the stakes are not that high with individuals, and if you can serve satisfactorily--when we had permanent staff members--

MR. TRACTENBERG: Isn't that an unusual standard to use? That is, you respond only to public dissatisfaction?

I thought the whole function of the Board of Examiners is to be above political and public pressures, to be there to preserve merit.

Now you've indicated that although this may not be a system particularly designed to achieve the most in merit, as long as nobody from the public cries out against it, there probably won't be any changes.

DR. GREENE: I'm not saying it is not designed to achieve the utmost in merit. I haven't said that. I have said that examination assistants were selected in a particular way for particular reasons.

MR. TRACTENBERG: One of the reasons didn't happen to be a premium on their specific capacity to construct exams?

DR. GREENE: That is a prime factor, that they had the ability in terms of our recommendations to do the job that we had to have done.

I didn't say anything that denied that. We're just talking about the way in which they were selected.

They were selected on an informal basis by recommendation for their part-time function.

MR. TRACTENBERG: But certainly the procedure outlined in this newsletter suggests that in fact anybody in the system who expresses interest will have a crack at--

DR. GREENE: Should be considered. The trouble was, who wrote in, was--

MR. TRACTENBERG: This says a system will be devised to involve all interested persons who have not been used to date and with availability as the only criterion.

DR. GREENE: To involve them to the extent of giving them an opportunity to present themselves.

We have been talking in reality of some testing situation for people who want to serve. That is, in our deliberations that followed it, Dr. Rockowitz and I were tentatively saying that we could set up a television interview and have the people who want to serve as interviewers write a critique of that interview and rate it and then observe them with recordings.

So we are thinking of a way. We are thinking, in the way of

preparation of short-answer questions, that we can easily ask people to write short-answer questions and we'll have them graded by test experts.

Our thinking following that meeting, and those are working minutes, and there is one sentence there that strikes me as being inaccurate that you read, is that, Dr. Rockowotz and I are considering this very business of examinations for the selection or qualification of our assistants.

MR. TRACTENBERG: I assume that recognizes some inadequacy in the current system.

DR. GREENE: We're always seeking improvements. We hope some suggestions for improvements come from these hearings.

MR. TRACTENBERG: Let me ask just a few more questions about the personnel who construct the exams. Are they specially trained by you in any way or are they simply high school principals who have some appreciation of what teachers should be like?

DR. GREENE: They may be supervisors or teachers who are recommended as knowing the subject or having the professional know-how, and we do, as I said, investigate them.

Then, if we use them for preparing written tests, they are brought in, given samples of test questions, they are given instructions, with reference to a booklet by Atkins, on composing test questions, Dorothy Atkins, and they're discussed and so on, and gradually, by experience, they develop greater know-how.

We have trial interviews in the interview situation, where we get a group together and they witness an interview. There is a discussion of the interview technique.

Prior to each testing session there is a briefing session in which the problems are discussed, the criteria discussed. We have written detailed criteria on the interview.

In written English we have a rating sheet, special briefing sessions, where they all rate the same paper and discussion and so on.

There is an extensive training program.

MR. TRACTENBERG: How many hours would you say is involved in this intensive training program?

DR. GREENE: It depends on the various stages.

The first training program in the interview might be a one-hour or two-hour training, plus reading that is done of a couple of hours, plus the first time they sit in on an interview to see how it's conducted. It runs to hours.

Then, each time they serve, there are further training periods.

MR. TRACTENBERG: At least the first time, the total training which they are given, excluding the amount of time reading, maybe three, four hours?

DR. GREENE: For an initial service, in preparation of test questions, plus their own background. You can't dismiss the background.

If you have a chairman of a department who has been interviewing teachers who want to serve in his school, seen beginning teachers, seen and talked about their problems, that all goes into the hopper when he is used to advise us on selection. He is drawing upon years of experience and training. We're just focusing his years of experience and training on our particular needs and techniques.

MR. TRACTENBERG: Could you estimate for me the percentage of those recommended to be temporary assistants who, in fact, are screened out, those who never serve as temporary assistants although they have been recommended?

DR. GREENE: It has varied at various times.

We have a standing body of people who have the experience, have the training; and as with other bodies, you tend to use experienced able people.

What we're talking about then is the percentage of new people that get into an examining situation. I used to feel, when we had a panel of seven people preparing a new test, it would be a good thing to get two new people or one new person out of the seven, surely, into the discussion phase.

So, the extent to which new people are worked in varies with the situation. In terms of using minority people--

MR. TRACTENBERG: I don't think you have answered my question.

My question was not whether you bring new people in, but how many people do you screen out by virtue of whatever procedures you use.

That is, let's assume Community Superintendent X from District Y gives you a list of 40 people within his district whom he is recommending as temporary assistants. You said you apply some screening procedures to that list. How many of that list do you typically screen out?

DR. GREENE: It would vary. I'll tell you exactly what happens.

We refer the list to the unit head and we say here's the list that has come in. To the extent you can, investigate these people and see which ones you can use and try to work them in.

If the unit is swamped with examinations for which they have to rely on experienced people, they might, of the 40, call in five people in a particular semester. If they are not swamped, they might call in ten.

MR. TRACTENBERG: Or they might use all 40.

DR. GREENE: It's extremely unlikely that they would suddenly bring in 40 new people and try to run ongoing examinations.

MR. TRACTENBERG: I'm not saying suddenly.

DR. GREENE: They might bring them in and decide some are not qualified or investigate and find they are not qualified. It varies.

MR. TRACTENBERG: To your knowledge, has any person recommended to be an assistant examiner ever been excluded from that possibility before he has served as an assistant examiner?

DR. GREENE: Yes.

MR. TRACTENBERG: But you can't estimate a percentage.

DR. GREENE: I'm not sure I understand fully the question.

MR. TRACTENBERG: I'm looking to your standards, basically. Are you suggesting that everybody who is a licensed teacher or supervisor in the New York City school system is competent to construct examinations, grade examinations, to give oral interviews with three or four hours of training?

DR. GREENE: No, I'm not saying they're all competent to do that.

MR. TRACTENBERG: How many do you screen out as incompetent to do that?

DR. GREENE: Again it's a question--we have a corps who are reasonably competent although we screen them too.

What we do is add additional people and then have a look at them. If we add five, we may decide we want to use only three of the five or we may decide only to use two.

The screening is directed to the newer people who are being recommended.

MR. TRACTENBERG: Earlier you said this isn't a career job, this concept of a corps of people which you used continuously makes it sound they have a--

DR. GREENE: The corps of people are not used continuously. They are used from time to time for a couple of hours, but they exist as a corps. Their names and addresses exist, and they have served before and they've had experience.

We may not call a person, if this is January, we may not call on a person until next March, and then we won't call him until next November.

MR. TRACTENBERG: Once on your approved list, forever on it. Is that right?

DR. GREENE: Not necessarily. We do visit the panels, we get statements from applicants, criticism, people who prepare questions for us in new areas may not be good enough and aren't used in those areas. There are some people about whom we find out things and we stop using them.

MR. TRACTENBERG: What percentage?

DR. GREENE: A very small percentage. I would say out of 100 whom we have been satisfied with, maybe one might be dropped because of reasons.

MR. TRACTENBERG: If I can summarize, you can't really point to any percentage of those who are recommended who are screened out without being given the opportunity to participate. And once having participated, only approximately one percent are subsequently eliminated.

DR. GREENE: I think your first statement on the initial screening, where we have people and we look into their record and background, I think the figures--if I have to make a guess-- of the newcomers that may be rejected, it may be one out of two, at that stage, that we do not use.

MR. TRACTENBERG: That's somewhat inconsistent with your statement as to the Association of Assistant Principals--all insiders will be included, with availability the only criterion.

DR. GREENE: That sentence there is the one I said I'm

amazed it is there. I would not go along with any such statement to any group.

I believe that it is wrong to say we will use insiders. I believe what we meant in terms of involvement is what I have indicated, that they ought to have an opportunity to apply and be considered in some reasonably objective way.

MR. TRACTENBERG: How large is the staff who does the screening?

DR. GREENE: We have a total of six units and there may be 50 people working in the units.

MR. TRACTENBERG: What percentage of their time is spent in screening assistant examiners?

DR. GREENE: In total time, eight-hour day or whatever the day is, or 40 hours, it might vary one week to another. I don't know if there is a fixed amount of time.

MR. TRACTENBERG: Not a great amount of time.

DR. GREENE: Over-all, no. I believe the procedure we have in mind would be an improvement.

MR. TRACTENBERG: Do you ever solicit recommendations?

DR. GREENE: Yes, several times, as recently as six months or so, after the Decentralization Law, we sent a letter to every community superintendent asking him to submit names to us of people, and we indicated in that letter the criteria of integrity, of understanding of people, sympathetic approach, rapport and all that.

MR. TRACTENBERG: Did you make any other efforts to solicit recommendations?

DR. GREENE: These went to the community superintendents. We have on occasions had meetings of chairmen and principals and have said if there are people in your department who are good, who have an understanding, we'll take their recommendation. And we've written to colleges and spoken to college people and out-of-town people as well.

I know a good many out-of-town people. When we have a situation where we want out-of-town people and can get them, I ask them to recommend individuals, and we bring them in too.

MR. TRACTENBERG: In this newsletter, there is a copy of a letter from Miss Gertrude Unser to an officer Farino of the Council of Supervisory Associations, asking him to recommend retired supervisors.

Is that also common practice, you canvas the CSA--

DR. GREENE: We canvas CSA or any organization that has some knowledge of staff because very often you can get insights about people from their colleagues as to whether they're good or whether they're bad.

All we do is get a pool of names. We have occasionally some special problems in which we may want to use retired people.

When a person retires it doesn't mean he is thereupon no good any more and should therefore cease to exist. There are some wonderful people whose services are useful to us because they are available during the day.

For example, on the out-of-town recruitment drive, if we didn't have good retired people, we would have to pull individuals out of schools. That would handicap the schools because we would be pulling out good people. Other things being equal, if we can get a good retired person as compared with a good person in service, we would have the retired person who could be sent throughout the country for a week or two or three or four or five and not drain the school.

That is an advantage. That's the only focus. It's not that we are saying the people in the school system aren't good, but given the practicalities, other things being equal, your retired person may be available for certain jobs.

MR. TRACTENBERG: I wasn't suggesting there was anything deficient about retired people. I was only using that letter as some evidence of the way in which you have sought recommendations.

DR. GREENE: I have indicated that I have asked individuals, groups, deans of colleges, wherever we can get names of good people as we need them.

MR. TRACTENBERG: Before I interrupted to pursue this line, you started to mention something about the ethnic breakdown of your staff.

I wonder if you would return to that, your full-time staff and your temporary examination assistants.

DR. GREENE: I think of our full-time assistants--I'm trying to recall, the figures were given to me yesterday and I have so many other figures in my mind--I think 13 percent of our staff --I think if we have 60 people, about nine--no, more than that-- about 11 or so are minority group people, of our own unit staffs.

MR. TRACTENBERG: Professional personnel?

DR. GREENE: Yes. We do have some problems in that solicitation you ought to be aware of because we don't use people in current examinations, and there are a great many excellent minority group people who are upward bound, in examinations. And we have interviewed some for vacancies who say we're going to be in the principal's exam and they can't be on our staff.

We have a number, as I have indicated, about 13 percent of our own staff.

MR. TRACTENBERG: How about the percentage with respect to the temporary assistants?

DR. GREENE: We don't have figures. We don't keep figures on the temporary assistants who are one faith, another faith, or one color.

I was able to give you the picture in terms of our own staff because we see them. They're right with us; we know who is who.

You asked the question and you have a right to ask the question and I gave you that. I just couldn't tell you what the figures are on the temporary assistants. I don't know.

MR. TRACTENBERG: Have you written to the Association of Black Supervisors and Administrators and asked--

DR. GREENE: We had a meeting with a committee of the Black supervisors about seven months ago and one of the topics discussed with them was the necessity for increasing the number of Black supervisors, and they were asked to submit recommendations either through the community superintendents or on their own.

Subsequent to that meeting, we took specific steps to increase the number by instructing all our unit heads to give high priority to adding minority group members to the examination assistants group which was going to function that month, the month after.

In other words, it was immediately, following that meeting.

MR. TRACTENBERG: You obviously have no way of determining the success of that effort since you don't know the ethnic composition before or after.

DR. GREENE: In response to a letter of Mr. Robinson, and this goes back, and I'll put that in evidence for you, I did indicate that following that we had an examination for bilingual teachers or supervisors, and we introduced 16 people of Puerto Rican background on the examining panel within one month after we decided to augment the efforts in that regard. And we indicated another area, I think another exam was in progress at that time, probably assistant principal of junior high and the unit head indicated to me he was able to involve eight, ten, or twelve minority group people, so I indicated in four or five areas where I made specific inquiry while I was chairman and I have a copy of that letter and I'll leave that also.

MR. TRACTENBERG: Before I move on, I think it is important to tie this whole discussion of personnel back into where we started, which is the question of content validity.

You agreed with me that content validity is meaningful only if two things follow. That is, one, there is a completely accurate and full description of the duties of the job, and two, the staff converting these duties into examination questions is fully expert.

We've gone on to discuss the expertise and character of the examination assistants who I gather play a very substantial role in creating the examination and administering it.

Obviously you are not completely satisfied since you and Dr. Rockowitz are a committee designed to improve the process by which you select examination assistants.

Are you reasonably satisfied with the level of expertise that you have available to you?

DR. GREENE: Yes.

MR. TRACTENBERG: Let me turn to a fairly broad policy question. As I am sure you are well aware, probably far better than I, there have been a significant number of studies conducted over the past 20 years which have been devoted either exclusively or largely to the question of personnel processes in the New York school system.

Virtually all of the ones I am aware of have recommended either abolition of the Board of Examiners in its current form or else rather substantial modifications of the way in which it operates.

I have reference, just to put those on the record, to the

Strayer-Yavner report which was done for the Mayor; the Cresap, McCormick & Paget study, done on behalf of the Board of Education; the Schinnerer report, done on behalf of the State Commissioner of Education; the Crewson report, conducted by a staff member of the State Education Department; the two Griffiths studies on behalf of the Board of Education; the Bundy report, done in conjunction with a legislative mandate.

In addition, I believe the past two State Commissioners of Education have gone on record as favoring drastic changes in the personnel system. And similarly the State Board of Regents; the prior New York City Board of Education, presided over by John Doar; former Superintendent of Schools Donovon; and the Mayor of the City of New York in the bill which was introduced to the Legislature.

Yesterday we heard the current President of the City Board favor drastic revisions in the system and the current Chancellor as well. A former Superintendent Dr. Theobald, a community board president, a community superintendent and others.

Against that range of authority, I wonder if you could point to any studies or other material which recommends the retention of the Board of Examiners in essentially its current form.

DR. GREENE: I would like to say to learned counsel the implication of his last sentence was that all the individuals to whom he referred advocated abolition of the Board of Examiners.

I don't think that's true to my knowledge.

There were some studies that recommended abolition of the Board of Examiners. There were some studies that recommended changes.

MR. TRACTENBERG: Changes such as, for example, making it a division under the Deputy Superintendent of Personnel.

DR. GREENE: There were studies that were made and changes recommended and, in some cases, abolition. Some of the people changed their minds.

You mentioned the Strayer-Yavner Report. We have a statement from Louis Yavner six months ago saying whereas he once was very critical of the Board of Examiners and believed changes should be made, he recognizes the contemporary Board of Examiners and procedures are far different than what they were. He believes the merit system must be protected, and that he has changed his opinion. He believes the Board of Examiners should continue to function and is in fact essential.

MR. TRACTENBERG: What was the nature of the study he conducted to reach that conclusion?

DR. GREENE: He reached the present conclusion on the basis of criticism that he and Dr. Strayer had made years ago, his recollection of that, and his evaluation of studies that were printed, which he read, his evaluation of procedures with which he was familiar and he has gone into detail and in fact he has been counsel representing litigants against the Board of Examiners, and through that has--

MR. TRACTENBERG: But there were no studies as formidable as the original study which ran some 1200 pages.

DR. GREENE: I don't think he blotted that study out of his mind. It was within the framework of that study which he had in mind.

I think you should be aware of the fact that the Board of Education that made the recommendation was not unanimous.

Mrs. Rose Shapiro, a prominent Board member, said the merit system should be maintained through the Board of Examiners. The Board President, Mr. Alfred Giardino, and I can read you a quote from what he said, indicated in writing that he believed the Board of Examiners must be continued--

MR. TRACTENBERG: Didn't he recommend--

DR. GREENE: You have quoted propaganda analysis and I'll toss in some names too.

MR. TRACTENBERG: Please describe the character of the study.

DR. GREENE: Former Superintendent of Schools, William Jensen.

MR. TRACTENBERG: What year was that?

DR. GREENE: I believe before Mr. Theobald.

Dr. Jensen joined the Committee for the Preservation of the Merit System through the Board of Examiners and he believed it should be maintained.

Board President Andrew Clawson also believed that way. So there are pros and cons.

MR. TRACTENBERG: Have there been any exhaustive studies of the kind I have described?

DR. GREENE: Let's look at the matter of studies.

Where you have a hostile Board of Education or where you have a desire for change--this is not a local phenomenon, it's a national phenomenon which occurs in many other communities-- there is a formula for this. You bring in a study group, and you have the study group which you pay usually come up with the findings you want.

Some of the studies, I'm not saying all, some of the studies were quicky studies. You mentioned the Schinnerer report. No examiner ever spoke to him. The Griffiths report was written in three months, from June through September when most of the staff wasn't there.

But we can bring in any group and they will turn up a proposal to abolish this group or be critical for a group. That's what they're being paid for. The question to be discussed is not whether study groups made studies, but let's talk about what our procedures are. If you have the studies, let's discuss procedures and not studies and not names.

THE CHAIRMAN: Dr. Greene, in the examination, I am going to allow counsel to ask you questions he is going to ask you. You can respond and elaborate, but I'm going to require you to be on the point.

If he asks you a question, I don't think the answer should be let's discuss something else. That's not fair.

Even as I allowed you to go on, I'll allow him latitude in asking questions.

DR. GREENE: I'm answering the questions to the best of my ability, but if counsel wishes to ask yes or no questions only and you order me to answer that way, I will do so, but I don't think that is the purpose of the Commission, which wants to hear--

THE CHAIRMAN: At this point we're all suffering under having been here for longer than we had anticipated. At no point has either counsel or I directed you to answer yes or no.

I am saying though, especially considering the lateness of the hour and we're going to go on with this examination until it is finished, that we try to keep our answers as directly on the point as possible. Whatever elaboration you require as necessary, you will be allowed to make.

At the same time, I may have to ask for more pointed answers unless we're going to go on for an hour or two and inconvenience witnesses who are now into the afternoon. I will ask for the same kind of consideration that I showed you.

DR. GREENE: I thank Madam Chairman for the consideration, but I think the record should show this too, that we indicated in advance that the nature of this inquiry was such that ten- to 15-minute presentation plus follow-up questions was not sufficient and not fair to the Board of Examiners, and we wrote that in a letter to each member of the Commission.

Now, we're talking about sustained studies that took months and weeks. If it is the intention of the Chairman of this Commission to have a quicky study of a couple of days and then come out with a report and then even to limit the members of the Board of Examiners to ten or 15 minutes, I'm just as fatigued as anybody but--

THE CHAIRMAN: Dr. Greene, not only have I not limited you to ten to 15 minutes, I allowed you to go on uninterrupted for an hour and 15 minutes.

All I am insisting here is that in the interest of economy and fairness to other witnesses, that you be as gracious to me as I have been to you by keeping your answers as brief as is consistent with thoroughness and that you try to be as direct to counsel and not engage in argument with counsel lest we be here with your testimony until 5:00 or 4:00 in the afternoon and keep other important witnesses such as the Vice-President of the Board of Education, such as community superintendents and other people who have come from responsibilities in schools.

I don't want to engage in a 15-minute colloquy, and I will instruct counsel to keep his questions as pointed as possible and omit what questions he might think can be omitted and to realize, obviously, Dr. Greene will wish to reply to questions as much as counsel wishes to ask them, and above all, that all sides be fair here. I think that we have been fair.

MR. TRACTENBERG: Dr. Greene, let me just restate the question.

Are there any studies of any character under any auspices, financed from any sources, which support the Board of Examiners in its current form or something substantially identical to its current form?

DR. GREENE: We have a study here, "Teacher Selection Methods," which I will leave with you.

MR. TRACTENBERG: Who conducted this study?

DR. GREENE: We invited people from all parts of the country to come in to evaluate our methods in a discussion and to present methods they were familiar with.

There is also a Kandell Report which is on record as being favorable.

There is also the New York State Department of Education Report, which focused on the Buffalo school system in 1968, and which drew the conclusion in Buffalo, which has an examining system--this is 1967-68 State Education Department sponsored--they have the clear statement the examining systems in Buffalo should be continued, although the time lag for issuance of lists should be changed.

I think that has an applicability to the New York City system.

MR. TRACTENBERG: Isn't it also fair to say that in 1968 the State Education Law was expressly amended to limit the requirements of an examination in Buffalo?

DR. GREENE: Nevertheless the study was made by the New State Educational Department. I can give you the exact quote and a copy of the report.

MR. TRACTENBERG: I think it's appropriate to put it on the record. It is unfortunate we did not have copies of these two reports available to us in the preparation for these hearings.

As I recall, there was a specific request for any studies which were pertinent. I will obviously accept at face value what you have just said about these reports. Nevertheless, there is a formidable array of opinion from a variety of educational sources which suggests that something is drastically wrong with the selection process in New York City as it has been in operation.

Do you have any idea why this rather broad ranging criticism? Are these people in favor of a spoils system? That seems to be one of your major defenses--if we do away with the Board of Examiners, we'll have no recourse but to resort to a spoils system.

DR. GREENE: I would say a number of the reports were directed to what we might today call weaknesses in the selection system and I indicated 15 areas of improvement. A number of those areas were properly the subject of earlier studies.

The other point I want to make, there were among those you have indicated individuals who were brought in, who did inadequate studies, who had hostile attitudes and the resulting reports could have been expected. And there is also a host of people in important positions who didn't accept those reports, or the extreme version of them, who said the extreme version was wrong and didn't go along with them.

MR. TRACTENBERG: Presumably on even less investigation.

DR. GREENE: On reading the reports and finding out how they were made.

MR. TRACTENBERG: Let me ask one more thing in this

line. You earlier characterized the Board of Examiners as a service agency to the Board of Education.

DR. GREENE: Yes.

MR. TRACTENBERG: That's a rather peculiar relationship, isn't it, if the agency being served wants to abolish the service agency?

DR. GREENE: The Board of Education itself is an agency of the State and the State in a sense creates the Board of Education and the State established the Board of Examiners to be a service agency to the city.

If there are individuals in the Board of Education who want changes for whatever reasons in the Board of Examiners and who are dissatisfied for whatever reasons, that still doesn't detract from our performing a service which may be an unpopular service with some Board members, which they may rebel against because they want to hand-pick or they want to see a greater flexibility which we see as hand-picking, doesn't detract we're--

MR. TRACTENBERG: Which is it, they want to hand-pick or--

DR. GREENE: I certainly don't think members of our Board of Education are interested in that, but perhaps some of them, if they advocate this, they may not be aware or be giving sufficient attention to the import of the hand-picking that would take place.

I know them. I have the utmost respect for them, and they've been doing an excellent job under very difficult conditions.

But, we are their service agency assigned by the State.

MR. TRACTENBERG: Whether they want you or not.

DR. GREENE: To try as best we can to meet--and we do try the best we can. We made changes in a number of our examinations including the elementary principals' examination as a result of meetings with them where they had expressed dissatisfaction and urged things. So we are obedient. Not fully compliant, because then there would be no reason for our existence, but we are obedient.

MR. TRACTENBERG: Let me touch on two other things.

Number one was your reference to the 40 percent provision in the Decentralization Law and your deference to legislative wisdom.

I don't know whether you were in Albany, Dr. Greene. I was in Albany during the entire period of the discussion of the Decentralization Act, and I find it incomprehensible that anybody can label the process that went on there as wisdom. But I do have a question, and that is, how do you know the legislative purpose?

You state a number of things the legislature must have had in mind when they they devised this 40 percent hiring provision.

So far as I know, there is no record of legislative history which surrounds bills that pass the State Legislature. How is it that you have insights into what the Legislature really intended?

DR. GREENE: For one thing, I have a deep respect for the Legislature and for the members of the Legislature as representatives of the people, and as people of intelligence, and I see their handiwork. And I say to myself why was this done? And I read the commentaries of the discussion at the time and questions were asked of me by people who did present viewpoints, cautions, and problems and so on; and so, seeing the handiwork and realizing the problems, I gave credit where I think it is due.

MR. TRACTENBERG: Just two final things in that connection.

One, I assume since you defer to the Legislature because it is elected by the people, you ought similarly defer to the expertise and integrity of community boards because they are elected by the people. Doesn't that necessarily follow?

DR. GREENE: Will you repeat that question, please.

MR. TRACTENBERG: If you place such deference in the Legislature because they are popularly elected and therefore you assume what they have done was wise, musn't it follow that the community boards, because they are popularly elected, should be treated with the same deference?

Your assumption should be: In handling the selection of personnel, the community boards will deal with integrity, honesty, and fairness and with an eye toward the quality--

DR. GREENE: I have faith in the community boards to do the right thing, but that doesn't mean that experience should blind me to the fact that in the matter of jobs there are pressures which are brought to bear as is true with the State Legislature.

I have great respect for their wisdom in setting laws and arriving at judgments, but you and I both know there is a great deal of patronage that emanates through the Legislature and I would say much the same thing about local school boards.

I respect them greatly. I think they represent the people. They ought to have as many facts, and we ought to cooperate and work with them. But the reality and practicality of the job situation is there are influences and pressures.

MR. TRACTENBERG: And these don't affect the Board of Examiners themselves, influences and pressures.

DR. GREENE: We have tried to set up a system where--

MR. TRACTENBERG: I'm talking about your own hiring practices, the discussion we had about the way in which temporary assistants were selected.

DR. GREENE: I did not disagree with you that we ought to have a formalized procedure.

MR. TRACTENBERG: Finally, just as a matter of logic, you suggest the compromise that was involved, was a compromise which in effect provided some greater flexibility, 40 percent flexibility for the community boards.

Isn't it equally as logical that the compromise achieved by the Legislature as a result of the variety of pressures on it was that the Board of Examiners should continue in existence despite a very substantial amount of public opposition?

DR. GREENE: I believe they probably had an equally substantial amount of public support of the Board of Examiners. They were weighing one as against the other, and this was a compromise.

I have indicated all along there are many supporters in terms of what we hear and see and places where we speak. We're naturally in the position of being a target. I know of no umpire in a baseball game who is popular per se.

As I said at the very beginning of the discussion this morning, our job is such we can't be very popular. We have to be attacked and criticized because we are making important decisions to the best of our ability. We can't be everybody's friend.

MR. TRACTENBERG: Just one final thing, and that is, you have indicated on a number of occasions, both here and in other public forums, that people were approaching the question of what should be done with the selection process in New York City illogically because what they were doing was considering replacing the Board of Examiners with something else simply on a showing that other cities who didn't have a Board of Examiners were doing as well.

It seems to me the logic could be turned around the other way, or the burden of proof, if you will. Why should New York City be spending three-plus million dollars a year to do through its selection process what apparently is done equally well in all the other school districts in New York State that don't have a Board of Examiners.

DR. GREENE: That's a matter of opinion. We believe it is done better here for reasons I detailed and I don't want to go into them again. In my initial presentation I listed a great many reasons why we believe our system is better.

One can't merely say why should we pay for having it just as good. That is your observation, not your observation, but you quoted the observation that someone else might make.

May I ask one question of the Chairman before I express my appreciation for your forebearance?

A number of the people who have testified and will testify are people whose names are not public, and I wondered how people get an opportunity to testify other than officials whom you have called.

There have been people or may be people who are not really officials. As we looked at the list of names of people, not officials particularly, it seemed most of them are people who had some opinion particularly contrary to the continuance of the Board of Examiners.

I would like you to consider, if you will, a list of names that you might invite, I'm not suggesting subpoenas, who may present the other side.

THE CHAIRMAN: We'll be happy to entertain any list you would like to provide.

The testimony is public. Anyone from the public has a right to come here and testify, and we have sent a mailing to the broadest cross section of people we could come up with, especially people who are on record as for the present system.

In addition, in order to accommodate the public, and especially people who may not be officials and not be able to get time off from work, we are having testimony today and tomorrow. We plan to go into the night as long as people wish to testify. There will be other testimony later in the week.

We've tried with respect to each issue to get people on both sides of that issue.

For example, there will be some testimony regarding testing. On the question of testing we have invited an expert the Board of Examiners has specifically relied upon as well as an expert who may disagree with that person.

We have tried very much in light of how controversial this matter is to be especially fair in the invitation of witnesses.

I wish to say, however, if the Board of Examiners will desire, if they will give us names, we'll contact those people.

DR. GREENE: Thank you very much.

THE CHAIRMAN: We are particularly pleased the Board of Examiners have come willingly to put its position on the record.

Many of the misconceptions on this matter flow from the fact the principal parties have not been on the record. The people who are very close to the issues or the people inside the school system may know about these things, but the general public does not.

The general public has a right to weigh both sides, and there are two sides. Anybody who believes this is a simple question, I think, fails to see its complexity.

I want to say for the record, in my view, Dr. Greene's testimony was able and factual and very important, since these hearings so far have been characterized by a high level of factual content on all sides. This testimony was very much in that tradition, and we are all sophisticated about the fact the more able the testimony, the more adversarial the cross-examination, and I want to congratulate Dr. Greene and Dr. Rockowitz and Miss Unser.

You may be excused. Thank you.

- - - - - - -

THE CHAIRMAN: The next witness is Mr. Isaiah E. Robinson. He is Vice-President, Board of Education, City of New York.

MR. ROBINSON: Commissioner Norton, Members of the panel, I would like to express my appreciation for the opportunity to participate in these hearings. I must apologize that I did not prepare a statement, because of time pressure for one thing.

But more particularly, because of the situation of examination and licensing procedures, from my prospective, wearing two hats over the past decade, most of the discussion, most of the opinions, most of the research has pointed to one direction about the Board of Examiners. And since 1969, March, there has been no drastic change in any of the assertions made. And, therefore, my testimony will be a brief reflection on some of my experiences as chairman of the Harlem Parents Committee, as well as discussions and reports about the same situation.

In 1964, after a great deal of movement in the city in mobilization of parents to bring about an equal opportunity in education, not only for young people, but for the Black and Puerto Rican professionals, the Board of Education urged Commissioner James Allen to appoint a committee to make recommendations to the Board on its desegregation policies. One of the major issues of this report was that of the recruitment, licensing, appointment, and promotion of Black and Puerto Rican professionals.

The Allen Committee noted that Black and Puerto Rican candidates have had more difficulty than others progressing through the system's hierarchy. In rejecting the Board of Examiners' attempt at rationalization for its procedures in the situation, the committee stated, and I quote:

"It is not enough that selection standards be high and objective. An equally important question is whether they are sufficiently relevant and flexible to obtain people with the qualities most needed in the schools. It should be possible in 1964," it went on, "to find more than the present group of fewer than ten Negroes who are competent to handle some of the system's more than 1,200 administrative positions. Surely more than the present two or three Negroes are capable of outstanding service among the 800 plus principalships."

There has been very little change in that number of minority educators in the administrative and supervisory appointments since the issuance of the Allen Report.

Given the historical bias against Black and Puerto Ricans, the Board of Examiners has until the very recent past made it very difficult for most minority applicants to scale the promotional ladder in the system. Because of this fact, the Board of Examiners has been under attack by public administrators, the Board of Education and various civic groups for nearly three decades, largely because of discrimination and inbreeding.

In 1959 the political scientists, Wallace Sayre and Herbert Kaufman, characterized the Board of Examiners as, and I quote, "a Civil Service reformer's dream, a bureaucrat's delight, and an official's nightmare." Their main criticism of the selection technique was that it limited the sensitivity about the work setting that people are being recruited for, and the examination was no more than a ritualistic device to promote insiders. Therefore, it is impossible for such techniques or procedures to be validated. Nevertheless, the Board of Examiners has been urged repeatedly to validate its testing procedures from the Kandell Report in the late 1930's to Strayer-Yavner in 1951, the Schinnerer report in the late 1950's, but obviously to no avail, as the answers to questions today suggested.

In 1963 and 1966 the Daniel E. Griffith research team commented on "the Board of Examiners' inefficiency in recuitment and promotion procedures" and on "the favored position of insiders." The Griffith recommendations were "the complete abolition of the Board of Examiners, setting up a personnel commission," and "using the National Teacher Examination as a basis for recruitment." It was this important study that gave Alfred Giordano, who was the President of the Board at that time, the clout necessary to push through legislation to reduce the size of the Board of Examiners from nine to five, as well as to change the administration to increase the recruitment of outsiders and to provide for more flexibility in promotion procedures. But the examination and promotion procedures have not changed that much since Giordano's compromise in 1967.

Let's look at the results of the highly touted meritorious recruitment, licensing, and promotional procedures of the Board of Examiners.

Licensed supervisory positions in the pedagogical service of New York City as of March 1969:

Principals: 790 white, 8 Black, no Puerto Ricans, no Orientals.

Assistant principals: 1,491 white, 114 Black, 4 Puerto Ricans, no Orientals.

Directors: 23 white, 2 Black, no Puerto Ricans, no Orientals.

Assistant directors: 50 white, 4 Black, no Puerto Ricans, no Orientals.

Assistant administrative directors: 40 white, 5 Black, no Puerto Ricans, no Orientals.

Teacher in charge: 18 white, 2 Black, no Puerto Ricans, no Orientals.

Department chairmen: 897 white, 26 Black, 1 Puerto Rican, no Orientals.

Guidance Counselor (could be characterized in this respect as a supervisory position): 967 white, 102 Black, 2 Puerto Ricans, 2 Orientals,

for a grand total of 4,276 white, 263 Black, 7 Puerto Rican, 2 Oriental, which means 94% of the supervisory staff in the pedagogical service is white, 5% Black, .1% Puerto Rican and .06% Oriental.

It seems to give the Board of Examiners a great sense of satisfaction and pride in achieving over 200% increase in the number of Black principals since the Allen Commission's report of May, 1964, where we have improved that situation over the five-year period from three to eight. This great achievement represents less than one appointment per year, while at the same time the percentage of Black teachers or Spanish teachers in this system has increased at the alarming breakneck speed of .7% per year.

And we hear so much about the success of our recruitment programs. This glowing record can only serve to reinforce the charges of racial bias in the examination and promotional procedures of the Board of Examiners. It also highlights the Kaufman-Sayre characterization of the Board as, and I quote again, "a Civil Service reformer's dream, a bureaucrat's delight, and an official's nightmare."

Certainly it has been a nightmare, but more so to the countless numbers of Black and Puerto Rican pedagogical aspirants who have received the curt notice, and I quote, "insufficiently meritorious."

What then is considered sufficiently meritorious? The most apt description that I have found is a bit brutish, but it was published in a student underground newspaper. I quote--and I think it also suggests, before I quote, the process and the phenomenon that most people have witnessed in the city school system of New York City.

The quote is from an underground newspaper:
"Our school is run by mummies. The principal creeps around looking busy and self-assured with two assistants respectfully following in his wake. What does this man mean in the universe? I don't think he's human. Sometime I think he's a Goddam android. Like all principals, they seem to be manufactured in a secret laboratory in the basement of the Board of Education by mad scientists and turned loose on our schools. Where else do they come from?"

While we may argue the merit and appropriateness of this caricature, we cannot escape the profound insight of this high school student as he ponders the mysteries of recruitment, licensing, and promotional procedures, the satirical and brutish candor he has laid bare, the harsh reality of inbreeding and nepotism.

The Griffith Report suggests that inbreeding has been promoted in three ways. Among others, little effort is made to really recruit outside the city. Examinations stress localized knowledge available only to insiders, with an informal system of prepping for examinations bringing inside candidates under the tutelage of other insiders who were already members of the administrative hierarchy.

For example, principals, department heads and superintendents prepare the questions for the examinations and provide the answers. Principals, department heads, superintendents, and Board of Examiners members have conducted coaching courses for a fee for selected candidates. Principals, department heads, and superintendents administering these examinations are paid in excess of $15 per hour. Principals, department heads, and superintendents mark the examination papers over the summer; or whenever available, participate in the interviews and evaluate and grade each candidate.

This obvious political and economical system has resulted in the proliferation of more than 1,200 specific separate licenses in the pedagogical service, a complete monopoly over school personnel.

While the Board of Examiners claims to have instituted many liberal reforms, the meritorious appointment and promotions have not sufficiently changed the blatant imbalance. As a consequence, today the New York City school system is not in compliance with federal law, which requires the integration of staff at all levels.

I think this would be enough, since I don't really have the time to crystallize a system that has existed for years, a system that is supported by many people, and most of them not of the system. I am certain that the greatest support for what is called "a merit system" is by other Civil Service employees--the police, the firemen, other uniformed services--who feel that they also have a stake in this kind of nepotism, not only for the Board of Education, but for other departments in city government.

The record is clear that obvious bias exists in the selection of personnel and that other options should be open to the school system for the selection of people who are professional and are committed to the service of the youngsters in New York City. As long as we have what I consider--and it's my own opinion, as most all of this testimony is--as long as we have this archaic system which, by its own testimony in answering questions posed in these hearings, has not demonstrated true validity, research, or any greater success than other systems which are more economical, I think it would be a disservice to the city to continue the system as it is presently constituted.

Thank you.

THE CHAIRMAN: Mr. Tractenberg.

MR. TRACTENBERG: Mr. Robinson, in the course of your work with the Board of Education in this area, have you formulated any ideas, any reasons why other large urban school districts have apparently been more successful in terms of attracting Black and Puerto Rican teachers and supervisors?

MR. ROBINSON: I think the basic question in New York City in terms of integration of schools or integration of staff, is one of commitment. There is no commitment. If there were commitment, we would have demonstrated, in the last three years at least, a better percentage increase.

It is true that recruitment teams go out of New York City. But I am willing to put the record, for example, of Westchester or Nassau or any surrounding community up against the success in selection, attracting, recruitment, and hiring of minorities in those school systems as compared with what's happening here. It is a dismal failure when all we can recruit is seven tenths of one per cent in the teaching service each year.

MR. TRACTENBERG: Doesn't the Board of Education or the Chancellor's office have to assume some of this responsibility since, I gather, recruitment is principally a function of the Board of Education or Chancellor?

MR. ROBINSON: There are many avenues open to the current Board of Education and the Chancellor under the new Decentralization Law.

Yet I do not feel that the flexibility within the law, or any liberal changes that would result from that law, gives the Chancellor or the Board of Education very much power in relation to the examining process. The law speaks only to teaching staff in those schools where 40% of them fall below a certain reading level where an alternative may be used. The law did not speak to any alternative in the selection of supervisors.

Now, if the leadership of a school is that important, and the system has demonstrated that it cannot really prove that it has used imagination and creativity in selecting a variety of individuals for this particular job, it cannot prove that selecting the ones it has selected are any better professionally than other systems, I cannot see that there is much hope under decentralization for community school boards or parents in selecting individuals, because the examinations result in lists with a life of four years. And the best candidate in the world can come along the next day after it is promulgated and cannot be hired in New York City until every name on that list is exhausted.

MR. TRACTENBERG: Do you think that the change from a ranked list for supervisory personnel to a qualifying list will substantially affect the situation?

MR. ROBINSON: I do not. I was opposed to the examination recently given for the simple reason that we cannot correct the imbalance in the system when we permit--and they claim it's democratic--open competitive examinations where only a small percentage of the candidates are Black or Puerto Rican.

The examination just passed had approximately 3,000 applicants, of whom approximately 250 were Black and Puerto Rican. Now, "So what," some would say. "On a list of whoever is certified there will be a substantial number of Blacks and Puerto Ricans from which to choose."

I submit that if what is claimed to be fact--that we will have great attrition this year and next--most of those who get through this examination who are Black and Puerto Rican will be placed the very first year. And there would be no opportunity after that for the next four years to place another Black and Puerto Rican supervisor.

MR. TRACTENBERG: That, though, is a function of the State Education Law itself, that is, the four-year life of the eligible list.

MR. ROBINSON: Correct.

MR. TRACTENBERG: Rather than anything that the Board of Examiners is itself doing.

MR. ROBINSON: It is true. But I am not aware of state certification of any candidate in the State of New York having a list, or a life that has to be exhausted before other candidates can be certified and screened or interviewed for appointments to a position. This option is not open in New York City to the community school boards or the Board of Education of the city.

MR. TRACTENBERG: Mr. Robinson, yesterday we heard testimony from various Boards of Education staff members about the recruitment and training area. And when pressed a bit with questions they seemed to feel the need of some kind of "guidelines," in the words of one of the witnesses.

Is the Board of Education entertaining evaluations of current efforts in the recruitment and over-all selection area toward the possibility of establishing some guidelines?

MR. ROBINSON: Because of the compromise, Giordano's compromise in 1967, there is a great opportunity for recruitment programs, different kinds of recruitment programs.

The law also suggests that it is possible community boards could be involved in their own recruitment programs. But the problem is that if recruitment takes place and you find an individual you like you cannot guarantee that individual a job.

For example, I am community school board aide. I go out to recruit candidates. I go to all the colleges I know. I have friends and relatives and fine good, worthy candidates. I cannot offer them a job if they first must pass an examination conducted by the Board of Examiners in New York City, and the several parts, which may go over several months. This individual who was looking for a job would be snapped up by any community around New York City.

MR. TRACTENBERG: Do you think the program, which I gather is now being launched, of having Board of Examiners officials accompany recruiting teams outside the state--

MR. ROBINSON: I didn't get that.

MR. TRACTENBERG: I understand that a program is in process under which Board of Examiners officials will go out of state with recruiting teams and administer an examination.

MR. ROBINSON: That occurred this year also.

MR. TRACTENBERG: Is that an improvement in your judgment?

MR. ROBINSON: If one feels that the major colleges in New York City provide enough white candidates for the teaching service, I cannot see two teams going out across the country selecting, or recruiting, both white and Black and Spanish applicants. It would appear that the inequity is in the recruitment, selection and promotion of Black and Spanish applicants, and that the recruitment effort should be aimed only at them, since the bulk of appointments made in New York City come from the six major teaching colleges in the city. We are not short of, and there's no need to spend the money on recruiting, white candidates; they are available here. But I think it's a waste of money to go outside to recruit whites.

MR. TRACTENBERG: So, you don't object to this program. You just think that the direction of it should be changed?

MR. ROBINSON: No. I think it's been ineffective.

MR. TRACTENBERG: It has been?

MR. ROBINSON: The emphasis, yes.

MR. TRACTENBERG: Ineffective in attracting Black and Puerto Rican candidates?

MR. ROBINSON: Yes. Because of the fact that while the team may go out and attract, it cannot offer positions, because there is uncertainty whether or not they'll ever get through the examination.

Now, under the provision for the 40% of schools who will have the NTE as the measure, it may be possible for some schools in some districts to attract, recruit, and hire on the spot some individuals, but it will not be universal in the system.

MR. TRACTENBERG: There is one technical thing I want to touch on, because it has occupied some of the discussion, and I'm not sure I understood a remark you made in your prepared statement about coaching courses.

MR. ROBINSON: Scribbled notes.

MR. TRACTENBERG: Scribbled notes.

I thought I understood you to say that there were coaching

courses run for private profit by Board of Examiners members and others engaged in the examination process.

MR. ROBINSON: Up until the reorganization of the Board that was one of the major issues. From the late or early fifties, or before that, up through 1967, that was the case.

MR. TRACTENBERG: That is--I want to make absolutely sure of this--that there were Board of Examiners staff people running coaching courses at the same time they were staff members of the Board of Examiners?

MR. ROBINSON: Well, I don't know whether it happened at the same time. If we have a closed system where the individual who is going to make out the questions and give the answers, who may also administer tests and do the interviews, I cannot see what the difference is if that same individual is going to coach some person who is on the inside to pass the examination already prepared.

MR. TRACTENBERG: I don't know very much about the history of the Board of Examiners--

THE CHAIRMAN: Counsel, I am going to rule this line of questioning is not fair, because you are asking the witness questions about history, and I believe he has indicated that there are some difficulties with that. You see, I don't think that he would want to go on the record with respect to precisely who was or was not giving courses unless he had an opportunity to research that. And on the other hand, we certainly wouldn't want to be unfair to the Board of Examiners and their staff because we have pressed our witness beyond what we fairly should.

MR. TRACTENBERG: Mr. Robinson, I gather from the closing of your remarks that you favor the abolition of the Board of Examiners?

Is that a fair characterization?

MR. ROBINSON: Yes. That's a fair characterization.

MR. TRACTENBERG: In your judgment, and based on your experience in the school system, both directly and when you were active with parents' organizations, is it your reaction that this might, if safeguards aren't taken, lead to a system of patronage?

MR. ROBINSON: No, it does not. The complaints and criticism had to do with a monolithic monopoly, if you will, that seems to be accountable only to God.

The recommendations, and the frustrations felt by most people, were based on the fact that there were no options available, that even that system was not accountable to the Board of Education, for which it claimed to be a service agent, that the Board of Education could only discuss eligibility requirements but not the scope of examinations, even though the jobs to be filled were under the jurisdiction of the Board of Education.

And, so, the effort is to make it possible for the Chancellor, and the Board of Education to at least influence the kind and quality of candidates that are certified in the city school system, and to have more than one option to do so, since it is claimed by the experts here, and elsewhere, that the Board of Examiners' tests cannot be validated as a predictor of success in the performance of the job.

MR. TRACTENBERG: That's all I have, Madam Chairman.

THE CHAIRMAN: Do the Commissioners have any questions they would like to ask?

Thank you very much, Mr. Robinson, for coming and for waiting so graciously.

I am going to note a slight change in procedure. The only lunch break that I am willing to recognize as valid is that of Counsel. I understand Counsel's lunch--and I am only allowing him a 15-minute lunch break--has not arrived. Therefor, until his lunch does arrive we will proceed, for we must bear in mind that there are witnesses who have been waiting here since rather early this morning. So I am going to call the next witness who is to be scheduled.

Mr. Philip Kaplan, Chairman, Community School Board No. 15, Brooklyn, New York.

Then we have this morning's witnesses, the following: Mr. Donaldson, Mr. Hayes, Mr. Hunter, Miss Lehrman.

Mr. Kaplan.

MR. KAPLAN: May I proceed?

THE CHAIRMAN: Yes.

MR. KAPLAN: Thank you.

My name is Philip Kaplan. I am President of Community School Board 15.

Community School Board 15 is located in Brooklyn, New York. We are one of the largest community school boards in the City of New York. We have approximately 27,000 children attending our district. In addition to that, we are also charged with certain responsibilities in the non-public schools, or the parochial schools, which have a registration of approximately 22,000 students.

In the district we have 20 elementary schools, of which 15 are Title I schools, or schools below the poverty level. We have five junior high and high schools, which are all Title I schools.

The district is composed of areas of Brooklyn called Red Hook, Sunset Park, Gowanus, South Brooklyn, Cobble Hill, Park Slope, Windsor Place, Kensington and parts of Borough Park. So, the makeup of the district is basically the makeup of New York City.

We have a school budget for the district of $23,800,000. We also have a Title I budget of approximately $4 million. So, we in District 15 are involved in big business, and the big business is education.

We are not corrupt. We don't see any corruption on our board. We don't see any corruption due to the fact that we were elected by the people in my community. We feel that we can legally, efficiently and with dedication run our district in the manner which we want.

I would like to cite certain examples. In the complex of District 15 we have various elementary schools. One school in particular is made up of a composition of 98% Puerto Rican. During the last six months, we have tried to retain the services of a Puerto Rican principal.

It is the feeling of our community school board that when you are dealing with the registration of approximately 1600 children, 90-some-odd percent Puerto Rican, that the individual who can best run this school is an individual who understands the problems of this minority group of our city, the Puerto Rican group. And we interviewed various principals, but we were told that it was illegal to select any principal who is not on a list, on a list that was prepared from an examination that was taken in 1964. We were told that we cannot hire any individual without interviewing the top three names on this list.

Well, the top three names were not of Puerto Rican descent. The top three names did not meet the requirements of the parents association as well as the community school board, but we had no choice. So, we finally did make a choice of one of the top three.

The parents have agreed to accept this individual, but I feel, and the board feels, and the superintendent feels, that the selection should have been one of an individual who would best fit the needs of our particular community and that particular school.

In the case of teachers, we have assignments directly from the central Board of Education, and we select teachers. We are blessed, however, with a fine teaching staff and a fine supervisory staff.

But times have changed. Our social needs have changed. The district has changed. And I feel that for an individual to best service a school which is predominantly of one particular nationality, or race, or heritage, he should have a feeling for that particular group of people.

We have students coming into our schools who do not speak English, who speak solely Spanish. And when they leave our schools, they go back to their homes and again they renew their Spanish-speaking ability. And if you do not have teachers and principals, who can understand their plight, and their problems of why they cannot speak, of why they cannot read--and you can't get this from a textbook; you have to get it from growing with the community; you have to get this from living with people and understanding their problems of translating and adapting to the needs of our City--these are the only individuals who can properly service this type of an area, and we have none to pick from. And I think that we should have some. The various community school boards need it. My particular school board definitely needs it.

In the hiring practices of the central Board of Education-- and I must say it is the central Board because we have no control over it--we must accept what they send.

We deal with a tenure situation also, where teachers are supposed to qualify within three years. However, we have recently held a principal's institute in District 15 where we met with all our principals, and the following question was raised and put to the principals. We asked them, in their years of experience, how many teachers were denied tenure within our schools?

One principal rose, who was in our service for 20-some-odd years, and who is claimed to be one of the most difficult principals--or I should say, one of the most efficient principals, in my viewpoint--and stated to me that she gave three bad ratings in her 20 years' experience. And of the three, she knows they are now teaching in other districts.

So, how do we commence to weed out those who cannot teach? How do we commence to pull away from the system, or extract from the system, those who do not qualify and meet the needs of our schools?

There is no method. The tenure method is a complete hoax. It doesn't accomplish anything because the professionals within the system will not earmark an individual as being inefficient or ineffectual in the system. And they are merely passed onto other principals, other teachers, other communities and other areas.

So, when we hear discussions by the Board of Examiners-- and I would like to preface my next remarks with the statement: that I myself have had no exposure to the Board of Examiners except my exposure in the last six months. I did not know where the Board of Education was located until nine months ago. I had no dealings with the educational process and functioning of the City of New York until I decided to become involved in the election of a community school board. The only exposure I did have is that I am a product of the public schools in the City of New York. I attended the elementary schools, high schools, colleges and eventually law school. I am an attorney. I practice here in New York. And I knew nothing about the Board of Examiners or the Board of Education prior to six months ago.

But I have done my homework, and I have done my research. I know what my problems are in my district. I know what the needs are in my district, and I'm trying to solve them. The board is trying to solve them. And we cannot solve them unless we are given the ability to hire the professionals who can best service our children.

And I call them "our children" because I live in this community and I have two children presently going through the school system. I have two children who I feel are getting a decent education basically because I am following up on their instruction.

But Puerto Rican parents who are first coming into the country don't have this ability, and they're not indoctrinated in our method of teaching, our methods of instruction. So, not only must we train children, we must also prepare parents; and we must also select those to prepare parents who are within the realm we are dealing with in the area where these parents come from. And, again, I speak to the minorities--let it be Black, let it be Puerto Rican, Arabic or what have you. This is the problem that we have on the local level, down on the street.

I am not a professional when it comes to education, nor do I profess that I have the answers. I know the problems. I know what I need. I know what I must have in my district.

I must have people who know the problems of the minorities. I must have people who know when you call somebody a "Black man," what it means. I must know and have in my district supervisors who know what it is to be Puerto Rican and not speak the language. They must know what it is to come to school as a

Puerto Rican, unable to speak the language, and have a teacher stand before them who says, "I cannot teach them," and when you go to transfer the teacher out of the system he is merely transferred to another school and presents the same problem.

The method of selecting teachers and supervisors seems to be one which the Board of Examiners wants to maintain.

If I and my board have the authority to prepare budgets, to spend $23 million to employ 1500-some-odd teachers, to run 30-some-odd schools, to educate 27,000 children, I think we should have the say about who we can employ to educate these 27,000 children. We should have the right to say who shall be employed under our budget of $23 million.

And I don't think that there is anything corrupt. I don't think there is anything immoral, I don't think there is anything under the table by giving this right to the local level where it belongs.

The whole theory of decentralization is one of involvement of the local constituents, local people. I think that it would be amiss to continue with a system which does not adhere to the needs of the pupils, needs of the community and needs of the local community school boards.

In my prepared address, which I have already submitted, I listed many alternatives, such as the National Teacher Exam, but I don't feel it is within my knowledge to go into these areas because I am not well versed with reference to them.

I speak to you not only as a parent, but as a president of a community school board who knows where the problems are. I know what's happening on the streets. I know what's happening within the schools.

We need to have the right to select our own. We need to have the right to select those who will be responsible to us. We have to have the right to go out and select supervisors and principals, who will adhere to the needs of our community and adhere to the needs of our children.

Thank you.

THE CHAIRMAN: Mr. Kaplan, I want to just question you a bit for the record, because there is always the tendency to misunderstand when we talk about the relevancy of ethnic and racial background when you are talking about school positions.

I notice in your example you referred again and again to Puerto Ricans, and you talked about a school that was 90% Puerto Rican. And when you have a school with Puerto Rican children, the language problem is an obvious one; the wholly different culture is an obvious one.

But you did not mean, did you, to suggest that only a person of Puerto Rican background or extraction could be a teacher or principal dealing with those children?

MR. KAPLAN: No. That was definitely not my intention.

THE CHAIRMAN: I am sure it wasn't. And I wanted you to be able to put that on the record.

MR. KAPLAN: But I do feel that the lack of proper supervisors and teachers within that school is a definite deterrent in the educational processes in that school. I am not saying it should be dominated by one particular race or nationality.

THE CHAIRMAN: I just wanted that to go on the record. I think often if we think closely about this issue, and we all have come to this city from different parts of the world and different parts of the country, that if we think back a generation or two we might think that children of, let us say, Italian or Jewish immigrants might have been more quickly assimilated into the school system if at that point there had been more Italian or Jewish teachers, and that in the same way each new immigrant or migrant group to a city has difficulties first of all with its children, who are absorbed into a new way of life. And the point is that life is obviously easier for children if someone who has some greater sensitivity and background in their culture and ways also has the opportunity to come into their schools and teach and supervise them.

Mr. Tractenberg?

Do you want to say something, Mr. Kaplan?

MR. KAPLAN: May I just make one remark.

I myself, when I started kindergarten, did not speak a word of English. I just spoke Jewish. When I started elementary school, the fact that there were teachers that understood Yiddish was a tremendous crutch. I think that's important to keep in mind, also.

THE CHAIRMAN: You mean, there were teachers in your public school who also spoke Yiddish as well as English?

MR. KAPLAN: That's right.

THE CHAIRMAN: And you found that to be a help to you in beginning your education?

MR. KAPLAN: It was a help to me and to my parents, who came to school to find out my progress, to speak to someone who spoke the same language as we did at that time.

THE CHAIRMAN: Mr. Tractenberg.

MR. TRACTENBERG: Mr. Kaplan, I just have a couple of questions.

You mentioned the problem of screening out teachers who don't meet satisfactory levels, and the fact that it is seldom done, and tenure is rather automatically granted.

Do you think that if a system replaced the current selection process with, for example, provisional licensing, it might improve the situation? A teacher has a one-year license and at the end of that time a decision would be made. Do you think under circumstances like that that the same principals who are now not eliminating incompetent teachers would do so?

MR. KAPLAN: I think if we start holding the principals accountable for the progress in their schools, they will start weeding out those teachers who cannot teach and meet the levels that they set. I think we have to start with the principals, not with the teachers, and we have to start on a professional level where the principals must be held accountable. And if their schools are not performing according to the standards set by the powers that be--let it be the community board or central board--

I think the principal is the one to come forth and say, "Why have you maintained this particular class at this particular level?"

Perhaps provisional licensing is the answer, where you give more power to principals and you request from them that they must so react if you give them the power.

MR. TRACTENBERG: Have you been able to identify with any kind of certainty the source of the problem regarding the great difficulty in getting bilingual teaachers? Is this basically a recruiting problem, or is it a problem with the length of time that lists take to be compiled, or is it a problem with people not being able to pass the examination?

MR. KAPLAN: Well, it's a problem that there aren't enough bilingual teachers in the City of New York. But we have attempted to solve it. We had a Title I coordinator who deals with special programs, federal programs. And one of our Title I programs involves bilingual training, or English to Spanish and Spanish to English. The individual who is charged with the responsibility of our Title I program never really had the feel of the plight of the Puerto Rican child.

And we hired as a Title I coordinator a Puerto Rican teacher who has been in the system in New York City for 20 years. And through the hiring of this Title I coordinator, we were able to obtain in our district additional bilingual teachers, additional teachers who have the feel of the problem of learning English from a Spanish background.

And the only way to really accomplish this is to hire individuals who know what the story is, know what the problems are. And you don't get them from the textbook. I didn't learn how to practice law from the textbook. I made my mistakes in the courtroom, just as teachers make their mistakes in the classroom.

MR. TRACTENBERG: Do you think that if a more flexible system of selection were in effect you would be reasonably likely to fill your needs for such kinds of people as bilingual teachers?

MR. KAPLAN: Yes, I do.

MR. TRACTENBERG: That's all.

THE CHAIRMAN: Thank you very much, Mr. Kaplan.

MR. KAPLAN: Thank you.

THE CHAIRMAN: It is now a quarter of two. I am calling a fifteen-minute recess until 2:00. And we will start promptly again at 2 p.m.

(Whereupon, at 1:45 p.m., there was a 15-minute recess; Whereupon, at 2:00 p.m., the hearing was resumed.)

THE CHAIRMAN: Begin taking your seats, please. This hearing is in session. Tell the people in the hall that the hearing is in session.

We have just had a 15-minute break. While the people are assembling here, let me announce once again to the members of the public who might wish to attend these hearings, but might be unable to do so because they have to care for small children, that we have arranged for a free day care center to be available around the corner, 225 Broadway, Room 27, 18th floor, for any parent who wishes to attend these hearings and leave his or her children at our facility, our day care facility which is located around the corner from these hearings. These hearings are taking place at 14 Vesey Street.

I want to apologize to all witnesses who are scheduled for our tardiness. We allowed Dr. Jay Greene of the Board of Examiners much more time than we had anticipated in the belief that, inasmuch as the Board of Examiners has been much criticized in this whole process, that it was only fair to give them the opportunity to say fully what it is they wanted to say. Thereafter, of course, Counsel had to ask them questions based on their testimony.

The Board of Examiners has given us names of other people from the public who they think might wish to testify. And we have consented to call these people and ask them to come in to testify during the public testimony this evening. I want to announce that there will be public testimony this evening and tomorrow evening.

The next witness, Mr. Andrew G. Donaldson, Community Superintendent, School District No. 9, the Bronx.

Mr. Donaldson.

MR. DONALDSON: Thank you, Madam Chairman.

First, I want to say that I consider it an honor and a privilege to have been invited and hope to be able to add information to the very valuable information you received this morning.

I speak as one of the community superintendents who was selected under decentralization last summer, but I also speak as the president of the New York Association of Black School Supervisors and Administrators, and we number within our ranks most of the Black supervisors in the New York City school system. And I believe my point of view reflects their feelings.

I also want to make it clear that most of us are products of the examination system. We are people who have taught in the school system. We are products of the school system, public school system. We have taken the examinations and passed them. So that there is no sour grapes attitude on our part.

We are very concerned about the Board of Examiners simply from the standpoint that it does not represent a merit system by any means. I think this is a catch phrase which has been publicized through the years, and many academic people take it to be synonymous. There is no merit to the Board of Examiners. It has discouraged people from coming into the school system.

The actual examination, as you have already heard this morning, is not done by the four members of the Board who are carefully examined in objective tests, but by an army of hundreds of assistant examiners, both permanent and temporary, who are paid and who actually create the tests, conduct them, and mark them.

I would suggest that the millions of dollars spent on this endeavor could be better spent on the children of the City of New York, and a fraction of this distributed among the school boards to enable them to determine objectively how best to select heads of the board and teachers to teach the children who are in need.

The great hue and cry of political patronage and interference exists right now and has existed in the Board of Examiners. And what appears to be merit is strictly a facade.

First of all, up until 1968, the Board of Examiners belonged to the Council of Supervisory Associations, was a member of the CSA, functioned as fellow members with the principals, with the superintendents, and most of the Board of Examiner members knew the officers of the CSA and the various allied associations.

There is no objective test to select assistant examiners. Now, here we have a Board which maintains its right, which upholds its right, to examine objectively all people and candidates who take positions in the school system virtually functioning with an army of people who do the actual examining, creating the tests and marking them, and which through 70 years has failed to produce an objective test by which to select the examiners. Now, there's a sheer contradiction.

I think one of the things that I have to emphasize within this is that there are people in the school system who have worked in the school system for 40 years or more, who were never called by the Board of Examiners, who have never served one day as assistant examiner. On the other hand, there are principals, assistant principals and others in the school system who have been called on regularly one exam after the other.

There are people in the school system who, having just passed an exam, were called upon while in probation to examine the next group of people coming through for the same exam. Now, the Board of Examiners has always taken the position that probation is actually a part of the examination. They maintain that the three-year probationary period is like the completion of the examination; and yet the Board itself has engaged these probationers to help examine other people to take license exams for the same level. I think this is a contradiction.

I think we should also emphasize that in many of these examinations there is an interview section conducted by assistant examiners who as Dr. Greene said this morning, were recommended by others in the system. They are well known, and they know the officers of the CSA and allied associations. Thus, it is virtually impossible for a person coming into an examination not to know some of the examiners present. It is a known thing in the coaching courses that you are told that if you recognize someone that you are supposed to declare that before taking the examination. And yet we were told in coaching courses, "If you recognize someone and he doesn't indicate that he recognizes you, say nothing."

Now, you can take a person who is the president of the Assistant Principals Association, which is the largest of the supervisory associations, or an officer in that, or a head of the Principals Association, or any one of the supervisory groups, and obviously that man upon walking into an examination for an interview is known immediately. There is very little likelihood that he could be unknown.

I think it also should be brought to your attention that the assistant examiners mark the examinations at home. It would be interesting to hear the reaction of the Board of Examiners to the suggestion that the candidates take the examinations at home.

But here you have examinations where ostensibly no one knows the name of the candidate. There is a number, a candidate knows his number. In many instances the candidate knows many of the examiners who are from the same system, and his paper is taken home by someone in the system, working day after day in the system, and marked at home. And the examiners all have telephones, and they probably have no difficulty calling one another. And I'm sure there is no difficulty in finding the number of a person whom you would like to locate. I know of one person who told me, in fact, that he knew the examiner who had his paper and who was marking it at home.

I think we are all aware of the examination jargon, the fact that there is a kind of language which has to be learned, rote-learned, to spew back on the examinations whether in written form or in verbal form; the fact that people make hundreds and hundreds of dollars writing these coaching books, thousands of dollars conducting the coaching courses, which still exist, in order to learn the jargon and spew it back.

I think it should be clearly known that even in the official coaching courses, which have just been begun recently by the Board of Education to prepare candidates for the exam, the phrase is used, as has always been used, "For examination purposes only."

At the time I took the examination, of course, there weren't any Board of Education coaching courses. You had to pay. And when they talk about minority group candidates, if I hadn't had the GI Bill of Rights, I probably couldn't have afforded the coaching courses. It cost $700. There were several hundred people in it. A principal, a practicing principal, was conducting it, a principal who made sure that he told us he made it a point to play golf on weekends with some of the examiners who are on the Board of Examiners.

I think the supervision test is another indication of how invalid the tests are, let alone unreliable. I think any teacher would have stopped testing years ago if they had to go by the standards which the Board of Examiners uses.

We know in supervision in the school system a supervisor attempts to bring out the best in a teacher, to diagnose the needs of that teacher, to discover the weaknesses and help the teacher to gain insight into her weaknesses and make corrections, and also to help the teacher understand that there is enough encouragement from the things she is doing well that she might feel that there is somewhat of a balance in criticism.

In the examination, for the supervision part you are taught to write as fast as you can, get down as many negative points as you can, make a recommendation for each negative point you find, because the negative point with the recommendation gives you twice as many points as finding the positive points, completely contrary to the practice. "For examination purposes only."

The Board of Education itself has varied requirements from time to time. At the point at which I took the junior high school principal's license, you had to have five years of supervisor experience before you could even take the examination. By the time the examination was completed this had been scaled down to three years. Therefore, a person who was ineligible at the time of the examination later on suddenly found himself eligible, although you had the same person with probably more experience than someone who had suddenly become eligible.

Years ago, a person could take the examination for principal while still a classroom teacher. Then the examination required that you have experience as an assistant principal or a supervisor before becoming eligible to even take the principal's exam.

Whenever a hurdle is built into the process it moves it that much more from minority group candidates. And then, of course, the old party line which the Board has used on us is that we don't see the people who wish to take the exam. They're not available. They don't come forward. Well, if we look at that carefully, we discover the reason. It's not very hard to find. If you build in enough hurdles, preliminary requirements, pretty soon you find that the person is filtered out from becoming even eligible to take the examination.

Years ago, minority groups were always failed on the speech part of the exam. You could take the written and pass it with flying colors; the teaching test, pass it with flying colors. And I know of two candidates right now who had never been to the South in their lives who were told in the speech test, "You speak with a Southern accent." It seemed if you were Black, you automatically spoke with a Southern accent.

They were gladly granted substitute licenses. The majority of minority group people in the system at that time had substitute licenses. And they were content to let you substitute for 20 years, but to get a regular license you had to pass the speech exam, and to get over that Southern accent seemed to be something impossible.

In order to take the assistant principal's examination, you had to have so many years of regular teaching experience. Even though you might have taught for 20 years full-time, every single day as a substitute teacher, doing the exact same job that a regular teacher did, you were ineligible to take the assistant principal's examination.

Therefore, being ineligible to take the assistant principal's examination, it is not very hard to discover why you didn't have many candidates rushing to take the principal's examination, because you couldn't take that unless you had had years as an assistant principal. Now, this contrived maze was not set up by accident. This was a carefully set up maze to prevent minority group candidates from getting into the school system, into supervisory positions.

The saddest part of this entire fiasco is that it has discriminated against whites more than it has discriminated against Blacks. Having gone through the coaching courses, having been one of the people who were successful in the examinations, I have no ax to grind. I presently possess several teaching licenses, a supervisory license, assistant director's license and a principal's license. So that I have done very well through the Board of Examiners. Having gone through this, having sat with the hundreds in the coaching courses and having heard the complaints, having heard the anguish, I can tell you most of the people who were discriminated against were not Black or Puerto Rican or Spanish. These were white people.

I have heard of the men who had to take their families up to the Catskills all summer and virtually abandon them so as to retire to cabins and cram and cram and cram, to learn the nonsense material in order to be able to regurgitate it on signal at top lightning speed from mnemonics which you learned. You learned hundreds of them so that you had ready pedigrees, ready jargon, with the ability to give it back as quickly as you could to get that miniscule portion of one point. The examinations are calibrated and marked two places beyond the decimal point. Your model answer is likely to have one-tenth of one point for a point that you dream up, and you have to get this down in lightning speed.

You are told in the coaching courses, "Write short declarative sentences." There is no mark for literary form. You are virtually trained out of doing every single thing you learned in school. Your whole orientation is "For examination purposes only." You are told this by the coach over and over again. This has nothing to do with running the school. This has nothing to do with reality. This is in order to pass the examination.

I want to also go into the point of what happens once the lists are promulgated. In my previous assignment as Deputy Superintendent in District 6, for two years we had a vacancy in a Harlem school. We went to the list. We went down 16 names on the list, the same list that the CSA insists that we consult in terms of the top three names. We went through the top three names, and we went down 16 names before we could even get a candidate who was willing to come to be interviewed, or to even see the school. Once he heard the school was in Harlem he said he was no longer interested. When we did get past the 16 names, and at least got three candidates to be interviewed--and we did interview them, and by great powers of persuasion convinced the parents that we had to go by the list--the candidate promptly refused to accept the assignment, even after having been accepted on the interview by the parents, you see.

Now this dilemma leaves us in a position where you virtually are programmed for conflict. You have schools which are already not functioning well, where people have used them as stepping stones to better schools. They have simply put in the three years --traditionally it is known as "done their time," as they call it, in these Harlem schools--and moved out to better schools. The system has promulgated this. And then, in order to get a replacement for the person, you are told you must go to this list with no one on the list who looks anything like the youngsters who go to the school, who doesn't live in the neighborhood, who has never understood the neighborhood, and who is only interested in

putting in three years in order to get out of the school. And then
you have to go down the list and virtually beg them to come for an
interview; and then after they are successful in convincing the
parents that they are at least competent, and the school board
selects them, then they refuse to even come to take the job. Now
this is amazing, to keep this system going on.

We had another school in which the very same thing happened, P.S. 192. I virtually had to beg three candidates to appear.
And out of the three, two of them told me they were doing me a
personal favor to come. Now these are the people who would insist
by lawsuit that we consult the list if we were to go beyond the list.
It just gives you an idea of the kind of relationship that exists
throughout this so-called "merit system."

I also want you to know of some of the by-products that go
with being bold enough to oppose the system, of showing any attempt to correct the system. There are subtle ways of disciplining.

Just two weeks ago I received my first salary as superintendent, and this was virtually after threatening Dr. Lang with a
lawsuit. I had one harassment after the other in order to get my
salary. He told the Board that he had to physically see my certificate, even though the coordinator of the School Board, Mrs.
Elizabeth Clark, said the contract was sufficient. Then, once the
certificate was sent, he said I had sent the wrong one, I had sent
him the candidate's copy and he was supposed to get the Superintendent's copy, which is an identical copy. That was another
way. And this was one harassment after the other until he was
summoned before my board and threatened with a lawsuit, and then
within a few days the first salary check came through.

We had requests in for assistant principals, which I was going to use in my district office--one white, one Spanish, three
Black. We put them in in accordance with our budget requests.
The budgets were delayed. I was notified by Dr. Lang's office
that they would not be appointed until the budget was approved.
And yet, as of December 1st, the white assistant principal was
appointed to a non-existent budget line. The Spanish and three
Black were not appointed. When I began threatening legal action,
15 days later the minority group appointments were made subject
to approval of the budget. The lines had existed from November
30th, the money had been there, the budget was in Personnel's
hands. The budget for the white candidate, to this day, has not
been approved, and yet he is appointed to a non-existent line on
the budget.

Now, if this isn't discrimination, I don't know what you call
it, but I see it as discrimination, and I see it as a direct outcome
of my position regarding the Board of Examiners.

We have 14 guidance counselors in our district who were
appointed without any consultation with the community superintendent or the community school board. The list appeared this
summer. It was never sent to the board, to the superintendent,
and out of the blue sky suddenly 14 appointments were made, not
only to the district, but in many instances to schools in direct
violation of the law. When Dr. Lang was challenged on this, he

said that there was a slight error, that they had used the wrong
form; they weren't technically appointed, but they were really
assigned. When asked on what basis they were assigned, he informed my board that they had been requested before decentralization, last spring, by principals. When the board reminded him
that the community school board and the superintendent were supposed to do the requesting, he indicated that since he hadn't heard
from us that he had gone ahead on the principals' recommendations.
When I reminded him that under the merit system, it was hard to
recommend someone for a job when the list hadn't even yet appeared, he said that the recommendations had been made in
anticipation of the list.

You have to realize that this system permeates the entire
school system. There is absolutely no way to trace down all of
the ramifications of it, but it's there.

And it's hard to believe that Dr. Lang who spent the last
few months of his tenure in the school system organizing administrative internships for future supervisors in the system now
plans to work in one of the colleges providing future supervisors
for New York City. I think it gives you a clear indication just
what type of system we intend to perpetrate.

I wanted just to make a correction in terms of Dr. Greene's
testimony this morning. He was careful to give the impression,
when he said that they did consult with the CSA, when they did ask
them for names of people, to use as assistant examiners; and
when Counsel asked if he also requested the same information
from the Association of Black School Supervisors, he said, "Well,
seven months ago we had a meeting, and at that time we did make
a verbal solicitation.'

What he forgot to say was, seven months ago we requested
the meeting after many, many frustrated attempts to get just this
done. And at that time, we questioned him at length as to why the
Board of Examiners so very carefully ignored our organization,
or ignored any attempt to consult with our organization in soliciting minority group candidates, while giving the public posture that
it was making such ambitious moves along these lines.

I think there are a few questions which at least should be
considered by the Commissioners. I would like to know if any
records are kept of the candidates who are not selected as assistant examiners, if any records are kept of those who are solicited
in the first place. It's interesting that a Board of Examiners
which is so meticulous in examining others for service in the New
York City system suddenly uses in the very substance of examining these people--the hundreds of assistant examiners--it uses
people who are recommended, who are referred, who are known
of and who have been 'tried out," to use Dr. Greene's words.

I wonder, in trying out someone on a candidate for a supervisory position, what happens to the candidate when they discover
the tryout wasn't successful? It strikes me that it is very unfortunate to try out people on others.

I would like to know--Dr. Greene calls it "the corps of
people," or "corps of consultants"; I call it "the in-club"--I would

like to know how many are dropped from the "in-club," and why, and if records are kept of those who are dropped? We have always insisted through the years that there is an "in-club," and this is how most of the people in the school system feel.

I think, within the last two years, the effects of the strike and the hysteria caused by the community versus union confrontations have given a kind of martyrdom to the Board of Examiners, which they have capitalized on to the public relations advantage. But before that the Board of Examiners were not friends of very many people in the school system who had not been able to survive their shenanigans.

I would like to know if there is a record kept of the probationers who are used as assistant examiners. They are certainly aware of their probationary service, because they are so recently licensed that it's amazing that they use probationers who are just in the jobs and pass up people who have never been used.

Do they have objective reasons for passing up others? Are these ever made clear to the people who have been bypassed? Are they aware that they have even been recommended? It strikes me as a kind of sinister undercover system for a group that claims that it perpetrates a "merit system."

I would also like to know if they keep a record of the temporary assistants who are used, and how often they are called, and how frequently they have been used through the years. I believe specific data along these lines will help you to truly discover how much merit there is in the Board of Examiners.

I maintain, with the millions of dollars presently spent, and I maintain, as a community superintendent who does not find it easy finding capable leadership to take over these schools which are non-functioning, that there is not much worry about political intrigue and patronage.

The public is there watching. The mothers and fathers are there at those schools nearly every day. These community school boards have been elected by a very aroused populace. The children themselves are aware of how well the school is run or misrun. And for us to assume that simple political patronage will move people into these positions and that no questions will be asked, I think is to assume the ridiculous.

Quite the opposite. What does obtain is when parents and community school board superintendents are all told, "You must select people from this list," this list of people they have never seen, whom they don't know the backgrounds of, who may not even be adequate to the job to be done, and they are locked into this by law, I would say the money might be better spent helping the school boards to find ways to gain leaders, to attract leaders to their districts, and certainly, much of that money might be better spent investing it in the schools to help the children learn.

Thank you.

THE CHAIRMAN: Mr. Tractenberg.

MR. TRACTENBERG: Excuse me. I have just a couple of brief questions.

Mr. Donaldson, do you have specific reactions from your

vantage point now as a community superintendent to particularly obvious roadblocks in the system? And by system, I don't mean just the examination process, but the recruitment process as well, and I suppose I may as well couple it with whether you have any specific suggestion for an alternate system or modifications in the present system?

MR. DONALDSON: Yes. First of all, in terms of reactions, my reaction is this, that if you want to be effective in the system, you go along with the system. If you are going to be a renegade, you pay the price of the renegade. The few items which I pointed out here of harassment are just a few of numbers of others which have come along.

I can cite another one. The Board of Examiners has granted for years what are called certificates of competency, particularly within the reimbursable fund areas, such as your Title I money and your state urban money. If you wish to have a special program going on in your schools, or in the neighborhood, say, on weekends or evenings underwritten by Title I funds, if you wish to have a ballet instructor for which there is no specific title, there is no specific title as teacher, you then have to send that candidate down to the Board of Examiners for an examination.

The examination is usually a kind of a cursory thing, the person examining the candidate usually knows less about the subject and the field than the person who is being examined. It sometimes takes a few months, usually a certificate of competency is given for the life of that program, and only for that specific position.

Now, as deputy superintendent, I noted that dozens of these were given simply on the superintendent's signature alone, this was just a matter of cost because the Title I programs were given. When I became superintendent in the district, the moment I sent for a second one in my first week in the job, I was told that there was a list that was in existence and that I could find a comparable candidate from the list to do the same job. You see, the subtle way of telling you that now you are going to gain a little more resistance. You find this comes through in many ways. You find that you are made to assume a posture which really doesn't exist.

A few weeks ago when I addressed the Synagogue Council in New York City along with Al Shanker and Walter Degnan, Mr. Warshaw, the principals' president and Mr. Rockowitz, who was here at this table earlier this morning, said to the rabbis assembled, "This gentleman's association objected to our going down to Puerto Rico to recruit Puerto Rican candidates."

And, of course, with this kind of inflammatory statement the rabbis were quite surprised, and they shook their heads as if to say, "We couldn't believe it." I said, when I was able to get the floor after his lengthy diatribe, I said, "What Mr. Rockowitz forgot to say was we also objected to any other junkets all over the United States to find capable people who are already sitting in New York City."

You see, if you want to go junketing, I think you should at least do it under a different guise than seeking candidates who are already here in the school system. Junketing is part of the game now. They suddenly have to go to Washington, D.C. to find Black candidates. They have been here in the school system all along. They have been effectively roadblocked from coming to the top.

Actually, the school system prevents candidates from coming to get into the school system. It has been well known. You go outside New York City, the word is "It's a closed system," a well-used phrase.

What is the point of coming here and waiting an entire two-year period to take an exam? The exams used to take at least two years if they were supervisory exams. Another year to promulgate the list, and you are likely to wait three, to four, to five years to be appointed. No one is going to put up with this nonsense. The examination discouraged people from coming into the system.

Now, this was known. Your teaching examinations were scheduled at the convenience of the Board of Examiners, not in terms of attracting candidates and utilizing them, strictly in terms of what was for the convenience of the Board. (There was one with parts that were scheduled, I believe, 14 years apart. You actually could go through an entire career before you were eligible to take another exam.) Therefore, you had a type who went in for the exams, and who put up with the nonsense. Yet despite this, we have actually been able to gain good people in the school system despite the examinations.

I can give you another little instance here, involving Mr. Rockowitz, when he was principal, when the list appeared in 1966 --the longest list in history by the way. As an appropriate advent for decentralization they simply decided they would give us as a present such a long list that we would be bottled up for the total decentralization period with candidates. And here, with the longest list in history, of over 400 names, a total of six Black candidates were on this list for principal. And yet, one person whose name took six months to get on the list, who was left off at the beginning, was an assistant principal who had worked in Mr. Rockowitz' school as an assistant to him, who disagreed with him on school policy, who had expressed her disfavor with the way he ran the school on a number of items and was effectively disciplined by being inconvenienced throughout this examination. She knew it. Everyone else knew it, particularly the Black supervisors. Only when she got legal counsel was she at least able to get the reason why she was being roadlbocked. And finally, when she got her license, there sat her name at the very bottom of the list with a 30-point leeway, which no one has been able to explain in terms of how they calibrate experience and how they calibrate the points granted. Thirty points could have practically put her at the top of the list. You see, this is part of the game.

Now, as for the solution. Within New York State, of course, we have state certification as the minimum essential. I am certainly not in favor of just inviting anyone who comes along to make him head of the school, or to invite him in to start teaching in the classroom. But I think we do have insight with these community school boards. And with their constant reference to parents groups who are in the schools, we do have the people who are most aware of the needs of that particular situation.

For instance, we have nearly 900 schools in the New York City system. With those 900 schools your variation is so wide that it's hard to even include them over one denominator. You may have a school with just a few hundred youngsters. You may have another school three times as large. You may have a person who is originally what is called a junior principal, now is a principal of a school where he has no assistant principal. You may have a person with the exact same license, exact same salary, who is supervising five assistant principals in one huge plant where thousands of youngsters come and go each day. Now, the needs of those schools, the turnover of staff, the background of staff, all of the pertinent information to get that job done, the people on the site know.

I think, therefore, we have to put into their hands the wherewithal to attract leadership for these schools, and to examine that. And I think this is where we at least give them some of the money which is being wasted on this central remote Board which is completely irrelevant, make it available to them to pull in consultants and let them do the selecting. I believe they should still be accountable. I think their methods of selection should be made public, and I believe they should be reported back to the central Board and to the Chancellor. But I think any other kind of confinement on their ability to function effectively will leave us in the dilemma in which we find ourselves, schools which no one wants.

It's a known thing now among the CSA people that they have written off certain schools, "We won't bother to fight for those." I think this perpetrates a racist system, where people feel, "Is this a minority school in Harlem no one wants? We'll allow a Black supervisor to take that." I think that's the worst kind of education you can give children.

So, I think the future movement has to be to give the people on site, the parents and the community school boards, the right and the flexibility to attract leadership, to recruit it, and then to examine for it, and then to report publicly as to the methods and means they have used and make this accountable back to the public. I think there alone, just knowing the nature of the job to be done, you don't have to worry about too much hanky panky. Believe me, you are going to find capable leadership. We have to do it despite the system and the confinements of it.

MR. TRACTENBERG: That's all I have. Thank you.

THE CHAIRMAN: I want to thank Mr. Donaldson for coming forward today. Just as we had this morning, we had testimony from the point of view of professionals who administer this system, based on the facts as they saw them. It's been particularly important to hear testimony of this force from a professional who, it should be noted for the record, is fully licensed, who comes here to testify not out of any personal inability to get through the system, but clearly is motivated by something else. He comes with particularly impeccable credentials.

The Commission takes note of and wishes more information

to be provided with respect to the very disturbing testimony about people on the list not wishing to go into these minority schools. It has been particularly anguishing to try to reconcile that testimony with testimony that the lists are so important. The Commission would regard the fact of minority parents being unable to get people on the list to accept jobs, while the school system insists that these people come from the list, as a situation fraught with such danger that it, quite apart from the underlying subject matter of these investigations, is of special interest to us. Therefore, I would ask Mr. Donaldson in his capacity as a community superintendent, in his capacity as the leader of his association, to provide us with more information on that particular phenomenon, which of all the facts that have been brought out here at these hearings, I must say I find the most disturbing. And I thank you very much for having come forward.

With apologies to Mr. Hayes, Mr. Hunter and Miss Lehrman, I have been notified that Mr. Victor Gotbaum has urgent business, and I am sympathetic with that. Many of the unions associated with District Council 37 are now in negotiations. If any other person has urgent business, which means that I should do what otherwise would be unfair, that is, put him ahead of someone, I wish you would send that information to me.

But I think we are fortunate that Mr. Gotbaum was willing to take time out of his schedule at what must be a terribly busy time for the Council. Therefore, I would like him to come forward now.

MR. GOTBAUM: It's terrible to start out with a disclaimer, Madam Chairman, but your previous speaker had impeccable qualifications. I have absolutely none in this field. And when Mr. David spoke to me, I told him I represented no teachers and no supervisors.

We are the largest public service union in the city, perhaps in the country, in terms of a single unit, but I am absolutely both hopeless and helpless in this particular area. I could only talk to a Civil Service system of hiring and promotion, and I do it apologetically. It's a terrible way to begin, but I must do this.

THE CHAIRMAN: Well, for the record, Mr. Gotbaum, I want to state that it is precisely your ability to look at the overall public service system that makes your testimony very much desired by us today. We are dealing with one large component of public service. And what we have not had until now is any notion of how it looks as compared with the overall picture of public service which is, of course, your domain.

MR. GOTBAUM: Well, let me run through this barefoot and just, you know, throw some general things on the table. And then, if you have any questions, I would be glad to answer them.

First and foremost, I think there is a terrible need for flexibility in terms of hiring and promotion, but I think this can be done within the Civil Service system.

I think it is a terrible mistake we make when we talk about doing away with the Civil Service system as a means for improving the hiring practices and the promotional practices. I don't think this has to be done. I think that you can keep the Civil Service system, and at the same time within that system provide the much-needed flexibility.

I would also state that I think you would be defeating the purpose of career development if you did away with promotion from within. Our union is a strong believer in this. We believe that once you deny people promotional opportunities you set up a demoralizing mechanism that will frustrate and hurt more than improve.

There is almost a magnificent shibboleth on the need for bringing in outsiders as though this is a tremendous cure, and it's really going to do the job. I think if attention is paid to the mechanism within, that promotion from within can provide what is needed in the system.

Now, I believe that the curse of Civil Service, the tragedy of Civil Service, is that attention has not been paid to the supervisors and the standards setting up supervisors. I hate to make this binding statement, but I would say that almost throughout the entire system we have supervisors who don't know a damn about supervision. They just don't know. They don't understand the span of supervision. They don't understand the delegation of authority. Not only that, they are not given the means and the ability to be able to do the job in this regard.

When you look at the system, and what happens there, we are a technical system. So that a teacher may grow full blown into a supervisor, but we do nothing about really making them a good supervisor. I am using that, although I am a little hesitant, because that's not my area.

But in our area, for example, we know in a hospital system, or in other areas of Civil Service, you can promote a person upward and then give him supervisory responsibility, but he doesn't have the ability to supervise. The administrator, the supervisor, is a very sensitive, tough, demanding job. And not only that. Regretfully, the system really hasn't provided him with enough ability to make decisions. By that I don't mean just he as an individual, but the system itself militates against giving him the flexibility, the ability to make decisions, to bring excitement to the job, to excite the people working with him, working near him. So, as a result, this promotional opportunity into middle echelon leadership is very bad indeed. And I really know of no system-- no system--that can rise above bad leadership, not even the labor movement, if I may add parenthetically.

As for hiring practices, it's almost impossible for me to talk in the whole area of credentials. Let me just generalize.

While we have to be concerned about the changing of credentials, we must be concerned about the changing of these credentials without diminishing standards. We have to try to define what does a person really do on the job. But even more important--even more important--how does he grow in the job? How does he obtain satisfaction in the job? How does he make a contribution in the job? And if in the changing of credentials you don't pay attention to this, you fail.

Let me give you a minor example of this in our field and

some of the difficulty we have had. They did away with the need for the high school credential for the entry level clerk. The union stood by when they did this because we felt it would not lower the standards for the entry level clerk, because it was a very simple job, with very simple tasks, and, frankly, you didn't need the high school credential.

So John Doe gets the job. He now does a simple task. He doesn't have his high school diploma. But where does he go? What has he got to look forward to? Because the next level, and the level above that, and the level above that, become more demanding. He then has to begin to make decisions, or he may become a supervisor. Without high school equivalency you are making a demoralized dead end worker out of this civil servant. You have taken away the credential need for the entry level, but he has no place to go.

I am happy to announce that the most forward-looking high school equivalency program is that begun by our union, which we got through collective bargaining, because the city really didn't provide it, because we were dismayed by the fact that when clerks came in there would be no opportunity for them for upward escalation.

So that I think you must look at, not so much the credentials --or let's say that you must look at the credentials--but you have to look at standards as well as the credentials and where the individual is going to go and what it means once you change the credentials. It's terribly important in both hiring and promotional practices. I will submit to you that we have to plan for a progressive transition that makes sense for all concerned.

And let me give you a subjective confession of a labor leader. And that is, as a labor leader, I must be terribly worried about the security of the people I represent. But also as a labor leader, in terms of my responsibility to the communities, I have to be dreadfully worried that the whole public service system makes sense to the very people we serve.

Now, this is a very sensitive, very, very difficult line that you have to walk. How do you equate the security of your members with the needs of the community, and can they merge? We can take lessons from other geographical areas. And I know they can be merged. There are Civil Service systems that are much more exciting than our own, that make a helluva lot of sense, where the worker gets paid and the community doesn't bitch half as much as they do here in New York.

In the federal system, for example, promotional opportunities are from within almost without exception. The British and French Civil Service systems are dignified systems, where the people in the systems have a great deal of prestige, where the community praises the system and looks upon it with a constructive attitude. So, I think it can be done, and it should be done.

I was going to finish off with the final note that all of the things I had to state really have nothing or little to do with decentralization. And I almost don't have the nerve to do this, because the previous speaker spoke far longer than I did and far more efficiently and proficiently, and he didn't even mention decentralization, because it really is not necessary.

I think if there is one beautiful thing about decentralization, it has brought all of these problems, all of these difficulties to the public scene. It's made us all a little more concerned. We are beginning to discuss them. We are beginning to plan around them. This is good. This makes sense. If only for that reason, I was very much in favor of decentralization, if it brings the problems closer to the citizens. If they begin to worry about them, if they begin to wrestle with them, it makes a lot of sense.

But if we sloganize the hell out of each other, if we talk about community control without understanding the responsibilities of community control, if we cling to a status quo--and finally, as a labor leader, let me talk to that--if we cling to a status quo in Civil Service that no longer makes any sense, in the long run we will kill and destroy Civil Service.

I know of no alternative to the system. Richard Joseph Daley in Chicago has given us an alternative. I don't think he really liked it. I don't believe that social patronage or political patronage has really been an answer. I think we have to revitalize the system. I think we have to understand necessary changes. I think we have to work with it. We can only work with it if we plan with it, if we stop Solomonizing with each other, and if we look at it in terms of what makes sense to the dispensers, to the workers, to the staff, and what makes sense to the public we serve.

I just throw these happy thoughts on the table. If you have any questions, I will be glad to answer them.

COMMR. COLGATE: Thank you, Mr. Gotbaum.
First, do the Commissioners have any questions?
Mr. Tractenberg.
MR. TRACTENBERG: I only have one question of Mr. Gotbaum.

You referred frequently to the Civil Service system. I just want to make sure I understand what you mean by that.

Does that necessarily imply a system based on written examination?

MR. GOTBAUM: No, not at all. In fact, I think the written exam, the written exam ought to be regarded as a diminishing vestige. In fact, the truth of the matter is, the person most negative about the written exam was the civil servant himself. I get more grievances about the written exam by civil servants than I do certainly from the public, who are not interested, because it just doesn't do the job. It can't define the job.

We know about the professional exam taker, the guy who spends hours studying for the exam, and then he may become a supervisor. And hell, he becomes a lousy supervisor. But, and this is the caveat, I must admit to you, before you can do away with the exam, as they have done in the federal service in the main, before you can do away with the promotional exam you have to substitute an enlightened middle echelon bureaucracy. And I am using the word "bureaucracy," in positive sense. You have to create an atmosphere in the system, whether it's the Board of

Education or whether it's the New York City Civil Service system, where a guy is rewarded for production, he knows his work is looked at.

What you have now, and what the exam very often does is this--one, two, three, four, five guys are working in the same place, and they're waiting for the exam to be given. So why attach a motor to your behind and really do a job and really work at it if this is what you have to wait for?

So, I think that sooner or later we need a transition away from the exam. But notice, I use the word transition, because you can't chop it away. And I really believe that the civil servant himself, who is the biggest and one of the best critics of the exam, should be brought into play on this.

MR. TRACTENBERG: Thank you.

COMMR. COLGATE: Mr. Gotbaum, thank you very much for your intensely revealing, candid thoughts. We appreciate very much your being with us.

May I call Mr. Lloyd B. Hunter, President of the Institute for the Advancement of Urban Education, and a former New York City teacher.

MR. HAYES: Sir, my name is Dennis Hayes. I was scheduled to speak after Mr. Donaldson, and I have been here. I was here yesterday morning because of an error in the assignment. I was here early this morning for my time, and I know that Mr. Hunter will be helpful, but I think--

COMMR. COLGATE: I will tell you what. Do you want to solve this, or should we do it with a flip?

MR. HAYES: I don't see what that has to do with it.

MR. HUNTER: If that is the problem, you want to speak, go ahead.

COMMR. COLGATE: Mr. Dennis Hayes, Program Director, Pre-Service Training Unit, the Board of Education.

Is that correct?

MR. HAYES: Yes.

THE CHAIRMAN: Just let me say that we have put a special burden upon all of today's witnesses, as we had yesterday, to some extent. They are all people who work hard for a living and feel about this issue such that they have taken time from their busy days to come here, and then they come here and find that they have been put over very long because of the way the testimony has been going.

I have tried to explain that the problem has arisen because of the special need to elicit lengthy testimony from the Board of Examiners and the need to examine them thereafter.

Then, on top of that, we have tried to make special arrangements for people who had emergencies, because we would feel very bad if somebody came to give testimony and didn't get to give it.

I am sorry for this misunderstanding. And I ask my staff to speak personally with each person to make sure no such misunderstanding occurs again, because once these two gentlemen got together there was no problem.

Go right ahead.

MR. HAYES: Thank you, Madam Chairman.

One of my duties at the Board of Education is to take care of the Professional Promotional Seminars, and I was called to speak on this topic. I will address myself to the eight items that were listed in the letter about which you wanted information.

The first was about the history, philosophy of the program and description of any similar programs that are supported by the Board of Education.

Yesterday Dr. John B. King gave a very eloquent description of the beginning of the professional seminars, and I certainly don't expect to give a better description. But I would like to say that after the initial program was started, which Dr. King described, the seminars were expanded to include not only the assistant principals' exam, which was the first one that was taken into consideration, but many other licenses.

The question about the length of these: These seminars were usually not as long as that first one, which stretched out over 18 months. But the seminars do take care of the written test, the interview test; and sometimes there are other tests, conference tests, classroom teaching tests, and so on; and if so, then these are included in the seminars.

Traditionally in New York City, private individuals have conducted courses to help train applicants for supervisory licenses. These are usually referred to as the coaching courses. Dr. King explained, and it was mentioned here again today, that the fees for these are rather high. And hoping that the professional seminars, by eliminating the high fees, would attract a greater number of minority group teachers, these courses were started.

Now the promotional seminars aimed at bringing the benefits of the coaching courses to all the candidates for supervisory licenses without great fees having to be paid. Besides the low fee, other steps were taken to insure that minority group teachers would be able to take advantage of these courses. The seminars were to be held in all five boroughs, wherever practicable in areas of high concentration of Blacks and Puerto Ricans. Special efforts were made to recruit minority group members.

One aim of these seminars was to give the applicants as thorough a training and preparation as possible both for doing well in the examination and for carrying out the responsibilities of the new position. Several of the instructors were staff members who had formerly conducted private coaching courses. The outline of the course and the notes prepared for distribution were written by a team of experienced supervisors. These supervisors also conducted the seminars at the various centers.

Among the people who played important roles in the planning of this program were four Black supervisors, all of whom hold the rank of superintendent. Dr. John B. King was Deputy Superintendent, Mr. Frederick Williams was Assistant Superintendent, although at that time he was Director of Inter-Group Education, I think it is called. Dr. Edythe Gaines and Dr. Henrietta Purcell were principals during the planning period and both have since been elected community superintendents.

The promotional seminars are one of the many programs sponsored by the Board of Education to assist people seeking supervisory and teaching licenses. For decades the in-service education program has offered courses that help teachers in their daily classroom work, as well as preparing them for supervisory licenses. Most of these courses were accepted as equivalent to university courses toward meeting the requirements of state certification. These courses are still being conducted as the Voluntary After School Professional Development Program, and they are joining up with the State College Proficiency Examination System so that they will get the college credit.

The Office of Personnel also conducts classes for oral and written English. These courses are offered to assist applicants who have been rated as unsatisfactory in either the oral or written part of the teaching exams. Applicants who are trained in foreign countries and for whom English is a second language are also encouraged to enroll in these courses.

Yesterday Dr. Lang and Mr. Williams had pointed out that most of the people enrolled in these courses come from minority groups. During the past five years, the Board of Education has also sponsored the Intensive Teacher Training Program to train liberal art graduates for teaching. This program has not been in operation since the 1968-69 school year because the need for teachers has been less severe.

In addition to these courses, under the supervision of the pre-training unit, the Board of Education sponsors several programs aimed at recruiting qualified personnel for the New York City school system with an emphasis on training staff members from minority groups. You have heard from some of these. Mrs. Hicks of the Bureau of Teacher Recruitment was here yesterday to speak for them. Mr. Atwell was here to speak from the paraprofessional program. I don't know if anybody was here to speak from the bilingual teaching program, but details of these particular programs would be available from the several bureaus involved.

A second question that was asked was the total budget allocation for this program of professional seminars. I have the figures for the last three years. In 1968-69 there was $101,749 for personnel services, and $1,550 for other than personnel services. In 1969-70 the personnel services was increased to $104,152, other than personnel services remained at $1,550. And for '70-'71 it was increased to $118,862 for the personnel services, and the other figure remained the same.

The third question concerned the staff of the promotional seminars. You wanted to know about the full-time staff and the regular positions of any part-time personnel assigned.

The following people are on the full-time staff: there is an elementary school principal, one assistant principal, one personnel examiner, and two stenographers.

The part-time staff is a much larger staff. Now, this part-time staff is fluid and changes with each seminar. Some members have a long record of service, but new members are recruited regularly. During the period from January 1st, 1970, to December 31st, 1970, this part-time staff included four high school principals, four junior high school principals, ten elementary school principals, five attendance supervisors, two other supervisors, six guidance supervisors, twelve school secretaries, and one acting director. Whenever feasible, minority group instructors are involved in these seminars. Of those listed above, seven are Black, but no Puerto Rican supervisors were involved during the last year. Not all of the Black supervisors served during the entire period.

One difficulty in recruiting staff for these seminars is the policy of the Board of Examiners that disqualifies seminar instructors from any service as examination assistants. This continues for two years. After completing work in the seminars most supervisors, including Black and Puerto Rican, prefer to serve with the Board of Examiners than with the seminars.

The next question concerned the supervisory licenses covered by the seminars. For the elementary schools we have conducted seminars for the license of assistant principal, for principal, and also for guidance counselor.

We have in the junior high schools the assistant principal exam, and the exams for chairman, and teacher trainer. And we have had the seminar for principal, and also for guidance counselor.

In the high schools we have had seminars for assistant principals in administration and assistant principals in supervision. This type was formerly chairman. And we have had seminars for guidance counselor.

For the several bureaus of the Board of Education, we have had the supervisor or CFRMD, supervisor of early childhood education, supervisor of education for the physically handicapped, supervisor of educational and vocational guidance, and supervisor of school social workers. We have also had district attendance supervising officer, and we have had seminars for the Assistant Director for the Bureau of Hearing Handicapped Children, and also for the Bureau of Visually Handicapped Children.

The next question concerned the numbers who have participated in the various seminars including the percentage of Black, Puerto Rican, and other. And also the question was asked about the percentage of those who were not already employed by the New York City school system.

Well, these seminars are sponsored by the Board of Education as an in-service training program. They were never intended to be open to the public at large, as college and university extension courses might be. Accordingly, all participants were already employed in the New York City school system. There have been a few exceptions to that, but generally that was the rule.

Now I have a table here showing the various licenses or seminars that were conducted in the last few years with the numbers of Black, Puerto Rican, and other candidates, and the percentages. I don't see any point in going through this unless you are interested in any particular one. And you have copies of this already.

Now, the sixth item that was asked, several questions about the seminars, the time required for participation in them, procedures by which it was made possible for applicants to participate in the seminars.

As far as the duration of the seminars, these vary in length. For the interview test we generally have arranged for three two-hour sessions. For the written test we have had as few as four two- or three-hour sessions, and as many as fourteen two- or three-hour sessions. These are the more recent seminars, not the one that was described yesterday by Dr. King. For the classroom teaching test we hold generally just a single two-hour session.

As far as the timetable is concerned, we try to offer as many choices as possible. If large numbers are involved we plan for sessions to be held on Tuesday, Wednesday, Thursday in the late afternoon, and on Saturdays, with at least one session in each borough. This schedule permits options to teachers who are taking university courses or who have other responsibilities. Sabbath observers are not penalized, since parallel courses are given on other days.

As far as publicizing the seminars, these seminars are always announced in special or general circulars that are distributed regularly to all schools, bureau offices, district superintendent offices and to some private organizations, such as the Urban League, that are on the mailing list of the Office of Information Services. Mr. Mark Price, editor of the Staff Bulletin, publicizes these courses in his paper, which comes out about 13 times a year. The Chief and the Civil Service Leader carry stories of the program, as do sectional papers and those that serve minority groups, for example, the Amsterdam News. Recently the seminar for the license of district supervising attendance officer was publicized widely by a news release to newspapers and professional organizations. After the initial part of the seminar, applicants who registered for the original seminars are usually notified of subsequent sessions of the seminar. Sometimes this can't be done because of pressure of time.

Now accommodations are made to attract as many teachers as possible. Many high school teachers, for instance, work late sessions. Some seminars are geared to the high school teachers, which are, therefore, scheduled for the early evening hours rather than starting at 4:00. Attendance teachers generally work until 4 p.m. The seminar for district supervising attendance officer was accordingly scheduled for 4:45 p.m.

Recruiters are employed to inform minority group eligibles of the opportunity available and to help them take advantage of the various course offerings. These recruiters are minority group supervisors who have already successfully completed promotion examinations.

The next question referred to the percentage of participants in the seminar who were successful as compared with the overall percentage of successful candidates.

Well, it was very difficult to determine accurately the percentage of successful candidates. I don't have that information, because many people sign up for the seminar who do not eventually apply for the examination. Some drop out because they find they do not qualify for the license, others because they cannot devote the time to study. Some who do apply for this examination do not appear for the test. This may be because of illness or other personal reasons. So I don't have the information that was requested. However, if it is needed, I will be able to spend some time and hopefully get that information.

The last question referred to the relationship between the promotional seminars and the Board of Examiners. "If any," it says. That is, any cooperation with respect to describing the contents of the seminar and also the relationship between the promotional seminars and the private coaching courses, if any.

Generally, the only information I get from the Board of Examiners is what is already available to the public. The list of exams is published early in each term and sent to all the schools, sent to many other officers. And notices for an exam, when it is finally officially announced, are also sent out to the schools, and so I get the information at the same time as the general public.

Each announcement of an examination by the Board of Examiners contains two parts that are of particular interest to the Professional Promotional Seminars unit. One is the scope of the examination, and the other the duties of the position. The scope of the examination informs all interested parties of the various phases of the examination--the written test, what type it will be, the total interview, field test, conference test, teaching test, evaluation of record and so on. In the duties of the position the responsibilities are listed, those responsibilities that must be assumed by all appointees under the particular licenses. We try to prepare the applicant for the performance of these duties. We do this because they may well be discussed in the examination, but also because we feel obligated to help the applicants assume the responsibilities of the position.

The Board of Examiners has traditionally held itself aloof from coaching courses that prepare candidates for license examinations. It maintains this same attitude toward the Professional Promotional Seminar instructors. The instructors are restricted from serving as assistant examiners for a period of two years after participating in a seminar.

Whenever we announce a seminar in a special or general circular, I almost immediately get a letter from Miss Unser or Dr. Greene asking for the list of instructors. As a matter of fact, although my position as director of the program does not bring me into close contact with candidates, and even though I do not receive any special compensation from this position, I have been excluded from any assignment as an assistant examiner. Furthermore, although the promotional seminars are concerned only with promotional opportunities, I am not even allowed to interview teachers for giving teachers' licenses.

The Professional Promotional Seminars Unit has no relation with any private coaching course. As a matter of fact, in the last two years, I have direct knowledge of only one such course.

I happened to notice on one of the bulletin boards at 65 Court Street the announcement of a course for the interview. Earlier witnesses have testified about the great number of these courses, but I personally have no idea how many such courses are now being held.

Now, I have addressed myself, Madam Chairman, to the topics that you have indicated were of interest to the Commission. I realize that the Professional Promotional Seminars have been prominently mentioned in some of the earlier interviews conducted in this inquiry. I shall be very happy to try to clarify any other aspects of the program about which you may desire further information.

THE CHAIRMAN: Thank you, Dr. Hayes.
Mr. Tractenberg.
MR. TRACTENBERG: Yes. I have just two questions.

Mr. Hayes, first of all, Dr. King yesterday described the philosophy of the promotional seminars, at least at the inception when he had a role in them, as basically designed to teach people to take the promotional test, and not as designed to teach them to be good supervisors.

Is that still the philosophy?

MR. HAYES: No. We continue to give people help in examination techniques. For instance, in the last seminar for elementary school principal, we had 14 sessions, and at each session, three or four different topics were considered. During the first session, we had this unit on examination techniques preparation for the short-answer test, and so on.

Now, during the course of the seminars, the instructors do point out--give the applicants help in answering the questions, but to say that it is our prime objective is no longer the case. We do make a very special effort to help the people to become good supervisors. If it's a supervisor of guidance, they learn about the borough. These seminars help them to learn how to work with beginning teachers, or new people in the position, how to supervise, how to have a training program, how to innovate in the program and so on.

So that I would say that 90 percent of our emphasis is on the duties of the position, the curriculum. For instance, for the elementary school principal or for the assistant principal, we would spend a great deal of time on the curriculum, the objectives of the various curriculum areas, the social studies program, the reading program, and so on, so that the people who are taking the examination not only will be able to pass the exam, but they will know what is expected of a reading program, what is expected of a math program and so on.

MR. TRACTENBERG: The other question is of interest to me because of the long colloquy this morning with Dr. Greene and that is your statement that you have difficulty getting supervisors to work with you in the promotional seminars because they seem to prefer to serve as assistant examiners.

Have you identified any reasons for this preference?

MR. HAYES: Well, if we are going to have a seminar, say,

for the interview test--for the elementary school principal, we had 17 different centers for the interview and this was going to call for three sessions. Now that means that if somebody served on that seminar for the three sessions, for the next two years he wouldn't be able to serve as an assistant examiner, and economically it would be much more to his advantage to serve as an assistant examiner.

That isn't the only reason. I have several--well, I am thinking of one Black supervisor in particular--who feels that she can do a much better job as an examiner than she could as a teacher and instructor in the seminar; and, therefore, she preferred not to work with the seminars but to continue to work with the Board of Examiners.

MR. TRACTENBERG: Is your pay scale the same, though, the same hourly compensation?

MR. HAYES: No. The instructors in the seminars from the beginning have been getting $25 an hour for the instructional period. The Board of Examiners, I think, now pays about $13, but I am not sure of what the rate is. By the way, that fee, or that sum, was determined in the last bargaining contract. The professional seminars are still paying the fee that John King instituted when he started this in 1963.

I must say, however, that we do give additional time for preparation, more than was given in the original program.

MR. TRACTENBERG: Thank you.

THE CHAIRMAN: All right. Thank you, Mr. Hayes. I appreciate your testimony. I want to now call Mr. Lloyd B. Hunter. And I want to say a special word of tribute to Mr. Hunter for his graciousness in allowing Mr. Hayes to testify before him. Mr. Hunter is obviously as busy as everyone else. He is President of the Institute for the Advancement of Urban Education. He is a former New York City schoolteacher.

MR. HUNTER: Thank you, Madam Chairman.

Before giving my brief statement, I have one request. Actually I still find myself somewhat in ignorance as to the basic action component, or components, being thought of by this Commission in terms of bringing about some change, whether in fact it is for legislative relief or some other kind of relief. So, my statement might be somewhat harried. However, it will reflect my experience in the New York City Board of Education dating back to 1963. Furthermore, I would also like to be kept in touch with the action done, whatever that should be.

I have been a teacher of Spanish, French, English, and English as a foreign language, both in and outside the New York City public school system. I received my regular high school Spanish teacher's license from the New York City Board of Examiners in 1963. I taught junior high school and high school Spanish in the city system until 1966, at which time I served as Special Assistant to the Board of Education until 1967, whereupon I served as Assistant Director for ESEA Title III programs until 1968.

I am, in many respects, a product of the New York City

public school system. Having left my native Jamaica in my early teens, I attended William Howard Taft High School in the Bronx, from which I was graduated. I was admitted to the City College of New York on the strength of my high school average in 1952. I was graduated from City College three and one-half years later with a Bachelor of Arts degree in Spanish.

Upon graduation from college, I completed certain education courses at night and sought a New York City teacher's license in high school Spanish. I passed the written exam and failed the oral on the basis of, and I quote, "traceable foreignisms" in my speech. I was advised to attend a special speech clinic, which I did.

While undergoing special exercises designed to "correct foreignisms" in my speech in 1957, I entered competition for and was awarded a Fulbright Scholarship to attend the National Autonomous University of Mexico. There, I earned a masters' degree in Spanish language and literature and returned to the United States to apply for my teaching license once again. I failed the oral once more in 1959. I enrolled in Hunter College at night and eventually completed the Masters in Teacher Education.

I taught high school Spanish on Long Island from 1960 to 1963, where one did not have to take an exam to be considered qualified.

I finally got through both sections of the New York City teacher's license exam in 1963. If I recall correctly, this was the year of a massive drive spearheaded by the NAACP, the Urban League, and the Amsterdam News to increase the numbers of minority persons licensed by the Board of Examiners. To this day, I don't know if I really finally passed, or if I was merely the recipient of "preferential" treatment for minorities at the time.

In the three years of teaching in the New York City public schools that followed, I failed to see the relationship between the ritual of the exam, the struggling through the very many cryptic questions, the elimination of foreignisms in my speech, and performance in the classroom, let alone success with the youngsters. Furthermore, I soon learned that very often many holding very important supervisory and policy-making positions did not even have to take such an exam. I believe these were referred to as the certificates of competency.

Now, I have participated in similar inquiries before as to the effectiveness of the Board of Examiners. In fact, I believe the record will indicate that these inquiries have been conducted regularly in one way or another for the last ten years. I have made available to this Commission a paper which I authored in 1966 giving a brief history of the relationship between the Board of Education and the Board of Examiners from 1961 to 1965. I trust that the Commission will find this paper helpful in its endeavors.

All in all, my experiences with the subject leads me to the conclusion that much of the inconclusiveness of the previous inquiries has resulted from the fact that the question has been posed incorrectly.

The question has usually been asked, should the Board of Examiners be abolished? This question is usually doomed to failure, since it immediately invokes all the reverence of the merit system, competitiveness, quality, minimum standards, the American flag and apple pie.

Neither should the question be centered upon the number of minority groups the Board of Examiners has or has not licensed. For, if one focuses on the fact that it is an institution in this society, one can already conclude that it is discriminatory, reflecting the restricting biases and narrownesses of the larger society.

I submit that the real question must focus upon whether or not the Board of Examiners serves a valid purpose for any teacher, Black, white, or in between, and whether indeed that purpose serves the goal of assuring quality educational programs and products for the clients of the New York City public schools.

When compared with all the large cities which do not give competitive exams, there is no clear advantage to the City of New York in terms of teacher qualities and pupil achievement. In fact, a report prepared by the Board of Examiners in 1966 entitled, "Teacher Selection Policies and Procedures in Large Public School Systems in the United States," tends to support the view that written teacher exams appear to be more a function of the size and the "bureaucratic development" of the school system than anything else. The larger the system the more tendency to give written tests. Only 12.8% of 382 large public school systems studied gave written teacher exams.

Now, either we admit that 88% of the large public school systems in this country do not have meritorious systems subject to graft and corruption, or there is some serious questioning or inquiries to be made as to exactly how they attract teachers of quality.

I support the position that the examining function of the Board of Examiners through the use of written exams should be abolished. Any agency maintained should have as its basic function the major task of rendering service on an on-going basis for teacher training, teacher renewal, and the development of new professionals. This service should be closely related to the community and under jurisdiction where the needs are more greatly or more closely understood. This service would be available to the administrators, teachers, parents, paraprofessionals and students of the New York City public schools.

I would recommend the creation of such an agency with the fictitious title of the New York City Staff Development Agency. This agency would have three basic units and functions: first, a certification unit, which should have a small staff to continue the function of certifying as to the paper requirements of the teacher, which could be the city or state certification requirements which have been recommended, to my knowledge, repeatedly within the last ten years; secondly, there should be a medical unit which shall examine the potential teachers' physical and emotional stability and his or her ability as to the requirements of the position within which he or she intends to teach; finally, the basic function of this agency should be maintained by a unit for carrying out staff development and training functions. This unit would be staffed by practitioners, theoreticians and identified successful teachers, or master teachers, and, as stated before, would provide teacher training, teacher renewal, and staff development functions for new professionals on an ongoing basis. It would employ the latest techniques and training formats of staff development and differentiated staffing.

Some ideas of the specific functions of such a unit could be team teaching, individualized instruction, classroom management, career development, development of individual instructional objectives for students, flexible modular scheduling, individual skill development, nongraded formats, mechanisms for tapping student interests and relating the curriculum more closely to the students' interests, diagnostic and prescriptive methods for determining individual problems of each student and preparing teachers to meet those problems, utilizing the total community as an educational resource, use of instructional aids, such as videotapes and other audio-visual equipment, development of communication skills, and other types of administrative concerns.

I believe there are many persons in this city who can contribute to such a function if, in fact, this were to be seen as a possible alternative in attempting to certify the teachers' ability in the classroom prior to service, which the record indicates, I believe, has been a dismal failure on the part of the New York City system.

Thank you.

THE CHAIRMAN: Counsel.

MR. TRACTENBERG: Mr. Hunter, just a couple of questions.

First of all, could you advise us, in your current capacity as President of the Institute for the Advancement of Urban Education, what school districts you work with around the country?

I gather you have worked with many.

MR. HUNTER: Gary, Indiana; Washington, D.C.; San Francisco, California; Los Angeles, California; Ravenswood, California--

MR. TRACTENBERG: I'm sorry, I can't hear you.

MR. HUNTER: Gary, Indiana; San Francisco, California; Los Angeles, California; Ravenswood, California; Sacramento, California; Washington, D.C.; did I say--District 5 in New York City; District 3 in New York City. And I can go on.

MR. TRACTENBERG: Part of your function in serving those districts has been in the personnel area?

MR. HUNTER: No. Usually my function is in the area of staff training. Not personnel recruitment as such, but training of teachers once they are on the job.

MR. TRACTENBERG: All right. Would you mind telling us why you left New York City school system after struggling so hard to get into it?

MR. HUNTER: Basically, I think, because the New York City school system requires one to consider the system as a defensible and preservable, or worthy of being preserved, unit. And I think--for example, one of my functions as special assistant was to service a committee that was chaired by Mr. Aaron Brown, then Vice-President of the Board, to upgrade minorities in the school system. But by occupying this position I became aware of the fact, very early, that I was the--well, I guess--the "house nigger" to keep certain Blacks happy that were doing something, but at the same time to sort of be a go-between. For example, there was a specific demand placed on the table by CSA and several other unions that you could not go above a certain percentage of Blacks in any position because it would destroy the merit system.

Well, I think this led to certain frustrations. I think it is an old story. It's really quite well experienced by anyone who has been in this position. It's a question, really, whether or not you wish to continue to be a figurehead, to be a stopgap, or to choose other options. And I chose other options.

MR. TRACTENBERG: And finally, your recommendation provided for a vastly revised, but nevertheless, a central unit, as I understand it.

MR. HUNTER: Well, a central unit. It's really a skeleton. The emphasis is not on a central unit. I did not pretend to give you today a proposal in full detail. I am saying the function needs to be different.

I think the hiring should be local, should be related to each community. I think also the determination of those skills needs to be determined locally.

MR. TRACTENBERG: That's all I have.

THE CHAIRMAN: All right, thank you very much.

Miss Lehrman deserves a medal. Although she was due to go on at 12 o'clock, she waited through to this time.

MISS LEHRMAN: Eleven-thirty.

THE CHAIRMAN: We thank you for your patience.

MISS LEHRMAN: I am going to speak to you in acceptable New York City Board of Education speech--

THE CHAIRMAN: Please speak into that mike. (Indicating)

MISS LEHRMAN: I am going to speak to you in acceptable Board of Education speech. And I want you to know this New York accent is around me and has been since I attended elementary school and public high school and college. That is how I got to this, and I hear it every day. I don't like it, but I am stuck with it.

I just want to say that if there is any connection between the way teachers are recruited or selected for our school system and the paucity of minorities on our school staffs, then you really have to prove that the system we use is so wonderful that every other alternative is inferior.

As an elementary school teacher, I am somewhat aware of how tremendously this white face affects the children in our school.

For example, we had one Black teacher a few years ago when the population of our school was, at that time, I think, 45% Black and Puerto Rican, and the rest of it was "other." And this little Black kid came to school and saw the Black teacher and said, "You the cook?"

"No, I'm a teacher."
"You're not a teacher."
She took him to her room to show him around.
"Well, maybe you say you're a teacher, but I still think you're a cook."

Now, any system that permits that kind of perception by any child, whether the child is Black or white or Spanish, or whatever, has a great deal of defending to do as to its excellence.

Mr. Greene spoke about the fact that he was worried that if the examinations or if the qualifications were to be presented by local school boards, that the supervisor's image would be reflected in his staff. It seems to me the image I see reflected in my school and all the schools around me is some image that is not relevant to what the kids are. So Mr. Greene has to explain that image away, if he doesn't want another image to come in.

My experience in becoming a teacher--you heard this ad nauseum today--but I will say that I was a teacher in private schools in New York for a few years. I went out of the country for a few years, and when I came back, I decided I wanted to teach in a public elementary school in 1959. And I went to a friend of mine. I used his pull to introduce me to a principal he knew.

I was interviewed by this principal, very briefly, who then requested that I be given an emergency substitute examination.

Now, Mr. Greene said there are no such examinations any more, but there is something very similar now, because I know teachers in my school can go; and they have requested an examination and have gotten something.

I was very worried about whether or not I could pass this examination, but I was told by those--the old hands--that if I could inhale and exhale, I couldn't fail. And that was true of the examination, very simple and stupid, and I passed very easily. They didn't check any reference for anything except time served, and that was in order to establish my level of pay.

After two years, during which time I was on my own except for a few brief supervisory observations--and those were formal, I was warned of those--I decided I couldn't take it any more. I didn't like the teaching or the learning atmosphere and I wanted to leave, but the UFT then came in and won bargaining rights and I thought that gave promise that conditions would improve, so I stayed and decided to apply for a permanent license.

Passing this, I was told, would require more than an ability to breathe, and I was told where to go for this coaching thing. And I am not going to go through all that, but it was memorizing. They gave us old examinations and told us old answers and we were told that we mustn't stray from or challenge the status quo. There were certain answers to be expected from us. We weren't to use multi-syllabic words or complex sentences in writing them down because we might misspell them, or do anything to increase the statistical chance of error.

We were given the key vocabulary in fad that year in order to incorporate it into as many answers as possible. I spent two weeks memorizing meaningless phrases and sentences, all reminiscent of my long forgotten college courses.

It was apparent that I was neither expected to be intellectually or morally committed to, or capable of carrying out, any of the answers. This is just the kind of practice to which Albert Shanker objects so strongly in his criticism of performance contracting by local school boards--this kind of--coaching children to pass examinations. We are going and went through exactly the same thing, and it is reflected in our teaching of children.

I passed the examination, and there was no way they could tell whether I could communicate with children or not, because there were no children there for that examination. And while everybody was talking, I thought, all those examiners were white, they all were my people--and I don't mean that in an ethnic sense. I mean, they were New York City College people, the kind of people who talked the way I did; and that made me less afraid of them. I suppose if I was faced by a Black or Puerto Rican board, I might not feel as comfortable as I felt then, although I must admit I was slightly nervous.

Anyway, I passed the examination. And then I was observed, once more, again by appointment. The supervisor came into my room, with a lot of prewarning, and I prepared that lesson very carefully, and he complimented me very highly on that one observation. And, another thing, the United Federation of Teachers' Vice-President in charge of the elementary schools told us to discourage any visits other than these formal visits to the classroom. Those are prescribed observations.

There was no other substantial involvement on my part in any procedure except for the terrible, but routine, tangles at 110 Livingston Street, which I am not going to tell you about because that is irrelevant.

My probationary period ended that year and I became a teacher in the New York City school system for the rest of my working life, with the assurance of a pension at the time of my retirement. Now, should I become dissatisfied with teaching or should I find that in spite of a sense of fulfillment in my work, I lack sufficient money or status, I can go through a very similar routine to become a principal.

Now that is all the merit there is to the merit system. With small exceptions, all the teachers in New York City went through this routine, and it doesn't--well, just talking with my colleagues just to question this charade arouses a storm of indignation that, you know, it is the American flag and it is apple pie and it is all these things.

And I really can't understand why we feel that way about it, in a sense, because the whole procedure, from the irrelevant college courses through the testing, through attendance at the in-service courses, which have not been mentioned but which you need for salary increments--but they are insane, the courses are ridiculous--the whole process is so meaningless and so degrading that the very act of having submitted to this makes you feel that you are entitled--I mean, it is something that somebody owes you something for having done this to yourself. It is a case of sour grapes in reverse. The fruit proved to be so hard to swallow that we have to save face by proclaiming it, at least, nutritious.

Is it Mr. Gottlieb--

MR. TRACTENBERG: Gotbaum.

MISS LEHRMAN: Mr. Gotbaum says the people who object most to the Civil Service are the civil servants. And yet they are offended at efforts to change it, I think, simply because of this psychology: I have been through it, now you go through it.

But no teacher can seriously believe that this trial by fire has equipped him for the awesome responsibility of educating children.

Now, in order to educate a child, I must give him a sense of his own integrity and at the same time I've got to give him a sense of his connection, a reasoned connection with the world around him. Certainly the whole selection procedure doesn't even touch on this. I didn't have to believe one answer that I gave. I didn't have to be committed to it morally or intellectually, and I didn't have to believe that I was capable of carrying out anything. It was just a matter of memorizing. As a matter of fact, I was not committed to many answers that I gave.

In today's world, especially, for teachers to support the witless rituals of the Board of Examiners, as an assessment of their ability to meet that challenge, is either tragic or comic, depending upon one's quota of cynicism. If we are going to support a Board of Examiners' definition of our competence, we are victimizing ourselves as teachers as well as victimizing the children because, contrary to public opinion, our occasional successes and the warming thought of a guaranteed paycheck cannot compensate for the deep, personal sense of hopelessness and self-doubt which plagues practically every teacher. We are not happy. It is not an easy thing to fail day after day. But if we support the system's measure of success as valid, we only have ourselves to blame for our failure to educate such great numbers of children.

We can't say that the children aren't educable, even for the most liberal of sociological reasons, because then what do we need licensing for if we can't educate them? Anybody can baby-sit.

We won't accept the thesis that our failure is rooted in racism, for then it follows that we are cunningly selective in using our teaching skills; teaching the white kids and not the Black kids deliberately.

But it is also impossible that all the teachers of past and present generations of functional illiterates could have turned out to be, even by random chance, much less by deliberate design, fundamentally incompetent.

Now, the answer must be sought in a system which thwarts the potential of its teachers by freezing performance standards at the very low level of the granting of the license to teach. A system which confers the lifetime title of "teacher" upon us before we have had a chance to become teachers, and then slams the book shut, has failed in its responsibility to permit us to develop beyond second-rate professionals.

Many of us do go on trying to prepare ourselves for teaching long after we have been licensed and given tenure. That is when it starts, but that is when the system leaves us. There is all this elaborate procedure going on now--I didn't know about the seminars--but there is the three-million-some-odd dollars spent in testing and then it is finished; the responsibility of the whole Board of Education stops.

No longer am I talking about the Board of Examiners. But the Board of Examiners defines us, and by defining us as teachers at a certain point and then dropping everybody, that is the end.

The nature of our work requires that each school staff develop as a purposeful body with coherent relationships among all staff members and between staff members and the community in which they serve. No amount of isolated work or study can satisfy those needs. By isolated, I mean out of school, in strange places.

The members of the staff of my school have exerted Herculean efforts in an attempt to communicate with each other in an environment free from distractions and the pressures of time. But nothing of that nature can occur as one teacher passes the other on the way in and out of the classroom; or during the once-a-month, 40-minute staff meeting; or while rumaging around for lunch out of a brown paper bag; or after school when some of us are attending college courses, training courses, dreamed up somewhere, unrelated to our school and our community, and others are moonlighting as taxi drivers or housewives, and all of us are exhausted after a hard day of teaching, which would be hard even if we were all succeeding happily, which we are not.

Extensive, or even routine conferences, among teachers in our school, are infrequent. We can't talk about a child who was in our classroom or was going to be in our class. There is no routine conference, unless you happen to grab somebody at lunchtime. There are too few planning sessions with paraprofessionals.

There is no possibility of on-going consultations with poets, mathematicians, linguists--and I think the Board of Examiners ought to find out something about language and that all people don't have to talk in a certain way to communicate beautifully, but that is another question--carpenters, doctors or parents. We have to select books, practically at a moment's notice from a tremendous list that is confusing and doesn't tell us anything. In all my years of teaching, I have never been approached by a publisher for my opinion of a book. And the Board of Examiners has never come to me to ask, in my opinion, what I think teacher qualifications are, nor has the Board of Education.

I do not mean me, I mean teachers are not considered as a very important part of the system. We make very few decisions about changes in curriculum or methods which are foisted upon us by outside researchers and professional grant writers, without regard to our perceptions. In fact, several programs with contradictory methods and goals operate at one and the same time. As a unique school staff, we cannot even articulate our problems in the total absence of the opportunity to systematically examine and evaluate our own methods and goals.

By contriving to make it so difficult for teachers of a school to develop consistent professional relationships once we have been licensed, the bureaucrats of the central Board, our union, and lately the local school boards and the burgeoning education industries are not only expressing their contempt for, and low expectations of us, but in doing so are maintaining their power basis at our expense and the expense of the city's children.

Education is, and should be, everybody's business. And when we talk about the merit system and the spoils system, I think it is important to clarify the fact that the spoils system can exist if a man is in a big business and he can somehow wangle to get a guy into the Federal Tax Office who is going to make it easy for him in some way with taxes. But how can we speak of a spoils system when the parents of children who are attending school, when--yes, they have a self-interest. But the interest is a valid interest, and you can't refer to that as a spoils system.

If a principal wants me in a school or parents want a certain teacher and they say we really want her, and, so, forget that she's got a slightly Jewish accent or forget that she's got a slightly Spanish accent, or forget whatever you have to forget. We want her; we think she will be good for the children. That is not a spoils system.

And, on the other hand, if you are going to have the response of the community and local control, as Mr. Gotbaum says, it is terribly important that there be some stabilized lines, because I, for one, as much as I am for even smaller community school boards than we have, I want some guarantee of stability. I would feel uncomfortable if every time there is an election I would have to worry about whether or not my methods and myself is at stake. So there have to be some guidelines set, but I don't see why they can't be set once and for all by the community and maintained. And for a contract, or whatever it is that has to be dealt with, deal with the community.

But the point I really want to make is that this licensing procedure has made us impotent. Then, on top of that, the attitude of the Board of Education has furthered our impotency. And an impotent teacher cannot teach children to be independent, cannot give the power to learn to children. And it may seem a contradiction, but I feel that the Board of Examiners has removed power from us, and therefore, I would like to have it abolished.

That is all I have.

THE CHAIRMAN: Counsel?

MR. TRACTENBERG: Just one question, Miss Lehrman. Do you think that your perception of the selection practices and the ways the schools function is typical of the perception of a substantial number of your fellow teachers?

MISS LEHRMAN: No, and the reason I think that is that there is an atmospheric climate of being low man on the totem pole. It is built in from the time of the examination, by the examination; and from there on in, to think of being independent is incredible.

When I say that teaching and administration are two different things, that I don't think there should be higher salaries for administrators than for teachers, everybody thinks I am some raving maniac. When I compare elementary school teaching to university teaching--I teach at New York University--I think that the demands on the elementary teacher are tremendous intellectual demands. But very few elementary school teachers believe that, and this is the root of the kind of education we are giving to the children. We have no faith in ourselves.

MR. TRACTENBERG: Thank you.

THE CHAIRMAN: This is testimony from a teacher. We have been waiting a long time to hear from a teacher who can talk straight from the very heart of the firing line.

Thank you very much.

One second, please.

Next is Mr. Ira Glasser, Executive Director of the New York Civil Liberties Union.

MR. GLASSER: My name is Ira Glasser, and I am the Executive Director of the New York Civil Liberties Union. I testify here today in order to bring to the Commission's attention, two areas of special concern to NYCLU: racial discrimination in hiring and violations of teachers' rights.

We believe that the Board of Examiners' hiring procedures result in a pattern and practice of racial exclusion, unrelated to the needs and requirements of a merit system, and in many cases inconsistent with the needs and requirements of a merit system.

We also believe--and we have incontrovertible evidence to prove this--that the Board of Examiners is the single greatest violator of teachers' rights in the city. No one who truly supports teachers' rights could possibly fail to speak out vigorously against the Board of Examiners, whose arbitrary and unconstitutional procedures are the most persistent source of teachers' complaints to our office.

During the past year, more than 50 teachers have sought our help, alleging that their licenses were delayed, denied, or revoked for arbitrary and unjust reasons. NYCLU's investigations of these complaints have generally substantiated them, and we are currently representing several teachers in lawsuits against the Board of Examiners.

The most flagrant denial of due process that the Board of Examiners inflicts upon teachers is the so-called "records hearing." The teacher is called down to the "records hearing" without knowing why the Board wishes to see him. He has no idea what the "records hearing" will be about. He receives no notice of charges, no right to counsel, no right to confront evidence against him, no right to present evidence in his own behalf. He merely appears, is told orally that he has received "bad ratings," is asked whether or not he has anything to say, and then has his license revoked. This procedure, utterly without even minimum requirements of due process, has victimized many teachers. We are currently representing one such victim in an effort to impose standards of due process upon the Board of Examiners.

The procedures for denying licenses in the first place are as barren of due process as the revocation hearing is. We have evidence that licenses have been denied for the following reasons:

1. Refusal to release confidential Selective Service records.
2. Allegations of homosexuality.
3. Allegations of psychiatric disabilities.

It is important to note that these allegations are nowhere reviewable, or subject to a fair hearing. Once the Board accuses you, you are guilty. In one case, a woman who once saw a psychiatrist for a few months during the time she was getting divorced, was disqualified on psychiatric grounds, without a hearing and despite letters from private psychiatrists testifying to her health.

4. Membership in the Communist Party, or other controversial political beliefs. (Questions about such beliefs actually exist on Board of Examiner reference forms, which are sent to former employers or university placement offices.)

5. Illegal arrests, where no conviction occurred, in civil rights demonstrations. (NYCLU is currently representing a teacher who was denied her license due to an arrest during a civil rights march in the South many years ago. Another teacher has had his license denied due to a single conviction for putting his feet on a subway seat.)

6. Youthful offender convictions, where supposedly sealed records have been obtained by the Board, making it impossible for an adult to ever escape even a single mistake made during his youth. Needless to say, there is no right to a fair hearing in order to inquire into the particular facts of the case.

7. Physical irregularities, such as leg braces as the result of polio, the use of a cane or crutches, overweight, and underweight. The Board of Examiners even has a category on one of its forms called "excessively short stature" as a disqualifying factor.

These violations of the free speech and due process rights of teachers by the Board of Examiners are widespread, and are part of the pattern of arbitrary and irrational procedures that characterize the Board's conduct. Even though these hearings are not primarily addressed to the subject of teachers' rights, NYCLU's concern in this area compels me to bring it to your attention.

We believe that the Board of Examiners is the largest source of violations of teachers' rights, and we think that these violations flow from the same patterns of arbitrary conduct that result in racially exclusive hiring practices.

I would now like to address myself to racial discrimination in hiring, since that is the main purpose of these hearings.

During the past few years, there has been a great deal of conflict over the methods for selecting principals and teachers in the New York City school system. The conflict has been everywhere: in the courts, where dozens of lawsuits have been filed; in the State Legislature, where fierce lobbying efforts have taken place; in the media, where charges and countercharges have been hurled; and, tragically, in the schools themselves.

A great deal of the conflict has focused on the effort to abolish or substantially change the Board of Examiners. This is not the first time that such efforts have been made in this city.

In 1951, the Strayer & Yavner report was severely critical of the Board of Examiners. So was the Schinnerer report of 1961, and so was the Griffiths report of 1966. All these independent studies were commissioned by the Board of Education. All recommended either eliminating the Board of Examiners or radically changing its powers and procedures.

Similar recommendations have been made since the 1930's, and at least one president of the Board of Education, Max Rubin --who is now a member of the Board of Regents of New York State --made a substantial effort to change the Board of Examiners during the early 1960's. I know of no independent study that on educational grounds alone has not recommended either abolition or radical change of the Board of Examiners.

Despite the weight of independent educational opinion, however, the Board of Examiners has managed to resist such recommendations each time they have been made. Pressures for reform have usually been met by a rather successful scare tactic. Each time recommendations are made, the Board of Examiners launches a campaign of fright that says, in effect, that any change in the current procedures will eliminate the merit system of hiring, and sweep us all back to the dark ages of politics and patronage.

In fact, the reverse is true. The Board of Examiners itself is the single greatest obstacle to merit hiring, as every independent study of its procedures has concluded.

The response of the Board of Examiners and its supporters to this generation of critics is no different than past responses. We, too, are charged with seeking an end to merit hiring and a return to patronage. These charges are as false and as self-serving today as they have been throughout the years. As Dr. Harvey Scribner said in a speech accusing the Board of Examiners of "unduly limiting the choice of talent" available to the NYC schools.

"No one is against merit; no one is for favoritism.

"The point is that merit is not the exclusive possession of the present licensing system....

"The issue is not the scrapping of merit, the issue is the development of alternative and more valid means of reaching a common end." (Address, Anti-Defamation League of B'nai Brith, New York City, New York, October 29, 1970.)

This generation of critics, however, differs from previous generations. We are not only criticizing the Board of Examiner's educational results; we are criticizing its racial results. Unlike past critics, we accuse the Board of Examiners of perpetuating procedures that result in patterns of racial exclusion in hiring.

That such exclusion exists is beyond any factual dispute. According to a recent study commissioned by the Puerto Rican Forum, only 3.8% of principals and 9.1% of teachers in the New York City school system are Black. For Puerto Ricans, the situation is even worse. Puerto Ricans occupy only .4% of principals' positions, and only .8% of teachers' positions in the New York City schools. These figures are especially alarming when one realizes that since 1957, the percentage of Black and Puerto Rican pupils in the New York City schools has increased from 31.7% to 53.7%. Clearly, the Board of Examiners' procedures have not managed to change in response to changing student populations.

This refusal to change, this rigid incapacity to hire more than a vanishingly small number of Blacks and Puerto Ricans, contrasts sharply with the records of other comparable cities. To mention just a few, Philadelphia, Cleveland, Detroit, and St. Louis have not been anywhere near as restrictive in their hiring practices as New York.

One curious reason for New York City's restrictive procedures is that the Board of Examiners' systems were developed in the 1930's to keep out applicants because at that time there were many more applicants than available positions. To continue to use essentially the same hiring systems during the 1960's, when the schools were facing severe shortages of qualified and experienced teachers and principals is typical of the ossification that afflicts the Board of Examiners. What is worse, the people kept out through these obsolete procedures have been primarily nonwhite.

The response of the Board of Examiners to these charges of racial exclusion has been predictable. They have charged in return that those of us who want to end racial discrimination in hiring by abolishing or radically changing obsolete procedures are merely seeking to inject "ethnic" considerations into hiring procedures, thereby destroying the merit system.

That charge is both untrue and dishonest. The truth is that by relying primarily on written examinations that only test general levels of knowledge, no one can predict meritorious performance. There has never been any evidence that performance on a test is significantly related to performance on the job. Moreover, this school system--which now seeks to brand any injection of ethnic considerations as racist and irrelevant--has always in the past considered ethnic background as a highly relevant factor in assessing merit, especially in a city so heavily and variably ethnic as ours.

In fact, many of those school officials who now vigorously contest the appointment of principals on the basis of their sympathy and ability to work with a particular community, were themselves appointed many years ago for precisely similar "nonobjective" reasons.

Consider this evidence:

Twenty years ago, in the case of Barrett v. Fields, 196 Misc. 339, 92 N.Y.S. 2d 117 (1949), aff'd. 276 A.D. 907 (1950), aff'd. 301 NY 543 (1950), the then Superintendent of Schools, William Jansen, made the following sworn affidavit before the court:

"The personal qualifications of the candidate for the specific type of high school to which appointment is to be made is the paramount consideration in filling the position of High School Principal. If choice were limited to the first three persons on an eligible list in making appointment to a particular high school, the person selected might be utterly unable to cope with the problems, curriculum and type of school that would confront him, although he might be particularly well qualified to fill a vacancy arising at a later date in an entirely different type of high school....

"In every instance attempt is made to select as principal of a high school the person who appears to be preeminently qualified to fill the particular vacancy from the point of view of the special curriculum, social or racial problems and type of school involved."

Superintendent Jansen then goes on to give specific illustrations of what he means:

a) Haaren High school, where the particular principal was selected because Haaren was an industrial arts school and the principal selected was, as Jansen put it, "a good shop man."

b) Stuyvesant High School, which concentrates on mathematics and engineering, and where the particular principal was selected because "of his mathematics background.... and also because he held a B.S. degree in Engineering and had had practical experience in that field."

c) Morris High School, which according to Jansen "presented serious social and racial problems" and where the principal, Jacob Bernstein, was selected because of "his particular sympathy with and demonstrated ability to deal with the problems involved."

d) Benjamin Franklin High School, where Leonard Cavello was selected because "he spoke Italian and had a knowledge of and sympathy with the problems in an Italian neighborhood." (This example is particularly ironic. Last November, the Council of Supervisory Associations sued Dr. Harvey Scribner because he appointed Melvin Taylor, a Black educator, as principal of Benjamin Franklin at least partially on the grounds that Taylor had a special sympathy with and knowledge of the problems of the community, which had in the years since 1949, changed from predominantly Italian to predominantly Black.)

e) DeWitt Clinton High School. This example is the most revealing of those that Jansen used in his statement to the Court 20 years ago. As he said then, "This is a boys' school that presented serious disciplinary problems. (The principal) was selected because he was a health education man with a fine athletic background, and because of his sympathy with and proven ability to handle these boys." Thus, this principal was chosen not by a mechanical, written, "objective" examination that tested only general standards of knowledge, but by nonobjective standards, including a standard of actual performance, that met the particular needs of that particular community.

That principal's name was Walter Degnan, the same Walter Degnan who now opposes selecting principals by any means other than a written, "objective" examination testing general academic knowledge, who now opposes selecting principals based on their "sympathy with and proven ability" to work with a particular community.

There are many Blacks in this city who believe that the rules always manage to change when it comes to them. This shameful history does little to dispel that belief, or the bitterness that goes with it.

The truth is that the merit system for hiring principals has always relied on qualifications that could not be tested by a general examination. As Stephen Bayne, another New York City Superintendent of Schools, said in that same court case 20 years ago:

"It cannot be reiterated too strongly that the efficient management of the educational system in New York City requires freedom and flexibility to ascertain the special traits and qualifications of candidates for... the high school principalship, and which cannot possibly be ascertained by a general examination.... It is an educational necessity to assign... as principals individuals who are particularly suited to meet the particular problems of given schools. The particular qualities required of the principal in a given situation cannot possibly be revealed in a blanket examination for the general position of high school principal.

"It would be detrimental to secondary education in New York City if the academic high school principals had to be assigned... on the basis of standards that might be called the general standards for a high school principalship."

The point should be clear. The effort to resist the appointment of Black principals to predominantly Black schools on the ground that "sympathy and ability to work with the community" is not a legitimate criterion flies in the face of the methods that have been used in this school system for over 20 years.

Walter Degnan, Leonard Cavello, Jacob Bernstein and Melvin Taylor were all appointed for qualities that were not measurable by a general written examination. Nonetheless, those qualities have always been and continue to be deeply related to merit.

The Board of Examiners' methods of hiring need to be radically changed. They are without merit, and they have resulted in a destructive and inexcusable exclusion of Blacks and Puerto Ricans.

Thank you.

THE CHAIRMAN: Counsel?

MR. TRACTENBERG: Just one question, Mr. Glasser.

This goes back to the earlier part of your remarks about teachers' rights.

You mentioned that you have handled a number of court cases involving teachers. Are there any that have resulted in decisions in favor of the teachers or are they all in the process?

MR. GLASSER: They are all in process, except one that has resulted in a decision.

We represented a teacher last spring who was a probationary teacher, had a license, was not a tenure teacher and was called down for a records hearing, of the kind that I described. He did not know what the subject of the hearing was. He received nothing in writing in advance. He was brought down, he had no right to a lawyer, had no right to get himself together to get any kind of a defense going. He was told orally, for the first time, what the problems were, he was told in vague terms that he had had some sort of unsatisfactory rating or allegations of bad performance against him.

He was asked if he had anything to say in his own behalf and under the situation, I suppose, he stammered something. There was no transcript kept, so it is difficult to say what happened exactly, and his license was later revoked.

We appealed that revocation on due process grounds to the Commissioner of Education who subsequently handed down a decision agreeing with us, that those kinds of hearings were totally without due process and in which he ruled that not even a probationary teacher could be stripped of his license by such methods. He mandated that nothing like that could happen unless there was written notice of charges in advance, unless there was a right to counsel, unless there was a right to cross-examination, unless there was a right to confront the evidence and to present additional evidence in your behalf.

Now, the interesting thing, and the thing that reveals the arrogant, arbitrary attitude of the Board of Examiners, as best as I can, is that they did not even accept that decision.

Normally, when a decision comes down from the Commissioner of Education, that is it; and while you may have problems of enforcing it, it usually ends the legal process.

The Board of Examiners petitioned for a rehearing before Commissioner Nyquist, even though the statute clearly says that a petition for rehearing can only be entertained if facts occur between the time of the opinion and subsequent to the petition for rehearing which substantially changes the facts that were before the Commissioner in the first place.

No such facts changed, no new information occurred, nothing was different. But they have continued to fight this in order to continue to be able to do all these things, as near as I can tell, pending the final disposition. The case is still in process because of that petition of rehearing. But the significant thing is, one, the Commissioner has agreed that the procedure is arbitrary and unconstitutional; and, two, they have continued to fight to maintain that kind of total power.

MR. TRACTENBERG: Thank you. That is all.

THE CHAIRMAN: The next witness is Mr. Louis Nieves, Executive Director of Aspira.

MR. NIEVES: I represent the Puerto Rican organization by the name of Aspira. We provide educational services to Puerto Rican students, about 4,000 students a year.

Puerto Ricans are a very young community in many ways, not only in median age but the time they have been in New York City. We are not an articulate community. We have not had as many opportunities to communicate our concerns and to describe our conditions. I think our pain has been a silent one and the cries of agony generally have been silent.

But what stands between us and our ability to communicate is an educational system which does not allow our students, our people, to achieve the kind of equity in education that is necessary for us to partake in these kinds of events with a significant degree of effectiveness.

I pulled together some information which I hope will testify that the Puerto Rican is, by far, the most discriminated against community in terms of the Board of Education.

Just recently we conducted a survey of information available in regard to the Puerto Rican community, and the conditions in the high schools and in the Board of Education, in general. I would like to communicate some of the findings from this.

In recent years almost as much, if not more, attention has been focused on the public school educator in New York City as on the achievement levels of students. More and more pressure is being exerted to force the schools to assume responsibility for the failure of students to meet basic educational standards. Parents are questioning the professional quality of teachers, principals, and higher administrators, employed by the school system.

It has been demonstrated that particular attitudes toward minority group students, such as the assumption that they cannot learn, may create the most serious obstacles to success in school. Unfortunately, the New York City Board of Education has made no attempt to investigate these kinds of attitudes among teachers and principals, and, consequently, no such data is available. It is not surprising, however, given the defensive posture of the school system, that critical gaps exist in gathering and reporting such material.

The employment practices of the New York City Board of Education regarding minority groups are of considerable importance for at least two reasons. First, it is widely accepted among educators and behavioral scientists that a student's self-image and feelings of personal value are influenced by the adults with whom he has contact. If the Black, Puerto Rican, or other minority group student has little contact with teachers and principals sharing his ethnic background, he loses a source of positive identification with the education system. The widely publicized study, "Equality of Educational Opportunity" (The Coleman Report) points to the feeling of control over one's environment as a critical element in the attitude of successful students. What it fails to investigate is the importance of school characteristics such as similar ethnic background between teachers and students for the development of this attitude.

The second reason why the ethnic composition of school employees is significant is somewhat less directly related to the delivery of good education, but equally important. As one of the largest employers in New York City (last year approximately 130,000 people), the Board of Education has the same responsibility as any other institution or organization not to permit discriminatory hiring practices. As the chief socializing institution, the school system is doubly bound to observe fair employment practices.

The most recent analysis of New York City public schools employment is available for March 1969. In only two categories, paraprofessionals and school lunch employees, was the percentage of Black employees equivalent to, or greater than, the percentage of Black students in the New York City school system (32.2%). In no instance was the percentage of Puerto Rican employees equivalent to the percentage of Puerto Rican students in the school population (21.5%).

Not surprisingly, the proportion of Puerto Rican and Black employees is largest in the lower paying, less prestigious positions, while it is a fact that the Board of Education headquarters employs a negligible percentage of Blacks and Puerto Ricans in top administrative positions. Two of approximately 50 Assistant Superintendents are Black; none are Puerto Rican. All of the four key positions are occupied by whites: Chancellor of Schools, and the Deputy Superintendents for Personnel, Business Administration, and Instructional Services.

It is clear that the employment picture last year was anywhere from six to 22 times worse for Puerto Ricans than for Blacks.

These conditions of employment existed during a school year when 173 elementary and junior high schools had more than 50% Black students, and 124 more than 50% Puerto Rican students.

While no one can deny that the conditions of employment in the New York City school system suggest both discrimination and disregard for the educational environment of minority students, some people might perhaps claim that conditions are the same everywhere else.

Lest no illusions be falsely maintained, when New York City is compared to four other major cities, it is highlighted as the most discriminatory system. The appalling state of the matter is that when comparing the ratio of Black students to Black principals with a similar ratio for whites, one discovers New York City to be over three times more underrepresentative of Blacks than the next worse city.

These kinds of figures attack the argument that New York City employs so few minority group members because the number of applicants is small. While no one is heralding the conditions of employment in the other four cities as ideal, their current proportion of Black principals suggests that we could be doing at least three times better in New York City with the existing supply of potential candidates.

New York City has the smallest representation of Black and Puerto Rican teachers of the five major cities. The percentage of Black teachers in cities other than New York is at least one half as large as the percentage of Black students. While these proportions do not represent an equitable distribution, they are much better than the 33%/9.2% ratio found in the New York City school system.

For Puerto Rican students the picture is much worse, although all cities have a greater underrepresentation of Puerto Rican teachers than Black teachers. In New York City and Detroit, where the percentage of Puerto Rican students is about the same, the percentage of Puerto Rican teachers is four and one half times larger in Detroit. New York City, with all its claims of progressivism and leadership in education, is, in fact, the slowest to accommodate its teaching staff to the characteristics of its student enrollment.

The point of the excerpt from this report is that in New York City, while it's bad to be a Black student, it's even worse to be a

Puerto Rican student. All of the standard reading and achievement scores have proven this in the past and continue to demonstrate it to be true today. There are about eleven times as many Black teachers as Puerto Rican teachers while there are fewer than three Black students for every two Puerto Rican students. This disparity in teacher representation and the low achievement rate of our students, we are convinced, are intimately related.

The documentation of these patterns of discrimination is ample as I'm sure you have heard and will continue to hear throughout these hearings. I would like to look beyond the current picture to a possible approach toward the resolution of the fundamental problem of getting more Puerto Rican personnel into the system.

During the past eight years, the number of Puerto Ricans going on to college has been multiplied many times over. In 1963 perhaps 250 Puerto Ricans went on to post-secondary education. In 1970 that figure grew to 4,000. As of today, Aspira estimates there are 7,500 Puerto Ricans in colleges here and across the country. The vast majority of them are New Yorkers, and from our continuing work with them, the vast majority are deeply committed to working on behalf of their community.

The Puerto Rican college student and the recent graduate believes that he can make a difference in the lives of those who could follow in his footsteps. The field of education is the most direct and most obvious path for him to choose in order to fulfill this commitment. But there are barriers, obstacles which are keeping him out of the schools. For the most part, there are the same obstacles which have created the incredible situation we have now.

What I am saying is that in the Puerto Rican community the number of college graduates, a few hundred motivated, qualified young people wishing to contribute, is growing with each succeeding year. If the school system continues to cling to artificial and irrelevant standards, it will not attract these young people.

In our present crises, we must reach beyond just easing the employment picture for teaching staff. The New York City educational system needs an infusion of minority members in positions such as social counselors, young Puerto Rican and Black college graduates assigned to schools with high Puerto Rican or Black enrollment. These counselors will bring a skill that no university could offer; they bring a knowledge of the crisis of the young that no guidance counselor with ten years' experience could offer. They bring a sense of commitment that only the indigenous could offer. The rigid and artificial professionalism in the school system is laying to waste the precious young of the Puerto Rican and Black community.

The time is upon us when we must get beyond these barriers. The time is upon us when a new climate of openness needs to be created and a new affirmative spirit infused into the classrooms and school buildings of the city. The young, dedicated Puerto Rican has that spirit to contribute. He has the capacity to revive the American concept of public education as the way in which all society can make real progress as individuals, as communities, and as a nation.

And if our school bureaucracy and our laws and our public authorities and our courts do not give him the chance to use that capacity and dedication, he is very likely to seek other ways of changing and improving the conditions of his people.

That is the end of my testimony.

THE CHAIRMAN: Thank you.

Any questions, counsel?

MR. TRACTENBERG: Just one question, Mr. Nieves.

We have heard a fair amount in the past two days about the problems of staffing the schools with a sufficient number of bilingual teachers, and that is obviously a unique problem of the Puerto Rican community and Puerto Rican students.

Do you have the feeling that if it were not for the present selection process, there would be a reasonably adequate number of persons with the ability to teach bilingually?

MR. NIEVES: No, there wouldn't be adequate, but there would be a lot more.

What I am recommending is that the school system be opened up to young college graduates who are Puerto Rican, as our agency has been opened up to these people who are able, in a very short time, to have a tremendous effect on the young people.

What I am saying is no significant standards in terms of testing and licensing are going to help. What we need is something more than just teachers, more than bilingual teachers. We need to provide an opportunity for the young people at the schools to relate to college graduates of their own ethnic group.

They would not necessarily have to be counselors in regard to the school achievement, and so on, although, certainly, this is possible. But they would be able to bridge the gap of communication between what is now the school system and the failing Puerto Rican student.

MR. TRACTENBERG: Thank you.

COMMR. McDONALD: You made a very fine presentation, and I want to thank you for it, but I wonder if you have an opinion as to whether New York City's poor statistical showing is the result of indifference or a lack of effort to increase the number of Blacks and Puerto Ricans or whether you think or have an opinion as to whether there is a definite discriminatory pattern, designed to be discriminatory.

MR. NIEVES: Yes.

I think the discriminatory pattern is inbred into the system. It has been many years since there has been an opportunity for new groups to join the highly professionalized teachers and school administrators.

I think, yes, through the expression of the Board of Examiners and the Council of Supervisors that this discrimination, as subtle as it is, is very much definite and defined. There is no question about it.

I am not concerned with the motivation, willingness or desire to be discriminatory; but when the effect is discriminatory and it is harmful, that is the purpose, if you will, as far as we are concerned.

COMMR. McDOUGALD: Thank you.

THE CHAIRMAN: Thank you.

We are concerned about the Puerto Rican figures. We are looking for ways to remedy that.

Why don't we give the stenographer a 5-minute break. We will resume again in 5 minutes.

(Whereupon, a short recess was taken.)

THE CHAIRMAN: These hearings are about to begin. Please tell everyone in the hall that the hearings are about to begin.

There are a number of people who wish to testify and we do not wish to have any time problem. We want to make sure that everyone that came to testify today will do so. That is why I am going straight through dinner.

I announce that anyone who wishes to testify can testify during this evening session that we are about to go into, and a number of people have already signed up, so, consistent with time problems, we will allow testimony of any one of the public on any side of this question.

Let me announce that there will be available to parents who wish to attend this hearing a free child care center located around the corner from this hearing. The child care center is at 225 Broadway, 18th floor, Room 27. For any parents who wish to attend this hearing a free child care center exists.

These hearings are being held at 14 Vesey Street.

I welcome Dr. Eugene Callender, President of the New York Urban Coalition.

DR. CALLENDER: Thank you, Commissioner.

I am Eugene Callender, President of the New York Urban Coalition.

I'm not an educator but I am very much interested in the subject of education. I speak today as a Black man and one who has participated in what is now popularly called the "Black experience" in America.

America has never been a land of opportunity for Black people and racism has permeated this country ever since our foreparents were brought from their native soil of Africa against their wills and kept in chains. Racism still permeates every institution in this country. Racism exists in the system of New York City, and racism exists in and is perpetuated under the Board of Examiners in New York City.

No one can deny the obvious fact that Blacks do not have equality of opportunity in the New York school system. Anyone who has recently read the study in the Columbia Journal of Law and Social Problems on the merit system cannot help but be convinced by its very lucid demonstration that the so-called "merit system" is not only invalid but also not objective. How can one call a system objective when these examinations, and I quote from this article, "are based on and produce excessive inbreeding."

According to the Columbia study, the Board of Education's own figures show that we have a grand total of 11 licensed Black school principals in our school system and no licensed Puerto Rican principals. Slightly different figures circulated within the

Board itself also include acting positions. These raise the total for Black principals to 37 (26 acting) and for Puerto Rican principals to 4 (all acting). These 41 positions represent a magnificent 2.3% of the city's 968 regularly licensed and acting principals--in a student body almost 55% Black or Puerto Rican.

The yawning disproportion between the racial identities of the primary consumers served by the school system, its students, and the Board of Education people doing the serving narrows only minutely as we go down the hierarchy from principals to assistant principals, department chairman, teachers, guidance counselors, even school lunch employees. The point hardly needs further elaboration by me.

As your chairman Mrs. Norton has put it, "When more than one-half the school population is Black and Puerto Rican, it's incumbent upon the school structure to change whatever restrictions it has that prevent these minorities from being employed. Private industry devised methods to improve minority employment. Other school systems have done it, and I think New York can do it too."

That other school systems have indeed done it is amply documented in the Columbia Journal of Law and Social Problems article to which I referred earlier. In Detroit, for instance-- scarcely a citadel of racial progressivism--17% of the principals, 25% of the assistant principals, and 41% of the teachers are Black; contrasted with 1.3%, 7.0% and 9.2% in the enlightened and liberal city of New York.

The Board of Education itself has recognized the situation in a number of ways, despite occasional protestations that no discrimination exists. Last June, for example, it announced a new series of training seminars for aspirants to the position of elementary school principal, which it stated were "expected to attract a large number of applicants due to the revision of requirements for this position by the Board of Education, designed to qualify more Black and Puerto Rican teachers."

Also, early this month, Deputy Superintendent Lang announced a Joint Employment Recruitment Program between the Board and the United Federation of Teachers, and stated that one of its major goals would be "the recruitment of minority group personnel both in and out of town for the purpose of creating a better racial balance of the staff."

So the problem certainly exists, and everybody knows it and recognizes it. But, when we turn to remedies, we are immediately confronted with the fact that appointments to supervisory positions in elementary and junior high schools are now made, under our new Decentralization Law, by community school boards elected in each district. These boards, as I'm sure members of this Commission know, are allowed to pick and choose at will from an unranked qualifying list of all candidates for the position who have successfully jumped the initial hurdle of state certification for the position and then a secondary municipal hurdle--erected, in our state, only in New York City. In New York City, this secondary hurdle takes the form of tests given by our Board of Examiners, a body that may have had some merit when it was first established in the days of McKinley, but surely has none whatever today. I shall speak more about that in a moment.

Let me speak first about the community school boards themselves, as set up under our 1968 Decentralization Law. These bodies now have, undeniably, an important voice in hiring, and I believe that any inquiry into Board of Education hiring practices must include a look at the local boards.

I suggest first that some of these boards may be serving too large an area. For example, District 28 in Southeast Queens is sharply divided ethnically, with most of the district's white residents in the northern communities of Forest Hills, Rego Park, and Richmond Hills. The southern end of the district is Black. The governing District 28 Community School Board contains six whites, all from the north end, and three Blacks, all from the southern end.

This is the body that recently suspended--by a six-to-three, racially divided vote--the Black acting principal of a Black junior high school, Desiree Greenidge, and 17 of her teachers. This has led to a student boycott of the school, charges filed with the State Division of Human Rights, and various court actions as reported in the newspapers. I do not know all the particulars of this dispute in District 28, but I suggest that possibly the trouble would have been averted if the district were smaller and there were separate community school boards for its northern and southern ends.

The manner in which community school boards are elected should also be scrutinized closely. Neither slates of candidates nor duplication of signatures are allowed. There are built in advantages to such organized groups as political parties, the teachers' union and the Catholic church; and the spillover voting system occasionally elects nondesired candidates. In addition, suffrage in these elections is extended to all residents of the district, whether they have children in its schools or not.

Finally, I suggest that the community school boards are presently lacking four essential powers they should have:

First, supervision of their district's high schools as well as its elementary and junior high schools.

Second, increased authority over its budget, including power to monetarily reward teachers for doing a good job.

Third, some voice in curriculum content, in diagnosing the individual needs of their students and helping formulate a program to meet those needs, within proper educational guidelines.

Fourth, total power of selection of staff from state-qualified candidates, the right to grant or refuse tenure, and the power to terminate unsatisfactory performers, with appropriate provisions for appeal. Annexed to this must be the authority (with a budget) to recruit teachers and/or supervisors for their respective districts, either in the metropolitan area or throughout the country.

Now let's talk about recruitment. As previously noted, the Board of Education has, on at least two occasions, indicated some awareness of the racial disproportion that exists in the ranks of its employees. I fear, however, that the efforts it has made to overcome this disproportion fall far, far short of the mark. This despite a statement last month by Mr. Jack Frank, a spokesman for the Elementary Principals' Association, that he's been around for 45 years and feels the city is doing the best it can. This "best" is indicated by the fact that nearly half of all Black and Puerto Rican high school students fail to graduate. And fewer than 5 percent of those who do graduate get academic, college preparatory diplomas.

I'm not claiming for one moment, of course, that all Black and Puerto Rican students who find our schools irrelevant and drop out of them would automatically stay in and graduate if there were an appropriate representation of Blacks, Puerto Ricans, or Chinese on the faculty. I am insisting that the dropout rate would be substantially, overwhelmingly, smaller if the Board of Education were anything remotely like a so-called "equal-opportunity employer."

As just one example of the kind of recruiting effort that can be made if the good will is really there, I wish to cite the current project of the Afro-American Teachers Association in Brooklyn, a project I'm proud to say the New York Urban Coalition is helping to support financially.

Finding more than half the children in school District 13 reading two to five years below grade level, the association was convinced the primary cause was the high percentage of probationary and substitute teachers in the district--678 out of 1,106 elementary school teachers and 279 out of 400 junior high and intermediate teachers. These probationary, substitute, and out-of-license teachers generally have little or no expertise in the subject they are teaching, and do not meet the state's educational requisites.

The Afro-American Teachers Association embarked, jointly with District 13, upon an intensive campaign to recruit mature, intellectually capable, creative young people from minority groups who would be interested in teaching in District 13, and to train them to become effective teachers. They took maximum advantage of the so-called "40 per cent provision" in the Decentralization Law, which permits the local boards to recruit some teachers from among those who have passed the National Teacher Examination only.

Recruiters from this program traveled to colleges and communities of the Southern border states, Puerto Rico, and the greater New York area and registered 379 minority teachers as available, signed up 193 to take the New York City teachers' examination, and put 50 into on-the-job training in the district's schools.

I repeat my previous statement. This is just one effort, in one district, by one community group in conjunction with its community school board. But it clearly demonstrates what could be done by the educational establishment, if it were so minded.

What the system is doing in the way of recruitment is, while not exactly nothing, certainly too little. The Board's own recruiting appropriation for the current fiscal year is about $123,000, and the joint program with the UFT alluded to earlier is funded at just under $396,000. However, almost $205,000 of the $519,000 is for personal services. Moreover, 25% of the much-lauded Joint Recruitment Program with the UFT is, I think significantly, to be done right here in the metropolitan area, where 85% of the Board's own efforts are already concentrated, and where education conditions already alluded to virtually insure a dearth of qualified candidates. Thus, the evils of the system feed upon themselves.

Why, for that matter, set up a recruitment program with the very union whose membership is already, for whatever reasons, so ethnically disproportionate? Why not in partnership with, or at the very least including, community-based, education-oriented groups like District 13's Afro-American Teachers Association? There would be a recruitment effort that might have a chance of really getting somewhere.

This joint recruitment effort might be construed as a conflict of interest on the part of the UFT. Are they recruiting persons who will dedicate themselves to teaching our children? Or are they recruiting union membership to give them added muscle at contract time or at their next lockout?

We have a conservative, Mr. Nixon, the President of the United States, making an alleged call for "power to the people" in his State of the Union address which moves the presidency light years away from the McKinley years on the one hand, while on the other we have our bearers of justice and fighters against corruption in a fixed bayonets position warding off anyone attempting to become a teacher or a supervisor in New York City by means other than those designed in the last century. This to me conveys the thought of power vested in the power brokers--in this case, in the outmoded Board of Examiners.

Yes, members of the Commission on Human Rights, I finally turn, somewhat wearily I confess, to the subject of the Board of Examiners. All that can be said must surely have been said, and there it still sits, an intractable monolith left over from the days of McKinley, dedicated deep within its bureaucratic soul to preserving the status quo.

Others have said the Board should be modified. I, and many others, call for its total abolition. I join with Chancellor Scribner--who has just got to be the best thing that has happened to education in this city in this generation--in finding it totally inadequate to the needs of today's education crisis. I join with the NAACP, Legal Defense Fund's court suit in finding its examinations racially discriminatory and professionally invalid. I join with this very New York City Commission on Human Rights, with virtually all education-oriented organizations outside the system, and with Mr. Albert Shanker of the Teachers Union in questioning its role in determining who's going to teach my kids and your kids.

I welcome to our ranks State Education Commissioner Ewald B. Nyquist, who has recently proposed new state standards based on classroom performance rather than on what candidates remember and, all too predominantly, on the extent to which they reflect middle-class cultural values. In the words of the Times the other day, "The importance of Commissioner Nyquist's proposals for New York City is that they could put an end to the tired old debate over the Board of Examiners. If the State Education Department can come up with quality controls based on classroom performance, even the Examiners' most dedicated supporters would be a claque without a cause." I can only add a fervent "Amen," and a hope that it may be so.

For the record, let me just capsulize what I and others have said previously on many occasions about the Board of Examiners:

Its examinations and personal interviews favor--are designed to favor, really can't help favoring--those who come to them with racial assumptions that are in reality, however "benignly" they may be intended, racist. These are the people--white people-- who know the system and speak the language, the ones who successfully pass the examinations and thereby the only candidates community school boards can choose from. Yet the Board of Examiners' tests, in addition to being culturally biased, measure neither the competence nor the attitude of the candidates--to say nothing of how well he or she will stand up in the classroom.

One can quickly dispose of the McKinley era argument that only our Simon-pure, lily-white Board of Examiners can protect us from political power, patronage, and unlawful influence by asking one simple question: How is it that every other school district in this state manages to get by without a board of examiners? How is it that none except Buffalo interposes its own supervisory tests as an additional requirement for employment in its school systems?

Recently Buffalo, which had the same kind of examining system (screening-out system), dropped its examination for supervisory level personnel. Isn't this some kind of admission, or an awakening to the real world? Is it alleged that now all school systems in New York State except our own are cesspools of graft and corruption?

In conclusion, members of the Commission on Human Rights, let me quote Dr. Dan W. Dodson:

"The schools are the handmaidens of the power arrangement within the society. They are the chief instrumentality by which the skills and mores of dominant white society are taught. The input of the school system is all the children of all the people. The output (I would add, for those who are not pushed out early, as so many thousands are) are people who know their place."

What I advocate is not really revolutionary. It is, quite simply, that we genuinely demonstrate the truth of what we say when we pledge allegiance to the flag of the United States. If this Commission can bring closer the day when the New York City Board of Education's recruitment, selection, employment, appointment, and promotion of its teachers and supervisors is more truly color-blind and culturally reflective of the students it serves, you will have shown us, as Chinese, Blacks, and Puerto Ricans, a certain kind of honesty, a certain kind of integrity in the statement that here there is indeed "liberty and justice for all."

Thank you for your attention.

THE CHAIRMAN: Are there any questions from the Commissioners?

(No response.)

THE CHAIRMAN: Does counsel have any questions?

MR. TRACTENBERG: No, I do not.

THE CHAIRMAN: I want to thank you very much for taking time from your busy schedule to come down here, Dr. Callender, and to give your testimony.

Mr. Irving Chin.

MR. CHIN: Mrs. Norton, distinguished members of the Commission on Human Rights, at the outset, I wish to applaud the Commission's hearing into the educational system's discrimination; and, secondly, I wish to express my personal appreciation to the Commission for allowing me to testify today on behalf of the Chinese community which is oftentimes a silent passed-over minority group.

We have been silent for many years, for many reasons, and we are overlooked oftentimes by the establishment, by other minority groups, and we are now about to be a little more verbal and vocal in our requirements.

We have been quiet in the past because our people, the Chinese community, have been few in number. They have not had sufficient training to verbalize their grievances. They have been fearful of government repression, and philosophically they have accepted many of the injustices. But now we are about to reverse the tide, hopefully with the Commission's help, to resolve many of the injustices in the educational system which are happening to the Chinese people.

I come today as Irving S. K. Chin, the Chairman of the Educational Committee to the Borough President of Manhattan, in his advisory council. We are an organization composed of many Chinese community organizations which was formulated by the Borough President to more effectively express our needs and to elicit and solicit from the legislative bodies definite needs for the community. We have joined together to express our needs in this area and we have found sympathetic ears, but we are asking for action.

In the educational area, which I am dealing with, I have found, through my experience as Chairman of the Educational Committee, many subtle discriminatory practices exercised by the establishment. For instance, we have found, in terms of funding, that the Chinese community oftentimes has no funding because they use discriminatory testing.

For instance, the Metropolitan Reading Achievement Test is oftentimes cited by the Board of Education as the reason why the Chinese community does not need funding, and this was personally expressed to me by a very significant person in the Board of Education when I appeared and said we needed money to alleviate some of our problems. The answer was, it is too bad that the Chinese do so well on the tests so, therefore, they obviously don't need money.

Let me point out to the Commission that there has been a rapid change since 1965, as a result of the immigration revision, wherein, instead of 105 Chinese coming into the United States annually, we now have approximately 20,000 in the United States, of which 8,000 are coming into New York Chinatown. This is a tremendous growth, and we are having difficult times adjusting these people.

I would like to mention that this is revising discriminatory practices in Immigration Laws which previously kept families separated for 10 years, so this is something that at least has been a solution.

However, because of the tremendous number of people coming into one geographic area known as New York Chinatown, we are finding that the people themselves cannot solve all their problems as we have previously been able to do.

Instead of the situation where the family associations were able to assimilate these families that are coming in at the rate of 8,000 per year, we have been finding problems in housing, in employment, social areas, etc., which previously have been totally unknown to the Chinese people.

Therefore, we look to governmental aid and assistance. But when we find that they throw us this quasi-equality, we rebel, and we will assert all our legal means to rectify this system.

Now, in terms of the Metropolitan Reading Achievement Test, they point to this as the method for deciding who gets the money for funding. And upon further examination, I have found that the Metropolitan Reading Achievement Test does not test all the people. In other words, it tests only those selected by the teachers as being qualified to take the test and who have at least a qualified ability to read.

Now, assume, for example, that you have a hundred students in a class, of whom 90 are from Hong Kong and have no reading ability. Their reasoning would be, take the 10 who are able to read and test them, and these 10 then represent the other 90 people, or the total of one hundred people.

So this makes it quite obvious that you can stack the deck so that you select the people who are to take the test. Therefore, those who are selected may be able to perform well, but they do not represent the majority of the people.

Secondly, I wish to point out that having been involved with this area of education, that many of the schools have attempted to keep their records high by dropping the Hong Kong immigrants who have difficulty adjusting to the language by putting them into the nonregent classes, which makes them not in the same category as those being examined, and, in essence, they are put into a slow class which causes them great difficulties and deprives them of the opportunity to catch up with other people.

Many of the students who are not given an opportunity to assimilate their English comprehension are, therefore, high school dropouts.

As an example of what happens to these high school dropouts, we have had, recently, the situation where a 14-year-old teenager stabbed another teenager in a teenage gang fight. We had an example of a 21-year-old student from Hong Kong immolating and burning himself in Times Square.

This is totally abhorrent to the Chinese because they did not believe this could happen. All of this is directly traceable to the fact that if these people had some English training, they might be alive today.

For example, the 21-year-old had come from Hong Kong sufficiently trained in mathematics. He could take computer training, but his English was insufficient; and because of that fact he was considered a dropout; and, for many reasons, he had a mental breakdown which caused him to burn himself.

So what we are trying to do is give the language training to the people so that they can accelerate and be assimilated into the mainstream of American society which we are so proud of. We feel that once they are given the English training that they will quickly adapt themselves, as many of us who were unable to speak --I was able to learn English at the age of 5--and this is something which is a possibility. But without giving the opportunity to these people when they are at high school age, they immediately become very despondent dropouts, and get into social problems.

Now, the funding we find out is very difficult for the Chinese community because, number one, our community school district extends itself up to 96th Street, where it is very difficult for us to get adequate representation, for we are competing with many groups. We feel that this is very unfair. We should have our own separate school district because we are now getting to a point in the total population where we have special needs.

Secondly, in approaching the Board of Education for funding, we note that they use what I call bureaucratic chicanery, which, in the vernacular, is phoney baloney, because this is what they do. They dissipate your time by saying under the Decentralization Law you must go to the local district for your funding, write your proposals, get everything submitted. So we waste our time in doing this, and then find out, after we submitted proposals, that the central Board has already mandated 95% of the funds for previous programs. Therefore, how can we expect to compete with the other groups for the last 5%?

Secondly, the programs, as they are situated, do not help the Chinese acclimate themselves into special training. And we need a multi-service center, similar to the Hungarians and Cubans, who were brought into the United States under a situation similar to the Chinese, but they were given advantages to adjust. And we need this because the numbers of agencies in the community which are able to be bilingual, to handle the many needs of the community, are a handful. You can count them.

Now, we would also like to have changes so that the school board election laws are more equitable. I wish to point out that under this new school board election law, which was passed, the eligibility of those who are to vote is couched in terms of citizenship. In other words, permanent residents who are not yet citizens cannot vote legally.

Now, I got into a discussion with the Board of Education on this point, and they thought that they could vote and I said it was not possible because we had approached the Attorney General for an opinion and also the City Corporation Counsel, and what we found out was that the City Corporation Counsel has given a ruling that the Chinese or any permanent residents--this does not apply only to Chinese, it would apply to Italians, to Polish, anyone who has come to the United States who has a child in one school and who is not yet a citizen--cannot vote. It takes 5 years, as you know, to become a citizen. So during the 5 years, this person is denied due process of at least voting for his child's education, and this we feel is inequitable. They should change it.

And Senator Bookson and Assemblyman DeSalvio, in our district, have introduced legislation to do this. However, Senator Bridges and, evidently, Governor Rockefeller, have seen fit to block it, and we ask that some pressure be put on the politicians to change this inequitable situation. We feel every parent, whether he is a permanent resident or citizen, has the right to vote for his school representative, and this is where we are finding the difficulty.

Now, we hope that with some assistance from the politicians --and I use politician in a very good, generic sense--that they will help the Chinese.

But we are a practical people. We cannot generate the votes which are necessary to persuade a politician that it is better to give this person some additional funding as opposed to another minority. What we seek is de facto equality. We have been given de jure equality, which is in the law, under the Bill of Rights. But we find, when you go out looking for equality, that we are getting a lesser share.

Take, for instance, those Chinese who apply for scholarship assistance for minority groups. They are told it is too bad, you are not a minority group now.

I don't know where we fall, if we are a majority or minority. It seems somehow that we should fit into the scheme of things somewhat under our orderly process.

So what we are asking for is that we be given equality with other minorities. We are not asking for more or less. We are asking to be treated as equal minority groups, and that we at least be given the chance to adopt and adapt ourselves into the mainstream of American society.

And we are hoping that through the hearings of this Commission and through the Board of Education that funding will come to our community because I believe that the money which will be invested will be returned manyfold because I think the Chinese have established themselves as basically law-abiding, progressive, and very studious people. Once they are given this opportunity, they will be able to repay themselves as we have many people in NASA, in the governmental program under the Nobel Prize. They are all contributing to our American society.

I would also like to say that Senator Jacob Javits had the foresight to introduce, in his new education bill, which is S.3883, provisions specifically for minority groups. It is now pending before the U.S. Senate and will be acted upon. It was not possible to have a vote at the end of the 91st Session. However, Senator Javits, has for the first time given us statutory rights as a minority. He has defined minority groups to include Orientals.

Now I feel that the Commission should also urge our legislatures in minority bills to ask for the definition of minority groups to include Orientals and this is very basic to our concept of equal rights.

In closing, I wish to bring in a little bit of my Chinese heritage to the Commission, if I may be able to do that. The Chinese have a concept of the Yin and the Yang, which is an equal cosmology of dual forces which, if they are balanced, will create harmony such as male and female balancing each other, positive and negative. And, in doing so, we recognize that our society in America, our great democratic society, which is proud of its heritage of all minority groups in a melting pot, will be only successful when the majority is equated with the minority. Once this balance is broken, you will have difficulties, you will have trouble, and this is the problem.

Now, when you balance the majority versus the minority, this is also equivalent to giving opportunity based on equality for all minorities. This is the balance of the fulcrum, and unless every minority group is given the same opportunity to achieve success and adapt himself, we will never have peace or equality in America. The Orientals, and especially the Chinese, who I represent, feel very strongly that we have been overlooked and that we have been silent too long.

And I would like to close with two quick poems which express this.

On the one hand, we have a poem which is at the base of the Statue of Liberty, which says:

"Give me your tired, your poor, your huddled masses yearning to breathe free, the wretched refuse of your teeming shore. Send these, the homeless, tempest-tossed to me, I lift my lamp beside the golden door."

This is a great poem to immigrants who come to the United States for this opportunity. Once they are here, we have a concomitant duty that these immigrants be given the opportunity, as other minority groups in the past, for equality.

And the other poem says:

"We hold these truths to be self-evident, that all men are created equal, that they are endowed by their creator with inalienable rights, that among these are life, liberty and the pursuit of happiness."

And my message to this Commission today is search your consciences so that every minority group be given the same opportunity, and once we find this harmony we will have equality in the United States.

Thank you.

THE CHAIRMAN: Mr. Chin, may I say this testimony on behalf of the Chinese community is especially important because in all of the talk about minority groups in this city, I think you are perfectly correct that the average person, even if that person belongs to a minority group, does not think of Orientals and Oriental immigrants as belonging to a minority group.

Although the danger signals are clearly there, and all of the same pathology says that the traditional disadvantage minority groups have gone through in this country, all those signals are on the walls in Chinatown today, which is burgeoning with the greatest influx of immigrants this city has seen since the early part of the 19th century.

You say, and rightly, that the problems of Oriental people --of Chinese people, in particular--are very different and point up the fact that in dealing with the problems of different minority people we have to have different approaches. You, for example, in the Chinese community have a bilingual problem, such as the people in the Spanish-speaking community, but it is very different. It comes from a different source, and it is going to take different remedies; and we need the input from minorities whom we don't even think of as minorities.

Recently, the Chinese community has brought to our attention the anguish of not even being recognized as a minority and, therefore, not being treated as a minority, even when you suffer all the economic disadvantages and all the other disadvantages that flow from being a minority group. Not alone in the school system, which it should be noted has taken little, if any, note of the special problems of Chinese people in our city, but it would appear that the whole of the city has yet to see the Chinese community for what it is, a minority community in our midst. And we would all do well, before that community is added to the roster of angry alienated communities in this city, to try to find ways to deal with what is surely a burgeoning, dangerous problem in Chinatown, with young people coming into this city and with no way to learn English, token bilingual teachers, massive high school dropouts--all through the grades--among a people who did not have a tradition of dropping out of education.

What has happened to the Chinese community in this city is that they have come here and lost ground rather than coming here, as is supposed to be the tradition, to find new opportunities.

You mentioned that law, and the Commission has written to several assemblymen to get the law changed, so that parents of Chinese extraction may vote for the local school board and not be disqualified by virtue of a technicality of not yet being an American citizen, which ought not be relevant, at least in school board elections.

We hope, in this session of the legislature, that can be corrected, and we hope that members of the general public will bring pressure. As Mr. Chin says, there are not enough Chinese to bring the pressure. But we who are Black and all the other minorities should know how it feels to be left out. We should join with this minority which is so little recognized by any of us for the disadvantaged group they are increasingly becoming in our society.

I thank you for coming on behalf of that community which we know so little of.

MR. CHIN: I also wish to express my appreciation to the Commission and to you, personally.

Thank you.

THE CHAIRMAN: Mrs. Rhoda Karpatkin.

MRS. KARPATKIN: Mrs. Norton, members of the Commission, Mr. Tractenberg:

My name is Rhoda Karpatkin. I am a member and past Chairman of the School Board serving the West Side of Manhattan and South Central Harlem, formerly 5, now Community School Board 3.

My testimony today is in two parts: first, our experience for over two years with the supervisory structure as it was created for us by the central Board of Education and as we tried to change it; and, second, my perception of a most formidable enemy of districts seeking to appoint Black and Puerto Rican principals.

Even before the new Decentralization Law, local school boards had been involved in principal selection, first in an advisory capacity, and since 1968, with some actual power. Our board from the beginning shared this process with parents.

Over the years, I have had the opportunity to observe that the qualifications parents and communities want in their principals are those that all the wise folk in education say we must have in our schools: solid professional ability and leadership, respect and empathy for parents and community, and involvement of parents and community in decision-making processes. Over the years, I have been a participant in the dynamics in which ineffective principals have left our district and community supported principals have been appointed.

In previous years, as vacancies developed in our district, we developed two policies. First, parents and teachers should be involved in the selection of principals. Second, the dreadful imbalance between the high percentage of Black and Puerto Rican youngsters in our schools--85% and the almost all white supervisory staff should be corrected by recruiting Black and Puerto Rican supervisors who had the qualities I have just listed.

We have done and are doing both. Today, selection of the principal involves not only the superintendent and school board, but a screening panel with parents elected from the parent body, elected teacher and paraprofessional representatives, and a community corporation representative. While this method obviously does not guaranty the selection of perfect or even superior persons, it has improved the quality and commitment of our principals.

As for our ethnic policy, it too has seen major changes. When I became chairman of Local School Board 5 in September 1967, there was one Black principal in our schools. Today in twenty-three schools, there are ten Black principals and one Puerto Rican, three of whom serve in integrated West Side schools and eight in Harlem. Our superintendent is Puerto Rican.

In our struggle to find persons uniquely qualified to serve the needs of our district, we have found that a place on the Board of Examiners' eligible list provided neither assurance nor hope that the applicant could render satisfactory professional performance or demonstrate concern for our children. We have spent hundreds of hours interviewing candidates on eligible lists. We found, for example, candidates for elementary school positions whose entire experience had been in high school, candidates who

believed parents' roles in schools should be limited to little more
than cake sales, candidates with low expectations for our Black
and Puerto Rican children, candidates with no experience with or
understanding of our community life, candidates who had never
heard of the British infant school or other significant innovations.

We found that for our Harlem schools, few and sometimes
no persons on the eligible list would even apply. There have never
been, in my years of experience, any applications to transfer into
a Harlem school. Indeed, one applicant from the list, who we
were interested in, withdrew after he looked at the neighborhood
--Lenox Avenue.

We found, moreover, time after time, that persons who had
been appointed from eligible lists lacked the training, ability or
attitudes needed to deal with severe problems in our schools.

If you are wondering why our district has so many vacancies
available to be filled by community-oriented principals, you have
to examine the performance record of some of the Board of Examiner-qualified principals in our district. In the last few years,
this is it:

Two left their schools the moment they had a right to transfer out after the minimum 5 years of service, thus substantiating
the claim of Harlem parents that inexperienced principals learn
on the backs of their children and then give privileged children
the benefit of their experience.

Three transferred out with school board consent after the
1968 strike. Pressures were too much for them after they failed
to serve at their schools during the strike, choosing to disobey
the lawful directive of Superintendent Donovan and to obey instead
their guru, Walter Degnan.

One was rated unsatisfactory by the district superintendent
and was sent by the central Board to another school in another
district.

One was denied tenure and transferred to the district office.

One left after the parents association strongly called attention to his long-term failure to improve pupil achievement.

One was transferred to the district office after persistent
and documented parent claims of incompetence and after her resistance to implementing the British infant school program, now
New York's most promising innovation.

One left after parent charges of incompetent performance.
To warm up the cold statistics above, let me read a letter from
the parents association of that particular school.

"Local School Board, District No. 5
300 West 96th Street
"Dear Mr. Gang:

"It is urgent that the present principal be removed immediately and that a new principal of our choice who has the interest
and welfare of this school and community at heart be assigned to
this school.

"He has failed to cooperate with us in the following things:

"1. He has shown no interest in the welfare and safety of
the children.

"2. He has shown no interest in the academic achievements of the children.

"3. He has refused to cooperate in the matters of overcrowded lunch schedules.

"4. He has refused to give an accounting of such funds as:
  (a) Candy sale
  (b) G.O.
  (c) Senior dues
  (d) Booster Campaign

"5. He refused to support the community in reference to the Afro-American Day Parade sponsored by the New York Urban League.

"6. He has not administered the Title I funds properly in that jobs from last year went unfilled and, to date, most of the positions for this year remain unfilled.

"7. Many text books in use are outdated. Many classes do not have adequate books.

"8. He is insensitive to Black children and to the Black community.

"9. He showed total disrespect for the president of the P.T.A. by refusing to properly introduce her at the June 1969 graduation to the dismay of graduates, parents and dignitaries.

"10. He does nothing about:
  (a) Lateness--an acute problem
  (b) Pupil conduct--acute problem
  (c) Chaotic conditions in the gymnasium
  (d) Fosters poor staff morale--gossip between teachers, administrators and parents.

"P.T.A. Executive Board."

I think this record helps explain the disenchantment of our district with the concept that there is some relationship between merit and the eligible list.

My point here is that the eligible list was and is irrelevant to our needs. There are 31 school districts in our city, each one with its own distinctive characteristics and individualized prerequisites. It is obvious to us that the Board of Examiners' method of testing candidates for all 31 districts with one test can never produce a list relevant to the needs of our children.

Instead we found that the Fordham University-Ford Foundation Urban Administrators Program provided excellent academic preparation and a supervised field internship, and that service as an assistant principal in our district or a similar one was invaluable training. We rely on professional, parent, and community evaluation of on-the-job performance.

The final word on the relevance of the Board of Examiners' lists to districts such as ours, where the overwhelming majority of the children are economically and educationally disadvantaged, was stated by the New York Court of Appeals in the case of Council of Supervisory Associations v. Board of Education, 23 N.Y. 2d 458, 297 N.Y.S. 2d 547 (1969). It upheld the judgment of the New York City Board of Education that "the general training and competitive tests for principals were not addressed to the special needs" of slum area children, who had been failed by the public schools, and that new tests and standards were necessary.

In appointing principals we have been able to achieve some flexibility through the device called "plugging," described in the July 1968 Niemeyer Report (final report of the Advisory Committee on Decentralization). A temporary vacancy, which can be legally filled by a so-called "acting principal," is created when the regularly appointed or payroll principal is on leave, serving at the central Board, or otherwise unavailable. While the appointment of an acting principal has always been a device to afford flexibility to serve the convenience of regular principals, we have found it useful to serve the needs of our children and schools.

Over the last few years, the Office of Personnel of the Board of Education has been reasonably cooperative with us. They have matched their supply of surplus principals with our vacancies. I think this has probably helped save some parts of the city's educational system from total destruction by providing a legal method by which the legitimate needs of local school districts could be met.

Unfortunately and obviously, this is no way to run a school system. It is better to change bad laws than to circumvent them. Moreover, when we depend on plugging, we depend on the grace of the central Board and other incidental factors, and that is not a dependency which leaves anyone feeling comfortable.

As the First National City Bank report noted, as the Court of Appeals has discussed, and as everyone knows, the principal is the key to school success. What our school district wants is a lawful method of setting qualifications for and appointing principals whose merit is that they can serve the needs of our children.

The Board of Examiners, which was to have achieved this, has instead been an impediment. We believe that without this local right to select principals qualified by locally determined standards within state law and accountable to local communities, community school boards cannot be accountable to their communities and decentralization cannot succeed. We believe the Board of Examiners must be abolished.

This intimate connection between true decentralization and the selection of principals brings me to the second part of my testimony. I have found that the most intense and vigorous opposition to our appointment of Black and Puerto Rican principals has come from the Council of Supervisory Associations. It has shown itself to be an enemy of decentralization, of local selection of principals, and an enemy of those who believe our schools must have more Black and Puerto Rican supervisors. It has a staff and budget revved up to wage a long and hard battle against the implementation and spirit of the Decentralization Law, and especially in a district such as 3.

The CSA leadership is fighting for a return to the glorious days of yesteryear when local district actions could be reversed at central headquarters by a CSA Lone Ranger galloping on his white horse to the Superintendent of Schools. I have heard a lot of rhetoric since the new Decentralization Law went into effect but CSA president Walter Degnan is the only person I know in New York who this year urged the need for a "strong central authority" in our city school system.

I think the course of conduct of the CSA poses a formidable threat to the implementation of the Decentralization Law and especially as it relates to the selection of principals. This becomes clear if you read the CSA <u>Newsletter,</u> which has a number of messages to deliver.

First, the CSA has embarked on an extensive and vigorous litigation campaign to fight the local appointment of principals desired by and responsive to the community. When the Chancellor appointed Melvin Taylor, a Black, to the principalship of Benjamin Franklin High School, the CSA sued, advising its members that the appointment was "in violation of law" and was "sanctioning school hijacking."

The Court upheld the appointment as lawful.

The CSA went to court to prevent Community School Board 14 from appointing Claude Huntley, a Black, as acting principal, and later to seek to punish the board for contempt in appointing him. I understand the judge declined to do so and Mr. Huntley still serves.

The CSA has gone to court countless times, usually ex parte, to seek orders ousting Louis Mercado, a Puerto Rican, as principal of P.S. 75 in my district. A number of judges have declined to do so.

CSA has sued to remove Sidney Morison as principal of P.S. 84, and every other principal "similarly situated," which means almost all the acting principals in our district, and that matter is now under consideration by the Court.

CSA is also litigating in other districts. The CSA tried unsuccessfully to intervene in the case brought against the Board of Examiners. Thus, by its substantial litigation budget it seeks to thwart the efforts of community school boards and the Chancellor to appoint persons who, in their opinion, are qualified for the positions and responsive to the needs of the particular school.

Second, the CSA is making a last ditch fight against the personnel authority of community superintendents and community school boards. The new law gives them precious little, but even that is too much for the CSA. While the clear legislative and popular mandate is for decentralization, the CSA is perpetually demanding that the Chancellor centralize several schools where community superintendents have sought to exercise powers granted them by law in relation to principals.

Third, CSA counsel has advised at least one principal to act in flagrant disobedience of the lawful and proper transfer directive of a community superintendent. Abetting the principal in this insubordination were officials of the CSA who day after day loitered in the hallways and offices of the school from which the principal was transferred. While berating the absence of order and security in our city's schools, the CSA has made its own direct contribution to the physical disruption of one already disturbed junior high school. I wonder if all the principals who are CSA members would think it a good idea, if a teacher, who believed a principal's order was unjustified, responded by direct disobedience, with Albert Shanker and his staff hanging around the school to provide physical and moral support for the insubordination.

Fourth, the CSA Newsletter constantly misinforms its readers. Since the membership is markedly apathetic and apparently meets only three times a year, misstatements in the Newsletter can be made with virtual impunity. A steady stream of misinformation has been fed to the readers of the CSA Newsletter concerning legal requirements under the Education Law and the actions of various school boards and superintendents.

Fifth, while the press and legislature have praised the central Board for an orderly and cooled down transition to decentralization, the Newsletter has been an instrument for the CSA President to launch intemperate and inflammatory attacks against the Chancellor, central Board, community boards, and superintendents. Anyone reading the Newsletter would rapidly conclude that the entire fabric of New York school system is being destroyed with rapidity.

Listen to the language of the voice of the city's top educators.

When the community superintendents exercise lawful authority over principals, it is "potential dynamite," "outrageous action," and "a dangerous new precedent." When Chancellor Scribner made his lawful appointment of Melvin Taylor, Mr. Degnan said he was "deliberately flouting" the law, that he "virtually guaranteed further disruption in the city's schools," that he "surrendered to school hijacking" and "defied the Decentralization Law." The appointment is characterized as "an abdication of responsibility by the Chancellor of the Board of Education."

If anyone has dreams that the tensions of the 1968 strike are finally wearing away, Mr. Degnan is ready with a page one warning that today "the threat to the welfare of children, supervisors, and teachers is perhaps even greater" than in the 1968 school crisis. It is clear to me that he is struggling to blow something up to the frenzied pitch of 1968.

Sixth, the CSA and the Board of Examiners are warm bedfellows, with luminaries of the Board of Examiners playing a leading role in the CSA. Two of the four examiners, Chairman Gertrude Unser and member Murray Rockowitz, are involved with CSA policy-making and advocacy at the highest level.

In the light of this clear-cut record, it is small wonder that a CSA committee reported that the CSA had been "notably unsuccessful in attracting minority supervisors."

In the light of the CSA record and this admission, I think this Commission might question the status of the CSA as the sole collective bargaining agent for the city's school supervisors.

I also request that this Commission, in addition to inquiring into why there are so few Black and Puerto Rican principals in our city, also provide support for districts such as ours, where there are many such principals. I think these hearings are an important first step. With the quality of leadership Mrs. Norton and the Commission have provided, and with the legal talent contributed by Mr. Tractenberg, I feel justified in believing that our district has found a working ally.

THE CHAIRMAN: Are there any questions from the Commissioners?

(No response.)

THE CHAIRMAN: Counsel?

MR. TRACTENBERG: No questions.

THE CHAIRMAN: Thank you very much.

Mrs. Rose Falcon, United Bronx Parents.

MRS. FALCON: I have a very short statement.

We are very used to only getting two or three minutes at the Board of Education, so we are not used to the luxury of receiving all this time.

My statement is quite short.

I would like to address my comments to the discriminatory practices toward the Puerto Rican community.

Puerto Rican children are herded into "discipline" classrooms because they are not competent in English, but the Puerto Rican teacher is not allowed into the system. In the meantime the children become retarded in English and they start to lose their competency in Spanish. This system then can take credit for retarding the Puerto Rican child in two languages.

Thus the discrimination as far as the Puerto Rican is concerned is two-fold. The system excludes the Puerto Rican teacher who is best equipped to help our children and thus our children are discriminated against educationally. Every principal, district superintendent, and teacher knows this discrimination is taking place.

For years, we have had one bilingual teacher in some schools who are not even allowed in the classrooms, are used as translators, clerks and nose-wipers. For instance, in P.S. 65, 1355 students are Puerto Rican, in P.S. 161 and 18, 64% of the students are Puerto Rican. In P.S. 29, 1650 pupils are Puerto Rican. One bilingual teacher in a school with almost 2,000 students of Puerto Rican background is ridiculous. One bilingual teacher for all these students and parents is blatant discrimination.

In the entire city of New York there are only ten Puerto Rican guidance counselors. Improper guidance tends to discourage rather than guide. Children are advised that they only need two years of college and can get a good job, can work with their fathers, can quit at 17 without their parents' consent, and so on. Parents who cannot communicate with these counselors are powerless in trying to counteract their advice.

The Board of Education keeps saying it can't find Puerto Rican teachers or supervisors. Some even say we don't have any. Yet it is very interesting to note that when you do have a Puerto Rican principal, all of a sudden other Puerto Rican staff emerges. Alfredo Mathew became principal of Junior High School 98 and found Puerto Rican teachers and supervisors to help. The effort being made by the Board of Education is just not real.

Let's look at the teacher training programs of the Board of Education. In 1969-70, 125 Spanish-speaking teachers were recruited, but of these only 27 were finally licensed. The Board of Education pays Puerto Rican teachers who are already professionals $2.50 an hour for training, while it pays a generous wage plus increments and benefits to the English-speaking teachers for training. The Puerto Rican teachers come here with families and responsibilities and end up with $2.50 an hour, which helps to encourage them to leave the New York City system and go back to Puerto Rico or to work in factories. Some teachers have been in this program for 3 years. Even those finishing the course do not pass the test. Someone has to be discriminating. Why a Puerto Rican teacher should take an examination in English to teach in Spanish is beyond me.

The whole city knows this has been going on. I am very glad the Commission has decided to take on the Board of Education. However, I hope it will use its power to bring forth quick results and not just write another report. If you can use your power in housing, to force a landlord to stop discriminating, why can't the Commission use its power to stop the discriminatory practices of this system of education.

Thank you.

THE CHAIRMAN: I am interested in what you said about the $2.50 for training.

What kind of training is this that a professional is sent to?

MRS. FALCON: This is the bilingual teacher program that the city has, and it is a recruitment and training program for Spanish-speaking teachers.

They have something like, at this moment, I believe, about 250 or 300 teachers who are going through training who have been there for two or three years, and every time that they are about ready, you know, something happens and word comes down that they do not accept this credit that they had previously accepted from Puerto Rico, so they must go on and go on and go on.

They are paid $2.50 an hour, most of them, and what they do is go to the training in the evening and work during the day. The program will put them in a school like a paraprofessional and they will get $2.50 an hour, but this is the only payment they get for being on that program. It makes it very hard.

THE CHAIRMAN: Do you know if most of these teachers come from Puerto Rico or from Spanish-speaking communities in New York City?

MRS. FALCON: Most of them are Puerto Rican teachers.

THE CHAIRMAN: From the Island?

MRS. FALCON: Well, a lot of them are teachers that have been here already. They work at other things. You will find them in factories and you will find them, you know, almost everywhere, who have been teachers in the Island and have experience and everything. They come here and they just can't get into the system and they must do something else.

THE CHAIRMAN: I am interested in your saying that when Puerto Rican professionals get into the system, they have success where the Board of Education has admitted failure.

MRS. FALCON: They have success in at least finding somebody, in, you know, advertising for bilingual teachers, at least getting them on a per diem or a daily basis in the school. They have more success than other principals who don't even try.

THE CHAIRMAN: Counsel?

MR. TRACTENBERG: I have one further question.

You contrasted, in your statement, this $2.50 compensation with a different rate of compensation available to non-Puerto Rican teachers who are also being trained.

MRS. FALCON: When an English-speaking teacher goes into a training program, when they have a special program in the school and they take a teacher for training, she is usually paid from about $10.50 to $12.50 an hour. She gets her regular teacher's salary for training.

MR. TRACTENBERG: This would be a licensed teacher, in the second case?

MRS. FALCON: Not necessarily. She could be a per diem or a teacher not yet licensed.

MR. TRACTENBERG: Thank you.

THE CHAIRMAN: The Commission is concerned in having heard of a proliferation of programs set up by the Board of Education which do not seem to produce the Spanish-speaking or Black teachers. This must be the fourth or fifth program we have heard of today which does not bring in minority group teachers.

Have you any insight into why these programs which have been set up with taxpayers' money being spent are such dismal failures in turning out minority teachers? Do you think that the programs are not well conducted? Do you think they are not necessary? Where is the problem?

MRS. FALCON: I really think that the problem is that no one makes a real effort. You know, when you make a lot of noise, then everybody gets excited and they give you a program--you know, it is like a bandaid that nobody expects to work. And they don't try to make it work. And they put all the stumbling blocks that they have in this program.

THE CHAIRMAN: I think this is a very concise answer. We may begin to get to the key to some of the problems here. The fact is that the minority communities, Black and Puerto Rican, in particular, have been really fiery about this problem.

For some years now, some school systems have failed to put in any programs. But your criticism goes to commitment, I believe, because if we had found so far, you see, during the two days of this hearing, that there are no programs, we could feel a bit more hopeful. But a very serious question that is being raised at this point of the hearing is that we have heard--your suggested program is the newest one we heard of--of a rather good number of programs, some going over a number of years, and the Board of Education has admitted that these programs have not done the job which they desired them to do.

I wonder if, in your view of the decentralized school system, the local school board system presents any hope for the development of other programs which might be more successful.

MRS. FALCON: Definitely. I think if in all these programs, instead of being centralized, the local districts were allowed to do their own recruiting and do their own training right in their districts, there would be a great improvement. For instance, in

District 7, if you could set up a teacher training program right in the district, and have the teachers come in, they would have their requirements from Puerto Rico, they could work in the schools while they are training and they could get the same amount of money that a teacher, a normal teacher, gets in the school system so they can live. There are competent teachers over there, and they train and teach over there.

The system has found it cannot teach our children. That has been proven. It cannot teach the foreign child. They say he is retarded, a discipline problem. And I think that first, you have to be able to talk to him, to understand what he is trying to say. The largest majority of the children cannot communicate and the system does nothing to bring it about.

THE CHAIRMAN: I want to thank you very much.

MRS. FALCON: I also have with me two other people. I believe if they have any questions--

THE CHAIRMAN: If any of the rest of the group wishes to testify, they may also testify this evening.

It may be that, in light of the combination of some of the ideas that seem to come out of the local level and some of the failures that have been admitted by the Board officials at the central level, the answer may be an extra training program, maybe between the central people and the local people. If the local people are desperate enough about their children, they may have to devise programs that work, and maybe the central Board can learn from them.

MRS. FALCON: That is exactly what we would like to see.

THE CHAIRMAN: Let's take a 15-minute break. We will resume at 6:30.

We have been left some questionnaires for the record. I want these entered into the record.

(Whereupon, a short recess was taken.)

THE CHAIRMAN: This hearing is in session.

Will you inform the people in the hall that we are about to begin again. We want to make sure that everyone who has come this evening has a chance to put his or her comments into the record.

Since this is going over WNYC, anyone who wishes to speak on any side of this issue is invited tonight and tomorrow night, which are the hours we found most convenient for the public. We set aside the evening hours and are staying late to hear testimony from the public.

There is a child care facility which we have provided around the corner from the hearings. The child care facility is located at 225 Broadway, Room 27 on the 18th floor, for parents who might like to attend these hearings and who, we feel, should have some place to leave their children free of charge.

Mr. Louis Caban.

MR. CABAN: Yes.

I would like to start by finishing what Rose Falcon started giving, some statistics we found in the three districts, District 7, 8 and 12.

Many of the parents of these districts were asked by the United Bronx Parents to request information from the public schools concerning the ethnic breakdown of the children in the schools.

In District 12, which is over 55% Puerto Rican and 35% Black, only three principals agreed to give the information to parents, P.S. 211, Junior High School 98 and P.S. 50.

In District 8, only one school principal, P.S. 130, released the information. That district is 40% Puerto Rican and 30% Black.

In District 7, every school except three, P.S. 30, 31, and 37, released the information.

District 7 is 65% Puerto Rican and 33% Black. There are more than 22,000 Puerto Rican children in its schools. There is one bilingual school serving about 500 children.

In the other schools there is no Puerto Rican principal and only two bilingual assistant principals. Only 51 teachers out of 1,500 teachers are bilingual for 22,000 bilingual children. Only one guidance counselor out of a total of 40 is bilingual.

MISS CONKLIN: Also, in District 8, the one school we got the information from, we had to wait for quite a while and only because they were aware that we were going to put pressure on them.

THE CHAIRMAN: Identify yourself for the record.

MISS CONKLIN: Doris Conklin.

So out of all the schools in District 8 that was the only one we got it from, and that was only because the principal saw that we were pretty adamant and we wanted it, but he gave us the runaround.

THE CHAIRMAN: Did he give you any reason?

MISS CONKLIN: He said he did not know if he would have the information, so we waited a month, and the day I went there with a letter that I was going to send to you and different people around the city, that he was refusing to give out public information, he had the information available then. It just happened it was that day. But, you know, he was very uncooperative, just very uncooperative.

THE CHAIRMAN: Of course, the information must be available because the Board, itself, had taken that information and had to get it at the local level to get it. The Board, of course, did its own survey. That is how we know what the figures are.

There was a time in this country when people didn't want to know. We all assumed we should be color-blind and we ought not to ask how many people were of any particular race or ethnic background. And then we discovered that, by not knowing how many people were of what race or background, we had no way at all of knowing if people were being discriminated against.

I want to put this in the record, because there is a great deal of public confusion on this. It was, itself, a crime, and was made a crime in the 1970 Census, not to answer the question with respect to race. And, obviously, that is because if this country is to resolve its racial and ethnic problems, it is not going to get very far if it starts from ignorance. So today there is great danger in not knowing where minority groups are to be found in society, because then it means the problem simmers for a long time and then bursts open because no one took the time to find out where they are, whether they are progressing rapidly or slowly.

The Board took its own census and should be given some credit for wishing to know what the ethnic and racial breakdown is. I believe, however, this is the first census the Board has taken, and I find it very strange that we should have gone this long without knowing what the actual ethnic and racial breakdown was.

I find your efforts to be particularly laudable, inasmuch as what you attempted to do is to find out where it counts, on the local level, what that breakdown means, that is to say, what the ethnic and racial breakdown is. And it is that effect which, of course, the Board of Census does not get, and which it has been particularly hard for you to get.

MISS CONKLIN: Did you get that background about the schools?

THE CHAIRMAN: We were given a folder.

That will be turned over to the stenographer.

MISS CONKLIN: We wanted to cite an example of the sort of teacher that passes the licensing procedures. You get some dillies in there that you can't get out. There is no way for community people or for parents to get rid of a teacher they find unsatisfactory.

You have a copy of a note there. We went with a parent to a school and we found this note. It was unsigned and undated. It was in the child's permanent record. The child is eight now and this was written about him when he was seven years old, and this would have stayed with him until he graduated. And also we know that the Board of Education keeps the child's record for 50 years; so if he applied for a job, a copy of this could go to the employer.

Anyway, this is the note that we found in the child's file:

"A real 'sicky.' Absent, truant, stubborn and very dull." First of all, she is not qualified to call him a "sicky." Second of all, "very dull" is not backed up by any testing or anything else.

It says, "Is verbal only about outside irrelevant facts," which happens to be the child's life. You know, his everyday thing, his family.

"Can barely read," and then, in parenthesis "which was a huge accomplishment to get this far."

As a final insult to the child, it is signed, "Have fun."

We tried to get some action with the principal because of this note, and all we got was a lot of very polite faces and an informal meeting with the teacher that he had, and there was nothing. Right now we are still in the middle of trying to do something about getting this teacher out, but there is really nothing we can do.

We have just a few more things we want to say.

MR. CABAN: One of the things we wanted to bring out, as far as hiring practices, is how any teacher with this type of attitude gets into the system and a teacher who really cares about our children, who can communicate with our children and plan and hope to teach things to our children, is somehow kept out of the system.

Some of the parents whom we have talked to around this particular school would like to do something about this teacher, but there is no way of firing a tenured teacher, no way that the parents have, except by pressuring the school, and if the pressure is successful they transfer the teacher. I don't see how transferring a teacher to another school where there are other Blacks and Puerto Ricans suffering this type of punishment would get us anywhere.

THE CHAIRMAN: There has been some testimony from a teacher earlier today, that part of the problem with such teachers who fail with minority children is that they do not have adequate direction and preparation from supervisors and others in the school system, and they are left on their own to deal with children from another community and another way of life. This was a teacher who had taught minority group children herself and learned from them.

I wonder if you have found, in your local district, that there might be a basis for improving relations between a teacher not from the community and those children, if there were some way to orient and acclimate them to their different life styles and needs.

MR. CABAN: As a personal point of view, I think that there could be ways of maybe some type of teacher training, but just as students don't care to learn from after-school programs, I wouldn't imagine the teachers would, either, on a nonpaid basis.

THE CHAIRMAN: Don't you think this should be a part of one's actual on-the-job duties rather than something that is peripheral?

MR. CABAN: I certainly do.

MISS CONKLIN: I think someone made a very good suggestion, and it just sort of says a lot, and that is--it was Dr. Gaines --and she said that if people, prospective teachers, can go and have a few dinners with parents and get into the community, right there, if you sit down to eat with someone, that is like a real basic, human thing.

If you were to relate to people on a human level, then you can relate to their children and you can respect them on a human level. I think a lot is just getting into the community and being there and participating and being a person with the people whose children you are teaching and with the children themselves.

MR. CABAN: I want to make one last comment: when you were talking about the statistics on a local level, one of the reasons why we did this is because statistics, on a large area, can be very, very deceiving.

Thank you.

THE CHAIRMAN: For the record, the United Bronx Parents have done a survey in their own district, District 7. This was done through the volunteer efforts of parents and other community people, and I think it demonstrates the concern around this issue and the desire and commitment that people have to try and do something about it.

Chairman Norton   271

It was difficult, apparently, to do on a local level what computers did more easily on the more generalized level. We congratulate you for the kind of effort and commitment it takes to do a project like this, using volunteer help, and it will be inserted into the record when the record of these hearings is complete.

MR. CABAN: Thank you.

* * *

"HOW MANY BLACKS AND PUERTO RICANS ARE EMPLOYED IN YOUR CHILD'S SCHOOL?

"The New York City Commission on Human Rights is investigating the employment practices of the Board of Education. It wants to find out whether or not the school system discriminates against Blacks and Puerto Ricans. Hearings on this crucial subject will be held in January.

"The Board of Education has released a city-wide ethnic census of its staff as of March 1969. It is important for parents to find out the facts for their own child's school. Please ask your principal for the following information, and bring it into United Bronx Parents, or send it directly to Eleanor Holmes Norton, Chairman, Commission on Human Rights for the City of New York, 80 Lafayette Street, New York City.

"THE PRINCIPAL SHOULD MAKE ONE COPY FOR YOU AND ONE COPY FOR THE COMMISSION.

"SCHOOL: P.S. 5, Bronx.
"1. How many students are in your school? 1403.
    How many are Black? 522. Puerto Rican? 865. White? 16.
"2. Is your principal Black? ___ Puerto Rican? ___ White? X .
"3. How many assistant principals are there in your school? 3.
    How many are Black? 0 Puerto Rican? 0 White? 3.
"4. How many teachers are there in your school? 64.
    How many Black? 9 Puerto Rican? 1 White? 54.
"5. How many guidance counselors are there in your school? 1.
    How many are Black? 0 Puerto Rican? 0 White? 1.
"6. How many paraprofessionals are there in your school? 30.
    How many are Black? 13 Puerto Rican? 16 White? 1.
"7. How many lunchroom employees are there in your school? 12.
    How many are Black? 9 Puerto Rican? 2 White? 1.
"8. How many custodial employees are there in your school? 6.
    How many are Black? 2 Puerto Rican? 2 White? 2.
"9. School Aides? 14. Black? 4. Puerto Rican? 4. White? 6.
"ANY OTHER COMMENTS:
    "Need more bilingual teachers in schools."

"SCHOOL P.S. 161, Bronx.
"1. How many students are in your school? 1619.
    How many are Black? 32%. Puerto Rican? 64%. White? 4%.
"2. Is your principal Black? ___ Puerto Rican? ___ White? X.
"3. How many assistant principals are there in your school? 2.
    How many are Black? 1 Puerto Rican? ___ White? 1.
"4. How many teachers are there in your school? 80.
    How many are Black? 11. Puerto Rican? 4. White? 65.
"5. How many guidance counselors are there in your school? ___
    How many are Black? ___ Puerto Rican? ___ White? ___

"6. How many paraprofessionals are there in your school? 34.
    How many are Black? 10. Puerto Rican? 23. White? 1.
"7. How many lunchroom employees are there in your school? 14.
    How many are Black? 10. Puerto Rican? 3. White? 1.
"8. How many custodial employees are there in your school?
    How many are Black? ___ Puerto Rican? ___ White? ___

SCHOOL: 1 X.
"1. How many students are there in your school? 1350.
    How many are Black? 450. Puerto Rican? 875. White? 25.
"2. Is your principal Black? ___ Puerto Rican? ___ White? X.
"3. How many assistant principals are there in your school? 3.
    How many are Black? ___ Puerto Rican? ___ White? 3.
"4. How many teachers are there in your school? 65.
    How many are Black? 8. Puerto Rican? 2. White? 55.
"5. How many guidance counselors are there in your school? 2.
    How many are Black? ___ Puerto Rican? 1 White? 1.
"6. How many paraprofessionals are there in your school? 39.
    How many are Black? 17. Puerto Rican? 15. White? 7.
"7. How many lunchroom employees are there in your school? 13.
    How many are Black? 5. Puerto Rican? 1. White? 7.
"8. How many custodial employees are there in your school? 6.
    How many are Black? 1. Puerto Rican? 3. White? 2."

"SCHOOL: P.S. 65X.
"1. How many students are in your school? 1910.
    How many are Black? 548. Puerto Rican? 1355. White? 7.
"2. Is your principal Black? ___ Puerto Rican? ___ White? X.
"3. How many assistant principals are there in your school? 4.
    How many are Black? ___ Puerto Rican? ___ White? 4.
"4. How many teachers are there in your school? 95.
    How many are Black? 11. Puerto Rican? ___ White? 84.
"5. How many guidance counselors are there in your school? 2.
    How many are Black? ___ Puerto Rican? ___ White? 2.
"6. How many paraprofessionals are there in your school? 43.
    How many are Black? 19. Puerto Rican? 22. White? 2.
"7. How many lunchroom employees are there in your school? 16.
    How many are Black? 7. Puerto Rican? 5. White? 4.
"8. How many custodial employees are there in your school? 5.
    How many are Black? ___ Puerto Rican? 3. White? 2.

"ANY OTHER COMMENTS:
    "We have four bilingual people on our staff. One is Ecuadorian, one is Dominican and two are Cuban."

"SCHOOL: P.S. 18.
"1. How many students are in your school? 970.
    How many are Black? 35%. Puerto Rican? 64% White? 1% - other.
"2. Is your principal Black? ___ Puerto Rican? ___ White? X.
"3. How many assistant principals are there in your school? 1.
    How many are Black? ___ Puerto Rican? ___ White? X.
"4. How many teachers are there in your school? 44.
    How many are Black? 4. Puerto Rican? 0. White? 40.
"5. How many guidance counselors are there in your school? 1.

How many are Black? ___ Puerto Rican? ___ White? X.
"6. How many paraprofessionals are there in your school? 16.
How many are Black? 9. Puerto Rican? 7. White? 0.
"7. How many lunchroom employees are there in your school? 5.
How many are Black? 3. Puerto Rican? 2. White? 0.
"8. How many custodial employees are there in your school? 6.
How many are Black? 2. Puerto Rican? ___. White? 4."

"SCHOOL: P.S. 29, Bronx.
"1. How many students are in your school? 3040.
How many are Black? 1200. Puerto Rican? 1650. White? 190.
"2. Is your principal Black? No. Puerto Rican? No. White? Yes.
"3. How many assistant principals are there in your school? 6.
How many are Black? None. Puerto Rican? None. White? 6.
"4. How many teachers are there in your school? 145.
How many are Black? 10. Puerto Rican? 2. White? 133.
"5. How many guidance counselors are there in your school? 3.
How many are Black? None. Puerto Rican? None. White? 3.
"6. How many paraprofessionals are there in your school? 63.
How many are Black? 33. Puerto Rican? 28. White? 2.
"7. How many lunchroom employees are there in your school? 20.
How many are Black? 13. Puerto Rican? 2. White? 5.
"8. How many custodial employees are there in your school? 12.
How many are Black? 2. Puerto Rican? 6. White? 4."

"SCHOOL: P.S. 27, Bronx.
"1. How many students are in your school? 1135.
How many are Black? 224. Puerto Rican? 903. White? 81.
"2. Is your principal Black? ___ Puerto Rican? ___ White? X.
"3. How many assistant principals are there in your school? 3.
How many are Black? ___ Puerto Rican? ___ White? 3.
"4. How many teachers are there in your school? ___
How many are Black? 1. Puerto Rican? 2. White? ___.
"5. How many guidance counselors are there in your school? 1.
How many are Black? ___ Puerto Rican? ___ White? 1.
"6. How many paraprofessionals are there in your school? 25.
How many are Black? 6. Puerto Rican? 18. White? 1.
"7. How many lunchroom employees are there in your school? 7.
How many are Black? 1. Puerto Rican? 6. White? 0.
"8. How many custodial employees are there in your school? 5.
How many are Black? 2. Puerto Rican? 2. White? 1.

"ANY OTHER COMMENTS:
"We have sent down several Black candidates for emergency licensing, we are now in the process of securing 3 Puerto Rican teachers who have passed the tests."

"SCHOOL: IS 38X.
"1. How many students are in your school? 1200.
How many are Black? 400. Puerto Rican? 790. White? 10.
"2. Is your principal Black? ___. Puerto Rican? ___. White? 1.
"3. How many assistant principals are there in your school? 3.
How many are Black? 1. Puerto Rican? ___. White? 2.
"4. How many teachers are there in your school? 80.

"How many are Black? 11. Puerto Rican? 2. White? 67.
"5. How many guidance counselors are there in your school? 2.
   How many are Black? 1. Puerto Rican? . White? 1.
"6. How many paraprofessionals are there in your school? 5.
   How many are Black? 3. Puerto Rican? 2. White? 0.
"7. How many lunchroom employees are there in your school? 8.
   How many are Black? 4. Puerto Rican? 2. White? 2.
"8. How many custodial employees are there in your school? 5.
   How many are Black? 2. Puerto Rican? . White? 3."

"SCHOOL: P.S. 43.
"1. How many students are in your school? 1353.
   How many are Black? 368. Puerto Rican? 965. White? 20.
"2. Is your principal Black? . Puerto Rican? . White? X.
"3. How many assistant principals are there in your school? 3.
   How many are Black? . Puerto Rican? . White? 3.
"4. How many teachers are there in your school? 79.
   How many are Black? 4. Puerto Rican? 3. White? 72.
"5. How many guidance counselors are there in your school? 2.
   How many are Black? 1. Puerto Rican? 0. White? 1.
"6. How many paraprofessionals are there in your school? 34.
   How many are Black? 14. Puerto Rican? 19. White? 1.
"7. How many lunchroom employees are there in your school? 7.
   How many are Black? 3. Puerto Rican? 2. White? 2.
"8. How many custodial employees are there in your school? 5.
   How many are Black? 0. Puerto Rican? 4. White? 1.
"ANY OTHER COMMENTS:
    "There is a need for more Puerto Rican and Black professional personnel in District 7.
                                        "Daniel F. Grayson."

"SCHOOL: P.S. 49.
"1. How many students are in your school? 1502.
   How many are Black? 677. Puerto Rican? 829. White? 16.
"2. Is your principal Black? X. Puerto Rican? . White? .
"3. How many assistant principals are there in your school? 3.
   How many are Black? 2. Puerto Rican? . White? 1.
"4. How many teachers are there in your school? 70.
   How many are Black? 11. Puerto Rican? 1. White? 58.
"5. How many guidance counselors are there in your school? 2.
   How many are Black? 1. Puerto Rican? . White? 1.
"6. How many paraprofessionals are there in your school? 31.
   How many are Black? 18. Puerto Rican? 13. White? .
"7. How many lunchroom employees are there in your school? 20.
   How many are Black? 6. Puerto Rican? 8. White? 6.
"8. How many custodial employees are there in your school? .
   How many are Black? 1. Puerto Rican? 2. White? 3.
"ANY OTHER COMMENTS:
    I found the principal (Mr. Grant) very cooperative.
                                        "Mrs. H. Long."

"SCHOOL: P.S. 51 Bronx.
"1. How many students are there in your school? 874.
   How many are Black? 223. Puerto Rican? 620. White? 2.

"2. Is your principal Black? __. Puerto Rican? __. White? X.
"3. How many assistant principals are there in your school?
3 A.P.'s and 1 A.P. paraprofessional coordinator.
How many are Black? 1. Puerto Rican? 1. White? 2.
"4. How many teachers are there in your school? 65.
How many are Black? 8. Puerto Rican? 0. White? 57.
"5. How many guidance counselors are there in your school? 1.
How many are Black? __. Puerto Rican? __. White? 1.
"6. How many paraprofessionals are there in your school? 27.
How many are Black? 11. Puerto Rican? 16. White? 0.
"7. How many lunchroom employees are there in your school? 14
How many are Black? 12. Puerto Rican? 1. White? 1.
"8. How many custodial employees are there in your school? 6.
How many are Black? 3. Puerto Rican? 1. White? 2."

"SCHOOL: BURGER 139X.
"1. How many students are in your school? 1371.
How many are Black? 28%. Puerto Rican? 71%. White? 1%.
"2. Is your principal Black? __. Puerto Rican? __. White? X.
"3. How many assistant principals are there in your school? 4.
How many are Black? __. Puerto Rican? __. White? 4.
"4. How many teachers are there in your school? 101.
How many are Black? 13. Puerto Rican? 6. White? 82.
"5. How many guidance counselors are there in your school? 2.
How many are Black? __. Puerto Rican? __. White? 2.
"6. How many paraprofessionals are there in your school? 5.
How many are Black? 3. Puerto Rican? 2. White? 0.
"7. How many lunchroom employees are there in your school? 12.
How many are Black? 8. Puerto Rican? 2. White? 2.
"8. How many custodial employees are there in your school? 5.
How many are Black? 2. Puerto Rican? 1. White? 2."

"SCHOOL: E.D. CLARK J.H.S. 149 Bronx.
"1. How many students are in your school? 1512.
How many are Black? 637. Puerto Rican? 854. White? 31.
"2. Is your principal Black? __. Puerto Rican? __. White? __.
(Mr. Rosenstein has been requested by community school board to serve as acting principal. We expect to have a principal assigned in the near future.)
"3. How many assistant principals are there in your school? 6.
How many are Black? 1. Puerto Rican? 0. White? 5.
"4. How many teachers are there in your school? 101.
How many are Black? 18. Puerto Rican? 4. White? 79.
"5. How many guidance counselors are there in your school? 3.
How many are Black? 1. Puerto Rican? __. White? 2.
"6. How many paraprofessionals are there in your school? 5.
How many are Black? 3. Puerto Rican? 2. White? 0.
"7. How many lunchroom employees are there in your school? 12.
How many are Black? 7. Puerto Rican? 2. White? 3.
"8. How many custodial employees are there in your school? 6.
How many are Black? 2. Puerto Rican? 0. White? 4."

"SCHOOL: 154.
"1. How many students are there in your school? 1315.

How many are Black? 552. Puerto Rican? 696. White? 67.
"2. Is your principal Black? ___. Puerto Rican? ___. White? X.
"3. How many assistant principals are there in your school? 3.
How many are Black? ___. Puerto Rican? ___. White? 3.
"4. How many teachers are there in your school? 62.
How many are Black? 7. Puerto Rican? 3, and 1 Cuban. White? 51.
"5. How many guidance counselors are there in your school? 1.
How many are Black? ___. Puerto Rican? ___. White? 1.
"6. How many paraprofessionals are there in your school? 27.
How many are Black? 12. Puerto Rican? 12. White? 3.
"7. How many lunchroom employees are there in your school? 17.
How many are Black? 5. Puerto Rican? 10. White? 2.
"8. How many custodial employees are there in your school? 6.
How many are Black? 4. Puerto Rican? ___. White? 2."

"SCHOOL: I.S. 155 Bronx.
"1. How many students are in your school? 1755.
How many are Black? 553. Puerto Rican? 1195. White? 7.
"2. Is your principal Black? ___. Puerto Rican? ___. White? X.
"3. How many assistant principals are there in your school? 8.
How many are Black? 1. Puerto Rican? 1. White? 6.
"4. How many teachers are there in your school? 127.
How many are Black? 12. Puerto Rican? 10. White? 105.
"5. How many guidance counselors are there in your school? 3.
How many are Black? ___. Puerto Rican? ___. White? 3.
"6. How many paraprofessionals are there in your school? 5.
How many are Black? 3. Puerto Rican? 3. White? ___.
"7. How many lunchroom employees are there in your school? 15.
How many are Black? 9. Puerto Rican? 3. White? 3.
"8. How many custodial employees are there in your school? 8.
How many are Black? 2. Puerto Rican? 4. White? 2."

"SCHOOL: C.J.H.S. 136X.
"1. How many students are in your school? 1604.
How many are Black? 795. Puerto Rican? 798. White? 10. Oriental? 1.
"2. Is your principal Black? Yes. Puerto Rican? ___. White? ___.
"3. How many assistant principals are there in your school? 7.
How many are Black? 2. Puerto Rican? 1. White? 4.
"4. How many teachers are there in your school? 120.
How many are Black? 31. Puerto Rican? 6. White? 83.
"5. How many guidance counselors are there in your school? 2.
How many are Black? 1. Puerto Rican? ___. White? 1.
"6. How many paraprofessionals are there in your school? 25.
How many are Black? 19. Puerto Rican? 4. White? 2.
"7. How many lunchroom employees are there in your school? 9.
How many are Black? 6. Puerto Rican? 1. White? 2.
"8. How many custodial employees are there in your school? 8.
How many are Black? 8. Puerto Rican? ___. White? ___.

"ANY OTHER COMMENTS:
"Please note that our school does not have a principal licensed as such by the New York City Board of Education. We

have an acting principal serving on an Assistant Principal license, assigned by Community School Board 12."

"SCHOOL: P.S. 130.
"1. How many students are in your school? 1011.
How many are Black? 269. Puerto Rican? 664. White? 79 (others).
"2. Is your principal Black? ___. Puerto Rican? ___. White? X.
"3. How many assistant principals are there in your school? 2.
How many are Black? 0. Puerto Rican? 0. White? 2.
"4. How many teachers are in your school? 52.
How many are Black? 6. Puerto Rican? 1. White? 45.
"5. How many guidance counselors are there in your school? 1.
How many are Black? 0. Puerto Rican? 0. White? 1.
"6. How many paraprofessionals are there in your school? 16.
How many are Black? 6. Puerto Rican? 9. White? 1.
"7. How many lunchroom employees are there in your school? 5.
How many are Black? 3. Puerto Rican? 0. White? 2.
"8. How many custodial employees are there in your school? 5.
How many are Black? 1. Puerto Rican? 2. White? 2.
"ANY OTHER COMMENTS:
"Aides--9. Black--1, Puerto Rican--7, Others--1."

"SCHOOL: P.S. 40, the Bronx.
"1. How many students are there in your school? 1419.
How many are Black? 388. Puerto Rican? 1010. White? 21.
"2. Is your principal Black? ___. Puerto Rican? ___. White? X.
"3. How many assistant principals are there in your school? 2.
How many are Black? ___. Puerto Rican? ___. White? 3.
"4. How many teachers are there in your school? 63.
How many are Black? 2. Puerto Rican? 3. White? 58.
"5. How many guidance counselors are there in your school? 1.
How many are Black? ___. Puerto Rican? ___. White? 1.
"6. How many paraprofessionals are there in your school? 28.
How many are Black? 16. Puerto Rican? 12. White? 0.
"7. How many lunchroom employees are there in your school? 17.
How many are Black? 6. Puerto Rican? 8. White? 3.
"8. How many custodial employees are there in your school? 6.
How many are Black? 1. Puerto Rican? 3. White? 2.

* * *

Extract from statement by Chairman Eleanor Holmes Norton:
"When more than one half of the school population is Black and Puerto Rican, it's incumbent upon the school structure to change whatever restrictions it has that prevent these minorities from being employed.... Private industry devised methods to improve minority employment.... Other school systems have done it and I think New York can do it, too."

UNITED BRONX PARENTS
December 1970.

791 Prospect Avenue	1679 Boston Road
842-1484	323-2955
563 E. Tremont	341 E. 149th Street
878-2055	665-3955

THE CHAIRMAN: Dr. Cecil Forster.
Dr. Forster is the Chairman of the One Hundred Black Men.
DR. FORSTER: My name is Cecil Forster.
I am the Director of Psychologist Services of the Harlem Inter-Faith Counseling Service and Assistant Professor of Psychiatry at New York Medical College.

The One Hundred Black Men thanks the Commission for the opportunity to make this statement.

Mrs. Chairman, members of the Commission:

The population enrollment in the New York City public schools is approximately 60% Black and Puerto Rican. For the sake of the self-concept of these pupils, the number of Blacks and Puerto Ricans in supervisory position should be substantially increased. It is generally recognized that supervisors of Black and Puerto Rican background understand the life style and learning styles, problems, interests, aspirations, and sensitivities of these Black and Puerto Rican pupils as a result of their having lived through the same kinds of discriminations, social pressures, economic and other denials of equal opportunity.

The present examination system followed in New York City and some of the requirements of licensure, either by deliberate design or otherwise, have clearly worked in practice to keep to an absolute minimum the number of Black and Puerto Rican supervisors in the public schools of the City of New York.

The number of Black and Puerto Rican principals over the past twenty years has never exceeded three out of the more than 900 licensed heads of schools despite the fact that hundreds of these schools have, for one reason or another, been predominantly Black or Puerto Rican. The licensing procedure has been such that the Examiners themselves have consistently claimed that the procedure results in the identification of those who have passed objective tests of an informational nature but fail to measure many of the personal and professional qualities required for success in administering schools where disadvantaged pupils predominate. These Examiners claim further that the test of such qualities must be made on the job through the probationary period and after. The test for licensure becomes a screening procedure of no greater validity than the acquisition of a state certificate and an interview conducted by a community board representing the pupils and parents comprised of the school population to be served by the candidates.

It is patently clear that a new procedure must be found to facilitate the selection and appointment of a very substantially increased proportion of Black and Puerto Rican principals and higher ranking supervisors in the best interests of pupils of Black and Puerto Rican background in the City of New York. To do less is an injustice to the Black and Puerto Rican communities as well as to the Black and Puerto Rican children and teachers of our city and will inevitably exacerbate the problems and failures of the public school system in this city.

The membership of the One Hundred Black Men, Incorporated, urges that every reasonable step be taken promptly by the appropriate governmental agencies to correct this malignant inequity. Sincerely yours, Cecil R. Forster, Ph.D., Chairman Education Committee. J. Bruce Llewellyn, President.

THE CHAIRMAN: Counsel, have you any questions?

MR. TRACTENBERG: No, I do not.

THE CHAIRMAN: Dr. Forster, I note your expertise and wonder if you believe that it would be possible to set up programs which might have the effect of transmitting to some teachers who do not come from minority communities, something of what it takes, something of the methodology and feel for better dealing with children from these troubled communities.

DR. FORSTER: Well, it would seem to me that some of the techniques that are presently utilized in sensitivity training would be one consideration.

It would seem to me, further, that the kind of instruction offered in programs like the Fordham University experiment that was subsidized by the Ford Foundation, that Dr. King developed, could be expanded to incorporate teachers.

Not having given this intensive thought, I would prefer not to comment further.

THE CHAIRMAN: Thank you for those comments. Thank you very much, Dr. Forster.

DR. FORSTER: Thank you.

MR. SELTZER: My name is Morris Seltzer. I was a past President and past Vice-President of the Junior High School Teachers for the New York City Teachers' Union and member of its Harlem Committee.

I came here in an effort to give some historical perspective to some of the things that I heard here tonight, and I think I have a few comments to make that would be very valid.

I was also a member of the Committee for Better Schools in Harlem. Both of the committees were set up in 1935 and 1936, after the first Harlem riot in March of 1935.

The Committee for Better Schools in Harlem set up in 1936 included parents and civic and religious leaders in Harlem, as well as a number of neighborhood organizations, and the Harlem Committee of the Teachers Union.

The committee was concerned with every aspect of education in Harlem, retardation, standards, buildings, teaching materials, truthful representation of Negro life and history, discriminatory attitudes and actions, and employment of Black teachers.

For years the Harlem Committee and the Committee for Better Schools complained about the disproportionately small number of Black teachers in the New York City public school system and were brushed off by school authorities.

If the number was small, the latter held, it was simply because there were few applicants. There could be no discrimination, they said, since neither application blanks nor records indicated whether applicants were Black or white.

Yet teachers knew that Blacks were being failed in the oral speech tests on the basis of "regionalisms in speech."

In an earlier period, Jewish teachers whose parents or

grandparents were foreign born were denied licenses for "foreignisms," lateral omissions and so on, but their speech patterns were no obstacle for securing substitute licenses and teaching at cut rates.

Toward the end of World War II, when a teacher shortage developed, there was some relaxation in the hiring of Black substitutes. However, the temporary licenses of some of them were canceled for no apparent reason in the years that followed.

By 1949 enough of the substitutes had come to the union for help to indicate a pattern of discrimination. It became possible to present irrefutable evidence of the cancellation of the license of Black substitutes with brilliant scholastic achievement and excellent teaching records at the same time that inexperienced white substitutes were being licensed.

Officers of the Teachers' Union presented more than a dozen specific cases of such revocation of license at a press conference in the fall of 1949. They charged also that discrimination was being practiced against Black applicants for regular license and that the number of Black teachers in the New York public school system, small to begin with, was falling.

The charges were vehemently denied. The Board of Examiners accused the union of "reckless demagoguery." The union nevertheless persisted in pressing for a change in the arbitrary and rigid speech patterns required by the Board of Examiners.

Since the Board claimed to have no record of the number of Black teachers in the schools, the Harlem Committee of the Teachers Union undertook its own survey. The results were sent to Superintendent Jansen in September 1951.

Remember all these years, and you realize how this problem has been with us for a great many, many years.

Answers to a union questionnaire from 104 elementary and junior high schools showed that Black teachers constituted 2.5% of the total, and only 1.5% regularly appointed. There were similar reports from 52 academic and vocational high schools, almost two-thirds of the total. In 26 of the high schools there was not a single Black teacher. Most of the few Black teachers were found in predominantly black high schools at that time.

The crudities in the speech tests were eliminated, but there was no effort to find additional Black applicants for teaching positions. A further survey of the union's Harlem Committee in 1954 showed that the increase in the number of Black teachers was insignificant. The Board of Education then declared that the small number of applicants kept the number of Black teachers down. This in addition to discrimination was undoubtedly a factor in the situation.

The union proposed that the Board encourage Black students in the New York City schools to train for the teaching profession, that it circularize colleges and universities with a large Black student body asking Black students to apply for positions in the New York City schools and assuring them of democratic treatment.

The results of the survey made by the Harlem Committee together with the union's proposals were sent to Black and other civic organizations and to trade unions with appeals for action. Conferences on the training and employment of Black teachers were held with state and city teacher training experts. Securing an increase in the number of Black teachers and supervisors became part of the integration program of civil rights and civic organizations.

There is no longer any secrecy about the number of Black teachers in the New York public schools. The measures proposed by the Teachers Union have in effect become official policies of the Board of Education.

At this point I want to indicate that in much of the above I've been quoting from the "New York Teachers Union 1960 to 1964," a history written by Celia Citron and published by Humanities Press.

Finally as a teacher myself of 13 years in a Harlem junior high school, I should like to state that while I felt I gave much to the young men that I taught, I always felt that Black and Puerto Rican teachers had something to give them that I couldn't.

We must increase their number. We must also increase the number of Black and Puerto Rican principals and supervisors. We can no longer afford "eliminatory examinations" in their case. On the contrary, because of necessity, even the Board of Examiners can work out ways to accomplish this, just as they have in the past, when they set qualifications so that only a handful, and if I remember correctly, even one person qualified. They once gave an examination where only one person qualified.

However, it is quite late for them to do so. Therefore, it seems to me that using state certification as qualification, coupled with acceptance by committees set up in each local school board, including not only local school board members but also parents of the children in their schools, should be very effective in solving the problem of more Black and Puerto Rican teachers and principals.

Basically the real test for all of them should be on-the-job performance before they get permanent tenure.

I might add as a final point that between 300 and 400 teachers were squeezed out of the school system during the witch hunts of the 1950's. I was one of them. These teachers were mostly teachers in the ghetto areas of the city who perhaps prematurely raised the very problems and solutions being discussed before this Commission.

The fact is that they were not premature and that if the problems of minority employment were met in the '40's and the '50's, and these teachers, Black teachers, Puerto Rican teachers and witch-hunting whites, were part of the school scene during the last 20 years, we wouldn't have as large a problem as we now have.

THE CHAIRMAN: Thank you, Mr. Seltzer.
Cynthia Jenkins.
MISS JENKINS: I'm Cynthia Jenkins from Southeast Queens.
New York has never educated its large Black and Puerto Rican student population in the same proportion as the white student population.

Therefore, the Blacks and Puerto Ricans as adults have not been able to return to the various professional ranks of employment in the Board of Education. In addition, the Board of Education has set up a selection policy in reference to personnel that keeps Blacks and Puerto Ricans who have been educated outside of New York City out of the professional positions.

This must be stopped. We cannot continue to support through tax funds an institution that continues to fail the majority of its students and which has standards for selection of personnel that keeps members of the majority student population's ethnic groups on tokenism representation.

Children of all ethnic groups, in order to develop a personal worth, must in their educational career see members of their ethnic group on all levels of employment. The Board of Examiners has prevented Black and Puerto Rican children from seeing this.

For example, I live in District 29, and 60% of the student population in District 29, Queens, is Black and Puerto Rican. Less than 5% is Puerto Rican. There are 26 elementary schools, two I.S. schools, two junior high schools.

In the junior high school there is one Black sitting in the principal's seat. Is he licensed? Is he sitting there as though someone is on the payroll as principal in the district office? We do not know that.

In the elementary level of the 26 schools there are three Blacks sitting in the principal's chair. Is someone else sitting in the district office who is principal on that line? We do not know that.

There are no Puerto Ricans in any administrative capacity in District 29.

Recently, there was a survey of all of the students who entered high school in 1965 in Southeast Queens. There were 5,000 students who entered high school in 1965. At graduation time in 1969, 2,000 Blacks and Puerto Ricans had dropped out. 3,000 graduated. Of the 3,000 that graduated, only 61 received academic diplomas. Something has to be done about this.

Recently the papers in New York City carried an article about the 1500 Black teachers and principals in the South who are no longer in those positions because of the integration of the school systems in the South. These Blacks have taught Blacks for years, have a technique, know how to teach Blacks how to learn, how to perform. Something has to be done about the Board of Examiners in order that the parents can recruit these Black personnel to come to New York City and other large cities and teach Black children how to perform. If the Board of Examiners remains, this can never be done.

THE CHAIRMAN: Thank you very much.

MRS. ANDERSON: I'm Dorothy Anderson. I live, I work, and my children attend school in Southeast Queens, District 29, specifically. I also happen to be the Director of Social Concern, which is an education and action group which is funded through Southeast Queens Community Corporation.

I would like to address myself to the programs that are

implemented because of the "educationally-deprived" children. Lines are drawn around communities that denote stigmatism carried while you have us and our children living within all these lines.

Programs in District 29 are really publicized. By that I mean that in the past we did not either as parent or community resident know what programs were being implemented in which school. Programs were written without due consideration to the youngsters they were implemented to serve.

Between the UFT and the Community Superintendent, there would appear to be a gentlemen's agreement with regard to hiring the administration of the programs. Programs have been recycled without evaluation so that tenure builds up, so that there again we have perpetuation of discrimination.

When dissatisfaction along with documentation causes a principal to be removed from a school, we find that a position that has never been publicized, along with qualifications for a position in the district office, has been created. We know of such actions because we know who has left our schools and who is sitting in the district office.

To add to the combination of the comedy of errors, whoever is used to replace the principal is not given the salary of the principal although the responsibilities of the position happen to be given to them. We never know whether the line has been vacated by that person who has left and gone down into the district office to a position that's been created. And oddly enough, that person that is used to supplant the principal happens to be a person of a minority group. However, he is never given the prestige of being principal. I have to repeat he gets the responsibilities but not the salary.

A case in point is the situation at I.S. 142 in Jamaica, Queens, where for 12 weeks we've had children out and nothing has been done by the central Board nor that community school board. And addressing myself to the community school board, I think we have to look at the lines for school districts as to how they're constituted to find out whether there can be minority control and I don't mean minority representation.

What I'm saying is we have positive lines that have been drawn by the federal government denoting us as a poverty area and we find we have been broken up, gerrymandered, into three different school districts so that in none of the districts do we have any control.

In District 27 we have one Black; in District 28, three; in District 29, two. And we know that in a democratic society the majority rules so that we find we have no control.

We find that our children are being miseducated continuously although funds that come from the federal government and from the state are poured into Southeast Queens. We find that the funds that come from the federal government and from the state only perpetuate the discrimination in the hiring practices and in the promotional policies of the Board of Education. This is evident. And we find too that both governments are slack in requiring accountability from the educational system.

Thank you.

THE CHAIRMAN: Thank you, Mrs. Anderson.

DR. VALLETUTTI: Madam Chairman, distinguished members of the Commission, for the record I would like to indicate that my name is Dr. Joseph F. Valletutti and that the group I represent, as Chairman, is the Congress of Italian-American Organizations, more commonly known as C.I.A.O.

On behalf of our teacher groups, we are pleased to add our voice to those of the other minorities present in protest against the composition of the Board of Education and the continued usefulness of the Board of Examiners. In this connection we believe that the present composition of the Board is not truly representative of the major minority groups in the city. Likewise, the Board of Examiners, as constituted, operates to keep the status quo, perpetuating across the board underrepresentation for all minority groups in all positions in the educational complex of the city.

Speaking for the Italians, we represent 20% of the student body in the public schools and 20% of the total population of the City of New York. Paradoxically, and by way of contrast, we Italians constitute only 10% of the total teaching staff. However, the picture becomes more vivid when we take a closer look at the component categories of underrepresentation. Please take due note of the fact that out of five members of the Board of Education, not one, and I repeat, not one is of Italian descent. Moreover, at Board headquarters there are no Italians in administrative policy-making positions. Consequently, at the top level positions, the Italians are batting zero.

The unresponsiveness of the Board of Education to the educational needs of the Italian population in this city is further demonstrated by disparities in the following categories:

There are approximately 90 high school principals. Only one, I repeat, only one is Italian.

There are about 146 junior high and intermediate school principals. Of this number only eight are Italian, a bare 4%.

There are approximately 607 elementary school principals. Of this number only 36 are Italian, a mere 6%.

Of all the assistant principals in all schools, including those in charge of subject areas (formerly known as chairmen), we Italians number less than 5%.

By way of illustration, we would like to point out how underrepresentation of Italian teachers discriminates against students of Italian descent. There is a high school in District No. 20 in Brooklyn where 60% of the students come from Italian homes. At that particular school neither the principal nor the administrative assistant principals are Italian. Of the eleven assistant principals in charge of subject areas, not even one is Italian. Among a staff of 18 guidance counselors and grade advisors, again we don't find any Italians. Of 180 teachers, 30 are Italian; that is approximately 16%. Of 250 foreign students, 150 are native Italians. Small wonder then, that at this school 90% of the dropouts are Italian, that the reading scores of the Italian students are low, and that the greater percentage of Italian students are general course students who do not go on to college.

It is therefore, the recommendation of the Congress of Italian-American Organizations, Inc. that in a concerted effort to eradicate these ills, it is necessary:

1) To abolish the Board of Examiners and substitute state certification to fill educational vacancies.

2) Appoint at least one Italian to the Board of Education, preferrably a person sensitive to the educational needs of the Italians.

3) Recruit and appoint immediately a representative number of Italians to policy-making positions at Board headquarters.

4) Establish an Italian ombudsman to investigate inequities.

In conclusion, I would like to thank the Commission for having had the opportunity to appear and to commend the Commission for its efforts to achieve a better balance in job opportunities in the field of education for all minorities.

Thank you.

THE CHAIRMAN: Thank you, sir. I would like to ask you some questions though. I'm interested in the figures because the survey that we got from the Board of Education did not reveal a breakdown of this order.

Where do these figures come from?

DR. VALLETUTTI: Let me preface my answer by telling you that we did ask the Board to make a survey a number of years ago, and they never did it, so that these figures are based on sources like the Red Book and based on speaking to principals and assistant principals, people in supervisory positions, teachers.

They come very close to a survey that we conducted ourselves in 1969. There have been slight modifications in that. We could probably make that available to you, but the validity is one that's based on actual statistics from the people in the field and the traditional sources. We do not actually have a survey from the Board.

THE CHAIRMAN: During these hearings we've been able to pinpoint complaints from various minority communities about where in the system they found problems. For example, some Spanish-speaking people have testified that there have often been problems with the oral exam because of the accent; some Black people testified that even though they weren't from the South, they were accused of Southernisms and disqualified from exams, in addition to color playing a part.

Can you, as best as you can, pinpoint where in the system and for what reasons you believe Italians have been disqualified?

DR. VALLETUTTI: I think the oral examination per se is a wonderful way of concealing and discrediting many people. It's a way of keeping the status quo.

I think the Board of Examiners has been guilty in this practice. I think it's a known fact. We've heard it said here tonight, and there are many court cases pending precisely on, hinging on, this point because heretofore there has been no way of examining or subjecting the oral to further examination. Now they're taping them so there is possibly a review. But, up until recently, that's been almost impossible.

So, it's been a way to discredit people and keep them from coming up in the ranks.

THE CHAIRMAN: This is interesting and helpful to us in that the Commission has been in the process of designing a questionnaire for some time so as to get at the concerns of the Italian-American community about anti-Italian bias and we're trying to get at its roots and nature. It's a different kind of bias from that experienced by some other minority groups, and therefore, we've had to draw up a different questionnaire.

In this regard I'm interested in whether or not it is your view that this practice which your testimony speaks to is a historical one, or is it one of recent origin which the Italian-American community in the city feels? Or have they felt it all along?

DR. VALLETUTTI: I think the Italian-American community has not been vociferous at all. They've been content to accept their fate and not do anything about it.

We have seen an awakening of the Italian-American conscience, and perhaps the Black people have taught us a great lesson in this respect. And we share this knowledge with them, that if you want something, you have to fight for it.

THE CHAIRMAN: I want to go on record in favor of a coalition between Italian-Americans and Blacks and Puerto Ricans in the City.

I want to thank you very much, Doctor, for coming forward. I think your testimony has been most valuable for the reason that whatever problems come out of the school system are always regarded as simply the problems of the traditional minority group people. There is a tendency to forget that this is a city of minority groups and that the minority group from which you come, like the minority group from which I come, is only a small part of this city, and that in many ways this city more than any other city has the great challenge of making sure that people of more different origins than you can find in any city in the world get their fair share of what there is in this great city. And perhaps not alone Blacks and Puerto Ricans, but other members of minorities, including white minorities, are not getting their share.

MR. TRACTENBERG: May I ask one question.

I'm just curious, Doctor, whether the same kind of defense has been made by the Board of Education in the case of Italian-Americans as in the case of Blacks and Puerto Ricans, that is, that there have been insufficient numbers of applicants and that, therefore, the number of Italian-Americans in the school system is really outside the control of the Board of Education.

DR. VALLETUTTI: I think that's hogwash.

MR. TRACTENBERG: Has that been their position?

DR. VALLETUTTI: I can't speak for the Board, but I think we have a member here who might enlighten us on that, if I can call on one of our members.

MISS LINQUIST: My name is Rita Linquist. I'm a member of C.I.A.O., also a staff member of the New York City Board of Education.

With regard to the question, is the number of Italians who

apply for applications to any teaching or administrative job or supervisory job small in number, one would have to look at the record and see the number of successful candidates.

The question in point or case in point is the recent principal, high school principal list that I had occasion to see today, 1969, I believe. On that list, there were no Italians.

The observation that can be made is that we come through the rigid examination and when we go to the subjective aspect, the oral, we do not survive. That is with regard to the number of applicants who do apply for the position.

THE CHAIRMAN: Clearly, the point where Italian-Americans feel that they are shut off is in the oral.

MISS LINQUIST: Right.

Without a reviewable record or transcript of what goes on within the panel, the interviewing panel, and with the freedom of the interviewers to take out of context what is said, one can be claimed to have said something or one can be told in the account that he said something which never took place. And we have some cases presently where we have Italians who have made the list for the Board of Examiners and have never been appointed, at least one. Never been appointed.

And, in certain subject areas, if you'll look at the record again, as Dr. Valletutti mentioned, on the high school level, there is less than 5% of the assistant principals of all high schools in charge of subject areas, previously designated as chairmen, less than 5% Italians. And these are in areas such as the school mentioned, the high school, District 20, where we have 60% Italians in the school, and we don't have any representation on the administrative staff or supervisory staff; and there 150 out of 250 foreign-born students are advised by a non-Italian adviser, where there is no identification with the cultural background of these youngsters.

THE CHAIRMAN: This testimony makes it clear that there is rather consistent concern on the part of a number of different groups with the oral examination and that will be something we want to study further.

While we can appreciate the need to have people at least in the lower grades speak fairly correctly in talking to young children, the indication from the testimony here is that the oral examination is very widely used to disqualify people.

We find that interesting in light of the fact that this is the home of all the immigrants of the people of the world where we might expect to find greater tolerance. If one went to Atlanta speaking with a Brooklyn accent, one might better expect to be disqualified; but in New York, one would think there would be a built-in tolerance, and people would be more sophisticated.

MISS LINQUIST: Along that line, I would like to mention too, while I have the opportunity, there is a series of books, four books, called "These Heroes," that talk about the inspiration of immigrants and their contributions to the culture of the United States, four different books being read by low-reading ability children.

In not one of 60 cases cited has an Italian been mentioned.

Although we have contributed as a minority to the greatest of this country, not one has been recorded in these books, so that this discrimination exists in curriculum. There are no in-service human relations books which encourages sensitivity to the Italians; where other courses are being given for all other groups, we don't have any for the Italian-American.

THE CHAIRMAN: I want to echo this with respect to the Oriental community.

This country has seen enough with respect to its classic minorities, its Black and Spanish-speaking people, so that you would think that we would wish to avert the problem of building up more disgruntled and angry minority groups, as is clearly going to be the case unless everyone feels his group is being relatively fairly treated.

The Oriental community feels it is an ignored community. Now we find the Italian community considers itself a classic discriminated against group. The city is taking cognizance of this and is moving before this becomes a crisis.

I would only reiterate that our experience with minority groups in this country in not taking recognition of their felt grievances is so awful that when we find coming on the horizon other groups who are feeling the same sort of things, we would do well to move early rather than late as we have classically done. Therefore I appreciate your coming forward now, rather than five years from now when this became a terrible problem in your community; and we'll take your testimony into consideration along with the testimony we've heard from other minorities here.

Let's also give a plug to a program next Sunday on the Commission Show, Open Circuit. We're doing a series of programs on the three largest white minority groups in this town, showing that there is great unawareness of the extent to which white minority groups feel themselves aggrieved.

Last week we discussed the Jewish community with Morris Abram; and this coming Sunday on NBC, Channel 4, we'll be discussing the Italian-American community; and the Sunday after that we'll be discussing with another guest the Irish-American community.

Mr. Zeitlin. Mr. Zeitlin is a principal at Louis Pasteur Junior High School.

MR. ZEITLIN: I want to thank you for this opportunity to speak. While I could say a lot about what has been going on, I would like instead to take up a matter which two years ago--when I had a sabbatical leave and wanted to do something worthwhile-- I prepared for Herbert Hill of the NAACP, and that is a study of the practices of the Board of Education in regard to its administrative employees.

As soon as I bring up this subject, everybody gets very sleepy because of course the administrative employees of the Board of Education do not have a direct relationship to the teaching situation and do not have much influence on whether or not individuals succeed.

But, I would like to point out that in this respect the discrimination is so open and so flagrant, though well hidden, that none of the argument I've been listening to in the last two hours can possibly be used to justify what's going on. I would even hazard a guess that if the reverse were true, and if the Blacks had all the jobs that the whites now had, everybody would see the injustice of the situation and it would take about five hours to a day to rectify the situation, which goes on year after year after year without being rectified.

Let me start at the top and work down. The Board publishes some years--by the way, I think Nader's Raiders would have more trouble finding out what's going on in the Board of Education than in U.S. Steel--I had to devote full time for two weeks and get several people to give me things that they had no right to give me and taking a chance of getting into trouble with that.

To begin with the top, it's not a generally known fact, it is a hidden fact--certainly true before, and I see nothing to indicate it isn't true now--that the highest paid person in the school isn't the principal at all. It's the custodian who in the past made two or three times the income of the principal, though this has been cut down somewhat.

In New York City according to the 1968 report of the Board which I have here--I got semi-legally the March 1969 report which is still not released for publication although two years old, and this is typical of difficulty in getting information on this--in New York City of 230 custodians, according to the 1968 report, eight were Black. Of 622 school custodial engineers, that's the higher position, ten were Black; six were permanently appointed and four provisional.

The picture has not changed substantially since then though I find it absolutely impossible to get the data. However, you members of the Commission have powers I don't have, and maybe you can.

The argument is given that this is a Civil Service examination, and it is unfortunate there aren't any Blacks who can qualify. But what is never stated is that the union which the custodians make up has so arranged things by nepotism and favoritism that each custodian takes under his wing one protege and lets him get the experience which is needed in order to qualify for the examination. And then, of course, the custodians give a course aimed right at the examination.

So the purpose of the Civil Service Law is completely subverted, and this goes on year after year after year. And the members of the Board who I don't think approve of this, though I have spoken to past members of the Board over past years and written them letters for several years, the members of the Board are so involved in these intense arguments or troubles with parents whose children are not learning anything, and the members of the Board come and go so fast, really, whereas we permanent civil servants stay on forever, they never even catch up with these things. I don't think they know they're going on. I'm not accusing them of bad faith.

I don't know whether you know it, but the Board employs

craftsmen, carpenters, plumbers, so on, who get union wages and who have one of the nicest jobs in the city. It may be one reason there are not more Italian teachers. This job may be better.

These men are really sitting pretty because unlike other members of the building industry they work 52 weeks a year, never miss a day and get straight union wages. 4.2% were Black two years ago. The number had declined from what it was four years ago. As Martin Luther King said, "Time is neutral. It does not cure all evils."

Let me give you some of the figures according to the last available report, figures which I had the utmost difficulty in securing.

There were four Negro carpenters out of 182, zero electricians of 63, eight laborers of 55, one machinist of 31, one machinist helper of 21, zero plumbers of 44, one steamfitter of 21, and of 30 foremen, zero Blacks.

Those are some of the worthwhile jobs in the school system.

For some of the other positions where I can't tell you as much, the Board of Education maintains the fiction that every custodian is an independent businessman who makes a contract with the Board to keep the building clean, keep it in order and so on. In fact the arrangement is such that I think it's attributable to the conscientiousness of the custodians that the buildings are in as good shape as they are. Therefore, I cannot give you the figures for another very good job, known as boilerman--well, the man in charge of the boiler. There is a term for it. The Board maintains that these are employees of the custodians and not their employees, and therefore, they do not maintain any figures on these people since they're not their employees. The same is true of the cleaners who have much less proper jobs.

Two more things and I'll be finished with my original presentation. I'm looking for the name of the men who are the first assistants for the custodians. Firemen, they're called.

Now, the over-all figures of the Board show that it employs more Blacks than are employed by other companies outside. That's true. But, they put all the figures together in all their public releases and don't point out that the overwhelming number of Black women employed by the Board are in the lowest category of clerk and the overwhelming number of Black men are very unfortunate people who work in school cafeterias who are not paid on an annual basis, laid off every summer, are only temporary people. And they balance the figures in this way.

Now, I submit that most Blacks in New York City work. And if you made up figures for the whole city and just lumped everybody together, you would naturally show that there are a great many Blacks employed in New York City by every employer in the city, however bigoted he may be, because there are certain positions where it pays to employ Blacks.

I'm not saying the Board is bigoted, but the general pattern of employment is distressingly like that of the general employers of the city.

Oddly enough if you want to find Black custodians, you can find them. They work in the parochial schools, getting very little money. Whenever there is a meeting called by the Police Department, there are Black custodians there, from the parochial schools. Judging from the way they dress, there is quite a difference between their salaries and the salaries of the employees of the public schools.

The Board announced, right after the Brown decision, that it was going to be a defender and a champion of its own graduates. I submit that now that most of the students in New York City are Blacks and Puerto Ricans, the Board is falling very short of this nobly stated purpose. It should be a model employer, and it isn't.

Of course, where does all this trouble come from? It comes from the unfortunate aspect of the role of the craft unions in New York City in keeping Blacks out of good positions. This is a union town and the Board says it will employ union labor and once it does that, it's lost the whole ball game.

I submit that the Board should use vocational schools and particularly evening trade schools to prepare competent minority people to fill these jobs, and then by genuine Civil Service examinations allow them to be filled.

Last of all, which I think is the most outrageous procedure of all and which I think is still going on--I know it was two years ago, but as I say, now I'm working again, I can't get all this information; it's a full-time job to get any of it, and now I'm active as principal of my school again--we should close down every private school in the public school system because we have them.

Under the Manpower Training Act and other laws like that, unions designate people who are being trained for jobs, and they are given courses in the Board of Education schools to which only those who are nominated by unions can attend. I think the Board is fully reimbursed for this by the federal government. This is something John Kennedy said he was going to do something about, and then decided he better not do anything about it after all.

I don't think it costs the taxpayers of the city any money, but there shouldn't be any course in any school, in my opinion, which isn't open to everybody who is competent to take it.

THE CHAIRMAN: When we announced this investigation, the matter you are speaking to was brought to our attention and we did find it quite a shocking situation.

It would appear no matter what level you're operating on, whether you're talking about garbage men, policemen, or janitors, this is a terrible problem in our society.

We're interested to see whether this matter can de dealt with through that machinery because if it cannot be, it does present a problem for this Commission, one which requires, it seems to us, separate and exclusive treatment on our part.

MR. ZEITLIN: May I point out the Board spends 30% of its money on its nonteaching personnel salaries. This is not a minor item I'm talking about. Additionally, you might include in that the money it spends on construction of new buildings and I don't have to tell you what's going on there.

I would like to point out that two years ago the Board still had in its contract, word for word, the same phrase which was used to stop a single Negro from getting employment when a billion in employment was spent building the World's Fair, a phrase which in my opinion is a guarantee to the union not to obey the Fair Employment Practices Act of the United States. This is a guarantee not to obey the law because it says that nothing will be done by the Board of Education during the construction of this building that will in any way embarrass or make difficulties for the unions that are involved.

This year the building program is cut down because of Mayor Lindsay's, the city's, financial difficulties.

It may not be 30% but two years ago I sat down and I figured out all the money the Board was spending on salaries, and I found that 30% came to over a half a billion dollars being spent on salaries for the so-called administrative jobs.

So, I'm not talking about some little corner which this Commission will neglect, I hope. If you don't neglect it, you'll be the first group that hasn't neglected it.

MR. TRACTENBERG: This isn't really a question, but perhaps Mr. Zeitlin has a reaction to it.

In earlier testimony, we heard from the Board of Examiners and Board of Education officials that virtually the entire professional staff of the Board of Examiners and the Personnel Office in the Board of Education consisted not of Civil Service personnel, but pedagogical personnel, ostensibly assigned on a temporary basis to these administrative types of jobs, but in fact, as it turns out, in most cases assigned there permanently and making their career in administrative capacities without having taken exams or being licensed in any way for those positions.

I think this ties in, in a kind of interesting way, with the suggestion that administrative personnel may really be rather intimately connected with the substance of the investigation.

MR. ZEITLIN: I think we've got a confusion of terms here, if I may be allowed to comment on that. I'm afraid you're going to go down a blind alley.

The Board uses administrative employees not at all in the sense of school administrators. The Board uses the term in the report made each year by the Deputy Superintendent in charge of business affairs to refer to all the people in maintenance, all the people in offices, all the people that have nothing to do directly with education.

The Board people could say that technically the overwhelming majority of their employees are educational and that I'm completely wrong in saying 30%. But I'm claiming when a custodian hires someone that he is an employee of the Board of Education, and it is a subterfuge to say he is an employee of the custodian.

When the Board spends half a billion dollars a year on construction, as it does in many years--and therefore is one of the largest constructors in New York City--it's a little ingenuous to claim, well, we just sign contracts with people, we know nothing about this.

Mr. Zeitlin

I have written the Board members for years and said they could break the whole logjam in the building industry if they would refuse to spend a single cent on building a new school until some of the problems were solved.

They build such a large part of all the construction there is, they could put enormous pressure on the building and trade councils to change these procedures.

THE CHAIRMAN: Thank you very much, Mr. Zeitlin, for coming forward with this.

MISS RINGGOLD: My name is Faith Ringgold. I was going to talk about the rights of women and to emphasize the right of Black women to rise in the system on the same par, as low as it is, with Black men.

Women teachers, as you know, in the system, comprise practically 85% of the teaching staff and men do all the administering. And this is true in the Black community as well as in the white.

However, taking precedence over this very important problem which is going to raise its ugly head very shortly, are the rights of children.

Let me give you a little background about myself. I have been a teacher of art in the public schools of New York City for the past 16 years. I have a B.S. and M.A. in art and education from City College. My license is regular fine arts teacher, day high schools.

I am unfortunately much prouder to be also a professional painter and lecturer. Presently I'm a lecturer in Black art at Wagner College, Staten Island and instructor in African and African-American art education at the Bank Street College for Teachers.

I am here tonight to focus attention on the obviously discriminatory practices at Brandeis High School. Brandeis High School has no Black or Puerto Rican or other nonwhite supervisors. Even the Black history courses at Brandeis High School, as meager as they are, are taught by white teachers only.

The annex where I teach has over 1500 students. To my knowledge, only two are white. The annex is located on 66th Street across the street from Lincoln Center. The pupils come mostly from the Harlem area.

There are six Black teachers in the school out of a staff of over 130 teachers. Of course this is just the annex picture.

The main building has over 5500 students, 99% of which are Black and Puerto Rican. The main building is located on 84th Street between Amsterdam and Columbus Avenue.

There are about 15 Black teachers in Brandeis High School out of a staff of 280 teachers. There are no Black supervisors in either the main building or the annex.

I've been teaching in the school for three years and the number of Black people employed as teachers in that school has not radically changed since I came there.

Recently, a student at Brandeis has been circulating a petition among the students to get a Black principal at Brandeis. He has been law-abiding and orderly about this. However, the events in his life since he and other students embarked on this project to get a Black principal at Brandeis make it quite clear that this school, which is predominantly Black and Puerto Rican, remains lily-white on the administrative and supervisory level.

Let me tell you of some of the events that have happened to the students. Students were told they would be suspended if they signed the petition or if they helped in any way to get petitions signed. Other deterrent tactics included that students were told the petition was poorly worded, that the school's name was misspelled, that the petition should include more of an explanation, that it wouldn't work.

Let me explain to you that our children have serious reading problems and I think the fact that they got a petition together that said simply, "Do you want a Black principal at Brandeis?" was a great accomplishment.

The kids were asked why do you want to get rid of the principal, he didn't do anything. To that, one student answered, "That's why we want to get rid of him, because he doesn't do anything."

All kinds of other insidious remarks were designed to forestall the students' determining their own destiny. However, the worst of the situation came when several students complained to me that they were being pushed around, harassed, and in other ways intimidated for no apparent reason by members of the faculty, obviously, with the intent of arousing them to strike back so as to involve them in an assault on teachers.

However, it didn't work. The students at that particular time, fortunately, because we've had violence at Brandeis but very small things have happened, the students in respect to the petitions have not resorted to any form of violence.

However, the students at Brandeis do need your help. I'm talking about the Commission. They need the help of the parents and teachers at Brandeis. These people, parents and teachers at Brandeis, must respect and cooperate in the students' right to participate in the so-called democratic process of petitioning.

Let me tell you more about what has happened at Brandeis High School.

On Thursday the young man who began the petition for the Black principal at Brandeis burst into my class in full view of my third period class, panting and shaking with fear, and threw himself across the threshhold of the door, exhausted from running away from two teachers who had been harassing him, pushing him, hitting him, slapping him and plucking him in his head, as well as threatening him with suspension and arrest if he did not stop his petition for his Black principal.

All of this was done in the presence of two uniformed policemen who sat by, obviously waiting for the student to strike back so they could beat or arrest him or both. These faculty members tried to take away his petition. They offered him freedom in return for the release of the petition. He refused. He was afraid, but obviously he was very committed. The student also, in another attempt to participate in the so-called democratic process, requested one of the policemen at the time he was being harassed to arrest the faculty member for harassing him and plucking him in his head. The policeman laughed.

When the student told me, along with the other students, the story, I have never felt more helpless to deal with the problems of students.

In an attempt to ascertain the rights of students when they are victimized by faculty or other school officials, since they obviously are not covered by the protective shield of New York's finest, I went to find out what agency, what recourse, to assure them to survive the oppressive sources.

I called the principal of the high school. He was out to lunch, pardon the expression. I spoke to his assistant, Mr. Halpern. He was not able to help me nor was he very interested in doing so.

I was obviously dialing the wrong number by calling the Board of Education.

I dialed the UFT for laughs, but they were busy and I didn't persist.

I contacted the City Commission and they put me in touch with the American Civil Liberties Union and I spoke to Mr. Summer who told me of a program of the Student Rights Project, located at 84 Fifth Avenue, 924-7800.

The only recourse students have, from my investigation among all the agencies, is the Student Rights Project of the American Civil Liberties Union. In the event a student is harassed, threatened or beaten, this Project seems to be the only available place for them to go. I have a handbook which lists students' rights and Mr. Summer is available to all students to help them insure their rights peaceably and under the law.

I am requesting the City Commission to look into the situation at Brandeis. The Commissioner just a few seconds ago said that it is very important to see things and to try to get them before they happen. At Brandeis we've had a fairly quiet situation. It would be very good to keep it that way and I think with the help of the Commission we can keep it that way.

It is important to look into the situation at Brandeis, both at the annex and in the main building, to speak with the students. Some students from Brandeis will be here tomorrow as well as teachers.

Many teachers are intimidated because of lack of tenure by oppressive tactics and have been, therefore, silenced. Black teachers at Brandeis are bought off and silenced through such plum jobs or programs as Reach Out, Look Up, really more like shut up, everything but speak up. If they had the security of the Commission, or another powerful City agency, maybe they would find their voices which the children so desperately need.

I too want a Black principal at Brandeis. I know this principal couldn't care less than the present one, nor could the principal possibly do less in the interest of Black people.

Maybe next year when Black solidarity comes, we can have

a program in the auditorium to celebrate the liberation of students and teachers at Brandeis High School. And maybe next year at Martin Luther King's birthday we can have a principal who will provide leadership in the observance of this great man because this year our principal had no program for Martin Luther King, Jr., although I understand he is planning to be principal of the school in his name.

THE CHAIRMAN: Thank you, Miss Ringgold.

I want to say for the record, we are going to continue to have a phenomenon of students and parents speaking out expressly for a specific minority group. We're never going to get back to normal, as it were, until we see sufficient numbers of all kinds of people in the system so that people can concentrate on other things.

It is interesting with all the problems you have, in other school systems in the country--and we keep in touch with those school systems--that their problems do not revolve around those questions. Those students are petitioning about other things. Because they see sufficient numbers of minority people around them, they focus their grievances on other things.

It's important to know that Miss Ringgold pointed out that this principal, for example, did not see fit to have a special program for Martin Luther King's birthday. One doesn't have to be Black to know what Martin Luther King means to Black people. One doesn't have to be Black to know Martin Luther King is indeed an ecumenical hero, maybe the first man to be a hero of both Black and white people living in the same country. But failure to be sensitive enough to know that, is important. One way to be sensitive is to be Black. But it ought to be possible to be human and to understand that if you lived through our times, you have seen perhaps the greatest hero of Black people shot down.

Part of what is driving young people who are not mature and don't have all the wisdom in the world, when they focus in on the question of ethnicity and color, is that they do not see enough people in the school system of various races and ethnic groups to discount the question of color or ethnic origin in whatever problem they happen to be dealing with. And they will not do it until they do see such people.

It may be that the problem at Brandeis High School would be less difficult if there were a Black principal; it might be less difficult if there were a sensitive white principal; it might be less difficult if there were a sensitive Puerto Rican principal.

Until you get representative staff throughout the system, people are going to focus their grievances around the color and ethnic personnel question. And it is very difficult to say to people lay aside racial and ethnic considerations when they are so numerous in the school system.

The purpose of these hearings is to try to take this question out of the many problems before the school system, so that it may focus on those questions it doesn't have any idea how to deal with.

This Students Rights Handbook is important, if for no other reason than that it indicates here is a lawful way to proceed. Therefore, it encourages people to use orderly processes.

Here, for example, is a petition, and as she said, here is the trouble in a ghetto school. Instead of running around and tearing up the building, they have done what is a very sophisticated thing, and what may ultimately be a very futile thing. They have signed a petition.

It takes us back to first principles of American democracy.

Carmen Snead and the other two witnesses with her, take the stand, please.

MISS SNEAD: I am Carmen Snead.

(Whereupon, at this point, Miss Snead commenced speaking in Spanish.)

THE CHAIRMAN: Miss Snead, you may speak in Spanish, but I want you to know it won't be taken on the record because, unfortunately, the stenographer writes only in English.

MISS SNEAD: I just did this on purpose. This is the way our people feel, the children and the parents feel, when they come into the school. They just talk Spanish and then here the supervisor, the principal, the assistant principal, the teacher, the paraprofessional--you name it--doesn't know even that he is a citizen of the United States. They look up and say, he must be mentally retarded, or something is wrong with him, he doesn't talk the same way we talk.

You see, that is the way--

You see he (pointed to reporter) moved his machine. He went over like this and he is trying to listen to me. Maybe I speak a little louder and maybe he can understand me.

The teacher will answer him very loud, "What are you talking about?" They think that he is deaf. You know, they just can't communicate.

They are very intelligent in their own language, but if they come over here--just like it will happen if you go to Russia or China and they won't understand--you won't be able to understand them. That doesn't mean the child or person is mentally retarded or disturbed. It means he has a different custom and background. That is all there is to it.

This is just me. I am kind of funny that way. I want to put my point across and I ask translation in here and somebody can translate. I don't want to be rude to anybody here. I just wanted to put the point across.

Another thing I want to say, we talk about--I jump from one place into the other, so you will have to bear with me. After all, I am deprived, too. Culturally deprived, that is what they call them--out at the Board of Examiners. I am going to talk about things that I saw myself.

I went to a school--a high school, for that matter--where there is no Puerto Rican teachers, principals, you name it. I don't think there is even a paraprofessional.

I went to talk to the principal and the door is closed. I am trying to say, it is funny there is no people there. Then I waited and picked up the intercom. He come out and there was two members of the Board of Examiners and they was giving the test for-- the principal's test--and he tells me, "Oh, Mrs. Snead, will you please wait a minute. We are in the midst of giving somebody a trial test and we have 15 more minutes to go."

And this assistant principal, which is a friend of the principal --I don't know--related or whatever, but she is there and taking a trial test with a clock and everything there to test.

After we got through, we went around and went to eat--I didn't want to be impolite--and we came back and he is sitting down. This principal is on the Board of Examiners. He starts talking about we have to keep the--keep this, because, you know, it--because it was--this was put into effect to stop the nepotism.

I say, "What are you talking about? Right here I am seeing this. This lady is so lucky that somebody will give her time for her to study this test, and all that, and then not only that, but I am sure this is not the first try that you give her. I am sure she had many other tries."

I mean, by the time they get to the Board of Examiners, they thought she could do it with her eyes closed.

Our Black and Puerto Rican people can't afford to do that. They must work in a factory, to work any place, but they can't afford to have anybody to do this.

"You say this is made to keep out nepotism? This is exactly what you are doing here."

He gave me--then the two more members were examined there.

This is one thing, that maybe because, too, maybe I am mentally retarded, too. Maybe I can't see. Maybe this is in the process of cultural background, like we were talking about, too.

Now, when I went to school as a child--this is just as simple as that--you know, we can't afford sometimes to buy a sharpener, but you must have a pencil and it must be sharpened, or else you get an "F." Then because you can't afford to have a pen, somehow you use a pencil all the way up to--I'm talking way back now, I don't know about now, if they still use it to sharpen the pencil-- but up to the 6th grade, until you can afford to get a pen, so now we use, what they use back home, what they call a Gem--we call it a brand name--it is a razor blade.

After everybody gets through with the razor blade, the boy takes it to school and that is his sharpener. A boy maybe carry a penknife, but it is not lady-like to carry a penknife, so you carry a razor blade. You have a razor blade to sharpen your pencil. It is clear a child comes from Puerto Rico and he is used to a razor blade, and he takes his razor blade to school.

Now, I know of an incident in this school where a boy was in the--a seven-year-old--in the second grade. Now, he took out his sharpener, his razor blade. So, right away, it was a big thing. He was suspended.

Now, the mother told me he--they don't speak the language. She just became a widow, and the boy was close with the father, very close--the boy go scared. They said it took three teachers to restrain this seven-year-old boy. I don't know what kind of teachers. Maybe they didn't have the men there that day, but it takes three to restrain a boy 7 years old.

This happened. I have--people like from the Bronx I have the same thing.

If a teacher there, a principal, or somebody knows or understands that this--they know, they went to school in Puerto Rico--that that is what they use it for.

I never heard of an incident back home of using that razor blade to hurt anybody. They always use their fists, but never use a razor blade, and I am sure it is the same way here. It is not part of the culture, but this is from the necessity of not having enough money to buy what you have to buy. And you use the next best thing you have.

About this program that the Board of Education, has about the bilingual teachers, that is one thing.

The other day I was there. I have some friend I went to visit, and they were talking about this one didn't pass a test because he doesn't speak enough English and he had an accent, and the other one didn't pass the test because he was raised here and he can't speak Spanish. So it is no good what side you are on. If you are Puerto Rican and Spanish-speaking, you lose out because you can't speak English or you have an accent; and if you're English, you can't get in because you can't speak Spanish.

I have a girl that came over to me and says, "I want to apply for this program." She says, "I just came from Puerto Rico."

She used to teach in Puerto Rico and they tell her she cannot teach here because of her language barrier. She taught in high school for 6 years and she was a principal. So here she says, "I don't want to go into a factory to work." And this happened last week.

And I say, "Well, did you go to this program that they have in the Board of Education?"

She said, "I went there when I came back last September and they told me that they would not be able to--I mean, they take my name and address, but let me know in January because now they are full, anyway. And I may not be able to get in."

How come they didn't take her name. If they don't take a name, how can they notify her?

Now, she went back again in November, and the same thing. She said, "The clerk, she didn't even look at me, but she told me they would not need me. When I give my name, I notice they don't take it down."

She went back a week before last, and the same thing happened again. So then I called up there and I says, "What happened?"

"Send her over. We don't have no room, but we can put her on maybe as an educational assistant, a paraprofessional and maybe she can work for $2.50 an hour until we can place her in a program."

My God, she has been in charge of high school students and has been a principal in charge of a school for 6 years. I think she could at least come over here and teach a third-grader.

And this is the way it goes over and over again. I can tell you that because I am there all the time--at all times.

I think a father went to school, in one of the schools, and the teacher herself came over and says, "Well, I can't talk to you now because I have to fill out some applications. First you must show me your passport."

Now, this is the end. If you don't know Puerto Rico is supposed to be a commonwealth of the United States, she has no business teaching in a school where the percentage is 99% Puerto Rican children.

So this is all I have to say.

Anything you want to add to it?

MRS. MOSES: Commissioner, my name is Mrs. Frances Moses, Chairman of the Educational Committee of the Tompkins Tenants Association, Incorporated, in the Williamsburg territory. I am a mother of four children. I am an inspector for the Board of Elections and also I am a family assistant in the Board of Education system.

I am deeply concerned about the unfair labor practices that has been placed on the only, we will say, so-called Black principal in the Williamsburg territory, District 14. This gentleman was appointed by the community board and also the parents approved in what we would consider a community meeting, due to the fact that the so-called CSA and, I will even say, the Board of Examiners, and also some of the--I don't know whether you call them the higher echelon of the UFT and the so-called people who have taken it upon themselves to say what would be good for the community.

Now, before this particular principal came into this particular school, IS 33, they happened to have had a principal who had been approved by the Board of Examiners who happened to have been of another ethnic group. The school had gone completely chaotic. The school had had six fires in the radius of, I would say, about 2 months.

Well, the parents were in an uproar with the conditions there, asking to please let us try somebody who could really help us. They sat down with the district superintendent and this, of course, was the PTA president, parents concerned, community leaders. And in sitting down with these people, having been given a list of some of the so-called principals who were supposed to be on this particular list that the Board of Examiners had, out of seven candidates, one showed up; and the one that showed up, of course, was not a Black person because there wasn't a Black person up on the higher part of the list. And, of course, he refused.

All right.

After many, many months of trying to see what they could do to help themselves, they finally came up with a gentleman who happened to have been established at one of the 600 schools. He was considered a person who had the certification of the state. He had certifications and qualifications that many persons perhaps would not even have who happened to be on the Board of Examiners so-called racist list.

After having been appointed by the Community Board since

August--if I am not mistaken it was an August meeting--this particular person--and I can give his name because, as parents, we have gone to court and we have been in and out; and the CSA and the Board of Examiners had brought it up to the Supreme Court-- this gentleman has been on the staff but he is being paid a teacher's salary.

Since he has been employed there, there have been no suspensions, the school is conducted in a different manner. But, yes, he is still on a teacher's salary. I don't know what you would call it, but I would call it not only racist but prejudiced to the utmost.

And I would state to the Commissioner that the New York City Board of Education should not celebrate any more Martin Luther King days because the principles for which he stood was that every child should be educated. And because he saw that the Blacks and the Puerto Ricans and all of the minority groups in the areas that he had traveled had been suffering from lack of education, he felt that something should be done. And when the schools practice the so-called Martin Luther King day, it is like a slur on our children. It should not be practiced, Commissioner, because, there again, my children and all the children in the City of New York are only practicing a farce.

Now, to get back again to this particular person, Mr. Claude Huntley. We have questioned and questioned again why should this person, who is carrying on the tasks of a principal, written into the so-called Red Book of the Board of Education, the 1971 issue, that he is a principal, but he is receiving a teacher's salary. If it were just because of the fact that this person was not on a particular list, but was able to contain the school in such a manner that anybody could be proud of. This particular person has made paraprofessionals, school aides and what-have-you, and he really went in there organizing, making children feel like they were somebody. And to see the Blacks and Puerto Ricans and I will say others, if there are any, going into this particular school--because somehow or other they do put others--it is a great pleasure, as a parent, to see a principal who will greet the children in front of the school in the morning. And this is an intermediate school where children have had a stigma placed upon them that there is nothing for you but the welfare.

The few that have happened to be selected to go, I would say, for what they would classify as the scholarship children or the intellectually gifted children that the Board of Education has set up, it is nothing but a fraud, because when he is gifted and he has many talents and he graduates from the so-called high schools-- which many of them find that they can't even pass the test for--it is rather sad. It is not just stealing the joy from the parents, but it is stealing so much from the youngsters that have not for many, many years felt that they were somebody.

Commissioner, I am asking you to check out, find out why many of these things have been happening. We have been down to the Board of Education, 110 Livingston Street, and many of us that were born and raised here in the State of New York almost have the feeling, and I--and I deeply, in my heart, state--that that place should be abolished because it would destroy--and when I say "destroy," I am speaking of the Board of Examiners, the UFT, the CSA--would destroy the one thing that God has given to all of us, that is, children. And this is what the Black and Puerto Rican people happen to be saying, and the children, these and others--and I say others, because there are many poor whites that happen to be in this city who are suffering, too.

This so-called racist mess has really been introduced, I will say, by the Board of Education and the Board of Examiners. And we know that they are racists, because if they were not racist, why isn't there a higher percentage of Blacks and Puerto Ricans on it. How could you say who has the proper diction?

We find, too, in working in many of these schools, that there are teachers, and believe me, they need to go back and get some speech. Many of them need help.

We find administrators we wonder about, for it is only tests that they have passed, and, believe me, tests do not make you have human relations to understand the needs of the children.

We feel that many of us in the community--because Williamsburg is one of the communities that people have said we haven't heard from--and what concerns us is the fact that a man, like Mr. Huntley, can have all these problems--and yet they can take a principal that was in one of the schools, and it was in all the newspapers, and place him in the district office and he is paid a principal's salary--and this principal, that is, only in name, so that the children can feel good, is receiving a teacher's salary. How pathetic.

I guess if you look at me, you would say, well, she is Black. Yes, I am Black. But I am also mixed with Shinnecock Indian. And I only have to go back to feel that my foreparents happen to have been swindled out of this great city, which was purchased for so little money, and yet many of you have taken it up and brought it into what we call an empire. And yet, what do you destroy? The children.

The Board of Examiners must be abolished. It is what one will classify as the Ku Klux Klan of New York City. Any other people who happen to say that it must continue, then they, too, are the men riding around and the women, also, without their hoods.

Many of us who have youngsters--and believe me, we are mothers to all the children--they question us. And when they say to us that children are tearing up the schools, Commissioner, just place yourself within the same walls that they have to be. People are saying, "You are mentally disturbed." "Oh, well, you can't be like this, because, after all, it is your home." "You can't do this and you can't do that" because of the fact that you are "poverty-stricken."

But I will tell every last one of you in here, we are all responsible and also I will tell you this, that anyone who takes it upon themself to say that they are a teacher and a supervisor, a Board of Examiners member, you are responsible for the corruption because you have the children more time than the parents.

When they leave us at 5 years old--and now you are taking them at 3--we don't have too much time, and the couple of hours that they come in the home, we have to try and do the homework that you have changed from the same system that many of us were educated under.

It is almost impossible, Commissioner, to try and relate to your children because everything has changed. You can't make one and one equal two any more. You must do it according to the concepts that the Board of Education is changing every day, and the poor teachers are confused. It is a new phonics system, a new this or a new that; and many of the youngsters are saying, "Mommy, we are looking to you, we are looking to our fathers," who happen to have to work sometimes two jobs. And many of them have become victims, Commissioner, because the City of New York is responsible, and I will say it again and again, the Board of Education is exploiting us, too, and in teaching our children that the welfare is the only system for them.

When a child has to come home and say to his mother, "Well, mommy, we know another child in the home is more money," and the child, too, is hearing it in the school and asks immediately, "Are you on welfare? You are going to the hospital?" It is the same thing. The Board of Education is saying again, "If you want lunch, you must be deprived."

The only thing, Commissioner, we are deprived of is fair treatment, and it has to be fair, because it is very pathetic to even see that many of our young men have to jump into poverty programs and many of our young women, who have different college degrees, they have to jump into it. And what is placed upon the child is a constant stigma, poverty, lack of this and lack of that.

As you can see, there are many of us willing to work on committees. We are not out completely to kill. But, believe me, we have also been frustrated, and when you are a mother--and you have to be a mother to so many, because the community, they rely upon us. They are relying upon us, too, Commissioner, because we do not want to feel that anybody, whether they are placed in any particular position, that it is again another sellout, because this has been placed upon us and we don't know who to trust.

If it is Black, if it is Puerto Rican and we do have--I mean, you know, you have to face it, we do have a few whites who are with us--but the main issue happens to be the youngsters, and I am asking you again, and I am asking everybody here, to see that this is no longer a game. Because you read it in the newspaper that the high schools are rebelling, they are rebelling in the elementary schools; and maybe if they took some of this money back and started all over again we would have a school system again.

MR. ROTHBAUM: Commissioner, my name is Arnold Rothbaum, and I am going to be speaking for the Education Committee of the Williamsburg Corporation.

District 14 has the honor of having the second worst reading scores in the city, and I have been told we are trying harder to become first. The district has approximately 29,000 children, of which 25% are Black and 65% are Spanish-speaking.

Of the approximately 17,000 Spanish-speaking children on the last test that I have seen--what they call an English proficiency test, which rates children's English, spoken English, on a scale of A through F, with C or below B considered great language handicaps--of the 17,000 Spanish-speaking children in the year 1968 through 1969, 40% were classified C through F. In 1969 through 1970, 44%. So there was a 4 per cent increase in one year.

There are exactly 21 Spanish-speaking teachers in the district. Not one teaches in a classroom. They serve--and I am not knocking these teachers, they are trying to do as good a job as they can--they serve as a buffer between the schools and the community. They serve as translators; they serve to quiet people, you know, if anything occurs. They really, in no way, serve except for parents to have someone to speak to, possibly. There is always that hope. They do not teach kids, as such.

This year was the first time that we got, in our district, one Black principal and one Puerto Rican principal. They are both off the list.

Miss Ceterio (phonetic) who is our principal at an MES school, which is 120, is an acting principal. Mr. Huntley, who is also at IS 33, is also at this point an acting principal. They are both not at this point receiving principal's salary, even though they are doing the work.

Let me just show you what a difference could make in the sense of things.

We have been talking about people like Claude Huntley. We have a 600 school in our district. It is called PS 36. As I said before, the ethnic composition of our district is 90% Puerto Rican and Black--65% Puerto Rican and 25% Black. The ethnic composition of that 600 school is 70% Black and 25% Puerto Rican. Yes, it is reversed.

We did a little investigation. Most of the children in PS 36 came from two schools--IS 33 was one of them. Again, as Mrs. Moses said, Mr. Huntley, who is Black and who worked at that school, has not yet this year suspended a child.

Let me give you some other specific examples of the cultural deprivation of the school system.

I have gone to suspension hearings and I have seen, practically in every case, where we are talking about a Spanish child, in the suspension hearing they have a thing which they claim is not part of the permanent record, but it travels with kids from school to school, all through their lives, and it is kept by the school system for 50 years. Practically every case where it involves a Spanish child, whether they are 9, 10, 11, there is a little note in there and it is usually something like this:

"Juan pays a lot of attention to girls."

All right. If there was any understanding of culture and what people call machismo in the Spanish culture, they would understand why.

When someone looks at this, when teachers put that in a record and you just look at it, it is a blank thing and, of course, these kids are classified as sex maniacs and you have to watch them.

There are other instances of where the cultural deprivation of the school system exists. I had another case with the suspension of a child at Junior High School 50. This kid has been here from Puerto Rico 2 years. His Spanish is beautiful. He speaks very well. He was placed in what they call a non-English-speaking section. Again, I gave you the statistics of how many Spanish-speaking teachers we have. It is not based on intelligence or anything else, just based on the fact they can't speak English. This kid, as a reward, was transferred up from this non-English section--and I say, "up," because it is looked like that to the lowest section, because we don't have heterogeneous groups, we have homogeneous groups. He was pushed up to the lowest section of the seventh grade.

He was bored. There was nothing there for him. There was no record from Puerto Rico, and the school system didn't ask for it.

We had a psychological test for the child, and they said he was tremendously bright. What did the school do? They put him back into the lowest section because they had no staff to really handle the problems of this child.

Another case. In Puerto Rico there isn't, as we have here, such a strict compulsory education law, so kids go to school, maybe some at five, some at six, some at seven, and some as much as eight. There was a case we had where this kid never went to school in Puerto Rico and he came here and he was 10 years old. They placed him in the fifth grade. Why? Because he is 10 years old. The kid couldn't read, couldn't write and still can't read or write. They now classify him as CRMD.

As to other things which have occurred, we once had two people come in from the Dominican Republic, two women. They were teachers down there. They were not bilingual. They only spoke Spanish.

We attempted something. We sent them into P.S. 19, which is 100 per cent--like a lot of our schools in our district--Spanish-speaking, which has in that C through F scale something like 74%. They asked to become paraprofessionals, not teachers. They wouldn't give them the application forms.

I just have two other incidents which I will relate to you.

One is that in our district, we have a school called P.S. 16, which has an assistant principal that nobody has ever seen. He has been on the payroll for 7 years.

Another is in Junior High School 57, which has a Puerto Rican assistant principal. This is in District 16. That Puerto Rican assistant principal is only receiving teacher's salary.

Some of the alternatives that the Education Committee has discussed--there are really two. One is that, first of all, the Board of Examiners should be abolished and, two, that we change things around. We have sufficient people in the city to really fill positions which are necessary now.

So, therefore, what we want is state certification. But another thing that we would like to request people to consider is the possibility of having, through our community, colleges, two-year colleges with an associate degree in teaching and with the possibility, after that, of a three-year internship program in our district.

And also for those who go to the four-year colleges, we would like to see a requirement at least for those teachers that come into our district, that they take Spanish.

And, also, as to those teachers, everybody knows that a test doesn't test teaching ability. It is what you learn on the job. We ask that those three years, prior to tenure, not be used for what it is now, which is basically that nobody is going to say, "I have trouble as a teacher because they can use it against me," and they will.

The whole philosophy of our school system, which is based on fear--whether it is fear of the parent or it is parents' fear of the teacher or the teacher's fear of the supervisor, and so on--that has to be erradicated so that it is really a learning process. And then, at the end, that should be like a graduation. It should be a great honor to get tenure. These people have gone through these things. They have gone through this intensive supervision and everything else, and possibly they will have a cure for some of the faults of the system that exist today.

Thank you.

THE CHAIRMAN: I want to thank the three witnesses who have testified about a single community.

I wonder if I might impose on those who are here. I will take it upon myself to say that I know Mrs. Buck is here with a tiny baby and it is likely that the baby is awake. I wonder if I might ask that she go before the others for that reason.

I think everyone is gracious enough and sympathetic enough to your problem.

MRS. BUCK: My name is Ruth Buck, and may I extend my thanks to everybody that let me go ahead because of my young baby.

I couldn't help it, but when I happened upon the radio program this afternoon on the investigation going on into the hiring practices of the Board of Education, I couldn't help but make my voice known, not just in the hiring practices but in the firing practices of the Board of Education.

I think that we have heard from many minority groups-- Blacks, Puerto Ricans, Italians, and others that I heard on the air this afternoon--but there is one minority group that I do not think you heard from yet, and that is the Christian in the New York City school system.

My name is Ruth Buck, as I said before, and I am a housewife, a mother of three children. One is 10, one is 3 and one is 2 months old.

I am a licensed teacher of Gregg stenography and typewriting in the New York City high schools. I am a licensed guidance counselor in the New York City high schools, and I am certified by the State of New York as a secondary school principal.

What happens in the Board of Education if one dares to act as though they follow the master, Jesus of Nazareth, without even so stating, but acting like they love, to the point that they will sacrifice on behalf of the students and the public who they serve? To myself, who always is willing and proud and never denies that I follow Him, I follow in the path that He would follow, as far as I can determine; and at the time of the strikes, I, if I stand alone, do not let down the public. What happens to someone like that?

Well, let's see. Twelve years in the system, excellent recommendations, a long history of one letter after another of satisfactory and superior service. But merely to cross the UFT or expose anything that a guidance counselor should be wise enough not to expose leads to the position that I am in now, fired from the system.

I would like to read part of a letter, dated November 29th, 1969, that I, as a guidance counselor at Franklin K. Lane High School wrote to Mr. Jacob Zack, Assistant Superintendent in charge of high schools at the time. And I wrote to him because I had grieved so many different ways, in and out and up and down the school system on behalf of the students and the injustices that were happening to them. And I make no apology at all for saying that I trust God in that if he gives me a housekeeper to take care of my children, that I go there free and that I am not worried about my children at home. And, therefore, I am, indeed, a mother to the children in my load. So let me read part of this:

"Dear Mr. Zack:

"This is to bring to your attention the matter of apparent wrongdoing against the following students at Franklin K. Lane High School: Amina McKnight, Charles Drew, Linda McMillan, Patricia ---"--I leave off her last name for her own benefit--"and Claude Miller. These students represent a sampling from my load of about 1,200 students. Injustices have apparently worked against these five and have similarly worked against many others; they are so prevalent now that such serious mistakes cross my desk daily."

And I would say, parenthetically here, that I am quite certain, at least, quite convinced, that of the graduating class in Franklin K. Lane High School, where I would be the counselor, that for at least half and probably three-quarters of the records of those students, they are seriously in error. That is, so much so, that some courses that they took were not recorded and that some courses that they did not take are recorded, that the wrong students' test records are entered on someone else's cards and so it goes at that school.

Now, I say to Mr. Zack in the letter that, "During the past 2 years I sought relief on behalf of other students by bringing cases through channels and up to the level of the Superintendent."

Then I went back to three; Albert, Carl Wade and Michael, and again I leave some of the last names off for the benefit of the students. I would just now summarize them briefly, because I know time will be going by.

Albert was known to psychologists since early elementary

grades and admitted setting fires in the school following seven fires in the preceding days. He was very promptly returned to the school without ample follow-up. There is detailed information about my supervisors pressing me to refer him to a particular private and unlicensed agency. The unlicensed agency cleared him on the first appointment, although they did not have information about his history.

Carl Wade was a well-behaved student, liked by his teachers and with excellent attendance and all passing marks. He was suspended from Lane for no valid reason and confined for 3 weeks to his house with his stepmother. The principal dismissed the matter with the statement that it did not happen and challenged me to show it to him in the records, although he had no intention of having it entered into the records.

Michael was a multi-handicapped student who had been admitted to Lane in September, 1967. In May, 1968, although he and his mother had passed through the office of the assistant principal, Mrs. Mary Cohen arranged matters in such a way that it resulted in him having no contact with any official teacher--and no valid record of his ninth grade attendance exists--and no contact with any grade advisor. He was placed in an academic course with a sixth grade reading level, and that with no contact with the guidance counselor. The principal handled the case, when the mother came to school threatening to bring a lawyer, by agreeing to change his course and all of his teachers in mid-May, resulting, of course, in all failures.

I received no satisfaction on any level concerning the above-mentioned cases. However, last term I brought other cases to the attention of Mr. Arthur Capson, who was assigned to a committee attached to the Superintendent's Office, to handle matters of alleged racial and/or religious discrimination. I brought to his attention the following six students, five of whom were Negro and one Puerto Rican, and this again represents a small sampling of many injustices to students in my load.

Shirley Jones was an academic senior, having been excluded from all classes from the end of January to March 7th, by mistake.

Linda Taylor, with a reading score of almost three years above grade level, was also excluded for many weeks by mistake, although I had especially offered my assistance as guidance counselor to help prevent such error but was forbidden by the assistant principal, Mrs. Mary Cohen, to go near the situation.

Richard Byrd was denied a fifth major by his grade advisor partly because he considered his ninth grade marks invalid because they had been received at Junior High School 271, which is Ocean Hill-Brownsville, and at the same time giving another student of a different racial and school background a sixth major.

Juan Vega, who was also formerly of Junior High School 271, was left waiting on a bench for five school days, February 20th, 21st, 24th, 25th and the 26th, although I brought this matter to the attention of the principal twice and the assistant principal three times.

Cynthia Cohen was a tenth grade commercial student who

was given a program of speech, family living, cooking, arts and crafts, music, lunch, health education and art appreciation and without business arithmetic, shorthand and typing. She had missed a term and the school is organized so that the latter classes were not available although Lane is a large school with about 5,000 students and has ample opportunity to organize so as to accommodate such students.

And finally, Donnie Broadway had been admitted to Lane from California and given a general course, although he was later recommended for academic work. It was found that detailed testing records from his former California school had been simply filed away without any notation of good test scores having been noted anywhere on his permanent record.

I have grieved inside of this system, I had grieved to the assistant principal, Mrs. Mary Cohen, the principal, Mr. Morton Selub, the district superintendent, Mrs. Elizabeth O'Daly, the Committee on Alleged Racial and/or Religious Discrimination, which is attached to the Superintendent's Office, Mr. Arthur Capson, and to the former Superintendent of Schools. At that time it would probably be Dr. Bernard Donovan.

I brought these new students, the ones that I mentioned in the beginning, where there was such serious error in each case. As a matter of fact, I don't know why we have to be afraid sometimes. I am adding, parenthetically again, why must we be afraid to state the truth?

Here is a girl, Patricia, who transferred from Lane to another New York City high school. Her record at Lane had been poor and in three terms she had passed nothing. However, the other school received a record indicating passing marks, passing regents examinations, and ready to graduate. The new school sent back a photostat of the record received. Patricia finally broke down and confessed to the new school and to us that she had paid $50 for a forged record from an adult employee at Franklin K. Lane High School.

I asked that something be done about it, or some investigation be made, and the result of this is that another--this was done on November 29th, 1969 and I was fired on December 5th, I think it was, 1969.

Now, of course, that would lead the Board of Education, I suppose, in their desperation, to get rid of someone who would expose them, to make up hearings and charges and false testimony, and that kind of thing. And I suppose that they did a thoroughly poor job of it, because none of their charges would stand up to anybody. So let me just tell you what the charges centered around. The fact that, after all, I was not--not the fact, I should say, but the fact that they had written records that, after all, I was not indicating--let me just word this so that I am exact--they had claimed that I would not go for a psychiatric, what they call, medical, but really, a psychiatric examination. And, of course, that isn't true, because--as I said, being Christian, we, who follow the Lord--every time they tried to call me or get me there, something happened. They sent it to the wrong address or they forgot to put stamps on it, or some silly things happened, so that I didn't even have a very valid firm appointment to go on.

But, you see, it is serious, is it not, when the Board of Education will take it upon itself, for those responsible, to single out one and say, if she is displeasing them, that she must go for psychiatric examination, because, after all, these actions question her mental competence.

There is one other thing that I would like to add.

At the time of the strikes, I went in alone, into Franklin K. Lane High School, when 300 teachers, approximately, and others were on strike. And, evidently, this irritated the supervisors, it seemed, more than the teachers around me. This was followed by their placing about 2300 students in my load and then, you see, the attempt would be to say that I wasn't able to perform satisfactorily.

There were other ways that I was harassed by the supervisors following the strike.

I would also like, Commissioner Norton, if you would take cognizance of this: that at a meeting of guidance counselors in 1965 there were about a thousand guidance counselors present. It was publicly stated by a man who we allege to be Dr. Eli Ginzburg, of Columbia University, I believe, who stated officially, I believe, because he was the invited speaker, that the Anglo-Saxon protest had done so much damage to our country that new people took over and the day of the WASP is over.

I did not come here to state my case on that, but rather to expose what I thought should be exposed in the manner of your delving into the hiring practices of the Board of Education. And, if it is appropriate, I would place with you now, Commissioner Norton, a memorandum, and for you to use that, if you may, to get into the matter of whether, indeed, white Anglo-Saxon Protestants are eliminated. I have looked and searched over the years for another white Anglo-Saxon guidance counselor, and I have found none. I asked some of my friends, of different racial and religious backgrounds, whether they would join me and look and see if they could find one, and they could not find any either.

May I ask the question, would you be able to take this case up in your commission?

THE CHAIRMAN: You can certainly leave your material with us, and we will see whether it falls within our province.

We thank you for coming forward.

I just want to say, for the record, that we need very much in this country to get back on the track. Unless we solve our racial and ethnic problems, we will end up with a country in which every man and every woman looks first at his origin and then makes a decision. Whereas, one's origin ought to be terribly irrelevant to everything; one's religion ought to be terribly irrelevant to everything. And unless these problems are solved, I am afraid they will become more and more relevant, which is a very dangerous situation.

I find it strange, indeed, when a person from what is considered to be the most favored group in this country raises this question, and I think the only time we will be able to get back to a sane state of affairs is when relatively all groups feel that they have a fair crack at it. We must remember that much of this is a matter of perceived fairness.

We in law understand the importance of the appearance of fairness, the appearance of justice, for it is very difficult to argue that a system is just if those who must participate in it do not perceive it as just. In this country the law is required to function, not only to mete out justice, but always to give the appearance of justice. I am afraid we have yet to get back to that first principle.

I hope that one of the by-products of this hearing will be that we will quickly solve the question of race and ethnic origin in the school system so that question can be taken out of the school affairs.

MR. WEINER: Members of the City Commission on Human Rights, my name is David Weiner. I am the Legislative Representative of the Teachers' Action Committee, the largest opposition caucus in the UFT.

The Teachers' Action Committee welcomes this opportunity to present its views on the employment practices of the Board of Education and the Board of Examiners and to offer some tentative proposals.

From our very inception a few years ago, we have been highly critical of the employment policies and practices of the Board of Education and also the policies and practices of the Board of Examiners.

After the NAACP Legal Defense and Educational Fund brought its suit to enjoin the Board of Examiners from proceeding with the elementary school principals' examination scheduled for this past November 3rd and other supervisory tests, TAC studied the issues raised and decided to take a public stand.

At its November 13, 1970 membership meeting, TAC voted in favor of abolishing the Board of Examiners, eliminating the present examination system and substituting state certification, with adequate safeguards to prevent abuse, as a basis for appointment and promotion.

TAC reaffirmed its position in its recently issued "Statement on Violence in the Schools." As part of its program to cope with violence in the schools TAC called on the UFT to support the hiring of Black and Puerto Rican personnel at all levels and in all capacities. TAC cited the fact that "compared to the next four largest cities, Chicago, Detroit, Los Angeles, and Philadelphia, and to Rochester, New York, where state certification is the basis for employment, New York City has the lowest percentage of Black and Puerto Rican teachers and supervisors and also the lowest ratio of minority group teachers and supervisors to minority group students."

TAC also urged the UFT to "join those seeking to eliminate the Board of Examiners and substitute state certification." "Irrelevant and discriminatory tests and procedures," TAC declared, "have for too long created difficulties in our schools." We favor the elimination of the Board of Examiners for many reasons but mainly because:

    1) Its policies and procedures have helped create the situation, or, at the very least, have not prevented the situation where:

        a. There is massive retardation in basic skills among poor and minority group students.

        b. As we have already stated, the proportion of minority group teachers, and even more so of supervisors, is far below those of other large cities.

    2) Many items tested have little if any bearing on the candidate's potential as a teacher or supervisor.

    3) Far from being objective, key parts of their tests such as oral interviews and evaluations by their very nature are highly subjective.

    4) Its policies and procedures have unduly promoted excessive inbreeding.

    5) Over a long period of time it has failed to respond to criticism and suggestions from a wide variety of sources.

At this point we want to make it clear that we support a merit system with tenure. However, we find that the present system is not a merit system. It is not doing the job. It is not providing the schools with the educational leaders they so sorely need. Instead it fosters and promotes a type that can best be characterized as "exam-takers." They prepare assiduously for the exams, take the coaching courses, avoid any association or action which may bring them in conflict in any way with the powers that be, and pass one examination after another up the occupational ladder. They are good exam-takers but unfortunately, too often, poor educational leaders. How many faculty and department conferences include educational items on their agencies? Where they are listed, how adequately are they treated?

Many young, idealistic people start teaching full of enthusiasm. Naturally they need help. Too often they do not get the help they need from their supervisors.

There is the story, and it is not apocryphal, of a young teacher who approached his chairman and asked him how to teach a particular topic. The chairman's response was, "How can I tell him how to teach?"

We disagree with UFT President Shanker's proposal that in addition to any state certification prospective teachers be tested for verbal ability, literacy and, in the high schools, for subject matter competency. It would seem to us that state certification by itself is adequate assurance on these scores.

We are aware that many teachers and others are concerned that the use of state certification may be accompanied by political patronage, favoritism, and provincialism in the process of selection, promotion, and dismissal. We too are concerned about this. It should be pointed out, however, that in large measure these abuses are present today in New York City and have been present all along. For years, teachers on a list would shop around for the so-called "most desirable" schools in the City and principals in these schools would "request" their appointment. Politics and nepotism were determining factors even though we have continued to use the term "merit system." On the other hand, teachers and supervisors at the bottom of the eligible lists or those with no influence were appointed to the ghetto schools, often against their will.

TAC has not been able to study and discuss the question of undesirable pressures in the hiring and promotion of personnel sufficiently to reach definite conclusions. We have been considering the proposal to set up committees of representatives of teachers, parents, and students on both district and school levels to interview and recommend teachers and supervisors to the Superintendent. It is far less likely that such committees will be subject to successful manipulation than the arbitrary decisions of one school executive or school board or even, for that matter, the arbitrary decisions of the present Board of Examiners. We are also weighing the establishment of review boards composed of parents, teachers, and students to hear complaints and make recommendations where staff members feel that they have been unfairly or unjustly treated.

At all events a most important role must be played by the teachers themselves and their organizations. A strong, democratic, forward-looking union sensitive to the needs of the communites is essential to maintain and protect the legitimate rights of teachers. Such a union is also essential to maintain and protect academic freedom, a basic ingredient in any healthy school system.

We hope that the outcome of these hearings will help to bring about the demise of the Board of Examiners and its system of examinations which have long outlived their usefulness.

For years, this examination system plodded along. Today, however, the massive problems facing public education in New York City have forced the whole situation out into the open. We can no longer afford to hide behind slogans like "merit system" when the system has long failed to produce meritorious leadership.

If I may add something about the present employment practices of the Board. I don't know if the members of the Commission are aware that there is a situation now in the schools where many, many vacancies are being filled by substitutes, and these are now what are called per diem substitutes, not regular substitutes, and as per diem substitutes, rather called per diem certificate holders, they don't get health benefits; they don't get vacation benefits; they don't get seniority or tenure; they don't come within the contract.

Many of these per diem certificate holders have already passed the examination. They are on lists. These very people are filling many jobs now which under the law--section 2573 of the Education Law--filling jobs which have been vacant for six months or more. They're doing it as per diem certificate holders when these jobs under the law should be filled by regular teachers.

We in TAC feel very strongly that these jobs should be filled by regular teachers and we're asking the UFT to take action, if necessary, to bring a lawsuit.

I also wonder if you are aware that 75% of all the above-quota teachers in the schools are going to be dropped at the end of this term. These are teachers who are filling day-to-day vacancies and in this way prevent classes from being uncovered. We had been told there will be no new appointments. The above-quota teachers will be fired, and in the high schools at this time we have seasonal unemployment because of a so-called "drop in register" and a few graduates and the fact that the number of students is very small.

There is a drop in register, and usually they take advantage of this drop. Although I can't substantiate it offhand, I would say they disproportionately drop and decrease the number of staff members of the school. For example, in my own school, Eastern District High School, we're losing ten teachers and one secretary. We can very well use those people for smaller classes and to carry on many activities that have to be carried on.

I hope you're interested in this and I hope, with all the other things you do, you consider this and see what can be done to get the people the permanent or regular jobs to which they're entitled and to get more people and teachers in the school.

THE CHAIRMAN: Thank you.

I have received word we are over our time in this building. I'm going to ask the speakers from here on in to try to keep their remarks to about five minutes.

MISS P. HILLMAN: Commissioner Norton and members of the Commission, I choose to speak because I am one of those teachers who came to New York City from the outside. I wish to add a new dimension to this discussion because I have not heard anyone discuss the topic as I shall discuss it.

Originally I taught in Philadelphia for quite a number of years and previous to that I had taught in Maryland, so that my experience extends over three areas, three states.

I came to New York City to take the test on three different occasions because the test is in three parts: written, oral, and physical, so that I had to come to New York City three different dates.

For some people, this might be a great inconvenience because it is inconvenient to come from long distances to New York City on three different occasions to take a test. However, if one wishes to take this test at the time I took it, I had no alternative.

At present though, there are some alternatives. The National Teacher Examination is now being given around the country. Candidates, as I understand it, may qualify by taking that preliminary part of the examination.

I find too that coming to New York City from the outside presents unique problems in housing. This is one of the problems that prevented my taking a position when it was first offered. I passed the examination, all three parts. I had no difficulty with the speech patterns. In fact, I think I rated higher on the oral than the written, having been out of school for quite a while. But, I found that the housing presented a great problem.

If you come into New York City, you might have your first experience of living in an apartment. This is new because most people outside of New York City who come from minority groups may not live in apartments. They might come from the open spaces where you live in houses, single houses, or you may have lived on a farm as I previously once did. So that there is apprehension as to living in an apartment, and there is also apprehension because the real estate in New York City is the most expensive in the country.

And so, if one looks at the expense of housing, one might say no to a new job in New York City. Outside of the City of New York, such systems as the Maryland system from which I came presented a unique problem in that it was a segregated system. Since it was segregated, it offered some benefits because of the segregation.

The University of Maryland was a segregated institution at the time, and so if you were a student in Maryland, you had to leave Maryland to get an advanced education.

So, in a sense, you were driven from that area in order to seek advancement; and so, many people from the South in education, who are Black, come to the North to seek advanced education. They did so because of the segregated patterns of the universities.

This was true in Baltimore, where you had Coppin, which developed the teachers for Baltimore City. This was also true in Washington, where you had a unique teachers' institution in Washington, D.C., including Howard University.

New York City, however, did not present this problem. You had de facto segregation so that opportunity seemed to be there, and yet it seemed to have been far away.

Also, in coming from out of town to New York City, there is another difficulty. The schools, unless they are new schools, in this city, do not look like the schools that most people outside of New York City are used to looking at. The schools here have bars across the windows. I can understand that because the supplies are stolen regularly. They present a drab, awesome appearance. These are what you call working appearance.

The working conditions in many of the schools for personnel are not too good unless you are in a new school. In the school in which I am now teaching, Junior High School 17, Manhattan, there is no lunchroom for teachers, there is no lounge for teachers. The only thing we have for a lunchroom is one classroom that has been converted and we've put in a few extra tables and chairs. We clean it ourselves; we arrange the tables ourselves; and we have no facilities planned for teachers.

So you see, working conditions, too, play a part in accepting jobs in New York City, especially in the very old buildings, and there seemed to be quite a predominance of those.

I came to New York City because there was a difference in the salary schedule. In some areas in the country, at that time, there were no salary schedules. There still aren't, in some areas.

There is no tenure in some parts of the country and teachers may be let go at a moment's notice. If they wish to cut the budget, if they don't raise the budget, or if they don't vote for a bond issue, then the teachers are just released. No security.

You see, there must be advantages if we are to attract teachers to New York City. There are some advantages and we in New York City must sell this to the rest of the country. And even with the disadvantages that exist, I think some of these certainly can be looked into and straightened out so that New York City can attract more minority group teachers to this system.

THE CHAIRMAN: Thank you, Miss Hillman. That testimony was important to us because we've been trying to see the extent to which programs of recruitment are focussed. You are one such product of recruitment.

Mr. Peter Saltz.

MR. SALTZ: I congratulate the Commission on its fortitude and patience. I wish to give specific testimony on the failure to appoint a Black principal at Shimer Junior High School in Queens.

In early 1970, a group comprised of Peter Saltz (then President of Jamaica NAACP), Richard Hansen (present President of Jamaica NAACP), Lawrence R. Bailey (Legal Redress Chairman of the New York State Conference, NAACP), and three other members of the Executive Board of the Jamaica NAACP appeared before Local School Board 28 and Dr. Hugh McDougall, District Superintendent.

The Board meeting was held at the Educational Testing Building on Merrick Boulevard and 89th Avenue. The Board was in executive session.

It is to be pointed out that the Board of early 1970 was not the same Board as elected in mid-year 1970, but that the District Superintendent, Dr. McDougall and the President, Mrs. Sophie Price, remained the same.

The purpose of the meeting with the Local School Board 28 in executive session was to seek the formal appointment of Mrs. Desiree Greenidge as principal of Junior High School 142, Shimer.

As an added and significant tangent, we pointed out to the Board that in the Borough of Queens, whose population equalled the sixth largest city in the United States, there was not a single Black principal in the schools of the Board of Education.

When we made this request to the Board in early 1970, Mrs. Desiree Greenidge had already been acting principal of the school for approximately a year and a half.

Dr. McDougall and Mrs. Price each stated very firmly that they were eager to have the appointment of Mrs. Greenidge as principal of Shimer, but a special course had to be taken and passed by Mrs. Greenidge and then her appointment would be made.

At no time during this session was it ever mentioned that Mrs. Greenidge might not be appointed because a Mr. Louis Butti was still listed on the line as principal of Shimer, even though he had not been at the school for the past year and a half.

In the following months, Mrs. Greenidge passed the necessary course. Dr. McDougall and Mrs. Price, however, never made an effort to appoint her principal despite their promises. It is certainly a lack of faith on their part.

The Borough of Queens is still without a Black principal and

Shimer, which did not have the cooperation and sensitivity of the local school board or the district superintendent, is now in a state of chaos, turmoil, and boycott.

This statement is issued on behalf of myself and Richard Hansen, President, Jamaica NAACP.

THE CHAIRMAN: Thank you very much.

This is a troubled school area. We are aware of that problem.

Again, we think that getting that ethnic question settled by getting more minority people in the system will itself have a meritorious effect on the problems in various districts such as yours.

MR. SALTZ: The point I wish to emphasize, Commissioner, is a lack of truth insofar as the District Superintendent and the Chairman of the Local School Board said they would do a certain act in bringing Mrs. Greenidge as principal, and they have never done that.

Thank you.

MR. GORDON: My name is Reuben Gordon.

Madam Chairman, Commissioners and citizens of New York City, I seriously doubt whether the City Commission of Human Rights has any real desire to do anything about ending discrimination on the part of the Board of Education, whether it be racial, religious, or political in nature.

If the Commission had any real desire to act, they would long ago have joined with citizens of all races, colors, and creeds in demanding a Grand Jury investigation of the criminal conspiracy of the Board of Education, of United Federation of Teachers President Al Shanker, and of the Council of Supervisory Association, in locking and barring the schools in 1968.

That illegal strike in violation of many city, state, and federal laws was vicious discrimination against all races, colors and creeds, not merely Blacks and Puerto Ricans.

I submit that this Commission appointed by Mayor Lindsay and owing political allegiance to him is staging a protracted public relations operation and filibuster with a view to delaying and preventing a Grand Jury investigation of the criminal conspiracy which long ago should have resulted in criminal indictment against the members of the Board of Education.

The fact that Mr. Shanker and Mr. Degnan were found guilty of contempt and were jailed briefly, proves beyond reasonable doubt that they are also guilty of criminal conspiracy against the public, in violation of the human rights of all pupils, parents, and teachers, by locking them out of their public schools.

These hearings have already provided voluminous evidence of the Board violation of many laws. This Commission would be derelict in its duty if it fails to demand and to obtain Grand Jury indictments against the criminals named thus far.

I urge that the City Human Rights Commission demand that the Grand Jury indict Procaccino, Shanker, and School Superintendent Donovan for conspiracy to defraud the public and to plunder the city treasury.

The following document presents facts about the school strike which have not been denied by any of the parties involved. Judge Bloustein has ignored a citizens' request to present this criminal conspiracy to the Rackets Grand Jury. The district attorneys have threatened with police arrest citizens who persist in their efforts to bring evidence of official crime to the attention of the Grand Jury.

To break through this protection of racket law enforcement officials, you are requested to forward this document to the Grand Jury who are your fellow citizens.

Dated December 8th, 1968, addressed to Justice Francis J. Bloustein, 4700 Independence Avenue, Bronx, New York 10471.

"Dear Justice Bloustein: On November 14, 1968, I brought to your attention a fraudulent memorandum of understanding entered into by the Board of Education and by Albert Shanker, President of the United Federation of Teachers.

"In this statement, to which I attached a copy of the fraudulent document, I pointed out that the several parties appearing before you in what purports to be an adversary action for a contempt citation are all deeply involved in a conspiracy to violate city, state and federal statutes.

"I shall specify the laws which the Board of Education, acting in collusion with President Shanker, have violated.

"1) They have violated the City Charter which forbids payment of salary to any city employee who failed to perform services for any period of time.

"The fraudulent memorandum of agreement was submitted to Comptroller Procaccino for the purposes of inducing him to pay a quarter of a million dollars of public funds to strikers in violation of the Charter.

"Comptroller Procaccino has informed me that he made payment of salaries to 300 teachers who performed those services under compulsion of the memorandum of agreement which was attached to the payroll submitted to him by the Board of Education.

"Comptroller Procaccino further stated that had he not paid these teachers on the basis of the Board submission of the payroll and the accompanying document, he could have been sued to compel payment as has been done in the past.

"With all due respect to Comptroller Procaccino's superior knowledge of the law, I submit that he has committed a misdemeanor in paying out public funds in violation of a clear prohibition of the City Charter.

"I have, in fact with the Comptroller's full knowledge, requested Governor Rockefeller to remove Comptroller Procaccino from office for violation of an express prohibition of the City Charter which is binding equally on all citizens and officials who come under its jurisdiction.

"This request has thus far not been acknowledged or answered. I assume that the letter has not been transmitted to Governor Rockefeller who is bound by his oath to act against officials who violate the laws.

"As a citizen who cannot expend the thousands of dollars to retain attorneys to initiate impeachment proceedings against the

Governor, I shall hold in abeyance such proceedings in the hope that action by the courts will render this action unnecessary.

"Failing such court action, however, I shall use whatever forums are available to me to enforce my rights as a taxpayer whose funds are illegally expended.

"Permit me to point out to your Honor that as a taxpayer you have equal standing with me to sue for removal of any and all officials whose nonfeasance deprives you of your property rights through illegal expenditures of your tax money.

"2) On the state level, the fraudulent memorandum of agreement between the Board of Education and President Shanker of United Federation of Teachers is a violation of the penal laws against conspiracy and embezzlement of public funds.

"3) On the federal level, all the citizens of New York State who paid taxes have been deprived of their property in violation of Section 242, Title 18 of the United States Code.

"This statute forbids denial to citizens under pretext of law of any right guaranteed them by the Federal Constitution or Federal Statutes.

"May I further point out that the Bill of Rights bans the states from abridging any right which a citizen may have under the Federal Constitution.

"Surely the founders of our country never intended to yield to labor unions, boards of education or to the courts the right to circumvent the ban imposed upon the states.

"Thus no fraudulent instrument or memorandum of agreement which is drawn up in violation of the New York City Charter can deprive a citizen of his power over the legal expenditure of taxes which he pays to the federal government.

"Such federal tax monies have been intermingled with state and city taxes which Comptroller Procaccino, acting illegally under duress, has illegally expended.

"All of the above statements are made on accepted principle that 'the common law is common sense.' I have seen that principle carved in the wall over the bench of a courtroom. I shall therefore forbear from citing the numerous cases which support the inferences drawn from the evidence of the fradulent memorandum of agreement.

"This memorandum I have brought to your judicial notice as part of the application submitted to you. That application to appear as a friend of the court in the contempt action against Shanker by his alleged adversary, the Board of Education, was submitted to the Supreme Court of the State of New York through your Honor. I was informed by your secretary that you had taken my application under advisement after having read the contents thereof.

"Permit me to point out that my application, disregarding any deficiencies in legal form, was submitted in good faith to be considered on its merits.

"May I further point out as I did in the original application that under the rules of equity, which were invoked by counsel in this action, the principle is recognized that petitioner or plaintiff may not bring an action in the matter in which his own hands are not clean.

"For one criminal to charge his criminal accomplice with violation of an illegal and fraudulent agreement to rob the public is to make of the courts the laughing stock of the citizens for whose protection the courts have been instituted.

"Just such a fraudulent agreement has been entered into by the Board of Education and the United Federation of Teachers through its president, Mr. Albert Shanker.

"The document embodying that agreement has not been brought before the court by any of the adversaries in this action for obvious reasons, because it incriminates both parties and mandates the court to scourge both adversaries from the courtroom for their violation of the principle that they must come before the court with clean hands.

"It is my contention that I as a taxpayer and as a member of the United Federation of Teachers am a party at interest in this contempt proceeding. I and all citizens have standing in court to expose the criminal conspiracy of both my employer, the Board of Education, and of President Shanker of the United Federation of Teachers.

"They are using this court as a sheltered sanctuary for their prolonged filibuster whose chief purpose is to conceal from the teachers and taxpayers the fact that both Shanker and the Board of Education are guilty of violation of all law.

"I submit to your Honor that the court in permitting this travesty of justice to continue is giving aid and comfort to a criminal conspiracy and is bringing further contempt upon the courts themselves.

"I have requested 'that the court turn over the fraudulent memorandum of understanding' now in your possession to the Rackets Grand Jury of the federal government, as evidence of the violation of the civil rights of citizens of this city regardless of race, color, and creed or of previous condition of servitude.

"This request is made in the belief that the action of a Justice of a Supreme Court in submitting evidence to a Federal Grand Jury would insure the Grand Jury would receive this document so they might consider it on its merits.

"As an ordinary citizen I have been blocked by officials from transmitting documents and information to the Grand Jury. Since I have received no word from your Honor who has now had the document and its accompanying applications under advisement for a month, I should like to turn over all documents submitted to you in this matter including this letter to the foreman of the Federal Rackets Grand Jury.

"I respectfully request the court's permission therefore to turn over all documents submitted to you to the Federal Grand Jury.

"Respectfully yours, Reuben R. Gordon. Enclosures."

I might add this letter to Judge Bloustein was never acknowledged and never answered and you might note other unions including the police of New York have subsequently gone on strike.

It is my belief that had this Commission and the responsible law enforcement officials brought before the Grand Jury the criminal conspiracy which blocked citizens from their rights of access to the schools two years ago, we might have avoided this current police strike, and the general tendency, apparently, to create a political general strike with the obvious intention of overthrowing the government, first of this city, then of the state, then of the nation.

Thank you.

THE CHAIRMAN: Thank you, Mr. Gordon.

As I close the hearings today, I would remind the public we're receiving public testimony on any side of this issue, this issue being the personnel practices of the Board of Education, during this week. Public testimony is being received tomorrow evening and night for the benefit of the working public.

In addition, there is a child care facility which we are providing for parents who have no other way to come to hearings of this kind for lack of someone to leave their children with. The hearings are at 14 Vesey Street. Around the corner we have provided a child care facility at 225 Broadway, 18th floor, Room 27.

These hearings will begin again tomorrow at 9:30 a.m.

(Whereupon, at this time, the hearings were adjourned until 9:30 a.m., January 27, 1971.)

- - - - -

HEARINGS HELD JANUARY 27, 1971

Witnesses in Order of Appearance

Testimony starts

Murray Rockowitz	page 322
Blanche Lewis	323
David Seeley	329
Albert Shanker	339
Walter Degnan	360
Lillian Weber	384
David Seeley	392
Hector Vazquez	394
Robert Thorndike	401
Richard Barrett	406
James R. Deneen	412
Stephen J. Pollak	422
Lloyd S. Mapp	433
Alfred Weinstein	434

Martin Frye	448	Seymour Samuels	483
Vincent Resta	452	Alvin Lashinsky	487
Marilyn Braveman	455	Doris Rosenblum	487
Marvin Bornstein	457	Helene Woolford	490
Nellie Jones	461	Patricia Seabrook	492
Herbert English	464	Anna S. Murphy	494
Bernard Friedman	467	John Hunter	496
Representative of Sonia Allen	469	William Degraffenreid, III	497
Charles Burton	471	Belle Bavine George	498
Linda Linton	473	Loretta James	499
Vincent Nassetta	475	Desdre Fleming	499
Steve Aiello	475	Barbara Washington	499
Judy Heumann	478	Esther Levenberg	500
Jorge Maldonado	480	Lalo Dextre	502
Anne West	482	Hal Koppersmith	502
		W. Rogers Gist	506

THE CHAIRMAN: These hearings are in session for the third day. I want to announce these hearings are being held at 14 Vesey Street, in Manhattan; that we will be taking testimony from the public this evening again at 4 o'clock and going until 9 o'clock, and any members of the public are invited to come and testify during those hours.

For people who would like to testify from the general public but have children and need some place to leave them, we have provided a free day care facility around the corner from the hearing. The day care facility is located at 225 Broadway, 18th floor, room 27, for parents who would like to attend these hearings but need some place to leave their children.

I want to announce that in addition to members of the public who may hear this and decide to come in and testify, we have tried to canvass a broad cross-section of the public in advance of these hearings by sending an announcement and invitation to speak to every principal in the city, every UFT chapter chairman and every parents association president as well as all organizations which are on record as having any interest whatsoever in education and every ethnic and racial organization in this city. I want to make that clear since I want the public to understand that we have, ourselves, taken the initiative to invite and are otherwise now inviting all members of the public to testify in these hearings regardless of their points of view.

We believe all sides of this question have not been adequately aired and the public confusion surrounding these issues comes from the fact that the various points of view have not been aired sufficiently publicly. I have been informed that Dr. Rockowitz of the Board of Examiners desires to give some testimony. I wish to offer him the opportunity to give some testimony at this time.

DR. ROCKOWITZ: Thank you, Madam Chairman.

It is my understanding that yesterday afternoon during the testimony of Mr. Andrew Donaldson, an unfortunate personal attack was directed at me with regard to a rating that I had given an assistant principal under my supervision who happened to be Black. What I am going to say should not be necessary with respect to that comment but I shall make this statement in any case.

My personal concern for human rights dates back to over a quarter of a century ago and I would like to cite a personal anecdote to indicate what I mean.

Mr. Rockowitz

I was Commanding Officer in 1945 of Radio Station Manila, WUQM. The staff consisted of 500 men, 250 of whom were Filipinos and 250 were American soldiers. When I assumed command of this station, there were segregated barracks, and men who worked in the same tricks--8-hour sessions in the radio station--slept in different barracks because they were segregated.

This made no sense to me, ethically, morally, and even on operational grounds. So I integrated the barracks even though it involved taking on some of the powers that be and transferring personnel who did not want to integrate sleeping quarters.

Furthermore, at the very same station, two different menus were being prepared. The Filipino men had a fish menu which went out in 1899, and the American soldiers were fed the usual better food that was provided for American troops. I abolished that type of discrimination in feeding of personnel and I made certain that everybody who worked at this station would receive the same kind of food.

As a result, when it came time for me to come back to the States, I received a citation for my concern for brotherhood, and the citation was by no means solicited.

In the instant case, Mr. Donaldson agreed to supervisors rating other supervisors on the basis of performance. When performance was mediocre or submediocre, he rated it as such. The rating he referred to was amply documented, and the person so rated received a copy of the rating with the documentation. That rating was never appealed by the person involved.

I prefer to mention the fact that there are numbers of Blacks and Puerto Ricans present whom I personally trained and helped to become supervisors, and I can cite among them Marjorie Williams and Mrs. Covington, serving in our public schools.

I don't think the attack was warranted, and I don't believe this is the place for a personal attack.

Thank you.

THE CHAIRMAN: We, of course, are pleased to announce that any witness who wishes to come back to the stand may do so. I do not personally recall the specific instance that Dr. Rockowitz refers to, but I do wish to say that this issue is terribly controversial and in the heat of testifying, it is inevitable that there will be some heat in the give and take. However, I congratulate the members of the public for the factual way in which the testimony thus far has been offered. I do think these hearings demonstrate that if there is a rational, high-level forum in which people who have different points of view can express their views, then even the most heated issues can be discussed rationally. And this hearing has lived up to my hopes in that regard. Above all, we wish to give everyone who has any point of view, any facts, any conclusions related to this subject matter, every opportunity to speak.

I would like to call Mrs. Blanche Lewis, President of the United Parents Association.

MRS. LEWIS: Good morning. I am Blanche Lewis, President of the United Parents Association.

Parents have moved into the front lines in the fight to reform and restructure public schools. And, like it or not, it is from here that we must wage our battle for the survival and success of our schools. Parents know that the effectiveness of our educational system cannot be assessed without recognizing that the key element in determining the quality of education provided is the professional personnel. Their training, their competence, their attitude, their dedication, or lack of these, have a telling impact on education.

We are well aware that the entire area of professional selection and licensing is a highly sensitive issue and one which arouses strong feelings. This is only natural, for what is involved is not only the staffing of our schools but individual job security and promotion.

I want to make it very clear that the United Parents Association is interested and committed to following due process procedures, to avoiding political patronage and discrimination. But what we cannot condone are the power strangleholds which squelch and cut off any possibility of improvement.

At this time we have a school system which is approximately 50% Black and Puerto Rican. Under the present licensing conditions, there are approximately 1,000 positions for principal. Only 12 are Black or Puerto Rican. The percentage is 1.3% Black and .6% Puerto Rican. As to teachers, 6.92% are Black and 1.0% are Puerto Rican.

The statistics show clearly that we must be doing something wrong. This problem didn't just spring up yesterday. The signs were there years and years ago. But how was the problem met? By facing it squarely? By intensive recruitment campaigns?

I am afraid not. It was met first by ignoring it. Then it was met by a form of subterfuge by a series of Board of Education resolutions. Then began the campaigns. We were told how the tests were being watered down so that they were becoming meaningless.

But parents who had been relegated to the back door began to demand to come in. The hope for decentralization and its promise was to give parents more say at the community level. This was clear at the public hearings. Therefore, the Board of Education in 1968 added to its decentralization resolution a specific requirement that community boards carry out their new roles with parents and parent organizations.

Unfortunately, parents are still viewed with suspicion when the role of parents in the selection of professional personnel is discussed.

Selection of principals and upper education leaders in the district is very much the concern of parents. It has been our experience that where parents have been involved they have acted very responsibly and, only after lengthy frustration, are they forced into taking more militant action.

Over the years there have been judicial decisions, Board of Education policy statements and directives, and the decentralization issue which have delineated the rights of parents in the public schools. All of these have been brought together in one document and submitted to the Board of Education. This document is called, "Parents Associations in the Schools," and I allude to it this morning because in your invitation for me to testify you asked for me to explain the significance of this document as to placement of personnel.

We feel this document is only the beginning and the minimum framework. It will be up to the parents and their community school boards to work together constructively to build on this framework, which does include the rights of parents to take part in the interviewing process of principals and district superintendents and does include the right of parents to be consulted on the granting of tenure to teachers.

This is just part of the answer. Parents know that there is much more in securing a quality staff than their role in selection, although that role is most important.

Our plan envisioned a sharing of responsibility between community school boards and the central Board of Education, with the central Board playing a minimal role. This central Board was to prepare lists of qualified eligibles, based on New York State certification and the National Teachers Exam or other suitable examinations. We were not wed to the National Teacher Exam, but we saw in it an opportunity of widening and broadening the scope here in New York City. The community school board would then interview the prospects from the central list to determine personal qualifications that they deemed important. They would appoint for a three-year probationary period, and they would supervise and rate all personnel and grant tenure after consultation with parents. Community boards would also have the option to recruit off of the lists, referring selectees to the central educational agency for qualifying certification.

At that time, as now, parents were convinced that a formal examination procedure, no matter how perfect, was not the only answer. Tests may measure an acquired knowledge and perhaps the ability to exercise judgment. They do not measure the qualities and personality characteristics which are important in teaching.

Therefore, we recommend that the probationary period be used far more effectively than it has been until now, with teacher training to consist of supervision and an honest rating of personnel leading to separation of those teachers and supervisors who cannot give our schools satisfactory service. Actual performance in the classroom must be considered the ultimate test of a teacher's ability. The probationary period must be made part of the examination procedure. An internship program for all new supervisory personnel must also be incorporated into the examination process. This would provide not only a more meaningful training on the job but a more efficient method of evaluating the applicant.

There is also an all too apparent need for massive retraining efforts to give both teachers and supervisors the help they need. Since what is involved is not merely a transmission of information, but changes in attitude and rethinking of some traditional practices, the training must call on modern techniques involving the dynamics of attitudinal change, and due process must be assured. This should involve every principal in every school and every community superintendent in every district. Those who are ineffective should receive whatever support they need, the tools to work with and the training, so that improvement can be achieved. Failing that, procedures must be established to make possible the removal of ineffective teachers, principals, and other supervisors.

Our experience indicates that under existing law and regulation, it is almost impossible to separate from service even the most incompetent professional. The solution has been one of two alternatives: assigning them to out-of-classroom duties--or to the Board of Education which by now has become known as 110 Hilton--or playing musical chairs by transferring them from one place to another.

Employees of the school system have their unions or professional organizations to protect them from abuse. The parents' concern must be for the children. We would hope that children would be the major concern of educators, but for far too many years we have seen only lip service given to children's needs. Parents want to play a supportive role, but they can no longer sit back and wait. Action must be taken now if the school system is to survive and, in effect, if children are to be able to go on in the New York City schools.

Thank you.

THE CHAIRMAN: Do the Commissioners have any questions?

MR. TRACTENBERG: I have a couple of questions.

In your statement you indicate that the position taken by the UPA delegate assembly was for the National Teacher Exam or another suitable examination in addition to state certification. I want to see if you can amplify the phrase "other suitable examination."

Must it be a written examination? As you probably know, the Board of Education gives, for certain examinations, review of records.

MRS. LEWIS: Our delegate position was taken three years ago and it represents a position of many different communities. As you know, we are a citywide organization with affiliates in every borough and every section of the city, so that it was not easy to come to a citywide position on this point and it was arrived at after many, many months of discussion. It just didn't rise up one night.

We were very upset with the examination procedures as they were then and are now being implemented. We knew very little of what was being done nationwide and we tried to find out. We did not know that much about the National Teacher Examination but, by its very name alone, its national implication, we felt it would give a broader base for recruitment. So, we were very careful not only to say the National Teacher Examination but to qualify that with the words "other examinations."

I think we were open to some oral test or some other kind of objective method of licensing. I must say that in every part of the city, parents were very much concerned with having the probationary period part of the examination procedure. They felt that this was the only thing.

At that time we were facing a very severe teacher shortage and the demand then was for a warm body. We didn't even care about the qualifications. At that time we had reports of children sitting in auditoriums for 84 days--and I have this documented--without instruction, because the teacher absentee rates and the shortage of teachers was so acute. So we were anxious to get more teachers into this system.

We were anxious that they get adequate training. We didn't want them just dumped into the classroom. We didn't want them to be sent to a school and get lost and become so frustrated that teaching for them would only become a revolving door.

We were open and are still open, therefore, to any kind of examination system which would provide for on-the-job training, an internship program, and would not license until after the probationary period.

MR. TRACTENBERG: A number of our earlier speakers have suggested, if I can capsulize it accurately, that the Board of Examiners ought to be abolished, that state certification or perhaps state certification plus some additional examination--perhaps an unwritten examination--should be the basis for the issuance of a kind of provisional license for a one-year period rather than three and that, as you have suggested, on-the-job performance ought to be evaluated before any permanent certificate was issued.

Is that consistent with your own view?

MRS. LEWIS: It would be our opinion if it was part of a total decentralization package.

We did not get the kind of package that we hoped for and so it was not essential. We recognized that somebody would have to do the testing, that somebody would have to prepare, to be the mechanical means.

It didn't matter to us whether they called themselves central licensing staff, Division of Personnel, or Board of Examiners. We wanted the inequities wiped out, and we wanted a better opportunity to improve the school system. We include in that the need for more Black and Puerto Rican people in the system.

MR. TRACTENBERG: Just a couple of more questions, if I may.

Along the same line, you said in your statement that the community board should also be able to recruit off of the central list and I believe you said, refer selectees to the central selection agency for qualifying certification.

Does qualifying certification in your judgment require a written test, or can it be a review of record?

MRS. LEWIS: It could be a review of record. It could involve some kind of oral interview. It could involve an interviewing process with the district superintendent and the community school board.

At this time I must say that we are open to any suggestions, any rational plan that can be presented to us, which would be studied very fairly by our delegates, and we would come to a speedy decision on it.

MR. TRACTENBERG: Two more things, Mrs. Lewis.

Do you have any reason to believe that if community boards and if their parents associations--functioning in the kind of consultive capacity that you described in your paper--were given greater flexibility, this would open the door to the spoils system or to political patronage?

MRS. LEWIS: I don't think it would be that at all.

Under current licensing procedures--and many of us have friends trying to get into the system who have passed the examinations, who are on the list and cannot get appointments to schools--appointees find that they are blocked because somebody else is suggested or recommended, or a principal asks for the appointment of the assistant principal that he knows. So we think that this kind of maneuvering is going to go on for a long time no matter how rigid the licensing examination system is.

What we believe is that the parents and the community school board together can meet the needs of their community because they know it best. They can see in a person the kind of personality characteristic or talent that is especially suited to their own needs, to their needs in that district. If they could have that kind of flexibility, then we feel we would see improvement in the system.

We know there are no hard and fast rules. I want to make this clear.

I know of a case where a high school parents association was actively involved in the selection of a principal. They set up criteria; they set up an interviewing process which could have served as a model for the entire city. After just a few months of seeing him on the job, both the parents and the teaching staff of that school felt that this man just did not meet their standards. Now it is almost a year and a half, and they have petitioned for his removal, they have petitioned for him to be rated, and nothing has happened.

So, it is not going to be a magic thing. We still demand from our professionals honest rating of the staff under their command.

But we do feel that with all parties involved there will be more support for this system. If you play a part in the selection of somebody, if you feel some kind of relationship to him, you offer more support and this, too, could mean an improvement in human relationships in our schools.

MR. TRACTENBERG: One of the participants at yesterday's session made some comments, which I know Chairman Norton found troublesome, about a problem which apparently existed in some of the Black and Puerto Rican community districts where an eligibility list existed.

They were told they must pick someone off the eligible list. They made inquiries of a number of people--perhaps everyone on the list--and could find no one even willing to fill the vacancy.

MRS. LEWIS: Yes, we have heard this from many parents. They have gone down the entire list.

Once or twice the people above them on the ranked list would waive their place, would say they didn't want to come to the school, so that they could go down the list and, other times, they would not waive and the parents and school administration were forced to take somebody who had a higher ranking on the list. I think the high school list with its limited number of applicants at this time poses such a problem.

MR. TRACTENBERG: I assume that puts both the community boards and the parents associations in a rather untenable position.

MRS. LEWIS: Of course, it does.

This is specially a problem where there is a great need for bilingual teachers. You have a list and you don't have anybody with the bilingual qualifications. They are not there.

The list, then, does become inhibiting even though it is qualifying and not ranked at this time.

MR. TRACTENBERG: Finally, a number of speakers yesterday talked about closer teacher-parent contacts as a way both to facilitate recruitment of teachers and obviously to make them more effective in the classroom.

A number of speakers of Puerto Rican ancestry said if only teachers can come to the community and have dinners with the parents, they would automatically develop a closer relationship.

Do you have any reaction to that?

MRS. LEWIS: I think there has to be a closer relationship between parents and teachers. For 50 years our organization has been dedicated to bringing the parents and the home closer to the teacher.

Some parties viewed this kind of familiarity as an intrusion on their privacy, so there has to be sensitivity shown in any of these situations. It is extremely difficult to make a blanket rule.

Certainly, during the school day and during the parents association functions, and as a result of the close liaison that the parents association has with its principals and teaching staff, there does develop a relationship. It can either be a very healthy and constructive one or, unfortunately, at times, a very unconstructive one. There is hope they will become close because, actually, their interest should be in educating the child; that should be the guiding interest that keeps people in the system. It is the vested interest that the parents have and it speaks in their activity. After all, parents are unpaid workers in the school.

MR. TRACTENBERG: That is all I have. Thank you.

THE CHAIRMAN: Thank you, very much.

I am going to call Mr. David Seeley, Director of the Public Education Association.

MR. SEELEY: Chairman Norton and Honorable Members of the Commission: Although the immediate reason for investigating the hiring and promotion practices of the New York City school system may be an entirely justified concern about racial discrimination, it is important to realize that serious questions have been raised both in and outside New York City about the educational merits of present school personnel practices.

Ironically, so far as ideas and proposals are concerned, New York City has been in the forefront of this movement to re-examine old practices. The Public Education Association has recently prepared a short summary of studies and reports over the past 20 years that have recommended major changes in our personnel procedures. I am attaching a copy of this summary for the record.

One of the most comprehensive of these reports, the so-called Strayer-Yavner Report, concluded that "in smaller school systems outside New York City farsighted superintendents are evaluating teacher competence against a set of standards much more meaningful" than those used by the Board of Examiners.

It also concluded that, "The Board has turned from truly significant problems enunciated 25 years ago and is dabbling in superficial research which involves counting, but little thinking."

The other reports, such as one by a respected large-city superintendent, Mark Schinnerer, commissioned by the State Department of Education, and one by a team from the N.Y.U. School of Education, conclude much the same thing. All of them call either for the abolition or major reorganization of the Board of Examiners.

The main criticism, both here and across the country, is that some of the most important qualifications for good teaching and good school administration--namely such personal qualities as commitment, initiative, and leadership--cannot be tested by most certification and examination procedure, so that people who have these qualities are often excluded in favor of people who have successfully completed the examinations or education courses of dubious relation to effective performance on the job. The more rigid and narrow the certifying procedure--and New York City's is almost a caricature in this direction--the greater these flaws become, to the point where some believe that the system not only fails to identify the kind of qualities and leadership needed but actually repels people of imagination and strong, independent character, and attracts and rewards those with a narrow outlook and dependent personalities, anxious to receive answers and authority from above.

What is particularly tragic about a personnel system that discourages or excludes people with the necessary teaching or leadership ability is that such qualities are in such short supply and are at the same time so desperately needed in this time of transition and turmoil in education. Thus the increasing impatience of the demands for change.

Our problem in New York City is that there has been no significant response to all of these pleas for reform. It has been a classic case of the failure of established institutions to respond to normal and reasonable pressures for change. We now find ourselves beset with the accumulation of several decades of unresolved problems, only one of which is the appalling, outrageous, trouble-breeding, and totally unconscionable shortage of Blacks and Puerto Ricans, particularly in the supervisory ranks.

I have no doubt whatever but that if our school system had responded in some reasonable way to the educational needs that studies and reports have emphasized for the past 20 years--the need for teachers and supervisors of strong character, community sensitivity, and leadership ability, rather than just those with ability to take highly rigid and structured tests--there would be today much less of a problem of minority discrimination. Blacks and Puerto Ricans would not only have been allowed into the system; they would have been actively sought out and encouraged for educational reasons. The minority population of the city would have been seen as an untapped resource of talents and commitment needed for the educational welfare of our school children.

Tragically this was not done, and indeed spokesmen for the system even today seem to rest content with the lame excuse that we have few Black teachers and supervisors because most school personnel have come from the city colleges, which themselves have had low minority group enrollment. This reveals an entirely passive view of personnel administration, one that sees no responsibility on the part of the school system to seek out and appoint those who can best help our children to learn. It is an indication of how far our present system has lost sight of its prime responsibility for educating children.

We are now at a point in the history of our city's public school system where the long-overdue reform of our personnel policies can no longer be put off if public education is to survive. We are also luckily now at a point where something can be done about it.

So long as we had a huge centralized system, responsible for selecting and promoting thousands of teachers and supervisors every year, it was difficult to escape from a bureaucratic and mechanistic system of hiring and promotion. Now there are 31 community school boards, each with a manageable number of schools and some responsibility so that school officials can be held to account for their performance.

It is clear that under decentralization there will have to be a two-layer structure of personnel selection, just as there is throughout the rest of the state and most of the nation, an initial screening or certifying process to determine the pool of eligible candidates, and then a selection process at the local level where the real work must be done, to find the best qualified candidate for each particular vacancy.

For initial screening or certifying, it would make sense to use the state certification process, thus offering a wider pool of selection and, at the same time, saving expense, trouble and turmoil for the city. Although this process is itself in need of improvement, as both the State Commissioner and Chancellor admit, it would allow us to escape from the even worse evils of the New York City System.

It should also be understood that no certifying procedure, by its nature, can claim perfection. In order to be broad enough to permit selection among the maximum number of good candidates, it will also inevitably admit a certain number of unsuitable candidates. This is not so much of a danger so long as we don't confuse a screening procedure with a selection procedure.

The claims about the illiterates and misfits with state certification we will be forced to hire if we abandon city tests are misleading. Unlike the city procedure, which almost guarantees appointment to those who pass an examination with high enough score, the state certification system only makes a person eligible to be appointed. The candidate still must convince a local school board that he is competent and qualified for a job before he is placed in contact with children.

There is also a difference here, by the way, from the licensing policies for doctors and lawyers, which are often used incorrectly and misleadingly as analogue to teacher certification. Doctors and lawyers hold themselves out to be hired by the individual citizen and the state tries to provide some assurance through licensing that each practitioner has the specific and highly technical skill that the citizen is expecting to get when he retains the doctor or lawyer.

Teachers are hired by public authorities, and, almost invariably, by other professional educators who work for these public authorities. They have the opportunity and the competence to check into the qualifications of those they hire. Furthermore, there are many characteristics other than technical knowledge that the hiring authority will want to examine before placing a person into intimate contact with children on a day-in and day-out basis. There is, unfortunately, no substitute for the judgment of local school authorities when it comes to building a strong staff.

It is at the local level, then, that the really important process of selection must take place. In other words, at this other level that has now come about in New York City. If the community school boards want to improve the quality of their schools, their first priority must be to develop aggressive and imaginative recruiting, training, and promotion programs. A mechanical examination system, which does not even pretend to measure some of the most important qualities of personality and commitment, and which is far from perfect even for measuring important intellectual qualities, simply will not do. There must be a much more open approach to recruitment, and then a much more careful examination of actual job performance during probation.

By the way, I would like to digress for just a moment to point out, in the summary of earlier studies that I gave to the Commission, that one was approved by the Public Education Association in 1952. Even at that time it recommended much the same thing that has been recommended today.

That report concluded that the committee felt supervision in the schools was poor, thus guaranteeing tenure to almost all teachers as a matter of course rather than competence; that the system was too inbred and therefore stagnant; and that expanded recruitment was necessary. A carefully structured three-year probationary period for supervisors was formulated.

Trainees would be involved in a two-pronged evaluative process: one-year assignments to three different schools staffed with specially trained and interested supervisors, thereby affording the trainee a comprehensive view of duties and responsibilities of school administrations, then combined evaluation ratings from the three schools. This rating profile would be weighed heavily in issuance of the final license.

I think it is extraordinary how uniform it has become in this city of shifting from the idea of using the initial certifying tests as a reliance for quality to the idea that we were putting forth 20 years ago of having on-the-job evaluation be the key to determining whether the person could do the job.

For both recruitment and on-the-job evaluation there must be a truly collaborative involvement of both professional and lay points of view. Teachers and supervisors must have the respect of both their peers and their clients for education to be effective.

What can we expect from the community school boards in meeting these important new responsibilities? The Public Education Association has been conducting a number of case studies of local selection procedures for school principals. The school professionals work with the local boards. We find some school people, in an effort to appear more "community minded," actually abdicating their professional responsibilities and withholding their professional judgments when they are badly needed.

These problems, however, are growing pains. In general, we are encouraged to think that the new community school boards can rise to the challenge now before them. We don't think they are going to accept old answers. They will continue to try new methods and invent new procedures until effective ways are found to recruit the best staff for our schools.

These trial-and-error efforts by our community school boards are, in my opinion, extremely important to education not only in this city, but throughout the country, for it is much more likely that practical and effective new answers will be found in the context of the realities of these districts than in abstract studies conducted by universities. We must make sure that our community districts have the freedom and get the necessary help to do this work well. If we tie them up in bureaucratic red tape, or continue to generate conflict and hostility by trying to force them to take unsuitable personnel produced by antiquated examinations and lists, we will not only cheat our own children, but we will miss an opportunity to make an important contribution to the improvement of educational personnel administration. That, I think, will be valuable.

Again, I am obliged to digress from my formal testimony here. This is really the first city that is trying decentralization on a major scale, and every other major city in the country is thinking about it, wondering whether they should do it and how it should be done. I think that, once again, New York City can move into the forefront, if we will see the implications, and not try to continue to hang on to the institutions that were developed for a single centralized system.

Now, what of the "merit system"? The reasons for change are hard to refute on logical grounds, but entrenched and irresponsible bureaucratic power is not the only reason why change has been so difficult. New Yorkers have been fearful that if the present examination system is abandoned, we will be engulfed by the type of corruption and political favoritism that was rife at the turn of the century. I think we have heard witnesses during these hearings say that over and over again.

Indeed, our Association was in the forefront of the fight for the original merit system, which was an important reform in its day, and it dates back 70 years ago. It is not irrational to continue to be worried about corruption in a city like this, but it is irrational to hold on to institutions that have outlived their usefulness, and which have now developed their own kind of internal corruption, as they become used more to protect the vested interests of those inside than to protect the quality of the education provided to our children.

The protections against corruption must now be applied to the selection procedures in the community school boards. Even without changing to state certification, the community school boards now have the responsibility for selecting from unranked lists for supervisors. If there is going to be corruption or favoritism it is in these selections that it will come.

Citywide tests are no longer a protection. The only effective protection will come from having professional and community groups work out procedures on the local level that will both protect against favoritism and at the same time insure the appointment of the most effective personnel. This will take ingenuity, but it should not be impossible, for it should be clear to both groups by now that they both share the same interests in this matter.

If ineffective personnel are appointed, the whole public school system will be in jeopardy, and the professional staff and their job security along with it. And if there is favoritism or cronyism, the morale of the staff, and hence the quality of the schools, will also suffer. The place for professional groups concerned with merit to apply their energies is in the development of these new local procedures, and not in trying to preserve ineffective central procedures that remove accountability from the local boards.

There is one particular fear about local selection that has stood as the greatest emotional force against change, namely, the fear that minority group parents will make racial factors the prime criteria for selection. From our studies so far, these fears are unfounded.

The cry that "We want a Black principal for Black kids" is made by a few spokesmen in certain cases, but this seems to be mostly a generalized expression of dissatisfaction with the kind of staff that has been produced by the "white controlled system." Once the actual selection procedure begins filling a particular vacancy, we have seen in every case examined that the parents' prime concern is to find the candidate who will do the best job for their children. As often as not the person selected is white.

Let me cite a few examples. At school A, with a student body 75% Black and Puerto Rican, the parents at first said they wanted a Black principal. A screening panel was established consisting of the parents association representatives, a paraprofessional and two teachers from the school, representatives of the local board, the UFT, and the community corporation. No principals indicated an interest in transferring to this school, and those on the regular eligible list who initially showed interest never came for the interviews.

It was a situation ripe for selecting an unlicensed Black candidate if this was what the community wanted. Yet the group finally selected the white acting principal of the school, who they felt was better qualified than any other candidate.

School B, with a 75% Black student body, also originally wanted a Black principal for the sake of developing the self-image of the students. A screening panel from the parents association and the local school board found none of the candidates who applied for the job from the regular list had the leadership ability they thought was needed for the school.

The Black parents then sought out and interviewed three additional Black candidates who had not previously applied. In the end, however, the panel, with the parents concurring, found a new white candidate who they felt was the best qualified.

In school C, two-thirds Puerto Rican and one-third Black, a large screening panel of 16 to 18 teachers, parents and local school board members were not favorably impressed with the regularly licensed principals who applied for transfer. After much consideration they chose a white assistant principal from a neighboring school, who they felt was doing a good job in his present position.

The prime concern of parents for qualifications, as shown in these examples, will tend to be the rule so long as there are adequate and open procedures for evaluating the needs of the job to be filled and for involving the parents. The only factor we can see that might change this situation is if white groups, out of fear of Black racism, continue to thwart the efforts of local communities to improve their own schools. This can only increase the influence of those demagogues who preach that Black communities must distrust all whites, regardless of qualifications.

Let me close by making a point that I hope will not be misunderstood. When I was in charge of the school desegregation program for the federal government, I was in contact with hundreds of Southern school officials who in various ways were trying to retain their segregated school systems in spite of the 1954 Supreme Court decision. From up North these people were looked upon as rednecks and bigots, who were viciously denying Black children their constitutional rights. They were not. They, by and large, were conscientious men and women who were convinced they were doing their best for the children under their charge. They could not see the injustice and harm they were doing to children.

Although, as Chairman Norton pointed out in her opening remarks, there are differences in the legal traditions of the North and South, there are not that many differences in human nature. Apparently racism and discrimination are much easier to identify from afar than when we are involved in them ourselves. I am sure this Commission will hear sincere pleas from New York school officials about why we cannot or should not change.

It is no disrespect for the sincerity of these men and women to say that their views must be disregarded. There simply is no defense in this day and age for an antiquated testing and promotion system that has set the worst record for minority group representation of almost any large city in the country and that is harming children every day it is allowed to remain in existence. If we cannot make such an obvious and long overdue reform as this through our machinery of government, how can we expect people to heed our pleas to "work within the system"?

Thank you.

THE CHAIRMAN: Thank you, sir.

COMMR. COLGATE: Mr. Seeley, you were talking about, if I recall your testimony, an initial screening examination. Did I understand you correctly to imply that as one went up the executive ladder in the school to the rank of assistant principal and various titles that one would also continue to have such a screening examination?

MR. SEELEY: Yes.

I think you would probably still have the same two-level process of some kind of initial certification.

COMMR. COLGATE: In other words, you would have a principal license?

MR. SEELEY: Yes.

I think, again, that the state license is the proper one. I think, if we can indeed shift more to an evaluation of on-the-job performance, then the initial process of screening ought to be a great deal more flexible.

I think that possibly might develop. We have been in discussions with the State Commissioner of Education and other people at the state level, and I can't say how they will come out on this, but I will speak for myself. I think what we really ought to do is have people come in on an initial pool by a number of different routes, maybe including that examination, maybe taking that examination. But there ought to be more flexibility to allow people with different kinds of backgrounds and different perspectives to have a try at these jobs since they cannot be actually hired without some public authority saying they are fit for that trial.

If we have good procedures, if we have the second stage, namely, on-the-job evaluation, it would seem more flexible.

MR. TRACTENBERG: Just a couple of questions, Mr. Seeley.

The President of the Board of Education, Murry Bergtraum, in the first day of these hearings, suggested his preference for the abolition of the Board of Examiners, in its current form at least, in favor of a statewide kind of certification test.

Do you have a reaction to that? Would you support that kind of certification and screening process?

MR. SEELEY: I do favor the statewide certification process, and I think it can be used. I don't think I favor a written test.

It seems to me foolish to spread to the whole state the idiocy of the New York City system. To the degree the people want to use a written test they might as well use something like the National Teacher Exam.

I wouldn't want them to limit themselves to that. That can be one way of people showing they have some minimal level of literacy and educational background. The National Teacher Exam is administered throughout the country. That can be one route.

People could take that and, based on whatever minimal score the state would set, it would say these people would be eligible or can be considered for a probationary period.

I think it would be foolish for the state to try to administer a statewide test. I noticed in the Times the other day, in recording the first day's hearing, it gave the impression that the Chairman of the present Board and the Chancellor favored this.

I was here at that time. I don't think the Chancellor was talking about a statewide test. He was talking about statewide certification.

MR. TRACTENBERG: A couple of other questions, Mr. Seeley.

One of the common charges against the examination process in New York City is that it is too academic, too intelligence oriented. I don't believe I remember the exact words.

I think you said you didn't believe it served that function adequately.

MR. SEELEY: This is a long story. I contemplated going into it in more detail and I think someone ought to do something more about it.

Looking at the tests I have looked at, there is only one conclusion I can come to. And that is, they are mindless. These are not even intelligence tests.

Let me read you one question, for instance; the very first question on the recent principal's examination. See what an intelligent person can make of asking a candidate this question.

This is a multiple choice question. This is the short-answer part of the test. I think there are a hundred short-answers. In each case the candidate is asked to check the correct answer.

"The curriculum may be best defined as (1) courses of study, (2) educational terms, (3) pupil experience, and (4) programs of study."

The candidate is supposed to know how you can best define curriculum.

Well, I participated in a discussion some time ago with a member of the Board of Examiners, a head of the Supervisors Association, and a number of other people, and a very eminent person raised this question. What is the correct answer to this question?

He was directing this to the Board of Examiners, a member present, asking what is the correct answer that you demand of candidates in order to say they are qualified to become a principal?

His answer was that it is unfair to pick out one question like that. But the head of the Supervisors said, "There is only one answer to that question. Obviously, pupil experience is the answer."

I think the mentality that is involved here is really what bothers me. This holds throughout the whole education establishment, as far as I am concerned, and goes not just to the question of these exams. This is the tendency for a kind of catechistic approach to this--whatever is in intellectual fad or whatever the current answer is. And this Supervisor was saying--he was liberal, progressive--because "in our view" curriculum is only defined as the experience of children, that has to be the answer.

It seems to me that that is a mentality that discourages anyone with any kind of desire to come to his own answers on things. You certainly could have a person who came from another system, which was an excellent system, who had a very high intelligence level, who didn't happen to take the cram courses to find out what the answers were, and who could very well answer, "courses of study" or "programs of study."

Yet with the mentality involved, you have to learn the current lingo of the educationist in order to be able to get through, and that exists throughout these examinations, as far as I can see. I don't think they even test real intellectual ability. They may test the rather unimportant intellectual ability of memorizing answers. They do not test initiative, and people who have a mind of their own fail.

MR. TRACTENBERG: How do you respond to the statement that you have selected only one out of many questions to subject to criticism?

MR. SEELEY: Well, although it would take all day, I think it would be extremely instructive to the Commission and public-at-large if all of the questions could be read.

I will pick out another one here. This is down the list a little ways.

"Of the following, the best defense for the call for a national policy for education is that, (1) it would result in equal education opportunity, or something like that; (2) the federal government would eliminate the necessity for local financial support by the public; (3) it would induce the federal government to include a defense amendment in order to assure legislative passage; (4) the associated economic forces in the society are not contaminated with school district to state boundaries."

An intelligent person can pick any one of two or three of those answers but, apparently, you have to learn the correct answer and that is the reason why the school principals and the people establishing the tests have this boondoggle of telling people what the correct answers are.

An intelligent, good principal hasn't got a prayer with this kind of an exam unless he has boned up or takes an expensive cram course to find out how to answer these questions intelligently. I would encourage the Commissioners to read through that last elementary principal examination and see if you can come to a conclusion as to its relationship to performance.

There is no objective way of evaluating the answers to the questions on this examination.

MR. TRACTENBERG: Just one final question, Mr. Seeley. There has been expressed at these hearings a good deal of sentiment for substantial change in the current system directed at Board of Education and Board of Examiners' officials.

Is the Board of Education properly subject to this criticism?

MR. SEELEY: There have been many, many suggestions for legislative change, including those by the State Board of Regents, itself, to abolish the Board of Examiners among many other things. And I realize, that there are legislative changes called for. But we have felt there were many, many things that the Board of Education could do under the current law.

I do not think they were required to go ahead with the present procedure. It is extremely expensive. Even today, tomorrow, the next day, last week, the Board of Education is paying 12 and 13 dollars an hour of the taxpayer's money to principals and assistant principals, earning 20 or 25,000 dollars a year. In addition, they are paying 12 or 13 dollars an hour to continue with the oral sections of this exam in the hope they may be thrown out in court and, even if it weren't, I believe the Board of Education could have held up this exam and continued.

One of the problems with it is going to be this--the Board of Examiners will go through the regular process of this examination, come out with a list of eligible principals which will then, under present legislation, be locked in for four more years.

It wouldn't make any difference how good a candidate arrived on the scene. If the best principal in the world arrived on the scene and wanted to be hired by a school district, a difficult school district, saying "I am willing to take it on," he couldn't be hired. He would be barred because this eligible list will come out and the supervisors will go to court and insist that people be hired from the eligible list.

Or the people on the list will say, "We passed the exam. We took all the trouble. We have been waiting all the time. Now we are on a list and you can't open it up any more."

Either the legislature won't be able to open it up or the Board would have to pay off eligible candidates, as they did two years ago with the then existing elementary school list when they were compelled to pay off all the people on it. There were virtually no Blacks on it either.

THE CHAIRMAN: We will call a 5-minute recess and the next speaker will be Mr. Albert Shanker.

(Whereupon, a 5-minute recess was taken.)

THE CHAIRMAN: May I ask Mr. Albert Shanker, President of the United Federation of Teachers, to please take the stand.

MR. SHANKER: I think that in discussing the question of employment practices in the Board of Education, I should make it very clear here that I am speaking not only as the President of the United Federation of Teachers, which is the official collective-bargaining agent for 82,000 employees of the Board of Education, but I am also speaking here on behalf of Harry Van Arsdale, Jr., on behalf of 1.2 million of the AFL-CIO employees affiliated with that body.

We do not wish to take a position that everything which the Board of Examiners has done is perfect or that the present Civil Service system, which has been in effect for over a half a century in the school system, has no faults. Undoubtedly, in a history that long, it will be possible to pick out examples and individual questions to quarrel with. There are questions of procedures and questions of judgment which are involved in these things which we are not interested in defending or in identifying ourselves with.

Furthermore, we do not take the position that the present Board of Examiners is necessarily the only institution that can ever be developed which would guarantee some sort of Civil Service system within the public schools of the City of New York. I don't think that these are the questions.

Other questions, however, are being raised, such as why should there be any form of written examination either for supervisors or for teachers coming into the school system in New York City.

I would like to point out here that we very strongly believe that there are aspects of the teacher's job and of the supervisor's job which require knowledge of particular subjects and that that knowledge can be tested on a written examination, and should be. I think it would be rather preposterous if we were to live in a state where you have to pass a written examination to become a barber, a hairdresser, where you need one to drive an automobile, to be a clerk, a stenographer, a real estate man, just about anything--an insurance salesman, an insurance agent, a broker.

There are literally hundreds of occupations where the state has asserted that the state has responsibility in maintaining particular levels of service and standards in terms of entry into that field, and I think it would be kind of ridiculous if the City of New York or the State of New York said that to drive an automobile and to sell real estate or sell insurance one needs a written examination, but to teach the children of the City of New York it is not required that there be an examination.

Let's not be fooled by the fact that the Board of Examiners exists in New York City but not in the rest of the State. Most districts of any size throughout the United States do use some form of written examination. If they don't have their own Board of Examiners, which in most cases they do not, than they use the National Teacher Exam or something similar to it.

Now, we are not here asserting that one can discern whether a prospective applicant is going to be a good teacher by giving him a test. I don't think that you can.

If he is going to be a mathematics teacher, you can tell if he knows mathematics. If he is going to be a French teacher, you can tell if he knows French. You can tell about any kind of teacher whether he is basically literate or illiterate.

So that the fact that one cannot measure all of the talents and skills necessary through a written examination does not mean that there should not continue to be examination for those particular skills and abilities and talents which can be measured.

I think the second very important thing which must be part of any school system, whether it is the present system or any future system which is set up, is that it be set up in such a way as to guarantee that there is no discrimination in employment because of race, religion, sex, union affiliation or non-affiliation, or anything of that sort. Now, in this argument, we would like to look at communities throughout the rest of the country and say, "They don't have Civil Service systems. Why do we need one?"

But, if we take a look at systems throughout the country, we will generally find that most school systems in small towns throughout this State have employed very few Blacks, a smaller number and a smaller percentage than the City of New York. Very few Spanish-speaking teachers or supervisors.

It is true that other cities may be slightly ahead of us, but that is usually due to a circumstance which, thank God, we do not have in New York City. Most other cities have had segregated Black colleges and universities in those particular areas which did produce teachers in those school systems. The fact we did not have such a segregated system in the City of New York has meant that we did not have a large number of Black college graduates to select from in this particular area.

Now, one thing ought to be said about one of the alternatives which is being proposed, and that is that state certification become the way of entry into a position in the City of New York. I think it should be pointed out that state certification at the present time means very little.

At one time a state certificate meant that the teacher sent credentials of various sorts to the State Education Department together with a list of references. It then took a number of years for the State Education Department to check on the background of the person and then either to issue the certificate or not. That practice, however, has been abandoned by the State Education Department because the work that it took to certify large numbers of teachers was too difficult for them, too time-consuming and expensive and, therefore, the State Education Department no longer asks for references, nor does it any longer even look at the transcript of the individual applying for a teacher's job.

Instead, it accepts from a college or university a self-serving statement that the student who may have graduated has substantially met the requirements established by the State of New York and a simple statement from a college or university. And, I might say, this includes not just colleges and universities in this state but in over a dozen other states where we now have reciprocity. A mere statement from the university that the student has taken something like what he was supposed to have taken will get the person a state certificate. It may very well be that five or 10 or 15 years ago such a letter from the university might have meant something. But given student unrest at various campuses today, we cannot tell whether a letter from a university represents a particular standard of achievement or accomplishment or whether it represents a negotiated settlement with a particular group of students during an uprising on campus.

I would also like to respond to one of the constantly recurring statements, which is that somehow the school system, as an employer, indicates that it has been discriminatory, or that it is a sign that it has been guilty of discriminatory practices, if the percentage of students in the school system who are Black and Puerto Rican is substantially different from the percentage of teachers and supervisors in the school system who are Black and Puerto Rican. I have been thinking about this for a good many months because this hearing is not the first place where that statement has been made. And I find it impossible to believe that any individual with a minimum amount of intelligence would use an argument like that.

We know that we live in a society in which the number of

years which one has been in the country, the amount of wealth or poverty that a particular group has, that these are factors in terms of what particular jobs in this society a group gets. And we know that there is an order in our large cities; that teaching is what might be called a relatively inexpensive profession to get into; and that, as various groups move into the cities, the first thing they start doing in their move towards upward mobility is to buy small businesses, become candy store owners, et cetera; and that their children, who are the first to go to college, then go into professions like teaching and then the teachers go into other professions. Therefore, it has almost always been that the teachers in urban school systems represented predominantly the immigrants of the previous generation who were teaching the children of the newer immigrants.

So, when the Irish came into the system, they were taught by WASPS; and the Irish then taught the Jews; and the Jews, the Italians; and I suppose the next group of Black and Puerto Rican teachers and administrators will be teaching the newly affluent grape-pickers, represented by Cesar Chavez, now moving up from the lowest to the next rung.

If we were to apply this very same question to other fields, then I think the Commission on Human Rights could very well extend their hearings and broader them. After all, why ask the Board of Education why the percentage of principals and teachers are different than the percentage of consumers of products in this area. Why not investigate the Daily News and the New York Times and Post since a much larger percentage of their readers are Black and Puerto Rican than is true of members of their editorial staff or, certainly, if we go into the area of ownership, why not ask the same thing of our large networks, CBS, NBC, and even of our smaller stations, as to why there is not the same percentage of minority representation on the board of directors, stockholders, and other management positions as there are television viewers and radio listeners of their particular stations, or why there isn't the same ethnicity in the pharmacy industry whether it be retail drugists or stores or people making the drugs, as there are minority groups consuming the various things in order to try to cure themselves of various illnesses.

The question, on the face of it, is ridiculous and I find it very hard to believe that speaker after speaker here has looked at the percentage of students, over 50% Black and Puerto Rican, and percentage of teachers, less, and has concluded that it proves something. If it does, I must urge you to go into these other fields and prove the same thing.

We can find much at fault with the Board of Examiners and with what it has done in the past, but some of it was not the fault of the Board of Examiners but of the city and the Board of Education. For a good many years the United Federation of Teachers has been urging that because the supply of Black and Puerto Rican college graduates in and around the City of New York was insufficient to provide ethnic balance on our staff, the Board of Education should provide a sufficient amount of money for a recruitment program so that instead of requiring graduates of the University of Puerto Rico and graduates of Black and integrated colleges in other parts of the country to fly into New York City to take an examination, that the Board of Examiners be given funds to go to the University of Puerto Rico and to these other universities to be able to conduct a recruitment program there. We first made this request in 1962, and we reiterated that request every year since. But neither the Mayor, nor the various bodies which approve the budgets of the city, nor the Board of Education have provided anything in the way of sufficient funds until 1969, when the United Federation of Teachers negotiated with the Board of Education, as part of our contract, a million dollar joint recruitment fund.

I am very happy to say that that joint recruitment fund has resulted in a program both in Puerto Rico and in other parts of this country which will bring to us over 1,500 Blacks and Puerto Ricans for our school system for the next school year. That is the program that ought to be expanded.

I think in any discussion of change in the present system there ought to be a consideration of what the alternatives are. At the present time in Scarsdale, in Plainedge and Plainview, in Lakeland and in Wappinger Falls, there are no parents, nor are there community agencies, nor are there local political groups placing their bodies in front of school doors and demanding that unless the particular candidate of their choice is employed something horrible is going to happen in the school. I am sorry to say that I can't make a statement like that about the City of New York.

At the present time, the alternative to an examination system--and to a system which gives people jobs on a basis of some objective criteria, regardless of whether they are the present criteria or new ones which would be adopted under some Civil Service system--is not a rational process of selection by school management which exists in those stable communities, but rather a process of confrontation and probably a process of selection extremely unrepresentative of the communities of New York.

Last night, one of New York City's 31 community districts, in trying to select a principal or an acting principal for one school, called their parents' meeting, an open meeting. This is a school with over 1,500 pupils. There are about 35 parents who came down and interviewed a number of candidates.

What it is that will emerge from that process I don't know. But I want to state very openly and very clearly that there really is no reason to believe that 35 people out of approximately 3,000 able to come down will make a selection based on any greater wisdom or intelligence than a process that could be arrived at through some sort of a testing program and Civil Service program.

I want to make it very clear that the mere fact that there is a Civil Service program and people are tested and placed on the basis of their rank on the list does not mean that local communities are denied a role in the process of selection. One of the products of the Decentralization Law is that we do have elected community boards. Those elected community boards do now employ their own community superintendent on a contract basis, and, therefore, he must be responsive to what it is that they want. And the community superintendent and community board now do pick their principals from qualifying, and not from competitive, lists, so that I assume the principals, too, will be more responsive to what it is that the community boards want.

Since both teachers and supervisors have a probationary period of three years, there is ample time for the community boards and community superintendents to see which candidates did well on the examinations but, in practice, do not function well on the job and to make sure that those who do not function well on the job are not retained during this probationary period.

So, even under the present system, if it were properly used, there is a system of checks and balances. There is an examination to make sure that the knowledge the person needs is there. There is a system of assigning people on a non-discriminatory basis. And there is also a system of weeding out people, if it is used by the community, who do not fit the needs either of that community or who are just not fit for the job anywhere.

I would urge very strongly, not that we retain everything that we now have. Teachers over the years and supervisers have felt a certain stuffiness about the present system. They have felt there was an over-reliance on the written test and an under-reliance on actual performance. I would tend to agree. There have been periods when there were extremely long delays in the processing of examinations which did result in many people just not waiting but going elsewhere. We are not saying that what has been has to be kept exactly as is. But the values of a system which tests what can be tested, which assigns on a non-discriminatory basis, ought to be combined with a recruiting program which seeks out minority group applicants to make sure our staff is integrated and with an on-the-job training program which finally weeds out those who cannot make it after we have given them all the help that we can.

I want to add one final thing, and that is that even without any radical changes the ethnic composition of our school staff will change; one, because of the nationwide recruiting program which we are involved in with the Board of Education; secondly, because of the open enrollment program in the City University which we strongly supported and which will produce large numbers of Black and Spanish-speaking college graduates who were not available before; and third, because of the career ladder program which has been negotiated for paraprofessionals in the school system in which thousands of paraprofessionals will now be enrolled in matriculated college programs, and, over a period of time, thousands of them will be entering the school system as teachers.

I would hope that one of the things that would come out of this Commission hearing is that you would urge the Board of Education to grant these college programs not just to the 4,000 paraprofessionals who are now recognized in collective bargaining, but to the 8,000 who are now being discriminated against by the Board of Examiners, paraprofesssionals doing exactly the same job, working side by side with those represented, who are now denied access to college education on a very highly artificial kind of basis as to what their title number has to be or something of that sort. We would very much want your support in that area where thousands of additional paraprofessionals could be going to college and preparing themselves for careers in teaching.

THE CHAIRMAN: Thank you, Mr. Shanker.

I want to go on record with this comment, since it is incumbent on us to hear all sides of this controversy. But it is also incumbent on this Commission to be especially responsible, when we are discussing a matter of percentages in a city which has more ethnic groups than any other city in the world and where each group has an identification with its own group. It is because this Commission has gone into private business, looked at their statistics with respect to groups of people who historically have been discriminated against in this country, and found them unsatisfactory, that we have been able to suggest ways that they might affirmatively change their program so as to attract more minority group people, change their recruiting processes. Because of the success we have had with such businesses, we thought we could not allow similar and lower percentages in public education and in public employment to remain without our trying to do something similar with respect to them.

It is very important that we all be responsible on this question since this city consists of Italians, and Poles, and Irish people, and Jews, and Blacks, and Puerto Ricans, and all of them feel that they deserve a part of this very rich pie called New York City. It is very important to make it perfectly clear that this Commission believes that every group deserves its chance in public employment.

Last night we had testimony from Italian-Americans who believed that the oral examination has discriminated against them. They have a right to come forward here even though they are not classically regarded as a group that is discriminated against.

It is important to understand why the percentages are regarded as things that must be improved upon with respect to the school system. It is important to understand that the Commission does not regard any percentage by itself as significant. It looks at the percentage in relation to a number of different factors according to the industry. Therefore, when we went to the major networks we were able to work out an agreement with them based on their industry, based on an understanding of specifically why minority groups are not found in that industry.

But the statistics with respect to Black and Puerto Ricans in the school system had to be looked at in the following context: that teaching has been the classic profession for Blacks in this country, both North and South. In every other state in the North, Blacks had been able to re-establish themselves in the teaching tradition they developed in the South, with the exception of New York. And some of these cities were not located near segregated colleges. Some were in the Far West, some in the Midwest.

In any case, it is a sad comment on New York City and on those of us who believe in integrated education if the places where

Blacks had been able to get employment in school systems were only where there have been segregated colleges. I cannot believe that that has been the single route into Northern school systems. I don't believe the figures show that. I don't believe the City showed that.

But, in any case, I think it is very important, especially for minority groups who have sometimes been discriminated against on the basis of quota systems which have kept them from opportunities because it was often thought that too many of them were in one place, just as Black and Puerto Ricans are saying too few of us are in some places, that quota systems have no place in this country or city and that, by the same token, minority groups who have historically experienced discrimination are not going to continue to find themselves represented in places where tax dollars go in token numbers.

MR. DAVID: Mr. Shanker you do not believe there is any relationship between the composition of the student body and the faculty. Why do you say that?

MR. SHANKER: Because we believe in an integrated school system. This is not restricted to Black and Spanish-speaking schools but throughout the school system it is true with white teachers and all ethnic groups.

We do feel there should be evidence of advancement and large numbers of Blacks and Puerto Ricans in the school system. We are saying we want more, and we have since 1962 been trying to get the funds. Recently we were successful in getting them to see to it that the numbers are larger. So, saying that we want more is true, and it is one thing. To say that there is discrimination is something that is quite different. We do not believe that there has been discrimination. We do believe that there has been an inadequate number of Blacks and Puerto Ricans in the school system and there are ways, in terms of recruitment, career ladders and so forth, of making sure that we do have a staff which is ethnically qualified.

I want to point out one other thing. The percentage of children in the school system who are Black and Puerto Rican is quite different from the percentage of adults in the city who are Black and Puerto Rican. There are a large number of middle class whites who have pulled their children out of public schools to go to either private or parochial schools. Family size is different among various ethnic and socio-economic groups within the city. Therefore, where you have almost 60% Black and Puerto Rican children in a city, it is not too significant since the teachers are not selected from the students but the adult population.

There ought to be a relationship between the adult population since the teachers are selected from that population. In addition, not only should it be confined to the adult population but the population of college graduates. It seems to me you would have to refine that even further and ask not what is the relationship between the Black and Puerto Rican teachers and the number of children, but between that and the number of adults in the population who are college graduates.

Now, given all of those, there will probably still be some discrepancy in the figures because, as I have said, while I believe there has been no discrimination, I believe there has not been an effort to reach out and to recruit, an effort which should be made. But that is a far different statement--saying that there has not been an effort to go out and recruit--from saying there is discrimination.

THE CHAIRMAN: Counsel.

MR. TRACTENBERG: A number of questions, Mr. Shanker.

You have gone on record in your remarks as favoring a written examination of some form. You then analogized it to certain state licensing examinations for beauticians, barbers.

MR. SHANKER: Even lawyers.

MR. TRACTENBERG: Does New York City have any examination for beauticians or barbers?

MR. SHANKER: You can't practice in the city without a state license.

MR. TRACTENBERG: Does New York City have an examination?

MR. SHANKER: Not to my knowledge.

MR. TRACTENBERG: Does that mean that you agree with the Board of Education President, Murry Bergtraum, that the Board of Examiners ought to be abolished, and that we should go to state examinations?

MR. SHANKER: If the state did set up an examination for teachers which would be as rigorous in this area as they are in other areas, I think it would be desirable to set a single standard for the state rather than to have different standards in different localities. I think that is highly desirable.

I find contradictory standards being proposed. For example, the Police Commissioner of the City of New York is saying that all the police ought to be college graduates and tested; and, at the very same time, the State Commissioner of Education says that teachers needn't be college graduates. I think that the trouble at the present time in setting up a state examination system is that the State Commissioner of Education has unfortunately already taken a public position which states not only that he isn't in favor of examinations, but that he doesn't believe teachers need a college education.

I think, unfortunately, this Commissioner is unlikely to set up the type of standards for teachers that have been set up in 60 or 70 or 80 other categories of employment careers in this State.

MR. TRACTENBERG: If there were adequate standards, a state examination would be preferable in your opinion?

MR. SHANKER: I would even favor federal certification. I favor more state and federal standards. I favor state and federal certification and state and federal financing of schools.

MR. TRACTENBERG: In view of that, would the National Teacher Examination be sufficiently reliable to ensure the minimum competency you talked about?

MR. SHANKER: I think for the most part.

We strongly supported the use of the National Teacher Examination. We supported its use in the current Decentralization Law for 40% of the elementary and junior high schools, and it may very well be that Educational Testing or some other such outfit which specializes in testing may be better equipped than a local unit for that purpose.

Furthermore, it has an advantage. People all over the country can take the same examination simultaneously, thereby avoiding the need for our own special recruiters hopping all around the country with all of the administrative problems attendant on really running a national program out of a local office.

I think that there are a great many advantages to using something which is available on a national basis, including the examination given by ETS.

MR. TRACTENBERG: If I may read from an article, dated November 23, 1966, in the New York Post, written by Bernard Bard. "In a blistering attack on the present teacher licensing system, Albert Shanker, President of the United Federation of Teachers, has called for abolition of the Board of Examiners which tests and certifies teachers and supervisors for the city's schools."

Further down in the article it says, "Shanker also asserted that the city teacher shortage was to go"--I assume the word is missing--"to go into the nationwide market."

MR. SHANKER: The position on the National Teacher Examination is still open. The abolition of the Board of Examiners is not because in the last four years we have seen the alternative very clearly. We did take the position some years back that the Board of Examiners should be abolished, but in the last four years, we have seen the alternative.

The alternative is not a selection process. The alternative is to decide which organized group is going to give out the goodies of various jobs.

We have seen the instances in New York. So far, we have been very, very lucky in this city. We have one group. What will happen if we have two or three groups, each with a different candidate, who decides that it will shut down a school, conduct a boycott or organize on that particular basis unless that candidate comes in? What I am saying is that we are not living in a very calm period. We are living in a period of confrontation. And bureaucracy, with all of its faults, may, during a period of time like this, be superior to the confrontations which are the only things likely to happen.

MR. TRACTENBERG: Interestingly, in the same article, you went on to talk about the way supervisory personnel ought to be appointed and the objective method you chose.

"Principals, assistant principals and department heads should be elected by senior teachers of each school instead of being put there by the present Board of Examiners system."

Is that to be contrasted with the procedures that community boards are carrying out or working toward carrying out?

MR. SHANKER: It depends on what your objective is. It also depends on what the job of the principal is going to be.

I think the unfortunate thing in discussions of this sort, is that we tend to assume that things have to remain as they are;

and even if the Board of Examiners were to be abolished, we are really talking about hiring principals for a job which they are now doing.

Actually, what is wrong is not so much the way principals are hired although it is not a very good way. However, nobody has found ways that are much better.

If you look across the rest of the United States, most principals and most school superintendents are ex-football and basketball coaches who happened to lead unsuccessfully their respective teams, and in order to bring a more successful coach in, they were given these jobs. That is the nationally approved method.

MR. TRACTENBERG: I should point out, incidentally, that our distinguished next speaker, the President of the Council of Supervisory Associations, was, I understand, an eminently successful physical education teacher.

MR. SHANKER: He didn't obtain his present position by virtue of failure in his previous one. At least, not to my knowledge.

THE CHAIRMAN: I think that is fair.

MR. SHANKER: I do, however, want to say this: The principal's job, as now constituted, really is an impossible kind of job. It includes within it 30 or 40 different and rather contradictory kinds of things. It includes, of course, being a chief clerk and answering correspondence, taking care of community relations with parents or community groups, being a kind of labor relations person and administering eight or 10 different contracts. It also includes supervising maintenance of the school in terms of custodial staff, administerial functions such as the scheduling of classes, and so forth. And finally it is supposed to include the development of an educational program, from curriculum to teacher training and evaluation.

What happens when you give a single person a range of duties which is so vast and so huge? What happens is that you will find there is a kind of pecking order among those duties, and that the principal tends to do some of these things first, others second, third and so on. What gets done first is the handling of correspondence. It is clean, fairly easy and gives one a sense of accomplishment, just as it does to appease parents which is taken as sort of a labor relations job. The things that do not get done are the educational things in the school.

Therefore, what you left out of your reading of my statement --which you had no other way of doing, since the article didn't go into very much depth on it--is that instead of having a number of functions, the principal's job should be divided. There should be an administrative function with a chief administrator hired to do some of the correspondence, the labor relations, some of the school maintenance type of things. That person need not be a teacher or educator at all. He could be some person who is good at hiring, buying and selling, and that sort of thing.

The principal, in terms of what we have been talking about, would be the equivalent of a department head in some of our better colleges and universities, who is generally selected by his colleagues for a period of time as a recognized expert in a particular field.

At the present time, one of the reasons a principal really cannot help a teacher is that a teacher is not going to go to a principal and say, "You know, I am very poor at the following five things. Will you please help me?" The reason she is not going to go to him is because at the end of the year he is going to rate her. Why should she confess her shortcomings to the fellow who has power to get rid of her?

We are talking about a department head, a colleague who would not stand in the threatening relationship of being a supervisor, but somebody who would be a recognized expert by the faculty and who would be responsible in a non-threatening way to bring about educational improvements in that particular department. We did favor that, and we do believe if that is the objective you want to accomplish, namely, to bring about change among a faculty, then that is an objective way of securing that objective.

MR. TRACTENBERG: That sounds almost identical, to some of the expositions we have heard from the community board level and from community superintendents about the very broad ranging responsibilities and demanding duties of school administrators, principals in particular. It doesn't, however, sound consistent with the kind of examination given. In fact, it was suggested by these witnesses that the examination process, involving as it does substantial preparation time for the series of exams given at every level of the system, is counterproductive. It deprives the supervisors of the very time they need to devote to helping teachers improve their performance in working with community groups.

Do you agree with that?

MR. SHANKER: I would agree. I would think that an examination which takes the amount of time to cram for, which some of the examinations have taken in the past, I would say that such an examination is counterproductive. In many cases, it might actually tend to attract a person who is most willing to sacrifice his reading of books, going to the theatre, and all sorts of cultural activities. It might actually select people less qualified for a job which is essentially political and social, rather than bookish and intellectual.

That doesn't mean though that examinations should be thrown out. It means that the one that is given ought to be thrown out and replaced with something for which cramming doesn't help you too much.

MR. TRACTENBERG: If a representative selection committee was instituted, consisting of community board members and, presumably, the community superintendent, representatives of parents' groups, and teachers, do you think that such a committee would have an adequate basis to evaluate the on-the-job performance of applicants for principalships and other supervisory positions?

MR. SHANKER: Let me say there are two things involved here.

One is, how does somebody come in? How does he get the job?

There I do not have very much faith in any sort of an interview process, whether it is by teachers or by committees or by anybody else. Anybody who has had to hire anybody for a job as complicated as being a supervisor or a teacher knows that the interview doesn't tell you anything, just as the present Board of Examiners' system doesn't tell you who is a good principal.

The procedure you are raising the question about merely tells you who is good at interviews and there are people who are terrific at interviews who make lousy teachers and lousy principals. I think you would do just as well if you had a lottery which is much less subject to manipulation. In order to secure nondiscrimination, appoint some people on a nondiscriminatory basis, whether it is by lottery or something else, rather than by the subjective screening procedure you are talking about.

I will tell you what I don't like about the screening procedure. Aside from my own experience--and I should reveal a couple of facts here, I did fail several Board of Examiners' examinations and had to take them over again.

MR. TACTENBERG: I assume you were told the reasons for your failure.

MR. SHANKER: Yes, I was.

MR. TRACTENBERG: Would you mind telling us what they were?

MR. SHANKER: I think it would be interesting. Poor speech patterns.

THE CHAIRMAN: I think you speak fine, Mr. Shanker.

MR. SHANKER: That's because I spent a year in front of a mirror saying, "Look at the lovely yellow lillies," and a few other things I don't remember as well.

That is one of my experiences with the examination system. The other is as an employer, and we are a rather large employer. The United Federation of Teachers, in trying to interview people, has made quite a few mistakes. I don't have any faith in my own or anybody else's ability to hire people on an interview basis.

Since you are involved in a question of discrimination I would like to raise a question. One of the problems we face here is how, under a system of state certification or a system of community screening, you are going to avoid new forms of discrimination.

Several weeks ago the Public Education Association held a forum which Dave Seeley chaired. With a Vice-President of Community School Board 13, Mr. Peter Fleming, the question was raised, "What do you find out about prospective applicants for principal in order to decide whether your community board hires him or not?"

Mr. Fleming answered that it was very simple--for the most part it was what their attitude was towards the strike in 1966, and if they supported the U.F.T. they are out. That was said at a public meeting by a vice-president of a community school board.

I would like to know, in view of the commitment of this Commission to preventing discriminatory practices, how a procedure which relies primarily on a community screening process would protect union members against that form of discrimination.

MR. TRACTENBERG: Is there anything under the present system involving eligibility lists that precludes that sort of screening?

MR. SHANKER: The present qualifying list would permit the kind of discrimination that I just described and I hope one of the things this Commission will address itself to, in view of the fact you are dealing with discriminatory hiring practices in the Board of Education, is an investigation of this particular statement made at a public meeting by an official of a school board, in which he announced the policy and practices of the school board which discriminates against applicants on the basis of their past union activity. I hope one of the things you will look into is precisely that form of discrimination.

THE CHAIRMAN: Unfortunately, discrimination on the basis of union membership is not within our jurisdiction under the law, but we do believe it is our duty to turn that information over to the Office of Labor Relations since it is in their jurisdiction.

MR. TRACTENBERG: I think you do agree with what I think is pertinent to this hearing. That is, it is not the system per se that would permit or prevent selection on that basis. That would obtain under the current system or under a system that placed greater reliance--

MR. SHANKER: There is some possibility at present. However, abolishing the system would probably create a greater amount of such discrimination.

MR. TRACTENBERG: Let me go back, if I may, to teacher examinations. To pull things together, I gather you favor a state-wide examination in preference to the city examination.

MR. SHANKER: Yes, I would very much favor the State of New York, the Education Department of the State of New York, setting up a system for professionals in the field of education which is parallel to what they do in the field of medicine, in the field of law, chiropractic, psychology, and dozens of other fields where there is a rather complicated division of labor. That is, generally, the Commissioner or the Board of Regents sets it up.

It is a public body. It is the professional group, itself, through a board, which establishes the examinations and sets the pass mark. It is the Commissioner or the Board of Regents that sets up a passing mark.

I think every other profession has a series of checks and balances which are built into it, and I think it is about time that in a field as important as education there should be a comparable and, I would say, identical system. I don't think there ought to be any differences. You see, in fields like medicine and law and chiropractic and psychiatry and others only licensed practitioners can practice.

I would favor a modification of the law which would say the same thing for public and for private schools. I don't see why we can say a half a million children in the City of New York have to be educated by a person without any certification at all.

MR. TRACTENBERG: I have a copy of a page of a publication called "The Instructor," which reports the results of a poll of teachers conducted in the spring of 1969, in which it is indicated that in answer to a question whether a National Teacher Examination should be required, the results were as follows: Yes, 20.5% No, 79.5%.

Is this proportion reflected in your membership in the U.F.T.? That is, do 79% of the teachers favor no examination for certification?

MR. SHANKER: No, I'm sure it isn't. I am sure it is probably accurate on the basis of a national poll.

We must remember on a national basis that when a student is in pre-med or pre-law or pre-engineering or liberal arts, when a student in the 40's and 50's and early 60's was flunking out of his school, that the usual practice of many universities was to say, "Are we going to kick you out of the university, or are you going to become a teacher?

It is not, therefore, surprising that a good many teachers on a national basis barely manage to get out of college because they were pushed out of every other institution. Colleges are notorious for passing everybody. It is precisely because of the low standards maintained by the colleges and institutions that it is so important for the government to maintain a standard of entry.

Just imagine, he can't become a doctor in this state though most of our medical schools are quite rigorous, just as law schools are rigorous. But the State of New York requires that despite the rigors of these schools an examination in addition to that has to be taken.

MR. TRACTENBERG: I think it may be interesting to read some quotes from teachers screened.

One said, "Wouldn't anything that could be tested in such an examination have already been taught, tested, and retested in the person's years in college?"

MR. SHANKER: Is the same to hold true for doctors? When a college gives him a ticket is he supposed to know everything? Therefore, there is no point in testing anybody any more?

I think that is ridiculous. The people who are doing typing here, before they get Civil Service jobs, are given tests for clerks, stenographers. This is precisely because we don't trust schools to evaluate their own people. In every industry in New York City, every company gives tests. Why are you trying to say that the only field in which a person can enter without your finding out whether a mathematics teacher knows math is the field of teaching?

If somebody knows it, by the way, why is he so afraid to take an examination? I wouldn't be afraid if I knew my job. The only ones that would be afraid are the ones who would not know their job.

MR. TRACTENBERG: I was going to say maybe your speech problem might be a question. I believe there are substantial questions that have been raised in the last few days about objective--

MR. SHANKER: I have no quarrel with raising the question of what should be tested. There is no question in my mind.

I haven't seen any of the recent examinations. I saw some of the late 50's vintage which I thought were atrocities. They required people to study for many months and cram a lot of vocabulary words which are not only not used by students, but adults would not use the words either. They were merely exercises and hurdles, and I am not here to defend that sort of thing. Therefore, the Board of Education should turn around to the Board of Examiners and say, in terms of setting up the requirements, that vocabulary is going to have a lower percentage. They should constantly criticize the examining in terms of looking at the examination and seeing what is a mere hurdle and what is it that the reasonably intelligent person is expected to know to teach the young.

The answer is not to say that because a given examination is a hurdle or is atrocious in terms of what it does, therefore you throw out the whole thing.

MR. TRACTENBERG: I believe it is the Board of Examiners' position that they have sole responsibility to determine the subject matter of the exam. So, in the example you have given, their position would be that the Board of Education could not order them to reduce the amount tested of one item or the amount tested of another item.

MR. SHANKER: The Board of Education sets qualifications and I think one of the things that ought to be looked into is whether the Board of Education, itself, has asserted its prerogative enough.

Obviously, the Board of Education can't make up the exams but, given a role in setting the standards which they have, it seems to me they do have more power than they have exercised up to now in this process.

MR. TRACTENBERG: You would favor a review and updating of eligibility standards?

MR. SHANKER: No question about it. I would favor constantly establishing a relationship between the examination and what one is to do on the job.

I have a good deal of sympathy for the criticisms that some of these examinations have gone beyond what is actually expected on the job.

That is, if somebody is going to be teaching mathematics in the seventh, eighth, and ninth grades, I think it is important that the person know that amount of mathematics and something above it. On the other hand, if the examination is so rigorous that you are really bringing in mathematicians at a very high level, the chances are you are being counterproductive because a high-level mathematician isn't going to be happy teaching seventh or eighth grade arithmetic.

I think the Board of Examiners has sinned in the past. I think criticism of the examinations ought to be continued to be leveled and, like most other institutions, if people keep hitting the Board of Examiners with things of this sort, I think that they will change. If they don't after a period of time, then I will be willing to reconsider my position as to whether they ought to remain in existence.

I would say one of the first things one does in a situation like this is to level a criticism and, if it doesn't bring about some sort of an improvement, further actions are always possible.

THE CHAIRMAN: Let me ask you a question, Mr. Shanker. Does the Union, as a matter of course, review the examination process or specific examinations so you might have a basis on which to make some judgment from time to time on the Board of Examiners?

MR. SHANKER: We haven't done it for a long time. We would be willing to. I think other groups should, too.

I think it might be a good thing to set up some sort of a watchdog which would take the exams or submit them to a rival group and, like Educational Testing, submit them to outstanding educators and then periodically look to see what is said. I think that would have a tremendous impact on the Board of Examiners as to whether they have justified what they do.

I don't think that a bunch of examination creators ought to lock themselves up somewhere and say everything they create is right. I think that there are avenues open to the public and to government other than abolishing the whole system. I think it is possible to straighten it out.

MR. TRACTENBERG: Isn't it true, Mr. Shanker, that, at least, for the last 20 years, if not substantially more than that, there has, in fact, been a series of studies of the Board of Examiners and the selection process which all of which virtually have resulted in the conclusion that the Board ought to be abolished or substantially modified and placed under the jurisdiction of the Department of Personnel, for example?

MR. SHANKER: They have been saying for 20 years that the Board of Examiners ought to be abolished. But it is very simple to get a report written on a subject when you hire somebody to do that job.

Each and every writer was asked before they came in to look over the system and was pretty much told what had to be put in the report. With any other employer, myself included, you would like to be able to run management without any kind of restriction whatsoever.

Did you ever meet a guy in a position of being a boss that preferred not to deal with the union, not to have Wages and Hours Laws, not to have anything else? Obviously, if I could run things exactly the way I want to, I would be much better off than if I am constantly hampered by having to provide justice for others.

Government is no different. Sure, the average community superintendent would like to go out and have his friends in rather than somebody who just passed an examination. The average teacher might want her friends next door rather than somebody sent in.

We are talking about political qualities here. If you abolish a Civil Service system in the field of education, you really ought to talk about abolishing it in the City and State of New York and the Federal Government, too. There is nothing that is more irrelevant in these examinations that you are talking about here than there is in any other given in Civil Service in this state or country.

I am willing to join with you to attack the whole thing, so far as it is irrelevant. But don't throw away the basis of objectivity that there is. Mainly, there are some things that can be tested and should be tested.

You have two separate problems. One problem is establishing a list, whether it is qualifying or competitive. I am not opposed to using the National Teacher Examination for that. That is only one of the jobs that the Board of Examiners performs, that is, creation of a list, whether it is qualifying or competitive.

The other function is to see to it that people who are on a list are employed without discrimination on the basis of whether it is friendship or whether it is race or union affiliation or something else. I am perfectly willing to say that the National Teachers Exam is the examination that people take. What we would still need is some sort of an institution to make sure that there is nondiscrimination in the hiring of those who are on those lists. That would have to be taken care of either by the Board of Examiners or some sort of an independent outfit which makes appointments.

MR. TRACTENBERG: As I understood the testimony we have received the last few days, under the State Education Law, the Board of Education has to decide that. That becomes the responsibility of the Board of Education's Office of Personnel rather than the Board of Examiners.

I gather you are saying it would be quite acceptable to you to have the National Teacher Examination as the basis for promulgating eligible lists so long as there is central assignment.

MR. SHANKER: I don't care if it is central assignment, as long as it is nondiscriminatory assignment.

I suppose one could have an assignment out of more than one center, out of a number of centers. There could be other mechanisms set up to provide for nondiscrimination. The important thing is nondiscrimination.

MR. TRACTENBERG: I think the important thing from our point of view is that you would find the National Teacher Examination perfectly acceptable as a basis of determining minimum competency, and it would not be necessary to give a separate New York City examination.

MR. SHANKER: That's right.

Of course, you could also require the Board of Examiners to use a National Teacher Exam. It is another way of accomplishing the same thing. They are doing it now in other exams.

I am not opposed to it being used in all cases.

MR. TRACTENBERG: That is an administrative detail and not a matter of substance. That is, in terms of substance, a National--

MR. SHANKER: As far as the examination, itself, is concerned, the answer is, yes.

The National Teacher Examination satisfies the requirements that I would set, and I do not believe that there is any reason for advocating a special examination by the Board of Examiners as a substitute for that.

MR. TRACTENBERG: I have just two more questions.

You mentioned the importance of the probationary period for screening out people who, in fact, did not measure up in terms of performance. Earlier this morning, Blanche Lewis said it was virtually impossible to screen out people. Would you favor any changes to make it more possible for community groups, community boards, to screen out incompetent people during the probationary period?

MR. SHANKER: I don't think you need any changes.

In the first place, let me say in your question you switched to three different groups in about 15 seconds. You started by saying that Mrs. Lewis found that her groups found it impossible to screen people. I would hope so.

I don't think it is the job of a parent to be screening people. Generally, a given student may have a run-in with a given teacher regardless of whose fault it is, and that parent can become very antagonistic. The mere fact she doesn't like a teacher doesn't mean a teacher is good or no good.

I don't want local groups deciding who to hire and who to fire. That would be equivalent to getting rid of the community board.

The community board hires a community superintendent. I think the community board ought to sit with the community superintendent and say, "How many probationers do we have? How many are good? How many aren't good? What are you doing to see to it that those who don't belong are dismissed?" I think that is the function of the community board, to bring pressure on the professional whom they hired, to make sure he is doing his job.

In turn, it is his job to translate that new pressure onto the principal. If that is done, you have a three-year probationary period in which the teacher and principals, I might say, have practically no rights at all. They can be dismissed without cause. In 99% of the cases, when somebody is no good, you can tell during the first few years.

By the way, quite a few of those teachers are let go. I don't know whether you realize it, but during the first two weeks of school, anywhere from three to seven hundred teachers leave the City of New York. They are ousted by some very capable people in the school system known as students. The least capable teachers can't take it, and in a short time they find out and they go.

There is a tremendous turnover in the first three years of teaching. We very rarely fire anybody. What happens usually is that the boss calls you in and says, "I think you would be happier elsewhere."

If you say, "I am going to work for you," he will say, "If you leave quietly, I will give you a good recommendation and you can bother the people next door."

That is how ministers and rabbis and union presidents get their jobs. There are an awful lot of people who are let go.

As far as tenure is concerned, it doesn't mean that you can't dismiss a person. It just means that the dismissal is appealable and it has to be based on evidence. Well, if somebody is no good, why shouldn't the principal have the evidence? Why shouldn't he show he has tried to help and, in spite of all this help, the teacher still didn't work out?

Do you really think that a judge is going to take a teacher's word against a principal's word as to who is competent? It is usual that the principal isn't really getting rid of an incompetent teacher. Usually it is because he gets into a fight with some teacher; a teacher would talk up at a faculty conference or something else.

He says, "You are fired."

The teacher then goes to the board and they find out this teacher has been teaching for 17 years. All of a sudden in the hallway the principal says, "Out you go."

In that case, the teacher wins hands down. The judge can obviously see that it was not a question of incompetence but a question of anger.

There is nothing wrong with the present procedures if they are used. They aren't used in many cases or, when they are, it is informal procedure that prevails, where the principal tells somebody to go voluntarily and they do.

I do believe an elected community board brings pressure to bear on a superintendent whom they hired and who is there for a contractual period of time. That is one element. They are bringing about accountability at this level.

The other is a difference in teacher supply. A couple of years ago, a principal, when he was faced at the end of the year with getting rid of an inexperienced incompetent, knew that he would wind up with another inexperienced incompetent. You had schools with five or six or seven teachers missing every day and students sitting around in the auditorium watching a movie. You could hardly blame the principal for saying that anybody willing to serve is better than nobody at all.

At least one can understand that in a period of shortage the standards obtaining necessarily go down. At the present time, while the newspaper records about an oversupply are somewhat exaggerated, we don't face the same condition of shortage that existed in the 50's and 60's.

MR. TRACTENBERG: You have gone on record recently as favoring the so-called British or informal classroom system, not, I gather, as a mandatory program but as an alternate. If there is a substantial movement towards informal classroom, don't you need different kinds of people to adequately handle an informal classroom?

MR. SHANKER: How are you going to know? You see, the informal program is not something somebody can pick up and walk into a classroom and do, nor can you interview a person and find out whether a person is going to do it well.

There is a certain setup. It is a style based on a precise knowledge of concrete materials which takes six months of training, which is rather lengthy and rather precise. If you think you are going to have some interview by a community board where some teacher walks in and says he is in love with the British system, and that proves something, it doesn't prove anything.

It is very easy to be informal in a classroom in a bad sense. A teacher can sit back, abdicate her role and let the children paint the room and repaint it a hundred times and throw toys at each other and proudly proclaim that all the noises and movements in the room are necessarily educational for children.

That isn't what it is all about. It is not freedom for the children. It does give children a great degree of flexibility in terms of talk and in terms of movement, but the types of experiences and the kinds of materials that are there are very much controlled. I would say that of either type--if you can divide teachers into two basic styles, one being a kind of performance which is a lecturer and the other being a different kind of performance where one is, in a sense, a planner of various experiences for children in a more open atmosphere--that you may find a handful of naturals. That is, you will find some natural performers that have the charisma, six hours and 20 minutes a day but not too many. And you may find a few naturals that are so attuned to children and parents that they can walk in and almost do it by sense, but very few in each case.

Both, whether one style or another, have to be trained for long periods of time and I know of no method at the present time which would enable you to know in advance whether a teacher is going to do well with one style or another.

MR. TRACTENBERG: Presumably, that applies to any written examination as well.

MR. SHANKER: No question about it.

Here we are talking about the performance characteristics which I do not believe can be tested or measured at the present time. We are not talking about whether somebody knows mathematics or knows French.

We are talking about a style of relating to other people and I think that we just don't have any way of measuring that at the present time aside from performance over a period of time.

MR. TRACTENBERG: If I understand you correctly, generally you feel that the probationary period is an important part of the selection process and may be even more important if we go to the British infants' type of school.

MR. SHANKER: Whether or not we go to the British infants' type of school, I feel we should have an internship program which parallels a period of clerkship of the young lawyer who goes to work for a firm. Really, the written tests merely state that you have a minimum knowledge you need to get into the field. They do not attest to whether you will be a capable practitioner in the field.

Since we are dealing with a complicated set of performance skills here, the real question of whether a person stays or does not stay has to be based on a period of time in which he gets help from more experienced people though an internship period. And the re-evaluation determines whether a person is a singer or not a singer. You can give him theory examinations but, finally, after a lot of training and a lot of help, he has to get up there and perform and he either does or doesn't. I think that is true here, also. I think the greatest amount of weight has to be given to on-the-job evaluation or an internship period.

MR. TRACTENBERG: No further questions.

THE CHAIRMAN: Thank you, Mr. Shanker.

I am going to call the next witness, Mr. Walter Degnan, President of the Council of Supervisory Associations.

VOICE FROM GALLERY Point of order. May I ask Mr. Shanker some questions?

THE CHAIRMAN: You are out of order. Ask your questions outside.

I understand Mr. Seeley wishes to have a conversation with respect to a matter that came up in Mr. Shanker's testimony after this witness and, because I was liberal with respect to Dr. Rockowitz, I will give Mr. Seeley the chair for a moment. I want to make it perfectly clear I am not going to make a habit of this.

In the case of Mr. Shanker, a serious charge was made that there has been discrimination although it is not of a kind within the jurisdiction of this Commission. Because of the seriousness of that charge, I will allow a response just as I allowed Dr. Rockowitz's comment on what he regarded as a personal attack on himself.

We will now hear from Mr. Degnan.

MR. DEGNAN: I will try to address myself to the question before the panel. Some of the things I have included here have already been said.

The solution to the problem to which these hearings are addressed--the low percentage of minority group personnel in the New York City school system--is within sight in the immediate future.

The low percentage of minority members of the school staff resulted from the small number of Blacks and Puerto Ricans in the City University, the fact that few Blacks and Puerto Ricans chose to go into teaching, and the fact that New York City's eligibility requirements for school staff were higher than those in most other cities in the nation. All these situations will have changed, and these changes will be reflected increasingly in a growth in the percentage of Blacks and Puerto Ricans on the school staff.

Unfortunately, many persons, whatever their reasons, refuse to recognize that fact and insist upon attributing the current situation to bias. Despite charges which are repeated constantly without proof, there has never been a shred of evidence to indicate, much less prove, that discrimination has been a factor in producing the present low percentage of Black and Puerto Rican supervisory personnel in the city's schools.

Today's licensed school supervisors are not drawn from today's student population but from the general population who meet the eligibility requirements and choose to enter the teaching profession. Thus, it is unrealistic and misleading to expect the staff and pupil populations to show the same ethnic proportions.

Until recently, relatively few Blacks and Puerto Ricans applied for teaching and supervisory positions in the New York City schools. As late as 1967, for example, Black and Puerto Rican students comprised only 8% of those attending the senior colleges of the City University, the source of about two-thirds of the teachers for the city's schools. The number of minority group graduates was far fewer, and relatively few went into teaching. Recruitment of minority group school personnel was impeded by the small supply and the more favorable conditions of employment for Black and Puerto Rican college graduates in other fields.

Furthermore, in the past, New York City teachers had to serve approximately 10 years--first as teachers, then as supervisors--before becoming eligible to take the principal's exam. Thus, ethnic changes in the college student population were reflected in the staff only gradually, over a long period of time.

It should be noted that New York City's high eligibility requirements for supervisors were not set by the Board of Examiners but by the Board of Education.

When the State Decentralization Law was passed, the Council of Supervisors and Administrators supported the change from ranked, competitive lists to qualifying lists, since we recognized that this change would provide increased flexibility in the choice of supervisory personnel and accelerate the rate at which qualified Black and Puerto Rican candidates would achieve supervisory positions.

The existence of qualifying lists, the recent broadening of eligibility requirements for supervisory positions, and the increased number of applications from minority groups signalled a rapid increase in the New York City schools. There are, for example, more than 300 minority group candidates in the current examination for elementary school principal. Previous results show that in New York City, as in other cities, Blacks and Puerto Ricans do as well on the examination as other candidates. On the 1965 elementary school assistant principal's examination, for example, 20% of those in the free Board of Education seminars preparing candidates for the test were Blacks and Puerto Ricans, and the same percentage passed.

Most large cities in this country select school administrators and supervisors from eligible lists resulting from competitive examinations. The reason is obvious: They recognize the potential dangers of favoritism, the pork barrel, and patronage in the selection of school personnel.

Since teaching is a profession, it should have professional standards. Why is there less reason for merit examinations for teachers and supervisors than for bar examinations for lawyers or medical boards for doctors and licensing examinations for accountants and pharmacists? Is it unreasonable to require teachers and supervisors to demonstrate competence in their field?

The charge that personnel selection in the city schools suffers from inbreeding is without justification. On the list of approved examination assistants are more than 1,000 persons from agencies outside the New York City school system, persons from colleges, state education departments, industry, and the professions. In planning sessions for examinations conducted by the Board of Examiners, I have sat with representatives from areas outside New York City.

Moreover, in examinations conducted by the Board of Examiners, there can be no glib coaching for pat answers. That is why an interview test is required.

Appointments to school supervisory positions should be based on proven merit; not influence, popularity, or muscle. Through the Board of Examiners, New York City has enjoyed an impartial, objective examination system for more than 70 years. Such a system protects everyone, including the members of the minority groups who will be entering the New York City school system in increasing numbers in the years just ahead.

That concludes my prepared statement. I hope I did not duplicate things.

THE CHAIRMAN: It is important to have your association's position on that.

Counsel?

MR. TRACTENBERG: Mr. Degnan, a couple of things about your remarks.

First, I gather that you would agree to a large extent that in New York City, the public school system has relied for its teaching and ultimately its supervisory staff on teaching institutions in New York City.

MR. DEGNAN: It isn't a matter of relying. This is the way of the world.

If one lived in Cleveland one would tend to teach in Cleveland. Many of the, shall we say, lower-middle class--and I fell into that category when I went into teaching--look upon teaching as a desirable profession and, if they can't afford to go to Yale, Harvard, and so on, they go to the City University. I think this accounts for the fact that teachers, by and large, in New York City, go to the New York City free colleges. I think that is a very important factor.

MR. TRACTENBERG: Do you agree that given the statistical data about minority teachers and supervisors in the New York City system as a result of this reliance, that continued reliance on New York City colleges is justified?

MR. DEGNAN: Most assuredly.

The people go from the community they know to a terrible place called New York City. I agree, if we can accomplish something in that direction, that is fine.

I think we have to basically accept the fact that our teachers are going to come from this area.

MR. TRACTENBERG: Do you think moving to a system which is based on the National Teacher Exam rather than a local examination would improve the possibilities of recruiting people from outside the New York City area?

MR. DEGNAN: I don't think that would make any difference at all.

I think, again, if you would analyze where people teach in these United States, they tend to teach in the home locale. They do not want to travel a thousand miles away unless they have a peculiar reason for getting away from it all. But, in general, they tend to teach where they live.

MR. TRACTENBERG: Do you think that the Joint Employment Recruitment Program is fated to dismal results?

MR. DEGNAN: I don't want to say that. I am simply indicating an obstacle. I know that other efforts made by the Board of Examiners to recruit people to come to New York have been relatively unsuccessful and, in some respects, a dismal failure. I am not sure of the statistics, but I am sure I am right.

There is one other thing I would like to say here that I think is terribly important. It is not a prepared text. I think, when we think in terms of the employment of minorities, we ought to look around us and get outside of New York City and ask ourselves how many minority group people throughout the state have been employed, whether they are Jewish, Irish, Black, or Puerto Rican. And I think you will be appalled by the fact that in most communities, not only in this state but in other states, there is a kind of closed corporation.

I know this, that if one were to go not too far from this city and happened to be a graduate of the City University and is competing with somebody from Harvard, he would have a very difficult time in getting the job because each of our communities has set up their own prejudice, or whatever you would call it. They set up in their minds the kind of person they want in their schools.

Very frequently, if you find that a person can make an effective appearance at an afternoon coffee klatch, the ladies say, "Isn't he wonderful? He is beautiful. We need him as a principal."

He becomes a principal. This is something we are overlooking. And I would like to stress the fact that for minorities, particularly, it is important that we have a system of selection that is fair and divorced from any sort of prejudice.

There is prejudice in every community in these United States of some kind or another. It is almost endemic to human behavior.

MR. TRACTENBERG: One of the major purposes of these hearings is to get behind rhetoric. Insofar as we have seen from actual statistics, of every major school district in New Jersey, New York, and across the country, New York City has the worst record of minority group teachers and supervisors.

MR. DEGNAN: That is not so. Detroit has the largest percentage of Blacks in the school system. I think it is 17%. But Detroit did an unusual thing. They set up two different kinds of examinations, one for Black and one for white. Then the community could pick from one list or the other.

I would hold that this would be something that I think the Blacks in our city would not want. I would hope they would not want it. This is not the answer to our problem. The answer to the problem is to get more people who are eligible to qualify, and this is coming. It is here.

I predict, by September, you will have 150 qualified elementary school principals who are Black, and then it will be up to the community boards to select them at their will. There is no reason why this situation should continue beyond this year.

MR. TRACTENBERG: I don't think that is really the issue. The question I posed is whether there is any statistical support to your assertion that in other communities discrimination runs rampant and, in fact, minority group members fare less well.

MR. DEGNAN: It is a kind of disguised discrimination.

It is a fact that in some of the suburban areas of our state you will find no Black employed, or maybe one Black employed because this is the way to respectability.

I recall a few years ago five Black teachers were invited to Darien, Connecticut. One approached me and asked me what I thought. I said, "What have you to lose?"

He came back and said that it was simply a showcase operation. They were, in his judgment, the most prejudiced people he had ever met.

MR. TRACTENBERG: I think it is more pertinent to talk, not about Darien, Connecticut, but about other urban areas that have major percentages of minority group children, and I have said that the statistics I have seen indicate that New York City has the worst record of any of those school districts.

MR. DEGNAN: Well, I think it all depends on what you mean by the worst.

If you are talking about five, 10 or 12, I don't think the variation is significant. I think it is true that fewer of our Black children have gone to college in New York City than is the case in some other communities.

It is a question of whether we have had more poor Blacks than other cities. I think there has been a migration from the deep South where poverty was a very real factor and I think they tended to come to New York.

I say, basically, the solution to this problem is to get Black and Puerto Rican children into college, and we are not doing that. We are doing something in that direction through open enrollment which is going to be useful, but I still think this is the great problem we face. It is akin to the problem the Irish faced when my father came here. It wasn't considered good manners for the Irish to go to college. It was sufficient if you went through high school.

The same thing as to the Italians and, for some reason, they thought girls should not go beyond high school, in any event.

I think the Blacks have responded well. I think the Puerto Ricans are not doing as well in this respect because we have more Blacks going to college percentage-wise than Puerto Ricans. It is a question of a change that, I suppose, has to be considered historically. I don't think you can do it overnight.

MR. TRACTENBERG: Would you agree that a much accelerated recruiting program--

MR. DEGNAN: I am completely in favor of that, but I am saying to you, realistically, I doubt whether it is going to be as successful as we would like it to be.

I think we ought to stress the fact that open enrollment and programs of that sort should provide increasing opportunities for Black children to go to college. As a high school principal, I know what the program is. I know it is not a question of talking to them about this.

They would say, "I can't even afford to go to city colleges."

If we have to support them financially to do this, I am for that. But I am saying, basically, we have to meet the poverty cycle. We have to break it and we have got to give them the means of going to college so that they can take their proper place in this society of ours.

MR. TRACTENBERG: What do you think about the trends that seem to be at work to eliminate the examination requirement for supervisors. I gather, in cities like Chicago, Cleveland, Detroit, Dallas, and Buffalo in this state, there has been a dramatic cutback in the extent to which written examinations are required for supervisory positions.

MR. DEGNAN: That isn't so. That is not so.

The fact is they still maintain competitive lists. They are behind us in this respect. If they do the intelligent thing, they will develop qualifying lists.

If their systems were decentralized as ours are--and, of course, Detroit is moving in that direction but most of them are not--I think there is no question that they ought to have qualifying lists.

They still maintain competitive lists and have difficulties because of this. They have trouble in Chicago because of this. They have competitive solicitation for principals and they have real difficulties where communities want a Black principal, for whatever reason. They have had very serious trouble.

I think we have the answer in the Decentralization Law. I think in the qualifying list we have the answer, and I'd say it is almost demonstrated in our intermediate ranges, and it will be demonstrated very shortly with the elementary school principal. I think what we are talking about today in a year will be an academic issue that has no great significance.

MR. TRACTENBERG: Let me respond for the record because I don't think your statement was truly accurate.

Dr. James D. Tanner, in Cleveland, says supervisory employees are appointed without any written tests.

MR. DEGNAN: There still is a test. They changed the test, perhaps.

MR. TRACTENBERG: I was careful to say no written tests.

MR. DEGNAN: You are talking now about whether this is a phase of a test that is necessary. I think it has a place.

I think in New York City, and certainly in the Board of Examiners, there has been a disposition to shorten it, to change it. When I took the high school principal's examination, written, it took five days. I think it is done now in a day. There are significant changes and I would not at this time want to say we ought not to have it. I think it has a place. Maybe it has been overemphasized. Maybe it hasn't.

I think the Board of Examiners has constantly tried to evaluate its procedures. Perhaps people haven't always agreed with their evaluation and believed in them, but I am convinced they act with good judgment and intent. Maybe they don't always provide the right answer, but it is not for want of trying.

MR. TRACTENBERG: You have been quoted publicly more than once as indicating that leadership potential and sensitivity to the pupil's behavior are very important characteristics for candidates for supervisory positions. Are you satisfied that the current examination process takes these things into account?

MR. DEGNAN: I think the examination simply separates the sheep from the goats. There is no proof that you're going to have good sheep.

But what you do on an interview, it seems to me, is get an evaluation of some of these qualities. If you examine some of the interview forms and the things that examiners look for and you consider some of the material of the interview, you will recognize that there are evidences disclosed sometimes of good human relations, of poor human relations, of leadership or lack of it. It is inherent in the interest you take.

Let me finish this. That is no proof of anything. The person who passes that test may not prove to be a good leader, but the person who fails it demonstrates that he can't be a good leader either.

I agree fully with the concept that the probationary period should be used wisely by the community boards, by superintendents, to determine whether or not what they thought was the case when the examination was given was true. If we have not exercised that sufficiently, it is our fault.

I don't agree entirely with Mr. Shanker about what he said. I think most principals are very much concerned whether a teacher is satisfactory or not. In many instances they are asked to leave, and in many other instances they are brought to trial. The trouble is today we are trying to fire people without due process.

We have two Black principals and one white principal who has been summarily discharged. No hearing. Two of them arrested. A very interesting development in decentralization and good human relations.

I think we have gone to the other extreme in some instances. If you don't like a person, cut his head off. That is far worse than keeping an incompetent around for a period of time until you are sure he or she is or is not incompetent.

MR. TRACTENBERG: Isn't it true that most of the supervisory personnel in the system come from within the system?

MR. DEGNAN: For the very same reason most of our teachers come from the City. It is perfectly reasonable to assume that a teacher is going to seek advancement. If you will go to Yonkers, you will see this.

The ones who hedgehop today are the superintendents, and the reason is rather simple. There are a number of them that don't do too well, and they don't stay too long because people begin to realize that they are not doing what they should do and so they move on. It is not true of supervisors other than superintendents.

MR. TRACTENBERG: How long, approximately, would a person who set out to pass an examination for elementary school principal have to serve in the school system?

MR. DEGNAN: I think it was reduced from five years to three.

MR. TRACTENBERG: Three years as a supervisor?

MR. DEGNAN: No, no.

The elementary school principal's examination is open to teachers now as well as assistant principals. This was another step to make it possible for more minority group people to be instantly eligible. Just how many, I don't know.

MR. TRACTENBERG: In any event, he must have served for at least three years. And most of these people have served in the New York City system?

MR. DEGNAN: Yes.

MR. TRACTENBERG: And they have been rated by their principal as teachers or assistant principals if, in fact, they come from that group?

MR. DEGNAN: Yes.

This would be minimal in terms of time. Frankly, I think that a teacher takes really a good 10 years to mature into a fully effective teacher and knowledgeable person.

I have no objection to lowering at this time but I think we have to be careful that we don't lower too far. My own personal judgment is that the best teachers I know are those who have had at least 10 years experience.

MR. TRACTENBERG: But, in any event, these people have been in the system a minimum of three years and have been rated periodically by principals?

MR. DEGNAN: Yes.

MR. TRACTENBERG: Yesterday, the Board of Examiners told us that their current philosophy is to separate out the incompetents. You, yourself, suggested that that was--

MR. DEGNAN: Let me give you an illustration that goes back into the Dark Ages.

When I came into the school system, my major was in mathematics and my masters was in English, and I took the health education examination because it was the first one that came along. At that time one could qualify for several different kinds of licenses.

There were 150 candidates and 10 passed. 10 passed. In those days it was a question of how do you get rid of people, not how do you qualify them. How do you get rid of them? Many of the practices of the Board of Examiners in those years were objected to because they were purely methods to get rid of people. You couldn't use them. During the depression you could do this. The whole philosophy has changed. Now it is not getting rid of people, but it is assuring they have minimal competence.

As a high school principal, when somebody comes into the school and teaches algebra and geometry and advanced mathematics, I want to know that they know it. I was a math major, and I know a little bit about it. And I know I meet a lot of people who teach math courses, but are they mathematicians? They get two or three years credit in math and they forget all about it.

This is the purpose essentially: To screen out those who are not qualified on the basis of what they know.

MR. TRACTENBERG: Doesn't this line of questioning suggest one of two conclusions--that is, either the rating system, itself, has not screened out those who are incompetent or the supervisory examination is redundant?

MR. DEGNAN: No.

The examination says to the community board--and by the way, they ought to want to know this--it says that as far as we can tell, this person has minimal competence.

MR. TRACTENBERG: Isn't that what the ratings are designed to do?

MR. DEGNAN: No, no.

The fact is that you can't afford to gamble with children's lives even for one year. The person who walks in has to know what he is doing.

MR. TRACTENBERG: It is a gamble but you rely on past ratings.

MR. DEGNAN: It is a gamble not to rely on anything. If you hire somebody--

MR. TRACTENBERG: I am talking about a supervisor. I am talking about a person who has been in this system for a minimum of three years.

MR. DEGNAN: It simply doesn't follow that that person has the qualities of the supervisor that are required.

He may be a good teacher. I have seen good teachers who didn't relate at all to their peers. I have seen teachers who could teach but to have them become assistant principal could be a tragedy because they don't have the qualities of leadership that that post requires.

MR. TRACTENBERG: Do you think there should be written tests for that quality of leadership?

MR. DEGNAN: I didn't say the written exam.

I said the examination tends to screen that type of person out. The interview test, the perusal of records, the written examination.

For example, I had an interesting experience the other day. Mr. Silverman criticized a question on the present principal examination. It happened to be a diary question where the principal came in on Monday morning and found certain things wrong. I think there were 29 windowpanes broken over the weekend.

He said, "Isn't that a silly question? You go to the custodian engineer and have them replaced."

I said to him, "You just failed that examination because if you did not have the insight to understand what that was symbolic of and what it might truly mean, then you failed the examination because this might well mean that your relationships with the community were at fault, that your relationship with the students was poor, that there was one child or a group of children breaking windows?"

A whole host of things go into a knowledgeable understanding of that symbol. And this is the kind of thing that I think we ought to have, and it can be tested on a written examination.

MR. TRACTENBERG: I have already used this, but I think it is pertinent and important here. It relates to coaching courses. Now this may not be a good coaching course, but it certainly reflects the views of an existing supervisor about the examination process. This course is run by people who are currently in the system. It pertains to what it takes to pass the written examination for the supervisor's position.

MR. DEGNAN: I don't think you have to mention it. I will tell you what it says.

It says, in effect, that we can insure the fact that you will pass this examination if you are properly prepared in each field.

MR. TRACTENBERG: It says more than that--

MR. DEGNAN: I must remind you that I have also been opposed to coaching examinations.

MR. TRACTENBERG: Have you taken any--

MR. DEGNAN: We have not had occasion to.

The coaching courses now are given by the Board of Education. I don't know of any others. There may be some but I don't know of them. I get no literature about them. I know nothing about it.

MR. TRACTENBERG: If you read the "United Teacher"--

MR. DEGNAN: Let me develop my thinking on this.

I remember when I took the junior high school's principal's exam--and it might have been a chairman's examination, I don't recall--there were several people, friends of mine, who took the coaching course. I refused to do it.

I said, "This is a waste of time and I am not going to spend money on it."

Two of us would sit down together and work out a problem. He had a sheaf of notes, and he said, "Wait. I think that is on page 900-something or other."

I said, "If you don't know what the answer to that is, how do you expect to use that on an examination?"

He failed. Lots of people who took coaching courses took them only because they thought it would do something for them that it didn't do.

There is no pat way of preparing anybody for an examination. He must develop his own understanding of the issues. He must have reflected on these things. He must have had some experience, at least, some insight into reasonable understanding of the problems and their solutions.

MR. TRACTENBERG: You must be aware that your testimony is not consistent with the testimony we have received from many people who have been through and are going through the licensing process.

MR. DEGNAN: I notice you have some people here who failed the examination. I wonder how they got here.

I failed the first time I took it, I know.

THE CHAIRMAN: Everyone so far who has appeared here is licensed.

MR. DEGNAN: I may be mistaken.

MR. TRACTENBERG: The only testimony we have had of failure on an exam was by Mr. Shanker this morning.

MR. DEGNAN: We can all testify to things we didn't like. I did. I failed, too. I failed the principal's exam the first time.

At that time I was irate about it. I thought I should have passed. I guess everybody--

THE CHAIRMAN: Mr. Degnan, I want to interrupt to say this. I have gone on the record with respect to some people who testified here in the last two days in order to make it perfectly clear that their criticism was not a product of their failure but two of them happened to be Black people who are now high administrators. I know you don't want to cast any disparagement upon the people.

MR. DEGNAN: No, no.

I suppose perfectly reasonable people react differently on the basis of their judgment of experiences.

I wonder why you didn't bring in the presidents of the principals associations. There are three or four or five of them.

THE CHAIRMAN: They were all invited to appear here.

MR. DEGNAN: Well, then, there is some communication lag because they told me they had not been.

THE CHAIRMAN: Who, specifically?

MR. DEGNAN: Well, Mr. Warshaw is the President of the Elementary School Principals Association. I saw him last evening, and when he heard I was coming he said, "I wonder why I wasn't invited."

THE CHAIRMAN: We sent invitations to every principal individually and to all the professional associations; and if there was any association that has not been invited, I want it to be called to my attention, especially since they want to testify.

Inasmuch as this is going over the radio, I want to announce that I received a list of names from Dr. Rockowitz. I had my staff call those people to invite them to come down.

I want to make it perfectly clear that any association and, indeed, any individual who has any point of view is invited here to testify.

MR. DEGNAN: I am sure Mr. Warshaw will be glad to do that. He told me only last evening that he was very anxious to testify and felt he has been overlooked.

I think that is probably true of Mr. Weinstein. As a matter of fact, I know it is true because he mentioned it to me.

MR. TRACTENBERG: If I can just return for a few more minutes.

I have here a page from the "United Teacher," dated September 13, 1970, advertising private coaching courses. I also have notes from a coaching course that was given for the elementary principals' exam this past fall

You tell me, on the one hand--

MR. DEGNAN: I think that may well be. I don't know about them.

I am saying that when something like that is really significant you hear about it from candidates. I think most of the candidates took the course that was given by the Board of Education, and anybody foolish enough to get involved in a private course gets no sympathy from me.

I always felt the coaching courses given by individuals constituted a sham and resulted in something that was wrong and almost immoral.

MR. TRACTENBERG: What percentage of the candidates for supervisor's examinations would you estimate have taken coaching courses in the past?

MR. DEGNAN: Are you talking about the total supervisory staff now of 4,000?

MR. TRACTENBERG: I am asking about a typical supervisory examination in the past, before the Board began its own Professional Seminars.

MR. DEGNAN: I would say, perhaps, one in 10. Perhaps, two in 10. No more than that. Most of us recognize that this is an inadequate way to prepare.

What did happen is this. If a person felt that he couldn't afford the time to prepare properly, that he had to go to Europe for the summer, he would say, "I will take that coaching course," and salve his conscience that he was prepared. The coaching course, in my judgment, wouldn't prepare him anyway. I think the person prepared is the one who did his own work and studied and worked with a group of three or four people and discussed issues and problems. It is not the person who sat in on the course and listened to somebody speak.

MR. TRACTENBERG: This ad says, "We have prepared hundreds of licensed supervisors."

MR. DEGNAN: If you want to sell something, that is the way you sell it.

MR. TRACTENBERG: Let me explore one more area with you, Mr. Degnan.

I assume that underlying your faith in the examination system is faith in its objectivity and in the experience of the people who are involved in preparing the examinations and giving them and grading them.

MR. DEGNAN: I have great respect for the examination system and for how it has served the school system. I think it is an acknowledged fact throughout the country that New York City has provided educational leadership, and that this has come from the supervisors and teachers who have been selected by this process.

Once again, I say that if there are ways in which the techniques and procedures can be improved, I think these are suggestions that the Board of Examiners will take seriously and always have taken seriously.

MR. TRACTENBERG: Do you agree with Dr. Greene that the selection process--

MR. DEGNAN: I don't know how you can do this in any other way. The assumption here is--let me see if I understand this.

MR. TRACTENBERG: I can give you some background. I gather there are no formal screening procedures, no stated requirements, and no written or other examination by which the supervisory personnel employed in the system are sorted out as to those who are qualified to be examination assistants.

MR. DEGNAN: Yes.

I don't know that you could conduct such an examination. Again, you want to know by performance.

MR. TRACTENBERG: If you can't tell about that, as to an examination assistant, how can you tell about a principal?

MR. DEGNAN: You know this. There are certain schools well run. The principal is well thought of .

Assistant principals are a variety of people, and principals can recommend some and not recommend others to assist in examinations.

MR. TRACTENBERG: Why is that better than the rating system?

MR. DEGNAN: The rating system is not accurate to screen out incompetents.

Let me say this, it isn't only principals who are assistant examiners. I have worked with college presidents on examinations. These are people selected by the Board of Examiners because they have confidence in their competence.

MR. TRACTENBERG: But on no particular basis have they been able to identify them except--

MR. DEGNAN: Not through recommendation. Through knowledge of the kind of schools they run. Through knowledge of the kind of people they are.

MR. TRACTENBERG: All I am asking is one simple question. Why is relying solely on performance to determine who should construct the exams, who should administer them, and who should grade them a better system than through examining for those skills?

MR. DEGNAN: I think this. If several principals are asked to submit material for a given examination, that is the way it is done.

There may be 15 or 20 or 50 principals who submit material. The examiner looks at the material and he sees, on the one hand, excellent material, well put together, well-conceived, and, next to that, something he considers ill-conceived and very poor.

The next time he runs an examination he doesn't call Mr. B in. He doesn't ask Mr. B to prepare materials. He continually asks for Mr. A and looks to Mr. C who is as good as Mr. A.

MR. TRACTENBERG: Does a candidate who has gone through the examination process and has been screened out by an examination assistant whose work you concede was not adequate have a right of appeal?

MR. DEGNAN: Wait just a moment. You are a step ahead of me.

I am saying, if the examiner gets material from me and from you and he says he didn't like your material and my material was all right, that is the end of you as assistant examiner.

The fact is that performance is the criterion for determining whether you serve on that examination or any other examination. Now, there are many people who have been ruled out because of their inadequacies as assistant examiners, as people who can submit real problems, who do not understand the role of the principal. This becomes obvious rather quickly.

MR. TRACTENBERG: I had read this into the record yesterday. The Association of Assistant Principals, I gather, is a unit of your association?

MR. DEGNAN: Yes.

MR. TRACTENBERG: Apparently, Dr. Greene and Dr. Rockowitz met with some representatives of this Association because of some dissatisfaction that not enough members of the Association were being appointed as examination assistants--

MR. DEGNAN: Let me say several things.

First of all, you can't employ everybody nor is it desirable that you employ everybody. Second of all, this is not employment. I have never looked upon it as employment. I look upon it as a service to the school system.

MR. TRACTENBERG: A service compensated at a certain rate.

MR. DEGNAN: It was $2 an hour. I don't know what it is now.

MR. TRACTENBERG: $100 a day.

MR. DEGNAN: It is an hourly rate.

MR. TRACTENBERG: It is approaching $14 an hour.

MR. DEGNAN: $14 an hour?

MR. TRACTENBERG: Right.

MR. DEGNAN: Teachers earn more than that.

$14 an hour? Why, I know that every time an examination was given and people outside the school system were called in, I can recall Examiners apologizing for the fact that they couldn't pay them at a rate that they thought it merited. What they said, in effect, was this is a service to the city and I hope you will approach it that way. That was said repeatedly.

Now, it is true that in the last contract there was an increase granted in this service. But anybody who serves the Board of Examiners looking for this as a job has no place in it.

MR. TRACTENBERG: You have been talking about pork barreling. How do you defend this system against the charge that it is pork barreling?

MR. DEGNAN: How many days? I don't know that anybody is paid a hundred dollars a day. For how many days of the year? Two or three?

Suppose a person works 10 hours a day on an examination. That doesn't happen very often. It can't

I would say this. At a time when I contributed my services --and there were times I was asked to do this and it was a burden to do it, I will tell you very honestly and very frankly--I had to do it during hours that I should have had for leisure time, but I did this. I don't think during any one year the Board of Examiners payed $1,200 at the most for all of that time. I could see the possibility of your having a hundred dollars a day but how many days can a person in the staff work during the year?

Maybe he works on a Saturday during the year or works an evening for two hours.

MR. TRACTENBERG: I would expect there are many people who would work seven hours a day for a hundred dollars.

MR. DEGNAN: If they have the talent that would be all right with me. I have no special hangup on this.

MR. TRACTENBERG: Aren't you, as the head of the--

MR. DEGNAN: When that group asked the question--

MR. TRACTENBERG: May I finish.

As the head of the Supervisors Association charging that to do away with the Board of Examiners would lead to pork barreling, to tolerate a system--

MR. DEGNAN: This is peanuts. We are not talking about a job of $25,000 or $30,000 a year. We are talking about peanuts in this.

MR. TRACTENBERG: Is that how you define pork barreling?

MR. DEGNAN: I am concerned about the 4,000 supervisory jobs in this city going to those who have the muscle, who can demand, shout, sit-in and insist. I am concerned about that. I am concerned about it, as I said before, because it is a disservice to all people when that happens.

MR. TRACTENBERG: Mr. Degnan, in your mind, isn't the integrity of this objective system that you prefer called into question in view of the way the most critical people in that system are selected, or is it your position that everybody who runs a school in New York City is competent to be called in as an examination assistant?

MR. DEGNAN: No. I say they are not competent to do that work.

MR. TRACTENBERG: Dr. Greene was hard-pressed to say on what basis selection was made and, in fact, agreed that there were deficiencies and that new procedures were going to be worked out.

MR. DEGNAN: I am not going to speak for Dr. Greene in this. He has a perfect right. He may have some better way of selecting examination assistants.

All I can tell you is of my experience. I know of my colleagues who have not been called because they did not demonstrate that they were competent people to submit questions, to conduct interviews, and the like, in an accepted way. That is all I can say about it.

I don't know how you would determine that except through some experience with the individuals. If you are saying, in effect, that everybody should be an examiner, I'd say, no.

I daresay that when the bar examinations are conducted, these examinations are run by--I don't know--I guess they are competent lawyers who make up the examination. People whom you have confidence in.

I am sure there are some lawyers you do not have confidence in.

MR. TRACTENBERG: All I am suggesting is that performance-based criteria are the sole basis of selecting people who conduct the exams.

MR. DEGNAN: In other words, you would gamble with lives of children--

MR. TRACTENBERG: You would gamble with all the candidates.

MR. DEGNAN: Oh, no.

I am saying this. If you have to select from 800 people, you have a wide selection to make and all the Board of Examiners has said is these 800 people meet the minimal examination qualifications. If you select somebody who hasn't gone through that process, you are endangering the lives of our children.

We are not in the business of providing jobs. We are in the business to educate children.

MR. TRACTENBERG: The minimum qualifications that you talk about are determined under a system of trial and error, you have said.

MR. DEGNAN: I didn't say that.

Let me be crystal-clear about this. I am saying that initially we separate out those who are not qualified.

MR. TRACTENBERG: And Dr. Greene was unable to tell us on what basis that separation was made.

MR. DEGNAN: On the basis of the examination.

Are you talking about the examination in existence now or supervisors in the school, or what?

MR. TRACTENBERG: I thought we were talking about selection of examination assistants.

MR. DEGNAN: I think this is a relatively unimportant element in this whole thing.

MR. TRACTENBERG: How can you say the people who make and grade the exams are relatively unimportant--

MR. DEGNAN: Let me get this straight.

The skills of assistants don't make the exams. They submit material.

If 25 people submit material to an examiner he has enough material in there for, perhaps, 50 examinations, but he is only to construct one.

MR. TRACTENBERG: When you say "examiner," do you mean one of the four members of the Board of Examiners?

MR. DEGNAN: I mean the examiner and his assistant.

There used to be more examiners, as you know. They are down to four people. They have assistants who assist them in this process.

MR. TRACTENBERG: Of course, we also heard from Dr. Greene that there are no particular objective standards by which their full-time assistants are selected.

MR. DEGNAN: I don't think that is quite true. There is an examination.

MR. TRACTENBERG: At least, at the current moment, there is no greater objectivity in the selection of the full-time examination assistants than the temporary.

MR. DEGNAN: I would say it is no more objective than the selection of a superintendent. Anybody can apply to be a superintendent. Then the district selects their man.

MR. TRACTENBERG: All I am suggesting to you is shouldn't there be a certain even-handedness? Either it is adequate for everybody or--

MR. DEGNAN: I agree that that position should be examined for. That is the present plan of the Board of Examiners.

They are examining for two licenses. I am not sure, I think one is called the senior assistant examiner and the other is called an assistant examiner, or something of that kind. That is proposed. The proposal, I think, is before the Civil Service Commission right now.

MR. TRACTENBERG: Aren't you troubled? It seems to me you represent 4,000 supervisory employees--

MR. DEGNAN: Yes.

MR. TRACTENBERG: --who have gone through this system which you now agree probably isn't the best system for selecting examination assistants.

Have you taken a public position before?

MR. DEGNAN: I think you are confusing things. I am talking now about people who help in the conduct of examinations.

MR. TRACTENBERG: That is what I am talking about.

MR. DEGNAN: They happen to be many in number.

MR. TRACTENBERG: Except for the four examiners, themselves, there are no examinations given to determine who is competent to make up examinations.

MR. DEGNAN: The Examination is a performance examination. You don't pick somebody who is a weak principal and put him in a position of making a judgment about whether this is a good candidate or not.

You select a principal who has made it, who is successful, who is well-regarded. And you select college professors in whom you have confidence, who have demonstrated capacity and ability. These are performance criteria, and I think they properly belong in this kind of selection.

MR. TRACTENBERG: Would you just answer very directly. Why don't performance criteria belong equally in the selection of supervisory personnel?

MR. DEGNAN: There are two things that may happen. First, those who are really qualified are closed out because there is no screening process, and it becomes a question of whether you know the right people. Outside of this system of ours, how do you get to be a principal? Has anybody looked into the ways and means of becoming a principal in Yonkers, for example?

I heard it directly from--

MR. TRACTENBERG: You keep raising it but I haven't seen any data on it. I am sure Mrs. Norton would--

MR. DEGNAN: When Al Shanker mentioned something about principals, football coaches, and unsuccessful ones, they were more often the successful ones. They were popular people in town. They knew the right people. They moved around the right circles. Maybe they attended the right bar.

MR. TRACTENBERG: In your judgment, that doesn't happen in the New York City school system?

MR. DEGNAN: No, sir, it hasn't. It is still happening in the other parts of the country.

Dr. Scribner says, "If it is good enough for New York State, it is good enough for Buffalo, New York."

It just isn't true. What is good enough for the state is not good enough for us.

MR. TRACTENBERG: Are we more corrupt in New York City?

MR. DEGNAN: No.

I think that if the rest of the State would adopt our procedures they would be better off. There would be much, much less political maneuvering. Minority people would have a much better chance in other communities--

MR. TRACTENBERG: Would you say all these other--

MR. DEGNAN: Wait a minute.

You are confusing something again. I am not talking about Cleveland and Detroit and other places that have an examination system. I am talking about rural communities, suburban communities, where, if you haven't gone to the right college, one of a group of 10, you don't become a principal in that town. Now, this is a fact.

I ask you once again: How many Jews are employed in teaching in the State of New York outside of the city? All right, that is a good question to look into. There aren't many. It has been notoriously the fact that the minority factors have--

MR. TRACTENBERG: All I can say--

MR. DEGNAN: You are talking about Cleveland and Detroit and Chicago. I gave you the answer to Detroit's problem. They solved it the way I told you.

That is quite different from going to one of your suburban communities in this area and finding out who is employed in those schools, what kind of people, where did they go to school, and you would find a predominance of White Anglo-Saxon Protestants in most of those communities.

MR. TRACTENBERG: I don't want to obscure one thing which I think is important that came out of your testimony and that is that you were satisfied and placed faith in the Board of Examiners--

MR. DEGNAN: Don't put words in my mouth. I am never completely satisfied with anything we do.

It is the best system we know. It is one that has worked. It is one that has protected the people. It is one that has given equal opportunity to every college graduate.

The fact of the matter is, as I said initially, we ought not to be emotional about this. We ought to look at the cold facts as to why we do not have more minority people.

I don't know anybody in this town who does not want more Black principals. I don't know of anybody. We know we have to have them. We want to get them in the right way. They will come. They will be here within a matter of months. They will be available in September through this examination process.

Let me bring in one other thing. When the Fordham internship was set up, there were 70 people, Blacks and Puerto Ricans largely, who were selected. There were 2,000 applicants. 70 were picked.

How did the 70 get picked?

MR. TRACTENBERG: Probably the same way the examination assistants are picked.

MR. DEGNAN: No, no. I know how they were picked, and I think most of us do. And most of the Blacks who were turned away know how.

MR. TRACTENBERG: I think you ought to--

MR. DEGNAN: They were picked because of various kinds of contacts that were there. There were Blacks who didn't get there because they didn't have that kind of contact.

I want a fair chance for everybody.

MR. TRACTENBERG: Let me read you an excerpt of a letter which appears in the Newsletter of the Association of Assistant Principals. It is on the letterhead of the Board of Examiners and it is signed by Miss Gertrude Unser.

"The Board of Examiners is interested in securing the services of examination assistants who are willing and able to conduct interview tests and assist outside of New York City. We should like to call upon recently retired supervisors. We seek your assistance in sending us names and addresses of recently retired members of your association whom you recommend for such service."

MR. DEGNAN: What is wrong with that?

MR. TRACTENBERG: A little bit of contact, I would say.

MR. DEGNAN: If you have people going back to Tuscaloosa to conduct an examination, you can't take them out of another area. If you know competent people you seek them out.

MR. TRACTENBERG: Competency, as determined by personal recommendation?

MR. DEGNAN: That letter indicates there is no guarantee they will hire them. I see nothing wrong in it.

MR. TRACTENBERG: I see nothing so different from that and the selection process of the Fordham interns, as you described it.

MR. DEGNAN: You don't see anything different when 70 out of 2,000 are selected?

I don't know how many people responded to that letter. I presume there were some. It was another way of trying to get some help. I have nothing to do with this. I would say, as a guess, very few responded. Most retired people do not stay in New York City. They leave it quickly. They go to Florida or some other place.

You might find a handful, but I would be very much surprised if you found many more. Many more of them have had it, and they don't choose to do anything except luxuriate.

MR. TRACTENBERG: One of the things your testimony has been helpful about is that there has been a charge made that there is a double-standard in the system--

MR. DEGNAN: Again, I object to your putting words in my mouth. If that is your conclusion, in my judgment, you have made the wrong conclusion.

MR. TRACTENBERG: I didn't say you have said that. I said some other people.

MR. DEGNAN: I'm sorry. I thought you said that about me.

MR. TRACTENBERG: That is all I have.

THE CHAIRMAN: Counsel, I don't know if I missed this. Did you question Mr. Degnan on the testimony received yesterday about unwillingness of supervisors--

MR. TRACTENBERG: Oh, no. I'm sorry.

Several community board members and, I believe, at least one community superintendent charged yesterday that they have had substantial problems living within the law.

The law, as you know, requires that supervisors, principals particularly, should be picked off eligible lists promulgated by the Board of Examiners. According to these people, there has been a number of occasions where they have scrupulously gone down the eligible list and contacted virtually everyone on it and have been unable even to get people to come in for interviews when they find out where this school was located.

MR. DEGNAN: Well, there is some evidence that people were not asked even though they were supposed to have been asked. I have on occasion given the superintendent a list of people who have said to me, "I haven't been called. I would like to be interviewed for that school." This works both ways.

I am sure there are some people who choose not to take a difficult school. They would be strange human beings, I suppose, if they felt otherwise. Some people are ready for anything and some people are not ready for anything. I don't hold any brief for that. If a person is on the qualifying list and he chooses not to take a job that he is offered, I don't take a brief on that.

If everybody said that, the superintendent ought to be free to make his selection in another way.

If you are talking about the difficulty of living within the law, when I am driving up the West Side Highway, I have to keep within the speed limit, and sometimes it is hard to live within the law. We all find it hard, but I think we have got to.

I think the community board has chosen to chase people out and not bothered to call and/or they say. "We are going to take somebody else regardless of the law"--

MR. TRACTENBERG: Isn't it in a most--

MR. DEGNAN: Mrs. Gaines said she won't take anybody from the list.

THE CHAIRMAN: I have been very liberal in allowing extraordinary latitude to go on at great length in answering counsel's questions, and I think counsel has been very restrained. I am not going to have counsel continually interrupted as he is trying to ask questions and, at the same time, not reprimanding you and allowing you to go on. I have been very liberal with you. He is not the most obstinate counsel you have ever encountered.

MR. DEGNAN: I am sorry. All I say is I am a little concerned when I am quoted as having said something by counsel or implied by counsel that I said something. I am a little bit annoyed when you get testimony from certain people and they tell you part of the story.

THE CHAIRMAN: We are all sophisticated about the nature of questioning by counsel. As a matter of fact, it is customary when witnesses are called for them to be asked questions based on prior testimony that they did not hear. That puts them at some disadvantage. However, there is no other way to do it, and one way to answer the question is, of course, to say that you don't accept that version of it.

The purpose of his summarizing of the testimony is to give you some basis to answer the question on. If you don't agree with his summary, then put that in the record.

MR. DEGNAN: All right.

MR. TRACTENBERG: What I was going to ask Mr. Degnan is whether it is not true that in the most current litigation decided by a court where the CSA brought a challenge against the appointment of a Black acting principal, the court did, in fact, sustain the appointment as quite lawful.

MR. DEGNAN: That's true. The court did and it is a question in my mind as to whether it will be sustained at a higher level.

I found in that statement a new definition of the word "exhaust." I didn't find it in a dictionary the way the judge used it. I am afraid the judge is going to back away from that position.

Could you not say when there were 500 people on the list that it was exhausted on the same line of reasoning that was used? I think it is a mistake.

MR. TRACTENBERG: Well, I am not going to second guess the judge.

MR. DEGNAN: We will find out.

MR. TRACTENBERG: But, at least, it is fair to say that you have not always been determined by the courts, in fact, to be stepping in to prevent unlawful acts by community boards.

MR. DEGNAN: I think we have all experienced the fact that Supreme Court Judges have been overruled at the appellate level or the Court of Appeals. That is why we have them.

MR. TRACTENBERG: Let me make sure that I understood one thing that I think I heard you say.

Did you suggest that people on an eligible list who refuse an appointment are dropped from the list?

MR. DEGNAN: That is presently the rule.

I believe the rule is that you may refuse an appointment once, but not twice.

MR. TRACTENBERG: Is that a rule, so far as you know, that has been enforced?

MR. DEGNAN: Yes.

MR. TRACTENBERG: So that you fully support a rule which is in force under which any potential supervisors on an eligible list who refuse an assignment are dropped from that list?

MR. DEGNAN: Thoroughly. I would say my personal view is that nobody has a right to refuse that job.

If he wants that job he should take it and not look for the easiest kind of a job possible. I reject that completely.

THE CHAIRMAN: Even that might be a little unfair to some supervisors. For example it may well be that a principal or a supervisor might find unsatisfactory a rigid system which would require him to take a job although his experiences might persuade him he is not qualified for it.

MR. DEGNAN: I don't mean he should be forced to go. He is asked whether he would consider it. I think that is wrong.

I have always held that every school deserves to have a principal. And if one is licensed, it follows, if he wants a job, he ought not to be thinking in terms of what school it is.

THE CHAIRMAN: Suppose he has been in such a school before, perhaps, not as an administrator but in some other capacity. Supposing he fails. He could not cope. He does not yet know how to cope.

Is it not inhumane for the system to require of all supervisors that regardless of temperament, background, experience, that they must deem themselves equally qualified to go to any school regardless of any special experience?

MR. DEGNAN: My assumption is that the community calls in an eligible and at the end of an interview offers that eligible the job and then he refuses it, or he says, "No, I won't come down for the interview."

I have no patience with that. Maybe it is my own personal conviction. I always felt there isn't any job that a principal ought not be able to face and be ready to face. I think that shopping around for something is not right to me. I can't accept it. I don't hold any patience with the person who says, "That is too difficult for me. I can handle an easy school but not that one."

That is a basic mistake.

THE CHAIRMAN: You don't feel it is realistic to bear--

MR. DEGNAN: What I am saying is that the community board calls people in and says to them, in effect, "How do you feel about this?"

The person says, "Well, I think maybe I am not quite up to doing this work."

That is one thing.

But we are talking about people who refuse to come down for the interview and, I presume, I don't know whether this is said or not, may even refuse after the offer is made.

THE CHAIRMAN: In all fairness, some of the examples given to us which were so distressing yesterday include examples of people who had been interviewed and had come into the neighborhood and made a judgment they were going to fail there. As much as that might indicate open bigotry on the part of some people that you and I would not condone, you and I are both prepared to be realistic. We recognize that there are disadvantages that have come to a large number of people, and there are those who do not have the background for that post. When a principal sees what the community is demanding; for example, that the principal's responsibility is to determine what would turn the pathology around in the school, he may feel he can not do so.

I am wondering if it is entirely fair to say he is shirking his duties if he says he doesn't want to go into that school.

MR. DEGNAN: Isn't it fair to say that if a person demonstrates to a community board that he would not want to come in the school, they will not invite him into the school?

THE CHAIRMAN: The situation we are aware of is that they

did not wish to invite these people, they said. They realized that these people were going to fail, and they were not holding them accountable for that.

There was nobody else because they didn't have the flexibility to go outside of this.

MR. DEGNAN: I think that business of failing is overstated in many people's minds, just as I think the hazards of teaching in New York City have been overstated. The difficulties that schools present have been overstated. It becomes a kind of popular fetish with people to say it was a terrible school.

Every teacher who talks about this says, "It is not true in my school. It is another school a mile down the road."

It is always the other school but the other school is rarely there and I think we tend, as a group, to magnify the difficulties that a school presents.

I am perfectly willing to agree that there may be situations in which the community board and the individual applicant come to the same agreement:

"This is not for you. This is not the school that you ought to be in."

I have no quarrel with that. That is why we have these interviews.

I am saying that if a person comes to an interview and then is offered a job and doesn't take it, I think that is reprehensible.

MR. TRACTENBERG: May I ask one more question.

As you heard Mr. Shanker in his testimony, he said he could find at least two acceptable alternatives to the Board of Examiners' system of licensing. One was a statewide examination to determine minimum competency and the other was the administration of the National Teacher Exam.

Are either of those acceptable alternatives to you?

MR. DEGNAN: There was something that should have been said, I think, that wasn't said.

The state is presently charged with certifying teachers. This is a purely mechanical thing.

When you take the college transcript and try to certify, I am told there are between 7,000 and 10,000 teachers in the State of New York who are not certified because the State Education Department hasn't been able to find the time to get this done. If they can't do that, I have very little confidence that they can set up an examination system. I have said this before.

I think the state would be well advised to set up an examination system comparable to New York City's. I would be very reluctant to give up our system on the promise that they would develop a comparable one when it can't be demonstrated that they have done it the rest of the state.

MR. TRACTENBERG: How about the National Teacher Exam, or whatever the supervisory component of it is called, as an alternative?

MR. DEGNAN: I think the National Teacher Examination, as long as standards are maintained, and I must explain there is no passing mark on that examination--60,000 people take it each year and you can be the last one but you have passed that examination.

Now, the National Teacher Examination doesn't indicate whether you have qualified or not. The local community then has to set its own standard, and that is where the problem rests. I think that it is a reasonable way of doing things except that the standards set by the community should be sufficiently high to insure getting adequately competent teachers.

MR. TRACTENBERG: If there were a reasonable standard set, then you would find that a satisfactory alternative to the current examination process?

MR. DEGNAN: I think it may well have to be supplemented. There is one other factor here. In New York City we give, I believe, somewhere in the neighborhood of a thousand different levels of examination. The National Teacher Examination, I think, has only 13. I know there is one for elementary school. I don't know what the others are. We are diversified in New York City to the extent that the National Teacher Examination couldn't possibly supply all of the necessary screening processes. For example, we have teachers of cosmetology, we have teachers in all sorts of vocational areas. None of these would be tested in that examination.

MR. TRACTENBERG: On the supervisory level, that is less of a problem, isn't it?

MR. DEGNAN: No. It is more of a problem because, I think, the standards of expectation throughout the country, in terms of what supervisors should know and be able to do, I think those standards are decidedly lower than in New York City.

MR. TRACTENBERG: That can be adjusted by the pass grade set.

MR. DEGNAN: I don't know.

It is like striking an average. Maybe we would lose out on this, and maybe we would do a much poorer job in the long run.

MR. TRACTENBERG: In any event, it is a possibility--

MR. DEGNAN: I think it has possibilities of exploration, yes.

MR. TRACTENBERG: Fine.

COMMR. COLGATE: Just a very small question to refresh my memory of your testimony.

As I recall, you testified that it was a certain amount of inconvenience to prepare those exams.

MR. DEGNAN: That might involve working either during the summer or something of the kind.

COMMR. COLGATE: I understand that. That was more or less talked about.

MR. DEGNAN: I can tell you for many years I felt it was a great contribution to society. The change that came didn't mean very much.

For many years there was a disgraceful amount paid.

COMMR. COLGATE: You also testified, as I recall, it was $2 an hour, or something like that.

MR. DEGNAN: Yes.

COMMR. COLGATE: Thank you, Mr. Degnan.
Counsel, will you note for the record that, at those rates, a person doing the same service for society as Mr. Degnan did would now be earning between $8,400 and $10,500 a year extra.

MR. DEGNAN: I think you misunderstood me.

I didn't say I earned $1,200 a year at the rate of $2. That rate went up.

I said it was $2 an hour for many years. It went up in the contract. It was a contract item.

I think, if my memory serves me, it went from $8 an hour to the sum you mentioned. When I earned $1,200 it wasn't at the rate of $2 an hour. Maybe they paid me $70 for the year or $80. It was a nominal amount.

MR. TRACTENBERG: Do you still serve as an examination assistant?

MR. DEGNAN: No, sir.

MR. TRACTENBERG: For how long?

MR. DEGNAN: Since I have been President of the CSA, I have not been involved in this.

THE CHAIRMAN: Thank you, Mr. Degnan.

- - - - -

THE CHAIRMAN: Dr. Lillian Weber next.

DR. WEBER: I'm Mrs. Weber. I'm one of those that the faculty of the City College of the City University in joint session and in going over my thesis for the University of London adjudged the equivalent of a doctor. I guess I didn't pass an examination, but was accepted on my merits on the basis of a qualitative decision.

In the second place, I'm not part of the Board of Education nor am I licensed and yet I work in schools by invitation of principals. Again my quality is being discussed rather than the question of examination.

In the third place, I would like to relate to this hearing, and I told Miss Aronson I would, not on the level of the question of examinations because I have, in teaching student teachers, found the examinations totally irrelevant to the question of performance. I was extremely interested to hear Mr. Shanker bear this out, that in fact so many teachers dropped out in those first few months, first few weeks even, I believe he said, and certainly in the first few years, and that the basic question is what happens to them in the school system in terms of performance. I would like to read you a statement that I prepared as a citizen to assist Chancellor Scribner with his questions and to assist Commissioner Nyquist, not really at their request, on the question of assessment and teacher education because I am a teacher educator and am, as you probably know, the designer of the open corridor programs in the City of New York.

I would like to make one more remark and that is to Mr. Shanker's statement on how long it takes to help anyone know how to handle open education programs--since I have never called them infant schools, and believe you me they're not. We should have the humility to know that anything that has existed for one hundred years in England could not possibly come to being overnight here.

In any case, he was relating to the question of retraining, not to the question of training. When we're talking about the question of training teachers, we should be talking to the point of training teachers first. The question of retraining teachers, those who have been trained in another way, all of whom have passed the examination, is another question, obviously.

Now, a question was posed by some of the people on the Chancellor's staff. This was put to a number of people: What, in your opinion, is the single most important change that should be made in the education and training of classroom teachers?

It seems to me this question is relative to the whole question of examinations because if you could feel that the training was right, then you would have perhaps, a different attitude toward the examining process.

Incidentally, and before I start, people are not admitted to the training program at City College before they have passed a written English examination and a speech examination. They are then admitted to the School of Education. This is on the undergraduate level.

There are many ways to become a teacher in New York City. There is the undergraduate full preparation way and then there was the shortage way represented by Alternate B examinations. The shortage way took people who were liberal arts trained; it was called the walk-in examination in common parlance. This was Mr. Shanker's point, as well, that if at one point they had 12 credits and later eight credits in education, with absolutely no practice in the schools whatever, and no indication of their performance, they passed the examination, and they were then hired. I'm sure this is common knowledge to all of you, that this was the case with Alternate B examination.

City College tried to remedy that situation by setting up TEMPUS programs for Alternate B examinees, which included supervised internships. ITTP people in intensive teacher training were given supervision on the job. And Urban Corps people, those in regular teacher training, and now those in the pilot project--which takes people both through open enrollment and regular admission--are in a combined program that takes them through four years of an integrated preparation.

Now, I'm relating to the piece of the City College program that I was instrumental in changing, and that I hope I'll be instrumental in changing even more.

The question was, as I said, what was the single most important change needed in Teacher Training. It seems impossible to answer in terms of a single change. Yet in fact, in 1967, I approached the problem in just this way. At that time it seemed to me that the single most important change was to create good practice situations that would end the discrepancies between theory and practice, that would end the washing out of all that the college courses had transmitted to the students by placement in situations where the realities were contradictions of everything learned in the college courses.

Of course, I'm taking my own stance, and I'll make a slight interjection there. I'm taking my own stance with the approval of the Chancellor and the Commissioner who are now coming out for alternatives in education. This is central to the question of how you regard the examining process.

I'm taking my own stance, a developmental stance, in defining a good practice situation as one supportive of the path of the child's development, one in which the teacher's role and school's role are clearly implementative of the child's growth. No such practice situation existed. Therefore, the entire education of the classroom teacher was washed out. She adjusted, feeling helpless to change things; and in isolation behind the closed door, she continued in education only by adjusting, only by employing survival techniques.

Incidentally, and I again refer to Mr. Shanker's evidence, he spoke about this principal who had complained about a teacher after 13 years, was it not. She had gotten all kinds of good ratings, but the principal had never seen her. That's the trouble. The supervisor may not have seen the teacher in the 13 years. Unfortunately, she had all kinds of good ratings.

I have described the necessity for good practice, mostly in terms of the child and the growth of the teacher. But in the old classrooms, there was even more that was damaging for teacher education. In whole class teaching the student teacher learned to be an assistant, never a teacher. The skills she was asked to learn were controls expressed mostly through routines. She was an assistant to the teacher helping with control while the teacher did whole class leassons. When her supervisor came, she herself performed with a 20-minute whole class lesson.

This way of student teaching is still prevalent and it is this way I thought destructive to any real preparation for teaching. The young teacher entered a classroom of her own with very little experience in even this kind of classroom management.

In the whole year placement that we at City College have created for our changed and reorganized areas, the student teacher is a full member of a teaching team, encouraged to try out many different things, encouraged to take responsibility for the extension and adaptation of the work of the children to whom she is relating. Her work changes all the time. She cannot prepare a nice tidy little lesson for her supervisor, but is partner to much more extensive planning. Over the period of a year, she is often called on to manage the entire room and to maintain and extend the environment.

May I say there was a UFT rule that only licensed personnel can take the classroom? This was also part of what we objected to. How can a student ever learn to manage a classroom if the only time she takes a classroom is for 20 minutes when her supervisor comes, and the rest of the time she isn't permitted to take the classroom on her own? These are asides.

Therefore, the single most significant educative force regarding the education or reeducation of teachers is to my mind the reorganization and revitalization of the schools themselves.

Nevertheless, this, of course, is an oversimplification. Since who is to do this, with what training and what rationale? The rationale must be joined to the practice. It must be modified and clarified by practice. It must find new possibilities and new formulations through the practice that we are talking about. But it must exist, be known, and be the substratum of the practice.

The classrooms cannot be reorganized except as guided by at least the first conceptualization of how, in fact, children learn. As I see it, working with teachers in the classroom, teachers need this conceptualization. They need an understanding of the development of language, of the development of mathematical conception; they need practice and skill in observing a child, and insights to help to interpret these observations.

When I said the single most important need was for change in practice, I was assuming teachers whose education had included these elements. Without these elements of the understanding of the learning of the child, skill in observing the child, and, I add a third factor, exploration of the possibilities of materials, the reorganization of the classroom will be nothing more than dogmatically asserted little gimmicks.

Up to now I've been considering the teacher, a person who draws the greatest source of her energies from her interest in children's growth and her role in this. If we consider the education of the teacher more broadly as a person, then the discussion becomes broader. I think it is this Commissioner Nyquist was talking about when he said colleges had not been daring enough and had not yet disregarded their three-credit approach. Obviously if a teacher is to understand the children's approach, the teacher should be a learning person. She must have contact with her own learning process and empathy with some other learning processes. She must have zest and enjoyment in the world.

I would think a good teacher education program should not offer separate courses. My experience is that almost nothing is retained, and this is at City College. I say nothing is retained from the junior year, from the earlier separate courses if they have not been linked in some way with the practice situation. I say nothing and I mean zero. Absolutely nothing. In the senior year we have to redo every ounce of child development that supposedly was taught because that must be linked with the practice situation. I know the foundations people will not be happy about this, but that's it.

Therefore, my conception of a good teacher education would include concurrent programs of practice theory and cultural resource courses, expressing the teacher's own need for knowledge and her interests in her own independent drives. These would cross over one from another using many connective paths. This would be continued over a three-year period with option for this course after the first college year. The present two-year teacher training courses are, I think, grossly inadequate.

If you would like to hear it, I have added the part that I'm sending to Commissioner Nyquist on assessment. This question of performance assessment is especially relevant to these hearings.

THE CHAIRMAN: You may proceed.

DR. WEBER: I want to relate now for a short time to the question of assessing performance, a question raised by Commissioner Nyquist.

I think that the state is obviously asking for flexibility of teaching programs and a recognition of variety in these. Both Commissioner Nyquist and Chancellor Scribner are stressing, in changing over from an inadequate and clearly unresponsive bureaucratized education system, the encouragement of alternatives. How then are alternatives to be assessed?

Commissioner Nyquist has suggested external assessment. But external assessment employed in England is employed within a common frame, a very basic agreement on goals, even within the variety that is encouraged in order to keep the paths of reexamination open.

At this point in our development it is important that we open up the long frozen dam and respond to the new opportunities for fluidity and for alternatives. One alternative cannot be assessed by the other alternative. It might be possible to pair two groups, each developing along a similar path to assess each other. But I think it is early even for that.

I think it is possible for the state inspecting programs to accept, as they now do, the validity of the many different alternative programs as good of their kind, and to inspect the practice situations as well.

There are good formal practice situations, I'm sure, though this is not my cup of tea, and good informal practice situations. Certainly I'm well aware there are inadequate informal practice situations.

I think that if on-site inspections were repeated from time to time, to see whether in fact the standard was maintained, one might have this combination or union of theory and practice whatever it was and good of whatever its kind.

I can conceive of some random double assessments, having particular teacher candidates compared for how well they reach the goals of their colleges. I think the Federal Taxation Bureau does some random kind of samples to determine whether people are honest or not, and I think it's possible to do random double assessments. Such external assessment would be within acceptance of the goal of the college and goal of the practice situation.

In addition, I think that the length of supervision must be taken into account. I have listed as ideal a three-year period of an integrated learning and developmental theory and practice situation with many opportunities for independent work. I think the young teacher's first year of truly independent work should be considered an internship under supervision. I prefer the word advisement.

I think final qualification--not tenure--should come only after three years work. I think only in these ways can one set up a situation where it is assumed that theory and practice are united and that learning is continuous.

I have not spelled out that the very nature of the practice that I have called good was premised on the need for teachers to have the support of learning from each other and of continuous advisement. It sets up the communities of teachers and children that have become known as "open corridors."

I then give an illustration which I think is better answered in questions. The advisors that work with me, for instance, come from a pretty high level from all over, and the reason I work with these advisors, each of whom supports one of these suggestions, two days a week, is because the present supervisory staff obviously is not within this goal. My advisors have been selected as a result of their background, after an interview and a period of three months of working with me in which I assess their performance.

Therefore, certainly I stand by the question of assessment.

As to a great pool of resources, I think the unfortunate backtracking in the process of integration in the South leaves us an amazing pool that I know about in the South of high level supervisors and principals, if we want to bring minority people to the City of New York.

THE CHAIRMAN: Counsel.

MR. TRACTENBERG: I just want to make sure I understand.

I think earlier in your remarks you suggested you didn't feel the examination process made a meaningful contribution to the development of teachers and the determination of who is a competent teacher.

Is that a fair characterization?

DR. WEBER: I think it is totally irrelevant. I think all of them may have passed the examination and I'm not relating to the question of minorities.

Half of my class is Black or Puerto Rican. This has been its composition for some time. They all passed the examination. But it is the focus in their training and the focus in the practice situation that determines whether they can grapple with one type of practice situation or another. And my basic judgment was that regardless of passing the exam, almost none of them could handle any practice situation in the past because in fact the whole process put them in the position of training as an assistant rather than a teacher. There was too little independence, too little anything.

What relevance has the examination? They can pass the examination, black, purple, tan or anything else. Yes, the examination is irrelevant to the process of selection of teachers, and I really do think Mr. Shanker said pretty much the same thing.

We do have everybody before entering the School of Education pass a basic very short competency test in written English and in speech.

MR. TRACTENBERG: In your judgment that's sufficient to determine the minimum competency.

DR. WEBER: If he is talking about the question of spelling and so on, which appeared in the newspaper the other day, I think the colleges take care of that. The School of Education doesn't administer that test. The liberal arts people who look down on the School of Education do, and may I say, they flunk quite a number.

But you see, I'm asking whether this is what you want to do. I see no reason not to have colleges to do that. I see no reason to have an expensive Board of Examiners do that.

MR. TRACTENBERG: I gather from what you say, assuming there was a substantial movement towards the informal or open corridor type of program, that really the test becomes even more irrelevant.

By that, I mean, I assume we're talking about basically a different kind of teacher.

DR. WEBER: I say provided you have new alternatives. But I say, even given the old program, the fact is we have many incompetent teachers in the schools who have passed the examinations. I think everyone is agreed on that. So that given any standard of reference, that's true.

The minute you have a voluntary system, which Mr. Shanker has supported, and the minute you have an alternative kind of thing, we want people who are far better trained than in the past and whom we will supervise far more because we know it's different. But what does the examination have to do with it?

I would like to read you, if I may, the questions that I would think would be relevant in assessment of one of my programs. The Educational Testing Service, incidentally, is working on this.

This is an illustration of an assessment that accepts the goals of my kind of reorganization. Incidentally, Chancellor Scribner said to a principal in my hearing the other day, "You have several things going in your school, write down the goals that you have in your school so that a parent coming in could say that's an intellectual exercise." I have submitted to that by saying what it is I've got. Therefore, you have the goals, and anybody coming in assessing it ought to assess within those goals.

Now, what's my thing? I suggest as possibilities asking these questions:

Is the environment charged? Has the grouping around common areas begun the process of developing community? Are there changed relationships? Is there easy discussion in a free social atmosphere?

Is the instructional mode changed to a teaching support of the child, independent, active, learning individually, and uneven in style and pace?

Has the teacher grown in understanding of how the child uses the environment?

What has the child experienced and understood of his experience?

Is the teacher guided by understanding of this to intelligent adaptation and extension of environment, and, in fact, does the child use it?

Is he active, curious and independent?

I could go on.

Are any of these on the examination or on any conceivable examination? None. It is this that has to be looked at if you would say, "Is this happening?"

We also have very carefully specified the goals--I'll leave all this with you--of what we expect the student to come out with from our program. This is given a student before she enters. We expect her to be able to plan; we expect her to be able to do this.

We are the only college in the City of New York, under the City University, in which there is an entire year of supervised student practice. I would like to know exactly what the examination thing, which all our students can pass, adds to this program in determining their competence.

I do think it is important, if a principal, following Commissioner Nyquist's suggestion, begins to act independently about what he has in his school and wants to select teachers trained in this. It seems to me the important thing is that he be able to select the teachers that fit his conception of the things that he wants going in his school.

Incidentally, I really don't see the pork barrel all over the City. I worked with people in Irvington, Greenburgh, White Plains, New Rochelle, Yorktown Heights, and those teachers are all very high caliber. I don't really know that New York City excels over these, and they don't have an examination system.

MR. TRACTENBERG: From the school authorities' point of view of certification you would favor, I gather, a performance-based kind of certification, an internship?

DR. WEBER: I would favor two things:

Inspection of a college's goals as to whether they were carefully and thoughtfully enough worked out, allowing alternatives, and inspection of the practice situations used by the college for whether they were really good of their kind and supported their goals.

MR. TRACTENBERG: Do you keep some kind of dossier of your students that could be made available to a school system that was interested in possibly hiring some?

DR. WEBER: Absolutely.

Incidentally, lots of students leave New York City and teach elsewhere, you know. It isn't true people in this day and age are immobile. I don't remember who described this, whether it was Mr. Degnan or Mr. Shanker, but that's a little absurd. Young girls go where their husbands are going.

May I also say not everybody submits to national examinations. My older son is an organic chemist hired by the University of Southern California, as an assistant professor. There isn't a national or even a local examination for organic chemists. The statement of the college is accepted.

The point is, if you don't think the college has a good program on inspection, drop it. If you dont' think the college is using good practice situations, which you reinspect from time to time, drop them.

But just be aware, if you're talking about alternatives, that alternatives mean that you must take into account the goal of a program and what it's about.

MR. TRACTENBERG: I would assume since better than 90% of the teachers in the New York City public school system come from New York City institutions of higher learning, the kind of evaluation you suggest would not be an undue burden.

DR. WEBER: The City of London is larger than this, and they do it.

The only thing I can say is that I don't take on my soul everything that's wrong with the New York City public school system because I have done everything in the world to try to change it.

Incidentally, I have spoken quite publicly, having led the course in City College that was somewhat critical of many administrative things in New York City and asked for a why not approach for two years.

But there is no way of working in this without dealing with supervisors and principals. Passing an exam doesn't make a supervisor able to help a teacher grow if most of the supervisor's work is using a bull horn in the lunchroom or being on the playground yelling at children or being in the hall patrolling. We must take a look at what the supervisors in fact do and realize that we need a very major program before we can even begin to use supervisors properly, utilizing their training for revitalization and reorganization of the schools. This is necessary, regardless of program.

As I have told the Commissioner and Chancellor Scribner, there are two elements. One is my program, which is very special, and the other is a general looking at the schools to make them more viable for everybody.

Let me tell you, as long as half of what people are talking about is control, you're not going to see anything happening.

I looked at that and said it wasn't good enough, let's change the situation so the teachers could teach and look at children. I wasn't looking at the supervisors. We had to bypass them entirely and bring in external advisors.

We are now working with half of the supervisors who want to learn the new way and half external, six from each side, learning a new way of advisement and support of teachers on the job. This isn't just an occasional walking in and looking at bulletin boards, but is an on-the-job working with them, which says that supervisors are not supposed to be in the office at all, but are supposed to take a section of the school, stay there, and relate to the teachers.

MR. TRACTENBERG: That's all the questions I have.

THE CHAIRMAN: Thank you very much.

We are a little behind, but not as much as I thought we would be.

This is Mr. David Seeley, Director, Public Education Association.

MR. SEELEY: I appreciate the Chairman's giving me this opportunity to come back to answer certain charges made by Mr. Shanker in his testimony.

Since I am answering certain charges I want to state for the record that by and large I agree with a great deal Mr. Shanker said and I think he evidenced an attitude of willingness to look for changes, which is quite hopeful. But I think he made certain statements which must be answered.

First of all, he did make a statement about these various studies over the last 20 years that recommended change in the Board of Examiners. He didn't just imply, he stated that the answer they all came up with had been bought.

I can't answer for the other organizations that made these studies for the last 20 years. They can answer for themselves.

I know our organization which did make one of these studies certainly was not bought because we are not paid for our studies. We're not publicly supported. We're a private citizens organization, and we came to that conclusion.

If we thought the Board of Examiners was good for children, we would be for them.

The important charge he made had to do with an incident which occurred in a meeting I was chairing and he related a situation where a community school board member had said that his board used as a test of a supervisory candidate that person's attitude toward the union, and if anyone is pro-union, he couldn't be hired.

That isn't what happened at that meeting. This is one of the questions the community board people asked, where the applicants stood on the 1968 strike.

Mr. Shanker did not point out that I vigorously objected to this kind of test. I think it is wrong to have this test.

The crucial thing that comes before us is how are you going to protect against this and this is the heart of the issue before this Commission which has not been revealed in the hearings so far. It comes down to this. If judgments are going to be made locally on the choice of supervisors and teachers, there is a danger those judgments will use factors such as the political test.

I would first of all say I think when that test is used, the cause of that is primarily because professional organizations instead of staying professional organizations have become political action organizations and, in fact, political action organizations fighting against community interests.

Although I vigorously oppose the kind of question the community school board member indicated, I ask you to think about the situation where you are a member of the community school board. You have two candidates, let's say. before you. One is to be chosen as principal, which is a very key position in that district. Now one of them gives every indication of being willing to work for the interest of that district, and the other one has been active in an organization fighting that community tooth and nail. I think you'll have to expect that community representatives are bound to want to take this into account. They do not want to appoint someone to a key administrative position who is their enemy.

That's what seems to me the tremendous mistake the professional organizations have made up until now. They have been putting themselves in a position of political action organizations that force this kind of choice.

There are only two ways in which we can guard against this. Those who would say the examination is the way to protect against this kind of thing can only mean one thing, and I would maintain my logic is irrefutable. If the central exam is going to protect the union from having communities pick antiunion people, then the central exam must be political.

That means it must screen out people at that level who have the wrong attitude, and I think that is the suspicion many of us have. It is not just racial, but it is found in the kind of judgments being made. As Mr. Degnan pointed out, they choose the examiners by saying is the man well thought of, does he run a good school. These are subjective judgments, and unless you are a member of the club you don't get chosen. If someone is viewed as being against the attitude of the current supervisor's association, he may never get on that list. That may be a protection if you root for pure political power, but it is not a protection that I think this city could ever accept.

The only way we can get protection is to have collaboration at the local level. I'm sure if the professional groups would collaborate, they will find communities do rely on professional judgments. And I do not think you'll get communities discriminating against candidates if they're union members unless they are seen as enemies of the community.

That is the most crucial thing that has come out. It comes to a fear of two contending political power groups, and if the one now in charge thinks they're going to maintain their power by keeping the judgments away from the community, there will be fights endlessly until the whole community is torn apart. That is not the way it can be done.

THE CHAIRMAN: Thank you, Mr. Seeley.

I want to say for the record I allowed Mr. Seeley that latitude in his answer. I felt I had to because I had allowed Dr. Rockowitz latitude in his answer when he alluded at some length to his record.

While I have allowed each of these people this latitude and have allowed latitude throughout the questioning, I wish we would all keep in mind that we will inevitably get behind.

Mr. Vazquez has been especially gracious in waiting and even allowing one or two others to go ahead of him, and I give him my personal thanks.

I want to say that after Mr. Vazquez--I don't have to worry about the stenographer, they have just changed--but out of humanity for counsel, I will allow a 15-minute break to allow him to eat a sandwich on the premises. After that 15 minutes, we will come back, and the first witness in the afternoon will be Robert Thorndike.

Mr. Vazquez.

MR. VAZQUEZ: Back in May 1970 the ADCA made a report called the Analysis of Puerto Ricans and Analysis of Puerto Rican Schools. It was as a result of that research that these hearings are being held today. And it is to the credit of Madam Chairman here and the Commission that they moved very quickly in bringing this out to the attention of the City and in continuing that interest. Sometimes these things are picked up and are quickly dropped. I hope out of these hearings something positive and meaningful will come.

Before I get into the main body of my presentation--incidentally, I have a very lengthy statement--I want to say I will be brief with it knowing that Mr. Counsel over here must be a little nervous.

The Board of Education should be required--this is a recommendation I make--to provide data, like the data we were able to obtain to put together this report. It is very difficult to gather this kind of information. As you know, this kind of information is very necessary for the advancement of our people, the minorities. Not having it on hand, you don't know a situation as drastic as this one exists. I think it is necessary that all of us should have made available information by the Board of Education about all problems and activities.

Another thing I would like to point out is that the Puerto Rican community has a great stake in these hearings. And I say that not only do we have the lowest ratio of professionals in the school system, but also the worst record of dropouts, lowest reading levels. Most of you have seen the New York Times today, the figures there.

Mindful that that only gives the rates of those who have been tested, and non-English speaking children are not tested, that points out the areas of South Bronx, East Harlem and Williamsburg in Brooklyn continue to have the lowest rate. Something like 22 schools in East Harlem, all the schools there, are below reading levels.

Another point I would like to make here which is very important is that we not only are underrepresented in the total professional setup of the Board, teachers, principals, but we also have no one at the top administrative level of the Board. And persons who have concerns of our community, problems that arise, find they have to go through three or four layers of bureaucracy. It is very necessary to get to the top in order to get solutions.

So, one of the recommendations we make further on is that someone be appointed in a position of Deputy Superintendent who deals mainly with the problems of Spanish-speaking Puerto Ricans. Then this becomes a positive and meaningful procedure of the Board.

It is true we have one superintendent in School District 3, and to us that represents a breakthrough. We hope there will be more breakthroughs in the future.

We have checked the reading level statistics for Puerto Ricans and they are very depressing. We have found in schools with 50% Puerto Ricans or more, 86% of the pupils are below grade level. Many of these are over two years behind by the fifth grade level.

The same thing happens in the junior and high school levels and here's when you find the dropout rate at the high school level is close to 57%. But that doesn't reflect the total dropout rate because if you go back and find out how many dropouts are in the junior high school before entering high school, we think the rate is around 85%, which is a tragic figure.

We have found out in researching programs which deal with

non-English speaking children--which compose about 121,000 in the school system, a little over 10% of the total, two-thirds being Puerto Rican--no effective program has been developed to meet this need.

This is nothing new to the Board of Education. In 1953 they spent a million dollars in research about the problem they were facing with the incoming migration of Puerto Ricans. And the recommendations that came out were very meaningful recommendations, but unfortunately none have been implemented so far.

We find that from the 121,000 non-English speaking children, only 10,000 get second-language training. We thought that maybe there might be some program that might be more effective, more complete. But only 4,000 or 3% of the non-English speaking children are attending these schools, and actually these schools are supported by federal funds. No city funds have been allocated for these types of programs.

We also notice the recommendations made in the 1953 study for screening and placement procedures have not been implemented. We have situations in which the placement procedures have been so bad that a deaf child has been seven weeks in class and nobody knew her problem. They figured she just didn't know how to speak the language. They couldn't determine she was deaf.

We also know of many parents who have problems communicating with the teachers and school administrators. So they can't get any answers or any results to any problem they have in the school with the children.

So, as you can see here, the plight of the Puerto Rican is not that he is not educated in Spanish or English, but that he is deprived of his right to learn. I think first fundamentally you have to accept that children have a right to learn.

How they learn is another question. There are two approaches here. You can take the traditional approach, put them in the classroom and see if they can absorb the subject matter. In the case of the children who don't speak or have a faulty knowledge of the language, this puts an additional burden on the child.

We feel a bilingual approach might be an approach. We believe the children can come into the system and can continue their education in Spanish, and English can be taught for a period until they can move into the classrooms with the other students and be able to maintain pace with English as the main language.

However, we would also like to see provision made that once the non-English speaking child learns to speak English and read and write it, he can continue with Spanish. We believe this is important for the self-image of the child, and he should have an opportunity to be proud of his heritage. Language is a skill and when he graduates, full knowledge of Spanish can be helpful in a career, either in teaching, foreign trade, or diplomatic service.

We believe there is a reason, a rationale for restructuring the educational system to meet this need, particularly since 22% of the enrollment are Puerto Rican students and, as I mentioned before, about one-half of those don't speak the language very well.

We also endorse the Chancellor's effort to recruit more bilingual teachers. The only problem we see now is that from the programs that have been developed, federally funded programs mainly, in two years of the programs helping persons to complete college, only 200 teachers have come out.

Also, the UFT has been operating a program with the Board of Education, apparently a one million dollar program, to recruit more teachers. So far they got less than 200 Puerto Rican teachers to apply as bilingual teachers. These applicants are required to pass the infamous Board of Examiners' exam.

I happen to have a copy of the exam that has been given for bilingual teachers, and it is very interesting to see the kind of questions that are asked to persons who are not familiar with the City:

"The Mayor of New York has the power to:
"1. Fix the annual tax rate.
"2. Appoint the President of the City Council.
"3. Budget.
"4. Appoint the head of the Fire Department."

You have to be very cognizant of the intricacies of the division of power in New York City, and I wonder if Mayor Lindsay knows the answers to these questions. But the fact is, these kinds of questions are not relevant to test the ability of a person to teach.

I found also a situation in which an incorrect question is being asked. The exam gives two answers that are incorrect. You are asked to pick the one incorrect answer. The question is as follows:

"All the dances are correctly paired with the country of origin, except the Tarantella, Spain; Troika, Russia; La Paspa, Mexico."

The Tarantella is danced in Southern Italy and not Spain. And La Paspa is not a Mexican dance. Whoever drew up this exam, possibly they don't have an up-to-date encyclopedia. This is the kind of thing a person might have to pass before he might be considered to take the exam.

It happens this exam has 25 questions out of 100 in Spanish. I found the Spanish questions are pretty good. Some of them do relate to education. But, this is 25 out of 100 which means, you know, 25%. And this test would only be 50 or 60% of the total examination score of one individual. So, the Spanish part of the test might only be worth ten or 15 points of the total exam.

If we are trying to recruit bilingual teachers, I would suppose we should have something close to 50/50. For we're trying not only to find people who have some teaching know-how, but people who are capable in the Spanish language.

This shouldn't be construed that we're trying to emphasize that anyone who is Puerto Rican should be approved as a teacher. But we believe there is a better way of testing people than these types of exams.

Interviews might be tried and evaluation of job performance by competent supervisors. We believe a person should be given an opportunity to come into the system. Be a little liberal there.

We would like to suggest several steps to be taken by the school system.

One is that schools be restructured so that all non-English speaking pupils be taught English as a second language for part of the day and the other subject matters in the native language until they become proficient in the English language.

Two, pupils shouldn't be placed in regular classes until it is verified that the pupil has an adequate knowledge of English, speaking, reading, and language.

Three, schools should be restructured so non-English speaking pupils who wish to would be able to continue learning their native language as a preferred subject.

Four, all prospective teachers must have at least two years of Spanish.

Five, special yearly reports be required in writing and arithmetic, of the non-English and Spanish-speaking child. These are not considered in the reading tests that are being given now.

Six, all teachers entering the school system must, beside knowing Spanish, be able to teach in another language. That has to be acquired as a skill and we don't think everybody can do it.

Bilingual personnel must be recruited with a goal of 10,000 Puerto Rican teachers and supervisors within four years. We urge and plan to recruit these three groups of Puerto Ricans in New York City to be trained as teachers:

One group, Puerto Ricans graduated from high school who would then go into college with the purpose of coming out as teachers.

Two, Puerto Ricans in college who can be recruited and asked if they would consider teaching as a career, not as a permanent career, but to try for a while in order to solve the problem.

Three, Puerto Rican paraprofessionals with a career ladder involved.

We believe persons who are either high school graduates or even dropouts, with the right incentives, can be attracted to the school system, can rotate, work on the job, doing different jobs in the schools and at the same time attending night school or day school. And we firmly believe these persons, once they graduate, would be better teachers than those who live in the suburbs, go to Columbia Teachers College and, when they go to the ghetto schools, throw up their arms and either get out or just accommodate in a way that isn't functioning.

We would like to see a training program for Puerto Ricans, so that in three years there would be at least 50 qualified as principals and 100 as assistant principals.

We would like to see the appointment by the central Board of a person on the level of a Deputy Superintendent reporting directly to the Chancellor dealing with the special needs of the non-English speaking and Puerto Rican pupils in the school system.

We would also like to see an increase in the number of bilingual teachers. About 200 of these personnel are there now, but they don't have any classroom functions, they deal with the relationship between the parent and community. We would like to multiply that number. As I mentioned to you before, the Puerto Ricans are not familiar with our school system. In Puerto Rico the system is more relevant to them, they speak the language, and it performs for them. They don't have the problems they face over here. These persons who have been working in community relations have been making people aware of the way they should go about solving problems. There should be at least one in every school with over 100 Spanish-speaking pupils. And we would like to see some of them put in high schools and junior high schools where now we don't have many or any.

We would like to see research performed on the problems of the Spanish-speaking and Puerto Rican child. We don't think an organization like ours should be the one that should be bringing this out to the public. The Board of Education has that responsibility to come out and provide this information so we can be able to participate and help along in changing the situation.

As I visualize it, with problems like this, the restructuring I mentioned is something that will have a cost. I would estimate it would cost about 40 million dollars to do a good, effective job. You might say that's a lot of money. Right now, we're spending close to 300 million dollars, and we would like to see two percent to go into that education, so the students don't have to drop out and the students will get sufficient credentials to go to college and we can get more teachers and professionals.

If we don't do that, I think we are doomed to see another generation of illiterates perpetuating the welfare cycle. We will see the Puerto Ricans in New York become like the Indians on reservations.

Now is the time to convince the Board of Education and state officials to do something. And, like I said, it's not a matter of more money, it is a matter of using money to do a more effective job.

THE CHAIRMAN: Thank you.

MR. TRACTENBERG: Do you think any of the programs that the Board of Education now has in the bilingual teaching area are likely to produce significant results?

MR. VAZQUEZ: I doubt so because the programs they have had so far can only scratch the surface.

First of all, I don't think they have developed an effective recruitment mechanism. I have seen them go in the wintertime to Puerto Rico to give tests, and frankly, you might interest teachers to come here, but I think the ones that might be interested would be turned off by the exams.

Secondly, I think it is just as unfair to try to get somebody who's pretty well established in some community to relocate and possibly then be placed in a difficult teaching situation. I could see that provides a sufficient amount of teachers to start, but not sufficient to meet the need.

What I think we need is to try to convince some of the Puerto Rican students of the colleges to go into teaching and provide some kind of a short but intensive training to do the job.

I think they have the basic qualifications. They know the people, know the language and I think they may even have the motivation.

Thirdly, I would like to see a program to get people who may not be as highly qualified as the Board of Examiners is trying to obtain, but who could be very effective. Like I mentioned to you, people are not being taught. And I would rather have someone not as highly qualified, but who would be able to teach my child than leave things as they are because you can't find qualified teachers.

I suggest the paraprofessionals, the high school students, high school graduates who can be convinced. They could even share some of the teaching roles, and this would accelerate it. We have to bring more people into the system. We have to open alternatives for these people and, more than that, I think we have to give the children an opportunity to learn. The only way we can do this is by bringing in more people.

We have seen examples of elders tutoring juniors. Recently, I saw in the Long Island Press, in Queens they have an influx of Spanish-speaking children, and they're asking for volunteer housewives to come into the schools. No requirements, high school education. If you work for nothing, it's okay. If you want to get paid, you have to have all these qualifications. But they thought this might be a solution, bring in volunteers.

I don't think the Board of Education has been able to develop a realistic approach, and I think people in the community will be able to be very creative in helping them. But the problem is there. Even if you deal with the bureaucracy, you have the problem of the stumbling block of the Board of Examiners.

MR. TRACTENBERG: Do you see that as a substantial roadblock both for out-of-town recruitment and moving people up through the ranks, paraprofessional and otherwise?

MR. VAZQUEZ: It's a very narrow bottleneck. But more than that, I see the problem of people not being interested in going into a teaching career.

How can you convince young Puerto Rican students to go into teaching courses when they know they're going to have a tough time getting a job? For a long time you don't have any Blacks going into engineering or any of those careers. There was a surplus of Blacks as ministers or in other professions because these were open to them. In the case of Puerto Ricans, I think we have a surplus of social workers. Very few go into other professions because the doors are closed to them.

I think if we bring out that we need teachers and we're going to do everything possible to get everybody in that meets the most minimal qualifications, if we provide training for them, and skills to do a job, and then they can go up the ladder, I think you'll be able to interest these people. It's better than pushing carts in the garment center or working in restaurants.

MR. TRACTENBERG: That's all.

THE CHAIRMAN: Thank you very much.

Counsel has been going since 9:30. We will have a break. I'm going to call a 15-minute break. It is now 25 minutes to 3:00. I will reconvene this hearing in exactly 15 minutes.

(Whereupon, at 2:35 p.m., a recess was taken; the hearing was resumed at 2:50 p.m.)

THE CHAIRMAN: This hearing is in session.
Would you tell the people in the hall that the hearing is in session again.

I am going to call Dr. Robert Thorndike, Professor of Psychology, Teachers College, Columbia University.

DR. THORNDIKE: My name is Robert Thorndike. I am a professor of psychology and education at Teachers College, Columbia University. I have taught courses in educational and psychological testing for over 30 years. I am the author or editor of four books and various articles on testing and personnel selection.

Tests used for selection and promotion are, in general, of two types. These may be designated, respectively, proficiency tests and aptitude tests.

A proficiency test undertakes to assess the extent to which a person has the actual skills required on a job. A good example of a proficiency test would be a typing test given to an applicant for a stenographer's job. Clearly, a person who is going to be employed to do typing requires typing skills, and the test is obviously and directly relevant as a measure of job performance.

The validity of a proficiency test such as this must be assessed judgmentally in terms of how well the tasks required in the test do match parts of the performance required on the job. The judgments can only be made competently by a person who has an intimate knowledge of the duties and demands of the job.

Obviously, no proficiency test covers all of the skills required on a job. Thus, the typing test doesn't indicate how well an employee will get along with other persons in the office, or whether she will be uniformly courteous to persons making inquiries over the telephone. A proficiency test can be expected to cover a certain limited range of job skills, and must be evaluated in terms of the importance of the skills that it covers and the fidelity with which it represents them.

In contrast to the proficiency test, an aptitude test undertakes to determine whether a person has the underlying abilities that are necessary if he or she is to acquire the skills of a job. Taking the example of typing, one might use a test of finger dexterity or speed of tapping to see whether a person is likely to learn quickly the skills of typing and whether the person would be a good candidate for a training program for a job as typist.

In the case of an aptitude test such as this, the evaluation of the test would be primarily empirical, and would be based on studies to determine whether in a substantial group of trainees the scores on the aptitude test were in fact closely related to some criterion measure of progress in the job in question. In the instance of the finger dexterity test, an appropriate criterion measure might be speed of learning how to type or level of proficiency in typing achieved after a standard period of training.

Again, no aptitude test will ever give a perfect prediction of progress of learning a job or of later success in it. All that one asks is that the test enable one to give a better prediction of progress in the training program, or of subsequent job performance, than would be possible without it.

It is my impression that most of the tests used by the New York City Board of Education to qualify individuals for positions in the school system should be thought of primarily as proficiency tests rather than as aptitude tests. That is, they should be viewed as attempts to assess acquired skills that are called for in performance on the job.

To the extent that this is true, evaluation of the tests must be judgmental and must be on evaluation of the relevance to job performance of the skills that are evidenced on the test. Under these circumstances, it is not appropriate to ask for empirical follow-up studies, though without doubt such studies would provide somewhat useful supplementary evidence on the effectiveness of the tests. Basically, one is not looking at the test as an indicator of whether the person will eventually grow into the skills required on the job, but whether he already has certain ones of those skills.

Clearly, any testing program will be incomplete so far as measuring all of the knowledge and skill that a job calls for. This is true because any test is a limited sample of behavior obtained under limited conditions. It is also true that the test is given in relation to a general category of job, such as elementary school principal, and specific positions within that category may well demand aspects of competence that are unique to the specific position. In this sense, a testing program can at best only indicate the possession of certain aspects of job competence and cannot be a complete assessment.

It is easy to criticize as imperfect objective testing devices used for personnel selection or up-grading. They are human instruments and will, inevitably, be less than ideal. Evaluation of existing selection procedures must be made in comparison with available alternatives.

One asks, if the present selection procedures are eliminated, what will take their place. Inevitably, it seems that some type of highly subjective and unguided impressions will be used as a basis for personnel decisions. At the very best, these impressions are likely to be inconsistent and unreliable. A long history of studying personal judgments, letters of recommendation, rating scales, and interviews has repeatedly demonstrated the extent to which these judgments are dependent upon the biases and whimsy of the particular judge.

At the worst, the judgments will become highly partisan and colored by the particular biases (be they political or otherwise) of the persons reporting those judgments. Judgments will be based on evidence having low reliability and questionable validity in relation to the decision to be made.

In acknowledging very real limits in formal testing procedures, I find it hard to be enthusiastic about the alternatives that I see as likely to take their place in a large, involved system like that of the City of New York.

THE CHAIRMAN: Counsel.

MR. TRACTENBERG: Dr. Thorndike, a couple of questions, if I may.

In your judgment, is it possible to design an aptitude test which could be used for teaching or supervisory personnel?

DR. THORNDIKE: You're saying an aptitude test?

MR. TRACTENBERG: Predictive test.

DR. THORNDIKE: That would identify the person's likelihood of acquiring and learning the skills and competencies that eventually would make him a good teacher or supervisor?

MR. TRACTENBERG: That's right.

DR. THORNDIKE: Obviously, this is not something which is answerable with yes or no. I think one could develop tests which would be better than chance, but I doubt they would predict very accurately and very precisely.

MR. TRACTENBERG: I understood you to say that you thought predictive validity studies would be pertinent to a determination of the adequacy even of a proficiency test. Is that right?

DR. THORNDIKE: I think they would have some supplementary relevance, yes. I think the primary consideration is the extent to which the test and tasks in it represent significant aspects of the job or job duties.

MR. TRACTENBERG: I would like, if I may, to read you a brief statement from another expert that the Board of Examiners has used. I think you may be saying the same thing. I want to make sure of it.

He said that "the approach used by the Board of Examiners in determining the validity or relevance of its tests consists essentially of a strategy which relies on the judgment of experts and consensus among them as to what constitutes an appropriate test item.

"The level of validity that may be achieved in this regard is implicit in the procedures used for developing the tests, that is, starting with a series of job specifications and assigning expert practitioners the task of writing appropriate items, but it is limited to the validity of the best guess of experts.

"Without studies of predictive validity, that is, assessments as to how well the tests select individuals who function successfully on the job, the very assumptions as to what constitutes expertise in any given field cannot be fully tested."

Is that essentially the position that you have stated, predictive validity would be necessary for a full establishment of the procedures?

DR. THORNDIKE: If I understand it, what this person is saying is it's not as easy to say what is required to be a good school principal as it is to say what's required to be a good typist, that the consensus would be fairly clear and unequivocal in the case of the typist, but there would be a good deal of disagreement as to what particular skills were essential in the competency of a school principal.

I suspect this is probably true, and the judgment on which the test content would be made would probably be more open to question in the more involved and intangible job in the schools than in the rather simple case I chose for my illustration.

MR. TRACTENBERG: Would that make it all the more important to use some kind of predictive validity study in this more complex situation?

DR. THORNDIKE: I'm not sure whether it makes it more important. It makes it at the same time more difficult because, just as it is difficult to agree in advance as to what skills are essential to the job of a principal, it will be comparably difficult to agree after the fact as to who is, in fact, a superior principal and who is not.

MR. TRACTENBERG: I understand the Philadelphia school system has just begun a predictive validity study which consists of hiring some 200 people who fell below their traditional eligibility line. They will be placed in teaching positions and followed through some kind of observation system. In that way the Philadelphia school system hopes to get at the question of predictive validity of teacher exams.

Is that a basic or fundamental kind of approach to establishing predictive validity?

DR. THORNDIKE: I'm not acquainted with the particular study. Given they can find an adequate solution to the problem of assessing which of the people do, in fact, become good teachers, this would certainly be an appropriate enterprise.

MR. TRACTENBERG: Let's turn for a moment, if we may, to the kind of tests the Board of Examiners now gives, that is, proficiency tests, and the way they apparently have sought to validate these tests. I understand that they have never conducted a predictive validity study of the teacher exams, so such studies as they have must be of the content validation kind.

Isn't it true there are really two important ingredients to determine the content validity of a test; number one, the adequacy and completeness of the underlying job description, and number two, the expertise of the people who decide which job tasks should be tested and then actually construct the particular questions?

DR. THORNDIKE: Yes, I would agree those would be the two main aspects of producing a valid proficiency test, yes.

MR. TRACTENBERG: We've heard in earlier testimony from an official of the Board of Education, the Deputy Superintendent for Personnel, who agreed he had the responsibility for preparing job descriptions, that, as to teachers, insofar as he knows, in the five and a half years he served in that position, there had been no updating of the job description.

The Board of Examiners says that it has sought to do some upgrading of its own, although it agrees this is not technically under its province.

Assuming the only official job description is at least five and a half years old, would you find that a sound basis upon which to construct an exam?

DR. THORNDIKE: Frankly, I don't know how much the job of teacher in the New York City schools has changed in five and a half years so I don't really feel qualified to express an opinion on that.

MR. TRACTENBERG: Assuming it has changed, it--

DR. THORNDIKE: Assuming the job has substantially changed, if the description refers to a previous job which is obsolete, it would not be very useful.

MR. TRACTENBERG: The other facet of content validity is the expertness of those who select tasks and actually construct the questions.

In your judgment, should those people, or some of them, have psychological, personnel, or psychometric skills to qualify them as experts in this task?

DR. THORNDIKE: I think the skills of preparing good test questions are, let's say, more an art than a science.

They certainly could appropriately and desirably have had practical experience and guidance and supervision by persons with a flair for this kind of composition to help in the preparation of the test materials.

MR. TRACTENBERG: Could you define, if you were asked, the kinds of background or qualifications that people who might be sufficiently expert to design content validity tests ought to have?

I gather it is difficult if you say it is an art and not a science. But if you were asked to undertake such a project, do you think you could, in effect, establish a job description for people who are going to construct these examinations?

DR. THORNDIKE: There is always a problem of getting the appropriate blend of expertise in the particular job and detailed knowledge about the job in question that makes one able to pick out tasks and situations that are really appropriate and highly germane to the job, and the type of editorial skills that enable one to phrase those in good test tasks. In the making of tests, this kind of cooperation between the expert of the subject matter and the person with a flair for the editorial aspect of it is one of the continuing problems.

Ordinarily these two kinds of skills don't exist in one person, so there is usually a collaboration and team effort.

MR. TRACTENBERG: You would then, if I understand you correctly, not be comfortable if the sole expertise available in the construction of these exams was on-the-job expertise, that is, if the people who were constructing the exams had only expertise based on first-hand knowledge, either from doing the job or supervising those doing the job?

DR. THORNDIKE: I would say this is only one-half of the kind of competence that would be needed on the team that was going to do the job.

MR. TRACTENBERG: As you may not know, we were advised yesterday by a representative of the Board of Examiners that there are no job descriptions for the examination assistants who play a substantial role, if not the principal role, in the construction of the exams, that the process by which these people are employed is a rather informal process of recommendation, that he couldn't give me any statistics about the number of people who have been screened out for somehow not meeting whatever standards were applied, that these standards are not written.

Would that tend to make you uncomfortable about the level of expertise of these people?

DR. THORNDIKE: The hypothetical situation, as you describe it to me, I think would tend to make me uncomfortable. I have no personal knowledge.

MR. TRACTENBERG: The hypothetical situation is a real situation, at least with the Board of Examiners.

MR. DAVID: Even if the job duties of teachers may not have changed in the last five or ten years, would you assume that a marked change in the racial composition in the student body would require a new job description and type of measurement?

DR. THORNDIKE: I think the five-year span is a narrow, narrow span.

Certainly the problems of teaching in the New York City schools in a 30-year span have very markedly changed.

THE CHAIRMAN: Thank you very much, Dr. Thorndike.

Dr. Richard Barrett, Office of Admissions Services, City University of New York.

DR. BARRETT: My name is Richard Barrett. I am currently employed at City University. My experience comes primarily from having been on the faculty at New York University for seven years, during which time I conducted courses in testing and consulted with various companies in the New York City area on their selection problems.

During this time I became interested in the possibility that our procedures, which seem to work to a greater or less degree with the kind of applicants we've been used to, might work unfairly toward minority groups, in this particular case toward Negroes. So I applied for and received a grant from the Ford Foundation and became the principal investigator of a study which resulted in a book entitled <u>Testing and Fair Employment</u>, in which we show there are no simple panaceas for the problem of using tests to select personnel so that we will be sure to be fair to everyone who is an applicant.

I plan in my discussion to give you a very short course in selection psychology and then compare the content of this course with some of the procedures of the Board of Examiners. Since a course of this nature can easily take a semester, there are many pieces that will be left out.

The first and, I think, most crucial step in developing a selection procedure is the job description. The job description should tell what a person does, why he does it, how he does it, what skills are involved, what kind of performance is likely to lead to success, what kind of performance is likely to lead to failure. Once there is a good job description, and this could take months for a complicated job such as that of a principal, the description will serve as a guide in the development of the rest of the selection procedures.

You may note I'm not using the word "tests" because I mean to include, in addition to tests, application blanks, observations of performance, interviews, and other selection devices.

When a selection procedure is being developed, the point of view that should be paramount in the mind of the person who is developing the procedure is that it should distinguish between those who are successes and those who are failures, and that the key answer to a test should at least seem to be consistent with the performance of those who are good on a job and inconsistent with those who are bad.

Once a test has been developed, it should be tried out and validated in some of the ways Professor Thorndike has mentioned.

But there is one point that is crucial, often overlooked in the discussion of tests. Not only should a test be valid for the selection of the people who are candidates, it must also provide a cutoff score which is realistic. We talk of selection tests. We really should talk of rejection tests. The tests are much better at saying who will not succeed than in saying who will. For this reason it is often possible to lower the cutoff score without removing too many successful candidates, but still maintaining a discrimination between those who will succeed and those who will obviously fail.

What I would like to do is to contrast this brief description of some of the salient points of selection with some of the procedures of the Board of Examiners that I have encountered in some of my work.

Let me read for you, for example, some of the items that have to do with a high school principal's work. One item is "to work to build and maintain high teacher morale." That is the end of the statement.

As it stands there, it is simply a platitude. Everybody wants high morale of the people that work for him. Everybody agrees, although there sometimes isn't proof of it, that high morale yields high production.

To exploit that one item means to find out what principals do to build morale, how morale is important to the children, what principals may do to lead to low morale, and what are the consequences of low morale, how much do high and low morale depend on things the principal has no direct control of.

In other words, this is the skeleton of a job description that does not give the kind of information that is useful for a person who is going to develop a test.

Let me just read three more as illustrations.

"To provide and supervise special programs for children in need of remedial reading, speech correction, et cetera."

"To organize and administer a modern audio-visual program."

"To organize and administer a co-curricular and extra-curricular activities program."

A person can make a career out of any one of those three statements and there is not enough flesh on the bones for a reader to understand what goes on.

The problem that comes up first, if we don't have an adequate job description, is that the person who is developing and scoring the tests, interviewing people, or giving them an observation, must then fall back on his experience. This means we have some senior person who has been in the system for a long time, whose experience is rapidly becoming out-of-date as circumstances change, who has probably had a very limited experience. In a system of 900 schools, he cannot have seen all of it. He falls back on his own experience and tends to perpetuate the conventional wisdom of the existing establishment. It is difficult for him to conceive of procedures that are going to allow for a change of any kind, particularly the kind of change that has to do with different kinds of people coming into the kind of job that he has been used to.

I said earlier that one of the important features of good development of selection procedures is that the right answer should be characteristic of the better performers and the wrong answer characteristic of poor performers.

Let me read to you excerpts from the directions for formulating standard answers and rating directions of the board of Education.

"1) First, give the matter of the appropriate answer some thought and study. Consult authorities. Make notes and lay out the general plan of the standard answer and rating directions.

"2) Then read through a representative sampling of answers, no less than 25, if possible. Draw up a tentative standard answer with rating directions, bearing in mind the applicability of your standards to the answers read."

I'll skip to "4."

"If you are one of a pair or committee of raters rating the same questions, confer with your co-workers before undertaking the rating itself. Compare notes with them as to standard answers and rating directions. Reconcile differences and arrive at a tentative agreement."

I can't read the whole thing, but I assure you there is not one word in it about what kind of answers are characteristic of people who perform well on the job. What it does, in fact, is not even put the development of the answers in the hands of the so-called experts who are doing the rating. It puts a large measure of the determination of the answer in the hands of the candidates who are taking the tests themselves because very directly it says what you do is read a bunch of examples, pick out good ideas from these examples, write them down, get a list of them, and use this as a way of scoring the examination. It is totally irrelevant to the need to develop people who are going to perform in certain ways.

I have heard many of these tests defended by principals in the school system by saying they're practical. When you read one of the test's items, it sounds like an expanded letter to Dear Abby or Ann Landers. They say this means a person who can answer it is going to be a good principal.

I submit this could be called the school marm's fallacy. There is a great difference between being able to write something and doing it. There is a difference between talking about doing something and actually going out and doing it.

Professor Thorndike called these proficiency tests, I immediately categorize this kind of question as an aptitude test because the principal's job is not to answer questions about what to do under these circumstances. His job is to do these things. It remains to be proven that being able to write answers to these questions is in fact related to performance on the job.

Another kind of selection device that is used is the interview. I have before me the interview test rating sheet which contains 21 items to be rated. The first four I shall read to you, all in the category of speech:

"1) Language usage and diction.
"2) Clearness and fluency of expression.
"3) Enunciation and pronunciation.
"4) Voice quality and inflection."

It is quite clear in the instructions that, although these four make up some 17% of the total ratings, they may be larger or less large than 17%. The person is not instructed to add up the rating in any direct way.

I submit there is a body of opinion that says that right now for people to communicate in the ghetto schools it is very desirable they be able to speak in the patois that may be current, whether the students are Black, Puerto Rican, or from other ethnic groups. It is quite apparent from the rise of community school boards and community interests, that there is some virtue in being able to talk to people in their own language. In fact, the diction of the proper Bostonian may be a drawback rather than an asset.

I would like to tell you about the experience of a friend of mine in the oral examination. He himself was somewhat of a Latin scholar, and knowing that one of the examiners was a thoroughgoing Latin scholar, he did all he could to avoid him and wound up being asked the derivation of a number of words. He couldn't answer the questions, and finally he said to the examiner that he thought the questions were trivial and asked him if he knew the derivation of that word.

It turned out the examiner did not, but he said, "Young man, I'm going to pass you because I like the way you stood up to me."

I think this might look good for a well-dressed white applicant, but the same kind of behavior, I suggest, might be considered to be overly aggressive on the part of a Black applicant. This kind of capriciousness leaves the door wide open to the expression of every individual prejudice that exists.

A large part of the tests that have been used, and I don't know if they still are, has to do with general knowledge, typically multiple-choice questions. These questions, I think, undoubtedly merit predictive validity. It is not part of one's job as a principal to define terms and so forth. Granted, he needs to have some minimum knowledge of what's going on in the academic area of the school, but we don't know what level of aptitude is required, nor do we know which areas are most crucial.

In looking over one of the examinations, I uncovered a number of words that seemed to me did not have a direct and obvious relation to the running of the school. For example,"sumptuary," "congeries," "beadle," and "plethoric." My favorite word is "amice." I have tested my friends at cocktail parties and other places and only one of them, who was formerly a priest, knew what it was. It is a vestment which is worn under the alb and crucifix. Clearly, this is a difficult item and there are other difficult items in the whole system.

Professor Irving Katz, who was a professor at New York University, did a study of testing behavior of minority groups.

He would have one situation in which there was one Black person taking a test and all the rest were white or the examiner was white. In other circumstances one Black person would have other Black persons in the room either as a tester or other examinees. He would also tell them that this was a hard test and very few people do well, or he would tell them this is an easy test and besides it doesn't make any difference.

The generalization that came out of this study is that threat had a more harmful effect on the Black persons taking the test than it did on the whites.

I have talked to various principals about how this testing procedure works, and it is loaded with threat. There are cram courses they take. Not only that, they meet and test each other. They practice writing out tests. One told me he even learned to use the abbreviation "T" for teacher so he could get that many more words down in the allotted time.

I suggest if Professor Katz' generalization is true, that threat has a more harmful effect on the Black candidates than on the white candidates, this whole system is going to discriminate against those people who will take the test poorly regardless how well they would have done on the job.

One other point I would like to make. I am not speaking about an empty academic exercise. Standard Oil of New Jersey was able to predict the success of executives by the means of tests. Robert Holt was able to predict the success of psychiatrists by taking tests. The Life Insurance Agency for Management Association has been able for years to select life insurance agents by the use of tests. It is possible to validate tests against performance.

I submit that in a school system where we have 900 schools, where we have 700 people as elementary school principals, there is an unparalleled opportunity to validate tests against performance in high level positions.

I would like also to suggest that merely putting aside one dollar for each student in school for a year, to study the possibility of producing valid tests, would be one of the wisest ways in which new money could be expended by the Board of Education.

THE CHAIRMAN: Counsellor.

MR. TRACTENBERG: I just have a few questions, Dr. Barrett.

If I understand you correctly, your questions about the validity of the examination process, to the extent you have had an opportunity to observe it here in New York City, go well beyond its discriminatory impact on minority groups.

That is, you question the underlying validity for separating out a good white candidate from a less good white candidate.

DR. BARRETT: It has many, many features in it which I think all lead toward slow change. When change is accelerating, the procedure should have a built-in mechanism to update itself. Otherwise, it is bound to become disfunctional.

MR. TRACTENBERG: I gather it is fair to say the likely impact on minority group applicants or any who are different from the prevailing pattern is going to be even more substantial if the test isn't job-related.

DR. BARRETT: Yes. As the candidates change, as the meanings of the positions change, as the impact of the community changes, anything that fails to change makes it harder on those who are going to be part of the change, certainly.

MR. TRACTENBERG: Just one final thing.

You touched on an area which I think is of great importance and about which we have not heard all that much. That is the area of the oral interview.

Is it fair to say, first of all, that an examination process is only as valid or as good as its weakest link?

DR. BARRETT: Well, that requires a fairly technical answer. I wouldn't put it quite that way, but if you are going to eliminate people by means of any procedure, such as the interview, and that interview has no validity or at worst has negative validity, moving out the good people, it detracts from the total quality of the selection process.

MR. TRACTENBERG: We have heard testimony--I don't think you were present for either of them--from two people who ultimately were licensed in the New York City system, but who failed the examination on one or more occasion because of the oral interview. In one case, it was because of traceable foreignisms in speech, and in the other, strangely enough, too much of a New York accent.

I gather that experience would not be atypical so far as your own observations and contacts suggest.

DR. BARRETT: The oral interview is generally one of the worst parts of the selection procedure. There are too many anecdotes about the greasy palm test. The interviewer shakes hands with a candidate. If the hand is greasy, the candidate is nervous and he is not to be considered further. It leads to the most rampant kind of individual prejudice.

I was told by a psychologist who worked for one of the largest employers that they checked the records of two of their college recruiters. He said one had a brilliant war record and the other a brilliant athletic record. The one who had a brilliant war record recruited more people than the other who had a brilliant athletic record.

MR. TRACTENBERG: Do you also share the disquiet which Dr. Thorndike expressed when I described the testimony of the Board of Examiners about how examination assistants are selected? Is this a crucial element in the over-all picture?

DR. BARRETT: I get the impression it is really a part-time job for a fairly few people who are selected by not very thorough means.

Again, all it is likely to do is to perpetuate the conventional wisdom, and that is going to exclude minority groups.

MR. TRACTENBERG: Do you have any sense, based on such knowledge of New York City as you have acquired, about how a more rational testing system might be developed here?

DR. BARRETT: That would be the subject of the three-hour

graduate course I ran through in three minutes. Job descriptions, building and trying out tests, refining the tests, discarding half or more of the tests, probably.

If there are going to be tests, have one actual job performance, such as the observation of an assistant principal acting as principal, making sure the people who do the observations record the important events.

Principals complain to me that when someone comes out for an evaluation they pay more attention to the quality of the files than the quality of the education. You can observe somebody doing something on the job very really but trivially.

MR. TRACTENBERG: Does a test, in your judgment, necessarily apply to a written, sit-down, pencil and paper test? Do you think it is possible to provide a valid examination process for teachers and supervisors which would not involve a written test?

DR. BARRETT: I carefully tried to use the word "selection procedure" except when I was referring specifically to tests.

I think there are many valid selection procedures. An evaluation of one's background, done carefully and systematically, can be a valid predictor. The interview, well done, can be a valid predictor.

There are all kinds of tests that are situational sort of tests. Many people have heard of the in-basket test. A person is given what purports to be an in-basket full of material he has to deal with in a short period of time. This is not the traditional paper and pencil test. This test seems to have some merit. It has been used in schools.

There are many different ways to select people, and I would like to keep all options open until we see which ones work and then use them.

MR. TRACTENBERG: Thank you.

THE CHAIRMAN: I will call Dr. James R. Deneen, Senior Program Director for Teacher Examinations, Educational Testing Service.

DR. DENEEN: Mrs. Chairman, I offer copies of my testimony, if you would like them.

THE CHAIRMAN: Yes.

Will you see that these copies are distributed.

Dr. James R. Deneen.

DR. DENEEN: Madam Chairman, my name is James R. Deneen. I am Senior Program Director for Teacher Examinations at the Educational Testing Service.

I have been asked to testify on three points, the validity of tests for selecting teachers, the uses and limitations of the National Teacher Examinations, which I will refer to hereafter as the "NTE," and the specific uses of the NTE authorized by the 1969 New York State School Decentralization Law.

By now the Commission has probably heard more than it cared to learn about the concept of test validity, but to assure common usage, I will briefly state that a test possesses validity to the extent that it measures what it claims to measure.

For the purposes of this testimony, two major kinds of

validity can be mentioned. One is content validity. This considers whether or not, in terms of topics and processes, a test item's content corresponds to the area it purports to cover.

A test maker seeking content validity for a standardized examination would consider such sources as widely used textbooks in the field, state and local courses of study, standards of accrediting and evaluation agencies, committees of representative teachers and supervisors, and special study commission reports.

Our second major interest is predictive validity. As the phrase indicates, predictive validity refers to the validity of a test to predict a given criterion, that is, a generally agreed upon standard of performance or achievement. The process of comparing the predictor with a criterion sounds deceptively simple. In fact, the problem of selecting an objective and stable criterion can be an exceedingly difficult one.

When the criterion lends itself fairly well to quantification, as, for example, grade point average in a given college, the predictive value of an examination like the Scholastic Aptitude Test of the College Boards is more readily established. But when the criterion is a complex of performance, whose determination involves highly subjective and often ill-defined judgments, for example, success as a lawyer, a nurse, or a teacher, then the professions tend to examine candidates for entry on the basis of knowledge gained in preparation programs.

Such examinations can possess content validity through the use of the sources above, but it is reasonable to ask what value they have in terms of prediction, particularly since the graduates of such programs have usually been granted some kind of state certificate or license. More specifically, what can a test that is properly content validated contribute to knowledge about and selection of teachers who are graduates of approved teacher training programs and are certified to teach?

One who is certified to teach is differentiated from the general population through having been exposed to certain courses in general education, professional education, and a teaching area specialty. The range of knowledge within this group is truly startling, as is the range of college standards and grading practices.

In New York City a sample of graduating seniors taking the National Teacher Examinations shows scores from the first to the 99th percentile range in terms of national norms.

Typically, the average score by college is notably higher for New York City and State than most other areas of the nation. In accepting certified teachers from other states, however, it would be possible for New York to receive students from teacher training institutions with average scores in the first percentile range on national norms, that is, on the National Teacher Examinations.

Thus, someone who is responsible for selecting teachers would learn something about the training of an applicant from the fact that he is certified, still more if he viewed the applicant's college grade point average, and still more from his performance on a standard test.

If it can be granted that a test yields additional information about an applicant's knowledge, how is this information useful in the selection of that individual for teaching?

Unless one is prepared to write off college learning as totally irrelevant to teaching, it seems that measures of that learning should contribute something to the teacher's selection process. To evaluate, for example, a prospective high school mathematics teacher's knowledge of math is surely reasonable, but to predict his overall performance as a mathematics teacher on the basis of a test score alone is not reasonable, nor would it be reasonable to make such a total prediction on the basis of any single criterion we now know, be it grade point average, teacher's certificate, oral interview, or receipt of references.

The process of predicting human behavior is inherently prone to error, and yet predictions in the sense of selecting one person over another to perform a given task can hardly be avoided. Some sort of standard will have to be used to select teachers at least if there are more applicants than there are positions.

An answer, one answer, to this problem is to recognize that selection of teachers will indeed take place on some bases, and these bases may be college degrees, test scores, personal friendship, appearance, and so on. The instrument that is used to determine them may be such devices as written tests, oral interviews or simply drawing names out of a hat. In regard to teaching, some of these appear at least somewhat more relevant than others. The most objective, the most helpful of them are still partial and fallible bases for decision, but they do advance the quality of these decisions to some extent.

Inability of educational research thus far to devise a predictor of teacher effectiveness cannot be attributed solely to a lack of effort. Very few researchers today speak about good teaching as though it were a single concept. Attempts to analyze the impact of different teaching styles on students with varying characteristics under diverse teaching conditions seem likely to prove helpful. The efforts of educational researchers to develop performance criteria, that is, measures of demonstrated teaching abilities encourage us to look for stable and practical measures within the next few years. They do not as yet exist.

Hopefully, these can be made feasible for selecting beginning teachers as well as evaluating those who are in service. And when they are joined to measures of teaching area knowledge, as well as formal and informal judgments of teachers' behavior by administrators, students, and others, these performance criteria should assist in substantially upgrading the quality of teaching.

The question of a test's validity is often raised in relation to its appropriateness for minority groups. The prevalence of low test scores within a given population may be an indication that the test is unfair for that population. Persons with little or no facility in English, for example, could not be adequately examined for their knowledge or professional education by an examination that was written entirely in English.

Low test scores in a given group, however, are not necessarily an indicator of poor test construction. The National Teacher

Examinations, for example, validly reflect the content common to undergraduate programs of teacher education. NTE scores of students in predominantly Black institutions of the South are notably lower than those of students in predominantly white-attended institutions of the same area. In fact, the test scores attest not to differential ability but to the often separate and almost invariably unequal education that is offered to Blacks and whites in this country.

This disparity of educational opportunity extends back through the college to the secondary school to the elementary school. We should expect valid educational measurement to reflect deprivation. Thus, test results may be a messenger of bad news to society and to individuals, and that role has never been a very popular one. Yet it seems wiser to heed the message than to kill the messenger.

The National Teacher Examinations were initiated in 1940 at the request of a number of school system superintendents who wanted a common measure of the academic accomplishment of teacher applicants.

The tests are designed primarily for the college senior level and are organized into twenty-four individual teaching area examinations, which evaluate the prospective teacher's preparation in specific subject fields, and a battery of common examinations.

The latter are designed to measure knowledge expected of every teacher. This knowledge embraces what teacher-training programs refer to as general education and professional education. It is evident from this description that the NTE are achievement tests which directly reflect college training and only indirectly can be used to predict teaching success.

If an agreement can be reached that knowledge of general and professional education and a teaching specialization are of value in the practice of teaching, then the tests may be determined partial and yet rather important predictors of teaching competence. Precisely because teaching competence cannot be predicted on the basis of college achievement alone, measures of such achievement should never be the only criteria for selection of beginning teachers.

Dr. Thorndike testified a few moments ago on the example, a relatively simple one in his terms, of selecting a secretary on the basis of performance on a typing test. And this is somewhat analogous.

Additional information from college grades and practice teaching records, references, and oral interviews can be weighed along with--I particularly wish to emphasize this--along with the special teaching needs of a given school district or school population.

Presently the most relevant but not, alas, very reliable way to measure your experienced teachers is by supervisors' ratings of their performance, since, finally, what a teacher does with his knowledge is the definition of his competence.

The chief value of the NTE, then, is that they supplement and to some extent standardize the academic records of a prospective teacher. The examinations help answer the question: What does the teacher candidate know?

In 1969, the New York Legislature authorized district boards in New York City to employ the NTE under certain circumstances, as an alternate to the qualifying examinations conducted by the New York City Board of Examiners.

The law requires that the teacher candidates who wish to qualify through the NTE must have, and i quote the law, "passed the National Teacher Examinations within the past four years at a pass mark equivalent to the average pass mark required of teachers during the prior year by the five largest cities in the United States which use the National Teacher Examinations as a qualification as determined by the Chancellor."

In fact, city school systems which employ the NTE as a factor in teacher selection do not have a minimum score, although some use a minimum on one part of the tests only. Probably--and this is my own guess--the resolution of the problem will result in a pass score on the NTE for New York City of around 1000 on the combined common and teaching area examinations. On the basis of the national norm, this score would place a candidate somewhere between the fourth and fifteenth national percentile rank, depending on his teaching area specialty.

For several years teacher candidates in certain instructional fields have had the option of taking the NTE instead of the New York City Board of Examiners' test. The pass score requirement places candidates between the seven and eighteen percentile rank on a national norm.

Last year some 2,300 teacher candidates for the New York City school system chose the NTE alternate battery of tests.

I will summarize my remarks this way:

First, examinations for teachers can possess content validity, the content in question being the information offered in teacher-training programs throughout the nation.

Second, these content validated tests can be predictive to the extent that competent performance requires the kind of knowledge gained in teacher training programs.

The National Teacher Examinations is a battery of tests which describe on a standard score scale teacher preparation in general education, professional education, and subject area specialization.

Results from the NTE say nothing about other factors which are absolutely critical to success in teaching, for example, physical skills, motivation, attitudes, ability to communicate with children, and so on. The NTE should thus be used as one of several criteria. In the selection of beginning teachers, the test results deserve consideration along with other objective criteria and on-the-job performance evaluations.

Finally, certain tests of the NTE have been used for several years as an alternate to the Board of Examiners tests. Under New York State law, this use may be expanded to permit local boards to hire teachers for schools with low reading scores.

MR. TRACTENBERG: Dr. Deneen, I have a number of questions.

Approximately how many school districts now use the NTE as part of their battery for selection of teachers?

DR. DENEEN: There are four states which use it throughout the entire state, so you have got to start with that many school districts.

MR. TRACTENBERG: Are any of them states that have large urban school districts?

DR. DENEEN: One of them, for example, is Texas, which does indeed have several large urban districts. Beyond that, I believe there are some eleven hundred--I'm really not sure--but I believe it is about eleven hundred school districts outside of these states.

MR. TRACTENBERG: And this includes some of the larger school districts?

DR. DENEEN: It does, indeed; yes.

MR. TRACTENBERG: How broadly is the examination offered? Is it given in testing centers around the country?

DR. DENEEN: It is administered four times a year in established test centers throughout the country. There are some four hundred such centers.

MR. TRACTENBERG: And approximately how many, or what percentage of the graduating class each year would tend to take this examination as a matter of course?

DR. DENEEN: About 40 to 45 per cent of all graduates of teacher training institutions.

MR. TRACTENBERG: So that would be a rather substantial number, a hundred thousand?

DR. DENEEN: About 120,000.

MR. TRACTENBERG: How much does the test cost? Is there a fee charged?

DR. DENEEN: Yes, indeed.

MR. TRACTENBERG: I assumed there was.

DR. DENEEN: The fees for each examination, or each of the two major parts of the exam are nine and ten dollars, respectively. The combined costs $15. Most candidates take the combined exam. This is the common examination and a teaching area specialty.

MR. TRACTENBERG: Do school districts ever assume the cost of the examination?

DR. DENEEN: Some school districts do, especially for those whom they ultimately hire. Most school districts require the candidate to bear the cost.

MR. TRACTENBERG: In New York City, as you may know, some 65 per cent of the teachers employed every year come from the City University system.

In your judgment, would it be possible to short-circuit the written examination route if reasonable and adequate evaluations could be carried out of the kind of teacher training program being offered in the City University? That is, could the kind of competency that your examinations test be assessed by actual evaluation of the City University program?

I am not sure whether you were here, but I think Dr. Weber,

who is associated with City College in its teacher training program, suggested that from her perspective, at least, she thought it might be possible for the Board of Education to do so.

DR. DENEEN: It is difficult to comment because I think you have indeed a specific example in mind which I'm not familiar with.

A good teacher training program, which has itself been solidly validated would provide an enormous help to anyone who is hiring teachers. You would know that the people who had gone through it had been exposed to certain kinds of good, valid training for teaching.

The problem we see in running teacher examinations is that colleges are rather generous in whom they graduate. I can't speak for the program you have in mind, but the range of abilities demonstrated by graduates of teacher training programs is, as I mentioned in testimony, rather startling.

MR. TRACTENBERG: Of course, it is possible that other components of this battery of selection mechanisms might get at incompetency or inadequacies as well as the written tests.

DR. DENEEN: If you are asking can the institutions do the selection, there is no question they can, certainly.

MR. TRACTENBERG: I gather that at City University there is a pre-screening, that is, a written test to establish English competency and certain basic knowledge. Would that in any way change your reaction? Again, I realize you don't know the specifics.

DR. DENEEN: No, I don't. What does it do to people who have modest English fluency? Against the problem of validating, against the need of the school system, this is important.

I am not challenging the City University system, but when you say there is a major component, a written English ability test, I'm wondering what you're doing then to help certain candidates with it.

MR. TRACTENBERG: Since you raise this, is there any version of the NTE which could adequately test candidates for bilingual teaching positions?

DR. DENEEN: No. We are talking with people about a Spanish version. That is not even quite correct. It is a different test, a test for two groups, for people who simply are more comfortable taking a test in Spanish than in English; and, secondly, for people whose preparation programs are very valid for teaching, for example, Puerto Rican immigrants in this country, but whose preparation programs, say, were taken in Puerto Rico. Our examinations would not be valid tests for these people.

MR. TRACTENBERG: So, presumably--and again I know you don't have any detailed knowledge of what the New York City Board of Examiners tests are like--any test constructed to evaluate United States teacher training, in your judgment, would not be valid to test the level of competence or basic knowledge of someone who was trained in a different tradition?

DR. DENEEN: No, your content validity would be severely compromised.

MR. TRACTENBERG: You have mentioned the desirability as well as the difficulty of predictive validity. Have any tests been carried out of the National Teacher Exam in terms of its predictive validity?

DR. DENEEN: Yes, we've had a few. I guess we're more suspicious than anyone else is of such tests. We disavow, very much, helpful predictive validity. Bear with me, please, while I explain that statement.

Let's start with a pupil. That's the place to begin. Children in school require certain kinds of help. They require help in a cognitive domain. They require it in an affective domain, and they require it in a social domain, in a physical domain, and there may indeed be others one could add.

If teachers are going to meet the needs of these kids, then their competencies must relate to these needs the kids have. So far, the only tests we have, and the only tests we know of which have very much reliability and validity are tests of the cognitive domain only. And that's why we are very hesitant.

I could design a study which would prove the NTE is a good predictive instrument for teaching performance, but it would not really be a good study, because I would design it so that the qualities I am getting at in the teaching situation would all be cognitive ones. Then our example would be very valid and show a terrific predictive validity, probably, but that would not predict, really, teaching performance. That would predict only one part of what a teacher should be in order to correspond with pupil needs.

I am sorry for the long-winded answer, but there have been studies which use the NTE to predict teaching performance as rated by supervisors. Some of them show a rather high correlation between NTE scores and supervisory ratings. We really do not think those are worth a great deal.

MR. TRACTENBERG: But it is possible to construct such a study?

DR. DENEEN: Yes, for predicting that which the examination fully examines.

MR. TRACTENBERG: Dr. Deneen, could you tell me in general the kind of staff that makes up the National Teacher Exam and revises it, the kind of expertise that is involved in this effort?

DR. DENEEN: I think I would divide it into two groups of people.

One is the people who are ETS, Educational Testing Service, itself. These are people like myself whose main task is to relate what is going on in education to the whole process of our company, that is, producing examinations, doing research, and so on. In other words, we try to keep our research people realistic. At ETS we also have a very large group of people who are psychometricians, people who are trained in testing measurements. That is one group.

The second group, when we come to construct an examination, is made up of people who are outside of ETS and indeed of no relation to ETS, and who are, by the best judgment we can make and others who advise us can make, the most knowledgeable persons in the field in which we are trying to construct a test.

We ask a committee of those persons to come to ETS, or we go to them, and they tell us what the domain is which is to be tested. They give us what we call specifications for the examination. They tell us what is to be tested, and how it is tested, that is, what things that you can observe would demonstrate that the qualities you are looking for are actually present in the person.

MR. TRACTENBERG: On that point, did you have any reaction to Dr. Barrett's brief description of the kind of job statement that is the basis for one of the New York City tests?

DR. DENEEN: We are talking about very much the same thing, yes.

MR. TRACTENBERG: In more detail? His criticism of it was that it made a rather general and broad statement of a particular facet of the principal's responsibility, and his judgment was that that was an inadequate basis on which to construct test questions.

DR. DENEEN: I may have answered your last question too quickly. I heard him describe what is needed to construct the test, that is, you must do a job performance evaluation, and I agree with that completely. I did not catch the reference directly to the Board of Examiners.

MR. TRACTENBERG: If I recall, he read as one of the statements on the job description for principal, that he has to encourage good morale in the school, and he thought that that was a rather meaningless statement from the point of view of one trying to construct a meaningful examination.

DR. DENEEN: I guess I would call that a goal, but as a goal it doesn't help you much until you specify it into objectives which are subject to some kind of measure.

How are you going to measure that kind of morale construction? You must specify it into observable behavior, or you have no test.

MR. TRACTENBERG: So the kinds of descriptions that you get from your specialists in the field would go well beyond the general statements?

DR. DENEEN: Yes. You cannot write test items on the basis of generalizations. You have to know what behavior you are looking for before you can possibly construct a measure for it.

MR. TRACTENBERG: I may have interrupted you. Were you finished about the personnel?

DR. DENEEN: Yes.

MR. TRACTENBERG: Obviously, from the ETS point of view, your point of view, the input of psychometricians and other experts in test contruction is important or indispensable in the construction of a valid exam?

DR. DENEEN: Yes.

MR. TRACTENBERG: How often is the National Teacher Exam modified? Is there a regular schedule of updating it, or is there some other mechanism by which new demands, particularly the kinds of demands that change the urban teacher's requirements, are reflected in the testing process?

DR. DENEEN: The common examination is updated every year. To be more specific, it is updated twice a year. The teaching area examinations are given minor updating every year, and major, that is, a complete new committee with a complete rewriting of possible specifications, every three to four years, usually every three years.

MR. TRACTENBERG: And have you done anything in the area of testing to try to come to grips with the underlying problems in urban education that are receiving wide publicity?

DR. DENEEN: I think we have. It is hard to know where to start because this occupies so much of our time these days.

One thing we have done, and I hope a very practical thing, is construct a test for teaching in the urban setting. People who advise us, especially Blacks and Puerto Ricans, have told us that our test is, to some extent, a test for suburban teachers. I am speaking now especially about parts of our common examination. We have taken that rather seriously and, under the process I have described of bringing in people who are experts in urban education, we have constructed a test for those who will be teaching in an urban setting. We hope that that test has more relevance to what these people will be doing, as they go into inner city schools.

Our tests have been subject to at least three reviews in the last year by minority group persons. We had a panel of Black educators a year and a half ago, and they cleaned up--I don't think that is too strong a word--some of what they perceived as subtly rascist items in the test.

We are conducting currently two studies in bias. On the tests that I am speaking of, the teaching area tests, is there bias against Blacks or other minority groups contained somewhere in the items in those tests?

I could go on and on. This is a problem of enormous importance to us.

MR. TRACTENBERG: But there is an on-going program, and I gather that you have made significant modifications in the National Teacher Exam as a result of it.

DR. DENEEN: I think that is absolutely correct.

MR. TRACTENBERG: That is all I have.

THE CHAIRMAN: Thank you very much, Dr. Deneen.

I would like to call Mr. Stephen J. Pollak, former Assistant Attorney General in charge of the Civil Rights Division of the Justice Department.

While Mr. Pollak is coming forward, I want to say that as of the end of the workday today, I am closing the Child Care Center for the ironic reason that it has not been used.

It may be that it has not been used because now many are able to hear us over radio, as these hearings are being broadcast live. But I rather suspect from our experience with the women's hearings which we held at the end of September, when our child care facility was little used, that it is not due to the fact that we are able to broadcast these hearings live, but it is due to the fact that in this country women are so unused to the availability of child care facilities that one does not know what to do when one hears that one can bring one's child out and come to a hearing.

One simply doesn't have the wherewithal, the methodology to put together one's self and one's child and come out, because one isn't used to dealing that way. In this country, you have to get a baby-sitter.

We are not going to be discouraged, though. We are going to try to have a child care facility available at each hearing in the hope that it will encourage the more general use of such facilities and thereby also encourage women, who we know earnestly desire such facilities, to change their life style, to the extent that is possible, to bring their children out with them when they go places, rather than relying exclusively on baby-sitters.

I am pleased to welcome Mr. Stephen J. Pollak.

MR. POLLAK: Madam Chairman and members of the Commission, I have a prepared statement, and I am prepared to speak initially from it, or proceed in any other way that is most useful to you.

THE CHAIRMAN: We would like you to speak from it initially, Mr. Pollak, if you would. Then counsel will, perhaps, ask you some questions.

MR. POLLAK: Thank you for inviting me to participate in the Commission's hearings on employment and promotion practices in the New York City public school system and their effect upon minority group professionals.

Following the suggestions of your Executive Director, Mr. Preston David, I will address my testimony to the legal obligations of school boards using standardized tests in the selection of teachers for employment, retention, and promotion.

I will review what school boards considering use of standardized tests as part of their selection processes must do to be certain that a particular test is a valid indicator and is nondiscriminatory.

Along the way, I will touch on a few other points which, I am advised, are of particular interest to you, including ways in which unvalidated tests may discriminate against members of minority groups; remedies courts have fashioned to correct such discrimination; and the characteristics of a legally valid selection process making use of standardized tests.

In the brief time available, I am certain to miss much that may be central to your particular concerns. I invite your questions during my direct testimony and thereafter.

I will turn first to the legal obligations of school boards with respect to the use and validation of standardized tests. My focus here, tailored to my experience, will be upon the nature of the obligations imposed by the United States Constitution and federal laws.

I must leave exploration of the requirements of the New York State Constitution and statutes and any pertinent ordinances of the City of New York to others.

I might add that the scope of these obligations, both state and federal, is at issue in the case of <u>Chance v. Board of Examiners</u>, now pending in the United States District Court for the Southern District of New York. The plaintiffs there are contesting the legality of the examination required by the Board as a precondition to the licensing of teachers for promotion to the position of principal in the city school system. The briefs in the case discuss the relevant laws. I have seen them and I think they would probably make a useful supplement to our record here.

Focusing then on federal law, the legal obligation of school boards with respect to the use and validation of standardized tests arise directly from Section 1 of the Fourteenth Amendment which, as you undoubtedly know, provides: "...nor shall any State deprive any person of life, liberty, or property without due process of law; nor deny to any person within its jurisdiction the equal protection of the laws."

School boards, as well as superintendents, principals, and other officials are arms of the state. Accordingly, they may not exclude any person from practicing his profession "in a manner or for reasons that contravene the Due Process or Equal Protection Clauses of the Fourteenth Amendment."

That is a quote from the U.S. Supreme Court decision in Schware v. Board of Examiners. The conduct of school boards with respect to employment matters must, then, afford due process. That is, it must not be arbitrary, capricious, or unreasonable.

Moreover, it must not deny equal protection of the laws which, since Brown v. Board of Education means that school boards may not discriminate, either directly or indirectly, either ingeniously or ingenuously, on account of race. Other cases, particularly Harper v. Virginia Board of Elections, extend this bar to discrimination on account of economic status.

Use, then, by school boards of standardized tests for the selection of teachers for employment, retention, or promotion must meet these constitutional requirements. There have been relatively few cases in the courts defining the precise limits of these constitutional mandates as they apply to the use of standardized tests by public bodies. However, we can draw from the decided cases a reasonably clear picture of the general outline of school board obligations in this field.

The Supreme Court has ruled that "any qualification must have a rational connection with the applicant's fitness or capacity" to perform an occupation or profession. That ruling was in Schware v. Board of Examiners.

In my judgment, this means that no school board may lawfully use a standardized test as part of its selection process, whether for hiring, retention, or promotion, unless that test is a valid and reliable measure of the candidates' capacity to perform well on the job for which they are under consideration. In fact, United States District Court for the District of Massachusetts has so held, in December of 1969, in the case of Arrington v. Massachusetts Bay Transportation Authority. It ruled there that the Authority denied rights guaranteed by the Fourteenth Amendment when it decided among applicants for drivers and collector positions on the basis of scores from tests which were not job-related.

Throughout my testimony I shall use the term "validation" or "job relation." By those terms, I mean to describe the steps which measurement specialists consider necessary to evaluate the appropriateness of the use of a particular test for the selection of candidates in the specific circumstances where it is to be used.

First, these specialists consider it necessary to evaluate the reliability of the test, meaning the degree to which it consistently measures whatever in fact it does measure, so that if you take it over and over again, the same people will get the same score.

Second, and more importantly, validation expresses the degree to which a test actually measures whatever it is used to measure.

I have been told by several measurement experts that reasonable testing practices generally require that studies be made to demonstrate that an examination to be used for teachers is valid and reliable for that use. Without test validation, and I am using the term to mean both testing its relatedness to the job and its reliability, there can be no assurance that a school board is acting rationally in employment decisions based upon test results.

Thus a typing test, to take a rather far-out example, may be a valid measure of some, but by no means all, of the skills required for candidates for a position as a teacher of typing. It would not be a measure of the skills required of candidates for a position as a teacher of physical education and could be expected to operate unreasonably, that is, to deny due process, if it was so used. For it would exclude good candidates with extensive backgrounds or training in physical education who are unable to type.

The thrust of the due process requirement is simply that school boards must act reasonably. If a board refuses to hire, retain, or promote a teacher because of his score on a test, the board should be able to show that the test is a reliable predictor of the capacity of those taking the test to perform on the job in that system. If the board cannot make this showing, its action, if challenged, will not be sustained.

To fulfill the mandate of the Equal Protection Clause, the standardized test must not burden or benefit candidates because of their race, economic class, or religion. This does not mean that the median score of Black candidates, for example, must be the same as that of white candidates in a particular system, using a particular test. Such scores can and, we know, do differ and will differ. The Constitution requires that the difference, if it is to be given any weight in the selection process, must reflect capacity to perform on the job rather than characteristics based upon race or past discrimination on account of race or class membership.

Let me give an example: In Mississippi studies show that as of now, as a result of past discrimination engaged in by governmental agencies including school boards, 90% of the graduates of Black Mississippi colleges can be expected to score below 1000 on the National Teacher Examinations, while 90% of the graduates of white Mississippi institutions can be expected to score above 1000.

One school board in Mississippi, maybe others, has set 1000

as a mandatory requirement for retention or hiring of teachers. On behalf of Black educators affected by the 1000 cutoff score, I have argued that the cutoff score classified teachers according to race, divided them into racial groupings.

Such racial classification, while not, per se, that is, ipso facto, unlawful, are suspect, as the Supreme Court has indicated in McLaughlin v. Florida and Korematsu v. United States, and other cases. To sustain a racial classification, the state or its agency must show "an overriding purpose independent of invidious racial discrimination which justifies this classification." That is from the case of Loving v. Virginia.

Further, where a test measures only a portion of the qualifications required for successful performance on the job--and that is really true of all tests I know of--and where members of a minority group uniformly score lower on the test, the Equal Protection Clause would preclude a school board from acting solely on the basis of the test.

Thus, the National Teacher Examinations are not designed to measure the capacity of candidates to perform in the classroom. Rather, the NTE is solely a measure of prior academic training.

Since Black teachers, in studies made by the designer of the test, uniformly score below white teachers trained in the Southern states, looking at that region, and since the test does not evaluate candidates' performance in the classroom, or their capacity to teach well--these being crucial issues to be determined--I believe that school boards have an obligation to use other measures of selection wherever they are available, either as substitutes for the NTE or as supplements to it.

Thus, for example, where selection is to be made from among in-service teachers, teachers in the system, the board has available to it direct observations in the classroom which will directly reveal capacity to perform on the job. Even when candidates are from outside the school district, school boards may have an obligation to set up practice teaching situations where candidates can be evaluated on a detailed, objective scale of required competencies by observers drawn from majority and minority groups. The best indication that a teacher can teach well is that he has taught well, and currently no paper and pencil test with which I am familiar measures this, or even is claimed to measure this.

My point is that where a standardized test has not been shown to be substantially related to the requirements for successful performance on the job and where that test disqualifies substantially more Black or minority applicants than white or majority applicants, use of the test is both unreasonable and discriminatory in violation of the Due Process and Equal Protection Clauses. I would read this in the decisions of the district court in the Arrington case, which I mentioned, and of the United States District Court for California in a case called Penn v. Stumpf, a 1970 case.

There is no requirement on plaintiffs to show that the school board has used the test purposefully to discriminate. This issue was recently considered by the United States District Court for the Eastern District of Louisiana, in a quite revealing case on these issues called Hicks v. Crown Zellerbach, an employment case, where the court struck down use of a standardized test that "substantially prefers whites over Negroes." Those were the words of the court.

If you will bear with me, I'd like to quote some of the statements of the court for their relevance to the legal issues that your Commission may wish to be considering. The court said--and I refer to the fact that it struck down the use of this test by Crown Zellerbach Company, and its statements go both to the validation requirements and to the non-discrimination requirement:

"No reason appears why the employer's use of tests should not also be governed by the rule that business necessity"--and we will interpolate "job relatedness or validation"--"must be shown to justify a practice which substantially prefers whites over Negroes.... The choice of appropriate tests for an employer is a difficult procedure requiring careful study and evaluation.

"Without such study, even experienced professional psychologists concede that they can do no more than make guesses which are often completely wrong.

"Moreover, the uncertainty surrounding test use is aggravated when tests are given to a mixed racial group which has been educated in segregated schools because tests assume that persons have had relatively equal exposure to educational materials. This makes careful professional study even more essential in such a situation. Without such study, no employer can have any confidence in the reasonableness or validity of his tests; and he therefore cannot in good faith assert that business necessity demands that these tests of unknown value be used."

That is the end of the court's statement.

A word of clarification may be in order with respect to the bearing of a case pending before the Supreme Court, Griggs v. Duke Power Company, upon the constitutional obligations I have been describing.

The issue in Griggs arises under Title VII of the Civil Rights Act of 1964, which requires private employers to afford equal employment opportunities but allows them "to give and to act upon the results of any professionally developed ability test provided that such test, its administration, or action upon the results is not designed, intended, or used to discriminate."

Those words are quoted from the pertinent section of the statute, Section 703h.

As stated by the Solicitor General of the United States in his brief to the Supreme Court, the Griggs case presents this issue:

"Whether it is unlawful under Title VII of the Civil Rights Act of 1964 for an employer to require completion of high school or passage of certain general intelligence tests as a condition of eligibility for employment in, or transfer to, jobs formerly reserved only for white employees, when:

"One, both requirements operate to disqualify Negroes at a substantially higher rate than whites; and

"Two, neither has been shown to be necessary for successful performance on the job.'

That is, there has been no validation study.

I believe the Supreme Court will conclude in Griggs that the test requirements of the Duke Power Company contravene Title VII. This would be consistent with the reading of the Act by the agency charged with its administration, the Equal Employment Opportunity Commission.

However, should the Supreme Court rule otherwise, I believe its ruling would stem from a reading of the scope of the exception in Section 703h for professionally developed ability tests. As such, such a ruling would not be determinative of the obligations of state agencies under the Fourteenth Amendment. Further, private employers have always had a freer hand in their dealings with employers than the arms of the state, here, the School Board.

I would turn now to discuss briefly what steps a school board is obliged to take in framing or selecting a test to make certain that it is valid and non-discriminatory. This, of course, is more a question for experts in the field of test measurement than attorneys, and in preparing my testimony for today, I have drawn particularly upon the views of your preceding witness, Dr. James R. Deneen, and Dr. Winton H. Manning, who are, respectively, Senior Program Director for Teacher Examination and Vice-President of the Educational Testing Service. These views I refer to were presented before the United States District Court for the Northern District of Mississippi in two pending cases challenging the use being made of the National Teacher Examinations and the Graduate Record Examinations in the selection of elementary and secondary teachers.

First, I do not believe that any school board can select a test out of a catalogue, give it to applicants, and hire or retain or promote those who score above an arbitrary line selected on the basis of national norms. Why not? Because there could be no assurance that the test will select those teachers who will possess the characteristics to meet the needs of the particular system and no assurance that the test will treat all candidates equally regardless of race, economic status, and other class.

Operating in this manner is a violation of the Fourteenth Amendment, giving an aggrieved teacher a cause of action under Section 1983 of the United States Code, and, if successful, the result could be an order barring the use of the test and awarding damages to the teacher.

Measurement experts advise that a program for validation of a test must address the specific conditions of the school district in which the test is to be used. Among other prerequisites, the school board should identify the strengths and weaknesses of its present staff and systematically determine the characteristics of the teacher preparation programs in those colleges from which successful teachers are normally drawn.

The composition and needs of the system's student body must be considered in relation to national and local educational goals. Once the district has ascertained these factors, it may proceed to identify existing tests which may be of aid in evaluating teachers who possess the characteristics to meet its needs successfully. Thereafter, the board should consult with the designers of the tests, such as the Educational Testing Service, to ascertain the functions each test can legitimately serve in its situation and the limitations of the test.

Let me say that the legal problems I have encountered relating to the use of standardized testing generally spring from the fact that employers here--potentially a school board--have more faith in the test than the designers of the test themselves. If the skepticism of the test maker were shared by the school administrators, I believe that many legal problems would be avoided. Moreover, I have found that the test designers generally are willing to counsel with the school boards in an effort to assure that their tests are not used in a manner contrary to good measurement practices.

In determining whether a test discriminates against members of a minority group who will be in the test population, the school board should make its own study using expert help as necessary. In this study it should determine how representatives of the minority group in its teacher population or from among the applicants fare on the test being considered as compared to the other candidates.

Where a test makes valid predictions for members of a majority group, but not for members of a minority, it should not be used in evaluating the latter group. Rather, other measures, possibly even other tests, should be substituted.

Where the test measures minor traits required of teachers rather than major ones, it should not be given significant weight, particularly if members of a minority group score below members of a majority group. Alternatives which measure critical traits should be sought and weighed more heavily.

Moreover, this process of validation and review for nondiscrimination should not be conducted once and then forgotten. Analysis of the effect of the test on minority applicants and review of the relationship of the test to the skills considered necessary to top performance on the job must be a continuing responsibility of the school administrators.

In conclusion, let me say that the scope to be given to standardized tests in the selection of teachers should not be hammered out in the courts but should be the product of cooperative efforts of educators and experts in test measurement. I fear that few, if any, school boards have made for their districts the studies necessary to insure that a test serves their legitimate needs without discrimination. These studies must be made and repeated as needs change, if tests are to be the servant of the boards rather than their master.

The selection process presents inscrutable challenges. Unless used within proper and careful limits, a test adopted as a part will become the whole of a selection process in what I believe will be serious risks of violations of the Constitution.

THE CHAIRMAN: Thank you very much.

Mr. Pollak, I guess this is rather crucial and extraordinary testimony for the reason that so much of it was devoted to the area of law, what is required under the court decisions and under the Civil Rights Act. I would just like to get this on the record--because of the tendency in the North to completely misunderstand the obligations of government to carry out discrimination laws and discrimination decisions. I think we only now are in the process, frankly, of beginning to educate ourselves in the North about what the obligations of Northern governments are--I wish you, before counsel begins to ask you questions, would state whether or not your testimony has any special reference to the Southern situation in the United States or whether that testimony can be considered to cover schools in other sections of the country as well.

MR. POLLAK: The testimony was drawn by me to try to describe the rules that apply in the North as well as the South. The requirements that action of governmental bodies conform to the Equal Protection and Due Process Clauses, requirements which in the context of tests demand that the tests be reasonably related to the job and treat persons equally, regardless of race, or other class, would be no different here in New York than they would be in a locality in Mississippi or anywhere else.

The factual context in which the problem has to be determined may differ, but the law, the legal requirements, will be the same. And, in my judgment, the question of whether a test is reasonably related to the purpose of selecting persons who can perform well on the job, that problem is not any different as it arises here or as it arises in Mississippi, where, as I say, I have litigated the question.

As I heard Dr. Deneen saying as I was awaiting my turn to testify, the Educational Testing Service, which distributes its tests nationwide, has apparently brought in experts and representatives of various minority groups, as he said, to clean up its test. And I presume that before the cleanup the test was having problems with respect to its treatment of minority groups, whether it was given in Boston or Buffalo or a couple of other places down South named "B."

MR. TRACTENBERG: I have questions of Mr. Pollak.

In your testimony, I think you said that if other measures were used in addition to the standardized test, that might improve the situation. Does that apply also if, in fact, failure on the standardized test would constitute failure in the whole process?

MR. POLLAK: No, and I am very much concerned. I guess I should speak like a lawyer. I am not a measurement expert. As a lawyer, I think that a school board is taking on serious risks when it adopts a flat cutoff score, in other words, a pass-fail line, on a test.

If you read what the people who make tests say about tests, and that, I guess, is the starting point, what they claim a test can do, I find that the designers generally make modest claims about what the test will show. It tells something about the applicant's past, what he has learned, predominantly what he has learned.

If you are thinking about teachers, as I mentioned in my testimony, most tests don't say anything--most paper and pencil tests--about whether the teacher is going to be effective in conveying knowledge and stimulating pupils. Therefore, if you take a flat cutoff point, you are cutting out of consideration all those who are below it, and giving no consideration to the possibility that some of those may have high potential in areas that are not measured by the test.

I tend to think that a strong case can be made for the position that the Due Process Clause requires a school board to take into consideration a number of factors and not merely a score on a test.

One of the things that concerns me, however, about that kind of position that I have just expressed is that if you have candidates who take a test, human nature will tend to have those who evaluate the personnel file of teachers weigh the test score very heavily. I mean, it might be that there will be ten items to be taken into consideration on paper. But if the applicants scored low on the test, even though the obligation of those who are making the selection is to consider ten items, and even though the evaluation in some of those other ten may be higher, the test score will be like a very bright light blinking on and off.

MR. TRACTENBERG: There are several things I want to bring to your attention, which may reflect an unusual situation this morning.

Number one, I am not absolutely sure it still applies, but I know that in many examinations given here in New York by the Board of Examiners, certainly recently if not currently, it was expressly provided that failure on any part of the total examination process would disqualify the applicant. In fact, we had testimony this morning from Albert Shanker that he himself failed more than one examination given by the Board of Examiners because of pronunciation problems on the oral interview.

If I understand you correctly, and if in fact it is still the practice of the Board of Examiners to fail someone simply on the basis of a test score which falls below a pass mark, you would feel that raises serious legal issues.

MR. POLLAK: You've got a case pending in the courts now --I am not in that case and I am not presuming to judge what issues are presented there or even try to comment on them outside of the court proceedings--but my experience in the cases I have looked at leads me to have serious question whether a flat cutoff score, which excludes everybody that falls on the other side, can be shown to be a reasonable part of a selection process.

The one consideration which has been suggested to me that has relevance to a large urban system, and I am sure would be suggested by those who would defend the reasonableness, has been that where you have a very large number of candidates to be considered and where the full consideration of their personnel files or applications is a time-consuming process, the Board may be able to defend the cutoff score as reasonable, not because it doesn't exclude qualified candidates, but because in the interest of administration, they have got to exclude some in order to get through the process. That would entail a careful weighing of whether that necessity to conduct the administrative program outweighs the arbitrariness of cutting out some qualified people.

MR. TRACTENBERG: We have also heard testimony here during the hearings from members of the Board of Examiners--I want to be very careful because I think your point is well taken about the pending litigation and we have established as one of the ground rules of the hearing that we would, when talking expressly about examinations, restrict it to the teacher examinations which are not in litigation.

A Board of Examiners member commenting on the teacher examinations said that they have never attempted a so-called predictive validity study, that is, they have never attempted to tie performance on the examination to subsequent performance as a teacher. They may have conducted some content validity studies.

Would the absence of any effort to conduct predictive validity studies raise legal problems insofar as you have determined?

MR. POLLAK: I would not say that I know of a case which would enable me to respond yes or no to that. Within the last fifteen months, the courts have been looking at the necessity for validation of tests. I think as far as they have gotten is that there must be a process of validation. Whether it must be validation by content or predictive validity, the courts have not determined. They just have not ground the flour that fine.

I think I can postulate a situation where the content validity study would produce some conflicting, or let's say, marginal indicators. It would perhaps not be really clear that the test was valid for the purpose for which it was used. In that event, I would think those who were challenging the test would come on and say the content validity study is not enough. You have to have indications of predictive validity.

It is just a question of whether all the signals are green. If it looks fine, why, then you have done enough. If they are not green, and the test is the sole determinant of the employment decision, then the courts may rule that you have to do more.

I think just how much has to be done in the validity area depends on how large a role is assigned to the test, and as Dr. Deneen said, again, in my hearing, as part of his testimony, or in response to your question, when you are considering teacher applicants who have had no prior teaching experience, then you may assign, or the school board may determine to assign, to a test a rather large role. In that event, I would think it would be held to a reasonably rigorous standard of validation in its district.

MR. TRACTENBERG: One final question, Mr. Pollak.

I assume, if a test in fact is to be job-related, that there has to be careful definition of what the job is. I would like just to read you a statement and see what your view is as to its legal import. This is a statement by William Enneis, who is a staff psychologist in the Office of Research at the United States Equal Employment Opportunity Commission.

He says as follows: "The job analyses should be conducted by independent persons trained in this activity, that is, job analysis. Otherwise, the results may be seriously biased by self reports which are completed by the incumbent assistant principals and principals.

"The reason for this potential bias is that many employees in administrative positions tend to report as important those work aspects which they most enjoy or those which they do well.

"Also, the frequency of reported job functions may be influenced by the extent to which the incumbent prefers to do them. Therefore, some critical components of the job may be slighted, even though they are matters of the greatest concern for teachers, pupils, the community, and the school system."

Is the kind of risk which this testing expert expresses here also a legal risk in your judgment? That is, if job analyses are not produced by the kinds of independent persons he describes, is there a serious legal problem as well as a testing problem?

MR. POLLAK: Again, I know of no decisions which have analyzed the strengths or weaknesses of a test validation program in such fine detail.

I think a couple of things occur to me. One, you have asked for an estimate of the legal risks, and I will come to that, but if you are setting up what school systems really want to do to set up their own best selection system, then that is a matter that they would like to do without the courts being involved. In that process, by the statement of Dr. Enneis, he seems to make good sense. You know, we have all experienced our own kind of personal view of any job we do, and it influences how we describe the job.

But if there is failure to have independent outside experts evaluating the jobs, I suppose the question I would have as to whether that would cause a legal problem would depend upon how the inside job holders' evaluations were dealt with.

I presume that you could not just have all of the people in the system evaluate their jobs. You would be inundated with job evaluations. And even if you did that, you would have to have some other people in the system collate those descriptions, and I think what is described there would be a good way of doing it, just as I think having outside test experts come in and help set up the system is probably good. But I don't know whether the failure to have outside people do it would really leave you with a hazard for having an adequate system.

I think probably it would be best. But whether failure to do it would be unreasonable in a due process sense, I think that is a bit down the road. One of the reasons I say that is that in cases that I have looked at, there were really no job analyses at all. A test like the National Teacher Examinations was selected to be used. A general inquiry around the area was made to find out what scores seemed to be a good minimum, and that was then the process. The kinds of things that needed to be done, like evaluation of the jobs, evaluation of the characteristics needed to perform the job, evaluation of whether it tests for those characteristics, and whether it does so reliably, those steps which seem reasonably simple are often not taken. And the first move in the right direction will be to take them, whether you take them with people inside the school system or with people outside.

MR. TRACTENBERG: Thank you.
I don't have any further questions.
THE CHAIRMAN: Thank you very much, Mr. Pollak.
I want to acknowledge that we have been indeed fortunate to have had testimony from a man who occupied the highest post in the Federal Government for civil rights work on the legal side during the past administration, when virtually all the law and guidelines with respect to this very difficult area of school desegregation were formulated.

I think it is a signal of the high importance of this very complicated area that we have been fortunate enough to have Mr. Pollak come here.

I thank you very much.

MR. POLLAK: I am pleased to have been able to come and glad to have been invited.

THE CHAIRMAN: We will take a five-minute break, after which we will meet Dr. Alfred Weinstein.

EVENING SESSION (3d DAY)

THE CHAIRMAN: There has been a substitution. Mr. Weinstein has graciously allowed Mr. Mapp to go ahead of him because Mr. Mapp has night court.

Lloyd S. Mapp of the East New York Community Corporation.

While Mr. Mapp is coming to the stand, I have been asked to announce again where these meetings are being held because some people, hearing this on WNYC, have believed that they were being held at City Hall.

They are being held close to City Hall, but not at City Hall. They are at 14 Vesey Street, the New York County Lawyers Association, on the second floor.

Mr. Mapp.

MR. MAPP: I would like to take the opportunity to thank Dr. Alfred Weinstein for allowing me to go first since I have an engagement that I have to get to as quickly as I can.

Mrs. Norton, members of the Commission, my name is Lloyd S. Mapp. I am here to testify on behalf of the East New York Community Corporation. We wish to extend our appreciation to this Commission for granting us the privilege to testify.

The issue of employment, retention, and promotion practices in the City public school system has been debated by associations, boards, committees, commissions, federations, and various organizations. It has been the subject of voluminous reports and studies.

Recommendations to the Boards of Education, Examiners, and Regents have been made by numerous organizations and agencies. Bills have been filed and refiled in the State Legislature, calling for amendments to the Education Law in relation to certification of staff to be hired in the City public school system. Yet the same discriminatory employment procedures are still being practiced.

It is hoped that out of these public hearings will come the

kind of legislative action needed to permit a school board the flexibility to employ pedagogical personnel suited for its schools.

Mrs. Norton and this Commission ought to be congratulated for having the courage to publicly examine the methods of the Examiners. This is a valuable public service that ought to be extended to other agencies of the City.

We know you have already heard the ills of the Board of Examiners, and therefore, we are not going to bore you further by documenting its discriminatory procedures.

What we would like to do is discuss alternatives to the current employment procedures.

First, the Board of Examiners should be abolished by legislative action. This is absolutely necessary in order to enforce a new code of employment, retention, and promotional procedures.

In setting up the new procedures, great weight ought to be given to such factors as a candidate's willingness and ability to understand the problems of students from troubled communities; a candidate's ability to deal justly with teachers, students, parents, and residents; a candidate's skill in detecting a possible explosive situation and moving to minimize its effect; a candidate's capacity to persuade, not command, others to work out solutions to conflicting problems; a candidate's ability in gaining the respect and support of students, staff, parents, and residents; a candidate's ability to try new innovative methods of teaching; a candidate's attitude with respect to a student's ability; a candidate's ability to create the kind of image that would assure students that they, too, can succeed.

We recognize that these factors in human quality are difficult to assess. We are living in difficult times that call for great efforts to stem the downward spiral of a large bulk of our students.

However, we do feel that the local community school boards can better assess these qualities than some distant central body. We also feel that the community school boards can best assess the formal educational background and practical experience of candidates seeking positions within their district.

We urge that the factors enumerated here be part of any recommended legislative action that this Commission proposes.

Thank you very much.

THE CHAIRMAN: Thank you, Mr. Mapp.

Counselor, any questions?

MR. TRACTENBERG: No questions.

THE CHAIRMAN: Dr. Alfred Weinstein, President, Junior High School Principals Association.

DR. WEINSTEIN: Madam Chairman, members of the Commission, thank you for the opportunity to present our point of view.

I am Alfred Weinstein, President of the New York City Junior High School Principals Association. I have served as a teacher of English in both junior and senior high schools. I have been an assistant principal in an elementary school, principal of two different elementary schools, and a principal of a junior high school.

At present, I am serving as a unit head with the Board of

Examiners, and my responsibilities are the preparation and construction of examinations through the selection of experts in various fields, the recommendation and selection of examination assistants for the construction and conducting of tests, the composition of panels for conference, interview, and inspection tests. All these are with the approval and aid of my consulting Examiner, Dr. Murray Rockowitz.

In these examinations, we draw on many disciplines, depending upon the license area in question. If it is in social work, for example, we will have professors of social work from different colleges and I will make sure that minority group representatives are on that panel. We will have supervisors in the field. We will have people from community health agencies and people who are in social agencies, so that a broad spectrum is brought into the composition and construction of tests, with selections in terms of the scope of the examination.

As someone who has gone through the New York City school system, and who has attained a modicum of success and is a member of a minority group, it has been my experience and deep personal conviction that it is through the unbiased and objective procedures of the Board of Examiners that applicants who are without any influence, political or otherwise, can become teachers and supervisors on the basis of ability, and without any kind of external influence.

Let me say, as an aside, that it has come up that since the Board of Examiners use assistants, in part, who come from the City system, that it is possible that there is an "in-group."

Let me say that during the briefing, and the sending out of the names of applicants for examinations, very careful attention is given to ensuring that examiners do not examine anyone they have any kind of personal knowledge of, or who serves in their school, or who in any way can exert an influence. We do not put that obligation upon the applicant to say he doesn't want a certain examination assistant, unless there is a reason for it that has some relevance, but upon the examination assistant's recognition of the candidate.

In the 72-year history of the Board of Examiners there has never been, to my knowledge, any case in which an applicant has been able to prove in the courts that he was denied license for reasons of discrimination, whether for ethnic, religious, or other reasons.

As one who has been deeply involved and committed to the pressing need for staffing our schools with Black and Puerto Rican teachers and supervisors, and who has helped many of them to prepare for and to pass examinations as teachers and for supervisory licenses, in my service as an assistant principal and principal in Bedford Stuyvesant, Brownsville, Bushwick, and Forest Hills, which was integrated in a pilot program when Dr. King was Deputy Superintendent, I know that the teaching and supervisory examinations are searching and valid in terms of those who are rated satisfactory by supervisors.

I know that there has not been any great study done or any

study done in terms of predictive validity, and I think that they should be done, and this is a criticism. I think that the Board of Examiners would be the first to accept this. I think there is a question of research funding and I would strongly urge that that be done.

You have heard testing experts on that. That is not my field of expertise, but I have been impressed with what I have heard and have read in the area.

Every group, immigrant or otherwise, which is new to the city, takes time to make its appearance, get into professions, and this is true of teachers.

The failure of Blacks and Puerto Ricans to emerge as teachers and supervisors in any significant numbers in New York City's school system is due, of course, to the history of American society, a system of laws and culture with separate and unequal education, which has existed in Northern cities as well as Southern cities.

We have heard about de jure segregation and de facto segregation, and it took the 1954 Supreme Court decision to spell that out.

The Board of Examiners itself is victimized by the kind of society which denies Black and Puerto Rican and other minority groups the kind of equal housing that affluent members of society have; the right to due process, which requires hiring lawyers, an expensive proposition in our society; good medical care; mental hygiene care; et cetera. And all this, of course, places a deficit upon the education of children.

Black people have been here in America longer than any other group, probably, but a repressive society has prevented them from getting a rightful place as leaders in all branches of government and leadership in society generally. I think we are on the verge of a great breakthrough in that area.

Let me say that the eligibility requirements are set by the Board of Education and not the Board of Examiners. And where minority group members have been excluded, it was because the requirements have been such that they were not eligible for the examination. Whether the supervisory level of experience was three years or four years, since they came into the system late or did not come into the system because of unequal opportunities for college, they couldn't take the examination.

The current elementary principal's examination has proven that, and as one who serves as a unit head, just in the past week I have seen more Black and Puerto Rican applicants than ever before. They are coming forth because of reduced eligibility requirements and because of programs which have encouraged them to enter teaching.

You have heard about this before, but I think it is worth repeating. Until recently, the small proportion of Blacks and Puerto Ricans who are college graduates have found that other professions were more profitable. College teaching, law, medicine, and the business world attracted most of them. Since 1954 we have had to compete with the business world for qualified college graduates. The few who have entered the public school system rose rapidly in proportion to their members.

I believe now that open enrollment in our City Colleges and the vast array of federally-funded and privately-funded programs will give us more and more Blacks and Puerto Ricans who will meet the eligibility requirements for teaching and supervisors. You see many more who are supervisors now and a great rise in the number of superintendents, many of whom have risen through the supervisory ranks.

Of all the proposals offered as alternatives to the Board of Examiners, none seems to me to meet the criteria of impartiality, of individual tests here to specify license requirement in terms of the duties of the job, of personal interviews in terms of criteria which have been established by the courts as valid. Appellants have gone to court on interview tests, and asked that their rating be reversed. In cases where they have gained it or not gained it, the criteria have stood up as valid. I think the most recent one was the assistant principal's examination in elementary school that was held up for a while. Nothing says that this should not be revised and tested and worked on, but I think it offers a good working model. There is no alternative that I have heard--I haven't heard all the proceedings of the Commission--and that I have read that guards against patronage or influence, which would determine an applicant's fate, either positively or negatively, irespective of the examination process.

I feel that state certification is inadequate. As a college instructor who taught fifteen years in Queens College in undergraduate work, four years in Hofstra, six years in Brooklyn, and graduate level courses, elementary and secondary, supervisory and teaching, I know that mere passing of a course is not searching enough to license a teacher.

A person might do very well in a course, do well on an exam, and still lack the kind of personal and inter-personal attitude that would make him a successful teacher. I do not have--nor does any instructor who has a hundred people or sixty people in a course--either the time or the ability to conduct the kind of searching examination he should to find out whether the person is qualified to have the potential of a teacher.

Previous speakers have charged that the examination assistants prepare the tests, conduct them, and have also acted as paid coaches to help applicants pass the examination.

Let me say for the record that I am against paid coaches. I think the purpose of coaching is important, and I think that the Board of Education waited too long to conduct and pay for Professional Seminars. There is no doubt that minority group people who prepared for exams were victimized by their lower income and couldn't pay for the courses, many of which were very expensive.

I must brand as absolutely false the charge that these examination assistants conduct courses. Anyone who gives a coaching course, whether it is privately conducted or one of the Professional Seminars, is on a do-not-use list, which is distributed to every unit head and circulated among all members of the professional staff of the Board of Examiners in order to assure the confidentiality of the examinations. Each year all the examination assistants receive notice of the conditions which would prevent them from serving: that they are on leave, that they are coaching, that they are on sabbatical. There are other qualifications.

Among previous speakers, there was one chairman of a local school board who seemed to feel that unsatisfactory teachers received tenure as the result of the testing procedures of the Board of Examiners.

The question of tenure rests with the community boards to accept or reject the recommendation of the principals and supervisors of teachers. Every teacher goes through a three-year probationary period. It is up to the supervisors to evaluate the effectiveness of the teachers under their supervision.

As a principal, I would feel I'm not worth my salt if I allowed a teacher to finish probation who was unsatisfactory or doubtful, or who has been rated negative in those aspects in which I want to see improvement. And I would think less of the principal who does not instruct his assistant principal and chairman to do the same thing.

But that is not the responsibility of the Board of Examiners. All the Board of Examiners can do is screen applicants to assess their potential as teachers and supervisors, and I believe that screening process and assessment can be improved. What procedure cannot be improved?

But it is up to the supervisors themselves and to the superintendents as well as the local school boards to exert responsibility for granting tenure. They must see to it that the people who are licensed do a job, a professional job in providing competent instruction, influencing attitudes and changes toward positive democracy, learning to live with their fellows, in, as Mr. Mapp said eloquently, learning to spot potential trouble and dispelling it, working with the students who have trouble, and raising those who are reading below grade or functioning below grade, whether in disadvantaged or advantaged areas.

Those are the province of administration, with the advice and final approval of the local school board.

I believe that local boards of education should have the right to select supervisors for their schools as they have. I have gone through the process myself. But I do not believe that the prior step of screening and assessing the potential of these professionals should be done by nonprofessionals.

Under the present Decentralization Law, community boards select all supervisors either by transfer or from eligible lists. When they reject an applicant, the applicant never knows why. It is not like an interview conducted by the Board of Examiners, or any board, maybe a medical board, or a law board, when an applicant fails--and I am not sure that that happens with a law board, but it happens with the Board of Examiners. I refer to the fact that when an applicant fails in a written examination or an interview test, he can appeal, he can obtain his reasons for failure in a rating guide, if he fails the written.

His record of performance is reviewable. This is not true when one appears before community school boards.

I believe that as time goes on, the community school boards can learn much from the history of the Board of Examiners in setting up standards for evaluating their own criteria in assessing the potential of supervisors they interview for positions in their district.

Let me just cite a few examples. There are friends of mine who have gone to three different schools in three different areas, competing against a group of experienced people and applicants off the list.

All different kinds of questions are asked and they differ with every school board. Some are profound, some superficial. Some interviews are twenty minutes and some are thirty minutes, and at the end of that, the applicant is told the result. That goes for superintendents, too, and I have gone through those interviews, so I speak from personal knowledge. You never know why you did not make it with one board and made it with another.

A friend of mine missed with two school boards and made it with a third, the school that was considered a good school situation in which there were twenty applicants. Yet he couldn't make it with the others.

I know of one case where a person did make an application for junior high school and was selected for a superintendency a month later.

I think that when you have that kind of preliminary screening, no matter how dedicated the laymen are, I don't think they have the background or the knowledge or the criteria. I think they can learn much from the Board of Examiners' procedures which could be updated.

Much of the criticism leveled at the Board of Examiners, and much of it that I've heard, such as the speech part, which has been eliminated, is very apropos. I have criticized that for years.

There used to be a separate speech examination which I felt had nothing to do with communication, and was artificial, but it stems from the practices and policies of the depression years. When I came back from the Air Force after service, it took me three times to pass a substitute teaching test in English, because I mispronounced words. You had to read lists of words. It was a ridiculous and absurd practice, and it was eliminated. It should have been eliminated sooner, and I have no brief for it. I would have no brief for any practice which is unnecessary and does not really test whether a person could be a good teacher.

Standards have been relaxed also on written tests and interview tests and written English grading. More errors per page are permitted. There is no longer a separate interview concentrating on the applicant's speech. Since the speech test has been dropped, there are far fewer failures.

In 1937 during the depths of depression--and I got this from people who have worked with the Board at that time, some of whom are retired--lists were promulgated with about 5% passing. Today 85% passing is the usual ratio.

I believe that there should be further change in the procedures of the Board of Examiners. The process for screening and evaluating examination assistants, which counsel asked members of the Board of Examiners about, should be intensified to insure a wider spectrum of knowledgeable, tactful, and conscientious people.

There should be an immediate examination held for unit heads and senior assistants, which should be open to all professionals in the field of teaching and supervision in our system.

At present, the qualifications prevent most teachers and supervisors from taking these examinations. They want people who work in industrial firms, who have tested personnel, selected personnel, and constructed tests, to serve for three years as a unit head. But one cannot serve for three years as a unit head, because the Board has dropped those who reached the three years on the basis of the decision by the State Commissioner that one having three years on the job receives tenure. I think Dr. Greene referred to the fact that it was difficult to operate the Board of Examiners because unit heads are constantly changing, and that is one of the reasons.

The adoption of tape recordings for all interviews, which was mandated by the Decentralization Law, is another improvement towards the goal of providing the applicant with a reviewable record.

I, myself, a number of years ago was a co-litigant challenging an examination. Our lawyer claimed that the notes provided by the examination assistants were insufficient to really review since they were not dictaphonic or stenographic. He requested the tape recording of all interviews. It took the Decentralization Law to do that and now one has a review of the record. I think it was unfair and it should have been done a long time ago. At that time, there was no tape recording and this has now been remedied.

I am certain that the members of the Board of Examiners, and the members of the supervisory and teaching staffs are going to update this procedure. Selection of testing personnel has been hampered by a lack of support in terms of funds for research and the establishment of a suitable staff.

No public body is perfect. A number of imperfections which are present in the Board of Examiners have been mentioned and gone into.

I think a body like this does a valuable service by opening it up so that people know what an examination process is. I think it is a healthy and a democratic process which is needed.

But as a service body, the Board of Examiners has functioned in such a manner that no bias has ever been proved against it, and these are qualities that must be maintained. In its history of selecting teachers and supervisors who are as good as, and I daresay better than most, other schools in large cities, the Board of Examiners is vital in performing a service.

As one who attends many conventions, the New York City teachers and supervisors and programs of instruction, which are written up in bulletins and presented at conventions, are respected and admired through the breadth of this land. I have heard administrators in Long Island say, after they hired New York City teachers that have gone through the testing process with us, "You have done well. You have completed the screening process for us."

There are a number of other things. I agree with Dr. Barrett that tests have to be validated.

I think counsel mentioned that it used to be that failure on one part would fail you on an entire test. I have lived through that, and I think that was absurd. You had to wait four years in between tests, and that was absolutely ridiculous, because it seemed to me that if you passed one part, just as you do, I think, with the CPA, you shouldn't have to take that part again. Why that was done, I don't know. It was a practice that grew up--I couldn't understand it--and it has now been dropped.

You had a change in that for a number of high-level tests. You have consideration zones, where a supervisor, in a supervisory test--and I don't want to get into law aspects--can score below, say, sixty, and still be considered within the test, if the other parts of his test bring him up. In other words, it is weighted.

One can also appeal. I would favor a system where one would be able to take only the part he failed again.

The Board has made some other improvements that people don't know about. The tests have been shortened and the kind of useless items that Dr. Barrett read, general culture and knowledge, have been dropped. They have been dropped for a number of years. Closer gearing of the tests to the job was done in '67, for example.

Some duty specifications were read today. When we start off a briefing, we go through the duties of the position, which are drawn up by the Board of Education through the Deputy Superintendent of Personnel, and the more explicit those duties are, the better you can gear the questions to the job. I think that should be done.

Just to say someone should have high morale is not enough. What is high morale? But when someone says, "You should have an up-to-date functioning or visual aids program," I think any principal knows that means all kinds of audio-visual aids, sound as well as silent, moving as well as fixed, using the latest kinds of equipment and knowing this is a supplement to teaching. You don't have to spell it out completely, but I think that is where the Board of Examiners has been concentrating and needs to do a lot more work.

THE CHAIRMAN: Dr. Weinstein, I don't want to cut you off, but there are so many people ready to testify.

DR. WEINSTEIN: I was about to conclude.

Madam Chairman and members of the Commission, thank you for allowing me to participate in this worthwhile interview and I think that this is a wholesome endeavor and is the very purpose of democracy in action.

THE CHAIRMAN: Counselor, do you have any questions?

MR. TRACTENBERG: I have some, but I am afraid to question the witness fully. It would involve probably the same three hours as with Dr. Greene, since he has raised many of the same issues.

I do want to focus on a couple of things which I think are important.

First of all, Dr. Weinstein, you indicated that you took no examination to qualify as a unit head.

DR. WEINSTEIN: That's right.

MR. TRACTENBERG: Was there a formal, written screening procedure which you went through?

DR. WEINSTEIN: As to the screening procedure, the unit that I am heading at present is a unit which has largely to do with guidance, social work, school psychologists, outside classroom activities, and special education, such as teachers of CRMD and hearing handicapped, language-impaired children. What Dr. Greene did was look for people who had had experience and training in some of those areas.

I have been assistant principal and principal of schools with many of the handicapped classes, and I supervised those classes. My doctorate was in secondary school administration. My postgraduate work was in the teaching of reading, in which I amassed thirty credits at Teachers College. I took post-doctoral work in psychology and was admitted to the advanced school in the New School for Social Work, and I worked in Hofstra Reading Clinic, giving intelligence tests, evaluating tests, so he felt I had the background. What other criteria he established, I don't know. The Board of Examiners did the screening.

MR. TRACTENBERG: But, so far as you know, there was no written set of specifications?

DR. WEINSTEIN: No, there was no written test.

MR. TRACTENBERG: Not a written test. Was there any written set of requirements for the position, a job description?

DR. WEINSTEIN: No, there was no job description.

MR. TRACTENBERG: Was there a public announcement made of the vacancy?

DR. WEINSTEIN: No, there was no public announcement.

MR. TRACTENBERG: Did you happen to know any of the Board of Examiners personally before you were appointed unit head?

DR. WEINSTEIN: I knew one of them who had begun teaching with me, but he wasn't the one I spoke to, and that was Dr. Rockowitz.

MR. TRACTENBERG: You are working as an assistant to Dr. Rockowitz now?

DR. WEINSTEIN: That unit was under Dr. Rockowitz, right. May I say something about that?

MR. TRACTENBERG: Certainly.

DR. WEINSTEIN: It was understood that I was coming on a temporary leave and was still assigned to my school, because a unit head had to leave on the basis of the three-year rule I told you about.

The Board of Examiners has asked for an exam and a job

duty description for about three or four years. There is a history of correspondence that Miss Unser has. I have seen some of it, so they wanted an exam for it. At one time they had eight examiners, one for each unit. Now they are reduced by law to four, and they had to have people who could carry on, maybe not in the best way possible.

But the exam was not announced and the requirements were not set by the Board of Examiners until two weeks after I got there. Then the requirements were set up and the descriptions were set up. And now it is in the process of qualifications being changed.

MR. TRACTENBERG: But at least your own appointment and presumably the appointment of other persons similarly situated in the Board of Examiners has not met with the kind of standard that you would require of the community boards, that is, there was no public announcement.

DR. WEINSTEIN: Certain people were called, but it was not a public announcement. A number of people were informed there was a possibility that there would be an opening for unit head.

MR. TRACTENBERG: Is the procedure for screening all full-time staff, who I gather are all pedagogical personnel assigned to the Board of Examiners, as well as the temporary assistants, similar to what you have described? That is, in terms of written announcements, written procedures?

DR. WEINSTEIN: No. As far as I know, the examination assistants who have come in, who are part of the staff, except for clerks, committee clerks, et cetera, are people who are experts in the field.

For example, a person might be a guidance counselor who has served and has been recommended by the Superintendent and approved by the Chancellor or the Superintendent.

MR. TRACTENBERG: But that expertise is an expertise which is common to many guidance counselors throughout the system?

DR. WEINSTEIN: That's right, but they would interview a number of people, just as they would interview a number of people for unit head and decide who they want.

MR. TRACTENBERG: But without written procedures?

DR. WEINSTEIN: That's right. There are no written procedures built into the law.

MR. TRACTENBERG: Doesn't that strike you as a bit inconsistent for a body which sets itself up as--

DR. WEINSTEIN: Yes, and I know that the Board of Examiners wants tests for these positions. The Board of Education has not seen fit to, they delayed, for example, tests for unit heads and senior assistants since the '60's or going back further.

So I think certainly a body that is a merit selection system should have people on it selected by merit, and I was willing to take the examination. Apparently now I am not even eligible for the examination. But I agree with you, and I know that the members of the Board of Examiners agree. It isn't something that they wanted.

MR. TRACTENBERG: Dr. Weinstein, are you knowledgeable about how many professionals in testing are on the full-time staff of the Board of Examiners?

DR. WEINSTEIN: Professionals in terms of the units?

MR. TRACTENBERG: Are there psychometricians, personnel psychologists?

DR. WEINSTEIN: Yes. I have only been at the Board of Examiners for three months, and I really haven't seen a breakdown. I know a number of unit heads and some of the people in there, so I really couldn't give you an accurate picture.

MR. TRACTENBERG: But they're all pedagogical people?

DR. WEINSTEIN: Well, some are not pedagogical. Some are research people. There are a few research people. One is a research assistant. One works with research and test items, but I really couldn't give you a knowledgeable answer. I don't have a breakdown and it wouldn't be right for me to say.

MR. TRACTENBERG: You mentioned that the Board of Examiners--I think these are your exact words--test the candidates' potential as teachers and supervisors?

DR. WEINSTEIN: Yes.

MR. TRACTENBERG: That strikes me as a somewhat different standard from what Dr. Greene and Dr. Rockowitz have talked about, which is that the test basically screens out incompetents. In fact, I believe Dr. Rockowitz, in answer to a specific question, said that there is no study to which he can point as to teacher exams which suggests that the exams in any way predict potential as teachers.

DR. WEINSTEIN: Well, they would have more knowledge of that than I. I would say that my understanding does not rule out the fact, and I have served as an examination assistant, that one does rule out incompetent information.

For example, supposing I was doing an interview examination on someone for a high supervisory license, principal of a school, supervisor of guidance, and I felt that their answer indicated they lacked tact and they were not sensitive and they didn't know how to work well with people and they slighted minority groups. All that would come out in the talking. Now the person might certainly be considered competent for that job and not demonstrate any potential.

I don't see the two as contradictory. You certainly get rid of the applicant who should not be in the public school, either in an assigned job or as a research assistant or psychologist or psychiatrist.

MR. TRACTENBERG: Doesn't that answer, though, reflect the very subjective nature of at least the interview part of the exam? You have a certain set of standards, and you have indicated if someone doesn't meet those standards, you would vote against him or score him low on the interview portion of the examination.

DR. WEINSTEIN: Yes.

MR. TRACTENBERG: Presumably, someone who brought to bear different personal standards than you would react differently to the same applicant.

DR. WEINSTEIN: There isn't anything in the world that

isn't subjective. Even astronomers are subject to how they feel that moment as they are looking through the stars. And, I think, people do differ.

Let me say that in a briefing--I don't know if people have talked about briefing--in a briefing session one goes over the criteria, and I have in front of me the interview test rating sheet that describes what we are looking for.

And after one does the general briefing on what the procedures are, for example, not that speech items are 17%--it is not rated that way--but that you take a profile of things, then we discuss what soundness of judgment is, that presentation of ideas should be in an organized sequence. Next, let's assume it is a psychologist examination, the subject speaker will meet with people from the colleges, an inter-disciplinary group, and a few supervising psychologists from the Board of Education. They will go over questions for this particular selection, which all the applicants have and are preparing answers to. They will discuss what would be possible answers; and there are alternatives, there are various options. There isn't one fixed answer.

After the candidate is through, the two examiners, or if there are three, write on this sheet either inadequate or passable, good, superior, whatever it may be, and then they can discuss it.

And so, individual assessment is involved so that one is not influenced by the other. Then between the two, sometimes there is a variation; and when people come together, very often there is a confluence, and subjectivity is taken care of there. But I think it has a subjective element in it. And I think in terms of what it can do, it assesses those who are competent in terms of their answers.

For example, someone said here, I think it was Dr. Barrett, that just because a person answers a question, one doesn't know if he can do well on the job. That is very true. We don't know about that, but, at least a candidate has to be able to answer what he would do if he were in such a situation, whatever kind of training program he had.

So although there is a subjective quality, because any interpersonal thing is subjective, it seems to me it is about as valid from my knowledge of it as any selection method. I am not talking about structural validity, because I am not expert at it. But it seems to me, the more panelists, the better--and very often there are three--because the three rate independently and then discuss it. They may or may not change their answer. A median mark is given in a case of three, an average in the case of two. But there is a careful briefing that takes an hour, an hour and fifteen minutes, in which this is gone over and this selection discussed.

MR. TRACTENBERG: I have heard this briefing described by an examination assistant, and I would be interested in how it accords with your reaction. The particular interview examination he participated in was administered by 400 examination assistants, who heard a briefing in an auditorium, all four hundred together, from a single principal, who had been given the questions to be discussed in the interview a day or so before. He gave his reactions to the kinds of answers that were appropriate.

I don't know how long it took, but is this consistent with the way in which these briefings are normally held?

DR. WEINSTEIN: That is not my experience. I am not saying it may not have happened. My participation in briefings--and I've been in them a long time on both ends--is that principals, let's assume it is a principal's examination, are on call, and if there are two groups, let's say, they are given the questions and have a chance to prepare notes. They review with the unit head what they are going to cover, and the unit head gives his procedures on explaining the items, even though it has been done many times before, and there are instructions. In addition to that, everyone has a set of instructions. And then the principal talks and usually it is a small group. I've never been with four hundred.

MR. TRACTENBERG: But there are a substantial number of examination assistants, aren't there, who conduct oral interviews? How many people applied for the last principal's examination?

DR. WEINSTEIN: The conducting, not the briefing?

MR. TRACTENBERG: That's right.

DR. WEINSTEIN: Yes, there could be a substantial number.

MR. TRACTENBERG: And those are the people who really do the interviews?

DR. WEINSTEIN: Yes, those are the people who do the interviewing. And, by the way, there is a tape recording now which means that everyone's voice is on it, everyone's opinion, so an examination assistant cannot make an arbitrary, capcricious judgment because he can't say the applicant failed to do something. The interview is on tape and the applicant has a reviewable record which he can go to. And as one who reads appeals as part of my job, many of them are upheld.

MR. TRACTENBERG: I am glad you raised this area, because that was the next question I was going to ask. You indicated that the tape recordings were done only when mandated by State law quite recently.

Is there any reason why the Board of Examiners could not have administratively determined to make tape recordings?

DR. WEINSTEIN: I indicated to you that a number of years ago, as a co-litigant in a suit, we asked for that through our lawyer. Many people who believe in the examination process believe that that would have made it much more valid, since, as I said before, there was no record except that kept by examination assistants, many of whom took copious notes. But these records were not dictaphonic or stenographic, and could not be reviewed.

MR. TRACTENBERG: Weren't there many criticisms of the absence of a record?

DR. WEINSTEIN: Yes, there were a number of appeals. One of the reasons given--and at that time I did not know any members of the Board--but one of the reasons I heard from people who had spoken to them was that it was impossible to get adequate recording equipment.

I'm not saying whether it was right or not. But since the obtaining of transistor recorders which made them portable, and

Dr. Weinstein

which go on even if there is no connection, because the batteries take over, it is easier to record the interviews. Before that, it was very difficult to do. They had these huge tape recorders, and it was a question of expense, too. But I think it should have been done. That is my personal opinion. I think it should have been done.

MR. TRACTENBERG: If it was not done until required by statute, why should one assume that the Board of Examiners will voluntarily make the numerous other changes in procedures which have already been identified in these hearings?

DR. WEINSTEIN: Because the Board of Examiners was also involved in the Decentralization Law. They made recommendations, and they did not oppose that. I think they were for that, too. I don't have personal knowledge of that.

MR. TRACTENBERG: In fact, the decentralization proposal of the Board of Education proposed the abolition of the Board of Examiners, so if the Board of Examiners had some input in the legislative process, it must have been inconsistent with the position of the Board of Education.

DR. WEINSTEIN: I'm talking about the Decentralization Law.

MR. TRACTENBERG: That is what I am talking about.

DR. WEINSTEIN: I don't understand your point.

MR. TRACTENBERG: I served as counsel to the Board of Education--

DR. WEINSTEIN: Yes.

MR. TRACTENBERG: --for the drafting of that statute and plan, and it proposed the abolition of the Board of Examiners.

DR. WEINSTEIN: Yes.

MR. TRACTENBERG: If the Board of Examiners was involved in the legislative process which resulted in the law continuing it, then it must have taken a position contrary to that.

DR. WEINSTEIN: To that provision, certainly.

MR. TRACTENBERG: That's right.

DR. WEINSTEIN: To that provision, yes.

MR. TRACTENBERG: So that its input was to seek to have the Board of Examiners extended?

DR. WEINSTEIN: Naturally, yes, because they think they serve a valuable function, and I would agree.

MR. TRACTENBERG: I am still not clear, and this is really the last question I have--

DR. WEINSTEIN: Yes?

MR. TRACTENBERG: --why you think one should place faith in voluntary changes by the Board of Examiners given the fact that you agree that in the past they have refused to make needed changes? In fact, you were a litigant in a suit which tried to change Board of Examiners procedures, and the procedures were changed only when the Legislature required it.

DR. WEINSTEIN: Well, there are a number of voluntary changes which the Board of Examiners made. These include: eliminating the speech part, which was done voluntarily; changing of the test items of general culture, which was done voluntarily;

detailing descriptions of job duties for more and more examinations, which was done voluntarily.

I don't think, very frankly, that any independent body can do that much by themselves. I think there has to be pressure from other groups, but done in a professional way. For example, it takes a long time for things to be done. It was through the system of supervision or rising through the ranks, which has been nondiscriminatory, I think, that changes were made possible. The changes took too long, but they were finally made.

Also, there are differences in the members of the Board of Examiners. I think the present Board of Examiners has been very flexible, very interested in making changes, and, I think, truly interested in selecting a broader spectrum of minority group members. I think all their efforts have shown that.

In the past, with a supply and demand system, and the kinds of practices I described, you had 5% of the people passing. That's a little before I came into the system. So I think the members of the Board themselves, as well as the democratic process plus voluntary changes, will help.

And I think the kind of Commission hearing you have here is very salutary. I think people should know about the practices of the Board of Examiners. I think that the practices and procedures stand up well when exposed under the searchlight.

MR. TRACTENBERG: Based on some of the concessions that have been made and suggestions that changes will follow, I'm not so sure.

Incidentally, I have one final thing. You made reference to Dr. Barrett's list of words and said those are no longer on examinations.

DR. WEINSTEIN: Yes.

MR. TRACTENBERG: I believe that list came from the 1970 elementary principal school's examination, which was given in November.

DR. WEINSTEIN: I did not see that exam. I was referring to the speech paragraph, that I think Albert Shanker referred to. When I first came in you were asked to read words, and I think I failed the word "schism." I think I pronounced it "skism." That is the kind of list I was referring to.

If those words appear, they should not appear and it is wrong. Such test items should be changed. As a constructor making tests for people to take, I have eliminated many things which I think are unnecessary and trivial.

THE CHAIRMAN: I want to thank you, Mr. Weinstein, for coming forward with that testimony in your dual role, representing the Board of Examiners and the Junior High School Principals Association.

THE CHAIRMAN: The next witness is Mr. Martin Frye.

MR. FRYE: Madam Chairman, panel members, I am Martin Frye, Community Superintendent, School District 4, which is in East Harlem. I have been superintendent of that district, which, before changes under decentralization, was part of Central Harlem for the past four years.

I have been through the examination procedures of the Board of Examiners going back to the year 1947. I hold seven licenses through the Board of Examiners, ranging from teacher of common branches through junior high school social studies, high school social studies, high school English, health education, elementary school principal, junior high school principal. I have had experience as an assistant examiner. I have examined hundreds of candidates for the Board of Examiners either through the oral process or by marking written papers. So that I feel that I have some background in regard to how they have operated in the past and, indeed, how they operate now, because I frequently refer people for examinations. And I see what the results are when the people come back either licensed or unlicensed.

Before I get into my presentation, I would like to react to some of what was said by the previous speaker in regard to change. Having watched the Board of Examiners for the past 23, 24 years, it is my feeling that they have never changed except as pressure was put on them to change. Yes, of course, it is voluntary. But it never comes from within, it comes from without. So that if there are criticisms of the kind we hear this week and changes come about, it is not because the Board of Examiners thought up the need for change. It is because others called it to their attention.

For example, the elimination of the word lists that Dr. Weinstein mentioned came about as the result of pressure from various groups that had suffered from them. I, too, failed an examination when I was asked to read a word list, and this goes back to 1947. The list was a group of words as follows: "fifty-six, fifty-sevenths; sixty-six, sixty-sevenths; seventy-seven, seventy-eighths." And by the time you hit the fourth one, nervous as you are, applying for a license, you can't get anything out. That went out only because of pressure from people who had been through that kind of torture.

The same is true of the tape. Dr. Weinstein indicated that "for a long time we were asking for tapes." Now, they did not finally yield, in my opinion, because the electronic kinds of materials improved. There were other ways of doing it. In the past, in fact, when hearings had been held on unsatisfactory teachers at the Bureau of Personnel, everything went on a plastic record before tape became as prominent as it is now. The hearings of those proceedings were always recorded. And I couldn't see that there would be any real difference in the procedure of setting up that kind of recording as opposed to tape. It could have been done.

The gearing of the test to the job came as a result of pressure, really. Because the Board of Examiners had been giving the same kind of test over and over, the test was, in many ways, no longer related to the kind of job the person was doing. And this was another objection that came from without. And so, the gearing of the test to the job was really because of outside pressure, not because of voluntary change.

Of course, every change you make is voluntary. I don't have

to do anything unless I really want to. But I will do it when the pressure is such that I say to myself, "Well, I have to do it or else get out of here, because I can't stand the pressure any more." In my opinion, that's the way the Board of Examiners has reacted.

I know there has been a lot of discussion during the past two days about the ability of minority groups to pass the tests. I don't think that I can add anything to that, to what has been said. I think it has all been said.

I come from a district where the pupil population is 100% minority group with a few exceptions. Our teaching staff ethnically does not represent anywhere near that in its breakdown. We have had problems in getting minority group people, Puerto Rican and Black people, on our staffs. We are located in Manhattan, and when a list comes out, particularly in common branches, the great majority of those on the list are residents of Queens, or in some instances Westchester, Nassau County, people who are not of minority group origin. Nevertheless, we must accept them under the existing system, or the system that has existed for so many years; because they are on the list they are entitled to the appointment.

When a vacancy occurs, that is not the fault of the Board of Examiners. It is not the Board of Examiners that does the recruiting. The recruiting is done by the Board of Education through its Personnel Division, and the Personnel Division is responsible for getting as many minority group people as is possible into these exams.

My personnel problems are such that when I go out and do personnel recruiting, I have problems getting the people licensed, even though they may be fully qualified by virtue of having taken the proper courses, having done student teaching perhaps outside New York, perhaps within New York City itself. But when we want a person licensed, we go through quite a rigmarole of getting in the proper papers and then waiting for the exam to be given. So, though we have the vacancies right then and there, we wait weeks, and sometimes months, before people are licensed and finally come to us. And by that time, out of desperation, we may reach out and take someone else who shows up with a license.

I would like to talk specifically about supervisory licenses within New York City. I think that the Board of Examiners has managed to get us many out-of-town people through the teacher exam procedure. But we have been accused of inbreeding within the New York City system, and there are statistics.

I did a study of my own district, as a matter of fact, where I discovered that a large percentage of our teachers came from out-of-town institutions and, indeed, were born out of town. I checked into places of birth. And I laid particular emphasis on what high school they graduated from to determine whether they were really out-of-towners or native New Yorkers. And I found that we do get many teachers from out of town, but when it comes to supervisors on the assistant principal level, the principal level in any level school, elementary, junior high, senior high school, that is where the inbreeding occurs.

If you check the statistics, I think you will find that perhaps 99% of our licensed principals, assistant principals, and chairmen came through the New York City system. Because of the way the exam system is structured for supervisory licenses, it is impossible--I don't even say practically impossible--I say impossible for someone from an out-of-town school system to pass our examination. And I will give the reasons.

First of all, when the written is given, questions are listed, essay questions, and we must answer those questions. I have taken this supervisory exam three times, and I know how to pass a supervisory exam. I have it figured out. Your style does not count for anything. You can give a literate, knowledgeable answer to an essay question and get maybe ten points out of a hundred. Your style is perfect, you dotted every i, crossed every t, the grammar is perfect, but there is a key that is used to mark that question. Style means nothing, the way you project your idea means nothing. What matters is how well your answer is matched against the key.

For example, if the question is on setting up a curriculum for third grade social studies, and on the key it says the first thing you do is determine objectives, and in your answer you have not written that you will determine objectives, you don't get credit for that. If you happen to mention it later, you might get two-tenths of a point credit. The odds are that if you have said something which is not on the key, even though it may be apt and applicable, you will not get credit.

Now, there is a trick to answering this in regard to style. You don't use flowery language, you don't show your education, you use the simplest language possible. The reason is, you have to take the number of points given at that particular time--let us say it is 300 in a three-hour exam--and subtract a certain number of minutes for reading questions and working up a little outline. Then you have to divide that by the number of points that the test is given to determine how much time you are going to spend on each essay, and then break that essay question up into other time blocks and try to answer each part of the question within the time block. If you are going to pay attention to style, you are not going to get all your ideas in. If you don't get your ideas in, you don't pass the exam. Your ideas have to conform with what the assistant examiners think the answer should be. The assistant examiners come from within the ranks of the New York principals. So that if you throw in an idea which you as a principal have used in Wanuskie, Vermont, or someplace out in the Midwest that we have never used in New York, it is not on the key, and you will not get credit. You have wasted time answering it. I daresay, any out-of-towner who comes in and takes our essay exam, if he can get a mark of ten out of 100, he is good, he is really good.

Now, what is the point in my saying this? We have one city here, New York City, and outside is a great big world, 49 states other than New York where there are excellent schools being run by excellent people, where there are people on teaching staffs who are upward bound--"upwardly mobile," as the saying is--who could well qualify and will at some time or another to be principal of a school, elementary, junior or senior high school. All these pupils who attend Cal-Tech, let us say, or M.I.T. or Harvard or any of what we come to think of as superior universities did not come from the Bronx High School of Science. Not every single one of them, they did not come from a New York City high school. And, in fact, if you look at the record, you will see, of course, that they come from every state in the union, and they come from cities where there are public schools, where there are teachers who are not licensed by the New York City Board of Examiners, where there are principals who did not go through our examination system, where there are programs which we never heard of in New York City and do not use.

The point is, that we should be able to hire such people to run our schools if they have proved themselves outside, either that they have the "potential" to use the word that Dr. Weinstein used, or that they have done the job elsewhere. There are people who would come to New York, and there are minority group people who would come to New York.

In my travels around the country, at conventions, in course work that I have done at universities, I have met scores of Black supervisors, Puerto Rican supervisors, who are superior people. Just in talking to someone you can make such a determination. Of course, you don't know what he actually does in his school. But how do we license supervisors in New York City? We talk to them. They come for an oral examination and we talk. So what would be different from giving someone an interview which is not an examination and making a determination? We will talk to people anyway before we hire them, jst as we do in an oral interview.

My point is simple enough, that if there are capable people outside New York who are qualified, and we can find them, and they happen to be minority group, we should be able to take them in, because they have proved themselves or because we think they have as much potential as one of our own might have. If we had that privilege, and that is a privilege afforded every school system in the country with the exception of a few like ours, I think that we could infuse some new blood into our schools, which would be a great advantage to us.

Thank you.
THE CHAIRMAN: Thank you, Mr. Frye.
Counsel, do you have any questions?
MR. TRACTENBERG: No.
Thank you, Mr. Frye.
MR. FRYE: Thank you.
THE CHAIRMAN: Rev. Vincent Resta.
REV. RESTA: Madam Chairman, and members of the panel, I am President of the Community School Board, District 4, the district where Mr. Frye is Superintendent. I am going to be brief. I don't have a large or long factual knowledge of the Board of Examiners. I have some reactions to some of the things that have been said about the Board of Examiners and their necessity.

First of all, it seems to me that there are--I know for a fact that there are--other large cities that have large numbers of minority group members in their population, and they have proportionate numbers of minority group teachers. In our city, and in our district, that's not true, proportions are way out of line. And if Chicago can do it, if other big cities can get some kind of proportion between the numbers of minority people and the number of teachers and supervisors of those same minority groups, New York should be able to do the same thing. The only obstacle that seems to exist has been the Board of Examiners.

Now, first of all, I want to react to the idea that the examinations are objective. I would believe an exam was objective if there were no oral component or no visual component, so that I could be perfectly sure that there was no judgment based on either the color of the person speaking or on his accent. I have seen examples of principals presently in the system whose accents are just as pronounced as some of the Puerto Rican people and some of the Black people I know, and yet who passed the Board of Examiners with no difficulty at all.

It also seems to me that perpetuation of the Board of Examiners is equivalent to saying that present supervisors are successful. Now I'm not trying to belittle all the supervisors in the City of New York, but when you consider the record, the education of minority groups, and failure to educate, I think we are perpetuating a system where supervisors whose methods of supervising have not proven to be a success test the ability of others to supervise schools. It's a perpetuation of methods that have not, at least to this point and with minority groups, worked.

And, of course, the other point was the point that Mr. Frye made. The Board of Examiners is not necessary in the employment of teachers in many other cities, even within New York State. Why it should be necessary in New York City as a method of obtaining objective or qualified teachers is beyond me.

Also, many times I have heard Mr. Degnan talk about the days when licenses were handed out in barrooms. I would suspect that so many people, remembering this so well, some of the supervisors who keep mentioning it, must go back to those days. They must have gotten their licenses that way, because I haven't seen any factual presentation on this except the often quoted story.

It also strikes me that "politics" here becomes a dirty word. You see, the school boards are all supposed to be political, and the presumption is that we care so little for the children under our care that we will hand out licenses to teachers and supervisors willy-nilly, suffer children to be abused by teachers and principals who are not qualified because we are politicians. I would suggest that politics is only a dirty word when you can't control the vote. If many of the teachers and supervisors live outside of the City of New York, and therefore have little or no effect on who is going to be elected to community boards, then politics becomes a very nasty thing in their opinion. And I resent, as a school board president and member, the implication that school boards care less about children than professional teachers and supervisors do.

Also, we have the charge, every time there is an issue about renewal of a principal, or appointment of a principal, we have the cute game played with us that minority group people are being racists when they look for Black and Puerto Rican principals. This came up first in I.S. 201. And at that time, sitting at a bargaining table with the then Superintendent of Schools, the answer that was presented to the charge that having a Black principal in 201 would be racist was, "All right. We'll guarantee that if you put a Black principal in Kew Gardens, we'll accept a white principal here."

P.S., the remark never got to the press. And there were no Black principals appointed in Kew Gardens. So, it seems, you are racist if you want it in your own neighborhood, and there is something wrong in wanting it in a neighborhood that is predominantly white.

One other thing, I think, is being overlooked. Right now we are talking about getting rid of the Board of Examiners. We are trying to get more Black and Puerto Rican teachers. But a situation is occurring which is going to frustrate many of the young people who are now in college under open enrollment and finally have the chance to make the ranks of teachers in New York City. That is, the flooding of the teacher market. All of a sudden, after years of teacher scarcities, we have many people who, for reasons of conscience, object to the war, and for other altruistic reasons, are entering the teaching ranks. And I am afraid those teacher ranks are going to be filled before the Black and Puerto Ricans graduate from college and look for those same teacher jobs. And I don't think this particular issue has been paid any attention at all.

One further remark about the Board of Examiners. You know, I am, as president of a school board, primarily concerned with public schools, but I must remark that my church has had a system of schools for a number of years which didn't employ a Board of Examiners, which has been eminently successful in guiding children through grammar school into high school and on into college. In fact, some of the teachers in the parochial schools didn't even have their degrees, and yet they succeeded in teaching.

Another point that has been made is that the Board of Examiners must check the subject matter competence of the teachers. Well, that would be fine, except for one thing, many of the teachers are not teaching the subjects they have their license in. You get the argument, "We must check whether he really knows his English," and he's teaching history.

And also--and this would be the last point--I want to tell a story about someone who was in the system, a principal with whom I used to argue frequently--he was a friend of mine--about this whole business of unqualified people. "These days," he argued with me, "you are fighting for the approval of unqualified personnel."

But I remember that some 20-odd years ago in his school there was a teacher who was a phys. ed. major, and he was teaching English. And the reason was that, the principal had explained very carefully, "Even though this man was only three pages ahead

of the students in the book, he was a good teacher," because he
had people with doctorates who used to come weeping at the office
that children had thrown erasers at them. And he had this man
who could maintain discipline and had some rapport with the students, who could teach.

So, I think there is an inconsistency in the posture that is
taken about qualified people. I don't see how tests really can test
your ability to teach. They may test your knowledge of a subject,
they may test your knowledge of procedures, but your ability to
communicate with students, your ability to capture their interest,
your ability to really be an educator, I think, in the last analysis
can only be tested in a probationary period. And yet, when we
have a probationary period and we find someone unsatisfactory,
those same unions that are highly incensed over the possibility of
the removal of the Board of Examiners would fight us on the removal of any probationers.

Thank you.

THE CHAIRMAN: Thank you, Rev. Resta.
Any questions, Counsel?
MR. TRACTENBERG: No questions.
THE CHAIRMAN: Marilyn Braveman.
MRS. BRAVEMAN: Commissioner, gentlemen, I am
Marilyn Braveman, Director of Education of the American Jewish Committee. I am speaking to day on behalf of the New York
Chapter of the Committee.

We believe that the effectiveness of the Board of Examiners
can be determined by the degree to which it enables community
school boards to place the best possible supervisor for each school
in that school, so that he in turn has access to the best possible
teacher to place in each class.

Now, we strongly support the concept of the merit system
to achieve this, but despite the changes made and described here
at length, that the Board of Examiners have made, we do not believe that the current procedures meet the criteria of a merit
system. A system of hiring and firing is not a merit system if
the standards do not take into account the full requirements of the
job. Merit has to be a two-way street, taking into consideration
not only individual qualifications but job demands.

The present job demand of the New York City schools has
been for more qualified Black and Puerto Rican teachers and supervisors. Now, although we reject the concept that belonging to a
particular group is an absolute qualification, we recognize that
minority group membership is a very relevant one. We make the
same kind of statement about merit, if it were large numbers of
Black and Puerto Rican professionals in the schools if the children
weren't learning, because they're not learning.

Now, we don't believe in any kind of double standard. We
believe in one single standard, and that is performance on the job.
Only those who have performed in the schools, with evaluation
based on objective criteria, should remain in the system, regardless of their race, creed or color. We believe that this Commission now has an opportunity to make recommendations that might
provide the best possible teachers for students.

At the same time, you should be protecting the rights of those teachers and supervisors who have demonstrated ability. It may be that right now their training just has not equipped them to meet the needs of the New York City schools. We still think they may have some skills and expertise that can be used, and we think that new ways to use them should be found. And I have a few suggestions there.

I would like to start off first with the Board of Examiners. The Board of Examiners has a large staff, they have long years of experience. And we think they could play a much more effective role if they didn't just spend all their time giving costly time-consuming examinations.

Now, among the things we think that they might be doing would be, first off, perhaps, helping the community school boards to develop objective hiring procedures, as the Chancellor has suggested, and in the continuing evaluation of those hiring procedures. They could serve as a resource to help community school boards set guidelines for developing personnel. There have never been effective systematic procedures for promotion within the system or within a school or school complex. Very often potential talent has gone unnoticed or wasted because supervisors just haven't the time to devote to training teachers and to use the skills developed by years of experience.

What we are saying, in effect, is that as teachers are recruited, simultaneously a talent search within the system should be undertaken so that outstanding teachers and administrators who have a record of performance could be brought to the attention of local school boards and superintendents very quickly so their skills can be utilized to the maximum benefit of the children.

We also would suggest that the Board of Examiners might be utilized to work jointly with the Personnel Division and with the community school boards in the preparation of some comprehensive personnel policies by which outstanding teachers would be promoted and unsatisfactory teachers would be retired to assure a true effective system, a merit system.

We think there are some roles for many teachers, too, some new kinds of roles. And we would like the community school boards to be able to call upon experienced teachers who have knowledge about teaching methods, expertise in the development and use of curriculum materials, and skill in working with parents and with the community.

We believe that full confidence in the schools will only be restored when the schools live up to the expectations of the supervisors, the teachers, the students, the parents, and the community at large. This will only happen when everyone, all involved, see that the Board of Education is seeking out, hiring, and promoting the best candidates available, those whose performance leaves no doubt as to what their qualifications are.

Thank you.
THE CHAIRMAN: Thank you. Counsel?
MR. TRACTENBERG: No questions.
THE CHAIRMAN: Mr. Marvin Bornstein.

MR. BORNSTEIN: Thank you.

Madam Chairman and members of the Board, I am from the West Side Parents Union in Manhattan. I want to bring to you some experiences relating to some of the things we have seen respecting teacher selection and opportunities for teaching in the New York City public school system.

Yesterday afternoon, after leaving here, I had an opportunity to be introduced to a young lady who was a graduate of a Southern college, who resides in the Harlem area. She has a background of eight years of work with youth on a professional level, and she sought employment as a teacher in the New York City school system. She had undertaken to meet the teacher requirements, for which her background was not adequate. She went from social work into teaching, and she had taken the examination given by the New York City Board of Examiners. She had already found principals in the Harlem area, where she had resided, who were very interested in employing her based on her background ability of working with young people of the same age group and on what they understood was her academic ability. She possessed a masters degree. She was told that according to the results of the examination she was not literate in English.

I think there are certain values that we haven't mentioned in the examination for literacy. It is not a content examination, but it's an examination of a person's supposed literacy. But what type of literacy are we examining? Are we examining standards set down by the Board of Examiners that most closely adhere to their concept of literacy, or standards that might be more applicable to a person who has a close understanding of and relationship to a community and to children, and who, having come out of a certain prior experience, possessed a different type of literacy, which is comparable, if not superior?

So, I think there are certain factors that have to be examined in this context. This was an aside, because it was not part of what I had prepared. But I just came out of this experience, was introduced to the person yesterday. I, by the way, referred her to Mr. Isaiah Robinson to bring this to his attention, and, of course, under the new State Decentralization ruling she would be, I believe, hirable at the present time.

I want to bring to the Commission's attention some other factors in hiring carried out by the New York City Board of Education. And what I want to bring to your attention now is the summer programs for children in the Youth Corps, which also lies within the domain of the Board of Education, as do programs in adult education and many other types of education. And I will bring to your attention one particular teacher's position that was open last summer in our neighborhood, the Mid-West Side Community Corporation area, for the Afro-American and Caribbean studies.

Resource teacher personnel were to be supplied by the Board of Education, and more expressly, the Title I program office of the Board of Education. This office was informed of the need for this teacher in this program, which was considered an essential one in terms of the large enrollment of Puerto Rican and Black students in this program. The Board of Education sent teachers for this position, but they just sent teachers who did not have a summer job. They did not examine or look for teachers to be sent to this position who had any relevancy or training in this area.

We were unable to accept these teachers in our area. They were licensed teachers who did not possess sufficient preparation or relevancy in these areas. And I think the question of relevancy is a very important one. When it seemed the Board didn't possess eligible candidates, the Community Corporation sought qualified candidates residing within the community.

This is a supposed option that lies with the Board. When candidates cannot be found for certain teaching positions, they will issue you what in quotes is called "a certificate of competency." Even if the person possesses a Ph.D., he must be certified as competent by the Board.

One person who was selected by the Community Corporation as a candidate for this particular resource teaching position was on a college faculty, was a doctoral candidate with a community fellowship in urban education. This person was sent to the Board of Education to be examined for competency.

When the candidate arrived at the office to be examined, she was kept waiting for a long period of time. And she observed that the people who had kept her waiting were just doing paperwork, and they did not really seem interested in examining her for this purpose. She was asked to fill out an application for a competency certificate and return with it on the following day. Having filled this out and returned, she was told by the person who had given her this form that the person in charge of the office was not in, and this was the only person who could issue a certificate of competency. When the teacher attempted--this person who is a teacher by profession, an educator--attempted to arrange for an interview to be examined on her competency, she was put off as to the exact time when she could be examined and certified. After several futile attempts along this line, the applicant returned to the director of the neighborhood program, and the head of the Community Corporation which was scheduled to begin this program at Teachers College, Columbia University.

When the Board of Education was pressed on certifying the candidate by the local community organization, they responded by saying that the candidate was not going to be given a certificate of competency--in other words, this was a sham--despite the fact that the candidate had not even yet been examined on her competence and/or ability. In fact, this office responded that no further candidates from the Community Corporation were to be certified because the Community Corporation was not playing ball, or meeting halfway the conditions of this office. What is to be implied, is that you hire a person supplied irrespective of their qualifications as long as they possess New York City licensing.

What was the net effect of the failure on the part of the Board of Education to allow for this particular position to be filled?

And this is just one example of many practices that have been to the detriment of the children in our community. Mr. Lipkins, who is the Assistant Director of the Neighborhood Youth Corps, and Acting Director of the Summer Enrichment Program, stated that filling this position would have improved the ability of the supervisory program teacher, who now had to assume a double responsibility to perform her tasks. An added burden was placed on her at the expense of everyone. She had two jobs to do, her supervisory duties as overall supervisor and her classroom duties as a reading teacher. She was helping teach pupils who were disturbed in reading, and as a result of not having this person who was to be sent she had to take on more than her task.

Incidentally, the curriculum teacher who had not been hired was meanwhile working as a volunteer in providing orientation to these same children for a community organization in a particular program in the community where they felt these children were not being given the type of supervision and the type of help they should have been granted.

I am illustrating this one example in hiring practices on the part of the Board of Education with the recommendation for the Commission that the powers in hiring that reside with the central Board of Education be granted, especially in instances as the above, to the needs of the community, either to the most applicable agency in the community, in this case the Community Corporation, or to the local community superintendent's office, with the adjunct assistance of the local board for evaluation either of the credentials of candidates or the preparation of persons serving ancillary teaching positions. That is, it would not be a prime necessity that a person be duly licensed by the Board of Examiners and the Board of Education.

The Board of Examiners' parallel with the old Board of Education is very interesting. From what I was able to ascertain yesterday by sitting here, it seemed to resemble the Board of Education, which, at one time, lacked essential minority group representation, or any minority group representation, in a city populated by large numbers of Black, Puerto Rican, and Hispanic pupils. It demonstrates to me and to many others in our community organizations the need to abolish the current Board of Examiners, or if this is not legally possible, to retire or replace some of their members with people who are more relevant to the educational needs of children in schools today. What I am talking about are the relevant needs, which are not the needs on paper or presented in curriculums which are never carried out in schools, but people who understand the day-to-day workings of a school by having assisted, or visited, or been intimately involved.

As an example, today I visited a local junior high school to discuss curriculum on a certain grade level. Walking in there, I saw in the hall a large child being utilized, a minority group child, to beat up, or restrain younger children, with teachers standing by in full view. And when I questioned this practice, they said these children are special children. I went from there directly down to the office of the administration of the school and was informed by a representative of the administration that "You have to understand the backgrounds from which these children come." This is the type of background they come from. This is what they bring to the school, and this is the way they are treated. And I told them I do not believe a word of what they are saying. So, I think there is a very relevant point here as to the inclusion of persons who really understand the people who live in the community, they work with the community, understand the needs of the community, and understand education.

And I also want to point out one other fact, the fact that I believe that the public education system in New York City must be infused with a number of other alternatives to education. That is, the infusion of persons with other skills and abilities. As I mentioned before, the teacher literacy testing examines for a specific set of values.

It was stated yesterday by Mr. Greene that these examinations are to screen out incompetents and illiterates and to screen in those with at least a minimal ability to begin teaching. We maintain, in essence, in many instances the opposite has occurred in the education of the minority group child, that many teachers have been barred who could have helped overcome the massive failure of this system.

THE CHAIRMAN: Do you have much more?
MR. BORNSTEIN: This is the end.

We believe that public education needs the infusion of many people who are not teachers by profession, but who could help immeasurably in the improvement of urban education. We are referring specifically to the leaves of absence from trade union groups, from other groups who work with these people, these young children after they get out of the schools, who come into many situations where they see these children intimately and work with them on a day-to-day basis as young adults.

We feel that junior high school and high school youths could be part of programs which could be developed by the community boards and the participating unions with relevancy to education and their future life. We feel that, much as a university infuses part of its resources into improving urban education, that there are many other factors that could be used for urban education, and that would be judged not on the basis of certain qualifications laid down by the Board of Examiners; that the statement by Mr. Greene--and this is the past page or so--that the examination process should evaluate the standing of the applicants or what would be the universal needs for teaching criteria, should be examined in depth to ascertain what in essence are the criteria necessary to improve public education in our city.

As the report of the Brooklyn Task Force indicates concerning academic failure in Brooklyn, it is not just a problem of minority group education. There's a problem of the failure of the system in all of its facets. This inability to educate children and motivate their development should be an essential criterion in the utilization and placement of professionals and supervisors in our public school system.

Thank you.

THE CHAIRMAN: Thank you, Mr. Bornstein. Do you have any questions, Mr. Tractenberg?

MR. TRACTENBERG: No questions.

THE CHAIRMAN: Let me just say that I tried to run this hearing not in the style of public hearings where people are given three minutes and then gaveled down for the reason that I understand the feelings on all sides of this issue. I am going to have to be a little more stringent, however, because I know that there are a number of witnesses, several of whom have gone to special efforts in preparing specific data for this hearing.

This is the last day that public testimony can be taken. And I therefore feel a duty to hold people to reasonably the time they were informed they can speak, which is five or ten minutes, lest some witnesses whose testimony is equally important not be able to speak. For we are leaving here tonight. This is not our building. We do have to get out on time, and I am determined that every member of the public who wishes to testify has a chance to come forward regardless of his point of view on this subject.

I want you to know that we are terribly behind, even though I have subjected my staff and fellow Commissioners to a schedule of no lunch and dinner breaks. Despite that, we have been unable to keep within the time we had set, largely because I have been overly liberal in the way I did the time. And I apologize to those, expecially Counsel and staff, who had to labor under that. But I think we all understand that this matter is of such importance that if we end up losing a little weight this week, perhaps we can bear up under it and be happy there was the opportunity to do it.

Let me call the next witness, Mrs. Nellie Jones.

One announcement. These hearings are being broadcast over station WNYC, and this is the last day for public testimony. We arranged public testimony in the evening and afternoon hours for two days, because the working public cannot easily come in the day. We do not have this room in the evening hours for the remaining days of the hearing, so anyone wishing to get his two cents in, come down now before 9:00.

Mrs. Jones.

MRS. JONES: Commissioner Norton and Commissioners, we were very happy to receive the invitation from you. And we thought about it a great deal and decided that we would like to present to the Commission some of the opinions of parents. And the opinions that I would like to present to you tonight are based on the qualities parents feel should be in an elementary school principal, because this happens to be an area of concern to a number of the parents to whom we relate.

We sent out in a random mailing 100 copies of a questionnaire that was developed as a result of a request from another community group. We received 65 responses to the 100 requests, and it is on the basis of this information that we will talk about certain things this evening.

The 65 responses represent opinions of parents in five school districts in Manhattan, two school districts in the Bronx, two school districts in Queens and Richmond.

First of all, the parents believe that an elementary school principal should be especially strong in program areas. In fact, 91% felt that it was an absolute must that he make sure there are good programs for children with special needs.

Equally essential to them were effective guidance programs, and 77% of the responses indicated this fact. 87% of the responses indicated it was essential, or preferable, for the principal to have a health education program. And it was interesting to note that they endorsed this for parents as well as children. And they also felt that it was very important to provide programs for teachers. Three-quarters of the responses indicated this.

Now, another area of emphasis in the questionnaire was the ability of the principal to provide supervision and educational leadership. Of the parents questioned, 84% felt that a principal must be absolutely sure that a good learning environment exists in each class, as well as in the whole school. And another 72% indicated a need for the principal to rate teachers by visiting the classroom on a regular basis.

The parents further indicated, 75% of them, that they were most desirous of having programs geared to help teachers improve and modernize their methods. They also wanted other kinds of training. They wanted training for the paraprofessionals as well as the teachers, on-the-job training. And more than half of them wanted the principal to provide teachers with special community orientation. I suppose this might be interpreted to mean they felt the teachers would better relate if they better understood what the neighborhood might be about.

Now, under "ability to communicate," the majority of responses fell into the "absolutely must" and "preferably should" categories. These parents, 97% of them, wanted parents and community clearly informed about the school's educational program. Another 77% wanted responses to requests to speak to community groups when these requests came into the principal. Another 87% thought that the principal should listen to discussions of staff regarding policy and programs. And it's interesting to note that 100% of the responses we received thought that the principal should listen to suggestions of parents regarding changes in school programs. And there were, all told, 77% who wanted community use of school facilities whenever it was possible.

We dealt with two other very small areas on the questionnaire. One had to do with personal qualities. And I think it is very interesting to note that 62% of the respondents had no particular opinion regarding the ethnic background of the principal. In response to the item which read "Be from the same ethnic background as the majority of the students," 62% of the respondents indicated that the principal "may or may not." And we thought this would be very interesting to share with the Commission, because we have heard from time to time some fear that if parents are participating in the selection process in any way, they might lean towards those of the same ethnic background.

Equally significant is the fact that respondents to the item "speak non-English language most common to the students," the response indicated that 33% stated "preferably should," and 50% stated "may or may not." But 93% of all the respondents felt that the principal "absolutely must" or "preferably should" be sensitive to the feelings of the groups and of the individuals with whom they were involved. So, I think it indicated this particular sampling of parents was very concerned about the sensitivity of the administrator.

Then there was a small space in which persons could write in some of the other items that were not asked. And I would just like to share with you one or two.

One item indicates under "personal qualities," that "the principal has to be a decision maker, not a middle-of-the-roader."

Another item indicated that they wanted the principal "to be aware of the community's necessities, and should be able to work with community, gathering their ideas," and it goes on and on. But one of the ones that appeared more frequently was "be willing to accept change."

Now, under "professional qualities," there certainly is something that has been discussed a great deal. The items regarding "source of licensing" produced a majority of responses in the "may or may not" category. 76% of these people wanted "previous administrative experience inside the school system," but didn't indicate how the licensing should come about. 62% wanted "past experience in similar situations," but did not especially care where the licensing came from, the city or the state.

On the last item on the questionnaire, which was "have a reputation for being a creative and innovative administrator," 26% of these persons felt this is "essential," while 63% believed this to be "preferable."

Now, in the write-in category, under "professional qualities," there are only three items. And they felt "the principal should have the courage to rate a teacher unsatisfactory if he is incompetent. The principal should go back to school from time to time to know what's happening and should have a thorough knowledge of the curriculum."

We thank you for this opportunity to share the opinions of 65 parents in New York City.

THE CHAIRMAN: Thank you.

Any questions, Counsel?

MR. TRACTENBERG: I have one question.

Mrs. Jones, I am just wondering if your personal experience in the school system in and around New York suggests to you that this kind of response may, in fact, be representative of the broader part of the population?

MRS. JONES: We would like to say that it is representative, but because of the areas that it represented, we thought that it was somewhat significant that we were getting groups of responses in particular categories.

THE CHAIRMAN: I don't know if the record shows that Mrs. Jones is the Director of the Center for Community Studies. I just want to note on the record your approach of doing a statistical study to get beyond stereotypes. I believe that this whole area is clouded by stereotypes.

I believe there are many stereotypes on the Board of Examiners, for example, some of which have been exposed here. And there are certainly stereotypes surrounding almost every issue about community control and what people will do in New York City once they have control over their schools.

I must say that Mrs. Jones's study is significant for the approach of attempting statistically to get at attitudes so that we might speak more knowledgeably about this whole problem with other bases than our preconceived notions of how people are going to operate. I appreciate your putting that in the record for us.

Mr. Herbert English.

MR. ENGLISH: Madam Chairman, my name is Herbert English. I am an assistant principal, acting, Junior High School 35 in Brooklyn, and I have been associated with the New York City system for thirteen years. I began teaching twenty-one years ago. I am here tonight to make a very brief statement.

It has struck some of my colleagues who are members of the African-American Teachers Association, some of the supervisors with whom I work and many of the teachers, that the Board of Examiners is following a deliberate policy; that the Board of Education is supporting that policy; that the United Federation of Teachers and the Council of Supervisory Associations, have joined hands, all together, in a deliberate, planned attempt to keep Black children ignorant.

This charge was made by me three years ago and I was charged over C.B.S. Radio with being paranoid. Since then a number of studies have been made by various people. Now I will refer to only one. A book was published either shortly before or after I made my particular statements, 110 Livingston Street, by David Rogers, which should be required reading for anyone who has testified here. And any listener who hasn't read it doesn't know what this hearing is about. 110 Livingston Street.

The pattern extends back something like sixty years, and it didn't begin with the current Board of Education. At that time we had an ethnic confrontation between two different groups, both white, Catholics versus Jews. This came to a head around World War I, progressed up to the time of the depression. The Jews trying to get higher positions, the Catholics were gradually phased out, as the children whom they educated went into various other areas.

With the Jewish control of the system, we see a repetition: the Catholics out, Jews in, Blacks trying to get in, Puerto Ricans trying to get in.

It would seem to us that we should put the cards on the table and admit that the system is not geared to teach the children now attending these schools.

There is no charge made by the African-American Teachers Association or by me that the people who control our system, who control the school system, are deliberately anti-Black "because Jews don't like Blacks." That statement is not made, and I have to state that categorically, because I have been misquoted before.

What I am saying is this, and I would like to be quoted correctly: Those who now supervise education in New York City are largely Jewish, 92%. Those who teach in New York City schools are largely Jewish, 85%. Those who are being crippled in the school system are something like 57% Black and Puerto Rican.

Therefore, all the prior statements that I have heard, sitting here, referring to minorities, irritate me no end. Blacks and Puerto Ricans are not minorities when you start talking about public school education in New York City. We are the majority. The minority is teaching us, or, misteaching us. We are the victims. And it's about time we put it in the record. This is open, blatant racism, and it has to be met on that basis.

The statistical analysis of the question has been made by experts today and yesterday, and I don't challenge most of the experts' testimony, except to say this much, that all that I have heard about testing and its validity and the way they measure tests and validate them, I have to reject all of it. And I reject it on personal experience.

There is no test that can be drawn up by anyone, however brilliant, and I don't give ground to anyone on knowing how to teach Black children. There may be greater teachers, there may be greater supervisors, and certainly there have to be better schools than where I am. But nobody that I know of has gone to school to learn how to teach Black children, so nobody knows how to teach Black children better than I do. And I am here to talk about my four Black children who have been crippled by this rotten system, and I am talking about the two thousand children that I help to supervise each day in Bedford-Stuyvesant. And I take no advice from anyone on that score.

Now, we have taken into our school system a revolving door process of teachers and supervisors from the Board of Education. All of them have passed Board of Examiners' tests. These are the people, the licensed people, and this is what I want to get across to the Commission. It is the licensed people, not the unlicensed people, who have brought the City of New York to its present state of educational chaos, the licensed people. It was done within the system. In other words, the system has failed, badly failed. Since it is such a tragedy, it needs drastic action. It needs drastic surgery.

It needs straight talk, and that's why I am here. I am talking to you real straight, since I am on the firing line out there, beyond the books, beyond the theory, beyond the rhetoric; since I am out there where the pushers are; since I am out there where the kids break the windows; since I am out there where the parents are angry and frustrated; since I am out there where the kids are dropping out, and stealing, and being unemployed, and wondering where they are going. I hear things that perhaps you at the Commission don't hear. I hope you do. But the one thing that I hear is a growing rumble of discontent.

What is happening in our high schools? You are reading in the newspapers what is happening in some of the junior high schools. You are reading about it. But I hear something else. I hear a general growing sense of resentment which I feel may result in racial explosion, unless something is done to stop this madness.

Nobody is asking for any person now teaching to be thrown out of his job. That is not our request, at least. What is asked for is that the present system of testing which merely screens out Blacks and Puerto Ricans be stopped. And one aside: Why has no Puerto Rican done something very dramatic to demonstrate their frustration? Because no schools that I know of in the city of the nine hundred schools, not one, is teaching Puerto Rican children, I mean, really teaching them so that they are learning. Not one school is teaching them because not one school is equipped with Spanish teachers to teach them. A statistic, just one statistic. Puerto Ricans comprise something like 37% of the population, the school population of New York City. Last year the statistics from the Board of Education were less than .5% of the teachers were Puerto Rican. That means that the teachers can't relate to the children.

What do we recommend? One, abolish all testing procedures. How is that to be done? We call on this Commission, that is, the African-American Teachers Association calls on this Commission to take immediate steps through injunctive processes, or any other legal processes, to see that all examinations are set aside forthwith, and that no more examinations, written examinations or oral examinations, for positions as teachers or supervisors in the City of New York, be held.

The second step that we recommend be taken immediately is that a study be inaugurated to determine whether a certain number of years of education need be prerequisites to one's teaching ability.

Much has been said here today before this microphone about how much education is required for one to become a teacher or how a person's teaching skills can be measured. We say they cannot be. And therefore, we claim four years of college, a degree, five years of college, a second degree, are perhaps not requisites to one's ability to teach.

We invite this consideration: The consideration of the idea of cadet teachers, that is, the high school cadet teacher, one who has not even received a high school diploma but who happens to be gifted and can establish rapport with children.

We feel that young children very often can teach younger children better than many of the adults whom I personally have seen become complete failures in the classroom.

Thank you.

THE CHAIRMAN: Thank you.

Dr. Bernard Friedman

Just let me say for the record again, because I think we have to be particularly sensitive to people's sensitivities and sensibilities, that the identification of people by their religion, I do not think in this case means criticism. We have to disassociate ourselves from indicating that anything these teachers do is related to their religion.

There is a tendency to identify the people in the school system in terms of the layers of immigrants who came to that system.

Just as at one point in history there were many people of Irish background in the school system, today there are, of course, many people of Jewish background in the system.

I would prefer that people not refer to people in the school system in this way, only because it is easily misunderstood by people in the Jewish community, not because evil intent is meant or because it is inaccurate. But we who are Black and Puerto Rican have always been supersensitive because of the way we have been treated historically. And I would, therefore, admonish us to be supersensitive about other people's sensitivities. And I, of course, can understand the sensitivity of the Jewish people. Therefore, we prefer not to speak of people in the school system by their religion.

But, of course, most of the people are white, and that, I think, encompasses all the people, or most of the people in the school system.

I wish to identify Dr. Friedman as District Superintendent, Bronx District 7.

DR. BERNARD FRIEDMAN: My name is Bernard Friedman, District Superintendent, 7, in the South Bronx, and I feel curiously juxtaposed after the last speaker, because I disagree with him and his arguments.

I think the salient question you have to ask each speaker who comes here is: If you abandon the Board of Examiners, and I am absolutely not making a plea for them, what will you substitute instead? Are you going to abandon any examination system, or are you going to substitute another one?

If you abandon the system completely, then you do a grave injustice to both the Black and Puerto Rican people and to the teaching profession. You, in a sense, say, on the one hand, that you have contempt for the intellect of Black and Puerto Rican people who will not be able to compete in an examination with all of the other citizens of the city or of the nation.

In other words, when Constance Baker Motley or Thurgood Marshall took the law examination to pass the bar, both of them competed as Black people with all of the white people. They didn't ask for no exam; they did not ask for an easier exam; they didn't ask for special privileges. When surgeons in Harlem Hospital, Suydenham Hospital, took their examinations as doctors, they took it in competition. They pitted their intellects against the intellects of all. That is on the one hand.

If, on the other hand, you say that the school system should have no examinations at all, then you show an open contempt for the profession as it is. Society, in a sense--

SPECTATOR: Come on--

DR. FRIEDMAN: Society, in a sense, puts its emphasis on a profession to the extent in which it examines it. If a person takes an exam to be a notary public, given by the state, he takes a comparatively easy one. If he wants to be a real estate operator, it gets a little harder. If he wants to become a lawyer, it becomes even harder. If he wants to become a doctor, it is comparable.

The fact remains that in this nation we value people by the

competitive qualities which they show. To take an examination like the school teaching one and say it should be eliminated must in any way be construed as having contempt for the profession and contempt for the people within it.

And, therefore, I say to you that the salient point of this entire study that you are conducting, and the question you ought to ask tomorrow to the people who are coming, is: If you abandon the Board of Examiners, then what will you substitute in its place?

SPECTATOR: Democracy!

DR. FRIEDMAN: And if, as I said before, you have no examination at all, then you must say, on the one hand, that you are afraid that Black and Puerto Rican people are inferior and cannot compete, or you say, on the other hand, that the profession has your contempt, it is not worthy of having any kind of examination procedure.

Now, I propose that if you really want to save the system, and if after examination, thorough and searching and critical, you appraise that the Board of Examiners has not fulfilled its function, then you have to think of another way of doing the examination system. You and I know that no lawyer can take a course in the New York University Law School and then get his bar degree by just taking it and getting his license, nor can a doctor get out of medical school and then practice. Why should a teacher who takes sixteen credits or so just be given a license for taking courses?

You and I know that that would be unjust, because if it isn't so, get all of these people off the wall whose pictures are here. They all went to schools and got their law degrees.

Secondly, for principals you would raise the entire principalships of the state if every principal had to take an examination given by the State Board of Regents. They then could give objective examinations, with examiners far removed from the New York City system, people taken from Buffalo or Oneonta or Plattsburgh, and license every principal in New York State. You would do away then with a great deal of the political chicanery and kinds of falsification you have, if principals in every town and hamlet and city of New York State would then have the same kind of credentials that a doctor or a lawyer or an architect or an engineer or a dentist has.

MR. DAVID: Dr. Friedman, it is important for the record to note that these five days of hearings were planned very carefully. The first day or two were spent in establishing the facts and spending some time on critically looking at the system. And we are encouraging all witnesses--indeed, we will be spending the last two days of the public hearing in trying to understand whether there are other methods of assessing merit, whether there are other models that worked in other parts of the state, and,' in fact, in other parts of the country. So that we are putting that question and asking the best minds we can find to respond to the specific question.

DR. FRIEDMAN: Then I think you are going to do what is very valuable to the school system, if you keep that in mind.

Thank you very much.

THE CHAIRMAN: Do you have any questions, Mr. Tractenberg?

MR. TRACTENBERG: No.

THE CHAIRMAN: Thank you, Dr. Friedman.

REPRESENTATIVE OF MISS SONIA ALLEN: Madam Chairman, Members of the Board: I am representing Miss Sonia Allen, Education Action Program, Bedford-Stuyvesant.

I would like to answer one comment made by the previous speaker when he referred to alternatives to the Board of Examiners. Previous speakers have made recommendations that we all listened to. On the other hand, in New York State only the Buffalo and the New York City school systems, which possess the poorest systems throughout the State of New York, as shown in the record, have Boards of Examiners. Therefore, we should take into consideration that other cities without Boards of Examiners are progressing. Then why shouldn't it be eliminated?

I would like to read something prepared by the Education Action Program, Bedford-Stuyvesant.

The competitive tests prepared by the Board of Examiners discriminate against Blacks and Puerto Ricans because they do not measure fitness and merit and because they do not indicate candidates' ability to perform the job.

It is therefore the position of the Education Action Program of Bed-Stuy, Youth in Action, that the city should eliminate its long-standing examination and licensing process for both teachers and supervisors and use state certification awarded on the basis of college programs and experience as a minimum requirement for appointment.

This would enable the 31 local community boards to develop their own specific hiring criteria.

The use of state certification instead of relying on a remote and centralized Board of Examiners would eliminate the selective principals' eligibility list and give the community board more freedom in choosing qualified candidates from any possible source.

The Board of Examiners is selected by the Board of Education. In early 1967 the Board of Examiners had nine members, all of whom had come up through the ranks. They were selected by examination, but it was generally understood that examinations at that level were tailored to applicants and that it helped to have political connections among top Board officials.

The Board of Examiners has four members who serve for life. By law, the duties of the Board of Examiners are to prepare and administer objective examinations, to determine the merit and fitness of all candidates for teaching and supervisory positions. These examinations are supposed to be open competitive and open qualifying. The Board may also establish an eligible list for positions when it finds an adequate number of qualified persons available.

Therefore, it is clearly seen that it is the Board of Examiners that determines who fills the teaching and supervisory positions in public schools.

The contents of the examinations are questionable. These

examinations are geared towards insiders, limited in scope, and discriminatory. Consequently, the ineffectiveness of the examinations is passed on to the communities, and children are the ones who suffer most, because the examinations are basically for subject matter mastery, based on memorization of factual data rather than practicality.

Leadership ability and professional competence are ignored. Therefore, teachers and supervisory personnel who can relate to the children of various communities are turned away. The exams are aimed at the white New York middle class.

The extent of racism on the part of the Board of Examiners can be seen by visiting the schools. The percentage of Blacks and Puerto Ricans are very low, although the percentages of Black and Puerto Rican students are much greater. Studies and recommendations have been made concerning the Board of Examiners and its effectiveness for over twenty years.

Some of the studies and recommendations by certain people like Strayer and Yavner in 1951, suggested changes to make the Board administratively accountable to superintendents and lay boards, questioned life tenure, and suggested legislation. Sayers and Kaufman reported that the Board of Examiners' powers, that is, the promotion from within, have made the New York City system more tightly closed than any other in the United States.

The New York University research team, headed by Dean Griffiths, comments on inefficiency in recruitment and promotion procedures that favor insiders. Little effort is made to recruit people from outside the city. Examinations are based on localized knowledge available only to insiders. Preparation for examination is supervised by insiders, already members of the administrative hierarchy.

Education Action recommends that, one, a cooperative effort between the central Board of Education and the Board of Higher Education for a teacher training exchange program be established.

Two: Southern Blacks who have experience and who have completed the requirements for state certification be recruited to teach in the schools.

Despite the recommendations and/or studies made, the Board of Examiners still exists, and large amounts of money and personnel are used for recruitment and examination administration. Generally, supervisors and principals, insiders, are used as assistant examiners.

It should be noted that the degree of selectivity is considerably less in examinations for substitute teachers than in tests for granting regular licenses. Yet the examiners are fully aware that most substitute teachers are employed on a permanent basis and are considered by the principals the equals of the regular license holders.

The elimination of the Board will give the community boards the duty of selecting, or, at least, having some say-so as to substitutes, teachers, and supervisors. Discrimination against Blacks and Puerto Ricans, who are qualified, will be alleviated.

The Board of Examiners has never represented and does not

now represent the majority of the citizens. Furthermore, there are only two cities in New York that do not use state certification alone as a means of licensing teachers and supervisor personnel, New York City and Buffalo. This, in itself, should help to support the idea that the Board of Examiners is a waste of money and personnel.

If the condition of the public schools in New York City is any indication of how a Board of Examiners affects the functioning of the school system, this in itself should support the idea that the Board of Examiners is a waste of money and personnel.

Thank you.

THE CHAIRMAN: Mr. Charles Burton.

I apologize to the witnesses who are having to wait much longer than expected.

Mr. Charles Burton, Education Committee of the Council Against Poverty.

MR. CHARLES BURTON: My name is Charles Burton. I am the Chairman of the Education Committee of the Council Against Poverty, which represents the two million poor in New York City.

We demand that the Board of Examiners be eliminated and that the community school boards be given the right to hire professional personnel based on state certification. We do so as a beginning step in eliminating the institutional racism which has characterized the personnel practices of the New York City Board of Education.

On every level and in every way possible, the hierarchy which controls the schools has systematically discriminated against Black, Puerto Rican, and Oriental professionals and also against Black, Puerto Rican, and Oriental children and their schools. We submit that the minority communities have been discriminated against by:

1) The Board of Examiners, which, through control by an "in group" of white professionals has kept minorities out of the system.

2) The Bureau of Personnel which has taken those Blacks, Puerto Ricans, and Orientals, who sifted through and segregated--

MR. DAVID: Mr. Burton, speak closer to the microphone, please.

MR. BURTON: 2) The Bureau of Personnel which has taken those Blacks, Puerto Ricans, and Orientals, sifted through and segregated them in the low-income schools, while the plush middle-income schools have been reserved for the white professionals.

3) The union contract which through its transfer plan provides a way out of low-income schools to middle-income schools.

With respect to the Board of Examiners, the examinations for licenses in the New York City schools are prepared and graded, in the main, by department chairmen and principals, all of whom are members of the Council of Supervisory Associations. These are the same people who give coaching courses for the very examinations that they administer. If there is a Black, Puerto Rican, or Oriental member of the CSA in New York City, we would be surprised.

With respect to the Bureau of Personnel, the favoritism, nepotism, and political wheeling and dealing is so Byzantine as to defy description.

It is alleged that we have an objective merit system. Yet we find that District 13, low-income, in Brooklyn, has hundreds of Black teachers, while District 22, middle-income, in Brooklyn a few miles away, has only a handful of Black teachers.

It is alleged that we have an objective merit system, yet District 20 in Brooklyn, the Bay Ridge area, is heavily staffed with Irish and Italian teachers and supervisors. For instance, for as long as one can remember, the principal of Bay Ridge High School has been an Irish Catholic. All of this is deeply ironic when one remembers the great hue and cry around I.S. 201 in Manhattan when the Black community requested that a Black principal be assigned instead of Mr. Stanley Lisser who had been assigned from central headquarters.

The fact is that in many ways the white communities have always had community control of the schools and that that community control has been exercised along the lines of color, religion and political clout. Community control never really became a problem until Blacks and Puerto Ricans asked in.

It is alleged that we have an objective merit system. But if the City Commission will investigate personnel assignments to the comfortable lily-white Districts 22 in Brooklyn and 26 in Queens, they will find hidden away the wives, sons, and daughters of the hierarchy of the Board of Education and the Council of Supervisory Associations.

It is alleged that we have an objective merit system. And although some teachers are assigned from a central list, the fact is that most teachers and supervisors in the so-called better schools, such as Bronx Science, Brooklyn Tech, and Midwood, are there because they were "requested" by the chairman or principal, and central headquarters merely rubber-stamped the appointments.

With respect to teacher transfers, it has been amply documented from many sources that the new, inexperienced teachers serve in the low-income schools and that the veteran, experienced, and high-priced teachers serve in the middle-income schools. The union negotiated transfer plan is the institutionalized method whereby teachers are trained in the low-income schools and then moved on to the middle-income schools. In fact, with respect to transfers, the transfer system gives a teacher two years of credit for every one year served in low-income schools. Needless to say, there is no system to reverse this flow with its consequent effect on the quality of education for minority children.

Another result of the concentration of veteran teachers in the middle-income, predominantly white, districts is that a disproportionately high share of the education budget is spent in these areas.

In summary, it is clear that the system is much more meretricious than meritorious and that radical reform is necessary.

THE CHAIRMAN: Thank you.

Mrs. Linda Linton, Association of Black Supervisors.

MRS. LINDA LINTON: Mrs. Norton, Mr. David, my name is Linda Linton, and I am a Vice-President of the New York Association of Black School Supervisors and Administrators. I am also one of the few Black acting principals in New York City.

I am sorry that the community superintendent has left, because I, too, am a part of the system, and I have some very serious questions that I would like to ask him.

I know that this past year I have tried very, very hard to staff my school with people who are competent or able to do a job of teaching children. All of these people have come through the supposedly objective examination, which is supposed to qualify them to do a job of teaching. I can say, without exception, that I have not found one superior teacher in the many teachers who have been assigned to my school in the past year and a half. I have found people who are inept, who are unqualified, who sometimes are not able to write the English language, who know nothing about Black children, who have very little empathy or understanding for them.

I am a product of this system, have taken eight examinations, passed seven of them. The eighth is now being marked. But I know that not one single one of these examinations had anything to do with my ability to be a good teacher, a good assistant principal, or a good principal.

I feel that the examination process is a process that gives the kinds of people who are able to pass examinations an opportunity to serve in our schools. I know of an assistant principal who has passed all kinds of examinations. He is one of the poorest, most ineffectual people that I have met in the school system in his inability to do his job. This is not an isolated instance.

We, the Black supervisors, feel that in some way the numbers of Blacks and Puerto Ricans who serve in supervisory capacities must be considered. We recommend New York State certification. We recommend for teachers the National Teacher Examination, so that we can be assured of getting people who are literate and who are able to read and write the English language.

We suggest for supervisors some similar type of national or New York State-wide examination. We feel that the Board of Examiners supports inbreeding. The Board of Examiners are a part of the Council of Supervisory Associations. The CSA has deliberately and frequently fought to keep Blacks out of supervisory positions. They have blocked every effort. They have brought lawsuits. They have lobbied in Albany. And they have done everything in their power to exclude Blacks.

In 1969, two short years ago, there were exactly three Black principals in this New York City school system. After a closed exam, which CSA fought bitterly to prevent, there were eleven Black principals. This city now has, actually, eleven licensed Black principals out of more than nine hundred schools. There are about forty to fifty acting Black principals, whose jobs are constantly being challenged, who serve with the thought that they may be removed at any minute.

I charge that the Council of Supervisory Associations has deliberately done everything in its power to exclude Blacks from supervisory positions. In 1941 the city had one Black licensed principal. In 1969 there were three.

I feel that if this organization had truly been a professional organization, concerned with improving education in the city, it would have conferred with organizations such as the Black Supervisors and worked out a way, that would be fair to all, to immediately increase the numbers of Black supervisors serving in the school system.

I feel that Blacks are not asking, as was implied by the community superintendent, for special privileges. They are not saying that they are unable to pass examinations. Because, while the Board of Education goes on jaunts all over the country to find Blacks who are qualified and Puerto Ricans who are qualified, there are, right here in this city, able, qualified--according to the Board of Education and the Board of Examiners standards-- highly qualified Blacks who could serve in supervisory positions.

I urge the Commission to recommend the upgrading and appointment and assignment of Blacks immediately in a number proportionate to the number of Black children in the schools. I'm not playing a numbers game, but, certainly, forty out of nine hundred schools, with a population of 55% Black and Puerto Rican, is an incredibly shameful condition. And if many of us had not fought very hard to increase the number to that very small number we would have perhaps just the three who were licensed in 1969.

NYABSA, then, urges you to recommend an examination procedure that perhaps would be a national examination, simply to be sure that people are literate. But the Board of Examiners, with its inbreeding, its lack of objectivity--because you cannot be a member of CSA which is fighting the promotion of Blacks and still be objective in giving examinations, in holding examinations, to increase the numbers of Blacks--must be immediately eliminated and other methods found of selecting as personnel people who are concerned, who have empathy for our children, who feel that our children can learn, and who are willing and able to do a job.

We suggest an internship for teachers; we suggest an internship for supervisors. We feel that no person should be given tenure without the strictest kind of on-the-job performance examination, so that those who head schools are doing it because of their ability to serve the children in the school and the parents, and not because of their ability to memorize formulas for passing examinations.

I have sat in on those cram courses, and they do give you formulas to pass examinations. And they do give you lists of words which will help you to pass examinations. And they do suggest, people who hold these examinations courses, that you use certain words, that you use the formula, that you use a certain pattern.

This has nothing to do with what I do every day in my school in the Harlem area. My ability to memorize all of that irrelevant material has nothing to do with what happens every single day in the school in which I am the principal.

Thank you.

THE CHAIRMAN: Thank you.

Mr. Nassetta. Mr. Nassetta is the Chairman of the Equal Employment Opportunity Committee of the Italian-American Civil Rights League.

MR. VINCENT NASSETTA: Madam, Commissioners, Mr. David, good evening.

May I make a preface before our presentation.

It was duly noted here this evening that the Commission responded quite quickly when an individual, providing testimony, used the word "Jewish." When another individual who used the word "Italian" and "Irish" mentioned the words "Italian" and "Irish," the Commission completely failed to respond whatsoever.

May we at this time take this opportunity to inform the Commission that we understand, possibly, the reasons why people in the United States of America have never had to be on their toes and worry about the sensitivity of Italians residing within this country. However, we respectfully request, at this time, that from now on the Commission would respond in equity and in all fairness, in due respect, to providing to Italian-Americans and Irish-Americans, and any other persons, the same basic, elementary courtesy which they are providing Jewish-Americans.

I will now start with my presentation.

My name is Vincent Nassetta. I am the Chairman of the Equal Employment Opportunity Committee for the Italian-American Civil Rights League.

This evening, the League is represented by myself and my colleague, the Chairman of the Education Committee, Mr. Steve Aiello, who will present his opening remarks to you.

MR. STEVE AIELLO: Ladies and gentlemen, Mrs. Norton. We won't take up that much time.

I am sure you all heard the words "relevant" and "self-image," and how important this is to the child in the New York City school system.

I also teach. I have been teaching for six years on the high school level in New York City.

I am Chairman of the Educational Committee of the Italian-American Civil Rights League, which, by the way, I think you should know, speaks basically for what we call the "grass-roots" Italian-American in this city. Within the past four months we have signed up approximately 35,000 members. The Italian-American community is finally becoming aware of some of the inequities in the educational system.

If you will, I would just like to present some facts, and I would like to preface the facts by saying that we support Chancellor Scribner in his recommendations dealing with the Board of Examiners.

To begin with, the Italian-American student in the State of New York, the public school system, represents anywhere from twenty to twenty-five percent of the school system. Very few studies have been done on this, and I leave that for whatever ideas you have.

As far as the Board of Education itself is concerned, the five-member board which supposedly represents the City of New York, at present has no Italian-Americans on it. As far as the Board of Examiners is concerned, in the last ten years there has not been an Italian-American. And, contrary to what one officer --I believe your second speaker--said, that is, in his knowledge no one was ever passed over, we have two people, Italian-Americans, who were on the Board of Examiners list, both of whom were passed over in preference for other people. We are thinking of instituting suit with your commission, for one of the individuals, after conferring with him.

As far as the high schools of New York City are concerned, at present there is one Italian-American principal in the high schools. He is on terminal leave. And since there are no Italian-Americans on the present list, that would mean that in September, one-fourth or one-fifth of the school population will have no representation on that level in the city high schools.

We have between 7 and 10% guidance counselors throughout the school system for, again, a population that constitutes from one-quarter to one-fifth of the school population.

And if one is to deal with self-image, and if one is to deal with the relevance of an education, the Italian-American dropout rate at high school is either first or second in the entire city. We are doing research on that right now.

Out of 1600 assistant principals throughout the City of New York, according to the Board directory of 1970, there are approximately 160 Italian-Americans. Seventy of those have not yet been appointed, and this is without counting the present list, which was just brought out by the Board of Education.

Again, at the junior high level, since we have been speaking of communities and meeting the needs of communities, in Italian-American communities, in districts such as 20 and 21, which are heavily Italian-American, we have, at the junior high level, in District 20, no principals: at the elementary school level, two. In District 21 we have no principals; elementary school level, one.

We are also following up a case where, in an Italian-American area, a junior high school refused to institute Italian as a language, in preference to Spanish and French, in an area that is over 75% Italian-American.

At the elementary school level we are fighting right now for the Flesch Program, which, for those of you who are not familiar, is the introduction of a foreign language at the fourth through sixth grade level. Again, in two districts which are heavily Italian-American, we are running into opposition by the supervisory staffs of those schools.

I was going to bring to your attention the recommended curriculum which is used for grades four through six in over eight hundred school districts, which excludes Italian-American contributions in the arts, literature, sciences, and the basic cultures of American history. These are the basic facts that we are dealing with, and we wanted to make your office aware of that.

Now, Mr. Nassetta, I believe, wants to follow that up.

MR. NASSETTA: When we speak of equal employment opportunity, we define it as access to the traditional levels of achievement. We are in a position where we know that the New York City Board of Education has discriminated against Americans of Italian origin.

It is the history of the New York City Commission on Human Rights to have taken no steps whatsoever in supporting and verifying and investigating and providing equal employment opportunity for Italian-Americans throughout the State of New York.

Equal employment opportunity to us means that there has to be access to every single grade level and grade step, from the porter within the school system to the principal, access to any particular job slot or occupational title that's available to anyone else.

Now, it is obvious through visible, very, very visible means, that since out of 91 high schools, there is only one Italian-American as a principal, the Commission has more than enough evidence, visible evidence, to institute a Commissioner's charge based on probable cause. We, at this time, demand from the Commission that it institute a Commissioner's charge of discrimination against the New York City Board of Education and the Board of Examiners, based on the probable causes which are visible, which need no written documentation whatsoever.

All too often, within the Italian-American communities, our youngsters, who are the youngsters of immigrants, who do have a language problem, are placed in the very same position as our African-American and Spanish-speaking brothers and sisters. They are kept on and on and on, until the point when they reach the ninth grade, and they read and speak and write on the third-grade level. They are now plunged into a general or vocational training situation.

It is by no means accidental that the highest dropout rate in the City of New York is enjoyed by the Italian-American. As a result, the Italian-American in this city and in this state has been dehumanized, emasculated, and brought to believe that he and she and their children are incapable of achieving the capacity to be able to function on a high school level and beyond.

This is criminal. And this criminality resulted because of the blatant discriminatory practices of the New York City Board of Education together with the Board of Examiners.

Once again, speaking for the Italian-American Civil Rights League, we demand from this Commission that it institute a civil rights case against the New York City Board of Education and the Board of Examiners, charging them with discriminatory labor practices based on probable cause.

I thank you very much.

THE CHAIRMAN: Thank you, Mr. Nassetta.

I think the record should be correct about the highest dropout rate. I believe the highest dropout rate in the City is the Puerto Rican dropout rate.

MR. NASSETTA: Check it out.

THE CHAIRMAN: In addition, I feel I must go on record with respect to the Commission's concern for the Italian-American community, since it was said the Commission has not taken any steps in that regard, to note that last summer the Commission did announce a full-scale investigation of anti-Italian bias in the city. Indeed, this received almost a full page in the New York Daily News.

Finally, while I admonished everyone earlier to be very sensitive to people's sensibilities, with respect to ethnic origin, I was not aware that anyone had referred to people in the school system as being Italians.

MR. NASSETTA: The previous speaker from the Council Against Poverty, spoke of Irish-Catholics--

THE CHAIRMAN: Let me make it clear that I was not aware that referring to someone by his ethnic background, such as calling him a Puerto Rican, or of Irish background, was considered objectionable. However, referring to people by their religion is not only considered objectionable but has been found over thousands of years to be an objectionable practice. So that if anyone wishes to refer to someone here, for example, as Catholic or Jewish or Protestant, he is bringing in to these hearings something that is totally irrelevant, because he is referring to people by virtue of their religion.

MR. NASSETTA: Madam Commissioner, if you check the record you will see indicated in the record that the gentleman from the Council Against Poverty had used the word "Catholic."

THE CHAIRMAN: If he used the word "Catholic"--

MR. NASSETTA: He certainly did.

THE CHAIRMAN: Let me go on record. He may certainly have done that. Calling people by their religion is a shameful practice. It has led to great conflict throughout history, and we won't tolerate that in these hearings. You were properly sensitive to that.

Now, let's go on in good humor.

Judy Heumann.

MISS JUDY HEUMANN: My name is Judy Heumann. I am Executive President of the Disabled in Action, an organization comprised of disabled and non-disabled individuals who are working for the improvement of human rights for the disabled.

We have long been a group which the Board of Education has discriminated against. As of today, I am the only physically disabled teacher that the Board of Education has employed. Since June, according to Dr. Scribner's office, no other disabled individual has been employed in the capacity of teacher.

When this sad story is taken in proper perspective, one begins to ask oneself: How can a system that educates the disabled be one of the systems that has a hiring policy of discrimination against the disabled?

According to Dr. Scribner's office, not only have no other disabled individuals been hired as teachers, but no work has been undertaken to improve the abysmal employment picture for the disabled. One must wonder why the Board of Education passed a resolution in December 1970 stating that as a result of a recent case the Board of Education was now going to start hiring qualified disabled individuals.

Why are the disabled continuously forced to beg for something which is rightfully ours? How can a system which educates the disabled and espouses equality for all expect these disabled youngsters to consider themselves equals in our society? I am teaching physically disabled students, and the reactions I have had from my students and from non-disabled students have been overwhelming. The disabled students have never had another individual who has similar problems to theirs sitting before them and teaching.

The solutions to these problems are quite easily derived once we rid our minds of an ideology which was started prior to the Middle Ages. We are supposed to live in a civilized society which recognizes an individual for what he or she is able to contribute. A teacher must be an individual who is capable of communicating new thoughts and ideas to a class.

We should not have to defend our rights to employment. However, we, as disabled individuals, find ourselves continuously forced to do so. The Board of Education must now begin to show good faith not only to the disabled but also to the public. The public has been led to believe that disabled individuals are now being hired.

Solutions must be immediately enacted.

1) Immediately re-examine all individuals who have been denied licenses because of a physical disability.

2) Immediately place these individuals in the classroom.

3) Immediately initiate programs of recruitment.

It is incumbent upon the Board of Examiners to seek out disabled individuals who have been afraid to seek employment in this field. I would like to make a correction. I don't mean the Board of Examiners. The Board of Education must contact all universities in the metropolitan area and inform their education departments and guidance counselors that they will now hire the disabled.

4) No unreasonable restrictions are to be placed on the hiring policies for the disabled.

Now that the disabled are graduating from universities, we are beginning to realize that a good education does not equal employment.

We are not going to be satisfied with merely being placed in positions as teachers. However, we realize that we all must start on this rung. We do, however, sincerely hope that the present discriminatory practices will not hold us back from attaining supervisory positions.

This Commission must realize the fact that the disabled are looking to you for help. We recognize that this Commission is the only commission in the country which specifically states that one is not permitted to discriminate against the disabled. We are looking towards you to help us find a solution to this problem.

We hope that in the future the disabled will no longer have to say that a good education does not necessarily equal employment.

Thank you.

MR. DAVID: Thank you very much, Miss Heumann.

I know that you know, but it is important for the record to point out that this Commission has for the past year and a half had jurisdiction over the physically handicapped. We have not had the amount of experience that we would have liked, but we are very serious about our finding that the physically handicapped are a disadvantaged group. And, as you know, because you have been helpful in it, we will, within the next month or two, have a major workshop at which we will bring together handicapped people to see where and how the Commission may be more valuable to this group.

THE CHAIRMAN: Thank you very much, Miss Heumann.

Mr. Maldonado. The next speaker, Mr. Jorge Maldonado.

MR. JORGE MALDONADO: Good evening. Before I begin reading what I have to say, I want to state I am firmly convinced New York City needs not the services of the present Board of Examiners, or at least not the way it is functioning now.

Our City is going through a tremendous financial crisis. This could be greatly alleviated with the elimination of a system which is not rendering the services which it is supposed to render. And, in addition, you have to see the red tape and the waste of money that we spend maintaining that system.

And now I am going to read my statement, which is very short.

My name is Jorge Maldonado. I am a graduate from the University of Puerto Rico. In addition, I have taken both graduate courses in the University of Puerto Rico and in the City University of New York. For salary purposes I am considered to have a master's degree equivalency in social studies.

I have had experience as a teacher in Puerto Rico and in New York City. I have been working as a teacher for the Board of Education of the City of New York since September 1964 on a regular substitute basis. I have applied, so far, for eight licenses, of which I have six. It is the eighth license that I applied for that I want to tell you about tonight. This is the license for regular Spanish teacher.

I took the examination in January 1970. The written part of the test, all in English, consisted of questions about Spanish and Latin and American history and culture. Instructions and questions were in English, as I have already said.

The test consisted of three parts. First there was a short-answer test, followed by a written essay. Then I was called for an oral interview, which was conducted in Spanish and English. In my opinion, the interviewers did not master the Spanish very well.

The test, in general, was an advantage for any applicant whose vernacular was English and who knew--in this sense it was an advantage to me, too--some Spanish and Latin American history and culture. In my opinion, just the knowledge of a few words in Spanish would have been enough for any applicant whose vernacular was not Spanish to pass the short part of the interview conducted in Spanish.

Sometime in May 1970 I got the result of the test. I had passed the short-answer test and interview. But I was disqualified for the license because my written English in the essay was found unacceptable.

I immediately appealed, but my appeal was turned down. I claimed the following:

1) To require of prospective Spanish teachers an exam which tests written ability in English but not written ability in Spanish is not only foolish but discriminatory against native Spanish-speaking people, mostly Puerto Ricans.

2) The method and standards employed by the Board of Examiners to grade my examination paper have the effect of discriminating against me because of a written Spanish accent. It is true that I may make grammatical errors, but these errors are no proof I cannot communicate with English-speaking students and parents.

In addition, the grading method and standard apparently provided no credit for the quality or the competence or the content or the color, tone, and expressiveness of language used by the applicant.

At this point I would like to read to you my examination paper, but in the interests of saving time I will not do so unless you ask me for its reading. If I would, I think you will agree that despite the grammatical errors, I can express my ideas adequately. Please notice, my gradings on the copy given to me by the Board of Examiners are not visible. So it is not possible to tell exactly why a specific demerit was given.

I filed a complaint with the New York City Commission on Human Rights. I understand that the Commission requested a copy of my examination with the grade marking clearly visible.

The Board of Examiners refused to comply with the Commission's request. They said, instead, that only I could get a copy of my examination paper. Then my attorney from the Workers' Defense League wrote this letter to the Board of Examiners on January 13, 1971, requesting the papers. As of today he has gotten no response. They never answered my letter.

3) I am under the impression that the teaching of foreign languages in the New York City public schools, and mostly Spanish, is very inadequate. If this is true, in my opinion, one of the reasons for it is the fact that the Board of Examiners does not seem to be interested in recruiting real, Spanish-speaking teachers to teach Spanish. I dare to say that in many schools Spanish teachers are not teaching any Spanish, but English. Only the Board of Examiners should bear the responsibility for this situation.

I think it is apparent that not only does the Board of Examiners maintain a testing system which discriminates against Puerto Rican-American citizens of this city, but also refused to face up to its public responsibility to account for its action.

I don't insist that when the tests of the Board of Examiners were created, they were intended to discriminate against Puerto Ricans, but that is their effect today. This is especially true when it is remembered that the emphasis in language education today, in any modern school system, is on audio-lingual and visual method.

Thank you very much for letting me testify tonight.

THE CHAIRMAN: Anne West.

MISS ANNE WEST: I am Anne Grant West from the National Organization for Women. I will be very brief.

Dr. Rockowitz has stated that the reason for the relative absence of minority group members in school supervisory positions is that as recently as 1967 less than 2% of the graduating class of the senior colleges of the City University was Black and even less was Puerto Rican; only a small fraction of these were education majors.

If the Board of Examiners wishes to justify its procedure by using this method of reasoning, the National Organization for Women would like to use the same method of reasoning for confronting the Board with the following facts:

In the 1967-68 term, women students at the senior colleges of the City University received 53% of the bachelors degrees, 61% of the advanced certificates, all of which were, of course, in education, and 62% of the masters degrees. Of these masters degrees received by women, 75% were in education. In the fall of 1969, women held 59% of the city's teaching positions but only 36% of the supervisory positions.

Furthermore, in the city's elementary schools, principals' positions are held by 619 men and only 185 women. In the junior high school, 127 men are principals: only 18 women are principals. In the senior high schools, the principals' positions are filled by 90 men, 15 women.

We have tried to get women principals and supervisors to testify here today to the kind of discrimination they have experienced in achieving their positions in the school system. However, all those with whom we spoke indicated they could not conclusively cite objective instances of discrimination, but that they had been more disturbed by a subtle sense of intimidation. They told of college advisors who warned them of difficulties they would face as women if they sought placement in administrative positions; and they spoke of male colleagues in the system who expressed disapproval of their being assigned to administration positions, and thus keeping men who presumably had families to support from holding these positions. It is understandable that none of these women wanted to offer such subjective evidence of intimidation as testimony at this hearing.

Even if the forms of discrimination against women in the school system are subtle, or admittedly subjective, we feel it is the responsibility of the school system to correct the present underutilization of women in administrative and supervisory positions. We recommend that the Board of Education issue well advertised publicity, stressing the right of women to apply for higher positions in the school system.

The Board must make a conscious effort to impress upon college advisors, as well as upon men and women in education, that women are as much entitled as men to support themselves and their families by filling high-ranking positions in the school system.

Finally, we support the right of communities to select as their school administrators and supervisors those who can deal best with the community's problems, regardless of the candidate's position on a ranked competitive list.

However, we see evidence that when the ranked competitive list is discarded, women are among the first to experience discrimination. Therefore, we urge that all districts be required to submit data on employment practices, listing by section the number of men and the number of women who hold positions at each level of status and salary.

We further urge that all information published by the city schools be classified by sex wherever personnel practices are concerned.

THE CHAIRMAN: Mr. Seymour Samuels, Queens Jewish Community Council.

MR. SEYMOUR SAMUELS: Mrs. Norton, Counselor, ladies and gentlemen: My name is Seymour Samuels. I am a Vice-President of the Queens Jewish Community Council. My responsibility with the Council is that of community relations and education.

The Queens Jewish Community Council represents through their respective organizations most of the Jewish residents of Queens. The officers and the board members of the organization are people of varied professions and occupations. We donate our time on a voluntary basis. Unlike other organizations, we do not have a paid staff or public relations people. We do not have access to mass media. But we do hear and we do listen to our member organizations and their members, who constantly express many concerns about the future of the city in which we live.

They are concerned about several things, Madam Commissioner. They are concerned about solving the sociological problem in which the majority of our public school children are either Black or Puerto Rican. And they are concerned about a professional staff which contains only 10% Blacks and Puerto Ricans. They are concerned about this school system, once the finest in the nation, and possibly still the finest.

I digress for a moment, because I draw attention to the fact that of forty Westinghouse finalists in the entire country, eleven come from the City of New York. With a population percentage of 4%, we produced 27% of the Westinghouse winners.

Our school system, though, has been deteriorating under the constant attack that it has been subjected to. It is being used as a scapegoat, we feel, for all the social ills of this city. Our people are concerned about what we do for the teacher and for the supervisor who is presently in a position of service and who is threatened with expulsion.

What do we do with communities concerned about growing children, married children, who are leaving their homes and their communities and departing from this city? How do we prevent this accelerating exodus of middle-class people from the city which we all love?

They are concerned about what we do with job opportunities for all the people in the City of New York. They are concerned about the terrible problems of narcotics addiction and the fact that dope is rampant and openly sold through the entire school system. They are concerned about the terrible problems of crime in our schools, attacks by students on teachers and upon administrators, and about the problems of crime in the streets.

At no point in these hearings has anyone really addressed themselves to the children of the city and what is best for the children in our schools. We have heard it said throughout the past three days that a Black child needs a Black teacher, a Puerto Rican child a Puerto Rican teacher. And I rather imagine that if we had polka dot children, it would require polka dot teachers.

Yet every study made--and several such studies have been reported in The New York Times and cited in the past three days at these hearings--such studies have shown that in Black universities and schools where the entire teaching staff is Black, the level of achievement is not noticeably different. As a matter of fact, the level of achievement is often below that attained in our New York City school system.

We also fear this play on numbers, and the insinuation that if 51% of our school population is of one ethnic group, then 51% of the teachers and administrators should be of that same ethnic group. This strongly suggests that a quota system is under consideration, and we are vehemently opposed to this. A quota system works aginst all minority groups. It suppresses able, qualified people from any ethnic group from getting a job if the quota of that group for the position is filled. Thus to maintain a quota system is clearly discriminatory.

We are concerned that the present attacks on the Board of Examiners are not so much attacks upon them as an attempt to destroy all objective determinations of professional competence. We ask you to consider the many other problems that will arise when teachers and supervisors are appointed without regard to tested competency.

What do we do to see that our children have competent instruction? How do we keep the school staff from being eliminated whenever a new school board is elected? How do we prevent nepotism or discrimination in any form? How do we guarantee that every person in this city be granted equal opportunity, and that no person be granted preferential opportunity?

On Monday night, I believe a gentleman by the name of Pemberton gave a chronology of his experience with the New York City school system. He described his attendance at the Fordham University administration course. If I may, I would like to tell you about one of our people. I will give you the name if you wish it, at the conclusion.

This chap spent twenty years in private industry, in the management field. He operated and ran several theaters, which meant that he was responsible for payrolls of up to 47 people, for the supervision of 47 and 50 people. He was responsible for the maintenance of buildings; he was responsible for what is ordinarily called showmanship; he was responsible for keeping order within the theater; he was responsible for almost everything that a good administrator should be responsible for. As a matter of fact, his business experience met the requirements of the Fordham University program.

He then left private industry and went into the teaching profession. This happened eight years ago. He qualified for the 1967 examination given for assistant principal to the junior high school. He took that test, passed the examination, was eventually placed on the July 1968 list for such position. That list now contains approximately eight hundred candidates. He subsequently took and passed the examination for administrative assistant in the high school division.

He has written to all 31 school boards in the city and has not been granted the courtesy of a single interview.

I bring this up, Madam Commissioner, to suggest that open-hiring practices of this kind may very well work against the very people that we all wish to help. What I have just cited is a statement of fact.

We would further suggest, Madam Commissioner, that the purpose of this hearing would be to influence the State Legislature, which is a valid purpose. We accept that, because the Board of Examiners is a creation of the State Legislature and of the State Education Law. And we anticipate that at the conclusion of these hearings, the legislative body will be given a statement of facts by your Commission, a complete report, with suggestions of what to do.

We suggest that in order for this report to be fair, that hearings be held throughout the entire state to examine the deficiencies in communities which operate merely on the granting of state certification.

We wish to ask, for example: Is there any nepotism throughout the state? Is there bribery? Is there discrimination? Does it exist in other school districts? I will hazard a guess that we will find that it does.

Before we experiment, Madam Commissioner, with a generation of our children, should we not be certain that we have absolutely accurate statistics on the supposed benefit of state certification?

It is our position that the best method is an objective system of testing for professional competence. This objective system must set forth the rules in advance. It must set the requirements in advance. And it must maintain these standards throughout the entire city. It must make such tests available to the entire population.

This is not an attempt to defend the Board of Examiners. There must be change, and we suggest the following change:

A test which now consists of the following items: A written part covering satisfactory competence in written English; and an interview examination. We feel that these should comprise only 50% of the test score. In addition to them, a performance test, based on a full year of performance under a temporary certificate, should comprise the other 50% of such testing procedure.

This will do two things. It will eliminate the difficulty of getting rid of the probationary teacher who holds that license in her hand.

What we are suggesting, Madam Commissioner, is that the actual license for teaching--or for supervision, or for administration--not be granted until the entire test is completed, the last half of the test being the performance part of the examination. But such performance must be evaluated by competent professionals and by the community that our administrators will be responsible to.

We hold that political, racial, and ethnic considerations must not be the criteria for choice of staff. We feel that parents and students deserve the best-qualified teachers that are available and that can be obtained. It is our opinion that this can be done by improving testing procedures, and that this will provide qualified personnel in an impartial, objective manner, free of discrimination.

Thank you.

THE CHAIRMAN: Thank you, Mr. Samuels.

I do wish to say I think you may do a service to the gentleman whom you mentioned in your testimony if you will tell him if he believes he has been discriminated against because of race, creed, color, sex, or origin, that he come to our office at 80 Lafayette Street to file a complaint. We will be happy to receive such a complaint.

MR. SAMUELS: Madam Commissioner, it wasn't discrimination. I am sure that there wasn't any discrimination involved. It is just the fact that now there is a pool of 800 people qualified by the Board of Examiners, 800 people, with possibly 100 or 150 available positions. And the only possible discrimination here is that I feel that many school boards may be missing a very able person by not granting him the opportunity of an interview.

THE CHAIRMAN: I see.

MR. SAMUELS: This is an important point, and that's why I say that this may work against everyone that we are trying to help.

THE CHAIRMAN: By not granting him an interview, they cannot make a judgment on him, personally.

MR. SAMUELS: Right, this is what I am stating. They are not making a judgment on him, personally, of course. So there is no discrimination. But, by the same token, they may be doing their community a disservice by not examining this individual.

THE CHAIRMAN: It is impossible to examine--

MR. SAMUELS: By interview.

THE CHAIRMAN: But it is impossible to interview eight hundred.

MR. SAMUELS: I would say that, yes.

THE CHAIRMAN: I think Mr. Samuels has a point. If a person isn't granted an interview, if he is a qualified person who wishes to teach, I think that does present some anguish. I am not sure what the answer to that is, but I am sympathetic with the person who writes to 31 places and doesn't get an interview.

I do want to say that I think a good point has been raised, one that we had to consider very seriously in planning these hearings, which is: What, in fact, does happen if one does not have a system like the one we have? We will be hearing testimony on this tomorrow. We will be examining very closely the experience of teachers from other states. (New York is unique in this respect.) We will be examining officials from other states, to see if there are problems of corruption. We have not underestimated the possibility of corruption and, if there are problems of corruption, how they have been dealt with.

I am sure that it is safe to hypothesize that the rest of the country isn't rampant with corruption, and we could, perhaps, learn what safeguards they have taken in this regard, and that will be our testimony tomorrow and the next day.

MR. SAMUELS: What we suggest by the other hearings, Madam Commissioner, is the fact that bringing in the professionals, bringing in the Board of Examiners--in effect, you will be bringing in boards of examiners or people that select personnel from other states--will not answer the question that we raised. It is bringing in those people, as you have done here, who have been screened out by the system that may be used out of New York City, or out of the State of New York. It is these people that could best tell us the shortcomings of whatever hiring practices are being used.

THE CHAIRMAN: It may be, though, that this issue is of sufficient interest around the state so that you will have others who are concerned. For example, we are inviting people from Buffalo. Buffalo has a similar system, and I think it is fair to ask them what they are doing.

Would you like to make a statement?

DR. ALVIN LASHINSKY: Alvin Lashinsky of the Queens Jewish Community Council.

I just want to add one other item, Madam Chairman. That is, when you do invite the people from other states and other cities, try not to invite the establishment. Try to invite the dissidents.

THE CHAIRMAN: I must admit that it is rather difficult, sitting in New York, to figure out who is the dissident in Iowa or in the State of Washington or in the State of Mississippi. We try to be fair in inviting people who know something about the overall school system. If there is someone whom you would like to suggest, we would be happy to invite them.

MR. LASHINSKY: Thank you very much for your courtesy and fairness.

THE CHAIRMAN: Thank you very much, and come again, sir.

Doris Rosenblum, P.S. 84, Parents Association.

MRS. DORIS ROSENBLUM: Just a bit of correction. I am not from P.S. 84; I am from P.S. 75. I am also the President of the Stryker's Bay Neighborhood Council on the West Side of Manhattan. And I want to thank you, Commissioner Norton, for holding these hearings. I think they are long overdue, and I think it's a service that you are performing for the entire city, probably the entire country.

I have just heard the testimony of the previous speaker, and I somehow feel there is a certain contradiction in some of the things he said. While he wasn't holding any brief for the Board of Examiners, at the same time he was talking about a long list of names on eligible lists of people waiting for appointments. And he indicated that the gentleman he was referring to was not able to be granted an interview, partly because of that long list.

But that is as a result of the Board of Examiners, and as a result of the fact that this special examination is required for all assistant principals and principals before they can take any office in any school.

I come from a school in the mid-West Side of Manhattan that has gone through all of this procedure, and we are very pleased that we now have a community principal. He is in an acting capacity, and we are trying like the devil to keep him to stay, because it's the parents in the community, together with the teachers and the paraprofessionals, whom we believe are the people who have and should have the voices in determining who should represent their children in terms of an education.

I have been a parent in that school for eight years, because my older kids graduated and have gone on. I have a younger one still in. I was Parent Association president before I even had a child in the school, because there was nobody to serve in that capacity, because parents have always felt, "By God, what can a parent association do?"

What can a person do when the beauracracy of the school system makes it impossible? All decisions are made for them. So I, nervously, as a new parent, said, "O.K., I'll try it." And, believe me, I learned it the hard way, but I fought, you know, and a lot was accomplished as a result of it.

I remember a couple of years ago when we had another principal, at the very beginning, telling me how wonderful it was that she was coaching loads of people to pass the principal's examination. She gave me some of the insight into how that was done, and I wouldn't want to repeat it. But, because she had some personal contact, she knew exactly what was to be given.

And I said, "But that's not nice; it's not right; it's not fair."

And she said, "Well, you know, we've got to have certain people in the capacity of principals and assistant principals because we've got to keep the tenure system alive," and so on.

I was a little naive at that time, and yet I said, "But it just doesn't sound right."

And, of course, as the years went on I began to see how really wrong it was, especially when everyone around me--and I live in a community where more than 50% of the children are nonwhite--was nonwhite, while every single supervisor, assistant principal, and principal was white. And, it began to dawn on me that something was wrong with this "merit system" of licensing and examination. And I began to do a little research in my spare time, as a working mother and as an active community person, and I began to realize that, by God, it was practically impossible for any minority group person, that is, nonwhite person, to pass this examination.

I heard Mr. Maldonado speak before, and I absolutely agree with him. I'm sure he is as competent, if not more competent, than any of the teachers in the system teaching Spanish, who are mostly non-Spanish people who have taken some Spanish courses in college and don't have the accents and are therefore killing the kids' use of the Spanish language, because I have seen my own kid go through it. It's abominable, having such teachers, rather than having a Mr. Maldonado in the school system teaching Spanish to children, be it Spanish children or non-Spanish children, who could have the opportunity to learn a language in the proper way.

And so we in Manhattan, in District 3, felt, "By God, it's about time we did something about the system, the Board of Examiners, and the fact that there has to be another examination" which we felt was not relevant or representative of what the needs of our community were.

And so we decided, when there was a vacancy, that we were going to have a screening panel which had representation from all the different aspects of the community, the parents, the teachers, and the paraprofessionals, and we went through a procedure of going over the list of the Board of Examiners. There were about 250 people on that list. We interviewed and we interviewed and we interviewed for months on end, while we had no regular principal in our school. And every single one of those people who came to us was completely irrelevant to the needs of our community. We found this in P.S. 75, we found this in P.S. 84, we found this in I.S. 44, and in a host of other schools in District 3 in Manhattan, and then we began to say, "Well, my God, perhaps there's another way. If these people aren't going to really meet the needs of our children, perhaps we have to do something about it."

Luckily, our community school board, which at that time was not a community school board but the local board for District 5, said, "You know, you can try to see if you can interview people outside of the list who have state certification, and see if any of these people could meet the needs of your kids. You can get them in on an acting capacity until possibly some kind of change in the law could be made."

We started to do that, and it took another period of time. But it's interesting that in each one of these schools we found the principals, and they are acting, who did fill the needs of our community and our children, who are not on the Board of Examiners' list and who did not take the examination.

Three of those principals are the ones who just recently, on November 3rd, when the last test was given, publicly defied that examination. One of them is Mr. Mercado from P.S. 75, where I am, and Mr. Morrison of P.S. 84, and Mr. Luther Seabrook of I.S. 44, and these three men said, "We will be judged by our performance in the schools." And the teachers, most of them, and the parents, practically all of them, and the students, practically all of them, agreed.

We felt this is the way to judge competence. If they are no good, then we don't have any problem in getting rid of them. But the list of the Board of Examiners and the tenure system would not permit us to get rid of an incompetent person in an administrative capacity.

I think it's high time that the parents and the community and the Commission on Human Rights realized that this is the way to make judgments, so that you are not stuck for life or, as in many cases, until they retire, and you have the opportunity of having people in these jobs who can be and who are judged by their performance. And if they aren't accountable to their communities, then, by God, let them go.

That's what the whole word, the whole idea of community control is about. That's what many of us in this city are working towards and are really going to spend the rest of our lives working for until we are assured that our kids are not going to have what we had as youngsters. I am a product of the public school system, and I was kicked up at fifteen out of high school, not because I was brilliant, but because I was questioning the system, and they wanted to get rid of me quickly. And believe me, it's made a dent, it's unfortunate. But I will not let my kids have the same problems that I had as a kid, and much more serious ones than that.

And I also, just for the previous speaker, wanted to mention, that part of the reason that some of your people from Queens may be leaving the city is because they have this kind of people in the system that are not relevant to their kids. They are going to places where only state certification is required for supervisory positions, like Great Neck and Roslyn, which are great systems. It is just in New York City and Buffalo, where this antiquated system of this kind of licensing still exists.

I think we have to begin to question it. And I think unless and until we all get involved in it, we won't realize that our children come first and not our political or our racial or our other kinds of views. And, by God, there are plenty of competent, competent people who are not white, who have been denied the possibility and the right to teach in this system. And if you call that a quota system, I don't agree with a quota system, but I surely agree that they have been denied the right to teach in our schools. And if that ain't right, I mean, if that isn't wrong, then take it from there.

MISS HELENE WOOLFORD: Madam Chairman and Councilman, thank you for the privilege of being here.

THE CHAIRMAN: You represent a special board?

MISS WOOLFORD: Yes. My name is Helene Woolford, and I represent the Corona East Elmhurst Community Corporation. I am their educational specialist and my topic is the abolition of the Board of Examiners.

The present Board of Examiners must be abolished. The promulgation of a Civil Service list is totally inadequate for filling the position of school principal. The criteria, as prescribed by the Board of Education, for qualifying for the position of principal and assistant principal is inadequate.

We are in the midst of a highly sophisticated technological age. Computers are here and here to stay. Let us take a look at the sophistry: What you put into the system is what comes out of the system. There is a trade acronym, GIGO, "Garbage in, garbage out," which epitomizes, specifically, the point I am making.

The revision of the criteria by which we select our school administrators is imperative. The method used by the Board of Examiners must be abolished. The Civil Service procedure does not reflect the ethnocentric balance of the school population.

For example, a survey revealed the following teacher-pupil ratio of just one school in our district, so you can imagine what the rest is. White teachers, 95%; pupil ratio, zero. Negro teacher, 1%; pupil ratio, 40%. Spanish-speaking teacher, 1%: pupil ratio, 55%. This sampling ratio is positive proof of an impersonalized teacher selection which does not attempt to respond to the undeniable need of the Spanish-speaking community for the young authority figure with whom they can identify.

The preponderance of minority children enrolled in the New York school system requires drastic changes in the procedure. The Decentralization Law should represent changes in selection criteria and/or methods for selecting administrators. It is not intended to eliminate existing positions or rob the incumbent of his or her livelihood, but the cry for quality education and innovation from school principals and assistant principals is unrelenting and must be responded to.

An interim design which will offer some alternative method for selection of school administrators is suggested for consideration, a design which would eliminate politics, political payoffs, a quota system. Parents and taxpayers have but one paramount concern, and that is high quality output from teachers and administrators, and maximum intake of education for their children.

Below is a quote from the Public Education Association Fact Sheet which will address itself to the unsatisfactory method of teacher and administrative selection used presently:

"For the past 20 years, the rating of all teachers and supervisors and candidates by the Board of Examiners has been a point of controversy. The practice has been defended as the only practical defense against political influence and favoritism in political appointments and has been attacked as irrelevant to competent on-the-job training performance and conducive to inbreeding of staff.

The central testing practices are now also being challenged in a suit filed in the Federal Court by the NAACP Legal Defense and Educational Fund on the grounds that they are discriminatory and violate the New York State constitutional requirements that all public appointments be made on the basis of merit and fitness.

"The new qualifying procedures of the Decentralization Law open a major new dimension in the old debate. It has given the community school boards the responsibility for making supervisory appointments for the schools under their jurisdiction, and has considerably changed the function of the Board of Examiners in the preliminary screening.

"Formerly, the Board of Examiners tested candidates and then ranked them in the order in which they were entitled to be appointed. Now, candidates take qualifying tests. All who pass the tests are placed on an unranked qualifying list and are eligible for appointment by community school boards or by the city Board, in the case of high schools.

"The change in procedure has also raised the question as to whether it makes sense to continue the present citywide screening role of the Board of Examiners, in view of the considerable cost and its questionable relationship to the most important qualities sought in supervisory candidates. The question is especially pertinent since state licensing already provides initial screening of candidates on their education experience, and a change in law now requires 31 community school boards to develop their own fair, objective procedures for selecting, from among those on the qualifying list, particular candidates who will best fill the vacancy.

"The necessity for change in the method of selecting school administrators and teachers is glaring, and it is evident among student-teachers, administrators, and praprofessionals, and organizations oriented to school programs and activities, that is, it is urgent that some new design for the function be projected and tested if the public school system is to survive."

I want to address myself to guidance personnel.

THE CHAIRMAN: Could you keep in mind as you are talking, unless everyone limits himself or herself very severely, there are going to be people who do not get to testify. Keep that in mind. There are other people.

MISS WOOLFORD: O. K.

We have a ratio for the Bureau of Child Guidance of Black personnel of 1 to 4; so that makes the percentile 17.2 in the schools. The ratio for guidance personnel under the Bureau of Child Guidance is three Puerto Ricans, 9.5 Blacks.

What does this mean in terms of selection of administrators in the schools? When they make decisions as to our children, and they find them disruptive, they rely upon the larger number of whites, which is 491, to make these referrals for suspensions. They do not give the parents due process, and the guidance personnel should be more representative. We should have more Blacks in that area so that they can relate the problems clearly and define them to administrators if they do not have the ability or do not understand the needs of the community.

THE CHAIRMAN: Thank you for that testimony.

Next is Patricia Seabrook.

MISS PATRICIA SEABROOK: Commissioner Norton, I would like to address this group in reference to the recent assistant principal's examination given in the high schools. I am a teacher in a New York City public high school.

This examination used to be a closed examination. The principal would arrange a special examination for one person in the school. The person would go to the Board of Education and take the examination. I never heard of anyone failing this examination, although there may have been one or two cases. There was great objection to this procedure. So an open and qualifying test was given.

However, a strange thing happened with this test. The principal still has the sole right of selection. The very same people who would have been chosen under the closed system are now being chosen under the so-called open system. But everyone is supposed to be happy, because an equal opportunity was given to all.

If history repeats itself, the appointments are to be made in February 1971. Then, again, however, there may be the possibility of frozen appointments. I hope there are, so you can investigate the situation.

If history repeats itself and a few women will be appointed to the all-girl schools, practically all men will be appointed to the all-boy schools, and mostly men will be appointed to the co-educational schools.

I have some figures to support my statement. The Board of Education, in a circular dated December 1, 1970, addressed to all principals of day academic and vocational high schools and assistant superintendents in the high school office, listed vacancies for the position of assistant principal. They also issued a four-page list of assistant principals acting and licensed in the New York City high schools.

In Manhattan, of 17 schools listed (and there is a possibility of error in my statement, but I would say they are 95% correct, because some schools are in a state of transition. For example, Stuyvesant High School has, I think, one girl admitted, so I would classify it still as a boys' high school.) there are five boys' high schools, one girls' high school. In the boys' high school, you have seven men, acting as assistant principals; one woman.

In the Bronx, there are 14 high schools, three boys' schools. Six men in the boys' schools; no women. In the girls' schools, two girls' schools, one man, two women.

In Brooklyn, there are 32 schools. Nine boys' high schools: 14 men, one woman. Four girls' high schools: three men, four women. The list goes on.

To summarize, of the 19 boys' high schools, there are 33 assistant principals, 31 men, two women. In the girls' high schools, there are eight girls high schools, 12 positions, five men, seven women.

Now, there are many people who took this exam, many people who passed it. There is no opportunity for anyone who disagrees, perhaps, with the views of the principal. The status quo, the system, again is operating.

I would suggest, Madam Chairman, that the high schools, in particular, be looked into. I feel very guilty in one respect, talking about the number of women, when I do not know of any Black assistant principal, and, as this list suggests, there are no Puerto Rican names on the list. Certainly, I hope this Commission lists this as its first priority.

I would hope that the parents, the community, the staff of the school, and one group that has not been mentioned tonight, the students of the school, would have a right to choose a competent assistant principal to serve them, so that the assistant principal will be responsive, not to the wishes of the principal, but to the community which he serves.

Thank you.

THE CHAIRMAN: Anna S. Murphy.

MISS ANNA S. MURPHY: Thank you, Commissioner. I will try to be as brief as possible.

My case is slightly different. It's discrimination against a program because it was started by citizens. That particular program is the All-Day Neighborhood School, and up until last month I was one of the assistant directors in charge of community relations between the All-Day Neighborhood School and its community.

Almost 30 years ago a group of parents of City and Country, which is a private school, decided that they would like to put into some of the public schools some of the programs that were carried out in private schools, and with the Public Education Association they secured a directive to set up a program in a public school. This started with W.P.A. workers under Dr. Del Franklin.

Dr. Del Franklin developed the All-Day Neighborhood School. Eventually, the P.E.A. said, "If this is a good program, the Board of Education must evaluate it and take it over." They could no longer finance it.

A survey was taken, an evaluation was made, and the program was adopted by the Board of Ed. about 28 years ago. In that length of time they have only found it convenient to extend it to 14 schools in the City of New York.

It also happens that in almost every budget hearing the Board of Education has found it necessary, if it had to make cuts, to make cuts in the All-Day Neighborhood School. Also, at almost every budget hearing, our citizens, our parents, the interested people from the P.E.A. have appeared and appealed that the cuts be restored, and our program has been restored. But we have had to fight for it every year. And the result was that we were able to maintain it. However, there still was not the support of the establishment, because it came from outside of the establishment, and because one main phase of our program was working with community.

Now the Board realizes that this is important and they have sort of taken an about-face and are encouraging the community. But our program was always held back because we involved community. It so happened--

THE CHAIRMAN: Miss Murphy, especially since this isn't on the topic of these hearings at all, I have given you fair time.

MISS MURPHY: Then I will go immediately to the point.

THE CHAIRMAN: All right.

MISS MURPHY: There were three of us who were acting directors in this program at teacher's salary. We were so involved in giving the best program to children in deprived areas, we never considered our position as being acting assistant directors.

When we decided that we should have a line in the Board of

Education budget for our positions, the Board of Education called an examination. There was no requirement to have any information or any knowledge about our program. The requirements said "three years of teaching." I want you to know that I have been in the program fifteen years. There is the acting director here, he was there 22 years, and the other person, 20 years, in developing and building this program.

They gave the examination; we protested. We said it should be a qualifying examination, with someone who knew the program. But they refused, the Board of Education refused to make it qualifying. It was open to the city, with "three years of teaching" as the only qualification.

The examination was held. They told us, "Go right ahead and take it. It's on your program. You made the program, you developed it, you worked in it."

I want to say that everyone of us who were in the program a minimum of 15 years failed that examination. Three people passed it; all three were assistant principals. One person bragged that he had never been in an all-day neighborhood school, and yet he passed the exam. Another person had visited some of the principals, she passed. The third one had been an assistant principal for a year in that particular program.

And we protested. We found out, of course, it cost us a thousand dollars to find out that you cannot protest the Board of Examiner's examination. But we appealed to the Commissioner of Education and told him, on the basis of our experience and our record, we were not even permitted to have an interview or discussion. And the Commissioner, who was then Commissioner Allen, upheld our appeal, and directed the Board of Education to appoint us into the positions that we had been holding for a minimum of 15 years.

Now, the Board of Education was very upset and took our case to a state court, which upheld the Commissioner. When the court upheld the Commissioner, it said we should have retroactive pay for two years, when the other persons were appointed, who, we told you, had never been on the program.

The result was, and I will make this very brief, in two months' time the Board of Education abolished our positions and told us this action was taken in the light of decentralization. That's it.

We wrote this booklet, the three of us, and there is Mary Thompson, who Dr. Donovan appointed as acting director. She failed the examination for a program that she created. We wrote this book and the Board of Education has our names.

THE CHAIRMAN: I appreciate your coming. I am glad you got to the second part of your testimony. It is very much of a nightmare, thinking of people--

MISS MURPHY: I retired last month from frustration.

THE CHAIRMAN: The use of exams in this way--people who spend fifteen or twenty years faced with that--should make all of us, regardless of color, stop and think. You have been doing something for 15 or 20 years, and they tell you at that stage of the game, "Take an examination," or you lose your job. I wonder what would happen to any of us in that case. I wonder if anyone could look at that situation and feel anything but anguish and sympathy for a person caught in the middle stages of life with having to take an examination to prove his fitness for a job he has been doing 15 or 20 years.

I simply have to put that in the record.

MISS MURPHY: I must say--

THE CHAIRMAN: I can't let this go on. There are seven more people. I believe I have been unfair to them because I have let the other people go on so long. I have a half hour, no more. I am risking that I won't get to them all. So, since we haven't disciplined ourselves, I am going to have to impose some discipline on the speakers that come up, because I am not going to have anyone who sat here all evening not get a chance to speak. And I will apologize to the people who came late that their time has been shortened by virtue of their brothers and sisters who have gone before. That's my fault. I am going to remedy that.

The next speaker is John Hunter.

MR. JOHN HUNTER: Commissioner, ladies and gentlemen. I am John Hunter, a teacher at Benjamin Franklin High School. At Benjamin Franklin High School we have special problems which teachers, students, parents, and community representatives feel must be dealt with differently.

I will give you a few examples, two to be exact, of the special problems that Benjamin Franklin High School has been confronted with, and still is.

One is the case of the dropout principals. In the last five years we have had no less than four principals at Benjamin Franklin High School. I think the reason for this is that principals, with the tacit approval of the Board of Education, have used ghetto schools as stepping stones to higher and better positions.

Two cases in point: A former principal became the acting Superintendent of the New York City school system.

Another case in point: A former principal of Benjamin Franklin High School was just recently assigned to a new school that was opened this past September.

Another example of a problem: In 1969, at Benjamin Franklin High School, a total of 257 diplomas were issued. 210 were general diplomas, 22 were certificates, 4 were commercial, and only 21 were academic. That is despite the fact that Benjamin Franklin High School is supposed to be an academic high school.

I think this leads us to question the competency of the teachers that are sent by the Board of Examiners to Benjamin Franklin High School and other "Franklins" in the New York City school system. I think it leads us to question the competency of the Board of Examiners to pass upon the competency of applicants for the positions at Benjamin Franklin High School and other such schools in the City.

As I said before, there are special problems. We have to deal with them differently. We need people who have special qualifications, who are specially competent in dealing with the type of problems that we are confronted with at Benjamin Franklin High School.

At this particular time I would like to mention a few other points of general information. Seasoned Black and Hispanic teachers from the South and Puerto Rico are denied licenses by the Board of Examiners because of accents and the lack of outmoded educational course requirements.

We further find that through an involved system of weighted scores, several applicants pass all individual parts of a test but still fail the examination, which, I think, is indicative of the fact that the Board of Examiners more often than not play a type of Mickey Mouse game when it comes to rating the examinations.

In addition to that, we find, as a number of speakers have pointed out, that questions and procedures that applicants have to tackle on an exam are too often irrelevant to skills necessary for doing the prescribed job. That being the case, I think that any time an examination is to be given for applicants for teaching positions in this city, a large stress should be placed on performance. And this performance should be for an extended period of time.

I further would like to point out that persons with experience, such as members of the Board or persons who have friends or associates in such capacities, set up coaching courses at handsome fees to prepare applicants for the exams. Others write letters of appeal for those who fail and want to be reconsidered. The fees for such letters range from $300 to $1,000, and the applicant still might not get the license. This compares favorably with the kickback system that everyone seems to fear if the Board were discontinued.

More often than not we talk about the so-called merit system here in New York City. Yet, we still find that more often than not the so-called Civil Service Laws are not strictly adhered to.

Examples of this: In New York City there are a number of acting positions. You have the acting principal position. You have the position of acting assistant principal. You have acting chairman. As a matter of fact, I think there is a case of one individual who has been an acting principal of a school in New York City for approximately thirteen years.

In addition to that, we find that there are many teachers in the high schools, in the junior high schools, who are actually teaching out of license. And this is the case here in New York City. Hopefully, something will be done about it. And I think that with the help of this Commission and people who are concerned there will be a positive change, a constructive change.

Thank you.

THE CHAIRMAN: Thank you, Mr. Hunter.

William Degraffenreid. How did a Black man ever get a name like that? I can't even pronounce it.

MR. WILLIAM DEGRAFFENREID: Good evening, everybody. My name is William Degraffenreid, III.

I attend Brandeis High School. I came to make a complaint

about Brandeis. My school doesn't have any Black representation at all. We have 99% Black students and 1% white.

MR. DAVID: What school?

MR. DEGRAFFENREID: Brandeis. We are supposed to be an integrated neighborhood, but there are not that many white students there at all. I was taking up a petition for a Black principal, and a lot of things happened to me. That's why I came to talk to you. Things like, when I first started, the teachers told me, well, the principal gave me a long story, and said, "Stop it."

THE CHAIRMAN: Get a little closer to the mike and talk a little bit more slowly so we can make sure we can hear.

MR. DEGRAFFENREID: He told me to stop. He told me, "Please be cool about it." He says that if I didn't be cool, he would throw me out of school, something like that. But, I did it anyway.

And when I started the petition again, some of the teachers gave me a hard time, like one of the gym teachers. He put me out of the gym because I had taken petitions around the room. The petitions were about a Brandeis Black principal. Well, I was in the room with him. I was scared, but I was in the room with him by myself. Then he told me to give him the book, but I wouldn't give him the book about the petitions.

So he took me down to the principal's office and told them I had written up charges on the principal, tried to get, you know, trumped-up charges. He threw me in the chair, he had his arms around me; cops were in the room. I told him to stop harassing me. I told the cops to do something. The cops didn't do anything but laugh. The dean came in the room and said, "You're going to be suspended if you don't sit down." So I told him, no, I didn't want to sit down. So he put his arms around my neck and tried to make me sit down, but I still didn't sit down. Someone in the background told him to leave me alone, so he walked away for a few minutes. I wanted to take the petitions up to one of the teachers for safekeeping, and when he came back, I actually tried to go to the bathroom, not to have to make an excuse. I said, "Would you take me to the bathroom?" He said "No." So I said, "All right, I want to go." He said, "You can go; leave the papers here." I said "No." He said, "Go ahead."

I ran up to Mrs. Ringel's room, a Black teacher in art. I ran up to her room; I fell into her room, giving her the papers. She said, "What's wrong?" I know I had the whole class, her class, excited. But I didn't mean to. But after a while, the class calmed down. I told her what happened. She said, "Go down, play it cool." So she took the petitions and put them away.

And that's what I came here to tell you. If I can't get a petition about my school, to do something about it, to change it, then there's no use for me to go to school to learn anything. They tell you this country is free.

THE CHAIRMAN: Thank you for coming down.

MISS BELLE BAVINE GEORGE: Good evening, ladies and gentlemen. My name is Belle Bavine George. I am a student at Brandeis High School. As William was saying, he was going around with a petition for the students of the school, not only the students but teachers of the school, to sign, so that we could have a Black principal.

We, the students of Brandeis High School would very much like to have a Black principal at that school. If this is not possible, then we would like to have some minorities, not only Black but Puerto Rican. Now, we, the students, we want a Black minority and Black principal at our school.

We do not want an Uncle Tom in either one of the offices. Now, if we're going to get an Uncle Tom for a Black principal or an Uncle Tom for any other higher office in Brandeis High School, well, then, we want to call this whole thing off, because right now we don't need anybody that's going to sink us.

We would appreciate it very much if you would look into the matter at Brandeis High School. If it's possible, we would like to have Black minorities and Puerto Rican minorities in our school. Thank you very much.

MISS LORETTA JAMES: My name is Loretta James. I'm from Brandeis High School. As William was saying about the principal harassing him, because of the Black petitions that he had, I don't think he had the right to harass him because he does have the right to have a petition around the place, you know. We wanted a Black principal in our school because we have a white principal, but the school is mostly Black and Puerto Rican. I don't know how we are going to come around, how the Black people in the school, Puerto Ricans, are going to come to a decision about who is going to be principal. But I feel that we should have a Black principal in our school.

THE CHAIRMAN: Is your problem that the principal is white or that he doesn't understand your problems?

MISS JAMES: It seems that he doesn't understand.

THE CHAIRMAN: All right, thank you.

MISS JAMES: Thank you.

MISS DESDRE FLEMING: My name is Desdre Fleming. I'm from Brandeis High School. I feel that we should have a Black principal because we have to go to the Black teachers with our problems; and if we had a Black principal, then we wouldn't have to burden the Black teachers with our problems. We could go down to the principal. Or if we had a Black dean, we could explain it to him. And if we have Puerto Rican teachers, too, because I feel if we tell our problems to our own kind, then maybe we will get somewhere.

That's all I have to say.

MISS BARBARA WASHINGTON: My name is Barbara Washington, and I am from Brandeis High School, and instead of having just a Black principal, I think, you know, we should have a principal that could understand our problems, know what we want. And, just like what she said, you know, we have problems with that principal. I want the principal changed.

That's all.

THE CHAIRMAN: Thank you.
Esther Levenberg.

Let me go down the names of the people I have: Lalo Destre, still here. Hal Koppersmith, still here. Marian Borenstein. W. R. Gist?

Now, remember I have got one, two, three, four people, and we have about fifteen minutes.

MISS ESTHER LEVENBERG: Madam Chairman, I am not here to testify about Brandeis High School, but let me add to the remarks the children have already made.

My name is Esther Levenberg. I taught at Brandeis High School. Not only does that principal not understand the problems of the children, he does not understand the problems of the teachers.

I was given an unsatisfactory rating from that school because, I believe, of a ten-minute observation. His observation and my letter are both public record now on file.

I am here to testify as, obviously, a white teacher, who feels competent, who looks, probably, like part of the establishment, but is actually, I think, a dissident. These days I am feeling rather like a saboteur.

I have been teaching at George Washington High School, using a variety of experimental and unconventional methods, with great success. And I have recently been excessed. It had nothing to do with numbers, but it had to do with the fact they just did not want me teaching in that school any longer.

The last day of class I made a tape with my children, showing the methods that I used. I call it "Encounter Methods in the Classroom: A Teacher Who Has Just Lost Her Job Evaluates the Term with Her Classes."

I would just like to read to you very, very briefly, some of the things the children say.

On the matter of the classroom:

"It's all right; this place is a death trap. In case of fire we got one big door to go downstairs; we have streets there where everybody can kill themselves trying to get out."

On the matter of the principal and the annex--by the way, this place is where that teacher was beat up:

"The boys do run over the principal. The principal calls those boys back and they just tell him to shut up. He don't know how to rule those boys. To tell you the truth, that principal is a real faggot, a stone-cold faggot."

I say, "George, what do you mean by a faggot?"

George says, "He's a weirdo."

I say, "Have you ever talked about these feelings in your other classes?"

The class says, "No."

I say, "Why not?"

They say, one girl says, "Ain't nothing to talk about in them. In my math class the man don't explain nothing and every time you look around there's a test coming up and he hasn't explained nothing. And in Miss G's class they run over her. My science class, he all right."

I say, "How do you feel about talking in this class about your problems, about your feelings?"

"I'll tell you why we talk in here, because we don't have a spy in here. We say something about the principal, and we know you won't go right down and tell him. Well, I'm telling you, we got somebody we can trust in this school. Like I can't say this--but, anyway--"

Then they say, "It's all right. It don't bother me. But you is the only teacher in here you can trust. That's the truth. You can't trust no other teacher. I can't stand some of these things walking around."

And then, on the matter of why I was let go:

I say, "Does anyone know why they probably did it?"

"You're not going to teach no more?"

The whole class is asking questions. George says, "You know, they probably doing that on spite because they know that half of all the students dig you in this school, and all the other teachers got ugly, boxed-up scabbed heads. They don't care about the students. They're here for a purpose, just to teach. They don't care about no one else's feelings."

These are by children.

I have passed the exams. I have passed the regular substitute license exam. Today I found out that I scored very high in the regular teacher's exam. Was I ever examined on my performance? I was not.

Ask the children about this, and they will verify it. I have no written observation from this school. I have observations from other schools. I could make your hair stand on end with the fatuousness represented therein. They do not represent any kind of relevance whatsoever in my opinion about a teacher's performance, be he Black or white.

My students were Black and I did relate to them. I had some of the worst problem children in that school. I had one boy last week who gave me probably the highest compliment I have ever gotten, a boy who was suspended, who hung around all day long to come to my class, because he wanted to let out some of the feelings that he had, and waited around to the sixth period class so that he could come in and talk to me. And there I was, running up against the system.

The other teachers did not, really, I think, understand what I was trying to do. We were rarely able to get together on it, and the last thing I heard was that I was going to be excessed.

The children's reaction was to write letters, which I showed the principal, to no avail; to get together a petition signed by a hundred students, brought before the principal. They got a runaround. I know they waited in his office for an hour and a half and got no place.

What happens to a teacher, be he white or Black, who is trying to relate to these children in a manner that they can understand, in a manner that they can appreciate? I ask you, Madam Chairman. I really do not know.

I know that I will be teaching, however, in another school next term. I am going to try my methods again. I am not going to stop. But I will not be surprised if I am excessed again.

THE CHAIRMAN: Lalo Dextre.

MISS LALO DEXTRE: I am President of the Parents Association, Intermediate School 44, in Manhattan. I do not represent a large organization. I am not an expert in education. I am just a parent.

I feel that the people who talk and show innumerable figures, they are trying to defend what is indefensible. I think that's been proven in this case, and by other people that testified before me. The bulk of the examiners and the undeniable record of systematical and institutionalized discrimination against minority groups is sufficient proof.

I have to say that our school is in District 3 in Manhattan. In our district we feel that the school should be controlled by the community.

In I.S. 44 for many years we have had principals that, for some reason or another, were white. They didn't relate to the Black and the Spanish-speaking children in this school. And parents in this school finally were given the approval by the local school board to screen people other than the ones on the list of the Board of Examiners.

We finally found a man who we thought was excellent, and we hired him. This man refused to take the test for the license for principal, because he said that he is accountable to the community, and therefore he doesn't need the approval of anybody else but the community.

What we suggest in I.S. 44 is the following:

1) The abolition of the anachronistic Board of Examiners.
2) The acceptance of state certification for teachers and principals.
3) Full authority to local school boards to hire and fire teachers and principals, provided that measures are taken to make sure that parents, parents' associations, students, and community organizations will have a principal and decisive role in the decision-making process of hiring and firing teachers and principals.
4) Teachers and principals shall be accountable to the community; and
5) the local school board shall be accountable to the community.

And I should point out the fact that the local school board should be limited, its power should be limited to the decisions of the community, because if we just delegate our power to the local school board and it is not accountable to the community, the only thing that we will be doing will be changing masters from one to another. There are some districts already that have a local school board that think that they are self-appointed do-gooders, patronizing Blacks and Puerto Ricans, and they don't have accountability to the community.

THE CHAIRMAN: Hal Koppersmith.

MR. HAL KOPPERSMITH: Commissioner Norton, my name is Hal Koppersmith, Education Ombudsman, Brotherhood of Parents, a teacher in exile and convict and welfare client for seven years. I ask that my testimony be postponed until tomorrow morning, because, I know you are a saint, Mrs. Norton, but this testimony has been arranged in such a way--I don't think it was done consciously--so that the people who know what the problems are do not get press coverage and do not get the time that is necessary. The people who are taking up all the time and almost all the space in the papers are the people who are responsible for the crisis in our classroom.

THE CHAIRMAN: They are not responsible for the press.

MR. KOPPERSMITH: I know you can't control the press, but, in terms of time, for example, Mr. Shanker was on for an hour and a half. I am sure that Mr. Tractenberg does as much homework as he can do, but not so much to catch every one of the racist lines that Mr. Shanker--

THE CHAIRMAN: You are taking up your time. This is the only time you are going to get.

MR. KOPPERSMITH: I am asking you, since this is citywide, I ask that my testimony be postponed to tomorrow morning.

THE CHAIRMAN: That is denied. I am not going to give to one member of the public what I don't give to another. I suggest you go on.

MR. KOPPERSMITH: I ask, what is the difference between Mr. Shanker and Blanche Lewis, and Mr. Koppersmith of the Brotherhood of Parents. I think each one of us is equally important.

THE CHAIRMAN: I think you are, too, but I have a decision to make.

MR. KOPPERSMITH: I am asking you, it is not so difficult. I am asking you to postpone the testimony until tomorrow morning.

THE CHAIRMAN: Denied.

MR. KOPPERSMITH: I worked three days on this testimony and to give it in three minutes, when you are tired, really doesn't make any sense.

THE CHAIRMAN: I am listening.

MR. KOPPERSMITH: If you insist on it, I will.

THE CHAIRMAN: Please go ahead. Go ahead with as much as you can, orally, and the rest we will incorporate in the record.

MR. KOPPERSMITH: It is impossible. Welfare clients don't have resources and secretaries to write up thirty pages. It is just impossible. Mrs. Lewis can do it; Mr. Shanker can do it. They can get their testimony that way, because they have the resources, but we don't.

THE CHAIRMAN: Mr. Koppersmith, if you feel strongly enough about this issue, get something into the record, because you are slowly using up your time--

MR. KOPPERSMITH: I just want it in the record, Mrs. Norton. I don't want to argue with you, but I have been in this thing for fifteen years, and there have been reports and hearings and reports and hearings, and when those hearings are finished, nothing happens. The power that was, still remains. And the same thing is going to happen here because of a lack of confrontation, because what we really need is an encounter, a confrontation with the prejudices that we all have. And part of the reason is because you are a saint. There are very few like you with very few prejudices, but what you did was suppress the prejudices people had. It wasn't the purpose of the hearings to bring them out in the open so that we can deal with them.

THE CHAIRMAN: We don't want to bring prejudice into the open in New York City. We are--

MR. KOPPERSMITH: This is why, Mrs. Norton, this is the reason that we have the crisis in our classroom today, because those prejudices have been hidden and manipulated and suppressed rather than brought out into the open so we can deal with them. And this Commission, in this sense, is doing exactly what the Board of Education has done.

Now, let me take the little time that I have. Whenever you stop me, you can. You can stop me whenever you want.

Part of the problem is that we talk about words, and particularly with influential people and intellectuals and professionals. And I know all the professionals you are calling tomorrow, and they don't know the problem in terms of talking to the people, that is, the poor people, white, Puerto Rican, and Black, who have to deal with the problem, because they attack it at an angle that the other people don't understand. The street people are the people who can talk to them, and the people who have worked in the community. But those are the people who only have five minutes' testimony.

One of the things I think we have to do is get a gut understanding of the basic problem we face, not only in the Board of Examiners, which is a microcosm of the macrocosmic problem in this society.

The Board of Examiners--and the best way I can think of dealing with it is by reading a short poem of five lines which tell us what the gut problem is that we face in the Board of Examiners, the city, jobs, and everything. and I want to quote this poem for you:

"What Happens?"
"What happens to a dream deferred?
Does it dry up, like a raisin in the sun,
Or fester like a sore, and then run?
Does it stink, like rotten meat,
On One Ten Livingston Street,
Or crust and sugar over, like a syrupy sweet?
Maybe it just sags like a heavy load.
Or does it just explode?"

Now, what Langston Hughes was trying to tell us is what is happening now. The Kerner Commission report is the essence of the whole problem in this Board of Examiners and in the Board of Education, but they've got the problem backwards. Because the Kerner Report said that the problem is that we are getting to a society that is divided between Black and white, and poor and rich. The problem is just the reverse: that we have had historically a society which is divided Black and white, and rich and poor.

The reason that we have the crisis now is because the Blacks and the poor, whether they be Puerto Rican or Italian, are trying to move into the system. And they are being prevented from moving into the system by the people, the affluent people, who presently control it. That is the source of the violence at George Washington High School and other places. And what happened this morning was an indication of how the powers that be, Mr. Shanker, Mrs. Lewis, manipulate the people, because a number of serious problems were not raised at all.

For example: On the question of whether these exams are merit exams or not, there were two state court cases which the papers played down, and that's not your fault.

A letter was written to James Allen, State Commissioner, in 1967, January 20, which said, as follows:

"Two State Supreme Court judges in the past two weeks have ruled that supervisors in the New York City School System were appointed by examiners who were illegal, a test that was unconstitutional, and methods based not on an objective standard of merit but individual, particular notions of the examiners."

In effect, what these judges ruled was that the whole system of examination was nothing but a political patronage pork barrel. And if you look at the principals chosen, then you're looking at people that have been feeding at this pork barrel.

Now, the interesting thing about these two cases, Mrs. Norton, is that one of them was brought by Mr. Shanker of the UFT. He was the one who charged that these cases were not cases of merit, but here he came and told you that supervisors were chosen on merit.

A number of years ago, the NYU-Griffith's Report--

THE CHAIRMAN: The bell has rung. There are two more people--

MR. KOPPERSMITH: --who asserted that promotion was based upon personal--I told you, Mrs. Norton, it is unfair. I am not going to--

THE CHAIRMAN: It is not only unfair to you, it is unfair to the next two people.

MR. KOPPERSMITH: I am saying, this issue is so important that, if you are serious about it, you will extend hearings until Monday, if necessary, or Tuesday.

I don't want to argue with you, Eleanor, because the hearings have played a purpose. There has been a lot of information but there is still a lot of mystery. It's partly the way you structured it, but more importantly it's the way the press has handled it.

For example, let me give you an example: The New York Times this morning carried the whole statement by Mr. Greene of the Board of Examiners, and mentioned that there are a few people who opposed it. They didn't mention the names of important people like Victor Gotbaum, who is a great labor leader, and Mr. Ira Glasser of the Civil Liberties Union. Now, in some way, I don't know what you can do, but I think that you should complain that these reports are inaccurate.

THE CHAIRMAN: The Civil Liberties Union was covered in another paper.

MR. KOPPERSMITH: But it wasn't covered in The Times, which is a very, very important paper. I don't want to argue with you. It is unfair in terms of structure, and I ask you, in all fairness, I am willing to come back in the morning. I am asking you to let me continue the testimony in the morning, because there is a lot of material that is involved.

THE CHAIRMAN: Thank you, Mr. Koppersmith.

MR. KOPPERSMITH: Thank you, Mrs. Norton. That was a short love.

THE CHAIRMAN: Mr. Koppersmith--

MR. KOPPERSMITH: Mrs. Norton--

THE CHAIRMAN: You have had the opportunity to read your testimony--

MR. KOPPERSMITH: May I read one thing that is crucially important?

THE CHAIRMAN: If you were Marian Borenstein, what would you do?

MR. KOPPERSMITH: I will tell you what I will do. You know what I will do, if you will permit me. There is one important thing that I do want to say. I am ready to let the Chair have Mrs. Borenstein and whoever else wants to testify, and give me three or four minutes afterwards when the others have testified. Is that fair enough?

VOICE: Ten o'clock!

MR. KOPPERSMITH: I really think it is only fair if I could have five minutes in the morning.

MRS. BORENSTEIN: If it's ten o'clock, I don't want to be rushed like that.

MR. KOPPERSMITH: I think you are being unfair.

THE CHAIRMAN: Mrs. Borenstein, if you want to put something in the record, you may. It is not quite ten o'clock yet.

VOICE: I think it is unfair.

THE CHAIRMAN: Mr. Gist may come forward if he wants to put something in the record.

VOICE: I do ask you for time tomorrow morning.

THE CHAIRMAN: I'm sorry. Tomorrow, it looks like we have to get out of the building at 4:30.

MR. KOPPERSMITH: If I stayed all afternoon and day, could I have the time, if you have some time left?

THE CHAIRMAN: If we have time left, I will take testimony from you. I certainly will.

MR. KOPPERSMITH: I will try and write the material. Otherwise--

MR. W. ROGERS GIST: My name is W. Rogers Gist. I represent the Community Teachers Association, and I have witnessed the practice of four different public school systems, and, comparatively, I think that the procedure by which New York City hires its teachers is one of the worst, one of the most unjust, semi-corrupt practices of hiring that I have witnessed.

The topic that I was given tonight is: If New York State

certification is adequate for the other cities in New York State, then what is so magical and so special and so superior about the New York City Board of Examiners' licensing of teachers to work in the public school system?

I would suggest and think that a look at the finished product that comes out of our schools, that has come out of our schools for the past twelve years, would tend to reflect that there is nothing so meritorious about the New York City Board of Examiners' means of selecting personnel for working with children. I would suggest that a review of the grade scores would tend to indicate that. And a comparison of these grade scores with other scores across the state and across the nation would tend to indicate that there is nothing so meritorious about the New York City system, our method for hiring teachers.

I have here three documents, dating back as far as 1961-- one published by Schinnerer, the so-called Schinnerer Report; another, the Allen, Commissioner Allen, Report, dated 1964; another called the Bundy Report, dated 1967--which contain professional suggestions, recommendations, and opinions in regards to the New York City public school system hiring technique.

All three of these documents indicate and suggest that the New York City public school system's method of hiring through the process of an examination and through the Board of Examiners is an incorrect, a most severely restrictive and limiting way of getting people into the system to work with youngsters.

As far back as 1961, the recommendations have been made by professional educators. Nothing was done. We have witnessed slow deterioration in performance of youngsters. And as a result of this retardation of youngsters' performance, we have witnessed parents beginning to become concerned and taking to the streets and being put in jail, in an attempt to correct this system and to get the staff of their choice and the staff which they feel will best service their youngsters.

THE CHAIRMAN: It is five minutes to ten.

MR. GIST: It is the opinion of my organization that the nucleus of the New York City public school system rests with the Board of Examiners, and that the control of the finances for one of the largest corporations in the country, and the control of sixty thousand teaching jobs, does not deserve continuation through the Board of Examiners. It does not deserve continuation for doing what it does to so many youngsters by limiting and restricting them from a wide variety of ideas from other people across the country, from other teachers who could come into the system if they didn't have to go through the Board of Examiners.

We suggest that the Board of Examiners serves as a closed door that discriminates, that restricts, and that breeds retardation by restricting outside participation and freshness. We also suggest that the well-known technique is designed to restrict people from advancing, designed to restrict people from earning their just and adequate salary increments through a procedure of yearly service on the job.

And we suggest that the Board of Examiners should be

abolished, and that, if it is not, it will continue to exercise the practice of genocide over the minds of the youngsters, a product which we think is the most delicate for the survival of a group. The control over the minds of youngsters and the molding of the minds of youngsters is the most delicate product for the survival of a group. And we think that this product of the mind is controlled for Black youngsters in this school system primarily through the way in which New York City hires its teachers through the Board of Examiners.

Therefore, we recommend strongly that it be abolished.

THE CHAIRMAN: Thank you, Mr. Gist.

I want to try to arrange extra time at the end of Friday's testimony. Actually, we have been marvelously successful in getting through. Tonight is the only night we had any people left over. We are trying to rectify that. Thursday, unfortunately, we have to end our hearing at 4:30 because the Bar Association has a meeting here and is evicting us early.

Friday we will do as we did Monday and Tuesday, that is, go on as long as we can, consistent with their rules, as long as people are here. I, of course, am still willing to accept testimony now, but this building is going to close. I am afraid that is the rule at the moment.

This hearing will convene again tomorrow morning at 9 a.m., 14 Vesey Street.

(Whereupon, an adjournment was taken to Thursday, January 28, 1971, at 9 a.m.)

- - - - -

HEARINGS HELD JANUARY 28, 1971

Witnesses in Order of Appearance

	Testimony starts
John H. Fischer	page 509
Laurence Iannaccone	517
Robert A. Dentler	522
Phyllis Wallace	529
Jeanette Hopkins	531
James Shields	537
Doxie A. Wilkerson	548
William Lynch, Jr.	552
Michael Usdan	556
Gary Calnek	561
Harold Haizlip	565
Marilyn Gittell	570
Judith Rothschild	576

THE CHAIRMAN: The hearings are now in session. They are being held at 14 Vesey Street.

May I call the first witness, Dr. John H. Fischer, President, Teachers College, Columbia University.

For those who may be listening on the radio, these hearings are ending early today, but we will try to go into the evening tomorrow.

Dr. Fischer.

DR. FISCHER: I am John Fischer, President of Teachers College. I have no formal prepared statement, but I would like to share with you some of my views on the general subject of the selection of professionals for service in education, and then to respond to such questions as you might want to put to me.

The chief reason that it is difficult to predict teaching performance is that teaching is, ultimately, an art, although, to be sure, it uses science in a variety of ways. The teaching procedure can be illuminated by the application of a number of sciences. In part, teaching can be studied by scientific analysis. But the process, finally, is a form of artistry. Hence, the best indicator of ability is proficiency in the practice of the art.

Like every art, teaching requires more than native talent if the art is to be practiced well. A certain element of discipline is required in teaching, as in painting or performance in music, or in dance, or in any other art.

It is necessary for us to try to predict competence in teaching, however, no matter how difficult it may be, because teaching, in addition to being art is, in our society, a profession. That is to say, it depends upon the possession of a body of specialized knowledge and expertise. It is carried on in the service and interest of the public. The practitioner is assumed to be personally responsible and accountable for the consequences of his actions. The practitioner is assumed to be in control of the situation in which he works; and the work is done within a setting of ethical assumptions and ethical standards.

Like the practitioner of any profession, the teacher should, therefore, be licensed; and, in our society, is licensed, typically, by the state, as all other professions are typically licensed in our society. This is to say, that the state, by means which it considers advisable and effective, identifies those who are likely to be able to teach responsibly and effectively and certifies them as competent to do so and worthy of trust for doing so.

But licensing is one matter and selection for employment is another. These two should not be confused, for the interests and responsibilities of the state, when it issues a license, and of the employing agency, when it selects a teacher or other professional for particular employment, are not necessarily congruent.

Hence it seems to me that in New York City we should make a distinction between the process of licensing, which I would argue belongs to the state, and the process of selection for employment, which I would argue belongs to the local educational authority, in our case, a responsibility which is divided between the central Board of Education and the district boards of education.

In view of the rapidly changing conditions in education and in society, I would argue that the arrangements for employment should include as much flexibility as is possible in order to enable employing educational agencies to bring into the schools the widest possible range of competencies, talents, interests, and capabilities.

In the process of selection for employment, tests of some kind inevitably must be used. They always are used as soon as one determines that Individual A rather then Individual B should be selected for a particular post. But this is not to say that the kinds of tests that we usually think of as objective, or written, tests are necessarily the ones to be used.

A great deal has been made of the system of written examinations, because it is said to be objective. If it is objectivity we want, then the way to get it in the greatest degree would be to measure the heights of prospective teachers to a thousandth of an inch and get their weight to a thousandth of a gram. And then we could formulate the most meticulous rating lists that would be objective.

Objectivity, however, is not the primary consideration in selecting the person to practice a form of artistry; validity is far more important. And it is by the measure of validity that all of our testing systems for the selection of teachers have been found to be wanting.

It has sometimes been argued that we need a system of objective, rigidly controlled tests in the New York City schools because the absence of such a system would open our schools to the hazards of favoritism, nepotism, corruption in various forms. If this were indeed the case, then we would be arguing that the systems of selection which are used in virtually all of the school systems of the United States suggest that in all of these other school systems the human beings making these selections can be trusted whereas in New York City, our people could not be trusted to be honest or competent or fair. I do not believe that the citizens or the public officials of New York City can be said to be so far below the moral standards, or other standards, of the school authorities in all the rest of the United States.

I have not talked about the special problems of selecting persons for leadership positions in the schools, and I would just say a word about that before concluding my statement and responding to such questions as you might have for me.

It becomes increasingly plain, at least to me, that it matters little in the long run how we organize the areas over which our boards of education preside. What ultimately matters is what occurs between the child and the teachers and other educators with whom he is associated in the schools that he attends. In the educational system, the action is in the individual school, increasingly, it seems to me. Therefore, we must focus our attention on the quality of leadership that determines the climate that prevails in any and every school.

I have been in education now for 40 years. In that time I have seen a wide variety of schools. I have seen them in beautiful, new buildings; I have seen them in ramshackle, old buildings, I have seen large schools and small schools. I have seen high-budget schools and low-budget schools. I have seen them from pre-kindergartens, nursery schools, through graduate, professional schools.

The one thing I have never seen is a good school without a good principal, or a good headmaster, or a good head, by whatever name called. If one can change but one element in a school, and one chooses to select the element with the greatest leverage for changing the school, it seems to me absolutely clear that that one element would be the principal of the school. I have seen schools that have literally been revolutionized in the course of a single academic year, with nothing changed in the year but the principal. Hence the selection of principals for our schools is a matter of the very greatest importance.

I am not attempting to depreciate the value of the teacher, but what I am arguing is that with an effective principal at the head of a school, a good teacher has a much greater opportunity to perform to the level of his ability. And with a good principal at the head of a school, the effect of a poor teacher can be meliorated.

In selecting persons for principalships in their schools--and, to an extent, the same statements could be made about those selected for supervisory and other administrative posts in the school system--the most important quality to be sought, I would argue, would have to do with the capability to understand the nature, the diversity, the variety, the force of those social influences to which the children in our schools are now subjected. And equal in importance to that set of capabilities would be sensitivity to the personal conditions, the personal promise, of the young people who come into the school. I know of no test that is likely to reveal, with any degree of reliability, the possession of the kinds of qualities, and the combination of these qualities, that seems to me essential that the leadership people in our schools possess.

Hence I would argue that the best basis for the selection of men and women to serve in leadership capacities in our schools would be evidence of effective performance in work as closely as possible similar to the demands of leadership in educational situations. Here, again, I am not attempting to discount the value of academic preparation, systematic professional preparation of the kind of background which distinguishes an intellectually capable individual from a mere well-meaning amateur. What I am saying is that academic training, though essential, is not sufficient. Understanding of the people with whom one works, understanding of the situations from which those people come, is at least equal in importance to possession of the traditional types of academic and systemized professional preparation.

And let me emphasize what I said a moment ago. I do not believe that we shall solve the problems of our schools by seeking to place in the key positions of leadership within them persons who are selected merely because they are committed, or merely because they are interested. The demands of the school system these days, the demands which our society places upon its educational institutions, are of such complexity that they cannot be well served, I am convinced, by persons of amateur status, no matter how willing, no matter how dedicated, no matter how eager they may be.

And so, I would be the last to fail to argue for professional competence. What I am suggesting is that we must expand the criteria by which we appraise professional competence, and not allow ourselves to be trapped by practices that were devised to meet the needs of a situation very different from the situation in which our schools must function today.

THE CHAIRMAN: Counsel.

MR. TRACTENBERG: Dr. Fischer, I have a few questions.

We have heard repeatedly during these hearings, in defense of the body of Examiners and the selection process in which it plays a substantial role, that the current function of the process is basically to screen out incompetence. And the question has been raised, in view of the fact that some 90% of all the teachers coming into the New York system come from New York City institutions of higher education, whether that is really necessary, whether graduation from these programs is a reasonable guarantee of minimum competency.

Do you have any reaction to that?

DR. FISCHER: Yes; I have two reactions.

I would argue that the most important task confronting us is not the screening out of incompetents, but the identification of those with the combination of capabilities that we need to move the schools and our children ahead. To emphasize the negative, which is to say the screening out of incompetents, is simply to attach an anchor to our educational institutions. What we need is a system that will identify, to the greatest extent humanly possible, those who have the relatively rare combination of talent and discipline that will provide a truly exemplary education.

Now, the second part of your question: do I think that the New York City higher education institutions can perform the screening function themselves. The answer is that I do. And I believe that if we assume that the possession of a bachelor's degree, or an advanced degree, is sufficient indication that the holder of the degree has met certain minimum requirements, I think we are making an entirely safe assumption.

I would not deny that there is a wide range in the quality of

American higher educational institutions. I think we all know that. But if the question is raised about higher education institutions in the City of New York, I think it is a safe assumption that the institutions here perform the, we will call it, negative screening function quite effectively.

MR. TRACTENBERG: I am not sure whether you have heard Dr. Greene. In his testimony, he actually read from some examinations which he said reflected the illiterates--I think that was his word--that were screened out, who had to his recollection, completed teacher training programs.

And Mr. Shanker yesterday, if I can paraphrase without distorting, said that we couldn't rely on state certification, because often people got degrees as a result of truces reached after student insurrections.

I gather from your remarks, that you don't find either of those arguments persuasive?

DR. FISCHER: I do not. I think that it is true, I know it is true, that our universities and colleges, being humanly designed and humanly managed institutions, fall somewhat this side of heavenly perfection. But so, I would submit, do the procedures of the Board of Examiners. And if we are going to concentrate our attention on the shortcomings of any system of selection, I am sure we can find them.

The problem is, where are the shortcomings of the greater consequence? And it strikes me that reliance on a system which is quite objective but of highly questionable validity--which is the way I would characterize the system of the Board of Examiners--is much the greater and more serious error.

MR. TRACTENBERG: I understand, Dr. Fischer, that teacher training institutions tend to compile rather voluminous dossiers about persons going through their programs. Is that true?

DR. FISCHER: Yes. The volume of material would vary from institution to institution. But most of our institutions do have substantial amounts of data on their graduates.

MR. TRACTENBERG: In your experience, are those dosdiers adequately used in the selection process by the Board of Examiners?

DR. FISCHER: I can't comment on what use the Board of Examiners makes of such dossiers, because I simply don't know.

MR. TRACTENBERG: I think in Dr. Greene's testimony, he indicated that while they did have access to them, they were loath to use them because, in his words, the dossiers contained secret information.

Do you have any response to that?

DR. FISCHER: Well, certainly confidential information should be respected and not used in any public sense. But it seems to me that any employing agency can obtain from a college or university, or from other reference sources, the information that it requires to separate incompetent or undesirable people from those who should be employed.

I return, again, to the assertion I made earlier, that the

vast majority, all but a very few, of the educational systems of the United States employ teachers who turn out, in the long run, by and large, to be competent and effective without resort to the elaborate machinery over which the Board of Examiners presides.

MR. TRACTENBERG: Just two more questions, if I may.

First of all, Dr. Fischer, in view of the rather unique circumstance that New York finds itself in--that is, drawing such a vast proportion of its teachers from within the city, and certainly the greater metropolitan area--do you think there could be more reliance by school authorities on observation of the teacher training programs or evaluation by school authorities of the caliber of the teacher training programs?

DR. FISCHER: Well, as you probably have heard already, the State Department of Education evaluates the programs offered in institutions of the state. And on the basis of its evaluation of those programs, it accepts and approves the recommendations of the individual schools with respect to their graduates.

In Teachers College, where we have a number of pre-service programs, we register each of these programs in advance with the State Department. The State Department looks into them and determines whether they meet the state criteria, and when they do, approves those programs and then, by implication, approves for certification those persons whom we certify as having completed the work which the state understands they will complete in our curriculum. This, in effect, says that the state takes our word for the quality of these graduates, once the state has gone through the preliminary steps of satisfying itself that the program is sound. And this, of course, applies to other institutions throughout the state.

MR. TRACTENBERG: If, however, New York City wasn't prepared to take the state's word--certainly Mr. Shanker and others have suggested that they had some serious questions about state certification--would it be reasonably possible, in your judgment, for the city to conduct its own observation of the caliber of teacher training programs?

DR. FISCHER: I see no reason why that would not be possible. And ultimately, I think, the observation of the actual program, is the most telling way of evaluating what goes on.

The other part of the process, of course, is to observe the performance of the individual concerned. As I said earlier, the best way to predict proficiency in the practice of any art is to observe the artist at work and to project from what one sees, what one may hope to expect.

I lean toward the practice, not lean toward it, I am strongly in favor of the practice of withholding final certification for all teachers until some period of time in the classroom, on the job. Three years might be a reasonable period. That is to say, once a person is appointed a teacher--call it, if you will, in probationary status, or use some other title--he or she should not be finally and fully licensed until after perhaps three years of demonstration on the job that he or she can, in fact, teach well enough to be licensed permanently as a teacher.

Beyond that, I lean toward the need for the renewal of license at periodic points, because it would be absurd to assume that because one is an effective teacher today he will necessarily be an equally effective teacher, or even an adequately effective teacher, 10 years from now. This may be the case, but it may not work out to be the case.

So, for the good teacher, a periodic review and renewal can do no harm. For the teacher who is not so good, periodic renewal and review could do a great deal of good.

MR. TRACTENBERG: Just one final question. You made some very interesting comments about identifying leadership potential for supervisory positions.

If, as I understand the case to be in the New York City school system, virtually all of the supervisory personnel come from the ranks, does it make any sense at all, in your judgment, to use a written examination when the tools for evaluating on-the-job performance are readily at hand?

DR. FISCHER: It would depend entirely on what one attempts to evaluate. If what one is getting at is technical knowledge in certain fields--for example, ability to work with statistics or specialized knowledge in physics or chemistry, or a foreign language, or any academic area--here, I think, written examinations have considerable value.

But if what one is seeking is ability to work with human beings, ability to release the potentialities of those with whom one is associated--ability, if you will, to inspire one's colleagues to better efforts, to reward, in a psychological sense, to encourage, to organize the efforts of a group of people to accomplish together something they might not be able to do working separately--tests for that kind of capability, so far as I know, are simply not available.

I certainly know of no test on which correlations between results on tests and performance on the job have been developed with any degree of persuasiveness. And so, I would argue one must determine what he is looking for. If it's technical knowledge, that's one thing; if it's the kind of artistry that is involved in working effectively with human beings, that's another. And for the second, written objective tests are of very limited, if any, value.

MR. TRACTENBERG: How might you distinguish between a department chairman, who may have to involve himself in rather technical subject matter, as opposed to a school principal, for example, with the kind of broader responsibilities and needs that you described?

DR. FISCHER: Well, the distinction here may be one of degree. It is not one of kind, I would argue. The department chairman ought to be able to work effectively with other human beings, in much the same way that the principal would. The principal would have a broader circle within which to do his work; he would face more kinds of problems, typically, than the department chairman would face.

And so, it may be that the generalization is that we do not yet have command of the technical, organized subject matter that the principal needs, to the extent that we might claim to have for certain aspects of the department chairman's job.

MR. TRACTENBERG: But certainly, in general, I gather your judgment is that much greater reliance ought to be placed upon on-the-job evaluation and other mechanisms that would tend to test a person's sensitivity and ability to relate to others rather than on written objective tests?

DR. FISCHER: Oh, yes, I agree with that. If I had to limit myself to using observations of actual behavior on the job or a written examination for selecting a principal, there would be no question in my mind; I would select the first. The written examination would strike me as a quite unpromising way of finding the best principal.

MR. TRACTENBERG: Fine. That's all I have.

COMMR. COLGATE: Dr. Fischer, I have a question which I would like to discuss with you--taken from your testimony-- about expanding the criteria for judging the professional competence about which you spoke.

Now, there appeared to be three areas of judgment which you have talked about. The first is the academic training content, which is, I think we both agree, essential. A teacher who is teaching French must know something about French, and a teacher who is teaching German has to know something about German, and a teacher teaching mathematics has to know something about mathematics.

Then you discussed the predictive testing of the capability or the quality of understanding the diversity, I believe, was one of your phrases, and the other was the sensitivity to the personal problems of the children in the instructor's care.

As I recall, you said in your testimony that you knew of no written test that could predict whether this budding artist now-- since we are talking about teaching as an art, the artist now has done the anatomy drawings in the art class--the budding artist is now about to start painting live models in his classroom. So now we have, in your words, the proficiency and competence of this artist. And, as I recall your testimony, you felt that the best way of judging this was watching the artist at work. When an artist at work is observed, we can therefore determine whether or not he is a good artist.

Now, I may be in disagreement with you here, because I don't believe that an artist's proficiency is measured by how neat he keeps his studio, but essentially by the results which come out of his studio.

Now, then, how do we measure the competence of a teacher by observing him at work as opposed to the results of the educated or noneducated children, which it is his or her job to produce?

DR. FISCHER: There is no difference between us, I think. When I referred to observing the artist at work, what I had in mind was observing the results of his work.

In teaching, we suffer from a condition which has a long history; we have never developed adequately a procedure for determining what difference the teacher or the school makes in the learning of a child. It is easy to measure how much a child knows, let us say, of arithmetic, or what his reading ability is in September, and to apply another test in June and to see what his or her status is at that point and to determine what the child has gained in so many months, as measured on standardized tests on reading or arithmetic. If the child has gained nothing in that time, it follows that the school hasn't taught him anything in those subjects in that time, at least nothing that is measurable by that test. But if he has learned a great deal, it by no means follows that he learned it in the school.

We have, for as long as there have been schools, credited schools with changes in the performance of students, without distinguishing between those changes that were induced by outside influences and those that were induced by what went on within the school. And so, what we need to do is to find far more effective ways than we have now of identifying what difference a teacher makes, or what difference a school makes in contrast to the differences that are observable in children, without regard to the causes that brought them about.

One has a better chance of determining what difference a teacher makes if one can observe the teacher at work. It's never easy, and there is no technique that I can suggest to you that will make it simple. But if one can see what goes on in the classroom, one has a far greater likelihood of being able to determine whether the teacher is making a positive difference with a class or with a child than if one simply stands off and measures this from some remote point by standardized instruments in the beginning and the end of the term.

THE CHAIRMAN: Thank you, President Fischer.

There has been a lot of discussion in these hearings about teacher's training. We have been, therefore, particularly fortunate in having a president of a teachers college here today and going on record in regard to these matters.

We appreciate your coming, Dr. Fischer.

DR. FISCHER: Thank you.

THE CHAIRMAN: We have very serious time problems today, and therefore I am going to be very much more rigid than I have been before, since 4:30 is our deadline today.

The next witness is Dr. Laurence Iannaccone, Professor of Educational Administration, University of Toronto.

Dr. Iannaccone.

DR. IANNACCONE: Before making my statement, maybe I'd better clarify my relationship to the questions you are concerned with.

My field is educational administration. I am particularly interested in the politics and research of education, and in 1963 was a member of a research team that looked at the personnel system of the City of New York, specifically selection and promotion, the examination pattern. This was done at the behest of the school district, after considerable pressure from the Legislature.

I was brought back in 1966 to make recommendations concerning examination procedures and personnel practices, which was in connection with work done at N.Y.U., once again, at the behest of the system. And I have had a rather long-standing interest in these kinds of problems.

Inevitably, if you do research on the personnel system in New York you turn to the Board of Examiners, because that is the center of the personnel system, realistically, at least. It is licensure and limits placed by the licensure process by New York City which become the constraints most often cited as the reason for not being able to do something--either make a change in practices, which more quickly adjust to the circumstances around, or more adequately meet the needs of the kids, for instance.

Discussion of the Board of Examiners and the examination processes of the New York City public schools is meaningless unless viewed in two contexts:

1. The Board of Examiners stands at the center of personnel practices in the city schools.

2. The personnel practices of the city's municipal bureaucracies, schools no less than any other, function to protect the vested interests of earlier arrivals, more established ethnic populations of the city, at the expense of more recent in-migrants or newer, upwardly mobile groups. The city schools' personnel system is so inbred as to be sociological incest. It functions to prevent any flow of teachers from outside of New York. The city's parochial monopoly of the teacher licensure function is separate from the rest of New York State even though its enormous costs increasingly fall upon the state's taxpayers.

The Board of Examiners and the examination processes depend upon the organized interests of school employees produced and protected by them, and upon the assumption that these processes prevent patronage. In turn, as I have pointed out elsewhere, the Board benefits from the belief that this presumed prevention of patronage carries with it, almost mystically, a guarantee of merit or quality.

Nothing could be further from the truth! At best, the pedestrian examination pattern rewards plodders. To teach in New York City, a teacher fully licensed by the State of New York would, in effect, have to surrender the meaning of his license. If a teacher in Scarsdale, Winnetka, or Beverly Hills, were inclined to accept the challenge of teaching in New York, he would have to begin with a substitute's license. Were such a teacher to exist, he ought to be re-examined for masochistic tendencies.

The evidence on the system's parochialism is clear. Less clear is what the city gains at this cost.

The personnel system, euphemistically called a merit system, does not evaluate critically its substitute or probationary teachers so as to promote the capable and separate the unfit. At best, it lives with the hope that somehow the unfit will drop away. As long ago as 1943, George D. Strayer, in the Interim Report of the New York City Subcommittee of the Joint Legislative Committee on the State Education System, a document paid for by the state, pointed out that no more than "two out of every thousand probationary teachers in recent years failed of permanent appointment."

There is no research which proves that the process produces better teaching. In fact, the absence of research on the validity of the examination system used in New York and the absence of research on the products of that process after all these years, places the burden of proof on the shoulders of those who would defend them.

Recommendations have been made since before World War II by study team after study team. Research concerning the validity of the examination process has not been undertaken, and the excuse of not enough money is ridiculous by 1970. It is one of the most expensive examination systems in America--and I don't mean only the examining systems in education.

On the other hand, look at what the personnel system does. It functions to reduce the rate of social mobility for each new group of migrants to the city and for each group beginning to fulfill the American dream of upward mobility. It results in fewer promotions to higher "licenses" for these populations than would be the case without the city's examination monopoly if the city, indeed, rested on state licensure.

I am citing from Chapter VI, an article entitled "The Racial Distribution of New York City Public School Teachers," done in 1963, in Teacher Mobility in New York City.

The journey, even only that portion which extends from substitute to regular teacher, moves along a lengthy, arduous road with a personalistic base. In each era of its history, ethnicity is the best predictor of examination success. In 1963, while doing research on the city schools' personal system, we found ourselves noting that the system was not particularly anti-Blacks; it was generally anti-new, upwardly mobile groups.

And in its actions, the system admitted the inequities of the examination system when it set up "cram" schools especially for its minority groups. In effect, this action said, despite the claim of merit in the exams, the cram school designed to "beat the tests" is a necessary element in the examination process. This is understandable, given the Mandarin marathon created by the test ladders.

And let me clarify this. We are not talking about a paper-and-pencil test. The exam pattern calls for a three-year testing cycle for most licenses after you leave the regular teacher's level. And that three-year testing cycle ranges from oral to written to observations and to supervisors' ratings, and yields people who pass the test and go on to a list for the next jobs, which list in turn can be held active for eight more years.

So, you can start a process of moving a young, vigorous teacher from the classroom into the principalship when he is 33 years of age, and finish him when he is 44.

By 1971, one should ask at least two questions:
1. If the merit system is so meritorious, why are books on how to take the exams and cram schools necessary to beat the test game?
2. Who benefits from the expense of cram schools? Has the examination system now become so necessary to the vested inter-

ests in expenditure of resources in giving them and beating the tests, that the support of these interests better explain their persistence than does any of the results claimed for them?

If this city is seriously interested in eliminating the inequities and inefficiencies of its educational personnel system, then it must abolish its monopolistic control of education licenses and re-enter the state licensure system.

I couldn't agree more strongly with your previous witness, Dr. Fischer. There is no point in this system remaining unique in its licensing.

THE CHAIRMAN: Counsel.

MR. TRACTENBERG: Yes. Just a couple of questions.

Dr. Iannaccone, Mr. Shanker yesterday, and I think others, have claimed that in the case of all of the studies of the Board of Examiners--some of which you have mentioned, dating back at least 20 years, if not longer--that the group which commissioned the study told the investigator in advance what it wanted; and, therefore, that the studies are subject to great scrutiny, if not to dismissal out-of-hand.

Do you have any reaction to that, as one of the principal investigators of one of those studies?

DR. IANNACCONE: That is kind of difficult, because Mr. Shanker has hired me a couple of times to make speeches at his union, and has never suggested what I should speak about.

That's an insult. And if it were stated under the proper conditions, you know, we might challenge it in the courts. But I don't think Mr. Shanker will see it that way.

To be specific, in 1963 the team that was brought together to do the job included people from outside of New York as well as inside New York. The dean at New York University who headed up that particular task is a man of impeccable scholarly ability. He and I would disagree on results on some things, for instance. But there is no question that I would trust his arrangements to be completely honest.

And, furthermore, I was one of a group of eight or ten senior men and research associates. You don't control the interviewing, or the data collecting of that many people in any way. We had no limits placed upon us, either in terms of the questions to be asked or in terms of the procedures to be used. The only limits we ran into were difficulties in getting data from the system, where the system didn't have them, for instance. But that's characteristic.

If that's an allegation, it's a good-sized one.

MR. TRACTENBERG: And the other question I have is with regard to state certification.

Another of the comments of Mr. Shanker and others is that reliance, even for the screening function, upon state certification would be misplaced because of several things: one, that the state seems to have administrative problems discharging its present certification responsibility; and secondly, that the kinds of course requirements imposed are not adequate to separate out illiterates from those who are literate, or to meet certain competence requirements.

Do you have a reaction to that?

DR. IANNACCONE: Yes, a couple of remarks.

First of all, as to the nitpicking about state administrative problems, I don't know of any, by the way. I'm sure they have them; it's a big state. But it can't possibly compare with the administrative problems of the city schools. That's number one.

Number two, you can't have it both ways. If the New York City schools provide for 12 years of public education, 4 years of graduate education, and still produce illiterates, one must ask the question about how it gets its teaching staff, too. The people who take those exams came almost entirely out of those schools.

Furthermore, all of this rests on the assumption of validity and reliability of those same exams.

Let me be specific. One of the cases we ran into--this just happens to be one from a file in New York City at the time we were doing the depth study in 1963--was the case of a teacher who was attempting to get a regular license to teach high school Spanish, also junior high school Spanish, which is a separate license with separate testing procedures, by the way. In the same year, she failed the oral portion for the junior high school but passed the written portion of that exam, and passed the oral portion for the senior high school and failed the written portion for the senior high school.

There is no reliability at all when you can do that in the same testing year.

Finally, on the other question, the rest of the nation--not just New York State, the rest of the country--is willing to depend upon state certification patterns, with minor testing in some of the smaller cities, such as Chicago, using the national standardized testing program, and it works relatively well. In the 1920's, one could argue, and did argue, that the New York City schools were producing better teachers than the rest of the nation. But certainly by 1970 nobody can argue that any longer.

MR. TRACTENBERG: Although I did say the other was the final question, let me try one more, if I may.

Do you have a reaction about how one might, in New York City, identify and obtain good teachers and supervisors, and could you relate that to the role of the community boards?

DR. IANNACCONE: Well, that's a kind of overloaded question.

MR. TRACTENBERG: You could separate it and treat it as two questions.

DR. IANNACCONE: One of the ways of doing it is to get your crucial decision-making as close to the action as possible. If what you want to do is observe people over a time, in terms of their work and in terms of what is coming out of it, the closer you could bring those decisions to the people involved, the better and more reliable those decisions.

By the way, the recommendations strongly urged the development of inside training and performance, not just examinations but observations over a lengthy period of time, to watch both internees and the administration perform and develop.

I guess what I'm saying is. I would rest very heavily on job performance, both in the teaching role and in other kinds of roles, which on another level is what the system is doing now, except it's compounding it in a variety of other ways, because nobody gets up the promotional ladder through the test system without first performing as an "acting" whatever--which is the system's internal means for beating the test, by the way.

THE CHAIRMAN: Do you have any questions, Mr. Colgate?

COMMR. COLGATE: No.

THE CHAIRMAN: Thank you very much, Dr. Iannaccone.

May I call Dr. Robert A. Dentler, the director of the Center for Urban Education.

DR. DENTLER: I would like to introduce my remarks, which are focused quite exclusively on conceiving an alternative to current procedures for certifying New York City school administrators, with a comment that my remarks are biased in a personal and professional respect, to wit: while I am the holder of four university degrees and have taught for over 20 years at all levels from grade seven through graduate school; while I am the author of over thirty articles on teaching and learning problems; and while I teach hundreds of teachers at Teachers College, Columbia; and while I have administered some $15 million of federal, state and local funds on behalf of improving educational practices, it is a fact that I would not qualify for a common branches teacher's license in New York City. In fact, it affects my testimony.

My remarks assume that current procedures for certifying and appointing public school administrators in New York City are undesirable, inequitable, costly, and unnecessary. My remarks do not test this assumption; that is the task of many others who testified yesterday and today.

However, those who have administered existing procedures also have a strong burden of proof to shoulder. In the past 20 years, the procedure has been under periodic, but severe criticism. The Board of Examiners and the Board of Education should have felt an obligation to put their procedures to an eventual test, to at least statistical if not fully experimental analysis. They have never done so, although they have researched the matter. That is to say, they have never tested empirically whether their procedures result in the appointment of administrators who perform better than persons who might have been appointed by mere chance.

The alternative procedure that I suggest here--and I advance it in order to be illustrative, or heuristic--is intended to meet certain standards which in themselves depart slightly from convention. These standards are:

1. That selection of principals should be applied uniformly, with no exceptions, no exemptive categories;

2. That procedures should cost no more, and preferably less than the present ones;

3. That those who pass the selection screen should be certified as competent to perform as school administrators for a period not to exceed five years from the point of passage;

4. That certified individuals should have full freedom of movement within the system, subject only to the class of their licenses.

Now, the aim of my alternative scheme, which again I offer as illustrative, is thus a set of procedures which offer some warranty of equity, economy, professional excellence and freedom of placement. I submit that these aims are of equal worth to the employing community and to the journeyman administrator as an individual.

My alternative would, of course, abolish the Board of Examiners and any vestige of its paper-and-pencil testing system. It would replace these with the following elements of my ideal alternative:

1. To qualify for any administrative post, a candidate would have to meet the state requirements for that type of post.

2. The State Education Department would expand its range of job definitions and minimum requirements. In the process, it would improve its mechanism for assessing equivalence much as our best university admissions departments have done in recent years in equipping themselves to adapt to transfer students and transfer credits. I am not proposing a state examination procedure, however, as will become clear later in these remarks.

3. The length and nature of previous work experience, plus not more than the bachelor's degree or its equivalent, should be the sole considerations entailed in Points 1 and 2 above. Written examinations, interviews, on-the-job ratings by supervisors and other special assessments should be wholly eliminated as immaterial to certification, as should specific courses of study or advanced degrees. None of these properties has ever shown in systematic research to have any ability to predict job performance for school administrators.

Teaching experience, by the way, is also no predictor of supervisory capabilities. Therefore, the work experience of the applicant must be evaluated in terms of its pertinence to school administration of the appropriate type, regardless of surface characteristics. For example, community organization work, youth agency work, education work in development or research or management, and governmental and military leadership service might prove highly pertinent as equivalent work experiences.

4. The most vital feature of my alternative would be the apprenticeship term. Applicants qualifying as candidates on my points above should seek employment as apprentice supervisors in any one of the schools or agencies registered with and specifically supported and monitored by the State Education Department as administration training sites.

The base apprenticeship would run one year and would require productive service or work in tandem with study.

5. Apprentices would either pass or receive no credit toward certification in the course of their apprenticeship. However, they would not be graded by trainers beyond this base selection. Trainers would have no special powers or privileges of the sort that accrue to examiners and university professors of educational

administration today; nor would the trainers become recommenders of apprentices, save in the capacity of ordinary supervisors of professional employees.

6. Apprentices who pass their base year would automatically be certified as qualified for employment as administrators anywhere in the school systems of the State of New York. As such, they could be hired without reference to any waiting list, or other temporal or quality controlled period.

7. Certification would be good within a category such as elementary school principal for not more than five years. Summer retraining--again, at a state-approved site; not a college or a university, but a work site--would be required for renewal thereafter, or for a changing of supervisory categories.

I don't intend that this brief sketch be taken as a literal brief of an alternative; instead, it's set out here starkly in order to urge upon the Commission consideration of what really pertains and what does not pertain to the selection of educational leaders.

My model is intended to convey these points. Conventional selection offers no valid or reliable means of locating education leaders. Conventional means may, therefore, be abandoned as immaterial.

Practical apprenticeship is pertinent and does predict leadership. Every school board in the state wishes to hire as administrators persons with proven direct experience. At this point, therefore, the stage of apprenticeship can serve to weed out incompetents without penalty to the individuals and at minimal cost, since the most magnificent thing about an apprenticeship system is that the apprentice does valuable work at public cost.

This model is designed to give maximum openness to leadership opportunities. It strips away not only examiners and layers of licensers, but college departments, consultants, employment brokers, placement specialists, and all who, in the words of Kenneth Clark, "presently cash in, however inadvertently and sometimes conscientiously, on the public quest for qualified leadership."

The model emphasizes the need for periodic retraining, renewal, and repassage of apprentice standards. In this way, I think it guards against obsolescence, as well as application of the Peter Principle, in which incompetence inexorably seeks its own level.

Currently, teachers are obligated to undergo periodic retraining, while administrators are not; obviously the reverse of the condition common to advanced industries, such as electronics firms.

The model that I have sketched gives no place to seniority. A given school board may wish to give the factor of seniority some weight, as it does with teachers. But managerial personnel can never expect advantage from more longevity. On the other hand, certified individuals who continue to renew their certification have every reason to expect to continue to be employable in the state as journeymen administrators.

What of our original cost criteria? My model involves two types of special cost: first, cost of developing and operating an improved state classifying mechanism; second, the cost of sustaining a state-funded apprenticeship system.

I submit that the first cost could be met in full by funding for the entire state for what the New York State Board of Examiners costs to operate in New York City alone. Once developed, the state classifying system would cost less and the difference could be expended on analyses of its effectiveness.

The second cost is already being borne by the state, and all local districts in this state, in the form of subsidizing college programs of educational administration. These generate hundreds of M.A.'s, or M.E.'s, M. Ed.'s and Ph.D.'s annually, with no demonstrable consequences of greater equity or excellence in administrative performance. These college programs may be invaluable. They should operate in response, however, to contractual demands from training agencies capable of combining direct work experience with study on an apprentice basis.

In California, a number of school districts, notably Berkeley, are already into this type of operation. And, I would add, in Scarsdale, New York, the Teachers Association now operates its own institute for teacher study, designed and conducted by the teachers, but with outside contractual terms through local board funding.

My model applies only to vice or assistant principals, principals, assistant superintendents, and to some classes of research and development leadership. It does not hold, I think, for guidance or curriculum supervisors or technical specialists who grow up from the ranks and who may require very specialized graduate studies. When staff, as against line leadership, seeks to move across to line positions, the model would apply, however, for a good guidance counselor who is often a poor school principal, and vice-versa.

This alternative of mine could be phased into being during a two-to-four year period. It need not disrupt or dislocate standing personnel arrangements nor should it be approached experimentally.

Administrative leadership selection is a matter for policy determination through implementation, though it should be evaluated vigorously. Good policies are not introduced abruptly, nor can they endure if they break too suddenly with the past.

Therefore, my alternative offers no remedy for a grave current wrong. As our Center reported to the United States Office of Education in 1969, "In Los Angeles, where 21% of the pupils are Black, only 6% of the administrators are Black; 20% of the pupils have Spanish surnames, but only 1% of the administrators have Spanish surnames. In Chicago, where 54% of the student body is Black, 33% of the teaching staff is Black, and 21% of the administrators are Black"--no, no, only 11% of the teaching force was Black and the proportion of Black administrators was, in that year, below 5%.

These data, which indicate that the condition obtains for several large cities, also further indicate that New York City is more remiss than its sister cities to the West. These data have changed very little since 1969, while pressure for remedies has built up swiftly under the aegis of decentralization. To make matters worse, the waiting list of licensed non-Black and non-Puerto Rican administrators has swelled greatly between 1967 and 1970.

The only conceivable remedy for use on an ad hoc basis is not my alternative, which is a gradual scheme and a complicated one. But the ad hoc scheme has been at hand since at least 1968, when Superintendent Donovan attempted to implement a policy of list-jumping and special selective and exemptive appointments. This policy, combined with liberal use of acting appointments, offers the only remedy for long-standing wrongs. It will continue to be opposed, of course, by those who are deferred from what they had assumed they had earned.

This expedient, this ad hoc arrangement, can best be applied, however, under conditions that guarantee teacher improvements over the long term in the whole selective system. For without deeper improvements of the kind implied in my alternative, the temporary expedient policy leads to cynicism and despair among those who came up the established line and to a debasing of the symbolic worth of the positions for those who are appointed under special or exemptive arrangements.

Above all, the city, and other cities like it in New York State, needs an overt policy of corrective action enunciated by the Board of Regents and by the local boards of education. Currently, our atmosphere in this respect is contaminated with equivocation, uncertainty, and an absence of candor which can only undermine public confidence in public education.

I am aware, finally, that neither my alternative nor my short-term remedies can be adopted without a substantial clash with established, powerful administrator organizations. These interest groups have ringed their positions securely, with laws assuring tenure and comparative immunity from public scrutiny. The Decentralization Law has already mitigated this condition. But deeper changes will be harder, not easier, to introduce when these groups feel threatened, as they do now, by the impact of even the modest pressures induced by decentralization. Only a combination of legal, along with state and local, political initiatives, would offer a prospect for change under these conditions.

THE CHAIRMAN: Mr. Tractenberg.

MR. TRACTENBERG: Yes. I have a few questions.

Also, I think, before I raise the questions, much of what you said at the end of your remarks raises an interesting colloquy that Mr. Degnan and I had yesterday, in which he, in substance, I think, accused the community boards of seeking to flaunt the law by using the very route you suggest, that is, the route of acting appointments.

And I asked Mr. Degnan if it wasn't true that in the most recent decision, involving Melvin Taylor's appointment, that the court had upheld as lawful his appointment on an acting basis, and Mr. Degnan said that was true, but I think implied that that may have been a fluke.

I just want to say for the record, that in this morning's

Times, there was reported a decision in a similar case, involving the appointment of a Black teacher as acting principal, Claude Huntley, and the court again found that a quite lawful exercise of authority, and, in fact, had an interesting comment, which I want to read into the record.

The Supreme Court justice said, and I quote: "continued experimentation with the program of intermediate schools seems indicated and further opportunity to develop them must be allowed. This court will not at this crucial point impose upon those who bear the responsibility of implementation the rigidity which petitioners ask in the filling of these significant positions."

And the court then went on to dismiss the petition--and this is a quote from the decision--"as without merit."

So, I think you are quite right; there is a political confrontation. I think to suggest that the community boards are acting outside of the laws is unfortunate, to say the least, and certainly not consistent with some of the judicial decisions that have been rendered in this area.

Now, there is an interesting conflict in your remarks with statements made yesterday by Mr. Shanker, who indicated that he felt it very important to establish a state examination, and that this was necessary to insure professionalism in the teaching profession. He analogized it to such other occupations as doctors, lawyers, barbers, and beauticians.

Is there any way to reconcile your remarks with Mr. Shanker's? I gather that you would change state certification and, if anything, reduce some of the state requirements, or at least provide for equivalency examinations; whereas Mr. Shanker feels it necessary to substantially increase the requirement imposed by state certification.

DR. DENTLER: Yes. I don't want to take on directly his point of view. I was not here yesterday and didn't hear them firsthand. I read of them in the New York Times this morning. But as you represent them to me now, there is a definite and pointed difference.

I would find it extremely embarrassing to recommend in 1971 that an obsolete system, such as bar examinations, be applied in what is still only a very incompletely emergent profession, the profession of school administration. I am not even taking on the topic here of the teacher as a professional. But the examination system for letterhead professions is fraught with absurdities in its own right. To transfer this and fit it to what is still an art and a craft, and only incompletely a profession, seems to me to invite further bureaucratization.

By the way, state examining systems still would have to fall back on the same sorts of criteria, which I have indicated research shows to be immaterial to predicting leadership. And what we want, in the case of school administrators, is effective leadership.

Now, knowing that, I can't imagine calling for a state examining system. I can imagine calling for a state-sponsored apprenticeship system of the sort I have advanced.

MR. TRACTENBERG: Some of your remarks raise, in my

mind, a possibility which I don't think has really been brought out in these hearings but perhaps is worth bringing out. And that is, your judgment about whether a career development ladder for teachers should be pointed to school administrative positions. We have had a lot of charges about inbreeding. If a teacher who wants to advance within the system can, really, look only to administrative positions and not to anything which would continue him in the classroom this may be an important source of inbreeding.

Do you have any reaction?

DR. DENTLER: Yes. I think there are forces at work in public education today which are breaking up that pattern, in any event. For example, with the impressive gains resulting from unionism, it is now the case that a male teacher can almost be a breadwinner; he can almost raise a family on a teacher's salary, without double or triple moonlighting. This will have consequences for ending the absurd stress of moving out of the classroom and into administration.

There are also other options becoming available for teachers that don't have to do with administration. But what I would like to emphasize is that leadership comes in many forms and can be found in many ancillary institutions around the world, of children and youth. And I just can't understand why schools would, in the future, draw their leadership exclusively from within the ranks of teachers.

I would even go so far as to argue that some of the research on this subject suggests that experienced, seasoned teachers may be the least likely personnel from whom to draw school administrators, that there are some personality distinctions here, matters of difference in life style.

And that is the reason I made my point, that a good guidance counselor is not at all necessarily a good school principal, or vice-versa.

MR. TRACTENBERG: Dr. Dentler, based on your experience in educational matters in New York City, do you think that giving the kind of flexibility you suggest to local communities, community boards, would lead inevitably to a system of patronage and nepotism and favoritism?

That is another of the allegations that we have heard rather frequently during these hearings.

DR. DENTLER: I think that was a very telling argument in the 1930's. I certainly would have subscribed to it then; I subscribe to it in retrospect. That is, historically the merit system made a contribution.

In the 1970's our problem is not the problem of corruption through patronage. Our problem is remedying long-standing wrongs, discrimination inside a racist institution--a public service institution which has racist characteristics--and the improvement of the means for locating effective leadership.

I am unexcited and unimpressed by the patronage argument. I never hear it being brought up by people except in that historical context.

MR. TRACTENBERG: That is all I have.

THE CHAIRMAN: Dr. Dentler, thank you very much.
I would like to call Dr. Phyllis Wallace and Miss Jeanette Hopkins of the Metropolitan Applied Research Center.

DR. WALLACE: There are a number of statistical tables and charts which have been included in the statement from the Metropolitan Applied Research Center.

When the recruitment and promotion of minority group teachers and supervisory staff in the top five cities in the United States are compared, it becomes apparent that New York City's record is, overall, the poorest.

Of the five largest cities in the country, New York City has, for example, the lowest percentage of minority group full-time classroom teachers. In New York City's public schools, 8.8% of these teachers are Black or Puerto Rican. But in Chicago, Detroit, and Philadelphia, the percentage of minority group teachers is at least three and one half times as great as New York City. Los Angeles, next lowest to New York City, has almost twice the percentage of Black and Spanish-surnamed teachers as New York City. These figures fail to reflect the actual relationship between certification procedures of the New York City Board of Examiners (and procedures in certain other cities) and the recruitment of Black and Puerto Rican personnel, since the old--now being abandoned--category of full-time substitutes, on which these figures are based, is included in official figures, and estimated to comprise roughly one-third of the total. Such substitutes were not required to have practice teaching and were not eligible for tenure.

New York City also has the poorest record among the largest cities in terms of percentage of minority group personnel in certain top supervisory staff positions: superintendents, principals, and assistant principals.

To take the position of principal as illustration, New York City has 4.7% Black or Puerto Rican principals, but Chicago has 6.9%; Detroit, 16.7%; and Philadelphia, 16.9%. In the category of assistant principal, New York is also lowest, with 12.4% Black and Puerto Rican staff. The other three cities have between two and three times as many as New York City in percentage terms.

New York City's figures, incidentally, are still more shocking if one excludes from the total of principals and assistant principals the number of acting principals and acting assistant principals, uncertified by the Board of Examiners. Roughly 78% of Blacks and Puerto Ricans serving as principals, for example, are in the "acting" category.

In terms of the ratio of minority group teachers to minority group students, New York City also ranks last among the five largest cities. There is one Black or Spanish-surname teacher for every 132 Black and Spanish children in New York City public schools. Each of the other four cities among the top five has a record of Black or Spanish teacher representation that ranges from about two to three times the New York City ratio.

There is one white teacher in New York City to every ten white students. In the other four cities, the white teacher-to-white-student ratio ranges from 1:14 to 1:18.

In terms of the ratio of minority group principals to minority group students also, New York City ranks last among the top five cities (Los Angeles cannot be included here because principals and assistant principals are combined in its figures).

However, there is one white principal for every 504 white students in New York City, compared with one Black (or Puerto Rican) principal for every 13,021 Black and Puerto Rican students in New York City. The references are to tables four and five in the MARC statement.

Of the five largest cities in the country, only Chicago and New York have boards of Examiners. But Chicago provides three alternative routes to teacher certification, relying on the National Teacher Examination (except for special skill areas, e.g., accounting), and with no exam required of full-time teachers with three or more years' experience and with satisfactory ratings. Principals in Chicago qualify on a written exam, the NTE, but its content has been recently revised to give more weight to child development and learning theory and to communications skills and human relations skills. The revised exam, as we will see later, immediately raised the number and percentage of Black principals passing.

Flexibility is characteristic of certification procedures for teachers in the other three top cities. In Detroit, for example, students graduating from the top half of their college classes are not required to take an exam. Other applicants take either a city exam prepared by ETS, or the NTE. For principals, a certifying examination based on the nature of the job is given in Detroit. Included are situational and administrative questions. In Los Angeles, principals are certified on the basis of a written exam and evaluation, but with reduced emphasis on the exam in the last two years. In Philadelphia, state certification, including a written exam, is required.

Claims are often made by defenders of the Board of Examiners that the percentage of Black and Puerto Rican teachers and supervisors is a function not of narrow or discriminatory licensing procedures, but a smaller "pool of eligibles." It is true that New York City has a slightly smaller percentage of Black and Spanish-surname population than the other largest cities. However, a "pool of eligibles" is as wide and deep as a city school system wishes it to be. Cities with aggressive recruitment programs among Blacks, like Cleveland, Philadelphia, Detroit, and Seattle, have significantly raised the percentage of Blacks on their staff in recent years.

In Detroit, for example, after a citizen advisory committee recommendation in 1962, Black faculty increased from 21.6% in 1961 to 39.6% in 1969. In Chicago, results of a new principal's exam showed a striking increase in total number passing and in numbers and percentage of Blacks passing, as compared with the previous exam. Almost one-half of those passing were Black; in the previous year, less than one-fifth were Black. On the new exam there were 73 Blacks, on the old exam 19 Blacks passing; on the new exam one Mexican-American, on the old exam no

Mexican-Americans; on the new exam, 75 others passing, on the old exam 60 others passing; on the new exam, all together, 150 passing; 79 passing on the old exam.

A striking example of effective recruitment and promotion in terms of ethnic mobility is Cleveland, with an ethnic enrollment distribution roughly similar to New York City. Cleveland has:

. more than four times as high a percentage of Black full-time classroom teachers (Cleveland, 38.9%; New York City, roughly 9%, including Puerto Ricans);

. more than three and one half times as many Black and Puerto Rican assistant principals (Cleveland, 46%; New York City 12.4%, though in New York City most of these are unlicensed acting assistant principals);

. about nine times as many minority group principals (Cleveland, 42.4%; New York City, 4.7%. If one subtracts Cleveland's "principals-in-training" from this total— 56 of 103--and New York City's unlicensed acting principals, Cleveland is even further ahead comparatively, 19.3% Black compared to roughly 1% for New York City).

These data are in Table 6 of the statement.

Seattle, on the other hand, is a forceful example of a city that has extended its pool of eligibles despite a high proportion of white total population (93%) and of white public school enrollment (88.6%). In Seattle, 4.2% of the principals and 13.2% of the assistant principals are Black. New York City, with five times the Seattle minority group enrollment, has almost exactly the same percentage of Black and Spanish-surname principals (4.7%, and most of these are unlicensed), and a smaller percentage of assistant principals (12.4%, and of these, most are unlicensed).

In summary, New York City ranks lowest of the top five cities in the country in terms of certain significant categories of representation of minority group teaching and supervisory staff. Further, New York City's certification and promotion procedures are, among these five, the most rigid and offer the fewest options.

The Metropolitan Applied Research Center does not cite statistics like those given above for their own sake, but as an indication that something is wrong. New York City has no reason to fall to the bottom in any aspect of education, as the above statistics suggest that it has. New York is the headquarters of the United States. It has the capability, the natural resources--intellectual, technological, economic--to lead in establishing equality of opportunity and access in all areas of public concern, particularly in education.

THE CHAIRMAN: Mr. Tractenberg.

MR. TRACTENBERG: I think they want to proceed with both their statements.

THE CHAIRMAN: Miss Hopkins has a statement.

MISS HOPKINS: My name is Jeanette Hopkins; I'm Vice-President for Editorial Affairs of the Metropolitan Applied Research Center.

MARC takes the position that the only significant test of the effectiveness of an educational system is its consequences in student performance. Therefore, it views the investigation of certification and promotion procedures in New York City as necessarily related to that criterion.

Do certification and promotion procedures reinforce effective education in this sense? Is there a relationship between ethnic imbalance in staffing and student achievement? In an attempt to explore this question, MARC has looked at New York City as it compares with other cities in the state which use the same or different procedures.

Take the Big Six cities in terms of pupil achievement. New York City and Buffalo both require a special city examination for teacher certification, in contrast with other state cities, all of which require state certification.

Of the six cities with the largest population in New York State, New York City and Buffalo have the largest percentage of public school enrollment achieving below-minimum competence as measured by reading achievement. This record holds for all three grades tested for 1969 and 1970. (See Table A.)

The reading readiness tests given in New York City in grade one showed a sharp and steady improvement in tested pupils' competence each year from 1965 to 1968-1969. This test was not given in 1969-1970). In fact, the figures released this last year show that more than two-thirds of the public school children who entered school in New York City (all but 29.5%) were above minimum competence in the first grade. But of the children tested at grades three and six that same year, more than 40% were below minimum competence. This year, performance declined for each grade tested. The percentage below minimum competence rose from 8 to 10% per grade in all grades tested in New York City—grades 3, 6, and 9.

Examining the New York City Board of Education figures for reading achievement released yesterday, based on a different test theory from the New York Test, and related to a national norm, we see that this year's second grade has been singled out in terms of performance improvement. The city average is one month above national norm. This progress is consistent with the state figures for last year's New York City first grade students, and both records suggest that students' potential is clearly more responsive to effective teaching than many have previously recognized. But even so, the city figures show that at the second grade level, as well as in every other grade tested in the city, more students were below the national norm for their grade than were above.

In the second grade, for example, 51.3% of the students were below the United States norm for this past year, according to figures released by The New York *Times* (December 20, 1970). But in grade three, 63.9% were below. That was no improvement from the past year, and a big jump from 1965. In each of the remaining grades tested, a significantly larger percentage was below norm for 1970 as compared with 1965, and grades 7, 8, and 9 were all further behind than they were in the previous year. All together, 63.3% of the pupils tested were below grade norm compared with 54.1% below in 1965.

And in arithmetic, New York City for 1969-70 was again the worst of the Big Six cities for every grade tested--3, 6, and 9. Buffalo was next lowest for grades 6 and 9.

In the comparison of New York City with all other public schools in the state, the discrepancy is even more plain. In 1968-1969, in these other schools in the sixth grade where the record was poorest, the average percentage below minimum competence in reading was only 18.9% compared to 42.9% for New York City for the same grade.

New York City also has a disproportionate record of minimum competence on the state tests. If one relates achievement figures to total enrollment, as for example in 1967-1968, one finds that 46% of all public school students in New York State below minimum competence were in New York City public schools, while only 24% of the total public school enrollment is in the city. In all other state public school systems, the percentage of educationally disadvantaged pupils and the percentage of the state-wide enrollment were about equal.

Skipping to the ethnicity of students and staff, when the percentage of minority group principals in the state's six largest cities are ranked, New York City and Buffalo, respectively, rank fourth and fifth. Albany is lowest in positions; but Albany has a higher percentage of minority group assistant principals (27.3% and, therefore, a greater pool of minority group professionals for future principal posts. Buffalo has the lowest percentage of assistant principals. Excluding unlicensed principals and assistant principals from the data on New York City would place the city at the bottom of the list in both categories. Both Buffalo and New York City have a larger "pool" of Black teachers in the system to draw on for supervisory posts (8.8% for New York City; 10.6% for Buffalo) than any of the other four cities, but the rest of the cities rely on state certification, not special city exams.

Now, of course, is there a causal relationship? A causal relationship cannot be assumed between low student achievement, low percentage of minority group professionals, and the procedures of the Board of Examiners. However, these factors do coexist and, perhaps, commingle in New York City. But, whatever the claims offered in support of the New York City Board of Examiners, there can be no claim that they have produced effective teachers, measured by student achievement. No positive relationship exists between the licensing procedures of the Board of Examiners and the demonstrable competence of supervisors and staff. Its tests have not proved predictive of classroom effectiveness. Tests may be "objective" in content, but irrelevant and invalid as a measure of actual performance.

This city can no longer afford licensed incompetency. The cost is too great for the city's students and taxpayers. From amounts gleaned from the Board of Education budget, the Board of Examiners operates on an annual budget of over $3 million: all but approximately $66,000 is paid for salaries. If the $32,000 paid to each examiner is subtracted, about $2.8 million is left for the Board of Examiners to disburse to assistants and consultants of their own choosing.

Overall, the budget of the Board of Examiners has increased about 233% during the 10 years between 1958-59 and 1968-69. By comparison, the total budget of the Board of Education increased 175% during the same period. For other comparisons, the budget of $3 million-plus of the Board of Examiners in the year 1968-69 approximates the money spent for libraries in all day schools, and exceeds that spent for adult education in evening high schools.

Now, as to alternatives, MARC recommends as alternatives to the present outmoded, discriminatory, and unproven city licensing system:

1. Abolition of the Board of Examiners, on the grounds that its function is unrelated to academic performance.

2. Prompt changes in state certification to focus on criteria based on classroom performance, as Washington State and Florida are attempting to do, with classroom performance to be tested over a three-year internship program to be administered by the city Board of Education in conjunction with universities of the city and state.

3. A three-year supervised internship program based on the medical model, with certification and tenure dependent upon effective classroom performance. Such performance criteria for teachers would include the ability to diagnose learning problems, the capacity to teach, and the capacity to stimulate children to learn.

We reject any system of licensing that justifies teaching failure by defining the child as a terminal case, as some do--not as a human being with potential, but as a cancer patient impossible to cure. Teachers or supervisors who, at the very least, do not believe in the capacity of children to learn have no business in the schools, and school systems based on such negative premises have no right to the taxpayers' dollars. Among the criteria for evaluation in principals' apprenticeship would be the capacity to stimulate academic achievement by reinforcing teacher and student motivation, and by parent involvement.

Various promising experiments in internships are now under way; some at the graduate level, some at the undergraduate level. Two examples are the Urban Teacher Preparation Program at Syracuse University, and the Wayne State Experimental Program in Detroit. In Syracuse, interns receive regular appointments as one-half time teachers combined with a full schedule of classes in the university. Able and experienced teachers released from teaching responsibilities serve as full-time supervisors of interns. The Wayne State Program concentrates on students in the junior year in college, with a full-time, 80% salaried, certified senior year teaching internship. We would recommend a program based on these models, but with an additional third year under advanced supervision in the school system before teaching certification and tenure are granted.

4. We would recommend, further, more rigorous recruitment within the city, including in the senior high school and early college years, as well as among teachers throughout the country.

5. In view of the past failure of the city school system to

educate minority group students effectively, and the consequent low percentage of Black or Puerto Rican graduates from the City University which now supplies most of the city's teachers, we recommend also:

    a. As a substitute for cram coaching courses to enable insiders to pass present exams, an intensive year-round training program focusing on basic cognitive skills, teaching methods, diagnostic techniques, and managerial and community skills, with stipend, sponsored by the Board of Education and the City University, to remedy the educational loss that discourages Blacks and Puerto Ricans from competing for teaching and supervisory posts. It must be the city's responsibility to compensate for its own past failures;

    b. The intensive pre-service and in-service programs will not be required for licensing, but satisfactory completion of the course in conjunction with two further years of a peer-evaluated teaching or administrative internship would lead to certification and tenure.

Professionalism is not an autonomous category, but bears a direct relationship to perceived effectiveness in terms of claims for performance. The public interest is paramount; the self-policing such as that undertaken by organizations like the state bar association and state medical societies is not alone adequate. The state, therefore, awards certification on the basis of legally defined criteria.

The task of the system is not to screen out or make do with the results of screening, or to justify the system on the grounds of 19th Century political patronage or on the grounds that there are few qualified Blacks and Puerto Ricans to fill top posts or on the subtly racist grounds that the children themselves are unqualified to learn. Rather, it is the task of the system to respond to need, to open up the system so that it responds to the people it is intended to serve. Professional educators can claim public support only when it is apparent to the public that the delegated responsibilities of teaching children have been met.

THE CHAIRMAN: Mr. Tractenberg.

MR. TRACTENBERG: Yes; a few questions.

I think you have hinted at it in your remarks but if you could, just for the record, state what you think are the principal reasons for New York City's poor performance in terms of recruiting and selecting minority group staff members as compared to other major cities.

DR. WALLACE: Well, I believe that the results in the City University, in terms of the small number of Black and Puerto Rican graduates, and the relatively few Black and Puerto Rican supervisors are both part of the same whole. They are both part of a reactionary racist system that has not compensated for its past failures; it has not adapted to the 20th Century.

MR. TRACTENBERG: Does that suggest that recruitment is one of the main areas in which this school system has fallen down in relation to the others that you have mentioned in your studies?

DR. WALLACE: I think that it's clear. All of the cities that we have examined pointed out that they had deliberately introduced vigorous recruitment procedures. And, in fact, they would laugh when the question would come up about the difficulties of New York City in finding qualified Black and Puerto Rican graduates.

MR. TRACTENBERG: I think that relates to what Mr. Degnan said yesterday, that one of the reasons for the success of Detroit in recent years in increasing its minority percentages in terms of staff, was that they give separate examinations for Black candidates.

From your inquiries of school systems, do you have any response to that?

DR. WALLACE: Well, we were listening to these comments yesterday, and we called Detroit and repeated the comments of Mr. Degnan to Mr. Anderson of the Office of Staff Relations, Office Personnel, and he just said two words: "Absolutely false."

MR. TRACTENBERG: Also, since we are bringing up prior testimony, the statement was made yesterday by some witnesses--at least one that I can recall--that there is some evidence, in fact, that Black teachers teaching Black children produce inferior results rather than superior results.

Is that information substantiated by any of the studies you have conducted at MARC?

MISS HOPKINS: No, it is not, by none of the studies we have at MARC.

DR. WALLACE: I might add, that Black teachers have been teaching Black students in the South for years, and the remark that it has not been effective, this is an extraordinary statement to make.

The South's educational system in the past has been a dual and segregated system, with proven inequities of facilities. And to suggest that we open up the New York City system to permit Blacks and Puerto Ricans on an equal basis, that this is equivalent to segregating them unequally is an extraordinary suggestion.

MR. TRACTENBERG: Out of these hearings have come a number of alternative suggestions. One is a state-wide written examination, theoretically along the lines, I guess, of the bar examination or the medical boards.

That is not what you have recommended. Would that be an acceptable alternative to the current New York City licensing procedures?

DR. WALLACE: Of course, we feel that state certification procedure is preferable, in principle, to the city system. But we don't feel that you can judge or predict classroom performance, particularly as it relates to student achievement, by any written exam.

I happen to have looked at some of the exams the other day, and I think, personally, as an editor and concentrating in English for many years, just on the basis of English alone, it is basically shocking and bad.

MR. TRACTENBERG: Have you had any experience or

occasion to study the National Teacher Exam? That was another one of the alternatives brought out by some of the other speakers.

DR. WALLACE: We have not.

MR. TRACTENBERG: One of your proposals was an internship program.

In view of the present low level of screening out of incompetent personnel, do you think an internship program can work effectively?

What kinds of changes would be necessary to insure that, in fact, incompetents are screened out during the internship period?

DR. WALLACE: Well, I think Dr. Fischer was right, that considerable research needs to be done on the criteria for effective teaching to demonstrate the direct relationship between teacher effectiveness and student achievement.

I think probably that for an effective internship program, the teachers who would be involved as supervisors should be involved in this in-service training themselves.

I don't know if your question suggested that.

MR. TRACTENBERG: Well, that was part of it. But what I really had in mind was the adequacy and effectiveness of an internship for screening out people who are not competent to be effective teachers.

The performance, as you probably know, in the New York City system, in using the probationary period, has been, by all odds, unsatisfactory; almost no one is screened out.

DR. WALLACE: Well, that's because it has been a very passive program. There has been no serious interest in supervision and no serious attempts to suggest that there is any relation of how students achieve and how teachers perform. It is easy to find out what students are achieving. And there is considerable evidence about particular procedures that can improve student achievement. The probationary period in New York City is far from adequate at present.

MR. TRACTENBERG: That is all I have.

THE CHAIRMAN: Thank you very much, Dr. Wallace. I think this is a particularly creative piece of research for us to have.

We are particularly fortunate that the Metropolitan Applied Research Center has chosen to put such an in-depth study in our record, and we thank you very much.

We will take a five-minute break, no more than that.

(Whereupon, a five-minute recess was taken.)

THE CHAIRMAN: These hearings are being held at 14 Vesey Street. Today will be a short day at the hearings. We will adjourn promptly at 4:30 today because of another meeting that is going to be held in this room. So, we are going to be thoroughly rigid in sticking to our schedule today.

I want to call Dr. James Shields, Professor of Education, City College of New York.

DR. SHIELDS: It is very difficult to know where to start, in talking about the whole process of teacher training and how it interacts with the operation of school systems as to hiring, promotion and retention and dismissal of teachers.

Let me start with a very short observation about teacher education, the colleges and the professions.

It turns out that the American college has taken on as one of its major functions, that of credentialing, not only in teacher education but in almost every other professional field you can think of. When a young man goes for a job today, as a seller of hosiery or yard goods in Macy's, he is asked if he has a college degree. If a man wants to practice law, he has to show evidence of a bachelor's degree, and usually a degree from a law school.

The same is true of teacher education and the teaching profession. If you want to become a teacher, you must present a bachelor's degree and some evidence of having taken courses in an institution that provides education courses.

Now, in teacher education, as in law, medicine, college teaching, selling hosiery, no one really expects that what goes on in that institution that provides for credentialing, which provides the access to the job, has anything to do with performance on the job. There is very little consideration of what the credential represents in terms of studying and training, of what it has to do with what the credentialled are expected to do. That is an observation that one has to think about.

Certainly a major alternative to the whole system would be for school systems, law offices, hospitals, not to ask for a degree before they ask a person if he wants to accept a position, but to ask him if he can perform the function which he is being hired to do.

This would mean, for instance, that people could, in teaching, come out of the community and assume a job as a teacher in a second grade classroom, or an older person who has worked with a large number of children, has experience with children, showed particular competence in dealing with children, could become a teacher without having to present the diploma or the education credits.

Now, when that happens, then I think a lot of the problems that we experience in schools of education will disappear, because then the schools of education will have to be competitive with other places that people can get the experience to become a teacher.

Does that make sense to you? Or is it a point of any relevance to this conference?

MR. TRACTENBERG: Certainly.

DR. SHIELDS: Just to make an aside right now. You see, the public school system has a monopoly on education. So the possibilities for reform and the betterment of the product they provide are very severely limited.

Let's say, in New York City, it costs $1,800 a year to educate a child. Let's take that as a figure. Well, if parents were given the $1,800 to spend any way they wish for their child's education, if they had the option of not putting their child in a local school or a school in a school district in which they lived but any place they wished, including a very wise man that lived down the street who could provide their child with a lot more beautiful educational experience, then the public school system would really have to shape up to attract people to its halls.

The same thing is true in teacher education and the providing of training for people to teach in the school system. If there were other alternatives than college and university credits and college and university credentials were not demanded by the school system as one of the requirements for teaching in the system, then the schools of education would have to be much better to survive.

I spent the years 1967-68 at Yale in the Department of Political Science doing studies on educational politics and power plays among educationists, and I came to City College following that. And I must say, I got into all this through the back door. I found my colleagues and the administrators and the people who were responsible for teacher education in the city universities, talking all the time about what was wrong with the New York City school system.

They were terribly aware of its problems and its deficiencies. And, of course, this was considered to be pretty avant-garde, to be even talking about it. But very rarely did any of them ask whether what they were doing had anything to do with the failure in the New York City school system. And I began to point out that right under the windows of City College is Harlem, where roughly 85% of the students who entered the school system drop out before they graduate, where as a child moves through the system he decreases in achievement. There is a regression. Not only doesn't the school system keep him where he is when he enters, but somehow or other, with the experience--I didn't say because of the experience, but with the experience--of the public school system he becomes less able.

I think the figures are roughly like this. In the second or third grade a child is roughly one year behind in reading; by the sixth grade his is 2 years behind; and by the ninth grade he is 3 years behind on the average. So that the experience has decreased his competitiveness in reading level.

And I am pointing out this occurs with the instructors, who are the teachers and the administrators of these people in the school system. As it turns out, the overwhelming majority of the teachers and the administrators are graduates of City College, people who have gone through our program.

Now, admittedly, it is what someone this morning called "sociological incest." And I think this is most evident. I don't know if it's just pure, nice physical incest. We don't even have to put any racial or religious or cultural overtones on it; incest isn't all of that.

But, in the New York City system, a child enters grade school. If he is very bright--this has been the case in the traditional definition of what brightness is, as defined by tests and the books used--he goes on to City College, and then he goes from City College back into the system to teach. This is incest. No input from systems and people outside of this little family.

And you know what has happened when they have tried to bring in a stud from the outside. Calvin Gross is a very good example. They decide that he is tormented and destroyed, and he finally limps away, never to be heard of again.

Have any of you heard of Calvin?

A VOICE: He has disappeared.

DR. SHIELDS: Yes. Perhaps even castrated. But this is the problem. So what do we do? How do we resolve it? As I said, the first one is a credential problem.

Now, the second one is what we do in teacher education. I am on the Board of NCATE, which is the National Council for the Accreditation of Teacher Education. This is a group that visits schools of education around the country and tells them whether or not they are in business for another year. It has been a group that has been traditionally controlled--a national group with offices in Washington--by people from the rural parts of the country, from the West and from small colleges and schools of education. And I very rarely, at meetings with them and in schools around the country, have run into professors of education who are terribly convinced that what they do has anything to do with creating a good teacher.

I would like you to invite one professor of education who feels that what he is doing he can really confidently say is making that person a better teacher. This doesn't even seem to enter the thinking of most people involved.

A couple of us at City College decided to really think hard about how to make the experience of education courses relevant to practicing teaching effectively. And we came up with a program which has limitations, but I think is a great improvement over the existing experience that most people have.

First of all, we have decided that every experience in teacher education should have a strong practical field aspect to it. So that we put most of the thrust of the program on having students go out to the schools and work.

Secondly, what happens now is a student takes, for instance, in most of the city universities, 12 hours of courses in the sociology of education, psychology of learning, child development, and adolescent development. And only after that experience are they allowed to have an experience in a school of any significance. But what they have been doing recently is providing two hours here and there haphazardly and calling it field work. And this is ridiculous. I have classes of students who have these 12 credits and then go into the schools and teach, never having been in a classroom, or never having been told what a reader is.

I was up at a school the other day, in the Bronx, and they were interviewing a young man for a job. And they asked him if he was familiar with the Basal Reader, and he said, no, he didn't know Mr. Basal--(laughter)--but he would try to look him up when he went home, so he would be ready to teach the next day.

Now, of course, we in the teacher training institutions can take part of the blame. This young man did know that Comenius said something about education in some century, a while back. And he knew that there is realism and there is experimentalism and there is Thomism; and that if you are a Thomist, you put the emphasis upon the intellect; and if you are a realist, or an experimentalist, you put the emphasis upon experience. He knew all that, and he could answer those questions in the teachers' examination.

But no one, of course--this is another aspect of the problem --really asks for too much evidence of whether or not a person can teach when he goes for a teaching job, or asks him to demonstrate it. Do they? He is given an examination, as I say, that asks for factual information largely, and then he is interviewed to see if he stutters or nots. He is given a physical to see if he is alive, and then he is given a certificate and he moves into the system.

The second aspect, as I said, the big thing, is field work. We have done away with all of the courses as they now exist. There are no courses except every week they have a two-hour seminar, or discussion period with people to observe them, and methods people to talk about that they observed, and what they did last week in the field. That is basically what the program is.

In the first year in this program--this is a 4-year program and we ask people to make a decision about becoming a teacher very early--they move into schools and just walk around the schools and go from class to class and they pick out six children they really think they could relate to, or want to help. And then they spend the rest of the first year, going to the classes of these six children and either working with them in the classes or outside the class, and developing a personal relationship with them.

Now, you see, instead of taking a course in child development, they work with children and watch their development over a year. This is organic learning. You don't read in a textbook, at age 7 most children do this, and at age 8 most people do that. You are with six children here and observe what they do, and you find out that not one of the children is "most children." he is a unique individual with special aspects and characteristics.

All we want to happen in the first year is that our teacher trainees develop the ability and facility for looking at an individual and seeing him as a unique person, a special unique individual, so that when they step in a classroom they are not looking, through their mind's eye, at disadvantaged children or Blacks or Jews or the bright class or the bad class. They are looking at 25 individuals, and they set up 25 individual relationships.

It is much less a stress for new teachers when they are working daily with setting up 25 relationships than if they are setting up a combat with a group of disadvantaged children, which is mostly what our teacher education programs gear people up to, getting ready for the battle in the ghetto.

The second year, they keep their six children and in their field time they go out into the community. They visit the parents of each of the six children. They visit the social agencies that have something to do with the children in this community, and then they try to ally themselves with an action group out to reform some aspects of the community. This could be a rent group, a little group that is trying to get a traffic light for outside the school.

All we want to happen in the second year is that they think of education as something bigger than a classroom; that they realize that most of the education that a child is receiving in the year that they have been there is outside the classroom and in the home, in the streets, in the community centers. And it might be, if someone really looked at it carefully, that if you used 100 as the full amount of experience and education a child received in any nine-month period from September to June, that 98 of it was outside the classroom.

And, also, we want teachers to think about moving the children outside of the classroom for education. Here we are; what you do is lock 30 children into a relatively small room and put all the chairs as they are here. Do you notice what happened here? The people in the first row are looking at the people in the second row; the people in the second row are looking at the next row, and so forth. It's an unnatural experience.

Most of us are full of energy and vitality, and particularly children. And we sit them down in a seat and say, "Stay there until 3 o'clock." And that is where all the education that is going to happen to you is going to take place, in that seat. When you walk into the classroom, get up out of your seat, the teacher says, "Get back to your seat. Get back to your seat. Sit down."
But what do you do when you're interested in something? You get up and you go to it; it doesn't come to you. Only a creative artist sits and a thought comes to him and he catches it.

We also want our teachers to feel responsibility for the lives of the children they are dealing with beyond the 9-to-3 experience.

In the third year they go back to the classroom and they try to find a classroom that has most of the children they have and they move into methods for completion. They learn about diagnosing reading problems and problems with mathematics, and that sort of thing, and what some of the techniques that have been developed to meet these are.

And in the fourth year, they do full-fledged student teaching, which is much more extensive than the normal one.

Well, this is the program we have developed. I think it's a move in the right direction. I don't know if it's the full answer. It certainly only touches a part of the problem, because most people at the moment who teach in New York City do not move through schools of education in programs of this sort.

Most people have had a very limited experience for about 12 education credits and then go into teaching.

Now, another big part of the problem is what you do with these inexperienced people when they get into the school system. Very little is done for them The union mandates a two-hour-a-week workshop on Monday afternoons or so for beginning teachers. And this has been a total failure. It seems to have nothing to do with anything. I have spoken to new teachers around the city about it, and mostly they try not to go. As a matter of fact, many of them just stop going.

The other attempt to solve the problem of the inexperienced teachers is--and this is a rather good idea--to provide a school teacher trainer. This is a program I have been evaluating for the state. That is why I have been getting into the schools. It is a program which the state funded under a fund called STINT. The State Department of Education gives a school enough money to pay the salary of an experienced teacher to go around and help out the new teachers in the school.

The unfortunate problem with this program, as I see it, is that the people who are the teacher trainers frequently have been successful in the system, and so they perpetuate some of the problems that exist: the ways of looking at Blacks, the traditional modes of retraining, and oppression of students. Many of them do, however, have access to curriculum supplies, readers and workbooks and things of that sort, which they do put in the hands of teachers. I find this a relatively effective program.

And, of course, the third thing that happens is that new teachers take education courses in our schools of education around the city in the afternoon. These, I would say, would be-- well, I was going to say totally useless, but maybe I should just say--useless, in terms of making or helping this new teacher become a better teacher. They do have some value in them; they provide these new teachers some place to do and talk to other people who are also having problems, and that makes them feel a little better.

Now, what should be done here? What would you say? I think Dr. Scribner's recommendation, as far as I understand it, that there be teacher training centers in each district, each borough, is a rather good one, because I think here you could integrate the STINT Program--that is, the teacher trainer in the school--with the kinds of experiences that they should be receiving in schools of education in these graduate programs, and also the union workshop. And, you see, you would have a training center where people could go which is close to the schools and the problems, not as isolated from the problems as the colleges and the universities are, and also close to the community and the observation of the local parents.

One of the problems with the university at the moment is that it's inaccessable for power groups in terms of influence. As I mentioned before, NCATE, which accredits institutions--most of you don't know about it, but yet this is the tune written by NCATE--determines the dance that the schools of education do in terms of the courses they offer. But if you localize the experience, I think it's an advantage in itself.

Now, let me conclude by saying my comments aren't all that dramatic. I think teacher education is, for most people, a rather boring, uninteresting sort of topic, and I think this partly explains why it's so neglected by everybody. It's a scandal. It's a downright scandal, and very few people are really giving much thought to it, I can assure you.

And let me tell you about this program. This program is not perfect. I have the proposal here for it. But when I submitted the proposal to the State Department of Education, someone called me up and said, "We're really going to support this proposal. We're going to tell you that"--and, as a matter of fact, about six other groups are interested in supporting it--"simply because it's just a little bit different from everything else that we receive regarding reforming teacher education."

And he said that most people, when they talk about reforming education, talk about the philosophical course here, taking the traditional philosophy of educational course and calling it the philosophy of urban education and using the same old professor, who probably hasn't been in school since his 14-year-old child was up in Darien, when he went to visit his elementary school teacher. That's the last time he has been in school. And this is the way it goes.

Now, do you have any questions?
THE CHAIRMAN: Mr. Tractenberg.
MR. TRACTENBERG: Just two questions, Dr. Shields.
First, does the selection process, as it now exists in the New York City school system, play any kind of meaningful role with respect to those that come out of the traditional background that you described and those deficiencies that you feel exist?

Other witnesses have suggested that the screening process to determine minimum competency, was necessary, in large part, because one could not place much faith on 12 education credits, or even a degree in education from a teacher training institution, and that therefore a written examination was the appropriate answer.

DR. SHIELDS: Wasn't or was inappropriate?
MR. TRACTENBERG: Was an appropriate answer.
DR. SHIELDS: They felt it was an appropriate answer?
MR. TRACTENBERG: They felt it was appropriate, yes.
DR. SHIELDS: Yes, because my feeling is exactly the reverse. I feel that a written examination should be one rather small part of the screening process.

Now, I thought what you were going to say is that there should be some way in the screening process where the school district requires that you demonstrate your ability to teach. You don't demonstrate your ability to teach by taking a written examination, do you?

Now, let me give you an example. If you were to go to Darien, let's say, or perhaps Scarsdale, or Evanston, maybe, and apply for a teaching job, the principal would interview you and chat with you and talk to you about your interests and where your head's at, and then he might do one of two things. He might take you around the school and introduce you to the other teachers; you would have lunch with the other teachers. He would then ask either if you could teach for 3 days in the school, or if a member of his staff could go to your school and observe you teach. Now, this kind of provision in the screening process is the first step towards testing whether or not a person can teach, really, watching how they interact with the students and how they feel about children.

You know, many teachers hate children. If there ever has been an exercise, in the history of mankind, in casual sadism, it has been what I observed practically every time that I walked into a school in the New York City school system. All right.

So, to go back, I am not all that big on written examinations. College professors don't take written examinations. No one tests them on their knowledge of nuclear physics.

Now, the question I thought you were beginning to ask was, do I think that if the school system changed its screening process, the way in which it screens teachers, the schools of education would change. And the answer to that is yes.

If New York City says they want you to have a course in lifesaving, or they want you to have a course in human relations--which is what they did say--then the schools of education introduce a course in human relations, because they want their graduates to be able to get jobs. So, you see, the school system does influence what schools of education do, at least in terms of courses offered.

Now, also, so does the state. You see the state following the lead of NCATE in certifying people; it has approached certification through parcels of courses. You know, you need three credits in Social Foundations of Education, three credits in Psychology of Education, three credits in Audio-visual aids. So, people have approached the training of teachers this way.

Now, I have been working a bit with the state and NCATE in trying to develop a program for testing competency of teachers. So what the state is now moving towards is saying, "Look, we want to stop thinking about courses; we want you to start thinking about how what you do changes this person."

No school of education, when they give a certificate, really goes too deeply into determining whether or not a person can teach, right? And certainly the screening process doesn't.

MR. TRACTENBERG: If I understand you correctly, you would agree that a degree from most teacher training institutions --at least from the traditional program--is not sufficient basis for school districts to rely on?

DR. SHIELDS: Definitely.

MR. TRACTENBERG: But, further, that the present screening process doesn't really add very much to the body of information?

DR. SHIELDS: Definitely. Absolutely.

MR. TRACTENBERG: The only other question I have is how you think the selection process, as it currently exists in New York City would affect people who come out of programs like yours.

Would it pose formidable obstacles because they don't have the traditional course work?

DR. SHIELDS: Well, there are two levels to consider. One, certainly for state certification, there is absolutely no problem. What most people don't realize, as I mentioned, is that the Department of Education on the state level has become very liberal about certification of teachers. So, if I present to the state this program, or a similar program and say, "This is the program we think is best for teachers," they will say, "Well, all right. It's quite acceptable, in lieu of the other traditional experience."

Now, on the local level, our teachers have a problem in passing some of the written tests.

MR. TRACTENBERG: I am told, for example, that the function of the written test--certainly the National Teacher Exam and, I gather--

DR. SHIELDS: Right.

MR. TRACTENBERG: --the Board of Examiners says--is not predictability in the classroom, to any extent--

DR. SHIELDS: Exactly.

MR. TRACTENBERG: --but rather to test past knowledge--

DR. SHIELDS: Exactly.

MR. TRACTENBERG: --which you learned in college.

DR. SHIELDS: Exactly.

MR. TRACTENBERG: And I would presume if you learned something different than the test constructor thinks you ought to have learned, that you may have some difficulty?

Is that a fair statement?

DR. SHIELDS: Exactly, exactly. There is not only that, but it's the ideological and philosophical mood that you can develop. You know, the traditional program is taught by traditional people for the traditional system. And if you are being interviewed, as most of our people know, for a job--and in our program you get very much committed to the community and helping the people in the local community, visiting parents, finding out what parents are really interested in--and you go for your interview for an elementary school license and you meet with the people there, they may say, "What do you think is the most important thing you can do as a teacher?"

And if you say, "Go out in the community and get a sense of the community and perhaps organize the community, to make the school better," well, you would not be hired.

As a matter of fact, interestingly enough, in our program this year I am having the worst--I'm involved in the second year of this program--problem imaginable, getting our young teachers, most of whom are Black and Puerto Rican, by the way, to go out in the community. Interestingly enough, even these Blacks and Puerto Ricans have gotten far, because they are the ones who have been most socialized into the very New York, middle-class, bureaucratic civil servant mentality.

They say, "No, no. We want to stay in the classroom and help our six children."

And they say, "No, you can't go in those houses."

And I say, "Why can't you go in those houses?"

Well, they say, "The principal of this school says, 'It's dangerous,' and the assistant principal says, 'Teachers don't do that sort of thing. It interferes with their teaching. Just stay in the school and tutor these kids.'"

So, there is the traditional program. Traditionality builds a tremendous mentality which is resistant to dramatic change.

And our program is not only different structurally, it's different ideologically and philosophically. So, this could be a hindrance to our people. Certainly the knowledge aspects could be a hindrance.

I don't really give a damn who Horace Mann is, or John Dewey is. Democracy isn't being able to recite the Constitution or the Declaration of Independence, or knowing who Abraham Lincoln is, or that he freed the slaves. Democracy is having the mentality and the attitudes of George Washington--if he was that democratic--and Abraham Lincoln. That is what we are interested in. As a matter of fact, it's a big defense mechanism, to spend all your time digging around in all these names and dates. I think Napoleon said, "History is a pack of lies told on the dead."

Anyway, the knowledge and the attitude aspect would be hindrances, I think, to the traditional programs. It's a problem. Reform is not as simple as it appears on the surface.

A concluding comment. As a political scientist, I am always interested in raising the question: If you really believe in reform, who can you depend upon to be with you when you are bringing about change?

I think normally people figure out what direction the winds are blowing and then lead the people in that direction. It's like the story from the French Revolution when one of the leaders was asked, "Which way are you leading the revolution?" He opened the window, and he saw the people going that way. He said, "I'm leading them that way."

But if you happen to be moving in a direction in which I hope the findings of this Commission will suggest to educators that they move, a very important question is: Who will you rely upon to bring about the changes necessary? Will it be the college liberals, university liberals, professional liberal types, or will it be the parents of the community?

A perplexing problem for me at the moment is that I find local community people in terms of educational reform--and this is very important--to be most resistant to the kinds of reforms I think about. I see it with my students in this program--85 or so per cent of whom are Black or Puerto Rican, 50% of whom didn't qualify for City College, under the traditional means.

In terms of selection, we decided that anybody who applied would be accepted. It just so happened that 100 people applied. We didn't ask whether they had a 70 average, or any of that sort of thing because, when you look at the program, you look at them and you see they have the right attitudes. But we do find that students from poor backgrounds, with parents from disadvantaged areas, who seem to be cooperative with the reform movement, most of them are those people who have been socialized most adequately out of that population to the traditional, middle-class civil servant mentality.

And so I am not terribly optimistic about the possibilities of bringing about significant reform. But I do think what you are doing is excellent, and it's encouraging to know that somebody, some place, on the city-wide level is talking about teacher education.

In that sense it's a revolution, at least in terms of the kinds of revolutions we have.

MR. TRACTENBERG: Thank you.
THE CHAIRMAN: Any questions?
COMMR. GLOVER: No questions.

THE CHAIRMAN: Thank you very much.

I now call upon Dr. Doxie A. Wilkerson who is Chairman of the Department of Curriculum and Information, Ferkauf Graduate School of Humanities and Social Sciences, Yeshiva University.

DR. WILKERSON: Perhaps I can best save time in this hearing by reading a document I prepared rather than speak extemporaneously and risk getting away from the subject.

I approach the issues before this panel as a professional educator whose main area of interest is the preparation of professional personnel for service in inner-city schools. Experiences in this work, including extensive contacts with the schools of New York City, afford some basis for at least tentative suggestions for improving the selection and promotion of educational personnel.

Let it be noted at the outset that the science of education has not yet developed to the point that firm conclusions from systematic research are available as guides for the selection of educational personnel; hundreds of empirical studies in this field are largely inconclusive. We simply do not know, for sure, what qualities and behavior patterns will lead predictably to effective performance in teaching and supervisory positions. Recommendations in this regard are based largely upon theoretical considerations and more or less informal observations, plus some evidence from systematic research. This is said not to disparage such recommendations, which are important and all we have, but to indicate that we are dealing in probabilities and not certainties.

With this disclaimer of absolute truth, permit me to outline several judgments and proposals that emerge from my experience.

I. The Problem

1. The mounting evidence that our public schools are largely dysfunctional for inner-city youngsters suggests that there is, indeed, a problem of professional personnel, in preparation or selection or utilization or all of these. The relevant systems currently operative are not producing the desired outcomes in the educational development of children.

2. Further evidence of a problem is seen in the disproportionately small numbers of minority group professionals entering the system, especially on the supervisory level. This certainly poses an important civil rights question; and, given the political climate of our city, it probably has important implications for the effectiveness of supervisory personnel in some neighborhoods. It may also have relevance, as is often asserted, to the effectiveness of classroom teaching; but evidence to support a generalization to this effect is lacking in my experience.

3. The current selection process for principals seemingly aggravates both aspects of the problem.

a. There appears to be no evidence to validate current selection procedures, which, in addition to examination of formal credentials, include an extensive paper-and-pencil test, a supervisory conference, and an interview; and the performance of a large proportion of supervisory officials selected by this procedure suggests that it is largely irrelevant. Such procedures may be reasonably effective in identifying applicants at the two extremes of the ability scale, but they are quite inadequate to differentiate among the great bulk of examinees who tend to cluster around the "passing" score.

b. The fact that two principals are included on each of the three-man interview panels used in the selection of principals affords unwarranted leeway for the operation of more or less consistent bias. Such panels could function--and many probably do--to approve applicants who would make "good members of the club," and to exclude others on non-professional grounds.

c. Whatever deficiencies there are in the selection of principals probably operate to the detriment of inner-city schools more than middle-class schools. Suggestive evidence in this regard is afforded by a study of Social Class and the Urban School, by Robert E. Herriott and Nancy St. John (Wiley, 1966). They found that the performance of the principal is far more closely related to that of his teachers in schools of low socioeconomic status than in schools of high socioeconomic status.

The importance of this relationship is emphasized by the crucial role of the principal in setting the "tone" of the school and the level of professional performance of the staff.

d. Current practices unduly restrict the pool of applicants available for appointment by community school boards, whose informal assessments of prospective leaders of schools in their neighborhoods are probably much more valid than those of the remote Board of Examiners.

4. Somewhat similar procedures currently used in the selection of classroom teachers--paper-and-pencil tests and interviews--are also lacking in demonstrated validity and open to the influence of systematic bias.

5. In the present state of knowledge in the profession, it is quite impossible to predict effective performance by principals or teachers on the basis of examinations conducted in an artificial situation over a period of one to three days, and only the most credulous could have confidence in such examinations as a basis for selecting professional personnel.

It is relevant in this regard to note that no large and successful corporation--IBM, Bell Telephone, et cetera--would consider for a moment the selection of middle-management personnel, even their educational directors, on the basis of an examination. Where competent leadership is imperative, as seems not to be so in our schools, demonstrably valid and reliable bases are used for the selection of personnel.

II. Suggested Approaches

1. Probably the only valid and reliable basis upon which school instructional and supervisory personnel can be selected is demonstrated performance on the job.

Suggestive of the irrelevance of some other conventional approaches is a comprehensive study by Neal Gross and Robert E. Herriott of "The Educational Leadership of Principals: Myths and Realities" (Harvard Graduate School of Education Association Bulletin, Vol. 10, No. 1, Spring, 1965). They found, among other things, that "executive professional leadership" by elementary school principals bears no positive relationship to type or length of previous teaching, previous administrative experience (e.g., as assistant principal), quantity of formal education, or sex. Age of appointment was found to be significant, the strongest leadership being demonstrated by principals appointed while they were no more than 40 years old, and the weakest by principals appointed at or beyond the age of 45. Especially notable among findings of the Neal-Herriott study are four personal characteristics that do have some value as predictors of executive professional leadership: high academic achievement in college, a high order of interpersonal skills, the motive of service, and willingness to commit off-duty time to the job. The first can be judged from academic records. None of the other three can be measured by an "examination"; performance on the job is the only valid and reliable basis for assessment.

2. Application of this "performance" criterion should begin with provisional certification of teachers and principals by the State Education Department on the basis of recommendations by colleges and universities with approved programs that include, as a minimum, carefully supervised internship experiences. Responsibility for evaluating such programs is that of the state.

Desirably, the accreditation of college and university programs for the preparation of educational personnel should be based also on additional performance criteria: the definition of specific competencies such programs seek to develop and evidence that they are, in fact, being developed. Happily, the State Education Department is moving rapidly toward the introduction of such criteria.

3. When a prospective teacher or principal receives provisional certification by the state, he should be eligible for appointment by local (i.e., district) school officials. There should be no intervention at this point by any central examining agency.

4. The provisionally certified teacher or principal's most important professional learnings will come during his early years on the job, and such preparation should be viewed as part of the selection process. Whatever special measures are required should be taken to assure that, from the outset, each such on-the-job trainee receives help and guidance from professionals who are competent to render such service.

This training function, carefully implemented, is of the utmost importance. It helps to protect the children and staff from the errors certain to be made by novice professionals, and it helps the school system to realize the developmental potential of such personnel.

5. The on-the-job performance of new teachers and principals should be evaluated formally each year, optimally by examiners from the staff of the school, the central Board of Education, and the community board of education. Those whose performance indicates clear inability to develop professional competence should be eliminated from the system, on the basis of such evaluation, at the end of the first, second, or third year. Those who demonstrate such ability should be awarded permanent certificates at the end of the third year.

Implicit in this suggestion, of course, is the necessity of developing--and validating on the basis of empirical evidence--an effective approach to on-the-job evaluation. This, in turn, requires clear definition of the competencies deemed essential for the different positions for which personnel is being selected and developed.

MR. TRACTENBERG: I have no questions.

COMMR. COLGATE: I have questions.

Dr. Wilkerson, you mentioned this performance criteria which led me to believe by your testimony, that as of right now there are no specific competencies which have been or can be measured in the teaching profession.

DR. WILKERSON: No.

COMMR. COLGATE: I am incorrect?

DR. WILKERSON: You are incorrect if you assume that is what I am saying. What I am saying is you cannot give me an examination on my competency in performance. You can observe my performance but to give me a pen and pencil test, then you have a most unreliable measure.

COMMR. COLGATE: How do I measure your performance by observing you?

DR. WILKERSON: I indicated in the testimony that systematic procedures for doing that should be worked out so there is some uniformity.

COMMR. COLGATE: Do they exist now?

DR. WILKERSON: They do not exist now. They exist in schools, in some institutions, but on a city-wide basis, or a statewide basis, no. The state is working on something of this sort because it is needed.

COMMR. COLGATE: In other words, you do not agree with Dr. Fischer who says that you need only go to the budding artist's studio and watch him in his work and then you can tell whether he or she is a good teacher. Is that so?

DR. WILKERSON: I am not quite sure that I know what you are saying.

COMMR. COLGATE: I am sorry, you were not here when Dr. Fischer made the analogy of a teacher being an artist.

DR. WILKERSON: A competent educator, a competent principal can observe the work of a teacher under him. He can observe his entire relations with his peers, his entire relations with pupils, the manner in which he organizes the learning experience, his reactions under stress. He can seek to judge whether he is accomplishing what he is supposed to accomplish and what are the objective results. These things can be observed because it is a process and it has nothing to do with a test, and to develop a system of such observation and judgment on the job is what I think would be infinitely more valuable and reliable than to rely on a test given in an empty room, given at 110 Livingston Street.

COMMR. COLGATE: Can you say that some sort of a prediction can be made as to that person's ability for the job of assistant principal or a principal?

DR. WILKERSON: I should think so. Note again my last

statement that I made because we are dealing with something that we do not have yet; we are proposing something. My last statement here was that there is the necessity of developing and validating on the basis of empirical evidence, which we do not have now, an effective approach to this on-the-job evaluation.

COMMR. COLGATE: Then, finally, it would appear that you would equate the ability to teach and the successful performance of that as either a prerequisite for, or as closely identified to becoming a principal or an administrator.

DR. WILKERSON: No, nothing that I said carries that implication.

COMMR. COLGATE: Thank you.

THE CHAIRMAN: Thank you very much. We are going to call a recess for as long as it takes the next witnesses to get here. We will schedule them this afternoon at 1:30. However, we hope that because of time problems some witnesses will be here in advance of that; they may be here earlier, at 1:15.

These proceedings are adjourned for the next half hour or 45 minutes.

(A recess was taken, and the hearing resumed at 1:30 p.m.)

THE CHAIRMAN: Mr. William Lynch, Jr., New Careers Laboratory, New York University.

MR. LYNCH: It is my belief, in appearing to testify before this Commission, that the criteria being used to consider the hiring practices of the Board of Education include at least two premises: (1) that there are too few good people in the school system; and (2) that the system does not educate children well, particularly Black and Puerto Rican children.

Trying, then, to respond to the Commission's request in a constructive context, I can only suggest an avenue which, to date, has been ignored and abused by the Board of Education, and which I feel is of immense value to the children who are supposed to be learning when they go to school every day.

There exists, within the Board of Education structure and on the Board of Education's payroll, a body of some 50,000 to 60,000 persons, 85% of whom are Black and Puerto Rican, who could be upgraded to be of assistance to children engaged in the business of learning. At least 15,000 of these persons are currently engaged in instruction-related activities as "paraprofessionals." These 15,000 persons, if the Board of Education were serious at all, could be given education through released time, and in-service training to enable them to be teachers, "minority teachers," in three to four years.

I must say in all sincerity that this simply won't happen, certainly not on the scale that I just mentioned, and probably not on any scale at all. I say this because the very feeble and faltering attempts the Board of Education has made in the direction of career development activities have been reluctant, at best. No released time was given to any paraprofessional employees until forced by contract negotiations last summer, and the time granted was a minimum. No career advancement was even attempted by the New York City Board of Education until it received special funds for this purpose, and then the implementation left a lot to be desired. No decent salaries were ever offered until forced by the unions--who represent only a small portion of the total number of nonprofessional and paraprofessional workers--and the Board threatened to fire half the workers so that they would have money to pay the remaining half. Who are we kidding when we offer constructive helpful suggestions to the Board of Education?

That paraprofessionals add to the learning of children in the classrooms is a fact. It is also a fact that with further training and education this body of workers can be a strong cadre of skilled and competent teachers. I shouldn't have to be the one to "reveal" this to the Board of Education in a public hearing. They must be aware of this.

If the Board was serious about improving its minority hiring practices--if that body of people really believed that Black and Puerto Rican, Oriental, Chicano, and other minorities could staff their own schools and could better educate their own children--and if they are serious about wanting our kids to have an education, then they might internalize some of the findings of this Commission.

If they are interested in some of the ideas I have merely alluded to, then:

(1) they might increase the amount of released time given to paraprofessionals to attend college--investing a major portion of time, money, and effort to reap better teachers and an improved system in the end;

(2) they might increase the number of workers who are included in the career development system;

(3) they might exert their strong influence on the New York college and university system so that persons who attempt to gain a degree on their own time while holding a full-time job might not find themselves in the midst of a maze with credits nobody will accept, and courses that are not transferrable to any senior college;

(4) they will abolish an examination for these persons, since they will have proven themselves twice over by their competence in the classroom.

I would like to believe that this might be implemented, but I am afraid that I cannot.

MR. TRACTENBERG: In your judgment is there anything the colleges and universities in this area could do to improve their own programs? Is it unlikely they will do this unless the Board of Education takes the lead?

MR. LYNCH: I think that colleges and universities all over the country are in a state of transition. I think one of the things they are faced with--if we are talking about paraprofessionals--are people who have been out of school and have had no education of any type for quite a number of years and do not have some of the things that the students have who leave high schools to go right into college. And I think a lot of their curriculum and other things could be modified and, if the Board of Education in the City of New York would take some kind of lead in this area, I think the

New York City universities and colleges would also be involved in making some kind of change and transition in this area.

MR. TRACTENBERG: You mentioned that there was only recently a released time provision and it was a modest one. How many hours of released time does a paraprofessional get?

MR. LYNCH: I think one hour for every eight hours of work; if they work 30 hours they get 3 hours of released time. I would like to say that the Harlem Rehab gives a paraprofessional at least 60% released time; and if you did studies of private industries, when they give released time to go to advance skills, they give much, much more time. And I think it would behoove the Board of Education to give at least 25% released time so that a person could at least take enough hours to be able to obtain a degree in five years. Right now, with three hours of released time, a person would take 10 or 12 years to get a B.A. degree.

MR. TRACTENBERG: Has the Board of Education program actually moved paraprofessionals into teaching jobs?

MR. LYNCH: Not to my knowledge and, if so, very few.

MR. TRACTENBERG: What kind of financial arrangements are there? I assume that a paraprofessional has further costs than tuition. Does the Board of Education provide those expenses?

MR. LYNCH: Only through special programs. I do not believe the city itself provides any funds. But if they really went about getting into the City University with the open enrollment, that would be a perfect opportunity to funnel people there.

MR. TRACTENBERG: At the moment, no Board of Education funds are being used?

MR. LYNCH: No.

MR. TRACTENBERG: You mentioned in your remarks that you thought the licensing examination was not necessary or appropriate for paraprofessionals who have been in the system for a while. Does that suggest the kind of experience that they could get in the classroom as paraprofessionals would qualify them to be teachers after a few years, in your judgment?

MR. LYNCH: The paraprofessionals, most of them, have instructional duties and they have proven themselves in two or three years, and a paraprofessional can do certain kinds of duties. Therefore, for them to go the whole college route and then take an examination is like putting the cart before the horse to prove themselves through an examination.

MR. TRACTENBERG: It is your belief then that paraprofessionals should be judged principally on a more extensive on-the-job evaluation?

MR. LYNCH: I hope so. I hope they do an on-the-job evaluation and that they get credit for on-the-job experience. If a teacher is working in the classroom and has acquired a lot of skills by picking them up, by being in in-service training or working with another teacher, that person should get college credit or certification from the City of New York for the kind of work they are now presently doing in the classroom.

MR. TRACTENBERG: As a paraprofessional acquires experience and also college credits, is there any formula that the

Board of Education has for advancing the paraprofessional's responsibilities in the classroom?

MR. LYNCH: There is a formula on paper now, but I think it is a very haphazard formula. It is based on the number of credits a person receives, which determines the kind of advancement in salary given. It is based mostly on salary and not on responsibilities in the classroom.

MR. TRACTENBERG: Finally, you suggested some measures that would improve the current formula for paraprofessional training and career advancement. Have you ever considered any entirely different procedures that might be even more expeditious in moving a paraprofessional up? Is there any thought being given to a totally different career ladder?

MR. LYNCH: I think there are many kinds of plans. I do not know any offhand. There are numerous kinds of plans around the country to make better use of paraprofessionals in the classroom. One of the concepts is of a team where there would be a master teacher and a green teacher to supervise a number of classes and the classes themselves could be controlled by a paraprofessional who had "X" amount of hours of training or credit.

MR. TRACTENBERG: I think one of the earlier speakers suggested that there was no particular magic to a college degree. Has any thought been given to permitting paraprofessionals to later become teachers through experience and on-the-job training even if they do not have a degree?

MR. LYNCH: I have no knowledge of what happens in public schools. I know that in federal programs, such as Head Start, when people have experience, they promote them to teachers, and the degree is waived for on-the-job experience. But, to my knowledge, I do not know where that is happening in a public school system.

MR. TRACTENBERG: Do you think this is something worth pursuing?

MR. LYNCH: Yes, I think definitely it is a proven fact that paraprofessionals can perform in the classroom and that they do teach the children. And one of these things that I feel, personally, is that most of the paraprofessionals that work in the New York City school system come from the community of that particular school in which they work and they have a kind of investment in it. If it is not their own children, it is the children of their friends, and they want to teach these children, and they are concerned about teaching the children.

I think that such a statement was made by someone who is not in the field of education. Dr. Horton, the former Assistant Deputy of Health Administrative Services, said that 90% of those students who attend college drop out after three years, but of those who come up the career ladder, only 10% drop out; and that they have a real commitment, let us say, to the nursing profession, for example.

We feel the same thing about paraprofessionals. For anybody to work for below poverty wages in the school system and come in every day, they have to have some kind of commitment to something. And I feel it is a commitment to teaching children.

THE CHAIRMAN: Thank you, Mr. Lynch. Thank you very much. We will now have a short recess.

(A short recess was taken and the hearing resumed.)

THE CHAIRMAN: I wish to reconvene the hearing, and I call upon Professor Michael Usdan, Head Designate, Instructional Programs in Educational Administration, CUNY; Coordinator, New York Component, National Program for Educational Leadership.

PROFESSOR USDAN: I thought that my remarks to the Commission might focus upon a brief description of a very atraditional and experimental national program to recruit and place educational leaders. This innovative effort is called A National Program for Educational Leadership (NPEL).

NPEL represents a systematic effort to provide a new cadre of leaders for American schools. The immediate goal is to recruit and train one hundred men and women during the next five years who will assume responsible positions in education, particularly urban school systems. They will be talented people, deeply committed to education, prepared in unconventional ways to meet unconventional as well as conventional needs.

The program should also have importance beyond these one hundred people and the positions they will assume, for another goal is to test alternative approaches to the selection, training, and placement of educational leaders. Knowledge produced by this experience will be shared and may have implications for many other individuals and institutions. The program is at once an effort to deal with the pressing leadership problems in public education and an experiment in higher education.

The NPEL began in 1970 at Ohio State University under the leadership of Luvern L. Cunningham, Dean of the College of Education; Richard C. Snyder, Director of the Mershon Center; and Raphael O. Nystrand, Associate Professor of Education. Supported by a grant from the U.S. Office of Education, the program was structured to include centers at The City University of New York, Claremont Graduate School, Northwestern University, and The University of Texas at Austin as well as Ohio State during its first year. I am the coordinator of the CUNY component where the first enrollees will start on February 1st.

Four assumptions undergird the NPEL. The most critical of these is that need exists for new leadership and corresponding support systems in public education. The problems in this domain are myriad and well known but often beyond our present capacity to resolve them. Some contemporary officials cope with them more effectively than others, and we must continue to rely upon them in the future. At the same time, there is need for new leaders who bring fresh approaches. The NPEL will be one source of such leaders.

A second assumption is that there exist very capable individuals who have made important contributions to fields other than education and whose present interests and talents mark them as potential leaders in education. Almost without exception, leaders in public education have begun their careers as teachers and progressed through the ranks. Persons lacking such background generally have not been considered for key administrative posts. This situation contrasts with other fields such as government service, business, and community development where top personnel are often recruited from diverse backgrounds. The qualities required for success in school leadership appear not to differ sharply from those possessed by outstanding persons in other fields. For such persons who seek new challenges and opportunities to contribute to society, education is an attractive field.

The third assumption is that persons who enter the NPEL will require program experiences which differ from those traditionally offered in administrative preparation programs. Candidates will have much less formal training and experience in education than most prospective school administrators. At the same time, many will be advanced in their general knowledge of administration. Some will have considerable experience in related areas such as business administration, law, or accounting. Thus, programs will build upon and supplement individual strengths while familiarizing candidates with the context and processes of schooling.

The fourth assumption is that some communities and professional associations of educators are now prepared to look to non-traditional sources of leadership talent. The severity of contemporary problems directs that we search for assistance wherever it might be found. A few cities have already indicated willingness to consider persons without formal experience in professional education as candidates for school superintendencies. The State of California revised its certification requirements in 1970 to allow non-educators to hold school administrative positions. It is likely that other states will follow suit.

The primary purpose of this special, national program is to identify, recruit, and train individuals who have not had work experience in school systems (the traditional recruitment source) as school administrators. Many of these persons will be members of minority groups.

The principal objective is to provide new leadership talent, prepared in unconventional ways, for educational leadership positions most of which will be in large city school systems. More specifically, it is expected that one hundred new administrators will be prepared over the next five years, 1970-75. The maximum period of preparatory work for one individual will be two years. The first NPEL Fellows will be available for placement in 1972. Such persons hopefully will be able to redirect institutions and communities and achieve improved levels of institutional performance.

A secondary purpose is to focus critical attention on the national educational leadership problem and to achieve a critical mass of thinking, resources, and commitment to leadership development in education.

Students were recruited in 1970-71 by seeking nominations

from a wide range of persons and institutional representatives. Publicity given to the program also generated many self-nominations. Brochures were printed and distributed to the following organizations and groups in the United States: 61 Community Action Program agencies; 500 of the largest corporations in the nation; 38 Urban Coalition centers; 150 Model Cities agencies; 93 Urban League headquarters; 11 regional chapters of the National Association for the Advancement of Colored People; 62 members of the University Council for Educational Administration; 100 predominantly black colleges; 50 state departments of education and superintendents of schools in cities of over 300,000 population. In addition to this mailing, brochures were distributed on a regional basis by each cooperating institution.

Besides the brochure, newspaper articles and editorials have stimulated much interest in the program. For example, on the day that a New York Times article about the program appeared, the City University of New York received more than one hundred telephone inquiries soliciting more information and/or application forms and materials. Moreover, national publications, such as Education U.S.A., the AASA Newsletter, and the National Committee for the Support of Public Schools Newsletter have published articles about the NPEL. A press release describing the NPEL was prepared and released for both local and national consumption.

Similar steps will be taken in 1971-72. In addition, efforts will be made to include articles in major new magazines and periodicals, especially those with wide circulation among minority groups.

An application and screening procedure was developed which calls for applicants to provide information about their background and to discuss their views about leadership and urban education. Further information about the leadership behavior and interests of applicants is obtained from personal references and through interviews with top-rated candidates.

The NPEL will award no degrees and the program will not result in formal certification in the traditional sense. Credentialing is not expected to be a barrier for persons who complete the program. This is partly because credentialing systems are changing and partly because it is hoped that persons who complete the program will be of such quality that school systems and other bodies will welcome them.

It is in this context that the program does not offer a degree. Student experiences will differ markedly from those typical of degree programs. The program inhibitions which degree requirements impose will be avoided.

The placement of NPEL Fellows in responsible positions is a continuing concern of the program and work has begun on identifying placement opportunities. The staff of the NPEL is working with professional organizations and state departments to insure acceptance of the Fellows. Discussions with some state department officials led the planners to believe some obstacles have been overcome and that progress will continue.

Although NPEL unfortunately can accept initially only a

handful of those who have applied, we have begun to assemble an impressive list of talented and diverse people who have manifested a strong interest in entering education. The Commission might be interested in a sorting out of the types and/or prototypes of people who have inquired about NPEL. The following rough classifications appear to surface:

(1) a number of business and professional types who through school board service or other community activities are attracted to public service;

(2) a good number of Blacks who have worked on the fringes of the educational establishment in OEO, Urban Coalitions, or Model Cities types of activities, who are unwilling to proceed up the traditional career ladders in urban school systems and want programs that will provide them maximum and rapid mobility into policy positions;

(3) retired or soon-to-retire successful executives and professionals looking for a second career;

(4) a number of very able women who have come up the PTA-school board route, talented women with grown children who are anxious to build educational careers at high administrative levels;

(5) a good number of young lawyers with superb academic credentials who evidently are interested in pro bono publico activities;

(6) a substantial number of people who are out of jobs;

(7) young clergymen and social workers who see urban school administration as a potential channel for their public service proclivities;

(8) a group of able people in their late twenties or early thirties who are undecided as to whether to follow the traditional credential route or a program like NPEL; and

(9) a large number of people who are "turned off" by the shibboleths of higher education and want flexible, individualistic programs like NPEL.

Our challenge, as I see it, is to tap this reservoir of talent and to generate flexible mechanisms to channel such persons to education and other forms of public service.

MR. TRACTENBERG: Would you say that this program is a direct result or reflection of the inadequacy of supervisory skills in urban schools?

DR. USDAN: Partially. I think it is also a reflection of the social revolution that has occurred, that extends beyond the schools, and the inadequacies of most social, educational and public institutions to respond to the severity of current urban problems and, yes, I think it applies to school supervisors throughout the country.

I know that these hearings are focused on the problems of New York City. The problems of New York City are dramatized by their size and scope, but one sees the same problems in all the big cities of the United States and, indeed, even in the smaller cities.

There is basic dissatisfaction with the responsiveness of

educational institutions to the need for very, very rapid change. To me the society is changing much, much faster than the educational institutions have changed.

MR. TRACTENBERG: Have you discussed your program with the New York City Board of Education?

DR. USDAN: Yes, we have discussed it. Chancellor Scribner is actually a member of a panel and, hopefully, will advise us.

We certainly hope that as part of the experiences of our Fellows, as the programs commence, we will be able to give these people experience in the New York City schools at all levels ranging from very necessary classroom teaching experience to administrative experience at the building, district, and central office level.

So, as our program evolves, and it gets underway in February, we are at the very embryonic stage of development and we hope to plug it into the New York City system, obviously.

MR. TRACTENBERG: Do you anticipate that if current school system selection processes are continued there will be problems after your Fellows graduate from the program if, for example, one wants to become a principal of one of the high schools in New York City?

DR. USDAN: I am not naive enough to believe that there will not be problems in regard to people who come up by such an untraditional route, but I am confident that these people will have enough ability to surmount this lack of training.

MR. TRACTENBERG: Can you characterize what type of qualities and characteristics you tend to look for in your Fellows?

DR. USDAN: Probably the most important criterion has been some kind of manifestation through their careers of social commitment. Particularly with the economic situation being what it is at this time and the fact that our stipend has been quite generous, one of our difficulties has been in sorting out people who are just unemployed and who see this as a viable opportunity now. And one of the things we look at quite closely is the history of social commitment and the involvement that a person has in the community, in the community action programs, and he must have been involved in general community activities of a historical nature. And we are convinced that we have found people of that type.

MR. TRACTENBERG: Did you use a written examination to identify these Fellows?

DR. USDAN: One of the difficulties is that in this section of the country, where you have such a population saturation, we were inundated with requests and inquiries for applications and what we decided to do was to establish a system whereby they would write out biographical essays and send it to our secretary in Columbus. We did have written materials submitted but it was not a form of examination.

MR. TRACTENBERG: I assume this was how you test social commitment which you said is really a prime personal characteristic.

DR. USDAN: Not only social commitment. Another prime

criterion for us was demonstrated by the success attained in whatever these people were doing. They are achievers and are people who are successful and continue to be successful in whatever they wanted to do to get involved in the educational field. And, number two, these are people that we felt would have the potential for rapid mobility in the educational field.

MR. TRACTENBERG: By and large, how was this test of success demonstrated? Can you tell this by references?

DR. USDAN: By references, these were people who held positions which reflected community involvement; and, in addition to our reactions to their papers, we had a kind of cross section of people interview these candidates rather extensively.

For example, we had the candidates react to case materials which were video taped and we tried to have a process where you assess a human being, which is an objective process to start with.

We used a number of techniques to broaden the amount of information we had on these people.

MR. TRACTENBERG: This might be an unfair question. I do not know how much you know about the current selection process in the New York City school system.

DR. USDAN: I know what I read.

MR. TRACTENBERG: Do you think the selection technique you have used might be equally applicable to the selection even of people already in the system, such as the selection of supervisory personnel?

DR. USDAN: I have more confidence in this process than I have in a written examination, if that is the answer to your question.

MR. TRACTENBERG: That is all.

THE CHAIRMAN: Thank you very much.

The next witness will be Gary Calnek, Central Coordinator, Public Service Careers Program, Manpower and Career Development Agency, Human Resources Administration.

MR. CALNEK: The Public Service Career Program is currently the largest paraprofessional training program in the country. We have been in existence since August 1967 and have trained people in a variety of fields, in health, education and in the welfare area, and we have been involved in both the public and private sectors.

In the spring of 1968 we became involved with the Board of Education in New York City and had a training program for 240 paraprofessionals. I offer this experience that we derived from the spring of 1968 through the present, and it is on that that I will be making comments today.

It is the intent of the program to improve the quality of services provided by relieving professionals of non-professional duties and freeing them to function in the areas of their specialization.

In addition, we tried to create means of access to credentialing for them in both the public and private sectors and we find that job-related skills and training are a satisfactory substitute for some, if not all, educational requirements on a pro-rated basis.

We tried to provide employment opportunities for the untapped and untrained resources and tried to give opportunities to persons who are currently unemployed and are perhaps unemployable and to establish for them a career ladder and in this instance on the education career ladder, for example, from the position of an E.D. assistant trainee through a teacher's position.

The original ladder was from an E.D. assistant trainee to an E.D. education associate and ultimately to a teacher's position.

In our efforts to achieve these goals we have encountered several obstacles with the Board of Education. They are as follows:

(1) There has been an unwillingness on the part of the administrative staff of the Board of Education to accept skilled training as a substitute for educational requirements.

(2) They have refused to waive the high school diploma as an employment requirement for the E.D. assistant's position. The E.D. assistant went through a 10 month skills training program provided by the Board of Education and it was supplemented by 15 hours of classroom experience per week.

(3) In addition, the E.D. assistant trainees are those who are successful in acquiring their high school diploma and in subsequently being hired by the Board of Education, and they found themselves in a job situation which offered a lack of security.

(4) The salary lines are funded through federal and state monies which are subject to cuts so that the first paraprofessional hired can be the first one fired. Thus, even if a paraprofessional meets requirements, he has no job security.

(5) Those E.D. assistants work from September through June, which is the work cycle, and if they wanted to work for the summer they must reapply for the summer months, and in the following September they must apply again to work from that September through June. So, in short, they have accrued no tenure in the formal sense of the word.

(6) In addition, the lack of meaningful financial assistance to the head of the household, men and women with families to support, was another obstacle to pursuing a career with the types of educational requirements outlined in order to eventually achieve a teacher's position.

During training, the trainees earn $2 an hour for a 35 hour week. On the E.D. assistant career ladder the E.D. assistant, after acquiring a high school diploma, would earn $2.25 an hour for 30 hours a week and when that is computed it comes out to $2.50 below what we would pay them as a trainee without a high school diploma.

In addition, there has been a limitation on the number of hours the paraprofessionals were authorized to attend college. That is, after the acquisition of the high school diploma they can now move on to the Associate Arts career. The current system allows for ten hours of released time per week and five of the ten hours are donated by the individual paraprofessional. The other five hours are jointly financed by the Board of Education which pays $2.25 an hour and an amount which pays the additional two and three quarters hours. Under this system there is approximately, taking a person who took those ten hours of released time, seven credits per semester for a period of about five years, if they had the tenacity to persevere under those conditions.

The released time provided by other agencies has been more extensive and has speeded the process.

The above requirements, from our experience, have not provided any particular opportunity for minority group persons to mature into teaching positions.

I would like to compare some of our experiences in other agencies to indicate how other public and private institutions have attempted, through their working force, to achieve more meaningful goals as I outlined in the beginning of my statement.

In the Department of Social Services, the administrative staff, with the Civil Service Commission, completely waived the high school diploma as a requirement. The employment requirement is six months of skills training provided by the Department of Social Services, which ends up in an entire salary of $5200 per year. Similar arrangements exist with the Housing Development Administration training people in hospitals, such as St. Vincent's Hospital, Columbia Dental Auxiliary Union, and Brookdale Hospital.

In addition, paraprofessionals in those other career programs receive $17\frac{1}{2}$ hours of released time as opposed to ten hours in the Board of Education. A person in most of the aforementioned agencies can maturate to the career ladder positions exclusively on experience. However, it obviously takes a long time since that experience is pro-rated. But this alternative is non-existent in the school system for a paraprofessional or in the paraprofessional program as it is constituted.

In addition, in the other agencies--those which are municipal agencies--the paraprofessional upon completion of his skills training and upon taking, quite often, an oral examination as opposed to a written examination is awarded probationary Civil Service status. This is uniform with other agencies. After completion of the six months probationary period there is accrued tenure and all of the compensatory benefits.

The most immediate reasons that I could provide as to the difference in the paraprofessional program which exists in the Board of Education and those which exist in other agencies are related to the administrative support, meaningful support. You can give lip service to something, or you can take the necessary administrative steps to accomplish it. There has always been significant union involvement and union support, and there is also the support of middle-management; but it is one thing to actively make a decision and it is another thing to have the decision implemented.

If middle management is not a part of the minority then they have no commitment to the program or to its goals. So therefore, somebody else has to guide it.

MR. TRACTENBERG: You have indicated that your agency has been in existence since 1967 or 1968?

MR. CALNEK: Spring of 1968.

MR. TRACTENBERG: Is your agency continuing to fund or otherwise support the Board of Education's career development program?

MR. CALNEK: Originally, we had our first contract for 240 persons as paraprofessionals. We were scheduled to have a second group of paraprofessionals beginning June 1969. But as a result of the experiences which I indicated that we had the Manpower Career Development Agency--even though we had funds allocated for that purpose--decided that it was not a meaningful use of the training funds and, therefore, they were rechanneled. Those funds were rechanneled into other program areas, such as health and welfare.

MR. TRACTENBERG: You actually experienced difficulty in implementing the objectives, and you ceased funding the programs after a year or a year and a half?

MR. CALNEK: We continued our commitment to those persons we originally recruited through the career ladder process. However, we did not bring additional persons into the system since we thought the system was inflexible and not responsive.

MR. TRACTENBERG: Was there any explanation for this by the Board of Education officials as to why they could not respond to what you thought were the reasonable needs of the program?

MR. CALNEK: There were several explanations. One was that the educational requirement was a necessity because the paraprofessional was having contact with the student educationally and could not function meaningfully without that training. It is significant to note that the paraprofessionals whom we have been involved with had functioned in grades, for the most part, one through three or kindergarten through grade three, and that amount of academic training and the abilities they applied had more than qualified them to look further. I feel, therefore, that those explanations had no relevance. They also indicated that the number of paraprofessionals was so large that it would be prohibitive to offer a meaningful training course through performance, and that gave concern to us regarding the sincerity of their intent to meaningfully integrate paraprofessionals into the staff apparatus.

MR. TRACTENBERG: So far as you know have any paraprofessionals made it up the Board of Education career ladder to become teachers?

MR. CALNEK: None of the paraprofessionals brought into our program.

There has been a significant pattern that developed in some instances. Some persons who persevered and acquired their high school diploma went into a variety of other fields because they initially entered our program with the intent of becoming teachers, but because of the lack of incentive and the lack of working wage, they were forced to pursue other careers.

MR. TRACTENBERG: We heard testimony from Mrs. Burton who has been a paraprofessional and indicated that she was dropping out of the program because she felt it was impossible for her to become a teacher if she continued in the program. I gather that is the experience your paraprofessionals encountered in the programs?

MR. CALNEK: Yes.

MR. TRACTENBERG: Do you think the union agreement in force now will subsequently change matters?

MR. CALNEK: The main impact is providing a higher living wage for the paraprofessionals. The union agreement does not at all deal with the entire area of tenure. The paraprofessional is theoretically vulnerable to not being rehired as he has not been in the past. The funds have come through the special federal and state programs as opposed to the regular educational expenditures.

MR. TRACTENBERG: And so far as the present procedure pertaining to this area applies, it would be necessary for a paraprofessional, even after six or eight years in these schools working with children in a class, who had obtained all the required academic credentials, to go through the regular Board of Examinations process?

MR. CALNEK: For what position?

MR. TRACTENBERG: In order to become a teacher.

MR. CALNEK: Yes, currently.

MR. TRACTENBERG: Have you ever had discussions with the Board of Ed. about the possibility of waiving those requirements?

MR. CALNEK: We have not pursued the waiving of the Board of Examiners since we were unsuccessful in waiving the high school diploma and the other things that were elementary, since we could not get E.D. assistant trainees into the E.D. positions. And if the E.D. trainees matured into that position and then left the entire career ladder process, we might end up without anyone who would attempt to apply for the teaching position. We are concentrating on focussing on this area which we felt was more important.

THE CHAIRMAN: Thank you, Mr. Calnek.

I would like to call Dr. Harold Haizlip, Headmaster, the New Lincoln School.

DR. HAIZLIP: Commissioner Norton, and members of the Commission, I feel somewhat like a fish out of water in addressing you in your hearing today because I come from a very small school of nearly 600 children, ages 3 through the 12th grade, here in Manhattan, where we think some very good things are going on. And, because of that, we have none of the trappings that are represented by the policies and procedures of the Board of Examiners.

I do not think that it is necessary for me to tell you how that system currently works but I would like to share with you some thoughts I have about the effects of the system on schools, on schooling or education, if you will, and most particularly on the children.

It seems to me that the structure of the Board of Examiners and the way it functions suggests a fundamental assumption with which we in private schools and many of us who consider ourselves enlightened disagree, and that is that the schools are for the adult rather than for the children. It seems as if we concentrate more on those factors which affect the security of the teachers rather than on their effectiveness in their jobs in teaching children.

The system as it functions now, I believe, fosters a lack of accountability on the part of the teaching staff to the administrators on the one hand, to parents on the other, and, if there is a third hand, most importantly to the student.

As you know, we have a way of saying, especially in our public schools, that students who fail are responsible for their own failure. I and many others fundamentally reject that. I do not think that students are responsible for their failure at all.

Secondly, I think this has become rather clear and I can adduce examples of this. There is a self-selection, pre-selection from the population of would-be teachers. That is, teachers who have prepared themselves for this profession and who are interested in it decide whether or not they want to go through some of the ridiculous routines spoken of and the silly activities surrounding the requirement for certification and subsequent employment.

It seems to me that teachers and many people who would become teachers tend to avoid the jobs in public schools because they feel that the examination, in and of itself, in terms of its content, is idiotic in terms of its relevance to the functions and responsibilitie of teachers and that it is absolutely insignificant as a tool to assess the capabilities, the knowledge, the commitment, which are perhaps the three most important criteria to find in a teacher. I think that many teachers select themselves out of the system or reject it insofar as becoming a part of the system because they do not want to become a part of the machine which they regard in many ways as impersonal, as uncaring, and as irrelevant, if not harmful, to a majority of the children.

Most good teachers in my experience are committed. They are committed to teaching as a career; they are committed to children; they are committed to a way of life which begins with what they think they can offer. What they look for in a school from the outside is a similar kind of commitment, a similar kind of interest in children.

This is a primary focus, and the first concern is not necessarily concern for one's own welfare as an adult. In the latter there is an impersonality and there is the absence of a human dimension. But a teacher's struggle to go on to find better ways is well known among people who are in the teaching field. And there are people who feel that way, who feel that these are the important criteria and the concerns that are necessary in educating children, and who feel that they tend to avoid doing this in the public schools. They sense that the Board of Examiners has a kind of self-perpetuating system which rewards rather than discourages a lack of concern for children.

Others who are or will be teachers, in my opinion, are functionaries. Their concern seems to be primarily money, more money, more money. They seem to have a considerable interest in obtaining a job in which there is security. In this profession, as you know, short of some certain sexual deviations, it is virtually impossible to terminate a teacher on the grounds of incompetency. It is virtually impossible to prove incompetency according to the standards and procedures which we now set.

I believe there are people in the profession who are aware of that, who sense through some sixth kind of perception that, as the system now operates, there is no need to be competent, there is not a likelihood of one being assessed in terms of his performance and that one can become a teacher and be a good teacher come hell or high water, but having the label and being called by the professional name is really the only thing that is necessary. One goes to work, avoids some major crime, if you will, and has a job forever. There is hardly ever any requirement in terms of being advanced in the job or being promoted to other positions of responsibilities for which one has demonstrated competency, ability, and success.

I also think that people are attracted to the schools because they sense, beginning with the examiners, the procedures of the Board of Examiners, that there is a lack of accountability to students. When students fail, I repeat, we normally say it is their responsibility, never that of the teacher. And, there is only focus on one's welfare, on higher salaries, fewer students, more assistants, larger rooms, anything, God help us, but more children. We are most happy if we have the least trouble with students, as the system now stands.

There is, I think, an inherent irrationality in this. Admittedly, bad teachers, by virtue of damaging the lives of numerous children over several years, have had priority in being considered for appointments over and above potentially better teachers. And I consider the Board of Examiners the gateway into the system.

The system is, finally, self-perpetuating. I think there is, as the evidence suggests, subtle, vicious racism as a result. It is the only way in which I can explain the absence of Black and Puerto Rican professionals in key positions in schools where children of these races predominate. I know that is the case in other schools and other systems in other cities.

I am not a native New Yorker. I spent many years in Boston and I can say that I am sure it is no accident that more than 75% of the teachers in Boston are white Roman Catholics. It cannot be accidental. I am sure it is not because Blacks and Puerto Ricans do not apply. Somehow or other they do not get there.

The system prevents rewards based on merit and performance and it has another critical factor: it fosters old age at the top. It takes many, many years for a person who is young, who has demonstrated capability, drive, competency, enthusiasm, to succeed in getting into positions of responsibility. One must wait his turn, go through the list as the list turns, with time passing every day until through some stroke of luck, whatever it happens to be, he may be or may not be considered for a job.

I believe that schools must be free. We attempt to run our own school in that way. We look for teachers who obviously meet minimal requirements in terms of formal training and education. Beyond that I feel that it is up to the person responsible for running the school and to those he reports to in the community, the parents. It is up to that person to create the kind of personality of the school, the kind of tone in the school, the kind of special programs in the school which are in the best interests of the students.

I do not feel that one can find out from an examination which kind of people do or do not have the potential. I do not think you can find through a written examination the kind of chemistry, the kind of enthusiasm to find and explore other methods of educating children successfully, of helping teachers to explore themselves, to explore what they know, reject what is not working. There is no way of finding that out on an examination but I think it is possible through careful interviewing of people to evaluate the willingness and the knowledge beforehand, even though mistakes are possible. But on the other hand, they can be correct, because they are evaluations which are necessary. And on that basis we will find better ways of improving our children's lives.

These schools are for children. The teachers are for the children. It seems to me that we have to find some way of enabling us to get into the schools people who are not looking for retirement, safety, and security on a professional basis early in life, after three years or two years.

Complacency is unwarranted. We know too little about how to educate any child, Black or white, poor or rich, to be complacent about what is going on as to the organization of schools, the programs of the schools, the people in them, and the school itself as a concept. We have to find ways to experiment with new ways, and it seems to me as we will not be able to begin to do that unless we turn around and look and investigate where the people come from, how they are screened, and what kinds of criteria are used. And I think that the results will speak for themselves. They will tell us what we are faced with.

There are children in the schools who are daily, essentially, wasting a good part of their time. Not all, but many waste a good deal of their time, and I hope that the changes that may flow from your conclusions promise well for all of us in this field. It is long, long overdue, I think, and we would welcome any change of this kind over what we now have. Thank you.

THE CHAIRMAN: Thank you Dr. Haizlip.

Counsellor, do you have any questions?

MR. TRACTENBERG: Have you, yourself, had any personal experience with the Board of Examiners?

DR. HAIZLIP: Yes.

MR. TRACTENBERG: Is there anything you could tell us that might shed some light on this system?

DR. HAIZLIP: I hesitate only because I would not want to give you one example as a basis for anyone to generalize about the entire system. It may be applicable and it may state something about the system, but it is a very personal experience.

I, several years ago, had completed my work in school administration. When I received my doctorate degree from Harvard University, I found that Dr. Gross had a considerable interest in me and he wanted me to join his central staff, but it turned out that that was impossible because I had had no previous experience in New York City, no teaching experience, no administrative experience, and there was some question about my age. That was a few years ago; today I am 34. And it seemed as if these things made it impossible so that the job offered, which had to be committed in writing, had to be withdrawn. Dr. Gross found he had gone too far too fast without the consensus of the system.

MR. TRACTENBERG: That is an interesting juxtaposition, I may say, to the immediately prior testimony of Professor Usdan about the way to bring into the system people of different backgrounds who have skills. Actually, your background was not that different since it was a Ph.D. in School Administration.

DR. HAIZLIP: I could not hear his testimony so I am not able to comment.

THE CHAIRMAN: Dr. Haizlip's background, for the record, is most unusual in that this is a Black man whose educational background included Amherst and Harvard, who wished to serve the public schools of New York and now is Headmaster of a distinguished private school, who found he was unable to serve the schools of New York.

I note this for the record because there has been testimony here that lamented the small number of Black people who had even graduated from college, much less come with the extraordinary credentials of Dr. Haizlip. The Commission can only lament the fact that the system was not able to find a place for such a competent professional, and we can only congratulate the private school system of the city that found a place for him.

MR. TRACTENBERG: Dr. Haizlip, could you describe briefly the selection mechanism you use at New Lincoln School to recruit the faculty?

DR. HAIZLIP: Whenever we have positions available we always make that known to the professional community, to people in the neighborhood, to parents in the school, to professional recruitment selection agencies and recruitment agencies, and so on, and we specify what it is for, the kind of job at a specific grade level or a specific subject area, and any other considerations that we think of importance to us, for example, prior teaching experience, experience in the neighborhood, or working with children of a particular background, any special kind of training that we would like to see.

After that we normally receive a flood of applications, sometimes from teachers in the public schools and sometimes teachers in other schools, sometimes from people not yet teachers but interested in becoming so. We screen those according to our base line criteria as to former training, prior expertise, the hardware, if you will, then we get in touch with them and ask them to come in and talk with us. We briefly tell them about the particular job we are interested in filling and ask them about themselves and ask them to spend one or two days in the school and in some instances we ask them to teach lessons so we can see them on the job for maybe two days, one day, or perhaps for a week, so that my faculty and I and other members of the administrative staff get a view of their ability to relate to students in the subject matter, and so on.

Following that we ask students, especially on the high school level, to give their reaction to a particular professional being considered for the faculty, and I get together with them and talk about the various candidates that have gone through that procedure and then we make the decision.

MR. TRACTENBERG: That kind of a procedure is certainly possible in a small private school but do you think it is feasible for a large public school system, like the New York City system, to incorporate some or all of those elements into its selection process?

DR. HAIZLIP: I feel it is absolutely insane to rationalize a difficult process because it depends upon the needs of children. If there are five million children in the city, it seems to me that there is no way to find out about a teacher other than by his spending time with people who care and by their talking with and finding out about his or her values above and beyond his or her knowledge.

This process is not just for the comfort or the security of the teacher. It is being done for the operation of the school that exists for children. If it takes 24 hours a day of work then that is what it takes, and we cannot compromise on the values we provide for our children, in my opinion.

MR. TRACTENBERG: Thank you, Dr. Haizlip; that is all I have.

THE CHAIRMAN: Tomorrow is the last day of the five days we have spent here taking testimony on the hiring practices and promotional procedures in the public school system as it exists today. We will have a short session this afternoon which will end at 4 o'clock.

Now we will hear from Dr. Marilyn Gittell, Director, Institute for Community Studies, Queens College.

DR. GITTELL: I originally indicated that I would not have a statement but I do so I will read that into the record.

Attracting qualified, sensitive school personnel for New York City schools has long been a problem. Study after study, hearing after hearing, have strongly recommended that New York City dispense with the present examination system. The importance of changing the criteria for recruitment and selection of school personnel cannot be overrated. Every effort at school reform has hinged on the personnel issue. Perhaps that is why we have been so unsuccessful in achieving any change. On the other hand, we should recognize that the defense of the examination procedure is essential to those who would maintain the status quo.

The Civil Service system which is falsely labeled a "merit" system functions just as the patronage system it replaced did (maybe less effectively because it does not respond to community pressures). It preserves a favored group, and it is inbred. The Civil Service system has become more than the sum of its parts, developing a reward structure and procedures of its own divorced from effective delivery of service and the basic needs of its consumers. Merit in this case would more accurately be defined as acceptance of the standards and values of those in positions of authority.

There is no evidence whatsoever to show that the examination procedure effectively selects teachers or principals who will succeed. It cannot even be proven that those who pass perform better than those who do not. Indeed, the evidence is otherwise. In the Goldhammer study, it was discovered that school personnel trained in educational administration were less competent than those whose training was in other fields. Yet those trained in other fields are automatically eliminated as even potential candidates for examination in N.Y.C. (and would also be disqualified in a state examination). Professor Ivar Berg, in a more general study, concluded that the academic credentialing system militates to a great extent against occupational success, and that the best criterion is on-the-job performance. Merit, he says, is clearly more related to performance than any other criteria.

We found in our study of six large urban school districts that supervisory personnel who had not come up through the ranks were the most innovative. Examination credentialing systems discriminate against such "outsiders" as they are referred to. Outsiders usually means those who do not support the system as it is constituted. I know of no examination that qualifies those who seek to change the very system the examination is there to defend.

Shaping an open and qualified school staff lies not with a rigid examination procedure and uniformity of recruitment but with flexibility and diversity of selection from a broader field according to local needs.

The Institute for Community Studies three-year evaluation of the demonstration school districts--Ocean Hill-Brownsville, I S. 201, and Two Bridges--concludes that whatever educational success these districts had was due, in large measure, to the community school boards being able to by-pass Civil Service standards in selecting key personnel. It was not only that these districts chose the first Puerto-Rican and Chinese principals and the first Black district superintendent in the city that was important, but that they clearly sought out teachers and supervisory staff who strongly believed in the educability of their children and were oriented to changing the character of a failing education process in their districts. Those people who were recruited (many with advanced degrees and a broad range of experience outside New York City) were not acceptable to those at the Board of Education not only because they did not meet the examination credentialing requirements, but because they were a threat to accepted practice.

I cannot emphasize too much that the examination system is the means for protecting those who are already in and keeping out those' who threaten the institution. Professionals are no less interested in power than anyone else, the difference is that they may argue their defense in terms of their expertise and know that the public will be wary of challenging them on that score. That is why we hear so much about "merit" yet have never been provided with any proof that indeed any one of the 1500-odd licensing examinations really do pick the most "meritorious" people.

Some have suggested that the state now administer an examination. That prospect would be no real alternative. Adding a state examination in lieu of a city examination would still work against minorities and outside qualified personnel.

We can project that the success or failure of the 1969 Decentralization Law will be determined by whether local boards will have the discretion to choose from a larger pool of talent. If the examination procedure remains intact the local boards will be sufficiently constrained as to assure their ineffectiveness.

A few examples of how inflexible the hiring process is may suffice. Recently, a local school board sought and hired a Spanish-speaking principal. Unfortunately, the pickings were slim since he was the only Spanish-speaking candidate on the Civil Service list. More than 30 schools in New York City now have acting principals. In many cases these people have proven themselves in active performance; they are supported by the parents who see them in action daily. Yet they must now scurry for credentialing or be lost to the school. Those district boards who may contemplate personnel changes are soon faced with the reality of the examination lists which severely limit their choice.

An essential element in decentralization was to secure local personnel policy which would be responsive to local needs and interests. As long as the determination of eligible candidates for teaching and supervisory posts is narrowed by a central examination procedure, local boards will not be able to fulfill their responsibility.

A corollary factor is the issue of accountability. If we continue to determine qualification by examination prior to performance rather than by performance itself (needless to say, performance as judged by those closest to the scene), we will not achieve meaningful accountability.

What seems to me most important to stress is that what is past cannot be corrected, but the future under decentralization is clearly at stake. If we look for any change in the practices which have made the school system unworkable, personnel policy is a key consideration. Unless and until local boards can choose people more directly responsive to their needs and identify more imaginative school types than those capable of passing examinations, there is not much chance that they will be able to change educational policy in any appreciable way.

MR. TRACTENBERG: You mentioned a larger pool from which community boards should be able to draw teachers and supervisors. Do you have some recommendations on the kind of pool and the basis on which the pool might be constituted?

DR. GITTELL: A simple proposition would be by state accreditation, and then you would automatically enlarge the pool.

MR. TRACTENBERG: How do you respond to the arguments that state certification does not screen out incompetents and illiterates?

DR. GITTELL: I read the press yesterday and I am still confused about what an illiterate means by the definition of the Board of Examiners. If they saw my spelling I would be in the same category. I am not qualified to teach in the New York City school system because I have not passed that examination, but it seems that the rest of us, as well as all the communities outside of Buffalo and New York City have been functioning on that basis. I doubt that they are doing any worse than we are, and I would question if they are not doing better than we are.

As to the definition of good teaching and what makes for a good teacher, I think the examination tends to bind us into a definition of good teaching and good administration which I would not agree with at all.

MR. TRACTENBERG: Another argument we have heard rather frequently is that the elimination of the Board of Examiners would lead to patronage and a spoils system. Based upon your experience in the demonstration districts, particularly, do you feel that that is a rational argument?

DR. GITTELL: Well, I think it is an unbelievable argument, frankly, the notion that the examination system, as I indicated in my paper, is anything different from what the patronage system has been. And, in fact, I myself feel that the so-called patronage system, which involves the selection of people qualified for the job and who have a shared interest with the person who is selecting them, is a much more desirable system.

It does not seem to me that it is possible that people who are looking for teachers or principals, who are concerned with the education of their children, are going to hire non-qualified people. The demonstration districts indicated just the opposite. In the screening of teachers that went on in each of those districts, particularly in Ocean Hill-Brownsville and in 201, they were concerned with the teachers' attitudes towards children--whether their attitude was that these children were educable which was a key factor at that time, and they were also concerned with their attitude towards the community, which was important to the people of the community on those boards.

The personnel that they chose, as indicated by studies to be published shortly, for the key posts were probably superior to most personnel in the city system. A number of years ago I did a study of district superintendents and reviewed what they did with their time, their qualifications, their background, et cetera. I would say that a comparative study of personnel in demonstration districts indicates a broad range of interests, a great sensitivity and more of the kind of people that Dr. Goldhammer talked about in his studies. He labeled good principals as people who were interested in their communities, that was the main criterion.

The people that I saw in the demonstration districts who were picked by the local boards out of the Civil Service examination lists were much more sensitively concerned with the community and they were much more dedicated to educating the children in those districts.

MR. TRACTENBERG: How predominant was racism in these schools? Was each ethnic group picking teachers from that particular group?

DR. GITTELL: Those of us who have been in the school

structure the last five or seven years under the decentralization controversy were told by the union that the poor ghetto schools would get no teachers since they did not have a formula for guaranteeing that teachers would go into the ghetto. That was not a valid argument because they had more applications than they could deal with at a certain point. It is quite clear now that you have a generation of students coming out of college whose major interest is "commitment," who would be attracted to these kinds of districts, and who are dedicated to doing a certain type of job. I have confidence that a community board and the parents would select people most competent to educate their children and if they were not competent they would get rid of them.

MR. TRACTENBERG: From your observations can you tell us what kind of background any ethnic group looks for in the selection of principals?

DR. GITTELL: In the selection of principals, well, in Ocean Hill-Brownsville they had a great many Puerto Rican and Chinese children and there were more Black principals in 201 than in the other districts. That is partially due to the fact that there are many discriminatory practices in other districts, and this was dealt with in those two districts. I would not say that people were hired because they were Black because what happened was that the qualifications of various candidates were judged together with the community interests of the particular person, and his background was also part of what was evaluated.

There were certainly many white teachers in those districts and you could argue that there was not enough of a supply of Black teachers in those districts so they were forced to hire whites but the figure was something like 70% in Brownsville. 70% of the teachers were Black throughout the whole district. The office staff was a predominantly Black staff, but a highly qualified staff.

If they just adhered to our credentialing system, the up and down and through the college graduation system, such a system would prevent what you are now talking about. I do not see any reason for us to assume or for anyone to prove that people who are looking for good educators to do a good job that is not being done now are going to hire incompetent Blacks. One of the arguments that was raised early in the demonstration districts was that they would fall apart. They did not, they were not going to fall apart and, in fact, they continue to function very well even while they were trying to put new programs into effect.

We did a study of parental attitudes as to whether community control or decentralization results in a major emphasis on Black interests and we encompassed the question of personnel.

On the question we asked "Do you think more Black personnel should be hired?" It was the one question where parents actually wrote in, a number of them, "We don't care whether teachers are Black or white; we just want them to teach our children." And we had basically a negative response on that question.

We asked about Black studies. "Do you think there should be more Black studies" and more than half the parents answered that they felt there were sufficient Black studies at that point.

That was in Ocean Hill-Brownsville where they adopted a program.

We concluded from our study that there was no indication there was any more excessive emphasis on that in Ocean Hill-Brownsville after the crisis than there was anywhere else, and all the evidence pointed to a contrary point of view.

MR. TRACTENBERG: The record at this point might well reveal that there is a court decision by the Third Circuit Court of Appeals arising out of a revision of the selection process in Newark and we will have the Superintendent of the Newark schools here tomorrow to tell us about that. The Court of Appeals said that race could be one of a number of criteria to be used in selecting staff. That is of some pertinence here.

I have one final question. You mentioned the importance of on-the-job performance as the basis for certification or licensing and, given the present record in terms of the elimination of probationers which is not very encouraging, do you think there can be meaningful screening under a selection system based on on-the-job performance?

DR. GITTELL: I do not see why not. In the course of my statement I am reminded of a situation in a middle-class white neighborhood school with an acting principal who has been there for over a year, and the parents have tried to get an examination scheduled for him so that they could keep him. They have been unable to convince anyone to schedule an examination, and I think they have the better judgment at this point. They can use better criteria for evaluating this particular principal than for them to go through this process and worry about an examination after a year or a year and a half since they are able to judge his competence and since they want him to stay. I do not see any major problem in judging performance. It puts a burden on community groups and forces people to pay more direct attention to performance, but I think that is the direction we have to move in.

THE CHAIRMAN: Thank you very much, Dr. Gittell.

I just want to say with respect to Counsel's comment that there is a court decision in Newark, to the effect that race is relevant in consideration as related to jobs such as teaching. Under the law of New York race may never be considered relevant to jobs, and we best wait until tomorrow to hear all of the facts and circumstances surrounding the Newark decision.

(Short recess taken at this time.)

THE CHAIRMAN: While we are waiting for the next witness, let me say that we have a short day today, we are stopping at 4:00. Tomorrow is the last day of these five days of hearings.

We have closed down the child care facility for the reason it was not used. The reason it was not used is because there is no tradition of using child care facilities in this country as yet because such facilities have not been available. Thus, parents are used to using baby sitters and have not organized their lives in such a way to bring their children out and leave them someplace.

We note that because we believe the failure to use the child care facility speaks not to the need for it, which is patently there, but to how far this country is from organizing itself around the concept of child care.

These hearings will begin tomorrow morning at 9:00 a.m., 14 Vesey Street, County Lawyers Association.

I would like to call Professor Judith Rothschild, Director of Urban Leadership Development Program, School of Continuing Education, New York University.

DR. ROTHSCHILD: In an effort to broaden recruiting practices, boards of education have initiated the practice of hiring paraprofessionals from among minority community people. These paraprofessionals usually start at the bottom rung of the career ladder. There exists, however, a group of experienced, trained paraprofessionals who might be tapped for points of entry above this bottom rung.

For the past five years Head Start has been providing not only rich practical experience in working with children and families, but also in-service courses including specially designed university-based intensive programs.

In the New York University Urban Leadership Development Program alone, 1150 paraprofessionals have completed a five to eight-week full time program. Our experience has convinced us that, given the willingness to create and implement new training models, it is possible to effectively prepare community people for teaching tasks and motivate them to further learning in shorter periods of time than we have heretofore thought possible.

Our first-hand experience leads me to raise two points that I think are pertinent to your hearings. The reservoir of existing talent in other child care agencies could be tapped. We need to develop in the city not only the career ladder, but the career lattice. The interweaving of program personnel offers the possibility of bringing talented individuals into the schools to serve children, teachers, and parents as well as providing career mobility to paraprofessionals.

Without trying to romanticize and without trying to minimize the problems involved, after five years of intensive teaching of paraprofessionals I am convinced that we have not yet begun to utilize their enormous talents. We have seen paraprofessionals accomplish unusual things after only a five-week program.

For instance, in many areas paraprofessionals have gone back to their agencies and have conducted workshops for teachers, other paraprofessionals, and parents.

In Buffalo we had a student who before she came to our program was afraid to travel outside of her own community. Today she is traveling all over Buffalo conducting workshops on the match and social studies concepts involved in block play.

Here is a note that a trainee from Boston prepared for her school upon her return:

"To: Teachers and Teacher Trainees

"I have just returned from one of the sessions at N.Y.U. in the Urban Leadership Development Program under Head Start which ran from November 10-December 12. I would very much like to share the information I have received with all of you, but I need your help.

"I would like to have some type of a seminar-workshop after

our vacation, in January, and I would like you all to help me limit my selection of what type of workshop would profit us all the most. Listed below are some of the main areas that were discussed in New York. I would appreciate it if you would check off those you are most interested in or feel you need help in. You may also add any that I may have omitted.

"1. Music and movement--sounds around us.
"2. Social studies concept as core to curriculum.
"3. Block-building.
"4. Trip experiences--first-hand experiences (i.e., space walk, market).
"5. New ideas for science.
"6. New ways of working with children (i.e., our attitude toward children, new ways of talking, listening).
"7. New areas of discipline (i.e., child with problems, interdisciplinary approach).
"8. Better room arrangement (importance of class climate).
"9. New ways to use old materials (i.e., teacher-made games, creative art experiences).
"10. Specific activities for and areas of language development.
"11. Poverty: who, what, where...
"12. Afro-American history and culture and Puerto Rican history and culture.
"13. Involvement, awareness--chain of command in Head Start (i.e., Secretary Finch-APAC's-ONC-HEW; other Head Starts and what they're doing; career ladder, our R.T.O.).
"14. Parent involvement: how, what, where; who's got the power?; working with PAC-APAC-ABCD; parents are teachers too at home.
"15. Other.

"Thank you very much for your help. I hope we can all profit together for the betterment of our Head Start children from my experience in N.Y.U."

Notice that she feels competent to discuss 14 areas with the staff. Reports from her director indicate that her confidence was not misplaced. Her workshop was extremely successful. Today in the Boston area many of the paraprofessionals have become paid consultants for the VOLT Corporation, a contractor providing training for high schools.

But perhaps the most important thing about the training is that in so short a time students develop insights into working with young children and are able to translate these insights into actual classroom practices. For a long time I have been troubled by the fact that even certified early childhood teachers coming from institutions that foster an open-ended form of education seem unable, once in the classroom, to implement anything other than a rigid, boring curriculum. I have come to the conclusion that what was possibly wrong in their training was that they did not really internalize the philosophy and were therefore unable to practice it.

How, then, do you train teachers in a more effective way? The goal in our intensive training program has been to put our students through a process on an adult level in order to convince them of a principle that we deem important.

Let me give you a very simple example. In Head Start programs lunch is served. Teachers and paraprofessionals had been inclined to be very punitive to children at this time. They are motivated by a real desire to see children eat the nourishing food, but they resort to unsuccessful forcing or disciplinary measures to try to accomplish this end.

In our program we take students on a trip to the market. There we make sure that we purchase some very strange looking foods that we are reasonably certain our students have not heretofore tasted. Squid, for example, was one of our purchases. At an afternoon class we forced, pressured, insisted that our students taste the squid. By the end of that afternoon they were really able to feel how children feel when they are faced with a food that seems as strange to them as squid might be to our adults. As a result of this type of experience we see real changes in their attitudes toward children and a developing ability to initiate appropriate curriculum.

Here is a letter that a student sent describing her experience upon returning to her own school. Note how she is able now to transfer from her own feelings to the feelings of children. Imagine how much more effective she will be in approaching new lessons with children.

"Monday morning was a morning of excitement and anticipation and a feeling of should I go or should I stay home. I finally decided I would go because prolonging it wouldn't make it any easier. I was glad that I did go.

"My first day back was only a half day. To add to my mixed feeling, Mrs. Munro called and said she wouldn't be in.

"Eight children came to school and they were very surprised to see me and wanted to know where I had been and about the school that I went to. I think the way they greeted me was one of the moments that I will never forget. They were so happy to see me, and I was so glad to see them that I forgot all about how undecided I was about coming to school. They wanted to know if it was a school just like the one they were going to and if there were other little boys and girls there and all about the teachers. I was eager and happy to answer their questions and to be back with them again.

"I was also thinking about how difficult it must be for a child to come to school for the first time to face the unknown and how hard it must be for a child to come back to school after being out of school for a long time or a short time. He wouldn't know what to expect. Would it be the same as he had left it? Would he have to learn something very different? Would some of the experiences he had at school be kind or so unpleasant that each time he stayed away it would be hard to come back?

"I really think we underestimate the feeling of children when we are introducing them to something new or when they have been away from something for awhile."

In addition to this process-oriented approach, we have also come to the conclusion that a reordering of the sequence of courses in college training programs may be necessary. Paraprofessionals have indicated to us that they feel many college courses are not relevant to becoming a good teacher. Our faculty, however, takes the position that to be a good teacher one must have a broad liberal arts background. How, then, to convince students of this and make the liberal arts background more relevant?

We have come to the conclusion that college programs should reverse their process and start first with the professional sequence and move from the professional sequence to the liberal arts.

Let me give you an example. We start with familiarizing students with children's art work. Then in a workshop situation we have students experience the art materials themselves. Discussion takes place around the fact that children's young art is nonrepresentational. Out of these two experiences grows an interest in abstract modern art. We then take our students to perhaps the Studio Museum in Harlem and from there to the Whitney Museum. Now seeing a connection between their own work, the children's work, and the work of great artists, they are more ready to explore the traditional art history courses.

We have had one student, for instance, who reported to us that she was studying French. When we asked why French she said that she had decided she simply had to read Piaget.

Open admissions programs at the colleges will bring into the teaching field many more minority persons. However, they tend to be young students. We feel that the life experiences of the middle-aged paraprofessional should not be lost, and we would like to see opportunities for these paraprofessionals to become full-fledged teachers because we feel that they offer one of the best hopes for the children of our city.

THE CHAIRMAN: Thank you very much, Dr. Rothschild. Counsel.

MR. TRACTENBERG: Dr. Rothschild, I have a couple of brief questions.

Have you in the course of your program working with paraprofessionals had to deal with the New York City Board of Education?

DR. ROTHSCHILD: Not with the New York City Board of Education because they have not been in Head Start in New York City. But we have dealt with paraprofessionals in the boards of education in other cities since our program deals with major cities from Washington to Boston on the northeast coast.

MR. TRACTENBERG: Have you experienced any difficulties in terms of paraprofessionals moving up any kind of career development ladder in the other educational systems?

DR. ROTHSCHILD: Yes, they have encountered a good deal of difficulty, because of the lack of credentials.

However, there have been many examples of paraprofessionals who have moved into teaching positions or assistant teaching positions in areas where coding and state regulations have not prevented them too much.

These however have not been with board of education programs. They have been in the main with private agencies.

MR. TRACTENBERG: Do you have any reason to believe that paraprofessionals are not competent to manage a classroom as teachers unless they meet the various formal certification requirements?

DR. ROTHSCHILD: I would not like to give you a flat answer. It would depend on the nature of the background.

If you're asking me whether I think certification alone is a criterion for good teaching, I would say no. If you're asking me whether I think I have seen many paraprofessionals who have the ability to do fine teaching, the answer is yes, even without the formal certification.

MR. TRACTENBERG: As I understand the paraprofessional career development program in the New York City Board of Education, a paraprofessional may be in the schools for six or eight years with responsibilities in the day-to-day operations and obviously being observable by others during that period and yet would have to take the formal licensing examination and go through the full licensing procedures.

Is that something you think is an unnecessary impediment to career development?

DR. ROTHSCHILD: I would like to personally see the licensing changed. I think that's held off competent people. The licensing alone is not the criterion for competency.

However, I want to qualify it by saying I don't believe a paraprofessional without any training is competent just to take over a classroom. I would like to see the Board develop a training program which capitalizes on both their life experience and the experience they've had in the classroom for these number of years.

MR. TRACTENBERG: Thank you.

THE CHAIRMAN: Thank you, Dr. Rothschild.

These hearings have one more witness. We will call a short recess.

(Short recess taken at this time.)

THE CHAIRMAN: I am going to call the hearings for today. The only remaining witness has had a problem emerge, so we are going to close the hearings for today.

This is the fourth of five days of hearings on the promotional and selection practices of the New York City public school system. Tomorrow will be the last day.

We will hear experts from other parts of the country concerning how their school systems select and promote teachers and supervisors.

It promises to be an important day of the hearings for the reason that it will look at some very vital issues which have been raised in the hearings, and in the testimony thus far, such as the very real issue of corruption, how do we insure that our school system will operate an objective way, free from corruption and favoritism.

It will look particularly at the experiences of other school districts, since a very real question is presented by the fact that our school system uses a system no longer used elsewhere.

Tomorrow morning at 9:00 a.m., the last day of these hearings. Adjourned.

(Whereupon, at this time, the hearings were adjourned until Friday, January 29, 1971, at 9:00 a.m.)

- - - - -

HEARINGS HELD JANUARY 29, 1971

Witnesses in Order of Appearance

	Testimony starts
Frank Riessman	page 582
Robert Poppendieck	589
Roy Edelfeldt	596
Ward Sinclair	601
Statement from Ewald B. Nyquist	608
Wendell Allen	612
Pat Goralski	620
Joseph Manch	632
Statement from George Dickson	642
Aubrey McCutcheon	644
Marina Brook	659
Anna Conigliaro	662
Vera David	665

Irving Ravin	667
Richard Parrish	671
Roy Sicular	675
LeRoy McMorris	679
Mrs. McIntosh	682
Roderick MacKenzie	685
Mildred Tudy	686
Joan Williams	690
Rose F. Sealy	692
Frank Pereira	694
Dorothy Joseph	697
Hal Koppersmith	701
David Salvadore	705
Mrs. Pullim	707
Juanita Cruz	707

THE CHAIRMAN: We are about to call the first witness. This is the last day of five-day hearings on the promotion and selection practices in the New York City public school system.

The first witness is Dr. Frank Riessman, Director, New Careers Development Center, New York University.

DR. RIESSMAN: Good morning. I will not read the testimony which I believe you have for the record, but rather summarize briefly the major things I want to say and go perhaps a little beyond the testimony that I prepared.

First of all, what needs to be said very clearly about the methods of certifying administrators and teachers in New York is that they display a frightful inadequacy in terms of any approach to validating these tests. Tests are utilized which have in no way been validated, in no way can tell us that the people who do well on these tests will do well as teachers or administrators, and the excuse is often offered that it is impossible to assess this to provide any validation.

There are a couple of very well-known scientific facts about this. One is that no test should be used unless it has been validated. This is a first principle in any introductory psychology course and, I repeat, as a psychologist I'm enormously disturbed about utilizing tests which have not been validated. There is no excuse to contend it is difficult to validate tests. This is true of all kinds of tests.

What is difficult to find is a pattern. Different methods can be set up to determine whether a test is valid or not. The test that is valid will tell you that people who have done well on the test are doing well on the job, and that people who have done poorly on the test are doing poorly on the job.

Secondly, it needs to be pointed out that the tests in themselves do not have at all what might be called face validity. That is, the questions on the tests are frequently ridiculous and this can be seen by just a brief sampling of them. For example, in the examination for assistant principal of junior high school, New York City, questions--these are not atypical in the least--such as "The French polish method of finishing wood involves the use of (a) varnish and turpentine, (b) wax and alcohol, (c) shellac and linseed oil, or (d) lacquer and pigment."

This brings me to the basic problem of what is involved in attempting to build a proper, a valid, a meaningful certification procedure. We are arguing that the most important way to do this is to have a performance-based certification procedure. Actually sixteen states are developing means for performance-based certifications of school personnel. Unlike efforts such as educational vouchers which seek by indirect means to affect the child's learning, it goes to the heart of what happens in the classroom.

The basics of it is an identification in precise terms of what must go on to enable a child to learn, what schools and knowledge a teacher needs in order to facilitate that process and then how to measure and assess these schools and knowledge.

In other words, what we need to have is a clear task analysis of what is required to be an effective teacher, to be an effective administrator. This is, I would suggest, a basic job that is going to face the teachers training institutions and our in-service programs in the United States in the next decade. We have never really done that. We have bypassed that job because it is very hard to find out what is required to be a good teacher and therefore we'll permit four years of college and taking certain courses which are vaguely related to teaching to suffice, or we'll construct tests such as the tests being utilized by the Board of Examiners which are at best intelligence tests, and there is some question about that, but we construct these very indirect and very poor means.

This occurs simultaneously with the fact that teachers throughout the United States are highly ineffective. This is true throughout New York City. There are many reasons for this. I am not in any way trying to suggest that we blame the teachers for this. They have been poorly trained. The tasks they do have not been well analyzed, their in-service training does not prepare them further to do this, they quickly lean back on the first thing they can do to keep order in the classroom. And teachers throughout this city, and in many parts of the United States, have focused on trying to keep order, which is very difficult to do without an understanding of what skills are involved, and the very best teachers we have are what I call the teachers who produce joy in the classroom. They make the kids happy, they keep them quiet, there is some entertainment and there is the new kind of informal education which is being raved about. This is simply a very first stage of teaching and not at all fundamental to children really learning and learning how to learn.

In other words, what we are doing here is permitting entertainment, which is sometimes called contact education, perfectly reasonable as a first step but it is only a first step. I'm suggesting the best teachers I've seen in New York City and around the country are no more than contact educators.

What we need to do, I'm arguing, is to assess very carefully the skills that are really required of teachers--the skills, the intelligence and the attitudes. This has to be built into their training, into their education, into their in-service training. We need to do this in order to then assess teachers who have acquired these skills and can be effective teachers.

State Commissioner Nyquist has put the issue very well. He points out that neither passing college courses nor the traditional exams are going to be the answer. What we need to develop is much more of an internship for new teachers, a clinical training of them, in which we find what skills they have, build in the required skills, assess and evaluate whether they have these skills and then, if they do have them, give them a permanent license. If they do not, they should be rejected from the system.

This is a very difficult kind of approach. It is fundamentally necessary to have an evaluation in a testing procedure. I'm not suggesting for a moment we simply let anybody teach who graduates from college. However, while we are developing that procedure, which needs to be done very carefully and can be done, I believe, in a very short period of time, there is no advantage in using the Board of Examiners' procedure over what is being done in most places in New York State and the United States. Neither of these procedures are good. Neither of them have been well validated, but with the Board of Examiners' procedure we're using a highly invalid procedure, expending millions of dollars per year doing it, picking teachers or supervisors who are good at test-taking and who have been highly coached who have a test-taking orientation which powerfully discriminates against minority and poor groups in New York, which is one of the basic reasons why an insufficient number of them have been involved in the system.

Let me just sum up what I've been trying to point out.

Fundamentally, the assessment and evaluation of teachers and supervisors have got to be related to our getting a clear job description of what they are to do. In other words, we have to know what the tasks are and what skills are required to do these things. These skills have to be taught in in-service and college training and have to be evaluated by very new kinds of procedures which have been called performance-based certification.

As I said before, this is occurring in over sixteen states in the United States which are making serious efforts to do this.

THE CHAIRMAN: Mr. Tractenberg.

MR. TRACTENBERG: Dr. Riessman, I have a couple of questions.

So far as you know, has there been any careful analysis either completed or in progress of the kinds of skills and attitudes that are required in teachers and supervisors?

DR. RIESSMAN: Very preliminary efforts are taking place. Our training laboratory is doing this. People working with differential staffing are doing this. The U.S. Office of Education is attempting to stimulate such work. At this moment, nothing full or complete has been done.

A number of states, as I indicated, the State of Washington, Minnesota, for example, are developing performance-based procedures, certification procedures based on such analysis. I think this is in the first stages of development and I would say it would probably be two years or so before they're fully developed.

MR. TRACTENBERG: In earlier testimony Dr. Lang, the Deputy Superintendent for Personnel of the Board of Education, indicated that during his tenure in that position, which is some five and a half years, there had been no updating of the statement of teachers' duties. Do you believe, based on your experience, that the conception of the kind of duties teachers should perform has changed sufficiently over five and a half years so it might be worthwhile to update, even given the limited state of the art in terms of analysis of these functions?

DR. RIESSMAN: There are a great many new models being developed of the skills and knowledge required. A great deal of attention has been given to them. So there has been some updating. But this updating has not been incorporated into the evaluation and testing procedures for the selection of teachers and supervisors.

As a matter of fact, there is a lot of new thinking about the nature of selection and I don't find any of that thinking reflected in the tests which really involve a high order of nonsense--I said nonsense--rather than the real issues. For example, the school administrator and supervisor in New York is going to have a lot to do with the community and relations with the community. Very few of the test items deal with that kind of question. As a matter of fact, they still seem to have a very out-moded notion of what is involved in administration, that you should have a lot of detailed knowledge of the specific field you are supervising. That is not good supervisory practice.

MR. TRACTENBERG: Earlier in these hearings the Board of Examiners, in responding to questions about the level or kind of validation of their examinations, indicated they have not attempted any predictive validity studies as to teachers' exams but argued that they were focusing on content validity instead.

You were referring in your remarks, I gather, to predictive and face validity and not to content validity.

DR. RIESSMAN: They think the tests prima facie, just looking at them, show something about the teaching process. I think there is no evidence for this and I think if you look at the items, in my testimony there are a number, you can literally get hundreds of these items which are patently absurd and have no direct validity. They are the typical kind of items which are used in very out-moded, intelligence testing. They are focused toward catching you on verbal nuances. They place a great deal of emphasis on small differentialities, meanings and words and so on. They are not related, in any way that I can see, to the content of the tasks to be done.

As a matter of fact, I must say I don't think the Board of Examiners has given much attention to what tasks are to be done. For example, if they were doing their proper homework and research, they would be looking at the teaching functions and making an analysis of the tasks that are involved and skills that are involved, and starting to build new kinds of procedures to assess these things. But, they have bypassed that completely with the age-old notion that teaching is a vague, total art, which can't be analyzed. Teaching is no more such an art than medicine or law or any other profession. All of these areas have very definite skills and intelligence that are required to do them. As a matter of fact, the great new thrust for accountability in the United

States is going to bring this home. Incidentally, this thrust comes principally from the poor and minority communities. They are concerned that teachers know how to do something related to teaching children and to children learning. They don't want teachers who simply know how to keep order in the classroom and entertain children. Joy alone is not going to do it, Dr. Silverman notwithstanding.

MR. TRACTENBERG: You spoke earlier of performance-based standards for certification and we will, I should add, have representatives of the state education departments of Minnesota and Washington among others to talk about the advances in this area, but in your judgment, based on your analysis of certification trends, do you think performance-based certification without the requirement of any written statewide examination ought to be adequate to certify teachers and supervisors?

DR. RIESSMAN: I think this is a complicated question. It is open to further analysis and research. I could see performance-based certification, including written tests, oral tests, interviews, observation, even films of the person who is being assessed. You might want a lot of different kinds of material to find in different ways whether he has the necessary competencies. I personally believe in a multi-approach way of dealing with them, because some people do not do well on a written test. They do better on an oral interview or in performance. I would like to be sure that we are having the person sufficiently at ease and in his own style assessing what he could do. I wrote about this, I hate to tell you, over 10 years ago, where I was originally concerned with the enormous inadequacies of the intelligence tests which are being used in a highly discriminatory way against poor and minority children, in many cases inadvertently.

Today this is more widely known but unfortunately it is not widely known about tests for teachers and supervisors.

To answer the question directly, we might want to use some written tests included in a battery of assessment tools.

MR. TRACTENBERG: I assume, from your remarks, that simply to take the kind of examination process that now exists in New York City and move it to the state level for all teaching candidates throughout the state is not what you have in mind as the basis of certification.

DR. RIESSMAN: No. It is an absurd displacement of something bad in the city to something bad in the state.

The newspaper report of Mr. Shanker's remarks the other day does not make clear how the state test is to be better than the city test. I don't want just to remove a highly invalid procedure that is functioning in the city and put it at the state level. I'm sure Commissioner Nyquist doesn't want to buy such a package. He is much more concerned, as I understand his remarks and ideas, with assessing through the internship the actual practices and work of the teacher.

By the way, teachers are not being trained at all in actual classroom procedures and problems. Teachers are given a lot of general knowledge about methods and then thrown into practice teaching, and then full teaching. What needs to be developed is a much more careful, we call it simulation design, where teachers in training have a great deal of opportunity in a protected setting to practice all kinds of skills they will ultimately use in the classroom. These practices can then be observed and new methods and approaches can be tried.

MR. TRACTENBERG: Earlier witnesses have spoken of the ultimate appointment of teachers, and of supervisors for that matter, as a two-stage process with initial screening at the state level in the form of certification and with selection at the local level. In New York City, that would mean by community boards and their community superintendents.

You indicated that it might take several years to create a sufficiently validated and informed alternate system. Do you think that, in the interim, even if the screening is of somewhat limited validity or doesn't sort people out very finely, as perhaps current state certification doesn't, that some of the deficiencies, perhaps all of them, could be taken care of at the local level?

DR. RIESSMAN: I do. In all kinds of communities, certainly in all kinds of middle- and upper-class communities, Scarsdale, Hartsdale where I live, New Rochelle and lots of other places in this state and all over the United States, it is standard practice to have the local community board interview prospective teachers and supervisors, and make this kind of selection.

It seems we only start to question this and talk about the silly patronage nonsense when it comes to poor communities doing it. Is it patronage when Scarsdale selects certain teachers to teach who pass, and in many cases have not passed, college exams? Many of these communities, it may not be well-known, will hire teachers who are in training who have not yet passed their college courses, have not yet received state certification. Is that special kind of patronage when it is done in upper-class communities? It seems we only get very up-tight about this when it occurs in communities of the poor who apparently don't know how to select teachers and supervisors.

What I am saying, to answer your question directly, is that in the interim period of course I would use screening by the local boards as we do all over the United States. There is nothing unique about that. And, screening should be by state certification, whether it be through passing a college course or getting a college degree, whatever it happens to be.

I know full well the limitations of that, but you won't solve the problem by using a test which has not been validated and which on the face of it seems absolutely absurd.

MR. TRACTENBERG: Thank you.

COMMR. COLGATE: I have one question.

Dr. Riessman, I enjoyed listening to your testimony, and I just wanted to ask you this question:

I noticed on the sheet in front of me you are the Director of New Careers Development Center of New York University. I am not an academician myself and I'm sometimes lost as to the growth of the universities and some of the things that they're doing and

I'm not sure whether this is wax and turpentine, linseed oil or shellac. I'm wondering, what is the New Careers Development Center?

DR. RIESSMAN: It is essentially concerned with training and research in connection with the utilization of paraprofessionals in the United States and with the possibility of paraprofessionals moving up what has been called a career ladder to become teachers.

Originally we talked about paraprofessionals moving up to aides, assistant teachers, associate teachers, and then to teachers based upon a combination of job experience, in-service training and college courses.

As you may know in 130 cities there is a program called the Career Opportunity Program which provides the possibility of recruiting teachers in a new way so aides can move up this ladder step by step to become teachers and they can do it in four years while acquiring a very relevant experience-based training, that is, by doing the job in the schools. Then you will get teachers who have not simply come out of nowhere but teachers who have come out of the earth, who have been trained in the classroom step by step and have acquired a lot of the skills we're talking about.

The New Careers Development Center has been concerned with doing research on those questions, puts out a newsletter and lots of other materials and does training of paraprofessionals and training of their trainers and supervisors.

COMMR. COLGATE: That is very interesting.

Would it be politically accurate to indicate that perhaps some of the teachers' colleges would not be sympathetic to what you were doing?

DR. RIESSMAN: What we're doing in NYU? Most teachers' colleges have been quite sympathetic. Of course, that is a selected group. But teachers' colleges are in a great crisis and are much concerned with revamping the education of teachers. They know that they have done a bad job of it. Paraprofessionals as you know are being admitted to colleges all over the country, in New York City very strikingly. There are at least a thousand of them going to school in New York City right now acquiring a college degree while working, and I don't particularly anticipate enormous resistance from teacher training institutions in this area.

COMMR. COLGATE: I thank you very much.

COMMR. FRENCH: These paraprofessionals have to take the Board of Examiners' examination finally?

DR. RIESSMAN: Yes. I'm not in favor of anybody taking it because it is an inane test.

MR. TRACTENBERG: We heard testimony yesterday and earlier about the judgment of some witnesses, including one of your staff members at the New Careers program, that certainly as to paraprofessionals who have been in the schools for four and more years, and completely observable there, requiring the examination made even less sense than for others.

DR. REISSMAN: Of course. They probably more than anybody else have had an experience and an on-the-job training which relates to the necessary skills in relation to the actual problems of the school. Again, they would have to be victimized, as everybody else is, by this test. When I say "victimized," this test isn't just a bad test. It is a negative test. I think it is quite likely if you did well on this test you have some negative characterictics for teaching. I don't have evidence for that because they don't test this out but the test favors a kind of mentality, a kind of bias, a kind of pickiness, a kind of small-mindedness, which is so inconsistent with everything we claim we want to do for the schools today--the new joy in the schools, informal education and a lot of other things which are small steps forward indeed, but which are completely inconsistent with the small picayune mind which will do well on those tests.

THE CHAIRMAN: Thank you very much, Dr. Riessman.

From the U. S. Office of Education, Dr. Robert Poppendieck, Director of Field Services, Bureau of Educational Personnel Department.

DR. POPPENDIECK: Good morning. I'm Robert Poppendieck, U. S. Office of Education, teacher, professor and, for the last 12 years, specialist for teacher education in the U. S. Office. My present title is Director of Field Services in the Bureau of Educational Personnel Development, the unit which is particularly concerned with teacher education.

My comments this morning will be drawn largely on personal insights and observations accumulated over some years of working particularly with the teacher education and certification people in the several states and territories, the people who are involved in teacher education within the institutions, and to some extent with those who are responsible in school systems where they actually employ the teachers.

Rather than give you a long introduction leading up to some comments and recommendations, I should like to start at the end with the points that I want to make, and then petition your favor to permit me to comment on the background from which my observations are drawn.

I have a strong bias in favor of performance-based teacher education and certification. I have a strong bias in terms of a continuity of pre-service and in-service continuing education of teachers. There needs to be a much more effective parity between the colleges that prepare and the schools that employ teachers, and the parity of decision-making and involvement in teacher education needs to operate through the career of the teacher.

The desirability of longer careers in education, the necessity for fewer temporary teachers and more career teachers, is a factor that needs to be taken into consideration in viewing recruitment, placement, and licensure of teachers. It needs also to bring into focus of differentiated staffing.

We live in a rapidly changing, complex society which imposes demands for many skills. We, as individuals, are better on some skills than we are on others, and the measuring of individual competence and interest has important implications for teacher placement and teacher certification.

The best observation of these then is not through some arbitrary objective measure, or a simple interview, but through a performance base of demonstrated behavior in a variety of educational situations, in which the neophyte applicant teacher, both while he is being prepared and while he is in a stage of application, is observed in a variety of instructional situations.

He should be observed by a variety of observers, who come from different backgrounds, professional and lay. By this means, the applicant will have an opportunity to show what he can do, and the observers can make recommendations about the kind of teaching assignment that this candidate is ready to take and about the kind of suplemental preparation and continuing education that he needs to have in order to perform more effectively in the situation.

This I see as a particular value we're going to realize in today's society of performance-based teacher education and certification.

Now let me back up to annotate the source of some of these concerns.

There is across the country considerable interest and some experimentation with the linkage of performance to behavior, both in teacher preparation and in teacher certification. We have not gone very far with experimentation in providing performance assessment for on-going career development. As this moves to licensure and certification, let me remind you that licensure is the prerogative of the governmental agency. It used to be localities and counties. It is now centralized in states, and a few cities like yours impose additional requirements beyond those of the state. Many cities move in on this. There is also a highly important concern of career teachers, the organized profession, who have a stake in the quality of the image of that profession and in continuing to raise its standards.

I have frequently observed foreign visitors as they come and inquire about our disparate educational patterns and many educational jurisdictions, that the governmental agencies establish minimum requirements the floor beneath which nothing can fall in order to protect the public from quackery while the organized profession is the agency continuously moving to raise standards.

I think it is difficult to clarify a process of teacher certification and teacher selection without being abundantly clear about the purpose of the enterprise. I think we know what we're driving at in society. I submit that we are interested in a society which is at one and the same time free, open, compassionate, which is non-racist, multi-cultural, and productive. I think we have an insight into how to achieve such a society. It is through schools which are free, open, and compassionate, through schools which are non-racial, multi-cultural and productive.

In such schools we require teachers who are both competent and concerned, competent in the specialization of interests which they're going to handle in their classes and educational situations, and competent in the human relationships of working with people whether it be fellow teachers, school board members, neighborhood people, parents or the variety of youngsters themselves. We need teachers who are concerned, and have a sense of dedication to the youngsters, teachers who are concerned about the people, the very individuality and human dignity of the people.

We don't know a whole lot about teaching yet. We know a few things about the functions of teachers. We know it is not to tell. I can tell people how to teach but it doesn't work. I can tell a student how to learn, but it doesn't work. I can set up a learning situation in which the student will have experiences by which he will grow, develop, learn. That works.

I see the three functions of teaching as being to stimulate, to endow and to release the developmental energies of the youngsters. It is a little bit hard to run this into an examination which we will provide for a candidate and say this one is much better at stimulating human potential, that one has a competence to release the possibilities that are hidden in a youngster.

The problem with tests is twofold: One is that a test can prove that a person doesn't know, but it can't prove that he does. If a person fails an item on the test, it is fairly sure that he didn't know it. If he gets it right, he may have guessed it or he may have known it. We never have conclusive proof that a test does say we've got it.

The other problem with a test is its relevance to the situation today in a changing society. I submit that tests validated 20 years ago in Minnesota on lumberjacks are not very valid in East Harlem this afternoon. This is why we have to move to the device of an educator-neophyte, visiting several instructional situations, showing what he would do by demonstrating his teaching in several different class activities, with different kinds of pupils with a variety of observers, professional and non-professional.

Let me move to the concept of linking this with an educational career. I am deeply concerned in government that of all the teachers we produce in our teacher preparing institutions, one out of six remains in education as a career, and five become dropouts from the teaching profession, some within the first year or two years or five years. I do not count as a dropout a woman who prepares to teach, teaches a while, marries, raises a family and comes back to teaching. She is a career teacher. I do not count as a dropout a man who prepares to teach and teaches for two years while he continues law study at night and moves into legal practice. My best recommendation for former teachers is that they are the kind of teachers I like to recommend for the school system which my own children attend. I wouldn't take my dog to a veterinarian if he was only going to be practicing for eight or nine months and then he was going to quit and do something else.

We need a sharper device for identifying among those in the teaching profession, the kind of people who have a sense of dedication to education that means they want to stay in it as a career.

I submit that preparation for teaching, as well as certification, gives us an insight into the probability of the candidate staying with the profession.

Let me move to the concept of pre-service, in-service continuity and link with that a concern for specialization, differentiated staffing. There are aspects of teaching at which I'm not at all good and there are others at which I'm reasonably effective. I think society gains if it pays me to do those things which I can do best and employs someone else in areas where I am less competent. Some teachers are very effective at working formally with large groups and they should have an opportunity to do that. Other teachers are much better at working with the assessment and diagnosis of learning difficulties of individuals or very small groups. They should have the opportunity to focus on that. So, as people come out of pre-service training with a general preparation for teaching, into their continuing educational growth and re-education, we need to move to differentiated staffing.

Differentiated staffing involves a team concept in part. It has a variety of guises but it does permit the teacher to give his primary efforts to those things which he can do best.

Also, with a teaching team concept and the introduction of paraprofessionals, multiple entry points are provided to the teaching profession and there is an opportunity, with performance-based observation of people, to observe the performance of helpers, and tutors. Thus, many can be accepted at that stage before they perform as teachers and are assessed for their competence as teachers.

As our way of life becomes more complicated, we will need a greater variety of people in the education profession. It has been said young people today will have to be re-educated for careers at least three times before they finally retire and if that is true for the world in general, then teachers will have to be re-educated at least four times in a career because they have much more important leverage.

Let me talk more specifically about performance-based criteria. I am not talking about just witnessing a teacher on one occasion and letting it go at that. I know it has been done that way in the past. Many of us who have been in the game for sometime are aware of any number of superintendents and principals who have interviewed an applicant for teaching and said, "Well, your papers look good, you are personable as I talk with you, there is a class in your subject going on right now, suppose I call the teacher out of the class and introduce you as a visitor and you go ahead and teach for a half hour and let me see how you behave in front of a class." That's not a new invention. Effective supervisors have used this device for years in innumerable situations.

What we have today is the possibility of not using just the bias of one employing principal, but the possibility of identifying critical devices, the criteria we need for the competencies a person can show in specific classroom situations, and having as observers some educators who represent the professional view, some educators who represent the immediate employer, some laymen, neighbors, parents and, if you please, a few students, to observe the behavior of the prospective teacher in the classroom and give their observations.

We have the opportunity of using video tapes. As a person is being taped in many situations, he gets accustomed to that camera and he can do it without a sense of embarrassment. As he has several visitors come in he is less apt to be annoyed.

I submit visiting to observe performance should be invited, the applicant should have an opportunity to tell the considering superintendent, "At 2:00 o'clock this afternoon I'm going ahead with a particular lesson for which I've been preparing the youngsters and I would like you to see it."

There should also be situations in which he doesn't know he is going to be observed and people come in by surprise. There should be routine cases when he knows there is going to be an observation and an opportunity for him to talk with the observers before he is observed and again to talk with them after he has been observed.

I submit the observer in the performance-based observation pattern should be required to make two kinds of recommendations: What are the kinds of teaching situations for which I would now recommend this candidate, what are the things I see him doing effectively now, and what are the recommendations I have for additional preparation experiences that he should have before he moves into a standard and general teaching assignment.

Years of experience accumulate. They are useful. But, experience of itself does not educate. It is only experience assessed that educates. I submit that the concept of performance-based teacher preparation and certification provides an opportunity for assessing experience at all stages of the game and making it possible to move a career teacher more strongly through his career observation and pattern. We have the involvement of the organized profession. We have the involvement of the neighborhood. We have the involvement of the responsible educational administration in the unit, and we have the involvement of the political jurisdiction, either local or state.

It is out of these kinds of experiences, contacts, observations, that I have come to the conclusion that a performance base of demonstrated competence leading to a recommended kind of assignment is the direction in which we should move in teacher certification.

I thank you for the opportunity of being here, commend the organization for the pattern of hearings that it is having and I express the regrets of my Associate Commissioner, and his immediate director of school programs, Dr. William Smith, that they could not be present and pleased to have been with you.

MR. TRACTENBERG: Dr. Poppendieck, a couple of questions, if I may.

In your experience, do written tests, even if objective and reasonably valid, in fact hinder development of professional standards? That is, do they test for the kind of sensitivities you described as being so important?

DR. POPPENDIECK: It can test the knowledge of the person for the field he is studying. The other skills are subjective and it is difficult to make them objective and reduce them to an objective test. We can test what a person knows by a written test, but in order to observe what he can do with what he knows and how he can draw out, stimulate and release the growth of the youngster, we have to observe a real live test rather than a written one.

MR. TRACTENBERG: Dr. Riessman, the prior witness, referred to some sixteen state education departments so far as he knew which are moving toward performance-based certification. Can you amplify that from your vantage point?

DR. POPPENDIECK: I indicated we have some biases. Last May we helped to fund a training conference in Florida, through the Florida State Department of Education, to which were invited teams of educators from ten or a dozen states and six or eight professional associations. It was a training conference focused on the problem of developing criteria for performance-base certification.

We didn't get as far as developing criteria but we did exchange enthusiasm about the performance-based approach. The State of Florida, in selecting the ten or twelve states involved, did send information to the fifty-seven states and territories to permit them to apply, asking them to indicate, number one, what they had already been doing with performance-based principles, number two, their hopes and aspirations and quality of interest. They had requests from some twenty-eight or thirty states, who wanted to be in on it at that time. We didn't have enough funding to provide for that many. We did provide for some ten or twelve. There is an interest in the majority of states and territories in exploring and possibly moving into the performance-based approach. It is not quite as organized as Dr. Frank Riessman implied.

You will have a representative from the State of Washington who will comment on their developments. The states of Oregon and California are interested as are the states of Minnesota, Michigan, Pennsylvania and New Jersey. The State of New York you are familiar with. It is one of the leading states moving in this direction.

The State of Florida has been developing small projects of teacher education linked with potential teacher certification on a performance base.

The State of Texas does have a massive project funded by us at the present time which involves a coordination of several institutions and the State Department in linkage with a national professional association, the American Association of Colleges for Teacher Education. There is strong interest, there is definite movement in this direction. States have not yet dropped the laundry list of courses and come up with an observation base, but they're moving in that direction. A problem is that it is more expensive, but it can be done gradually.

MR. TRACTENBERG: I would assume that for teachers already in a particular school system being considered for promotion performance-based information may be readily available but how about the beginning teacher, who applies from a teacher training institution to a school district? How would evidence of his performance be acquired?

DR. POPPENDIECK: I would like to think that as a freshman and sophomore in college he had a number of tutorial experiences in which he worked instructionally, that he moved into a live school system and served as a teacher-helper in a variety of situations long before he came to what we normally think of student teaching. I would like it if he moved beyond that to an actual paid internship while he is in a sort of entrance status. I would like to think that many prospective teachers, when they were still in school, acted as occasional teacher-helpers and occasionally substituted or actually took over instruction in the class while the teacher was present.

There is a host of opportunities along the route of preparation to teach, in which performance could be observed and rated. Recommendations should be developed about the student's strengths and weaknesses.

MR. TRACTENBERG: I assume, Dr. Poppendieck, that performance-based certification at bottom relies on the presence of satisfactory observation techniques. Are there any such techniques now in existence and in operation, to your knowledge?

DR. POPPENDIECK: They really haven't been widely formalized. There are very few school principals who don't drop in and visit teachers. They don't always have as much time as they like.

I think I had a good bringing up when I entered teaching. My superintendent used to see me teach and invite me to come into his office and talk with me about it and invariably he picked out one or two things that he thought were good and commended me about them and invariably the ax also fell. Yes, the observational techniques exist. It is of the essence of supervision, not only in education but in other fields. But it needs to be adapted right now to the process of certification.

MR. TRACTENBERG: There has been concern expressed though about the uniformity of observation techniques. In your judgment, is it possible to standardize or make uniform these observations?

DR. POPPENDIECK: I would be in horror and awe of having one observer with a checklist be the unique observer. I would favor that multiple biases be cancelled out by having several observers, professional and otherwise, see the individual on more than one occasion in a variety of situations.

This is where the variables move out and the essence of competence to meet the requirements of the job come in. Essentially it is subjective and needs to be done with a strong measure of subjective competence.

MR. TRACTENBERG: In your judgment, is this kind of technique workable in a school system the size of New York City where there are some 60,000 teachers and, I gather, six or seven thousand new teachers each year coming in to the system?

DR. POPPENDIECK: I think it is workable. I think it is expensive and I think unless it is built into the structure of supervision, including the observation of neophytes and applicants, we're going to have more crumbling within the structure.

I don't think it is possible to prepare a teacher, test, interview, observe him, admit him, put him in the classroom and go away. That is not the kind of world in which we live. Teaching is an on-going career and it is dynamic just as the world is dynamic.

MR. TRACTENBERG: Thank you.

COMMR. FRENCH: Do you think it would be possible to use parents or members of community boards as observers?

DR. POPPENDIECK: Yes. I think they should be used. I think they should not be used as the only observers but their voice must be in.

THE CHAIRMAN: Thank you very much, Dr. Poppendieck.

I'm going to call a short recess and give the stenographer a break.

(Short recess.)

THE CHAIRMAN: This is the last day of public hearings here at 14 Vesey Street, the County Lawyers Association. There have been five days of hearings on the selection and promotion practices of the public school system.

I wish to call next Dr. Roy Edelfeldt, Executive Secretary, National Commission on Teacher Education and Professional Standards, National Education Association.

DR. EDELFELDT: Good morning.

THE CHAIRMAN: Good morning, Dr. Edelfeldt.

DR. EDELFELDT: I think maybe my best service to you might be to speak very briefly and let you ask questions, because I think Frank Riessman and Bob Poppendieck have said a lot of the things that I would ordinarily say. I was thinking either they've read my stuff or I've been reading theirs.

THE CHAIRMAN: I'm glad there is some consensus in the profession.

DR. EDELFELDT: I think at least among some of us there is.

I'd like to hit another part of this and maybe some of my value to you would be the fact that in my job I am one of the fortunate people who has a chance to look at teacher education and personnel practices throughout the nation in all fifty states and, as a matter of fact, I just came back from Canada last week and have had an opportunity to look at the situation in a number of provinces in Canada. So I'd just like to make a short statement and hope that this prompts some questions from you.

I think we make some old assumptions today about people being qualified for jobs on the basis of credentials, or what college they've graduated from, or some other kind of hallmark which is framable and you can put on the wall, when there really may be very little relationship between their competence to do a particular job and the kind of credentials they hold. We've coined the phrase, the credential society, which I think we indeed are.

We also operate, I think, on 1920 notions of personnel practices in education and we tend to protect those practices of yesterday and we seem to lack the courage to make the changes that are needed. Now the inadequacies of the personnel policies and procedures are most clear, I think, in places where new people, new ethnic groups are getting into teaching or into sub-professional roles. The credentials game is most devastating to minority people who haven't acquired the middle-class veneer and standard verbal skills in test-taking, in polite society etiquette. Jobs often can't even be approached if a candidate can't acquire or produce credentials.

Now in contrast the essential skills for many jobs in education are hard to find. For example, it is difficult to find good teachers for poor children, or bilingual teachers for immigrant kids, or sensitive, aware teachers for people I call almost emotionally handicapped, or straightforward teachers to help alienated youngsters.

Now my illustrations aren't very polished nor are they precise, but I think you see what I mean.

We just don't have many people who can work with children, who are difficult, who don't conform to WASP, middle-class society values. And I might say parenthetically we probably don't even have many really effective teachers in middle-class settings either.

Now I don't blame the teachers for this. I blame the system. I blame it primarily because of the inadequate approach to personnel practices.

Everyone wants able people working with students. We've tried to assure competence through credentials. We call it certification. Certification is designed to guarantee to a parent that his child is working with a competent teacher. But certification now in some places seems to be designed mainly to protect teachers. When that becomes its major purpose, the process is outmoded. Now, even at its best, certification is an imperfect procedure for guaranteeing that a teacher is adequate. And this is where personnel practices become important and the two previous people have said very little about personnel practices, per se.

Certification may guarantee certain basic minimums. For example, that a teacher has studied in depth the subject that he will teach or that he has had a trial run under supervision in a school situation and that evidence can be presented that a certain person can work well with youngsters. But this doesn't mean that any teacher can work in any school and be successful, and I think that is one of the assumptions we've made.

I don't mean that any teacher can fit into any faculty and be a member of that team, and increasingly, as Dr. Pappendick indicated, we're looking at teachers in teams in differentiated roles. A teacher must fit into a faculty team effort if a comprehensive kind of coordinated educational program is to be achieved. And each teacher can't work in his own isolated room without regard to the other exposures the youngsters have in school. So, the circumstances of a particular assignment are as important as the whole question of competence by virtue of a credential. Many teachers succeed or fail, depending on their assignment. So there must be much more to the assignment process than just fitting a warm, certified body into an organization chart in P.S. whatever-its-number.

The business of fitting teachers--and this would apply to supervisors, because some of the concerns here are valid for both--into a job is difficult and it is time-consuming but I think it is worth doing. Dr. Pappendick indicated that it was expensive, but so is any new system. So is losing the large proportion of teachers we lose every year from teaching and finding new ones. If we could do a better job of assignment, we might keep people longer and cut out some of the expenses of recruiting. This whole procedure, I think, cannot be impersonal, even though in a large school district we seem to accept impersonality as inevitable. I submit it can be organized so that teachers and supervisors get matched with places or assignments that they are qualified for, places where they want to be, places where their best talents can be appreciated and used.

Now where these conditions don't prevail, there ought to be some chance for re-assignment. Unfortunately, too often we think of an individual succeeding or failing in terms of a job when the job in one situation may be one that a particular person cannot do, and there may be a job in another situation which he can do. So, it is a matter of placement. It is a matter of people. It is a matter of circumstances.

I think all of this requires good personnel procedures and records so that those who work with assignment and re-assignment know as much about a teacher or supervisor as is possible. Perhaps more important is that the assignment procedure is one the teachers themselves have a part in.

I think it is also important that teacher records not be like an FBI dossier. The teacher and the administrator should know and agree on the criteria for performance evaluation and they should both have a part in determining such criteria. Parents and students as well should have a part, even though their criteria may be different.

Now, ascertaining levels of competence fairly, and keeping and using records wisely and humanely, is complicated further by the recent introduction of sub-professionals into the schools. These are people new to the school setting. Educators are only beginning to learn how to select and train and assign such people. In most places, credentials aren't required as yet for sub-professionals. Many of these people are upward-bound in mobile professions. They're being trained largely on the job. Many of the people come from poor circumstances and they have incomplete educations in terms of middle-class values. Most do not do well on tests, although they may at the same time be very effective teachers or eventually supervisors.

Now many educators are committed to assigning people in schools on the basis of what an individual can do and that's a plain English way of talking about performance-based criteria. I'd rather say it in plain English. This assumes that performance can be measured fairly and by agreed-upon criteria, which is possible although not easy. It also assumes that assignment can and will be made on the basis of such evidence, and that's pretty important to underscore because we do have a lot of evidence that

Dr. Edelfeldt

this is not always done. That is difficult but not impossible and it assumes that defenders of the current certification and personnel practices will be willing to really try something new. I guess that is what you're wrestling with and you'll have to determine for yourself whether that is possible or impossible.

The point I'd like to leave with you is that we know much more about teaching and supervision and good personnel practices for dealing with people in jobs than we're using. If operating principles can be agreed on by the parties who are affected, and I think among them are certainly teachers' organizations, administrators, school boards, parents and students, it may be possible to improve personnel procedures. Certification is only one part of personnel procedures. I think there is a chance that we can make some drastic improvement. But I think there is probably no chance of much change if mutually agreeable operating principles can't be established. Worst of all, I think without operating principles, no one group will trust any other group, which I've been reading a little bit about in the papers.

Increasingly, I think, operating principles are being made part of negotiated agreements or collective bargaining contracts, and I predict that the main device for changing personnel procedures will be negotiating contracts.

Now this really marks a significantly new development in education in which teachers themselves, through their organizations, will have both the power and responsibility for determining the standards and the procedures to be employed to make judgments about their fellow members.

I'll stop there and see whether I've said anything that needs further explanation.

Thank you very much.

THE CHAIRMAN: Thank you, Dr. Edelfeldt.

Counselor Tractenberg.

MR. TRACTENBERG: Dr. Edelfeldt, you have indicated that you have rather broad experience with the various personnel procedures in states around the country. Have you formed any judgment about how unique the New York City procedure is, that is, having not only a Board of Examiners but also a Board of Examiners which creates, administers, and grades its own exams. For example, I understand a city like Chicago has a Board of Examiners, but generally it uses standardized examinations prepared by the Educational Testing Service. Is New York City really one of a kind?

DR. EDELFELDT: I think you can assume that it is one of a kind in that respect. But I think all the problems that go with it are experienced in most large school districts. It doesn't mean that they would have an exam or a Board of Examiners, but they have many of the same basic problems. For example, a basic problem right now is how to get people who can demonstrate that they're competent to do a certain kind of a job in the schools, to work especially with so-called disadvantaged youngsters. I think that is a problem in most of the large cities in the country.

MR. TRACTENBERG: Yet, if in fact, there is an extra

impediment in New York City, this may in part at least account for what motivates these hearings, that is, the poor showing of New York City in attracting minority group professionals as compared even to these other systems that, as you indicate, are not completely free from problems?

DR. EDELFELDT: Yes.

MR. TRACTENBERG: We've heard charges here at the hearings that it is not fair to children to place in a classroom a teacher who doesn't meet the kinds of licensure procedures that now apply. Do you have any reaction to that kind of argument?

DR. EDELFELDT: Well, yes. It isn't fair to children to put a person in a classroom who can't do an adequate job and I guess what I tried to say was that I don't think that in many cases, particularly when we're dealing with children you could call in quotes "difficult," that the credential is a guarantee that they're going to be adequate. I think we have a lot of documentation on that in different situations. Let's face it, most teachers either are or become middle-class by virtue of teacher training and when they get to that point many of them have only just come out of the lower middle-class background and they're probably the most ardent defenders of middle-class values alive, and so when they go into a class or school where there are lower-class children, there is a conflict between the value system of the teacher and the youngster, and if you don't establish some kind of relationship, warmth, rapport, whatever you want to call it, between teacher and youngster, if it is a constant rejection of what a child stands for and where he comes from on the part of the teacher, why, kids aren't going to be open and receptive to learning. So, that is part of the problem. But we don't test that at all in any of the written tests. We don't determine if a teacher will tell his students daily that they're dirty or uncouth or vulgar. If he does, you certainly don't get the kind of confidence that is going to make the teacher-student relationship very effective. Anybody who has been in any school situation where he found himself embarrassed by the teacher, and I think most of us have, know that at that point you're hardly receptive to learning and your ability to think is blurred.

MR. TRACTENBERG: Now, you talked about the importance of good assignment of teachers, and we have heard much in these hearings about the very high turnover of teachers in New York City. As I'm sure you know we now have a system with 31 community school districts, each with its own elected community board, and appointed community superintendent. In terms of your general expertise in this area, and your reaction to other systems, does it make any sense to you in a system like New York City to have central assignment of teachers from a central list or is this really the antithesis of the kind of good assignment practices you felt were important?

DR. EDELFELDT: Well, I think if it is central assignment in terms of really moving, as I said, warm, certified bodies into spots that are open, why, I think it is unreasonable and it is ineffective, and it doesn't make much sense. I think, as Frank Riessman indicated, where a great deal of care is given to individual appointments, and I know Scarsdale's procedure for years has been to bring people in for a day and they've been interviewed in the school where they hope they will teach, and they've talked to a lot of people who will be colleagues, and I think their holding power is good and I think it pays.

So I guess what I'm saying is I don't see a central assignment system merely saying, "You're going to be in P.S. so-and-so up on such-and-such a street next year" as being any more like a way to move cement blocks around, not teachers.

MR. TRACTENBERG: And finally, Dr. Edelfeldt, assuming that all the various forces which you quite properly identified as critical to making any kind of rational change in the system were receptive to change, can you estimate for us how long it might take to move to a more rational personnel procedure?

DR. EDELFELDT: No, I guess it depends on how much effort and money you want to put into it. It is a little bit like whether we continue, to use another example, to support prisons and welfare programs the way they are or whether we're going to put the money into the preventative dimensions of it so we don't have people in those situations. I think the same thing is true here.

I think initially, if you want to get into this phase, it will cost you money and some real time and effort, but the pay-off ought to be substantial because, in the first place, you have people placed where they want to work and, as you add new people to your staffs, you should have a much better quality of person. Adding those two together--if you have people who like what they're doing and who like where they're situated, and who are able-- you've already built some circumstances that makes for better performance. But better holding power, and as I understand it, holding power in New York City is not bad anyway. So I would say, I think you can move very quickly into this if you have the determination to do it, which of course has to be backed up with staff and with the money they cost.

MR. TRACTENBERG: Thank you.

THE CHAIRMAN: Thank you very much, Dr. Edelfeldt.

DR. EDELFELDT: Thank you.

THE CHAIRMAN: I'd like to call next Dr. Ward Sinclair, Associate Director, Office of Teacher Education and Certification, New Jersey State Education Department.

Dr. Sinclair.

DR. SINCLAIR: Madam Chairman, the office which I represent in the New Jersey Department of Education is concerned with teacher education and certification.

New Jersey, like other states, has granted teacher certification to individuals who have collected the prescribed number of courses to meet requirements. Unlike most states, New Jersey grants only one regular or standard certificate. That is once a person receives a standard certificate to teach in New Jersey, that certificate is good for life. There are no further hurdles for him to overcome.

The New Jersey certificates are issued by the authority

granted to the State Board of Examiners, which is a rather common title but I think has different powers from the Board of Examiners being discussed in different aspects here. According to Title 18A: 6-38 of the New Jersey Code, "The Board shall issue appropriate certificates to teach or to administer, direct, or supervise the teaching, instruction or educational guidance of, or to render, or administer, direct, or supervise the rendering of nursing services to, pupils in public schools operated by boards of education, and such other services as shall be authorized to issue by law based upon certified scholastic records or upon examinations or both and may revoke the same under rules and regulations prescribed by the State Board."

In January 1969, the New Jersey Board of Examiners conducted a two-day listening post, at which educators from across the state expressed their concerns, made recommendations, and raised issues regarding certification of teachers and other school personnel. One result of this two-day session was the consensus that the initial certification of teachers should be based on an individual's demonstrated ability to teach rather than only on his performance in college courses.

After approval of the State Board of Education, the Officer of Teacher Education and Certification undertook the responsibility for studying competence evaluation as a requirement for certification, and thus the Performance Evaluation Project was organized.

The objectives of this project are five-fold:
1. To identify performance criteria necessary to teach a given subject and/or age group.
2. To identify the common elements of competency, if any, which all teachers, regardless of subject areas or grade levels, should possess.
3. To develop a method for measuring the degree of competency of teachers.
4. To teach educators the proper use and interpretation of the method of evaluating teacher performance; and
5. To identify the level of performance required for initial regular certification.

Through their respective professional organizations, such as the New Jersey Art Educators Association, New Jersey Council of Teachers of English, etc., 16 task forces were organized on a state level in the following areas--I'll just run through the list. These are the 16 areas in which teaching certificates are issued in New Jersey: art education, business education, elementary, English, exceptional children, foreign languages, health education, home economics, industrial arts, mathematics, music, nursery school, physical education, science, social studies and vocational subjects.

Each of these 16 task forces is composed of the following types of people: four classroom teachers nominated by the respective professional associations; a department head or supervisor from the public school system; four college personnel, two from professional education and two from the related academic field; a curriculum specialist from the Department of Education; four people with general curriculum background, such as principals, college deans, superintendents, and lastly, a measurement and evaluation specialist.

An attempt was made to get a geographic distribution on each task force, to have representation from urban, suburban and rural schools, to involve teachers with less than five years of experience as well as those with more. And an attempt was made to add minority group representation on each task force.

All together approximately 260 New Jersey educators are directly involved in this project.

Recognizing that implementation of any recommendations resulting from this project will need backing, representatives from many organizations across the state have been asked to serve on an advisory committee. This body will offer criticism, suggestions and, in general, perform the traditional functions of any advisory group.

To show the scope of the representation on the advisory committee, I'd like to read the list of organizations which have representatives on the advisory committee of the Performance Evaluation Project. We have a member of the New Jersey Senate and one from the General Assembly; and the New Jersey Association of School Administrators, Congress of Parents and Teachers, Department of Education, New Jersey Education Association, Federation of Teachers, New Jersey Association of Private Colleges, State Chamber of Commerce, state colleges, New Jersey Taxpayers' Association, Rutgers, the state university, and the State Federation of District Boards of Education, all have representation on this advisory committee.

Since the organization of the task forces in May of 1970, each task force has met several times. They are now in the process of identifying the performance criteria which teachers must meet to be successful in their respective fields. A three-day training session was held this past November, to which two representatives from each task force were invited to learn to write behavioral objectives. These representatives have returned to their respective task forces to serve as experts in identifying and writing behavioral objectives. By June of this year it is planned that some of the task forces will develop their performance criteria to such a degree that they can be field tested.

This is the point at which we are now.

This Performance Evaluation Project is the one with which I am directly concerned but it is not the only agency in the State Education Department concerned with teacher education.

The Office of Equal Educational Opportunity, which is only two years old, is in the process of compiling some very interesting data. It has been discovered, for example, that there is one Black county superintendent in the state, one Black district superintendent, and approximately 12 Black secondary principals in the entire state.

When you consider that New Jersey has approximately 60,000 certified teachers, it becomes obvious that we have a problem in this area with minority peoples.

Although the Performance Evaluation Project is concerned now only with the initial certification of teachers, it does not take too much imagination to visualize that similar programs can evolve for the selection of principals and supervisors. In theory, what we are saying is that anyone who can demonstrate his competency to teach can be certified to teach regardless of where he learned to do the job.

More realistically, however, the one institution in our society which is geared to preparation of teachers is higher education. Consequently, it is my opinion that the significant changes we wish to see brought about among our teachers will have to occur in the teacher preparation programs on our college campuses. We have to be constantly aware of the dangers of developing criteria in connection with existing college courses. So far we have been and hopefully we can continue to be vigilant. Perhaps this isn't the ultimate to teacher certification, but there appear good reasons to expect that many persons may be certified as teachers who now find only obstacles in their way. College graduates who may have had a variety of experiences in the Peace Corps, VISTA, or similar programs, may be perfectly capable of performing duties, responsibilities and roles of teachers. They may be able to do this without one minute's instruction in a college or department of education. All we're saying with this project of ours is if they can teach, let them teach.

Having described the New Jersey Performance Evaluation Project, and some of its implications, I may be of better service by not taking more time with prepared remarks but answering some direct questions you may have.

MR. TRACTENBERG: Thank you.

THE CHAIRMAN: Thank you, Dr. Sinclair. Mr. Tractenberg.

MR. TRACTENBERG: Dr. Sinclair, you mentioned the existence of a State Board of Examiners in New Jersey. Does that imply that there is some form of state written examination administered by this Board?

DR. SINCLAIR: No, there is not.

MR. TRACTENBERG: Have you ever, in your consideration of a successful and appropriate certification procedure, considered a state written examination?

DR. SINCLAIR: A written examination?

MR. TRACTENBERG: Yes. I should say by way of background that several witnesses have suggested during these hearings that in lieu of a New York City examination, administered by the Board of Examiners, there might be some form of state examination.

DR. SINCLAIR: Nowhere in the Performance Evaluation Project are we talking about written examinations per se. However, let me expand a moment here. If a person is going to teach a discipline in a secondary school, history, English, mathematics or whatever, I presume that you could test his competency in that subject through a written examination. But, I don't see how a written examination can determine his competency for teaching the subject matter.

In other words, I am not in favor of the so-called written examinations which determine whether or not a person actually can teach.

MR. TRACTENBERG: Is there some way, under current certification or under future performance-based certification, in which the state tests this knowledge component or do you just rely on college background for that?

DR. SINCLAIR: This ties in with another whole movement in teacher certification of which, again, New Jersey is one of participating states. More states follow the program approval approach to teacher education than otherwise.

The way this works--and I don't know whether this has been brought up and I'm re-inventing the wheel for people here or whether this is something that might be of interest--is that if a college has a teacher education program, and a certain agency of the state of New Jersey--it happens to be the office I represent-- certifies that the program of that college is adequate to meet the needs or is adequate to prepare teachers in that given field, we, therefore, can approve that college. Any graduate from that program is automatically issued a certificate. It is the college's recommendation to the state. New Jersey is just moving into this so-called program approval approach to teacher education and certification. But it has been in operation for many years in many states. How it ties in with performance evaluation, as I visualize it, is as follows:

The teacher education institution, College A will have a list of criteria which have been predetermined through the task forces that are now studying the situation, College A will select its group of incoming students, go over the criteria with them and during a four-year period, or however long it takes to prepare a teacher, periodically review the skills of the prospective teacher to see how he is progressing. Right along in connection with this, some tests can be given to determine his academic competency. I see no necessity under our kind of certification program for a single day of testing for the candidates. This can be an on-going thing over a period of time. Now, a person who may not be in a situation in a college training program, may appear at a given point and time and say, "I want to be a teacher. I think I'm qualified. I studied the criteria. I think I can meet them." In whatever evaluation situation we would devise if he can demonstrate this, then I think he would be awarded a certificate.

MR. TRACTENBERG: It has been alleged earlier in these hearings that, although New York State has a similar approach to certification at the state level, unfortunately some people who pass through this process are nevertheless incompetent and, in fact, it was alleged that they were illiterate by whatever standard the particular witness used.

Has that been a problem in New Jersey? Have people who have completed these approved programs and been certified on that basis subsequently turned out to be incompetent or illiterate?

DR. SINCLAIR: No more so than those certified through any other means. And in fact, I would say less because if a college has a record of turning out people whom the professionals in the field judge to be incompetent, the marketplace effect, will come into being almost immediately. The superintendents won't hire the people from that school, etc., etc. I think if anything, it has tended to make the colleges much more cognizant of their responsibility, and do a closer job of supervision, not only in the traditional student teaching situation, but in all other aspects of the teacher preparation program. So that when the student is eligible for a degree and certification, the college can, with a greater degree of certainty, state, "Yes, this person, according to the standards and the measures we now are using, bears our stamp of approval. And therefore, we recommend him."

MR. TRACTENBERG: I assume state certification in New Jersey, as in New York, is only the first step toward ultimate appointment of a person. Are there any school districts, and I presume this would be limited to larger school districts, that have their own boards of examiners as New York City does, as part of the selection process?

DR. SINCLAIR: I'm not aware of any.

MR. TRACTENBERG: Just two more questions, if I may, Dr. Sinclair.

How long may the New Jersey evaluation of the performance-based approach to certification take in your judgment?

DR. SINCLAIR: We hope that by June of this year three or four of our 16 task forces will have workable criteria which we can field test. We plan to test these with two kinds of populations. One, undergraduate students who are in their student teaching programs, and we will use this not in place of but in addition to the regular on-going evaluation which student teachers receive. A second group--a captive audience, if you will--which we can use this criteria on are those people who have Bachelor's degrees in one subject field or another, and have decided to choose teaching as a career, subsequent to receiving their degrees. These are in what we call Masters of Arts teaching programs. These are more mature people for the most part and they have more of the traditional education behind them. We have these two groups that we can try our criteria on. That will be this coming fall, September to December. By June 1972 we expect all 16 task forces to have criteria developed. So that by September 1972 we ought to be able to field test this throughout all the teaching areas for which certificates are issued in New Jersey. I hope that by the end of that academic year, 1972-73, we will have been able to make some judgments. By July 1, 1973, we ought to be able really to implement the performance criteria.

MR. TRACTENBERG: So you are talking about a two or two and a half year testing period?

DR. SINCLAIR: Yes.

MR. TRACTENBERG: At the end of that time the performance-based approach could actually be implemented?

DR. SINCLAIR: We hope so.

MR. TRACTENBERG: Fine. That is all I have, Dr. Sinclair.

THE CHAIRMAN: Commissioner French has a question.

COMMR. FRENCH: Are you satisfied that this new system will bring into the teaching profession at all levels greater numbers of minority groups?

DR. SINCLAIR: I think so, Commissioner French, in that it opens many other avenues to teacher certification than just the single avenue of going through a four-year college preparatory program.

We have many students in New Jersey who are in a program called the Urban Education Corps and these are young people from all kinds of backgrounds, Spanish-speaking, Black, white, the gambit, who, after graduation from college, tried one or two different things. Many of them--I don't know what the percentage would be--are Peace Corps volunteers who have returned and who sometime since graduation from college, have developed a will or an ability to teach. If they have been in the Peace Corps, certification is no problem in Nigeria, Liberia or wherever they've been.

Now they come back and want to teach in New Jersey and they have to have a certificate and they haven't got credit one in teacher education. We do have the Urban Education Corps which works with four of our institutions and these people do one year internships plus a couple of summers of academic work in teacher education and so on. This could be short cut. I don't sound like a teacher educator.

For many of these people this is wasted time or a good part of it, and if they can demonstrate through their performance that they are capable of teaching we would certify them under our new proposal.

COMMR. FRENCH: Thank you.

THE CHAIRMAN: Thank you very much, Dr. Sinclair.

This testimony from a sister state so similar to our own has been particularly valuable, and we are able to see what is being done with respect to the programming process.

Before I call Dr. Wendell Allen, I'm going to call a five-minute recess.

(At 11:35 a five-minute recess was declared.)

THE CHAIRMAN: These hearings are in session. Tell those in the hall that the hearings are in session.

Before I call Dr. Allen, I've been asked to have read into the record the statement from the Commissioner of Education of the New York State Education Department, and I believe we ought to read that early into the record inasmuch as we shall be hearing today from several other states.

I'm going to ask Commissioner Gilbert Colgate to read the statement from Dr. Ewald B. Nyquist, New York State Commissioner of Education.

Commissioner Colgate.

COMMR. COLGATE: Thank you.

I'll start by reading the covering letter addressed to the Commision from Dr. Nyquist dated Thursday, January 28th.

"The University of the State of New York
The State Education Department
Office of the President of the University
and Commissioner of Education
Albany, New York 12224.

"Thursday, January 28, 1971

"Mr. Preston David
Executive Director
Commission on Human Rights
80 Lafayette Street
New York, New York 10013.

"Dear Mr. David:

"I very much appreciate your invitation on behalf of Eleanor Holmes Norton, Chairman of the Commission on Human Rights, to participate in your hearings on employment and promotion practices in the New York City public schools.

"As I have indicated by telephone, I cannot appear in New York on January 29th. I appreciate the opportunity to submit the statement that is attached. Should the Commission members have any questions regarding that statement, please send them to me and I shall be pleased to respond.

"The problems of recruitment, selection, appointment and promotion of educational personnel throughout the State continues to be of tremendous importance. We share your concern with the effects of these practices on the employment and promotion of persons in minority groups. We will appreciate receiving any reports and recommendations that result from your hearings.

"Faithfully yours,
"Ewald B. Nyquist"

The statement of Mr. Nyquist, Commissioner of Education, State Education Department, is as follows:

"Madam Chairman and Members of the New York City Commission on Human Rights:

"I appreciate your invitation to participate in your hearings on employment and promotion practices in the New York City public schools. I regret that I cannot be in New York City on January 29 and am grateful for the opportunity to submit a statement, even though I could not be present. Should any Commission members have questions regarding the statement, I hope that they can be transmitted to me for response.

"The problems of recruitment, selection, appointment and promotion of educational personnel throughout the State of New York are of vital interest to us. We share your concern for the effects of these practices on the employment and promotion of persons in minority groups. In the letter from your Executive Director, Preston David, inviting my participation in the hearings, Mr. David indicated that you would be examining current methods and alternative models of recruitment, selection, appointment and promotion. I believe that I can be of most help to the Commission by commenting on our statewide interests in these matters. I have divided my remarks into two parts. First, I should like to comment about proposed changes in the process of teacher certification. Second, I should like to comment about some projects we have sponsored in the recruitment, promotion, and certification of educational personnel in minority groups.

"Change in Certification

"I look for radical changes in the certification of teachers. The present system is archaic and really does not tell us much about the prospective competence of teachers. The completion of degrees and of a collection of courses does not fully inform us about a teacher, only that he is not intellectually inadequate and that he has some presumed interest in teaching. Future certification will undoubtedly depend on performance over a period of time, with tenure not granted until that performance is adjudged to be competent. I look, too, to the profession itself to be involved in the professional licensing of teachers, such as is now the case for all other professions.

"We are not alone in this criticism of the present system but we also have a responsibility to assume a measure of leadership to ascertain whether other alternatives can be developed.

"Certification today is an inadequate device to protect the public against incompetent teachers in the classroom. Few states, higher institutions, or professional associations are actively involved in developing viable alternatives to today's state certification pattern; however, all are quick to condemn the present practices.

"There are two basic criticisms of certification as we now know it. First of all, judging fitness for licensure is based on input--courses taken--rather than on output--classroom performance. Second, the decision about certification is made by agents far removed from the candidate for licensure himself. The decision should be made, using a State approved process, by persons much closer to the candidate.

"There are compelling reasons to seek changes in certification today, including the move to differentiated roles for school personnel, rapid developments in instructional technology and restructuring of long-standard curriculums.

"The State should be concerned with attracting people into teaching more than it is concerned, through certification, with keeping people out.

"Both the schools and the colleges can be developed as agents for more relevant licensure action. The college would recommend for initial certification at an entry. The school would recommend for final certification action based on an analysis of demonstrated performance. The State's role would be to help develop the new pattern for certification, and make possible the development of approved processes through which performance is judged for certification purposes. The State would grant approval both to schools and colleges to carry out their roles. The State would serve as the central record-keeping agency and furnish summary reports on teaching personnel for employees and for colleges seeking advice about new or expanding areas of need in teacher preparation.

"Development of the system(s), and their implementation

will permit the State to more adequately meet the public demand for some assurance of competency in those employed in the public schools. The process of gaining acceptance of the need to move away from the present basis is well underway. It is now essential that some further study be commenced and some pilot attempts be supported with the necessary research components.

"We are asking the Governor and the State Legislature to provide funds for the development of alternative certification processes. The requested funds would permit the initiation of some cooperative ventures between school districts and higher institutions in designing and implementing systems of appraising the performance of educational personnel.

"We place high value on change of the State certification system so that it is based more on performance than completion of a college degree and a certain number of specified courses. Such a certification system would be, of course, statewide. The focus would be on what the teacher accomplishes in the classroom rather than on his own paper and pencil testing. We believe that such a system would be more sensitive to assuring that the best qualified personnel, whether of minority groups or of the majority, are in education.

These statements about the present State certification system do not contradict my known views about the inadequacies of the certification system now in effect in New York City under the aegis of the Board of Examiners. The Board should be abolished and State certification substituted which, even with its own present inadequacies, offers more desirable flexibility and freedom to select competent teachers. Eventually, we shall have an improved overall State system.

"Projects to Promote Recruitment, Certification and Promotion

"Soon after Mr. Conant's book The Education of American Teachers (1963) was published, the Education Department instituted a program in five New York State higher institutions. This program freed the institutions from any regulations which might serve to restrict them in the design and implementation of programs in teacher education based on an all-university effort.

"While that three-year project may not be adjudged to have been a complete success, it did highlight some very significant needs for the improvement of teacher education. One of the findings was indication that the existence of specific requirements for certification served to inhibit creative program development.

"Since that study, the Department has been working to identify one or more systems of administering teacher education and certification in more appropriate ways.

"Proficiency Exams--One aspect of providing a measure of credit for certification purposes is the policy of accepting the satisfactory completion of a college proficiency examination in lieu of specific collegiate study. Since January 1970, almost 600 (579) examinations in Spanish have been given. A majority of the persons taking this examination have been from New York City. It is possible through this examination to satisfy all the language requirements for certification as well as part of the education requirements.

"The College Proficiency Examination Program office in the Department has recently completed an agreement with New York City which will tie the proficiency examinations to some of the City's in-service courses.

"Veteran Recruitment--Other Department activities are related to the issue. State funds have been made available for programs to help returning veterans prepare for public school service.

"Two programs, in New York City and in Buffalo, presently prepare veterans for professional roles in education. Both are directed specifically to the needs of minority group members. In both programs, veterans are recruited broadly, but with attention focused on residents of the model cities areas. The programs are carefully coordinated, supervised, and directed to the following broad objectives.

"a. Black and Puerto Rican veterans are recruited for teacher training through the career ladder concept to serve in ghetto schools;

"b. students are counseled individually to gain maximum educational advantage from work experience in the schools as paraprofessionals, while coordinating this effort with course work in cooperating universities and colleges;

"c. students are counseled individually in order to fully utilize services available through the G.I. Bill, and to receive such remedial services as are needed.

"In New York City, supervision, guidance and coordination are provided by the Office of Personnel of the Board of Education. Academic work is provided through various colleges and universities, with work experience provided through public schools in the Model Cities area.

"Urban Teacher Corps--During 1969-70 and 1970-71 the Department's Urban Teacher Corps program has sponsored several programs in New York City. These programs have had as their objective the preparation of teachers and/or paraprofessionals for the schools, or the in-service education of teachers and/or the in-service education of teachers and/or paraprofessionals to aid them to increase their competencies. During the two-year period more than eight thousand (8929) staff members have participated in these programs. Some of the programs were operated by the Board of Education and others were operated through various higher institutions in the city.

"Training Minority Group Administrators--In 1967 the New York State Education Department received Ford Foundation grants totalling $528,000 for the purpose of conducting a three-year program to provide training for 60 minority group members, serving in teaching positions in New York City public schools, to assist them in moving into administrative positions. The activities included academic training at Fordham University followed by an administrative internship in a New York City public school.

"The participants were divided into three groups. Each group of trainees spent a semester as full-time students at Fordham where they participated in specially designed classes in administration. This semester was followed by the internship where the trainee assumed administrative responsibilities in a public school under the supervision of the regular administrative staff and the Fordham University faculty members who were involved in the training during the academic semester.

"To date, all of the trainees have assumed and are maintaining administrative positions in the New York City public schools.

"I have briefly indicated statewide concerns for problems of recruitment, training, selection and promotion of educational personnel. We are constantly concerned with our responsibilities for improving these practices and to be assured that there is no discrimination in the application of these practices. In carrying out these responsibilities, we will be pleased to receive any reports and recommendations that result from your hearings. Thank you."

And on my own behalf, thank you, Dr. Nyquist.

THE CHAIRMAN: Thank you, Commissioner Colgate, for reading Dr. Nyquist's statement.

Counsel will prepare any questions based on that statement and we will mail such questions to Dr. Nyquist and later read them into the record after the close of these formal open hearings. And in time for our preliminary report and our final report.

Having heard the views of the Commissioner of Education for the State of New York, we are going to hear from other states as we've already heard from New Jersey, so that we might have some basis for judging our system in the context of others from diverse sections around the country.

To that end, we are particularly fortunate to have Dr. Wendell Allen, who has come all the way from the State of Washington. He is Assistant Superintendent, Division of Teacher Education and Certification, Washington State Education Department.

DR. ALLEN: Madam Chairman, members of the committee, on several occasions this morning, your counsel has inquired about the length of time necessary to move in some of the directions discussed toward performance-based certification. We began in the early part of the sixties--but have been actually engaged in the process of trying to change teacher preparation, statewide, since 1965. We adopted standards in 1968 for one part of our certification or preparation, namely, for what are sometimes called support personnel, people such as counselors. The material that has been given to each of you, dated January 14th, represents a revision, the latest revision of those standards which we are hopeful will go before the State Board of Education this coming June. It will revise those earlier standards for support personnel and will establish them for teacher and administrator preparation.

We are really engaged in a statewide attempt to reform teacher education. We're interested in this primarily as a first step toward changing education in the schools. Throughout all of our discussions it has gradually developed that there are four interlocking ideas in back of this approach to state standards.

One of these is that preparation of school personnel should be based and developed from performance expectations for those personnel in the schools. The second one is the view that preparation should be individualized. Thirdly, that preparation should be viewed as career long and developmental. The fourth idea is that there should be direct responsible involvement and in our case we've chosen three agencies which are closely concerned with the educational program, its operation and so on, namely, the professional associations of school personnel, the school organizations, and the colleges and universities which have in the formal sense had the sole legal responsibility for preparation of personnel.

The actual responsibility for the development of the substantive standards is delegated to these three agencies that I mentioned. At the state level the standards do not include any specific substantive standards regarding degree, or number of courses or emphasis. What the state then is concerned with, as this develops, is the working relationships, involvement and maintenance of equity among these three agencies working together to determine the standards that are to be applied. These programs are, of course, subject to the approval of the state and to state monitoring, and certification comes through recommendation from the consortiums that are developed after a person gets through various stages of preparation.

In our case there the certification structure involves a preparatory certificate, an initial certificate and a continuing certificate. The underlying idea is that throughout the career of the person in the schools, these three agencies will be involved.

I think in a few minutes we might turn to the criteria for state approval but I want to make several more comments.

First of all, we think of teacher preparation as a developing thing. As a person becoming. We don't start with assessment. Assessment, the process of determining competence, comes first of all, as we envision it, out of these three agencies making determinations at a given point in time of the roles in the school, the teacher roles, the administration roles, the support personnel roles. From a particular program they need to reach agreement on what are the competencies for this particular role. From that has to be developed the learning experiences that seem appropriate for preparation for that role.

One of the things that becomes apparent as you study these standards is that they are not statewide in the sense of uniform performance expectations for a particular role statewide. As we envision this, there can be any combination of colleges, universities, school organizations and professional associations working together to prepare personnel well for a particular school system. Performance expectations should be based on the needs of the students in this particular situation. This can become very complex. Part of what we're engaged in now is working out the bases for implementation.

The idea of an open system requires, too, that you literally do not have any across-the-board standards, such as that everyone must have so many years of experience in order to move to this or everyone must have a certain kind of degree. Eliminating this doesn't mean that the college courses or the degrees themselves are not important and desirable but rather that they are not the basis from which you start to develop a standard.

So, in Washington we are attempting to change our whole approach, to being concerned with the relationships, to realizing that a program has to be developed on performance expectations and that it must be individualized, to being concerned then with the agencies in the state who are directly involved in this whole process that they themselves perform well.

This requires a very thorough-going approach. It envisages the use of all sorts of techniques, including testing as far as that is concerned, but not as generally thought of as a single process.

Now, I want to emphasize that we see this system as it develops as one that has change built into it. One of the criticisms of standards generally as they exist today is that they are set up on a substantive basis at the state level, and based essentially on college courses plus some internship or laboratory experiences. And then they are only changed as state standards are changed (even in cases like ours where our present state standards give colleges a lot of leeway in their programming). The pressures toward uniformity, toward consequential programs that everyone takes are very great, so what we're engaged in in part, you see, is breaking through this tendency to think that preparation should be the same for everyone. We're setting up a process so it can be genuinely individualized and there can be varieties of learning experiences and there can be input from the individual and he is a key person in deciding first what he's going to go for, as it were, and in self-evaluation along with experience. One of the real problems of this is working out this business of how professional associations and school administrations and colleges can work together. It means changing roles of people. That is one of the traumas that we're going through.

We have a number of projects. We have a lot going on that is very good in experimenting with this. But it is a fundamental change in the whole approach to preparation and the state's role in connection with it.

Just to illustrate, in our January 14th statement, on the fourth page of the Criteria For Approval Of Preparation Programs we say, regarding the state approval of the programs, "Criteria re: the development of preparation opportunities and alternatives. The consortium shall:

"a. describe the role or roles which are to be assumed by the person who is to be issued a specific certificate;

"b. describe the competencies (knowledges, attitudes, skills, etc.) required of persons who plan to perform the described roles;

"c. describe examples of the kinds of experiences that will be provided to assist each candidate develop or demonstrate the required levels of competencies;

"d. describe the procedures which ensure that each

candidate participates in the design of his own program and the procedures which enable the candidate to achieve certification at his own rate of demonstrable accomplishments;

"e. specify examples of kinds of evidence that will be used to determine acceptable entry and exit levels of competence of the candidate; including, as appropriate, evidence of competence when working with clients;

"f. describe examples of procedures which will be used to provide positive, growth-providing feedback to the candidate and to the program;

"g. describe the procedures and arrangements which ensure continuing career development opportunities for persons holding initial and continuing certificates."

In addition to those kinds of criteria, there are criteria for the consortium with respect to their collaboration arrangements, and I'll run through this quickly.

The State Board will approve any program of preparation that meets the following criteria:

a. With respect to collaboration arrangements, the preparation program is developed and offered by a consortium of designated agencies, one or more colleges, universities, one or more school organizations, and one or more professional associations.

b. The consortium will specify the arrangements and processes it will use to formulate policy, develop program objectives, elements and characteristics; to gain input and involvement of students and citizens in model development; to implement the programs, administer the program, including monitoring candidate progress, reporting and recommending certifications and so forth; and to conduct program review and evaluation. Or, they may specify all of this in their plan in advance before the program is approved.

c. The consortium will give evidence also that it has the human and material resources to conduct and implement the preparation program.

I think from this kind of a brief description you can see that this sort of shift is something that takes time. What we plan to do and are doing, as a matter of fact, is that when these actions are taken, hopefully by next June, for completing the adoption, for application to all school personnel, we will continue with our present standards for a period of time, so that these standard programs will develop gradually as the resources are available, and so they aren't done on a token basis, now.

I haven't gone very far into the reasons for this. I mentioned uniformity of programs and the tendency to think of preparation as being the same for everybody. Also, many have been concerned that adults set the school climate. Yet if you think of schools as helping people to become, than the preparation of teachers should be the same kind of preparation that we're trying to work toward for children. We have to create the kind of climate that will permit schools to stimulate growth in teachers as well as children.

THE CHAIRMAN: Thank you, Dr. Allen.

MR. TRACTENBERG: Dr. Allen, could you briefly state your views as to why it has taken so long to implement this kind of program of performance-based certification? Obviously, this is a complex area, but if you could give us some reactions it would be helpful.

DR. ALLEN: Well, of course. I suppose what I have been saying here is more in relation to our particular process. But there is an absolute need for a climate of trust here. As I see it, the development of this, and of thinking of this process in terms of preparation rather than evaluation, are critical. Evaluation has to be regarded as feedback to the person to help him improve. All of the available resources must be brought to bear to help the individual and to relate the objectives in the teaching situation to his performance. This is going to call for a lot more joint participation of those involved--the individual, his peers, the school administration--in bringing technical knowledge to bear on the thing. This is a complex cooperative effort which the human element enters into. There must be an attempt to really develop cooperative working relationships. That makes it time consuming. Obviously any kind of a statewide testing program, although it can contribute a narrow element, can't really serve this broad purpose.

Everybody subscribes rather readily to these ideas that it should be performance-based and it should be individualized and career long but when you get to the implementation level the state has to be concerned with process and the working relationships to the people who do have the expertise and are close to the scene to work it out. And I don't think we're going to find any quick answer on this because it is a human thing. It is learning, it is a state of knowledge, and it is complex and it has to relate to values and so on, and all of these things come into the picture.

That's a long answer to a short question.

MR. TRACTENBERG: Do you think though that once states like your own, state education departments like your own, have gone through a lot of this pioneering work in revising the fundamental basis for state certification, that it will become somewhat easier and somewhat more quickly done by other states?

DR. ALLEN: Yes. Although they are not necessarily models that can be used intact I think that is true.

MR. TRACTENBERG: Under your performance-based system, what kind of role does the local school district play in terms of recruiting and ultimately selecting and appointing teachers and supervisors?

DR. ALLEN: As I've tried to make clear what I've been talking about directly has been concerned with preparation. But it sets up a frame of reference wherein this local school district, the local professional association, and the colleges which are cooperating with them are working together. And this carries with it, as Dr. Edelfeldt I think has suggested earlier, the necessity for these things to interlock. That is the personnel policies, the relationships, the actual selection of people, their assignment in the working situation where they can be productive and where they can be helped to grow.

We're concerned at the state level, of course, with state certification. Dr. Edelfeldt said he thought these improvements in personnel policies were so essential and should involve such a close relationship among the faculties, professional associations, and school districts that it will most likely be dealt with on a negotiation basis, and I think this is just the way it is going to be. Has to be.

MR. TRACTENBERG: I would assume though, if I understand your remarks correctly, that to have a performance-based certification process would not be consistent with having the kind of selection process that exists in New York City, for example. To certify people on a performance basis, on the basis of how well they can teach and have demonstrated their ability to teach, is not consistent with subjecting them to the kind of written examination approach that New York City now has.

Would that in your judgment be inconsistent and perhaps tend to defeat the purpose of performance-based criteria on the state level?

DR. ALLEN: I would be inclined to think so. It would hardly fit into the kind of dynamic development, that I've been discussing. We don't anticipate in our state system any uniform criteria. I want to comment on that a little bit because it might be misunderstood.

What we have been working on at the state level, and it is essentially informal, is various committees like committees of the Association of Counselors involving school and college people. They've given careful consideration to the role of counselors, and using national reference points to the work of the American Personnel Guidance Association and Counselors' Association they've come up with a definition of role, and with broad statements of competencies.

Now, these are reference points that are supposed to be helpful, that are intended to be helpful to groups working on actual preparation programs from which learning experiences and performance tasks and so on are developed. These are applied individually to people, with a focus on a particular role, in places like Seattle, for example. And there are people who say, "Well, my, isn't this terrible." There is no uniformity across the state, you see. What if this person moves from Seattle to Spokane. He has had a program that is tailormade to go into the central city of Seattle.

While there are differences in his preparation, I think the common elements, if you look at different teaching fields, different supporting role and different administrative positions, tend to be strong. So when you come to the point where you're talking about employment of someone who has been working in a particular school in Seattle and he or she decides to move to Spokane, Spokane has its own consortium and arrangement of people working in preparation over there, and the Spokane school district is involved in this. And this person will have state certification all right. He has gone through and is in a program of continuing development in Seattle. Spokane will be able to apply its particular local standards and needs essentially the way it does now in determining whether the person goes in there. So this aspect of it, the lack of uniformity in a detailed sense that can be applied in a given test, does not concern us. It is partly for this reason that I wouldn't advocate a statewide examination, although you might have a very good test which would cover certain aspects of the knowledge required.

I'm sorry I take so long to answer each of these questions.

MR. TRACTENBERG: That's all right.

Do you see any reason why the kind of system that you've described for Washington, and its urban areas like Seattle, would not be workable in a system as large as New York City? That is, could a system this size, even though it is broken into 31 separate community districts, respond reasonably to the kind of individualized performance-based criteria you've described?

DR. ALLEN: I don't see any reason why it couldn't. I would regard the 31 community districts as an advantage rather than a disadvantage in this process. This does not mean to imply in any sense that it would be an easy task.

MR. TRACTENBERG: But you think it is workable?

DR. ALLEN: Yes.

MR TRACTENBERG: Is there or has there ever been seriously considered any statewide written examination in Washington, either as a part of performance-based certification or as an alternative to it?

DR. ALLEN: No. We've had some examinations in the past for a particular little segment that have been in a requirement and we no longer have them, but, not on any broad basis such as that.

MR. TRACTENBERG: Has the development of reliable techniques for observations of performance caused you any problems? Do you have such techniques now, at least through your guidance counselor and related categories?

DR. ALLEN: Well, not generally, except there has been some good work done in our state and elsewhere, and there can be reliable and valid observation of specific functions. Of course, one of the things that I haven't stressed here, is this matter of getting at objectives and being specific and synthesizing. We have to move this way. I believe the marshalling of these resources will in due course lift our whole level of thoroughness, objectivity and helpfulness to the individual to a considerably higher level so that we can utilize the technology and the resources that we now have. And I don't think it is insurmountable. It is complex, it is difficult. I think we all, and perhaps the public generally, have been too prone to think we can solve these problems by some kind of panacea like some laying on of hands or some test that is going to pick out the competent as compared with the incompetent teacher.

We're finding out and have found out the hard way in our schools, and in teacher preparation, that this isn't the way to do it.

MR. TRACTENBERG: In moving away from the traditional uniform bases for certification, and in New York City licensure, toward performance, toward diversity of background, do you anticipate any problems of the kind that earlier witnesses have mentioned; that is, are you going to run into people who are incompetent, illiterate, somehow unsafe to put in classrooms with children?

DR. ALLEN: The development of definitions of roles and competencies and the appropriate learning experiences and so on, is necessary. All of these kinds of decisions have to be made. As I see it, this is not going to be easy, but requires many people to work together. It is going to be possible to make these determinations and it will literally be true in due course that persons with a variety of backgrounds, perhaps quite a range of experience and background, much of it possibly informal rather than in formal education, may be able to qualify in a short time, and others may have to take longer than they take under present programs to reach the criteria level of actual performance.

So the answer to the question boils down to why we are putting our stress on these criteria, the integrity of these working relationships and monitoring and moving slowly into it, because there are always going to be these charges or concerns about equity. As we've talked about this around the state one of the first questions a teacher will ask is, "Who is going to evaluate me?" We have to say, "Well, we can't say who is going to evaluate you. You're going to evaluate yourself, but there is going to be an arrangement worked out so that the decision will be made by a group working on your program." But we're recognizing the fact in dealing with the human condition and process, and we've already found through our experience, that setting up these spurious uniform standards doesn't do away with anything you're talking about.

MR. TRACTENBERG: So, presumably, if we try to bring it back to at least one facet of the New York City experience it might well be possible under the Washington certification procedure, as you've outlined them, for a paraprofessional who has worked in a classroom for four or five years, and has met performance standards to be state certified, even perhaps if he or she has no college degree or no requisite number of educational courses?

DR. ALLEN: That's right.

MR. TRACTENBERG: That's all.

THE CHAIRMAN: Dr. Allen, I wonder if you can tell me based on your experience in the State of Washington, using your present system and the system you're moving toward, whether or not teacher selection in your state has been affected by corruption or favoritism of any kind. There has been some concern on the part of people outside of New York City who do not know terribly much about safeguards in other states, but know only that local school boards in most states choose teachers, that leaving that decision to local school boards may result in some form of corruption or favoritism, even racism.

I wonder if in your experience any of these problems has been encountered and if so, how they have been dealt with.

DR. ALLEN: No. Not on anything like the scale that seems to be implied in your question.

THE CHAIRMAN: Do you find on the whole, then, that people

sitting on local school boards are as vigilant against corruption and other forms of favoritism as civil servants might be if they were in charge of those schools or others on a statewide or citywide level would be? Is there sufficient concern, in other words, on the part of parents to offer a deterrent to corruption, favoritism, racism and the like?

DR. ALLEN: Yes. I would agree with that. I think part of the picture is the need for a strong professional watchdog of the professional people themselves in our association.

My own view is that there has been too much tendency on the part of professional associations to be just that, instead of getting involved in the actual process of supporting and participating in sound personnel policies. I think at this stage it is still true in our country, that we need state certification. In our particular state, we have not a traditional tenure bill but a continuing contract sort of thing that requires due process for dismissal, for example. It is not unrelated to this.

There are some things sort of interrelated here, such as building up a favorable climate based on state and local standards and leadership. I think we're moving into a period of much broader participation by the community in these matters, but I don't regard that as a threat to the development of improved preparation and improved school boards.

THE CHAIRMAN: Dr. Allen, I want to thank you very much for coming here all the way from the State of Washington.

DR. ALLEN: I'm happy to have come, and these experiences always are helpful to us, too.

THE CHAIRMAN: I see you've traveled all the way across the country and it was important for us to hear from a state which is in the forefront in this area.

Thank you very much.

We are next going to be calling a witness from the State of Minnesota. We've tried to get representatives from a variety of states, which are working on these matters of evaluation. Most use certification alone. And the listening public may be interested to know that we, in deciding which states to invite, could only canvas as many states as possible to see what was being done in order to have some basis to compare our own situation with. Many states, of course, that we looked to were not doing anything new in this regard and were simply relying on existing state certification. So we have invited states that have either thought about new approaches or are working on them and there will be some more of them this afternoon, after lunch.

I would like to introduce at this time Dr. Pat Goralski, Director, Professions Development Center, Minnesota State Education Department.

DR. GORALSKI: Thank you, Madam Chairman, members of the Commission and others in the audience.

I am very pleased to have a chance to come here today to talk with you about some of the things that we're doing in Minnesota, some of the things we're trying to do and even more important, some of the things that we're thinking about. I think that we are just beginning to make some real strides. I believe that in order to put this into some kind of context, I should tell you a bit about where we're coming from.

Minnesota has long had what is called the program approval approach to teacher education. This means that the State Department of Education and my office in particular, the Professions Development Section, is responsible for looking at colleges and approving the college for teacher education, in much the same way as an accreditation visit. We also will look at specific programs that lead to certification.

We also work a great deal of the time with task forces and advisory committees which are made up of all segments of the teaching profession, the education professions and I think you'll be pleased to know that of recent years, we're starting to include members of the community in these kinds of meetings, because we feel that somehow or other their concerns for children are even greater than ours, and ours are very great indeed. So a great deal of our work in these task forces and communities is in giving voice to the State Board of Education. And the State Board of Education is a lay body. It does look to all the professional associations for voice, and I believe there is a great deal of evidence that the voice has been taken and followed for the most part. When our Board has questions, they're usually very penetrating kinds of questions and an accommodation is reached.

I've been in this job for two and a half years and I believe that we haven't had a standoff in all that time, that the Board and the education professions have been moving forward very well together. We then have a situation where programs are approved for the colleges by the state. Then when a student moves through this program in the college, the college recommends him or her to our certification officer. He is an administrative type of person and he's not in my office. He will then issue certificates based on the recommendation of the college that the person has completed an approved program to become a teacher or a counselor, and little by little we're beginning to call these people education personnel. Because in the State of Minnesota, we have a very important new adjunct to the education professions, an adjunct isn't a very good word. We have large numbers of paraprofessionals. We have 800 teacher aides in the City of Minneapolis alone. They have been serving very, very well since the beginning of the Title I programs. They were so successful during the first year or two, that Minneapolis even put hard money into it. That means local tax money in order to hire more teacher aides because the schools that were not able to get Title I money were very impressed with the kinds of services we were able to put into the Title I school district, and they did ask that there be some local money so that teacher aides could be added to the schools out of the inner-city area that was eligible for Title I.

We have large numbers of teacher aides in the City of Duluth and large numbers of them in the City of St. Paul. These are our cities of the first class. Throughout Minnesota, educators have been very impressed with the work that has been done by our paraprofessions and we have a large and growing program of teacher aides, both those who are paid by local systems and those who are volunteers working in the schools.

One of the kinds of things, of course, that people have asked us is what are we going to do to certificate these people and it is a very tough question, because if we move this way too fast there could be a danger of structuring people into very small boxes. This we wanted to avoid at all costs, and we felt that we needed to mature a little bit, as far as differentiating staff and seeing the kinds of things that aides could do. I think it is a very good thing that we did. Because we have long since left behind us the stage where teacher aides are only working as clerical assistants, and taking kids out to the playgrounds and these kinds of things. They are doing instructional tasks under the supervision of our certificated personnel.

I think that the statement that I forwarded to you earlier, and I have another copy with me if you don't have it, will pretty well define the area within which teacher aides work. In Minnesota it is almost anything that they can do with supervision from a teacher or someone who is certificated and this is a very wide latitude that we have.

Perhaps I should describe a bit about what we're trying to do to open our system in Minnesota, and it is a very open system anyway, but we want to open it still farther before we start to think in terms of a paraprofessional-professional situation. Incidentally, I'm convinced that those terms are going to drop out of use. I don't think they're going to have meaning for very much longer, at least I hope they don't.

One of the things that we're doing is trying to move to a system where we have only two kinds of certificates, by functions of course, teacher, counselor, principal. But as far as any gradings of certificate there will be an entrance certificate, and this has not been taken care of yet as far as moving through the State Board of Education, but we're thinking in terms of probably a two-year period on that for people who are new in any function in Minnesota. Thus, it could apply to a teacher who is experienced coming from another state. It could also apply to a teacher who has worked for a long time successfully in Minnesota who then wants to change functions and become a principal or a counselor.

Anyone, as he begins a function working in our schools, would have an entrance certificate for that particular role or function.

Now here again, this is our thinking. We're also thinking that there will be a continuing certificate, because we do not believe that anyone who works in education ever has his education completed. You are always in the process of growth and becoming and changing and accommodating to whatever is around you and trying to do a better job for the kids that you're serving. So the continuing certificate will very likely run for a five-year period.

We have had a task force very hard at work during the past year developing a continuing education proposal which is very interesting indeed. It has not come to our State Board of Education because we've had a political change in the State of Minnesota, and our Board is in flux right now. We have to wait until our new Board is there and bring this before them. But it is ready to be given to them for their consideration. Here there would be a state committee and a local committee in every school district and there are ways that larger districts can subdivide and smaller ones can combine to take care of the administrative business, but the important thing is that this committee is going to look at things that people do for certificate renewal. And on this committee there will be a member of the community as well as the various segments of the professional group in this continuing local situation. The same kind of thing will be true of the state committee which will hear appeals.

It will be these local committees, eventually, and the state committee or whatever structure is finally adopted which will begin to look with us at the local level, the state committee to provide some state coordination, to move toward performance standards that are meaningful. But, you see, the local committee will give us some way of working at the local level so that whatever is done is going to be appropriate for those kids in that community and for the parents who are sending their youngsters to the school.

So we have high hopes. This is a different kind of approach. I do not believe there are other approaches that have community representation. And over and over again, you'll be interested, on the task force professional people said they wanted that community person there to keep us all honest, to make sure that there could be input all the way as far as the qualifications of educational personnel who are working with youngsters from the community.

So we have high hopes for something that will be adopted such as this continuing education regulation. We're not sure that it will go through in the form that it is being recommended but something must go through because life certification was discontinued by our last legislature. This means that we have a void in our certification process which does give us a little bit of impetus to get something adopted and to get something that is workable.

So we think that as this begins that we're going to have a situation where there will be a place in this whole structure for people to work into the education professions, for them to work in one part of it, for them to move in a career ladder vertically, for them to move in a career ladder horizontally.

For instance, if someone started as a social worker aide in the City of Minneapolis, and was doing home visits with parents and so on, but as she works in the school and works with these people, she decided that she'd really rather be a classroom person or a counselor or something like this, then she would probably make a horizontal move to a teacher aide, and then begin a vertical move to full accreditation as a teacher.

Now we have another theory that comes in here. My job is to try to see that there are programs developed so that people can be trained to give the best possible service to the kids in the State of Minnesota. This is my fundamental role, and I have to assume that if people are criticizing colleges or if they're criticizing communities or whatever, that these people are doing the best they can.

What we need if we want to do something different is to get together with more people and say, "We all need more training. We all need a little more expertise in this area." And this is the way that we're trying to move in Minnesota. We're trying as best we can to set in motion kinds of devices that will open up relationships between colleges and the community. Our new human relations regulations, which I fully expect to be passed because I don't think that it is going to have any real opposition, require that any college that purports to train teachers for a community must have members of that community come in and talk with them at the college and become satisfied with whatever that college is doing about human relations in its program for training teachers. This results from having many people in our communities say, "We don't want any more teachers like certain ones who happen to be in our community. These people are not good for our kids." So at the state level, we're trying very hard to set in motion the sorts of machinery that will require that people interact with each other, thereby educating each other, thereby facilitating the kinds of changes that everyone in the state wants to see made.

This is the process that we're in. It is time consuming. But we are moving our regulations in this direction. Our new regulations all say that the college is to relate all of the areas of competency enumerated in the regulation to components in the college program. And then it is supposed to show how it is going to go about developing these competencies in people and how it plans to evaluate them.

Now, this is, I would say, a transitional kind of regulation. Our human relations regulation has the same kind of language in it. In other words, these are the things you want that the community and profession want you to do in training teachers. Whether it is media people or all teachers for human relations. Tell us where in your program you're going to do this, show us how you're going to evaluate it and then let's work together and keep an eye on this thing and see whether it was really done. As we evolve we may take two more generations of regulations before we come to one that is what a performance standard regulation would look like. At the same time, now that we're building this kind of capability into our colleges, you see this is an educative process and as people work together, both sides are going to learn a lot, we're also starting to work with people on another aspect. For if we go to performance standards and we're going to measure performance standards, we hypothesized that unless people have the capability to evaluate themselves, and engage in a rather sophisticated manner in talking about the evaluation of their performance with the evaluators or management or however you look upon the school board and the administration, that this thing is bound to fail because everyone will become extremely insecure. When people are threatened, they don't perform well and we could really set ourselves back instead of moving forward.

So one of the things we're also setting in motion is some kind of situation where people can work together, developing their expertise in self-analysis, and cooperative or mutual self-appraisal. It will require working closely with community people to have them say what is it they want for their kids, and how we set about doing this, and how we know when we've done it.

Last week we were in Tucson where we took the two directors of our Career Opportunities Programs from Minneapolis and Duluth. St. Paul wasn't lucky enough to get such a program so we took their staff development person with us, too. The workshop was to train participants in various means of self-appraisal so that they can become more effective in working in their school districts so that this whole business of performance standards is not the threat that it could very well be. We're all a little bit threatened by things like this.

I guess there is one more thing that I need to stress again. I alluded to it but I don't think I hit it head-on as much as I would like to. We hypothesized that whoever works with our kids should be excellent in that particular function or role. If you follow that through then the role of what is now a paraprofessional, as compared with a professional, is different from what I think most of us have grown up with. The distinction then between a professional and paraprofessional would become the range of the functions not how good you were at them, because you would be at satisfactory performance level with whatever you were doing professionally or paraprofessionally. This is why I think those two terms will drop away pretty soon, because I think the terms will become dysfunctional. So we would see that as someone moves from a beginning job, where there are probably two or three different functions that they were very good at, to a more advanced job what they would keep doing is increasing the range of the kinds of things that they could do until they have enough skills on a broad enough range so that they can engage in the kinds of decision-making about the education of youngsters that we have tended to think of as a professional function. And so I if I were to make a guess about what future certification might be like, I think it will change quite drastically.

I believe that we will make some kind of beginning where the certificate will be a cross between a record of training and a record of work experience, and it will start showing the competencies of the person that have been developed either through work or work experience, or through training and it will probably also be a combination of both and then move on, increasing the range of the things that the person is able to do. This is differentiated staffing. And it will no longer then be paraprofessional or professional. It will be, what is this particular person qualified to do and how do we know that he can do it at a satisfactory level.

How we come to the problem in performance standards, identifying the critical kinds of performance that are necessary to deliver to the kids the services that we in our community decide they ought to have. That is our number one problem, and we must say these things with enough precision because we've been very unprecise in our language in education. It is no wonder we're under attack. We must be precise enough in our statements as to what this is all about so that any one of us can watch any one of us perform with youngsters and say, either that person can do or can't do and if he isn't doing, I think the assumption is he needs more training. We will--and this sounds a little wild but it is true--move out of the time frame. We've had the normal curve distribution in education for many years. One of the things that has kept all of our characteristics distributed on this bell curve that all of us in education have been very enamored about over the years is we held people in a time frame. If we take the time frame out and let people have more chances to learn something, then we're going to have a different kind of a situation from any that we have had in the past. We will stop doing things such as keeping records of people's failures. We will start only caring about what they can do. I think one of the great things about getting out of the formal education is knowing that nobody is keeping a list any more of the things we can't do. We can try them and put them behind us until there is a time when we can do them. And so I think this has many, many ramifications for education, beyond just certification of teachers.

You know, I heard a fellow say one day that schools are pretty mean to kids but they're awful mean to teachers, too, and I think this is probably quite true for many of us. So we're moving ahead, and the last thing we're involved in that I'd like to mention deals with our chance to become nationally involved with one another that will make a pay-off here eventually.

I came on my job two and a half years ago. If I had just been able to stay in Minnesota and not known what Wendell Allen was doing out in the State of Washington and what the people in Texas and other states were doing, it would have been very difficult. But we have our EPA (Educational Professional Act) programs that allow us to take eleven people down to a training session in Florida last May, that are allowing us to say people need to know how to go about self-evaluation so they can't be completely victimized by somebody else coming and saying that you're doing that all wrong, so that they can engage in dialogues with these people, that allow us to take six people from Minnesota to another conference to learn about self-appraisal and so we can have follow-up conferences at home.

These kinds of things are very important and we have several national committees that really should help us to stay in touch. If you people find out some things that will be helpful to us, maybe if we trade information we can make a go of it.

Thank you.

THE CHAIRMAN: Thank you, Dr. Goralski. It is more likely that we'll find out things from you that will be helpful to us.

Mr. Tractenberg.

MR. TRACTENBERG: Dr. Goralski, I want to ask you some things that will sound very familiar and very much like the things I've asked Dr. Wendell Allen, because I think how the two of you, one in relation to the other, view these questions is of great importance to us as we try to move toward some kind of a more rational system here.

Is there in your current or proposed system of certification a place for written examinations?

DR. GORALSKI: No. And the only thing I'd like to say about that is, if you want to know how well someone can write an examination that is a good thing to give them, but if you want to know how they're going to relate to kids, then you really have to watch that person perform. That's why we have that two year--or it may turn out to be three--entrance certificate. It permits us to find out whether that person relates to kids. If it is an American history teacher you could give him an examination to know if he's competent in his field, that is a possibility. But maybe the college can attest to that, too. That is one thing that we have all been very good at in the past, you know.

MR. TRACTENBERG: You have, at least up to this point, relied on the approved colleges to tell you which people are competent in their fields?

DR. GORALSKI: Right. They know them at that point. When they get out into our school districts we'll start to know even more.

MR. TRACTENBERG: What role does the local school district have in this over-all process? Is it your anticipation that the local districts will rely very heavily on your determination of performance ability or will they make their own determination?

DR. GORALSKI: It will have to be made at the local level. We can't possibly have enough state personnel to do something like this, so largely it becomes then an enabling activity from a state level, doing the kinds of things that will enable people at the local level to make better and better judgments. And when we no longer have life certificates, we won't always have to worry about if someone gets through, you're stuck with him forever.

Now we will have some people on life certificates, those issued prior to June 1, 1969, but beyond that point, we will have five year reviews. So we look at it as building people to become ever more competent in their jobs and to be ever more competent in making these judgments. Local school districts could expect to work with people from my office in upgrading in-service education. In-service training has had a bad name because it hasn't been very well done and our colleges are concerned about it, and so are we. So we are making available the kinds of training people need to become truly functional at that level.

In Minnesota, though, whether someone is competent--this is bad language because when you talk about competencies, you're talking about developing a person to become more competent, but you turn that coin over and you come into all our legislation about incompetence--is an administrative, management, State Board, superintendent kind of decision.

If someone is incompetent, that in the last analysis moves back to a management decision. But up to the point where we're trying to work with people to make them more competent, this is the area we're working in.

MR. TRACTENBERG: So if, for example, the New York State Education Department moves in the direction of your State

Education Department, and we've tried to zero in on New York, a largely white community district in New York City and a largely Spanish-speaking district and a largely Black district might well make a very substantial input in terms of evaluating the particular kinds of performance that they valued, and that that would be quite consistent with your state approach?

DR. GORALSKI: Yes. After educational personnel come out from the colleges having completed an approved program, we have to open up some options because we have some silly things going on right now in our COP program (Career Opportunities Program) that we haven't been able to break loose. We think we have one of the best in the country but we have a very hard time getting one of the colleges not to put people who have worked very well as aides right into practice. But we really see the college making the determination. For instance, when a person who wants to teach social studies really has the subject matter background, we're saying that that is an important thing and colleges probably can best figure that one out. However, we're also saying that equally important are many other kinds of skills in working with kids, and I don't think we have any longer to set up this dichotomous situation where the person who has one kind of skill doesn't need another. I think we can have people with all kinds of combinations of skills working with our kids so that they develop better.

MR. TRACTENBERG: Is there any city school district in the State of Minnesota that has any kind of licensure process like New York City?

DR. GORALSKI: No, and that is not envisioned.

MR. TRACTENBERG: You've indicated that your State Legislature did away with life certification. I assume there are some reasons which you could articulate for us about why that was done?

DR. GORALSKI: It is the idea that people working in education are never finished. It is an evolutionary process. It has to remain open. The way we were trained 20 years ago isn't too appropriate now, and we feel that people need some impetus to stay up on top of their professions. Also, there are things such as our human relations regulations that apply to all people and there has to be a vehicle to have this apply. It is very hard to have things that are very important now, that perhaps were always important, but people somehow didn't deal with them. How do we reach the people who have life certificates with things that today we know are so terribly important?

MR. TRACTENBERG: Do I understand you then to say that legislative change resulted from a recommendation of the State Education Department or was this supported by the State Education Department?

DR. GORALSKI: This was supported by the State Education Department certainly and it was also supported by the entire education community, our professional organizations, our colleges, everyone. But our colleges know that they're going to be having a very difficult time servicing all the in-service needs that are coming.

MR. TRACTENBERG: Do you anticipate that new certification procedures and principles will dramatically increase the diversity and backgrounds of teachers and other personnel?

DR. GORALSKI: Yes.

MR. TRACTENBERG: Do you anticipate that it will have some effect on the ethnic composition of the education force? That is, is it likely that there will be more Spanish-speaking and more Black teachers?

DR. GORALSKI: We expect so and we have evidence of that. I'm sorry I didn't bring my statistics but we have recruited as many veterans and members of various ethnic minority groups in Minnesota and we have large numbers of American Indians in Minnesota, too, into our Career Opportunities programs. And we have tripled the programs. We have made a real effort to have these people participate both as members of boards, and as participants in the programs, and I think we've made some progress. At the same time, we have more of those and it should help.

MR. TRACTENBERG: But do you see the new certification approach as having as one of its significant benefits a likely increase in the number of minority group professionals?

DR. GORALSKI: Right. Yes.

MR. TRACTENBERG: That's all.

THE CHAIRMAN: Dr. Goralski, I was intrigued at your description of the Minnesota system as a quite open system already, and as one which you're trying to open even further. I'm going to put the same question to you, therefore, that I put to Dr. Allen, because of the concern that opening up education systems of this kind may lead to corruption, favoritism and racism, that this concern is not altogether unfounded in this city because there was a time, particularly in the thirties, when there was a shortage of jobs, and when there was corruption and there was favoritism in this city, although not racism, as I understand it.

From the viewpoint of a state officer who, I take it, is in touch with various cities large and small around your state, first, have you encountered such practices up until now, and if so, how are you dealing with them; and, secondly, do you anticipate that further opening of your system will result in such practices if you don't take safeguards to ward off such practices?

DR. GORALSKI: I have kind of an old view that if a system is really open the chance for corruption is almost nil. It is by getting some of it blocked off into private little domains of various groups where it really can offer an opportunity for corruption. The major criticism that has been leveled at our system is that it is an administrative monstrosity and that is absolutely correct. It is an administrative monstronsity.

If you are going to make opportunities available to everybody on the most equitable basis you can, and if you're going to try to maintain an open system where everyone has a chance to participate in decision making, you have an administrative monstrosity. It isn't neat. No matter how you go about it, you can't make it neat. You just have to have people trained--and another thing we're trying to do is give our state people some training in what it is like to be under fire all the time.

If we're going to work in an open system, if we're going to have change, the people who are in target positions such as mine and many others in state agencies, and in city agencies and so on, have to be willing to stand out there and take the responsibility for decisions, for getting people to participate with them in decisions, and say this is the best I can do. Now, help me to do better. We can't close up the system and say, "Okay, we'll have another little situation where we'll only let these people in or we'll only let another group in."

But I think the danger is there, and I think it is always there, where you have groups of people and individuals who are vying for power. And I guess if you can do it in New York, we can do it in Minnesota and we'll have to help each other to try to see what we can do to have a truly open system.

THE CHAIRMAN: Well, we haven't done it in New York. Indeed, when you speak about the possibility of it, the danger really is not so much with the open system but from groups getting control over certain parts of it. Could that be interpreted to include, for example, local school boards in some of your communities?

DR. GORALSKI: Yes.

THE CHAIRMAN: And if so, how would you go about keeping such a system from becoming corrupt, from the state's point of view? How would you keep that system from becoming inbred to the point of corruption, let us say, with respect to favoritism or racism of some kind?

DR. GORALSKI: Local school board members in Minnesota are elected. I don't know what your system is here.

THE CHAIRMAN: We have an elected system in the community school boards.

DR. GORALSKI: Now we think that our committees will help. I think it will keep people more vigilant, more involved in things. You know, not vigilant from a negative standpoint of being a watchdog, but vigilant from a standpoint of active participation in the kind of decisions that are relevant to schools. But if our school boards are taken over by people who are of just one group, it either means that that is a total constituency or some of the people who are voting aren't doing their jobs, and we really have to wake them up somehow. Am I answering your question?

THE CHAIRMAN: Would state law become applicable through the State Department of Education if such practices were deep enough to amount to corruption of some kind? Would your department have any responsibility?

DR. GORALSKI: No, this comes through the State Attorney General and that becomes a legal problem. We're an educative body and we make regulations about training teachers and so on.

MR. TRACTENBERG: Considering the openness of your system, I'd be interested to know whether you know of any instances where matters have either been referred to the State Attorney General or where the State Attorney General has had to take action on his own.

DR. GORALSKI: I'm very sorry that my two and a half years

is showing now. I've been so busy working in the area where I have been, that although I'm sure there probably are some cases I don't know about them. The person in our State Department of Education who handles things where legalities start to come up is one of our assistant commissioners in the Division of Administration, and if you would want to direct something to Mr. Farley Bright, I'm sure he would know this immediately, but it is not an area that I'm responsible for.

MR. TRACTENBERG: I may be asking the same thing in a different way. You've presumably, in developing the criteria and beginning to work toward cooperation between local communities and the state in certification, had personal contacts with local school board members and others from local communities. Is there anything based on that experience which raises concerns of the kind Mrs. Norton was talking about in your mind?

DR. GORALSKI: No, I think as a matter of fact the system will provide more effective avenues to influence the system. In other words, to make our whole system, and by that I mean our department, our boards, both local and state, more responsive to the will of the people, rather than less. Because what we're having is a group of people now participating very actively who essentially were silent before. And it seems to me that this is adding to the way our system serves everyone rather than opening a chance for corruption.

Now am I dealing with what you mean?

MR. TRACTENBERG: I think that last comment is particularly pertinent because if many of the statements we've heard suggesting there may be corruption or a spoils system are borne out at all even by charges, they involve people trying to get around a system they allege is not an open system. Thus, for example, there has been the use of acting appointments instead of regular appoointments because they can't find anybody on the eligible lists that met their needs.

DR. GORALSKI: We have people who say they can't find qualified personnel through the system. During the days of teacher shortages, one could get around this by hiring late or something of the sort. But we don't have a shortage of qualified personnel so our policy is no provisional certification of any kind. But this does not apply to paraprofessionals and we're trying to hold this open until we get the system changed enough so that it accommodates to them in a way I described earlier.

We're not there yet and I would want to reiterate that. We've been talking about where we're trying to move.

MR. TRACTENBERG: Of course the situation in New York City is somewhat different.

DR. GORALSKI: You bet.

MR. TRACTENBERG: Local New York City communities say, "We're quite prepared to accept or appoint only people who meet state certification requirements as do local school boards in virtually all other districts in New York." But they argue that the special and different requirements imposed only within New York City are unduly restrictive. I gather you don't have a situation like that in Minnesota.

DR. GORALSKI: No.

MR. TRACTENBERG: Have any of your cities additional standards which have restricted the eligible pool?

DR. GORALSKI: No. And you see we only have about 4,000,000 people in the whole state, too, which is very different from your problem here, I suppose.

THE CHAIRMAN: Any further questions?

(No response.)

THE CHAIRMAN: Let me thank you again, Dr. Goralski, for coming all the way from the State of Minnesota.

We're going to call a luncheon recess for about 45 minutes or an hour. And these hearings are adjourned until about 2:00 o'clock.

- - - - -

THE CHAIRMAN: This is the Friday afternoon session of a 5-day series of hearings on the hiring and promotional practices of the City's public school system.

We spent the first two or three days having the facts laid out by the various principal parties in the school system. We then heard criticism from various community and educational associations and we have been spending the last day or so hearing about all the alternative models, both underway and proposed.

Today's testimony has been from people mostly from other states and cities who are informing us about the kind of system they use for selecting and promoting teaching and supervisory personnel in their school system.

I would like to call to the stand Dr. Joseph Manch, Superintendent of Schools, Buffalo, New York.

DR. MANCH: I am pleased to be here. I want to make it very clear at the outset that I am not here to tell the New York City school system how to run its school system. I know that you have a great many problems, as all of us do in large cities, but when I received a phone call followed by a letter my understanding was that I was asked to come to explain how we have changed some of our practices in recruitment and employment which has made it possible for us, I think, to employ a larger number of administrators who may be identified as members of a minority group, largely Black administrators.

I said that if I could arrange my schedule I would be happy to do it with the understanding that I would merely be describing what we do in Buffalo in our school system without any inference that you may adapt it in the New York City school system. I do think that what we have done may be of special significance in New York City because before we effected the changes New York City and Buffalo were the only two systems required by the Education Law to give examinations for certain categories of employees. I am talking about the promotion of employees from teachers to administrators. And I was aware for a long time that surrounding communities and surrounding school districts accepted applications from graduates who were certified as having taken the appropriate courses and having met state certification requirements for various positions. We, on the other hand, employed them on a probationary basis and in most cases we had to give an examination and derive an eligibility list from that examination. And then, for practical purposes, in terms of procedure, we have always appointed them in rank order.

It was my feeling some years ago--and I might say that I am in my 14th year as Superintendent of Schools--as I saw changes taking place in the school population, as well as the population of the city, that we had to have a broader opportunity to employ people and to assign people so that there would be fair representation.

Shortly after I assumed the superintendency, I sent memoranda to our administrative staff who were responsible for assigning administrative personnel and teachers. The first memorandum went as follows--I issued this on April 19, 1966 several years after I began as Superintendent and as I became aware of a certain kind of polarization--

"As assignments for 1966-67 are now being prepared, it is appropriate to recall our long-standing policy on teacher assignments to your attention at this time. Briefly stated, it is our policy that care is to be taken in assigning staff to schools in order to insure a favorable balance of experienced and new teachers in every school.

"It is recommended that you review the present teacher assignments for which you are responsible to see how well they reflect this policy.

"You are requested to continue to take appropriate and effective steps to adhere as closely as possible to the policy on assigning teachers to maintain and improve staff balance."

Actually, that was a follow-up memorandum to the first one I issued March 13, 1961, where I called attention of this need to the staff who had responsibility for assigning teachers and others, and one sentence in that original memorandum, which I should have read first, reads as follows:

"This is especially important in areas of the city where there are large numbers of children who, because of certain environmental and related factors, require every opportunity possible to help them achieve their fullest potential."

Three or four years ago I began to realize that we were not getting capable employees as a result of our examination procedure and were unable to appoint and assign persons and most particularly of the minority community, Black teachers and administrators, in a way in which we could feel we were maintaining a good balance and, in reviewing the law, I felt that some changes might be made that would be helpful.

We did go to work on that and the minutes of the Buffalo Board of Education meeting of January 24, 1968, indicate that, based on recommendations made to the Board for changes in the law, the Board approved the recommendations after a considerable debate. It was not a unanimous vote--it was a 5 to 2 vote of a 7-member board. We went ahead with that authorization and proceeded to effect changes in the law. Let me just read a very brief description of the process we followed and then I will touch on the effect that this had:

"In the late fifties and early sixties our examination procedures for administrative personnel especially principal of an elementary school and supervisor of elementary education consistently failed to produce candidates of background and experience to meet the demands of all schools in the City of Buffalo. Consequently we were compelled to transfer administrative personnel throughout the city in order to meet the taxing demands of some schools. The Superintendent and other Central Office administrators recognized that we had to attract to our schools persons of high competence and diverse background in order to meet the total demands of the Buffalo public schools. A change in the existing law, Section 2573, was necessary in order to widen our administrative selective process. One, the effort to change the Education Law applicable to the City of Buffalo was started in the early 1960's, but it wasn't until 1968 that this became a reality; two, the proposed amendment of the law was presented to the division heads for comments and modification; three, this proposal was given to the corporation counsel for approval as to the form of the proposed amendment; four, at the January 24 meeting of the Board of Education, the proposed amended law was presented to the Board for approval; five, Dr. Dwight E. Beecher, Executive Secretary, Conference of Large City Boards of Education, was asked to follow through with legislators on the proposed amendment and Mr. John Doerr, who was then the legislative representative for the City of Buffalo, was asked to seek favorable action in both houses on the bill; six, Senator Glinski introduced proposed amendment Senate No. 4937; seven, telegrams were mailed to the Speaker of the House and the President of the New York State Senate and other senators and assemblymen from the district; eight, see attached list of Black administrators appointed since the change in the law."

The law was modified. I do not think it necessary for me to read the law. In essence, what we did was to change the law so we no longer were required to give examinations for certain positions for which we had, up until that time, been required to do so. For example, we had to give examinations just as I believe New York City still does for teachers, supervisors, elementary school assistant principals, elementary principals and high school principals, and other positions up to the associate superintendent category. I felt we had to give the opportunity for many people who have not been able to find entry to the level of elementary principalship and up to that point there should not be an examination procedure.

The law has changed and made it possible for us to appoint people directly on the Superintendent's recommendation with the approval of the Board--for example, elementary school principals and those in a supervisory capacity--without an examination. Before this change these categories required an examination. As far as teachers are concerned, we effected a change in the law which made it possible to give a kind of continuing examination; candidates can walk in and apply, and after taking the teacher's examination and whatever else is required and after an interview, it might be possible almost immediately to add these names to the list in rank order. It made it possible for people who were interested in teaching in Buffalo to get on the list without waiting for the new examination, and without serving as temporary teachers or without probationary status. It meant that if they qualified--they had to have the qualifications required by the Board of Education and the State--they could be immediately appointed and their names added to the list as probationary teachers. Prior to that, many teachers would not come to Buffalo because they had to wait until the list ran out which in some cases was three years, and in the interim they could only be sure of temporary assignments. Elsewhere all they had to do was be quickly but thoroughly interviewed, and then be appointed as probationary teachers. That was not possible in Buffalo. It is now possible without waiting three years and it is a kind of a continuing list.

I believe this has helped us. I asked our personnel office to give me some figures yesterday. They show that we now have on our regular staff approximately 10% Black teachers, and approximately 10% of the total Black administrators. For the Federal programs we have no figures on the number of Black teachers, but 35% of the administrators are Black. And in the Central Office, 11% of the administrators are Black. I think that if you examine the figures which I do not have at this point as to what the situation was five years ago, it was a good deal different then.

All candidates, regardless of background, race, or whatever criteria you want to apply, must be qualified, they must be able to present credentials from recognized institutions of higher learning in courses of studies they have pursued which indicate that they are qualified in terms of state education requirements and the requirements of the Board of Education for those positions. But it means now that anyone who wants to be an elementary school principal does not have to take an examination for that position. We still have the examination for elementary assistant principal. When the position of principal is open we advertise for that position--I am using those two positions as an example at the moment --and applications are received, a committee interviews those who appear to be well qualified in terms of the credentials they submit and on their experience, and the committee makes a recommendation to the Superintendent of several who appear to be very good choices, and the Superintendent makes a selection and recommendation to the Board of Education.

I must point out that in the City of Buffalo the Superintendent is, in a sense, the Chief Examiner. He is authorized by law to recommend to the Board of Education, after appropriate procedures are followed, those approved for these positions. We do not have a Board of Examiners in the same sense that you have one in New York City. The Superintendent is the Examiner, so to speak.

Well, that in essence is what we have been doing. I might tell you that at every Board meeting one of the Board members raises the question, which now he does not even phrase in detail. He merely says, "I am raising the same question I raise regularly as to whether or not we take race into consideration in the appointment and assignment of teachers or administrators," and my response is "No, we do not in terms of appointment; all have to be qualified in accordance with criteria set up." I do take into consideration Board recommendations on assignments that they approve. I might pause at this point for any questions you may have.

MR. TRACTENBERG: Do you know offhand the approximate ethnic breakdown among both the student body and the general population in Buffalo?

DR. MANCH: The student body population is 36% non-white, the balance is white. Non-white means largely Black. We have some Puerto Ricans and others among the students. As far as the city as a whole is concerned, I think it is about 20% non-white at this time, maybe a little higher.

MR. TRACTENBERG: So that if my recollection is correct, the statistics you gave us both as to teachers and more especially those on a supervisory or administrative level, the percentage of non-whites is rather substantially higher than here in New York City in those categories and you attribute that in substance to some changes you made in the Education Law giving you broader powers in the selection of personnel.

DR. MANCH: I don't know what New York City's statistics are--I gave you ours and if you check the same figures I gave you in terms of what these figures would have been three or five years ago or even longer than that, you will find that the record is substantially higher for non-white administrators at this time and I think it is attributable to the fact that we did have these changes made in the law and we do give great consideration to the need for people of certain abilities in the appointment of personnel.

MR. TRACTENBERG: You said you do not have a Board of Examiners as it exists in New York City; you also mentioned, I think, that the National Teacher Exam has been used as the written examination. Does that mean that there is no longer a locally created examination?

DR. MANCH: Part of it is locally created; a few years ago we created all of our own examinations and then some years ago we used a national examination for basic testing and, of course, we have generally created some of our own examinations for special areas.

MR. TRACTENBERG. Do you find the National Teacher Examination, at least as to basic skills, satisfactory enough to fill your needs?

DR. MANCH: We think it is satisfactory.

MR. TRACTENBERG: Then you mentioned at one point that since the early 1960's you had been striving to make certain changes in the basic state law. Does the change that was finally made in 1968 fully meet the various changes you sought to have made or would you have preferred more substantial modifications?

DR. MANCH: Well, we were considering this. I thought very seriously of going further. I thought of the possibility of doing away with teacher examinations. For a variety of reasons.

it seemed to us it would not be wise to attempt that at that time.

I have from time to time raised the question as to whether we shouldn't now go further than we did. I think in a short time we probably will consider that. We still have examinations for teachers. I indicated the changes we made. We still have examinations for the appointment of an elementary school assistant principal and that is about as far as it goes. For administrators we have no examinations. Did I say elementary school assistant principal? We also have examinations for high school assistant principal. We have no examination for elementary school principals or high school principals and we have no examinations for supervisor.

MR. TRACTENBERG: If I read you correctly your experience with the elimination of some of the examinations previously required would make you favorably disposed toward a recommendation in the future to cut back still further on the examination requirements.

DR. MANCH: I have been considering it. I want to look at the decision to see whether it is working well. There is some feeling among some people that it is not a bad idea to have an examination for assistant principalship to be based on the experience of the individual because there we have some basis to consider experience for a high school principalship. My own feeling is that testing is not sacrosanct or sacred. I think intelligent people sitting on a committee to review candidates can make pretty good judgments about their experience and capabilities. Some candidates who come to us with certification have already been through a program of education certified by some college or university which is accredited legally and otherwise to be able to do what we have been doing in our large cities. I do not know how many large cities outside of New York State do this at the moment, but certainly New York City and Buffalo have been going beyond what other communities do in examining candidates and appointing them.

I am aware that years ago these laws were passed because there was some feeling that we needed to have protection in terms of examinations. We got away from and are avoiding any possible political persuasion in the appointment of people and I think that this depends on who is running the business. If a school system is going to have in positions of responsibility people who would be persuaded on the basis of political interference to appoint people instead of doing it on the basis of merit, then you have a problem and I am not saying you have it or we have it. I have felt no interference of any kind since doing away with the examinations I referred to. There are referrals because we go through regular procedures. Sometimes candidates are brought to me, and other candidates are examined through interview, and I usually ask for six names before I make a selection. I usually bring in the folders and examine them myself and sometimes decide to interview some of the candidates because in the City of Buffalo it is still possible for the Superintendent to know many of the teachers and many of the administrators based on his own observation. I still find time to visit many schools--I did so yesterday--but it is getting more difficult all the time. Anything is possible in a city of the size of Buffalo--more possible than in New York City--but I know from my own experience that what we have done is working well.

MR. TRACTENBERG: In New York City under the Decentralization Law, we have 31 community school districts with each of the community districts having an elected community Board and an elected community superintendent and each of them is not much different in size than the Buffalo school system.

DR. MANCH: I have had occasion to refer to the New York City decentralization procedures at our own Board meetings and the Board of Education in Buffalo is considering a preliminary study on what I have presented to the Board about decentralization. The point is well taken and I should tell you that I have some feeling about this because about 16 years ago I served on a committee at Teachers College in Columbia dealing with decentralization. What we did at that time was recommend a decentralized system of six school districts. But we were ahead of our time and it was not accepted.

You do have about 30 districts and I know that each one of the 30 is probably between the size of Rochester and Buffalo. It is feasible on that basis but I do not know if the boards representing the decentralized districts have the authority to employ personnel. I do not recall whether they do or not.

MR. TRACTENBERG: They do but with more limited authority than you have.

DR. MANCH: I think it would work on that basis, judging from our own experience.

MR. TRACTENBERG: Do you anticipate, if in fact you decide to recommend that teacher examination requirements be eliminated, that you would have a problem with patronage or persuasion as to those appointments or do you think your experience would be comparable to the one you described for the supervisory positions?

DR. MANCH: I can only tell you on the basis of my experience I have felt no pressure based on our present system. I hate to talk personally, but I think it is pretty well known that I do not yield to this type of persuasion. People have called and if they ring me up, fine, I have a standard response. I say, "The candidate will receive full and fair consideration," and that phrase is pretty well known in Buffalo. And I think you certainly have administrators here who would take the same position.

May I make another comment about the teacher situation. In time, when there are plenty of openings I do not think there would be any problem anyway because you need all the teachers you can get. At this time there may not be when a great many people are seeking positions with a few openings, and this is why I think it is important that the Board of Education make it very clear what its policy is and that merit will prevail.

MR. TRACTENBERG: We have heard testimony earlier in the hearing from community board members, community superintendents and others who have expressed the feeling that their careers would be very unsafe if ever it was to be known they were making appointments on the basis of personal relationships or any kind of pressures when, in fact, whatever popular pressure they felt was the pressure to appoint the most highly qualified and meritorious person for the particular position. I gather that has been your experience.

DR. MANCH: What do you mean they would be unsafe--I did not catch that.

MR. TRACTENBERG: That such pressures as they have felt have been directed at making it absolutely certain they pick people for the positions who, in fact, were most meritorious.

DR. MANCH: Very good.

MR. TRACTENBERG: And I gather that has been your experience.

DR. MANCH: Yes. I do not recall a single instance in which there has been any critical reaction in terms of the recommendations I made and the appointments I made. I find that people recognized that these were good appointments. I get a letter now and then from people who do not sign their names telling me I am favoring Black people and so on--many of us get those letters--and I get sanctimonious calls. I happen to be a superintendent who puts his family in a very difficult position. My wife is here and she knows what I am talking about. I have my phone number in the book and 99% of the people who call are a delight to talk with and 1% I would rather not speak to.

MR. TRACTENBERG: So the problem is not substantial?

DR. MANCH: No.

MR. TRACTENBERG: Do you think state certification as it presently exists, or as Dr. Nyquist talked about trying to revise it, might be an adequate basis for allowing certain people to select personnel?

DR. MANCH: If it isn't, then we better look at the colleges and universities. I agree with what Dr. Nyquist said on it.

THE CHAIRMAN: We are very impressed to hear about Buffalo and, of course, of the similarities between your system and our similar procedures. I am impressed particularly with the careful yet responsible way in which you have proceeded and the responsible judgments you told us about. I am particularly interested in your comment, about the use of race and that race becomes relevant sometimes in respect to assignment. You prefaced those remarks with, as I recall, something about the nature of the times in which we live--everyone of course knows that. There are minority children who present the greatest challenge to the school system these days because of the difficulties they have had learning in our schools, and that in our school system it is probably the greatest challenge to find a way to provide a breakthrough to these children who come to school handicapped. What I would like to know is a little bit more in addition to what you said about the process of assignment. You said it has been of some value to be able to send a principal to a Black school if he happens to be Black, or do I take it you would not necessarily find a Black principal should go to a Black school or a white principal to a white school.

DR. MANCH: There are many factors to be considered in assignment. Someone told me that we had the first Black high school principal appointed in New York State. When I recommended him for East High School, I didn't know if it was true, but he was certainly the first Black high school principal in Buffalo; this is practically an all-Black school.

There were a number of candidates in addition to this gentleman to consider for the position but I thought it was very important that he be considered. I thought at the time of that appointment that it would be very, very good to have a qualified person there who is also able to identify with the community and the children; and I thought that they needed some models. But a few years earlier I deliberately recommended a Black elementary school principal in a school in an all-white area because I thought the children there needed to see a Black principal. That man happens to be my Deputy Superintendent at the moment. But, it depends on the situation and I think it is relevant at times.

I once responded at a Board meeting to a question always put to me, "Do I recommend people to certain positions despite their race?" And this is the answer: I think the thing to consider is not so much the race but what does this person have in terms of identification, does it make him a valuable person at that school; and if he happens to be Black and because he is Black he can identify with the children and with his environment in the community and with the population, fine, then it is relevant; and we start with people who have qualified.

I have never recommended a person for a position, white or Black, who did not have the necessary requirements prescribed by law.

Have I answered your questions?

THE CHAIRMAN: Yes.

COMMR. DAVID: Counsel has already asked you most of these questions. Frequently, when there is a discussion of licensing above state standards, New York City and Buffalo are held out as if they had the same systems. As I understand your testimony, one, you want through legislation to get rid of some of the titles; two, where you give examinations you bank heavily on national testing; three, you are considering other possibilities; and, finally, you yourself, through the Board of Education, have the authority that the New York City system has assigned to the New York Board of Examiners. Those are four important differences. Are there other elements?

DR. MANCH: The element of size. That may have a considerable relevance. The fact that you have a decentralized situation of about 30 districts, each being approximately the size of some of the large cities in the state, makes our situation more relevant. I can offhand think of no other elements unless you want to suggest them.

COMMR. DAVID: The whole tendency you indicated is to pull away from the system that exists in this city.

DR. MANCH: Yes, I think it is discriminatory in terms of large cities. Why should New York City and Buffalo be singled out? The important thing is that the villages or the suburbs of Buffalo or other areas, when they go through their examination procedures, are able to select people who are qualified and relevant to a particular situation and to select the one that they would want to appoint. I indicated before that if the concern is the entry of politics into situations then we have to have people who are immune from that; particularly, you have to have people who are not worrying about their jobs.

MR. TRACTENBERG: One more question which occurred as you were talking. I would assume that part of the reason you have been successful in increasing the number of minority professionals is because you have been recruiting more people from the minority groups from which to select. We have heard many times in testimony here what a deterrent it is to put up with the delay in promulgating a list which has been, I gather, one of the changes Mr. David referred to. The continuous list is a substantial change, from a recruiting point of view, as compared to New York City's.

DR. MANCH: Yes, this applies of course only to teacher examinations. I asked about this yesterday and I asked if this in any way meant that there were people who would be hurt by new people coming in and being listed in rank order and I was told that we had not had that problem and that it has worked out quite well. I was concerned about that problem. On the other hand, it has helped us because it means that if a person wants to come to Buffalo and work there rather than in a suburb he can apply. For a long time we had a system that was pretty competitive, but we are not competitive--it means they can come in and be examined on the spot, having already received their credentials in terms of National Teacher Examination--that is the one we are using--and they may be appointed very quickly at the next Board meeting; and, if appointed, it is as a probationary teacher. To be a temporary means you have an assignment that can only hold through the balance of the school year.

MR. TRACTENBERG: We have heard much on the phasing out of the substitute license in New York City but apparently it has been replaced to a large extent by what is called a per diem certificate.

DR. MANCH: It is a rose by any other name.

MR. TRACTENBERG: So that you apparently feel from a recruiting point of view you are able generally to recruit capable people and capable minority people. The change you were able to effect permits you to appoint people rather quickly and this change has been an important one.

DR. MANCH: Yes, perhaps we did improve our salary situation. I was able to say to the press that for the first time in years I was able to walk down the hall and see people in line waiting to become teachers in Buffalo. I think that is a good sign.

THE CHAIRMAN: Thank you very much. I want to spread on the record my thanks to one of the highest officials of the City of Buffalo for taking time to come here. No testimony we received here has been more valuable than this testimony coming from the only other city in the country that has a plan similar to ours.

This record would have been most incomplete without your testimony, your evaluation and the facts you brought to us. I want to give you my personal thanks.

DR. MANCH: Thank you for inviting me and I must make it very clear for the record that I am not saying that we have succeeded wholly or that we do not have some problems. We certainly do. I have one more apology. If I sound rather tired it is because I have been up since 5:30 a.m. checking the weather. I have been checking the weather three mornings in a row before making a decision--a decision has to be made by 7 o'clock in the morning as to whether the schools will be open or closed because of the weather and I received a lot of calls telling me that I did not know what I was doing--when I left the sun was shining. I would like to apologize for being a little late.

COMMR. DAVID: He rearranged his schedule to be in New York.

THE CHAIRMAN: I am going to ask Commissioner Eleanor Clark French if she will read the statement of Dr. George Dickson, Dean, School of Education, University of Toledo.

COMMR. FRENCH: Dr. Dickson's statement pertains to teacher's certification procedures and is as follows:

"In the interest of brevity and clarity, I shall limit my comments to the 'what' of certification, leaving the 'how' to others. If this seems reminiscent of Mark Twain's position on the submarine menace, I can only assure you that there are, in this case, ways to boil the water. When asked for his solution to the dangers of submarine attack during World War I, Twain advised 'Boil the water.' When asked how he would do this, Twain is supposed to have replied that it was his task to think of a solution, someone else's to carry it out.

"There are historic reasons for a lack of precision concerning the 'what' of certification. We are now able to remove one important obstacle and are on the verge of a major breakthrough.

"I think we can agree that teacher certification, as it has been conceived in the past, has dealt with knowledge. We have required evidence--very questionable evidence, but that is another issue--that teachers know something. College credits are counted or programs of teacher preparation are approved. Clearly, this approach requires that we assume that 'knowing' is not the only prerequisite to, but is operationally effected by behaving in accordance with that knowledge.

"We have also, of necessity, acted as though 'knowing'--whatever was deemed essential--when followed--apparently automatically--by behaving in right ways would make the desired change in pupil behaviors.

"Obviously, we cannot continue to support these assumptions. Just because someone knows something is no indication that he can necessarily apply the knowledge. We cannot continue to ignore the specification of what a teacher must accomplish in terms of skills and various competencies--his ability to behave in specified ways and to carry out the function for which he is responsible in a skill.

"In fact, the Assistant Commissioner for Higher Education of your State, Dr. Alvin P. Lierheimer, has said that for certification we must ask, 'Does this person have understanding of the situation and the ability to diagnose the problem? Does he have in his kit the right kind of techniques to view, evaluate, feed back and alter his behavior accordingly?'

"We are now able to specify the knowledge, skills, attitudes, competencies, et cetera, that teachers should possess at the time of entry to our profession or at the completion of a pre-service program. And we can do this in operational, observable ways. This is what our own Elementary Models Teacher Education Project at the University of Toledo is about, and there are others working in this direction.

"Teacher certification operations are not now relying on such ability or teacher education developments although consideration of performance-based teacher education and its application to certification procedures is being discussed in several states, notably Florida, Texas, Washington and including New York.

"But it is again one thing to achieve behavior in certain ways from prospective teachers and still another to be assured that they will be able to perform tasks confronting them in the real world of their classroom.

"And so we must focus on teachers being able to demonstrate that they can bring about desirable pupil outcomes prior to certification. To be absolutely honest with you we may not at the University be able to deal adequately with the third ingredient of certification: changes in the pupils. Such change is probably situationally specific. I do firmly believe that in any given situation one could prescribe minimal and optional changes in pupil behavior. I am not certain yet that this can be done in a pre-service program. Perhaps it must wait for demonstration--this being the ultimate certification process--as the primary component of in-service teacher education. Then the state education agency and the teaching profession may or may not draw upon university resources in the process.

"Each way of determining a teacher's ability to succeed has merit, and we cannot yet abandon any. What I am saying is that we do not have a continuum of ways of determining certification from least valid: knowledge; through behavior: skills; to outcome: changes in pupils. A better way of conceptualizing the problem is to consider all three as important predictors of probability and success which should be used in concert.

"What I have hoped to suggest briefly today is a new model for certification which is competency-based and is anchored in three sources of data: knowledge, teaching behavior, and changes in learners. I advocate an immediate shift to in-service certification based upon compentencies from the first two areas to be followed by verification competence to be drawn from the third area by the state department of education in cooperation with others: education associations, teachers' unions, et cetera, during the specific situation it governs--the pre-service phase.

"I am about to support my argument at some length for the

first two areas and to urge you to take the lead in assuring our ability to determine success in the third, and most important, area--changes in learners.

"We must meet the ultimate test of program and teacher accountability by providing an absolute criterion of teaching effectiveness. This has to be accomplished while accommodating individual differences in teaching performance and style in achieving pupil outcome. While we may not be completely clear about all of the specific teachers' behaviors that bring about specific outcomes in pupils, we must continue with efforts and programs that promote such development and utilization. Such efforts will force our educational system to clarify further the goals and objectives of education and how such goals are realized and, finally, the guesswork will be taken out of pre-service selection, teaching hiring and teacher retention when teachers fully understand and demonstrate that their final certification is based on what they can or cannot do for and with pupils in terms of pupil outcomes.

"The performance-based criteria concept is necessary in teacher certification. The pupil has taken a stand on the subject of teachers being held accountable in terms of the products of their behavior. The education profession must soon come to the same stand."

THE CHAIRMAN: Thank you, Commissioner French, for reading the statement of Dr. George Dickson.

I am pleased to welcome now from the City of Detroit, Mr. Aubrey McCutcheon, Deputy Superintendent, Division of Staff Relations, Board of Education.

MR. MC CUTCHEON: Thank you very much.

Needless to say, I am pleased to be able to be here and contribute whatever I can to your understanding of some possibilities, if you are serious in New York City about attempting to increase substantially the number of minority school administrators and supervisors in the New York City school system.

I say that because I think that what I might say to you at this hearing, after reading a few newspaper accounts of some of the testimony given over the past days, speaks well for the future.

I kept saying to myself that if there are a lot of excuses that, traditionally, an educator uses in not deviating from the so-called norm, perhaps my testimony would not be of any use to you whatever. But, if on the other hand there is some sincere desire to increase the number of minority administrators--technically, of course, you do not increase the number of minority group administrators without increasing the number of those people at the lower levels--and to help them get the training and certification that Dr. Dickson spoke of in his paper that was just read then I submit to you it is a very simple task. I think we have shown that in the City of Detroit. Like Dr. Manch, we are not entirely satisfied that we have done all we can do even with decentralization. But we do not feel we are going to be seriously hampered in doing something about the number of Black administrators. I emphasize administrators because in the letter which I received from the Commission it was stated that you desired I address my remarks more to the selection and assignment of principals than other administrators.

You should know that I am not an educator at all, although I hold the rank of Deputy Superintendent of Schools in Detroit. I am a lawyer and I came to the public school system as a lawyer in the field of labor relations at the time the public act in Michigan had just been passed authorizing collective bargaining for public employees. The Supervisor who hired me, Dr. Sam Brownell, knew at the time he hired me for this role that if I branched out into other areas of educational administration, there would be some difficulty with various institutions and organizations which would not look too keenly on the idea of a non-educator assuming a high position in the education system.

The Superintendent who promoted me to the position of Deputy Superintendent in charge of staff relations, which includes the office of personnel and office of labor negotiations, literally had to make a fight about the appointment. This is a case of what can be done if you want to do it.

I would submit that every good personnel administrator knows how to apply the ingredients of whatever relations he is faced with in order to come up with a menu to his liking. If he wants to do it he can find a way to do it even within the framework of those regulations which may appear to be somewhat restrictive. Flexibility, of course, does help, and we are fortunate in the State of Michigan, and in Detroit particularly, to have a great deal of flexibility with respect to how we select administrators and how they are assigned.

There have been several instances I should point out to you in which we have indeed looked at race, not only in determining how and where we are to assign personnel but even in determining whether or not they were qualified for what we called an eligibility list.

I can recall in 1968, during the spring and summer of 1968, when the Detroit public school system had an old eligibility list for secondary principals which did not include the names of any Black assistant principals, how we found a way to establish a list which consisted of a substantial number of Black secondary assistant principals who were promoted in September 1968.

During the same summer we had a list of candidates for elementary principal. That list contained approximately 19 white candidates. We were able to find a way during that summer to establish a brand new list of more than 21 Black candidates. Twenty-one exactly were appointed in the Detroit public school system to principalships in elementary schools in September 1968.

Our flexibility helped us to do that, but I submit that even within the constraints imposed upon us by tradition and by various rules, the dedication to do the job, the dedication of the Superintendent of Schools to have the job done, the public declarations that have been made that we indeed were going to do the job, helped us to find the way to do it; and I want to reiterate again that we, of course, are not saying that in Detroit we have done all that we should do.

You should know a few statistics in the Detroit public school system in 1966, the time at which Superintendent Drachler assumed the acting superintendency, and where I was first employed, we had a total staff, including faculty and administrators, which was approximately 30% Black and of that number we had less than 11% Black administrators.

In August of 1970, we had a total staff which was in excess of 40% Black and we had within our administrative ranks approximately 40% administrators who were Black.

Again, we do have flexibility and we look for additional flexibility and we look for ways because we are dedicated to finding ways to work within whatever restrictions there may be and, again, every good personnel administrator, every dedicated superintendent of a board of education or board of examiners or the legislature who wants to see this job done can find ways to have it done.

Just last week we established a list of candidates for secondary school assistant principal. Those candidates took examinations, written examinations, and the list contains approximately 95 names. Of those 95 names approximately 69 of the persons listed are Black.

Now, the people in Detroit expect this today. They know that this is going to happen. We do not make statements that we are recommending that we increase the number of Black administrators or that we request certain people to do certain things to enable us to have additional Black administrators in the school system.

We talk about balanced staff but we do not say things like we want to have balanced staff. We say we are going to have and we require that there be an increase, a substantial increase, in the number of Black administrators in our school system. We declare that publicly and we stated at our Board meeting to the members-- we answered the Board members to that effect.

Our School Superintendent has on more than one occasion made it very clear to the public that he has hired a person to do a particular job and he expects that job to be done and he admits publicly sometimes that he may know before the community knows that they have a new minority group administrator but he also says that he expects that the person he has hired to do this job is not going to put someone in any job who is not qualified to do that particular job. He stated to our Board members, just a couple of months ago, with respect to a particular appointment to an executive level position, a position which is a higher rank than an assistant superintendency rank in our school system, that he did not know any longer than a hour before they knew who the particular person was who was selected for the job. That happened to be a Black candidate who was selected, a person whose credentials almost reminded me of the Sidney Poitier role in the "Man Who Came to Dinner"; and yet we had some criticism from some people because they did not know in advance who this person was and what his credentials were.

We have a Superintendent of Schools in the Detroit public school system who is willing to say to his Board, "I have someone in charge of that and that is the person who will address you on the subject as to the qualifications of the person."

What I am trying to say is that what you have to do first, I believe, in any school system is to make up your minds that you do want to increase the number of minority group administrators in your system. You have to declare that publicly, you have to be willing to take the criticism that is so often blurted out about reverse discrimination, and things of this sort and yet go about doing the job. Then you have to hire somebody to do that job and give them the power to do that job, reminding them that if they do the job unfairly they are the ones to be subject to the criticism so there is not any cop-out for any Superintendent of Schools or the Board of Education, who have the primary responsibilities, but it is a recommendation by them because they cannot do all things themselves.

I do not know a lot about the rules and regulations and restrictions under which the people in the City of New York have to labor in trying to overcome this problem, but, as a lawyer, my guess is that even if those in the New York City school system are unable to change the requirements of a Board of Examiners, you can look at that law and even within that law if the dedication is there you will be able to substantially increase the number of minority school administrators and supervisors in your system. You can go a little bit further by perhaps changing small parts of the law which give you greater flexibility. You might even take such a small step as to have the law amended to include a statement that the law is to be read in such manner that it is designed to increase the number of minority administrators in the New York City school system and that, I believe, in itself will go a long way toward helping the system to work not only with its supervisors and administrators union --we have one in Detroit--we have had to deal with them on this subject. We have been able to get their cooperation first of all because they recognize that we are serious and we were going to do it, and, second, because fortunately we do have some people sensitive to the kind of needs we have in the Detroit system, a system which is reaching 65% Black pupil population at this moment.

Perhaps you have questions you would like to ask, and I will attempt to answer those questions. I am not sure that my remarks are going to be beneficial to you in view of the kind of restrictions you may have, except for the fact that a close look at those restrictions I think will show that there are ways within the regulations themselves to improve your situation in New York City.

THE CHAIRMAN: Your testimony is particularly valuable for the very reason that you do come from a large and troubled city like our own with a large minority group population in the public schools.

Let me ask Counsel to proceed with the questions.

MR. TRACTENBERG: I think it would be very useful if you could just describe to us briefly the kind of flexibility that you have in the Detroit system. Perhaps I can give you a 30-second background about New York City. There is a statutory provision for a Board of Examiners and for virtually all appointments to professional positions within the school system, both teaching and supervisory, to be made from eligibility lists constituted by the Board of Examiners through an examination process.

I think that is probably the only frame of reference that is necessary.

MR. MC CUTCHEON: Let me state some of the flexibility we do have but keep in mind first that you might place your Board of Examiners in the Detroit Public School System as being the authority for determining what criteria are going to be used within certain prescriptions of the law.

I recognize that that means I am saying that the Board of Examiners then would be somewhat in the power position of a Superintendent of Schools, but perhaps they have even greater power than the Superintendent of Schools. Maybe they have to make up their mind to exercise whatever degree of flexibility they have to help the New York City school system in the same way those within the Detroit public school system exercise flexibility in an effort to increase the number of minority group administrators.

Someone has to find out what kind of a written examination is going to be given. We have that responsibility in Detroit. Somebody has to attempt to find out how much weight that written examination has as opposed to the weight given an oral interview by persons who constitute a selection committee. We have that flexibility and that responsibility in the Detroit public school system. Someone has to determine who is going to be on the selection committee. I can tell you we are not reluctant in Detroit to have an all-Black selection committee just as we know for many, many years there were all-white selection committees reviewing the credentials of both Black and white candidates. So, we sometimes have all-Black selection committees.

We almost always have, since 1967, a selection committee which is composed of a majority of Black members and they do not all think alike, they do not all act alike, but they are there and I think it gives a greater assurance to Black candidates coming through because they know they are going to get a very fair evaluation and any personnel administrator will have to admit that there are many, many opportunities for you to make decisions which might sway the selection one way or the other.

I am saying that someone has to be in the position to make that decision who is sensitive to the need to have a larger number of Black administrators in your school system. If you do not have someone who has the power to make that decision then you are going to be a few steps removed from getting the job done.

We also have the power to determine how many people are going to be on the list and that may mean that you look at the rank order--and we have the power to ignore the rank order--but you may like to look at the rank order to see the composite score based on the written examination, based on the oral questioning, based upon ratings and other things, and you may find you just do not have within that group a large enough number of Blacks, people of Slavic ethnic background, white females, for instance.

We had a severe problem recently with respect to our secondary school assistant principals in that we did not have enough white females on the list and we exercised the same kind of flexibility to increase the white females on the list that we exercised in order to increase Black administrators.

We recently had a group coming to us and saying that we are ignoring people of Slavic descent and they have been able to point out the very few people in high administrative positions of Slavic descent. They were not accusing us of obvious discrimination and the next day after they made this particular plea to our Board --it was an attack more than a plea--something came across my desk in my role of Deputy Superintendent of Staff Relations which enabled me to make a decision as to whether or not there were going to be X number or Y number of people placed in an eligibility pool for consideration for a particular position and the next three names on that list--and this is where determining qualifications and using race in determining qualifications plays a part--the next three names, as I understood and as I had been informed, were people of Slavic descent. I can assure you that their three names appear today in that eligibility pool.

The degree of qualification is something that someone has to determine and now, with decentralization, our regional boards are going to be making the selection. Since some of our regional boards have a large number of schools with large Slavic pupil population, it may be intentional that they would want to select more qualified Slavic teachers for their particular school because the teacher would be a person who understands the language so why shouldn't that be taken into consideration in establishing the pool. But this is some of the flexibility we enjoy and maybe to some degree even the Board of Examiners can exercise flexibility --they have to be sure that they do have on their list a larger number of people from minority groups than they already have to give their examination.

THE CHAIRMAN: Often, they have to give their examination at particular times to make certain they have a large number of Black supply.

MR. MC CUTCHEON: The story is always told--we have been looking but nobody applied--so maybe when the applications are in and you find out you do not have a large number of Blacks or others who have applied and you are looking for a particular group to be represented on an eligibility list, maybe you have to decide you have to do some greater advertising or you will extend the time for people to apply for a particular job--and these are all things personnel administrators have done for many, many years for a number of reasons and I see no better reason for exercising this kind of flexibility than to achieve a greater minority group membership within the administrative group structure.

MR. TRACTENBERG: What is the nature of your examination? That is, the New York State constitution expressly requires appointment to civil service positions, including teaching and supervisory positions, to be based on merit and fitness to the extent practicable and that it has to be determined by competitive examination to the extent practicable. But I think it is clear that within the law a competitive examination does not necessarily involve any written component and that there can be a simple and uniform examination consisting of a review of the record and an oral interview.

I gather you said that for certain positions you used that type of examination process rather than the formal examination process.

MR. MC CUTCHEON: We have used formal examinations for certain positions but we no longer use them for principals; we use them for department heads, supervisory positions, and also for assistant principal. But, again, even though we use them, the flexibility is there for us to determine, number one, what the examination is going to be, and I would guess that somebody in New York is responsible for putting that exam together, and if those persons are dedicated to being certain that larger numbers of minority group people can qualify, they can include factors in the examination to achieve that--it could be relevant if it asks the kinds of questions that people brought up in the ghetto are able to answer without doing anything detrimental to our society.

I am saying we have used essay exams; we have asked our School Community Relations Department to put together questions which really measured more the potential of the person to relate to certain types of communities than anything else, but these are people who have been teaching for several years; we require in our system that a teacher must have been a teacher for at least four years and cannot be promoted until they serve five years and we require that before they can be promoted, they must have served in a variety of school experiences, at least one of them in a low socio-economic area. We put that requirement in in 1967, and it means Black or white administrators who qualify must meet this particular requirement; and our School Community Relations Department has come up with a set of essay questions which we have asked rather than the kind of ETS format that is generally followed in school systems. So whoever has the opportunity to determine what a test is going to be used for, I submit, can, if they are dedicated to this type of substantial increase of Black administrators in their school system, have an objective test which enables them to have a larger number of minority people who succeed on these exams.

MR. TRACTENBERG: Has the kind of flexibility you described led to charges that you have been discriminating in reverse and, if so, what is the answer you have given and how do you feel about it?

MR. MC CUTCHEON: I start out with the premise that I think everybody agrees with--that public education generally has not done the job by its traditional standards. I said a few moments ago that in a way I am fortunate that as a lawyer I did not come to the schools with these traditions so sometimes people will excuse what I say on the basis that I do not understand the need and that is all right also. But we get those charges and we do not say that all discrimination is reprehensible. I think if we look at what goes on in our society, we will recognize that fact. There are a lot of discriminatory acts in which we engage that have a positive value. One example is the manner in which we treat the poor medically. We do not deny people medical services because they do not have money and maybe we ought to be doing a better job on that. That is discrimination also but it is positive. We say you do not have to pay but your neighbor does have to pay because he has money.

So I say to people who make the charge that this is reverse discrimination and that we are lowering standards that we will see whether in the long run we really have lowered standards or whether we really produce a better education system than we had a hundred years ago or more. We tried out the old way and we know that we have not done the job. Now we will try it this way and then measure it in a hundred years and then make a statement as to whether or not we have truly lowered the standards in order to end all discrimination.

MR. TRACTENBERG: It has come up repeatedly during the hearings that if you get more flexibility this will lead to political patronage and pressures leading to a spoils system.

Is this another kind of charge that was made to you when you exercised flexibility?

MR. MC CUTCHEON: That charge has also been made. I think I have to say to you that there is that possibility. A person does have to be really of high integrity and dedicated to do the job. But I think there are some factors now that exist in public education which diminish substantially the kind of political impact or pressure that might be put on an individual to do things which he or she should not do, and that is the existence of collective bargaining. There is a procedure now by which a person can make a claim of violation of rights with respect to collective bargaining agreements and this sort of thing helps even though court decisions have clearly pointed out that discrimination of the kind that ensures a higher number of minority members in administrative positions is not something for which a person can recover if he is overlooked in some way. Yet, if it can be proven that the decision was political then I think that a person would be able to prove his claim. So, that safeguard is there as well as the pressure that ordinarily will come from collective bargaining groups which will be able, if this happens frequently, to show that the responsible individual is not doing the proper job.

I pointed out that we did find a way in 1968 and have since established a new list of eligible candidates. We did that partly by sitting down with our administrative organization and pointing out the problem to them in several meetings over a period of about two months and making it clear to them that we were going to do this job. Now, it was not all just a matter of total agreement quickly. We did have to exercise a threat once in a while. For instance, we have the flexibility in our system, and did have it for a long time, to strike from the eligibility list the name of a person who, having been offered an assignment or two, turned them down. Unfortunately, before we do it the total concurrence of our administrative organization is necessary. We did have to remind them that we did have the power and also had to remind them that in the City of Detroit no white administrator will accept certain appointments because that person would know that he would not have an opportunity to survive.

I think that when they realized this they said to themselves "Are we going to subject any person to this risk?" And we said we will establish a new list and in time there will be promotions and they decided it was better to go along with us.

Now, we did live up to the commitment and we set a deadline date and said that anyone who was skipped over on the old list while we appoint people on the new list will be promoted by a certain date even if we have to find a special assignment for them. We met our deadlines and we met with some criticism from some people who were not selected and who thought we were discriminating against them, but I do not think those charges were valid charges in view of the superior purpose that had to be accomplished.

MR. TRACTENBERG: I gather there has been an effort and you have been ultimately successful in getting the cooperation of the supervisory associations.

MR. MC CUTCHEON: Yes, they now work very well on the whole matter and we, for the first time, included one of their representatives on the advisory committee established in concert with the organization of superintendents. That committee makes its recommendations to the Superintendent or his designee. I happen to be his designee. And a person is put on the eligibility list and put into a particular assignment. We have had tremendous cooperation from the administrative group. That did not come easily, but it did come after they realized that we were indeed going to do this job. We preferred to do it with their cooperation, but the job was going to be done.

MR. TRACTENBERG: I think it is important to emphasize, as you yourself stated, that your motivating impulses are for educational reasons and reflect the educational problems in the system.

MR. MC CUTCHEON: Absolutely.

MR. TRACTENBERG: I have no more questions.

THE CHAIRMAN: I want to thank Mr. McCutcheon for giving us his testimony about his school system. It has been technically valuable to us and you have the personal thanks from me and the rest of the Commission.

- - - - -

THE CHAIRMAN: After I make a statement, I'm going to ask counsel to read something into the record.

I do want to say for the record, many who are listening and who are here may not know I am the only full-time paid Commissioner and fourteen other Commissioners serve without pay and give their time free of charge, in a word, to the City of New York. They have, at some sacrifice sat with me throughout these hearings listening to the public, almost totally listening, receiving testimony, and I believe it is only fitting to call attention to who they are.

The Commissioners who have been able to sit during these hearings include Eleanor Clark French, who is here to my right today, and Frank Mangino, who is here to my left today. Commissioner Mangino was here to my left late through the evening one cold night when we heard public testimony. Commissioner French has been particularly faithful in coming to sit through these hearings.

In addition, several of the other Commissioners were in attendance throughout this week--Commissioner Gilbert Colgate, Commissioner Jerome Becker, Commissioner Murray Gross, Commissioner Rabbi Harry Halpern, Commissioner Cornelius McDougald, Commissioner Archibald Glover.

I think we are fortunate that the City of New York is able to have the services of citizens of such high public spirit as to give their time in this fashion to human rights' work.

Yesterday there was a comment concerning the Newark, New Jersey public schools. They had been invited to testify here concerning the use of race by that school system in conformity with a decision of the Third Circuit Court of Appeals, the highest court next to the United States Supreme Court.

We had wished Mr. Franklin Titus, the Superintendent, to be here, particularly to explain how race could be legally and constitutionally used as apparently the court had said it could so as to avoid confusion on this matter, since for most people race is known to be an irrelevant factor legally.

Mr. Titus, we have learned, is unable to be with us today because of an emergency that has arisen with respect to labor negotiations in which he is now involved. I understand that there is a court decision from this state which explains in great part the legal use of race in a school situation and I thought for purposes of clarification, I would ask Mr. Tractenberg to read that decision in, and I think we might consider that that decision, from which he will be reading, explains the use of race here in New York City and that it probably conforms with the decision in the Third Circuit Court of Appeals as well.

I am going to ask counsel to read the statement now.

MR. TRACTENBERG: This is an excerpt from an opinion rendered on December 26, 1970, by Supreme Court Justice Pino, in Kings County, in a case called In the Matter of the Application of Council of Supervisory Association v. The Public Schools of the City of New York.

It was a case about which we heard testimony earlier in the hearings involving the appointment as acting principal of Benjamin Franklin High School of Mr. Melvin Taylor.

The CSA argued that Mr. Taylor, because he was not on the Board of Examiners' promulgated eligible list, was not eligible for appointment.

The Court, speaking through Justice Pino, found against the CSA and indicated that in its judgment Mr. Taylor's appointment as an acting principal was quite valid and lawful.

I think there is one thing in the Court's opinion that bears particularly on the question of the use of race and I will read it. It is as follows:

"The implications that Mr. Taylor has been chosen because

of his race should be put to rest. Mr. Scribner states that the appointment was made on the basis of Mr. Taylor's extensive teaching and supervision experience. As head of one of the largest educational systems he is entitled as a minimum to the presumption that his official acts are honestly motivated. There is no doubt that Mr. Taylor's ethnic experience played an important part in this appointment. However, as Judge Bergen states in <u>Council of Supervisory Associations v. Board of Education</u>"--I should add that was an earlier decision--"in a case upholding the respondent's temporary designation of four acting principals to pose in a demonstration of school districts, the position could not lawfully be filled on the basis of race but experience in the race problems should become an objectivably and measured standard for the position. Mr. Taylor's appointment is in all respects lawful and will not be enjoined at this time."

THE CHAIRMAN: Thank you, Mr. Tractenberg.

I should say for the record it is unfortunate that some words so quickly become euphemisms for others in our society. It is clear from that decision that we need to get more precisely what we're talking about in this often inflammatory area, that the word "race" is being used as a euphemism for other traits and characteristics such as experience, such as background and commitment.

It seems perfectly clear that the decision from which Mr. Tractenberg read would equally have allowed the appointment of a white principal in that school, if that principal had the background, the commitment, the support, that is required in a hard-core ghetto school where no one knows the answers. As it turns out, a large proportion of people these days who have that commitment come from the race of the children who are involved. There is nothing short of a missionary zeal in the minority communities concerning the almost total failure of children in public schools.

If the Black and Puerto Rican teachers believe that their children are not educable, they have lost their entire future. So, they often bring to schools a very special commitment to teach those children.

Similarly, we have been favored in this school system with large numbers of white people who bring that kind of missionary zeal where only missionary zeal will succeed. That was of course clear in Ocean Hill-Brownsville where numbers of young, white people found their way to that demonstration district. Large numbers of young white people came because they had that special commitment and the Ocean Hill-Brownsville board was quick to recognize them for that commitment and zeal regardless of their color.

The record should make it clear we're not talking only about young people, that Harlem, for example, over the last three or four decades has always been fortunate to have a small cadre of committed white teachers and principals who went into teaching for much the same reasons that many people go into medicine, because they are driven by some higher idealism, because they want to cure, and these white teachers and administrators are often found in ghetto schools because they wished to go there.

It is a sad comment on the failure of that missionary zeal that in order to get teachers to go into these districts, there had to be a part of the contract that required teachers to serve in those districts. Failure of that missionary zeal is no better pointed up than by the fact that the only way to staff schools in these districts today is by virtue of that provision which requires teachers to go into them.

When a teacher is required to go into a school district which she may vitally feel she cannot handle, I ask you whether you believe those children have even a minimum chance of learning. I do not put this on the record to criticize those teachers. I do not believe most Black people know how to teach Black children today, who come with the handicap of generations of slavery and discrimination and I do not believe most Puerto Rican people know how to teach most Puerto Rican children today, who come with the handicap of late migration to this country in a time of receding economy and therefore have been the most unfortunate immigrants to come to these shores.

I do not know that most Orientals could teach Orientals coming in large numbers into Chinatown today, Hong Kong immigrants, dropping out of school left and right because they lack the bilingual facilities to help them learn English so that they can learn anything else.

I put this on the record because I think the relevance of race has to be made precise and accurate, so that in this city where we have so many people of so many ethnic backgrounds, we all come to the deepest and most sophisticated understanding of what we're talking about.

The city can't afford a period of demogogic rhetoric around the race and religious issue. As long as I am chairman of this Commission, it will not happen. No one will be able to say he didn't know what we meant by the relevance of race. Those are not words to be played with or used demogogically by any race or religion of people in this city. I want that to go on the record.

I want to say that two other large cities had pledged to come here today and they have sent us their regrets--serious problems arose to keep them from coming here and they said they would have the statements read into the close of the hearings. We hope to get them next week. That is from Rochester and Cleveland.

We endeavored to get a cross-section of cities and states which were meeting various problems of our own. Before I go to public testimony, I must read into the record one other matter, relating to the way in which these hearings have been possible.

At the risk of embarrassment to two people I shall now cite, I feel I must cite them. Although she is on my own staff, I think I must say for the record that Miss Brooke Aronson, the chief of the Research Division, has had the enormous task--in my mind, when I gave it to her, I thought it a virtually impossible one--of putting together inside of a month and a half or two objective hearings that would look at this issue. Her mission read, in three ways:

First, to set out the facts concerning the school system. The facts could be set out not by the partisans but only by those within the school system. So, she was to assemble the top leadership of the school system. We spent the first two days hearing from both the Board and staff of the public school system and the Board of Examiners.

Then, in fairness because it is a controversial issue, she was to assemble critics of the school system's record in this regard and she assembled a cross-section of critics.

Finally, and perhaps the most creative part of the task, a cross-section of the possible alternatives and models for doing what we do in New York, for we felt it only fair if we were going to subject the public school system to criticism to put on the record what other ways there were of doing it.

This Commission takes no position with respect to which of those ways is the best way to do it, at least not at this point before we have analyzed the record. We did feel the duty to put forward for the public school system and for the public a variety of ways and we have been particularly fortunate in this last day of hearings to hear from a number of states and cities whose experience has been different and as different as ours.

I think what Miss Aronson has done is close to the impossible. It is the highest level of staff work.

Finally, I think I must say something about counsel, for these hearings would not have been hearings at all, without special counsel. These are not hearings where it would have been possible for Commissioners to make anything like a helpful or fact-finding record without the benefit of counsel with special expertise and brilliance. We are particularly fortunate that we acquired the services of Paul Tractenberg, who is grossly underpaid and much overworked. I can't tell you the kind of enormous preparation it took to ask relevant questions of people who were discussing the largest and most complex school system in the world, a bureaucracy, and I say this not in criticism, but as a matter of fact, I believe, that is more complex than almost any other in this or any other city. In part, by virtue of the fact that it has jurisdiction over 1,000,000 children. A lawyer without background and experience, I say to you in all truthfulness, could not have handled this assignment. But even with background and experience, a lawyer with less skill and brilliance could not have brought to these hearings what Mr. Tractenberg has brought to it.

With amazing skill and with a style that was incisive but marvelously uninflammatory and gentle, he examined and cross-examined witnesses who had all of the information there is to have about the school system, people whose actual knowledge must surely have over the years been greater than his but which he over the period of some month and a half began to learn so that he might be in some position to ask them questions.

Of course, it is true that he was once a counsel for the Board of Education when he was in private practice for a large law firm in this city, though he is now a professor of law at Rutgers Law School. I can't say enough about his performance here. I believe the success these hearings have had, and I believe they have had some success, is due almost entirely to the way he has conducted the examination of witnesses.

Let me say finally in clarification of our role here, though we had counsel and though we called witnesses and though we were prepared to use our subpoena powers, be it necessary, these were not hearings in the court sense. We are not a court. This is an advocacy agency on behalf of those groups of people in this city who still encounter discrimination. The law suffers us to go out and find ways to reduce discrimination against them in this society and bring them in to this society's institutions. However, no hearing, even an exploratory one of this nature, is a hearing unless it is a fair hearing and we have tried to be fair by giving as much time to those who defend the system as we thought they required, even though we often felt we had to more drastically limit the time of the witnesses who criticized the system for there are so many of those. We would not have ended these hearings any time sooner if we would let them go on, but we had to do anything we could to get on the record the data and views of those within the system.

In all fairness, I think myths have surrounded every part of the hiring and promotional part of this system and myths have surrounded the Board of Examiners. I think that one very valuable purpose it served was to give the Board of Examiners more time than any other witness here to make it perfectly clear that we weren't dealing with the primitive bias, as the Board of Examiners has been characterized, but with an institution which moved perhaps too slowly but at least moved, and it was important to get on the record the degree to which they have moved and the degree to which they are willing to move and what it took to make them move and what their attitudes were on these questions. I congratulate them for coming forward as well as others in the school system who, after all, have a task which is mammoth and which if you gave me today, I could not guarantee you I could perform terribly much better.

I think it is important to realize the enormous complexity of the school system in this city, bigger than most cities in the world, the school system itself. We shall, taking that into account of course, nevertheless, write a report which we think is one in keeping with our mandate under the law. We shall at all times be fair and be called accountable when we are not fair. But, this Commission shall never regard it as anything less than its duty to move vigorously against all kinds of discrimination. We will never trample upon the rights of others but we will not be timid in moving forward in aid of minority group people who on the one hand are criticized if they are a burden on the state and on the other hand are criticized when they seek opportunities into existing institutions.

As long as we are on this Commission, we're not going to force minority people to meet that cruel dilemma of being cursed for not carrying their load in society and being cursed when they try to enter the institutions in the regular way which has been set up for everybody in this society.

Finally, I want to thank the members of the public. No issue in this city today is more volatile than the personnel question of the public school system. We went into these hearings at some risk because some of the volatility flows from deep vested interests --some who have felt that through hard work they have made it into the public school system on one hand, and, on the other, the vested interest of parents in the ghetto community who sincerely believe if their children do not make it in the school system then it is all over for them, and people will not survive. I warn you that is a demoralized view of minority group parents in this city. It behooves all of us to understand that every group of people which has come to these shores in the history of this country, has seen improvement with each generation except Black people and Puerto Rican people.

No matter what ethnic group you belong to it is probably the case that you are better off than your grandfather was. I would not like to say the extent to which that is not the case for people who live in the slum areas of our city. I would not like to say what happens when a people sees every other group of people doing well, some better than others, for whatever reasons, in a land where progress is the rule of other people but themselves. No democracy can afford that situation, no school system will survive that continues that way.

This Commission will issue a report in the near future, we hope within the next six weeks or so to have a preliminary report, a basis for action, a basis for sitting down with the school system.

We are not the adversary of the school system. We are a service agency wishing to offer our expertise and experience to help cure what every official of the school system says has distressed them.

Finally, we believe the material that has come forth from these hearings is truly significant. We don't believe there has been amassed any place else the kind of data on such matters as test validity and relevance, the legality in the northern situation of low minority groups, and the like.

The members of the public who suffered through these hearings, both on the radio and sitting here, and held themselves on all sides when they heard someone speak in a way with which they disagreed, I can only give you my great tribute and compliments. I think what it reveals is that people are willing to discuss rationally any issue when there is a high enough level for all with jurisdiction to do something about the issue. But when issues of this kind are left to be settled in the streets, they will be settled there. Make no mistake about it. They will be settled there. The purpose of this hearing was to offer an alternative to the streets for settling an issue of concern to every parent in this city, and I compliment the members of the public for the way in which they have attended and accepted these hearings with the rational dialogue which we had wished to occur and which turned out to occur.

After that long soliloquy, I do hereby call the public to public testimony.

(Applause.)

COMMR. FRENCH: Before we begin the public testimony, this is Commissioner Eleanor Clark French speaking.

Those were very inspiring remarks of Commissioner Norton and those were very kind tributes which she gave to those of the staff who have made these hearings such high level hearings. It has been a great privilege to have been here. But those remarks would not be complete, if something further were not said. I have taken the responsibility to do so, on behalf of the Commissioners --to say what I am sure all those of you who have been here and observed the hearings and all those of you who have heard the hearings during this week must realize, that it is mostly the magnificent leadership given these hearings and everything else that the City Commission on Human Rights has been doing the last months by Commissioner Eleanor Holmes Norton to which we can credit whatever good will comes out of these hearings.

As she has said herself, we have embarked upon an investigation and study of what we can do to improve the lot of the children of this city and thereby citizens of this city, and I want to pay tribute to the way in which Chairman Norton has chaired these hearings. She is a brilliant young woman, as you know. It is her sense of dignity, justice and complete integrity that has dominated these five days of hearings, and I speak on behalf of all of the Commissioners, I'm sure, in paying great tribute to our Chairman.

Thank you.

(Applause.)

THE CHAIRMAN: I want to assure you only professional courtesy kept me from calling my fellow Commissioner out of order. I want to thank Mrs. Eleanor Clark French for her terribly over-generous remarks.

Because there was such interest among the public although we didn't anticipate public testimony today, we will sit today until those members of the public who didn't have an opportunity to testify will be given one.

I have been given names of people who have signed up and I will call them in the order they signed up.

Marina Brook.

MRS. BROOK: Commissioner Eleanor Holmes, Commissioner Mangino and Commissioner Mrs. Eleanor French, I am most happy to be here this afternoon to be able to try to testify to a certain extent of what my feelings are about the education that our Puerto Rican children are receiving in the public schools of New York City. However, my English has an accent and I could not express myself fully and be properly understood the way I want to, unless I speak in Spanish. With all due respect to the Commissioners, and to the public present, I would like to speak Spanish.

THE CHAIRMAN: You have our permission to speak in Spanish and you are welcome to speak in Spanish. We do want you to know the reporter doesn't speak Spanish but you are welcome to speak in Spanish.

MRS. BROOK: I would like this to be on the record if my accent doesn't mean much. The accent is what stopped Puerto Rican teachers to pass the test of the Board of Examiners.

THE CHAIRMAN: You pass our test. You can speak in English.

MRS. BROOK: Going back, a few years back, I would say about eight or nine years back, we all, the Black and Puerto Rican mothers, were getting so desperate because their children were not learning; they were, according to the statistics, three or four years behind in reading. Everybody started trying to get together to be able to ask, from the Board of Education of the City of New York, to try and see in which way they could help the children to be able to reach a better level. But, we did go many, many times to the Board of Education, patiently and orderly, but we were not heard. The teachers--I am not accusing the teachers of not teaching, naturally, but our children needed someone to understand them a little better. The teachers that the Puerto Ricans and other Spanish-speaking children had were at a little disadvantage with the Black children although the problem was the same, ghetto schools and supposedly they had the worst teachers or the teachers who did not have the experience they've supposed to have to be able to deal with children who are poor.

Then, after that came the school boycott, marches to the Board of Education, 110 Livingston, the Board of "Miseducation" we used to call it.

Now, something has happened after we sat and moved, and we moved the system by sitting for three days at the Board and after finally being arrested, fifteen citizens were arrested. After that the Mayor, who had said before that the Board of Education was an autonomous body, not even he could dictate to them what they should do, finally got in and started moving something. I don't know what he moved but he moved a little bit. Whatever it was, it did help a little to start moving things toward a better understanding at least with the Black and Puerto Rican mothers and fathers and educators, too, because we also had educators that were disgusted with the way the children were being taught.

It was not only the teachers were not so very good, but the teachers themselves claimed they have not enough textbooks, they do not have enough classrooms, and that it was very difficult. Classes were so large that it was impossible for the teachers to take care of such a large class. They didn't have gymnasiums, no libraries and at the time there was $1,500,00,000 allocated for the fiscal year. Finally we did get to the bilingual processes and the demonstration districts and decentralization, which hasn't been too much really because there is a lot to do yet. It is not a reality.

The decentralization, the way I see it, is only to keep your mouth shut, because the beautiful demonstration projects failed not because they wanted to fail but because the system made them fail. Now I hear such beautiful things in these hearings, and I am so happy to have been here, just a few times because I could not make it the whole time, but I have followed the papers and the radio, that everybody is in agreement. All the educators from the other cities and even the Board of Examiners, and everybody is happy, too--we need bilingual teachers, and there can be no discrimination and the Board of Examiners must go, and so and so and so forth.

Now I would like to ask one question:

What does the Commission on Human Rights intend to do to give the responsibility to the Board of Education to change or to come up with the promises that should have been ours and we have been denied. We need more Puerto Rican teachers. The accent seems to be very bad but I see that in the South the Blacks and the whites speak with the same accent. I spoke with a white, beautiful girl in Florida and then with a Black mammy, and they both spoke in the same manner. I couldn't understand them very well, but they couldn't understand me either. But then comes the Irish brogue, and the Israeli brogue, what you call it, if there is such a thing, and they all have little mannerisms that are so pretty, you know.

What does the child lose by listening to a beautiful teacher, an educated teacher, who may have a little different way of speaking, the same language but a little different accent. I don't think the child loses anything at all. On the contrary, he gains a world of knowledge because then he will know how the Irish have their little ways of speaking, how the Mexicans have their little ways of speaking, how the Blacks from the South have a different way of speaking, how the Blacks from the North and from the East speak.

So, I would like to really see that this will be, for some reason, the last time that we should see discrimination against Blacks and Puerto Ricans or Irish or Jews, or whatever it is, because really, in a democracy like ours, I think we should already have learned that we all have to live together, play together, work together and study together.

Now, another little point that I will have to say is, that it surprised me that at the table, whatever you might call it, the Commissioners' table I didn't see a Puerto Rican person or a Spanish name at the table, and I looked over it three times and I didn't see a Puerto Rican at the jury table.

I know this is a hearing and the Board of Education was sitting here and he was cross-examining them, so this is almost a court, and a beautiful court it has been, and I only hope from this something beautiful will come for the Puerto Ricans and the Black teachers in the City of New York.

Thank you very much.

THE CHAIRMAN: Thank you. I understand a question was raised about Puerto Rican Commissioners on this Commission. I think that is a fair question.

This Commission has had Puerto Rican Commissioners. We are unfortunate that the active Puerto Rican Commissioner is now the Manpower Commissioner, Commissioner Erazo. We are unfortunate that the other Puerto Rican Commissioner has not been active. The Mayor of the City of New York is now considering appointments to this Commission, and I expect this discrepancy, the fact that we ironically are momentarily and only temporarily without a Puerto Rican Commissioner, can be rectified, with not only one but several Puerto Rican Commissioners.

I would like to call next Anna Conigliaro.

We are pleased to welcome a former member of the Board of Education. We are pleased to have you testify here.

MRS. CONIGLIARO: Thank you very much, Commissioner Norton. I thank you for this opportunity to give my views on this point. I'm sorry that I have come at such a late time, but I hope that I may bring some specific information which might be of some use.

By now you have heard all about the stories and statistics and relevant points of legality and irrelevancy and so forth, pointing to the fact that there is discrimination in the Board of Examiners. I will speak to you about discrimination on the basis of my experience as a former member of a local school board, a former member of the Board of Education, and as a concerned parent and citizen. Last, but not least, as someone with personal experience and knowledge from having gone through the entire process of examination and having acquired a license of substitute bilingual assistant in community and school relations.

I submit that the Board of Examiners' tests, practices and procedures result in discrimination, and not only, and I would like to emphasize that, not only against Blacks and Puerto Ricans. It fosters in some instances racism and also by the very nature and through the rigidity of both requirements and questions with the corresponding expected responses and answers prevents a number of persons, especially Blacks and Puerto Ricans but also members of other ethnic groups, from entering the system and especially reaching the higher rungs in the hierarchy.

The Board of Examiners furthermore, is supposed to run on the merit system and civil service principles. Supposedly, it is the embodiment of fairness and impartiality--a machine which possesses the right people in a system which rewards with promotions those people who not only can give the right answers but also behave the right way. A few Blacks have made it to the top.

On the other hand, the Puerto Ricans have not made it yet. Only one Puerto Rican has been given the examination of assistant administrative director and passed it. The Board of Examiners gave him the examination one and a half years after he was recommended for this position, and two and a half years after he was in charge of the program with a license and the pay of a supervisor. I will elaborate on that point later.

Ladies and gentlemen, let me present to you the bilingual program of bilingual assistants in community and school relations. This program has a fancy and impressive title and license vested by the Board of Examiners, but let us see what it has actually done.

From 1949 until recently, this program was the only door, the only door, through which Spanish-speaking professionals could enter the system. For twelve long years, the only license they could take was a substitute auxiliary teacher.

In 1962, they were allowed to take the regular license for the same position, and they were appointed officially one year later, 1963.

By the way, this is standard procedure. It takes approxi-

mately a year to process applications, from the moment you take
the examination to the moment you get an appointment, unless you
have special permission to take the test under emergency situations or a recommendation of the Board. So, naturally, people
who can't afford to wait this long, may just be eliminated, they
don't come back. This happens not only to Blacks and Puerto
Ricans but to other people as well, and that is one way we lose
people. I know of cases like that, and you have interviewed at
times to avoid situations where a person who is a potentially good
teacher doesn't get into the system.

But, getting back to the bilingual program, which is the only
program which the system has had and that still has the largest
number of Spanish-speaking professionals. Let us take a look at
the examination.

I took the substitute license, so I took the test and I can
assure you that it is not difficult. Originally, and until 1968, this
license required knowledge of both English and Spanish, with a
ratio of 85% English and 15% Spanish, and a test was given to
measure this knowledge. In 1968 it is supposed to be 50-50 per
cent. I am sure many people have failed the test for varied reasons, but one basic reason for failure by many, I submit, has
been the fact that these tests were given and rated or scored without a real knowledge by the examiner of the applicant's language
and culture.

A clear case of culture gap on the part of well-intentioned
examiners, at best, and possibly of latent racism, at worst. Also,
even though bilingual assistants will have to deal largely with
Spanish-speaking children, parent and community groups, the
examiners have been more exacting on examining and scoring the
85% or 50% English section of the test which they knew best and
the applicant knows less well, and much less exacting or capable
to examine fairly on the Spanish section, which generally speaking
the examiners know less well and the applicant better.

I will give you an example of this. I know of people who lost
points in the scoring because they translated "cake" the way we
translate it, using the word "biscoche torta." The two words are
perfect Spanish. "Biscoche" is a perfectly correct word in Spanish as everybody who has a rudimentary knowledge of Spanish
knows.

Let's see how the program has done. In 1965, sixteen years
after the program had been in existence--it started with ten and
then went progressively to 20, 50, 70 or whatever, until presently
there are 234 bilingual assistants in 24 districts. The people who
wanted to be supervisors were given an opportunity. In 1965, 60
people took the supervisory examination and only 11 made it, only
11, and to this day there are only 11 supervisory positions. This
test was given in 1965, and even though it has been requested by
the director, I must put it in quotes, of the program, no action
has been taken.

Let's see what is happening to the program which is supposed
to represent at least the best effort in dealing with the Spanish-
speaking community and in affording the opportunities for employing Spanish-speaking professionals.

Since 1967, the person in charge of the program has been performing all the duties of director, without authority, and with the pay and title of supervisor. Why? It took the Board of Examiners about a year and a half or so to give him the examination. He has passed it. He is eligible, so why has no formal appointment been made? Do I need to tell you the effects on the morale of the staff, and on the effectiveness of the program?

Now I would like to present a few examples to substantiate some of the things that I said at the beginning. I would like to read to you a question used in the examination for the position of teacher of English as a second language. I am quoting:

"While you are teaching, an irate parent storms into the room screaming that nothing is being done to help the Spanish-speaking children. What procedures would you follow in this situation?"

This is a teacher of English as a second language teaching Spanish-speaking children. I don't think I have to say who the teacher thinks the parent is who comes storming in screaming. Why this question? Is it relevant? How is it rated?

Let me give you another example. A principal of an intermediate school had a vacancy for a graphics teacher in his school. He found a candidate whom he liked and felt was acceptable, and sent him to the Board of Examiners to be examined. This man is a Puerto Rican who has lived here for many years and has worked in the graphics department of the Daily News. According to the Board, he didn't pass the English test, he needed to take a course, and he also had to take the practical test. The man lives in Staten Island and he had to go to Far Rockaway, that is the only shop. But the thing is, he had to take a test on all the industrial aspects of the license, and all he was going to teach was graphics. The man being a Puerto Rican who takes no nonsense, left and never came back. Let's see, who was that man?

Three years have passed and yesterday I called him to find out what had happened to him. I learned that he has been serving at Staten Island College, has approached 35 credits in English, economics and speech and everything without any difficulty, and we missed the opportunity of using that man, who is an expert in his field of graphics, and the children didn't get graphics during that year because that vacancy remained unfilled.

Another example. I know of a young man from Puerto Rico with a classification of 1-Y. This is a medical deferment on the basis of a chronic sinus condition, as has been found out. He took the examination for bilingual assistant for community and school relations. He passed it with a very high mark, but then since the time that he took it, the ruling of the board has changed so no longer can a man with a 1-Y classification be accepted. So, he has been denied appointment.

So, rules change, ratios change, names change, divisions in which the programs belong change, but essentially a situation continues. We have the largest program which employs Puerto Ricans, and yet doesn't have personality, identity, it doesn't have a sense of direction.

Considering the lateness, I have just tried to bring to your attention certain cases which I thought might be useful for your consideration.

I would like to conclude this presentation by making just a few recommendations. As many people before me have recommended, I believe that state certification should be the requirement for hiring in the public school system just as it is in the private and public school systems in the State of New York. I also feel that a clearly defined procedure for community school boards to recruit and hire personnel must be established, taking into consideration the special needs of the districts.

A training program must be instituted at the local level, and I hope that the Commission on Human Rights, which has done this before through the leadership programs, would continue to do it, at this particular time at which decentralization is being tested.

I think it is extremely important at this point that we attempt to educate and train our parents and our community people in the exercise of their duties as participants in this new decentralization process. This may sound ridiculous to some who may say, aren't the people entitled to some mistakes, but my dear friend, we cannot forget that a double standard exists and will continue to be with us for some time. It is my feeling that we may be on borrowed time even with the little power that decentralization is offering now if we don't take steps to insure that this little power, this opportunity for people to participate in the decisions which affect their lives and their children's lives, is maintained. People must be made aware of their sense of responsibility in keeping the policy and decision-making and the control at the local level. They must understand that we have a responsibility to put our resources to maximum use and benefit, and together seek other resources and avenues to achieve the goal that will unite us, the improvement of the education of our children.

I thank you very much.

THE CHAIRMAN: Thank you.

I want to call Vera David.

MISS DAVID: Good evening everyone, and thank you very kindly, Mrs. Norton. I tried very hard to get here the first of the week but I couldn't until today.

I have heard quite a bit of talk this afternoon about the school system but I haven't heard any talk as to how any of us can get to the children to make them better students.

I find that we fight against each other so much in the school system--I'm working there, I know. When we come into the school system to get jobs to teach the children, we come in there with a mind to take the children and mold them and make them into the best citizens in the world. Then, after we get into the school system, we sort of feel that we are going to join the others that have been in the school system for a very long time before we got in. But, this doesn't help the children at all.

I've seen situations where you walk into a classroom and you look at a child, a child is standing there, giving you a very, very blank look. The blank look is almost saying, "Will you help me,

I can't talk to anyone, no one hears me," while the person that is supposed to be teaching the child is somewhere talking with her coworker about "I wonder how much that job pays, I wonder do I have enough credits, can I go over there and talk with Mr. or Mrs. So-and-so? Do you think that I can get in?" That time they are devoting to that particular person talking about the amount of credits that they have, or "Do you think I can get this job," during that time this child is running around the wall just like a fly. I have seen that many, many times.

Then I walk over and they'll say to you, "Something is wrong with this child," if you question why the child is running all over the place. What is wrong with the child? They'll say this child has a problem. The problem this child I think really has is that no one is sitting there directing her or him or giving instructions.

I am going to get off that, and I want you to listen to me about something that happened with a young man who was an educational assistant who came into the school to help the children to become better children and to be extra hands and eyes for the teacher in the school.

The young man's name I won't quote but the young man had worked for the school system for three and a half years. Because he was young, he just didn't think like the older teachers, but he did come in and teach the children to read better and to play together better, and to make them feel that they were children in the classroom, and someone was watching, helping and taking care of the children.

If I seem a bit nervous, I am sorry. I have an impediment of speech in the jaws, so please excuse me.

This young man came in and he worked for three and a half years. After three and a half years of working, they decided they didn't want him to work with the children any more, because he didn't get to school on time. I'm not saying that the young man was right or wrong. I'm not arguing about the right or wrong of the young man for not getting to school on time as he should do. What I'm trying to convey to you is that because the young man didn't come through all the time, they got rid of him.

After they got rid of the young man at this particular school, the young man was out of work from September until January. When you work for the Board of Education you can't draw unemployment. This young man had to go to someone to talk about getting another job. So, when he came down to the Board to speak to someone about another job, they just said to him, "We don't have a job for you." That was very bad for a young man at this particular time to have someone say to him, "We don't have a job for you."

Now, he was supposed to go back out into the district and look for a job, so that he could be with children, to teach them the things that he thought he should teach them. When he went back out there into the school, they said, "We are very sorry, we just don't have an opening for you," so he batted around for four months.

The day before yesterday, the man got a job at a particular

school, and went back into the school with the children. I feel that four months is much too long for a person who wants to help children, knows how to help children, and can help children, to be out of a job. Don't you?

I won't take any more of your time because I have so much to say and I may sound scattery.

I myself have had quite a lot of uncomfortable things happen to me in the Board but my purpose is to try to help all of the children, whether the children are Black, white, or have stripes all over them, Puerto Rican, Irish, German, Jewish, or whatever language they speak. All mankind I'm willing to help any time, any place, anywhere, within the Board of Education system that I can.

I thank you very kindly.

THE CHAIRMAN: Thank you.

I want to call Irving Ravin.

MR. RAVIN: My name is Irving Ravin. I would like to thank you for the opportunity to speak, Commissioner Norton, all the other Commissioners.

I am theoretically a teacher. I'm changing occupations at midstream, age 49. Since October I have had offers from seven principals and four community superintendents to teach in the New York City school system, but have been stymied by, let's say, foolish procedures at the Board of Examiners. My latest per diem offer is right here, and the Board of Examiners won't touch it.

However, my own problems I would say are minimal as compared to the problems of the pupils of the City of New York, insofar as they're being denied good education by the practices of the Board of Examiners. I believe that the Board of Examiners is not actively trying to discriminate, but I believe also that you have a system which is so bureaucratic, and so insufficient, and so foolish in so many of its procedures, that it can't help having some of the worst systems possible in hiring practices, which, in effect, does discriminate.

I think that if any of us were to go to the offices of the Board of Examiners, and see and interview any of the people taking tests or waiting around and ask them about their experiences, there would be almost unanimous agreement about the inefficiencies and foolishness of the Board of Examiners.

I think also, when the state has decided to appoint four people to the Board of Examiners at $32,000 a year and give them lifetime jobs, the tendency is for the organization to become rather inefficient. There is no great incentive to keep up with standards. I think Commissioner Norton, if she were appointed for life at a healthy salary and all the Commissioners had lifetime appointments at good salaries, within twenty years or even in ten years the Commission of Human Rights won't be worth what it is today or anywhere near that.

Various people have said from time to time that New York City has more stringent hiring practices than the state, under state certification. In actual practice, I don't think that is the case. The city requires twelve education credits for a provisional license, the state requires twenty-four credits. However, the matter of college credits in education, I believe, is one of the big faults of the Board of Examiners and is unrealistic so far as determining qualifications to teach in New York City schools or possibly for any other school system as well.

Last summer I took twelve credits in education at St. Francis College along with sixty other people, mostly youngsters, and I personally doubt very much whether more than five of that sixty were any better qualified to teach as a result of having those twelve credits in education. In the meanwhile, I've had nine more credits. The principals and community superintendent who are willing to hire me, I believe, had no concern over the education credits or anything else in education that I might be qualified for but were concerned that I, as a person, was able to give something to children, that I would like children to learn these days on an individualized instruction basis.

The Commissioner of Education Nyquist, the Chancellor, Dr. Scribner, and United Federation of Teachers' president, Albert Shanker, have all come out in favor of open classrooms, individualized instruction of children learning at their own speeds and in their own styles. I think in view of this, the Commission and the people of New York should question extremely seriously the whole licensing procedure as to whether it is applicable to the new type of teachers that are wanted because the type of teachers that are wanted are not the specialists in certain branches of knowledge that were wanted ten years ago. Right now the trend for the future apparently is for people who can be expediters of knowledge, who can be facilitators of knowledge, who can help children to learn themselves from various materials on hand, can help them in individual discovery programs.

From the tests I took, I took both the temporary and permanent test, given by the Board of Examiners, I was appalled not by how difficult the tests were but how simple they were. I believe, I would say, 50% of any graduating class of the High School of Music & Art and possibly 25% of the graduation classes of the High School of Science could pass these tests for teaching without any education courses, without any college credits whatsoever, if they were to spend about ten hours studying previous tests and about five hours looking into the answers the Board of Examiners wanted on oral questions on the methods of teaching. The passing marks the Board of Examiners have allowed, 50% on both written and oral tests, is also appalling because this again is not any type of real qualification or evidence that the person is really ready to teach. Other people in these hearings have pointed out that written examinations do not give much evidence of ability to teach. Even the person from the National Teacher Examination pointed out that his examination, the NTE, only measured a certain small portion of teaching aptitude, that of the amount of general knowledge a person has, and that a tremendous amount of other things were needed to choose teachers.

The fact that high school graduates could pass the Board of Examiners' test does not mean, in my opinion, that they would be ready to teach. I believe that we should revise drastically our idea of who should be teaching in our classrooms. I think that one of the reasons that the UFT supports the Board of Examiners right now in their licensing procedures for teachers, is that if we were to really come up with criteria for teachers in how much learning children were doing under tutelage, that somewhere around 25% of teachers with tenure in the New York City school system would be found unqualified by any really objective test, and the union doesn't want to have that brought out to light.

I believe that the type of tests which would be valid would be a fairly elementary oral examination first to see that the applicant has the ability to convey his thoughts in an organized, coherent manner; a basic written examination, to show that he was able to write in clear, coherent English. The fact that the Board of Examiners has disqualified many people in the past, has flunked people because they didn't in their written exams put in subordinate clauses in their essays, is I think a very shameful one, and many people who were not used to writing English with subordinate clauses flunked the test just for that particular reason, I believe.

In addition to these two qualifications, I do not believe that a college degree, even in itself, is necessary to function effectively as a facilitator of learning in the city school system because what is needed are people who are able to reach young children--I'm talking about elementary teachers, but I think this would apply to junior high school or high school teachers. I believe that in the new system of teaching and facilitated learning, that Nyquist and Silberman have responded to, and which Lillian Weber is organizing, a very qualified background is necessary.

It should be borne in mind that in the British school system the least qualified of their teachers are in the elementary schools and they pay them the least. Most of them, I believe, do not have the educational requirements, educational courses, that are required in the New York City school system, and yet the British elementary school system is something which is highly admired in this country and apparently the model for most of the progressive thinking in this country.

What I would suggest then is that for people who do want to become teachers, who have the ability to demonstrate to their local school boards these abilities, we can do away with both the city licensing and state certification because I think these certification credits are for the birds. If you talk to the teachers' college graduates, down at NYU, and the less prestigious at St. Francis or Yeshiva, and you talk to people who have been graduates of these colleges and have been teaching a while, they will tell you ninety to one hundred per cent of the education courses were of no real practical value in helping them reach the children.

I would suggest the basic test would be one where you put these prospective teachers into classrooms with twenty-five children, and ask them to prepare a lesson which would keep the children interested for a forty-five minute period. I think that you can easily equip classrooms with two-way mirrors, and the children, even if they know the mirrors are there and there are observers, will be able to function in their regular way. I have been in classrooms during open school week in which my stepson was present, where there was a substitute and where the kids had no compunction about half a dozen parents being in the room, and they were engaged in throwing spitballs and throwing paper airplanes and running around the room, and in general not paying any attention to the teacher. This was in a good upper middle-class classroom, not an inner-city classroom.

I've visited the inner-city classrooms, worked as a volunteer and have seen classrooms where twenty-five to fifty per cent of the kids in a fifth and sixth grade classroom are still on first or second grade reading and math level. So whenever these lovely organized teachers, selected by the Board of Examiners, go through their regular lesson plans, the kids cannot keep up with them, they have no idea what is happening; they are bored, restless and they climb the walls. So if the local community boards have the responsibility of selecting their own teachers to fit their own classrooms, based on these tests within sample classrooms, I would suggest also that the applicant have an opportunity to go to three different classrooms if they flunk in the first one, because the class is too wild, and I think there are sufficient classes where this could easily be done.

I believe that the community school boards can choose the candidates fairly. I think one of the big points in favor of community school boards acting in a fair manner without discrimination is the fact that many of these school boards, as a result of proportional representation, did elect, I believe, a rather high proportion of Catholic people as members of the community school boards. I have attended a number of community school board meetings in two different districts and have seen several occasions when there were religious matters brought up in relation to Catholic issues, such as special bus service for private Catholic schools, using the city bus system, where these boards which were heavily Catholic, didn't lean over in any greater degree than I, with a Jewish background, might have decided in a similar situation.

I believe that these people who are willing to serve on community school boards without pay are extremely public spirited and I don't think there is much of any likelihood they would be doing anything in their hiring practices to choose people who would be all of one religion or ethnic group or political group, or nationality group.

As I say, I see no reason for even needing college graduates. If there are college graduates who wish to apply, you might give them priority because you have had rules in the past about college graduates and education credits, but I don't see that education credits have been helping to provide good teachers for the school system.

I just want to summarize now because I've been speaking quite a while. I believe that there is an overwhelming minority of teachers in the school system selected by the Board of Examiners who are unfit to teach because they do not have the rapport that is necessary to reach young children. They don't have the feeling, they don't like children, they're afraid of them, they're not willing to meet them with respect, to meet them at whichever level they are, to work with them on an individual basis, to try to help them learn what they're interested in--and I'm not talking about a lot of crazy things in the curriculum which make no sense and will have no bearing for their later lives.

I think that the Board of Examiners has failed miserably without any bad intentions and that they have in effect discriminated without bad intentions. But I believe if we give the matter over entirely to the community school boards now, without city certification, without state certification, they will be able to choose teachers who will be able to reach the children and give them the break they have been missing until now.

THE CHAIRMAN: Thank you.

For those still wishing to testify, please keep in mind that this is for the evening and this is a special session and there are other people who are waiting to testify.

I am pleased to welcome Mr. Richard Parrish.

MR. PARRISH: Thank you, Madam Chairman; I should say, Commissioner Norton, and members of the Human Rights Commission and members of the audience.

The United Black Caucus of Teachers recommends the demise of the Board of Education's Board of Examiners because it has been an ineffective recruiter and/or selector of minority teachers or supervisors and, more importantly, it more than any other Board of Education group serves to perpetuate, legitimatize and rationalize racism in the school system.

My name is Richard Parrish. I represent the United Black Caucus of Teachers. I have been also asked to represent the Greater New York Division of the National Afro-American Labor Council whose views on this matter are the same as the United Black Caucus of Teachers.

I am a classroom teacher with 22 years experience, now employed as a teacher of Special Education at P.S. 70 in the Bronx. From 1956 to 1965 I was President of the first Black teachers protest group, the Community Teachers Association, and the concerns I express here can be also said to be substantially those of this organization as well.

The United Black Caucus of Teachers wishes to commend the Commission for these timely hearings which are likely to project into full national view the deplorable status of minority workers in the school system as partially reflected in the 3.8% and 9.1% figures for Black supervisors and teachers respectfully.

When one looks at the few fully licensed Black principals in the system, one can hardly appreciate, let alone comprehend, the 3.8% unless there are many white supervisors passing for Black. As a matter of fact, Black teachers have been blacked out of principal positions for more than 60 years.

Our investigation, statistics and analyses reveal that from 1900 to 1960, the latest year for the U.S. census report, the total number of fully licensed Black principals at any one time was less than 5; that for most of this period there was either no Black principals, or, at best, one or two.

And I have, as an appendix to these remarks, the census figures.

Just to give you some idea of how they go, because I did make a rather definite statement and I don't want to call an organization or a group racist unless I think it has historic evidence for it, if we were to start at the year 1900, which was about the time when the schools became incorporated into the New York public school system and the Board of Examiners came into being, in New York City at that time there were 60,666 Blacks, to be exact. Of course, you had, in New York City at that time, I guess no more than about four million people. It might be understandable at that point that there were less than three Black principals.

But, by 1910, the figure had risen to 91,709 for Blacks, and still less than three.

In 1920, the same thing, less than three Black principals.

Now, as I was doing research and trying to find out specific evidence of Black supervisors, so hard because the records do not reveal candidates or teachers by race. You have to refer to the memory of those oldtimers who have been in the system, people like Mrs. Gertrude Ayers, the first Black principal; or the retired Dr. Frances Turner, former Board of Examiner member, whom I have consulted; Dr. James E. Allen, now retired, former coordinator in Central Harlem. The evidence I got was that you may talk about a William Buckley--no relationship, I am sure, to the present personage in the Senate--in the 1920's, maybe around World War I, and then neither in literature nor in the memories of these people now in their 70's and 80's, can they give me definitely the name of any other Black supervisor before this time. And then, if you go all through the 20's you have none.

Then, when you come into the 30's, just one name comes up, Mrs. Gertrude Ayers, first Black principal in Central Harlem, and I can talk extemporaneously like this, because I can almost go on for hours and name every Black licensed principal on my two hands. Even up until this day, until this moment. There are no more than 11 fully licensed Black principals that have been accredited by the Board of Examiners now. There are certainly acting Black principals. There may be as many as 20 or 21, so added to those fully licensed, it would be about 31.

Our investigation then revealed that as the population rose, from 1930 to 1960, Black population went from 142,176 to approximately 1,087,931. All during this time there has been nothing going on in the minds of the Board of Examiners.

Despite these developments over these 60 years, the urban revolution accompanying two world wars and the emergence of New York City as the political and cultural capital of Black America, abundant with talented manpower, there have been no comparable or significant changes in the racially restrictive employment policies of the Board.

One obvious outcome of these policies is that 98%, or more, of the public school students of our school system have never been permitted to seek or experience the educational leadership of a capable Black principal. Another outcome was the demoralization of Black college graduates and teachers who upon trying to break into the system were frustrated, sidetracked and deluded by bureaucratic red tape, superficial interviews and oral examinations.

Two cases stand out in my mind: The first was that of Mrs. Gertrude Ayers who, in the course of the examination for principal, was told she had failed because she had a southern accent. Mrs. Ayers was born and had lived in New York City all her life. Actually, she had never been farther south than South Ferry, Manhattan. After threatening the Board with a court suit, she was finally passed and became the first Black woman principal.

The other flagrant case of discrimination practiced by the Board was that of Miss Layle Lane who was told that she could not qualify for a teacher's examination because she had attended an unaccredited college, Howard University.

She fought back. It took her several years of hard work to make Howard University an acceptable Class A college to the Board of Examiners. She went on to become an eminent social studies teacher at James Monroe and Benjamin Franklin High Schools and later to emerge as an equally eminent National Vice President of the American Federation of Teachers.

Now, I quote these two cases merely to indicate that, despite their almost autocratic, capricious attitude, the Board of Examiners actually held in its hands the careers of outstanding Blacks who tried to break the system, and only those who had something-- I don't know what you would call it--the gumption and the guts and the courage to fight back, have been able to make it, and even they, most of the time, didn't.

Now, while these two courageous teachers made it into and within the system, there have been countless hundreds of others who have been shunted aside or defeated. In the opinion of the United Black Caucus of Teachers the methods and procedures of the Board of Examiners have been anything but fair, have, in all honesty, constituted a devilish ordeal for most Blacks, a 70-year-long nightmare.

In proposing the elimination of the Board of Examiners, and also that this Commission likewise make such a recommendation to the local and state bodies responsible for these decisions, the United Black Caucus of Teachers can hardly view with favor such substitutes as have been tossed around, such as the National Teacher Examinations or state examinations. The folly of these examinations is that they do not predict with enough accuracy or validity whether a person can be a successful teacher or not, and the even more devilish thing about it, this Board of Examiners, once it has made a decision, the rest of the ring of supervisors-- I conceive of the Board of Examiners as being the hub of this ring-- reinforces the racist decision of the Board of Examiners. So that you would have, based upon an invalid test, the perpetuation of the error by principals and supervisors who had to pass upon the candidate during the first three years of his or her service. That is, during his or her probationary period.

It is like saying if I went through--this is the Board of Examiners saying this was right. Now I have the right to weed you out and bring you into the club if you can play the game, and if you play the game the way we have set it up, then you are given a stamp. Since most of them were white and mostly middle-class, 99% of them fit into the club. Very few were weeded out.

This you don't find in any business enterprise or any industry. There is no predictive instrument given by any industry which can say, with more than 50 to 60% validity, that this person will succeed. But with our Board of Examiners, they hire 99% and 98%.

Rather than these superficial tests, the N.T.E. or the state or any other device which they may put together to test or screen out candidates, the United Black Caucus of Teachers would rather support the idea that state certification, a realistic internship program, properly funded and with final approval residing in local school boards, are sufficient procedures to recruit, train and upgrade teacher personnel in this City as in any other community in New York State.

We believe that the New York City metropolitan area is teeming with untapped teacher talent. Recruitment programs for teachers and supervisors alike might concentrate here at home before more of our promising prospects accept jobs in New Jersey, Westchester County, Long Island, Pennsylvania and other states as they have been doing over the past few years. Prompt action is of the essence.

I know personally of people, teachers in this City, who could not make it and become supervisors after 10 years of working here, and they have gone as far west as Seattle, Evanston, Chicago, Detroit, and you find them in Montclair, in Englewood, Teaneck, you will find them in White Plains, you will find them on the Island. If these same candidates can be supervisors in white, middle-class suburbs, upper middle-class cities like Evanston, something is wrong that they couldn't make the grade here in New York City.

Finally, I would say that the time is running out. Time is of the essence. The United Black Caucus of Teachers proposes that in the event that state certification becomes a reality in New York City, Black teachers, supervisors and others concerned be organized and deputized by the Board of Education and the City of New York to take the lead in making an all out effort to change the shameful historic blackout of competent minority principals from the school system.

Now, this we feel is absolutely necessary because Black people throughout this Nation, in the professional field of education, are not going to come to New York. Black people right here in New York City are not going to go into the field of administration unless they can visibly see successful Black supervisors confronting them, face to face, telling them that the racist system is over, if you qualify, like any other person in New York State, you have an honest chance of working and using your talents for all the children of New York City.

I want to thank you very much.

THE CHAIRMAN: I want to call Mr. Roy Sicular.

Please, those who come on now, remember that there are

people waiting and I would like everyone to keep his remarks, as much as possible, to five or 10 minutes at the most.

MR. SICULAR: My purpose in being here is to--

THE CHAIRMAN: Speak into the microphone.

MR. SICULAR: --is to point out the discrimination and harassment that is brought to bear against radical teachers, against teachers who believe in a different philosophy of education, against teachers who believe in change, which perhaps is one thing that most of the administrators and most of the people who run the Board of Education are afraid of.

I am a school teacher. This is my third year. My name is Roy Sicular.

I am certified by the state to be a regular social studies teacher. However, I have had much difficulty in getting my regular license from the Board of Examiners. I have taken tests four times. On one occasion I failed the written part, because of some grammar errors, basically. On two other occasions I failed the oral interview because I told them I didn't think they had a right to interview me, and I told them it was my opinion that they had no right to interview me. But, apparently, they held that against me as well as my other ideas on education with which they didn't agree.

Now, on my last attempt I passed everything. I feel that you tell them what they want. All right. So I passed everything.

However, in the process of teaching on my regular substitute license, I acquired a rather bad record and, therefore, my license was denied on the basis of record, which I am appealing. But I do not think I have much of a chance because, in the process of my three years I can document how a person can be harassed out of a job and how a person can be framed, so to speak.

Let me begin with the specifics.

Specifically, there are certain schools in this city that have marking policies that say students--let me read from it--it says:

"Slow classes. Those in which most people are reading two years or more below-the-grade level, no mark higher than 80 should be given in academic areas without the approval of the subject teacher and the assistant principal."

This was in my later school.

This goes against all the educational philosophy that I have learned, because it creates basically a failure syndrome, and what you are doing is actually--before open enrollment--condemning these poor students to a non-academic future.

I disregarded that marking policy and I got a letter from an assistant principal.

"While you did revise your grades twice, it remains an inordinately long list of exceptions to our school marking policy in your grading for your slower classes. I reviewed the reasons for our school marking policy..." and it goes on--I don't want to take up the time here--but, basically, it is something that I defy.

Another bone of contention, the giving of citywide examinations to classes that are incapable of reading these examinations.

Now, in this last occasion in this particular school, these

poor little kids couldn't read the examination. I was helping them read the examination and I was helping them with a few of the questions. Their science teacher told the principal that the test was invalid later and, of course, this was, you know, considered unprofessional.

Also, another very interesting point in the giving of these examinations, the students are supposed to be dismissed at a certain hour. After the students had finished the exam, I dismissed them because I saw no purpose in them having to stay when they are only getting restless and can be dangerous to themselves.

I got a note:

"Mr. Sicular, you were proctoring a class at 10:40 yesterday. I came around to the various classrooms before 12 o'clock. I arrived at room 301 where you were supposed to be at 11:55, but the class was gone. Please let me know in writing where you were and who, if you dismissed early, had given you permission to leave early."

Okay, you know, this is unprofessional to disregard school rules. You know, it is illegal. They can fine you. And I have been in three schools. I have been in South Jamaica, I have been in the Bronx in my career, and I see what goes on. If they don't like you, they can find ways to get rid of you.

Another note is:

"Dear Mr. Sicular, I was by your room the other day. Your class control is such that the classroom is excessively noisy. I have frequently found students walking around the room, sitting by the piano, also too many students leave the room."

This is another thing. So-called school rules.

In some schools one person is supposed to go out on a pass, in other schools two people. It is such a degrading thing, you can't even go to the bathroom when you want to.

To the students, it is dehumanizing. Their lives are regulated to such an extent, it is quite unhuman. I don't want to go into this.

The point is, there is a certain educational philosophy, and if this is a public school, there is no reason why a person with a certain educational philosophy that may be different than the standard shouldn't be able to implement it. No one can say at this point exactly what a valid educational experience should be, and the point is that I am certified by the state. I graduated from Queens College in 1968. I should have the right to practice my profession without harassment, without discrimination.

I have already collected three U ratings because I won't compromise my principles, and I will tell assistant principals and principals when I think they are wrong and there is one thing that most of these people, who I call ball-less wonders, are afraid of. That is defiance, because they emasculated themselves on the altar of obedience and they want everybody else to be obedient, and if there is one thing that the schools teach, it is obedience. And if there is one thing that can't be stood, it is defiance.

But the people who have been alienated from their minds, the people who have been turned off and made to feel docile, suddenly find their minds and say, why should I, and they are saying it all over and these people are rising up.

Here is just one newspaper article:

"Students on rampage. Police were called to I.S. 72 in Rochdale Village after about 30 students, some of whom have been barred from graduation exercises this week because of their conduct, went on a destructive rampage according to school officials. Two youngsters were picked up by police who referred them to the Youth Division."

I was at that school briefly.

The point I am trying to make is when the police were around there was a concern that the schools would have to be closed because they have two policemen in many schools on a regular basis. And it is a very sad commentary on the state of education. Very sad.

I would like to continue with my few things.

Quite frankly, the last depressed class in our society is the children these days. Everybody has to take so much. And it is passed on to the poor little children.

Now, unfortunately, it is an accepted thing. It is an accepted value of the society. Unfortunately, I have very little sympathy for the parents I meet, who I find unduly hostile. They reflect their world and the children pick up the attitudes of the parents.

Now, either you are going to change the children before they get into the school or you are going to have intensive pre-school education, you are going to have intensive parent education, or you change the schools and you change them.

A lot of people are able to put up with the schools, but now people are saying, "Why should I?" You know, they don't have the motivation of other people. There are classes in certain schools with--I will be specific--in Junior High School 310, I have a friend called Larry Kantrowitz who tells me two of its lowest grades do not have a regular teacher. They have substitutes every day. They can do that because these are the slower parents and the parents aren't concerned, so they can get away with that.

Unfortunately, there is a tremendous amount of latent, subconscious racism and sadism on the part of personnel, and the discussions in the school rooms are, we against them, the animals, and keep them down and keep them in control, unfortunately. And it is a very sad situation.

I recommend people to read authors like Paul Goodman and Eric Fromm and Holt, Silberman and Cole, and get an insight into what is going on and what is happening.

Let me tell you one other thing, and that is in Nazi Germany only 1% of the teachers had to be eliminated by Hitler, and teachers are generally a conservative lot.

Albert Shanker is interested in the teachers. He is interested in his main vital interests, unfortunately. The "Fuehrer" has, in his own organization, eliminated four of his U.F.T. field representatives. And when this happens you have to begin to think of what is happening to our organization.

Finally, in closing, I brought a few things which I am going to burn to symbolize the deeper trends and the deeper things that are wrong with our system.

I have a report card--a grading system perpetuates the failure syndrome. I have my old report card on which I did quite well --a ninth grade report card, 12.2 reading level, you know, all good marks and everything is very nice and jolly. But I had to give a student a report card which had all low grade marks, all failures, and the student said to me, "Cram it up your ass." And I can understand why, because we are telling the student you are a failure, we are telling him you are not worth anything, and the student rejects it. The student rebels. The student says, "I am worth something." And marks perpetuate a failure of psychology alienating these people from their minds.

This will take too long to burn. I will just rip it up.

Now, what is the next item I have here--

THE CHAIRMAN: How much longer will you be?

MR. SICULAR: I will be finished soon.

I have here one of my U ratings, which is completely arbitrary and completely capricious and completely against what I have been taught to believe in, and I will just rip that up. Actually, maybe I should burn it, but since you are in a rush, you know, I will try and be compliant.

What else do I have here. I have here a copy of my student transcript of marks, 130-some-odd credits, most of which were taken by taking examinations which have been described as follows: "It's like taking a shit in which you just wait and when the time comes you let it out." The exam is like a piece of toilet paper, and it all comes out and you give them back what they want to know. And that is how you get by. That is how you get through the system. It is like a big game. So that is what it is all about.

And I thought I was putting in time to make it count. When I came out, I thought I would be able to help. I volunteered to work in a disadvantaged school, and I was at one time a little idealistic and I thought I would be able to help, but it is just not really worth too much right now because I am not even able to practice my profession. I was terminated in my last school. So that is that.

What we have here is very representative of this country. It is a dollar bill. And the U. S., the dollar bill, is an imposition of two signs, a U and S. If you look at the dollar sign, it is an S with a very thin U. And that exactly is what this country stands for, a dollar bill. In other words, the buck, the dollar. Now, I am going to burn it right now. Well, I think money is what is messing this country up, quite frankly.

Well, let's see. What is this--an old substitute license from the City of New York, which isn't worth much because I haven't been able to get a job with it because of my record, and the whole concept of formal education is really farcical.

What else do we have here. I have a couple of U. F. T. cards, which I don't think are worth much either. Actually at one time the organization was very vital, but they did some things. Sherman Junior High School 142, they called them a bunch of militants. I think I'm going to rip up these cards because--maybe some day the organization will become revitalized.

All right.

And, last but not least, and this is the most important card. There comes a time when people have to take a stand, when they have to become political prisoners and there comes a time when, like people in Germany, only 1% of the teachers ever spoke up, the rest were concerned with their own self interest. Now, there comes a time in which you really have to become a political prisoner, and I intend to burn my draft card right now, because of the priorities of this country.

THE CHAIRMAN: I have been quite liberal with you, and you are getting way beyond your 15 minutes and your time will be up in a few minutes.

MR. SICULAR: That is the last one.

THE CHAIRMAN: Don't take advantage because I am not an authoritarian.

MR. SICULAR: Maybe if this money was spent on education, maybe if this country, you know, got its conscience, maybe 8,000 aircrafts lost at a cost of maybe 30 billion dollars is enough to put two more people in every classroom and it is enough to build an awful lot of houses.

So that is the end of my testimony.

THE CHAIRMAN: Thank you, Mr. Sicular.

- - - - -

MR. McMORRIS: My name is LeRoy McMorris.

Madam Chairman, Commissioners, I am speaking probably from the other side of the fence. I'm from a white, middle-class neighborhood. We have only one school. However, that school is predominantly Puerto Rican.

THE CHAIRMAN: Where is your school located, please?

MR. McMORRIS: P.S. 140, District 20.

THE CHAIRMAN: In what borough?

MR. McMORRIS: In Brooklyn, Bay Ridge, Bensonhurst, Flatbush, the southern end of Sunset Park and so forth.

I know that P.S. 140 has been seeking a principal. They sought two people that they liked, one who is Puerto Rican, another who is not, but who knows Spanish, and has rapport. Neither one of the two could be hired because they were not high enough on the list.

I am mainly here as a parent, but I am an adult lightning rod for the Bay Ridge Youth Organization, a group of formerly alienated young people who have been turned around and have been brought back, at least temporarily into the system, a group of young people I was a little concerned about, who I love very much and would put my life on the line for.

I am a member of the Public Action Committee for Education, in District 20, known as PACE 20. I am a member of the Public Education Association and a member of its high school field team. I will refer back to that a little later.

There are three classes of people in this country who have no means to fight back. These are the prisoners in penal institutions, those hospitalized, and our young people from 9:00 to 3:00 or during whatever time the school is open.

It has been stated earlier here today, and in the past week, that perhaps a panacea would be if in more Black schools, there were more Black teachers, in predominantly Puerto Rican schools, there would be more Puerto Rican teachers.

I don't think I need to explain that in most of the public high schools in Brooklyn most of the teachers are white or in euphemism of the Board of Education, 'other."

The Board of Education now has four categories, speaking of students: Negro, Puerto Rican, Other and South American, which I learn is Spanish-speaking; so somebody from the country of "Ifno," or Spanish Sahara where they speak Spanish on the continent of Africa would be considered as "South American," but somebody from Brazil who speaks Portuguese would be tossed into the "Other" category which also includes whites, American Indians, Chinese, Japanese, anything that does not fit into the other three.

I think this type of a category shows the thinking within the Board of Education, but I got off of a previous point.

Th high schools in Brooklyn have predominantly white teachers. In a study issued by the Brooklyn Education Task Force about the failure of academic high schools in New York City, for the graduating class of 1970, June, New Utrecht High School, showed 95.5% "Others" in the graduating class, and 38.2% academic diplomas, the only type of a diploma which would guarantee you at that point to get into a college.

Lafayette High School: 92% of the graduating class, "Other," but of course that would mean predominantly white; and 49.5% academic diplomas.

Abraham Lincoln High School: 92.5% "Others," and 63.5% academic, the diploma.

It begins to sound right.

Then we go to Sheepshead Bay High School: 87.4% "Other"; 48.3% academic diplomas. These are white children being taught by white teachers.

Midwood High School, and this fits what is put out as propaganda as the pattern, I should say: 84.6% "Other" in the graduating class, 70.8% academic diplomas.

Then we come to the high school, close to where we live, where my daughter in junior high will have to go if she cannot get into another high school--84.6% of the graduating class, "Other," predominantly white; and academic diplomas, 36.6%. 19.5% refused diplomas in the final year. That principal has been removed recently, fortunately.

I would like to contrast that with Bushwick High School to which I went as a member of the high school field team. You will feel that the attendance record there is low. The school is 170 per cent utilized. Classes begin at 7:40 a.m. and the last class ends at 3:30 p.m.

Built into the educational structure and into the mentality of some of the businesses, is the idea that if a young person has to work as well as go to school, he has to work after school. This means that the 11th and 12th grades go to school in the morning, and the 9th and 10th grade students go in the afternoon.

At Bushwick, they also have to follow this, because that is policy. The attendance for the 9th and 10th grade is beautiful from September through the end of October. Then there is a sharp drop and that sharp drop continues from the end of October, when we go off daylight-saving time, until daylight-saving time comes back in the spring, and then many of these young people if they have not been turned off because they have not been attending, and I'll come to the reason why, they come back and in the last couple of months they try to catch up.

Many of their parents are working parents, so they are not home in order to come to the school at 5:30. The area around Bushwick is dangerous to walk in. The kids naturally value their lives, even higher than a possible education. So, they cut, so they don't come.

If we're talking about human rights, we can make a perfect system within the school of the best possible teachers from whatever imaginable formula anybody can conceive, but if the young person, when he walks out that door knows that he or she runs the danger of being killed, beaten up or molested, or forcibly given drugs, no school is worth that, I submit.

A teacher, the one evening I was there late, told me when I went out there again, that he had walked with me, making up things, so that if there was any trouble, there would be two of us, and I said, "Do you do this with the students, because you're here late?"

"Yes," he said, "at times I do, when I can."

I said, "But you have to walk back as you're going to have to walk back tonight."

And he said, "But these are my kids."

There is a valuable teacher but he has been moved out of teaching now to be the human relations coordinator. It follows.

I know of another high school, the one I'm assigned to now. Forty-one % Black students, 13% of the faculty Black--18% last year--but there are better jobs, and there are better opportunities opening up, and it's an awfully hard job to get out to Springfield Gardens, which is the other high school.

After the Kent State and Cambodia demonstrations, there were no riots there, but a group had formed outside the school, and one young man was arrested. Another young man was about to be, and the Dean of Boys saw and went and heard the second one saying, "How come you are arresting the first one?" at which the second one was threatened with arrest.

The Dean of Boys then took the side of the students and asked the police the same way. Need I add, he was arrested.

I have the feeling too, we can make changes, but I have lost all hope--the November 1969 Board of Education meeting soured me quite honestly.

I was supposed to be speaking on what was to have been the first item. There had been disturbances at Franklin K. Lane, and other high schools. That item was moved up to first on the agenda. I was already standing in line to speak when they moved the other one up.

Other people were then of course allowed to speak. Many of the students spoke, some of them using language that you might not expect in genteel society, granted.

I have never seen five people--the Board members--look more bored. This was to be expected, but just about opposite where I was standing, there were three rows of young whites. The men looked as though they could have gotten their clothes out of Brooks Bros. And the young ladies were also nattily dressed.

Up go the arms of all of these at the same time in the revolutionary salute. They begin yelling things like "Don't harass the students."

The five-member Board reacted. There was hasty whispering. I looked down at my notes to hear them move for adjournment. I looked up.

Now, this was on a place with a rather wide stage, but when I just looked up, Murry Bergtraum, Joseph Montserrat, and Dr. Mead, were nowhere to be seen. I don't know how they could have moved that fast, but they were gone.

Why? Because unfortunately this is built into our whole system, I guess, or our whole attitude in the city. When I read figures last year on the low academic diploma percentage at a Board meeting, I was advised by a member of the district, "Please, even if those are true, don't, don't get the white middle-class aroused. You know history."

I said, "Yes."

"You know who began the American Revolution and the Russian Revolution."

And I said, "Yes."

He said, "You arouse them, you will be swept away."

I think though we have come past that. I think we're seeing around the world, that when most of the revolutions occur, they occur from the middle-class, regardless of color, et cetera.

This was what the Board was afraid of. There are more and more of us in District 20 and in other middle-class areas. I include among those as well as Bay Ridge, as well as Bensonhurst, as well as Riverdale, Crown Heights, certain parts of Bedford-Stuyvesant, Springfield Gardens. We finally are beginning to wake up. We finally are beginning to be aroused, and if history, which I heard downgraded here by some of the witnesses, is any criterion, built into our system, built into our government now, our government in Washington, is a middle-class orientation.

I did not add that the same person that spoke to me at that Board meeting also said, "We can expect noise, reaction from 'them.' We can handle them. Please, not from within us."

That's a pretty sad commentary, and maybe the only thing we have left is fear. If so, then we have to start building out of that fear, because otherwise hearings like these will be band-aids, where a much worse infection festers under the surface. We need, on the social level now, antibiotics, not band-aids.

Thank you.

COMMR. FRENCH: Thank you very much, Mr. McMorris.

MRS. McINTOSH: I am here today as a concerned parent,

and recently--in fact, this is a memorandum of January 28th--this came in through my twins who attend a public school in the Bronx, in District 9. It was written by the Community Superintendent of our district, Andrew G. Donaldson, and was addressed to all principals, all UFT Chapter Chairmen, all Staff, all Parents, and all District 9 Community. It stated this:

"Yesterday I received a copy of a telegram signed by Albert Shanker, Mario Ramo and Howard Block of the UFT, addressed to the Mayor, the Chancellor and Members of the Board of Education, alleging harassment and intimidation of teachers and UFT Chapter Chairmen in District 9.

"It came as a complete surprise to me. There has been nothing of the sort nor has there been any complaint of such.

"The Chairman and Vice Chairman of my Community School Board and I attended the UFT Conference at Harrison House in Glen Cove over the past weekend. During that conference, Mr. Shanker, Mr. Ramo, and Mr. Block engaged in several friendly conversations with me. No one gave any hint of displeasure or of any grievance.

"Mr. Shanker and I sat at the same breakfast table last Sunday. As a result of our conversation I was invited by him to address the entire assembly with respect to the performance contract project in District 9. There was no complaint made of any kind.

"I have worked assiduously to insure that each teacher is guaranteed due process whenever a grievance has been appealed to this office. Each case has been weighed on its own merits.

"Today, every single grievance has been found in favor of the teacher complainant. To my knowledge, neither the Community School Board, the parents, the community, nor I have any wish to recreate an Ocean Hill-Brownsville in District 9 in the Bronx. New York City learned that no one wins in that type of confrontation."

My twins brought this letter home from school. As a concerned parent, I am appalled because I have no vested interest except to feel that my children deserve the best education that I as a taxpayer, and my husband, can afford.

I don't think it can be done, if we have any kind of difference between principals, UFT staff, parents and the District 9 Community. I feel that we must have unity, we must strive for unity because the sufferer is the child.

As far as I can tell you about District 9, our District is a multi-ethnic group. Formerly it was Irish and Jewish and now we are in the process of decentralization, and therefore we are now in the sort of transition to Black, Puerto Rican, some Yugoslavians, some Haitians, some Spanish outside of Puerto Rico, plus from Puerto Rico.

Our School Board is also multi-racial. You have Black, white, Puerto Ricans, et cetera, on the School Board.

Recently they had a Discovery Day at Taft High School for the Puerto Ricans, a great big thing. The next thing they had Martin Luther King Day at Taft High School.

I feel that our School Board is trying. It's not easy. Decentralization is not easy. It's a transition that's very difficult, but it deserves the open participation of everyone, without hatred, without bitterness, without vested interest.

True, we do have a shortage of funds. We have severe overcrowding in District 9. Again, as I stated, there is difficulty because of the ethnic transition of students.

The reading level is low, but I feel there must be unity, there must be a high ethical concept where all are concerned, and all are involved toward elevation of our children, and also elevation of the school system to a higher level and degree of consciousness.

We just don't have that in New York City. We have too many vested interests and if we don't watch out, particularly in our district, there will be polarization, and I feel one of the things we should do, when you think of discrimination, is to anticipate it and prevent it before it starts. Not just on the higher level, but also among the children.

I feel that's what we should do. That was number one. Therefore, I want to state that as a parent, I am for unity of all factions toward better education of our children in District 9.

The other part is this: Recently I attended a debate which was given by the Society for Experiments in Education, and was held at the High School of Art and Design. The debate centered around pro and con, whether we should have school examiners and whether we should have assistant school examiners, because they don't have to take an exam in order to test those who wish to come into the school system.

While there, during the debate, at which Dr. Theobald, Dr. Eugene Callendar, and Mr. Donaldson from our district were against the Board of Examiners' system, and for the Board of Examiners were Mr. Degnan, Dr. Greene, Mr. Sanders. Mr. Degnan is with the supervisory people of the Board, Dr. Greene is the head of the Board of Examiners--

COMMR. FRENCH: They both testified here.

MRS. McINTOSH: Granted, we have not had sufficient Black and Puerto Rican supervisors within the school system. This has been going on a long, long time as Mr. Richard Parrish just mentioned.

However, in their zeal, during the debate, from the podium of the stage, Mr. Sanders of the UFT stated that he understood that over 3,000 people took the principal exam, and out of 3,000, about 300 were Black.

As a parent who sat there listening to this debate, I was in the audience and they threw open the questions to the audience, and I questioned the validity of his statement.

Number one, how did he arrive at that number, what is the validity of his figures that he knew that so many Blacks took the exam against so many whites. Where did he get his figures?

In their zeal to correct the paucity of Black and minority principals in the school system and to correct the distribution of this, how did they come to this figure?

Meanwhile, what about the validity--remember, when you take

the principal's exam, you are given a number, you're supposed to be given a number and therefore, in other words, the written exam is all by number.

I questioned the validity of coming about with any kind of figure regardless of where it was obtained, while the exam was still in progress, because quite a few of those people were still waiting for interviews when this figure was given, and I question the ethics, regardless where the figures come from.

If there is an exam being given, I feel that no information should leak out until the end of the total exam period.

Again, let me state as a parent, I feel that New York City is lost if we aren't multi-racial or multi-ethnic and if we don't get together and correct the wrongs of our decadent system. If we don't try to work together, principal, staff, UFT, community, parents and all district people, we are going to be in a pretty bad fix.

COMMR. FRENCH: Thank you so much for coming.

Mr. Roderick MacKenzie.

MR. MAC KENZIE: My name is Roderick MacKenzie.

Madam Chairman, I was just putting the finishing touches on what I wanted to say here and, if it is all right with you, I would like to read most of it because I want to be able to make the points I would like to make.

A major point I must open my testimony with is that most of the complaints we hear about blatant bias against Blacks and Puerto Ricans in the New York City Board of Education personnel selection procedures are invalid today. I could support this contention with a number of specific illustrations. I will limit it, however, to one.

A list for assistant principal in the junior high schools has been in existence for almost two years. A high percentage of the Blacks on the list have already been appointed to positions through politicking, friends who are district superintendents and community school board members, et cetera. Few, if any, of the whites have.

Two white people in my school were high on the original ranked list, which was changed to an eligible list, after it had been promulgated, to satisfy the demands of the loudest complainers. They had written to every school district in the city, as they tell me. Most district superintendents did not even answer their letters and not one invitation to come for an interview was received.

It is pretty clear that the discrimination in personnel selection now is in favor of the Blacks, and is anti-white. This does not refute the possibility of socio-economic discrimination against Blacks, Puerto Ricans and poor whites from birth. The more important and larger thought that this brings to me is what should our goals be. To build a viable, healthy society?

There can be little question that discrimination has existed, and exists today, in personnel selection procedures, due to bias in favor of those familiar with the vocabulary and other tools required to score well in the tests, bias in favor of those skilled in paper-and-pencil test behavior, and the fact that man has, as yet, been unable to devise culture-free tests.

Yet, as Dr. Thorndike so ably stated here, no more objective methods of selection have been devised.

This does not mean that all the present tests used by the Board of Examiners are highly valid. Inbreeding probably does find its way into the test construction, and coaching of friends and hangers-on results in reward of these not so concerned about justice. But, concentrating on justice and honesty, which I consider essential as both goal and tool toward building a healthy society, will the elimination of tests or a Board of Examiners lead to a more just and honest society?

Politicking will fill the vacuum. Politics is defined in political science as the pursuit of power. Recalling that power usually corrupts, the effect of which we can see throughout our land, do we want to continue to teach our children that it pays to be dishonest and aggressive. Do we want to set the example that teaches that acquisition is more valuable than ethical behavior or peace of mind? Do we want to pursue power, to have such a need for power and money that we would rather appear as the repulsive politician than the educator and scholar?

We can have an equitable distribution of the wealth and an honest testing system. Or we can have new politicking and fratricide.

If we have a corrupt testing system, it is because people have made it. Corruption will not diminish by abandoning the attempts to build an honest testing system and replacing it with politicking and the rawest favoritism.

I would like to end my efforts here by asking if there are any questions.

THE CHAIRMAN: Any questions?

(No response.)

THE CHAIRMAN: Thank you very much, Mr. MacKenzie. I now call Mrs. Joan Williams and Mrs. Mildred Tudy. I want to compliment these two young women for having the fortitude that they have. They have now been sitting through these hearings and waiting very patiently. I want to say that I, personally, appreciate it.

MRS. TUDY: I am a parent. My name is Mildred Tudy. I want to thank the Commissioner for allowing us the time, as well as the others, to present our views on what might be termed racism in the schools.

I would say if it is racism in the hiring practices of the school system, it is just reflective of our society. All of our institutions are reflecting our society and we are living in a racist society.

We speak of power. Education plus opportunity is power. It is power to pick ourselves up by our bootstraps and to become productive citizens. And this is what we, as parents, are striving so hard to do, so that our children might have better opportunities than we had, to have more doors open, and they might be able to take their stand, producing for themselves, as well as for the society as a whole.

Now, we know that the educational system has perpetuated racism in various forms. I have heard mentioned today a lot about the hiring practices of teachers and supervisors. These are just two categories.

We have school secretaries who do their thing. I have seen principals appointed in school districts, minority Black principals and Puerto Rican principals, and watched how their operations were fouled up by secretaries who were part of the racist system, who withheld information. You know, the secretaries receive the information first, because they are right at the phones. And they withhold information, oftentimes very pertinent information, until the close of the school day, or maybe they never share it all with the principal. We do know of school secretaries who have delayed transcripts for students going to college because they were doing their thing, you see.

This society has promulgated a lot of racist things at all levels.

We have also in the school system a very wonderful development--paraprofessionals. These paraprofessionals came about through Title I, through the offices of the Office of Economic Opportunity. And here is a wonderful opportunity for bringing community people, community parents, into the school system so that they might understand the system and they might help take some of the clerical work away from the teacher and they might help share some of the teaching situations so that they might break down the adult-to-student ratio in the school system. But we have watched over the years--over the past few years--how bringing in community people as paraprofessionals has ended. In so many instances many of our parents have become another part of the bureaucracy. And I have seen a ludicrous thing where Black parents have stood in the door barring Black students, because the principal has made this person feel no longer a part of the community, concerned about the individual child's rights or the individual child's needs, but he was there, instead, as a racist principal, you see.

That is another area that I hope we get into.

I hope that we can get the community school boards operating in the areas with the paraprofessionals so the paraprofessionals can get support through the school boards and through the community so they will have no need for job security, to just lean on a decaying system and rely and become, themselves, part of that system.

In our school system, another element that is reflective of racism is the guidance system. We have guidance teachers who do their thing to perpetuate the racism in our society. They will most often relegate Black and Puerto Rican students to their old general course, that non-doing course, just a record of attending school.

Too few of our children know about the SEEK program, know about the College Discovery Programs, and too few of them know about College Bound.

Once in a while, a few of us trickle through, a little tokenism.

Our guidance system is a perpetuation of racism.

We also have local school boards which are very political

and also very reflective of our racist society. Very few of them are doing anything about the minority groups in the particular district.

However, if we are going to say bad things, we should say some of the positive things that are happening, too. In our own District 14, we do have a school board that is mainly white, middle-class, from Greenpoint, Brooklyn, in domination over the multi-ethnic group of families in Williamsburg. Seven of the nine members are from Greenpoint. But they have done something positive, one thing positive, and that was in the appointment of Claude Huntley as temporary principal of IS 33.

If you read yesterday's paper, you saw that that appointment was upheld by Justice Pino in Supreme Court, Brooklyn. He said that this school board had the right to appoint a principal who was not on the list.

We have no Black principals in that school district now, besides Mr. Huntley, and really he is only temporary, because that is the ruling of the Court. He is not permanently assigned yet. He is another one of those temporaries.

This school district has a school pupil population of over 60% Puerto Rican and over 30% Black. We have about 6 or 7% whites. But we have never had a Black or Puerto Rican principal until these past few months.

At the present time the school board has appointed a temporary principal in the elementary school, Miss Marie Cetera, so that board is doing something positive. That is one of the only things they are doing positive, because they are leaning over backwards doing other things that speak of racism.

We have also to look into this problem of ID cards. I know, Commissioner, you are knowledgeable about these ID cards that are given to young people when they have had infractions of the law. We had help from Legal Services in establishing that this was discrimination.

Youngsters who were involved in some altercation, or some sort of infraction outside of the school building, oftentimes had the police enter this on their permanent school record, and we had a ruling in court, last July, 1970, that there was going to be a moratorium on this, that no longer were the police officers to enter these infractions that were not happening in the school building, or on school grounds. At least for a year they could no longer enter these infractions on their permanent records.

You know, this is very damaging when they want to get civil service jobs and your permanent school records go on until you pass on, and they are still down in the school basement. Racism.

We also have to abolish this Board of Examiners because we all know and we hear repeatedly it is not relevant. They are there to perpetuate a closed shop.

We have the people who have the power that be, and they have the power to keep a closed shop.

It does not matter if the products that are being produced--and these are school children--are not the kind of products we want; if these children are not able to read. The fact is, you are keeping jobs for teachers, for closed-shop teachers.

We must get on with the job of hiring more Black and Puerto Rican teachers and administrators so that they might be able to work positively with the students, the many Black and Puerto Rican students. This is not to say that we don't have dedicated white teachers. We do have. I know of quite a few. But we don't have nearly enough. And we have too many who are there for just the salary and are there just to perpetuate a racist thing.

Now, if we look also at the category of adult education, we have many, many parents who are striving to go to school for their high school equivalency. For various reasons they weren't able to stay in school and to get it when they were young people. And a very, very sickening thing, over the years, is to have been watching people going night after night, through all kinds of weather, trying to get equivalencies and they have been going into a system where so few are able to get them because they weren't taught to get them.

Many of the teachers have not been teaching relevant material, they have not been teaching the adults so that they might pass these examinations and, oftentimes, when they have accumulated years of learning in preparation for a high school equivalency test, they were sent out into the hinterlands to take the test.

These kinds of systems are not likely to encourage people to get the kind of education that we all need to live in this kind of society. That smacks of racism.

We must use funds--when I say "we," I mean the local school board--to help Black and Puerto Rican parents learn the school system, to learn budgeting, to learn curriculum, to learn about tenure and what makes for tenure, to learn how to evaluate. We must use some of the school funds to do this.

And last, but not least, what the Chancellor has proposed, the abolition of the Board of Examiners, having teachers licensed based on state certification plus the requirement of the parents in any particular community. These should be the criteria so that we might get on with the job of educating our children.

And I am hoping, Miss Norton, this is not just another hearing, that just a lot of testimony will go into the record.

People have come up and bared their chests, on whatever behalf they did it on, and I hate to think that nothing concrete will come out of this, because we have over a million children in the school system now. I know I have a daughter at Science. There is not one Black teacher in Science. There are too few Black students in Science, too few Puerto Ricans in the High School of Science. But we must get on with the job because if we are screaming about the welfare rolls now, what are we going to do with the population explosion, what will we do in the next decade, build bigger prisons, build bigger mental institutions? We can't contain it. It is boiling over now.

Let's not have this as another public hearing. And I believe, knowing a little bit about how you have operated in the past, you and the other Commissioners--I do know some of the other Commissioners there--that you will mobilize the community because, in the end, it will have to be community people getting on the

Board of Estimate, getting on all of these institutions to make them do the job.

In District 14, the parents are very active. We are trying very hard. We have now had a principal in IS 49 who was involved in these insensitive promotions, dumping the kids out from junior high to high school when they were reading on a second grade level, putting them into the eighth and ninth grades and then on into high school, just to get rid of them. We have had him suspended and he has a hearing coming up now.

We, in District 14, mean to go on with this. We mean to make it better so that most of our children can get the kind of education they need. And I am begging you here today, don't let this go off into the record as a lot of testimony. We want to be involved and we want to see something concrete come out of this, because it is a racist system.

THE CHAIRMAN: Mrs. Williams.

MRS. WILLIAMS: Good evening.

Commissioner Norton, Commissioner French, and ladies and gentlemen.

I am just a lay member of the community. I have no important position except that I am a parent, and I think that is quite important. I have six children. My youngest is three and my oldest is 18.

Now, I have been living in a ghetto community for 12 years, with my children, having to get to schools and having been bussed out, and I can give you some of the results of what has happened.

My 18-year-old is going to Kings County Hospital to be an RN. She didn't do this coming out of a ghetto school only. She did this by me bussing her to Fort Hamilton out in Bay Ridge. That is when they had the bussing program.

And my other dauther followed behind her.

They came from this school now that we were talking about, IS 33, when they had a principal that, you would say, had a system there that wasn't conducive to learning. When we got into Fort Hamilton, they were making 65's, 70's, for about two to three years. It took them at least two solid years to catch up with the white type, or, higher type curriculum where they could really grasp what they were doing.

They are not dumb children by far. They have me and their daddy to prove this.

I will say this much, when the oldest daughter got to be a senior, all of a sudden she blossomed out, like 95's, because I guess she had incentive, she knew what she wanted to do, and she was getting an education. Her guidance teacher asked her, when she was getting ready to see what she was going to do, "Why are you taking Latin? Nobody takes Latin any more."

But, in all probability, my daugher is going to become a nurse and Latin happens to be a valuable thing for her to know.

And my older daughter, who is smarter than the other one, was supposed to be in Arista in Fort Hamilton High School, and they said she made an 88% average. All the children that were Black got a letter saying that they didn't have enough room for everybody to become an Arista.

THE CHAIRMAN: Arista is the honor society?

MRS. WILLIAMS: Yes, Arista is the honor society of Fort Hamilton.

But then I looked around and there was a boy that made 88 and there was a boy that made 85%, and he was white and he was in Arista and she and the other Black students that live in Fort Greene were promptly notified, by a polite letter, that they didn't have any more room.

Now, I belong to the PTA out there in Fort Hamilton, and I attend the meetings--most of the time but not all of the time, because it is a trip. But sometimes I get the guile up and I go and I act very nice to people and everything. But I noticed that they just have a select group of Black students. They don't want too much of an influx of Black students.

Now, getting back to 33, I have another in 33. He is 13.

He is under the jurisdiction of Mr. Claude Huntley. When Mr. Claude Huntley wasn't principal there, 33 used to rage like hell and fury, big fights from Tompkins Avenue up to Throop Avenue. I mean, the whole school was involved. It was just like a madhouse. Fires and everything, and all kinds of destruction. And then, finally, here, when my son was admitted to 33, Mr. Claude Huntley came as acting principal.

Well, I am not just trying to flower-up anything, but you should see the change in the decorum, you should see the cooperation between the community.

The man, if he is good enough to act as principal, should be good enough to be principal. Maybe they like for you to be principal on teacher's pay. You know, you can do the duties and you can handle the other things, but we won't pay you a principal's price.

Now, this man has been, like Mrs. Tudy just went through, and I won't go into all that. We haven't much time.

He has been upheld by the courts, but he is still not legally a fully authorized principal.

I think that what we need in ghetto schools, instead of me bussing out my children to get a decent education is to let the community be involved and trained. Until we get training we are not going to go in there flatfooted, and say we know how to run the school. We know what it takes.

There is a whole lot of things going into education. Even the teachers can't put across things any more. So, all of us need training in this field.

If we could just band together, like other speakers have spoken about, and try to utilize all of the factions we might make some progress. There is something about the old curriculum that when I went to school I learned how to read and I learned how to write, I had penmanship, I learned geography, knew my fractions in the fifth grade, had English grammar in the fourth grade. They don't teach that any more.

Maybe I am backwards, maybe I am stupid, but I know this for a fact, when I took a test for Manpower, she said, "Mrs. Williams, you have a reading score of second year college."

I only went to high school, and I am 38 years old--or will be.

And, just the same, I feel that I had a darn good education. And I was raised in Brooklyn. I was raised in Bedford-Stuyvesant, Pacific Street, between New York and Brooklyn Avenue.

All of a sudden after I got out of school, the school went haywire. Everybody stopped learning. Everybody stopped reading. Everybody stopped writing.

I even tell my 18-year-old daughter, write, don't scribble.

The whole system is not just with the Board of Examiners. Maybe it starts there, or with college and how they teach teachers but the whole curriculum is too permissive and it is off-dated. It is not outdated because you can't even come up with it because it is so far gone.

Thank you.

- - - - -

MISS SEALY: Commissioner Norton and Commissioner French, I am Rose F. Sealy, and I have been a regularly licensed teacher and counsellor and supervisor with the New York City Board of Education for a long time.

I was educated in Bedford-Stuyvesant and I have served in the schools in Bedford-Stuyvesant. I am currently on leave to teach in the City University of New York.

I have observed the effects of racial discrimination and I have personally experienced racism in the New York City schools many times during the years I've served.

However, I will limit my statement to my observations over the last five or six years, to point out that despite stated policies to integrate schools, to recruit minority staffs, and to initiate compensatory programs, discriminatory attitudes and practices continue.

Differential practices result in a double standard in hiring staff, and in operating programs which serve minorities. This double standard serves to exclude and penalize competent Black staff, denying them equal access to decision-making positions and, on the other hand, accepts programs designed to serve minorities which are of low quality in accordance with the standards established by the Board of Education itself.

In February 1965, I was licensed as an assistant director in the Bureau of Educational and Vocational Guidance, and since there was no opportunity for appointment to the position, I requested appointment to a lower position as supervisor of guidance.

Although there are numerous precedents for appointment to a lower position where there are no openings for candidates at the higher level, my request was denied.

At that time, when there were no licensed Black supervisors from the Bureau of Educational and Vocational Guidance serving in the schools of New York City, I was never appointed and the list has now expired, although I still hold the license.

I accepted a supervisory responsibility on assignment without the salary and working conditions which would have accompanied a regular appointment and, as an acting supervisor, I was forcibly assigned by the Board of Education to integrate teams of observers made up of appointed white supervisors sent to Ocean Hill-Brownsville. The Black supervisors, mostly serving without appointment or supervisory salary, objected to this role.

We were threatened with dismissal and ordered to serve. While we served there, we were systematically excluded from meetings and decision-making and our voices were only heard in a minority report which, in frustration, was finally submitted to the Superintendent of Schools by the Black observers.

I voluntarily served for four years on assignment as Citywide Supervisor of Guidance for the Manpower Development Training Program operated by the Board of Education which uses Federal funds and other monies to operate programs designed to provide basic education and vocational training to adults.

The MDT Act requires that minority groups be served by these programs. The director of the program, Mr. Herman Kressell, held no Board of Examiners supervisory license. He is a plumber and a union member. The double standard does not require him to have a supervisory license although he supervises persons who hold supervisory licenses such as myself.

He hired, as supervisors in this special program, at the same rate I was paid, and I am on a pre-doctoral level, non-Black friends who had not even attained college graduation, he hired relatives, his operation was so biased that at least six cases have been filed against him at the State Division of Human Rights and 14 charges of unfair labor practices have been filed at the Public Employees' Relations Board.

There is a double standard when it comes to programs which serve primarily Black and Puerto Rican people. While maintaining the inviolability and impartiality of licenses and credentialing the Manpower Program creates positions, hires whomever they like without regard to competency, without a review by any elected board.

The double standard of the Board of Education is apparent in this program. Mr. Kressell has hired as supervisors friends at $10.10 an hour, without credentials, who in turn hired college-trained Puerto Rican graduates, who cannot get employment because they do not speak English well enough. They are paid $4.50 an hour to do work that the supervisor has never been trained to do.

The Manpower Development Training Program resists establishing professional relationships with poverty agencies such as MCDA, which serve the poor and has not adopted their procedures such as meaningful community representation, or learned their sensitivity.

And I cite here the fact that the program for training duplicates efforts made by Manpower Career Development Program, and the Manpower Training Program. The Board of Education was directed to come up with a joint training program, and they declined to do so. One of the reasons they cited was that they would not go along with community representation.

An additional example of the insensitivity of this program toward minority people whom they are mandated to serve, is a publication called the "Information Booklet on the Puerto Rican

Trainee for MDT Staff Members,' by the Board of Education, Herman A. Kressell, Director, which is not only historically inaccurate, but which is insulting to Puerto Rican citizens.

It describes them as a dancing people, and says that they don't understand time in the same way that the rest of us do. Most of the people who come from New York, come from a poorer class, that marriage in this type of family is not a question primarily of love, but a hasty solution to an economic problem. Puerto Ricans tend to be somewhat dependent, unable to make decisions; "Puerto Ricans like to show off"--these are quotes-- "Puerto Ricans are a dancing pecple. A party is not a party without music and dancing."

This is the double standard to which I think we must all object, and to which we must all direct ourselves and I think the mere existence of the kinds of double standards which I have cited, cited, results in a program which is high in cost, and low in service, characterized by unfair hiring and promotional practices, and demonstrated insensitivity to the people who are to be served. Its mere existence is an example, a flagrant example, of what we are here to correct.

Thank you.

THE CHAIRMAN: Thank you, Miss Sealy.

MR. PEREIRA: My name is Frank Pereira.

This is one of the difficulties in racial classification. The name, you see, is not associated with Black people, and of course Beaumont who was with Dr. Toqueville on his visit to the United States in the 1830's went to Louisiana where people were segregated according to race and he looked into the Black section and saw a woman who was very light and said why is she in the Black section and he said in her ancestry there is African.

Then he looked over in the white section and saw someone who was darker than the white-looking girl in the Black section and he said in her ancestry there is Spanish.

This is Beaumont, by the way.

Secondly, since people have been maligning history, one person was talking about the French Revolution. While it is difficult to state what the underlying causes of such a large movement as the French Revolution were, certainly the immediate causes are very clear.

The middle-class had very little to do with it because at that particular time in France, in 1789, France was divided into three classes: The nobility, the clergy, and what we would call "others."

The immediate cause of the French Revolution was the fact the nobility did not want to give up its privileged position of not being taxed and the clergy did not want to give up its privileged position and you must remember of course the clergy is divided, the higher clergy was chosen from the nobility.

It was this inability during the time when the French monarchy, not the nation, but the monarchy, was in financial trouble, that sparked off the events that led to the French Revolution, which perhaps is a nice way to start off here; that is, it is the inability sometimes of those who have privileges to give up their privileges that spark off the events that many times lead to, shall we say, persons who were hitherto silent becoming more vocal.

In my particular case, I will read two letters and that is all.

"June 30th, 1960. Dr. Samuel S. Treicher, Committee on Appeals, Board of Education, 110 Livingston Street.

"Dear Dr. Treicher: On May 2nd, 1960, I asked that I be allowed to appeal the declination of my application for a position as substitute social studies teacher on physical and medical grounds, specifically psychiatric disorder."

As you can tell by this letter by 1960 they could not refuse me on grounds of either spoken or written English.

"I was given until May 10, 1960, to make such an appeal. Yet a letter under Mr. Wayne's signature, dated May 10th, 1960, indicated that my time had run out. The Easter recess was not taken into account.

"There are many reasons for my believing that I deserve a rehearing and reexamination. For 11 years I have tried to get into teaching."

This is 1960 and I graduated by the way from Brooklyn College, one of the best schools, presumably the Harvard of New York, and in the day session, not the evening session.

"For 11 years I have tried to get into teaching. The one thing I can do well.

"My first break came in 1950, when I went to Nigeria. I did an excellent job there under extremely difficult conditions.

"The medical examination came at an extremely inauspicious time and the follow-up was even more unfortunate from my point of view. Many of the conditions present at the time have been removed.

"I sincerely believe that a reexamination will result in my being allowed to teach.

"Finally one should not be judged in performance of a job that conflicted with one's education and career. I did a good job in Nigeria, I can do a good job here. All I need is a chance to prove myself as teacher."

That was 1960.

1966: "Mr. Alfred A. Giardino, President, Board of Education," et cetera, "Reference: Exam No. 69135701310 (1951) and 6913 and 5539 (1966)."

"Dear Sir: In 1959 and again in 1960, I took and passed a written test for a position as substitute teacher of social studies in the secondary schools, but was disqualified for "medical" reasons. The explanation was 'The findings of the medical doctors that there is 'psychiatric disorder' involved.'

"In vain did I ask for a review of my application and for a statement of what exactly was the justification for the disqualification.

"My feeling is that I am a victim of racism pure and simple. When all other excuses are exhausted, the Board of Examiners can fall back on this psychiatric disorder. Such a term is about as useful as a respiratory inflammation.

"If I have a persecution complex, it is because I am imagining the almost daily instances of racist attitudes I face. I am begging you to open my case, make a complete investigation, and remove the stigma which the examiners have placed upon me.

"Finally let me note that my case and thousands like it is more eloquent than all the statements to the contrary.

"Here is a Harlem man, raised under difficult circumstances, brutalized in the Army, struggling to rise above his station in life, whose family even now is replete with a struggle just for survival, who graduates from high school, goes on to college, avoids the road traveled by the author of Manchild in the Promised Land"-- this is no adverse criticism of him, but the reception of him by white people and by some Blacks also--"finds that he is shut out of doing the job that he had trained himself to do because of another technicality.

"What incentive is this for others who choose the easier path or at least the path which seems easier."

Since then I have taught at the New York City Community College, and the reason why I give you this lesson in history is to point out what Black people have to go through. This is not a person who is arguing that the tests are irrelevant, which may well be--I don't care much for tests myself but you have to have some standards--but, this is a person who has passed--this wasn't the first time. When I went to Brooklyn College, they told you you had to take a test in speech and I could not take the courses necessary for teaching especially at that time, student teaching, high school level, because I had an "S" defect, you see.

What I'm saying is, we're talking about what we call career models, and in my opinion in this country Black people, especially mainland people, have better models than any other group of people in the sense that they're models themselves.

The persons that they're supposed to look up to, are themselves humiliated, you see, and I can give examples, not in my case, but in public, the case of Dubois who was shackled, of Nat King Cole and Roland Hayes. These are public figures, you see.

How can I go into the classroom now, any classroom, and say, "If you work hard for the job that you want to do, you will have a chance to do that job," when in my own case, and in the case of many others, it is not true.

These two letters constitute my case history--of course it is more complicated than that--and the other material indicates how deeply rooted this question of racism and racial attitudes of human beings who live and breathe like us is. These things are more deeply ingrained than we realize, and many Black people, especially young people, are under the illusion that white people are different and therefore good.

Let me remind you, I saw Intruder in the Dust this morning on television, when I should have been listening to you. But, in it this Black person was supposed to stand by while a white person called him names.

Of course, that was quite clear, but the argument, of most white people who say things that make Afro-Americans feel badly is, "Well, we didn't know, we don't know how you feel."

Let me remind you the police react in the same way, white and Black, when they are called pigs, and Mr. Kahane is crying about the persecution of Jews in Russia.

So that these racial attitudes of white people cannot be excused by just 200 years of experience. I as a historian know that not one of these persons in this room has lived that long.

It cannot be argued on grounds that we didn't know and we don't know how we would react because, if you read the newspapers you will find you react in the same way. Some of you are scared and some of you are not. These things don't know any color line, bravery, fear.

Then, to be more germane to this, and I use the French Revolution very advisedly, there are perhaps thousands of cases like this, in which those who presumably are in privileged positions do not want to share that privilege, you see, and find themselves in a position where the whole house comes falling down.

COMMR. FRENCH: Thank you, Mr. Pereira.

THE CHAIRMAN: Mrs. Dorothy Joseph.

MRS. JOSEPH: My name is Dorothy Joseph. I have been an employee of the New York City Board of Education since September 1955 and served as a teacher in the day elementary schools until June 1965. I hold two additional licenses--guidance counselor and assistant principal. I was licensed as an assistant principal in December 1965 and appointed under this license in September 1968.

My assignment in the Manpower Development Training Program began in January 1965 when I was employed for 15 hours a week as a teacher of basic education at the Brooklyn Adult Training Center. I subsequently served as basic education supervisor, teacher-in-charge of a training center and coordinator.

My last assignment in the Manpower Program was as coordinator of high school redirection, a Board of Education program designed to redirect potential high school dropouts.

While I presently coordinate this program under the supervision of the High School Division, I am no longer a part of the Manpower program. This was at the request of Mr. Herman A. Kressel, Director, for reasons as indicated by him in writing, "No funds to pay salary." However, it is interesting to note that my service in the Manpower program from June 1965 was as a supervisor with the pay of a classroom teacher. I became eligible for pay on my assistant principal's license in September 1968 and in June 1969 when Mr. Kressel indicated his inability to continue me because, "You make too much money."

It is also interesting to note that a number of white supervisors who had been maintained in the Manpower program on supervisory pay ever since its beginning in 1965 were being retained even though I was the only Black Board of Education licensed supervisor receiving supervisory pay.

My concerns in terms of the practices of the Manpower program are, however, larger than personal involvement regarding my own assignment.

As a professional person, born and raised in the Bedford-

Stuyvesant section of Brooklyn, I had been particularly impressed with the need for the Manpower program to establish and implement methods by which the large number of underachieving Black and Peurto Rican residents of areas such as Bedford-Stuyvesant and Harlem might make full use of the offerings of Manpower. It was difficult to give an honest answer to the many inquiries which came from individuals and organizations regarding the possibility of entering the training program within a reasonable time after application.

While it is recognized that the majority of trainee recruitment is handled by the New York State Employment Service there are opportunities for direct community recruitment and referrals. The Manpower program offered this service to residents of the Chinatown area on two occasions. The professional staff went to Chinatown, interviewed and enrolled interested male and female applicants who were then able to enter the training program within a few weeks. Other applicants for Manpower training have had to wait as long as two years, and, in some cases, they have never been called. There has been no such recruiting effort made in other communities where large numbers of Black and Puerto Rican people live.

The challenge in the Manpower program is to provide an opportunity for economic mobility for the poor and the disadvantaged. There There is need for all staff to understand the philosophy and practice of effective service in this area. It is particularly important for those of us who serve as supervisors and, therefore, affect and influence the performance of other staff members to grow in the area of sensitivity and effective communication. This training on an initial and/or an on-going basis has been lacking. The need was particularly apparent to me in my position as coordinator of the high school redirection program. The students in this program, who were potential school leavers, represented the alienated and disaffected youth who were desperately in need of help in restoring their faith and confidence in themselves and in society. It was extremely difficult to work with these young people in a constructive and positive way because of the constant negative attitudes displayed by the teacher-in-charge and supervisors toward the students.

A booklet written by a Puerto Rican supervisor and distributed under Mr. Kressel's direction, ostensibly prepared to help Manpower staff understand and better serve Puerto Rican trainees, is a typical example of the insensitivity demonstrated by the Manpower administration. Mrs. Seeley has already referred to the booklet. I had listed some of the same statements, in quotes, that Mrs. Seeley has, so I won't repeat them, except to indicate, "The average Puerto Rican spends a lot of time visiting friends and attending weekly dances," and, "The Puerto Ricans are a dancing people," and there are these and other stereotyped statements that reflect the level of generalized insensitivity prevalent in the Manpower program. I would also indicate to you that this booklet has the seal of the Board of Education and it was put out by Mr. Kressel. I think the saddest part of this is that the booklet has had wide circulation and even though it was brought on many occasions to the attention of the Board of Education, those responsible for it still continue to function in their assignments and nothing has been done to remove or educate the people involved.

The efforts of a cross-section of Manpower staff to point out and change these and other negative practices in the program were unsuccessful and resulted in either request for removal of these employees from the program and/or treatment which was so degrading and harassing it forced concerned staff to leave the program.

I would like to include, in the record, a letter written by Bedford-Stuyvesant Youth in Action, in July of 1969, which clearly states their concerns regarding discriminatory practices in Manpower, and it reads:

"Dear Mr. Monseratt:

"The Bedford-Stuyvesant Youth in Action Community Corporation vigorously protests the recent series of reprisals against Black supervisors and other Black employees in the Manpower Development Training Program. It has been reported that these reprisals are one in a series of effronteries that have taken place against the participants in the Manpower program in particular and the Black Community in general.

"Another part of this report is that a few weeks ago two Black supervisors, Mrs. Dorothy Joseph and Mr. Edward Hightower were reassigned to 'other professional duties.' These supervisors have, as others have done in the past, protested the continuous inequities in the program and have called for changes. The reassignments were the only result of these protests. These inequities are serious and cannot be overlooked.

"First, the program as it now functions, suffers from a lack of leadership, a clear direction and goal, insufficient and unrealistic training for Black and Puerto Rican participants, and poor service from white professionals who cannot relate to the problems, needs, and aspirations of Blacks and Puerto Ricans.

"Second, equipment which has been purchased at great expense to the program has been permitted to remain in storage, thereby depriving the participants of the opportunity to utilize it and familiarize themselves with its operations. This limits the development of marketable skills of the participants.

"Third, the cumbersome and bureaucratic procedures used to enroll new participants have resulted in a long waiting list. Participants generally wait one to two years after the initial processing before they are enrolled in the Manpower courses. Only once did the wheels of bureaucracy turn faster. This was to permit the enrollment of recent immigrants from Hong Kong who had the protection of their families for financial security and employable skills.

"Fourth, the Director of the Program, Mr. Herman Kressel, lacks sensitivity, is unresponsive to changes needed in the program, and exhibits an attitude toward participants that can be described as ignorant and racist. He has permitted material to be distributed to staff members that purports to be a psychological study of the Puerto Rican community, but in reality is a statement of the reactions, beliefs, and experiences with the Puerto Ricans of one individual staff member. Grievously, this material has been widely circulated to the various Manpower training centers for use by staff. Unfortunately, this material bears the seal of the Board of Education and has been cited by the Black and Puerto Rican community as another example of the educational system perpetuating discriminatory practices. A director of the Manpower Development Training Program must surely possess an ability to work with the Black and Puerto Rican community, have experience in administration and supervision, possess training in sociology and psychology of minority groups, as well as some experience in the different aspects of the employment process - namely, interview, intake, aptitude testing, counseling, placement, follow-up and evaluation. Mr. Kressel did not bring this kind of varied background to this position.

"The concept underlying the Manpower Development Training Program is sound and is urgently needed for the salvation of the inner-city. Changes must be made, however. The program designed to implement the concept needs restructuring. The professionals must be more carefully selected. Up-to-date equipment must be continuously used and repurchased. Participants must be admitted promptly after a recycling of the program activities in order to maintain their level of interest and enthusiasm. These changes will not occur under the present Director, Mr. Herman Kressel, and he should be reassigned to another program which does not serve Blacks and Puerto Ricans. Finally, the Black supervisors who were reassigned must be retained in the program and additional Black and Puerto Rican supervisors employed throughout the centers in the city.

"The Black and Puerto Rican community has had many experimental programs designed to deal directly with unemployment and the development of skills. Failures of these programs have been cited as 'proof' that Blacks and Puerto Ricans cannot learn. These programs were poorly organized and poorly staffed at the outset and doomed to failure. Bedford-Stuyvesant Youth in Action Community Corporation now requests that you and other members of the Board of Education take immediate steps to make the changes enumerated herein and to strengthen the Manpower program. In this way, needed Manpower can be provided toward self-determination and self-help in the Bedford-Stuyvesant and other Black communities.

This is signed, "Very truly yours, Vernelle Albury, Chairman, Education Committee, Board of Directors," with copies to Dr. Bernard Donovan, Dr. Seymour Lachman, Mr. Isaiah Robinson, Mrs. Mary E. Meade and Mr. Murray Bergtraum. It is dated July 31st, 1969.

I would say to you that the situation in January of 1971 remains the same. Nothing has changed.

Since 1965 and to the present, the program has trained building maintenance men. This course qualifies trainees for, at best, glorified porter jobs. It would seem that the facilities of this program might have extended themselves to provide training on a skill level high enough so that Blacks and Puerto Ricans might enter the building trades as plumbers, carpenters, painters, electricians, et cetera.

As coordinator of high school redirection, even though the program has been removed from the jurisdiction of the Manpower program and is now under the High School Division -- it is housed in a Manpower center and has suffered lack of positive support on a continuing basis -- I cannot help but feel that my activity as part of a concerned group of staff who sought to bring about constructive changes in the Manpower program has subjected me and the program which I coordinate to continued harassment.

The Manpower program is conceptually one which could make important changes in the lives of many poor people. The practices which I have described limit severely this possibility.

I hope the City Commission will be able to recommend meaningful changes so that the large amount of Federal funds appropriated for this program can begin to do the job for which they are intended.

Thank you.

THE CHAIRMAN: Mr. Hal Koppersmith.

MR. KOPPERSMITH: Commissioner Norton, Commissioner French, I just wish to say that if everybody in the city was as beautiful as you two, it would be a heavenly fun city.

Now, when I was 17, I played a rabbi in a play called Winterset. And there is one scene where my 16-year-old daughter meets a boy under the bridge and says to him, "What hurts you, Mia?"

And this boy, the son of the great Italian martyr, Bartolomeo Vanzetti, says to her, "Love, honor, integrity, justice, these are words on paper. It is good to have them there. You will get them nowhere else."

And she says, "What hurts you, Mia?"

And he says, "Just that. You will get them nowhere else."

Now, I suggest to you the problem we are having in the high schools and in the schools, in general, is the youngsters want love, honor, integrity and justice, and what they find from the adults in the school system is hypocrisy, and the youngsters have enough dignity left to fight back to maintain their spiritual and mental life.

My name is Hal Koppersmith, with a "K," teacher-in-exile-for seven years, a convict for inviting fifth graders to riot, and a welfare client.

Now, I think it is important to people listening to remember that this is a welfare client speaking, because there are stereotypes about what welfare clients are, so I would suggest to you that the welfare mothers of this city are doing a very much more productive job than the guy who is writing appeals. I also have the signal honor of being the only teacher ever expelled, illegally, from the United Federation of Teachers. And I would like to say that case is coming up soon.

And I would like to tell Mr. Shanker, if he is listening, a Uganda proverb which says, "Those with too much ambition don't sleep in peace." Sweet dreams, Mr. Shanker.

Now, incidentally, I would like you to know that my license was taken away without any due process and I was removed from the Union without any due process. In fact, I wasn't even given a reason for my license being taken away. And how this thing happens was explained by the honorable John Kenneth Galbraith, when he wrote, "A bureaucracy" -- the Board of Education, the Council of Supervisory Associations, the United Federation of Shankers -- "is governed not by the truth but by its own truth. It defends its truth against the reality. Those who question it are discounted for eccentricity, ignored for ineffectiveness or excluded for unreliability."

Now, I suggest to you that some of the most creative teachers in the schools, as you have heard in the community testimony, have been eliminated by this kind of operation.

My thesis today is really quite simple -- that the present system of examinations is not objective, is bureaucratically biased, is professionally and humanly demeaning and racially discriminatory. That, in effect, it screens out teachers of merit, creativity and charisma in favor of civil service, mental midget mediocrities with dehumanized computer memories, who are joyless, sexless and humanless, and Albert Shanker is their leader, and leads them -- and leads them in a struggle against the powers, the poor, the minorities and the young.

But it is written in the bible that, "The first shall be last, and the last shall be first," and Shanker cowers in fear whenever he remembers this biblical prophecy. While, for the people, hope soars that soon they will be able to sing with the kings, "Free at last, free at last, thank God Almighty, we are free at last."

A great libertarian-psychoanalyst has written, "The fundamental conflicts in human life are not between competing ideas, one true and the other false, but rather between those who hold power and use it to oppress others and those who are oppressed by power and seek to free themselves of it."

The crises we face in the school system today are the result of the oppression established by the Council of Supervisory Associations, and the United Federation of Teachers against parents and the students of this school system. Now, this test, let me make clear, is not objective at all. In fact, it starts with a bias, and let me show you how the bias works very nicely. The fact of the matter is that this whole civil service system is nothing but a political patronage pork barrel, and let me show you how it works, and then they call it objective.

For example, Commissioner French and Commissioner Norton, if I asked you who is the well known Spanish-speaking poet who wrote "Snaps," Jose Torres, Albisek Campos, Jose Marti or Victor Hernandez Cruz, chances are you wouldn't know. Or if I asked you the question from which country does the following proverb come, "The humble pay for the mistakes of their betters," Uganda, Basutoland, Tanzania or Kenya.

Now, I can set up a test with all these very objective questions and I can set up any kind of test you want. One that will eliminate Puerto Ricans, one that will eliminate Blacks, one that will eliminate Blacks and Puerto Ricans and one that will eliminate whites.

Now, what you have in the school system right now is a group of white affluents who are not familiar with the culture of the Blacks and, furthermore, who are far more involved in other things. For example, today the Black community and Black students in colleges and high schools are very much concerned with their identity. And so they are reading everything that comes out in Black literature, Black history, et cetera, and they are not reading Shakespeare. The whites, on the other hand, are reading Shakespeare and are very sure that western European culture is the ultimate and are not concerned with this. So that you find when the test is made up, the test is made up of those kinds of petty information which the whites think are important in terms of education in 1970, and which the Blacks do not.

This is shown very clearly, for example, in the Louis Harris book on Blacks and whites where, in terms of almost any poll you take, the position of the Blacks and whites are quite different. For example, although most Blacks are not Black Panthers, 80% of the Black people are sympathetic to the Black Panthers, whereas, 80% of the teachers are not sympathetic to the Black Panthers, and this puts the Black children down.

Another thing that happens, if you look at the "United Teacher," you will find out that there are trips to Italy, to Israel, to London, to France, to Germany, et cetera, et cetera. There are no trips to Africa, despite the fact that 30% of the students are Black and are very concerned with Africa. So that even if there isn't racism, there is a kind of concern that Black people have that stimulate the interest of the Black children, because I am sure that if 30% of the teachers were Black, the Black teachers would be going to Africa and when they came back, they would have experiences which they could give to the Black children, which are important to their identity. This doesn't happen because of the structure of the school system.

So the first question is the question of objectivity and it is just a lie that there is anything objective about these tests.

As far as merit is concerned, these tests test nothing but the ability of a person to memorize garbage that means nothing, that is utterly irrelevant and which they forget one day after they take the exam. It doesn't test knowledge at all.

That is nonsense.

The question then is, why are they fighting for this kind of thing. Because, what we have, is a real political patronage pork barrel, and the way it works is very simple. In 1898, the political parties were the ones that had the power and were handing out the patronage. In the 1970's, one of the big political outfits is the trade union movement and the Council of Supervisory Associations. The patronage is being handled, not through the political parties, but through the other big institutions. Any adult who has any sense at all will understand that the choices that the council of Supervisory Associations and the United Federation of Teachers will make in terms of appointing principals are not going to favor appointments of guys who support the community and, in fact, Mr. Shanker charged that if the community had control of the selection and firing of teachers, they would get rid of some of the union people in favor of those who are anti-union. A lot of people are anti-union, but they are pro-community.

The fact of the matter is that in 1968 the UFT, in collusion with the Council of Supervisory Associations, fired the teachers who were pro-community. They not only fired them but they made sure, through assignments, that there was never a nucleus in any school or district of pro-community teachers that could threaten the UFT. The whole meaning of Ocean Hill-Brownsville was to destroy the independent power base of a Black community that threatened, not the Union, but the racist policies that were followed by Mr. Shanker. Basically, Mr. Shanker does not represent the interests of any teachers in the City of New York; basically, he represents the interests of the supervisors.

One other question that came up. Mr. Shanker and Mr. Degnan always liked to compare themselves to doctors and lawyers. I would like to read something in relation to that.

The "United Teacher" headline for January 24th reads:

"Charles Silberman will receive John Dewey Award at UFT Spring Education Conference."

Then, the headlines of the New York Times story of these hearings on January 28th, reads:

"Shanker would use lawyers' license method," and the first sentence reads:

"Albert Shanker, President of the United Federation of Teachers, called yesterday for State teachers and supervisory examinations similar to those given in law and medicine instead of those now administered by the controversial Board of Examiners."

Charles Silberman eminently deserves the honor of the UFT John Dewey Award for his brilliant book, Crisis in the Classroom; that he has to accept it from the hands of Tom Dewey Shanker is obscene, that Shanker's proposals for the hiring of teachers and supervisors for the New York City school system would prevent this John Dewey Award winner from teaching in New York is ironic, that Shanker is trying to parasitically cash in on Silberman's educational prestige for his own totalitarian political purposes is a crime against integrity, that the advertising sheets, the New York Times, the Post and the Daily News permit Mr. Shanker to cash in his counterfeit credentials is a crime against all the parents, the students, the teachers and the taxpayers and a subversion of honest journalism, that Shanker has not read either John Dewey or Charles Silberman with any comprehension or understanding is clear.

Listen to Charles Silberman discussing John Dewey in his Afterword and then compare it with Shanker's statement in the New York Times.

Charles Silberman: "It is one of the complaints of the schoolmaster that the public does not defer to his professional opinion as completely as it does to that of practitioners in other professions, Dewey wrote in one of his last published works. While this might appear to be a defect in the way education is organized, he argued, it in fact is not, for the relation between professionals and the public is different in education than in any other profession. Education is a public business with us, in a sense that the protection and restoration of personal health or legal rights are not. The reason is simple To an extent characteristic of no other institution, save that of the state itself, the school has the power to modify the social order. An under our political system, it is the right of each individual to have a voice in the making of social policies as, indeed, he has a vote in the determination of political affairs. If this be true," Dewey concluded, "education is primarily a public business, and only secondarily a specialized vocation."

That is the opinion of Mr. Silberman and Mr. John Dewey. It is not the opinion of Mr. Shanker. Mr. Shanker, with his professional elitism, has contempt for the elected and accountable community school boards and this is indicated where in the New York Times he said:

"If the local community school boards had the power to hire and fire, they would just get the goodies,"

and Mr. Shanker wants the goodies for himself.

Before I conclude, I would like to discuss, very quickly, the problems of personnel policy.

I completely support state certification with the local school board doing the hiring and firing. In fact, state certification itself is not really necessary because a written exam doesn't make any sense for teachers because teaching is a performing art, much closer to acting, singing, dancing, then it is to medicine or law. There is no body of knowledge for teachers as there is a body of knowledge for law and professions and the only way to test a teacher is in the act of teaching and the only way of accountability is in terms of whether the student learns or not. And this could only be done in the classroom.

I am just tired. Thank you.

THE CHAIRMAN: That was a lovely way to end.

MR: KOPPERSMITH: You think that was a lovely way to end, that I am tired?

THE CHAIRMAN: Yes.

MR. KOPPERSMITH: All right. I think I am tired.

THE CHAIRMAN: Because that means that you threw your whole self in your testimony and we thank you for it.

MR. SALVADORE: Madam Chairman, Commissioner and ladies and gentlemen, my name is David Salvadore and I come from Cuba. I am here tonight to speak in front of this Commission and to inform of something that happened to me once I decided to be a teacher in this country.

I had a formal education in Cuba that led me to hold a Doctor's Degree in Education. When I moved to this city, I just tried to commit myself to do what I considered my best opportunity to society or community where I'm living, so I decided to go into teaching.

After struggling up and down, finally I got the right information and channels to proceed to get my license in the city public system. It was required for me to have a test at the Board of Examiners in Livingston Street.

The City and the Board of Education provide a lot of projects to help the development of the Spanish-speaking community in town, and projects that are really very helpful. They are not the solutions to all the problems that we are facing now in this country, but they will help and they are a real way to help to solve these problems.

So, I was involved in one of these projects. I got to know the

District Superintendent, I got to know the young lady who was in charge of this particular project, and they issued me a letter asking or requesting the Board of Examiners to give me a test.

I went there and I had an interview, which I passed, but then comes the written part of the test. It was not a complete failure. I must tell you I wrote about 800 to 1,000 words, and I had 22 wrong spellings, plus six diction and other few, four or five grammar construction.

I am a foreigner and English for me is a second language, that I did not devote in my country more than what we used to have in high school. I feel very proud of my command of English and also the letter that the superintendent of the district sent to the Board of Examiners stated clearly I was going to be hired for a very special project in which they required a teacher with a very fluid and solid knowledge of Spanish because they have hundreds of students which only know Spanish and they need to be taught in this language until they can, you know, raise to a certain level and with this, they can be incorporated or assimilated to the normal English curriculum.

The project was beautiful. I doubt if it would work because they were having trouble to recruit the teachers for this project.

Well, this was my first experience in this city trying to pursue a certificate and I gave it up. I got a nice opportunity for work for a company, I'm doing it at the moment. I am satisfied with my work, but still I am out of my field, and I consider myself to the development of the Spanish community in New York.

Either I have to suffer again another test, a written test, through the Board of Examiners, and I know I would fail. Because, this is asking a person, whose first language is not English, to have an efficiency of an English-speaking graduate. I think this is not fair, and it is less than the opportunity of the Spanish community that we have already in New York.

Later, I kept on, and I went to a test -- this was more formal, because this was a temporary license -- then I went to a test on teacher of Spanish in junior high school, and there I again had failure in the written part of the test, in English, you know, and disqualified myself.

Then I took another test for the bilingual teacher in school and community relations. You see, both are specific projects in which the city has spent thousands and thousands of dollars and that we see the need this city has for this kind of Spanish-speaking people to advance to a level in which they can integrate into society, in which they can be positive in the full extent of their own life to the life of this nation.

So, again this was part of my failure, the written test.

I just only want to point out as a final statement, this discrepancy between the projects of the city in this field and the means the Board of Examiners has to fulfill the projects, is a complete failure, and it hurts the Spanish-speaking community in New York.

Thanks very much for your kind attention.
THE CHAIRMAN: Thank you.
Mrs. Pullim.

MRS. PULLIM: Mrs. Norton, Mrs. French, it's nice to talk to you because I have a lot of trouble.

I've been unemployed for four years and on relief and the one thing you can say about relief, the rent gets paid but, you know, you can't go to movies or go to church or buy any clothes. I buy stockings, you know, and so it's a constant worry.

A person being unemployed for four years, well, I was with the school system and I had trouble with the children. I was at P.S. 62 in the Bronx and my job was taken away from me.

The thing about that job, the principal knew that I had trouble because she could hear the children, the noise they were making, but she was willing to give me a chance, you know. And so I was trying and the principal was, you know, she was trying to help me.

Somehow, I don't know how, I had to go to the psychiatrist but, anyway, I went to the psychiatrist and we talked for about two minutes, and the next couple of days, I had a letter from the psychiatrist saying I should turn my license in.

I was nice and obedient, took my license down to Livingston Street and turned it in, something I had worked for, you know. I turned the license in.

What makes me so worried, when people inquire into my employment history, what did you do such and such a time, I have to bring up the episode with the school board.

Well, what happened? She saw a psychiatrist, something is wrong with her. And so, it just put me, you know, in a shadow I just can't seem to get out of.

And so that is why -- I don't know why I'm coughing -- that was the gist of what I wanted to say, and so, you know, I need the right person to tell me something.

Thank you.

THE CHAIRMAN: Thank you, Mrs. Pullim.

The next witness is Juanita Cruz.

MRS. CRUZ: Good evening. My name is Juanita Cruz --

THE CHAIRMAN: I believe Mrs. Cruz is the last witness. I want to thank her because Mrs. Cruz has been here several days before.

MRS. CRUZ: I think it is commendable that the Commission has taken the responsibility to try to bring some light to the issue of education in the City of New York for the benefit of the life of the City and although I have worked very hard, just like everybody else has and I'm completely drained of energy. I tried to put something together because I feel it's my responsibility as a member of this society and mother and so-called professional person to try and bring what I feel could be done in this city, to save the city, and primarily to save our children.

I do it because as a mother I know what it is to have children, although you don't have to have them physically. I do it for all the young people in the high schools that either go into drugs or dying because of overdoses or are being turned off, because we're living in such a stage of fright and paralysis that it is just completely covering this whole city and we must try to do something.

So, I begin. More of our children need to accept the challenge of the current times and help make changes rather than give up hopelessly on society and themselves, drop out of school or resort to other things that find their imagination and sense of adventure. They should not need to seek an escape hatch from frustration in their positive self-image by resorting to drugs or antisocial behavior. So many of our children have met their deaths due to narcotics in many cases.

The adventure with drugs started without fully realizing that ultimately it might mean violence, a drug-related disease or an overdose.

Where does the role of the school enter. In order for the city's Black and Puerto Rican children to understand the society in which they live, they would need to have teachers besides their own parents that have been properly trained by the colleges.

This has not been the case. Colleges, as well as the school system, need to cease perpetuating their system and maintaining their image. If the school system does not expect teachers to relate to the parent and the community from which the pupils come, how can teachers understand or teach our children. What support does the white, dedicated teacher get under the present system.

We are all the products of our environment and the society which we live in. This society was predetermined for us before our birth. How we understand this will determine how we will in great measure live our lives, relate to others, and rear and guide our children to prepare them to function in society as well as contribute to the positive growth of society.

This city as part of the greatest society is failing to develop the institutions of learning that will adequately foster human growth and intellect. This hearing bears this out.

We are also living in a vastly changing society, which requires that agencies and professionals respond to this society's needs.

My recommendations: It must be made possible for Blacks or Puerto Ricans who are in the cities to have an opportunity to train, to become teachers if they choose.

These are the people that our children could relate to and learn from. Under these conditions, the enlightened, motivated, white teachers would receive the cooperation, direction and support many of them are seeking and fail to get in their well-meaning but futile attempts to teach our children.

Human values and human beings are more important than maintaining hollow institutions which only serve to perpetuate the racism which this country was built upon. We were born into this racism, but others after us should not have to be.

Thank you.

THE CHAIRMAN: Thank you.

These hearings have finally come to a close. I just want to note for the record my thanks to various segments of the school system and public who came to testify, the Board of Education and the Board of Examiners and their staff.

I appreciate that they willingly came forward to present the facts about their operation as they see them. I think their testimony was deeply factual and probing and was important not only for the way this educated the Commission and the public, but for the very salutary effect their testimony has regarding some myths the general public has concerning their operation.

I want to thank the numerous interested individuals and organizations in the city who came here to testify with respect to their own experience.

I want to thank those who came from other cities and states, kind enough to lend us the aid of their advice and views and experience.

I want to thank the minority people of this city who too have misconceptions and stereotypes about the system but also have great anguish, and who in the face of that anguish conducted themselves as totally rational people committed to search for sound solutions.

In the face of the continuing failure of their only hope, their children, in a school system, their conduct at these hearings has been so superb that I cannot say enough for it or about it.

I want to thank the general public which consists of more different kinds of people, ethnic groups and races, than can be found anyplace in the world, with the attention they paid at these hearings, the tolerance they have shown during this time when an issue of great controversy in the city was being aired and I'm going to finally thank those of you have have sat here to the final end of these hearings for doing so.

These hearings are adjourned.

(Whereupon, at this time, the hearings were adjourned.)

APPENDIX A

SUMMARY OF TESTIMONY AND CONCLUSIONS
AND RECOMMENDATIONS OF THE COMMISSION

The Commission's investigation of the current personnel practices of the New York City school system yields one inescapable conclusion--that change is urgently demanded. This was the clear consensus of five days of public hearings. For even the defenders of the current system recognized its deficiencies in selecting school personnel. The essential issue raised by the hearings was whether the system that now prevails can be further modified to meet the divergent needs of all the individual schools and districts in the city, or whether more drastic change is required.

A few of the many who testified, principally the representatives of the Board of Examiners, consider the current system fundamentally sound. They assert that the examination process, with its emphasis on a written proficiency test, screens out incompetents and provides an objective merit system under which selection is free from patronage and political pressure. They point to the significant number of recent modifications as evidence of the system's responsiveness to changing needs, and predict that, in time, the number of minority professionals will increase.

The view of the vast preponderance of witnesses, however, was that the current selection system has certain fundamental flaws which cannot be completely corrected except by wholesale reform. At the heart of the problem, as they see it, is a complex and rigid examination process presided over by the Board of Examiners. But problems with recruiting, establishment of eligibility requirements and the use of the probationary period, all of which are the responsibility of the Board of Education and the Chancellor, were seen as having considerable impact.

Critics of the system attack it on two levels--underlying theory and implementation. They contest the merit of the basic premise articulated by members of the Board of Examiners--that the primary function of a selection process is to screen out incompetents. Although it must do that, they say, the major problem confronting the schools is to identify candidates with real teaching and supervisory talent, and especially those with ability to educate inner-city children who are now most inadequately served. What is needed, therefore, and what is being sought actively in many areas of the country are methods to screen *in* the best potential talent. In the words of Dr. John Fischer, President of Columbia University's Teachers

College,"...[T]he most important task confronting us is not the screening out of incompetents, but the identification of those with a combination of capabilities that we need to move the schools and our children ahead." Indeed, many witnesses said if emphasis were placed on identifying such people, the number of Black and Spanish-speaking professionals in the school system would increase substantially.

Even if screening out incompetents were the most important objective for a selection system, many witnesses criticized the way New York City has sought to achieve this goal. The criticism falls into six principal areas.

1. Outmoded. An elaborate, formal examination process may have served an important function more than 70 years ago, when the Board of Examiners was created and when the requirements to teach consisted of one year of teacher training school beyond high school, but, according to many witnesses including Chancellor Harvey B. Scribner, it is now "...antiquated, outmoded and inconsistent with both contemporary educational requirements and the concept of decentralized schools." Members of the Board of Examiners responded by pointing to modernization in the process and to evidence that, even today, such a process is necessary to prevent a spoils system.

2. Delay and Deterrence. Delays in promulgating eligible lists based on the examinations discourage many from ever applying to the school system and cause some who have applied to accept jobs elsewhere, according to Board of Education officials who are in charge of recruiting efforts. Aside from the delays, the examination process also reportedly deters many applicants because its procedures are confusing and offend some minority applicants. Moreover, Theodore Lang, until recently Deputy Superintendent in charge of the Office of Personnel, said problems in the promulgation of eligible lists cause difficulties in assigning teachers to fill vacancies. Defenses offered by members of the Board of Examiners included a description of recent innovations to reduce delays, such as testing seniors before graduation and giving one-day walk-in examinations in certain circumstances.

3. Rigidity. Board of Education President Murry Bergtraum said the present selection system's "emphasis on formalistic training, formalistic requirements, long periods of service" is both a reason why the New York City school system has a low percentage of Black and Puerto Rican professionals and a disservice to all applicants. Chancellor Scribner, Community Superintendent Edythe Gaines and many other witnesses bemoaned the limited pool of eligible candidates available under the current system. Dr. Jay Greene of the Board of Examiners, on the other hand, argued that "flexibility" often is just another name for the spoils system, and, in any event, the current selection process actually provides a larger, rather than smaller, pool of eligibles.

4. Cost and Patronage. Many witnesses criticized the high direct and indirect costs of the examination system. The Board of Examiners' annual budget is now more than $3.5 million, with all but a very small portion going to salaries. For example, more than

$2 million is paid, at a per day rate of almost $100, to temporary examination assistants, most of whom are also full-time professional employees of the school system. An indirect cost of the examination process which many witnesses found objectionable is the cost of private coaching courses usually conducted by current supervisory personnel. The registration fee alone is substantial; but witnesses also spoke of the cost in time and energy expended on an exercise with limited, if any, relevance to performance of the job. Dr. Greene responded to these criticisms by asserting that another written examination, such as the National Teacher Examination, would be more expensive, and that decentralized recruiting and selection by the 31 community boards would be still more costly. The bases for these predictions were, however, challenged.

5. Invalidity and Bias. The most frequent and serious of the critical comments about the current selection process is that it lacks validity and objectivity. Two types of validity are pertinent-- predictive and content. According to the testing experts who testified, predictive validity refers to an examination's ability to identify who will perform well on the job. Content validity, on the other hand, deals with how well an examination tests for specific knowledge or skills required on a job and how important the knowledge or skills tested for are to total performance. Many witnesses charged the Board of Examiners' examinations have no predictive validity-- that is, there is no evidence a high scorer on the examination will perform better than a lower scorer. And members of the Board agreed that they have no basis for making such a prediction, and that, in fact, for teacher examinations they have never attempted a predictive validity study. Their explanation is that predictive validity is very elusive, especially when good performance is difficult to define. Moreover, they rely on content validity. According to Dr. Robert Thorndike, Professor of Psychology at Columbia Teachers College and a testing consultant for the Board of Examiners in current litigation, content validity depends upon two main ingredients -- adequate job descriptions from which to select key job skills, and the necessary expertise to construct examination items which will effectively test for those skills. Many witnesses, including several testing experts, charged that neither of these ingredients is present in the school system's examination process. According to Dr. Lang, during his five and one-half years as Deputy Superintendent in charge of the Office of Personnel, there was no updating of job descriptions for any teaching positions. And Dr. Richard Barrett, a test expert, said that the job descriptions for supervisory positions which he had recently seen were "mere skeletons" not providing the kind of information useful for the test constructor. Lack of expertise in constructing test items was also charged by a number of witnesses. All the expert witnesses agreed that psychometric skill is indispensable to the construction of a valid examination. Yet, according to members of the Board of Examiners, their entire permanent professional staff consists of pedagogical personnel from the school system assigned to them by informal procedures with no requirement that any of these personnel have expertise in test construction. The Board also has a large

corps of temporary examination assistants which is selected by equally informal procedures. Some of these assistants are from outside the school system and presumably provide psychometric expertise. However, members of the Board of Examiners testified that much of the test construction is actually done by personnel whose principal expertise is their experience as supervisors within the school system. The four regular members of the Board of Examiners (the Chancellor or his designee is the fifth member) are required to take a Civil Service examination which covers test construction, among many other subjects, but none of the current members' main background is in psychology, test development, personnel management or a related field. All four are former English teachers who have been supervisors in the New York City school system.

It should be noted that if an examination lacks validity in the sense that it is not job-related, serious legal issues will be raised under the United States Constitution and federal statutes and regulations as well. Stephen Pollak, former Assistant Attorney General in charge of the Civil Rights Division of the U.S. Department of Justice, described in detail the legal requirements which pertain. Among other things, he testified that "no school board may lawfully use a standardized test as part of its selection process, whether for hiring, retention or promotion, unless that test is a valid and reliable measure of the candidate's capacity to perform well on the job." Members of the Board of Examiners did not deny that more validation should be made. Dr. Greene said, "I agree we should have more research and go into matters of validity whether predictive or content." The defense offered was that in its budget of more than $3.5 million only about $40,000 was available for research.

Many witnesses charged that the examination process is not only invalid but also discriminatory, in effect if not in purpose. And the bias alleged is not racial or ethnic alone; it operates against all outsiders, against all who think differently. One witness, Dr. Laurence Iannacone, Professor of Education Administration at the University of Toronto, described the personnel system of the New York City schools as "so inbred as to be sociological incest." Most of the critical witnesses said the examination process has two main sources of bias -- cultural and geographic bias in the written test and subjectivity in the oral interview and review of record. Some of the most compelling testimony about alleged bias came from Spanish-speaking witnesses. If, in fact, the examination process discriminates against Spanish-speaking teachers it would be especially unfortunate in view of the critical need for bilingual teachers. With close to 300,000 Spanish-speaking students in the school system, there are reportedly far fewer than 1,000 Spanish-speaking teachers. Witnesses representing the Chinese and Italian communities also testified about the exclusionary effect of the examination process. Members of the Board of Examiners respond to charges of bias by enumerating the safeguards built into the system to ensure objectivity. These include openness in terms of ability to take the examinations and to be apprised of the qualifications, scope and pass marks, full documentation and reviewability, right of appeal,

Summary and Recommendations

confidentiality during the examination process, and professional development and administration of the examinations. What the critics maintained was that these criteria, however laudable, are not being fully met. Members of the Board of Examiners conceded that there have been "hazards" in parts of the examination, but denied that this is still true, pointing to recent changes in their procedures.

6. Inconsistency with Decentralization. Finally, many witnesses said that a selection process with such great emphasis on centrally created, administered and graded examinations leading to centrally promulgated eligible lists from which personnel have to be selected around the city is inconsistent with meaningful decentralization. Chancellor Scribner in particular expressed the hope that community boards would soon have real selection authority without "a form of city certification.. laid on top of state certification." Until they do have such authority, he said, "these boards will operate with severe and undue constraints. They will not be fully responsible for the total management of the schools under their jurisdiction and no mechanism for holding these boards fully acountable for the effectiveness of their schools can be devised." Frustration with a highly centralized selection mechanism and the belief that largely local selection would be more effective were expressed by community board members, community superintendents and school principals. Defenders of the current system argued that a more completely decentralized personnel system would be costly and duplicative. Also, they said, local pressures would produce a spoils system under which those in power handpicked appointees.

Much of the testimony presented at the Commission's hearings dealt with flaws in the current New York City personnel system, especially the selection facet. But, the hearings were designed to be more than a forum for those with particular grievances. Exploring possible alternatives to the current system, based on developments around the country, was an important goal. To achieve this, a wide range of expert witnesses was brought together because of their leadership in teacher education selection techniques, especially testing and innovative programs preparing school personnel on all levels; or because they represent state education departments or urban school systems actively engaged in developing new forms of personnel screening and selection. Moreover, all witnesses, and particularly those serving in leadership roles in the New York City school system, were asked to assess the merits of possible alternatives.

The consensus which emerged from this testimony was one of general dissatisfaction with traditional selection methods, relying as they do upon as assessment of pre-employment preparation and giving little attention to effective measurement of actual performance. Thus, the criticism and demands for change within New York City are part of a nation-wide reaction against and reevaluation of the philosophy of personnel selection and professional development epitomized by the Board of Examiners and its emphasis on the written proficiency test.

Recently, for example, the United States Supreme Court held in the case of Griggs v. Duke Power Co. that standardized tests which are not sufficiently job-related cannot be used for employment purposes if they have the effect of disproportionately screening out minority group candidates. Within various professions, criticism of traditional licensing tests, such as bar examinations, on the grounds of bias and invalidity is growing. Leading educators throughout the country are concentrating on the development of systems of performance-based criteria for selection of school personnel which would largely replace traditional methods. This effort is intimately connected with a total remodelling of teacher training to focus on in-school skill development. Such changes must go hand in hand with restructuring of certification or licensing procedures, and imply close cooperation among the professionals, the certifying or licensing authorities, and the community.

Most educational leaders favor a dual process of selection consisting of a highly flexible and open initial screening, with final selection on the local level, preferably after a period of service or internship sufficient to allow critical and objective observation and evaluation. A variation suggested by some witnesses is a system of two-stage certification, provisional and permanent.

Given this preference, it is not surprising that the principal alternative proposed for New York City was reliance on state certification for initial screening and on community board and superintendent for final selection without the intervention of a substantial city-wide process. Although state certification has certain limitations, it is being improved and, even now, provides an openness and and flexibility which many witnesses believe is essential. Freeing the city school system -- which has about one-third of the State's pupils -- from preoccupation with the process of written tests for 1,200 licenses, would be a powerful stimulant to accelerated development of new standards and approaches throughout the State. New York City, with its enormous and varied school population and its array of colleges and universities, could be a fertile source of new ideas and programs. Decentralization, if more fully utilized, would offer a unique opportunity to measure and compare differing selection techniques.

Local selection is however not without some potential problems. According to a number of witnesses including community board members, community boards and their superintendents will have to develop their expertise in selection techniques, and adequate safeguards against favoritism will have to be incorporated. (Because this is a matter of special concern to the Commission, it will be discussed in more detail later in this section.)

As more reliable performance-based criteria for selection are developed, state certification and local selection both will rely on them. To what extent there should be continued reliance on written tests was discussed by many witnesses. Most witnesses criticized substantial reliance on written tests which focus on acquired knowledge. In the view of many experts, written tests are costly to administer and process, and require continual assessment and revision to assure validity. In addition, even if intended as only one facet of the selection process, written tests frequently become the whole of it because test scores appear more conclusive and incontrovertible than the judgment of peers, supervisors or observers. Evidence of this tendency is manifest in New York City where the probationary period -- ostensibly a critical element in selection of personnel -- is grossly underutilized and, in fact, serves only to disqualify those who display totally unacceptable behavior. Other witnesses said formal written tests may actually be counterproductive in assessing capacity if they place undue emphasis on test-taking skill at the expense of qualities such as ability to communicate knowledge, creativity, commitment, and the ability to grow in sensitivity to the needs of children and parents. Studies of test performance, according to one expert witness, suggest this may pose special problems for minority candidates. And, more generally, witnesses stressed that standardized written tests create a clear potential for discrimination, whether intentional or not, against minorities or "outsiders" to any given locality or system. Finally, according to witnesses, even partial reliance on a written test would impede the development of more valid performance-based selection criteria.

These objections, together with the lack of evidence that the few school systems in the country currently using locally developed written tests have superior teacher quality or pupil achievement, led some witnesses to favor elimination of such tests from the selection process. Only New York City and Buffalo are expressly required to rely on competitive examinations which include a substantial written test, and Buffalo's examination requirement was reduced in 1968. That city's school superintendent favors elimination of required examinations altogether.

Other witnesses favored elimination of all written tests, whether locally developed or not, because, in their judgment, written proficiency tests generally do no more than confirm college grades. In New York City -- where approximately 65% of new teachers are graduates of City University and many more come from other local institutions -- such confirmation would seem especially unnecessary. Moreover, since New York City promotions are generally awarded to those with substantial years of experience in the city's schools, written tests for supervisory and administrative positions are perhaps even more superfluous than those for teacher applicants.

Some witnesses suggested that written tests may have a continuing place in well-conceived selection procedures in conjunction with other selection techniques, but only to the extent that test scores can be demonstrated to have a clear and consistent relationship to performance. The National Teacher Examination of the Educational Testing Service, which is already used in some circumstances within New York City, or a state-wide certification examination, were proposed by some witnesses as the most logical written test component of the process. Other witnesses were critical of both. The NTE was portrayed as yet another culturally biased test. The Educational Testing Service is aware of this concern and has taken steps to eliminate biased material on the advice of panels of minority educators. It is also designing special examinations for teaching in an urban setting and for Spanish-speaking applicants.

Even with these efforts, ETS representatives stress carefully the limited role the NTE is designed to play in the selection process and the potential for abuse. But if used within those limits, the NTE has certain advantages. It is offered frequently across the country and is ordinarily taken by many prospective teachers. Its designers have shown an openness to change and an awareness of the danger of bias. A state-wide written examination was criticized largely on the ground that it would impose on all professional personnel throughout the State a system which has proven unsatisfactory in New York City.

Despite the broad consensus favoring an employment system based on improved state certification and local selection, two concerns voiced at the hearings warrant careful consideration. Fears were expressed that the process will degenerate into pure patronage and that vigilante action by special interest groups will control decision-making. Proponents of the city-wide examination see it as protection against such abuses.

Little evidence has been presented to support this assumption, and extensive testimony at the hearings by supporters of the examination system failed to lend credibility to fears of corruption and disorder. Nonetheless, the Commission does not take these fears lightly, because they have often been linked in public debate to valid issues of due process.

The essence of due process in the American system is that law, rules and custom should err always on the side of zealous protection of individual rights. The Bill of Rights is not just important in case of massive threat to civil liberty; it is important as a constant safeguard against the slightest possible abridgement of any citizen's rights. Proof of possible large-scale abuses in the city school system is not, therefore, necessary to justify strict safeguards to ensure fairness and due process. Adequate safeguards, along the lines discussed in Recommendation #3 below, should be an integral part of any selection process whatever its potential for bias or corruption. This is essential even though testimony at the hearings generally failed to support the oft-stated fears that local selection actually leads to bias or corruption.

In communities where local selection, unhampered by an elaborate written test, is the rule, patronage and related problems have not become concerns. Witnesses from other cities and states reported that they are not plagued by such problems. Teachers in districts which do not use local written examinations are neither demonstrably inferior nor less secure in their jobs. Here again, the appraisal of Dr. Joseph Manch, Superintendent of Schools of Buffalo which has the only system in the State comparable to this city's, is most persuasive. He reports that there have been no incidents involving such interference in Buffalo since examinations were eliminated for supervisors and principals.

The testimony presented reveals that the belief that corruption would follow if selection were handled by community boards in New York City is speculation based on the view that intergroup problems in this city are so serious that irrelevant considerations would dominate concern for an improved educational system with its concern for objective employment criteria based on performance. Albert Shanker, President of the UFT, for example, considers what is feasible elsewhere, in more homogeneous and stable communities, impossible in New York. He and the UFT favored abolition of the Board of Examiners until just five years ago, but now regard it or some other written examination process as a necessary bulwark against open confrontation between teachers and community groups. There was no indication that such critics had studied other means to prevent bias that might not at the same time have a deleterious effect on recruitment and mobility in the public school system.

New York does face undercurrents of racial and ethnic tension which have in the past spilled over into dangerous and frightening conflicts. It would help little, however, in efforts to prevent future conflicts, if fear or speculation were sufficient reason to perpetuate a system which has had other harmful effects. It is not asking too much of an employment system to <u>both</u> afford significant participation across racial and ethnic lines <u>and</u> assure freedom from bias and unfairness.

To be sure, change, almost by definition, carries some unpredictability or risk. In this instance, the tasks of all concerned are to reduce the unpredictability by conscientiously appraising the facts and experiences at hand, and by dealing specifically with the actual risks.

The facts relating to other communities are not alone in contradicting the fears of favoritism. New York City's own experience to date with decentralization indicates that concern with the quality and effectiveness of education is more intense and more generally held by an alert and sophisticated public than in any previous period. This was manifested not only by the widespread and high quality participation and interest in the hearings, but also in the testimony of witnesses, which included community board members, community superintendents, and parent and community spokesmen.

In Community Superintendent Andrew Donaldson's words, "The public is in there watching. The mothers and fathers are at those schools nearly every day. These community school boards have been elected by a very aroused populace. The children themselves are aware of how well the school is run or misrun. And for us to assume that simple political patronage will move people into these positions and that no questions will be asked, I think is to assume the ridiculous."

Less explicit, but clearly present in the minds of those who oppose decentralized selection, is the possibility that race or ethinc identity, in response to local pressure, will become the overriding factor in selection. This would be persuasive indeed if the fear were realistic. But the actual experience indicates otherwise.

Dr. Marilyn Gittell, Director of Queens College's Institute for Community Studies, reported that a recent study of the three demonstration districts shows that screening of staff was thorough and careful and those selected were generally superior candidates. Parents who participated in screening were concerned with teaching ability and not race and ethnic background.

A study of parental attitudes in the choice of principals conducted by the Center for Community Studies at Columbia Teachers College found the majority of parents - 62% of those surveyed - ready to identify qualities they considered essential, but with no opinion on the merits of ethnic factors.

This finding was confirmed by Public Education Association studies of individual schools, cited by David Seeley, its Director. His opinion, supported by an analysis of numerous individual schools' procedures, is this:

> The cry that we want a Black principal for Black kids is made by a few spokesmen in certain cases, but this seems to be mostly a generalized expression of dissatisfaction with the kind of staff that has been produced by the white-controlled system. Once the actual selection procedure begins filling a particular vacancy, we have seen, in every case examined, that the parents' prime concern is to find the candidate who will do the best job for their children. As often as not, the person selected is white.

The Commission is impressed that the only empirical studies of which we are aware indicate that corruption has not become a factor in the school system as decision-making has gravitated to the local level.

Clearly, however, race or ethnic background is not a matter which the school system may ignore. Assuring both equal opportunity and effective education will require affirmative action to upgrade the role of minorities in the system -- the kind of affirmative action routinely required of private employers by federal, state and local law. This does not imply the establishment of onerous quotas or preferential hiring. It does acknowledge the importance of achieving better racial representation as a goal of all personnel policies and practices in a country where such equalization has been tragically delayed.

Race has been an explicit factor in making more fair the school personnel policies in such cities as Detroit and Buffalo where significant improvements in providing fair employment opportunity have occurred. For example, according to Aubrey McCutcheon, Deputy Superintendent in charge of staff relations in Detroit, "We say we are going to have, and we require that there be, an increase, a substantial increase, in the number of Black administrators in our school system." In addition, numerous witnesses testified to the deficiency in the education of Spanish-speaking and Chinese-speaking children, a case where ethnic factors as they relate to the ability to speak a language in addition to English attain particular significance.

If commitment to teach children (especially those who have difficulties in the school system), sensitivity to the needs of a community, ability to communicate effectively with children and their parents were accorded appropriate weight, along with subject matter knowledge, literacy and the like, undoubtedly a higher proportion of those selected would come from minority groups.

Under such an approach, the number of bilingual persons on the professional staff of the school system would undoubtedly increase significantly. Also, other serious problems arising from undue restriction of eligibility would be alleviated. Current lists of eligibles, especially in the case of principals, offer few choices to many schools, since those on the lists often decline to consider schools where openings exist. Inexperienced teachers are often in effect "drafted" to what are considered difficult assignments, where they mark time until they are eligible for transfer. Several community superintendents and principals testified to their ability to find well-qualified persons, eager to serve in the very assignments rejected by many of those on the eligible lists. Flexible local selection would lift many barriers of this kind that now disadvantage further the disadvantaged schools.

This does not mean that race or origin standing by itself as a qualification, or any form of arbitrary exclusion, can ever be tolerated. The aim of change must be to improve the quality and effectiveness of personnel and to equalize employment opportunity through greater openness and flexibility. Any resort to the narrow criterion of race or origin would not only do violence to basic concepts of human rights but would undermine the purpose of reform. Adequate safeguards against this kind of abuse must accompany any new system.

Members of community boards were among the first at the hearings to recognize the need for a range of supportive services to permit them to discharge adequately their obligations to all their constituents. They pointed to their need for assistance in developing sound recruitment and selection practices and expertise in evaluating performance. Several recommended specifically that local selection be required to be open and readily reviewable and that adequate protection against favoritism be developed.

It should be noted that the Board of Education and the Chancellor already have certain statutory powers which can be used in this connection on a city-wide basis. For example, the Chancellor has the power and duty to establish minimum education and experience requirements for professional personnel. The Board of Education has the authority to develop city-wide personnel and procedural policies which the Chancellor has the power and duty to enforce. Moreover, the State Commissioner of Education has broad authority to hear controversies arising in the schools. And, of course, recourse to the courts is always possible and frequently used in school matters, as for example in a suit now pending in a New York federal district court against the Board of Examiners and Board of Education on the grounds that the supervisory examinations are discriminatory and invalid.

Although the needs of individual schools vary, even under a local selection system there would be elements common to all districts and all schools that could be handled most efficiently by a central body. For this reason, many witnesses saw a new role for the Board of Education, perhaps by using the permanent personnel of the Board of Examiners, among others, in the (Board of Education's) Office of Personnel as an advisory and review agent. This central agency could provide information to all applicants interested in New York City, help to put them in contact with community boards whose needs matched the applicant's skills and interests, investigate and review data concerning all applicants, develop guidelines for selection procedures, train community board members in interviewing and observation techniques, design performance criteria and measurements for evaluation, and supply outside experts in training, selection and evaluation to consult with community boards. In addition, such a central agency could design and administer internships and in-service training programs, and conduct systematic research to measure the effectiveness of personnel and to compare different selection and training techniques. This is a challenging assignment, far more demanding than designing and administering standardized written tests. Upgrading selection procedures will require not only greater flexibility and innovation but also careful research and evaluation.

However, the transition to a new selection system might pose problems beyond the ability of the central agency to handle immediately. The Commission has taken this into account in shaping its recommendations (see #2 below).

RECOMMENDATIONS

The Commission, after careful study of the testimony and based on the foregoing conclusions, makes the following recommendations:

1. The Board of Examiners in its current form should be discontinued and its permanent staff transferred to the Board of Education's Office of Personnel. This action, we believe, is critical if a narrow concept of merit, based largely on written proficiency tests of questionable validity, is to be replaced by a more realistic appraisal of merit. In any reorganized selection system, however, the Commission believes the presence of adequate due process safeguards is indispensable (see #3 below).

The current Examiners' system is costly, cumbersome, and, regardless of intent, restricts the opportunities available to many who might contribute ably to the education of this city's school children, especially inner-city children. Such professionals and aspirants include members of minority groups and, as the testimony revealed, many others as well.

In their testimony, even the members of the Board of Examiners claimed only that the testing system screens out incompetents and protects against extraneous influences in selection. They were not, however, able to present any evidence of a relation between test achievement and performance on the job. The Commission believes that this minimal proficiency can be ensured under a system which also places greater emphasis on local application of performance-based criteria than does the Board of Examiners system. We believe also that, although the testimony does not support the fear that favoritism and corruption would increase under a new system, protection against such influences can best be provided by specific due process requirements.

The background knowledge of the city's school system undoubtedly possessed by the members of the Board of Examiners in conjunction with the expertise of qualified specialists could be untilized in conducting much-needed research on selection criteria for use by the City Board of Education and community boards. As part of the Office of Personnel, they might also carry out such functions as channeling applicants to appropriate community boards, investigating and reviewing data about applicants, training members of interested community boards in selection techniques and developing panels of experts to be available to assist community boards on selection matters.

2. The New York City school system -- like virtually all other school districts in New York State and the rest of the country -- should rely on state certification for initial screening of professional staff. Community boards should have the ultimate responsibility for the second and crucial stage in the employment process -- actual selection of staff based upon sound and objective selection criteria and procedures geared to the needs of individual boards. To assist community boards while they are developing their expertise in selection matters, a special, temporary panel of education experts appointed by the Board of Education should provide community boards with pertinent information and with advice about specific problems.

State certification can and should be improved, but as a limited tool confined to screening, it is less costly and more open and flexible than a city-wide licensing system. There is no evidence from its use throughout the State that it compares unfavorably with the present New York City system either in terms of teacher competence or pupil achievement. Its use would enlarge significantly the city's pool of potential teachers and supervisors in a way that would permit community boards needed flexibility, subject to adequate due process safeguards.

As is true of virtually every other board of education in New York State, community boards should have authority to select from among state-certified candidates. The special, temporary panel appointed to assist community boards should include, among others, recognized experts whose experience relates to the use of state certification in combination with flexible local standards. The panel would provide community boards, teachers, parents and all concerned with relevant information and expert advice on specific problems, including those which may arise during the changeover of selection systems.

3. At the earliest date, the Board of Education should develop appropriate policy guidelines to ensure protection of due process for all applicants and personnel. Detailed administrative regulations for enforcement of the guidelines should be promulgated and enforced by the Chancellor.

Despite the lack of factual evidence that systems not employing formal local examinations with written tests have special problems of corruption and favoritism, the possibility is one which the Commission does not treat lightly. Only through the most precise application of due process guidelines can the system ensure protection of individual rights and prevent such problems from arising in the first instance. Current collective bargaining agreements and Board of Education by-laws provide grievance procedures which apply throughout the city school system. They will, of course, continue to be enforced. But they do not adequately cover applicants for employment whose rights should be protected by appropriate Board of Education policy guidelines and more detailed regulations promulgated by the Chancellor. The Chancellor already has the power and duty to enforce throughout the city all prevailing policies, by-laws, rules and regulations, and contracts by means including, if necessary, suspension, removal or supersession of community boards.

Protection through due process is the foundation of a democratic society and all its institutions -- its schools certainly no less than any other.

4. The City Board of Education and the community boards, directly and through the many institutions of higher learning and other educational organizations with which they have working relationships, should assume a leadership role in developing performance-based training and selection techniques. This can serve both as a spur and a resource to the State in its ongoing effort to incorporate meaningful performance-based criteria into the certification process. Redistribution of the power of selection is not enough. Unless, both at the state and local level, strides are made toward better training and assessment of performance, the schools will not meet the needs of the children or the community. Moreover it is unfair to expect teachers to perform well under today's difficult conditions in the deteriorating urban environment without the guidance that will enable them to improve their performance.

In these efforts, special attention should be paid to those with experience in developing performance-based criteria, such as educators in Oregon, Washington, California, Minnesota, Michigan, Pennsylvania, New Jersey, Texas and Florida, states which have already made significant progress in this area.

5. The City Commission on Human Rights will take steps to develop an affirmative action program, in cooperation with the school system, specifying certain recruitment, selection and promotion measures, to be undertaken by community boards and the City Board with a view toward overcoming the low representation of minorities.

Many private employers have made agreements of this kind with the Commission as part of their obligations under the law. Such an agreement would provide the school system with the kind of minority group hiring guidelines (based on the valuable experiences of others who have required highly trained personnel in this city) which several Board of Education staff members said are desperately needed if real progress is to be achieved. The school system has sufficient flexibility to make a meaningful start at such affirmative action regardless of any legislative steps. Legislative action, however, is still vital if a personnel system is to be structured which provides maximum assurance of equal employment opportunity and which is most likely to produce professionals best qualified in every way to educate the children of the city.

* * * * *

The basic recommendations of the Commission require legislative action. And these statutory changes are absolutely necessary for thorough reform of the selection process that now prevails in New York City. There are, however, many areas where changes can be made in the interim, changes to better integrate the several parts of the selection process and to make the whole more responsive to the needs of children and the community. Avenues open to the Board of Education could be used to greater effect and the Board of Examiners itself has the power to restructure the content and form of its examination process.

Much of the current attention, especially toward increasing the opportunities for minority personnel, is focused on recruiting. The limited success, thus far, of out-town-recruiting suggests that substantial problems are created by the complexities and rigidities of the examination process. Those in charge of the Office of Personnel's recruiting programs suggested that attracting outsiders was difficult not only because immediate job offers cannot be made on the spot, but also because New York City has a negative image, a reputation of limited opportunities for minority persons. A vast reservoir of capable manpower remains untapped, both within the city and without, in large part because entry and promotion hinge on a series of separate examinations, each of which can involve substantial pre-examination preparation and expense, and substantial post-examination delay. One interim measure for alleviating this problem is the use of simplified examinations -- either so-called unassembled examinations, which consist of review of record without written tests, or one-day walk-in examinations with short-form written tests - especially for those being recruited on campuses outside the New York metropolitan area. There are already precedents within the New York City system for using either unassembled examinations or one-day walk-in examinations. Alternatively, the National Teacher Examination, which many prospective teachers take as a matter of course, could be used as a part of the selection process instead of a local written test. This simplified procedure could enable New York City to compete on more equal recruiting terms with city school districts like Detroit whose recruiters are authorized to offer jobs on the spot to applicants who rank in the upper half of their class and who make a favorable impression during the interview.

An interim change in recruiting emphasis might also help. Virtually no effort has been made to recruit candidates for supervisory positions from outside the system. This contributes to New York City's reputation as a closed school system, especially for minority groups. If outside candidates were actively sought (and if the selection process did not make it more difficult for them, as many witnesses testified was the case) the reputation would begin to change.

Further beneficial changes could result from modifying eligibility requirements. The first step in the selection process is the determination of eligibility for examination. The Board of Education has been moving in the direction of changing the qualifications largely by reducing the number of years that must be served on one job level to be eligible for examination for promotion. Because most minority personnel are relatively new to the system, reducing the time requirements probably will accelerate the rate of their promotion, and there is no evidence that this will adversely affect quality. If the content and form of the examination are unchanged, however, the impact is likely to be limited. Moreover, upgrading remains a lock-step progression through the ranks. What is needed is the determination of qualifications based on skill, demonstrated capacity, and personality rather than on strict and substantial quantitative measures of time in grade. This approach would be consistent with current developments in educational circles regarding the identification of urban school administrators. For example, Professor Michael Usdan of City University described a program under which mid-career people from various professions are being specially trained to lead school districts without the traditional educational or experience background.

Another important facet of the selection process, which can be the subject of interim change, is the development of job descriptions. Analysis of functions for all job titles clearly needs updating and refinement. The consensus of testing experts was that a precise job description is the crucial element in designing an effective selection method. The Board of Examiners, in theory, designs tests to meet job descriptions given them by the Office of Personnel. For teachers, a new and continually revised job description is an urgent need. According to Dr. Lang, there has not been a new job description for teachers in at least five and a half years. He stated, "I guess we assume we have a knowledge of what a teacher does and the Board of Examiners has a knowledge of it." Such an assumption is unfounded in the face of criticism of the teachers' examinations. For supervisory and administrative positions, new job descriptions are prepared when a new examination is scheduled, but outside test experts consider them inadequate bases for sound test construction. Dr. Barrett characterized current descriptions of principals' functions as a "skeleton of a job description that doesn't give the kind of information that is useful for a person who is going to develop a test." Job analysis is a sensitive and demanding task, one that requires expert skill. Furthermore, community school boards and their superintendents should be involved in the process to assure relevance to local school needs. It is important that where new criteria are being developed parents and other community representatives, as well as professional educators, make a substantial contribution to the process. The Board of Examiners cannot be faulted entirely, if the tests they design are based on out-of-date and overly broad statements of duties rather than timely and specific skills and qualities.

The next element in the selection process, and the focal issue of the hearings, is the design and administration of tests, written and oral. The most obvious deficiencies result from the limited resources of the Board of Examiners in designing selection instruments and in assessing their validity. A consensus emerged that far more research is needed into all facets of the examination process. If simplified local examinations or the NTE were used instead of the current, more elaborate examinations, the Board of Examiners would have more manpower for its research efforts. Such an immediate shift in its priorities would be an important first step toward its ultimate role as the research arm of the Office of Personnel's staff recruitment and selection activities.

The final element in selection, the probationary period, requires careful restructuring. Optimally, it should serve as a carefully observed internship. Increased local initiative arising from decentralization may focus more attention of the probationary period, but this cannot be left to chance. The Board of Examiners correctly asserts that its tests do not predict performance. Those with the responsibility for rating new personnel must be given the tools for reliable appraisal of performance. Effective use of the probationary period requires staff time and planned involvement of colleagues, supervisors and community board members, as well as training of all those who take part. Satisfactory use of the probationary period could, in fact, provide significant feedback about the testing process itself.

On balance, the preeminence in professional personnel matters accorded the Board of Examiners results largely from the fact that other elements, intended as important parts of selection, have been neglected. The Examiners' apparent autonomy is partially a reflection of inadequate performance by those responsible for preparing job descriptions and for following those who succeed on the tests through the probationary period. Even an adequately staffed Board of Examiners can only serve as intended, as a resource to the Board of Education and, therefore, to the schools, if all parts of the selection process are well handled and properly articulated. Until the current system is replaced, it is imperative to close the gaps exposed during the hearings. Moreover, the Detroit experience indicates that commitment from the top is the essential ingredient. The number of minority group members within the professional staff can be increased considerably, within the confines of any system, if that is the clear intent of those in charge.

What is required, above all, is the formulation of a positive plan for hiring school personnel, and this can begin even before legislative changes are effected. Many witnesses commented on the lack of guidelines for recruiting, selecting or evaluating personnel. Such guidelines need to be developed for the system at large, identifying the broad general qualities to be sought and how they best can be measured, as well as a specific program addressed to increasing minority employment. It is not enough to think only in terms of recruiting minority candidates, especially when this amounts to lining up people who become discouraged at the complexity of procedures or for other reasons never materialize as additions to the staff of the school system. Procedures for facilitating their appointment and promotion are the indispensible concomitants. It is time for the Board of Education to identify specific employment goals and the means by which such goals will be achieved within a specified time period.

Two specific areas, susceptible to some immediate improvement without legislative action, so urgently demand attention, that they warrant being singled out for special mention. They are the career development of paraprofessionals and the employment of bilingual teachers and supervisors.

Paraprofessionals

Currently, some 15,000 paraprofessionals are employed in the city in a variety of job titles, mostly as educational assistants. The UFT, through its involvement in the paraprofessional program, has probably made its most significant contribution to equal employment opportunity in this aspect of the school system. Gardner Atwell, head of the Board of Education's Auxiliary Educational Career Unit, "estimates that 48% of the paraprofessionals are Black and 16% are Puerto Rican." Although many have been working in the schools for three years or more, less than one-third are enrolled in career development programs in local colleges. The career ladder designed for paraprofessionals predicates progress on college course credits. Under current released time provisions, it will take, on the average, eight years of combined work and study to acquire a Bachelor's Degree. To date, none, except five who had prior college credits, have achieved the Associate Arts Degree, a level on the ladder providing a small pay increment, but no clear enlargement of function. No provision has been made to evaluate or accredit the years of experience and the skill acquired in in-school work, except where college programs accord experience some weight in counting total credits.

Witnesses, both paraprofessionals themselves and those who plan and conduct training for them, testified to the hardships endured, especially by the many who are mothers of young children, in the long years of working and studying, in the lack of job security, of transferability of experience, in the unequal and often unsupervised quality of work experience, the insufficient in-service training, and the seeming irrelevance to career aspirations of many college requirements. On the other hand, those who have trained paraprofessionals for work in schools outside New York City, or for jobs in other public services, report that with new forms of intensive training focused on and directly related to on-the-job activity, paraprofessionals have progressed more rapidly. Where traditional requirements were modified to accept new combinations of experience and study, paraprofessionals have been able to assume greater responsibility and make an important contribution to the service.

Until very recently, little tax-levy funds have been used for either employment or career development of paraprofessionals in the city's schools, and a staff of only three persons has been assigned to handle all aspects of their employment. Early in 1971, the Board of Education made its first allocation of a significant sum to finance college education for additional numbers, a noteworthy step because it indicates an on-going commitment to them. But the same limited hours of released time exist, and much more remains to be done in regularizing, standardizing and supervising their work so that formal recognition can be given to experience, where merited. Indications are that many -- perhaps many of the best qualified and most ambitious - become discouraged by the slow pace and leave the schools for jobs in other service sectors, where progress is less dependent on college credits, and where released time provisions are more generous.

The paraprofessionals' major significance could be to serve as a pilot group for the development of performance-based criteria. Experimental teacher-training programs essentially use a paraprofessional model for the first and most important part of training -- in-school experience carefully structured to allow for skill development and understanding of teaching problems -- with theory and academic subject matter following and related closely to experiential development. Because the majority of paraprofessionals are minority group members who are mature adults strongly committed to working with children, especially the urban ghetto child, and are experienced in working within their communities, they represent a manpower resource that warrants fuller utilization. If career development were structured to focus on in-service training and development, selection of teachers from among the paraprofessional ranks could be made with far greater reliability than from among the recent graduates of teachers' colleges and at a far more rapid rate than is now the case. This group is a logical source from which to infuse the system with increased minority personnel of demonstrated aptitude for, and strong attachment to, teaching as a vocation.

Special attention should be given to the Puerto Rican and, for the first time, to the Oriental paraprofessional, at a time when one of the school system's most urgent needs is for more bilingual personnel. In Chancellor Scribner's words, "I feel that one should be able to put into that classroom [those with children for whom English is a second language] first of all, a bilingual person." With an estimated low of only several hundred bilingual teachers in the schools serving close to 300,000 Spanish-speaking children, paraprofessionals could play an important role. One need is to increase the numbers of Puerto Rican paraprofessionals and the second is to increase the opportunities for them to move to full professional status. Few Puerto Ricans, of the small total number employed, are enrolled in career development programs. And almost no attention has been paid to the rapidly developing need for Chinese paraprofessionals at a time when that community is experiencing tremendous pressures from a new round of immigrants who speak only Chinese.

Bilingual Teachers and Administrators

Bilingual teaching cannot depend entirely on paraprofessionals, however. Teachers and administrators of Puerto Rican and Chinese descent are grossly under-represented in the schools, not only to serve the needs of Spanish and Chinese-speaking children and their families, but also as role models to encourage these children to stay in school, aim toward college, and consider teaching as a viable occupation. Spokesmen working in schools with large Puerto Rican enrollments in particular, attested to the special difficulty of employing bilingual personnel because so few become eligible through the existing selection channels. According to many witnesses, examinations give undue emphasis to English and to areas of information irrelevant to the immediate job and with which non-New Yorkers would be unfamiliar. They fail to emphasize the ability to communicate with the bilingual child. Federally funded bilingual projects and recruiting addressed to Puerto Rican colleges meet with only limited success in attracting Spanish-speaking candidates. Freedom from conventional requirements would enable many community districts to find bilingual persons of high quality, who do not now seek teaching jobs, or who might not now succeed on the examinations. As Community Superintendent Gaines said, "In a district where close to 60% of the children come from Spanish-speaking homes, we have a talent pool of people who can teach Spanish, although they may not have the other qualifications. We would not ask that they be fully licensed - but only given a certificate of competency to teach in Spanish." The alternative to this has been an inexcusable failure to minimally communicate with thousands of children who do not speak English well.

Because reading scores and other measurements of pupil achievement, such as the drop-out rate, indicate that the schools are serving least well the large numbers of children of Puerto Rican background, special methods must be devised to meet their needs. Philip Kaplan, Chairman of Community School Board No. 15 in Brooklyn, spoke of how important it was to have bilingual teachers when he was a child in a New York City public school; "I, myself, when I started kindergarten, did not speak a word of English. I just spoke Jewish [Yiddish]. When I started elementary school, the fact that there were teachers who understood Yiddish was a tremendous help. I think that's important to keep in mind. ...It was a help to me, and to my parents, who came to school to find out my progress, to speak to someone who spoke the same language as we did at that time."

It is estimated that bilingual programs now reach only about one out of every four Spanish-speaking children (and a far lower percentage of Chinese-speaking children). Hector Vazquez, former Board of Education member and Executive Director of the Puerto Rican Forum, estimates that only about 10,000 Puerto Rican children are receiving as much as one period a day in English as a second language. Certificates of competency, or exemptions from some of the normal requirements for native English-speaking candidates, in favor of ability to speak Spanish or Chinese as well as in-service training and other supportive measures, are only some of the possible measures that might help to meet the needs of the bilingual child.

APPENDIX B: PREPARED TESTIMONY SUBMITTED IN WRITING

Testimony by Dr. Mortimer Kreuter, Professor of Education and Director of Teacher Preparation at State University of New York at Stony Brook.

TEACHER PREPARATION AND CONTINUING PROFESSIONAL TRAINING IN THE DECADE AHEAD: COMMENTS ON THE TEACHER TRAINING COMPLEX AS A SPECIAL PLACE FOR SKILL TRAINING OF EDUCATIONAL PERSONNEL

Ladies and Gentlemen of the Commission on Human Rights: My name is Mortimer Kreuter, Professor of Education and Director of Teacher Preparation at the State University of New York at Stony Brook. From 1948 to 1965, I was a teacher and principal in the New York City schools and have some familiarity with the problems the Commission is grappling with.

The testimony which I am presenting today represents my own professional viewpoints on teacher education and not necessarily those of the State University at Stony Brook.

It seems clear when discussing the employment and promotion of teachers that not enough attention is given to the rapid change in the larger society which require the smaller school society and its personnel to respond to those changing conditions. Indeed, all of the factors that have impacted upon the larger society have entered the school-house and are part of its latent if not manifest curricula. This generation of children who will inhabit the 21st century is growing up in a society conflicted in the presense of instant mass communication, the tension of living in the megalopolis, and the disparities between national goals as stated by political leaders as against those declared by groups seeking individual rights. Further, many are children of parents who are demanding participation in the life of the schools and an accounting by the school as to its stated goals of equal education for all.

Technology and tradition, the future and the past, and the demands of both sides of the generation gap meet in the schools. The schools must find teachers and retrain veteran teachers to live with and find their way through the ambiguities of this situation.

A major response of educational policy makers to changing social conditions, especially in the cities but increasingly in the suburbs also is the construction of modular buildings to fit the planning of new organizational systems to humanize the school enterprise. These new schools are coming to be called "open" schools and they refer to schools which are child-oriented, flexible rather than fixed, based upon the principle that children have human rights as well as parents and teachers, and that children must be involved in the decisions about teaching and learning on their own ability levels, not competitively.

Less easy to engineer are the programs for the new types of teachers and educational personnel who will be required to operate within open systems. What will be required of the teachers who will work in these emerging systems? How will such teachers be identified and evaluated?

It seems obvious from the available research and evaluation literature that personnel requirements for manning the open schools of the next 15-20 years will specify a teacher trained to deal with human strengths, sensitivities and sanity rather than with subject matter alone. In consequence, we will have to invent a system of teacher training sharply different from the past 20 years which has been obsessed with teaching teachers to package the curriculum and to sort children as test takers and products. It is no wonder teachers regard tests as inevitable; they have been constantly tested themselves and can only get to be teachers if they are tested yet one more time.

The aspiring teacher is trained in the testing system -- commonly having a relatively retrograde model of teaching-testing during the pre-college school experience, perhaps a course model in college itself, and then a short period of imitating another teacher-tester in practice teaching. The student teacher enters a classroom and is told by the senior teacher under whom he is to learn - "Teach, test, teach, retest, and keep 'em quiet. Your job is discipline." This folklore is passed along as insider's wisdom to counteract "theoretical" training.

In fact, the whole teacher evaluation procedure must be changed. From his training period on, the new teacher will have to learn that tests are not a religion and that children can learn with and without tests and he himself can be judged on various professional criteria other than tests; namely, the way he performs in classrooms. The new teacher must be able to (1) make instructionally sensible and accountable decisions by using analytical methods; (2) manage the educational inputs of a widening cast of players in the open school scene -- paraprofessionals, community persons, mental health workers, consultants, specialists, parents; (3) guide children to teach themselves and their peers; (4) fit into a team of teachers when that approach is needed; (5) foster throughout the entire school experience the non-punitive attitudes conducive to children's development.

This kind of new teacher training will require the re-training also of the current teacher staff. Nothing less will do than a drastic re-shaping of pre- and in-service teacher training for carefully articulated and publicly stated objectives leading to an open school concept which lets in the world outside. In my judgement, the on-the-job evaluation of teachers to work in this context will be a necessary component of the teacher training changes which must come about in this decade. The almost total reliance of teacher evaluators on tests scores will inevitably give way in this movement to the more difficult to determine but much more powerful techniques of performance evaluation. Nobody cares what his doctor scored on his boards but whether he is able to doctor well.

In addition, we will have to re-teach the public that test scores are not really absolute indicators of children's intellectual status. There is no test maker in the country who really thinks that a grade of 75 or 80 is better than one of 70 and so on. Can children read and think and feel capable about themselves is the real goal of the open school. That is where the teacher training effort must go; then the ways in which the capabilities of children are measured will be in how well they perform life tasks appropriate to them, not how they rank.

There is currently widespread discussion about which institution should conduct teacher education for the changing schools of the next two decades. Some contend that teacher training should be moved totally to the public school sector; others that only in a university atmosphere where knowledge is being created can teachers be trained to transmit the subject matter of a discipline. The difficulty with the either-or concept is that each agency has its own primary mission; the public school to teach children, the university to accrue new knowledge and speculate upon it. Neither institution is primarily disposed to train teachers and where they do take up the training role, too often the result is often second-rate treatment of it. Moreover, the community and other interested agencies rarely can affect either the university or the public school training effort even though they have vital stakes in the outcomes.

Therefore, since teacher training lies between the two first institutions, and affects the others, an interface structure must be created for the pooling of resources and talents to produce effective and up-to-date teachers. This priority is important to all school systems, but to the city schools in particular because if educators fail in New York and other urban centers, the surrounding suburban areas will immediately suffer as the failure of the system radiates outward.

The interface structure for teacher training must take the view that there is a profession of teaching which is learnable as a set of conscious and purposeful behavior rather than a mystical talent born only to some; accountable for its outcomes to its clients; and that relevant others can contribute to a child's learning. In order for this view to become actualized, the university level teacher training would have to move beyond the usual academic course practice teaching stage. The public schools would have to offer teachers an opportunity to gain continued training in a non-authoritarian setting, separated from the supervisory reports and ratings which get in the way of their training programs. The community and other agencies would have to help to guide as well as to monitor an interface type of training organization. Critical to this entire concept is the building of confidence among teachers that they will gain skills which are useful to them in the classroom practice of the open, non-competitive school.

The extraordinarily useful volume Teachers for the Real World prepared by Smith and his associates for the American Association of Colleges of Teacher Education discusses such an organization for teacher training. Called teacher training complexes, these organizations recapture to some degree the best of old normal school practices for teachers, but go beyond this pre-teaching stage to include long-term training of career teachers as their needs for new skills emerge. The teacher training complex is a special and neutral setting for the training aspects of teacher preparation to take place and includes the combined talents of universities, schools, communities, and other agencies. For example, if the schools were to try to create a new position for the human relations aspects of a school, a training complex could employ a training specialist in this field from agencies like this Commission.

The financial supports for the training complex are as yet undefined. At first, to give it the independence to get started, federal funds are being sought. Ultimately, a mechanism for the permanentizing of funds for the training complexes would probably come from the federal government to the states in the same way that farm bureaus and local social security offices are financed to serve regional needs in the human needs areas they encompass.

At the present time, four simulation projects founded by the U.S. Office of Education Bureau of Educational Personnel Development are being modeled in different parts of the country to gain the experience necessary to install on a full scale basis the concepts of the teacher training complex. These teacher training complexes each driving towards its own destination but with implication for the directions to be taken by the others: Southeastern Oklahoma University (affiliated with the Dallas, Texas public schools); Appalachia State University (affiliated with Western North Carolina schools); Clark University (affiliated through University of California with the Berkeley schools and through West Virginia University with its regional schools); and Stony Brook affiliated with the Middle Island (Long Island) school system. All of these teacher training complexes aim to do their work in newly developing organizational forms with one overriding purpose -- the shell training of educational personnel. Much of what these complexes will be doing is based upon research; each accepts the assumption that enough research already exists with respect to teacher training and that what is critically important now is for the research and evaluation findings to be engineered into a training system. The inputs of the community, teacher associations, and other universities are built into the complex.

At Stony Brook, the teacher training complex is in its sixth month, based in school practice and offering pre-student teaching, student teaching, and in-service training toward the goal of preparing the three levels of teacher-trainees to teach in the middle schools. The essential points of this and the other teacher training complexes which might be useful to the New York City planning efforts in teacher training and selection are as follows:

Teacher Training Complex

1) <u>Training Orientation</u> - The training complex model is performance oriented and asserts that the training of teachers requires a specialized learning situation which assumes the following set of conditions. (a) That there is superior practitioner level competence on the part of the training staff and intellectual capability on the part of students and experienced teachers to be trained. (b) The model asserts that professional training patterns can be constructed to train professional nurses, surgeons, airline pilots, engineers, social workers, pharmacists, and others to perform highly specialized sets of tasks. Similarly, teachers who are required to work in the exceptionally difficult and complex area of human relations to be found in open classrooms can and should be trained to perform the professional skills requisite to such challenges.

2) <u>Training Objectives</u> - This model proposes to train students to develop the skills requisite to the following set of <u>abilities</u> identified by Smith and his associates (American Association of Colleges for Teacher Education, 1969) in the work mentioned previously:

    (a) Perform stimulant operations (question, structure, probe)
    (b) Manipulate different kinds of knowledge
    (c) Perform reinforcement operations
    (d) Negotiate interpersonal relations
    (e) Diagnose student needs and learning difficulties
    (f) Communicate and emphasize with students, parents and others
    (g) Perform in and with small and large groups
    (h) Utilize technological equipment
    (i) Evaluate student achievement
    (j) Judge appropriateness of instructional materials
    (k) Work effectively in a team teaching role
    (l) Employ individualized, continuous progress resource materials
    (m) Work with teacher aides, peer group tutors, and other assistants
    (n) Teach students from diverse populations

One essential feature of the teacher training complexes is that they are places to which teachers and others may come to learn how to function more effectively in the operation of schools. Since the schools interact with the communities and their agencies, it would be possible for judges, police, and probation officers to attend training sessions on selected topics like school organization; the teachers roles, ethnic and social issues in the high schools, the yough sub-culture,...Parent groups and civic association representatives could be trained to do school district policy making, supervise financial matters, share in the introduction of new curriculum. The main point is that the training complex sees itself as making all and any educational personnel and those close to them more capable in managing and teaching schools and classrooms.

The current discussion about teacher training cooperatives to be started in each borough seems to point in this direction. From the experience gained by those involved in the training complexes described here, it would seem appropriate to suggest that the training cooperatives link themselves with the institutions affecting them but at the same time to find a way to maintain the special identity essential to a training center.

In that regard, I am appending to this presentation for your perusal an article prepared by me based upon a planning project dealing with the establishment of a teacher training college in the Harlem district. This research was conducted in 1968 and conceptualizes a specialized City University College of Urban Teacher Education which serves the community by operating a school district, training educational personnel, and researching the educational needs of the neighborhoods from pre-school through continuing education of adults.

The points raised in the training complex model are elaborated in the Harlem Teacher College master plan available to you in its detailed form from the Center for Urban Education, 105 Madison Avenue, New York City, under whose supervision this research was conducted. The impressions of Harlem leaders, parents, and high school students towards this concept were analyzed and reported as being generally favorable, especially since the available housing stock and community-serving structures and services would be included rather than being displaced by a teachers college.

Performance Evaluation of Teachers

A final point must be made in the discussion of the teacher trained in a performance context and that is the absolute necessity of evaluating the teacher against stated criteria. As I am sure this point has been raised by others appearing before the Commission, I will not elaborate it lengthily.

The training complex is in the process of developing criteria for evaluating a teacher's performance as the measure of its own effectiveness. Some educators are talking to Teacher Assessment Centers to which candidates could go to assess their performance capabilities. It is one of the most exciting teacher education developments currently being tired out in the states of Washington, Oregon and Florida. Unquestionably, the training complexes would be involved in the performance evaluation movement but whether a teacher assessment center should be independent of the complexes, universities, and school systems is yet to be worked out. Probably a combined effort of educational institutions and state education departments will develope.

As professionals, teachers need to write less about their fields than do librarians, social workers, and others of equivalent education. Teachers have to shape subject matters by the behavioral interactions of communicating orally or by demonstration or guidance. If written evidence of subject mastery is required, surely a more efficient route is to accept the National Teacher Examination, or the Graduate Record Examination, or a college major, or a master's degree comprehensive examinations and essay, or the equivalent.

The uses of the performance evaluation for teacher selection are many, not the least of which is that they are relatively inexpensive to conduct since they are carried in schools on school time by supervisors and others. Time does not permit much discussion of this point, but it should be pointed out that the New York City Board of Examiners could provide very useful data and clinical judgment on the performance assessment of teachers. The Examiners have given tests on classroom teaching; school, conference, and assembly management; technical skills. Given the increasing decision-making role of students and parents in the schools, these field-type tests should be expanded in appropriate ways to include this clientele in assessing teacher and supervisory capabilities.

As we move in the decade ahead to connect teacher training closely to the effective delivery of instructional and interpersonal services, in an open system, all of us, teacher educators, teachers, community and social agencies can make a distinctive contribution to the quality of educational life for the new generation by demonstrating that we are willing to perform our tasks and to be evaluated on them.

Thank you for the opportunity to express my views on this topic.

Statement by Mrs. Nathan W. Levin, Chairman, Education Section of Citizens' Committee for Children of New York, Inc., 112 East 19th Street, New York, N. Y.

NEEDED: GOOD TEACHERS

The search for good teachers for our public schools has been a priority of Citizens' Committee for Children ever since the Committee was established some twenty-five years ago. As we worked in the schools, we became increasingly convinced that many good teachers are either not attracted, are screened out in the hiring process, or forced out by the discouraging lack of support during the first, often difficult, teaching years.

As the demographic changes in our City became obvious, the teacher trainers on our Committee, Dr. Alice Keliher, Dr. Roma Gans and others, warned us twenty years ago that unless the process of selecting teachers was overhauled and a recruitment program to attract teachers from other states was undertaken the schools were on a downhill course to gigantic failure. Teachers at that time (the late 40's) were being screened out because of their accent, a sibilant 's' or other miniscule distinctions which were labelled speech defects. We need teachers, we said, who have not only professional knowledge but love and respect for children, who understand them, their families and their cultural backgrounds. It was obvious that the screening procedures of the Board of Education were not geared to detect and hire teachers with these vital human qualities.

THE FACES OF DISCRIMINATION

In 1948, CCC secured permission from the Examiners and the Board of Education for an ambitious research program on testing teachers' attitudes. After two years of concentrated work, we were stopped and our records impounded because it became clear that out of our work there really might emerge a tool to test teachers' attitudes.

The lack of concern on the part of those responsible for teacher training and assignment, their refusal to face reality, the insidious racism in the staffing, were exposed in a lawsuit which two parents brought and won against the Board of Education in 1958 (now referred to as the Polier decision) which showed "a city-wide pattern of discrimination in staffing schools whose pupil population was predominantly Negro and Puerto Rican."

In a report on "DeFacto Segregated Schools," Citizens' Committee for Children found "overwhelming difficulties and deep staff discouragement.... Everyone in these schools had concrete suggestions on how the Board of Education could help to get more regularly licensed teachers in the 'special service school', among which changes in Board of Examiners' procedures and timing were given high priority."

Discrimination against minority groups over the years has had many faces and the small number of Black and Puerto Rican teachers, supervisors and principals is only one of them! Discrimination against ghetto schools was also evidenced by the fact that the ratio of fully licensed teachers to substitute teachers in "special service schools" was less than half that in other schools.

A Teacher Recruitment Unit, organized in 1962, conducted a drive to recruit new teachers, both within and outside of New York City and State, and an advisory committee for the Unit (on which CCC was represented) gave special emphasis to the need to recruit more "minority group teachers and principals." Its results were minimal largely because applicants found "the examination processes unnecessarily time-consuming and degrading." It was then that CCC first suggested that "teachers who have completed approved training programs might be licensed to teach in New York City on the basis of State certification without further examination." We pointed out that ghetto schools were largely staffed by substitutes and the New York City requirements for the substitute license were below qualifications for New York State certification. This step would thus constitute great progress. As the present situation shows, the system of securing teachers for our schools has remained unchanged.

GROWING ALIENATION BETWEEN TEACHERS AND STUDENTS

We are submitting "A Report on New York City High Schools" done by a special Task Force of CCC and issued just a year ago. You will be interested in the report in its entirety if you have not already seen it, but the following excerpts will highlight for you the complex problems which arise from inadequate, insensitive policies. We found:

Appendix B

"...The climate for learning in New York City's public high schools has been dangerously polluted by an increasing estrangement between students and faculty...which heightens racial tension...and encourages a mutual distrust between student and teacher."

"...High school faculty and administrators work in fear for their physical safety and regard many of the students as alien forces. Most teachers and all but two principals are white and have been trained to appreciate only achievement measured by rigid intellectual standards."

"...Most senior staff members are not encouraged to solve the problem of reaching the ever-increasing number of students who do not respond to existing programs. They are more interested in students with high academic records and in their school's record of awards, honors, and admissions to good colleges."

"...Far from considering their responsibility to get through to this growing portion (unreached majority)..., many staff members resent the changing student composition as 'lowering the school's standards'."

"...Repeatedly, students complain that teachers are not interested in them...Students want to talk with those who are teaching them, but feel that barriers...in their teachers' attitudes make such communication impossible."

WE MUST REACH OUT

We recount some of the things we have learned over the past years simply to show that the present situation could have been avoided many times over. That it was not, is due not to the lack of realistic proposals but to the refusal to consider them. Half-hearted attempts have been made from time to time during the teacher shortage to attract Black candidates from the South, but the self-righteous insistence that they must meet tests for which they are not educated or prepared, cast doubts on the integrity of these attempts.

The current excuses for the small number of Black and Puerto Rican teachers in our schools, used during the present hearings, sound painfully familiar: you cannot license Black candidates if the City University does not graduate Black students. It signifies not only smug passivity but frightening irresponsibility. There is no more important aspect of education than the task of finding the teachers we need for our children. We cannot simply sit and wait for them -- and discourage those who do appear!

THE CASE FOR FLEXIBLE HIRING PRACTICES

A review of the Principal's examination shows clearly the attitude of the Board of Education. What is being tested is the breadth of _theoretical_ knowledge that presumably has been accumulated during years of taking courses in administration. However, from my own personal experience, I know that this is no measure of the administrator's ability to perform on the spot in the system day to day. For some twenty years, I was intimately involved in the operation of a school system close to New York City. Thirteen of those years I served as the president and a member of the Board of Education where I had the unique experience of functioning as an additional full-time administrative assistant to the District Superintendent, who was recognized as one of the most inspired, creative and forward-looking educators of a central school system. From her I received post graduate level on the job training while participating in recruitment, supervision, evaluation of personnel, curriculum development, community relations, and every other aspect of school administration essential in the operation of a district wide program for 7 schools: kindergarten through junior and senior high school. During that period, I participated in the interview process of dozens of candidates. If I learned anything from that invaluable apprenticeship it was the difficulties in personnel selection. Two candidates who shone most brilliantly, with all the right written answers and those most poised and articulate bearing during the orals, turned out to be our most dismal failures. On the other hand, the weakest applicant, a compromise, whom we took temporarily out of desperate need during the shortage, turned out to be one of our most gifted elementary school principals, producing an outstanding "esprit de corps" among students, teachers and other school personnel, as well as parents in the school community. It mattered little to the running of that school, that he had yet to complete his administrative course work and was only provisionally licensed by the State.

As for the selection of classroom teachers: along with the recruiters, I never learned to recognize any obsolute indicators to help in screening, but I do know that often a reject by one school principal could number among the most successful in another's school.

This experience has reconfirmed for me, again and again, the need to continue CCC's crusade for better selection, training and supervision of teachers; for new ways of attracting the young and dedicated; and for helping them understand and conquer the difficult classroom problems they will face.

The search for the best teachers is the task which must be given highest priority. We propose that the New York City Commission on Human Rights designate a Task Force, consisting of representatives of teacher training institutions, responsible leadership in the Board of Education and the local districts, concerned and knowledgeable citizens called together to develop a program for recruiting and training teachers and that the implementation of such a program become the first priority on the agenda of every group that cares about education.

Appendix B 741

NEW YORK CITY ELEMENTARY SCHOOL PRINCIPALS ASSOC.
JULIUS WARSHAW, PRESIDENT
1077 REMSEN AVENUE, BROOKLYN, N.Y. 11236

Remarks by Julius Warshaw, President, New York City Elementary School Principals Association, 1077 Remsen Avenue, Brooklyn, N.Y.

I welcome the opportunity as President of the New York City Elementary School Principals Association to address the Commission today.

I have listened to some of the excerpts of radio programs and the testimony and have been impressed with the variety of statements and information which have been disseminated. But, in very simple terms I would like to express to you what I think is the major problem. In the selection of teachers and supervisors, we are really engaging in a game. In most games there are winners and losers. Sometimes the losers become winners. Sometimes we must make adjustments so that the losers who feel that they have not had equal opportunities are given an opportunity to make up for some differences. In the parlance of sports, we call this a handicap. If we were to apply this concept in the selection of teachers and supervisors, "that of a handicap," I think we would be perpetrating the greatest hoax and insult on the minorities. It is only necessary to ask Black and Puerto Rican teachers and supervisors whether they feel that in their selection there was an element of discrimination. If anything, the presence of the Board of Examiners helped them to maintain their rights. We must accept the contention that Negro and Puerto Rican teachers are just as capable as any other group to develop and become competent teachers and supervisors. It is our opinion that the attempt to abolish the Board of Examiners and substitute in its place the simple principle of State tenure, would deprive all potential teachers and supervisors to a fair and equal chance to serve.

The developments that have taken place in the last few days illustrate what is the most difficult problem in most educational systems. That problem is how we can attract, select, maintain, and develop the most competent teachers and supervisors for our school system. Let us briefly consider the importance of pre-service education, licensing, and appointment, on-the-job training and retraining. The failure of the educational system is our inability to mold these factors into a well organized integrated program. Briefly, we depend upon college courses to develop teachers, which are out of line with the needs of the particular position. We then select those we feel are qualified to be licensed and do very little to provide sufficient time, depth and training for the teacher who has been appointed. We then allow little time after five or ten years of service to retrain the teacher and the supervisor. The training and retraining of teachers and supervisors should be a year round operation.

I am happy to see that Mrs. Norton stated the fact that no one is accusing the Board of Examiners of overt discrimination. There is also little covert discrimination. If anything, major modifications have been made in the practices of the Board of Examiners to meet the great need for Black and Puerto Rican teachers and supervisors. The next few examinations will definitely increase the number of such personnel to at least 100%. With the advent of decentralization, it then becomes possible for Community Boards to select from this pool of licensees those they consider most qualified. It is therefore, to the interest of all concerned to be able to support the basic principles of the merit system and that additional modifications be made which will attract even more and better teachers and supervisors from the minorities.

The subtelties of the problem, that of attracting many Black and Puerto Rican teachers and supervisors, direct our attention from our major problem, that of providing a better education for all the children of New York City. If we do that, we may accomplish one objective and drive many competent teachers and supervisors, from ever wanting to serve in our school system again. Thank you.

Statement by Elaine Gaspard, Educational Specialist of Neighborhood Board #5, and Chairman of the P. A. Presidents Council of Central Harlem.

Good evening; my name is Elaine Gaspard - Educational Specialist of Neighborhood Board #5, and Chairman of the P.A. Presidents Council of Central Harlem.

I feel that the time for the Board of Examiners existency is at an end. The methods they have been using for testing and employment have become obsolete.

The Board method of testing has not provided us with qualified teachers, it has only served to close the door on people with an ethnic background. I have listened to your allegation that the Board of Examiners have changed their method of testing. Their equestions are supposed to be more relevant to open the door to more ethnic groups: But you and I know that as long as you have an oral test as well as a written test we are still depriving a large segment of any ethnic group from passing. Too much importance has been placed on an accent which will be found in most ethnic groups or race, and in many cases a slight, a very slight speech impediment. I can only conclude that this policy is put into practice to eliminate those who do not have friends in high places or those who do not meet your bogus requirements.

Therefore, I recommend that the Board of Examiners be abolished, and that upon graduation of a student from College, this student may be eligible to teach. I would propose that the following guidelines be adopted:

Appendix B

1. Each District be allowed to screen their own teachers.
2. Each school Advisory Council or Parent Body is also given the right to screen the teacher and make the final decision.

Explanation:

Each community is unique, and their needs are not the same as another geographical area. They have found from experience that some teachers suit the need of the community more than others. This should not cause confusion amongst the opposite, for when two persons are agreeable it tends to form a perfect marriage.

3. The Parent Council have a right to mandate any teacher to submit to a test of narcotic addiction.
4. A teacher should agree to submit to a psychiatric examination before hiring.
5. The community should decide on tenure, less than the (3 years) allotted time.
6. The delegate agencies under C.A.P. should be members of Advisory Councils as has been our practice at Neighborhood Board #5, in our assigned schools in Central Harlem, to offer any assistance in the schools requested by the supervisory or parent body.
7. C.A.P. should set up workshops to educate interested groups on the decentralization laws.
8. We should develop a city wide mechanism for firing incompetent teachers and administration personnel, and determine teacher accountability.

APPENDIX C: STATEMENTS SUBMITTED AFTER THE HEARINGS

2/8/71

Miss Eleanor Norton, Commissioner
Human Rights
80 Lafayette Street
New York City

Dear Commissioner Norton:

    I want to express my admiration for the well researched and conducted hearings on the Board of Education's hiring practices. I heard most of them on WNYC's excellent coverage, however, I am most distressed by the almost total black-out (or white-out, if you will) which you received everywhere else.

    I sued the Board of Examiners for my present job of chairman of department and charged, among other things, racial discrimination. The court did not rule on the discrimination charge but I think you may find the attached review of the case of interest.

Sincerely,

Charles Allen
33 68 21 Street
LIC, N.Y. 11106

Civil Service Law & You
By William Goffen

(Mr. Goffen, a member of the New York Bar, teaches law at the College of the City of New York, is the author of many books and articles and co-authored "New York Criminal Law.")

Review of Ratings

    It has long been established by the Courts of New York that a candidate for civil service appointment has the right to judicial review of the rating on his examination. Yet, examining agencies persist in making this right difficult to exercise by failure to supply the information necessary for meaningful judicial review.

    A recent case of an agency's reluctance to cooperate with a candidate's efforts to obtain judicial review of his examination is Allen v. Board of Examiners of Board of Education of the City of New York (New York Law Journal, Oct. 31, 1968, page 14). The petitioner, an applicant for licensure as chairman of Fine Arts

Appendix C

Department in day high schools, passed the written and interview parts of the examination but failed the teaching test. Such test consists of an actual class lesson under observation of the examiner.

In his Article 78 proceeding, the petitioner demanded annulment of his teaching test and an order directing that he be given a new teaching test. Among other contentions, he asserted that his teaching test lacked objectivity. As the Court of Appeals well stated in Fink v. Finegan:

> A test or examination, to be competitive, must employ an objective standard or measure. Where the standard or measure is wholly subjective to the examiners it differs in effect in no respect from an uncontrolled opinion of the examiners and cannot be termed competitive.
>
> An examination cannot be classed as competitive unless it conforms to measures or standards which are sufficiently objective to be capable of being challenged and reviewed, when necessary, by other examiners of equal ability and experience.

The teaching test assesses various capabilities of the candidate specified in a rating sheet used by each examiner. The examiner makes running notes as an aid to his determination. The conduct of the test accords with the Board's guidelines.

In accordance with its custom, the Board furnished the petitioner only with a summary statement of reasons for failure in the test. It did not supply the rating sheets, thereby making it impossible for the petitioner to ascertain whether the alleged weaknesses were supported by the running comments of the examiners.

Justice Abraham J. Multer directed the Board to submit the rating sheets so that they would be available for inspection. Justice Multer cited, among other authorities for his order, Schwartz v. Bogen and Gassner v. Board of Examiners. These were Second Department cases. As held in the Schwartz case:

> In our opinion, the refusal of respondents to permit petitioner to examine the standard against which her performance was measured was unreasonable and substantially impaired her right of appeal. The results of the examination should be so stated that the applicant can "check up the conclusions by some objective comparison."

The Civil Practice Law and Rules expressly authorizes the Court to compel the Board to make available the rating sheet. Section 7804(3) states that after directing the agency to file its answer to the petition the Court may order the agency "to supply any defect or omission in the answers." In accordance with this statutory authority, Justice Multer directed the Board to serve copies of the rating sheets used in the petitioner's teaching test as well as copies of the Board's written instructions or guidelines for the conduct of the test.

One may think that the Court's determinations in the Gassner and Schwartz cases would have made amply clear even before the Allen case that the Board of Examiners is expected to cooperate in the requests of candidates for full disclosure of the basis for their grades. Even without court direction, an administrative agency ought not add to the difficulties of an employee who is attempting to enforce his civil service rights. Indeed, the agency should gladly offer its employees full cooperation in their legitimate efforts through approved procedures to protect their rights.

Civil Service Leader, November 26, 1965
Reprinted with permission

Education Committee for The Upper West Side
501 W. 125th St. Room 104, New York, N.Y.10027

Jan. 28, 1971

Mrs. Eleanor Holmes Norton
Chairman City Commission on Human Rights
80 Lafayette Street
New York, New York 10013

    The Local Education Committee for the Upper West Side takes the position that:
    The Board of Examiners for the City of New York which license the teachers and supervisors of our schools should be abolished. The facts and figures show that only 5% of the supervisory positions are held by Black's and Puerto Ricans. It is obvious to us that the Board of Examiners are biased in their hiring procedures. We disagree with the statement made by Mr. Shanker that the Board of Examiners could administer State or Federal tests to applicants and serve to see that personnel discrimination did not take place in hiring teachers. We know that the Board of Examiners has discriminated for years. Why give them another chance to do the same? We say abolish the Board of Examiners. Who said that they were qualified to license teachers? Were they tested for their qualifications before being appointed to judge others? Take a look at the damage that has been done to our children by incompetent teachers placed in our schools by the Board of Examiners. This alone proves that they should be abolished.
    We have taken this position on the behalf of the community we serve from 122nd St. to 181st St. Upper West Side Poverty Area.

Dorothy Brown
Chairman, Upper West
Side Education Committee

Appendix C 747

2186 Fifth Ave. Apt. 16E
New York, N.Y. 10037
January 26, 1971

Mrs. Eleanor Holmes Norton, Director
State Human Rights Commission
270 Broadway
New York, N.Y.

Dear Mrs. Norton:

Enclosed is a copy of an article which appeared this week in The American Teacher which is The National Publication for The American Federation of Teachers.

The fact that the Supreme Court read my appeal and upheld my contention on the insufficiency of the Board's denial is significant.

I have been acting Chairman for three years with excellent training and experience in the field of Speech, Drama and Communications.

Very truly yours,

Mrs. Marian P. Jones

(Article from The American Teacher)

DRAMA TEACHER CHARGES PROMOTIONAL-EXAM 'BIAS'
New York, N.Y.

"Mrs. Marian P. Jones, a member of the United Federation of Teachers, AFT Local 2, and acting Chairman of the speech and drama department at Benjamin Franklin High School in East Harlem, has had her petition to the state supreme court upheld in her appeal to the city's board of examiners regarding what she intimates may be racial bias in a promotional examination.

"The court held the board of examiners' denial was insufficient, and is waiting to set a date for a hearing until she gathers additional outside evidence.

"Mrs. Jones took a written English examination for chairman of speech in day high schools in April, 1968, and was given an unsatisfactory rating. In her appeal, which the examiners denied, she reports 'numerous instances where the ratings violated 'Direction to Readers' issued by the board of education; numerous instances where the petitioner (Mrs. Jones) was penalized more than once for the same alleged error; and that the standards employed by the rating officers were not always in accord with those currently accepted by reputable sources.'

"A former assistant professor of drama and speech at Morgan State College, Baltimore, Md., and Hampton

Institute, in Virginia, Mrs. Jones has been teaching in the New York City system since 1956. She notes that 'there is not a black or Negro person duly licensed by the board of examiners for such a position (chairman of speech) in New York City.' Her attorney, William J. Williams, won a precedent-setting case three years ago when he secured a court order to the examiners to release model answers to a supervisors' examination. (Williams reports, though, that the courts refuse to hold the board in contempt for not supplying the information, even though it was ordered to do so, and thus relief for his client is still pending.) Eugene Kaufman, UFT house counsel, reported that the UFT used this case not long ago as precedent to get the board to release medical records in a questioned decision.

"Appeals from board of examiners decisions, Kaufman said, have a 50-percent chance of success in the medical part of the examination; a 10- to 15-percent chance for a written examination; and 'a very remote' chance of success when the interview part of a test is concerned."

ELEANOR HOLMES NORTON, CITY COMMISSION ON HUMAN RIGHTS, 80 LAFAYETTE ST, NYK   01/28/71

REGRET INABILITY MAKE PERSONAL APPEARANCE AS THE ONLY PROFESSIONAL OF PUERTO RICAN BACKGROUND TO HAVE BEEN LICENSED AND APPOINTED AS A JUNIOR HIGH SCHOOL PRINCIPAL AND TO HAVE ATTAINED THE POST OF COMMUNITY SUPERINTENDENT I AM VERY AWARE OF BOTH THE NEEDS OF THE SCHOOL SYSTEM AND THE WAY THE IRRELEVANT EXAMINATION WORKS I NOT ONLY HAVE TAKEN AND PASSED SOME THREE TEACHER EXAMINATIONS AND FOUR SUPERVISORY EXAMINATIONS I HAVE ALSO SERVED AS AN ASSISTANT EXAMINER FOR THE BOARD OF EXAMINERS UNDER SEPARATE COVER I AM SENDING YOU DOCUMENTATION WHICH PROVES THE HYPOCRISY AND SUBJECTIVITY OF THE EXAMINATION FOR SUPERVISORS WE IN DISTRICT THREE AND I AS A PROFESSIONAL DEDICATED TO PERFORMANCE AS THE ONLY CRITERIA FOR JOB SECURITY FULLY ENDORSE THE ABOLITION OF THE BOARD OF EXAMINERS FOR SUPERVISORY SELECTION AND THE OPENING OF OUR EDUCATIONAL SYSTEM TO ALL
ALFREDO MATHEW JR., COMMUNITY SUPERINTENDENT DISTRICT 3 MANHATTAN

Appendix C

IN THE

UNITED STATES DISTRICT COURT

FOR THE

SOUTHERN DISTRICT OF NEW YORK

BOSTON M. CHANCE and
LOUIS C. MERCADO, et al.,

Plaintiffs,

v.

BOARD OF EXAMINERS, et al.,

Defendants.

CIVIL ACTION
No.
Civ.

AFFIDAVIT IN SUPPORT OF
MOTION FOR PRELIMINARY INJUNCTION

STATE OF NEW YORK)
) ss.:
COUNTY OF BRONX)

ALFREDO MATHEW, JR. being duly sworn, deposes and says:

1. My name is Alfredo Mathew, Jr. and I reside at 50 Orange Street, Brooklyn, New York 11201. I am the regularly appointed principal of Junior High School 98, 1619 Boston Road, Bronx, New York 10460.

2. I graduated with a B.A. degree cum laude from City College of New York in 1955. I earned a M.A. from City College of New York in 1961 and I am presently a Ph.D. candidate in Educational Sociology at New York University.

3. I have been continuously employed in the New York City school system since 1954. I hold the following New York City licenses: Regular Teacher of Social Studies, Junior High School; Regular Teacher of Social Studies, Senior High School; Assistant Principal, Elementary School; Assistant Principal, Junior High School; Social Studies Chairman, Junior High School; and Principal of Junior High School. I also hold New York State certification as Principal and as District Superintendent.

4. I served briefly in 1969 as an assistant examiner for defendant Board of Examiners in which position I helped to administer the examination for assistant principal of junior high school. Just prior to my serving in that position, when I was working at the Board of Education as a supervisor of bilingual teachers, I was horrified to learn that the personnel at the Board of Examiners who prepared the examination for this position were almost totally deficient in either a knowledge of the job of bilingual teacher or of the Spanish language and the Puerto Rican-Hispanic culture. My dis-

taste for the crudeness and unimaginativeness of the examination system was confirmed by my subsequent experience as an assistant examiner. I was shocked by the pat answers which were prepared by the Board of Examiners' chosen experts as guides for the assistant examiners such as myself in evaluating the candidates.

    5. It is my opinion that the examination techniques place pressure on the assistant examiners to pass candidates who have mastered the mnemonical approach to supervision. Not only is it my feeling, based on my experience, that the Board of Examiners' system does not produce tests which measure the capacity of the candidates to do the job being tested for; but I further believe that this system and the kind of "successful" candidate it produces is in large measure responsible for the failures of our school system.

    6. I would further emphasize the fact that questions and interviews of Board of Examiners' tests are composed by the very supervisors whose failures have in large measure precipitated our current educational crisis. Thus, the Board of Examiners' system is specifically geared to "inbreeding" and therefore, to perpetuating the inadequacy of the system. There is no question in my mind that the Board of Examiners' procedures do not measure merit and fitness, but rather that they sustain expediency and cynicism.

                                       ALFREDO MATHEW, JR.

Signed and sworn before me
this _____ day of _____, 1970.

_____
Notary Public

(The material below refers to testimony on p. 172.)

NATHAN HALE JUNIOR HIGH SCHOOL
163 Butler Street
Brooklyn, New York 11231

January 29, 1971

Mrs. Eleanor Holmes Norton
Chairman Commission on Human Rights
80 Lafayette Street
New York, N. Y.

Dear Mrs. Norton,
    I would like to reiterate the contents of a telegram which I sent to you earlier today:

"An unfortunate error in my minutes of Meeting with the Board of Examiners created a false impression. Never was the availability of examination assistants considered the sole criterion for employment. The discussion, as indicated earlier in the minutes, emphasized ability and experience with availability, of course, as an added consideration.
Please have your counsel introduce this correction into the record."

I know that in your attempt to present the truth to the public you will make every attempt to rectify this error.

Yours truly,

Beatrice Neu

c.c. Mr. Jay Greene, Board of Examiners
Dr. M. Rockowitz, Board of Examiners

1415 New York Avenue 6A
Brooklyn, New York 11210
March 27, 1971

Mrs. Eleanor Norton
Commission on Human Rights
80 Lafayette Street
New York, N. Y.

Dear Mrs. Norton:

This letter is in reference to New York City's Board of Examiners. I had really taken the attitude that the bureaucracy is united too tightly to even mention justice. Later I decided that informing you of this complaint could not endanger the commission.

I began my services in the New York City school system as a regular substitute teacher of social studies (363122) in junior high schools on November 10, 1965. I took the short answer test for a regular teaching license as a teacher of social studies in junior high schools in May 1970. In October 1970, I was administered an interview test. The interview test was administered by a male and a female examiner. The examination was conducted in the presence of a tape recorder. The passing score is 60.0. I received my results which read 57.76 weighted average on January 6, 1971.

This is my sixth year working in this system as a regular substitute teacher of social studies in junior high schools. In my utmost opinion I find the Board of Examiners to be very biased, unjust, and discriminating toward black teachers. No matter how excellent the work is, many black teachers neither receive top credit nor receive positions on the basis of their performance. There appears to be top rewards accorded to teachers who give low performance.

I challenge the validity and reliability of the Board of Examiners. (1) Why is it necessary for a teacher to take both substitute and regular tests? Teachers who take the regular examination are allowed a certain period of time to accrue 30 credits above their B.A. degree to meet the requirements. The fallacy is that some teachers who have achieved 30 credits are denied regular licenses while teachers who have not achieved 30 credits may be administered regular teaching licenses. There are no qualitative requirements to be met after one has been denied regular license - the applicant simply takes the test over and over again until he has been successful in receiving a license as a regular teacher. This action does not provide measures to develop a more qualified applicant. (2) The interview test is conducted by two examiners and a tape recorder. I question the validity and reliability of two subjective examiners. Under such examining conditions, two people determine whether an applicant will receive a regular license. The fallacy is that applicants have already passed through a college of professors who have given approval of their work and performance with the stamp of the institution, yet two people determine to a degree whether the same applicants should become a regular licensed teacher. It is highly possible that the examiners do not perform well as teachers. Traditionally, teachers in New York City have been promoted to higher positions when they could not perform well in the classroom. The system appears to reward poor performance and punish or suppress teachers who perform well. Nepotism exists within the system. Many teachers receive positions because they have relatives on the board, therefore, they have good connections. There are some teachers who are more qualified than the examiners, yet are denied regular licenses by them.

The denial of regular licenses has certain financial and political implications. A teacher may reach the maximum salary step (C6 $\neq$ promotional) before receiving a regular license. After reaching the seventh step a teacher of this calibre does not receive the annual salary increment. This action saves money for the Board of Education, yet the teacher is rendering top services.

Observing another point, a regular license is a requisite to move into higher positions. In order to take tests for licensed supervisory and/or administrative positions, one has to have regular license experience. Yet the cry is that there are no qualified black people to take positions - the truth is more laws are contemplated and passed to keep blacks out of these positions.

Appendix C

Personally, I classified myself as a very good teacher. My performance has extended beyond the call of duty because of my interest in the wholesome and total development of children. I have worked in three junior high schools in Brooklyn. I challenge any chairman, supervisor, assistant principal, and principal to deny my good performance as a teacher. My performance in the previously mentioned schools has led administrators to place me in some acting administrative capacity (especially when such work would enhance their position). I have served as social studies advisor, special guidance teacher for the most difficult students, coordinator of Afro-American history, chairman of Afro-American history department, and acting guidance counselor. Social studies awards have been won by my students when they were not in top SP classes. I have received many commendations for my performance. (A number of letters of commendation and favorable evaluations from supervisors were enclosed as well as the writer's 810 rating report of February, 1968 for an examination for which she filed but did not take.)

I have a master's degree in guidance, secondary education and state certification (more than 60 credits beyond my BS degree). I am on the highest salary step offered with the New York City school system (C6 ǂ promotional). I do not receive the annual salary increment because I have been denied regular license. Whereas I am taking time to write about these conditions, there are many teachers affected who believe that nothing can be done. Teachers fear that they will be blackballed and blacklisted if they speak out against the unfairness and discrimination which exist in the New York City school system.

It is evident that the New York City school system caters to inadequate teaching performance by evaluating the products which are produced. Many children become psychological dropouts as early as the age of seven and wait upon the time when they can become physical dropouts. These children find the system very meaningless—they depend on teachers who do not concern themselves with neither their interest nor their development. Children are confronted with teachers who identify with the self-fulfilling prophecy theory. Some teachers assume that these children cannot learn, therefore, they do not make an effort to teach them, hence the children do not learn. I, myself, have been confronted with teachers and administrators who made and still make verbal remarks to the effect that the children cannot learn. I maintain that any educator who expresses this velief has no place in schools. However, this type school system preserves and protects these teachers. New York City may find it advantageous to have education controlled by the State - evaluation of record and annual evaluation according to performance. It is hard for me to survive in this system where day in and day out I must watch the decay in schools (teacher who does precisely nothing to benefit a student, but receives a pay check and mosttimes with regular license) not to mention the children.

Appendix C

    Since America purports to be a country of democracy with freedom of expression, I took the time to express some of my feelings and experiences centered around bias, injustice, and discrimination in the New York City school system. I do not know the value of my expression, but I do know from experience that this is not even a sample of the corruption in the New York City school system.

Respectfully,

Dorothy Rutledge

Enclosures
cc: NAACP 261 W. 125th St.
    Harvey Scribner 65 Court Street

BOARD OF EDUCATION OF THE CITY OF NEW YORK
J.H.S. 57, 125 Stuyvesant Avenue, Brooklyn, New York 11221
              OFFICE OF THE PRINCIPAL

Miss Dorothy Rutledge   June 17, 1969
Afro-American Coordinator

Dear Miss Rutledge:
    I want to thank you for the work that you did for our school this term. The contributions that you made in the field of Afro-American history were a great help to members of my department. The programs you put down were appreciated by the children and the members of the staff.
    The material you provided for the teachers was a great help in integrating American history with the history of the Afro-American.
    My personal thanks for your cooperation and aid. I hope that you will be with us next year.

Very truly yours,

Neil Lefkowitz
Chairman, Social Studies Dept.

NL:js

cc: Mr. Frederic Sorkin, Principal
    Dr. Abraham P. Tauchner, District Superintendent
    Mr. Matiwane Manana, Coordinator, African Cultures
    File

Appendix C

1010 LAFAYETTE STREET
BROOKLYN, N.Y. 11221

ABRAHAM P. TAUCHNER
DISTRICT SUPERINTENDENT OF SCHOOLS

June 26, 1969

Miss Dorothy Rutledge
Teacher Coordinator
Whitelaw Reid JHS 57
125 Stuyvesant Avenue
Brooklyn, New York 11221

Dear Miss Rutledge:

    Within a short time you have done a commendable job in your school as teacher-coordinator in the African-African American Studies Program.
    You have shown great creativity in the resource materials you developed and gave an excellent demonstration lesson when the State Evaluators were here. The performance of the play "Ethiopia, At the Bar of Justice", by your children on the 8th of June, 1969 was well done.
    Your cooperation in assisting in the training of the inexperienced teacher-coordinators has helped our program, and you have also helped our children to gain some of the insight necessary to make them good men and women.
    We would find you a great asset to our program next term.

                              Yours truly,

                              Matiwane H. E. Manana
                              District Coordinator
                              African-American Studies
                              District 16

MHEM:ca
    cc: Dr. Abraham P. Tauchner
        District Superintendent

        Miss Loretta U. Boyce
        Title I Coordinator

Appendix C

Enrico Fermi Junior High School
35 Starr Street
Brooklyn, N.Y.

Alvin L. Kulick　　　　　　　　　　　　Donald Singer
Principal　　　　　　　　　　　　　　　Assistant Principal

　　　　　　　　　　　　　　　　　　　Meyer Markon
　　　　　　　　　　　　　　　　　　　Acting Chairman

TEACHER　　　　　CLASS 7-446　　DATE 3/20/67

MOT: Miss Rutledge
AIM: "Today we are going to discuss how the early settlers....."
"To learn how the early settlers began their way of life along the Atlantic Coast."

THE LESSON: Miss Rutledge began the lesson by introducing the aim. A student then listed the southern colonies. The problems faced by the settlers was discussed, and notes were placed on the board. Indian influence (farming, hunting, etc.). The class then discussed the settlers' customs which they brought from Europe; Colonial trade was then discussed; Colonial skills - carpenters, blacksmiths, etc.; the need for a labor force and the subsequent importation of Negroes was then mentioned. A student was asked to summarize the lesson. Miss Rutledge reviewed homework assignment and collected day's assignment.

MATTERS FOR COMMENDATION:
1. The lesson was very well organized - it had an Aim, Motivation, Summary and homework assignment.
2. The room appearance was excellent - evidence of student work, etc.
3. The board was used to great advantage - it was neat and well organized.
4. Students were involved effectively - most participated in the lesson, one listed southern colonies, one summarized lesson, etc.
5. Teacher was well prepared and organized for lesson - planning was complete; Miss Rutledge walked through room checking on pupils' work.
6. Important Social Studies vocabulary ("musket") and concepts (slavery began as an economic necessity) were well developed.
7. Wall map was used effectively - students pointed out areas.

Appendix C

RECOMMENDATIONS:
1. Lesson might have been improved if the students were involved in a more meaningful manner. For example, use a situational approach to the above lesson. "If you were a colonist, which problems would you face?" Or, "How would you attempt to solve your problems if you were new to an area?" This would enable the students to relate from their own experience and make the lesson more "real" and "alive." This would also permit the students to move the lesson from one topic to another - problems, solutions, etc.
2. Try to use more diagrams on the board - showing trade routes, etc.

GENERAL COMMENT:
Miss Rutledge has an excellent rapport with her students. Her manner is gentle and sincere. She has obvious respect for her students and their needs.

SUPERVISOR: D. Singt
CONFERENCE HELD: 3/21/67
FOLLOW UP: TEACHER (SIGNATURE)

MR. WILLIAM H. HARRIS, Principal

   ASSISTANT PRINCIPALS

      A. BOYCE
      R. McFADDEN
      S. McNAIR
      R. ADAMS
      B. QUSIM   April 14, 1970

Dear Mrs. Rutledge:

   Just a little note to express to you my appreciation for sending me a copy of the Afro-American Newspaper. I am very proud of the paper and offer my sincere congratulations to you for putting out such a fine piece of work. Congratulations to you and to the people of your department for the fine work that you are doing.

                                                    Sincerely,

WHH/la   William H. Harris
                                                     Principal

Appendix C

THE ENRICO FERMI JUNIOR HIGH SCHOOL 111 K.
35 Starr Street
Brooklyn, N. Y. 11221

March 17, 1966

Dear Miss Rutledge:

I was quite pleased at the condition of class 8-1 on my little visit yesterday. The students seemed interested, and the degree of instruction was at a high level.

I was also quite impressed with the way the students derived the meanings of such concepts as "freedom" and "nationalism."

Yours truly,

M. Markon
Acting Assistant Prin.

THE ENRICO FERMI JUNIOR HIGH SCHOOL 111 K.
35 Starr Street
Brooklyn, N. Y. 11221

November 10, 1966

Dear Miss Rutledge:

Thank you for participating in the P.T.A. meeting at 8:00 P.M. on Thursday, November 3.

This was appreciated by the many parents and members of the community.

Sincerely,

Alvin L. Kulick
Principal

ALK:mmm

A copy of this is being placed in your file.

Miss D. Rutledge
Teacher - Class 7-326

Appendix C

BOARD OF EDUCATION OF THE CITY OF NEW YORK
<u>J.H.S. 111</u>   <u>Brooklyn</u>
  School   Borough Zone   Address   Telephone

OFFICE OF THE PRINCIPAL

June 14, 1967

Dear Miss Rutledge,

    The eight year review for the seventh grade assemblies was enjoyed by all the students.
    I know that it took time and effort on your part to assist the students. This extra work, which you do so well, is greatly appreciated by me and by the students.

                                    Thank you,

                                    Dan Wohl
                                    Assistant Principal

Copy for file

BOARD OF EDUCATION OF THE CITY OF NEW YORK
<u>J.H.S. 111</u>   <u>Brooklyn</u>
  School   Borough Zone   Address   Telephone

OFFICE OF THE PRINCIPAL

Alvin L. Kulick
Principal   November 3, 1967

Miss Dorothy Rutledge
Students in United Nations Play

Dear Miss Rutledge and boys and girls,

    On behalf of the 6th grade, and the members of the Social Studies Department, permit me to thank you for your United Nations program this past week in the grade assemblies.
    In addition to being timely, your presentation was colorful, interesting and educational. You proved that various peoples, working together, could live and work in harmony.
    Thank you very much.

                                    Sincerely yours,

                                    D. Singer
cc:ALK   Assistant Principal

Appendix C

THE ENRICO FERMI JUNIOR HIGH SCHOOL 111 K.
35 Starr Street
Brooklyn, N. Y. 11221

Alvin L. Kulick
Principal

March 20, 1968

Miss Dorothy Rutledge
Advisor, Social Studies Magazine
Students of classes 8-106, 114, 231, 233

Dear Miss Rutledge, boys and girls,

    After having read your latest magazine, "The African Heritage," Mr. Kulick and I would like to compliment you on an extremely well-organized and readable publication.
    The Social Studies department of our school is committed to the goal of improving the teaching of Minority History. Your magazine is a further indication that this goal is beginning to be achieved.
    We look forward to reading further issues of your publication.

                        Sincerely yours,

                        D. Singer
                        Assistant Principal

cc: Mr. Kulick

THE ENRICO FERMI JUNIOR HIGH SCHOOL 111 K.
35 Starr Street
Brooklyn, N. Y. 11221

Alvin L. Kulick
Principal

May 6, 1968

Dear Miss Rutledge:

    The efforts of you and your class on behalf of a recent 810 candidate were extremely cooperative. It insured the proper climate for the visiting teacher's classroom teaching test.

                        Thank you.

                        Sincerely,

                        D. Singer
                        Assistant Principal

CC:ALK

Appendix C

BOARD OF EDUCATION OF THE CITY OF NEW YORK
J.H.S. 111   Brooklyn   June 27, 1967
—————   —————————   ———————————————
 School   Borough Zone   Address   Telephone

OFFICE OF THE PRINCIPAL
Alvin L. Kulick

Dear Miss Rutledge:

The work you did with the bulletin boards and the shows you put on for the assemblies shows the interest you have in the school and the students.
I do wish you a happy and healthy summer.

Sincerely,

Dan Wohl
Assistant Principal

C.C. for file

ENRICO FERMI JUNIOR HIGH SCHOOL
35 Starr Street
Brooklyn, N.Y.

Alvin L. Kulick   Donald Singer
Principal   Assistant Principal

                               Joseph Smith
                               Social Studies Coordinator

TEACHER: Miss Rutledge   CLASS: 8-231   DATE: 12/8/67

AIM: "To learn how the common man won a share in the governing of the nation."
MOTIVATION: "Describe the cover of your Social Studies textbook."
THE LESSON: Aim written on board. Homework assignment also on board. Students were asked to describe their textbook's cover - discussion of how U.S. democracy has progressed from one era to another (Declaration of Independence, N. W. ordinance, etc.). Medial summary - "today we are also discussing changes. Discussion of President Jackson - life on frontier, his respect for the common man; his influence on the political party system." Final summary - "Why was Jackson's election considered a revolution?" Discussion of National and State conventions.

MATTERS FOR COMMENDATION:
1. Good routines - students took notes; had textbooks, raised hands, etc. - class well organized.
2. Room well decorated and used for Social Studies lesson - maps, etc.
3. Important concept developed - U.S. democracy a cumulative series of events.
4. Previous lessons and work recalled and used during lesson.
5. Students encouraged to improve their reading skills.
6. Teacher well-organized and prepared - lesson planning, scholarship, etc.
7. Board work orderly and in outline form.
8. Students well behaved and well mannered.

RECOMMENDATIONS:
1. Homework assignment might be more effective if given at end of period.
2. Greater effort should be made to involve the girls in the lesson -- greater use of their personal experience - life on frontier, etc.
3. Students should evaluate each other's readings, responses, etc.

GENERAL COMMENT:

SUPERVISOR: D. Singt

CONFERENCE HELD: 12/8/67   TEACHER (SIGNATURE)
FOLLOW UP:

Miss Rutledge's classes are working on scrapbooks on American History. She has also recently completed an excellent Social Studies magazine, entitled "Understanding our World."

---

435 Convent Ave., #44
New York 10031
Feb. 5, 1971

Hon. Eleanor Norton, Chairman
City Commission Human Rights
80 Lafayette Street
New York

Your Honor:

Regretfully, because of a severe attack of Virus, I was incapacitated for more than two weeks and therefore I was unable to attend The Hearings. By doctor's orders I am still confined to the house.

I believe the enclosed materials will serve to illustrate a glaring example of discriminatory practice by the Board of Education.

Thank you for your interest, cooperation and assistance.

Yours truly,

Adele W. Timpson

Encl.

EDUCATION DEPARTMENT REPORTS

JUDICIAL DECISIONS

OF THE

COMMISSIONER OF EDUCATION

VOLUME 9

OFFICIAL EDITION

The State Education Department

Office of Counsel

Albany

1970

In the Matter of the appeal of ADELE W. TIMPSON from the refusal of the BOARD OF EDUCATION OF THE CITY SCHOOL DISTRICT OF THE CITY OF NEW YORK to recognize petitioner's tenure status*

Decision No. 8122
(March 30, 1970)

Warren I. Susman, Esq., attorney for petitioner

Hon. J. Lee Rankin, Corporation Counsel, attorney for respondent

NYQUIST; Commissioner. - Petitioner has served for the last nine years as a principal of a day elementary school. Petitioner, however, is admittedly not licensed for this position and has not passed the competitive examination conducted by the Board of Examiners. Notwithstanding lack of licensure, respondent has wilfully and knowingly continued petitioner's assignment. She has, in fact, rendered satisfactory service for three times the normal probationary period for such a position. This fact pattern clearly falls within the scope of my decision in <u>Matter</u> of <u>Murphy, et al.</u> (8 Ed Dept Rep 101 (1968), petition to review dismissed, Supreme Court Albany County (1969) and this appeal must therefore be sustained.

It is ordered that the Board of Education of the City School District of the City of New York adjust petitioner's title in accordance with this decision and that hereafter it compensate petitioner at a rate in conformity with her adjusted title.

*Bd. of Educ., City School Dist, City of N.Y. v. Nyquist; Supreme Court, Albany County, Special Term; Pitt, J.; Motion to dismiss petition granted; Sept. 11, 1970; n.o.r.

Office of Superintendent
SCHOOL DISTRICT 6
P. S. 192, Manhattan
500 West 138th Street
New York, N. Y. 10031

October 19, 1967

Dr. Bernard E. Donovan
Superintendent of Schools
Board of Education
110 Livingston Street
Brooklyn, New York 11201

Re: Mrs. Adele Timpson
Acting Principal,
P-100-M

Dear Dr. Donovan:

Since 1961, Mrs. Adele Timpson has compiled an excellent record of pupil improvement as acting principal of M.E.S. 100, Man. As her District Superintendent, I can readily bear witness to her tireless devotion to the interests of her pupils and the needs of her school-community.

In fact, her unwillingness to sacrifice these upon the altar of examination preparation may have been an important factor in her failure to achieve placement on the current eligible list for principal of day elementary schools.

Such failure, however, should be more than counterbalanced by her consistent and long-time success as the head of M.E.S. 100. For six long years she has conclusively demonstrated her ability to guide the destinies of an elementary school. It is manifestly unjust to continue to deny her principal's salary for doing a principal's job, and it would be unthinkable and ungrateful to remove her from her present position. This is particularly true in view of recent action in granting full principal's salary to newly assigned acting principals of demonstration elementary schools.

I, therefore, propose as an act of simple justice to Mrs. Timpson, that our Board of Education pass a resolution granting principal's salary to any assistant principal who for five or more years has rendered satisfactory service as acting principal of a Special Service or More Effective School. Precedent exists, by analogy, in the Board's decision some years ago to grant Associate Superintendent's salary to those Assistant Superintendents who had served as Acting Associate Superintendents for a given length of time.

I strongly urge that at least this belated salary recognition be given to Mrs. Timpson's outstanding service, even if she cannot be given a principal's appointment.

    Yours truly,

    SIDNEY ROSENBERG
    District Superintendent

SR/s

cc: Dr. Aaron Brown
    Dr. Nathan Brown
    Mrs. Margaret S. Douglas
    Rev. John J. Hicks
    Dr. Theodore H. Lang
    Dr. Seelig Lester
    Miss Trude T. Weil

Appendix C

BOARD OF EDUCATION
OF THE CITY OF NEW YORK
110 Livingston Street
Brooklyn, N. Y. 11201

BERNARD E. DONOVAN
Superintendent of Schools

November 9, 1967

Dr. Sidney Rosenberg
District Superintendent
500 West 138 Street
New York, N. Y. 10031

Dear Dr. Rosenberg:

You wrote to me on October 19 concerning Mrs. Adele Timpson, Acting Principal of P-100-M. I am well aware of Mrs. Timpson's abilities and her contributions to the system. However in the absence of an examination for the license of principal, I am unable to appoint Mrs. Timpson as a principal.

I shall keep Mrs. Timpson in mind in case other jobs open as we go into our demonstration and experimental work.

Sincerely,

Bernard E. Donovan
Superintendent of Schools

BED:al

December 11, 1967

Hon. Bernard E. Donovan
Superintendent of Schools
Board of Education
110 Livingston Street
Brooklyn, N. Y. 11201

Re: Mrs. Adele W. Timpson
P. S. 100, Manhattan

Dear Dr. Donovan:

Permit me as a resident of Harlem and one vitally concerned with the processes and quality of education throughout the City to urge upon you the adjustment of the salary of Mrs. Adele W. Timpson, Acting Principal of P. S. 100 in Manhattan to that of Principal; as is permitted in Demonstrations Schools.

I know of Mrs. Timpson's good record and the high regard in which she is held in Harlem's educational and civic community, and would suggest that this salary adjustment within the law would be a salutary act.

            Yours truly,

            Percy E. Sutton

PES:rs
cc: Corres. BPM RS
   Timpson Gordon Wingate

BOARD OF EDUCATION
OF THE CITY OF NEW YORK
DISTRICT 16
1010 LAFAYETTE AVENUE
BROOKLYN, N.Y. 11221

ABRAHAM P. TAUCHNER
DISTRICT SUPERINTENDENT OF SCHOOLS

            March 11, 1968

Dr. Bernard E. Donovan
Superintendent of Schools
Board of Education
110 Livingston Street
Brooklyn, New York

Dear Dr. Donovan:

  I have known Mrs. Adele W. Timpson for many years, as a teacher, as an Assistant Principal, and as Acting Principal of Public School 100 in Manhattan. As a matter of fact, when I was asked by the then Superintendent of Schools, Dr. John Theobold, to become principal of Public School 100 in Manhattan, I immediately requested Mrs. Timpson to join me as a supervisor at this school.
  At that time Public School 100 in Manhattan was facing most serious problems. The school, reopened as an elementary school the previous year, was completely upset. The principal who had served for one year was transferred to another school, and I was asked by the Superintendent of Schools to take over the leadership.

Appendix C

After working with Mrs. Timpson for a few weeks in June and July, I became seriously ill with peritonitis and was unable to return to school until November. Mrs. Timpson took over the leadership of the school completely and has continued to move Public School 100 in Manhattan ahead ever since.

Justice and equity request that Mrs. Timpson be compensated at the salary of an elementary school principal, and I know you will do everything you can to make this possible.

Sincerely yours,

Abraham P. Tauchner
District Superintendent

APT:dm

BOARD OF EDUCATION OF THE CITY OF NEW YORK
SCHOOL DISTRICT 6
500 West 138th Street
New York, N.Y. 10031

SIDNEY ROSENBERG
DISTRICT SUPERINTENDENT

March 20, 1968

Dr. Bernard E. Donovan
Superintendent of Schools
Board of Education
110 Livingston Street
Brooklyn, New York 11201

Re: Mrs. Adele W. Timpson
Acting Principal P-100-M

Dear Dr. Donovan:

I received from Dr. Abraham P. Tauchner a copy of his letter to you in which he sets forth very logically and conclusively the rationale for compensating Mrs. Timpson at the salary of an elementary school principal.

Mrs. Timpson has for almost seven years been performing and continues to perform with dedication and distinction the job of elementary school principal in a very difficult situation.

I wish to urge once again that Mrs. Timpson's compensation be raised to the salary of an elementary school principal.

Yours sincerely,

SIDNEY ROSENBERG
District Superintendent

SR/s

Appendix C

BOARD OF EDUCATION OF THE CITY OF NEW YORK
DIVISION OF SPECIAL SERVICES
BUREAU OF COMMUNITY EDUCATION   DISTRICT OFFICE
District 6, Manhattan

EDWARD J. CLARK, SUPERVISOR   P. S. 192
500 West 138th Street
New York, N.Y. 10031

September 12, 1968

Mrs. Adele W. Timpson
Acting Assistant Superintendent
District 6
500 West 138 Street
New York, New York 10031

Dear Mrs. Timpson:

    I would like to take this opportunity to congratulate you on your appointment as Acting Superintendent in District 6 Manhattan. I wish you great success in this very challenging position. As Supervisor of Community Education and one of your regular staff members, I will do everything I possibly can to assist you.

                                       Sincerely yours,

                                       Edward J. Clark
EJC:pd   Supervisor

BOARD OF EDUCATION
OF THE CITY OF NEW YORK
110 LIVINGSTON STREET
BROOKLYN, N.Y. 11201

Mrs. Morris Shapiro
PRESIDENT

September 17, 1968

Mrs. Adele W. Timpson
Acting District Superintendent
District No. 6
500 West 138th Street
New York, New York 10031

Dear Mrs. Timpson:

    I was delighted to learn that your Local School Board has designated you as Acting District Superintendent of District 6.

Appendix C

My only hope is that schools will be operating soon and that your community will enjoy the great contribution you have to offer.

My best wishes to you in this new and challenging post.

Sincerely,

Rose Shapiro

RS:tn
CC: Mr. Kenneth Josey
    Chairman, Local
    School Board #6.

BOARD OF EDUCATION
OF THE CITY OF NEW YORK
110 LIVINGSTON STREET
BROOKLYN, N.Y. 11201

NATHAN BROWN
Executive Deputy Superintendent of Schools

November 6, 1968

Mrs. Adele W. Timpson
435 Convent Avenue (Apt. 44)
New York, N.Y. 10031

Dear Mrs. Timpson:

Thank you for writing to me.

You filled in for your district at a very difficult time. I know that you must derive great satisfaction in the outpouring of support which took place when you and the Local School Board were under attack.

You are still tops with us here and we look forward to your continuing service to the children in your area.

All good wishes.

Sincerely,

NATHAN BROWN
Executive Deputy Superintendent

Appendix C

HERBERT H. LEHMAN COLLEGE Office of the President
Of the City University of New York

Bedford Park Boulevard West
Bronx, New York 10468

August 8, 1969

Mrs. Adele Timpson, Principal
P. S. 100
21 West 138th Street
New York, N. Y.

Dear Mrs. Timpson:

    Please permit me to express my thanks to you for your graciousness during my visit to P. S. 100 as a part of the evaluation team for Title 1 Summer Program in District #6. Although extremely busy, you took the time to give me a fascinating tour of your summer programs, and a thorough briefing on the objectives and results of the several programs at your school. The dedication and professional competence of you and your staff were clearly exhibited in the happy faces of involved students and in the general tone set throughout the school. Indeed, it was a refreshing experience for me.
    I commend you, and extend my best wishes for your continued success.
    Again, many thanks.

                                  Very truly yours,

                                  James B. Miller
                                  Executive Assistant
                                  to the President

JBM/ep

Appendix C

MATTHEW A. HENSON SCHOOL
MORE EFFECTIVE SCHOOLS PROGRAM
21 W. 138 St., N. Y. 10037

Re: Adele W. Timpson, Acting Principal 1961 - 1971

Mrs. Timpson received a temporary assignment in late July 1961, effective September 1961, to P.S. 100, Man., to replace the Board of Examiners licensed principal who had to be transferred at the end of his first year.

Mrs. Timpson later learned that the District Superintendent Charles Shapp had been unable to prevail upon any principal or any licensed assistant principal in the district to accept assignment to P.S. 100, M. in the spring of 1961.

Although Mrs. Timpson had served creditably as an assistant principal in P.S. 91, Bronx - District 21 under Superintendent Johanna M. Hopkins - and could have refused the temporary (1961 - 1971) assignment, in the interest of the children she bent to the task.

Later, Mrs. Timpson requested the termination of the assignment but was prevailed upon by Dr. John King, Associate Superintendent at the time and later Miss Truda Weil, Acting Associate Superintendent, to remain because, "You are doing such a fine job." "You have made '100' an outstanding school to which visitors are referred."

Many letters of praise from visitors and evaluators are on file. More than five hundred petitions from parents and community representatives were sent to Dr. Bernard Donovan, Superintendent. These asked that I receive compensations and title of principal.

In August 1966 at the close of the Intensive Teacher Training Program and again at the Northside Center Luncheon in October 1966, the late Isidore Bogen, Chairman of the Board of Examiners said, "Adele, I think your trouble is that you devoted time and energy to running that school instead of taking time out to study."

Mrs. Timpson asked him if he thought the applicant should be penalized for doing a good job in a school to which she had been assigned continuously against her wishes.

He asked Mrs. Timpson if she had appealed the rating.

Upon receiving an affirmative reply he suggested that she write him a letter including dates and data.

Mrs. Timpson wrote to him but unfortunately she did not hear from him because he was ill. He succumbed to a fatal illness.

Some months later I received an acknowledgment of my letter but no hope from Dr. Denn.

Mrs. Timpson has received commendatory evaluations from all of her supervisors, teams of evaluators sent in by the Board of Education during the years 1961 through 1971.

On June 25, 1966 at a testimonial luncheon held at the Concourse Plaza Hotel in the Bronx, Mrs. Timpson was praised by parents and teachers, "She has changed a Blackboard Jungle into a More Effective School."

Appendix C

    Doesn't the nine year record of Mrs. Timpson and the retention by the Board of Education prove that she has evidenced the ability to function as a competent principal and therefore should have her title adjusted?
    Ewald B. Nyquist, Commissioner of Education of the State of New York in the matter of my appeal from the refusal of the Board of Education of the City of New York has ordered the Board of Education to adjust my title and to provide compensation in conformity with the adjusted title (March 30, 1970).
    To date - July 18, 1970 - the board of Education has failed to comply.
    Since my case is without parallel - continued assignment for nine years of satisfactory service - and as so many of my colleagues - superintendents, directors, principals, assistant principals, etc. - have said, "It's about time." "It's long overdue," and since the decision upon which my appeal is based was appealed and decision #8941 dated October 18, 1966 was rendered and petition review dismissed - Supreme Court, Albany County 6/16/69 - may I enlist your good offices on my behalf?

                                        Adele W. Timpson

Encl.

    The Board of Education appealed the Commissioner's decision, Supreme Court, Albany County, Special Term in September 1970. Petition was dismissed September 29, 1970.
    It is interesting to note that C.S.A. (Council Supervisory Associations) president Walter Degnan and other officers have orally said, "Adele, you certainly are entitled to be granted the title, license, tenure and salary." They have not had the intestinal fortitude to put their statements in writing.
    Letters of commendation received from Superintendents, Special Evaluators sent in by the Board of Education, City and Community officials, etc.

                                        Adele W. Timpson
                                        May, 1971

1. Education
    1.1 Graduated with honors from P. S. 6, Man.
    1.2 Graduated from Hunter College H.S. - State Scholarship
    1.3 Graduated from N. Y. Training School Teachers, 3rd out of 287.
    1.4 Graduated from Hunter College - B.A. Education Major
    1.5 Masters Program Hunter College - M.S. Ed. (Supervision)
    1.6 Completed specialized courses in curriculum, organization and administration in the graduate schools of Hunter College,

Appendix C

Fordham University, N. Y. U., City College and Teachers College, Columbia University.
2. Organizational Affiliations
    2.1 Association of Administrative Women in Education
    2.2 N. Y. Association Black Supervisors and Administrators
    2.3 Association of Assistant Principals
        2.3.1 Member, 1952-1970
        2.3.2 Vice President, 1958-1963
        2.3.3 President, 1963-1965
    2.4 N. Y. Society Experimental Study of Education
    2.5 Association Study Negro Life and History
    2.6 7/10 Life Member N.A.A.C.P.
    2.7 Member Phi Delta Kappa Sorority
    2.8 Catholic Teachers Association Archdiocese N.Y.
        2.8.1 Member, 1948-1970
        2.8.2 Executive Board, 1964-1968
    2.9 Participant - Catholic Interracial Council
    2.10 Community
        2.10.1 N.Y. Mission Society - Minisink
        2.10.2 Y.M.C.A. 135 Street
        2.10.3 Utility Club
        2.10.4 H.A.N.A.
        2.10.5 Harlem Teams Self-Help
        2.10.6 32nd Precinct Community School Committee
        2.10.7 Utility Club
        2.10.8 Northside Center
        2.10.9 Hope Day Nursery
        2.10.10 Harlem Hospital
        2.10.11 Bank Street College
        2.10.12 N.Y.U.
        2.10.13 Brooklyn College
        2.10.14 College Mt. St. Vincent
        2.10.15 Harlem Institute Teachers
        2.10.16 Bowery Savings Bank
        2.10.17 N. Y. Bank for Savings
        2.10.18 Cadets, Scouts, Urban League, et al
3. Professional Experience
    3.1 Teacher J.H.S. 139 M - Grade 2 (1928-1930) Substitute
    3.2 Teacher P.S. 119 M - Grades 2, 4 (1930-1933) Regular
    3.3 Teacher P.S. 90 M - Grades 2,4,5,6 (1933-1937)
    3.4 Teacher P.S. 67 X - Grades 5, 6 (1937-1952)
    3.5 Acting Assistant Principal, P.S. 67 X (1947-1948)
    3.6 Licensed Assistant Principal, P.S. 91 X (1952-1961)
    3.7 <u>Drafted</u> - Acting Principal, P.S. 100 M (1961-1971)
    3.8 Supervisor - Tutorial and Remedial Programs (1963-1970)
    3.9 Acting District Superintendent, District 6 (9/68-10/68)
    3.10 Supervising Principal District 6 (1964-1970)
    3.11 Board of Examiners
        3.11.1 Assistant Examiner - examination of candidates teaching positions City of N. Y. interview tests, written and classroom performance.

Appendix C

3.11.2 Assistant Examiner - examination candidates for supervisory positions (assistant principal)
4. Teacher Education
    4.1 Supervising Principal (district-wide) Teacher Training In-Service Workshop, 1965-1970.
    4.2 Instruction - Hunter College City of N.Y. Graduate Courses - Elementary School Ed., 1961
    4.3 Prepared 5 Teachers for successful candidacy for promotion to Assistant Principal
    4.4 In-Service Courses
        4.4.1 Appointed instructor Bureau of In-Service Training - Board of Education N.Y. Conducted courses for teachers and supervisors in the areas of Science, Mathematics, Social Studies (including Negro History), First Aid.
    4.5 Chairman, Committee Assistant Principal, District 21-22 for the Organization and Supervision of Learning Materials and Experiences in Mathematics and Science.
5. Publications
    5.1 Co-author Board of Education, City of N.Y. curriculum bulletins, Science Curriculum Bulletin, Mathematics Curriculum Bulletin.
    5.2 Member of the Superintendent's Committee to evaluate curriculum materials for use in the public schools throughout City.
6. Projects Completed
    6.1 Chairman following committees involving coordination among teachers, pupils, parents, and community.
        6.1.1 Curriculum Committee, P.S. 67 X (1940-1952)
        6.1.2 Teachers' Interest Committee P.S. 67 X (1940-1952)
    6.2 Organized one of the ten original schools in the More Effective Schools Program.
    6.3 Organized In-Service Course in Afro-American History in District 6 in cooperation with the African-American Institute
7. Honors
    7.1 Citation from National Sorority Phi Delta Kappa, 1966
    7.2 W.W.R.L. Award - Celebrity Field of Education, 1967
    7.3 Guest of Honor Cooperative Committee of Staff, Parents, Pupils, Community, June 1966
8. Licenses and Certificates
    8.1 Teacher of Common Branches (28th out of 800 ≠)
    8.2 Assistant to Principal (11th on women's list)
    8.3 Junior Principal
    8.4 N.Y. State Certification - Principal

(See copies of numerous letters of commendation from supervisors, e.g., "She (Mrs. Timpson) has changed a Blackboard Jungle into a more effective school.")

See record of pupil academic growth 100 M. Overwhelming majority of substitute teachers took and passed regular examination. Invariably asked for regular assignment to 100.

Appendix C

STRASSER, SPIEGELBERG, FRIED & FRANK
120 Broadway, New York, N. Y.

February 3, 1971

Mrs. Eleanor Holmes Norton, Esq.
New York City Human Rights Commission
80 Lafayette Street
New York, New York

Dear Mrs. Norton:

In cooperation with the New York Civil Liberties Union we have represented Miss Joyce Thomas in connection with her efforts to obtain reinstatement of her substitute teacher license which was terminated by the Board of Examiners of the Board of Education of the City of New York in January 1970. We believe that her case is highly relevant to the hearings the Human Rights Commission is currently holding into the alleged racial discrimination practices of the Board of Examiners.

Although, at the present time, we cannot establish with certainty that Miss Thomas' license was terminated by the Board of Examiners because she is black or because of her past civil rights activities, we strongly suspect that this is the case. At the very least the termination of her teaching license was wholly arbitrary and capricious and provides an all too common example of the kafka-esque procedures of the Board of Examiners which necessarily discourage qualified new entrants into the teaching profession in the New York City public schools.

Miss Thomas is a graduate of Florida A&M University and has taught with distinction for serveral years in the Newark, New Jersey public schools. The three principals there for whom she has served have all given her good ratings.

Miss Thomas took and passed the New York City examinations for a substitute early childhood teacher license in the Fall of 1968. On May 9, 1969, after apparently no more than the usual Board of Examiners' bureaucratic delay, Miss Thomas was issued a substitute license by the Board of Education.

Subsequently in the Fall of 1969, she was called in by the Board of Examiners for a further interview "on her record." On January 14, 1970 she was sent a notice by the Board of Examiners terminating her license as of February 1, 1970 for "unsatisfactory record." The sole basis for Miss Thomas' alleged "unsatisfactory record" arises from her failure to acknowledge in her application for a license that in 1963 while a student at Florida A&M University she had been arrested in peaceful demonstrations protesting segregation of a movie theatre in Tallahasse and the jailing of the leaders of an earlier protest. I enclose a "summary statement of reasons for unsatisfactory record" furnished Miss Thomas by Unit 5 of the Board of Examiners.

On March 5, 1970 Miss Thomas appealed the Unit 5 decision

to the full Board of Examiners, and on June 16, 1970 the Board sustained her appeal indicating, however, that she "will be notified when and where to appear for a continued interview test (on record)."

Despite repeated contacts by Miss Thomas and ourselves, the Board of Examiners did not schedule Miss Thomas' further interview until October 16, 1970. The interview was scheduled then only after Dr. Seymour Lachman, one of the members of the Board of Education, made a written inquiry to the Chairman of the Board of Examiners as to the reasons for the delay.

On October 26, 1970 Miss Thomas was interviewed by two examiners who refused to give her their names. The examiners also refused, over our objection, to permit Miss Thomas to have counsel present at the interview. In a telephone inquiry prior to the interview, I was advised that Miss Thomas could not present any character witnesses on her behalf.

Although more than three months have now lapsed since Miss Thomas' interview, the Board of Examiners has not announced any decision. Indeed, the only communication Miss Thomas has had from the Board is a letter within the past week asking for additional character references.

The Board of Examiners' termination of Miss Thomas' license is patently arbitrary and illegal.

Miss Thomas' "unsatisfactory record" arises solely from civil rights activities protected by the First Amendment of the United States Constitution. Under Section AA51-2-0 of the New York City Administrative Code, arrests or even criminal convictions arising from such activities cannot legally be a basis for disqualifying a person from public employment in New York City. Denying public employment on the grounds of such arrests or convictions also violates the Federal Civil Rights Act of 1964 (42 U.S.C. A2000(a)).

It is also clear that Miss Thomas did not intend any deliberate "untruthfulness" or "lack of candor" in failing to disclose her civil rights arrest or arrests on her application for a teaching license. Miss Thomas is proud of the events out of which these arrests arose, and it is inconceivable that she would have deliberately hidden them in applying for her license. She has repeatedly explained to the Board of Examiners in 1970 that her failure to note these arrests on her application was simply an inadvertent omission.

It is interesting to note that, until last week when the Board of Examiners wrote her with regard to names of character references, the Board made no effort whatsoever to make any inquiry into Miss Thomas' character and relied instead on the wholly subjective impression of the examiner at her interview in the Fall of 1969. Even now, the Board has only asked her for references and has not indicated that she will be afforded any opportunity to present character witnesses on her behalf.

I am not writing to you primarily with the view to obtaining relief from the Human Rights Commission in Miss Thomas' individual case, but because I fear that her experience is only too typical of the experience of many teacher applicants with the Board of

Examiners -- particularly applicants who are black or have had the initiative to be active participants in the Civil Rights Movement or in other out-of-the-ordinary events of our times.

Although we are confident that Miss Thomas' right to get a teaching license will ultimately be vindicated, nearly three full school years have elapsed since she first applied for her license and she doesn't have it yet. Obviously, the power of the Board of Examiners arbitrarily -- and perhaps on the basis of racial discrimination -- to force an applicant to expend three years or more of time and effort in obtaining a teaching license is a matter which should be of concern to the Human Rights Commission.

If you desire any further information on this matter please telephone me. I can assure you that Miss Thomas and I would be pleased to cooperate in any inquiry which the Commission might wish to make into the facts of Miss Thomas' case.

Very truly yours,

Lewis A. Stern

LAS:smc

Board of Education   Board of Examiners   City of New York

Thomas, Joyce
Sub. E.C. October 1968 exam.

SUMMARY STATEMENT OF REASONS FOR UNSATISFACTORY RECORD - Nov. 22, 1969

Miss Thomas stated that she felt the question on the application regarding court actions was ambiguous and that, since she had never had any traffic violations, she felt free to answer "No." She had also not listed her arrest on the fingerprint card, which says clearly, "Have you ever been arrested..... for any offense ......?" Moreover, she had great difficulty recalling the incidents reported by the Deputy Sheriff at Tallahassee, Florida (contempt of court 5/63 and trespassing 9/63). One of the two incidents, she did not recall at all.

She had been a participant in a protest against a theatre while a student at Florida Agricultural and Mining College but could not remember ever appearing in court. She had a recollection of having been in jail, and of paying a bondsman $10.00, but maintained that, to the best of her knowledge, she had never been fined. As a matter of fact she was given a sentence of 30 days or a fine of $50.00. The fine was paid on January 13, 1964. The incident that led to her being jailed occurred, she said, outside of the jail where she and others were protesting the incarceration of leaders of a previous protest.

The applicant showed a serious lack of candor in explaining her apparent failure to be truthful on the application form and we, therefore, recommend that the record be deemed unsatisfactory.

Unit 5

COMMISSION ON HUMAN RIGHTS ATTN MRS ELEANOR NORTON
80 LAFAYETTE ST NYK   Jan 29 1971

THE BOARD OF EXAMINERS HANDICAPS OUR SCHOOL SYSTEM.
WE ENDORSE ABOLISHMENT.

PTA PS 163 WEST 97TH ST MANHATTAN

TOPIC GUIDE

Major topics too broad to break down in the Subject Index are listed here in capital letters. Under each are listed all the Subject Index headings that refer to aspects of the major topic. For example, under BILINGUAL TEACHERS, below, the reader will find Bilingual personnel, NYC: data; Bilingual personnel: need for; etc. The Subject Index refers the reader to the pages on which each of these subjects is discussed.

ACCOUNTABILITY OF EDUCATIONAL SYSTEM AND PERSONNEL
See: Administrator training and apprenticeship programs
Community involvement, training and certification recommendation
Community superintendents, NYC, selection and responsibilities
Continuing education of teachers
Decentralization, NYC: community districts
--------------------: recruitment
--------------------: selection system inconsistencies
--------------------: teacher and administrator selection
Due process rights, teachers' and candidates'
Fair employment practices, racial data as measure of
Internship training
Local selection: need for assistance to effect
-------------: objections to
-------------: worth of
Performance-based criteria: for assignment
-----------------------: objections to
-----------------------: for promotion
-----------------------: for selection
-----------------------: for training and certification
Principals: responsibilities and impact
Probation period
Race and ethnicity, criteria for placement
Selection system, effects on children
Supervision and inservice training, paraprofessionals
Supervision of teachers
Teacher accountability, justification and implementation
Teacher training programs: relationship with education systems
Tenure: teachers', and accountability
Training, certification, and differentiated assignment of paraprofessionals, program alternatives

BILINGUAL TEACHERS
See: Bilingual personnel, NYC: data
----------------------: need for
Bilingual program, NYC: criticism
Bilingual teachers: recruitment, NYC
---------------: selection of, testing for
Cost: minority recruitment, NYC
Dropout rate: minority students
Joint Recruitment and Training Program, NYC
Minority student achievement
Minority teacher recruitment, NYC: criticism
-------------------------------: history and effectiveness
-------------------------------: among paraprofessionals
Non-English speaking students, NYC, placement and achievement
Oral interview: criticism
Puerto Ricans: data, teachers and administrators, NYC
-------------: student achievement, NYC
-------------: teacher recruitment, NYC

Race and ethnicity, criteria for placement
School districts, NYC, racial composition
Selection system: effects on children
Students, teachers, and principals, racial data: NYC
--: NY State
--: other large cities
Training, certification, and differentiated assignment of paraprofessionals, program alternatives

BOARD OF EDUCATION, NYC
See: Board of Examiners, NYC: relationship to Board of Education
Chancellor, NYC, duties and powers
Custodial employees, discrimination in hiring
Examinations, NYC: preparation for
-----------------: walk-in
Inservice professional training programs
Job descriptions: NYC examinations
Joint Recruitment and Training Program, NYC
Manpower Development Training Program, discrimination in hiring for
Paraprofessional program, NYC
Practice teaching, training component
Principals: placement by NYC Board of Education
Professional Promotional Seminars, NYC
Recruitment Division, staff, NYC Board of Education
Supervision of teachers
Teacher training programs: NYC Board of Education cooperation with

COMMUNITY BOARDS OF EDUCATION, NYC
See: Acting principals, NYC: placement, number, race and use
Community involvement, training and certification recommendation
Community superintendents, NYC, selection and responsibilities
Decentralization, NYC: community districts
--------------------: National Teacher Education use
--------------------: recruitment
--------------------: selection system inconsistencies
--------------------: teacher and administrator selection
Ford Foundation fellowships
Fordham internship program, NYC
Local selection: need for assistance to effect
-------------: objections to
-------------: worth of
Minority schools, NYC, white principals' and teachers' attitude toward
Principals: responsibilities and impact
Race and ethnicity, criteria for placement
School districts, NYC, racial composition

DATA
See: Acting principals, NYC: placement, number, race, and use
Bilingual personnel, NYC: data
Black teachers and administrators: data
Custodial employees, discrimination in hiring
Dropout rate: classroom teachers
-----------: minority students
Italian teachers and administrators, NYC

Jewish supervisors and administrators, NYC
Minority student achievement
Non-English speaking students, NYC, placement and achievement
Paraprofessionals: number and race, NYC
Puerto Ricans: data, teachers and administrators, NYC
------------: student achievement, NYC
Recruitment Division, staff, NYC Board of Education
School districts, NYC, racial composition
Students, teachers, and principals, racial data: NYC
---------------------------------------: NY State
---------------------------------------: other large cities
Women: as administrators, NYC

MINORITY RECRUITMENT SYSTEM, NYC
See: Bilingual teachers: recruitment, NYC
Black teachers: recruitment
Board of Examiners, NYC: relationship to Board of Education
Coaching courses
Cost: minority recruitment, NYC
Decentralization, NYC: recruitment to fill vacancies under
------------------: teacher and administrator selection
Eligibility requirements for promotion
Examinations: NYC, preparation for
------------: walk-in
Field examinations, NYC
Ford Foundation fellowships
Fordham internship program
Inservice professional training programs
Minority recruitment, outside NYC
Minority teacher candidates, NYC area colleges
Minority teacher recruitment, NYC: criticism
-------------------------------: history and effectiveness
-------------------------------: among paraprofessionals
Professional Promotional Seminars, NYC
Puerto Ricans: teacher recruitment, NYC
Race and ethnicity, criteria for placement
Recruitment bar, NYC selection system
Recruitment division, staff, NYC Board of Education
Recruitment policy, minorities
School administrators, NYC: major source
-----------------------: recruitment of
Teacher training programs: NYC, Board of Education cooperation with
Teachers, NYC, major source of
Training, certification, and differentiated assignment of paraprofessionals, program alternatives

PARAPROFESSIONALS
See: College training, paraprofessionals
Minority teachers recruitment: among paraprofessionals
Paraprofessional program, NYC
---------------------------: funding
Paraprofessionals: justification for use
---------------: number and race, NYC
---------------: salary scale
---------------: Teachers' Union representation
Supervision and inservice training, paraprofessionals
Tenure: lack of for paraprofessionals

Training, certification, and differentiated assignment of paraprofessionals, program alternatives

PROMOTION OF SCHOOL PERSONNEL
See: Acting principals, NYC: placement, number, race, and use
Administrator training and apprenticeship programs
Coaching courses
Community superintendents, NYC, selection and responsibilities
Decentralization, NYC: selection system inconsistencies
----------------: teacher and administrator selection
Eligibility requirements for promotion
Ford Foundation fellowships
Fordham internship program
Inbreeding, NYC
Internship training
Local selection: need for assistance to effect
-----------: objections to
-----------: worth of
Minority schools, NYC, white principals' and teachers' attitude toward
Performance based criteria: for promotion
----------------------: objections to
Principals: placement of by NYC Board of Education
--------: responsibilities and impact
Professional organizations, impact on selection and promotion
Professional Promotional Seminars, NYC
Race and ethnicity, criteria for placement
School administrators, NYC: major source
-----------------------: recruitment of

SELECTION SYSTEM, ALTERNATIVES
See: Administrator training and apprenticeship programs as alternative
Certification requirements, state changes
Examinations: national use
Local selection: need for assistance to effect
-----------: objections to
-----------: worth of
Minority recruitment: outside NYC
National Teacher Examination: objections to
--------------------------: scope and use nationally
--------------------------: selection alternative
Performance based criteria: for assignment
----------------------: for promotion
----------------------: for selection
----------------------: for training and certification
----------------------: objections to
Probation period
State certification: eligibility alternative
---------------: unreliable alternative
State examinations: selection alternative
----------------: unreliable alternative

SELECTION SYSTEM, CRITICISM
See: Bilingual teachers: selection of, testing for
Board of Examiners, NYC: studies of
Cost: selection system, NYC

Decentralization, NYC: selection system inconsistencies
Discrimination (various entries)
Due process rights, teachers' and candidates'
Examinations: national use
----------: NYC, invalidity and bias
----------: NYC, processing
Fair employment practices, racial data as measure of
Inbreeding, NYC
Invalidity and bias, NYC examinations
Irrelevant and outmoded, NYC selection system
Minority recruitment: outside NYC
Minority schools, NYC, white principals' and teachers' attitude toward
Oral interview: criticism
Patronage, NYC
Recruitment bar, NYC selection system
Rigidity, NYC selection system
Selection system, effects of on children

SELECTION SYSTEM, NYC
See: Assistant examiners, NYC
    Bilingual teachers: selection of, testing for
    Board of Examiners, NYC: justification for
    ----------------------: membership and qualifications
    ----------------------: relationship to Board of Education
    ----------------------: staff
    ----------------------: studies of
    Chancellor, NYC, duties and powers
    Coaching courses
    Community superintendents, NYC, selection and responsibilities
    Cost: selection system, NYC
    Decentralization, NYC: National Teacher Education use
    -------------------: teacher and administrator selection
    Due process rights, teachers' and candidates'
    Eligibility requirements for promotion
    Examinations: justification
    ----------: NYC, content, structure, changes in
    ----------: NYC, preparation for
    ----------: NYC, processing
    ----------: walk-in
    Fair employment practices, racial data as measure of
    Field examinations, NYC
    Fordham internship program
    Job descriptions: NYC examinations
    Minority teacher candidates, NYC area colleges
    Oral interview: use in selection process
    -------------: validity of
    Probation period
    Professional organizations, impact on selection and promotion
    Professional Promotional Seminars, NYC
    School administrators, NYC: major source
    Substitute teachers
    Teachers, NYC, major source
    Test validation: content and predictive

TEST VALIDITY, DETERMINATION OF
See: Job description, key to test validity

Oral interview: validity
Test construction
Test limitations
Test validation: content and predictive
------------- : legal obligations
Testing, impact on minorities

TRAINING OF EDUCATIONAL PERSONNEL
See: Administrator training and apprenticeship programs as alternative
Certification requirements, state changes
College training, paraprofessionals
Community involvement, training and certification recommendation
Continuing education of teachers
Dropout rate: classroom teachers
Ford Foundation fellowships
Fordham internship program
Inservice professional training programs
Internship training
Joint Recruitment and Training Program, NYC
Minority teacher candidates, NYC area colleges
Performance based criteria: for training and certification
Practice teaching, training component
Probation period
Supervision and inservice training, paraprofessionals
Supervision of teachers
Teacher training programs: criticism
- ---------------------- : NYC, Board of Education cooperation with
---------------------- : relationship with education systems
Training, certification, and differentiated assignment of paraprofessionals, program alternatives

SUBJECT INDEX

Names in parentheses following the page numbers identify the speakers. Please refer to the preceding Topic Guide for explanation of the topics printed in capital letters.

ACCOUNTABILITY OF EDUCATIONAL SYSTEM AND PERSONNEL, See Topic Guide
Acting principals, NYC: placement, number, race and use 103-104 (King); 246-247(Callender); 260-261(Karpatkin); 283(Anderson); 316-317(Saltz); 473-474(Linton); 488-490(Rosenblum); 497(J. Hunter); 521-522(Iannacone); 526 (Dentler); 526-527(Tractenberg); 572(Gittell); 672(Parrish)
Administrator training and apprenticeship programs, as alternative 99-101, 103-104(King); 121-124 (Pemberton); 260(Karpatkin); 332 (Seeley); 523-525(Dentler); 550-551(Wilkerson); 556-561(Usdan); See also School administrators
Assistant examiners, NYC 26, 28, 29-30(Unser); 39(Scribner); 60, 62(Flinker); 171-180, 187(Greene); 171-172(Tractenberg); 192(Robinson); 209-210(Donaldson); 221, 223, 224-225(Hayes); 361-362, 371-379, 383-384(Degnan); 405 (Thorndike); 411-412(Barrett); 435, 437-438, 439-440, 443, 444-446(Weinstein)

Bilingual personnel, NYC: data 97 (King); 264(Falcon); 304(Rothbaum); 663-664(Conigliaro)
-------: need for 37-40(Scribner); 54-55(Gaines); 64-65(Flinker); 197-198, 199-200, 201-202(Kaplan); 253-254, 257(Chin); 266-267 (Falcon); 297, 298-300(Snead); 304-305(Rothbaum); 328-329(Lewis); 396-397, 398-400(Vazquez)
Bilingual program, NYC: criticism 304-305(Rothbaum); 395(Vazquez); 662-664, 664-665(Conigliaro)
BILINGUAL TEACHERS, See Topic Guide
Bilingual teachers: recruitment 68-69(Lang); 83, 85(F. Williams); 109-110(Hicks)
-------: selection or, testing for 181 (Greene); 299-300(Snead); 396-397 (Vazquez); 418-419(Deneen); 480-481(Maldonado); 662-663, 664 (Conigliaro); 705-706(Salvadore)
Black teachers and administrators: data 69-70, 71(Lang)
-------: recruitment 21-22(Unser); 66-67(Lang); 93-94, 95-96(King); 104-105, 105-106(Hicks)
See also Discrimination: against Blacks
Blacks: discrimination against 205-206(Donaldson); 225-227, 228-229(L. Hunter); 246(Callender); 279-281(Seltzer); 283(Anderson); 456-457(Bornstein); 671-674(Parrish); 694-697(Pereira); 697-698, 699(Joseph); 702-703(Koppersmith)
BOARD OF EDUCATION, NYC, See Topic Guide
Board of Examiners, NYC: criticism, See Selection System, NYC: criticism
-------: justification for 15(Unser); 140-164, 164-189(Greene); 339-341, 343-344, 348, 355-356 (Shanker); 362, 365-366, 367 (Degnan); 435, 437, 438-439, 440-441(Weinstein)
-------: membership and qualifications 12(Bergtraum); 18, 27-28 (Unser); 144, 154(Greene); 164 (Rockowitz); 469-470(S. Allen); 667-668(Ravin)
-------: relationship to Board of Education 11-12(Bergtraum); 16 (Unser); 37-40(Scribner); 49-50 (Strauss); 73-74, 76-78(Lang); 144, 145-146, 148, 154-155, 170-172, 185-186(Greene); 196(Robinson); 222-224(Hayes); 338-339 (Seeley); 353-354(Shanker); 361 (Degnan); 436(Weinstein); 469 (S. Allen)
-------: staff 28-29, 31(Unser); 164 (Rockowitz); 169, 180(Greene); 439-440, 441-443, 444(Weinstein); 667-668(Ravin)
-------: studies of 181-182(Tractenberg); 182-186(Greene); 190-192 (Robinson); 236-237(Glasser);

246(Callender); 329-331, 332 (Seeley); 355-356(Shanker); 392-393(Seeley); 470(S. Allen); 507 (Gist); 517-519, 520-521(Iannacone); 522(Dentler)

Certification requirements, state changes 9(Bergtraum); 147-149 (Greene); 250-251(Callender); 388-389(Weber); 543-544, 545-546 (Shields); 557,558(Usdan); 584-585(Riessman); 593-594(Poppendieck); 602-604, 605-607(Sinclair); 609-610, 610-612(Nyquist); 613-616, 619(W. Allen); 620-623, 625-627(Goralski); 632, 633-635, 636-637(Manch)

Chancellor, NYC: duties and powers 33-34, 37-38, 39-40(Scribner); 46-47, 49-50(Strauss); 123(Pemberton); 173-174(Greene); 193-194, 196(Robinson)

Chinese, discrimination against 252-258(Chin)

Coaching courses 24-26(Tractenberg); 85-86(F. Williams); 93-95, 102-103(King); 145-146(Greene); 205, 207(Donaldson); 219, 223-224 (Hayes); 368-369, 371(Degnan); 437-439(Weinstein)

College training, paraprofessionals 125-126, 127-129(Atwell); 129-130, 131-135, 136, 137-138(J. Burton); 552-553, 554(Lynch); 561-563, 565(Calnek)

COMMUNITY BOARDS OF EDUCATION, NYC, See Topic Guide

Community involvement: training and certification recommendation 55-56(Gaines); 266-267(Falcon); 270(Conklin); 329(Lewis); 541-542, 546-547(Shields); 597-598(Edelfeldt); 616-617(W. Allen); 620-621, 622-623, 624-625, 630-631 (Goralski)

Community superintendents, NYC: selection and responsibilities 33 (Scribner); 157-158, 173(Greene); 208(Donaldson)

Continuing education of teachers 269-270(Caban); 279(Forster); 325-326(Lewis); 535(Hopkins); 543 (Shields); 589-590, 590-591, 594 (Poppendieck); 612-613, 615-616 (W. Allen); 622-623, 627, 628-629 (Goralski)

Cost: minority recruitment, NYC 72-73(Lang); 106-107, 108(Hicks); 249(Callender)

-------: National Teacher Examination 152-153(Greene); 417-418 (Deneen); 480(Maldonado)
-------: selection system, NYC 61-62, 62-63, 65-66(Flinker); 93-95 (King); 153, 169, 188(Greene); 339 (Seeley); 399(Vazquez); 497(J. Hunter); 533-534(Hopkins)
Custodial employees, discrimination in hiring 288-293(Zeitlin)

DATA, See Topic Guide
Decentralization, NYC: community districts 64-65(Flinker); 248-249(Callender); 254-255(Chin); 316(Saltz); 688(Tudy)
-------: National Teacher Education use 33, 36-37(Scribner); 49 (Strauss); 56-58(Gaines); 67-68, 74-75(Lang); 109, 114-115(Hicks); 152, 157, 186-188(Greene); 347-348(Shanker); 415-416(Deneen)
-------: recruitment 8-9(Bergtraum); 74-76(Lang); 89-90(F. Williams); 106-107, 109(Hicks); 194-195(Robinson)
-------: selection system inconsistencies 33-35, 36-37(Scribner); 46-48, 49-50(Strauss); 50-56(Gaines); 60-62(Flinker); 193-194(Robinson); 197-199(Kaplan); 207-208, 208-209, 210, 212-213 (Donaldson); 233-234(Lehrman); 247(Callender); 257-261(Karpatkin); 324-325, 328-329(Lewis); 331, 339(Seeley); 450(Frye); 457-459(Bornstein); 489-490(Rosenblum); 491-492(Woolford); 502-503(Dextre); 572(Gittell); 660-661 (Brook); 679(McMorris)
-------: teacher and administrator selection 32-35(Scribner); 46-47 (Strauss); 51-53(Gaines); 74, 78-80(Lang); 85(F. Williams); 122-124(Pemberton); 150-151, 157-158, 162, 173(Greene); 193-194, 195 (Robinson); 343-344(Shanker); 361, 364-365(Degnan); 437-438 (Weinstein); 486-487(Norton)
Discrimination: against minorities, NYC 14(Bergtraum); 46, 47 (Strauss); 190, 193(Robinson); 206, 208-209(Donaldson); 235, 236-237, 237-238, 239-240 (Glasser); 278(Forster); 281 (Jenkins); 330-331, 335-336 (Seeley); 409(Barrett); 433-434 (Mapp); 453(Resta); 464-465, 465-466(English); 469, 469-470(S.

Allen); 471-473(C. Burton); 488-489, 490(Rosenblum); 493-494 (Seabrook); 496-497(J. Hunter); 502(Dextre); 535-536(Wallace); 567(Haizlip); 584, 586, 587(Riessman); 660-661(Brook); 662(Conigliaro); 692-694(Sealy);
See also Blacks; Chinese; Italians; Puerto Ricans; Women—discrimination against
-------: against outsiders and disabled, NYC selection system 55 (Gaines); 478-480(Heumann); 519 (Iannacone); 571(Gittell)
-------: through written examination 100-101(King); 494-496(Murphy); 662-663(Conigliaro); 705-706 (Salvadore)
See also Oral interview: criticism
Dropout rate: classroom teachers 357(Shanker); 384(Weber); 591-592(Poppendieck); 598(Edelfeldt)
-------: minority students 282 (Jenkins); 476(Aiello); 477(Nassetta); 477(Norton)
Due process rights, teachers' and candidates' 144(Greene); 235-237, 240-241(Glasser); 357(Shanker); 366(Degnan); 423-425, 430(Pollak); 437-438, 440, 441, 446-447 (Weinstein)

Eligibility requirements for promotion 8, 12(Bergtraum); 15(Unser); 69, 76-77(Lang); 205-206(Donaldson); 360-361, 366-367(Degnan); 436-437, 439-440, 441, 446-448 (Weinstein); 449-450(Frye)
Examinations: invalidity and bias 47 (Strauss); 59-61(Flinker); 204-207 (Donaldson); 230-232(Lehrman); 235-237(Glasser); 250-251(Callender); 330-331, 337-338(Seeley); 472-473, 474(Linton); 582, 583-584, 584-585, 585-586, 588-589 (Riessman); 701-702(Koppersmith)
-------: justification for 18, 20-21, 23-24(Unser); 141, 149-152, 161, 162-164(Greene); 339-341, 347-348, 352-353, 355-356(Shanker); 361-362, 363, 365-366, 367-369, 371(Degnan); 401-402, 403-404 (Thorndike); 414(Deneen); 435-436, 437, 444-445(Weinstein); 467-468(Friedman); 483-486 (Samuels); 685-686(MacKenzie)
-------: national use 33(Scribner); 227(L. Hunter); 361, 365(Degnan); 364-365(Tractenberg); 469, 471 (S. Allen); 510-511(Fischer); 521 (Iannacone); 530-531(Wallace); 531-533(Hopkins); 599-600(Edelfeldt); 604-605, 605-606(Sinclair); 626-627(Goralski); 634-635, 635-636, 636-637(Manch); 645-646, 648-650, 651-652(McCutcheon)
See also National Teacher Examinations; State examinations; Test construction, limitations, etc.
-------: NYC, content, structure, changes in 29-30(Unser); 140, 142-143, 159-160, 176, 186 (Greene); 365(Degnan); 440-446 (Weinstein)
-------: NYC, preparation for 68-69(Lang); 83-84(F. Williams); 219-220(Hayes)
See also Coaching
-------: NYC, processing 58-59, 62-63(Flinker); 79-80(Lang); 111-112(Hicks); 141-142, 143, 169-170 (Greene); 164(Rockowitz); 212 (Donaldson); 344(Shanker); 664 (Conigliaro)
-------: walk-in 87-88(F. Williams); 145, 162(Greene); 211(Donaldson); 385(Weber); 649-650(Tractenberg)

Fair Employment practices, racial data as measure of 1(Norton); 155-156(Greene); 191-192(Robinson); 242-244(Nieves); 246-247 (Callender); 268-269(Norton); 341-342, 345-347(Shanker); 360-361, 363-364(Degnan); 452-453 (Resta); 470(S. Allen); 473-474 (Linton); 476-477(Nassetta); 484 (Samuels); 548-549(Wilkerson)
Field examination, NYC 105-107, 108-109, 111-112(Hicks)
Ford Foundation fellowships 91(F. Williams); 100(King); 121(Pemberton); 260(Karpatkin); 611-612 (Nyquist)
Fordham internship program 17, 18 (Unser); 91-92(F. Williams); 99-101, 103-104(King); 121(Pemberton); 156-157(Greene); 260(Karpatkin); 377-378(Degnan); 611-612 (Nyquist)

Hearings, Human Rights Commission, purpose 1-4, 189, 202-203 218-219, 285-286, 288, 291, 322, 323, 360(Norton); 468-469

(David); 503-506(Koppersmith); 580, 620, 632, 656-657(Norton); 659(French); 708-709(Norton)

Inbreeding, NYC 190-193(Robinson); 450-452(Frye); 469-470(S. Allen); 473-474(Linton); 490-491(Woolford); 518-520(Iannacone); 537-539, 546-547(Shields); 570(Gittell); 627-628(Goralski); 688-689 (Tudy)

Inservice professional training programs 84(F. Williams); 219-220 (Hayes); 231(Lehrman); 264-266 (Falcon); 521-522(Iannacone); 534-535(Hopkins); 542-543(Shields); 611-612(Nyquist)

Internship training 44, 45(Scribner); 101(King); 279(Forster); 386-387, 388(Weber); 536-537(Wallace); 542(Shields); 550-551(Wilkerson); 583-584, 586-587(Riessman); 674 (Parrish)

Irrelevant and outmoded, NYC selection system 35(Scribner); 40-43(Theobald); 58-59(Flinker); 217-218(Gotbaum); 230-233(Lehrman); 238(Glasser); 247-248, 250, 251(Callender); 260-261(Karpatkin); 312(Weiner); 333, 335-336 (Seeley); 350-351, 353-355 (Shanker); 384, 389-390, 390-392(Weber); 407-408, 409-410 (Barrett); 469, 469-470(S. Allen); 474-475(Linton); 506-507(Gist); 518-519, 520, 521(Iannacone); 528 (Dentler); 533(Hopkins); 546-547 (Shields); 584-585(Riessman); 596-597(Edelfeldt); 609(Nyquist); 667-669(Ravin)

Italian teachers and administrators, NYC 284-285(Valletutti); 287 (Linquist); 475-476(Aiello)
------: discrimination against 284-286(Valletutti); 286-287(Linquist); 475-476(Aiello); 476-477 (Nassetta)

Jewish supervisors and administrators, NYC 464-465(English)

Job description: key to test validity 404-405, 405-406(Thorndike); 423-424, 427-428, 431-432(Pollak); 419-421(Deneen); 406, 407-408(Barrett); 431-432(Tractenberg); 582-584(Riessman)
------: NYC examinations 76-78 (Lang); 170-172(Greene); 350-351, 353-354(Shanker); 405-406 (Thorndike); 407-408, 410-411 (Barrett); 419-420(Deneen)

Joint Recruitment and Training Program, NYC 67(Lang); 107-111 (Hicks); 246(Callender); 342-343, 344-345(Shanker); 362-363 (Degnan)

Local selection: need for assistance to effect 47-48, 49-50(Strauss); 102-104(King); 227-228, 229(L. Hunter); 233-234(Lehrman); 312-313(Weiner); 324, 324-325, 326 (Lewis); 332, 333-335(Seeley); 456(Braveman); 482-483(West); 492(Woolford); 665(Conigliaro); 691-692(J. Williams); 689(Tudy)
------: objections to 149-151, 154, 157-158, 186-187(Greene); 343-344, 348, 350-352, 358(Shanker); 376-377(Degnan); 402(Thorndike); 484-485, 486-487(Samuels); 685, 686(MacKenzie)
------: worth of 55-56(Gaines); 63-64, 65-66(Flinker); 99-100, 100-101(King); 196(Robinson); 197, 199(Kaplan); 210, 212-213(Donaldson); 281(Seltzer); 434(Mapp); 453-454(Resta); 461-463(Jones); 469, 470-471(S. Allen); 471(C. Burton); 487-488, 489-490(Rosenblum); 493-494(Seabrook); 502-503(Dextre); 522-526, 528 (Dentler); 549, 550(Wilkerson); 567-568, 569-570(Haizlip); 571-575(Gittell); 583-584, 587-588 (Riessman); 592-593, 595-596 (Poppendieck); 622-623, 627-628, 629-632(Goralski); 637, 638-639 (Manch); 650-651(McCutcheon); 670-671(Ravin); 705(Koppersmith)

Manpower Development Training Program, discrimination in hiring for 692-694(Sealy); 697-700(Joseph)

Minority recruitment, outside NYC 20-21(Norton); 87(Tractenberg); 340-341, 343(Shanker); 363-364 (Degnan); 530-532, 535-536 (Wallace); 632-635, 641(Manch); 644-652(McCutcheon)

MINORITY RECRUITMENT SYSTEM, NYC, See Topic Guide

Minority schools, NYC, white principals' and teachers' attitude toward 207-208, 213(Donaldson); 213-214(Norton); 258-261

(Karpatkin); 312-313(Weiner); 334 (Seeley); 378-382(Degnan); 381 (Norton); 492(Woolford); 496(J. Hunter); 654(Norton); 699-700 (Joseph)

Minority student achievement 248-250(Callender); 312(Weiner); 496-497(J.Hunter); 506-508(Gist); 531, 535(Hopkins); 539(Shields); 660, 661(Brook); 680-681(McMorris); 689(Tudy)
See also Puerto Rican student achievement, NYC

Minority teacher candidates, NYC area colleges 15, 19(Unser); 70-71 (Lang); 115(Norton); 115(Hicks); 244(Nieves); 342, 344-345 (Shanker); 360-361, 364-365(Degnan); 435-437(Weinstein); 454 (Resta); 569(Norton)

Minority teacher recruitment, NYC: criticism 94-95, 102-103(King); 104, 113, 114-115(Hicks); 193-195 (Robinson); 211-212(Donaldson); 248-250(Callender); 264, 265-266, 266-267(Falcon); 330-331, 332 (Seeley); 342-343, 347(Shanker); 389(Weber); 396-397, 398, 399-400(Vazquez); 470(S.Allen); 473-474(Linton); 534(Hopkins); 535-536(Wallace); 674-675(Parrish)
-------: history and effectiveness 71-72(Lang); 82-85(F.Williams); 95(King); 104-115(Hicks); 362-363 (Degnan)
See also Black teachers: recruitment; Puerto Ricans: teacher recruitment, NYC
-------: among paraprofessionals 70-71(Lang); 84(F.Williams); 126-130(Atwell); 344-345(Shanker); 398, 399-400(Vazquez); 553, 554-555(Lynch); 579(Rothschild); 611 (Nyquist); 627-629(Goralski)

National Teacher Examination: objections to 114(Hicks); 151-154 (Greene); 673-674(Parrish)
-------: scope and use 151-153, 164 (Greene); 314(Hillman); 347-348, 352-353(Shanker); 382-383(Degnan); 415-416, 416-417, 418-421 (Deneen); 424-425(Pollak); 530 (Wallace); 634-635, 636-637 (Manch)
-------: selection alternative 62-63 (Flinker); 81-82(Lang); 325, 326-327(Lewis); 336-337(Seeley); 347-348, 355-357(Shanker); 473 (Linton)

Non-English speaking students, NYC, placement and achievement 253-254(Chin); 264(Falcon); 303-304, 304-305(Rothbaum); 395-396(Vazquez); 477(Nassetta)

Oral interview: criticism 59-60 (Flinker); 206(Donaldson); 225-227(L.Hunter); 230-231(Lehrman); 279-280(Seltzer); 286(Valletutti); 286-287(Linquist); 287 (Norton); 312(Weiner); 350-351 (Shanker); 408-409, 410-412(Barrett); 453(Resta); 456-457(Bornstein); 548-549(Wilkerson); 659 (Brook); 673(Parrish)
-------: use in selection process 24(Unser); 142-143, 143-144 (Greene); 365-366(Degnan); 439-441, 445, 446-447, 447-448 (Weinstein)
-------: validity 100-101(King); 669 (Ravin)

Paraprofessional program, NYC 124-130(Atwell); 552-554(Lynch); 561-565(Calnek)
-------: funding 126(Atwell); 552-553, 554(Lynch); 563-564(Calnek)

PARAPROFESSIONALS, See Topic Guide

Paraprofessionals: justification for use 54-55(Gaines); 245(Nieves); 398, 399-401(Vazquez); 460(Bornstein); 466(English); 538-539 (Shields); 553, 555-556(Lynch)
-------: number and race, NYC 124-125, 127(Atwell); 130-131, 137-138(J.Burton); 242-243(Nieves); 552(Lynch)
-------: salary scale 130-131, 137-138(J.Burton)
-------: Teachers Union representation 125-126(Atwell); 137-138(J. Burton); 344-345(Shanker); 565 (Calnek)

Patronage, NYC 49(Strauss); 203-206, 209-210(Donaldson); 312, 312-313(Weiner); 471-472(C. Burton); 488(Rosenblum); 528 (Dentler); 570-571, 573-574(Gittell); 693(Sealy)

Performance-based criteria: for assignment 589-590, 591-592 (Poppendieck); 597-599, 600-601 (Edelfeldt); 609(Nyquist); 621-622, 623-624, 625-626, 628 (Goralski)

-------: objections to 147, 156-157 (Greene)

-------: for promotion 43(Theobald); 217-218(Gotbaum); 238-240(Glasser); 261(Karpatkin); 332-333, 336 (Seeley); 348-350(Shanker); 474-475(Linton); 511-512, 515-516 (Fischer); 522-526, 527-528(Dentler); 549-551, 551-552(Wilkerson)

-------: for selection 42-43, 45 (Theobald); 63-64, 65-66(Flinker); 129-130(Atwell); 358-359(Shanker); 412(Barrett); 414-415(Deneen); 455-456(Braveman); 485-486(Samuels); 497(J. Hunter); 510-511, 513, 514-515, 516-517(Fischer); 521-522 (Iannacone); 544-546(Shields); 549-551, 551-552(Wilkerson); 570 (Haizlip); 572, 575(Gittell); 583-585, 585-586(Riessman); 589-591, 592-593, 594-596(Poppendieck); 604, 606-607(Sinclair); 669-671 (Ravin)

-------: for training and certification 305-306(Rothbaum); 386-387, 388, 388-389, 391-392(Weber); 474-475(Linton); 509-510, 510-511, 514-515, 516-517(Fischer); 533-534(Hopkins); 536-537(Wallace); 550(Wilkerson); 583-585(Riessman); 589-593, 593-596(Poppendieck); 601-607(Sinclair); 609-610 (Nyquist); 612-620(W. Allen); 620-623, 624-627, 628-629, 630-631 (Goralski); 642-644(Dickson)

Practice teaching, training component 43-44(Theobald); 385-386, 391(Weber); 540-541(Shields); 586-587(Riessman)

Principals: placement by NYC Board of Education 283(Anderson); 302 (Moses)

-------: responsibilities and impact 201-202(Kaplan); 258, 261(Karpatkin); 300-302(Moses); 304(Rothbaum); 334-335(Seeley); 348-350 (Shanker); 434(Mapp); 438(Weinstein); 461-463(Jones); 489-490 (Rosenblum); 502(Dextre); 511-512 (Fischer); 549(Wilkerson); 560-561(Usdan); 568(Haizlip); 574-575 (Gittell); 689-690(Tudy); 691(J. Williams)

Probation period 9-10, 13-14(Bergtraum); 42-43(Theobald); 65-66 (Flinker); 81(Lang); 198-199, 201-202(Kaplan); 325, 326-327, 328 (Lewis); 343, 356-360(Shanker); 366, 366-367, 368, 372(Degnan); 437-438(Weinstein); 518-519(Iannacone); 536-537(Wallace); 566-567 (Haizlip)

Professional organizations, impact on selection and promotion 171-172, 178-179, 179-180, 180-181 (Greene); 203-205, 207-208, 209 (Donaldson); 228-229(L. Hunter); 239(Glasser); 249-250(Callender); 260-261, 261-264(Karpatkin); 279-281(Seltzer); 283(Anderson); 300-301, 301-302, 303(Moses); 311-312 (Weiner); 317-321(Gordon); 342-343, 355(Shanker); 348(Tractenberg); 372-373, 378-379, 380(Degnan); 378 (Tractenberg); 393-394(Seeley); 455 (Resta); 464(English); 471, 472-473(C. Burton); 473-474(Linton); 526(Dentler); 599(Edelfeldt); 613-614, 616-617, 620(W. Allen); 647, 651-652(McCutcheon); 668-669 (Ravin); 673-674(Parrish); 702, 703-705(Koppersmith)

Professional Promotional Seminars, NYC 24(Unser); 68-69(Lang); 83-84(F. Williams); 97-98(King); 205 (Donaldson); 218-225(Hayes); 247 (Callender); 361, 368-371(Degnan); 519-520(Iannacone)

PROMOTION OF SCHOOL PERSONNEL, See Topic Guide

Puerto Ricans: data, teachers and administrators, NYC 242-244 (Nieves); 395-396(Vazquez)

-------: discrimination against 241-242, 242-243, 245-246(Nieves); 264-266(Falcon); 299-300(Snead); 480(Maldonado); 659-660, 661 (Brook); 693-694(Sealy); 697-699 (Joseph)

-------: student achievement, NYC 303-305(Rothbaum); 395-396(Vazquez); 465-466(English)

-------: teacher recruitment, NYC 66-67(Lang); 90-91(F. Williams); 96-97(King); 109(Hicks); 264, 265-266, 266-267(Falcon); 396-397, 398, 399-400(Vazquez)

Race and ethnicity, criteria for placement 10-11(Bergtraum); 48-49(Strauss); 100-101(King); 197-199, 199-200, 200-201, 202(Kaplan); 200-201(Norton); 229-230(Lehrman); 238-240(Glasser); 242, 244 (Nieves); 278-279(Forster); 281 (Seltzer); 281-282(Jenkins); 295-296(Ringgold); 296-297, 310-311 (Norton); 298-299(Snead); 334-335

(Seeley); 380(Tractenberg); 398-
399(Vazquez); 452(Frye); 453-454
(Resta); 455(Braveman); 462-463
(Jones); 464-465(English); 471-473
(C.Burton); 475(Aiello); 484, 485-
486(Samuels); 496(J.Hunter); 497-
498(Degraffenreid); 499(George);
499(James); 499-500(Fleming);
536(Wallace); 574-575(Gittell);
575(Tractenberg); 575, 639(Norton); 635-636, 639-640(Manch);
645-646, 648-649, 651(McCutcheon); 653(Norton); 653-654(Tractenberg); 654-655(Norton); 674-
675(Parrish); 688-689(Tudy); 703
(Koppersmith); 708(Cruz)
See also School districts, NYC,
racial composition
Recruitment bar, NYC selection
system 87-88(F. Williams); 93-97
(King); 194-195(Robinson); 203
(Donaldson); 314(Hillman); 399-
400, 400-401(Vazquez); 566-567
(Haizlip); 662-663(Conigliaro)
Recruitment Division staff, NYC
Board of Education 82-85, 88-89
(F. Williams); 106-107(Hicks)
Recruitment policy, minorities 66-
67(Lang); 82, 84-85(F.Williams);
106-108(Hicks)
Rigidity, NYC selection system 9-10,
14(Bergtraum); 33(Scribner); 53-
55(Gaines); 108-109(Hicks); 330,
336(Seeley); 451-452(Frye); 510
(Fischer); 568-569(Haizlip); 662
(Conigliaro)

School administrators, NYC: major
source 90-91(F. Williams); 362,
366-367(Degnan); 450-451(Frye);
537(Shields)
-------: recruitment 90-91(F. Wil-
liams); 222-223(Hayes); 325, 327-
328(Lewis); 522-528(Dentler)
School districts, NYC, racial com-
position 46-47, 48(Strauss); 66
(Flinker); 197-198(Kaplan); 258
(Karpatkin); 267-268, 270-278
(Caban); 282(Jenkins); 293-294
(Ringgold); 304(Rothbaum); 450
(Frye); 476(Aiello); 490-491, 492
(Woolford); 679-680, 681(McMor-
ris); 683(McIntosh); 688, 689
(Tudy)
SELECTION SYSTEM, ALTERNA-
TIVES, See Topic Guide
SELECTION SYSTEM, CRITICISM,
See Topic Guide

Selection system, effects on children 7-8(Bergtraum); 32-33
(Scribner); 50, 53-54(Gaines);
191-192(Robinson); 232-233(Lehrman); 241-242, 244-245(Nieves);
249(Callender); 264(Falcon); 269-
270(Conklin); 281-282(Jenkins);
282-283(Anderson); 294-296(Ringgold); 298-299(Snead); 301-304
(Moses); 304-305(Rothbaum); 395-
396(Vazquez); 453(Resta); 459-
460(Bornstein); 465-466(English);
472-473(Linton); 481-482(Maldonado); 489, 490(Rosenblum); 492-
493(Woolford); 496(J.Hunter);
500-501(Levenburg); 506-508
(Gist); 531, 535(Hopkins); 544-545
(Shields); 548-549(Wilkerson);
565-566, 566-568, 569-570(Haizlip); 597, 600(Edelfeldt); 659-661
(Brook); 664-665(Conigliaro); 687,
688-689(Tudy); 690-691(J. Williams); 697-700(Joseph); 707-708
(Cruz)
SELECTION SYSTEM, NYC, See
Topic Guide
State certification: eligibility alternative 33,38(Scribner); 42-43, 45
(Theobald); 65(Flinker); 101(King);
213(Donaldson); 281(Seltzer); 285
(Valletutti); 311-313(Weiner); 331-
332, 336-337(Seeley); 388, 389-
390, 391-392(Weber); 469(S.Al-
len); 471(C. Burton); 506(Gist);
520-521(Iannacone); 572-573(Gittell); 583-584, 587-588(Riessman); 609, 610(Nyquist); 636-638,
639(Manch); 664-665(Conigliaro);
674(Parrish)
-------: unreliable alternative 146-
149(Greene); 340-341, 352-353
(Shanker); 417-418(Deneen); 437
(Weinstein); 597, 600(Edelfeldt)
State examinations: selection alternative 9, 13(Bergtraum); 347-348,
352-353(Shanker); 468(Friedman)
-------: unreliable alternative 147,
156-157(Greene); 336-337(Seeley);
382-383(Degnan); 527(Dentler);
571-572(Gittell); 586-587(Riessman); 617-618(W. Allen)
Students, teachers, and principals,
racial data: NYC 191(Robinson);
242-243(Nieves); 280(Seltzer);
324-325(Lewis); 473-474(Linton);
492(Woolford); 671-673(Parrish)
-------: NY State 533(Hopkins);
635, 636(Manch)

-------: other large cities 3(Norton); 237-238(Glasser); 242-244(Nieves); 246(Callender); 311-312(Weiner); 525-526(Dentler); 529-530(Wallace); 603-604(Sinclair); 645-646, 647(McCutcheon)
Substitute teachers 62-64, 66 (Flinker); 76(Lang); 83(F. Williams); 145-146, 161-162(Greene); 206(Donaldson); 230(Lehrman); 279-280(Seltzer); 313-314(Weiner); 470(S. Allen); 677(Siculair)
Supervision and inservice training, paraprofessionals 125-127(Atwell); 133, 135-137(J. Burton); 552-553 (Lynch); 611(Nyquist)
Supervision of teachers 205-206 (Donaldson); 231(Lehrman); 270 (Norton); 312(Weiner); 323(Rockowitz); 325-326, 328(Lewis); 386, 392(Weber); 501(Levenburg); 518-519(Iannacone); 537(Wallace); 566-567(Haizlip)

Teacher accountability, justification and implementation 48(Strauss); 233-234, 234-235(Lehrman); 248-249(Callender); 456(Braveman); 515, 516-517(Fischer); 585-586 (Riessman); 592-593(Poppendieck); 601-607(Sinclair); 613, 619(W. Allen); 622-623(Goralski); 643-644(Dickson)
Teacher training programs: criticism 10(Bergtraum); 43-45(Theobald); 385, 387, 388, 389-390 (Weber); 537-541, 543(Shields); 577-579(Rothschild); 582-584, 586-587, 588(Riessman); 591-592 (Poppendieck); 667-668, 669-670, 670-671(Ravin); 691-692(J. Williams)
-------: NYC Board of Education cooperation with 67-69, 72-73 (Lang)
-------: relationship with education systems 43-45(Theobald); 160-161 (Greene); 385, 390, 391-392 (Weber); 417-418(Deneen); 470(S. Allen); 513-515(Fischer); 545 (Shields); 553(Lynch); 589-590, 590-591, 594(Poppendieck); 604, 605-606(Sinclair); 613-615, 616-617(W. Allen); 620-621, 624, 628 (Goralski)
Teachers, NYC, major source of 45 (Theobald); 45(Tractenberg); 70-71, 80-81(Lang); 160(Greene); 362 (Degnan); 537(Shields)

Tenure: teachers', and accountability 13-14(Bergtraum); 198-199, 201-202(Kaplan); 231, 232-233 (Lehrman); 240-241(Glasser); 269 (Conklin); 269-270(Caban); 295-296(Ringgold); 315-316(Hillman); 325, 325-326(Lewis); 332(Seeley); 357-358(Shanker)
-------: lack of for paraprofessionals 132(J. Burton); 437-438(Weinstein); 562, 563, 565(Calnek); 687(Tudy)
Test construction 404-405(Thorndike); 419(Deneen)
Test limitations 406-407, 407-408 (Barrett); 415-416(Deneen); 424-425, 427-428, 429-431(Pollak)
Test validation: content and predictive 143, 163-164, 168-169, 181-186 (Greene); 164(Rockowotz); 167-168 (Tractenberg); 401-405(Thorndike); 403-404(Tractenberg); 410 (Barrett); 412-415, 418-419 (Deneen); 422-428, 431-432(Pollak); 510, 513, 515(Fischer); 548-549, 551-552(Wilkerson); 582-583, 584-586, 586-587, 587-588(Riessman); 591, 592-594(Poppendieck)
-------: legal obligations 422-433 (Pollak)
TEST VALIDITY, DETERMINATION OF, See Topic Guide
Testing, impact on minorities 409-410(Barrett); 421(Deneen); 586 (Riessman); 596-597(Edelfeldt); 648(McCutcheon)
Training, certification, and differentiated assignment of paraprofessionals, program alternatives 398(Vazquez); 462(Jones); 552-556(Lynch); 561-562(Calnek); 576-580(Rothschild); 587-589(Riessman); 592(Poppendieck); 598 (Edelfeldt); 619(W. Allen); 621-622, 623-624, 625-626, 628(Goralski)
TRAINING OF EDUCATIONAL PERSONNEL, See Topic Guide

Women: as administrators 340 (Shanker); 482(West); 493-494 (Seabrook)
-------: discrimination against 482-483(West); 492-494(Seabrook)

INDEX OF WITNESSES

Aiello, Steve, 475-476
Allen, Sonia, 469-471
Allen, Wendell, 612-620
Anderson, Dorothy, 282-283
Atwell, Gladstone, 124-130
Barrett, Richard, 406-412
Bergtraum, Murry, 7-14
Bornstein, Marvin, 456-460
Braveman, Marilyn, 455-456
Brook, Marina, 659-661
Buck, Ruth, 306-310
Burton, Charles, 471-473
Burton, Joan, 129-138
Caban, Louis, 267-278
Callender, Eugene, 246-251
Calnek, Gary, 561-565
Chin, Irving, 252-258
Conigliaro, Anna, 662-665
Conklin, Doris, 269-270
Cruz, Juanita, 707-708
David, Vera,
Degnan, Walter, 360-384
Degraffenreid, William, III, 497-498
Deneen, James R., 412-421
Dentler, Robert A., 522-528
Dextre, Lalo, 502-503
Dickson, George, 642-644
Donaldson, Andrew, 203-213
Edelfeldt, Roy, 596-601
English, Herbert, 464-466
Falcon, Rose, 264-267
Fischer, John H., 509-517
Fleming, Desdre, 499-500
Flinker, Irving, 58-66
Forster, Cecil, 278-279
Friedman, Bernard, 467-468
Frye, Martin, 449-452
Gaines, Edythe, 50-58
George, Belle Bavine, 499
Gist, W. Rogers, 506-508
Gittell, Marilyn, 570-575
Glasser, Ira, 235-241
Goralski, Patricia, 620-632
Gordon, Reuben, 317-321
Gotbaum, Victor, 217-218
Greene, Jay, 140-164, 168-189
Haizlip, Harold, 565-570
Hayes, Dennis, 218-225
Heumann, Judy, 478-480
Hicks, Daisy, 105-115
Hillman, P., 314-316
Hopkins, Jeanette, 531-535
Hunter, John, 496-497
Hunter, Lloyd B., 225-229
Innacone, Laurence, 517-522

James, Loretta, 499
Jenkins, Cynthia, 281-282
Jones, Nellie, 461-463
Joseph, Dorothy, 697-700
Kaplan, Philip, 197-202
Karpatkin, Rhoda, 257-264
King, John B., 93-104
Koppersmith, Hal, 503-506, 701-705
Kreuter, Mortimer, 731
Lang, Theodore, 66-82
Lashinsky, Alvin, 487
Lehrman, Wendy, 229-235
Levenburg, Esther, 500-501
Lewis, Blanche, 324-329
Linton, Linda, 472-475
Linquist, Rita, 286-288
Lynch, William, Jr., 552-556
McCutcheon, Aubrey, 644-652
McIntosh, Mrs., 683
MacKenzie, Roderick, 685-686
McMorris, LeRoy, 679-681
Maldonado, Jorge, 480-482
Manch, Joseph, 632-641
Mapp, Lloyd S., 433-434
Moses, Frances, 300-304
Murphy, Anna S., 494-496
Nassetta, Vincent, 476-477
Nieves, Louis, 241-246
Nyquist, Ewald B., 609-612
Parrish, Richard, 671-675
Pemberton, Vernal, 84, 121-124
Pereira, Frank, 694-697
Pollak, Stephen J., 422-432
Poppendieck, Robert, 589-596
Pullim, Mrs., 707
Ravin, Irving, 667-671
Resta, Vincent, 452-455
Riessman, Frank, 582-589
Ringgold, Faith, 293-296
Robinson, Isaiah E., Jr., 190-196
Rockowitz, Murray, 164-169, 323
Rosenblum, Doris, 487-490
Rothbaum, Arnold, 303-306
Rothschild, Judith, 576-580
Saltz, Peter, 316-317
Salvadore, David, 705-706
Samuels, Seymour, 483-487
Scribner, Harvey, 32-40
Seabrook, Patricia, 492-494
Sealy, Rose F., 692-694
Seeley, David, 329-339, 392-394
Seltzer, Morris, 279-281
Shanker, Albert, 339-359
Shields, James, 537-547
Sicular, Roy, 677

Sinclair, Ward, 601-607
Snead, Carmen, 297-300
Strauss, Peter J., 46-50
Theobald, John J., 40-45
Thorndike, Robert, 401-406
Tudy, Mildred, 687-690
Unser, Gertrude, 15-31
Usdan, Michael, 556-561
Valletutti, Joseph F., 284-286
Vazquez, Hector, 395-401
Wallace, Phyllis, 529-532, 535-537
Washington, Barbara, 499
Watkins, James, 115-121
Weber, Lillian, 384-392
Weiner, David, 311-314
Weinstein, Alfred, 435-448
West, Anne G., 482-483
Wilkerson, Doxie, 548-552
Williams, Frederick, 82-92
Williams, Joan, 690-692
Woolford, Helene, 490-493
Zeitlin, Elliott, 288-293